The Princeton Review®

NO LONGER PROPERTY OF
SEATTLE PUBLIC LIBRARY

# 10 Practice Tests for the
# SAT®

## 2019 Edition

Jonathan Chiu and the Staff of The Princeton Review

PrincetonReview.com

Penguin
Random
House

The Princeton Review
110 East 42nd St, 7th Floor
New York, NY 10017
Email: editorialsupport@review.com

Copyright © 2018 by TPR Education IP Holdings, LLC. All rights reserved.

Published in the United States by Penguin Random House LLC, New York, and in Canada by Random House of Canada, a division of Penguin Random House Ltd., Toronto.

Terms of Service: The Princeton Review Online Companion Tools ("Student Tools") for retail books are available for only the two most recent editions of that book. Student Tools may be activated only once per eligible book purchased for a total of 24 months of access. Activation of Student Tools more than once per book is in direct violation of these Terms of Service and may result in discontinuation of access to Student Tools Services.

ISBN: 978-1-5247-5787-8
ISSN: 2377-7273

SAT is a trademark registered by the College Board, which is not affiliated with, and does not endorse, this product.

The Princeton Review is not affiliated with Princeton University.

Permission has been granted to reprint portions of the following:

*Art, Mind, and Brain: A Cognitive Approach to Creativity.* Gardner, Howard. Copyright © 1982. Reprinted with permission of the author.

"At Pluto, the End of a Beginning." Billings, Lee. Excerpted with permission. Copyright © 2015 Scientific American, a Division of Nature America, Inc. All rights reserved.

"A New Billion-Mile Journey for New Horizons." Scharf, Caleb A. Excerpted with permission. Copyright © 2015 Scientific American, a Division of Nature America Inc. All rights reserved.

"Does media multitasking always hurt?" Kelvin F. H. Lui, Alan C.-N. Wong, *Psychonomic Bulletin & Review.* August 2012, Volume 19, Issue 4, pp. 647-653. http://www.psychonomic.org

From *The New England Journal of Medicine,* Arias, Cesar A. and Murray, Barbara E., "Antibiotic-Resistant Bugs in the 21st Century--A Clinical Super-Challenge," Vol. 360, Pages No. 439-443, Copyright © 2009 Massachusetts Medical Society. Reprinted with permission from Massachusetts Medical Society.

Excerpt from "Noblesse Oblige? Social Status and Economic Inequality Maintenance among Politicians." Kraus, MW, Callaghan B (2014). PLoS ONE 9(1): e85293. doi: 10.1371/journal.pone.0085293.

Excerpt from "No Rest for the Weary: Migrating Songbirds Keep Their Wits without Sleep." (2004) PLoS Biol 2(7): e221. doi:10.1371/journal.pbio.0020221.

"Report Cards Give Up A's and B's for 4s and 3s." From *The New York Times,* March 24 © 2009 The New York Times. All rights reserved. Used by permission and protected by the Copyright Laws of the United States. The printing, copying, redistribution, or retransmission of this Content without express written permission is prohibited.

Excerpt from "A Sensory-Motor Control Model of Animal Flight Explains Why Bats Fly Differently in Light Versus Dark." Bar NS, Skogestad S, Marçal JM, Ulanovsky N, Yovel Y (2015). PLoS Biol 13(1): e1002046. doi:10.1371/journal.pbio.1002046.

Excerpt from "Bring on the Hipsters: Gentrification is good for the poor." © The Economist Newspaper Limited, London.

Excerpt from "Identifying the Volcanic Eruption Depicted in a Neolithic Painting at Çatalhöyük, Central Anatolia, Turkey. Schmitt AK, Danišík M, Aydar E, Şen E, Ulusoy İ, Lovera OM (2014). PLoS ONE 9(1): e84711. doi:10.1371/journal.pone.0084711.

Reprinted by permission from Macmillian Publishers Ltd: *Nature News,* "Where in the world could the first CRISPR baby be born?" Ledford, Heidi, Vol. 526, No. 7573, (C) 2015.

Excerpt from "It's the Thought That Counts," Belk, Russell W. (C) 1976. Reprinted with permission from the author.

"Fracking's Future" originally appeared in the January-February 2013 issue of Harvard Magazine (115:3; 24-27). Permission granted by the authors: McElroy, Michael B. and Lu, Xi.

"Unchecked Fracking Threatens Health, Water Supplies." © 2015. Reprinted with permission from the Natural Resources Defense Council.

"The Current Political World-View, Education and Alienation," Murphy, John W. and Pardeck, John T. *International Journal of Adolescence and Youth,* Vol. 3, No. 1-2, 1991. Excerpt reprinted by permission of the publisher (Taylor & Francis Ltd, http://www.tandfonline.com).

Excerpt from "Processed foods: contributions to nutritions." Republished with permission of American Society for Nutrition, from *The American Journal of Clinical Nutrition,* Weaver, Connie M.; Dwyer, Johanna, Fulgoni, Victor L.; King, Janet C.; Leveille, Gilbert A.; MacDonald, Ruth S.; Ordovas, Jose; Schnakenberg, David, Vol. 99, No. 6, 2014; permission conveyed through Copyright Clearance Center, Inc.

Excerpt from "Big Food, Food Systems, and Global Health." Stuckler D, Nestle M (2012). PLoS Med 9(6): e1001242. doi:10.1371/journal.pmed.1001242.

Excerpt from "Hey, What about the 24th?" From Slate, May 2 © 2008 The Slate Group. All rights reserved. Used by permission and protected by the Copyright Laws of the United States. The printing, copying, redistribution, or retransmission of this Content without express written permission is prohibited.

"Arctic Sea Ice: What, Why, and What Next" originally appeared as a guest blog on Scientific American's website, September 21, 2012. Permission granted by the author, Naam, Ramez.

"Forcing Gas Out of Rock With Water," originally published on the National Geographic website by Marianne Lavelle, October 23, 2010. Reprinted with permission.

"Like in Humans, Genes Drive Half of Chimp Intelligence, Study Finds," originally published on the National Geographic website by Virginia Hughes, July 12, 2014. Reprinted with permission.

"Ecosystem experiment reveals benefits of natural and simulated beaver dams to a threatened population of steelhead (Oncorhynchus mykiss)." Nicholaas Bouwes, Nicholas Weber, Chris E. Jordan, W. Carl Saunders, Ian A. Tattam, Carol Volk, Joseph M. Wheaton & Michael M. Pollock. Scientific Reports 6, Article number: 28581 (2016). doi:10.1038/srep28581. This article has been abridged from its original format.

"The F.D.A.'s Blatant Failure on Food," from The New York Times, July 30 © 2014 The New York Times. All rights reserved. Used by permission and protected by the Copyright Laws of the United States. The printing, copying, redistribution, or retransmission of this Content without express written permission is prohibited.

June 4, 1945 speech from Winston Churchill reproduced with permission of Curtis Brown, London on behalf of the Estate of Winston S. Churchill. Copyright © The Estate of Winston S. Churchill.

Excerpt taken from "Why Socialism?" by Albert Einstein in *Monthly Review* vol. 1, no. 1, May 1949; reprinted with permission by *Monthly Review.*

"Has the U.S. Really Reached an Epic Turning Point in Energy?" originally published on the National Geographic website by Wendy Koch, February 4, 2016. Reprinted with permission.

"Balance as bias: global warming and the US prestige press," reprinted from Global Environmental Change, Volume 14, Issue 2, Maxwell T Boykoff and Jules M Boykoff, pages 101–194, Copyright 2004, with permission from Elsevier.

"Sustainable Earth: Water" originally published on the National Geographic website by Brian Handwerk. Reprinted with permission.

"Food: How Altered," originally published on the National Geographic website by Wendy Koch, February 4, 2016. Reprinted with permission.

Excerpt from "Some Salt with Your Statin, Professor?" © 2014 Malcolm Macleod. PLoS Biol 12(1): e1001768. doi:10.1371/journal.pbio.1001768.

"Reclaiming Our (Real) Lives From Social Media," from The New York Times, July 17 © 2014 The New York Times. All rights reserved. Used by permission and protected by the Copyright Laws of the United States. The printing, copying, redistribution, or retransmission of this Content without express written permission is prohibited.

Excerpt(s) from MY LIFE ON THE ROAD by Gloria Steinem, copyright © 2015 by Gloria Steinem. Used by permission of Random House, an imprint and division of Penguin Random House LLC. All rights reserved. Any third party use of this material, outside of this publication, is prohibited. Interested parties must apply directly to Penguin Random House LLC for permission.

"Stanford researchers uncover patterns in how scientists lie about their data," by Bjorn Carey, originally published by Stanford University, and retrieved from the following website on October 4, 2017: http://news.stanford.edu/2015/11/16/fraud-science-papers-111615/. Text used with permission of Stanford University and may not be reproduced without their permission, © 2017.

"The Story of YInMn Blue," originally published by Mas Subramanian, Joseph Tang, and Oregon State University, and retrieved from the following website on October 4, 2017: http://chemistry.oregonstate.edu/content/story-yinmn-blue. Text used with permission of the authors and may not be reproduced without their permission, © 2017.

"Zombie ant fungi 'know' brains of their hosts," originally published on August 22, 2014, by Chuck Gill, Penn State College of Agricultural Sciences, and retrieved from the following website on November 17, 2017: http://news.psu.edu/story/323688/2014/08/22/research/zombie-ant-fungi-know-brains-their-hosts. Text used with permission of the author and may not be reproduced without his permission, © 2017.

**Editorial**

Rob Franek, Editor-in-Chief
Casey Cornelius, Chief Product Officer
Mary Beth Garrick, Executive Director of Production
Craig Patches, Production Design Manager
Selena Coppock, Managing Editor
Meave Shelton, Senior Editor
Colleen Day, Editor
Sarah Litt, Editor
Aaron Riccio, Editor
Orion McBean, Associate Editor

**Random House Publishing Team**

Tom Russell, VP, Publisher
Alison Stoltzfus, Publishing Director
Jake Eldred, Associate Managing Editor
Ellen Reed, Production Manager
Suzanne Lee, Designer

Editor: Aaron Riccio
Production Editors: Liz Rutzel and Jim Melloan
Production Artist: Maurice Kessler

Printed in the United States of America on partially recycled paper.

10  9  8  7  6  5  4  3  2  1

2019 Edition

# Acknowledgments

This edition would not have been possible without the extraordinary talent of and tireless effort by Amy Minster, Elizabeth Owens, and Alice Swan.

Special thanks to Brian Becker, Chris Chimera, Anne Goldberg, Jim Havens, Bobby Hood, Tony Krupp, Spencer LeDoux, Aaron Lindh, Stefan Maisnier, Leah Murnane, Kay Robinson, and Steve Voigt for their outstanding contributions to this title.

Many thanks also to Chris Aylward, Zoe Gannon, Anne Goldberg, Cat Healey, Douglas McLemore, Sara Soriano, Jess Thomas, and Christina Torturo for their invaluable input into the development and review of the content in this title.

Thanks to John Berry, Ian Brown, Lori DesRochers, Jay Hilsenbeck, Krissi Leslie, Lindsay Maxwell, Michelle McCannon, Scott O'Neal, Ian Persits, Rebecca Scott, Tyle Stelzig, and Susan Swinford for their contributions to this project.

The Princeton Review would also like to recognize the sharp eyes and dedicated attention brought to this project by our outstanding production team of Liz Rutzel, Jim Melloan, and Maurice Kessler.

With this book, we honor Nicole-Henriette Pirnie, whose enduring vivacity will live on through all the instructors she trained and all the students she mentored here at The Princeton Review.

# Contents

# Get More (Free) Content

**1** Go to **PrincetonReview.com/cracking.**

**2** Enter the following ISBN for your book: 9781524757878.

**3** Answer a few simple questions to set up an exclusive Princeton Review account. (If you already have one, you can just log in.)

**4** Click the "Student Tools" button, also found under "My Account" from the top toolbar. You're all set to access your bonus content!

## Need to report a potential **content** issue?

Contact **EditorialSupport@review.com**.
Include:

- full title of the book
- ISBN number
- page number

## Need to report a **technical** issue?

Contact **TPRStudentTech@review.com** and provide:

- your full name
- email address used to register the book
- full book title and ISBN
- computer OS (Mac/PC) and browser (Firefox, Safari, etc.)

## Once you've registered, you can...

- Take a full-length practice SAT and/or ACT

- Get valuable advice about the college application process, including tips for writing a great essay and where to apply for financial aid

- If you're still choosing between colleges, use our searchable rankings of *The Best 382 Colleges* to find out more information about your dream school

- Download additional bubble sheets and score conversion tables

- Check to see if there have been any corrections or updates to this edition

# Chapter 1
# Your Guide to
# Getting the Most
# Out Of This Book

## WHAT'S INSIDE

Welcome to *10 Practice Tests for the SAT*. As you've probably already guessed, his book contains ten full-length practice tests for the SAT, which we at The Princeton Review have created based off the information released by the College Board. We've rigorously analyzed available tests, and our content development teams have tirelessly worked to ensure that our material accurately reflects what you will see in terms of design, structure, style, and most importantly, content on test day. We continually evaluate the data on each question to ensure validity and to refine the level of difficulty within each test to match that of the SAT even more closely, and you shouldn't hesitate to reach out to us at EditorialSupport@review.com if you feel something's amiss.

We are confident that if you work through these tests and evaluate your performance with our comprehensive explanations, you'll improve the skills that you need to score higher on the SAT. Use the included score-conversion tables to help you to assess and track your overall performance so that you get the most out of your test-prep, as well as in-depth explanations that not only explain how to get the right answer but also why the other choices are incorrect. Through careful self-assessment, you can correct any recurring mistakes, as well as identify any weaknesses or gaps in knowledge that you can then focus your attention on studying.

**What Is The Princeton Review?**

The Princeton Review is the nation's most popular test-preparation company. After thirty years in the business, our goal is to help students everywhere crack the SAT and a bunch of other standardized tests, including the PSAT and ACT as well as graduate-level exams like the GRE and GMAT. We offer courses and private tutoring for all of the major standardized tests, and we publish a series of books to help in your search for the right school. If you would like more information about how The Princeton Review can help you, go to PrincetonReview.com or call 800-2-Review.

## HOW TO USE THIS BOOK

Each test is laid out as you'll encounter it on the SAT. While we recommend that you take each test in full, in accordance with the allotted times, and under conditions similar to those that you'll face on the day of the examination, you're welcome to focus on specific sections on which you'd like more practice.

Don't forget to carefully review our detailed explanations! Whether you get a question right or not, its explanation is packed full of our powerful SAT strategies and techniques, and might help you to save time on future questions, or to clarify where you might have gotten a right answer for the wrong reason.

## WHEN YOU TAKE A TEST

Here are some suggestions for working through this book:

1. Keep track of your performance. Whether you're working through individual sections or taking each test as a whole, be sure to score yourself with the diagnostic tables beginning on page 957. Include the time and date with each entry so that you can track your progress.

2. The SAT is a timed test. You may be a star test taker when you have all the time in the world to mull over the questions, but can you perform as well when the clock is ticking? Timing yourself will ensure you are prepared for the constraints of the actual test, just as our strategy-filled explanations can help you to discover faster methods for solving questions.

3. Don't cram it all in at once. It's hard enough to concentrate through-out one SAT—don't burn yourself out by taking multiple tests in a row. You wouldn't run two marathons back-to-back, so why treat your brain (which is like a muscle) in that way? Give yourself at least a couple of months before your anticipated "real" test date so that you can learn from any mistakes that were made on these practice tests.

4. Accordingly, take time to analyze your performance between tests. As you actively review your work, your mind will be subtly taking notes and tweaking the way it handles future questions of a similar nature, shaving seconds off its processing time as it grows more accustomed to particular wordings or presentations.

## Filling In Answers

It's not enough to get the right answer on the SAT quickly—you also have to accurately bubble it into a separate scantron sheet, and a surprisingly large number of mistakes can be made at this point, especially if you're skipping over certain questions along the way. To that end, we've included sample scantrons at the end of each test, which you can rip out of the book so that you get into the habit of rapidly transferring answers from the test itself to the scantron. (We've also included this in your online student tools, in case you'd rather print out a fresh copy.)

The SAT also includes Student-Produced Responses (grid-ins) for the two math sections. We've replicated those on the scantrons, so that you can practice correctly filling them in now. A version of the following directions should appear on the test itself, but rather than waste valuable time reading it later, take a moment to familiarize yourself with it now.

**Directions:** A Student-Produced Response question requires you to solve the problem and enter your answer by marking the circles in the special grid, as shown in the examples below. You may use any available space for scratch work.

Answer: $\frac{7}{12}$

Write answer in boxes. → 7 / 1 2 ← Fraction line

Grid in result. → 

Answer: 2.5

2 . 5 ← Decimal point

Answer: 201
Either position is correct.

2 0 1   2 0 1

**Note:** You may start your answers in any column, space permitting. Columns not needed should be left blank.

- Mark no more than one circle in any column.

- Because the answer document will be machine-scored, **you will receive credit only if the circles are filled in correctly.**

- Although not required, it is suggested that you write your answer in the boxes at the top of the columns to help you fill in the circles accurately.

- Some problems may have more than one correct answer. In such cases, grid only one answer.

- No question has a negative answer.

- **Mixed numbers** such as $3\frac{1}{2}$ must be gridded as

  3.5 or 7/2. (If 3 1 / 2 is gridded, it will be

  interpreted as $\frac{31}{2}$, not $3\frac{1}{2}$.)

- **Decimal Answers:** If you obtain a decimal answer with more digits than the grid can accommodate, it may be either rounded or truncated, but it must fill the entire grid. For example, if you obtain an answer such as 0.6666..., you should record your result as .666 or .667. **A less accurate value such as .66 or .67 will be scored as incorrect.**

Acceptable ways to grid $\frac{2}{3}$ are:

2 / 3   . 6 6 6   . 6 6 7

# GOOD LUCK!

We know that the SAT may seem intimidating at first glance—but then again, after using this book, you'll be taking it on at tenth or eleventh glance, so you're headed in the right direction. Also, as you prepare, whether you're stressed or relaxed, remember this key point:

**The SAT doesn't measure the stuff that matters.** It measures neither intelligence nor the depth and breadth of what you're learning in high school. It doesn't predict college grades as well as your high school grades do, and many colleges know there is more to you as a student—and a person—than how you fare on a single four-hour test administration on a random Saturday, Sunday, or Wednesday morning.

This is a high-stakes test, and you should absolutely work hard and prepare. But don't treat it like it's some mythical monster or world-ending catastrophe. It's just a test, and we at The Princeton Review know tests. We're here for you every step of the way.

# Chapter 2
# What You Need to
# Know for the SAT

# GENERAL INFORMATION ABOUT THE SAT

Let's take a moment to discuss some SAT facts. Some of them may surprise you.

**Wait, *Who* Writes This Test?**
You may be surprised to learn that the people who write SAT test questions are NOT necessarily teachers or college professors. The people who write the SAT are professional test writers, not superhuman geniuses, so you can beat them at their own game.

## Who Writes the SAT?

Even though colleges and universities make wide use of the SAT, they're not the ones who write the test. That's the job of Educational Testing Service (ETS), a nonprofit company that writes tests for college and graduate school admissions, and the College Board, the organization that decides how the tests will be administered and used.

They've changed the SAT twice in the last ten years, and they've admitted that students can and should prepare for the test, which means that the test *can* be beaten, and as they say, practice helps to make perfect.

## What's on the SAT?

**"Optional" Is as Optional Does**
Though the SAT refers to the essay as optional, there are some colleges that may require it. Before planning your test-day strategy, make sure you've researched each of the colleges you plan on applying to, and take the essay only if you have to.

The SAT is 3 hours long, or 3 hours and 50 minutes long if you choose to take the "optional" essay. It includes four tests (and the essay).

- Reading Test: 65 minutes, 52 questions
- 10-minute break
- Writing and Language Test: 35 minutes, 44 questions
- Math Test (No Calculator): 25 minutes, 20 questions
- 5-minute break
- Math Test (Calculator): 55 minutes, 38 questions
- 2-minute break
- Essay; 50 minutes, 1 prompt

With the exception of the open-ended essay prompt and a few grid-in problems in the math section, everything else is multiple-choice, with four options for each question. Here's a brief rundown of what to expect.

## Reading Test

Your score on the Evidence-Based Reading and Writing section of the SAT is comprised of your scores on the Reading Test and the Writing and Language Test. The Reading Test is 65 minutes long and consists of 52 questions, all of which are passage-based and multiple-choice. Passages may be paired with informational graphics, such as charts or graphs, and there will also be a series of questions based on a pair of passages. The selected passages will be from previously published works in the areas of world literature, history/social studies, and science. Questions based on science passages may ask you to analyze data or hypotheses, or to read graphs, while questions about literature passages will concentrate more on literary concepts like theme, mood, and characterization. The main goal is to measure your ability to both understand words in context and find and analyze evidence.

## Writing and Language Test

The Writing and Language Test is 35 minutes long and consists of 44 questions, which are also multiple-choice and based on several passages. However, instead of asking you to analyze a passage, questions will ask you to proofread and edit the passage. That means you'll have to correct grammar and word choice and make larger changes to the organization or content of the passage.

## Math Test

You'll have a total of 80 minutes to complete the Math Test, which, as we mentioned earlier, is divided into two sections. The No-Calculator portion is 25 minutes, and has 20 questions, while the Calculator portion is 55 minutes, with 38 questions. Most questions are multiple-choice, but there are also handfuls of student-produced response questions, which are also known as grid-ins. (Instead of choosing from four answer choices, you'll have to work through a problem and then enter your answer on your answer sheet by bubbling in the appropriate numbers.) Exactly 13 of the 58 math questions will be grid-ins.

## Optional Essay

Unlike other essays you may have seen on standardized tests, this one does not require you to write about a personal experience or to argue for or against a position. Instead, you'll have to read a short passage and explain how the author effectively builds his or her argument. The test writers want to see how you comprehend an idea and demonstrate that understanding in writing, using evidence from that author's text.

**Table of Content**
If you're super curious about the content that the Math Test covers, the test developers have cryptically designated the four main areas as (1) Heart of Algebra, (2) Problem Solving and Data Analysis, (3) Passport to Advanced Math, and (4) Additional Topics in Math.

## The Experimental Section

The College Board is not straightforward with whether there will be an experimental section on the SAT, and, if so, whether any of the questions within it will actually count toward your score. One vital consideration is that only students who do not take the optional essay might find themselves facing down this fifth section. Therefore, in order to better prepare those students who may see this optional section, the tenth test in this book has an experimental section instead of an essay prompt. This way, you can be more familiar with the test structure if in fact you are one of the "lucky" ones.

One final twist: while we know, at least as of the printing of this book, that the experimental section is 20 minutes long, we also know that this section can be on reading, writing, or math. Resist the urge to peek at which one we've included with Practice Test 10; as with each of the tests in this book, you want to emulate testing conditions as closely as possible, and in this case, you're also making sure you're ready to deal with potential testing fatigue. You've got this!

## Scoring on the SAT

The SAT is scored on a scale of 400–1600, and also introduces a series of cross-test scores and subscores that analyze various proficiencies. Here's the breakdown:

- **Total score (1):** The sum of the two section scores (Evidence-Based Reading and Writing and Math), ranging from 400 to 1600
- **Section scores (2):** Evidence-Based Reading and Writing, ranging from 200–800; Math, also ranging from 200–800
- **Test scores (3):** Reading Test, Writing and Language Test, Math Test, each of which is scored on a scale from 10 to 40
- **Cross-test scores (2):** Each is scored on a scale from 10 to 40 and based on selected questions from the three tests (Reading, Writing and Language, Math):
  1) Analysis in History/Social Studies
  2) Analysis in Science
- **Subscores (7):** Each of the following receives a score from 1 to 15:
  1) Command of Evidence (Reading; Writing and Language)
  2) Words in Context (Reading; Writing and Language)
  3) Expression of Ideas (Writing and Language)
  4) Standard English Conventions (Writing and Language)
  5) Heart of Algebra (Math)
  6) Problem Solving and Data Analysis (Math)
  7) Passport to Advanced Math (Math)

**A Note on Essay Scoring**

If you choose to write the essay, you will be graded by two readers in three areas: Reading, Writing, and Analysis. You will be scored on a 2-to-8 point scale for each of the three areas.

## Scoring Tricks

You will not be penalized for wrong answers on the SAT. This means that you should always guess, even if this means choosing an answer at random. With only four answers to choose from, your odds of getting a right answer are decent, and only get better if you use Process of Elimination (POE) to eliminate an answer choice or two.

Because time is at a premium on the test, don't be shy about bubbling in a guess on a question that you don't fully understand so that you can move on to questions that you feel more confident you can answer correctly (and quickly). That said, try to indicate which questions you've done this on so that if you have time left at the end of a test, you can return to those tricky questions and try to get a few extra points.

## WHEN IS THE SAT GIVEN?

The SAT schedule for the school year is posted on the College Board website at **www.collegeboard.org**. There are two different ways to sign up for the test. You can either sign up online by going to **www.collgeboard.org** and clicking on the SAT hyperlink, or sign up through the mail with an SAT registration booklet, which may be available at your school guidance counselor's office.

Try to sign up for the SAT as soon as you know when you'll be taking the test. If you wait until the last minute to sign up, there may not be any open spots in the testing centers that are closest to you.

If you require any special accommodations while taking the test (including, but not limited to, extra time or assistance), **www.collegeboard.org** has information about applying for those. Make sure to apply early; we recommend doing so six months before you plan to take the test.

**Stay on Schedule**
Although you may take the SAT any time starting freshman year, most students take it for the first time in the spring of their junior year and possibly retake it in the fall of their senior year. In addition, you may also need to take SAT subject tests (many competitive colleges require them), so don't leave everything to the last minute. You can't take SAT and SAT Subject Tests on the same day. Sit down and plan a schedule.

# Chapter 3
# Practice Test 1

# Reading Test

## 65 MINUTES, 52 QUESTIONS

Turn to Section 1 of your answer sheet to answer the questions in this section.

---

### DIRECTIONS

Each passage or pair of passages below is followed by a number of questions. After reading each passage or pair, choose the best answer to each question based on what is stated or implied in the passage or passages and in any accompanying graphics (such as a table or graph).

---

### Questions 1–10 are based on the following passage.

This passage is excerpted from Mary Shelley's *Frankenstein*, originally published in 1818.

My journey was very melancholy. At first I wished to hurry on, for I longed to console and sympathize with my loved and sorrowing friends; but when I drew
*Line* near my native town, I slackened my progress. I could
5 hardly sustain the multitude of feelings that crowded into my mind. I passed through scenes familiar to my youth, but which I had not seen for nearly six years. How altered every thing might be during that time! One sudden and desolating change had taken place;
10 but a thousand little circumstances might have by degrees worked other alterations, which, although they were done more tranquilly, might not be the less decisive. Fear overcame me; I dared no advance, dreading a thousand nameless evils that made me
15 tremble, although I was unable to define them. I remained two days at Lausanne, in this painful state of mind. I contemplated the lake: the waters were placid; all around was calm; and the snowy mountains, 'the palaces of nature,' were not changed. By degrees the
20 calm and heavenly scene restored me, and I continued my journey towards Geneva. The road ran by the side of the lake, which became narrower as I approached my native town. I discovered more distinctly the black sides of Jura, and the bright summit of Mont
25 Blanc. I wept like a child. "Dear mountains! My own beautiful lake! How do you welcome your wanderer? Your summits are clear; the sky and lake are blue and placid. Is this to prognosticate peace, or to mock at my unhappiness?"

30 I fear, my friend, that I shall render myself tedious by dwelling on these preliminary circumstances; but they were days of comparative happiness, and I think of them with pleasure. My country, my beloved country! Who but a native can tell the delight I took
35 in again beholding thy streams, thy mountains, and, more than all, thy lovely lake! Yet, as I drew nearer home, grief and fear again overcame me. Night also closed around; and when I could hardly see the dark mountains, I felt still more gloomily. The picture
40 appeared a vast and dim scene of evil, and I foresaw obscurely that I was destined to become the most wretched of human beings. Alas! I prophesied truly, and failed only in one single circumstance, that in all the misery I imagined and dreaded, I did not conceive
45 the hundredth part of the anguish I was destined to endure. It was completely dark when I arrived in the environs of Geneva; the gates of the town were already shut; and I was obliged to pass the night at Secheron, a village at the distance of half a league from the
50 city. The sky was serene; and, as I was unable to rest, I resolved to visit the spot where my poor William had been murdered. As I could not pass through the town, I was obliged to cross the lake in a boat to arrive at Plainpalais. During this short voyage I saw the
55 lightning playing on the summit of Mont Blanc in the most beautiful figures. The storm appeared to approach rapidly, and, on landing, I ascended a low hill, that I

> CONTINUE →

might observe its progress. It advanced; the heavens were clouded, and I soon felt the rain coming slowly in
60 large drops, but its violence quickly increased.

While I watched the tempest, so beautiful yet terrific, I wandered on with a hasty step. This noble war in the sky elevated my spirits; I clasped my hands, and exclaimed aloud, "William, dear angel! This is
65 thy funeral, this thy dirge!" As I said these words, I perceived in the gloom a figure which stole from behind a clump of trees near me; I stood fixed, gazing intently: I could not be mistaken. A flash of lightning illuminated the object, and discovered its shape
70 plainly to me; its gigantic stature, and the deformity of its aspect more hideous than belongs to humanity, instantly informed me that it was the wretch, the filthy daemon, to whom I had given life. What did he there? Could he be (I shuddered at the conception) the
75 murderer of my brother? No sooner did that idea cross my imagination, than I became convinced of its truth; my teeth chattered, and I was forced to lean against a tree for support. The figure passed me quickly, and I lost it in the gloom.

## 1

Which choice best describes the developmental pattern of the passage?

A) A lighthearted description of an adventure

B) A dramatic response to a request for help

C) A profound analysis of an ancient curse

D) A melancholy recounting of a doomed homecoming

## 2

Which choice best describes what happens in the passage?

A) One character returns home to avenge the death of his brother.

B) One character fears his future in the hometown he left.

C) One character is afraid to return to a city haunted by an unknown monster.

D) One character worries that he won't be welcome at home.

## 3

Which emotion does the narrator most feel?

A) He feels joy at returning home.

B) He feels antagonism for the daemon.

C) He feels dread concerning his fate.

D) He feels sorrow over William's death.

## 4

Which choice provides the best evidence for the answer to the previous question?

A) Lines 34–36 ("Who but . . . lake")

B) Lines 42–46 ("I prophesied . . . endure")

C) Lines 58–60 ("It advanced . . . increased")

D) Lines 74–75 ("Could he . . . brother")

## 5

As used in line 28, "placid" most nearly means

A) palatial.

B) dull.

C) peaceful.

D) divine.

## 6

The main purpose of the first paragraph is to

A) represent a journey.

B) embellish an emotion.

C) provide a context.

D) establish a mood.

CONTINUE

**7**

Why does the narrator mention "a thousand little circumstances" (line 10)?

A) He fears a natural disaster and its aftermath.

B) He dreads the effects of a devastating incident.

C) He knows he could have stopped a tragedy.

D) He has incited a revolution to take down the government.

**8**

Which of the following provides the best evidence for the answer to the previous question?

A) Line 8 ("How altered . . . time")

B) Lines 9–13 ("One sudden . . . decisive")

C) Lines 50–52 ("The sky . . . murdered")

D) Lines 64–65 ("William, dear . . . dirge")

**9**

In the passage, the narrator addresses the tempest with

A) awe, but not fear.

B) ebullience, but not rage.

C) disconsolation, but not anger.

D) insanity, but not regret.

**10**

As used in line 66, "stole" most nearly means

A) loomed.

B) pinched.

C) wrapped.

D) displaced.

CONTINUE

**Questions 11–20 are based on the following passage.**

This passage is an excerpt from Howard Gardner, *Art, Mind and Brain*. © 1982 by Basic Books.

Twenty years ago psychology seemed a rather remote and sterile area to individuals interested in the full and creative use of the mind. The field harbored a trio of uninviting specializations. There was academic psychology, featuring the use of contrived laboratory apparatus to study the perception of visual illusions or the memorization of long lists of nonsense syllables. Such lines of study bore little evident relationship to human beings engaged in thought. There was behaviorism, the approach that emerged from work with rats and pigeons. Behaviorists claimed that we act in the way we do because we are reinforced for doing so and, given their focus on overt activity, these scholars denied inner life—no thought, no fantasies, no aspirations. Finally, there was psychoanalysis, which offered not only a controversial method of treatment but also an overarching theory of human nature. While psychoanalysis had a grandeur and depth that eluded both academic psychology and behaviorism, it strongly accentuated human personality and unconscious problem-solving.

The cognitive revolution came in two parts. First, there was the frank recognition that one could—one must—take seriously human mental processes, including thinking, problem-solving, and creating. Study of the mind once again became a proper scientific undertaking. Second, there was the demonstration by several researchers that human thought processes were characterized by considerable regularity and structure. Not all of this cogitation took place in full view, nor could such cognitive processes always be either related to external stimuli or confirmed by introspection. But there was structure to thought processes, a structure the careful analyst could help lay bare.

Many of us who were studying the behavioral sciences in the 1960s were swept up—and have remained inspired—by this revolution. For some, the appeal lay in computer programming and artificial intelligence—the design of machines that display intelligence. For others, the thrill came in conducting careful laboratory experiments in which one could trace, on a millisecond-by-millisecond basis, an individual's mental process as he carried out a multiplication problem, reasoned through a logical syllogism, or rotated an image of geometrical form in his head. Still others took roads that went through pedagogy, through anthropology, or through the neurosciences. In my own case, I found especially appealing the approach to the mind put forth by structuralists working in the cognitive regions of several social sciences.

In the opening set of essays I lay out the principal assumption of this structuralist approach as it is exemplified by the developmental psychologist Jean Piaget, the linguist Noam Chomsky, and the anthropologist Claude Levi-Strauss. These thinkers share a belief that the mind operates according to the specifiable rules—often unconscious ones—and that these can be ferreted out and made explicit by the systematic examination of human language, action, and problem-solving. There are many intriguing differences among their approaches as well, and I review several of these: still, one finds throughout a surprisingly (and reassuringly) common vision of what the human mind is like and how it can best be described for scientific purposes.

The structuralist approach to the mind has limitations. Those that are more germane, given my own concern with artistic knowledge, derive from the essentially closed nature of structuralist systems. Though creative thought has not escaped their attention, each of the major cognitive structuralists views the options of human thought as in some way preordained, limited in advance. This makes their work especially problematic for a study of mind where the major focus falls on innovation and creation, as in the fashioning of original works of art.

To my mind the limitation implicit in the standard structuralist stance can be circumscribed by the recognition of one special feature of human thought—its ability to create and sponsor commerce through the use of various kinds of symbol systems. These symbol systems—these codes of meaning—are the vehicles through which thought takes place: by their very nature they are creative, open systems. Through the use of symbols the human mind, operating according to the structuralist principles, can create, revise, transform, and re-create wholly fresh products, systems and even worlds of meaning.

CONTINUE →

**11**

The main purpose of the passage is to

A) review a set of essays on structuralism and creativity.

B) convince scientists to abandon behaviorist thought.

C) emphasize the limitations present in psychology.

D) present the author's view that structuralism allows for creativity.

**12**

The central claim of the passage is that

A) psychology has evolved since the 1960s before which it was too sedate and impractical for modern scientists.

B) traditional structuralist principles can allow for the possibility of human creativity.

C) behaviorists are limited in their scientific processes and have preordained views that humans act largely on their operant conditioning.

D) the author's opinions on creativity are revolutionary and supported by research in traditional psychology.

**13**

The author describes the different branches of psychology throughout the passage mainly to

A) guide the reader through a complete historic progression of a science.

B) establish his prominent and novel role within the psychological community.

C) highlight a difference that makes structuralism inferior to behaviorism.

D) show how the revolution of the 1960s affected psychology.

**14**

Gardner indicates that the cognitive revolution he describes in the passage was

A) a motivation for the author's exploration of creativity and structuralism.

B) a pertinent factor in revitalizing a dying field of science.

C) beneficial for interjecting thoughtful scientists back into the field of psychology.

D) more effective than previous changes to the perspective of psychologists.

**15**

Which choice provides the best evidence for the answer to the previous question?

A) Lines 8–9 ("Such lines . . . thought")

B) Lines 27–30 ("Second, there . . . structure")

C) Lines 36–38 ("Many of . . . revolution")

D) Lines 38–41 ("For some . . . intelligence")

**16**

The author characterizes the branch of psychology that became popular after the cognitive revolution mentioned in line 22 as using both

A) problem-solving and creating.

B) meticulousness and mathematics.

C) regularity and structure.

D) fantasy and aspiration.

**17**

Which lines best support the previous answer?

A) Lines 11–15 ("Behaviorists claimed . . . aspirations")

B) Lines 23–26 ("First, there . . . creating")

C) Lines 41–47 ("For others . . . head")

D) Lines 64–67 ("still, one . . . purposes")

**CONTINUE** ➡

According to the passage, the author references Jean Piaget, Noam Chomsky, and Claude Levi-Strauss because they

A) represent different approaches to a unified belief about the mind.

B) present work that is inherently problematic when used in psychological discussions.

C) are psychologists who support his assumptions about structuralism.

D) published works that do not support the author's opinion on creativity.

The "original works of art" mentioned in line 78 mainly serve to emphasize how

A) admiring of artistic knowledge and endeavors the author is.

B) distorted the views of the structural psychologists are.

C) restricted the traditional structuralists' views on creativity are.

D) closed-minded and limited psychology is regarding artistic ability.

Which choice most closely captures the meaning of the "symbol systems" referred to in line 84?

A) Thought processes

B) Problematic methods

C) Structured principles

D) Representative expressions

**CONTINUE**

**Questions 21–31 are based on the following passages.**

Passage 1 is adapted from Lee Billings, "At Pluto, the End of a Beginning." © July 2015 by *Scientific American*. Passage 2 is adapted from Caleb A. Scharf, "A New Billion-Mile Journey for New Horizons." © August 2015 by *Scientific American*. Lee Billings is a science journalist. Caleb Scharf is the Director of Astrobiology at Columbia University.

**Passage 1**

Early this morning, if all has gone well, the first golden age of interplanetary exploration will have come to a close. At 7:49 Eastern time, NASA's New
Line
5 Horizons spacecraft was slated to reach its primary target, Pluto and its moons, concluding what some call the preliminary reconnaissance of the known solar system.

Though it was conceived in the late 1980s, New Horizons wasn't launched until 2006, after long years
10 of delays, redesigns, and even near-death cancellations. Its unlikely five-billion-kilometer voyage to Pluto has been the work of decades. And yet today, at the climax of its mission, the spacecraft was expected to traverse the expanse of Pluto in less than three
15 minutes, whizzing 12,500 kilometers above the surface at nearly 50,000 kilometers per hour. From the start, the spacecraft was custom-built for speed. Carrying enough fuel to crash into orbit at Pluto would have made New Horizons too bulky, expensive, and slow to
20 even launch in the first place, so instead it will flyby and continue outward, on an endless journey into interstellar night.

During its brief close encounter, New Horizons will be too busy gathering data to immediately phone
25 home, instead using those precious moments to scrutinize the planet with a suite of seven instruments all running on a nightlight's share of electricity. Mission planners will only learn of the flyby's success later tonight, via a radio signal. Or, they could learn of
30 its failure by hearing nothing—the spacecraft has an estimated 1 in 10,000 chance of suffering a destructive high-speed collision with debris while passing through the Plutonian system.

Presuming New Horizons' flyby is successful, its
35 confirmatory signal traveling sunward at the speed of light will reach Earth some 4.5 hours after being transmitted, and is expected to arrive at 8:53 PM. Though the primary encounter is best measured in minutes and hours, the slow data-transmission rate

40 imposed by such vast distances ensures that New Horizons will be beaming its archived images home well into 2017.

**Passage 2**

What do you do when you've flown 3 billion miles through interplanetary space?
45 You keep going.

Although NASA's New Horizons mission has only just begun to transmit the bulk of the detailed scientific data from its history-making encounter with the Pluto-Charon system (at an excruciatingly slow 2 kilobits per
50 second) the spacecraft team has been hard at work on a critical, and time-sensitive, decision.

It had long been hoped that New Horizons would be able to deploy its instruments to study further objects in the Kuiper belt. But back in early 2014 it
55 wasn't clear that astronomers and planetary scientists were going to be able to find any suitable candidates within the range of trajectories that the mission—with its limited on-board fuel resources—could reasonably adjust to. Despite searching with Earth-bound
60 telescopes it was clear that our understanding of the number of objects smaller than Pluto (but still large enough to study) was incomplete, as candidates were in short supply.

Using the Hubble Space Telescope in the summer
65 of 2014, in what was a bit of a last-ditch attempt, there was huge relief as just five plausible targets finally revealed themselves, with two later confirmed to be good for an intercept.

The first of these, called PT1 (potential target one)
70 or more officially 2014 MU69, has now been chosen as the next goal for New Horizons.

This object is thought to be at most 30 miles across —akin to a cometary nucleus on steroids—and barely 1% the size of Pluto. In other words, it's an entirely
75 different beast than Pluto, but it may be the kind of body that helped form Pluto itself some 4.5 billion years ago, and it's within reach for New Horizons at a mere billion miles further along the interplanetary road.

CONTINUE

**21**

In line 10, the author of Passage 1 mentions "delays, redesigns, and even near-death cancellations" primarily to

A) indicate why the ship was built for speed.

B) predict that not all may go well with the mission.

C) express concern that the ship may crash.

D) explain the period of time between the plan and its execution.

**22**

The author of Passage 1 indicates that the flyby over Pluto could have which outcome?

A) Scientists could receive data beginning at 7:49 Eastern time.

B) Scientists could receive no data from the ship.

C) Scientists could learn of the mission's failure through a radio signal.

D) Scientists could receive data after a delay of 3 minutes.

**23**

Which choice provides the best evidence for the answer to the previous question?

A) Lines 3–7 ("At 7:49 . . . system")

B) Lines 28–29 ("Mission planners . . . signal")

C) Lines 29–33 ("Or, they . . . system")

D) Lines 34–37 ("Presuming New . . . 8:53 PM")

**24**

As used in line 26, "suite" most nearly means

A) jacket.

B) room.

C) array.

D) candy.

**25**

What function does the discussion of the measurement of the primary encounter in lines 38–39 serve in Passage 1?

A) It supports a claim made earlier in the text.

B) It undermines an assumption made in the previous paragraph.

C) It emphasizes the relativity of time in measuring space.

D) It highlights the brevity of the encounter vs. the slow pace of the documentation.

**26**

The central claim of Passage 2 is that New Horizons has started to transmit information about Pluto but

A) it will then continue on an endless journey into night.

B) it is also on the way to its next observation.

C) plans for its next task need to be decided upon soon.

D) the preliminary reconnaissance of our solar system is complete.

**27**

As used in line 53, "deploy" most nearly means

A) mimic.

B) utilize.

C) release.

D) negate.

CONTINUE

**28**

Which statement best describes the relationship between the passages?

A) Passage 2 expresses concern about the dangers mentioned in Passage 1.

B) Passage 2 revises the interpretation of events described in Passage 1.

C) Passage 2 describes the next chapter in the story depicted in Passage 1.

D) Passage 2 provides qualified support for the successes celebrated in Passage 1.

**29**

The author of Passage 2 would most likely respond to the discussion of New Horizons' continued journey in lines 21–22, Passage 1, by claiming that the journey

A) will involve at least one further stop.

B) will not take place on a literal road.

C) will be endless.

D) will take a long time before return is possible.

**30**

Which choice provides the best evidence for the answer to the previous question?

A) Lines 46–51 ("Although NASA's . . . decision")

B) Lines 52–54 ("It had . . . belt")

C) Lines 69–71 ("The first . . . Horizons")

D) Lines 74–79 ("In other . . . road")

**31**

Which statement about New Horizons' journey is true about both passages?

A) Passage 1 contains an exaggeration, while Passage 2 contains an ironic understatement.

B) Passage 1 utilizes a metaphor, while Passage 2 relies on strict realism.

C) Passage 1 relies on allegory, while Passage 2 makes use of personification.

D) Passage 1 presents a history, while Passage 2 presents an anecdote.

**CONTINUE**

**Questions 32–42 are based on the following passage and supplementary material.**

This passage is adapted from Kelvin F. H. Lui and Alan C.N. Wong, "Does Media Multitasking Always Hurt? A Positive Correlation Between Multitasking and Multisensory Integration." © 2012 by Psychonomic Society, Inc.

Humans often engage in multitasking—that is, performing more than one task simultaneously or in rapid alternation. We can effortlessly talk to each other while walking and watch television while eating. Certain multitasking situations are more challenging because the tasks involved are more difficult or they concurrently engage overlapping processes and, thus, interfere with each other more. Talking on cell phones while driving is a good example. Sometimes, such difficulties can have serious consequences.

One way that modern technology has transformed human living styles is through the invention and popularization of various media of communication and interaction, including radio, television, telephone and text messaging, video games, computers, and the Internet. Media multitasking has thus grown into a popular phenomenon and even a way of life, especially among young people. The high accessibility of computers, in particular, has cultivated obsessive multitasking, due to the ease of switching between instant messaging, music, Web surfing, e-mail, online videos, computer-based games, computer-based applications, and so forth.

The immediate effects of media multitasking on one's memory, learning, and other cognitive functions have been a focus of recent research. It was found that watching TV while doing homework decreased participants' performance on the recognition of TV content. Besides, Furnham and Bradley found detrimental effects of background music on participants' performance in various cognitive tasks. Armstrong and Chung showed a negative effect of background television during science article reading on subsequent recall and recognition. Similarly, reading and watching video simultaneously impaired participants' performance on the reading task. Moreover, Hembrooke and Gay found that opening laptops and engaging in media multitasking behaviors during a lecture impaired students' memory for lecture contents.

Research also has examined the chronic effects of media multitasking. Kirschner and Karpinski found that heavy Facebook users reported having lower grade point averages (GPAs) and suggested the possible deleterious effect of simultaneously using Facebook with other activities. Besides, the amount of time spent on instant messaging was found to be negatively correlated both with cognitive performance in lab tasks and with GPA. While these two studies assumed that Facebook usage and instant messaging often co-occur with other activities and, thus, represent multimedia usage, they did not, however, exclude the simpler possibility that Facebook usage and instant messaging simply occupy the time that could be used for studying.

A recent large-scale study compared the way in which heavy media multitaskers process information differently from those who do not. Participants completed a self-report questionnaire in their study to indicate their level of media multitasking. It was found that heavy media multitaskers performed worse than light media multitaskers in several cognitive tasks that involved working memory, selective attention to task-relevant information in visual search, and surprisingly, task switching. It was suggested that heavy media multitaskers have developed the habit of simultaneously consuming information from multiple media and, thus, "breadth-biased cognitive control." As a result, heavy media multitaskers could not precisely differentiate between important information and distractors. They readily spread their attention to different sources of information regardless of whether they were relevant to the primary task at hand. This is why they were inferior to light media multitaskers in tasks that required one to disregard irrelevant information in the environment and in memory.

An intriguing possibility, however, is that their breadth biased cognitive control will lead to better performance if a task contains some unexpected information that is important to the task at hand. When a media multitasker reads, for example, he or she may more readily detect an SMS ringtone from a mobile phone, although the ringtone does not carry information useful for the primary task of reading. In fact, situations like that may actually be more representative of what happens in real life.

CONTINUE

In this study, our aim was to measure the potential difference between high and low media multitaskers in this tendency to capture information from seemingly
90 irrelevant sources. Specifically, we accessed how much one can integrate visual and auditory information automatically, using a visual search task in the pip-and-pop paradigm. In this paradigm, participants made speeded responses to indicate which of a horizontal
95 or vertical line segment was present among a number of oblique line segments of various orientations. Both target and distractor lines in the display changed color between red and green continuously. Participants performed the same search task on both tone-
100 absent (baseline) and tone-present trials, but only in tone-present trials was each target color change accompanied by a short auditory tone (the pip).

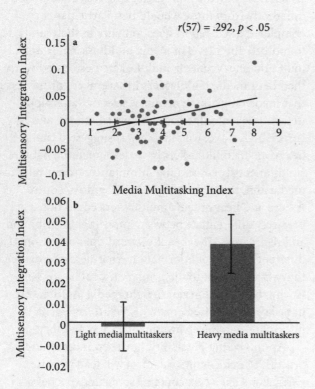

a) Scatterplot between the multisensory integration index for accuracy and the media multitasking index.

b) Multisensory integration indices for light and heavy media multitaskers. Error bars indicate standard errors of the means.

**32**

The authors most likely use the examples in lines 3–9 of the passage to highlight that

A) multitasking is usually difficult and dangerous.

B) multitasking is a fairly common occurrence.

C) students who want to increase their grades should not multitask.

D) multitasking is an instinctual habit.

**33**

In line 7, the word "engage" most nearly means

A) marry.

B) capture.

C) employ.

D) absorb.

**34**

The study authors mentioned in paragraph 3 (lines 24–40) would likely describe "media multitasking" as

A) focused.

B) disadvantageous.

C) multifaceted.

D) chronic.

**35**

The authors indicate that Kirschner and Karpinski suggest grades decreased because students

A) used a social media platform while studying.

B) performed badly on tests due to fatigue.

C) spent too much time on Messenger.

D) spent too much time on Facebook in general.

CONTINUE

**36**

Which choice provides the best evidence for the answer to the previous question?

A) Lines 26–29 ("It was . . . content")

B) Lines 42–46 ("Kirschner and . . . activities")

C) Lines 49–55 ("While these . . . studying")

D) Lines 56–58 ("A recent . . . not")

**37**

In the fifth paragraph (lines 56–76), the author indicates that, compared to heavy media multitaskers, light media multitaskers are more

A) distracted.

B) focused.

C) scholarly.

D) discriminating.

**38**

Which choice provides the best evidence for the answer to the previous question?

A) Lines 56–58 ("A recent . . . not")

B) Lines 65–68 ("It was . . . control")

C) Lines 73–76 ("This is . . . memory")

D) Lines 77–80 ("An intriguing . . . hand")

**39**

As used in line 57, "process" most nearly means

A) filter.

B) share.

C) digitize.

D) retain.

**40**

The authors refer to the pip-and-pop paradigm (lines 92–93) in order to

A) question a technique.

B) support a claim.

C) offer a clarification.

D) introduce a method.

**41**

In the graph following the passage, the line of best fit demonstrates that

A) light media multitaskers get good grades.

B) Kirschner and Karpinski's study was correct.

C) Facebook usage leads to lesser cognitive functions.

D) a weak data correlation exists in the study.

**42**

The authors of the study would likely attribute heavy media multitaskers' increased Multisensory Integration, as represented in the graph, to an ability to

A) discern important information in context.

B) spread their attention to multiple unrelated tasks.

C) display an increased level of sensitivity.

D) observe all details during a stressful event.

CONTINUE

**Questions 43–52 are based on the following passage and supplementary material.**

This passage is from Cesar A. Arias, M.D., Ph.D., and Barbara E. Murray, M.D., "Antibiotic-Resistant Bugs in the 21st Century—A Clinical Super-Challenge." © 2009 by *New England Journal of Medicine*.

In March 1942, a 33-year-old woman lay dying of streptococcal sepsis in a New Haven, Connecticut, hospital, and despite the best efforts of contemporary
Line medical science, her doctors could not eradicate her
5 bloodstream infection. Then they managed to obtain a small amount of a newly discovered substance called penicillin, which they cautiously injected into her. After repeated doses, her bloodstream was cleared of streptococci, she made a full recovery, and she went
10 on to live to the age of 90. Sixty-six years after her startling recovery, a report described a 70 year-old-man in San Francisco with endocarditis caused by vancomycin-resistant *Enterococcus faecium* (VRE). Despite the administration, for many days, of the best
15 antibiotics available for combating VRE, physicians were unable to sterilize the patient's blood, and he died still bacteremic. We have almost come full circle and arrived at a point as frightening as the preantibiotic era: for patients infected with multi-drug
20 resistant bacteria, there is no magic bullet.

It is difficult to imagine undertaking today's surgical procedures, transplantations, cancer chemotherapy, or care of the critically ill or HIV-infected without effective antimicrobial agents.
25 Bacteria are champions of evolution, and a few microbes have adapted to a point where they pose serious clinical challenges for humans. Among the gram-positive organisms, methicillin-resistant *Staphylococcus aureus* (MRSA) and *E. faecium*
30 represent the biggest therapeutic hurdles. The evolution of MRSA exemplifies the genetic adaptation of an organism into a first-class multidrug-resistant pathogen. After the introduction of penicillin and, later, methicillin, *S. aureus* quickly developed
35 resistance to the β-lactam compounds, and by 2003 more than 50% of *S. aureus* isolates recovered in U.S. hospitals were MRSA.

Then MRSA began developing resistance to glycopeptides, first evolving, through largely undefined
40 mutations, low-level resistance to vancomycin, which was associated with a thickening of the pathogen's cell walls. Such isolates were designated VISA (or GISA), for vancomycin (or glycopeptide) intermediately resistant *S. aureus*. VISA is difficult for clinical
45 laboratories to detect, but its presence is associated with the therapeutic failure of glycopeptides. The break-points for susceptibility to vanomycin have therefore been changed, screening tests for VISA have been proposed, and much debate has ensued regarding
50 the usefulness of vancymycin in the treatment of serious MRSA infections.

Next, strains of MRSA with true, high-level resistance to vancomycin (vancomycin-resistant *S. aureus* or VRSA) emerged. Such resistance is due to
55 the acquisition of the *vanA* gene cluster, originally described in enterococci. Fortunately, fewer than a dozen such isolates have been reported (mostly in Michigan), and their dissemination appears to be limited, at least for now. VRSA, like other
60 strains of health-care associated MRSA, is often resistant to multiple drugs, including clindamycin, aminoglycosides, trimethoprim-sulfamethoxazole, rifampin, and fluoroquinolones.

CONTINUE

| Antibiotic family | | | | |
|---|---|---|---|---|
| Penicillin | Aminoglycosides (including streptomycin) | Macrolides (including vancomycin) | Aminopenicillins (including methicillin) | Fluoroquinolones (including amikacin) |
| **Bacteria** **Resistance of bacteria to antibiotic family** | | | | |
| *E. faecium* | | 75% | 19% | |
| *M. tuberculosis* | | 9% | | 47% |
| *P. mirabilis* | 9% | | 22% | 28% |
| CoNS | | 63% | | 50% |
| *C. difficile* | | 3% | | |
| *P. aeruginosa* | 15% | | | 27% |
| *E. coli* | 9% | | 22% | 33% |
| *Shigella* | 56% | 14% | 78% | 0.2% |
| *S. aureus* | | | 51% | 0.8% |
| When Introduced | 1940s | | 1950s | 1960s |

**43**

Based on the passage, the authors' statement "We have almost come full circle ... for patients infected with multi-drug resistant bacteria, there is no magic bullet" (lines 17–20) implies that

A) antibiotics are no longer used to treat bacterial infections.

B) the medical sciences have finally come around to antibiotic treatments and therapies.

C) there is currently no solution for how to treat multi-drug resistant bacteria.

D) vancomycin-resistant *Enterococcus faecium* is no longer treatable.

**44**

A student claims that antibiotic use has never been 100% effective in the treatment of a bacterial infection. Which of the following statements in the passage contradicts the student's claim?

A) Lines 8–10 ("After repeated . . . 90")

B) Lines 14–17 ("Despite the . . . bacteremic")

C) Lines 33–37 ("After the . . . MRSA")

D) Lines 56–59 ("Fortunately, fewer . . . now")

**45**

The authors use the word "evolution" in lines 25 and 31 to indicate that

A) only one type of bacteria, methicillin-resistant *Staphylococcus aureus*, has demonstrated significant resistance to antibiotics.

B) multi-drug resistant bacteria was an inevitable outcome of the evolution of medical science and prescription drug development.

C) antibiotics are not effective at treating specific strains of bacteria as those strains are significantly altered from their original presentation.

D) strains of bacteria previously known to scientists have entirely disappeared and been replaced by drug-resistant versions.

**CONTINUE**

### 46

In the second paragraph (lines 21–37), what do the authors claim to be a result of antibiotic resistance?

A) The disappearance of methicillin-resistant *S. aureus* (MRSA) and *E. faecium*.

B) The creation of a "magic bullet" antibiotic to treat patients infected with multi-drug resistant bacteria.

C) A significant increase in the numbers of deaths from bacterial infection in the United States.

D) The majority of clinically observed cases of *S. aureus* were resistant to at least one antibiotic treatment.

### 47

The authors' main purpose of including the information about MRSA's glycopeptide and vancomycin resistance is to

A) review the history of medical research, specifically antibiotic development and therapy.

B) present the progression a specific bacteria demonstrated to alternate treatment options.

C) provide a list of the most common antibiotics that are used to battle certain bacteria.

D) confirm the broad resistance of *S. aureus* to all known antibiotics

### 48

The authors' use of the words "appears" and "often" in lines 58–60 in the final paragraph functions mainly to

A) confirm that the levels and types of antibiotic-resistance of MRSA and VSRA are well known.

B) counter the claim that based on clinical results antibiotic resistance is slowing for MRSA and VSRA.

C) support the authors' call for greater attention and research funding for multi-drug resistant bacterial research.

D) emphasize the lack of certainty that surrounds our existing knowledge of multi-drug resistant bacteria.

### 49

Based on the table and passage, which choice gives the correct description of penicillin?

A) Penicillin was initially introduced for medical use in the first half of the twentieth century.

B) *Streptococcal sepsis* has not developed antibiotic resistance to penicillin.

C) Fewer bacteria have demonstrated resistance to penicillin than to fluoroquinolones.

D) More bacteria have demonstrated resistance to penicillin than to amikacin.

### 50

Do the data in the table support the authors' assertion that *S. aureus* and *E. faecium* represent the biggest therapeutic hurdles?

A) Yes, because collectively they show some level of resistance to three antibiotic families, which is more than any other single bacteria listed.

B) Yes, because the highest level of resistance either bacteria exhibits is 75%, the largest percent of resistance listed.

C) No, because the lowest level of resistance either bacteria exhibits is 0.8%, the smallest percent of resistance listed.

D) No, because collectively they show some level of resistance to three antibiotic families, which is fewer than any other single bacteria listed.

**CONTINUE** ➡

According to the table, which of the following bacteria provides evidence in support of the answer to the previous question?

A) *M. tuberculosis*

B) *CoNS*

C) *Shigella*

D) *P. aeruginosa*

Based on the table, is Aminopenicillin-resistant *S. aureus* resistant to at least one member of the Fluoroquinolones family or none, and which statement made by the authors is most consistent with that data?

A) At least one; "Then MRSA . . . walls" (lines 38–42)

B) At least one; "VRSA, like . . . fluoroquinolones" (lines 59–63)

C) None; "Fortunately, fewer . . . now" (lines 56–59)

D) None; "VRSA, like . . . fluoroquinolones" (lines 59–63)

# STOP

**If you finish before time is called, you may check your work on this section only.**
**Do not turn to any other section in the test.**

# Writing and Language Test

## 35 MINUTES, 44 QUESTIONS

**Turn to Section 2 of your answer sheet to answer the questions in this section.**

---

**DIRECTIONS**

Each passage below is accompanied by a number of questions. For some questions, you will consider how the passage might be revised to improve the expression of ideas. For other questions, you will consider how the passage might be edited to correct errors in sentence structure, usage, or punctuation. A passage or a question may be accompanied by one or more graphics (such as a table or graph) that you will consider as you make revising and editing decisions.

Some questions will direct you to an underlined portion of a passage. Other questions will direct you to a location in a passage or ask you to think about the passage as a whole.

After reading each passage, choose the answer to each question that most effectively improves the quality of writing in the passage or that makes the passage conform to the conventions of standard written English. Many questions include a "NO CHANGE" option. Choose that option if you think the best choice is to leave the relevant portion of the passage as it is.

---

**Questions 1–11 are based on the following passage.**

### "Made-Up" Science

When we hear about the opinions of "ten scientists" or "ten dentists," or we hear that things are "clinically proven" or "lab-tested," for **1** example, and we might expect to be reading scientific journals. However, these phrases and statistics are well-known outside of scientific circles because they are so commonly used in a less likely place: advertising. It's not enough for, say, a shampoo to promise clean hair: it seems the only way to sell shampoo is **2** by lowering the price and offering special deals and coupons,

**1**

A) NO CHANGE

B) example, consequently we

C) example: we

D) example, we

**2**

Which provides the most relevant detail?

A) NO CHANGE

B) to merge into larger corporations and reduce the number of shampoo brands.

C) by comparing the product to other products customers buy more regularly.

D) to promise 40% more volume and bounce or 60% fewer split ends than other brands.

**CONTINUE** ➡

These claims are part of what has been called, since 1961, "cosmeutical" science. The word itself combines "cosmetics" and "pharmaceutical." Since the term was coined in 1961, cosmetics companies have been under more pressure to innovate, as competition grows and markets expand outside the United States. This pressure has led to an increased reliance on scientific data as a way to back up the advertisers' claims.

[1] But where exactly do these claims come from? [2] However, if these claims seem absurd at times, it's because they may come from nowhere at all. [3] A recent study of these scientific claims appears in the *Journal of Global Fashion Marketing*. [4] In this study, the researchers looked at over 300 advertisements from fashion magazines like *Elle*, **3** *Vogue*, and *Vanity Fair*. [5] The obvious answer would seem to be "the lab." **4**

To anyone who has ever **5** believed the truth-value of these advertisements (or of advertisements in general), the researchers' findings are probably not surprising. The researchers found that a mere 18% of the claims made in these advertisements were true. 23% of the claims were classified as "outright lies." **6** 42% were considered too vague to classify.

**3**

A) NO CHANGE
B) *Vogue* and,
C) *Vogue*; and
D) *Vogue*: and

**4**

To make this paragraph most logical, sentence 5 should be placed
A) where it is now.
B) before sentence 2.
C) before sentence 3.
D) before sentence 4.

**5**

A) NO CHANGE
B) pondered
C) questioned
D) skepticized

**6**

The writer is considering deleting the underlined portion. Should the writer do this?
A) No, because it demonstrates the most surprising of the researchers' findings.
B) No, because it completes the discussion of the data and is mentioned again in the passage.
C) Yes, because it is a reminder of how subjective the researchers' study truly was.
D) Yes, because the reader could deduce this information through simple mathematics.

CONTINUE →

These findings are good for a laugh, but **7** they may have more serious implications as well. Although everyone knows that the Food and Drug Administration can **8** reign what goes *into* food and drugs, what is less known is that the FDA can also punish false advertising claims. That sizable 23% that is telling "outright lies" may have a federal agency investigating its claims, and these investigations **9** might have resulted in significant fines and lawsuits.

While this has obvious ramifications for the "outright lies," what can the FDA do **10** from that much larger share of "too vague" claims? These may be safe for the simple reason that they are too vague to be disproven. Whatever the FDA may decide to do, this research should still remind consumers about the potential perils of trusting the word of advertisers. **11** Thus, the claims are often harmless, but consumers want to believe that they are giving their hard-earned money to trustworthy organizations.

**7**
A) NO CHANGE
B) will have
C) may have
D) might be having

**8**
A) NO CHANGE
B) regulate
C) name
D) administrate

**9**
A) NO CHANGE
B) have resulted in significant fine's
C) may result in significant fines
D) may result in significant fine's

**10**
A) NO CHANGE
B) to
C) by
D) with

**11**
A) NO CHANGE
B) On the other hand,
C) True,
D) Nevertheless,

CONTINUE

**Questions 12–22 are based on the following passage and supplementary material.**

### Gerry's Salamander

The United States is often lauded for its contributions to democracy in the world. When the process is allowed to work, democracy in the United States is truly admirable, and all of those who vote can feel that they are participating in the process in a significant way. **12** This being the case, there are some abnormalities in the history of U.S. elections that fall short of these expectations.

[1] One notable instance came in a state senate election in Massachusetts in 1812. [2] Unfortunately, it was not the last. [3] Shortly before this election, Elbridge **13** Gerry, then governor of the state, called for a redistricting that was supposed to reflect demographic shifts within the city. [4] To anyone paying attention, however, it **14** will become clear that this redistricting would benefit Gerry's own party, the Democratic-Republicans. [5] It was one of the first and most infamous works of political trickery in the history of the country. **15**

**12**
A) NO CHANGE
B) Happily,
C) Politically,
D) Unfortunately,

**13**
A) NO CHANGE
B) Gerry then governor of the state,
C) Gerry, then governor of the state
D) Gerry, then governor, of the state

**14**
A) NO CHANGE
B) would have become
C) became
D) becomes

**15**
To make this paragraph most logical, sentence 2 should be placed
A) where it is now.
B) after sentence 3.
C) after sentence 4.
D) after sentence 5.

**CONTINUE**

Gerry's tactics gave birth to a new term. The *Boston Gazette* poked fun at Gerry's redistricting **16** <u>plan. This newspaper said</u> that the newly created South Essex electoral district resembled a salamander on the map. This image, combined with the governor's name, came to be known by a very specific **17** name: gerrymandering. The practice unfortunately continues to be a tool of political manipulation to this day.

Particularly on the state and local levels, gerrymandering can have a tremendous influence on the outcome of an election. As the below graphic shows, gerrymandering can turn **18** <u>voters against some of the legislative bodies in their state.</u> In a population of 50 people, in which voting blocs lived in contained areas, different districting can result in vastly different outcomes, even where there is a clear advantage for one party. In the redistricting shown below, **19** <u>40% light gray voters can become 60% dark gray districts</u> through the careful manipulation of the districts.

**Gerrymandering, explained**
Three different ways to divide 50 people into five districts

| 50 people | 1. Perfect representation | 2. Compact, but unfair | 3. Neither compact nor fair |
|---|---|---|---|
| 60% light gray 40% dark gray | 3 light gray districts 2 dark gray districts **LIGHT GRAY WINS** | 5 light gray districts 0 dark gray districts **LIGHT GRAY WINS** | 2 light gray districts 3 dark gray districts **DARK GRAY WINS** |

---

**16**

Which choice most effectively combines the two sentences at the underlined portion?

A) plan, when the paper said

B) plan, at which time the paper said

C) plan, saying

D) plan and they said

**17**

A) NO CHANGE

B) name: which was

C) name;

D) name. And it was

**18**

Which choice best completes the description of the purpose of gerrymandering?

A) NO CHANGE

B) a series of political factions against one another.

C) elections into long processes with delayed results.

D) electoral disadvantages into electoral advantages.

**19**

Which choice most accurately and effectively represents information in the figure?

A) NO CHANGE

B) 60% dark gray voters can become 60% light gray districts

C) 40% light gray voters can become 100% dark gray districts

D) 60% light gray voters can become 60% dark gray districts

**CONTINUE**

Gerrymandering almost always benefits the parties in [20] power, not those out of power, because those are the parties that have the influence necessary to redistrict. Many perfectly viable candidates have been shut out by cruel and unfair districting practices. In this and in other political arenas, it is much easier to stay in power than to gain power.

The real victims of gerrymandering, however, are the voters. The process is used quite often to disenfranchise certain voters by making [21] they're votes less valuable. In "majority-minority" districts in particular, districts with large non-white populations, gerrymandering can discount the importance of particular races or classes of voters, many [22] of whose voting interests may go against those in power. The American voting system works, but only when all voters are given an equal say in the outcome of an election.

[20]
A) NO CHANGE
B) power usually,
C) power
D) power for the good

[21]
A) NO CHANGE
B) their
C) there
D) they are

[22]
A) NO CHANGE
B) voters'
C) of their
D) DELETE the underlined portion.

**Questions 23–33 are based on the following passage and supplementary material.**

### The Original Condition

If you've ever been to an art museum, you know the basic layout: long hallways and large rooms with paintings hung a few feet apart. You know how the paintings are **23** by certain means marked, and you know that the paintings have been arranged chronologically or thematically.

There's one thing, however, which you've definitely noticed even if you can't quite articulate it. Particularly when looking at old paintings, **24** paintings all have that vividly *new* look, whether they were painted in 1950 or 1450. Even where the subject matter is older, the colors are vibrant, and you're never forced to wonder exactly what the painting must have looked like in its original state. **25** The history of painting is nearly as long as the history of mankind.

A)  NO CHANGE

B)  marked,

C)  being marked in a way,

D)  by so means of marking,

A)  NO CHANGE

B)  you've surely noticed how *new* all the paintings look,

C)  noticing the *new* look of all the paintings is something you can do,

D)  the paintings always strike you as very *new* looking,

The writer is considering deleting the underlined sentence. Should the sentence be kept or deleted?

A)  Deleted, because it strays from the paragraph's major focus by introducing an irrelevant fact.

B)  Deleted, because it restates a historical detail that is provided in a later paragraph.

C)  Kept, because it is a useful introduction to the topic of this paragraph.

D)  Kept, because it provides a humorous anecdote regarding the work of art restorers.

**CONTINUE**

This incredible feat is the work of a highly specialized group: art restorers. Despite this specialization, the profession has exploded in recent years. **26** Art restoration has been growing steadily since 1930. While the job of an art restorer may seem fairly straightforward **27** when looking, the job is in fact quite complicated. Sometimes, as in the case of Michelangelo's famous sculpture David, the cleaning and restoration of artworks is a simple **28** matter, applying chemicals, washing away grime, and scrubbing off the dirt.

**26**

At this point the writer wants to add specific information that is consistent with the focus of the paragraph.

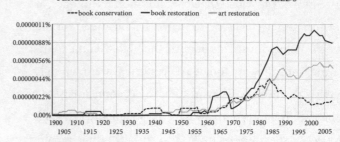

PERCENTAGE OF AMERICAN WORKFORCE IN 3 FIELDS

Which choice most effectively provides a sentence with relevant and accurate information from the graph above?

A) NO CHANGE

B) The number of book restorers who became art restorers tripled in 2000.

C) By the year 2020, it is predicted that art restoration will even eclipse art conservation.

D) From 1970 to 2005, the percentage of people working in art restoration has roughly tripled.

**27**

A) NO CHANGE

B) beholden,

C) at first glance,

D) under your gaze,

**28**

A) NO CHANGE

B) matter

C) matter:

D) matter;

CONTINUE

[29] With most paintings, however, the process is a good deal more involved because it is not necessarily just a matter of "cleaning" the older paintings. One cannot merely take a scrub brush to a centuries-old great work. Because of the wide range of restoration techniques, art restoration itself can be controversial business. For many years, before museums became the high-volume tourist attractions they are today, art "restorers" were typically artists themselves. They would project some image of what the painting must have looked like originally and apply a variety of techniques, up [30] to and including: repainting, to preserve this "original."

[1] Now, however, more attention is paid to the historical quality of the artworks. [2] Some art historians [31] who is writing today even go so far as to say that dirt and grime themselves are parts of the historical fabric of a painting and thus should be left in. [3] Others argue that the purity of the painting is all that matters. [4] They will restore the original look of a painting, even if that means "fixing" the painting by some non-paint means. [32]

Whatever methods they use, art restorers are more needed [33] for ever, but their work is also less permanent. In order to retain the integrity of the artwork in case the restorers make a mistake, all restoration must now be reversible, a reminder that art "history" is very much a thing of the present and the future.

**29**

A) NO CHANGE
B) Anyway,
C) In this sense,
D) Alongside cleaning,

**30**

A) NO CHANGE
B) to, and including,
C) to and including
D) to, and including:

**31**

A) NO CHANGE
B) who are
C) whom is
D) whom are

**32**

The writer wants to add the following sentence to the paragraph.

> For example, a recent restoration at Harvard's Art Museums involved precisely calibrated lights that would correct the color damage to a series of murals done by Mark Rothko in the 1960s.

The best placement for the sentence is immediately

A) after sentence 1.
B) after sentence 2.
C) after sentence 3.
D) after sentence 4.

**33**

A) NO CHANGE
B) by
C) what
D) than

**CONTINUE**

**Questions 34–44 are based on the following passage.**

**The Rise of *Hyperion***

Literary critics have always paid the most attention to "serious" authors. The great authors of recent memory, especially in American literature, have been distinctly "literary" authors: Toni Morrison, Philip Roth, Thomas Pynchon, and Jonathan Franzen. Often overlooked in this pantheon of great authors are the contributions of authors in non-traditional [34] modes. Specifically overlooked is the genre of science fiction. In some ways, the novel that has hearkened back to the great authors of the Victorian nineteenth century is not Morrison's *Beloved* or Roth's *American Pastoral* but *Hyperion* by Dan Simmons.

Simmons's novel was published in 1989, and it won the Hugo Award for best science-fiction novel that year. [35] All things considered, it is regularly listed among the greatest science-fiction novels of all time. The novel [36] that spawned a series of novels dealing with the same fantastic universe, the first of which was *The Fall of Hyperion*, published in 1990. *Hyperion* tells the story of seven pilgrims who travel to the distant world of Hyperion in an attempt to avert a galaxy-wide war between hostile factions. Because the pilgrims are [37] not sure in a complete way why they've been recruited for this

**34**

Which choice most effectively combines the sentences at the underlined portion?

A) modes, which notably include

B) modes, and overlooked in particular is

C) modes, specifically

D) modes, and one genre suffering neglect is

**35**

A) NO CHANGE

B) For all that,

C) To this day,

D) Check this out,

**36**

A) NO CHANGE

B) which,

C) is that which

D) DELETE the underlined portion.

**37**

A) NO CHANGE

B) not sure in their entirety

C) not entirely sure

D) lacking a complete sureness

CONTINUE ➡

"pilgrimage," they spend the long journey to Hyperion sharing 38 your stories, each of which illuminates the journey 39 while explaining this new fantasy world to the reader.

If this structure 40 of sound familiar, that's because it draws on some of the great classics of literature, most notably *The Canterbury Tales*, which itself is a kind of travel narrative, as it follows 41 pilgrims travel together to the Canterbury Cathedral. The name of the novel draws on a long literary history as well: poems by John Keats

38

A) NO CHANGE
B) their
C) our
D) everyone's

39

A) NO CHANGE
B) when
C) though
D) as if

40

A) NO CHANGE
B) and sounding
C) sounding
D) sounds

41

A) NO CHANGE
B) pilgrim's travels
C) pilgrim's traveling
D) pilgrims traveling

CONTINUE

and novels by Friedrich Hölderlin and Henry Wadsworth Longfellow. **42** With all of these literary tributes, if great works of literature are expressions of, as T.S. Eliot says, "tradition and the individual talent," then *Hyperion* is certainly a great work. **43**

In addition to its incredible achievements in terms of literary history, *Hyperion* is also a truly incredible work of science fiction. The future world it imagines is vivid, and its continuities with the contemporary world **44** is clearly defined. *Hyperion* is awash in literary laurels, but it is also an entertaining novel—quite a combination!

The fact that *Hyperion* is not as well known as some of the more accepted "classics" should make us wonder what we mean by this term "classics." We should also wonder what else we've been missing because it hasn't met our traditional criteria for greatness.

**42**

Which choice most effectively sets up the information that follows?

A) Dan Simmons must have studied the poems and essays of T.S. Eliot at some point in his life.

B) Even beyond these nominal debts, *Hyperion* pays homage to countless genres, including the war story and the detective novel.

C) But don't worry, there are still plenty of lasers and space ships in the book too.

D) Although the critics of the early twentieth century probably would've loved it, many of them died before *Hyperion* was published.

**43**

At this point, the writer is considering adding the following sentence.

Some of T.S. Eliot's most famous poems are *The Waste Land* and "The Love Song of J. Alfred Prufrock."

Should the writer make this addition here?

A) Yes, because it helps to put the literary quality of *Hyperion* into its appropriate context.

B) Yes, because it names another series of works that are overlooked for being non-traditional.

C) No, because it introduces a new set of information that does not have a clear link to the rest of the passage.

D) No, because it disagrees with the passage's central claim that *Hyperion* is the greatest work of science fiction.

**44**

A) NO CHANGE

B) has been

C) being

D) are

# STOP

**If you finish before time is called, you may check your work on this section only.
Do not turn to any other section in the test.**

# Math Test – No Calculator

## 25 MINUTES, 20 QUESTIONS

**Turn to Section 3 of your answer sheet to answer the questions in this section.**

---

### DIRECTIONS

**For questions 1–15,** solve each problem, choose the best answer from the choices provided, and fill in the corresponding circle on your answer sheet. **For questions 16–20,** solve the problem and enter your answer in the grid on the answer sheet. Please refer to the directions before question 16 on how to enter your answers in the grid. You may use any available space in your test booklet for scratch work.

### NOTES

1. The use of a calculator **is not permitted**.
2. All variables and expressions used represent real numbers unless otherwise indicated.
3. Figures provided in this test are drawn to scale unless otherwise indicated.
4. All figures lie in a plane unless otherwise indicated.
5. Unless otherwise indicated, the domain of a given function $f$ is the set of all real numbers $x$ for which $f(x)$ is a real number.

### REFERENCE

$A = \pi r^2$
$C = 2\pi r$

$A = \ell w$

$A = \frac{1}{2} bh$

$c^2 = a^2 + b^2$

Special Right Triangles

$V = \ell wh$

$V = \pi r^2 h$

$V = \frac{4}{3}\pi r^3$

$V = \frac{1}{3}\pi r^2 h$

$V = \frac{1}{3}\ell wh$

The number of degrees of arc in a circle is 360.
The number of radians of arc in a circle is $2\pi$.
The sum of the measures in degrees of the angles of a triangle is 180.

---

**CONTINUE**

**1**

During a certain week, Jan worked $j$ hours each day for 3 days, and Noah worked $n$ hours each day for 5 days. Which of the following represents the total combined number of hours worked that week by Jan and Noah?

A) $3j + 5n$

B) $5j + 3n$

C) $8jn$

D) $15jn$

**2**

If $\dfrac{y + 2}{5} = c$ and $c = 4$, what is the value of $y$ ?

A) 16

B) 18

C) 20

D) 22

**3**

For $i = \sqrt{-1}$, what is the sum $(10 - 4i) + (3 + 6i)$ ?

A) $13 - 10i$

B) $13 + 2i$

C) $7 - 10i$

D) $7 + 2i$

$$\left(10 - 4\left(\sqrt{-1}\right)\right) + \left(3 + 6\left(\sqrt{-1}\right)\right)$$

**4**

$$(ab^2 + 4a^2 + 6a^2b^2) - (-ab^2 + 2a^2b^2 + 4a^2)$$

Which of the following is equivalent to the expression above?

A) $-2a^2b^2$

B) $-2a^2b^2 + 8a^2$

C) $2ab^2 - 2a^2b^2 + 8a^2$

D) $2ab^2 + 4a^2b^2$

**CONTINUE**

**5**

$$w = 3{,}150 + 450l$$

A marine biologist uses the equation above to estimate the weight, $w$, of a mature great white shark, in pounds, in terms of the shark's fork length, $l$, in feet. Based on the equation, what is the estimated weight increase, in pounds, for each foot of growth in fork length in a great white shark?

A) 3,150

B) 2,700

C) 1,350

D) 450

**6**

Juan is a book editor who is given a book to edit. The number of pages that he has left to edit at the end of each hour is estimated by the equation $P = 326 - 12h$, where $h$ represents the number of hours spent editing the book. What is the meaning of the value 326 in this equation?

A) Juan edits pages at a rate of 326 per day.

B) Juan edits pages at a rate of 326 per hour.

C) Juan is given a total of 326 pages to edit.

D) Juan will finish editing the book in 326 hours.

**7**

If $\dfrac{x}{y} = 3$, what is the value of $\dfrac{12y}{x}$ ?

A) 4

B) 6

C) 8

D) 12

**8**

$$2y + x = -17$$
$$5x - 4y = -15$$

What is the solution $(x, y)$ to the system of equations shown above?

A) $(-7, -5)$

B) $(-4, -1)$

C) $(-3, 0)$

D) $(5, -11)$

**CONTINUE** ➡

9

$$c = \frac{\dfrac{r}{1,200}}{1 - \left(1 + \dfrac{r}{1,200}\right)^{-N}} M$$

In order to buy a house, a couple takes on a mortgage of $M$ dollars at an annual rate of $r$ percent to be paid off over $N$ months. If the equation above is used to determine the monthly payment, $c$, that the couple needs to make to pay off the loan, which of the following expressions gives the value of $M$, in terms of $c$, $r$, and $N$?

A) $M = \left(\dfrac{r}{1,200}\right) c$

B) $M = \left(\dfrac{1,200}{r}\right) c$

C) $M = \dfrac{1 - \left(1 + \dfrac{r}{1,200}\right)^{-N}}{\dfrac{r}{1,200}} c$

D) $M = \dfrac{\dfrac{r}{1,200}}{1 - \left(1 + \dfrac{r}{1,200}\right)^{-N}} c$

10

A line in the $xy$-plane has a slope of $\dfrac{2}{3}$ and passes through the origin. Which of the following points lies on the line?

A) $\left(0, \dfrac{2}{3}\right)$

B) $(2, 3)$

C) $(6, 4)$

D) $(9, 4)$

11

$$f(x) = cx^2 + 30$$

For the function $f$ defined above, $c$ is a constant and $f(3) = 12$. What is the value of $f(-3)$?

A) $-12$

B) $-2$

C) $0$

D) $12$

**CONTINUE**

**12**

$$A = 240 - 20w$$

$$B = 320 - 30w$$

In the equations above, $A$ and $B$ represent the price per night for a room in Hotel $A$ and Hotel $B$, respectively, $w$ weeks after September 1 last autumn. What was the price per night in Hotel $A$ when it was equal to the price per night in Hotel $B$?

A)  $80

B)  $160

C)  $180

D)  $220

**13**

If $a - 4b = 18$, what is the value of $\dfrac{3^a}{81^b}$?

A)  $81^2$

B)  $9^6$

C)  $3^{18}$

D)  The value cannot be determined from the information given.

**14**

If $(ax + 3)(bx + 5) = 35x^2 + kx + 15$ for all values of $x$, and $a + b = 12$, what are the two possible values for $k$?

A)  46 and 50

B)  15 and 35

C)  21 and 25

D)  5 and 7

**15**

If $y > 5$, which of the following is equivalent to

$$\dfrac{1}{\dfrac{1}{y-4} + \dfrac{1}{y-3}} \ ?$$

A)  $2y - 7$

B)  $y^2 - 7y + 12$

C)  $\dfrac{y^2 - 7y + 12}{2y - 7}$

D)  $\dfrac{2y - 7}{y^2 - 7y + 12}$

CONTINUE

## DIRECTIONS

**For questions 16–20**, solve the problem and enter your answer in the grid, as described below, on the answer sheet.

1. Although not required, it is suggested that you write your answer in the boxes at the top of the columns to help you fill in the circles accurately. You will receive credit only if the circles are filled in correctly.

2. Mark no more than one circle in any column.

3. No question has a negative answer.

4. Some problems may have more than one correct answer. In such cases, grid only one answer.

5. **Mixed numbers** such as $3\frac{1}{2}$ must be gridded as 3.5 or 7/2. (If  is entered into the grid, it will be interpreted as $\frac{31}{2}$, not as $3\frac{1}{2}$.)

6. **Decimal Answers:** If you obtain a decimal answer with more digits than the grid can accommodate, it may be either rounded or truncated, but it must fill the entire grid.

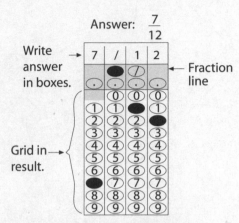

Answer: $\frac{7}{12}$

Write answer in boxes. Fraction line. Grid in result.

Answer: 2.5

Decimal point

Acceptable ways to grid $\frac{2}{3}$ are:

Answer: 201 – either position is correct

**NOTE:** You may start your answers in any column, space permitting. Columns you don't need to use should be left blank.

CONTINUE ▶

**16**

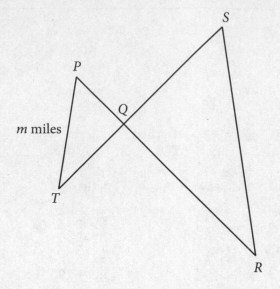

In a certain park, the layout of the six bicycle paths is shown in the figure above. The lengths of $\overline{PQ}$, $\overline{QT}$, $\overline{QS}$, and $\overline{SR}$ are 3 miles, 4 miles, 8 miles, and 10 miles, respectively. Paths $\overline{PR}$ and $\overline{ST}$ intersect at point $Q$, and $\angle TPQ$ is congruent to $\angle QRS$. What is the value of $m$ ?

**17**

If $y > 0$ and $y^2 - 36 = 0$, what is the value of $y$ ?

**18**

In a right triangle, one angle measures $d°$, where $\cos d° = \dfrac{5}{13}$. What is $\sin (90° - d°)$ ?

**CONTINUE**

**19**

If $c = 3\sqrt{5}$ and $5c = \sqrt{5z}$, what is the value of $z$?

**20**

$$a + b = -10$$
$$2a + b = -33$$

What is the value of $b$ in the system of equations shown above?

## STOP
**If you finish before time is called, you may check your work on this section only.**
**Do not turn to any other section in the test.**

# Math Test – Calculator

## 55 MINUTES, 38 QUESTIONS

**Turn to Section 4 of your answer sheet to answer the questions in this section.**

### DIRECTIONS

**For questions 1–30,** solve each problem, choose the best answer from the choices provided, and fill in the corresponding circle on your answer sheet. **For questions 31–38,** solve the problem and enter your answer in the grid on the answer sheet. Please refer to the directions before question 31 on how to enter your answers in the grid. You may use any available space in your test booklet for scratch work.

### NOTES

1. The use of a calculator **is permitted**.
2. All variables and expressions used represent real numbers unless otherwise indicated.
3. Figures provided in this test are drawn to scale unless otherwise indicated.
4. All figures lie in a plane unless otherwise indicated.
5. Unless otherwise indicated, the domain of a given function $f$ is the set of all real numbers $x$ for which $f(x)$ is a real number.

### REFERENCE

$A = \pi r^2$
$C = 2\pi r$

$A = \ell w$

$A = \frac{1}{2} bh$

$c^2 = a^2 + b^2$

Special Right Triangles

$V = \ell wh$

$V = \pi r^2 h$

$V = \frac{4}{3}\pi r^3$

$V = \frac{1}{3}\pi r^2 h$

$V = \frac{1}{3}\ell wh$

The number of degrees of arc in a circle is 360.
The number of radians of arc in a circle is $2\pi$.
The sum of the measures in degrees of the angles of a triangle is 180.

**CONTINUE**

**1**

In the figure shown above, lines $a$ and $b$ are parallel and lines $k$ and $\ell$ are parallel. If the measure of $\angle x$ is 75°, what is the measure of $\angle y$ ?

A)　15°

B)　75°

C)　105°

D)　165°

**2**

The graph above shows the number of customers per hour at a coffee shop. Over which of the following intervals is the number of customers strictly decreasing then strictly increasing?

A)　From 9 A.M. to 12 P.M.

B)　From 12 P.M. to 2 P.M.

C)　From 2 P.M. to 5 P.M.

D)　From 3:30 P.M. to 6:30 P.M.

**3**

If $y = \dfrac{x}{k}$, where $k$ is a constant, and $y = 5$ when $x = 30$, what is the value of $y$ when $x = 42$ ?

A)　6

B)　7

C)　10

D)　17

CONTINUE

---

**4**

| 1 kilogram = 1,000 grams |
| 10 decigrams = 1 gram |

A pharmacy sells a certain type of medication in 1-decigram doses. Based on the information shown in the box above, three kilograms of medication contain how many 1-decigram doses?

A)  300,000

B)    30,000

C)     3,000

D)      300

**5**

If $6x - 4$ is 11 less than 25, what is the value of $9x$ ?

A)   3

B)   8

C)  18

D)  27

---

**6**

Which of the graphs below best illustrates a strong positive correlation between $h$ and $p$ ?

A)

B)

C)

D)

**CONTINUE**

---

**Questions 7 and 8 refer to the following information.**

$$p = 101 + 10.094d$$

The total pressure on an object submerged in the ocean depends on the depth of the object beneath the surface. The formula above shows the relationship between $p$, pressure, in kilopascals, and $d$, depth, in meters.

**7**

At which of the following depths will the total pressure be closest to 200 kilopascals?

A) 8 meters

B) 9 meters

C) 10 meters

D) 11 meters

**8**

Which of the following formulas expresses depth in terms of pressure?

A) $d = \dfrac{p}{10.094} - 101$

B) $d = \dfrac{10.094}{101 - p}$

C) $d = \dfrac{p + 101}{10.094}$

D) $d = \dfrac{p - 101}{10.094}$

**9**

Wind Turbine Operation in Five Counties

The number of wind turbines in use in five counties is shown in the graph above. If there are a total of 3,750 wind turbines operating in these five counties, which of the following is an appropriate label for the horizontal axis of the graph?

A) Number of wind turbines (in tens)

B) Number of wind turbines (in hundreds)

C) Number of wind turbines (in thousands)

D) Number of wind turbines (in tens of thousands)

**CONTINUE**

**10**

For how many values of $k$ is it true that $|k - 3| + 2$ is equal to one?

A) None

B) One

C) Two

D) More than two

**11**

Number of Residents in Each of 14 Apartments

Number of apartments

According to the histogram shown above, which of the following is closest to the average (arithmetic mean) number of residents per apartment?

A) 3

B) 3.25

C) 3.5

D) 4

**12**

Which of the following integers CANNOT be a solution to the inequality $6x - 4 \le 7x - 3$ ?

A) 1

B) 0

C) –1

D) –2

**13**

| Weights of potatoes (in ounces) | | | | | | | | |
|---|---|---|---|---|---|---|---|---|
| 2 | 3 | 3 | 4 | 4 | 4 | 5 | 5 | 6 |
| 6 | 7 | 7 | 7 | 7 | 8 | 8 | 9 | 9 |

An agriculture class harvested 18 potatoes from the school garden and compiled the weights of the potatoes in the table above. If the 2-ounce measurement is removed from the data, which of the following statistical measures of the values listed will change the least?

A) The mean

B) The median

C) The range

D) The total

**CONTINUE**

14

$$p + x > y$$
$$r - x < -y$$

In the $xy$-plane, $(2, 2)$ is a solution to the system of inequalities shown above. Which of the following must be true about $p$ and $r$?

A) $p < r$

B) $r < p$

C) $p + r = 0$

D) $|p| = |r|$

15

| | Political Party | | | |
|---|---|---|---|---|
| | Liberal | Conservative | Independent | Total |
| Men | 59 | 74 | 62 | 195 |
| Women | 82 | 63 | 55 | 200 |
| Total | 141 | 137 | 117 | 395 |

A group of voters in country $X$ responded to a poll that asked which political party they planned to vote for. The table above shows the results of the polling data. Which of the categories below accounts for approximately 15 percent of all poll respondents?

A) Men voting Liberal

B) Men voting Independent

C) Women voting Conservative

D) Women voting Liberal

CONTINUE

**Questions 16 and 17 refer to the following information.**

Total Cost of Renting a Car by the Day

The graph above shows the total price $P$, in dollars, to rent a car for $d$ days.

What does the slope of the graph represent?

A) The total number of cars rented

B) The initial cost of renting a car

C) The average increase in price to rent a car for each additional day

D) The total number of days for which a car is rented

Which of the equations below shows the relationship between $d$ and $P$?

A) $P = 25d$

B) $P = d + 30$

C) $P = 10d + 30$

D) $P = 20d + 30$

**18**

The figure above shows the complete graph of the function $f$ in the $xy$-plane. For which of the following values of $x$ is $f(x)$ at its maximum?

A) −4

B) −3

C) −2

D) 3

**19**

The price of a train ticket purchased in the train station or from a conductor is 15 percent less during off-peak hours than it is during peak hours. If a ticket is purchased from the conductor, an 11 percent surcharge is added to the price. Alec purchased a ticket from the conductor during off-peak hours and paid a total of $t$ dollars. Which of the following, in terms of $t$, represents the price he would have paid if he had purchased the ticket in the train station during peak hours?

A) $\dfrac{t}{0.96}$

B) $0.96t$

C) $\dfrac{t}{(0.85)(1.11)}$

D) $(0.85)(1.11)t$

**20**

Number of Exercise Sessions per Week

|  | 0–2 | 3–5 | More than 5 | Total |
|---|---|---|---|---|
| Group 1 | 13 | 22 | 15 | 50 |
| Group 2 | 11 | 18 | 21 | 50 |
| Total | 24 | 40 | 36 | 100 |

The table above was compiled by a nutrition researcher studying how often people exercise when asked to keep a log of their exercise sessions. Group 1 was comprised of people who regularly eat snacks, and Group 2 was comprised of people who rarely eat snacks. If one person is randomly chosen from among those who exercise fewer than six times per week, what is the probability that this person belonged to Group 1 ?

A) $\dfrac{35}{64}$

B) $\dfrac{50}{64}$

C) $\dfrac{29}{100}$

D) $\dfrac{35}{100}$

**21**

A service station sells gasoline for \$3.25 per gallon and diesel fuel for \$3.00 per gallon. On Monday, the service station's revenue from selling a total of 131 gallons of gasoline and diesel fuel was \$404.25. How many gallons of diesel fuel did the service station sell on Monday?

A) 35

B) 55

C) 76

D) 86

**CONTINUE**

**Questions 22 and 23 refer to the following information.**

Total Budget Spending in One U.S. State by Category, 2010–2014

| Year | K-12 education | Higher education | Public assistance | Medicaid | Corrections | Transportation |
|------|------|------|------|------|------|------|
| 2014 | 3,635,265 | 3,099,112 | 29,450 | 2,990,415 | 930,525 | 1, 556,244 |
| 2013 | 3,677,428 | 2,734,615 | 45,873 | 3,005,188 | 820,855 | 1,873,618 |
| 2012 | 3,715,853 | 2,550,665 | 55,645 | 3,020,012 | 773,420 | 1,721,682 |
| 2011 | 3,747,921 | 2,309,789 | 54,321 | 2,984,375 | 694,011 | 1,388,904 |
| 2010 | 3,785,200 | 2,104,214 | 55,787 | 3,001,650 | 632,350 | 1,434,006 |

The table above summarizes annual spending, in thousands of dollars, for six categories of spending in one U.S. state, 2010–2014.

**22**

Of the following, which category's ratio of its 2010 spending to its 2014 spending is nearest to the higher education category's ratio of its 2010 spending to its 2014 spending?

A) K-12 education

B) Medicaid

C) Corrections

D) Transportation

**23**

Which of the following is the best approximation of the average rate of change in spending on public assistance from 2012 to 2014 ?

A)  $6,000,000

B)  $10,000,000

C)  $13,000,000

D)  $26,000,000

CONTINUE

**24**

A fish leaps vertically upward from the surface of a lake at an initial speed of 9 meters per second. The height $h$, in meters, of the fish above the surface of the water $s$ seconds after it leaps is given by the equation $h = 9s - 4.9s^2$. Approximately how many seconds after the fish leaps will it hit the surface of the lake?

A) 2.0

B) 2.5

C) 3.0

D) 3.5

**25**

A circle in the $xy$-plane is centered at $(3, 0)$ and has a radius with endpoint $\left(1, \dfrac{8}{3}\right)$. Which of the following is an equation of the circle?

A) $(x - 3)^2 + y^2 = \dfrac{10}{3}$

B) $(x + 3)^2 + y^2 = \dfrac{10}{3}$

C) $(x - 3)^2 + y^2 = \dfrac{100}{9}$

D) $(x + 3)^2 + y^2 = \dfrac{100}{9}$

**26**

A square lawn has a length of 8 feet and a width of 8 feet. Eight researchers each examine a randomly chosen region of the field; all regions are square with length and width of one foot. The researchers count the number of seedlings in each region that have reached a height of at least 2 inches. The table below shows the resulting data.

| Region | 1 | 2 | 3 | 4 |
|---|---|---|---|---|
| Number of seedlings | 82 | 87 | 95 | 99 |
| Region | 5 | 6 | 7 | 8 |
| Number of seedlings | 102 | 106 | 111 | 115 |

Which of the following best approximates the number of seedlings that are at least 2 inches high in the entire lawn?

A) 80

B) 640

C) 800

D) 6,400

**27**

A zoologist is studying the reproduction rates of two different breeds of chinchillas in country $Y$. He discovered that the Eastern chinchillas in his study produced 30 percent more offspring than the Western chinchillas did. Based on the zoologist's observation, if the Eastern chinchillas in his study produced 143 offspring, how many offspring did the Western chinchillas produce?

A) 100

B) 103

C) 110

D) 186

CONTINUE

**28**

When polynomial $g(x)$ is divided by $x - 4$, the remainder is 3. Which of the following statements about $g(x)$ must be true?

A) $g(-4) = 3$

B) $g(4) = 3$

C) $x - 4$ is a factor of $g(x)$.

D) $x + 3$ is a factor of $g(x)$.

**29**

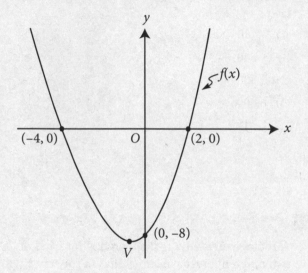

The figure above shows the graph in the $xy$-plane of the function $f(x) = x^2 + 2x - 8$. Which of the following is an equivalent form of the function $f$ that includes the coordinates of vertex $V$ as constants in the function?

A) $f(x) = (x + 1)^2 - 9$

B) $f(x) = x(x + 2) - 8$

C) $f(x) = (x - 2)(x + 4)$

D) $f(x) = (x + 2)(x - 4)$

**30**

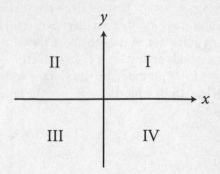

If the system of inequalities $y \geq x + 2$ and $y \geq \dfrac{1}{3}x - 1$ is graphed in the $xy$-plane shown above, how many quadrants will contain solutions to the system?

A) 4

B) 3

C) 2

D) 1

CONTINUE ➡

## DIRECTIONS

**For questions 31–38**, solve the problem and enter your answer in the grid, as described below, on the answer sheet.

1.  Although not required, it is suggested that you write your answer in the boxes at the top of the columns to help you fill in the circles accurately. You will receive credit only if the circles are filled in correctly.

2.  Mark no more than one circle in any column.

3.  No question has a negative answer.

4.  Some problems may have more than one correct answer. In such cases, grid only one answer.

5.  **Mixed numbers** such as $3\frac{1}{2}$ must be gridded as 3.5 or 7/2. (If $3\ 1\ /\ 2$ is entered into the grid, it will be interpreted as $\frac{31}{2}$, not as $3\frac{1}{2}$.)

6.  **Decimal Answers:** If you obtain a decimal answer with more digits than the grid can accommodate, it may be either rounded or truncated, but it must fill the entire grid.

Acceptable ways to grid $\frac{2}{3}$ are:

Answer: 201 – either position is correct

**NOTE:** You may start your answers in any column, space permitting. Columns you don't need to use should be left blank.

CONTINUE →

**31**

### Amount of Greg's Heating Bill Each Month from January to June

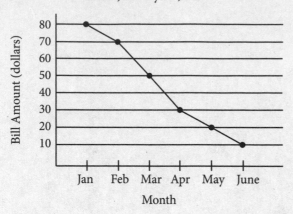

The line chart above shows the amount of Greg's monthly heating bill from January to June. The amount of his bill in April was what fraction of the amount of his bill in February?

**32**

A worker at a shoe factory is required to box at least 8 pairs of shoes per minute, but is not allowed to box more than 12 pairs of shoes per minute. According to this information, what is a possible amount of time, in minutes, that it could take the worker to box 168 pairs of shoes?

**33**

Safety regulations in a certain building require that the elevator not carry more than 1,600 pounds. A delivery driver will enter the elevator with a pallet containing a certain number of identical cartons that weigh 45 pounds each. If the combined weight of the delivery driver and the empty pallet is 250 pounds, what is the maximum number of cartons that will be allowed by the building's safety regulations?

**34**

├── 9 inches ──┤

An aluminum can in the shape of a right circular cylinder has a <u>diameter</u> of 9 inches and a volume of 81π cubic inches. What is the height of the can, in inches?

CONTINUE

**35**

For what value of $x$ is the expression

$$\frac{2}{(x-6)^2 + 4(x-7) + 8}$$ undefined?

**36**

A train passes through the Appleton train station every 20 minutes. The first train each day passes through at 6:00 A.M., and the last train passes through at 10:40 P.M. How many trains pass through the Appleton station in one day?

**Questions 37 and 38 refer to the following information.**

Helene purchased a $50 savings bond, issued by city $A$, which earns interest that is compounded annually. She uses the expression $\$50(1.03)^t$ to find the value of the savings bond after $t$ years.

**37**

What is the annual interest rate, expressed as a percentage, earned by the savings bond? (Disregard the percent sign when gridding in your answer.)

**38**

Helene's sister Carolyn purchased a $50 savings bond issued by city $B$. Carolyn's bond has an interest rate, compounded annually, that is 1 percent greater than the interest rate earned by Helene's bond. After 12 years, the value of Carolyn's bond will be how much greater than the value of Helene's bond? (Round your answer to the nearest cent and disregard the dollar sign when gridding in your answer.)

# STOP

If you finish before time is called, you may check your work on this section only.
Do not turn to any other section in the test.

# SAT Essay

## DIRECTIONS

The essay gives you an opportunity to show how effectively you can read and comprehend a passage and write an essay analyzing the passage. In your essay you should demonstrate that you have read the passage carefully, present a clear and logical analysis, and use language precisely.

Your essay must be written on the lines provided in your answer sheet booklet; except for the planning page of the answer booklet, you will receive no other paper on which to write. You will have enough space if you write on every line, avoid wide margins, and keep your handwriting to a reasonable size. Remember that people who are not familiar with your handwriting will read what you write. Try to write or print so that what you are writing is legible to those readers.

**You have <u>50 minutes</u> to read the passage and write an essay in response to the prompt provided inside this booklet.**

## REMINDER

—    Do not write your essay in this booklet. Only what you write on the lined pages of your answer booklet will be evaluated.

—    An off-topic essay will not be evaluated.

CONTINUE →

As you read the passage below, consider how Eleanor Roosevelt uses

- evidence, such as facts or examples, to support claims.
- reasoning to develop ideas and to connect claims and evidence.
- stylistic or persuasive elements, such as word choice or appeals to emotion, to add power to the ideas expressed.

**Adapted from Eleanor Roosevelt, "The Struggle for the Rights of Man." The speech was delivered to the United Nations in Paris, France on September 28, 1948.**

1    I have come this evening to talk with you on one of the greatest issues of our time—that is the preservation of human freedom. I have chosen to discuss it here in France, at the Sorbonne, because here in this soil the roots of human freedom have long ago struck deep and here they have been richly nourished. It was here the Declaration of the Rights of Man was proclaimed, and the great slogans of the French Revolution—liberty, equality, fraternity—fired the imagination of men. I have chosen to discuss this issue in Europe because this has been the scene of the greatest historic battles between freedom and tyranny...

2    We must not be confused about what freedom is. Basic human rights are simple and easily understood: freedom of speech and a free press; freedom of religion and worship; freedom of assembly and the right of petition; the right of men to be secure in their homes and free from unreasonable search and seizure and from arbitrary arrest and punishment.

3    We must not be deluded by the efforts of the forces of reaction to prostitute the great words of our free tradition and thereby to confuse the struggle...

4    There are basic differences that show up even in the use of words between a democratic and a totalitarian country. For instance "democracy" means one thing to the U.S.S.R. and another the U.S.A. and, I know, in France. I have served since the first meeting of the nuclear commission on the Human Rights Commission, and I think this point stands out clearly.

5    The U.S.S.R. Representatives assert that they already have achieved many things which we, in what they call the "bourgeois democracies" cannot achieve because their government controls the accomplishment of these things. Our government seems powerless to them because, in the last analysis, it is controlled by the people. They would not put it that way —they would say that the people in the U.S.S.R. control their government by allowing their government to have certain absolute rights. We, on the other hand, feel that certain rights can never be granted to the government, but must be kept in the hands of the people...

**CONTINUE**

6   I think the best example one can give of this basic difference of the use of terms is "the right to work." The Soviet Union insists that this is a basic right which it alone can guarantee because it alone provides full employment by the government. But the right to work in the Soviet Union means the assignment of workers to do whatever task is given to them by the government without an opportunity for the people to participate in the decision that the government should do this. A society in which everyone works is not necessarily a free society and may indeed be a slave society; on the other hand, a society in which there is widespread economic insecurity can turn freedom into a barren and vapid right for millions of people.

7   We in the United States have come to realize it means freedom to choose one's job, to work or not to work as one desires. We, in the United States, have come to realize, however, that people have a right to demand that their government will not allow them to starve because, as individuals, they cannot find work of the kind they are accustomed to doing, and this is a decision brought about by public opinion which came as a result of the great depression in which many people were out of work, but we would not consider in the United States that we had gained any freedom if we were compelled to follow a dictatorial assignment to work where and when we were told. The right of choice would seem to us an important, fundamental freedom.

8   The place to discuss the issue of human rights is in the forum of the United Nations. The United Nations has been set up as the common meeting ground for nations, where we can consider together our mutual problems and take advantage of our differences in experience... It is now as always our hope that despite the wide differences in approach we face in the world today, we can with mutual good faith in the principles of the United Nations Charter, arrive at a common basis of understanding.

---

Write an essay in which you explain how Eleanor Roosevelt builds her argument that the United Nations should create a Universal Declaration of Human Rights. In your essay, analyze how Roosevelt uses one or more of the features listed in the box above (or features of your own choice) to strengthen the logic and persuasiveness of her argument. Be sure that your analysis focuses on the most relevant features of the passage.

Your essay should not explain whether you agree with Roosevelt's claims, but rather explain how Roosevelt builds an argument to persuade her audience.

**END OF TEST**

**DO NOT RETURN TO A PREVIOUS SECTION.**

Completely darken bubbles with a No. 2 pencil. If you make a mistake, be sure to erase mark completely. Erase all stray marks.

**1.**

YOUR NAME: _____
(Print)
           Last           First          M.I.

SIGNATURE: _____      DATE: ___ / ___ / ___

HOME ADDRESS: _____
(Print)
           Number and Street

        City        State        Zip Code

PHONE NO.: _____
(Print)

**IMPORTANT:** Please fill in these boxes exactly as shown on the back cover of your test book.

**2. TEST FORM**

**6. DATE OF BIRTH**

| Month | Day | Year |
|---|---|---|
| ○ JAN | | |
| ○ FEB | ⓪ ⓪ | ⓪ ⓪ |
| ○ MAR | ① ① | ① ① |
| ○ APR | ② ② | ② ② |
| ○ MAY | ③ ③ | ③ ③ |
| ○ JUN | ④ | ④ ④ |
| ○ JUL | ⑤ | ⑤ ⑤ |
| ○ AUG | ⑥ | ⑥ ⑥ |
| ○ SEP | ⑦ | ⑦ ⑦ |
| ○ OCT | ⑧ | ⑧ ⑧ |
| ○ NOV | ⑨ | ⑨ ⑨ |
| ○ DEC | | |

**3. TEST CODE**      **4. REGISTRATION NUMBER**

**7. SEX**
○ MALE
○ FEMALE

**The Princeton Review®**

**5. YOUR NAME**

First 4 letters of last name   FIRST INIT   MID INIT

(A–Z bubble columns)

**Test ①**   Start with number 1 for each new section.
If a section has fewer questions than answer spaces, leave the extra answer spaces blank.

## Section 1—Reading

1. Ⓐ Ⓑ Ⓒ Ⓓ
2. Ⓐ Ⓑ Ⓒ Ⓓ
3. Ⓐ Ⓑ Ⓒ Ⓓ
4. Ⓐ Ⓑ Ⓒ Ⓓ
5. Ⓐ Ⓑ Ⓒ Ⓓ
6. Ⓐ Ⓑ Ⓒ Ⓓ
7. Ⓐ Ⓑ Ⓒ Ⓓ
8. Ⓐ Ⓑ Ⓒ Ⓓ
9. Ⓐ Ⓑ Ⓒ Ⓓ
10. Ⓐ Ⓑ Ⓒ Ⓓ
11. Ⓐ Ⓑ Ⓒ Ⓓ
12. Ⓐ Ⓑ Ⓒ Ⓓ
13. Ⓐ Ⓑ Ⓒ Ⓓ
14. Ⓐ Ⓑ Ⓒ Ⓓ
15. Ⓐ Ⓑ Ⓒ Ⓓ
16. Ⓐ Ⓑ Ⓒ Ⓓ
17. Ⓐ Ⓑ Ⓒ Ⓓ
18. Ⓐ Ⓑ Ⓒ Ⓓ
19. Ⓐ Ⓑ Ⓒ Ⓓ
20. Ⓐ Ⓑ Ⓒ Ⓓ
21. Ⓐ Ⓑ Ⓒ Ⓓ
22. Ⓐ Ⓑ Ⓒ Ⓓ
23. Ⓐ Ⓑ Ⓒ Ⓓ
24. Ⓐ Ⓑ Ⓒ Ⓓ
25. Ⓐ Ⓑ Ⓒ Ⓓ
26. Ⓐ Ⓑ Ⓒ Ⓓ
27. Ⓐ Ⓑ Ⓒ Ⓓ
28. Ⓐ Ⓑ Ⓒ Ⓓ
29. Ⓐ Ⓑ Ⓒ Ⓓ
30. Ⓐ Ⓑ Ⓒ Ⓓ
31. Ⓐ Ⓑ Ⓒ Ⓓ
32. Ⓐ Ⓑ Ⓒ Ⓓ
33. Ⓐ Ⓑ Ⓒ Ⓓ
34. Ⓐ Ⓑ Ⓒ Ⓓ
35. Ⓐ Ⓑ Ⓒ Ⓓ
36. Ⓐ Ⓑ Ⓒ Ⓓ
37. Ⓐ Ⓑ Ⓒ Ⓓ
38. Ⓐ Ⓑ Ⓒ Ⓓ
39. Ⓐ Ⓑ Ⓒ Ⓓ
40. Ⓐ Ⓑ Ⓒ Ⓓ
41. Ⓐ Ⓑ Ⓒ Ⓓ
42. Ⓐ Ⓑ Ⓒ Ⓓ
43. Ⓐ Ⓑ Ⓒ Ⓓ
44. Ⓐ Ⓑ Ⓒ Ⓓ
45. Ⓐ Ⓑ Ⓒ Ⓓ
46. Ⓐ Ⓑ Ⓒ Ⓓ
47. Ⓐ Ⓑ Ⓒ Ⓓ
48. Ⓐ Ⓑ Ⓒ Ⓓ
49. Ⓐ Ⓑ Ⓒ Ⓓ
50. Ⓐ Ⓑ Ⓒ Ⓓ
51. Ⓐ Ⓑ Ⓒ Ⓓ
52. Ⓐ Ⓑ Ⓒ Ⓓ

## Section 2—Writing and Language Skills

1. Ⓐ Ⓑ Ⓒ Ⓓ
2. Ⓐ Ⓑ Ⓒ Ⓓ
3. Ⓐ Ⓑ Ⓒ Ⓓ
4. Ⓐ Ⓑ Ⓒ Ⓓ
5. Ⓐ Ⓑ Ⓒ Ⓓ
6. Ⓐ Ⓑ Ⓒ Ⓓ
7. Ⓐ Ⓑ Ⓒ Ⓓ
8. Ⓐ Ⓑ Ⓒ Ⓓ
9. Ⓐ Ⓑ Ⓒ Ⓓ
10. Ⓐ Ⓑ Ⓒ Ⓓ
11. Ⓐ Ⓑ Ⓒ Ⓓ
12. Ⓐ Ⓑ Ⓒ Ⓓ
13. Ⓐ Ⓑ Ⓒ Ⓓ
14. Ⓐ Ⓑ Ⓒ Ⓓ
15. Ⓐ Ⓑ Ⓒ Ⓓ
16. Ⓐ Ⓑ Ⓒ Ⓓ
17. Ⓐ Ⓑ Ⓒ Ⓓ
18. Ⓐ Ⓑ Ⓒ Ⓓ
19. Ⓐ Ⓑ Ⓒ Ⓓ
20. Ⓐ Ⓑ Ⓒ Ⓓ
21. Ⓐ Ⓑ Ⓒ Ⓓ
22. Ⓐ Ⓑ Ⓒ Ⓓ
23. Ⓐ Ⓑ Ⓒ Ⓓ
24. Ⓐ Ⓑ Ⓒ Ⓓ
25. Ⓐ Ⓑ Ⓒ Ⓓ
26. Ⓐ Ⓑ Ⓒ Ⓓ
27. Ⓐ Ⓑ Ⓒ Ⓓ
28. Ⓐ Ⓑ Ⓒ Ⓓ
29. Ⓐ Ⓑ Ⓒ Ⓓ
30. Ⓐ Ⓑ Ⓒ Ⓓ
31. Ⓐ Ⓑ Ⓒ Ⓓ
32. Ⓐ Ⓑ Ⓒ Ⓓ
33. Ⓐ Ⓑ Ⓒ Ⓓ
34. Ⓐ Ⓑ Ⓒ Ⓓ
35. Ⓐ Ⓑ Ⓒ Ⓓ
36. Ⓐ Ⓑ Ⓒ Ⓓ
37. Ⓐ Ⓑ Ⓒ Ⓓ
38. Ⓐ Ⓑ Ⓒ Ⓓ
39. Ⓐ Ⓑ Ⓒ Ⓓ
40. Ⓐ Ⓑ Ⓒ Ⓓ
41. Ⓐ Ⓑ Ⓒ Ⓓ
42. Ⓐ Ⓑ Ⓒ Ⓓ
43. Ⓐ Ⓑ Ⓒ Ⓓ
44. Ⓐ Ⓑ Ⓒ Ⓓ

Completely darken bubbles with a No. 2 pencil. If you make a mistake, be sure to erase mark completely. Erase all stray marks.

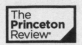

Test ❶  Start with number 1 for each new section.
If a section has fewer questions than answer spaces, leave the extra answer spaces blank.

## Section 3—Mathematics: No Calculator

1. Ⓐ Ⓑ Ⓒ Ⓓ
2. Ⓐ Ⓑ Ⓒ Ⓓ
3. Ⓐ Ⓑ Ⓒ Ⓓ
4. Ⓐ Ⓑ Ⓒ Ⓓ
5. Ⓐ Ⓑ Ⓒ Ⓓ
6. Ⓐ Ⓑ Ⓒ Ⓓ
7. Ⓐ Ⓑ Ⓒ Ⓓ
8. Ⓐ Ⓑ Ⓒ Ⓓ
9. Ⓐ Ⓑ Ⓒ Ⓓ
10. Ⓐ Ⓑ Ⓒ Ⓓ
11. Ⓐ Ⓑ Ⓒ Ⓓ
12. Ⓐ Ⓑ Ⓒ Ⓓ
13. Ⓐ Ⓑ Ⓒ Ⓓ
14. Ⓐ Ⓑ Ⓒ Ⓓ
15. Ⓐ Ⓑ Ⓒ Ⓓ

16. 17. 18. 19. 20.

## Section 4—Mathematics: Calculator

1. Ⓐ Ⓑ Ⓒ Ⓓ
2. Ⓐ Ⓑ Ⓒ Ⓓ
3. Ⓐ Ⓑ Ⓒ Ⓓ
4. Ⓐ Ⓑ Ⓒ Ⓓ
5. Ⓐ Ⓑ Ⓒ Ⓓ
6. Ⓐ Ⓑ Ⓒ Ⓓ
7. Ⓐ Ⓑ Ⓒ Ⓓ
8. Ⓐ Ⓑ Ⓒ Ⓓ
9. Ⓐ Ⓑ Ⓒ Ⓓ
10. Ⓐ Ⓑ Ⓒ Ⓓ
11. Ⓐ Ⓑ Ⓒ Ⓓ
12. Ⓐ Ⓑ Ⓒ Ⓓ
13. Ⓐ Ⓑ Ⓒ Ⓓ
14. Ⓐ Ⓑ Ⓒ Ⓓ
15. Ⓐ Ⓑ Ⓒ Ⓓ
16. Ⓐ Ⓑ Ⓒ Ⓓ
17. Ⓐ Ⓑ Ⓒ Ⓓ
18. Ⓐ Ⓑ Ⓒ Ⓓ
19. Ⓐ Ⓑ Ⓒ Ⓓ
20. Ⓐ Ⓑ Ⓒ Ⓓ
21. Ⓐ Ⓑ Ⓒ Ⓓ
22. Ⓐ Ⓑ Ⓒ Ⓓ
23. Ⓐ Ⓑ Ⓒ Ⓓ
24. Ⓐ Ⓑ Ⓒ Ⓓ
25. Ⓐ Ⓑ Ⓒ Ⓓ
26. Ⓐ Ⓑ Ⓒ Ⓓ
27. Ⓐ Ⓑ Ⓒ Ⓓ
28. Ⓐ Ⓑ Ⓒ Ⓓ
29. Ⓐ Ⓑ Ⓒ Ⓓ
30. Ⓐ Ⓑ Ⓒ Ⓓ

31. 32. 33. 34. 35.

36. 37. 38.

# Chapter 4
# Practice Test 1:
# Answers and
# Explanations

# PRACTICE TEST 1 ANSWER KEY

## Section 1: Reading

| | | | |
|---|---|---|---|
| 1. | D | 27. | B |
| 2. | B | 28. | C |
| 3. | C | 29. | A |
| 4. | B | 30. | C |
| 5. | C | 31. | A |
| 6. | D | 32. | B |
| 7. | B | 33. | C |
| 8. | B | 34. | B |
| 9. | A | 35. | A |
| 10. | A | 36. | B |
| 11. | D | 37. | D |
| 12. | B | 38. | C |
| 13. | D | 39. | A |
| 14. | A | 40. | D |
| 15. | C | 41. | D |
| 16. | B | 42. | B |
| 17. | C | 43. | C |
| 18. | A | 44. | A |
| 19. | C | 45. | C |
| 20. | D | 46. | D |
| 21. | D | 47. | B |
| 22. | B | 48. | D |
| 23. | C | 49. | A |
| 24. | C | 50. | D |
| 25. | D | 51. | C |
| 26. | B | 52. | B |

## Section 2: Writing & Language

| | | | |
|---|---|---|---|
| 1. | D | 23. | B |
| 2. | D | 24. | B |
| 3. | A | 25. | A |
| 4. | B | 26. | D |
| 5. | C | 27. | C |
| 6. | B | 28. | C |
| 7. | A | 29. | A |
| 8. | B | 30. | C |
| 9. | C | 31. | B |
| 10. | D | 32. | D |
| 11. | C | 33. | D |
| 12. | D | 34. | C |
| 13. | A | 35. | C |
| 14. | C | 36. | D |
| 15. | D | 37. | C |
| 16. | C | 38. | B |
| 17. | A | 39. | A |
| 18. | D | 40. | D |
| 19. | D | 41. | D |
| 20. | C | 42. | B |
| 21. | B | 43. | C |
| 22. | A | 44. | D |

## Section 3: Math (No Calculator)

| | | | |
|---|---|---|---|
| 1. | A | 11. | D |
| 2. | B | 12. | A |
| 3. | B | 13. | C |
| 4. | D | 14. | A |
| 5. | D | 15. | C |
| 6. | C | 16. | 5 |
| 7. | A | 17. | 6 |
| 8. | A | 18. | $\frac{5}{13}$ |
| 9. | C | 19. | 225 |
| 10. | C | 20. | 13 |

## Section 4: Math (Calculator)

| | | | |
|---|---|---|---|
| 1. | C | 20. | A |
| 2. | C | 21. | D |
| 3. | B | 22. | C |
| 4. | B | 23. | C |
| 5. | D | 24. | A |
| 6. | A | 25. | C |
| 7. | C | 26. | D |
| 8. | D | 27. | C |
| 9. | B | 28. | B |
| 10. | A | 29. | A |
| 11. | D | 30. | B |
| 12. | D | 31. | $\frac{3}{7}, \frac{6}{14},$ .428 or .429 |
| 13. | B | | |
| 14. | B | | |
| 15. | A | | |
| 16. | C | | |
| 17. | D | | |
| 18. | C | 32. | Any value from 14 to 21, inclusive |
| 19. | C | 33. | 30 |
| | | 34. | 4 |
| | | 35. | 4 |
| | | 36. | 51 |
| | | 37. | 3 |
| | | 38. | 8.76 |

For self-scoring assessment tables, please turn to page 957.

# PRACTICE TEST 1 EXPLANATIONS

## Section 1: Reading

1.  **D**   This question asks about the developmental pattern of the passage, so it should be answered after the specific questions. Look for clues in the text that indicate the mood and story of the passage. This particular passage moves from glum to foreboding. The narrator is nervous on his journey, but he states that when he sees the city he foresees his bleak future. Since the narrator discusses the past, he goes further to confirm it: *I prophesied truly, and failed only in one single circumstance, that in all the misery I imagined and dreaded, I did not conceive the hundredth part of the anguish I was destined to endure.* Choice (A) refers to the joy he felt at seeing his native land, but that is only a half-right answer because it does not address the negative mood and events. The passage says nothing about the narrator responding to a request for help, so (B) is incorrect. The author describes the daemon, but the passage does not mention an ancient curse, so (C) is incorrect. Choice (D) accurately describes the narrator's mood and final despair. Choice (D) is the correct answer.

2.  **B**   This question asks about what happens in the passage, making it a straightforward question to answer after the specific questions have been answered. Choice (A) goes beyond the information in the passage, since there is no mention of any plans the narrator has to avenge his brother's death. Choice (B) accurately addresses the feeling of anxiety the narrator has throughout the passage, as seen in the fourth paragraph when he says, *The picture appeared a vast and dim scene of evil, and I foresaw obscurely that I was destined to become the most wretched of human beings.* Keep (B). Choice (C) describes the narrator's fear of returning home to the monster, but the passage discusses how the narrator seems to be more afraid of what has changed and how his future may be affected, so it can be eliminated. Choice (D) addresses how the narrator becomes anxious about returning home, but he says he *longed to console and sympathize with my loved and sorrowing friends*, so it seems that he isn't afraid he will not be welcome. Choice (B) is the correct answer.

3.  **C**   The question asks which emotion the narrator *most* feels. Because the question uses the word *most*, this indicates there may be more than one emotion the narrator feels. The answer to this question is the one that the narrator feels most strongly. Notice that the following question is a best evidence question, so this question and Q4 can be answered in tandem. Look at the answers for Q4 first. The lines in (4A) mention *the delight [the narrator] took*, so look to see if those lines support any answers in Q3. Choice (3A) mentions the *joy...at returning home.* Connect those two answers. Next, consider the lines for (4B). The narrator says that he *prophesied truly... all the misery I imagined...anguish I was destined to endure.* He's looking into the future and seeing terrible things. Consider the answers to Q3. Choice (3C) mentions *prescience concerning his fate*, which is a paraphrase of *looking into the future.* Connect (3C) and (4B). The

lines in (4C) mention the coming storm, which is not referenced in any of the answers to Q3. Eliminate (4C). Choice (4D) mentions the narrator's reaction to the daemon, but does not reference any emotion. Eliminate (4D). Without any support from Q4, (3B) and (3D) can be eliminated. Consider the remaining pairs of answer choices in the context of the passage. The emotion the narrator feels *most* is negative, so (3A) and (4A) can be eliminated. Choices (3C) and (4B) are the correct answers.

4.   **B**   (See explanation above.)

5.   **C**   This is a Vocab-in-Context question. Use the context to substitute another word based on the clues in the text. The passage says *all around was calm; and the snowy mountains, 'the palaces of nature,' were not changed. By degrees the calm and heavenly scene restored me, and I continued my journey towards Geneva.* Therefore, *placid* must mean something like *peaceful* or *calm*. Choices (A), (B), and (D) can all be eliminated. Choice (C) is the correct answer.

6.   **D**   The question asks about the *main purpose* of the first paragraph, so the correct answer will accurately summarize the paragraph. The author starts the passage by saying *My journey was very melancholy* and later describes his *painful state of mind* to set a tone for what will come. The author's choices create a negative mood for the reader. Choice (A) is incorrect, since the paragraph isn't written to represent anything. Choice (B) says that the author exaggerates the narrator's emotion, but the narrator is feeling a profound sort of dread, so there's no exaggeration. Choice (C) says that the paragraph is there to give context, but the narrator doesn't mention his brother's death explicitly or the daemon until later in the passage. Choice (D) best explains that the paragraph is there to establish the mood as the narrator returns home. Choice (D) is the correct answer.

7.   **B**   This question asks why the narrator uses a particular phrase. Carefully read the window to look for clues to indicate the narrator's meaning. His focus is on how things may have changed in the six years he's been gone (*How altered everything might be during that time*). Although *one sudden and desolating change had taken place*, the narrator goes on to say that *other alterations* had possibly been worked by those *thousand little circumstances*. Of these little circumstances, he says that *although they were done more tranquilly, [they] might not be the less decisive.* Therefore, although there was only one major change, significant changes could also have come from smaller events that were individually less traumatic but still added up to something big. Choice (A) can be eliminated because the change that happened (the loss of the narrator's brother) was not connected to a natural disaster. Choice (B) is a good paraphrase of the prediction, so don't eliminate it. The narrator never mentions his role in the murder or any way he could have affected the outcome, so eliminate (C). Choice (D) can be eliminated because there is never any mention of politics. Choice (B) is the correct answer.

8.   **B**   This is a best evidence question with a clear window. Simply consider the lines used to predict the answer to question 7. The textual evidence used to answer Q7 was in the lines *One sudden and desolating change had taken place; but a thousand little circumstances might have by degrees*

*worked other alterations, which, although they were done more tranquilly, might not be the less decisive.* Choice (B) is the correct answer.

9.   **A**   This question asks about how the narrator addresses the tempest. Find evidence in the text to support how the narrator feels about the storm. He states, *While I watched the tempest, so beautiful yet terrific, I wandered on with a hasty step. This noble war in the sky elevated my spirits; I clasped my hands, and exclaimed aloud, "William, dear angel! This is thy funeral, this thy dirge!* Although the rain is pelting him and lightening is flashing, his spirits are high. Thus, the *awe but no fear* in (A) looks good. Don't eliminate it. He describes the storm as *violent* and *terrific*, so a word that means overjoyed is too positive, making (B) incorrect. While he is sad about William's death, he is not sad about the storm, making (C) incorrect. It is possible that the narrator is a little dramatic, but there is no evidence to prove that he is crazy. Therefore, (D) is incorrect. Choice (A) is the correct answer.

10.   **A**   This is a Vocab-in-Context question. Use the context to substitute another word based on the clues in the text. The passage says, *I perceived in the gloom a figure which stole from behind a clump of trees near me.* The figure is emerging from behind the tree, so *stole* must have something to do with how the figure is moving. Put in *emerged* or *stepped out from behind*. Eliminate any answers that have nothing to do with that prediction. That eliminates (B) and (C). To *loom* means to *come into view in indistinct and enlarged form*, and *displaced* means *to move out of the usual place*. Based on the context, it would make more sense for the monster to move out from its position behind the trees. Choice (A) is the correct answer.

11.   **D**   This is a main purpose question, so even though it's the first question for the passage, it should be done at the end. It asks about the main purpose, so the correct answer should address why the passage was written. In the fourth paragraph, the author does mention *a set of essays*, but this passage is an introduction for those essays, not a review of them. Eliminate (A). Choice (B) is incorrect because the author does not use persuasive language, nor is there an argument for or against any field in this passage. Eliminate it. Choice (C) can be eliminated because, while the author does mention the limitations of Piaget and others, he goes on to reconcile those limitations with his own scientific views, so that's not the main purpose of the passage. Choice (D) sums up the information that the author provides in the passage. He introduces psychology and its fields of study to get to the point of how structuralism has influences on his own work. Choice (D) is the correct answer.

12.   **B**   This question asks about the *central claim* of the passage. This is a general question, so it should be answered after all the specific questions have been answered. The central claim of the passage is related to the main purpose: What is the most important part of the author's argument? The author's main point is that structuralism provided a wider range of avenues for psychologists to explore the mind. Choice (A) does not match this prediction because, while it might make sense that the author thinks pre-1960s psychology was *sedate and impractical,* that isn't actually in the text. Eliminate (A). Choice (B) is supported by the final paragraph, so keep it.

Choice (C) is partially true in that behaviorists believe that humans *act in the way we do because we are reinforced for doing so,* but that is not the central claim in this passage. Also, there is no evidence their views are *preordained,* so this choice can be eliminated. Choice (D) can be eliminated because there is no evidence that the author's work is revolutionary. Although that word appears earlier in the passage, it does not refer to the author's work. Choice (B) is the correct answer.

13.  **D**   This question asks about the reason the author *describes different branches of psychology* throughout the passage. In the first paragraph he mentioned *academic psychology, behaviorism, and psychoanalysis.* He labels these three as *uninviting specializations.* Then he mentions the *cognitive revolution* in the 1960s in the second paragraph, and he goes on to further describe how the revolution *inspired* those in the field who became and remained interested in the *structuralist approach.* The correct answer should address this shift. Choice (A) does not match the prediction because the author's goal is to present the shift, not to simply lay out the history. Choice (B) does not match because there is no evidence that the author is in any way prominent in the scientific community. It can be eliminated. Choice (C) can be eliminated because the author never makes any reference to structuralism being *inferior to behaviorism.* In fact, the author seems to feel more positively about structuralism than behaviorism. Choice (D) is consistent with the prediction and is the correct answer.

14.  **A**   This question is in a paired set with Q15. This question asks what the author indicates about the *cognitive revolution* in the passage. The author is positive about the revolution, mentioning that the revolution made the study of the mind *a proper scientific undertaking.* He also says the revolution provided a *structure to thought processes.* In the third paragraph, he says many in the behavioral sciences in the 1960's were *swept up—and have remained inspired—*by the revolution. Choice (A) matches the idea that the author was *swept up* by the revolution, so keep that answer. Choice (B) can be eliminated because there is no evidence that psychology was ever a dying science. Choice (C) can be eliminated because while the author hints at a revitalization of psychology due to the revolution, the thoughtfulness of previous psychologists was not mentioned or questioned. Choice (D) does not match any of the predictions because there is no mention of changes prior to the 1960s. Choice (A) is the correct answer.

15.  **C**   This is a best evidence question, so consider the lines used to predict the answer to Q14. Choice (C) is the correct answer.

16.  **B**   This question and Q17 are a general paired set, so they can be answered in tandem. Consider the lines given in Q17 and see if those lines can be used to support any of the answers in Q16. Choice (17A) supports (16C), so draw a line to connect those answers. Choice (17B) might initially look good because the words *problem-solving* and *creating* also show up in (16A), but those words describe mental processes, not the psychology. Eliminate (17B). Choice (17C) supports (16B), so draw a line connecting those answers. Choice (17D) does not support any of

the answers for Q16, so that answer can be eliminated. Look back at the answers for Q16. Neither (16A) nor (16D) has support, so both of those can be eliminated. This leaves two pairs of answers: (16C)/(17A) and (16B)/(17C). Look back at the question. It asks about the branch of psychology that became popular *after the revolution*. The description of behaviorism in (17A) is from before the revolution. That pair can be eliminated, leaving (16B) and (17C) as the correct answers.

17.  **C**  (See explanation above.)

18.  **A**  This question asks about the author's reason for mentioning Piaget, Chomsky, and Levi-Strauss. In the fourth paragraph, the author says these scientists *(psychologist, linguist, and anthropologist) exemplify the principal assumption* of the structuralist approach. Choice (A) matches the prediction, so keep it. Choice (B) can be eliminated because their work is not *inherently problematic*; it is just not fully in line with the views of the author. Choice (C) can be eliminated because the author notes that these men are not all psychologists: Chomsky is a linguist and Levi-Strauss is an anthropologist. Choice (D) can be eliminated because there is no evidence that these men have published anything that would not agree with the author's conclusions about creativity and structuralism. Choice (A) is the correct answer.

19.  **C**  This question asks about the author's use of the phrase *original works of art.* In the fifth paragraph, the author discusses the *limitations* of the structural approach. He uses the *original works of art* as an example in which the structuralists' ideas about human thought were *problematic for a study of mind where the...focus falls on innovations and creativity.* Choice (A) does not work because it does not address the *limitations*. Eliminate it. Choice (B) can be eliminated because the author makes the point that the structuralists' view are *limited*, but he never argues that the views are *distorted.* Choice (C) is a good paraphrase of the text, so keep it. Choice (D) is too broad in its mention of *psychology* and incorrect in its assessment of psychology as *closed-minded.* Choice (C) is the correct answer.

20.  **D**  This question asks about the meaning of the *symbol systems.* The author states that those systems are *codes of meaning* and *vehicles through which thought takes place.* Choice (A) is incorrect because while the symbol systems are used in thought processes, they are not the thought processes themselves. Choice (B) is incorrect because symbol systems reconcile the issue with creativity and structuralism. Choice (C) is incorrect because the author does not refer to the systems as *principles,* but as a *feature of human thought.* Choice (D) is correct because the symbols are the way the human mind makes meaning. Choice (D) is the correct answer.

21.  **D**  This question asks about the author's purpose in mentioning *delays, redesigns, and even near-death cancellations.* Use the given line reference to find the window in the passage. The earlier part of the sentence makes a contrast between the conception of New Horizon *in the late 1980s* and its launch in *2006,* so look for an answer choice that deals with a time delay. Choice (A) deals with speed, not a span of time. Choices (B) and (C) deal with possible problems with the mission, and are thus irrelevant to time delay. Choice (D) deals with a time delay between

a plan and its execution. Plan matches *conception*, and execution matches *launch*. Choice (D) is the correct answer.

22. **B** This question asks what outcome the author says could result from the flyby over Pluto. Use the key word *flyby* to locate the window at the end of paragraph 2. The following paragraphs both describe possible results of the flyby, so look for an answer there. Choice (A) mentions 7:49 Eastern time, which is from paragraph 1. Choice (B) states that no data might come in, which matches *its failure by hearing nothing*. Choice (C) contains *mission's failure* and *radio signal*, which match phrases from paragraph 3, but (C) is deceptive—the text states that scientists will learn of the *success* through *a radio signal*. Choice (D) mentions receiving data after a delay, which matches paragraph 3, but (D) specifies the delay as 3 minutes, a number mentioned in paragraph 2. Choice (B) is the correct answer.

23. **C** This question asks for the best evidence for the answer to Q22. Since the sentence in paragraph 3 containing *its failure by hearing nothing* supported that answer, eliminate answer choices from other paragraphs, then compare the remaining answer choices to select the best match. Choice (C) contains the phrase *its failure by hearing nothing*, so that is the correct answer.

24. **C** This is a Vocab-in-Context question, so find the word *suite* in line 26 and cross it out. Replace it with another word that makes sense in the context of the text. A word like *group* or *collection* would make sense, so use such a word to compare to the answer choices. Choice (A) may recall suit, which looks like *suite*, but has a different meaning. Choice (B) is one meaning of *suite*, but not in this context. Choice (C) means arrangement. Keep any unknown words, just in case they are correct, and only eliminate ones that are definitely incorrect. Choice (D) may recall sweet, which has the same pronunciation as *suite*, but not the same meaning. Since (A), (B), and (D) are wrong, the correct answer must be (C), even if this was a previously unknown word. Choice (C) is the correct answer.

25. **D** This question asks why the author discusses the measurement of the primary encounter. Use the given line reference to find the window. The sentence containing *primary encounter* begins with *Though*, so the author is establishing a contrast. Although that encounter *is best measured in minutes and hours*, the sentence goes on to emphasize how long it will take for the data to all be sent to Earth. Look for an answer choice that makes a contrast between a short amount of time and a long amount of time. Choice (A) references an earlier claim that could be supported by this discussion, but no earlier claims are supported by this discussion. Choice (B) refers to an undermined assumption, but there is no assumption and nothing is undermined. Choice (C) is about time, but does not match the prediction. Choice (D) is about time, and it matches the prediction, since it indicates a contrast between something fast and something slow. Choice (D) is the correct answer.

26. **B** This question asks about the main idea of Passage 2. Because it is a general question, it should be done after all the specific questions. It begins with the first part of a contrast, that *New Horizons has started to transmit information about Pluto*, but then the question ends with a *but*.

Find something in the text that contrasts with the idea of New Horizons reaching Pluto. The end of the passage mentions another target for New Horizons *a mere billion miles further along the interplanetary road*. The correct answer will have something to do with further goals for New Horizon. Choice (A) might initially look attractive because New Horizons is going to *continue on…into the night*, but (A) has nothing about the next mission. Choice (B) is a solid paraphrase of the prediction, so don't eliminate it. Choice (C) might be true, but it isn't the contrast given in the passage. Eliminate it. Choice (D) is not mentioned in Passage 2. Choice (B) is the correct answer.

27. **B** This is a Vocab-in-Context question, so find the word *deploy* in line 53 and cross it out. Replace it with another word that makes sense in the context of the text. A word like *use* would make sense. Look for an answer choice that matches this prediction. Choice (A) might recall the word *decoy*. Choice (B) matches the prediction. Choice (C) does not match the prediction. Choice (D) might recall the word *destroy*. Choice (B) is the correct answer.

28. **C** This question asks how the passages relate to each other. Because it is about both passages, it should be done after all the specific and general questions about the individual passages. Both passages inform readers about the objects New Horizons will encounter and study (Pluto, and then something beyond), and both have a positive tone. Choice (A) mentions *concern* and *dangers*, which do not match the prediction. Choice (B) mentions a revision, but there is no revision. Choice (C) is a possible match to the prediction: The *story* could be *the first golden age of interplanetary exploration*, and the *next chapter* could be the search for new objects beyond the solar system. Choice (D) mentions support, but there is no *qualified* support of Passage 1 by Passage 2. Choice (C) is the correct answer.

29. **A** This question asks how the author of Passage 2 would most likely respond to something specific in Passage 1. Note the main idea of Passage 2, and use the given line reference to find the window in Passage 1. The continued journey is referred to in Passage 1 as an *endless journey into interstellar night*. Passage 2 describes the journey as having a target, rather than lacking an end or a goal, so look for an answer that fits this prediction. Choice (A) is possible, since New Horizons will now head toward *PT1 (potential target one) or more officially 2014 MU69*. Choice (B) is a true statement, but one that does not answer this question. Choice (C) fits Passage 1, not Passage 2, and (D) makes a statement not supported by either text. Choice (A) is the correct answer.

30. **C** This question asks for the best evidence for the answer to Q29. Since paragraph 6, which contains *PT1 (potential target one) or more officially 2014 MU69*, supported that answer, eliminate answer choices involving other paragraphs, then compare remaining answer choices to select the best match. Choice (A) is from paragraph 3. Choice (B) is from paragraph 4. Choice (C) is from paragraph 6, and contains the predicted phrase. Choice (D) is from paragraph 7. Choice (C) is the correct answer.

31.   **A**   This question asks which statement is true about New Horizons' journey in both passages. Passage 1 depicts an *endless journey into night*. Passage 2 names a stopping point located *a mere billion miles further*. Choice (A) could be true, since the journey could end and since a billion miles is described with the word *mere*. Choice (B) mentions metaphor and strict realism, neither of which have textual support. Choice (C) mentions allegory and personification. Although Passage 2 may personify the spacecraft as a person (*What do you do? ... You keep going*), no allegory appears in the text. Choice (D) may be tempting, due to the mention in Passage 1 of *a golden age*, but Passage 2 does not present an anecdote. Choice (A) is the correct answer.

32.   **B**   This question asks what the authors intend to highlight with their examples. Use the given line references to find the window. Choice (A) contradicts that we can *effortlessly* talk and walk. Choice (B) fits the claim that *Humans often engage in multitasking*. Choice (C) does not match the first paragraph. It is deceptive, because later there is discussion about multitasking and lower grades, but this is a correlation. Choice (C) suggests that doing one thing can cause the other. Choice (D) does not match the first paragraph. Later, the authors suggest that multitasking could have some evolutionary benefits, but this is not the same as instinctual and is not why the examples of multitasking are mentioned. Choice (B) is the correct answer.

33.   **C**   This is a Vocab-in-Context question, so find the word *engage* in line 7 and cross it out. Replace it with another word that makes sense in the context of the text. A word like *use* or *require* would make sense, so use such a word to compare with the answer choices. Choice (A), *marry*, recalls a different meaning of *engage*. Choice (B), *capture*, does not fit the prediction. Choice (C), *employ*, matches the prediction *use*. Choice (D), *absorb*, does not fit the prediction. Choice (C) is the correct answer.

34.   **B**   This question asks what the authors would most likely say about media multitasking. Use the line reference provided to find the window, and locate something the authors actually did say. Paragraph 3 begins by mentioning that *recent research* has examined effects of *media multitasking*. The rest of the paragraph presents results that are described as *detrimental* and *negative* and twice the word *impaired* is used. Thus, select an answer choice that summarizes these meanings. Choice (A), *focused*, is positive. Choice (B), *disadvantageous*, fits the prediction. Choice (C), *multifaceted*, is either neutral or positive. Choice (D), *chronic*, is negative, but fits the prediction less well than (B). Choice (B) is the correct answer.

35.   **A**   This question asks for something specific the author says about Kirschner and Karpinski, namely: what do they suggest is the reason that grades decrease? Use the names as lead words to locate the window. This is paragraph 4. The second sentence reads: *Kirschner and Karpinski found that heavy Facebook users reported having lower grade point averages (GPAs) and suggested the possible deleterious effect of simultaneously using Facebook with other activities.* Thus, look for an answer choice that closely matches this sentence. Choice (A) could fit, since Facebook is a social media platform. Keep it for now. Choice (B) could be true, but it does not fit the prediction because

there is no mention of social media. Choice (C) could be true, but it does not fit the prediction because there is no mention of Messenger in the prediction. Choice (D) mentions Facebook, but the prediction was about using Facebook while doing other things, like homework, not about spending too much time on Facebook in general. Choice (A) is the correct answer.

36. **B**   This is a specific best evidence question, so simply consider the lines used to predict the answer to Q35. Lines 43–46 were used to predict the answer to Q35, so (B) is the correct answer to this question.

37. **D**   This question asks what the large-scale study authors assume to be true about light media multitaskers as compared to the heavy media multitaskers. Use the lines provided to find the window. Much of the paragraph is about heavy media multitaskers, but the final sentence says that heavy media multitaskers are *inferior to light media multitaskers in tasks that required one to disregard irrelevant information in the environment and in memory.* Thus, look for an answer choice showing that light media multitaskers are better at disregarding irrelevant information. Choice (A), *distracted*, suggests the opposite of this prediction. Choice (B), *focused*, fits this prediction. Keep it for now. Choice (C), *scholarly*, has nothing to do with this prediction. Choice (D), *discriminating*, fits this prediction. Compare the remaining answer choices. Choice (B) is further away from the text's focus on sorting through relevant information. This choice also doesn't work because the heavy media multitaskers are focused, just on broader information. Choice (D) is closest in meaning to the text. Choice (D) is the correct answer.

38. **C**   This question asks for the best evidence for the answer to Q37. Since the prediction came from paragraph 5, eliminate answer choices from other paragraphs first. Choice (38A) is from paragraph 4; eliminate it. It supports (37C), but it is not relevant here. Choices (38B) and (38C) are from paragraph 5; keep them for now. Choice (38D) is from paragraph 6; eliminate it. Also, it supports nothing from Q37. Choice (38B) is about heavy media multitaskers, but Q37 asked about light media multitaskers; eliminate it. Choice (38C) is about light media multitaskers, and it contains the phrase used to predict the correct answer to Q37. Choice (38C) is the correct answer.

39. **A**   This is a Vocab-in-Context question, so find the word *process* in line 57 and cross it out. Replace it with another word that makes sense in the context of the text. Given the focus of the rest of the paragraph on sorting, distinguishing or discriminating between relevant and irrelevant information, use one of these verbs as a prediction. Choice (A), *filter*, fits this prediction. Choice (B), *share*, does not fit because the passage discusses how multitaskers bring in information, not how they send it out. Choice (C), *digitize*, makes no sense. Choice (D), *retain*, does not fit the prediction. Choice (A) is the correct answer.

40. **D**   This question asks why the authors refer to the *pip-and-pop paradigm*. Use the line reference provided to find the window. In paragraph 7 the authors state what they were trying to measure, then mention the pip-and-pop paradigm, then go on to describe how the paradigm works.

Choose an answer choice that fits this outline of paragraph 7. Choice (A) does not fit, since the authors are not questioning a technique. Choice (B) does not fit, since there is no claim that would be supported. Choice (C) can be eliminated because the authors are introducing the pip-and-pop paradigm, not clarifying it. Choice (D) could fit, since the paradigm is an experimental method, and since they are introducing it before explaining what it is. Choice (D) is the correct answer.

41. **D** This question asks for the most accurate interpretation of the line of best fit on the graph following the passage. Notice that the line has a positive slope, and that $r = 0.292$. The term $r$ represents the correlation between the two factors on the $X$ and $Y$ graphs. Also notice what the $X$ and $Y$ axes represent: media multitasking and multisensory integration. Choice (A) is incorrect, because neither the graph nor the text indicate what grades light media multitaskers get. Choice (B) is incorrect because the study in question deals with a different topic than Kirschner and Karpinski's study. Choice (C) is incorrect, because neither the graph nor the text discuss cognitive functions. Choice (D) is true: The data are not tightly grouped around the line of best fit, so although there is a correlation, it is weak. Choice (D) is the correct answer.

42. **B** This question asks how the study's authors would interpret a specific finding presented in the graph. First, look at the graphs, both of which indicate that heavy media use is positively correlated to multisensory integration. To answer the question of how the authors would interpret this finding, look at the passage. Paragraphs 5 and 6 discuss heavy media multitaskers. Paragraph 5 focuses on their weaknesses in distinguishing between data, while paragraph 6 focuses on their strengths in being aware of multiple data. Heavy media multitaskers may have *better performance if a task contains some unexpected information that is important to the task at hand. When a media multitasker reads, for example, he or she may more readily detect an SMS ringtone from a mobile phone, although the ringtone does not carry information useful for the primary task of reading.* Choice (A) describes a strength of low media multitaskers, rather than heavy media multitaskers. Choice (B) fits the prediction, since reading and hearing a ringtone match *multiple unrelated tasks.* Choice (C) could be true, but it is too general to fit the prediction. Choice (D) is more specific, but it claims too much. The passage mentioned reading and ringtones. Choice (D) claims that heavy media multitaskers observe *all* details, and during a *stressful* event. This does not fit the passage. Choice (B) is the correct answer.

43. **C** The question asks what the authors' statement implies. Use the given line reference to find the window in order to answer this question. This sentence summarizes the paragraph, which begins by describing a woman who was surprisingly cured by the use of antibiotics early in the 20th century and a man who wasn't cured six decades later. The authors' statement *we have come full circle* indicates that we are medically back to pre-antibiotic days, and the fact that there is *no magic bullet* indicates there is no solution to this problem. It does not indicate that antibiotics are no longer used to treat bacterial infections, only that antibiotics are increasingly ineffective; eliminate (A). Based on the paragraph it is clear that doctors were on board

with the use of antibiotics before this article was written, which eliminates (B). Choice (C) is supported as the author states there is *no magic bullet*, or solution, as to how to treat antibiotic-resistant bacteria as illustrated in the paragraph. Keep it. Choice (D) is deceptive; although this paragraph does mention *E. faecium*, it does not say that it is no longer treatable at all; it only states that one case was not treatable with antibiotics. Eliminate (D). Choice (C) is the correct answer.

44.   **A**   This questions asks which statement would contradict the claim that *antibiotic use has never been 100% effective in the treatment of a bacterial infection*. Use the given line references provided in the answer choices to find a statement that contradicts this statement. Choice (A) describes a successful use of antibiotic treatment for a bacterial infection, which would contradict the idea that antibiotics have never been 100% effective. Choice (B) describes an unsuccessful application of antibiotics to treat a bacterial infection; this supports the claim in the question, so (B) should be eliminated. Choice (C) discusses how bacteria developed resistance to certain antibiotics, but it does not indicate the success rate of those antibiotics prior to that resistance. As this choice neither supports nor contradicts the claim, eliminate (C). Choice (D) can be eliminated for the same reason; it does not contain any specific information about the success, or lack thereof, of antibiotic treatments against bacteria. Choice (A) is the correct answer.

45.   **C**   This question asks what a word, *evolution*, indicates in the passage. Use the given line references to find the windows in order to answer this question. The sentences that contain *evolution* in them are discussing *adaptation*, with the first sentence focusing on bacteria as a group and the second focusing on MRSA specifically. As it is not only one bacteria discussed in both lines, (A) should be eliminated because it is too limited. Although the sentences do discuss evolution and drug-resistant bacteria, neither indicate that the evolution was *inevitable*, so (B) should be eliminated. These lines do indicate that it is the adaptability of bacteria that enables them to resist antibiotic treatment, which supports (C). Keep (C). While the passage does say that bacteria have adapted and evolved, there is no indication that any specific strains have disappeared, eliminating (D). Choice (C) is the correct answer.

46.   **D**   This question asks about a specific claim. As the window given is very large (an entire paragraph) and antibiotic resistance is the main focus of the passage, it is likely that the authors say there are many things that could be a result of antibiotic resistance. In this case, it would be most effective to check each answer choice against what is stated in the passage and use POE. Choice (A) can be eliminated as the paragraph indicates that those strains have actually become more difficult to overcome, not that they have disappeared. Choice (B) can be deleted as it is a reference to an entirely different paragraph (paragraph 1), and it is incorrect—there is no *magic bullet* according to the passage. Choice (C) can be eliminated as deaths are not mentioned in this paragraph. Choice (D) is supported by the paragraph as it states that *S. aureus quickly developed resistance to the β-lactam compounds*, which fits that *S. aureus* is resistant to at least one antibiotic treatment. Choice (D) is the correct answer.

47.  **B**  This question asks why the author included information about MRSA's glycopeptide and vancomycin resistance. As no reference is included, use chronological order and lead words to locate the window of the passage in which these terms appear, which is in the third paragraph. This paragraph reviews MRSA's history of resistance in relation to glycopeptides and vancomycin and medical changes that resulted from that resistance. Choice (A) can be eliminated as it is much too broad and the paragraph does not contain information about the medical research that went into developing antibiotics. Choice (B) correctly reflects the fact that a history of a bacteria's resistance to differing antibiotics is reviewed. Keep (B). Choice (C) is not supported by the paragraph; not only is there no reference to these being the most common antibiotics used, the information indicates that they are no longer effective at treating a specific bacteria. Eliminate (C). Choice (D) is another choice that is too broad because it refers to all antibiotics, but only certain ones are mentioned. Eliminate (D). Choice (B) is the correct answer.

48.  **D**  This question asks about the function of the words *appears* and *often*. Use the reference window, the final paragraph, to read these words in context. The author uses *appears* when referring to the fact that the dissemination of certain *isolates appears to be limited, at least for now* and *often* when referring to the fact that VRSA is *often resistant*. These sentences indicate a lack of certainty and specificity: strains of a bacteria are referred to as having *true* resistance, rather than *100%* or some other resistant measurement, spread *appears* to be limited rather than is or isn't limited, a bacteria is *often* resistant rather than a specific percent resistant. All of these words indicate a lack of certainty. This best matches (D). Choice (A) is incorrect, as no levels of anything are confirmed in this paragraph. Choice (B) is incorrect as clinical results are not discussed in this paragraph. Choice (C) is incorrect, as there is no call for greater attention or funding for this area of science. Choice (D) is the correct answer.

49.  **A**  This questions asks for an answer that is supported by both the table and the passage. Locate where penicillin is discussed in the passage. In the first paragraph, penicillin is discussed in the context of curing a woman of streptococci in 1942. The only answer that is supported by this is (A), since the passage refers to penicillin as a newly discovered substance when it was administered in 1942. This is also supported by the chart as the "when introduced" row indicates it was introduced in the 1940s, or in the first half of the 20th century. Choice (B) is supported by the passage, but is not supported by the graph. Eliminate it. Choice (C) is supported by the graph, but not the passage, so it can also be eliminated. Choice (D) can be eliminated, because there isn't any data about the bacteria's resistance to amikacin specifically. Choice (A) is the correct answer.

50.  **D**  This question asks if the data in the table supports the authors' assertion that *S. aureus* and *E. faecium* represent the biggest therapeutic hurdles. In order to be the biggest therapeutic hurdles, this would mean that they have great resistance to many antibiotics. Check each answer choice against the information provided in the graph. Choice (A) can be eliminated, as other bacteria demonstrate levels of resistance to more than three antibiotic families. Choice (B) can be eliminated, as 75% is not the greatest percentage of antibiotic resistance listed on

the graph; Shigella has a 78% resistance to aminopenicillins. Choice (C) is incorrect, as there is an even lower percentage of resistance, 0.2%, found on the table. Choice (D) stresses that *S. aureus* and *E. faecium* do not represent the biggest therapeutic hurdles because other bacteria demonstrate resistance to many more antibiotics than these do. The number of antibiotics other bacteria are resistant to create a greater challenge in treatment, based on the general information contained in thc passage. Choice (D) is the correct answer.

51.　**C**　This questions asks for a bacteria on the table that supports the answer to the previous question. As the answer to the previous question was (D), *S. aureus* and *E. faecium* do not represent the biggest therapeutic hurdles because other bacteria demonstrate resistance to many more antibiotics than they do, the correct answer choice will be a bacteria with resistant to a greater number of antibiotics than *S. aureus* and *E. faecium*. These two have a combined resistance to three antibiotics families. Choice (C), *Shigella*, shows resistance to four families of antibiotics. Choice (C) is the correct answer.

52.　**B**　This question asks whether or not something is true based on the table, and then what line from the passage also supports that information. First, determine if Aminopenicillin-resistant *S. aureus* is resistant to at least one member of the Fluoroquinolones family. Looking at *S. aureus* on the table, it is clear that it shows resistance to the Fluoroquinolones family, even though it's only a small percentage. Eliminate (C) and (D). Between (A) and (B), only (B) contains any information regarding the Fluoroquinolones family. Choice (B) is the correct answer.

# Section 2: Writing and Language

1.　**D**　This question has answers with STOP punctuation, so use the vertical line test. In this sentence, the idea before the punctuation is *When we hear about the opinions of "ten scientists" or "ten dentists," or we hear that things are "clinically proven" or "lab-tested," for example* is incomplete. Therefore, it cannot precede a colon, eliminating (C), nor can it precede the combination of a comma and a coordinating conjunction, eliminating (A). Choice (B) adds an unnecessary word, thus making (D) the best answer.

2.　**D**　The following paragraph refers to *These claims*, suggesting that there must be some claim in the sentence in question, preferably one that refers back to some of the pseudoscientific claims at the beginning of the paragraph. Choices (A), (B), and (C) offer irrelevant pieces of information that do not support these claims, so they can be eliminated. The most *relevant* detail, therefore, comes from (D), which offers one of *these claims*.

3.　**A**　In this sentence, *Elle*, *Vogue*, and *Vanity Fair* comprise a list of three things. On the SAT, that list needs to be separated by commas, including one before the word *and*. Choice (A) is the only one of the answer choices that provides this comma in the appropriate spot.

4.　**B**　Sentence 5 refers to an *obvious answer*, suggesting that the sentence will come after a question. Look for question marks! Only sentence 1 contains a question (real or implied), so sentence

5's *obvious answer* must follow sentence 1's question. Choice (B) best captures this positioning within the paragraph.

5. **C** This sentence states that the researchers' findings are *not surprising*. The paragraph goes on to describe how deceptive many of these advertising claims are. Who, therefore, would not be surprised to find that a set of ads is deceptive? Not someone who believes the ads, eliminating (A), nor someone who has merely thought about those ads, eliminating (B). Choice (C) provides the hint of skepticism that the question needs. Choice (D) would seem to provide this skepticism as well—the only problem is that *skepticized* is not actually a word, thus eliminating (D).

6. **B** The previous sentences in this paragraph provide the first parts of the researchers' findings. With the categories of *true* and "*outright lies,*" it is not necessarily clear what the third category will be. Therefore, the sentence should be kept because it completes the researchers' findings, as (B) suggests.

7. **A** This sentence is separated into two parts by a comma and a coordinating conjunction. This combination requires two complete ideas on either side of it. The only answer choice that creates a complete idea after the conjunction is (A), which completes the sentence to say *they may have more serious implications as well*.

8. **B** Choose the word that has the most specific and consistent meaning within the context. In this sentence, that word is *regulate*, (B), because the word clearly describes what the FDA is capable of doing. Choices (A) and (C) don't make sense in the context. While it might seem logical that the Food and Drug Administration would *administrate*, as in (D), there is not proof from the passage that the FDA *administrates* what can go into makeup.

9. **C** The early part of this sentence contains the verb *may have*, which suggests a hypothetical situation happening in either the present or the future. Choices (A) and (B) place the verb in the past tense, which is not consistent with the rest of the sentence. Choice (D) can be eliminated because it introduces an unnecessary apostrophe. Choice (C) provides a consistent verb without excessive apostrophes.

10. **D** Choices (A) and (C) can be eliminated immediately because those prepositions do not pair idiomatically with the verb *to do*. Choice (B) can also be eliminated because the FDA is not doing anything *to* the claims. Instead, as (D) implies, the FDA may do something *with* the claims, such as punish or correct them.

11. **C** Choice (A), *Thus*, implies causation, but there is no causation between this sentence and the last. Choices (B) and (D) imply a contrast where there is no contrast. The best answer in this case comes from (C), *True*, which suggests a kind of concession on the part of the author.

12. **D** There is a contrast in the previous sentence between something *truly admirable* and something that *fall[s] short of these expectations*. The word that links the ideas, therefore, must imply some

kind of contrast. Of the answer choices, only (D) does so. While the essay is about politics, there is no need for the word *Politically* in this sentence.

13. **A**    The phrase *then governor of the state* describes *Gerry*, but it does not restrict either the meaning or completeness of the sentence. In this sense, the remark is unnecessary in that it provides information parenthetically. As such, the remark should be offset with a pair of commas, as in (A).

14. **C**    The action described in this sentence occurs in 1812, which is to say, the past. Therefore, the verb should reflect this past tense, thus eliminating (A) and (D). Of the remaining two verbs, (C) is more concise, and (B) rather wordily implies that the action described in the sentence may not have happened.

15. **D**    The sentence *Unfortunately, it was not the last* should follow a sentence that mentions some *first*, which sentence 5 does. While sentence 2 may sound fine where it is now, there is no good reason to keep it there. It separates the *election* mentioned in sentence 1 from the *election* reference in sentence 3. Sentence 5's use of the word *first* provides a much better reason for the placement of sentence 2, which should therefore go after sentence 5, as (D) states.

16. **C**    The question asks for a way to combine the two sentences. In questions like these, look to the shortest option first, particularly because the desire to combine sentences is fundamentally a desire for conciseness. In this case, (C) is the shortest, and it is not missing any information that the other answers possess. Therefore, (C) can be said to provide the most effective combination of the two sentences.

17. **A**    Choices (B) and (D) should be eliminated right away because they provide a number of words that are unnecessary and make the wording of the sentence awkward. One of the remaining answers has STOP punctuation, so use the vertical line test. In order to choose between a colon and a semicolon remember this: A semicolon joins two complete ideas, whereas a colon only requires a complete idea before. In this case, the single word *gerrymandering* is not a complete idea, so the semicolon can't be used, thus eliminating (C) and leaving (A) as the correct answer.

18. **D**    As described by the passage, the desired effect of gerrymandering is the acquisition of political advantage through demographic redistricting. While the events described in (A), (B), and (C) may be outcomes of gerrymandering, they do not describe its purpose. Only (D) describes the purpose, as it cites the desire to gain political advantage.

19. **D**    Follow the percentages carefully. The un-districted figure on the far left shows 60% light gray voters and 40% dark gray voters. The distribution of these voters does not change, but the method of division on the far right of the figure shows how these voters can be rearranged in such a way as to create 3 dark gray districts and 2 light gray districts, or 60% dark gray districts from 60% light gray voters. Choice (D) best captures these percentages.

20. **C** Choices (A) and (D) give information that is implied by the words *benefits* and *in power*. Because those choices give redundant information, they can be eliminated. Then, (B) adds another unnecessary word, so it too can be eliminated. This leaves only (C), which is more concise than the other choices but accomplishes the same basic goal.

21. **B** This sentence describes the votes *belonging to* the voters. Therefore, the sentence requires the possessive form of the word *their*, as it is given in (B).

22. **A** While it may seem desirable to DELETE underlined portions whenever possible, doing so here would create a grammatical error, namely a comma splice between two complete ideas. Choices (B) and (C) would create the same problem. Only (A) correctly situates the idea within the sentence's given punctuation.

23. **B** All of the answer choices say essentially the same thing, so choose the answer that does so most concisely and clearly. Choice (B) provides this answer in that it says in a single word what the longer answers say with more words.

24. **B** This sentence begins with the modifier *Particularly when looking at old paintings*. The thing that this modifies should come directly after the modifier. The *paintings* cannot be *looking at old paintings*, thus eliminating (A) and (D). Choice (C) can be eliminated because *noticing* is not what is *looking at old paintings*. Only (B) provides a viable answer in suggesting that *you* are *looking at old paintings*.

25. **A** On the SAT, every sentence should have a clear, definable role within a paragraph, a role that is consistent with the theme of that paragraph. While the sentence in question is interesting, it does not have a clear role within the paragraph, so it should be deleted, thus eliminating (C) and (D). Then, the sentence should be deleted because it is irrelevant to the topic of the paragraph, as (A) states.

26. **D** Check the answer choices against the graph shown in the question, and use POE. The light gray line given in this figure represents the percentage of the workforce that works in art restoration. This line has a small bump from 1900 to 1910 and then disappears until approximately 1945, after which time it generally rises. Choice (A) is incorrect because the field did not begin growing in 1930, nor can it be said to rise steadily at any point after that. Choice (B) can be eliminated because it states that book restorers became art restorers, which is not supported in the graph, nor would the doings of book restorers be relevant to this passage. Choice (C) can be eliminated because the curves shown in the graph do not extend to 2020, nor is there any indication that the art-restoration line will overtake the art-conservation line at any point. Choice (D) is therefore the correct answer—it describes what is shown in the chart. In 1970, the percentage of people working in art restoration was just under 22 (leaving out all of the zeros) and by 2005, the number was just under 66, or roughly triple.

27. **C** Choice (A) can be eliminated because it is not clear whom or what the phrase *when looking* is meant to describe. Choice (B) does not make sense in the context. Choice (D) does not contain a meaning consistent with the sentence's intended meaning. Only (C) can work in the sentence, which indicates a contrast between the simplicity the viewer may see *at first glance* and the true *complicated* nature of what the viewer is seeing.

28. **C** The word *matter* is not part of the list at the end of this sentence, thus eliminating (A). The word *matter* is an introduction to the list. It should therefore be offset by some punctuation, eliminating (B). One of the remaining answers has STOP punctuation, so use the vertical line test. In order to choose between a colon and a semicolon, remember that: a semicolon requires complete ideas both before and after it, whereas a colon only requires a complete idea before. In this case, the list after the punctuation is not a complete idea, so only a colon will work, making (C) the correct answer.

29. **A** The previous sentence refers to what happens *sometimes*. This sentence describes what happens more often. The transition between these two ideas must therefore include some transition from *some* to *most*, as only (A) does.

30. **C** A colon must be preceded by a complete idea. The idea *They would project some image of what the painting must have looked like originally and apply a variety of techniques, up to and including* is not complete and therefore cannot precede a colon, eliminating (A) and (D). Then, if there is no particular reason to use a comma (or any punctuation, for that matter), don't use that punctuation. Choice (C) contains no punctuation, and none is needed, thus making (C) the correct answer.

31. **B** The subject *some art historians* is plural, so it requires a plural verb, thus eliminating (A) and (C). Then, because the word *who* is the subject of the verb *are*, it should be kept in the subject form, as in (B). The object form *whom* would not apply in this case (because one would not say *them are writing today*), eliminating (D).

32. **D** The sentence in question provides an *example* of something that must be described in the preceding sentence. The best option for that preceding sentence must be sentence 4, which describes restoring paintings by *non-paint methods*. The sentence in question describes fixing a painting by relighting it, one example of these *non-paint methods*. The sentence should therefore be placed after sentence 4, as (D) indicates.

33. **D** The word *more* in this sentence implies a comparison. The word in the underlined portion must therefore indicate some comparison, as only (D) does.

34. **C** The question asks for a way to combine the two sentences. In questions like these, look to the shortest option first, particularly because the desire to combine sentences is fundamentally a desire for conciseness. In this case, (C) is the shortest, and it is not missing any information that the other answers possess, so (C) provides the most effective combination of the two sentences.

35. **C** The previous sentence describes an event in the past. This sentence describes an event in the present. Therefore, the transition should somehow address this shift in time, which only (C), *To this day*, does.

36. **D** When given the option to DELETE the underlined portion, it is usually best to choose that option unless there is a very good reason not to. In this case, the information in the underlined portion and its alternatives are not needed. In fact, deleting the underlined portion fixes what would otherwise have been a sentence fragment. As a result, (D), DELETE, is the best possible answer.

37. **C** All of the answer choices say essentially the same thing, so choose the answer that does so most concisely and clearly. Choice (C) provides this answer in that it says in fewer words what the other answers say with more words.

38. **B** When unsure which pronoun to use, find the original noun to which the pronoun is referring. In this case, that is actually another pronoun, *they*, which refers to the noun *pilgrims*. The only pronoun consistent with both words is therefore *their*, or (B).

39. **A** This sentence states that two things are happening simultaneously: the pilgrims figure out why they have been chosen for the pilgrimage as the reader learns more about the fantasy universe. Therefore, the underlined portion should contain some indication of this simultaneity. Of the available choices, only (A) does so. Choice (B) also provides some indication of time, but it implies a cause-and-effect that is not contained in the meaning of the sentence.

40. **D** The word *If* implies some complete action or thought. Of the available answer choices, only (D) completes that thought, creating the idea *If this structure sounds familiar*.

41. **D** There are only two reasons to use apostrophes: possession and contraction. Neither of those reasons apply here, thus eliminating the answers with apostrophes, (B) and (C). Then, within this sentence, the word *traveling* should describe the pilgrims. The word without the *-ing* ending is either a verb or a noun, so it cannot fulfill this function. Only (D) has the appropriate ending and the appropriate lack of apostrophes.

42. **B** The next sentence begins *With all these literary tributes*. Therefore, this sentence should contain more literary tributes, a continuation of the list begun earlier in this paragraph. The phrase *pays homage* in (B) best indicates these literary tributes, so (B) is the only one among the answer choices that has a discernible connection to the following sentence.

43. **C** While the information in the proposed sentence is true, this is not an essay about T.S. Eliot, so additional information about Eliot would not contribute in a substantial way to the essay as a whole. Therefore, the sentence should not be included, thus eliminating (A) and (B). Then, the sentence should be excluded because it is irrelevant, not because it contradicts any of the essay's claims, making (C) the best answer.

44.　**D**　When a question is testing verbs, check the subject. In this case, the subject is the word *continuities*, which is plural. Therefore, all singular verbs, as in (A) and (B), can be eliminated. Choice (C) creates a sentence fragment. Therefore, only (D) completes the sentence and is appropriately consistent with its subject.

# Section 3: Math (No Calculator)

1.　**A**　Write an expression for the number of hours each of the two people has worked. Jan worked $j$ hours a day for 3 days, so she worked a total of $3j$ hours. Noah worked $n$ hours a day for 5 days, so he worked a total of $5n$ hours. Therefore, the total hours worked by Jan and Noah combined is the sum of these two, which is $3j + 5n$. These are not like terms, so they cannot be combined or simplified further. The correct answer is (A).

2.　**B**　Plug $c = 4$ into the right side of the equation to get $\dfrac{y + 2}{5} = 4$. Multiply both sides of the equation by 5 to get $y + 2 = 20$. Subtract 2 from both sides to get $y = 18$, which is (B).

3.　**B**　Even though this looks complicated, start by combining like terms. Add the real terms, 10 and 3, to get 13. Then, add the imaginary terms, $-4i$ and $6i$, to get $2i$. Add these two to get $13 + 2i$, which is (B).

4.　**D**　Simplify this expression by combining like terms in bite-sized pieces. Start with the $ab^2$ terms. The $-ab^2$ term from the second polynomial is subtracted from the $ab^2$ in the first. $ab^2 - (-ab^2) = ab^2 + ab^2 = 2ab^2$. Eliminate any choice that does not include $2ab^2$: (A) and (B). Now look at the $a^2$ terms. The $4a^2$ term from the second polynomial is subtracted from the $4a^2$ term in the first. $4a^2 - 4a^2 = 0$. Therefore, the correct answer cannot have an $a^2$ term. Eliminate the remaining choice that does, which is (C). The correct answer is (D).

5.　**D**　The weight of a mature great white shark is estimated by $w = 3{,}150 + 450l$, where $l$ is the fork length in feet. The question asks for the estimated weight increase in pounds for each foot of growth. To determine this, plug in values for $l$ that show a one foot increase. First, plug in $l = 2$. If $l = 2$, then $w = 3{,}150 + 450(2) = 4{,}050$. Then plug in $l = 3$. If $l = 3$, then $w = 3{,}150 + 450(3) = 4{,}500$. The increase is $4{,}500 - 4{,}050 = 450$. Therefore, the correct answer is (D).

6.　**C**　The number of pages Juan has left to edit is represented by the equation $P = 326 - 12h$, where $h$ represents the number of hours worked. The question asks for what 326 represents in this equation. Since $P$ is a number of pages, 326 must also be a number of pages, so eliminate (D). Choices (A) and (B) each deal with a rate. In order to turn a rate into an amount, the rate must be multiplied by time. Since $h$ represents time, the coefficient on time, 12, must represent the rate rather than 326. Therefore, eliminate (A) and (B). Only (C) remains, so it must be correct. To understand why it is correct, plug in $h = 0$. If $h = 0$, then $P = 326 - 12(0) = 326$.

Therefore, after working for 0 hours at the start of the project, he has 326 pages left to edit. Therefore, the correct answer is (C).

7. **A** The question says that $\frac{x}{y} = 3$. Plug in values of $x$ and $y$ that satisfy this equation. Let $x = 6$ and $y = 2$. Plug these values into the expression $\frac{12y}{x}$ to get $\frac{12(2)}{6} = \frac{24}{6} = 4$. Therefore, the correct answer is (A).

8. **A** To solve this problem, plug in the answers. Test the points in the answer choices by plugging them into the two equations. In order to be the solution of the system of equations, a point must satisfy both equations. Start with (A): (–7, –5). Plug these values into the first equation to get $2(-5) + (-7) = -17$. This is true, so plug the values into the second equation to get $5(-7) - 4(-5) = -15$. Since this is also true, the correct answer is (A).

9. **C** The equation includes a very complicated fraction. However, the equation asks for the value of $M$, which is not part of the fraction but rather the value that is being multiplied by the fraction. In order to isolate a variable that is multiplied by a fraction, multiply both sides by the reciprocal. On the right side of the equation, the fractions cancel, isolating $M$. On the left side, the reciprocal is multiplied by $c$ to get $\dfrac{1 - \left(1 + \dfrac{r}{1,200}\right)^{-N}}{\dfrac{r}{1,200}} c$. Therefore, the correct answer is (C).

10. **C** The question asks about a line in the $xy$-plane. Any such line can be defined by the equation $y = mx + b$, in which $m$ is the slope and $b$ is the $y$-intercept. The question says that the slope is $\frac{2}{3}$, so $m = \frac{2}{3}$. The question also says that the line passes through the origin, which is the point (0, 0). Since the $y$-intercept is the point at which the $x$-coordinate is 0, the origin must be the $y$-intercept, so $b = 0$. Thus the equation of the line is $y = \frac{2}{3}x + 0$, or $y = \frac{2}{3}x$. Plug the points in the answer choices into this equation. Start with (A). Plug in the values from (A) to get $\frac{2}{3} = \frac{2}{3}(0)$. Since this is false, eliminate (A). Try (B). Plug in the values from (B) to get $3 = \frac{2}{3}(2)$. Since this is false, eliminate (B). Try (C). Plug in the values from (C) to get $4 = \frac{2}{3}(6)$. Since this is true, select (C).

11. **D** Since $f(3) = 12$, plug this into the function equation to get $f(3) = c(3)^2 + 30 = 12$. Therefore, $9c + 30 = 12$. Subtract 30 from both sides to get $9c = -18$. Divide both sides by 9 to get $c = -2$.

Plug this into the original equation to get $f(x) = -2x^2 + 30$. The question asks for $f(-3)$, so plug in $x = -3$ to get $f(-3) = -2(-3)^2 + 30 = -2(9) + 30 = -18 + 30 = 12$. The correct answer is (D).

12. **A** The question asks for the price per night when it is the same for both hotels. Since the two equations given are for the price per night in the two hotels, set the two expressions for the prices equal: $240 - 20w = 320 - 30w$. Add $30w$ to both sides to get $240 + 10w = 320$. Subtract 240 from both sides to get $10w = 80$. Divide both sides by 10 to get $w = 8$. This represents the number of weeks, but the question asks for the price per night. Plug this value of $w$ into the equation for $A$. $A = 240 - 20(8) = 240 - 160 = 80$, which is (A).

13. **C** The question asks for the value of $\dfrac{3^a}{81^b}$. To divide numbers with exponents, the bases must be the same. Convert the denominator to a base of 3: since $81 = 3^4$, $81^b = (3^4)^b$. When raising a number with an exponent to an exponent, multiply the exponents, so $81^b = (3^4)^b = 3^{4b}$. Therefore, $\dfrac{3^a}{81^b} = \dfrac{3^a}{3^{4b}}$. When dividing numbers with exponents and the same base, subtract the exponents, so $\dfrac{3^a}{3^{4b}} = 3^{a-4b}$. The question also says that $a - 4b = 18$, so $3^{a-4b} = 3^{18}$. Therefore, the correct answer is (C).

14. **A** The question gives a quadratic in both factored and expanded form. Get them in the same form by expanding the factored quadratic on the left side. Use FOIL on $(ax + 3)(bx + 5)$. Multiply first terms to get $(ax)(bx) = abx^2$. Compare this to the $x^2$ term on the right side, $35x^2$. Therefore, $ab = 35$. Since $ab = 35$, consider the factors of 35. There are two pairs of factors: 1, 35 and 5, 7. Since the question says that $a + b = 12$, $a$ and $b$ must be 5 and 7, but there is no way to determine the order. Therefore, consider both $a = 5$, $b = 7$ and $a = 7$, $b = 5$. If $a = 5$ and $b = 7$, the equation becomes $(5x + 3)(7x + 5) = 35x^2 + kx + 15$. To get the value of $k$, determine the coefficient on the $x$-term of the quadratic expression on the left. To do this, find the product of the outer terms and the product of the inner terms, which are $25x$ and $21x$, respectively. Add these products to get $25x + 21x = 46x$, so, in this case, $k = 46$. Eliminate any choice that does not include 46: (B), (C), and (D). Therefore, the correct answer is (A). (To determine the other possible value, plug in $a = 7$ and $b = 5$ to get $(7x + 3)(5x + 5)$. Multiply outer terms to get $35x$. Multiply inner terms to get $15x$. Add the products to get $50x$, so $k = 50$.)

15. **C** Rather than dealing with complicated fractions, simplify the fractions by plugging in. The question says that $y > 5$, so plug in $y = 6$ to get $\dfrac{1}{\dfrac{1}{6-4} + \dfrac{1}{6-3}}$. The fraction simplifies to $\dfrac{1}{\dfrac{1}{2} + \dfrac{1}{3}}$. Now, add the fractions in the denominator, using the bowtie method.

$$\dfrac{3 \quad + \quad 2}{\dfrac{1}{2} \diagdown\!\!\diagup \dfrac{1}{3}} = \dfrac{5}{6}$$

Therefore, the original fraction is equivalent to $\dfrac{1}{\frac{5}{6}}$. When dividing by a fraction, flip the bottom fraction and multiply. Therefore, $\dfrac{1}{\frac{5}{6}} = \dfrac{\frac{1}{1}}{\frac{5}{6}} = \dfrac{1}{1} \times \dfrac{6}{5} = \dfrac{6}{5}$, so $\dfrac{6}{5}$ is the target number. Plug $y = 6$ into the answer choices and eliminate any choice that is not equal to $\dfrac{6}{5}$. Since (A) and (B) are not fractions, eliminate them immediately. Try

(C). $\dfrac{y^2 - 7y + 12}{2y - 7} = \dfrac{6^2 - 7(6) + 12}{2(6) - 7} = \dfrac{36 - 42 + 12}{12 - 7} = \dfrac{6}{5}$, so keep (C). Try (D).

$\dfrac{2y - 7}{y^2 - 7y + 12} = \dfrac{2(6) - 7}{6^2 - 7(6) + 12} = \dfrac{5}{6} \neq \dfrac{6}{5}$, so eliminate (D). The correct answer is (C).

16.  **5**  First, label the figure. Label $\overline{PQ}$ with length 3, $\overline{QT}$ with length 4, $\overline{QS}$ with length 8, and $\overline{SR}$ with length 10. When a question involves two triangles, determine whether they are similar. Similar triangles, by definition, have three pairs of congruent corresponding angles. However, since the measures of the angles in all triangles have a sum of 180°, it is only necessary to show that two pairs of corresponding angles are congruent. The question says that $\angle TPQ$ is congruent to $\angle QRS$. Also, $\angle PQT$ and $\angle SQR$ are vertical angles, so they are also congruent. Thus, the two triangles are similar. Similar triangles have a consistent proportion between corresponding sides (sides that are opposite congruent angles). The question asks for the value of $m$, or the length of $\overline{PT}$, which corresponds with $\overline{SR}$. Use the lengths of another pair of corresponding sides, $\overline{QT}$ and $\overline{QS}$, to set up a proportion: $\dfrac{m}{10} = \dfrac{4}{8}$. Cross-multiply to get $8m = 40$. Divide by 8 to get $m = 5$. Therefore, the correct response is 5.

17.  **6**  To solve the equation $y^2 - 36 = 0$, add 36 to both sides to get $y^2 = 36$. Take the square root of both sides to get $y = \pm 6$. However, the question specifies that $y > 0$, so $y = 6$.

18.  $\dfrac{5}{13}$  Draw the right triangle. Label one of the non-right angles with measure $d°$. Since $\cos = \dfrac{adj}{hyp}$ and $\cos d° = \dfrac{5}{13}$, label the side adjacent to $d$ as 5 and the hypotenuse 13. Using the Pythagorean Theorem (or the 5-12-13 Pythagorean triple), the missing side has length 12. Since the

angles in a triangle have a sum of 180, label the missing angle $x$ and set up the equation $d + x + 90 = 180$. Subtract 90 from both sides to get $d + x = 90$, and subtract $d$ from both sides to get $x = 90 - d$. The question asks for the sine of this angle. Since $\sin = \dfrac{opp}{hyp}$, find the side opposite this angle, which is 5, and the hypotenuse, which is 13, to get $\sin(90° - d°) = \dfrac{5}{13}$. Alternatively, note that the angle of measure $(90° - d°)$ is the complement of the angle of measure $d°$. The sine of an angle is equal to the cosine of its complement. Therefore, $\sin(90° - d°) = \cos d° = \dfrac{5}{13}$. Either way, the answer is $\dfrac{5}{13}$.

19. **225** The question asks for the value of $z$. The second equation, $5c = \sqrt{5z}$, is in terms of $c$ and $z$, so plug in the value of $c$ to get $5\left(3\sqrt{5}\right) = \sqrt{5z}$. Simplify the left side to get $15\sqrt{5} = \sqrt{5z}$. Since the equation involves square roots, square both sides to get $\left(15\sqrt{5}\right)^2 = \left(\sqrt{5z}\right)^2$. Square each factor to get $(15)^2\left(\sqrt{5}\right)^2 = \left(\sqrt{5z}\right)^2$ and $(225)(5) = 5z$. Divide both sides by 5 to get $225 = z$. The answer is 225.

20. **13** To determine the value of $b$, stack the equations and cancel the $a$ terms. To do this, make sure that the $a$ term coefficients are opposites. Multiply the first equation by $-2$ to get $-2a - 2b = 20$. Stack this below the second equation, $2a + b = -33$, and add the two equations.

$$\begin{array}{r} 2a + \phantom{2}b = -33 \\ \underline{-2a - 2b = \phantom{-}20} \\ 0a - \phantom{2}b = -13 \end{array}$$

Therefore, the new equation is $0 - b = -13$ or $b = 13$. Thus, the correct response is 13.

## Section 4: Math (Calculator)

1. **C** When two parallel lines are intersected by a third line, or by two or more parallel lines, remember this simple rule: All the small angles are the same; all the big angles are the same; and any small angle + any big angle = 180°. "Small" angles are less than 90°, and "big" angles are greater than 90°. In this question, $x$ is a small angle, and $y$ is a big angle, so $x + y = 180°$. Substitute the given value: $75° + y = 180°$. Subtract 75° from both sides to get $y = 105°$. The answer is (C).

2. **C** Work through the answer choices one at a time. For (A), the number of customers stays the same from 9:00 A.M.–11:00 A.M., then increases from 11:00 A.M.–12:00 P.M., so eliminate (A). For (B), the number of customers stays the same from 12:00 P.M.–1:00 P.M., drops suddenly, then stays the same from 1:00 P.M.–2:00 P.M., so eliminate (B). Choice (C) looks good; the number

of customers decreases from 2:00 P.M.–3:30 P.M., then increases from 3:30 P.M.–5:00 P.M. Finally, in (D), the number of customers increases from 3:30 P.M.–5:00 P.M., then decreases from 5:00 P.M.–6:30 P.M. This is a trap answer that does the opposite of what the question asks for, so eliminate (D). The correct answer is (C).

3.  **B**  Start by plugging in the values given for $x$ and $y$, then solve for $k$. If $5 = \dfrac{30}{k}$, then $5k = 30$ and $k = 6$. It is given that $k$ is a constant, which means that its value doesn't change (whereas $x$ and $y$ are variables, so their values do change). Now plug in the values for the second scenario: $y = \dfrac{42}{6}$, so $y = 7$, which is (B).

4.  **B**  Set up a proportion. First, convert the 3 kilograms into grams: $\dfrac{1\,\text{kg}}{1{,}000\,\text{g}} = \dfrac{3\,\text{kg}}{x\,\text{g}}$, so $x = 3(1{,}000) = 3{,}000$ grams. Next, convert the 3,000 grams into decigrams: $\dfrac{1\,\text{g}}{10\,\text{dg}} = \dfrac{3{,}000\,\text{g}}{x\,\text{dg}}$, so $x = 10(3{,}000) = 30{,}000$ decigrams, which is (B).

5.  **D**  The simplest way to solve this problem is to translate it into an equation and solve for $x$. The statement *6x – 4 is 11 less than 25* can be translated as $6x - 4 = 25 - 11$. Simplify the right side: $6x - 4 = 14$. Add 4 to both sides: $6x = 18$. Divide by 6: $x = 3$. Be careful not to fall for (A); read the full question! The question asks for the value of $9x$, and $(9)(3) = 27$, so the answer is (D).

6.  **A**  When a question contains a scatterplot, draw a line of best fit through the dots, so that roughly half the dots are above the line, and half are below. If the line of best fit has a positive slope, it means that $h$ and $p$ have a *positive correlation* (the question might say "association" rather than "correlation"). If the line has a negative slope, it means that the two quantities have a *negative correlation*, as in (B). If there is no clear relationship between the variables, there is *no* correlation. If the dots in the scatterplot are packed relatively closely, the correlation is *strong*; if they are far apart, the correlation is *weak*. Fortunately, there's no need to choose between strong and weak here. The answer is (A).

7.  **C**  Plug in 200 for $p$ and solve for $d$: $200 = 101 + 10.094d$. Subtract 101 from both sides: $99 = 10.094d$. Divide both sides by 10.094 to get $d = 9.808$. The question asks for the closest answer, so round to the closest integer, which is 10. The correct answer is (C).

8.  **D**  The fastest way to solve this question is to use algebra. Start by isolating the term that contains $d$ by subtracting 101 from both sides: $p - 101 = 10.094d$. Divide by 10.094: $\dfrac{p - 101}{10.094} = d$. Now simply write the expression in reverse so that $d$ is on the left side: $d = \dfrac{p - 101}{10.094}$. This matches (D), so that's the correct answer. As an alternative, plug in to solve the problem.

Plug in 2 for *d* and solve for *p*: 101 + (10.094)(2) = 121.188 = *p*. Now plug these values into the answers and pick the one that works. Only (D) matches.

9. **B** Add up the number of wind turbines shown on the graph: 9 + 11 + 3.5 + 8 + 6 = 37.5. Now try the answer choices. Start with (B) or (C), then move higher or lower if the first choice doesn't work. Try (C): 37.5 × 1,000 = 37,500, which is too big. Try (B): 37.5 × 100 = 3,750, which is correct.

10. **A** When the SAT mixes math symbols and words, try translating the words into a math equation. In this question, the phrase $|k - 3| + 2$ *is equal to one* translates to $|k - 3| + 2 = 1$. To isolate the absolute value expression, subtract 2 from both sides to get $|k + 3| = -1$. Here's the tricky part of the question: An absolute value expression can never be negative, so no values of *k* would make this expression true. Therefore, the answer is (A).

11. **D** Read carefully! There are 14 apartments: 1 apartment with 6 residents, 2 with 4 residents, 4 with 5 residents, and 7 with 3 residents. Add up all the residents: 6 + 4 + 4 + 5 + 5 + 5 + 5 + 3 + 3 + 3 + 3 + 3 + 3 + 3 = 55. Divide by the number of apartments: $\frac{55}{14}$ = 3.929. This is closest to 4, so the answer is (D).

12. **D** There are two ways to tackle this problem: solve algebraically or plug in the answers. To solve algebraically, subtract 6*x* from both sides to get $-4 \le x - 3$. Then add 3 to both sides to get $-1 \le x$ or $x \ge -1$. Since *x* must be −1 or greater, −2 cannot be a solution, so the answer is (D). To plug in the answers, start with (B) or (C). Here, it makes more sense to start with (B), because 0 is a very easy number to plug in. Plugging in 0 gives $-4 \le -3$, which is true, so eliminate (B). Now try (C): $-10 \le -10$, which is true, so eliminate (C). Finally, try (D): $-16 \le -17$, which is false, so the answer is (D).

13. **B** To calculate (or estimate) mean, median, or range, it's best to save mean for last, since it's usually the most time-consuming to calculate. Start with the easiest part: the total. If 2 is removed, the total will change by 2. The range is the difference between the largest and smallest term. The range now is 9 − 2 = 7, but if 2 is removed, the smallest term will be 3, so the range will be 9 − 3 = 6, and the range changes by 1. To find the median in a set with an even number of terms, take the average of the two middle terms. Here, the two middle terms are both 6, so 6 is the median. If 2 is removed, there will be 17 terms, so the 9th term will be the median. Since the new 9th term will be 6, the median will not change at all. This makes it unnecessary to calculate the average. The average is the total divided by the number of things, so if 2 is removed from the total and 1 from the number of things, the average will change. Therefore, the answer is (B).

14. **B** Plug (2, 2) in for *x* and *y*, and solve for *p* and *r*. In the first inequality, $p + 2 > 2$, so $p > 0$. In the second inequality, $r - 2 < -2$, so $r < 0$. Since *r* is negative and *p* is positive, *r* must be less than *p*, so the answer is (B).

15.  **A**  When a question says approximately, go ahead and approximate. The total, 395, is close to 400, so 15% of 400 = $\frac{15}{100} \times 400 = 60$. Often this would be enough to find the correct answer, but in this case there are two answers, 59 and 62, that are very close, so try them both. $\frac{59}{395} \times 100 = 14.94\%$. That looks good, but try (B), just to be safe: $\frac{62}{395} \times 100 = 15.7\%$, which rounds to 16%, which is not correct. The correct answer is (A).

16.  **C**  Slope is rise divided by run, or vertical change divided by horizontal change. For each additional day, the price increases by $20, so the slope, $\frac{20}{1}$, is equivalent to the average daily price increase. The correct answer is (C).

17.  **D**  When the SAT asks for the relationship between two variables, they are asking for an equation. In this case, it's the equation of a line, and all the answer choices are in slope-intercept form. The slope is 20 (as calculated for the previous question). Notice on the graph that when $d = 0$, $P = 30$, so the $y$-intercept is 30. The equation of a line in slope-intercept form is $y = mx + b$, where $m$ is the slope and $b$ is the $y$-intercept. In this question, $m = 20$ and $b = 30$, so the equation is $y = 20d + 30$, and the answer is (D). Plugging in values from the graph can also determine the correct equation.

18.  **C**  Remember that $f(x) = y$. The maximum $y$-value on this line graph is 3, and when $y = 3$, $x = -2$, so the answer is (C). In this type of question, if they ask for an $x$-value, the corresponding $y$-value is likely to be a trap answer (in this case (D) is the trap).

19.  **C**  When there are variables in the answers, plug in. Start from the simplest price, which is a peak ticket bought in the station. Let's say that price is $100. In that case, an off-peak ticket purchased in the station will be 15% off, or $85. For an off-peak ticket purchased from the conductor, there is an 11% surcharge, so $\frac{11}{100} \times 85 = 9.35$, and $85 + $9.35 = $94.35. This is the value of $t$, and the question is asking for the value of a peak ticket bought in the station, which is $100. Now plug $t = $94.35 into the answer choices, and choose the one that equals $100; the correct answer is (C).

20.  **A**  In most SAT questions, all the information matters. But, once in a while, there will be unnecessary information designed to create confusion. In this question, it is not necessary to know the total number of people, nor whether they eat snacks or not. A person is being randomly chosen from *among those who exercise fewer than six times per week*, so only the first two columns in the table matter. There are a total of 24 + 40 people who exercise fewer than 6 times per week and, of those people,

$13 + 22 = 35$ of them are in group 1. Use the probability formula: *probability* $= \dfrac{want}{total} = \dfrac{35}{64}$. The correct answer is (A).

21.  **D**  This question can be solved two ways: as a system of equations, or by plugging in the answers.

To solve with equations, start by assigning variables. Make $g$ the number of gallons of gasoline and $d$ the number of gallons of diesel. Now write two equations: $3.25g + 3d = 404.25$ and $g + d = 131$. To get the value for $d$, try to make the $g$ values disappear. Multiply the 2nd equation by $-3.25$ to get $-3.25g - 3.25d = -425.75$. Stack and add the two equations to get

$$
\begin{aligned}
3.25g + \quad 3d &= 404.25 \\
\underline{-3.25g - 3.25d} &= \underline{-425.75} \\
-0.25d &= -21.5
\end{aligned}
$$

Divide by $-0.25$ to find that $d = 86$, so the correct answer is (D).

A safer method is to plug in the answers. Start with (C). If the station sold 76 gallons of diesel, then the station sold $131 - 76 = 55$ gallons of gasoline. The revenue from diesel would be $76 \times \$3 = \$228$, and the revenue from gasoline would be $55 \times \$3.25 = \$178.75$, for a total of $\$228 + \$178.75 = \$406.75$, which doesn't match the total sales of $\$404.25$ given by the problem. Since the total was too high, move to (D), where more of the cheaper diesel fuel was sold: If the station sold 86 gallons of diesel, then the station sold $131 - 86 = 45$ gallons of gasoline. The revenue from diesel would be $86 \times \$3 = \$258$, and the revenue from gasoline would be $45 \times \$3.25 = \$146.25$, for a total of $\$258 + \$146.25 = \$404.25$, which matches the total sales given by the problem. The correct answer is (D).

22.  **C**  With the ugly numbers in the chart, approximation is helpful here. The ratio of 2010 higher education spending to 2014 higher education spending can be estimated as 2.1 million to 3.1 million, or even more approximately as 2:3. The only other column that is close is corrections, which can be estimated as 630,000 to 930,000, also fairly close to 2:3. The correct answer is (C).

23.  **C**  When questions ask for an approximate value, round the numbers to avoid unnecessary math. Round public assistance spending in 2012 to $\$56,000$ and round 2014 spending to $\$30,000$. Subtract to get an approximate difference of $\$26,000$. Divide by two to get an average of $\$13,000$. Read carefully: The chart values are in *thousands of dollars*, so multiply by 1,000 to get the actual rate of change of $\$13,000,000$, which is (C).

24.  **A**  When the fish hits the surface of the lake, the height will be 0, so plug 0 into the equation: $0 = 9s - 4.9s^2$. From here, the easiest thing to do is plug in the answer choices. Start with (C): $(9)(3) - (4.9)(3^2) = 27 - 44.1 = -17.1$. This negative value means that the fish has gone 17 meters below the surface. Choice (C) is too big, so try (B). It's also too big, so the answer must be

(A). Double check to be sure: $9(2) - (4.9)(2^2) = 18 - 19.6 = -1.6$. The question is asking for an approximate answer, and (A) is closest, so that's the correct answer. The problem can also be solved by factoring $h = 9s - 4.9s^2$ into $h = s(9 - 4.9s)$. The solutions for $s$ in this equation are $s = 0$ (the time when the fish began the leap) and $9 - 4.9s = 0$ (the time when the fish hit the water). Solve the latter for $s$: $9 = 4.9s$, so $s = \dfrac{9}{4.9} = 1.84$ seconds, which is closest to (A).

25.  **C**  The equation of a circle centered at $(h, k)$ is $(x - h)^2 + (y - k)^2 = r^2$. Therefore, the left side of the equation must be $(x - 3)^2 + y^2$. Eliminate (B) and (D). To narrow it down further, find the radius by drawing a triangle and finding the legs to plug into the Pythagorean Theorem (this is safer than trying to remember the distance formula).

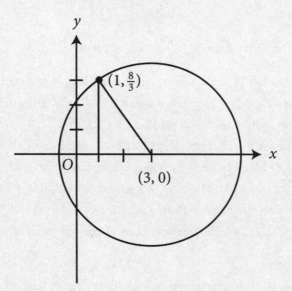

The base is 2 and the height is $\dfrac{8}{3}$, so use the Pythagorean Theorem to find the radius. $2^2 + \left(\dfrac{8}{3}\right)^2 = r^2$, so $4 + \dfrac{64}{9} = r^2$, or $\dfrac{36}{9} + \dfrac{64}{9} = \dfrac{100}{9} = r^2$. It's not necessary to take the square root, because the only piece missing from the circle formula is $r^2$. The correct equation is $(x - 3)^2 + y^2 = \dfrac{100}{9}$, which is (C).

26.  **D**  When dealing with area questions, always calculate the areas—don't make assumptions. The area of the lawn is $8 \times 8 = 64$ square feet. There are 8 samples, and each sample is $1 \times 1 = 1$ square foot, so the total area sampled is $\dfrac{8}{64} = \dfrac{1}{8}$ of the total area. Next, since the question asks for approximation, approximate the total number of seedlings. Notice that the middle values are very close to 100, and

the highest and lowest values are almost equidistant from 100, so the average number of seedlings in a sample is about 100. Therefore, the total number of seedlings in all the samples is approximately $100 \times 8 = 800$, and the total number of seedlings in the lawn is approximately $800 \times 8 = 6,400$. The correct answer is (D).

27.  **C**  The easiest way to solve this question is to plug in the answers. Start with (B). If there were 103 Western chinchilla offspring, then the Eastern chinchilla produced $103 \times \dfrac{30}{100} = 30.9$ more offspring than the Western chinchilla, totaling 133.9. Since 133.9 does not match the 143 offspring specified by the problem, eliminate (B) and move to a larger number. Try (C): If there were 110 Western chinchilla offspring, then the Eastern chinchilla produced $110 \times \dfrac{30}{100} = 33$ more offspring than the Western chinchilla, totaling 143, which matches the number specified in the problem. Therefore, the answer is (C).

28.  **B**  The opening sentence, *when polynomial g(x) is divided by x – 4, the remainder is 3,* means that if an $x$-value of 4 is plugged into the polynomial, the corresponding $y$-value will be 3. This fact can be represented with the equation $g(4) = 3$, so (B) is correct. Without knowing this, the question is pretty tough. However, it is possible to plug in, with a little knowledge about how remainders work. Consider an easier question: When a number is divided by 5, the remainder is 3. What is one value for the number? It's fairly easy to come up with an answer to this question, such as the number 13. A simple way to find a quotient with a certain remainder is to double (or triple, etc.) the number, and add the remainder. So, double 5 and add 3, and the result is 13. The same thing can be done in this more difficult question. The divisor is $x – 4$, so double it and add 3: $2(x – 4) + 3 = 2x – 5$. This polynomial meets the requirements of the question and can be used to test the answers. For (A), plug $x = –4$ into the polynomial: $2(–4) + 5 = –3$, so (A) is false. For (B), $2(4) – 5 = 3$, so (B) looks good, but be sure to check all four answers. For (C), remember that if $x – 4$ is a factor of $g(x)$, then 4 is a solution, and plugging 4 into the equation should yield zero. But working through (B) already demonstrated that $2(4) – 5 = 3$, so (C) is false. For (D), plug –3 into the equation: $2(–3) – 5 = –11$, so (D) is false, and the answer is (B).

29.  **A**  The question gives an equation in *standard* form, which is $y = ax^2 + bx + c$, and asks for the equation in *vertex* form. The vertex form of a parabola is $y = a(x – h)^2 + k$. It's called vertex form because the vertex of the parabola is at $(h, k)$. The $x$-coordinate of the vertex will always be the average of the $x$-coordinates of any two points that have the same $y$-value. The graph gives two points on the $y$-axis (these are the *solutions* or *zeros* of the equation), so find the average of the $x$-coordinates:

$\dfrac{-4 + 2}{2} = -1$, so $h = -1$. From the graph, it also looks like the $y$-coordinate of the vertex is $-9$, so $k = -9$, making the vertex $(-1, -9)$. Now look at the answers. Choice (A) is in vertex form, and the vertex it shows is $(-1, -9)$, so the correct answer is (A).

30. **B** To answer this question, use the provided quadrant drawing to make a quick sketch with both equations drawn. It is not necessary to make a perfectly accurate graph; just get the general idea. For this system of inequalities, any solutions must be above *both* lines (because the solutions must be greater than both $y \geq x + 2$ and $y \geq \dfrac{1}{3}x - 1$), so shade in this area as shown below:

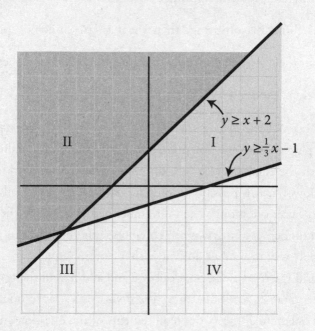

As the sketch shows, there are solutions in Quadrants I, II, and III, but not in IV. Therefore, the answer is (B).

31. $\dfrac{3}{7}$, $\dfrac{6}{14}$, $\dfrac{9}{21}$, **.428 or .429**

Locate the values for April and February, and write them as a fraction: $\dfrac{30}{70}$. This fraction won't fit into the grid-in box, so either reduce it or convert it into a decimal.

32. **Any value from 14 to 21, inclusive**

If the worker boxes 8 pairs of shoes per minute, it will take $\dfrac{168}{8} = 21$ minutes to box all the shoes. If the worker boxes 12 pairs per minute, the same task will take $\dfrac{168}{12} = 14$ minutes. Therefore, any answer from 14 to 21 is valid. An easy way to solve a question like this is to just plug in a value within the given range. Suppose the worker boxes 10 pairs per minute. In that case, it will take $\frac{168}{10} = 16.8$ minutes to complete the task. This is a valid answer, and it is faster than finding the boundaries of the range.

33. **30** Begin by subtracting the weight of the driver and the pallet: $1,600 - 250 = 1,350$. Now divide by the weight of the boxes: $\frac{1,350}{45} = 30$. Therefore, 30 is the maximum number of boxes that can be safely loaded into the elevator.

34. **4** The formula for the volume of a cylinder is $V = \pi r^2 h$, so plug the given information into the formula. The radius is $\frac{9}{2}$, so $81\pi = \pi \left(\frac{9}{2}\right)^2 h$. Divide both sides by $\pi$ and square the fraction on the right: $81 = \frac{81}{4}h$. Divide both sides by $\frac{81}{4}$ to get the correct answer, which is 4.

35. **4** A fraction is undefined if the denominator is zero, so set the denominator equal to zero: $(x - 6)^2 + 4(x - 7) + 8 = 0$. Now solve for $x$ by using FOIL and distributing where necessary: $x^2 - 12x + 36 + 4x - 28 + 8 = 0$. Combine like terms: $x^2 - 8x + 16 = 0$. Factor the equation: $(x - 4)^2 = 0$. Take the square root of both sides: $x - 4 = 0$. Add 4 to both sides: $x = 4$. The correct answer is 4.

36. **51** The trains arrive at 6, 6:20, 6:40, then 7, 7:20, 7:40, then 8, 8:20, 8:40, and so on. There are three trains per hour, so count the number of hours—using a pencil to keep track if necessary. There are 17 hours, and $17 \times 3 = 51$, so the correct answer is 51.

37. **3** For this question, it helps to know the compound interest formula, which is $A = P\left(1 + \frac{r}{n}\right)^{nt}$, where $A$ is the total amount, $P$ is the principal or initial amount, $r$ is the interest rate (expressed as a decimal), $n$ is how many times per year the rate is compounded, and $t$ is the number of years. That may seem complicated, but usually the interest is compounded once a year, so $n = 1$, and the formula can be simplified to $A = P(1 + r)^t$. Therefore, the interest rate expressed as a decimal is 0.03. Multiply by 100 to express the interest rate as a percentage: $(0.03)(100) = 3$, which is the correct answer.

38. **8.76** It helps to solve question 37, the easier question of the pair, before solving this one. Helene's interest rate, from the answer to question 37, is 3%, so to find her total after 12 years, use the formula above: $A = 50(1.03)^{12} = 71.29$. Carolyn earns 1% more, so her total is $A = 50(1.04)^{12} = 80.05$. Subtract the first total from the second to get 8.76, which is the correct answer.

# Chapter 5
# Practice Test 2

# Reading Test

## 65 MINUTES, 52 QUESTIONS

**Turn to Section 1 of your answer sheet to answer the questions in this section.**

---

### DIRECTIONS

Each passage or pair of passages below is followed by a number of questions. After reading each passage or pair, choose the best answer to each question based on what is stated or implied in the passage or passages and in any accompanying graphics (such as a table or graph).

---

### Questions 1–10 are based on the following passage.

This passage is excerpted from Miguel de Cervantes, *Don Quixote*, originally published in 1605 and translated by John Ormsby in 1885.

At this point they came in sight of thirty or forty windmills that are on that plain.

"Fortune," said Don Quixote to his squire, as soon
Line as he had seen them, "is arranging matters for us better
5 than we could have hoped. Look there, friend Sancho Panza, where thirty or more monstrous giants rise up, all of whom I mean to engage in battle and slay, and with whose spoils we shall begin to make our fortunes. For this is righteous warfare, and it is God's good
10 service to sweep so evil a breed from off the face of the earth."

"What giants?" said Sancho Panza.

"Those you see there," answered his master, "with the long arms, and some have them nearly two
15 leagues* long."

"Look, your worship," said Sancho. "What we see there are not giants but windmills, and what seem to be their arms are the vanes that turned by the wind make the millstone go."

20 "It is easy to see," replied Don Quixote, "that you are not used to this business of adventures. Those are giants, and if you are afraid, away with you out of here and betake yourself to prayer, while I engage them in fierce and unequal combat."

25 So saying, he gave the spur to his steed Rocinante, heedless of the cries his squire Sancho sent after him, warning him that most certainly they were windmills and not giants he was going to attack. He, however, was so positive they were giants that he neither heard the
30 cries of Sancho, nor perceived, near as he was, what they were.

"Fly not, cowards and vile beings," he shouted, "for a single knight attacks you."

A slight breeze at this moment sprang up, and the
35 great vanes began to move.

"Though ye flourish more arms than the giant Briarus**, ye have to reckon with me!" exclaimed Don Quixote, when he saw this.

So saying, he commended himself with all his
40 heart to his lady Dulcinea, imploring her to support him in such a peril. With lance braced and covered by his shield, he charged at Rocinante's fullest gallop and attacked the first mill that stood in front of him. But as he drove his lance-point into the sail, the wind whirled
45 it around with such force that it shivered the lance to pieces. It swept away with it horse and rider, and they were sent rolling over the plain, in sad condition indeed. Sancho hastened to his assistance as fast as his ass could go, and when he came up found him unable
50 to move, with such a shock had Rocinante fallen with him.

"God bless me!" said Sancho, "did I not tell your worship to mind what you were about, for they were only windmills? And no one could have made any
55 mistake about it but one who had mills of the same kind in his head."

CONTINUE →

"Hush, friend Sancho" replied Don Quixote, "the fortunes of war more than any other are liable to frequent fluctuations; and moreover I think, and it is
60 the truth, that the same sage Friston*** who carried off my study and books, has turned these giants into mills in order to rob me of the glory of vanquishing them, such is the enmity he bears me; but in the end his wicked arts will avail but little against my good sword."

* seven miles
** a hundred-armed giant from Greek mythology
*** the magician (El Sabio Frestón), an imaginary character who Quixote imagines as the thief of his books and the enchanter of the windmills

**1**

Which choice best summarizes the passage?

A) An adventure goes awry when two young men decide to pretend they are in a great battle due to their longing for adventure.

B) A great warrior and his faithful steed single-handedly vanquish an army of giants in a mystical tale.

C) Two knights find themselves in an argument over what is really happening in their immediate surroundings.

D) A knight with an altered perception of reality engages in what he believes to be a battle of good versus evil.

**2**

The main purpose of the opening sentence of the passage is to

A) inform the reader of the true setting of the story for later plot purposes.

B) elaborate on the importance of technological advances during the Middle Ages.

C) describe the field on which a great battle is about to take place.

D) provide detailed imagery to enhance the mood of the following story.

**3**

During the course of the first six paragraphs (lines 1–24), the main character's focus shifts from

A) recollection of past victories to the prospect of imminent defeat.

B) reflection on the role of money in warfare to the role of God in battle.

C) generalization of how to wage a successful battle to specific rules of combat.

D) evaluation of an enemy before him to an argument with his faithful companion.

**4**

The phrase "sweep so evil a breed from off the face of the earth" at the end of the second paragraph mainly has which of the following effects?

A) It establishes the story as a horror story that will primarily focus on the evil in the world.

B) It informs the reader that Don Quixote is in fact a prophet who receives orders from God to go into battle.

C) It indicates the grandiose view that Don Quixote has of the battle he is about to undertake.

D) It demonstrates to the reader the dangers of taking religious fanaticism to the point of violence.

**5**

The passage indicates that Don Quixote would characterize his charge into battle as

A) ridiculous.

B) insane.

C) unexceptional.

D) brave.

CONTINUE

**6**

The passage indicates that Sancho views Don Quixote as a

A) boss who endangers his employees.

B) superior who needs looking after.

C) skillful leader to follow into battle.

D) pious man who requires help.

**7**

Which choice provides the best evidence for the answer to the previous question?

A) Lines 20–21 ("It is . . . adventures")

B) Lines 21–24 ("Those are . . . combat")

C) Lines 25–28 ("So saying . . . attack")

D) Lines 41–43 ("With lance . . . him")

**8**

The passage indicates that Don Quixote does not believe Sancho's description of the "giants" (line 17) because

A) Sancho's eyesight is not as good as Don Quixote's.

B) Don Quixote claims Sancho is not as brave as he is when it comes to battle.

C) Don Quixote knows more about Friston's schemes than Sancho does.

D) Don Quixote believes Sancho is too busy praying to pay attention.

**9**

Which choice provides the best evidence for the answer to the previous question?

A) Lines 13–15 ("Those you . . . long")

B) Lines 16–19 ("Look, your . . . go")

C) Lines 21–24 ("Those are . . . combat")

D) Lines 32–33 ("Fly not . . . you")

**10**

At the end of the passage, the reference to Friston mainly has the effect of

A) giving the reader greater insight into how Don Quixote perceives reality.

B) revealing the evil in the world that Don Quixote is fighting his battle against.

C) explaining to the reader the detailed history of how Don Quixote came to see things.

D) illustrating for the reader the evil that can come from personal misunderstandings.

**CONTINUE** ➡

**Questions 11–20 are based on the following passage.**

This passage is adapted from Susan B. Anthony's 1873 address to Post Office Districts of Monroe on women's suffrage.

*Friends and Fellow-citizens:* I stand before you tonight, under indictment for the alleged crime of having voted at the last Presidential election, without
Line having a lawful right to vote. It shall be my work this
5 evening to prove to you that in thus voting, I not only committed no crime, but, instead, simply exercised my *citizen's right,* guaranteed to me and all United States citizens by the National Constitution, beyond the power of any State to deny.
10     Our democratic-republican government is based on the idea of the natural right of every individual member thereof to a voice and a vote in making and executing the laws. We assert the province of government to be to secure the people in the
15 enjoyment of their unalienable rights. We throw to the winds the old dogma that governments can give rights. Before governments were organized, no one denies that each individual possessed the right to protect his own life, liberty and property. And when 100 or
20 1,000,000 people enter into a free government, they do not barter away their natural rights; they simply pledge themselves to protect each other in the enjoyment of them, through prescribed judicial and legislative tribunals. They agree to abandon the methods of brute
25 force in the adjustment of their differences, and adopt those of civilization.

    Nor can you find a word in any of the grand documents left us by the fathers that assumes for government the power to create or to confer rights.
30 The Declaration of Independence, the United States Constitution, the constitutions of the several states and the organic laws of the territories, all alike propose to protect the people in the exercise of their God-given rights. Not one of them pretends to bestow rights.
35     "All men are created equal, and endowed by their Creator with certain unalienable rights. Among these are life, liberty and the pursuit of happiness. That to secure these, governments are instituted among men, deriving their just powers from the consent of the
40 governed."

    Here is no shadow of government authority over rights, nor exclusion of any from their full and equal enjoyment. Here is pronounced the right of all men, and "consequently," as the Quaker preacher said, "of
45 all women," to a voice in the government. And here,

in this very first paragraph of the declaration, is the assertion of the natural right of all to the ballot; for, how can "the consent of the governed" be given, if the right to vote be denied. Again:
50     "That whenever any form of government becomes destructive of these ends, it is the right of the people to alter or abolish it, and to institute a new government, laying its foundations on such principles, and organizing its powers in such forms as to them shall
55 seem most likely to effect their safety and happiness."

    Surely, the right of the whole people to vote is here clearly implied. For however destructive in their happiness this government might become, a disfranchised class could neither alter nor abolish it,
60 nor institute a new one, except by the old brute force method of insurrection and rebellion. One-half of the people of this nation today are utterly powerless to blot from the statute books an unjust law, or to write there a new and a just one. The women, dissatisfied as
65 they are with this form of government, that enforces taxation without representation,—that compels them to obey laws to which they have never given their consent,—that imprisons and hangs them without a trial by a jury of their peers, that robs them, in
70 marriage, of the custody of their own persons, wages and children,—are this half of the people left wholly at the mercy of the other half, in direct violation of the spirit and letter of the declarations of the framers of this government, every one of which was based
75 on the immutable principle of equal rights to all. By those declarations, kings, priests, popes, aristocrats, were all alike dethroned, and placed on a common level politically, with the lowliest born subject or serf. By them, too, men, as such, were deprived of their
80 divine right to rule, and placed on a political level with women. By the practice of those declarations all class and caste distinction will be abolished; and slave, serf, plebeian, wife, woman, all alike, bound from their subject position to the proud platform of equality.

CONTINUE

**11**

The central problem that Anthony explains in the passage is that women have been

A) prevented from voting, which is a violation of their human rights.

B) prevented from participating in Congress, which has led to the creation of unjust laws.

C) too kind and just, while men are cruel and unfair.

D) denied equal access to schools, which has prevented them from attending college.

**12**

Anthony uses the phrase "grand documents" (lines 27–28) mainly to refer to the

A) paper the Declaration of Independence was written on.

B) letters from a grand jury.

C) President's personal notes.

D) important legislation the country was founded on.

**13**

Anthony claims that which of the following was a purpose of the Declaration of Independence?

A) The protection of human rights

B) The bestowal of human rights

C) The creation of human rights

D) The prevention of violence

**14**

Which choice provides the best evidence for the answer to the previous question?

A) Lines 4–9 ("It shall . . . deny")

B) Lines 27–29 ("Nor can . . . rights")

C) Lines 30–34 ("The Declaration . . . rights")

D) Lines 50–55 ("That whenever . . . happiness")

**15**

As used in line 33, "the exercise" most nearly refers to

A) an activity.

B) a workout.

C) a use or application.

D) a process.

**16**

It can be reasonably inferred that "natural right" (line 47) was a term generally intended to

A) describe the right of men and women to vote.

B) criticize the right of women to run for office.

C) advocate for the right to bear arms.

D) introduce the origin of the fifth amendment.

**17**

As used in line 59, "class" most nearly means

A) subject.

B) group.

C) genus.

D) stylish.

**18**

Anthony contends that the situation she describes in the passage shows that the U.S. Government has

A) established laws denying women's suffrage.

B) denied participating in an unjust system.

C) considered women superior to men.

D) dethroned kings for political equality.

CONTINUE

**19**

Which choice provides the best evidence for the answer to the previous question?

A) Lines 1–4 ("Friends and . . . vote")

B) Lines 35–40 ("All men . . . governed")

C) Lines 50–55 ("That whenever . . . happiness")

D) Lines 75–78 ("By those . . . serf")

**20**

Lines 61–75 of the seventh paragraph are primarily concerned with establishing a contrast between

A) those with power and those without.

B) poor men and rich men.

C) social customs and religious customs.

D) laws and guidelines.

**CONTINUE**

**Questions 21–30 are based on the following passage and supplementary material.**

This passage is adapted from the U.S. Geological Survey, "Ground Water." © 1999 by the U.S. Department of the Interior.

Although there are sizable areas where ground water is being withdrawn at rates that cause water levels to decline persistently, as in parts of the dry
*Line* Southwest, this is not true throughout the country. For
5    the Nation as a whole, there is neither a pronounced downward nor upward trend. Water levels rise in wet periods and decline in dry periods. In areas where water is not pumped from aquifers in excess of the amount of recharge to the aquifer—particularly in the
10    humid central and eastern parts of the country—water levels average about the same as they did in the early part of the twentieth century.

A major responsibility of the U.S. Geological Survey is to assess the quantity and quality of the
15    Nation's water supplies. The Geological Survey, in cooperation with other Federal, State, and local agencies, maintains a nationwide hydrologic-data network, carries out a wide variety of water-resources investigations, and develops new methodologies for
20    studying water. The results of these investigations are indispensable tools for those involved in water-resources planning and management. Numerous inquiries concerning water resources and hydrology are directed to the Survey and to State water-resources
25    and geological agencies.

To locate ground water accurately and to determine the depth, quantity, and quality of the water, several techniques must be used, and a target area must be thoroughly tested and studied to identify hydrologic
30    and geologic features important to the planning and management of the resource. The landscape may offer clues to the hydrologist about the occurrence of shallow ground water. Conditions for large quantities of shallow ground water are more favorable under
35    valleys than under hills.

Rocks are the most valuable clues of all. As a first step in locating favorable conditions for ground-water development, the hydrologist prepares geologic maps and cross sections showing the distribution and
40    positions of the different kinds of rocks, both on the surface and underground. Some sedimentary rocks may extend many miles as aquifers of fairly uniform permeability. Other types of rocks may be cracked and broken and contain openings large enough to carry

45    water. Types and orientation of joints or other fractures may be clues to obtaining useful amounts of ground water. Some rocks may be so folded and displaced that it is difficult to trace them underground.

Next, a hydrologist obtains information on
50    the wells in the target area. The locations, depth to water, amount of water pumped, and types of rocks penetrated by wells also provide information on ground water. Wells are tested to determine the amount of water moving through the aquifer, the
55    volume of water that can enter a well, and the effects of pumping on water levels in the area. Chemical analysis of water from wells provides information on quality of water in the aquifer.

Evaluating the ground-water resource in developed
60    areas, prudent management of the resource, and protection of its quality are current ground-water problems. Thus, prediction of the capacity of the ground-water resource for long-term pumpage, the effects of that pumpage, and evaluation of water-
65    quality conditions are among the principal aims of modern-day hydrologic practice in achieving proper management of ground water.

Ground water, presently a major source of water, is also the Nation's principal reserve of fresh water. The
70    public will have to make decisions regarding water supply and waste disposal-decisions that will either affect the ground-water resource or be affected by it. These decisions will be more judicious and reliable if they are based upon knowledge of the principles of
75    ground-water occurrence.

CONTINUE ➡

**21**

According to the Geological Survey, the capability to assess the nation's water supplies is significant primarily because

A) the study of such water supplies will provide critical information to plan future infrastructure.

B) the study of water supplies will allow agencies to plan and manage all water resources.

C) it will enable researchers to assess the quantity and quality of nationwide hydrologic data.

D) it will enable scientists to verify the depth and location of ground water.

**22**

Which choice provides the best evidence for the answer to the previous question?

A) Lines 6–7 ("Water levels . . . periods")

B) Lines 20–22 ("The results . . . management")

C) Lines 47–48 ("Some rocks . . . underground")

D) Lines 56–58 ("Chemical analysis . . . aquifer")

**23**

The third paragraph serves mainly to

A) propose a new method and detail its efficacy.

B) explain different methods for finding a natural resource.

C) address a need for making a discovery.

D) describe how a hydrologic instrument is implemented.

**24**

As used in line 32, "occurrence" most nearly means

A) plan.

B) happening.

C) event.

D) presence.

**25**

As used in line 52, "penetrated" is closest in meaning to

A) drained.

B) inserted.

C) excavated.

D) breached.

**26**

Based on information in the passage, it can reasonably be inferred that ground water occurrence

A) is produced only by the flow of rain water through permeable rock in a valley.

B) could be located by proximity to landscape features such as hills and existing wells.

C) might be relatively constant across large landscapes but is affected by many seasonal variables.

D) achieves roughly the same depth regardless of the occurrence and persistence of surface water.

**27**

Which choice provides the best evidence for the answer to the previous question?

A) Lines 6–12 ("Water levels . . . century")

B) Lines 26–31 ("To locate . . . resource")

C) Lines 31–35 ("The landscape . . . hills")

D) Lines 36–41 ("As a . . . underground")

**28**

In the figure, which hydrologic or geologic layer holds only moisture with molecular attraction?

A) Unsaturated zone

B) Surface water

C) Creviced rock

D) Water table

**CONTINUE**

Which concept is supported by the passage and by the information in the figure?

A) Rock orientation can affect mapping the occurrence of ground water.

B) Rock orientation changes based on the type and orientation of the rock.

C) Rock orientation is determined by the folds and crevices in a rock.

D) Rock orientation is fairly uniform for some sedimentary rocks.

How does the figure support the author's point that rock orientation affects aquifer characteristics?

A) It presents numerous types of rocks folding and turning to block or allow ground water to pass through.

B) It depicts the variation in rock orientation on ground water supplies in a certain cross section.

C) It demonstrates how rock orientation is the best ground water indicator out of many other landscape features.

D) It shows that rock orientation allows ground water to extend as aquifers for miles.

**CONTINUE**

**Questions 31–41 are based on the following passage and supplementary material.**

This passage is adapted from Chester Lloyd Jones, "Bananas and Diplomacy." © 1913 by *The North American Review*.

To those in world-trade, names of countries and regions suggest their products. It has always been so. The East Indies four hundred years ago meant spice;
*Line*  two hundred years ago China meant silks and tea;
5  Canada meant fur. The Caribbean to Queen Elizabeth meant gold—it was the route of the treasure ships of Spain—to Washington it meant sugar and molasses, and to our children it will mean bananas.

The Panama Canal has so occupied our attention
10  for the last decade that we have overlooked a significant economic change taking place independently of the forces which promise so radically to change the transportation routes of world commerce. Economists tell us that the trend of Caribbean diplomacy will be
15  determined by the banana crop. At the beginning of the twentieth century, there are food products that will exercise an influence upon international politics unconnected with the Panama Canal and of an importance which can be measured only in prophesy.

20  The market for bananas in the United States was developed largely through the efforts of one man. Forty years ago, Captain L. D. Baker was engaged in trade between the Orinoco River and Boston. On one trip he called at Port Morant, Jamaica, for a cargo of
25  bamboo for paper-making and carried back a few bunches of bananas, then a curiosity in the New England markets. The venture proved profitable and the captain thereafter made several trips a year to Port Antonio, Jamaica, to take cargoes of bananas to
30  Boston.

How important the trade has become is illustrated by the figures of exports. In 1911 there were sent from Caribbean countries in the export trade 52,936,963 bunches, which, on the average of 140 bananas to
35  the bunch, represents a total of over 7,400,000,000 bananas. In 1912 the continental United States alone consumed 44,520,539 bunches, or over sixty bananas for each man, woman, and child. Two facts appear from the following figures: with the exception of the
40  Canary Islands, all the countries producing large quantities of bananas for export border the Caribbean, and the United States consumes 85 percent of all bananas exported—five times as much as all the rest of the world.

**Banana Supply of the United States 1912**

| | |
|---|---:|
| Jamaica | 15,467,918 |
| Honduras | 7,151,178 |
| Costa Rica | 7,053,664 |
| Panama | 4,581,500 |
| Cuba | 2,478,581 |
| Nicaragua | 2,270,100 |
| Guatemala | 2,017,650 |
| Colombia | 1,542,988 |
| Mexico | 817,006 |
| British Honduras | 557,160 |
| Dominican Republic | 304,000 |
| Dutch Guiana | 261,548 |
| Others | 17,246 |
| Total | 44,520,539 |

**The world supply in 1911 as shown by the same records was:**

| Country of Origin | Quantity (Bunches) |
|---|---:|
| Dominican Republic | 404,000 |
| Mexico (Frontera Province) | 750,000 |
| Honduras | 6,500,000 |
| Costa Rica | 9,309,586 |
| Jamaica | 16,497,385 |
| Colombia | 4,901,894 |
| Panama | 4,261,500 |
| Canary Islands | 2,648,378 |
| Cuba | 2,500,000 |
| Nicaragua | 2,225,000 |
| Guatemala | 1,755,704 |
| British Honduras | 525,000 |
| Dutch Guiana | 387,516 |
| Others | 250,000 |
| Total | 52,915,963 |

45  The business, especially when the fruit must be sent long distances, demands organization for collecting fruit from small planters and large capital for steamers with refrigerating appliances. In fact, reliance on private planters has proven unsatisfactory and the
50  big banana-marketing companies now own extensive plantations throughout the West Indies and on the mainland.

**CONTINUE** ➡

The increased production of the banana in its natural state and the diversification of its uses promise
55 to introduce a new and hitherto neglected factor in our food supply. If present development continues, it will raise the Caribbean region from its dependence on foreign markets for food to one of the regions from which an important part of the world's food-
60 supply will be drawn. The wheat fields of the Dakotas and Manitoba will meet as one of their competitors in feeding the world the banana plantations of the American Mediterranean.

These figures show that the world is just awakening
65 to the value of the banana as food. If the present development continues, the acreage devoted to banana-growing must rapidly increase. Improved refrigeration and quick steam service will continue to widen the area in which the product can be marketed.
70 The development of the banana-flour industry also promises to open a market for the product of areas too distant to profit by the demand of fresh fruit, just as the perfection of the manufacture of copra, the dried meat of the coconut, has opened up a new industry reaching
75 to the farthest islands of the Pacific.

Great as the blessings of the Panama Canal will be to the trade of the world and to that of the United States in particular, we must not let the new markets which it will develop beyond the Isthmus make us
80 forget that region so rich in possibilities which lies this side of the continental divide and so much nearer our own markets. Friendship with our near neighbors is no less important than the good will of people over wide seas. One of the most important, and from our past
85 experience let us remember, one of the most delicate problems with which our men of state have to deal is the diplomacy of the Caribbean.

---

**31**

The main purpose of the passage is to

A) examine the impact of an export on the global economy.

B) posit that bananas will become the new gold standard.

C) consider a dilemma brought about by global economics.

D) argue that international politics bars the Caribbean from gaining financial independence.

---

**32**

The main purpose of the second paragraph (lines 9–19) is to

A) illustrate how exports will skyrocket with the completion of the Panama Canal.

B) introduce an idea not widely associated with a familiar region.

C) prove that bananas will dominate the economy of the twentieth century.

D) provide support that economists correctly prophesy that the Panama Canal will radically change world commerce.

---

**33**

As used in line 17, "exercise" most nearly means

A) operate.

B) exert.

C) train.

D) maneuver.

---

**34**

Which choice best supports the author's claim that bananas are likely to play a significant role in the global economy?

A) Lines 1–5 ("To those . . . fur")

B) Lines 13–15 ("Economists tell . . . crop")

C) Lines 42–44 ("United States . . . world")

D) Lines 60–63 ("The wheat . . . Mediterranean")

---

**35**

As used in line 82, "friendship" most nearly means

A) affection.

B) fondness.

C) collusion.

D) cooperation.

**CONTINUE**

**36**

The main idea of the final paragraph (lines 76–87) is that

A) friendship is important and often overlooked in the global economy.

B) the Panama Canal has proven to be a great blessing in international trade.

C) new markets will emerge beyond the Isthmus, calling for change in the global economy.

D) the Caribbean may prove to be an important component of the global economy in coming decades.

**37**

In the passage, the author anticipates which of the following potential difficulties for the banana industry?

A) Transporting bananas large distances requires certain technology to be successful.

B) Steamers are the best way to transport large quantities of bananas.

C) The banana flour is produced in areas too distant to be reached.

D) The banana industry will be surpassed by copra exports.

**38**

Which choice provides the best evidence for the previous question?

A) Lines 15–19 ("At the . . . prophesy")

B) Lines 45–48 ("The business . . . appliances")

C) Lines 48–52 ("In fact . . . mainland")

D) Lines 70–75 ("The development . . . Pacific")

**39**

Data in the tables provide most direct support for which idea in the passage?

A) Countries other than the United States are beginning to learn about bananas as food.

B) The increased production of the banana is the beginning of an economic revolution in the Caribbean.

C) Acreage toward banana-growing must increase to accommodate increased production.

D) The export numbers in the tables show an upward trend in banana consumption.

**40**

Data in the tables indicate that the greatest difference between U. S. banana supply exports in 1912 and world banana supply in 1911 is from which country?

A) Honduras

B) Panama

C) Jamaica

D) Nicaragua

**41**

Data in the table of the world supply in 1911 most strongly support which of the following statements?

A) Panama and Columbia combined supplied more bananas than did Jamaica in 1911.

B) The profits earned from bananas did not fluctuate.

C) Dutch Guiana produced the fewest bananas in 1911.

D) Colombia exported more bananas in 1911 than did Cuba.

CONTINUE

**Questions 42–52 are based on the following passages.**

Passage 1 is adapted from Jonah Lehrer, "The Neuroscience of Music." © 2011 by *Wired*. Passage 2 is adapted from Jeanette Bicknell, "Musical Thrills and Chills." © 2011 by *Psychology Today*.

## Passage 1

Why does music make us feel? On the one hand, music is a purely abstract art form, devoid of language or explicit ideas. And yet, even though music says
Line little, it still manages to tickle some universal nerves.
5 When listening to our favorite songs, our body betrays all the symptoms of emotional arousal. The pupils in our eyes dilate, our pulse and blood pressure rise, the electrical conductance of our skin is lowered, and the cerebellum, a brain region associated with bodily
10 movement, becomes strangely active. Blood is even re-directed to the muscles in our legs. (Some speculate that this is why we begin tapping our feet.) In other words, sound stirs us at our biological roots.

We can now begin to understand where these
15 feelings come from, why a mass of vibrating air hurtling through space can trigger such intense states of excitement. A new paper by a team of Montreal researchers marks an important step in revealing the precise underpinnings of "the potent pleasurable
20 stimulus" that is music. The scientists asked ten individuals who experience chills to instrumental music to bring in their playlist of favorite songs— virtually every genre was represented, from techno to tango—and played them the music while their brain
25 activity was monitored.

Because the scientists were combining methodologies (PET and fMRI) they were able to obtain an impressively precise portrait of music in the brain. The first thing they discovered is that music
30 triggers the release of dopamine in both the dorsal and ventral striatum. This isn't particularly surprising: these regions have long been associated with the response to pleasurable stimuli.

The more interesting finding emerged from a
35 close study of the timing of this response, as the scientists looked to see what was happening in the seconds *before* the subjects got the chills. In essence, the scientists found that our favorite moments in the music were preceded by a prolonged increase of
40 activity in the caudate. They call this the "anticipatory phase" and argue that the purpose of this activity is

to help us predict the arrival of our favorite part. This subregion of the striatum has been typically implicated in learning of stimulus-response associations and
45 in mediating the reinforcing qualities of rewarding stimuli such as food. In other words, the abstract pitches have become a primal reward cue, the cultural equivalent of a bell that makes us drool.

## Passage 2

People who are strongly affected by music
50 sometimes claim that it gives them chills down their spine and makes their hair stand on end. (The technical term is "piloerection.") When we are affected in this way by music, art, or by the grandeur of nature, what exactly is going on? Can some kind of
55 evolutionary explanation help us make sense of the experience?

One of the most intriguing explanations for music's "chill" effect has been offered by neuroscientist Jaak Panksepp. Panksepp found that chills and piloerection
60 were most likely to be associated with sad music, and with the bleak simplicity of a solo soprano voice or instrument emerging from a relatively richer musical background. A great example occurs in Whitney Houston's version of Dolly Parton's song "I Will
65 Always Love You," when the words of the title are repeated at the beginning of the third rendition of the chorus. Panksepp offers an evolutionary explanation for the origin of the chill phenomenon, whether the music involved is a popular song, operatic aria, or
70 instrumental work. He argues that chills may emerge from brain dynamics associated with the perception of social loss, specifically with separation calls. Separation calls are cries by young animals that inform parents of the whereabouts of offspring that have become
75 lost. The "coldness" of chills may provide increased motivation for social reunion in the parents.

Recent experimental work by Mathias Benedek and Christian Kaernbach offers some support for Panksepp's hypothesis. Subjects listened, on
80 headphones, to four short musical selections and four short audio excerpts from film soundtracks. Researchers monitored their physical responses, including skin conductivity, and cardiovascular and respiratory measures, and set up a camera to record
85 piloerection. They found that some of the listeners'

CONTINUE

responses, specifically short-term increases in heart-rate and in respiration depth, were consistent with the physiological reactions usually associated with non-crying sadness. While the existence of a connection
90 between piloerection and sadness lends some support to Panksepp's ideas, researchers did not find much evidence for any connection between piloerection and a sense of coldness.

**42**

The author of Passage 1 indicates which of the following about the caudate?

A) It emerges from a close study of response times.

B) It is involved in learning associations.

C) It causes the chill experience.

D) It helps reinforce qualities of food.

**43**

Which choice provides the best evidence for the answer to the previous question?

A) Lines 6–10 ("The pupils . . . active")

B) Lines 29–31 ("The first . . . striatum")

C) Lines 37–40 ("In essence . . . caudate")

D) Lines 42–46 ("This subregion . . . food")

**44**

The author of Passage 1 indicates that music

A) may preclude feeling states.

B) often derives from feeling states.

C) can evoke feeling states.

D) could contain ideas of feelings.

**45**

As used in line 5, "betrays" most nearly means

A) demonstrates.

B) turns against.

C) undermines.

D) misleads.

**46**

The author of Passage 2 refers to "coldness" (line 75) primarily to

A) outline the chill effect of music.

B) illustrate an evolutionary explanation.

C) associate it with sadness.

D) trace the origin of piloerection.

**47**

According to the author of Passage 2, what do Panksepp and Benedek and Kaernbach have in common?

A) They undertook experiments to study the chill effect.

B) They argue for an evolutionary explanation of the chill effect.

C) They draw a connection between piloerection and sadness.

D) They draw a connection between piloerection and happiness.

**48**

The reference to the song "I Will Always Love You" has primarily which effect?

A) It exemplifies when piloerection is likely to occur.

B) It serves to console young when they are separated from their parents.

C) It provides support for Benedek's hypothesis.

D) It shows an example of bleak repetition.

**CONTINUE**

**49**

The main purpose of both passages is to

A) highlight recent methods of learning music through neuroscience.

B) show the superiority of neuroscience over merely psychological analysis of responses to music.

C) explain how music can evoke feelings in scientists.

D) show the relevance of neuroscience to understanding responses to music.

**50**

Which choice best describes the relationship between the two passages?

A) Passage 1 examines an evolutionary explanation of piloerection, while Passage 2 considers the findings of a study of the chill response.

B) Passage 1 considers positive emotional responses to music, while Passage 2 considers the relevance of negative emotions to musical responses.

C) Passage 1 reviews recent research, while Passage 2 reviews more established theories.

D) Passage 1 relies on the methods of neuroscience, while Passage 2 considers only theoretical work.

**51**

On which of the following points would the authors of both passages most likely agree?

A) Although music is generally abstract, it can affect us in quite concrete ways.

B) The use of tests such as PET and fMRI is a superior way of obtaining a precise understanding of the role of music in the brain.

C) The neuroscience of emotion and the study of musical response can both help illuminate phenomena such as the chill response.

D) The chill effect of music can be seen along with the expression of both positive and negative emotions.

**52**

Which choice provides the best evidence that the author of Passage 1 would agree to some extent with the argument attributed to Panksepp in lines 70-72, Passage 2?

A) Lines 1–3 ("On the . . . ideas")

B) Lines 12–13 ("In other . . . roots")

C) Lines 29–31 ("The first . . . striatum")

D) Lines 46–47 ("In other . . . cue")

## STOP

**If you finish before time is called, you may check your work on this section only.
Do not turn to any other section in the test.**

**No Test Material On This Page**

# Writing and Language Test

## 35 MINUTES, 44 QUESTIONS

**Turn to Section 2 of your answer sheet to answer the questions in this section.**

### DIRECTIONS

Each passage below is accompanied by a number of questions. For some questions, you will consider how the passage might be revised to improve the expression of ideas. For other questions, you will consider how the passage might be edited to correct errors in sentence structure, usage, or punctuation. A passage or a question may be accompanied by one or more graphics (such as a table or graph) that you will consider as you make revising and editing decisions.

Some questions will direct you to an underlined portion of a passage. Other questions will direct you to a location in a passage or ask you to think about the passage as a whole.

After reading each passage, choose the answer to each question that most effectively improves the quality of writing in the passage or that makes the passage conform to the conventions of standard written English. Many questions include a "NO CHANGE" option. Choose that option if you think the best choice is to leave the relevant portion of the passage as it is.

**Questions 1–11 are based on the following passage.**

**Streaming Something Beyond Hard Work**

There is no question that the American workforce has changed, regardless of whether one believes it has changed for better or worse. In the 1940s, the United States led the world in most economic categories, and its businesses were some of the most praised in the world. By the 1980s, however, the dominance of the United States had been challenged by industries the world over, and the economy was measured in terms of global effects rather than national ones.

This **1** growing and enlarging competition has unfortunately led to a loosening of companies' responsibilities toward their employees. Retirement

**1**

A) NO CHANGE

B) increased competition

C) increased competing among countries

D) larger spirit of competitiveness for all

CONTINUE ➡

pensions are largely a thing of the past. **2** Moreover, whereas someone born in the 1940s might have expected to spend his or her entire career with a single company. Many of whom now swap through four or five "careers" throughout a single working life.

This trend has intensified recently, particularly in **3** Silicon Valley startups. One of the major success

Which choice most effectively combines the underlined sentences?

A) Moreover, whereas someone born in the 1940s might have expected to spend his or her entire career with a single company; many workers now swap through four or five "careers" throughout a single working life over the course of it.

B) Swapping jobs is, moreover for instance, a thing that new workers do now, whereas those in the 1940s would have been more likely to work for a single company for their entire careers.

C) Moreover, whereas someone born in the 1940s might have expected to spend his or her entire career with a single company; many workers now swap through four or five "careers" throughout a single working life.

D) Moreover, whereas someone born in the 1940s might have expected to spend his or her entire career with a single company, now the norm has workers swapping through four or five "careers" throughout a single working life.

At this point, the author is considering adding the following information.

the fast-paced, forward-thinking, occasionally ruthless world of

Should the writer make the addition here?

A) Yes, because it shows the author's ability in finding apt adjectives.

B) Yes, because it creates a richer description of the company discussed in the essay.

C) No, because it lengthens the sentence unnecessarily with information that is given elsewhere.

D) No, because it is not the kind of thing that would be acceptable to say in the workplace.

stories from among these many-sided companies [4] that is Netflix, the streaming and DVD-mailing giant, who may have been singlehandedly responsible for ending the lifespans of both the video store and the DVD in only a few short years. Netflix's compulsively innovative methods have changed the way that those living in the United States and in many other parts of the globe interact with visual media, especially in movie theaters, on home entertainment systems, and on [5] computers.

[6] For all this, Netflix has become famous (or infamous) for changing its employees' relationship to the workplace. Netflix's staff is relatively lean, and employees are incredibly well treated. Their salaries are higher than those of other Silicon Valley businesses, and the employees are given *unlimited* (yes, you read that correctly) vacation time. Furthermore, as Netflix continues to push beyond the traditional boundaries of film and TV, the company affords its employees the opportunity to be on the cutting edge of change.

4

A) NO CHANGE
B) that are
C) is
D) are

5

A) NO CHANGE
B) machines used for computing.
C) PCs and Macs with the capacity to stream.
D) intelligent machines.

6

A) NO CHANGE
B) Irregardless,
C) Thus,
D) Furthermore,

CONTINUE

All of Netflix's success comes at a price, however. **7** Just putting seriously all of it right out there, employees at Netflix are warned not to think of the job as one that they will keep "for life." Netflix is not concerned with traditional ideas of "hard work:" **8** to come to work on time, staying late, and showing loyalty to the company. Instead, Netflix is concerned only with *results*. Just ask the computer programmers who started Netflix's streaming service and then were let go when the service became so successful that Netflix had to use Amazon.com's servers instead. While these employees had done about as good a job as one could do, **9** yet they were fired the moment they were no longer needed.

Indeed, as companies continue to tighten their belts and their responsibility to be profitable remains, they will demand more of their employees and withdraw some of the comfortable **10** premising that the employees of earlier eras relied on. **11** This may be the workplace of the future, and we can only hope that employees will adapt as well as they have to past changes.

---

**7**

Which choice most effectively sets up the idea given in the second part of this sentence?

A) NO CHANGE

B) Turned off by the company's rudeness,

C) Having no idea what they're walking into,

D) From the first day on the job,

**8**

A) NO CHANGE

B) coming

C) come

D) workers coming

**9**

A) NO CHANGE

B) and

C) because

D) DELETE the underlined portion.

**10**

A) NO CHANGE

B) premise

C) promises

D) promising

**11**

Which statement most clearly ends the passage with a restatement of the writer's primary claim?

A) NO CHANGE

B) This is the end of employment as we know it, and we should all head for the hills.

C) You can try to get a job at Netflix, but they're not really hiring all that often.

D) If you've ever been fired or laid off from a job, you know how difficult it can be.

**CONTINUE**

**Questions 12–22 are based on the following passage.**

**Television—Not So Bad After All?**

— 1 —

A mere ten years ago, surveys recorded data that showed the average American viewer to watch four hours of television a day. Television was a central part of the American household. Now that the Internet has come to supplant television's central role in American culture (as people spend more time watching six-second videos on Vine, reading short posts on Facebook and Twitter, and **12** they send quirky photos and videos on Snapchat), the complaints that had always been made about television can seem rather quaint. Those who critiqued television as a dangerous influence on society have since changed to new and, as they would see it, worse targets on the **13** web and are not much interested in television anymore.

— 2 —

Television certainly had its harmful effects on those who watched it for that frankly inconceivable four hours a day. There could be no "couch potatoes" without TVs, and the scourge of reality TV might never have been thrust upon the American viewing public. **14** As aforementioned, shining light in your eyes for many hours at a time can wreak havoc on one of **15** your most important senses: vision.

**12**

Which choice most closely matches the stylistic pattern established earlier in the sentence?

A) NO CHANGE

B) the sending of quirky photos and videos features prominently on Snapchat),

C) sending quirky photos and videos on Snapchat),

D) they send quirky photos on Snapchat and videos),

**13**

A) NO CHANGE

B) web,

C) web, they

D) web, the images on the Internet

**14**

A) NO CHANGE

B) However,

C) That said,

D) Moreover,

**15**

A) NO CHANGE

B) you're most important senses,

C) you're most important senses;

D) your most important senses;

CONTINUE

— 3 —

However, television accomplished some incredible things as well. Drawing on the networks that **16** radio creates throughout the entire country, television provided something truly national for the first time. During the first American performance of The Beatles on *The Ed Sullivan Show*, there was not a single crime committed in the United States. **17** Everyone, literally everyone, was watching TV.

— 4 —

A large component of this "big world" was the presence of non-white faces. **18** Especially African Americans, non-white people, who parroted and parodied the patterns of black speech, were represented on the radio by white actors. While African Americans were the most frequently targeted group, Asian Americans and those of all ethnicities were similarly lampooned in the national media. The popularity of television actually ended up forcing these media into a kind of progressivism: the

**16**

A) NO CHANGE
B) radio created
C) radios' create
D) radio's creation

**17**

At this point, the writer is considering adding the following sentence.

> The Beatles had many hits, including "She Loves You" and "I Wanna Hold Your Hand," that continue to influence the course of rock and roll to the present day.

Should the writer make this addition here?

A) Yes, because it helps to explain why the music of The Beatles can help to prevent crime.

B) Yes, because it gives the reader additional context that helps to explain the importance of television.

C) No, because it suggests that television's only function was to broadcast musical performances.

D) No, because it adds a detail that is irrelevant to the paragraph's main focus.

**18**

A) NO CHANGE

B) For many years, non-white people, especially African Americans, were represented on the radio by white actors, who parroted and parodied the patterns of black speech.

C) African Americans were non-white people especially who for many years parroted by white actors and parodied in speech patterns.

D) White actors parroted especially African Americans from non-white actors in their patterns of black speech, which were parodied for many years.

CONTINUE →

Chinese-American character on *Have Gun Will Travel* **19** and some of the other shows set in the old West would no longer work as racial masquerades. As a result, some of the earliest leading roles for non-white actors and actresses came on television, earlier than in film and theater in many cases.

— 5 —

Television may not play the central role in American culture that it once did, but many of the things that it achieved, both good and bad, remain in the culture today.

— 6 —

This national reach could occasionally lead to conformity and sensationalism, but it also showed **20** many in the American public, just how diverse the American scene had become. People still had to have a certain amount of wealth to travel physically outside of their **21** hometowns. They were usually filled with citizens who had the same basic backgrounds and attitudes. Television could show them just how big the world outside was.

**Question 22 asks about the previous passage as a whole.**

**19**

Which choice gives a second supporting example that is most similar to the example already in the sentence?

A) NO CHANGE

B) who was played by Ben Wright on the radio show

C) and even some of the shows that weren't so popular on radio

D) or the African-American character on *The Beulah Show*

**20**

A) NO CHANGE

B) many, in the American public

C) many in the American public

D) many, in the American public,

**21**

Which choice most effectively combines the sentences at the underlined portion?

A) hometowns: they

B) hometowns, and theirs

C) hometowns with what

D) hometowns, which

**Think about the previous passage as a whole as you answer question 22.**

**22**

To make the passage most logical, paragraph 6 should be placed

A) where it is now.

B) before paragraph 2.

C) before paragraph 3.

D) before paragraph 4.

CONTINUE ➡

**Questions 23–33 are based on the following passage and supplementary material.**

### The Noise Is Not for the Birds

Even if you love the vibrant life of the city, you probably still love to come home to a nice, quiet spot. Even the busiest lives need some calm once in a while for some of life's basic, private tasks. In fact, this doesn't only describe human lives. While untouched nature is usually prized for the way it *looks*— 23 there greenery, scurrying animals, and placidity—nature is actually just as much characterized by the way it *sounds*.

24 Thus, when we build highways through thriving natural habitats, we don't just change the way they look. 25 You've certainly been somewhere remote enough that there aren't any cars around, or you've been woken up some morning by the sound of a car horn or a revving engine. Although the sound of the car is the sound of our day-to-day life, that does not change the fact that car traffic is remarkably loud.

---

**23**

A) NO CHANGE
B) their
C) it's
D) its

**24**

A) NO CHANGE
B) Thence,
C) Whereas,
D) This being so,

**25**

At this point, the writer is considering adding the following sentence.

> We also change the way they sound.

Should the writer make this addition here?

A) Yes, because it reminds the reader of the beauty of birds' songs.
B) Yes, because it completes the idea started in the previous sentence.
C) No, because it shifts the emphasis of the paragraph to sound rather than sight.
D) No, because it disagrees with the thesis developed in the paragraph as a whole.

**CONTINUE** ➡

Furthermore, while we have become relatively [26] weakened to the sounds of cars on our "quiet" residential streets, not all animals have. A recent study checked the effect of [27] raising the highway volume on local bird populations. This might seem like an easy study with all the new highway construction going on in the United States all the time, but the researchers [28] at the Intermountain Bird Observatory in Idaho and wanted to study the effects without becoming part of the problem. Instead of building new roads, the researchers opted to produce the *sound* of roads, creating a fake, [29] or, a "phantom," road with 15 pairs of speakers playing the sounds of traffic noise.

**26**

A) NO CHANGE

B) inured

C) hip

D) keen

**27**

A) NO CHANGE

B) the noise being more on highways

C) increased highway noise

D) highways exhibiting more noise levels

**28**

A) NO CHANGE

B) who work at the Intermountain Bird Observatory in Idaho, where they wanted to

C) at the Intermountain Bird Observatory in Idaho wanted to

D) at the Intermountain Bird Observatory in Idaho, they wanted to

**29**

A) NO CHANGE

B) or a "phantom," road

C) or a "phantom"; road

D) or a "phantom" road,

CONTINUE

[1] The results were telling. [2] According to the study, the mere *sounds* of 30 traffic, "reduced avian populations by a third and cut species diversity by a significant amount." [3] Birds, it seems, need to spend as much time as possible with their heads down—hunting and pecking, feeding their young, and fattening up for their various migrations. [4] This is bad news for avian life in the deep South, where the Interstate Highway Commission 31 has announced plans to eradicate avian and other wildlife populations between Natchez, Augusta, Savannah, and Knoxville. 32

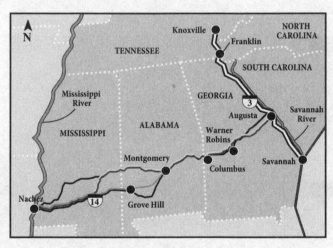

**Proposed Interstate Routes**

While this study will, the scientists hope, discourage new road construction within the national parks and other forested areas, it can also have effects where the roads are already present. With lower speed limits and rubberized asphalt, 33 the roads won't be quite so noisy, and the native fauna might feel just a little bit freer to roam.

30

A) NO CHANGE
B) traffic reduced
C) traffic, reduced
D) traffic—reduced

31

Which choice offers an accurate interpretation of the data in the figure?

A) NO CHANGE
B) will push avian populations northeast into North Carolina and northwest into western Tennessee.
C) has planned an east-west route from Savannah to Knoxville and a north-south route from Augusta to Natchez.
D) has planned a north-south route from Savannah to Knoxville and an east-west route from Augusta to Natchez.

32

Where is the most logical place in the paragraph to add the following sentence?

When there is so much distraction from outside noise, however, birds are more likely to be looking up than down, casting a cautious eye on their potentially perilous surroundings.

A) After sentence 1
B) After sentence 2
C) After sentence 3
D) After sentence 4

33

A) NO CHANGE
B) there won't be so much noise,
C) they won't be so noisy,
D) there won't be all the noisy roads,

CONTINUE

**Questions 34–44 are based on the following passage.**

A "Failed" Search for the American Southwest

Sometimes it really *is* about the journey rather than the destination. Francisco Vázquez de Coronado, an early Spanish explorer and [34] conquistador; died believing that he had failed in his mission, but his pursuit of that mission has been just as significant to history as it would have been had he achieved his goal. Coronado's experience is an excellent window into the difficulty of assessing the Spanish explorers, [35] but also we can see the blurring of the line between hero and villain. In much the same way that Columbus is still praised as being the "discoverer" of the United States but reviled for the atrocities he [36] eviscerated against the native populations, Coronado presents a historical challenge.

Coronado's aims were [37] fewer than noble. He didn't particularly care about making history. He was

---

**34**

A) NO CHANGE
B) conquistador
C) conquistador,
D) conquistador—

**35**

A) NO CHANGE
B) wherein
C) just as
D) so too

**36**

A) NO CHANGE
B) did
C) committed
D) manifested

**37**

A) NO CHANGE
B) less, then
C) less then
D) less than

CONTINUE

much more interested in making something **38** else, altogether: money. Coronado, **39** who grew up in a noble family in Spain, came to New Spain (present-day Mexico) when he was 25 years old. Within four years of his arrival, Coronado had become intoxicated by the circulating rumors of the Seven Cities of Gold. **40** They merely lay in wait for someone to claim the bounty, these cities, or so the rumor had it, were richer than any place in the world.

Of course, there were no such places, neither in Cíbola, a city just west of modern-day Albuquerque, nor in Quivira, a town in central Kansas. Coronado's disappointment was absolutely unforgiving and vicious: many fellow travelers died on these expeditions, and **41** many Zuni families in the region were slaughtered as a result of Coronado's greed.

**38**

A) NO CHANGE
B) else:
C) else, nevertheless:
D) else, and it was:

**39**

A) NO CHANGE
B) he grew
C) growing
D) whom grows

**40**

A) NO CHANGE
B) Merely lying
C) They merely lie
D) While laying merely

**41**

Which choice provides information that best supports the claim made by this sentence?
A) NO CHANGE
B) the journeys were long and arduous.
C) medical care was very limited at the time.
D) no one stopped to see the sites.

**CONTINUE**

[1] However, Coronado's journey was not entirely without merit. [2] That's a lot of territory to cover in the middle of the sixteenth century! [3] Notice how far we have traveled in this short essay alone. [4] We started in Spain, then went to Mexico, then to New Mexico, then to Kansas **42** after that. [5] Thus, while Coronado's tactics were vicious and his goals less than noble, he was nonetheless one of the first to provide reliable information on the terrains of vast stretches of the American West. [6] His expedition provided the first European sightings of the Grand Canyon, the Colorado River, and many of the lands along his route. **43**

Though Coronado's expedition may have been fraught with unpleasantness and we may balk at the idea of calling his sightings "discoveries," Coronado's contributions to the course of American history were nonetheless significant. His influence is all around us. **44** While Coronado may not have achieved his stated goal, we have his "failure" to thank for a large swath of the contemporary United States.

**42**

A) NO CHANGE

B) en route.

C) while we were there.

D) DELETE the underlined portion, and end the sentence with a period.

**43**

To make this paragraph most logical, sentence 2 should be placed

A) where it is now.

B) before sentence 3.

C) before sentence 4.

D) before sentence 5.

**44**

At this point, the writer is considering adding the following sentence.

> A small island off the coast of San Diego bears his name, as does a high school halfway across the country in Lubbock, Texas.

Should the writer make this addition here?

A) Yes, because it names some of the places of which Coronado was most fond.

B) Yes, because it cites some of the contemporary places that were influenced by Coronado.

C) No, because it disagrees with the paragraph's central claims regarding Coronado's cruelty.

D) No, because it introduces a tangent into the American Southwest that is not further elaborated.

**STOP**
**If you finish before time is called, you may check your work on this section only.**
**Do not turn to any other section in the test.**

**No Test Material On This Page**

# Math Test – No Calculator

## 25 MINUTES, 20 QUESTIONS

**Turn to Section 3 of your answer sheet to answer the questions in this section.**

---

### DIRECTIONS

**For questions 1–15**, solve each problem, choose the best answer from the choices provided, and fill in the corresponding circle on your answer sheet. **For questions 16–20**, solve the problem and enter your answer in the grid on the answer sheet. Please refer to the directions before question 16 on how to enter your answers in the grid. You may use any available space in your test booklet for scratch work.

### NOTES

1. The use of a calculator **is not permitted**.
2. All variables and expressions used represent real numbers unless otherwise indicated.
3. Figures provided in this test are drawn to scale unless otherwise indicated.
4. All figures lie in a plane unless otherwise indicated.
5. Unless otherwise indicated, the domain of a given function $f$ is the set of all real numbers $x$ for which $f(x)$ is a real number.

### REFERENCE

$A = \pi r^2$
$C = 2\pi r$

$A = \ell w$

$A = \frac{1}{2} bh$

$c^2 = a^2 + b^2$

Special Right Triangles

$V = \ell wh$

$V = \pi r^2 h$

$V = \frac{4}{3}\pi r^3$

$V = \frac{1}{3}\pi r^2 h$

$V = \frac{1}{3}\ell wh$

The number of degrees of arc in a circle is 360.
The number of radians of arc in a circle is $2\pi$.
The sum of the measures in degrees of the angles of a triangle is 180.

CONTINUE

**1**

The cost $C$, in dollars, that a catering company charges to cater a wedding is given by the function $C = 20wt + 300$, where $w$ represents the number of workers catering the wedding and $t$ represents the total time, in hours, it will take to cater the wedding using $w$ workers. Which of the following is the best explanation of the number 20 in the function?

A) A minimum of 20 workers will cater the wedding.

B) The cost of every wedding will increase by $20 per hour.

C) The catering company charges $20 per hour for each worker.

D) There will be 20 guests at the wedding.

**2**

If $12x + 4 = 20$, what is the value of $6x + 5$ ?

A) 4

B) 6

C) 10

D) 13

**3**

$$5x - 4y = 36$$
$$-x - y = 0$$

Which of the ordered pairs $(x, y)$ below is a solution to the system of equations shown above?

A) $(-5, 4)$

B) $(-4, 4)$

C) $(4, -4)$

D) $(5, -4)$

**4**

In the equation $y - \sqrt{4x^2 + 28} = 0$, $x > 0$ and $y = 8$. What is the value of $x$ ?

A) 3

B) 4

C) 5

D) 6

**CONTINUE**

**5**

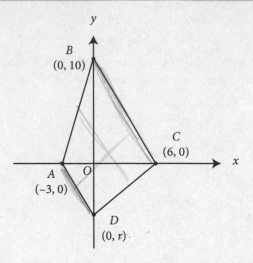

The figure above shows quadrilateral $ABCD$ in the $xy$-plane. If $\overline{BC}$ is parallel to $\overline{AD}$, what is the value of $r$ ?

A) −6

B) −5

C) −3

D) −2

**6**

Which of the following expressions is equivalent to $16x^6 - 24x^3y^3 + 9y^6$ ?

A) $(16x^2 - 9y^2)^3$

B) $(16x^3 - 9y^3)^2$

C) $(4x^3 - 3y^3)^2$

D) $(4x - 3y)^6$

**7**

$$S = 180(n - 2)$$

The measure $S$, in degrees, of the sum of the angles in a polygon is related to the number of sides, $n$, of the polygon by the formula above for all $n > 2$. If the sum of the angles of a polygon is greater than 2,000°, then what is the least number of sides it can have?

A) 11

B) 12

C) 13

D) 14

**8**

The graph of line $k$ in the $xy$-plane has a $y$-intercept of −8 and contains the point $(4, 4)$. The graph of line $m$ contains the points $(1, 5)$ and $(5, -3)$. If lines $k$ and $m$ intersect at the point $(s, t)$, what is the value of $s - t$ ?

A) 2

B) 3

C) 4

D) 5

CONTINUE

**9**

$$\left(k^{x^2 + xy}\right)\left(k^{y^2 + xy}\right) = k^{25}$$

In the equation above, $k > 1$ and $x = 3$. What is the positive value of $y$ ?

A) 1

B) 2

C) 4

D) 5

**10**

$$F = \frac{D}{E - D}$$

A factory tracks quality control by using the formula above to determine a fault rating, $F$, based on the number of defective parts, $D$, and the number of acceptable parts, $E$. Which of the following expresses $D$ in terms of $F$ and $E$ ?

A) $D = \dfrac{E}{1 - F}$

B) $D = \dfrac{E}{1 + F}$

C) $D = \dfrac{FE}{1 - F}$

D) $D = \dfrac{FE}{1 + F}$

**11**

The graph in the $xy$-plane of the function $g$ has the property that $y$ is always greater than or equal to –2. Which of the following could be $g$ ?

A) $g(x) = x^2 - 3$

B) $g(x) = (x - 3)^2$

C) $g(x) = |x| - 3$

D) $g(x) = (x - 3)^3$

**12**

Which of the following complex numbers is equivalent to $\dfrac{1 + 10i}{6 - 3i}$ ? (Note: $i = \sqrt{-1}$)

A) $\dfrac{1}{6} + \dfrac{10i}{3}$

B) $-\dfrac{1}{6} + \dfrac{10i}{3}$

C) $\dfrac{8}{15} + \dfrac{7i}{5}$

D) $-\dfrac{8}{15} + \dfrac{7i}{5}$

CONTINUE

**13**

The estimated value of a truck declines at an annual rate of 7 percent. If the original value of the truck was \$35,000, which of the functions $v$ best models the value of the truck, in dollars, $t$ years later?

A) $v(t) = 0.07(35,000)^t$

B) $v(t) = 0.93(35,000)^t$

C) $v(t) = 35,000(0.07)^t$

D) $v(t) = 35,000(0.93)^t$

**14**

$$\frac{6x - 1}{x + 4}$$

Which of the following is equivalent to the expression above?

A) $6 - \dfrac{25}{x + 4}$

B) $6 - \dfrac{1}{x + 4}$

C) $6 - \dfrac{1}{4}$

D) $\dfrac{6 - 1}{4}$

**15**

$$3k^2 - 18k + 12 = 0$$

What is the product of all values of $k$ that satisfy the equation above?

A) 3

B) 4

C) $3\sqrt{5}$

D) $6\sqrt{5}$

**CONTINUE**

## DIRECTIONS

**For questions 16–20**, solve the problem and enter your answer in the grid, as described below, on the answer sheet.

1. Although not required, it is suggested that you write your answer in the boxes at the top of the columns to help you fill in the circles accurately. You will receive credit only if the circles are filled in correctly.

2. Mark no more than one circle in any column.

3. No question has a negative answer.

4. Some problems may have more than one correct answer. In such cases, grid only one answer.

5. **Mixed numbers** such as $3\frac{1}{2}$ must be gridded as 3.5 or 7/2. (If [3 1 / 2] is entered into the grid, it will be interpreted as $\frac{31}{2}$, not as $3\frac{1}{2}$.)

6. **Decimal Answers:** If you obtain a decimal answer with more digits than the grid can accommodate, it may be either rounded or truncated, but it must fill the entire grid.

Answer: $\frac{7}{12}$     Answer: 2.5

Write answer in boxes. ← Fraction line

Grid in result. → Decimal point

Acceptable ways to grid $\frac{2}{3}$ are:

Answer: 201 – either position is correct

**NOTE:** You may start your answers in any column, space permitting. Columns you don't need to use should be left blank.

**CONTINUE** ➡

**16**

In the equation $3(x - 5)^2 + 7 = ax^2 + bx + c$, $a$, $b$, and $c$ are constants. If the equation is true for all values of $x$, what is the value of $c$ ?

**17**

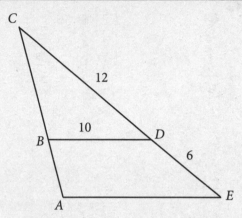

In the figure above, $\overline{BD} \parallel \overline{AE}$. What is the length of $\overline{AE}$ ?

**18**

At the end of a card game, Eve has a pile of red and blue chips that is worth \$120. If red chips are worth \$5 and blue chips are worth \$20, and Eve has at least one red chip and at least one blue chip, what is one possible number of red chips Eve has?

**19**

$$\frac{1}{2}x + ay = 16$$
$$bx + 4y = 48$$

In the system of equations shown above, $a$ and $b$ are constants. If there are infinitely many solutions for this system, what is the value of $a + b$ ?

CONTINUE

20

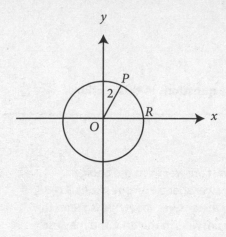

The *xy*-plane above shows the circle with center *O* and radius 2. If the measure of $\angle POR$ is $\dfrac{\pi}{3}$ radians, what is the *x*-coordinate of point *P* ?

**STOP**
**If you finish before time is called, you may check your work on this section only.**
**Do not turn to any other section in the test.**

# Math Test – Calculator

## 55 MINUTES, 38 QUESTIONS

**Turn to Section 4 of your answer sheet to answer the questions in this section.**

---

### DIRECTIONS

**For questions 1–30**, solve each problem, choose the best answer from the choices provided, and fill in the corresponding circle on your answer sheet. **For questions 31–38**, solve the problem and enter your answer in the grid on the answer sheet. Please refer to the directions before question 31 on how to enter your answers in the grid. You may use any available space in your test booklet for scratch work.

### NOTES

1. The use of a calculator **is permitted**.
2. All variables and expressions used represent real numbers unless otherwise indicated.
3. Figures provided in this test are drawn to scale unless otherwise indicated.
4. All figures lie in a plane unless otherwise indicated.
5. Unless otherwise indicated, the domain of a given function $f$ is the set of all real numbers $x$ for which $f(x)$ is a real number.

### REFERENCE

$A = \pi r^2$
$C = 2\pi r$

$A = \ell w$

$A = \frac{1}{2}bh$

$c^2 = a^2 + b^2$

Special Right Triangles

$V = \ell wh$

$V = \pi r^2 h$

$V = \frac{4}{3}\pi r^3$

$V = \frac{1}{3}\pi r^2 h$

$V = \frac{1}{3}\ell wh$

The number of degrees of arc in a circle is 360.
The number of radians of arc in a circle is $2\pi$.
The sum of the measures in degrees of the angles of a triangle is 180.

---

**CONTINUE** →

## 1

A contractor creates a mosaic floor pattern in which there are 9 blue tiles for every 80 tiles in total. At this rate, how many blue tiles will there be in a floor pattern of 4,800 tiles?

A) 700

B) 620

C) 540

D) 480

## 2

$$c = 120 + 75d$$

A couple rents a car for their vacation. When a particular car is rented for $d$ days, the total cost will be $c$ dollars as shown in the equation above. What is the value of $d$ when $c$ is 345 ?

A) 25,995

B) 354

C) 75

D) 3

## 3

An artist creates prints of her latest painting to sell. The artist earns $50 for each large print she sells and $35 for each small print she sells. Which of the following expressions represents the amount, in dollars, that the artist earns for selling $l$ large prints and $s$ small prints?

A) $50l + 35s$

B) $50l - 35s$

C) $35l + 50s$

D) $35l - 50s$

$$50l + 35s$$

## 4

When 6 times a number $y$ is subtracted from 15, the result is 33. What number results when 3 times $y$ is added to 19 ?

A) −3

B) 7

C) 10

D) 28

CONTINUE

**Questions 5 and 6 refer to the following information.**

A television store's revenue is directly proportional to the number of televisions it sells. The store earns $1,440 in a day in which it sells 6 televisions.

**5**

The store pays the factory 39% of the money earned from the sale of each television. The rest of the money earned is the store's profit. What is the profit the store makes on a day in which it sells 6 televisions?

A) $390.00

B) $561.60

C) $690.00

D) $878.40

**6**

How much revenue will the store earn on a day in which it sells 9 televisions?

A)     $960

B)    $2,160

C)    $8,640

D)   $12,960

**7**

A record collector is looking to buy records that cost either $20 or $35 each. Let $a$ be the number of $20 records and $b$ be the number of $35 records. The collector can buy a maximum of 25 records and can spend up to $750. Which of the following systems of inequalities accurately describes this relationship?

A) $\begin{cases} a + b \le 750 \\ 20a + 35b \le 25 \end{cases}$

B) $\begin{cases} 20a + 35b \le 750 \\ a + b \le 750 \end{cases}$

C) $\begin{cases} \dfrac{a}{20} + \dfrac{b}{35} \le 750 \\ a + b \le 25 \end{cases}$

D) $\begin{cases} 20a + 35b \le 750 \\ a + b \le 25 \end{cases}$

**8**

$$y = x^2 - 12x + 35$$

The equation above is a quadratic equation. Which of the following equivalent forms of the equation displays the $x$-intercepts of the parabola in the $xy$-plane as constants or coefficients?

A) $y + 1 = (x - 6)^2$

B) $y - 35 = x^2 - 12x$

C) $y = (x - 5)(x - 7)$

D) $y = x(x - 12) + 35$

CONTINUE

**9**

In a certain quiz game, each player begins with $p$ points, loses 3 points for every question answered incorrectly, and cannot increase his or her score. If a player who answers 15 questions incorrectly has a score of 165, which of the following is the value of $p$?

A)  210

B)  180

C)  140

D)    0

**10**

| | |
|---|---|
| Number of hours per day Albert expects to devote to typing the document | 4 |
| Number of units in the document | 21 |
| Number of words Albert types per minute | 85 |
| Number of sections in the document | 145 |
| Number of pages in the document | 725 |
| Number of words in the document | 181,235 |

Albert needs to type a long, prewritten document. The table above shows information about the document, Albert's typing speed, and the number of hours he expects to devote to typing the document each day. If Albert types at the rates provided in the table, which of the following is closest to the number of days Albert would expect to take in order to type the entire document?

A)      9

B)     36

C)    148

D)  2,132

**11**

At 9:00 A.M. Monday, a trash can with a capacity of 20 cubic feet contains 8 cubic feet of garbage. Each day after Monday, 3 cubic feet of garbage are added to the trash can. If no garbage is removed and $d$ represents the number of days after Monday, which of the following inequalities describes the set of days for which the trash can is full or overflowing?

A)  $12 \geq 3d$

B)  $8 + 3d \geq 20$

C)  $20 - 3 \leq d$

D)  $20 \leq 3d$

**12**

In function $m$, $m(4) = 6$ and $m(6) = 10$. In function $n$, $n(6) = 4$ and $n(10) = 2$. What is the value of $m(n(6))$?

A)    2

B)    4

C)    6

D)  10

**CONTINUE**

**13**

The circumference of Earth's equator is approximately 40,000 kilometers. Earth rotates completely around its axis in one day. Which of the following is the closest approximation of the average speed, in kilometers per minute, of a point on Earth's equator, as the Earth rotates about its axis?

A) 18

B) 20

C) 28

D) 56

**14**

A theater owner wanted to determine whether local residents were more interested in seeing operas or symphonies. The theater owner asked 85 people who were in a shopping mall on a Sunday and 5 people declined to respond. Which of the following factors is the greatest flaw in the theater owner's methodology in reaching a reliable conclusion about the local residents' performance-viewing preferences?

A) The size of the sample

B) The location in which the survey was given

C) The population of the area

D) The residents who declined to respond

**15**

Population of Town T from 1990 Projected Through 2035

According to the line of best fit in the scatterplot above, which of following best approximates the year in which the population of Town T is projected to reach 5,000 ?

A) 2017

B) 2022

C) 2028

D) 2033

**16**

The half-life of an unknown isotope is approximately 25% less than that of carbon-14. The half-life of carbon-14 is 5,730 years. Which of the following best approximately the half-life, in years, of the unknown isotope?

A) 1,400

B) 4,300

C) 5,705

D) 7,200

**CONTINUE**

**17**

A company's accounting department took a survey of its employees' salaries and found that the mean salary was $80,000 and that the median salary was $45,000. Which of the following could explain the difference between the mean and the median salary in the company?

A) Many of the employees' salaries are between $45,000 and $80,000.

B) The employees have salaries that are close to each other.

C) There are a few employees with salaries that are much lower than the rest.

D) There are a few employees with salaries that are much higher than the rest.

**18**

Results of Interview for Applicants to College C

|                          | Accepted by College C | Rejected by College C |
| ------------------------ | --------------------- | --------------------- |
| Completed interview      | 15,700                | 34,300                |
| Did not complete interview | 9,300               | 40,700                |

The table above summarizes the results of the 100,000 applicants to College C. If an accepted student is randomly chosen, what is the probability that the student did <u>not</u> complete an interview?

A) $\dfrac{93}{1,000}$

B) $\dfrac{1}{4}$

C) $\dfrac{93}{250}$

D) $\dfrac{157}{250}$

**19**

Mathias saves an average of $d$ dollars per month, where $d > 300$. The actual amount he saves per month varies, but is always within $20 of the average amount. If this month Mathias saved $k$ dollars, which of the following inequalities expresses the relationship between $k$, the amount he saved this month, and $d$, the average amount he saves per month?

A) $d - k < 20$

B) $d + k < 20$

C) $-20 < d - k < 20$

D) $-20 < d + k < 20$

**CONTINUE**

**Questions 20 and 21 refer to the following information.**

The class president chose 200 students at random from each of the junior and senior classes at her high school. Each student was asked how many hours of homework he or she completed in an average school night. The results are shown in the table below.

| Number of hours | Junior class | Senior class |
|---|---|---|
| 1 | 25 | 30 |
| 2 | 80 | 70 |
| 3 | 50 | 60 |
| 4 | 35 | 35 |
| 5 | 10 | 5 |

There are a total of 600 students in the junior class and 400 students in the senior class.

Based on the survey data, which of the following statements accurately compares the expected total number of members of each class who complete four hours of homework?

A) The total number of students who complete four hours of homework in the junior class is 35 more than in the senior class.

B) The total number of students who complete four hours of homework in the senior class is 35 more than in the junior class.

C) The total number of students who complete four hours of homework in the junior class is 200 more than in the senior class.

D) The total number of students who complete four hours of homework is expected to be the same in both classes.

What is the median number of hours of homework in an average night for all the students surveyed?

A) 2

B) 3

C) 4

D) 5

The equation of circle $P$ in the $xy$-plane can be represented as $x^2 + y^2 - 6x + 8y = -9$. What is the radius of circle $P$?

A) 2

B) 4

C) 8

D) 16

**CONTINUE**

**Questions 23 and 24 refer to the following information.**

$$G = \frac{ab}{d^2}$$

The gravitational force, $G$, between an object of mass $a$ and an object of mass $b$ is given by the formula above, where $d$ represents the distance between the two objects.

### 23

Which of the following expressions represents the square of the distance between the two objects in terms of the masses of the objects and the gravitational force between them?

A)  $d^2 = \dfrac{Gb}{a}$

B)  $d^2 = \dfrac{Ga}{b}$

C)  $d^2 = \dfrac{G}{ab}$

D)  $d^2 = \dfrac{ab}{G}$

### 24

Objects $k$ and $m$ have the same masses, respectively, as do objects $a$ and $b$. If the gravitational force between $k$ and $m$ is 9 times the gravitational force between $a$ and $b$, then the distance between $k$ and $m$ is what fraction of the distance between $a$ and $b$ ?

A)  $\dfrac{1}{243}$

B)  $\dfrac{1}{81}$

C)  $\dfrac{1}{9}$

D)  $\dfrac{1}{3}$

**CONTINUE**

**25**

The figure above shows the complete graph of the function $g$ in the $xy$-plane. Which of the following must be true?

I.   $g(-3) = 2$

II.  $g(2) = -3$

III. $g\left(\dfrac{1}{2}\right) = g(2)$

A) III only

B) I and II only

C) I and III only

D) I, II, and III

**26**

Two athletes have their pulses, in beats per minute (bpm), monitored while they exercise. One athlete alternates brisk running with walking, while the other athlete jogs at a constant pace. The graph above shows the athletes' heart rates at 30-second intervals. Which of the following statements accurately compares the average rates at which the pulses of the two athletes change?

A) In the interval from 1 to 2 minutes, the rate of change of pulse for the athlete who alternates running and walking is of lesser magnitude than the rate of change of pulse for the athlete who jogs only, whereas in the interval from 3 to 4 minutes, the rate of change of pulse for the athlete who jogs only is of lesser magnitude.

B) In the interval from 1 to 2 minutes, the rate of change of pulse for the athlete who jogs only is of lesser magnitude than the rate of change of pulse for the athlete who alternates running and walking, whereas in the interval from 3 to 4 minutes, the rate of change of pulse for the athlete who alternates running and walking is of lesser magnitude.

C) In every 30-second interval, the rate of change of pulse for the athlete who alternates running and walking is of lesser magnitude than it is for the athlete who jogs only.

D) In every 30-second interval, the rate of change of pulse for the athlete who jogs only is of lesser magnitude than it is for the athlete who alternates running and walking.

**CONTINUE**

**27**

The graph in the *xy*-plane of linear function *g* has an *x*-intercept at $(s, 0)$ and a *y*-intercept at $(0, t)$. If $t - s = 0$, $t \neq 0$, and $s \neq 0$, which of the following must be true about the graph of *g*?

A) It has a positive slope.

B) It has a negative slope.

C) It has a slope of zero.

D) It has no slope.

**28**

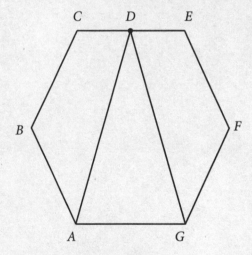

In the figure above, *ABCEFG* is a regular hexagon and *D* is the midpoint of $\overline{CE}$. If the area of the hexagon is $864\sqrt{3}$ square feet, what is the area, in square feet, of triangle *ADG*?

A) 144

B) 432

C) $288\sqrt{3}$

D) $432\sqrt{3}$

**29**

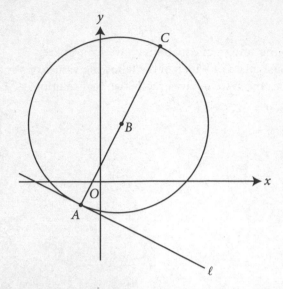

In the *xy*-plane above, $\overline{AC}$ is the diameter of the circle centered at *B*, and the coordinates of points *A* and *C* are $(-1, -1)$ and $(3, 7)$, respectively. If line $\ell$ is tangent to the circle at point *A*, which of the following is an equation of line $\ell$?

A) $y = -\dfrac{1}{2}(x + 3)$

B) $y = -\dfrac{1}{2}x + 3$

C) $y = -2x + 1$

D) $y = -2x - 3$

**CONTINUE**

**30**

$$y = rx^2 + s$$
$$y = -2$$

In the system of equations above, $r$ and $s$ are constants. For which of the following values of $r$ and $s$ does the system have exactly two real solutions?

A)  $r = -2, s = -1$

B)  $r = -1, s = -2$

C)  $r = 2, s = -2$

D)  $r = 3, s = 1$

CONTINUE

## DIRECTIONS

**For questions 31–38,** solve the problem and enter your answer in the grid, as described below, on the answer sheet.

1. Although not required, it is suggested that you write your answer in the boxes at the top of the columns to help you fill in the circles accurately. You will receive credit only if the circles are filled in correctly.

2. Mark no more than one circle in any column.

3. No question has a negative answer.

4. Some problems may have more than one correct answer. In such cases, grid only one answer.

5. **Mixed numbers** such as $3\frac{1}{2}$ must be gridded as 3.5 or 7/2. (If [ 3 1 / 2 ] is entered into the grid, it will be interpreted as $\frac{31}{2}$, not as $3\frac{1}{2}$.)

6. **Decimal Answers:** If you obtain a decimal answer with more digits than the grid can accommodate, it may be either rounded or truncated, but it must fill the entire grid.

Acceptable ways to grid $\frac{2}{3}$ are:

Answer: 201 – either position is correct

**NOTE:** You may start your answers in any column, space permitting. Columns you don't need to use should be left blank.

**CONTINUE**

### 31

If 560 minutes is equal to $z$ hours and 20 minutes, what is the value of $z$ ?

### 32

A climate scientist estimates that a certain state's average snowfall is decreasing by 0.4 inches per year. If the scientist's estimate is accurate, how many years will it take for the average annual snowfall to be 6 inches less than it is now?

### 33

Dave was charged a fine for returning a number of overdue books to the library. Each week after he incurred the fine, he paid the library a fixed amount until the fine was paid off. The equation $C = 12 - 1.5w$, where $C \geq 0$, models the amount $C$, in dollars, that Dave owes $w$ weeks after he incurred the fine. According to this model, how much money, in dollars, did Dave initially owe the library? (Disregard the $ sign when gridding in your answer.)

### 34

$$g(x) = 2x^2 - kx + 14$$

In the $xy$-plane, the graph of the function above contains the point $(4, -2)$. What is the value of $k$ ?

**CONTINUE** ➡

**35**

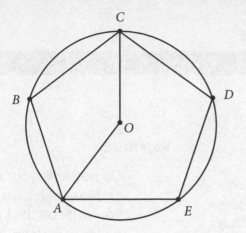

In the figure above, the circle is centered at point O, ABCDE is a regular pentagon, and ABCO is a quadrilateral. If the length of arc $\overset{\frown}{ABC}$ is 24, what is the circumference of circle O ?

**36**

Satya ate a breakfast sandwich and an order of fried potatoes and consumed a total of 910 calories. If the breakfast sandwich contained 240 more calories than the fried potatoes, how many calories did the breakfast sandwich contain?

**Questions 37 and 38 refer to the following information.**

$$P_{t+1} = P_t + 0.3(P_t)\left(1 - \frac{P_t}{C}\right)$$

A certain species of deer on an isolated island has a current population of 4,200. The estimated population of deer next year, $P_{t+1}$, is related to the population this year, $P_t$, by the formula above. In this formula, the constant C represents the maximum number of deer the island is capable of supporting.

**37**

Suppose that environmental conditions on the island changed suddenly, and there was a resultant decrease in the maximum number of deer the island is capable of supporting. If the number of deer increases from 4,200 this year to 4,704 next year, what would be the maximum number of deer the island is capable of supporting?

**38**

If C = 10,500, and the given formula is accurate, what will the population of deer be 2 years from now? (Round your answer to the nearest whole number.)

## STOP
**If you finish before time is called, you may check your work on this section only.**
**Do not turn to any other section in the test.**

# SAT Essay

**DIRECTIONS**

The essay gives you an opportunity to show how effectively you can read and comprehend a passage and write an essay analyzing the passage. In your essay you should demonstrate that you have read the passage carefully, present a clear and logical analysis, and use language precisely.

Your essay must be written on the lines provided in your answer sheet booklet; except for the planning page of the answer booklet, you will receive no other paper on which to write. You will have enough space if you write on every line, avoid wide margins, and keep your handwriting to a reasonable size. Remember that people who are not familiar with your handwriting will read what you write. Try to write or print so that what you are writing is legible to those readers.

**You have <u>50 minutes</u> to read the passage and write an essay in response to the prompt provided inside this booklet.**

**REMINDER**

— Do not write your essay in this booklet. Only what you write on the lined pages of your answer booklet will be evaluated.

— An off-topic essay will not be evaluated.

CONTINUE ➤

As you read the passage below, consider how Martin Luther King, Jr. uses

- evidence, such as facts or examples, to support claims.
- reasoning to develop ideas and to connect claims and evidence.
- stylistic or persuasive elements, such as word choice or appeals to emotion, to add power to the ideas expressed.

**Adapted from Martin Luther King, Jr.'s "Letter from a Birmingham Jail," written April 16, 1963.**

1   My Dear Fellow Clergymen:

2   While confined here in the Birmingham city jail, I came across your recent statement calling my present activities "unwise and untimely." Seldom do I pause to answer criticism of my work and ideas. If I sought to answer all the criticisms that cross my desk, my secretaries would have little time for anything other than such correspondence in the course of the day, and I would have no time for constructive work. But since I feel that you are men of genuine good will and that your criticisms are sincerely set forth, I want to try to answer your statement in what I hope will be patient and reasonable terms.

3   I think I should indicate why I am here in Birmingham, since you have been influenced by the view which argues against "outsiders coming in." I have the honor of serving as president of the Southern Christian Leadership Conference, an organization operating in every southern state, with headquarters in Atlanta, Georgia. We have some eighty five affiliated organizations across the South, and one of them is the Alabama Christian Movement for Human Rights. Frequently we share staff, educational and financial resources with our affiliates. Several months ago the affiliate here in Birmingham asked us to be on call to engage in a nonviolent direct action program if such were deemed necessary. We readily consented, and when the hour came we lived up to our promise. So I, along with several members of my staff, am here because I was invited here. I am here because I have organizational ties here.

4   But more basically, I am in Birmingham because injustice is here. Just as the prophets of the eighth century B.C. left their villages and carried their "thus saith the Lord" far beyond the boundaries of their home towns, and just as the Apostle Paul left his village of Tarsus and carried the gospel of Jesus Christ to the far corners of the Greco Roman world, so am I compelled to carry the gospel of freedom beyond my own home town. Like Paul, I must constantly respond to the Macedonian call for aid.

5   Moreover, I am cognizant of the interrelatedness of all communities and states. I cannot sit idly by in Atlanta and not be concerned about what happens in Birmingham. Injustice anywhere is a threat to justice everywhere. We are caught in an inescapable network of mutuality, tied in a single garment of destiny. Whatever affects one directly, affects all

CONTINUE ➔

indirectly. Never again can we afford to live with the narrow, provincial "outside agitator" idea. Anyone who lives inside the United States can never be considered an outsider anywhere within its bounds.

6    You deplore the demonstrations taking place in Birmingham. But your statement, I am sorry to say, fails to express a similar concern for the conditions that brought about the demonstrations. I am sure that none of you would want to rest content with the superficial kind of social analysis that deals merely with effects and does not grapple with underlying causes. It is unfortunate that demonstrations are taking place in Birmingham, but it is even more unfortunate that the city's white power structure left the Negro community with no alternative...

7    You may well ask: "Why direct action? Why sit-ins, marches and so forth? Isn't negotiation a better path?" You are quite right in calling for negotiation. Indeed, this is the very purpose of direct action. Nonviolent direct action seeks to create such a crisis and foster such a tension that a community which has constantly refused to negotiate is forced to confront the issue. It seeks so to dramatize the issue that it can no longer be ignored. My citing the creation of tension as part of the work of the nonviolent resister may sound rather shocking. But I must confess that I am not afraid of the word "tension." I have earnestly opposed violent tension, but there is a type of constructive, nonviolent tension which is necessary for growth... The purpose of our direct action program is to create a situation so crisis packed that it will inevitably open the door to negotiation. I therefore concur with you in your call for negotiation. Too long has our beloved Southland been bogged down in a tragic effort to live in monologue rather than dialogue.

---

Write an essay in which you explain how Martin Luther King, Jr. builds an argument in response to the claim that the protests in Birmingham were "unwise and untimely." In your essay, analyze how King uses one or more of the features listed in the box above (or features of your own choice) to strengthen the logic and persuasiveness of his argument. Be sure that your analysis focuses on the most relevant features of the passage.

Your essay should not explain whether you agree with King's claims, but rather explain how King builds an argument to persuade his audience.

---

**END OF TEST**

**DO NOT RETURN TO A PREVIOUS SECTION.**

Completely darken bubbles with a No. 2 pencil. If you make a mistake, be sure to erase mark completely. Erase all stray marks.

**1.**

YOUR NAME: _____
(Print)
         Last          First         M.I.

SIGNATURE: _____ DATE: ___ / ___ / ___

HOME ADDRESS: _____
(Print)
         Number and Street

_____
    City         State         Zip Code

PHONE NO.: _____
(Print)

**IMPORTANT:** Please fill in these boxes exactly as shown on the back cover of your test book.

**2. TEST FORM**

**6. DATE OF BIRTH**

| Month | | Day | | Year | |
|---|---|---|---|---|---|
| ○ JAN | | | | | |
| ○ FEB | ⓪ | ⓪ | ⓪ | ⓪ | |
| ○ MAR | ① | ① | ① | ① | |
| ○ APR | ② | ② | ② | ② | |
| ○ MAY | ③ | ③ | ③ | ③ | |
| ○ JUN | | ④ | ④ | ④ | |
| ○ JUL | | ⑤ | ⑤ | ⑤ | |
| ○ AUG | | ⑥ | ⑥ | ⑥ | |
| ○ SEP | | ⑦ | ⑦ | ⑦ | |
| ○ OCT | | ⑧ | ⑧ | ⑧ | |
| ○ NOV | | ⑨ | ⑨ | ⑨ | |
| ○ DEC | | | | | |

**3. TEST CODE**

| ⓪ | Ⓐ | Ⓙ | ⓪ | ⓪ |
| ① | Ⓑ | Ⓚ | ① | ① |
| ② | Ⓒ | Ⓛ | ② | ② |
| ③ | Ⓓ | Ⓜ | ③ | ③ |
| ④ | Ⓔ | Ⓝ | ④ | ④ |
| ⑤ | Ⓕ | Ⓞ | ⑤ | ⑤ |
| ⑥ | Ⓖ | Ⓟ | ⑥ | ⑥ |
| ⑦ | Ⓗ | Ⓠ | ⑦ | ⑦ |
| ⑧ | Ⓘ | Ⓡ | ⑧ | ⑧ |
| ⑨ | | | ⑨ | ⑨ |

**4. REGISTRATION NUMBER**

| ⓪ | ⓪ | ⓪ | ⓪ | ⓪ | ⓪ | ⓪ |
| ① | ① | ① | ① | ① | ① | ① |
| ② | ② | ② | ② | ② | ② | ② |
| ③ | ③ | ③ | ③ | ③ | ③ | ③ |
| ④ | ④ | ④ | ④ | ④ | ④ | ④ |
| ⑤ | ⑤ | ⑤ | ⑤ | ⑤ | ⑤ | ⑤ |
| ⑥ | ⑥ | ⑥ | ⑥ | ⑥ | ⑥ | ⑥ |
| ⑦ | ⑦ | ⑦ | ⑦ | ⑦ | ⑦ | ⑦ |
| ⑧ | ⑧ | ⑧ | ⑧ | ⑧ | ⑧ | ⑧ |
| ⑨ | ⑨ | ⑨ | ⑨ | ⑨ | ⑨ | ⑨ |

**7. SEX**
○ MALE
○ FEMALE

The **Princeton** Review®

**5. YOUR NAME**

| First 4 letters of last name | | | | FIRST INIT | MID INIT |
|---|---|---|---|---|---|
| Ⓐ | Ⓐ | Ⓐ | Ⓐ | Ⓐ | Ⓐ |
| Ⓑ | Ⓑ | Ⓑ | Ⓑ | Ⓑ | Ⓑ |
| Ⓒ | Ⓒ | Ⓒ | Ⓒ | Ⓒ | Ⓒ |
| Ⓓ | Ⓓ | Ⓓ | Ⓓ | Ⓓ | Ⓓ |
| Ⓔ | Ⓔ | Ⓔ | Ⓔ | Ⓔ | Ⓔ |
| Ⓕ | Ⓕ | Ⓕ | Ⓕ | Ⓕ | Ⓕ |
| Ⓖ | Ⓖ | Ⓖ | Ⓖ | Ⓖ | Ⓖ |
| Ⓗ | Ⓗ | Ⓗ | Ⓗ | Ⓗ | Ⓗ |
| Ⓘ | Ⓘ | Ⓘ | Ⓘ | Ⓘ | Ⓘ |
| Ⓙ | Ⓙ | Ⓙ | Ⓙ | Ⓙ | Ⓙ |
| Ⓚ | Ⓚ | Ⓚ | Ⓚ | Ⓚ | Ⓚ |
| Ⓛ | Ⓛ | Ⓛ | Ⓛ | Ⓛ | Ⓛ |
| Ⓜ | Ⓜ | Ⓜ | Ⓜ | Ⓜ | Ⓜ |
| Ⓝ | Ⓝ | Ⓝ | Ⓝ | Ⓝ | Ⓝ |
| Ⓞ | Ⓞ | Ⓞ | Ⓞ | Ⓞ | Ⓞ |
| Ⓟ | Ⓟ | Ⓟ | Ⓟ | Ⓟ | Ⓟ |
| Ⓠ | Ⓠ | Ⓠ | Ⓠ | Ⓠ | Ⓠ |
| Ⓡ | Ⓡ | Ⓡ | Ⓡ | Ⓡ | Ⓡ |
| Ⓢ | Ⓢ | Ⓢ | Ⓢ | Ⓢ | Ⓢ |
| Ⓣ | Ⓣ | Ⓣ | Ⓣ | Ⓣ | Ⓣ |
| Ⓤ | Ⓤ | Ⓤ | Ⓤ | Ⓤ | Ⓤ |
| Ⓥ | Ⓥ | Ⓥ | Ⓥ | Ⓥ | Ⓥ |
| Ⓦ | Ⓦ | Ⓦ | Ⓦ | Ⓦ | Ⓦ |
| Ⓧ | Ⓧ | Ⓧ | Ⓧ | Ⓧ | Ⓧ |
| Ⓨ | Ⓨ | Ⓨ | Ⓨ | Ⓨ | Ⓨ |
| Ⓩ | Ⓩ | Ⓩ | Ⓩ | Ⓩ | Ⓩ |

**Test ❷**   Start with number 1 for each new section.
If a section has fewer questions than answer spaces, leave the extra answer spaces blank.

## Section 1—Reading

1. Ⓐ Ⓑ Ⓒ Ⓓ
2. Ⓐ Ⓑ Ⓒ Ⓓ
3. Ⓐ Ⓑ Ⓒ Ⓓ
4. Ⓐ Ⓑ Ⓒ Ⓓ
5. Ⓐ Ⓑ Ⓒ Ⓓ
6. Ⓐ Ⓑ Ⓒ Ⓓ
7. Ⓐ Ⓑ Ⓒ Ⓓ
8. Ⓐ Ⓑ Ⓒ Ⓓ
9. Ⓐ Ⓑ Ⓒ Ⓓ
10. Ⓐ Ⓑ Ⓒ Ⓓ
11. Ⓐ Ⓑ Ⓒ Ⓓ
12. Ⓐ Ⓑ Ⓒ Ⓓ
13. Ⓐ Ⓑ Ⓒ Ⓓ
14. Ⓐ Ⓑ Ⓒ Ⓓ
15. Ⓐ Ⓑ Ⓒ Ⓓ
16. Ⓐ Ⓑ Ⓒ Ⓓ
17. Ⓐ Ⓑ Ⓒ Ⓓ
18. Ⓐ Ⓑ Ⓒ Ⓓ
19. Ⓐ Ⓑ Ⓒ Ⓓ
20. Ⓐ Ⓑ Ⓒ Ⓓ
21. Ⓐ Ⓑ Ⓒ Ⓓ
22. Ⓐ Ⓑ Ⓒ Ⓓ
23. Ⓐ Ⓑ Ⓒ Ⓓ
24. Ⓐ Ⓑ Ⓒ Ⓓ
25. Ⓐ Ⓑ Ⓒ Ⓓ
26. Ⓐ Ⓑ Ⓒ Ⓓ
27. Ⓐ Ⓑ Ⓒ Ⓓ
28. Ⓐ Ⓑ Ⓒ Ⓓ
29. Ⓐ Ⓑ Ⓒ Ⓓ
30. Ⓐ Ⓑ Ⓒ Ⓓ
31. Ⓐ Ⓑ Ⓒ Ⓓ
32. Ⓐ Ⓑ Ⓒ Ⓓ
33. Ⓐ Ⓑ Ⓒ Ⓓ
34. Ⓐ Ⓑ Ⓒ Ⓓ
35. Ⓐ Ⓑ Ⓒ Ⓓ
36. Ⓐ Ⓑ Ⓒ Ⓓ
37. Ⓐ Ⓑ Ⓒ Ⓓ
38. Ⓐ Ⓑ Ⓒ Ⓓ
39. Ⓐ Ⓑ Ⓒ Ⓓ
40. Ⓐ Ⓑ Ⓒ Ⓓ
41. Ⓐ Ⓑ Ⓒ Ⓓ
42. Ⓐ Ⓑ Ⓒ Ⓓ
43. Ⓐ Ⓑ Ⓒ Ⓓ
44. Ⓐ Ⓑ Ⓒ Ⓓ
45. Ⓐ Ⓑ Ⓒ Ⓓ
46. Ⓐ Ⓑ Ⓒ Ⓓ
47. Ⓐ Ⓑ Ⓒ Ⓓ
48. Ⓐ Ⓑ Ⓒ Ⓓ
49. Ⓐ Ⓑ Ⓒ Ⓓ
50. Ⓐ Ⓑ Ⓒ Ⓓ
51. Ⓐ Ⓑ Ⓒ Ⓓ
52. Ⓐ Ⓑ Ⓒ Ⓓ

## Section 2—Writing and Language Skills

1. Ⓐ Ⓑ Ⓒ Ⓓ
2. Ⓐ Ⓑ Ⓒ Ⓓ
3. Ⓐ Ⓑ Ⓒ Ⓓ
4. Ⓐ Ⓑ Ⓒ Ⓓ
5. Ⓐ Ⓑ Ⓒ Ⓓ
6. Ⓐ Ⓑ Ⓒ Ⓓ
7. Ⓐ Ⓑ Ⓒ Ⓓ
8. Ⓐ Ⓑ Ⓒ Ⓓ
9. Ⓐ Ⓑ Ⓒ Ⓓ
10. Ⓐ Ⓑ Ⓒ Ⓓ
11. Ⓐ Ⓑ Ⓒ Ⓓ
12. Ⓐ Ⓑ Ⓒ Ⓓ
13. Ⓐ Ⓑ Ⓒ Ⓓ
14. Ⓐ Ⓑ Ⓒ Ⓓ
15. Ⓐ Ⓑ Ⓒ Ⓓ
16. Ⓐ Ⓑ Ⓒ Ⓓ
17. Ⓐ Ⓑ Ⓒ Ⓓ
18. Ⓐ Ⓑ Ⓒ Ⓓ
19. Ⓐ Ⓑ Ⓒ Ⓓ
20. Ⓐ Ⓑ Ⓒ Ⓓ
21. Ⓐ Ⓑ Ⓒ Ⓓ
22. Ⓐ Ⓑ Ⓒ Ⓓ
23. Ⓐ Ⓑ Ⓒ Ⓓ
24. Ⓐ Ⓑ Ⓒ Ⓓ
25. Ⓐ Ⓑ Ⓒ Ⓓ
26. Ⓐ Ⓑ Ⓒ Ⓓ
27. Ⓐ Ⓑ Ⓒ Ⓓ
28. Ⓐ Ⓑ Ⓒ Ⓓ
29. Ⓐ Ⓑ Ⓒ Ⓓ
30. Ⓐ Ⓑ Ⓒ Ⓓ
31. Ⓐ Ⓑ Ⓒ Ⓓ
32. Ⓐ Ⓑ Ⓒ Ⓓ
33. Ⓐ Ⓑ Ⓒ Ⓓ
34. Ⓐ Ⓑ Ⓒ Ⓓ
35. Ⓐ Ⓑ Ⓒ Ⓓ
36. Ⓐ Ⓑ Ⓒ Ⓓ
37. Ⓐ Ⓑ Ⓒ Ⓓ
38. Ⓐ Ⓑ Ⓒ Ⓓ
39. Ⓐ Ⓑ Ⓒ Ⓓ
40. Ⓐ Ⓑ Ⓒ Ⓓ
41. Ⓐ Ⓑ Ⓒ Ⓓ
42. Ⓐ Ⓑ Ⓒ Ⓓ
43. Ⓐ Ⓑ Ⓒ Ⓓ
44. Ⓐ Ⓑ Ⓒ Ⓓ

The Princeton Review®

Completely darken bubbles with a No. 2 pencil. If you make a mistake, be sure to erase mark completely. Erase all stray marks.

**Test ❷** Start with number 1 for each new section.
If a section has fewer questions than answer spaces, leave the extra answer spaces blank.

## Section 3—Mathematics: No Calculator

1. Ⓐ Ⓑ Ⓒ Ⓓ
2. Ⓐ Ⓑ Ⓒ Ⓓ
3. Ⓐ Ⓑ Ⓒ Ⓓ
4. Ⓐ Ⓑ Ⓒ Ⓓ
5. Ⓐ Ⓑ Ⓒ Ⓓ
6. Ⓐ Ⓑ Ⓒ Ⓓ
7. Ⓐ Ⓑ Ⓒ Ⓓ
8. Ⓐ Ⓑ Ⓒ Ⓓ
9. Ⓐ Ⓑ Ⓒ Ⓓ
10. Ⓐ Ⓑ Ⓒ Ⓓ
11. Ⓐ Ⓑ Ⓒ Ⓓ
12. Ⓐ Ⓑ Ⓒ Ⓓ
13. Ⓐ Ⓑ Ⓒ Ⓓ
14. Ⓐ Ⓑ Ⓒ Ⓓ
15. Ⓐ Ⓑ Ⓒ Ⓓ

16. 17. 18.

19. 20.

## Section 4—Mathematics: Calculator

1. Ⓐ Ⓑ Ⓒ Ⓓ
2. Ⓐ Ⓑ Ⓒ Ⓓ
3. Ⓐ Ⓑ Ⓒ Ⓓ
4. Ⓐ Ⓑ Ⓒ Ⓓ
5. Ⓐ Ⓑ Ⓒ Ⓓ
6. Ⓐ Ⓑ Ⓒ Ⓓ
7. Ⓐ Ⓑ Ⓒ Ⓓ
8. Ⓐ Ⓑ Ⓒ Ⓓ
9. Ⓐ Ⓑ Ⓒ Ⓓ
10. Ⓐ Ⓑ Ⓒ Ⓓ
11. Ⓐ Ⓑ Ⓒ Ⓓ
12. Ⓐ Ⓑ Ⓒ Ⓓ
13. Ⓐ Ⓑ Ⓒ Ⓓ
14. Ⓐ Ⓑ Ⓒ Ⓓ
15. Ⓐ Ⓑ Ⓒ Ⓓ
16. Ⓐ Ⓑ Ⓒ Ⓓ
17. Ⓐ Ⓑ Ⓒ Ⓓ
18. Ⓐ Ⓑ Ⓒ Ⓓ
19. Ⓐ Ⓑ Ⓒ Ⓓ
20. Ⓐ Ⓑ Ⓒ Ⓓ
21. Ⓐ Ⓑ Ⓒ Ⓓ
22. Ⓐ Ⓑ Ⓒ Ⓓ
23. Ⓐ Ⓑ Ⓒ Ⓓ
24. Ⓐ Ⓑ Ⓒ Ⓓ
25. Ⓐ Ⓑ Ⓒ Ⓓ
26. Ⓐ Ⓑ Ⓒ Ⓓ
27. Ⓐ Ⓑ Ⓒ Ⓓ
28. Ⓐ Ⓑ Ⓒ Ⓓ
29. Ⓐ Ⓑ Ⓒ Ⓓ
30. Ⓐ Ⓑ Ⓒ Ⓓ

31. 32. 33. 34. 35.

36. 37. 38.

# Chapter 6
# Practice Test 2:
# Answers and
# Explanations

# PRACTICE TEST 2 ANSWER KEY

## Section 1: Reading

| | | | |
|---|---|---|---|
| 1. | D | 27. | A |
| 2. | A | 28. | A |
| 3. | D | 29. | A |
| 4. | C | 30. | B |
| 5. | D | 31. | A |
| 6. | B | 32. | B |
| 7. | C | 33. | B |
| 8. | B | 34. | B |
| 9. | C | 35. | D |
| 10. | A | 36. | D |
| 11. | A | 37. | A |
| 12. | D | 38. | B |
| 13. | A | 39. | A |
| 14. | C | 40. | C |
| 15. | C | 41. | D |
| 16. | A | 42. | B |
| 17. | B | 43. | D |
| 18. | A | 44. | C |
| 19. | A | 45. | A |
| 20. | A | 46. | B |
| 21. | A | 47. | C |
| 22. | B | 48. | A |
| 23. | B | 49. | D |
| 24. | D | 50. | B |
| 25. | C | 51. | C |
| 26. | C | 52. | B |

## Section 2: Writing & Language

| | | | |
|---|---|---|---|
| 1. | B | 23. | D |
| 2. | D | 24. | A |
| 3. | B | 25. | B |
| 4. | C | 26. | B |
| 5. | A | 27. | C |
| 6. | D | 28. | C |
| 7. | D | 29. | B |
| 8. | B | 30. | B |
| 9. | D | 31. | D |
| 10. | C | 32. | C |
| 11. | A | 33. | A |
| 12. | C | 34. | C |
| 13. | A | 35. | B |
| 14. | D | 36. | C |
| 15. | A | 37. | D |
| 16. | B | 38. | B |
| 17. | D | 39. | A |
| 18. | B | 40. | B |
| 19. | D | 41. | A |
| 20. | C | 42. | D |
| 21. | D | 43. | D |
| 22. | D | 44. | B |

## Section 3: Math (No Calculator)

| | | | |
|---|---|---|---|
| 1. | C | 11. | B |
| 2. | D | 12. | D |
| 3. | C | 13. | D |
| 4. | A | 14. | A |
| 5. | B | 15. | B |
| 6. | C | 16. | 82 |
| 7. | D | 17. | 15 |
| 8. | A | 18. | 4, 8, 12, 16, or 20 |
| 9. | B | | |
| 10. | D | | |

19. $\dfrac{17}{6}$ or 2.83

20. 1

## Section 4: Math (Calculator)

| | | | |
|---|---|---|---|
| 1. | C | 20. | A |
| 2. | D | 21. | A |
| 3. | A | 22. | B |
| 4. | C | 23. | D |
| 5. | D | 24. | D |
| 6. | B | 25. | C |
| 7. | D | 26. | B |
| 8. | C | 27. | B |
| 9. | A | 28. | C |
| 10. | A | 29. | A |
| 11. | B | 30. | A |
| 12. | C | 31. | 9 |
| 13. | C | 32. | 15 |
| 14. | B | 33. | 12 |
| 15. | B | 34. | 12 |
| 16. | B | 35. | 60 |
| 17. | D | 36. | 575 |
| 18. | C | 37. | 7,000 |
| 19. | C | 38. | 5,741 |

For self-scoring assessment tables, please turn to page 957.

# PRACTICE TEST 2 EXPLANATIONS

## Section 1: Reading

1. **D** This question asks for the main idea of the passage. Look for an answer choice that describes the passage in general; beware of answer choices that are true for only part of the passage. Choice (A) mentions *young men*, but the text does not mention their ages, and neither Don Quixote nor Sancho Panza *decide[s] to pretend* that he is entering battle. Choice (B) might—rather generously—describe Don Quixote and his horse, but Sancho Panza is not mentioned, and the giants are not actually there. Choice (C) might initially look good, because the two men do have an argument. However, the text identifies Sancho as Don Quixote's squire. Remember that Mostly Right is All Wrong. Since the two men are not both knights, (C) can be eliminated. Choice (D) includes the battle of the second half of the passage as well as the different perception of reality of the first half (and the very end). Choice (D) is the correct answer.

2. **A** This question asks about the function of the opening sentence. First, review that sentence: *At this point they came in sight of thirty or forty windmills that are on that plain.* The author tells the reader that these are windmills, not giants, as Don Quixote thinks. Choice (A) mentions the true setting (vs. the setting Don Quixote imagines), which could fit this prediction, so keep it for now. Choice (B) mentions technological advances and their importance, which are not discussed in this passage. The beginning of (C) sounds good in that it describes the field, but the second part of the choice does not match the text. There was no battle. Eliminate (C). Choice (D) says this sentence provides detailed imagery, but there are no details about the windmills, beyond a rough estimate of their number. Thus, (A) has the strongest support and is the correct answer.

3. **D** This question asks what changes in the main character's focus from paragraph 1 to paragraph 6. Review that part of the text and summarize what happens. For example: "Don Quixote says he's going to attack the giants; Sancho Panza says they're not giants; Don Quixote disagrees." Choose an answer that fits this summary. Choice (A) mentions *recollection* and *prospect*, which do not fit this prediction. Choice (B) mentions *money* and *God*, which do not fit this prediction. Choice (C) contrasts general and specific issues concerning battle, which does not fit this prediction. Choice (D) mentions an *evaluation* (they are giants) and an *argument* (no, they aren't). Choice (D) most strongly matches the prediction and is the correct answer.

4. **C** This question asks about the effect of the phrase *sweep so evil a breed from off the face of the earth*. First, locate the phrase and read it in context. It occurs at the end of Don Quixote's explanation that he intends to rid the world of these giants. In the next line, Sancho Panza asks, *"What giants?"* Panza's question deflates the inflated heroic tone that Quixote established. So look for an answer choice that supports the idea that Quixote establishes an inflated heroic tone. Choice (A) says the theme is a horror story, which does not fit this prediction. Choice (B) can be eliminated because Don Quixote is not, in fact, a prophet and has not received any

communications from God. Choice (C) could fit, since *grandiose view* matches inflated heroic tone. Choice (D) has no textual support: Quixote is not presented as a religious fanatic. Choice (C) is the correct answer.

5.  **D**   This question asks how Don Quixote would view his charge into battle. To answer this question, look at what Don Quixote actually says or thinks about this battle. In paragraph 6, he says he plans to *engage them in fierce and unequal combat*. The battle will be *unequal* because there are 30 or 40 of them, and he is only *a single knight*. He also calls the giants *cowards*. Look for an answer choice that fits these parts of the text. Choice (A), *ridiculous*, is what the reader and/or Sancho Panza might think about Don Quixote, not what Don Quixote thinks about himself. Choice (B), *insane*, is an even more extreme interpretation of what the reader and/or Sancho Panza might think. Choice (C), *unexceptional*, does not match the tone of Don Quixote's statement at all. Choice (D), *brave*, fits the prediction. Choice (D) is the correct answer.

6.  **B**   This question asks how Sancho Panza views Don Quixote. Notice that this is a best evidence question, so Q6 and Q7 can be answered in tandem. Look at the answers for Q7 first. The lines in (7A) show Don Quixote passing a judgment on Sancho Panza, so it cannot help answer Q6. Eliminate (7A). Choice (7B) again shows how Don Quixote views Sancho Panza, so it can be eliminated. Choice (7C) is the only one to actually include Sancho Panza, who cries out that Quixote is about to attack windmills, not giants. Look at the answer choices in Q6 to see if (7C) supports anything. The terms *boss* and *employees* from (6A) are more modern than language Sancho might use, plus Don Quixote never *endangers* Sancho. He actually tells him to stay back if he's frightened. The term *superior* and the phrase *needs looking after* from (6B) fit (7C), so draw a line connecting those answer choices. Sancho definitely does not follow Don Quixote *into battle*, so (6C) can be eliminated. The phrase *who requires help* from (6D) seems right, but Quixote is not portrayed as *a pious man* in the lines from (7C). Now look at (7D). It supports nothing from Q6, so eliminate it. At this point, the only options for correct answer choices are (6B) and (7C). Choose them! Choices (6B) and (7C) are the correct answers.

7.  **C**   (See explanation above.)

8.  **B**   This question asks why Don Quixote does not listen to Sancho Panza's description of the "giants." Panza says they are windmills, and in lines 21–22 Quixote says that Panza is *not used to this business of adventures* and suggests that he might be *afraid*. Choice (A) mentions *eyesight*, which does not fit the prediction. Choice (B) mentions *not as brave*, which could match *afraid*. Keep it for now. Although Don Quixote mentions Friston's schemes, he never indicates whether he believes Sancho also knows about the schemes, so (C) can be eliminated. Choice (D) can be eliminated because Quixote suggests that Panza might start praying, not that he is doing so now. Only (B) has support. Choice (B) is the correct answer.

9.  **C**   This is a best evidence question, so simply refer back to the lines used to predict the answer to the previous question. Lines 21–22 were used to answer the question, so (C) is the correct answer.

10.  **A**  This question asks about the main effect of referring to Friston. Use that name as a key word and locate a window. Quixote says that this same Friston *who carried off my study and books* has also *turned these giants into mills in order to rob me of the glory of vanquishing them.* The effect of referring to Friston seems to be to show how Quixote can maintain his delusions in the real world. Even though he can now see that the things he attacked are really windmills, his fanciful view of the world has not changed. Choice (A) mentions that the reader gains insight into how Quixote perceives reality, and this fits, so keep it for now. Choice (B) says mentioning Friston reveals the evil in the world. Since it is unclear whether Friston is even real, and since the author does not say Friston is evil, eliminate (B). Choice (C) may be tempting in that the reader might want a detailed history of how Quixote came to see things, but that history is not present in this passage. Choice (D) again mentions evil as well as how evil results from personal misunderstandings. This has no support. Choice (A) is the correct answer.

11.  **A**  This question asks about the main idea regarding a problem women have had. Since this is a general question, do it after completing all specific questions. Look for an answer that finds support in several parts of the passage. Choice (A) seems possible, since paragraphs 1, 2, 5, and 7 all explicitly treat the issue of women's right to vote. Choice (B) does not have support in the text. Choice (C) has nothing to do with the text. Choice (D) raises an issue not explicitly discussed in the text. Choice (A) is the correct answer.

12.  **D**  This question asks what the author means by *grand documents*. Use the given line reference to find the window. The sentence following the one containing this phrase mentions the *Declaration of Independence, the United States Constitution*, and other documents, so choose an answer that means *important documents from U.S. history*. Choice (A) is too literal and too specific. Choice (B) does not match the prediction. Neither does (C). Choice (D) refers to *important legislation* and matches the prediction. Choice (D) is the correct answer.

13.  **A**  This question asks about a purpose of the Declaration of Independence. Use the lead words *Declaration of Independence* to find a window. The third paragraph says that the Declaration, and other documents, *propose to protect the people in the exercise of their God-given rights.* This fits (A), so keep that answer choice for now. The same paragraph says the opposite of (B), as well as of (C) so both of those answers can be eliminated. There is no support for (D). Choice (A) is the correct answer.

14.  **C**  This question asks for the best evidence for the answer to Q13. Since the prediction comes from paragraph 3, eliminate answer choices from other paragraphs first. Choice (A) is from paragraph 1. Choices (B) and (C) are both from paragraph 3; keep them for now. Choice (D) is from paragraph 6. Now compare the remaining answer choices. Choice (B) does not contain the phrase used to predict the correct answer to Q13. Choice (C) does contain that phrase. Choice (C) is the correct answer.

15.  **C**  This is a Vocab-in-Context question, so go back to the text, find the phrase *the exercise* in line 33, and cross it out. Replace it with another word that makes sense in the sentence based

on the context of the passage. Something like *the use* makes sense. Use that prediction to work through the given answers. Choice (A) seems relevant, so keep it for now. Choice (B) makes no sense. Choice (C) fits the prediction exactly. Choice (D) does not make sense. Although (A) might have looked good initially, when compared with (C), (A) loses strength. The people are not doing *an activity* with their rights. They are simply *using* them. Choice (C) is the correct answer.

16.   **A**   This question asks for a logical inference regarding the general function of the term *natural right*. Use the given line reference to find the window. The complete phrase is *natural right of all to the ballot*, and the sentence ends with a mention of the *right to vote*. Choice (A) fits this prediction perfectly. Choices (B), (C), and (D) do not fit this prediction. Choice (A) is the correct answer.

17.   **B**   This is a Vocab-in-Context question, so go back to the text, find the word *class* in line 59, and cross it out. Replace it with another word that makes sense in the sentence based on the context of the passage. A word like *group* or *part* would make sense, so use those words to work through the answer choices. Choice (A) does not fit the prediction, but (B) does. Choice (C) may seem possible, but is also overly scientific. Choice (D) is another meaning of *classy*. Between (B) and (C), (B) fits the prediction best. Choice (B) is the correct answer.

18.   **A**   The question asks what the author concludes about the U.S. government, given the situation described in the text. Notice that the following question is a best evidence question, so questions 18 and 19 can be answered in tandem. Look at the answers for Q19 first. The lines in (19A) mention that the author is accused of the *crime of having voted … without having a lawful right to vote*, so look to see if those words support any answers in Q18. Choice (18A) mentions *laws denying women's suffrage*. Since suffrage means the right to vote, connect those two answers. Next, consider lines for (19B). The speaker quotes selections from the Declaration of Independence about being *created equal* and having *rights* such as *life, liberty, and the pursuit of happiness*. This is not referenced in any choices in Q18, so eliminate (19B). The lines in (19C) refer to the need for revolution when any government becomes repressive. This may weakly support (18D), so connect those two answers. Next, consider lines for (19D). These lines very clearly support (18D), so connect these two answers. Without any support from Q19, (18B) and (18C) can be eliminated. Consider the remaining pairs of answer choices in the context of the passage. While both (18A) and (18D) seem to be something that the author says that the government has done, the question asked what the author says about the government given the situation described in the text. Since that situation is the government unjustly barring women from voting, eliminate (18D) and its support in (19C) and (19D). Choices (18A) and (19A) are the correct answers.

19.   **A**   (See explanation above.)

20.   **A**   This question asks for the primary contrast in paragraph 7. Scan paragraph 7, and notice that it begins with *the whole people* and then states that *one-half of the people* have been made powerless by *the other half*. Choice (A) involves people and fits the main idea of the entire text.

Choice (B) involves people and a contrast, so keep it for now if you don't see a clear reason to eliminate it. Choices (C) and (D) do not involve people. Now go back to the text to find evidence to best support either (A) or (B). The text does mention rich men and poor men, but the main focus of the paragraph is the contrast between the *one-half of the population* that is *utterly powerless* and *left wholly at the mercy of the other half*. Choice (A) is the correct answer.

21. **A** The question asks why it is important to be able to assess the country's water supply. Find and read the window where the passage mentions the Geological Survey. The text states that water supply assessments *are indispensable tools for those involved in water-resources planning and management*, so the correct answer should deal with planning and management. Choice (A) mentions *plan[ning] future infrastructure*, so keep it. Choice (B) also uses the words *plan* and *manage,* so keep it for now. Choice (C) mentions researchers assessing data, not *planning* and *management,* so eliminate it. Choice (D) also does not relate to the prediction. Go back to the text now and find evidence to keep or eliminate either (A) or (B). When the two choices are compared, the wording of *all water resources* should stand out as more extreme than the wording in (A). Because there isn't matching extreme wording in the text, (B) can be eliminated. Choice (A) is the correct answer.

22. **B** The question asks for the best evidence to support the answer to the previous question. The text cited previously states that water supply assessments *are indispensable tools for those involved in water-resources planning and management*. Find the lines in which this statement is made and select the choice that matches. Choice (B) is the correct answer.

23. **B** The question asks why the information in the third paragraph is included. Read above and below the third paragraph to determine how it links the ideas together. Paragraph 2 discusses the importance of assessing water resources. Paragraph 3 mentions how to locate ground water, and paragraph 4 continues to discuss locating ground water with clues from rocks. So paragraph 3 is included because it introduces how a water resource can be found and assessed. Choice (A) mentions a *new method*, which could be tempting but the passage does not specify a method for finding ground water as *new*. Eliminate it. Choice (B) matches because it mentions *finding a natural resource*. Choice (C) does not match since it describes a *need*. Paragraph 3 introduces how a water resource can be found. Eliminate it. Choice (D) mentions a *hydrologic instrument* that is not mentioned in the passage, so eliminate it. Choice (B) is the correct answer.

24. **D** This is a Vocab-in-Context question, so go back to the text, find the word *occurrence* in line 32, and cross it out. Replace it with another word that makes sense in the sentence based on the context of the passage. Since the text discusses how to find ground water and the sentence states that *the landscape may offer clues to hydrologists*, the intended meaning of the word must have to do with the *existence* of ground water. Choice (A) does not mean *existence*. Neither does (B) or (C). Choice (D) means *existing* or *occurring*. Choice (D) is the correct answer.

25. **C** This is a Vocab-in-Context question, so go back to the text, find the word *penetrated* in line 52, and cross it out. Replace it with another word that makes sense in the sentence based on

the context of the passage. The sentence mentions *depth to water* in its description of wells. So wells must be dug underground. The intended meaning of the word is something like *dug into*. Choice (A) does not mean *dug into*. Eliminate it. Choice (B) is similar in meaning to *penetrated*, but does not mean *dug into*. This choice is a trap answer. Eliminate it. Choice (C) means *dug into*. Choice (D) is also similar in meaning to *penetrated* but not similar to the prediction of *dug into*. The correct answer is (C).

26. **C** This question asks what the passage states about the occurrence of ground water. Since much of the passage is about ground water occurrence, this is a general question. Because this is also a paired set of questions, the best evidence question can be answered in tandem with this question. Look at the best evidence answers first and see if any of them support any of the answers for Q26. The lines for (27A) reference how water levels *rise in wet periods and decline in dry periods* and *average about the same as they did in the early part of the twentieth century*, especially in the *humid central and eastern parts of the country*. This supports (26C), so connect those two answers. The lines for (27B) discuss techniques for finding ground water. These lines don't support any of the answer choices for Q26, so (27B) can be eliminated. The lines for (27C) mention using the *landscape* and *hills* to find ground water. Choice (26B) mentions using landscape features to locate water, so connect (27C) and (26B). The lines for (27D) discuss *locating favorable conditions for ground-water development* by mapping the *distribution and positions of the different kinds of rocks*. This evidence does not support any of the choices in question 26. Eliminate it. Look at the remaining pairs of answer choices and use the text to make a decision about which pair is best supported. Choice (26B) is not actually supported by the text, because the *landscape features* mentioned in the text are *hills* and *valleys*. *Existing wells* are not mentioned until later. This eliminates (26B) and (27C). Choices (26C) and (27A) are the correct answers.

27. **A** (See explanation above.)

28. **A** This question asks which hydrologic or geologic layer in the figure holds moisture with molecular attraction. First, reference the figure to determine if it describes moisture held by molecular attraction. It does. *Water (not ground water) held by molecular attraction* is labeled by arrows pointing to types of rock above the *water table*. The only two layers depicted above the water table in the figure are the *unsaturated zone* and the *land surface*. Choice (A) is one of those zones. Choice (B) is not depicted above the water table. Eliminate it. Choice (C) is shown both above and below the water table, so it would not hold only moisture with molecular attraction. Eliminate it. Choice (D) is not above the water table, so eliminate it. The correct answer is (A).

29. **A** This question asks which concept is supported by both the passage and the figure. The figure depicts two types of rock orientation that result in differences in ground water. The passage, in paragraph 4, discusses how *positions of the different kinds of rocks* could provide *clues to obtaining useful amounts of ground water*. The correct answer should discuss rock orientation and locating ground water. Choice (A) matches the prediction. Choice (B) is not supported by the figure, so eliminate it. Choice (C) is not supported by the figure either. For (D), while the

passage states that *some sedimentary rocks may extend many miles as aquifers of fairly uniform permeability*, it does not equate *permeability* with rock *position*. Eliminate it. Choice (A) is the correct answer.

30. **B** This question asks how the figure depicts the effect of rock orientation on ground water. Reference the figure for information on rock orientation. The figure shows two columns of rocks with different orientations and differences in ground water. Choice (A) mentions *rocks folding or turning*, which is not depicted in the figure. Choice (B) matches the figure. Keep it. Choice (C) mentions a best water indicator, which is not in the figure. Eliminate it. Choice (D) claims the figure shows many miles of aquifer, which it does not. Eliminate it. Choice (B) is the correct answer.

31. **A** This question asks about the main idea of the passage, so it should be done after all the specific questions. The passage describes the impact of exports on the global economy, specifically focusing on the banana and its potential impact on the Caribbean. This supports (A). Choice (B) is incorrect because it takes the idea of the passage too far and cannot be proven. Be cautious about answer choices with strong words like *must* or *will*, as these words can make the choice too extreme. Answer choices with strong wording aren't necessarily wrong, but there must be equally strongly-worded support in the passage. This passage does not contain that type of strong wording, so (B) can be eliminated. Eliminate (C) as well because it does not mention exports or bananas. Finally, (D) is incorrect because the Caribbean is not barred from gaining economic independence. Choice (A) is correct.

32. **B** This question asks about the main purpose of the second paragraph. Carefully read the second paragraph to determine what's going on in that paragraph. In the first sentence, the author says that the Panama Canal has *so occupied our attention* that we have *overlooked a significant... change taking place.* The paragraph goes on to describe that change. The correct answer will have something to do with a new change in economics or the emergence of the banana as an influential economic player. Choice (A) recycles *the completion of the Panama Canal,* but it is not the main idea of the paragraph, nor is it a true statement based on the passage, so it can be eliminated. Choice (B) matches the prediction, so don't eliminate it. Choice (C) is extreme because the passage never indicates that bananas will *dominate the economy,* and (D) is not the main point of the passage. Both of these choices may be eliminated. Therefore, (B) is correct.

33. **B** This is a Vocab-in-Context question. Find the word *exercise* in the passage and cross it out. Use context clues to put in another word that fits the meaning of the passage. The passage mentions the food products having an *influence upon international politics,* so *exercise* could be replaced with something like *exert* or *influence.* While (A), (C), and (D) are all synonyms for *exercise,* based on the context and prediction, (B) is the only answer that works. Choice (B) is the correct answer.

34. **B** The question asks for which lines best emphasize the potential importance of the banana as a product. Choice (A) can be eliminated because the lines do not mention bananas. Choice (B)

could work because those lines refer to economists' predictions that Caribbean diplomacy will be determined by the banana crop. Choice (C) does not answer the question, though it seems as though the banana has gained popularity in the United States. A lot of Americans eating bananas doesn't automatically mean bananas play any kind of significant role in the global economy. Eliminate (C). Choice (D) is also off-topic, as it describes how the Caribbean can become self-sustaining with the banana. Therefore, (B) is correct.

35. **D** This is a Vocab-in-Context question. Find the word *friendship* in the passage and cross it out. Use context clues to put in another word that fits the meaning of the passage. The passage mentions *near neighbors* and *diplomacy of the Caribbean*, so the missing word must mean something like *positive relations with neighboring countries*. Choices (A) and (B) might be good synonyms for *friendship*, but neither matches the context of the passage. Eliminate both of those choices. *Collusion* does mean working together, but with an illegal or fraudulent goal. This doesn't match the prediction, so it can be eliminated. Choice (D) matches the prediction and is the correct answer.

36. **D** This question asks for the main idea of the final paragraph. The final paragraph highlights the importance of the Caribbean and the diplomatic importance of exports. Choice (A) is incorrect because it is too literal. While the word *friendship* does show up in the final paragraph, it is not a literal reference to being friends. It's a reference to diplomacy, which is not mentioned in (A). Eliminate (A). Choice (B) is mentioned, but it is not the main point of the paragraph. Choice (C) recycles words, so it might look good at first glance. However, a careful reading of (C) shows that although the words look familiar, they aren't put together in a way that matches the prediction. Eliminate (C). Choice (D) matches the prediction and is the correct answer.

37. **A** This question is a general paired question, so look at the next question first to find connections between evidence and the answer choices for this question. Choice (38A) does not support any of the choices in question 37, so eliminate (38A). Choice (38B) supports (37A), so connect those two answer choices. Choice (38C) does not support any of the choices for question 37, so eliminate (38C). Choice (38D) could potentially support (37C) or (37D), so keep these answer choices. Since (37B) is not supported by any of the evidence in question 38, it may be eliminated. Now, look at the question to see which of these pairings answers question 37. The question asks for *potential difficulties* that the author anticipates. Choice (37A) outlines the need for certain technologies to work, which is a potential difficulty. Choices (37C) is extreme and recycles the words in a way that makes the statement untrue. Therefore, eliminate (37C). Choice (37D) is also untrue, so (37D) and (38D) can be eliminated. This leaves (37A) and (38B) as the correct answers.

38. **B** (See explanation above.)

39. **A** This question asks about data in the tables and ideas in the passage. The correct answer will connect the two. Choice (A) links the idea of the United States importing the majority of the

world's bananas with the data showing that the world's banana crop isn't going completely to the United States. Keep (A). Choice (B) may be true based on the text, but there is nothing in the table to support that answer. Eliminate (B). Choice (C) is also true based on the text, but again, does not also connect to the tables, so it can be eliminated. Choice (D) might initially look good, but the tables measure two different things (U.S. Banana Supply and world banana supply), so no trends are indicated. Choice (A) is the correct answer.

40. **C** Simply check the exports from each of these countries to see which shows the greatest increase or decrease in exports to the United States. Jamaica has the greatest difference between those two data points, making (C) correct.

41. **D** Use the chart to answer this question. Choices (A), (B), and (C) are untrue statements according to the chart. From the numbers in the chart, (D) is true because Colombia exported more bananas than Cuba in 1911. Choice (D) is correct.

42. **B** This question asks what Passage 1 says about the caudate. Use this key word to find the window in paragraph 4. The caudate seems to be a brain area that is active during music listening and before the chill response. The next sentence states that *this subregion* is involved in *learning of stimulus-response associations, and in mediating the reinforcing qualities of rewarding stimuli such as food.* Choice (A) suggests that the caudate emerges from study, which makes no sense. Eliminate (A). Choice (B) says the caudate is involved in learning associations, which is strongly supported by the prediction. Choice (C) is deceptive: The caudate activation takes place before the chill response, but it does not cause it. Choice (D) is deceptive: The caudate does not help reinforce qualities of food. Choice (B) is the correct answer.

43. **D** This question asks for the best evidence for the answer to Q42. Since the prediction comes from paragraph 4, eliminate answer choices from other paragraphs first. Choice (A) comes from paragraph 1, and (B) comes from paragraph 3. Both (C) and (D) come from paragraph 4. Choice (C) does not contain the phrases that supported the prediction. Choice (D) is the correct answer.

44. **C** This question asks what the author of Passage 1 says about music. Notice that all four answer choices contain the word *feelings*. Now focus the search for statements the author makes about music and feelings. The text opens asking *Why does music make us feel?* It continues by explaining that music can stimulate certain brain areas, after which we experience certain feelings. Choice (A) says music *may preclude feeling states. Preclude* means something like exclude, so (A) is not supported. Choice (B) suggests that feelings cause music, rather than the reverse. Choice (C) fits the prediction well. Choice (D) is deceptive because the individual words in the answer may look familiar, but the answer actually contradicts the text's claim that music is *devoid of ... explicit ideas.* Choice (C) is the correct answer.

45. **A** This question is a Vocab-in-Context question, so go back to the text, find the word *betrays,* and cross it out. Now read the complete thought, and insert a word that makes sense based on the

context clues. A word like *expresses* or *shows* would make sense, so use such a word to compare to the answer choices. Choice (A) has a similar meaning, so keep it for now. Choices (B), (C), and (D) are all different meanings of *betray*. Choice (A) is the correct answer.

46. **B**   This question asks the main reason the author of Passage 2 refers to coldness. Find the window and read to determine why the author is talking about coldness. *The "coldness" of chills may provide increased motivation for social reunion in the parents.* The correct answer should have something to do with social reunions or families. Choice (A) is deceptive, mentioning the chill effect, but the author is not outlining anything here. Choice (B) is not obviously right, but is also not obviously wrong. Keep it for now. Choice (C) refers to sadness, which is in another part of the passage. Choice (D) is deceptive, since it mentions *piloerection*, but the text says there is no connection, not that one helps trace the other's origin. With three choices eliminated, the correct answer must be what is left. Paragraph 2 is about Panksepp's *evolutionary explanation*, and the description of *coldness* as providing *motivation for social reunion* can be called an illustration. Choice (B) is the correct answer.

47. **C**   This question asks what the author of Passage 2 says that Panksepp and Benedek and Kaernbach have in common. Use those names as lead words to locate the relevant parts of the passage. Paragraph 2 states that Panksepp is a *neuroscientist* and shows him as providing an *explanation*. Paragraph 3 says that Benedek and Kaernbach have done *experimental work* that *offers some support for Panksepp's hypothesis* and *lends some support to Panksepp's ideas*. Choice (A) is true for Benedek and Kaernbach, but it is not true for Panksepp. Choice (B) strongly matches Panksepp, and it could weakly match Benedek and Kaernbach. Keep it for now. Choice (C) strongly matches Panksepp in paragraph 2, and Benedek and Kaernbach in paragraph 3. Choice (D) contradicts the passage entirely. Between (B) and (C), (C) has much stronger support in the passage. Choice (C) is the correct answer.

48. **A**   This question asks about the effect of the reference to the song "I Will Always Love You." Use the lead words to locate the window. The song is called *a great example*. The previous sentence clarifies that the song is an example of *chills and piloerection* being *associated with sad music*. Choice (A) is very close to this prediction, so keep it. Choice (B) is deceptive, referring to a later part of the paragraph. Choice (C) refers to a researcher mentioned later in the passage. Panksepp is the one who references the song, not Benedek. Choice (D) is deceptive, incorrectly combining terms used in the paragraph (*bleak, repetition*). Choice (A) is the correct answer.

49. **D**   This question asks about the main idea of both passages. Passage 1 reports on the findings of Montreal researchers who used brain scan technologies in their experiments. Passage 2 relays a neuroscientist's evolutionary explanation and then reports on the findings of two other researchers who measured physiological responses. Both passages are interested in exploring how music and feelings are connected. Choice (A) mentions methods, but also says the passages focus on *learning* music, which is not the case. Eliminate (A). Choice (B) sets up a false opposition that is not supported in either text. Choice (C) may seem possible, but the use of the word

*scientists* makes the answer too specific. Eliminate it. Choice (D) says that the passages mean to inform us that neuroscience (the study of the brain) can help us understand responses to music. Since feelings can be responses to music, this fits the prediction. Choice (D) is the correct answer.

50.  **B**  This question asks about the relationship between the two passages. Think about what is similar and what is different between the passages. Choice (A) attributes the evolutionary explanation to Passage 1, but that is actually in Passage 2, so (A) is flawed. Choice (B) says that Passage 1 considers positive emotions and Passage 2 considers negative emotions in relation to music. This matches the *intense states of excitement … pleasurable stimulus …* and *favorite part* in Passage 1 and *sad … bleak … loss …* and *cries* in Passage 2. Keep (B). Choice (C) contrasts research in Passage 1 to theories in Passage 2. It's true that Passage 1 is about research, but Passage 2 has both theories and research, so that answer doesn't match what's in the text. Eliminate it. Choice (D) correctly states that Passage 1 relies on methods of neuroscience, but then says Passage 2 considers only theoretical work. This is not true, so eliminate (D). Choice (B) is the correct answer.

51.  **C**  This question asks about a point on which both authors would agree. Although this question asks about both passages, don't forget to POE one passage at a time. Go through the answers considering just Passage 1. Choice (A) is supported, so keep it. Choice (B) might initially look good because those tests are mentioned, but there's no indication that the author thinks those tests are *superior*, so (B) can be eliminated. Choice (C) is supported by the text. Choice (D) looks mostly right, because Passage 1 does discuss music and the expression of *positive emotions*, but Passage 1 does not mention anything about *negative emotions*. Eliminate (D). Only (A) and (C) are left. Use Passage 2 to compare the two remaining choices. Although Passage 2 does address *concrete ways* music affects us, there is no acknowledgement in the text about music being *generally abstract*. Eliminate (A). Choice (C) is supported and is the correct answer.

52.  **B**  This question asks what in Passage 1 best fits a specific part of Passage 2. To tackle this question, start by identifying the exact relevant part of Passage 2. It is an argument attributed to Panksepp. Using the line references provided, locate that argument: *He argues that chills may emerge from brain dynamics associated with the perception of social loss, specifically with separation calls.* Now consider each answer choice to see which one best fits the idea of social loss or separation. Choice (A) is about music being abstract. This does not fit the prediction, so eliminate it. Choice (B) is about music causing a deep reaction. This could fit the prediction, so keep it for now. Choice (C) is about dopamine and some brain areas. It is very specific, and doesn't connect with the ideas of loss in the prediction. Choice (D) talks about sounds functioning as a reward cue. This involves positive emotions, whereas the prediction had a negative emotion. Thus, (D) is not as good a fit for the prediction. If *sound stirs us at our biological roots*, then *sad music* evoking an association with *loss* seems like a good example of being so stirred. Choice (B) is the correct answer.

# Section 2: Writing and Language

1. **B** Notice that all four answer choices have essentially the same meaning: *increased, growing, larger spirit of…* all mean roughly the same thing in this context. When this is the case, choose the shortest answer that makes sense in the given context. In this sentence, that answer is (B), which contains all the information the other answers do in the fewest words.

2. **D** While all four choices technically "combine" the sentences, only (D) does so in an effective way. Choices (A) and (C) change the punctuation and some of the words, but this punctuation is not appropriate in context because the first of the two sentences is incomplete. Choice (B) can also be eliminated because it creates awkward combinations such as *moreover for instance* and states, awkwardly, that *swapping jobs is a thing that new workers do now*. Therefore, (D) is correct.

3. **B** The proposed addition helps to clarify business practices in Silicon Valley by explaining how that place is *fast-paced, forward-thinking,* and *occasionally ruthless*. This phrase should be added to the sentence because it enriches the paragraph's description of Silicon Valley and why a business model like Netflix's would be effective there. Choice (B) most effectively captures this reasoning. In addition, check the reasons to find opportunities for POE.

4. **C** Choices (A) and (B) create sentence fragments, so they can be eliminated. Then, since the subject of the remaining verb is the singular noun *Netflix*, the verb too must be singular, making (C) correct.

5. **A** The earlier parts of this sentence mention *visual media* and *home entertainment systems*. In order to make the underlined portion consistent with the earlier parts of the sentence, eliminate (B), which is unnecessarily wordy and (C), which is too specific. Choice (D), *intelligent machines,* may describe something relevant to the sentence, but it does not do so in language consistent with the rest of the sentence, and the term is somewhat broad. Only (A), *computers,* captures the tone of the rest of the sentence without adding unnecessary words or using weird terms.

6. **D** The previous paragraph discusses Netflix's technological innovations. This paragraph discusses Netflix's innovations in the business world. As such, the word or phrase that links the two ideas should indicate some continuation of the discussion. This eliminates (A), which has no obvious relation to either paragraph, and (B), which is not a word. Choice (C) can also be eliminated because it implies a cause-and-effect relationship that is not present in the passage. Only (D), *Furthermore,* appropriately links the two paragraphs.

7. **D** This sentence discusses Netflix's openness about how it conducts business. Choice (A) captures this idea, but it does so in language that is too informal and grammatically incorrect. The sentence is not concerned with Netflix's *rudeness,* eliminating (B). Choice (C) actually contradicts the idea of Netflix's forthrightness. Only (D) effectively sets up the second idea in this sentence.

8. **B** Notice that the underlined word is part of a list. The other parts of the list are *staying late* and *showing loyalty to the company.* As such, the word in the underlined portion should be consistent with *staying* and *showing*. Choices (B) and (D) both contain the word *coming*, which is consistent with the remainder of the list, but (B) is more effective because it does not introduce unnecessary words.

9. **D** When given the option to DELETE the underlined portion, give that option serious consideration: It is often correct. In this case, all of the proposed choices interrupt the idea unnecessarily, so the best option is to delete those words altogether. Choice (D) is therefore the best from among the possible answers.

10. **C** A *premise* is a statement or proposition that provides the basis for a conclusion. While that could potentially work in this context, the word *promise* is much more precise because the passage as a whole is about Netflix's unwillingness to *promise* all the long-term benefits of a typical job. As such, (A) and (B) can be eliminated because they use the wrong word. Then, of the remaining two, (C) is consistent with the given context, which calls for a noun.

11. **A** The passage as a whole is about how Netflix represents a new frontier in how employees interact with the companies for which they work. The passage is not concerned with apocalyptic scenarios like the one described in (B), with helping readers to get jobs at Netflix as in (C), or in losing a job in general as in (D). The most effective restatement of the passage's main claim comes from (A), which refers to Netflix's practices as indicative of a potential *workplace of the future.*

12. **C** The *stylistic pattern established earlier in the sentence* is that of a list. The other two items in this list are *watching six-second videos on Vine* and *reading short posts on Facebook and Twitter.* The format of each of these items is an *-ing* word describing an activity followed by the site on which the activity is conducted. Choices (B) and (C) both follow this format, but (C) adheres more closely to the pattern of the other two items in the list.

13. **A** This sentence is very long, but make sure that there is a good reason to add punctuation. Choices (C) and (D) add commas, but they also add words that create comma splices. Choice (B) adds a comma, but removing the word *and* creates an awkward phrase with no obvious relationship to the rest of the sentence. As such, (A) provides the most effective connection of this part of the sentence with what has come before it.

14. **D** This paragraph is all about TV's *harmful effects*, so this sentence about *shining light in your eyes for many hours at a time* is in keeping with that discussion. Choices (B) and (C) suggest a contrast, so they can be eliminated. Choice (A) suggests that the information has been mentioned before (*aforementioned*), which it has not. Choice (D) is therefore the best answer in that it provides a transition that preserves the continuity of the ideas in the paragraph.

15. **A** This sentence discusses the *senses* belonging to *you*, or *your* senses. Choices (B) and (C) can be eliminated because *you're* is a contraction of *you are*. Then, (D) can be eliminated because it

contains a semicolon, which would require complete ideas both before and after. The single word *vision* is not a complete idea, making (A) the best answer.

16. **B** The sentence and paragraph are in the past tense, so the verb in this underlined portion should be in the past tense as well. This leaves only (B). Choices (C) and (D) are also wrong for introducing apostrophes in text which contains neither possession nor contraction.

17. **D** This paragraph is about television's national reach. It mentions The Beatles, but it is not particularly concerned with The Beatles. As a result, this sentence would add information that is not obviously connected to the paragraph's main focus. Therefore, the sentence should not be added because it is irrelevant to the paragraph's main focus, as (D) states. To help determine "Yes" or "No," check the reasons to use POE.

18. **B** This is a complex sentence, so use the context. The following sentence refers to African Americans as a *targeted group*. The previous sentence refers to a new presence of *non-white faces*, suggesting that *non-white* groups were not represented in quite the same way before. Choices (A) and (C) do not establish the link between the sentences clearly, and while (D) contains all the words the other choices do, it doesn't actually make any sense. As a result, the only choice that correctly positions the parts of the sentence relative to one another is (B).

19. **D** The other example given in this sentence is *the Chinese-American character on* Have Gun Will Travel. Choice (D) gives an example in a similar format and is in fact the only one of the answer choices to provide a second example. The others provide irrelevant information or elaborate on the first example.

20. **C** If there is no specific reason to use commas, don't use them. In this case, setting off the phrase *in the American public* with commas would imply that that information is not necessary to the meaning of the sentence. However, the word *many* is not adequately specific without this information. As such, this phrase should contain no commas at all, as in (C).

21. **D** Choice (A) merely changes the punctuation of the sentences—it does not exactly combine them. It also preserves the ambiguity of the word *they*, which could refer to either *hometowns* or *people*. Choice (B) also preserves this ambiguity. Choice (C) creates a new mistake by introducing words that have no clear role within the sentence. Only (D) correctly links the two parts of the sentence, as the word *which* clearly refers back to the word *hometowns* that precedes it and is offset by a comma.

22. **D** Paragraph 6 begins with *This national reach*, suggesting that the paragraph that precedes it must discuss something about a *national reach*. Paragraph 3 discusses this national reach and how television *provided something truly national for the first time*. Therefore, paragraph 6 should be placed after paragraph 3, or before paragraph 4, as (D) states.

23. **D** The answer choices provide a variety of pronouns, so find the original noun. In this case, the original noun is *nature*, which is singular, thus eliminating (A) and (B). Choice (D) is the

more effective of the remaining choices because it shows possession: *nature's greenery* is *its greenery*, whereas (C) would say *it is greenery*, which doesn't make sense in the context.

24. **A** The previous sentence discusses how nature *looks* as well as how it *sounds*. This sentence continues that discussion, introducing the idea that highways don't just change how nature *looks*, they change how it *sounds*. Choices (A) and (D) indicate that continuation, but (A) does so more concisely and precisely, without adding the potentially ambiguous pronoun *this*.

25. **B** Everything so far in the passage has taken special care to emphasize how nature *sounds* as well as how it *looks*. This sentence would continue to provide that crucial emphasis, so it should be added here. Choice (B) effectively states the reason: It completes the idea stated in the previous sentence that *when we build highways through thriving natural habitats, we don't just change the way they look*.

26. **B** When unsure of what word to use, fill in the blank with a word that makes sense. In this case, something like *accustomed to* would work. Choice (A) certainly does not mean that. Choice (B) does—*inure* means "to grow accustomed to something unpleasant." Choices (C) and (D) don't work in the context at all—*keen* means "eager" and *hip* means "aware" and/or "stylish." Only (B), therefore, works in this context.

27. **C** All four choices say essentially say the same thing, so choose the one that does so most concisely and precisely. Choices (B) and (D) add awkward *-ing* constructions, so those choices should be eliminated. Choice (A) makes the highway sound like a radio or stereo system, so that too should be eliminated. Choice (C) works best—it says precisely what the other choices say imprecisely.

28. **C** When so many words are changing in the answer choices, ignore the part that stays consistent (*at the Intermountain Bird Observatory in Idaho*) and focus specifically on what is changing. In this case, the word *and* in (A) and the word *who* in (B) create awkward sentence fragments. The word *they* in (D) restates the subject unnecessarily. Choice (C) states the proposed idea most directly without adding new errors.

29. **B** In this sentence, the phrase *or a "phantom"* is a rewording or clarification of the word *fake*. The phrase is not necessary to the meaning of the sentence and should therefore be offset with commas, as in (B). Choices (A) and (D) misplace the comma, and (C) uses a semicolon, which cannot work in this context.

30. **B** If there is not a good reason to use punctuation marks, don't use them. Nothing is being quoted here, so there is no need for quotation marks, as in (A). No information is being offset as unnecessary, so there is no need for a comma, as in (C). The idea up to and including the word *traffic* is not complete, so a single dash cannot be used, as in (D). Therefore, only (B), which contains no punctuation, can be used.

31. **D** The figure shows proposed highway extensions in the American South. The Interstate Highway Commission has no particular plans to eradicate avian life in these regions, thus eliminating (A) and (B). Then, the route from Savannah to Knoxville goes roughly north-south, and the route from Augusta to Natchez goes roughly east-west, as indicated by the map. Therefore, (D) is correct.

32. **C** The proposed sentence describes what birds do when they are unable to act as they usually would. The word *however* implies a contrast with some previous sentence that describes normal bird behavior. Sentence 3 does so in describing how birds *need to spend as much time as possible with their heads down*. The new sentence describes how highway noise prevents those birds from doing so, so the new sentence would be best placed after sentence 3, as suggested by (C).

33. **A** Notice the modifier at the beginning of this sentence: *With lower speed limits and rubberized asphalt*. This modifier describes *the roads*, which should follow the modifier, thus eliminating (B) and (D). Also, (C) can also be eliminated because the pronoun *they* is ambiguous in the context. Choice (A) places the subject close to its modifier and does so without introducing an ambiguous pronoun.

34. **C** The underlined word is part of a larger phrase, *an early Spanish explorer and conquistador*. With the comma after the word *Coronado*, the passage has already indicated that the phrase should be set off with commas. Choice (C) provides the second comma and does not change the punctuation unnecessarily, as (A) and (D) do, nor remove it, as (B) does.

35. **B** Use POE to eliminate bad answer choices, especially when the choices don't follow an obvious pattern. The phrase *but also* is typically paired with the words *not only*; therefore, because the sentence does not use the phrase *not only*, it should not use *but also* either, eliminating (A). The same pairing happens with the phrase *just as* and *so too*, which are listed separately in (C) and (D) and can both be eliminated. Only (B) works in the context, with the word *wherein* referring back to the word *window*.

36. **C** This question is testing word choice, or idioms. Choices (A) and (D) can be eliminated because the words they contain are not idiomatically consistent with the word *atrocities*. Choice (B) suffers from the same issue, though it is a bit closer in meaning to the correct word, *committed*, as in (C). In short, one *commits atrocities* but does not *do atrocities*.

37. **D** Because the adjective *noble* cannot be counted (one cannot have, for example, five noble), it takes the word *less* rather than the word *fewer*, eliminating (A). Then, because the word *than/then* is being used in a comparison rather than in a sequence, *than* is the correct choice, eliminating (B) and (C). Only (D) remains, which uses the correct forms of each of the words and does not introduce unnecessary punctuation.

38. **B** All four choices contain the word *else* and the colon. Choices (A), (C), and (D) give additional words, but none of these words have a clear, essential role within the passage. As such, (B)

gives the same information as the others and does so in the fewest words. Choice (B) is therefore the best of the available answer choices.

39. **A** Choices (B) and (D) introduce words to the underlined portion, creating awkward sentence fragments that don't make sense. Choice (C) suggests that Coronado was *growing up* in Spain at the moment that he arrived in New Spain, which can't be true. Only (A) remains, therefore, to start the phrase that describes Coronado's upbringing.

40. **B** Choices (A) and (C) begin with the word *They*, which creates a comma splice with the sentence's two ideas: *They lay in wait for someone to claim the bounty* and *these cities were richer than any place in the world*. If these ideas were to remain complete, they would need to be separated by a period or some other kind of STOP punctuation. Choice (D), however, introduces the unnecessary word *While* and breaks up the phrase *lying/laying in wait*. The best of the answer choices is therefore (B), which is concise and fixes the comma splice.

41. **A** The claim made by this sentence is as follows: *Coronado's disappointment was absolutely unforgiving and vicious*. With a specific detail, (A) effectively communicates the *unforgiving and vicious* aspects of Coronado's journey. Choices (B), (C), and (D) may all be true, but none are as specific as the claim made in this sentence.

42. **D** When given the option to DELETE the underlined portion, give that option serious consideration: it is often correct. In this case, all the choices add some redundant or unnecessary detail to the sentence, so it is best to end this sentence at the word *Kansas*, as (D) suggests.

43. **D** Sentence 2 states, *That's a lot of territory to cover in the middle of the sixteenth century!* This sentence thus clearly refers to some previous sentence that describes covering *a lot of territory*. Sentence 4 describes a journey from Mexico to Kansas, the most specific possible referent for the phrase *a lot of territory*. Sentence 2 should therefore be placed before sentence 5, as indicated in (D).

44. **B** The previous sentence says, *His influence is all around us*, but the remainder of the passage does not give any specific instances of where this *influence* can be seen. Therefore, the new sentence should be added to the sentence because it provides examples of Coronado's *influence*. Choice (B) best captures this reasoning. Choice (A) may be true, though the passage does not indicate what Coronado's favorite places were.

# Section 3: Math (No Calculator)

1. **C** Use Process of Elimination. The $w$ represents the number of workers, and $t$ represents the total time in hours. Therefore, the 20 must have something to do with the cost of the workers' hourly wage. Eliminate (A) because nothing is mentioned about a minimum number of workers. Eliminate (B) because it is unrelated to the workers. Choice (C) relates to the hourly wage, so keep it, but check (D) just in case. Choice (D) can be eliminated because the number of wedding guests is unrelated to the cost and unrelated to the workers and their time. Choice (C) is correct.

2. **D** Subtract 4 from both sides of the equation to get $12x = 16$. Divide the entire equation by 2 to get $6x = 8$. Therefore, $6x + 5 = 8 + 5 = 13$, which is (D).

3. **C** Plug in the answers, starting with (B). In (B), $x = -4$ and $y = 4$. Plug those values into the first equation to get $5(-4) - 4(4) = 36$. Solve the left side of the equation to get $-20 - 16 = 36$, and $-36 = 36$. Since the values do not work in the first equation, eliminate (B). Next try (C). In (C), $x = 4$, and $y = -4$. Plug those values in the first equation to get $5(4) - 4(-4) = 36$. Solve the left side of the equation to get $20 - (-16) = 36$, and $36 = 36$. Next, try the same numbers in the second equation: $-4 - (-4) = 0$. Solve the left side of the equation to get $-4 + 4 = 0$, and $0 = 0$. The coordinate pair works in both equations, therefore, the correct answer is (C).

4. **A** Plug $y = 8$ into the equation to get $8 - \sqrt{4x^2 + 28} = 0$. Therefore, $\sqrt{4x^2 + 28} = 8$. Plug in the answers to see which value of $x$ works. In (B), $x = 4$, making the square root $\sqrt{4(4)^2 + 28} = \sqrt{4(16) + 28} = \sqrt{92}$, which is not equal to 8. A smaller number is needed, so eliminate (B), (C), and (D). The answer is therefore (A).

5. **B** Parallel lines have the same slope. Since the question asks for the $y$-coordinate of a point on $\overline{AD}$, which is parallel to $\overline{BC}$, start by finding the slope of $\overline{BC}$. Use the slope formula $\dfrac{y_2 - y_1}{x_2 - x_1}$ to get $\dfrac{10 - 0}{0 - 6} = \dfrac{10}{-6} = \dfrac{5}{-3}$. Now use this slope to find the value of $r$: $\dfrac{5}{-3} = \dfrac{0 - r}{-3 - 0}$ or $\dfrac{5}{-3} = \dfrac{-r}{-3}$. Therefore, $5 = -r$, so $r = -5$, and the answer is (B).

6. **C** Use Bite-Sized Pieces and Process of Elimination. Focus on just the first term in the expression given, which is $16x^6$. In (A), the first term in the expanded version of the expression would be $(16x^2)^3 = 4{,}096x^6$. Eliminate (A). In (B), the first term in the expanded version of the expression would be $(16x^3)^2 = 256x^6$. Eliminate (B). In (C), the first term of the expanded expression would be $(4x^3)^2 = 16x^6$. This is correct, so either expand out the rest of (C) or check the first term on the expression in (D) to be sure. The second option is easier: $(4x)^6 = 4{,}096x^6$, so (C) is correct.

7. **D** When a question asks for the least possible value, plug in the answers, starting with the smallest answer choice. Plug in $n = 11$ from (A) and see if $S > 2{,}000$ as stated in the question. The equation becomes $S = 180(11 - 2) = 1{,}620$. This is not greater than 2,000, so eliminate (A). A larger value for $n$ is needed to make the sum of the angles greater than 2,000. Try (C) to get $S = 180(13 - 2) = 1{,}980$. This is still too small, so (D) must be the correct answer.

8. **A** First, define the equations for both of the lines. The slope-intercept form of a line is $y = mx + b$, where $x$ and $y$ are the coordinates of a point on the line, $m$ is the slope, and $b$ is the $y$-intercept. Plug in the point $(4, 4)$ and a $y$-intercept of $-8$ into the slope-intercept equation to get $4 = (m)(4) - 8$. Solve for $m$ to get $12 = 4m$ and $m = 3$. Therefore,

the equation for line $k$ is $y = 3x - 8$. Next, find the equation of line $m$. Given two points, use the point-slope formula to find the line: $y - y_1 = m(x - x_1)$. To find the slope, $m$, use the slope formula $\dfrac{y_2 - y_1}{x_2 - x_1}$. For line $m$, the slope is $\dfrac{-3 - 5}{5 - 1} = \dfrac{-8}{4} = -2$. Therefore, plugging the point $(1, 5)$ into the point-slope formula results in $y - 5 = -2(x - 1)$. Distribute the $-2$ to get $y - 5 = -2x + 2$. Solve for $y$ to get $y = -2x + 7$. Set the two line equations equal to each other to get $3x - 8 = -2x + 7$. Solve for $x$ to get $5x = 15$, and $x = 3$. Plug $x = 3$ into the equation for line $k$ to get $y = 3(3) - 8 = 1$. Therefore, the point of intersection $(s, t)$ is $(3, 1)$ and $s - t = 3 - 1 = 2$, and the answer is (A).

9.  **B**  When multiplying variables with the same base and different exponents, add the exponents. The equation becomes $k^{x^2 + xy + y^2 + xy} = k^{25}$. Combine like terms to get $k^{x^2 + 2xy + y^2} = k^{25}$. Therefore, $x^2 + 2xy + y^2 = 25$. Factor the quadratic to get $(x + y)^2 = 25$. Take the square root of both sides to get $x + y = \pm 5$. Substitute 3 for $x$ to get $3 + y = \pm 5$. Since the question asks for the positive value of $y$, the equation to use is $3 + y = 5$, so $y = 2$, and the correct answer is (B).

10.  **D**  Plug in. Let $D = 2$ and $E = 5$, so the equation becomes $F = \dfrac{2}{5 - 2} = \dfrac{2}{3}$. Plug these values for $D$, $E$, and $F$ into the answer choices to see which answer works. Choice (A) becomes $2 = \dfrac{5}{1 - \dfrac{2}{3}}$. Solve the right side of the equation to get $2 = \dfrac{5}{\dfrac{1}{3}}$, and $2 = 15$. Eliminate (A). Choice (B) becomes $2 = \dfrac{5}{1 + \dfrac{2}{3}}$. Solve the right side of the equation to get $2 = \dfrac{5}{\dfrac{5}{3}}$, and $2 = 3$. Eliminate (B). Choice (C) becomes $2 = \dfrac{\dfrac{2}{3}(5)}{1 - \dfrac{2}{3}}$. Solve the right side of the equation to get $2 = \dfrac{\dfrac{10}{3}}{\dfrac{1}{3}}$, and $2 = 10$. Eliminate (C). The answer must be (D). And indeed, plugging in the values gives $2 = \dfrac{\dfrac{2}{3}(5)}{1 + \dfrac{2}{3}}$. Solving the right side of the equation results in $2 = \dfrac{\dfrac{10}{3}}{\dfrac{5}{3}}$, and $2 = 2$.

11.  **B**  Since calculator use is not allowed on this section, graphing and checking each function is not an option. Plug in instead. Usually, zero is a number to avoid, since it messes things up, but the goal here is to find what could be true, so messing things up helps. If $x = 0$, (A) becomes $0^2 - 3 = -3$. This is not greater than or equal to $-2$, so eliminate (A). Choice (B) becomes $(0 - 3)^2 = 9$, which is greater than $-2$, so keep it for now. Choice (C) becomes $|0| - 3 = -3$, and (D) becomes $(0 - 3)^3 = -27$. Neither of these values is greater than $-2$, so eliminate them and choose (B).

12. **D** When a fraction has imaginary numbers in the denominator, multiply the fraction by the com-

plex conjugate of the denominator. The complex conjugate of $(6 - 3i)$ is $(6 + 3i)$. The original ex-

pression becomes $\dfrac{(1 + 10i)(6 + 3i)}{(6 - 3i)(6 + 3i)}$. Use FOIL to multiply it out to get $\dfrac{6 + 3i + 60i + 30i^2}{36 + 18i - 18i - 9i^2}$.

Combine like terms to get $\dfrac{6 + 63i + 30i^2}{36 - 9i^2}$. Since $i = \sqrt{-1}$, $i^2 = -1$. Plug this into the ex-

pression, which becomes $\dfrac{6 + 63i + 30(-1)}{36 - 9(-1)} = \dfrac{6 + 63i - 30}{36 + 9} = \dfrac{-24 + 63i}{45}$. Split this into two

fractions, as seen in the answer choices, to get $\dfrac{-24}{45} + \dfrac{63i}{45} = \dfrac{-8}{15} + \dfrac{7i}{5}$, which is (D).

13. **D** The decay formula states that $decay = original(1 - r)^t$, where $r$ is the rate of decay and $t$ is time. Therefore, the value of the truck after $t$ years is $35{,}000(0.93)^t$, which is (D).

14. **A** Rather than trying to do some messy algebraic manipulation, plug in a simple number like

$x = 2$. The expression becomes $\dfrac{6(2) - 1}{2 + 4} = \dfrac{11}{6}$. Now plug $x = 2$ into the answer choices to see

which one equals $\dfrac{11}{6}$. Choice (A) becomes $6 - \dfrac{25}{2 + 4} = 6 - \dfrac{25}{6} = \dfrac{36}{6} - \dfrac{25}{6} = \dfrac{11}{6}$. That matches,

but check the other answer choices to be sure. None of them equals $\dfrac{11}{6}$ when $x = 2$, so the

answer is (A).

15. **B** The product of the roots of a quadratic $ax^2 + bx + c = 0$ is $\dfrac{c}{a}$. In the given quadratic, $c = 12$ and

$a = 3$, so $\dfrac{12}{3} = 4$. Without this handy trick, another way to solve this is to use the quadratic

formula to find the roots, then multiply them together. Either way, the answer is (B).

16. **82** Expand the left side of the equation to get $3(x - 5)(x - 5) + 7$. FOIL the quadratic to get $3(x^2 - 10x + 25) + 7$. Distribute the 3 to get $3x^2 - 30x + 75 + 7 = 3x^2 - 30x + 82$. Therefore, $c = 82$.

17. **15** Because $\overline{BD}$ and $\overline{AE}$ are parallel, triangles $ACE$ and $BCD$ are similar triangles (all of their cor-

responding angles are equal to each other). Therefore, the lengths of their sides are proportional.

To solve for the length of $\overline{AE}$, set up the following proportion: $\dfrac{10}{12} = \dfrac{\overline{AE}}{18}$. Cross-multiply to

get $12\overline{AE} = 180$. Solve for $\overline{AE}$ to get $\overline{AE} = 15$.

18. **4, 8, 12, 16,** or **20**

Plug in. Start by testing whether a single red chip could work. If Eve has one red chip, then she has $120 − $5 = $115 worth of blue chips, which does not divide by 20 for an integer number of blue chips. If Eve had 2 red chips, she would have 110 worth of blue chips, which still won't work. If Eve had $20 worth of red chips, though, she would have $100 left for exactly 5 blue chips. She would need 4 red chips to equal $20, so 4 is one possible answer. Any number of red chips that gave Eve a multiple of $20 would also work, so 8, 12, 16, and 20 are also acceptable answers.

19. $\dfrac{17}{6}$ or **2.83**

If the system of equations has infinitely many solutions, it means that the two equations are the same line. Therefore, seek to make the two equations look the same. Multiply the top equation by 3 to get $\dfrac{3}{2}x + 3(ay) = 48$. To make the bottom equation the same, it must be true that $b = \dfrac{3}{2}$, and $3a = 4$. Solve for $a$ to get $a = \dfrac{4}{3}$. Therefore, $a + b = \dfrac{4}{3} + \dfrac{3}{2} = \dfrac{17}{6}$.

20. **1**  Convert $\dfrac{\pi}{3}$ radians to degrees by multiplying by $\dfrac{180}{\pi}$. $\dfrac{\pi}{3}\left(\dfrac{180}{\pi}\right) = 60$. Therefore, the angle $POR = 60°$. Next, draw a straight line from $P$ to the $x$-axis, and mark the angles as follows:

Remember that the sides of a 30-60-90 triangle are in a ratio of $1 : \sqrt{3} : 2$. Given that 2 is opposite the 90° angle, the length opposite the 30° angle is 1, and the $x$-value of $P$ is therefore also 1.

# Section 4: Math (Calculator)

1. **C**  There are 9 blue tiles for every 80 tiles. The question says *at this rate*, so set up a proportion. Make sure to have like units on the top and like units on the bottom:

$\dfrac{9 \text{ blue}}{80 \text{ total}} = \dfrac{b \text{ blue}}{4,800 \text{ total}}$. Cross-multiply to get $80b = 43,200$. Divide both sides by 80 to get $b = 540$. The correct answer is (C).

2. **D**  The question asks for the value of $d$ when $c = 345$. Plug this value of $c$ into the equation, $c = 120 + 75d$, to get $345 = 120 + 75d$. Subtract 120 from both sides to get $225 = 75d$. Divide both sides by 75 to get $d = 3$. The correct answer is (D).

3. **A**  The question states that the artist makes \$50 for each large print. Since the artist sells $l$ large prints, she earns a total of $50l$ for all the large prints. The artist also earns \$35 for each small print. Since the artist sells $s$ small prints, she earns a total of $35s$ for all of the small prints. The question asks for the amount she earns for both the $l$ large prints and the $s$ small prints. This is equal to the sum of the two amounts, which is $50l + 35s$. The correct answer is (A).

4. **C**  Translate the first sentence into an equation. The expression *6 times a number y* translates to $6y$. This term *subtracted from 15* translates to $15 - 6y$. The term *the result is 33* translates to $= 33$, so the whole sentence translates to $15 - 6y = 33$. Solve for $y$. Subtract 15 from both sides to get $-6y = 18$. Divide both sides by $-6$ to get $y = -3$. The question asks, *What number results when 3 times y is added to 19?* The term *what number* translates to a variable. Use $x$. The term *results* translates to $=$. The term *3 times y* translates to $3y$. The term *is added to* translates to +. Therefore, the question translates to $x = 3y + 19$. Since $y = -3$, plug this into the equation to get $x = 3(-3) + 19 = -9 + 19 = 10$. The correct answer is (C).

5. **D**  The question asks for the profit the store makes when it sells 6 televisions. It also defines profit as the amount of money left after paying 39 percent of the money earned. According to the information given, the total revenues from selling 6 televisions is \$1,440. To determine how much the store paid the factory, take 39% of this by entering $\dfrac{39}{100} \times 1{,}440$ on a calculator to get \$561.60. To find the profit, subtract this amount from the revenue: \$1,440.00 − \$561.60 = \$878.40. The correct answer is (D).

6. **B**  The information given for this set of questions uses the term *directly proportional*, so set up a proportion in the form $\dfrac{x_1}{y_1} = \dfrac{x_2}{y_2}$. The question asks for the revenue when the store sells 9 televisions, and the information above the question says the store makes a profit of \$1,440 when the store sells 6 televisions. Set up the proportion: $\dfrac{\$1{,}440}{6 \text{ televisions}} = \dfrac{x}{9 \text{ televisions}}$. Be sure to put like units in the numerators and like units in the denominators. Cross-multiply to get $6x = \$12{,}960$. Divide both sides by 6 to get $x = \$2{,}160$. The correct answer is (B).

7. **D**  The question asks for a pair of equations. Use Bite-Sized Pieces to determine each equation. The question says the collector can buy a maximum of 25 records, so the total number of records must be less than or equal to 25. Come up with an expression to determine the total number of records. The number of \$20 records is $a$ and the number of \$35 records is $b$, so

the total number of records must be $a + b$. Therefore, the correct choice must include the inequality $a + b \leq 25$. Eliminate any choice that does not include this: (A) and (B). The other equation in both remaining answers involves an expression set less than or equal to 750. Find 750 in the problem. The question states that the collector can spend up to \$750, so come up with an expression for what the collector spends. To find the cost of the \$20 records, multiply the number of these records, $a$, by 20 to get $20a$. Similarly, to find the total cost of the \$35 records multiply $b$ by 35 to get $35b$. Therefore, the total cost of all the records is this sum: $20a + 35b$. This sum must be less than or equal to \$750, so the answer must include the inequality $20a + 35b \leq 750$. Eliminate the remaining choice that doesn't include this inequality: (C). Therefore, the correct answer is (D).

8.  **C**  The $x$-intercepts, by definition, are the $x$-coordinates of the points at which $y = 0$, so set $y = 0$ in the equation above to get $0 = x^2 - 12x + 35$. Factor the right side of the equation by finding a pair of numbers with a product of 35 and a sum of $-12$. This pair is $-5$ and $-7$. The factored form of the equation, therefore, is $0 = (x - 5)(x - 7)$. Set both factors equal to 0 to get $x - 5 = 0$ and $x - 7 = 0$. Solve each equation to get $x = 5$ and $x = 7$. Select the answer that includes both the numbers 5 and 7, which is (C). Alternatively, know that the $x$-intercepts are the same as the solutions. To find the solutions, put in the equation in factored form, which is (C).

9.  **A**  A player loses 3 points for every question answered incorrectly. If a player answers 15 questions incorrectly, he or she loses $15 \times 3 = 45$ points. If this player has 165 points remaining, he or she must have started with $165 + 45 = 210$ points. Since the player started with $k$ points, $k$ must equal 210. Therefore, the correct answer is (A).

10. **A**  Not all the information in the table is relevant. The question asks for the number of days it would take Albert to type the entire document. The table provides the number of pages, sections, and units in the document. However, it does not provide any way to determine the amount of time it would take to type a page, section, or unit, so ignore this information. The table does, however, provide the number of words in the document and the number of words Albert can type per minute. Use the formula: *Amount = Rate × Time*. The amount is 181,235 words, and the rate is 85 words per minute. Set up the equation $181{,}235 = 85t$. Divide both sides by 85 on a calculator to get approximately 2,132 minutes (it's okay to round a bit, since the question asks for the *closest* answer). However, the question asks for days. Each day, Albert expects to devote four hours to typing the document. 2,132 minutes is equal to

$\dfrac{2,132}{60}$ = 35.533 hours. At 4 hours per day, 35.533 hours of typing can be completed in $\dfrac{35.533}{4}$ = 8.88 days. Select the closest choice, which is (A).

11. **B** The capacity of the trash can is 20 cubic feet, and the question asks when the trash can will be full or overflowing. In other words, it asks when the amount of garbage in the trash can is at or above capacity. First, come up with an expression for the amount of garbage in the trash can. Each day 3 cubic feet is added. Therefore, after $d$ days, $3d$ cubic feet has been added. This amount is added to the original amount, which is 8, so the amount of garbage in the trash can after $d$ days is $8 + 3d$. The question asks for when this amount is at or above capacity, which is 20. Therefore, the inequality is $8 + 3d \geq 20$, which is (B).

12. **C** The question asks for the value of $m(n(6))$. For compound functions, start on the inside and work to the outside. The inside is $n(6)$. According to the information in the question, $n(6) = 4$. Therefore $m(n(6)) = m(4)$. According to the information in the question, $m(4) = 6$. Therefore, $m(n(6)) = m(4) = 6$, so the correct answer is (C).

13. **C** The question asks for the average speed in kilometers per minute, so determine distance and time in kilometers and minutes, respectively. The circumference of Earth's equator is about 40,000, so this is the distance. Earth completes a rotation in one day, which is 24 hours. However, the question asks for minutes, so convert hours to minutes with the proportion $\dfrac{1 \text{ hour}}{60 \text{ min}} = \dfrac{24 \text{ hours}}{x \text{ min}}$. Cross-multiply to get $x = 1,440$. To determine speed, divide distance by time to get $\dfrac{40,000 \text{ km}}{1,440 \text{ min}} \approx 28$. The correct answer is (C).

14. **B** The theater owner is trying to determine whether local residents would prefer to see operas or symphonies by surveying people at a mall on a Sunday. Go through each choice and determine which one describes the cause of a flaw in the theater owner's methodology. Choice (A) is the size of the sample. While it's possible that this sample size is too small, there is no information about the area's population to determine whether this is a sufficiently or insufficiently large sample. Eliminate (A). Choice (B) is the location in which the survey was given. The location causes a flaw, because it creates a bias toward people who are likely to visit a shopping mall. Keep (B). Choice (C) is the population of the area. There is no information about the population of the area, so it is impossible to determine whether this creates a problem. Eliminate (C). Choice (D) is the residents who declined to respond. There is no reason to think that this significantly hurts sample size or creates a bias. Eliminate (D). The correct answer is (B).

15. **B** The question asks for the year the population is projected to reach 5,000. Population is expressed by the vertical axis, so find 5,000 on that axis. Trace the line across the graph until reaching the line of best fit. Then, follow downward until reaching the horizontal axis somewhere between 2020 and 2025. The only choice between these two is (B).

16. **B** The half-life of the unknown element is approximately 25% less than that of carbon-14. Take 25% of the half-life of carbon-14, which is $\frac{25}{100} \times 5{,}730 = 1{,}432.50$. Since it's 25% *less*, subtract this number from 5,730 to get $5{,}730 - 1{,}432.50 = 4{,}297.50$, which is closest to (B).

17. **D** The question states that the mean salary of the employees is $80,000 and the median salary is $45,000. The mean refers to the average (the sum of the salaries divided by the number of employees), and the median refers to the middle salary when listed in order. If the median is $45,000, there must be an equal number of employees with salaries greater than $45,000 and less than $45,000. If the average is greater than the median, it must mean that the salaries at the top half have a greater effect on the average and the ones at the bottom half, which would happen if a few employees had significantly higher salaries. This is (D). Alternatively, come up with a simple example that describes the situation. For example, there could be three employees with salaries $20,000, $45,000, and $175,000. The median is $45,000 and the mean is $80,000. Go through the choices and eliminate any choice that doesn't describe this situation. Choice (A) says that many employees' salaries are between $45,000 and $80,000. In this case, there are no salaries between $45,000 and $80,000. Eliminate (A). Choice (B) says the employees' salaries are close to each other. In this case, the salaries are far apart from each other. Eliminate (B). Choices (C) and (D) are opposites. Choice (C) says a few salaries are much lower than the rest and (D) says a few salaries are much higher than the rest. In this example, the low salary is much closer to the median than the high salary, so eliminate (C) and pick (D).

18. **C** The question asks for probability, which is $\frac{want}{total}$. The question says *an accepted student* is chosen, so the *total* is the number of accepted students, which is $15{,}700 + 9{,}300 = 25{,}000$. The question asks for the probability that *the student did not complete an interview*, so this number represents the *want*. Make sure to only count the students who did not complete an interview and were accepted, which is 9,300. Therefore, the probability is $\frac{want}{total} = \frac{9{,}300}{25{,}000} = \frac{93}{250}$, which is (C).

19. **C** Plug In. Let $d = 400$ and $k = 390$. Plug these values into the answer choices to see which answer works. Choice (A) becomes $400 - 390 < 20$, which is true. Keep (A). Choice (B) becomes $400 + 390 < 20$. This isn't true, so eliminate (B). Choice (C) becomes $-20 < 400 - 390 < 20$. This is also true, so keep (C). Choice (D) becomes $-20 < 400 + 390 < 20$. Eliminate (D). Now plug in some different numbers to try to eliminate (A) or (C). Try $d = 390$ and $k = 400$. Choice (A) becomes $390 - 400 < 20$, and (C) becomes $-20 < 390 - 400 < 20$. Both of these are still true. When that happens, try plugging in some numbers that *don't* work—the correct answer will prove false and an incorrect answer may still be true. Try $d = 400$ and $k = 450$, which don't work because they are more than $20 apart. Choice (A) becomes $400 - 450 < 20$, which is still true, so eliminate it. Choice (C) is false for the numbers that don't work, so it is correct.

20. **A** The median is the middle number when all the numbers are listed in order. However, in this case, there are too many numbers to list them in order. Instead, think in terms of what the middle number would be. Half the numbers should be greater than the median and the other half of the numbers should be less than the median. Since the president polled 200 students each from the junior and senior classes, a total of 400 students were polled. Therefore, in this case, there should be 200 greater than and 200 less than the median. Therefore, the median is the average of the 200th and 201st numbers. Find the 200th and 201st numbers in the ordered list. Start with the smallest numbers. In the combined junior and senior classes, there are 25 + 30 = 55 students who complete one hour of homework a night. The median must be greater than this. In the combined junior and senior classes, there are 80 + 70 = 150 students who complete two hours of homework. Therefore, there must be a total of 55 + 150 = 205 students with 1 or 2 hours. Since the tally is greater than 201, the 200th and 201st students must be part of the group of students who complete two hours of homework. Therefore, the average of the 200th and 201st (the median) must be 2. The correct answer is (A).

21. **A** The question asks how to compare the number of students who complete four hours of homework in the two classes. The number in the table for both classes is 35, which would seem to point to (D). However, these numbers do not represent the entirety of the two classes but rather a random sample of 200 from each class. Use proportions to determine the actual expected amounts. Since there are 600 students in the junior class, set up the proportion $\frac{35}{200} = \frac{x}{600}$. Cross-multiply to get $200x = 21,000$. Divide both sides by 200 to get $x = 105$ students in the junior class who complete four hours of homework per night. Since there are 400 students in the senior class, set up the proportion $\frac{35}{200} = \frac{x}{400}$. Cross-multiply to get $200x = 14,000$. Divide both sides by 200 to get $x = 70$ students in the senior class who complete four hours of homework per night. Therefore, the junior class has $105 - 70 = 35$ more students who complete four hours of homework than does the senior class. The correct answer is (A).

22. **B** The equation of a circle is $(x - h)^2 + (y - k)^2 = r^2$, where $r$ stands for radius. Start by reordering the equation to get $x^2 - 6x + y^2 + 8y = -9$. To solve for the radius, it is necessary to complete the squares. Remember what gets added to one side of the equation must be added to the other: $(x^2 - 6x + 9) + (y^2 + 8y + 16) = -9 + 9 + 16$. Therefore, $r^2 = -9 + 9 + 16 = 16$, and $r = 4$, which is (B).

23. **D** Solve the equation for $d^2$. First, multiply both sides of the equation by $d^2$ to get $Gd^2 = ab$. Then, divide by $G$ to get $d^2 = \frac{ab}{G}$. Therefore, (D) is correct.

24. **D** Start by plugging in the same mass for $k$, $m$, $a$, and $b$. Let $k = m = a = b = 2$. The gravitational

force between $k$ and $m$ is 9 times the force between $a$ and $b$, so plug in $G_{km} = 81$ and $G_{ab} = 9$. Square

numbers will work well here, since the distance is squared in the formula. Use these values in the

formula to find the distance between the given objects. The gravitational force for $k$ and $m$ becomes

$81 = \dfrac{(2)(2)}{(d_{km})^2}$, so $81(d_{km})^2 = 4$, and $(d_{km})^2 = \dfrac{4}{81}$. Take the square root of both sides to get $d_{km} = \dfrac{2}{9}$.

Follow the same steps to find the gravitational force for $a$ and $b$: $9 = \dfrac{(2)(2)}{(d_{ab})^2}$, then $9(d_{ab})^2 = 4$, so

$(d_{ab})^2 = \dfrac{4}{9}$, and $d_{ab} = \dfrac{2}{3}$. Now make the fraction: $\dfrac{d_{km}}{d_{ab}} = \dfrac{\frac{2}{9}}{\frac{2}{3}} = \dfrac{2}{9} \times \dfrac{3}{2} = \dfrac{1}{3}$, which is (D).

25. **C** Remember that $f(x)$ or $g(x) = y$. The graph shows that when the $x$-value is $-3$, the $y$-value is 2. Therefore, statement (I) is true. Eliminate (A). The graph shows that when the $x$-value is 2, the $y$-value is 2.
Therefore, statement (II) is false. Eliminate (B) and (D). The correct answer is therefore (C).

26. **B** Use Process of Elimination. The graph of the athlete who only jogs is linear, which is to say the
rate of change is consistent throughout time, while the rate of change for the athlete who alternates
running/walking is represented by a curve—it flattens out during minutes 3 and 4. Based on this,
eliminate (C) and (D) since the rate of change is not consistent for the running/walking athlete.
Eliminate (A) because the rate of change is greater for the athlete who jogs during minutes 3 and 4.
The correct answer is therefore (B).

27. **B** Plug in values for $s$ and $t$ that make the statement $t - s = 0$ true, such as $t = 5$ and $s = 5$. Therefore, the

points $(0, 5)$ and $(5, 0)$ are on the line. The answers all refer to the slope of the line, so plug these points

into the slope formula: $\dfrac{y_2 - y_1}{x_2 - x_1}$. This becomes $\dfrac{0 - 5}{5 - 0} = \dfrac{-5}{5} = -1$, making (B) the correct answer.

28. **C** Rather than trying to remember the formula for the area of a hexagon, ignore triangle $ADG$ for
now and divide the hexagon up into triangles, like this:

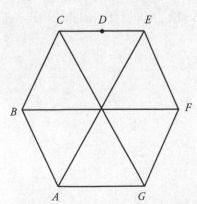

Because the hexagon is a regular one, each of these six triangles is the same. The area of each triangle is $\frac{1}{6}$ of the hexagon, or $144\sqrt{3}$. Each internal angle in a regular hexagon is 120°, so each triangle is equilateral. Use this information to find the length of a side of the hexagon. Isolate one triangle to work with, and divide it in half to form two 30°-60°-90° triangles.

To more easily use the relationships of the 30°-60°-90° triangle's sides, label $\overline{AG}$ as $2x$, so the height of the equilateral triangle is $x\sqrt{3}$.

The area of a triangle is $A = \frac{1}{2}bh$, so plug the information into the formula to get $144\sqrt{3} = \frac{1}{2}(2x)(x\sqrt{3})$. Simplify the right side to get $144\sqrt{3} = x^2\sqrt{3}$, then divide both sides by $\sqrt{3}$ to get $144 = x^2$. This means that $x = 12$, and $\overline{AG} = 2x = 24$. This is the base of triangle $ADG$.

To find the height, go back to the hexagon divided into equilateral triangles. The height of each equilateral triangle is $x\sqrt{3}$ or $12\sqrt{3}$, and the height of triangle $ADG$ is equal to 2 of these heights, or $24\sqrt{3}$.

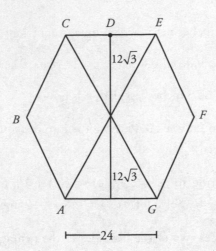

Plug these values into the area formula to get $A = \frac{1}{2}(24)\left(24\sqrt{3}\right) = 288\sqrt{3}$, which is (C). Another way to approach this question is to ballpark—the area of triangle $ADG$ is about one-third of the area of the hexagon. Dividing $864\sqrt{3}$ by 3 results in $288\sqrt{3}$, which is—not just approximately—(C).

29.  **A**  Start by using Process of Elimination. The diagram shows that line $l$ has a negative slope and a negative $y$-intercept. All the answers have lines with negative slopes, but only (A) and (D) have negative $y$-intercepts. Eliminate (B) and (C). Since line $l$ is tangent to the circle at point $A$, line $l$ is perpendicular to the line containing $\overline{AC}$. Perpendicular lines have slopes that are opposite reciprocals, so find the slope of $\overline{AC}$. The slope formula is $\frac{y_2 - y_1}{x_2 - x_1}$, which becomes $\frac{7 - (-1)}{3 - (-1)} = \frac{8}{4} = 2$ for $\overline{AC}$. Therefore, the slope of line $l$ is $-\frac{1}{2}$, so (A) is the answer.

30.  **A**  The solutions to a system of equations are the points the equations share. The line $y = -2$ is the straightforward equation, so $y$ must be $-2$ in the other equation. Plug the values given in each answer choice for $r$ and $s$, along with $-2$ for $y$, into the first equation, and solve for $x$. The answer that yields two real solutions for $x$ will be the correct answer. Choice (A) becomes $-2 = -2x^2 - 1$. Add 1 to both sides to get $-1 = -2x^2$. Divide both sides by $-2$ to get $\frac{1}{2} = x^2$. Take the square root of both sides of the equation to get $\pm\sqrt{\frac{1}{2}} = x$. Therefore, (A) has two real solutions: $\left(-\sqrt{\frac{1}{2}}, -2\right)$ and $\left(\sqrt{\frac{1}{2}}, -2\right)$, so (A) is the correct answer.

31.  **9**  There are 60 minutes in an hour. To convert minutes into hours, divide the number of minutes by 60. $\frac{560}{60} = 9.\overline{3}$ or nine and one-third hours. Therefore, 560 minutes is equal to 9 hours and 20 minutes, and $z = 9$.

32. **15** The rate of decrease is 0.4 inches per year. Set up a proportion: $\dfrac{0.4 \text{ inches}}{1 \text{ year}} = \dfrac{6 \text{ inches}}{x}$. Cross-multiply to get $6 = 0.4x$, then divide by 0.4 to get $x = 15$ years. Therefore, it will take 15 years for the average annual snowfall to be 6 inches less than it is now.

33. **12** Dave incurred the initial fine at week 0. Plug 0 for $w$ into the equation to get $C = 12 - 1.5(0)$. Solve for $C$ to get $C = 12 - 0 = 12$.

34. **12** Plug $(4, -2)$ into the function to get $-2 = 2(4)^2 - k(4) + 14$. Simplify the equation to get $-2 = 32 - 4k + 14$, and $-2 = 46 - 4k$. Solve for $k$ to get $-48 = -4k$, and $k = 12$.

35. **60** Because the angle $COA$ faces two of the five sides of the pentagon, angle $COA$ is $\dfrac{2}{5}$ of the circle. The length of the arc made by this angle is 24, so set up an equation: $24 = \dfrac{2}{5} \times circumference$. Multiply both sides by $\dfrac{5}{2}$ to get $circumference = 60$.

36. **575** Let $b$ represent the number of calories in the breakfast sandwich and $f$ represent the number of calories in the fried potatoes. The information in the question can then be translated into the following equations: $b + f = 910$ and $b = f + 240$. Solve the second equation for $f$ to get $f = b - 240$. Plug this value for $f$ into the first equation to get $b + b - 240 = 910$. Solve for $b$ to get $2b - 240 = 910$, $2b = 1,150$, and $b = 575$.

37. **7,000** According to the question, $P_t = 4,200$ and $P_{t+1} = 4,704$. Plug these values into the equation to get $4,704 = 4,200 + 0.3(4,200)\left(1 - \dfrac{4,200}{C}\right)$. Simplify the right side of the equation to get $4,704 = 4,200 + 1,260\left(1 - \dfrac{4,200}{C}\right)$. Subtract 4,200 from both sides of the equation to get $504 = 1,260\left(1 - \dfrac{4,200}{C}\right)$. Divide the equation by 1,260 to get $0.4 = 1 - \dfrac{4,200}{C}$. Solve for $C$ to get $-0.6 = -\dfrac{4,200}{C}$, $-0.6C = -4,200$, and $C = 7,000$.

38. **5,741** According to the question, $C = 10,500$ and $P_t = 4,200$. Therefore, $P_{t+1} = 4,200 + 0.3(4,200)\left(1 - \dfrac{4,200}{10,500}\right)$. Solve the equation to get $P_{t+1} = 4,200 + 1,260(1 - 0.4) = 4,200 + 756 = 4,956$. That's the deer population after one year, but the question asks for the population after two years, so do it again. Plug 4,956 into the equation as the new $P_t$ to get the deer population two years from now: $P_{t+1} = 4,956 + 0.3(4,956)\left(1 - \dfrac{4,956}{10,500}\right)$. Solve the equation to get $P_{t+1} = 4,956 + 1,486.8(1 - 0.472) = 4,956 + 785.03 \approx 5,741$. Only round at the last step to make sure the answer is as accurate as possible.

# Chapter 7
# Practice Test 3

# Reading Test

## 65 MINUTES, 52 QUESTIONS

**Turn to Section 1 of your answer sheet to answer the questions in this section.**

**DIRECTIONS**

Each passage or pair of passages below is followed by a number of questions. After reading each passage or pair, choose the best answer to each question based on what is stated or implied in the passage or passages and in any accompanying graphics (such as a table or graph).

**Questions 1–10 are based on the following passage.**

This passage is adapted from Oscar Wilde, "Lord Arthur Savile's Crime." Originally published in 1887.

It was Lady Windermere's last reception before Easter, and Bentinck House was even more crowded than usual. Six Cabinet Ministers had come on from the Speaker's Levée in their stars and ribands, all the
5 pretty women wore their smartest dresses, and at the end of the picture-gallery stood the Princess Sophia of Carlsrühe, a heavy Tartar-looking lady, with tiny black eyes and wonderful emeralds, talking bad French at the top of her voice, and laughing immoderately
10 at everything that was said to her. It was certainly a wonderful medley of people. Gorgeous peeresses chatted affably to violent Radicals, popular preachers brushed coat-tails with eminent sceptics, a perfect bevy of bishops kept following a stout prima-donna from
15 room to room, on the staircase stood several Royal Academicians, disguised as artists, and it was said that at one time the supper-room was absolutely crammed with geniuses. In fact, it was one of Lady Windermere's best nights, and the Princess stayed till nearly half-past
20 eleven.

As soon as she had gone, Lady Windermere returned to the picture-gallery, where a celebrated political economist was solemnly explaining the scientific theory of music to an indignant virtuoso
25 from Hungary, and began to talk to the Duchess of Paisley. Lady Windermere looked wonderfully beautiful with her grand ivory throat, her large blue forget-me-not eyes, and her heavy coils of golden hair. *Or pur* ("pure gold") they were—not
30 that pale straw colour that nowadays usurps the gracious name of gold, but such gold as is woven into sunbeams or hidden in strange amber; and they gave to her face something of the frame of a saint, with not a little of the fascination of a sinner. She was
35 a curious psychological study. Early in life she had discovered the important truth that nothing looks so like innocence as an indiscretion; and by a series of reckless escapades, half of them quite harmless, she had acquired all the privileges of a personality. She had
40 more than once changed her husband; indeed, Debrett credits her with three marriages; but as she had never changed her lover, the world had long ago ceased to talk scandal about her. She was now forty years of age, childless, and with that inordinate passion for pleasure
45 which is the secret of remaining young.

Suddenly she looked eagerly round the room, and said, in her clear contralto voice, 'Where is my chiromantist?'

'Your what, Gladys?' exclaimed the Duchess, giving
50 an involuntary start.

'My chiromantist, Duchess; I can't live without him at present.'

'Dear Gladys! you are always so original,' murmured the Duchess, trying to remember what
55 a chiromantist really was, and hoping it was not the same as a chiropodist.

'He comes to see my hand twice a week regularly,' continued Lady Windermere, 'and is most interesting about it.'

**CONTINUE**

60   'Good heavens!' said the Duchess to herself, 'he is a
sort of chiropodist after all.  How very dreadful.  I hope
he is a foreigner at any rate.  It wouldn't be quite so bad
then.'

'I must certainly introduce him to you.'

65   'Introduce him!' cried the Duchess; 'you don't mean
to say he is here?' and she began looking about for a
small tortoise-shell fan and a very tattered lace shawl,
so as to be ready to go at a moment's notice.

'Of course he is here; I would not dream of giving
70   a party without him. He tells me I have a pure psychic
hand, and that if my thumb had been the least little bit
shorter, I should have been a confirmed pessimist, and
gone into a convent.'

'Oh, I see!' said the Duchess, feeling very much
75   relieved; 'he tells fortunes, I suppose?'

'And misfortunes, too,' answered Lady Windermere,
'any amount of them. Next year, for instance, I am in
great danger, both by land and sea, so I am going to
live in a balloon, and draw up my dinner in a basket
80   every evening. It is all written down on my little finger,
or on the palm of my hand, I forget which.'

---

**1**

Which choice best summarizes the passage?

A)  A woman tries to introduce a guest to the practice
    of chiromancy.

B)  A woman hosts a large party and engages another
    woman in conversation.

C)  A detailed description of a party and its host.

D)  A woman hosts her last party before fleeing
    danger.

---

**2**

As used in line 5, "smartest" most nearly means

A)  most fashionable.

B)  most clever.

C)  most painful.

D)  brightest.

---

**3**

The passage most clearly implies that Lady
Windermere is

A)  nearing the end of her hostessing days.

B)  uninterested in discussions of political economy.

C)  less gracious than the Duchess of Paisley.

D)  less serious about fortune-telling than she claims.

---

**4**

Which choice provides the best evidence for the
answer to the preceding question?

A)  Lines 1–3 ("It was . . . usual")

B)  Lines 46–48 ("Suddenly . . . chiromantist")

C)  Lines 69–70 ("Of course . . . him")

D)  Lines 78–81 ("I am . . . which")

---

**5**

The description of "gorgeous peeresses … violent
Radicals, popular preachers … eminent sceptics"
and "a perfect bevy of bishops" (lines 11–14) mainly
serves to

A)  contrast political and artistic types of people.

B)  illustrate the variety of people attending the
    reception.

C)  compare the women to the men.

D)  underscore the discrepancy between social classes.

---

**6**

As used in line 50, the word "start" most nearly means

A)  opening.

B)  commencement.

C)  twitch.

D)  procedure.

---

CONTINUE ➡

The narrator indicates that Princess Sophia, the Radicals, and the Royal Academicians are

A) violent, yet disguised.

B) as immoderate as the other guests.

C) more popular than those who had not been invited.

D) an interesting combination of different types of people.

The narrator implies that Lady Windermere will

A) be unable to live without her chiromantist.

B) relocate to a hot-air balloon.

C) get another divorce.

D) enjoy her reception.

As presented in the passage, the Duchess of Paisley is best described as

A) innocent but indiscreet.

B) proper but curious.

C) youthful but experienced.

D) saintly but sinful.

Which choice provides the best evidence for the answer to the preceding question?

A) Lines 32–34 ("and they . . . sinner")

B) Lines 35–37 ("Early in . . . indiscretion")

C) Lines 60–63 ("Good heavens . . . then")

D) Lines 65–68 ("Introduce him . . . notice")

**CONTINUE**

**Questions 11-20 are based on the following passage and supplementary material.**

This passage is adapted from Michael W. Kraus and Bennett Callaghan, "Noblesse Oblige? Social Status and Economic Inequality Maintenance among Politicians." ©2014 by Public Library of Science.

The United States is in the midst of unprecedented levels of economic inequality. These large scale economic disparities place the most strain on those at the bottom of the social hierarchy—poor and working class families—who must contend with increased poverty, unemployment, problems with health and social support, and homelessness. Americans have few options to combat economic inequality, but they can turn to the democratic system to enact social and fiscal policies that protect individuals from growing wealth disparities. Given that political participation is one of the only avenues available for individuals to combat this economic trend, investigations into the factors that predict whether politicians will support the reduction or increase of economic inequality remain an important area of research.

Social status is broadly defined as the rank-based value of individuals, and can be measured by one's leadership role in organizations, by assessing levels of socioeconomic status (SES; e.g., occupation prestige, annual income), or by one's membership in one or more social categories—such as one's race or gender. However social status is measured, most research finds that higher status confers greater benefits than lower status. For example, when compared to high SES individuals, men, and European Americans, lower status individuals (i.e., low SES individuals, women, and African Americans) experience stereotype threat —anxiety about confirming negative stereotypes about their low status group—that impedes their academic performance. In general, individuals belonging to higher status positions in society benefit from greater access to material and social resources, increased workplace opportunities, and reduced discrimination based on their social status. High status individuals also tend to hold public office more than their low status counterparts, and as a result, have unique access to decision-making power on matters related to economic policy and wealth distribution.

Status disparities force high status individuals to explain why they hold a potentially unfair advantage in society relative to their low status counterparts. Recent research indicates that when faced with explaining their elevated social positions, high status individuals endorse meritocratic beliefs. Specifically, high status individuals, motivated to maintain their elevated social positions and the benefits they bestow, are particularly likely to explain their many social advantages in terms of a fair application of effort, talent, and skill.

Several lines of empirical evidence suggest that high status individuals endorse meritocratic beliefs more than their low status counterparts. For instance, people with higher status are happier when they believe that positive outcomes in society are based on merit and high-performing members of a group are more likely to advocate dividing resources based solely on merit. In a recent online survey, individuals with higher income and who subjectively ranked themselves higher in the social class hierarchy in society— using rungs of a ladder based on ascending levels of education, income, and occupation status—reported a greater belief that the world is fair and that society's structure is based on merit than did their lower status counterparts.

The present research aligns with mounting evidence suggesting that an individual's social status is a reliable predictor of support for economic inequality in society. That social status predicts support for economic inequality among members of Congress—individuals with direct access to creating and implementing policies that shape the future of economic inequality in the US—is a potentially important piece of information for US citizens to consider in future elections.

CONTINUE

Panel A

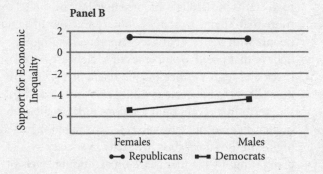

Panel B

Relationships between social status and the tendency to sponsor legislation supporting economic inequality

What function does the first paragraph (lines 1–16) serve in the passage as a whole?

A) It advocates embracing the trend supported by subsequent research in following paragraphs.

B) It illustrates a practice favored by the authors that should be implemented according to correlational research.

C) It acknowledges that a discrepancy exists and offers solutions to the problem based on research results.

D) It gives an overview of a discrepancy and indicates why research on that discrepancy might be important.

Which choice do the authors explicitly cite as an advantage of individuals with higher socioeconomic status?

A) Stereotype threat

B) Increased workplace opportunities

C) Political activism

D) Discrimination

Which choice provides the best evidence for the answer to the previous question?

A) Lines 23–25 ("However social . . . status")

B) Lines 25–31 ("For example . . . performance")

C) Lines 31–35 ("In general . . . status")

D) Lines 40–42 ("Status disparities . . . counterparts")

The central idea of the third paragraph (lines 40–49) is that

A) some individuals with higher socioeconomic status cite reasons other than SES for their perceived advantage.

B) the world is fair and society's structure is based on merit for both high and low SES individuals.

C) individuals of high socioeconomic status seek to keep those of lower socioeconomic status from succeeding.

D) SES predicts social inequality in most societies.

CONTINUE

**15**

Which choice provides the best evidence for the answer to the previous question?

A) Lines 35–39 ("High status . . . distribution")

B) Lines 40–42 ("Status disparities . . . counterparts")

C) Lines 42–45 ("Recent research . . . beliefs")

D) Lines 57–64 ("In a . . . counterparts")

**16**

As used in line 47, "bestow" most nearly means

A) withhold.

B) grant.

C) earn.

D) promote.

**17**

As used in line 65, "aligns" most nearly means

A) arranges.

B) straightens.

C) agrees.

D) focuses.

**18**

Which choice best supports the conclusion that an individual's social status is a reliable predictor of support for economic inequality in society?

A) Lines 35–39 ("High status . . . distribution")

B) Lines 50–52 ("Several lines . . . counterparts")

C) Lines 57–59 ("In a . . . society")

D) Lines 68–74 ("That social . . . elections")

**19**

Which choice is supported by the data in the figure?

A) Males are slightly less likely to sponsor legislation supporting economic inequality than females.

B) The number of individuals polled who identify as low SES is higher than the number of individuals who identify as high SES.

C) The number of Republicans endorsing legislation that supports economic inequality and the number of Democrats supporting such legislation is roughly the same.

D) A female Democrat self-reporting a lower wealth status is most likely to vote for legislation reducing economic inequality.

**20**

Taken together, the two figures suggest that most people who are likely to sponsor legislation supporting economic inequality

A) are employed and have upward mobility with increased work opportunities.

B) are from all socioeconomic backgrounds and social categories.

C) are Democrats who identify as female and low wealth.

D) are Republicans, regardless of gender.

CONTINUE

**Questions 21–30 are based on the following passage.**

This passage is adapted from PLoS, "No Rest for the Weary: Migrating Songbirds Keep Their Wits without Sleep." ©2004 by Public Library of Science.

Every spring and fall, billions of songbirds fly thousands of miles between their summer breeding grounds in North America and their wintering
*Line* grounds in the more hospitable climates of southern
5 California, Mexico, and Central and South America. While some birds fly during the day, most, including the white-crowned sparrow, fly under cover of night. Many aspects of this remarkable voyage remain obscure, especially if, and how, nocturnal migrators get
10 any sleep at night.

A tracking study of the Swainson's thrush found that the roughly seven-inch birds flew up to seven hours straight on six of seven nights, racking up over 930 miles. While the study didn't track their daytime
15 behavior, the birds' migratory pace—as well as the increased activity required to sustain migrations— suggests little time for sleep. Yet field observations indicate that presumably sleep-deprived fliers appear no worse for wear, foraging, navigating, and avoiding
20 predators with aplomb. Researchers are left trying to reconcile this observation with the vast body of evidence linking sleep deprivation to impaired neurobehavioral and physiological function. How do songbirds cope with so little sleep? Do they take power
25 naps? Have they taken "sleep walking" to new heights? Or have they managed to selectively short-circuit the adverse effects of sleep deprivation during migratory stints?

To investigate these questions, Ruth Benca and
30 colleagues studied cognitive and sleep behaviors in captive white-crowned sparrows over the course of a year. The sparrows fly nearly 2,700 miles twice a year between their Alaska and southern California homes. In laboratory cages, the birds' migratory instincts
35 manifest as increased restlessness at night during the migratory season, with lots of hopping around and wing flapping.

Niels Rattenborg et al. characterized the birds' activity levels with motion-detection measurements
40 and video recordings, and placed sensors on their brains to monitor their seasonal sleep patterns. The brain recordings showed a marked seasonal difference in both the amount and type of sleep during a 24- hour period. Cognitive tests—birds performed a task

45 that involved pecking a key in exchange for seed— revealed that birds in the nonmigrating state suffered cognitive deficits when sleep-deprived but displayed an "unprecedented" ability to maintain cognitive function in the face of ongoing sleep loss in the migratory state.

50 These results suggest that wild songbirds drastically reduce sleep time during migration, though Benca and colleagues concede it's impossible to know for sure without recording the birds in action. Such an ability to temporarily circumvent the need for sleep, however,
55 could prove useful for humans in situations that demand continuous performance.

Whatever the mechanism, the unprecedented imperviousness of migrating songbirds to sleep deprivation, the authors conclude, clearly warrants
60 further testing. But it also raises interesting questions about the role of sleep, which recent studies suggest is required to incorporate novel perceptions into the brain's memory banks. If this is true, how do songbirds consolidate memories of migratory events with so little
65 sleep?

Understanding the mechanisms that power the sleepless flight of songbirds promises to unravel one of the longstanding mysteries of their improbable journey. It may also shed light on the origins of sleep-
70 related seasonal disorders and the much-debated role of sleep itself.

---

**21**

Which choice best reflects the overall sequence of events in the passage?

A) A phenomenon is observed and a series of experiments seek to explain it, yet further research is necessary to fully understand the data found.

B) An anomaly is observed and recorded; the results are analyzed and declared inconclusive.

C) A new discovery revolutionizes a current theory, disproving old assumptions, and a new hypothesis is formed.

D) An unexpected finding arises during a study, spawning a secondary study; both studies are interpreted and summarized.

**CONTINUE** →

**22**

As used in line 21, "reconcile" most nearly means

A) reunite.

B) appease.

C) clarify.

D) integrate.

**23**

Which statement best captures Ruth Benca's central assumption in setting up her research?

A) The acquisition of sleepwalking from their evolutionary ancestors allows songbirds to travel great distances while migrating.

B) The tendency for songbirds to hop and flap their wings indicates their tendency towards migration.

C) Songbirds in a controlled research setting will be less likely to exhibit migration behavior than those in the wild.

D) Songbirds' ability to fly long distances without sleeping has little effect on their cognitive abilities.

**24**

Which choice provides the best evidence for the answer to the previous question?

A) Lines 11–14 ("A tracking . . . miles")

B) Lines 14–17 ("While the . . . sleep")

C) Lines 17–20 ("Yet field . . . aplomb")

D) Lines 34–37 ("In laboratory . . . flapping")

**25**

In the fourth paragraph (lines 38–49), the results of Niels Rattenborg's findings mainly serve to

A) show how unexpected results can upset an entire hypothesis.

B) reinforce the findings of Ruth Benca's laboratory research and previous field observations.

C) introduce a component of previous research on the songbirds' migration patterns.

D) underscore certain differences between other researchers and Benca's research.

**26**

After researchers noted the "'unprecedented' ability to maintain cognitive function" during migratory state, (line 48), they

A) concluded that it was impossible to know how the birds maintain normal levels of cognition during migratory seasons.

B) acknowledge that the correlation raises other questions about how the birds function during migration.

C) observed the birds' cognitive deficits when sleep-deprived in a nonmigratory state.

D) consulted other researchers in the field to compare their results.

**27**

The passage identifies which of the following as a factor necessitating that the team of researchers concede that further research is necessary?

A) The speed at which the birds flapped and hopped

B) The birds' increased activity levels

C) The controlled environment of the study

D) The decreased cognitive levels during sleep deprived, nonmigratory states

**28**

As used in line 68, "improbable" most nearly means

A) dubious.

B) unconvincing.

C) remarkable.

D) supposed.

**CONTINUE**

**29**

What can reasonably be inferred about songbirds from the passage?

A) Their activity levels may correlate to migratory seasons.

B) Their activity levels while migrating are similar to those of sleepwalkers.

C) Their mechanisms of migration are impossible to fully understand.

D) Their cognition and memories increase during migration.

**30**

Which choice provides the best evidence for the answer to the previous question?

A) Line 25 ("Have they . . . heights")

B) Lines 34–37 ("In laboratory . . . flapping")

C) Lines 50–53 ("These results . . . action")

D) Lines 60–63 ("But it . . . banks")

CONTINUE

## Questions 31–41 are based on the following passages.

Passage 1 is adapted from Carol Boston, "High School Report Cards. ERIC Digest." Originally published 2003. Passage 2 is adapted from Winnie Hu, "Report Cards Give up A's and B's for 4s and 3s." Originally published 2009.

### Passage 1

Most states have embraced standards-based education, a process that requires them to identify what specific knowledge and skills students are
Line expected to master at each grade level and then align
5 curriculum, teaching, and testing with those standards. Some schools are now experimenting with changes in their report cards to better reflect student progress toward achieving the standards.

Rather than the familiar A through F in each
10 subject, standards-based report cards might feature numbers or phrases that represent whether students have reached, exceeded, or not yet met various specific performance expectations. As an example, a third-grade mathematics grade might include a number or
15 phrase that would denote whether students exceed, meet, approach, or begin to achieve standards in comparing, adding, and subtracting fractions and identifying place values. Such a report card actually provides more detailed, specific information than a
20 traditional grade, though parents and students may find the change disconcerting, and concerns have been expressed about how colleges might evaluate report cards that don't show traditional grade point averages (Manzo, 2001).
25 Report cards that combine traditional grades and information about progress toward standards are also an option. Wiggins (1994) advocates a performance-based report card that plots overall student achievement against norms and standards,
30 identifies strengths and weaknesses in specific areas, and also includes teacher judgments about students' academic progress, growth, intellectual character, and work habits. Marzano (1998) shows an example report card that includes a transcript indicating how many
35 times each standard has been assessed, the average score obtained, as well as the highest, lowest, and most recent scores.

### Passage 2

Thomas R. Guskey, a professor at Georgetown College in Kentucky and an author of *Developing*
40 *Standards-Based Report Cards*, a book that is soon to be released, said the new approach was more accurate, because it measures each student against a stated set of criteria, rather than grading on a curve, which compares members of a class with one another. "The
45 dilemma with that system is you really don't know whether anybody has learned anything. They could all have done miserably, just some less miserably than others."

The executive director of the National Association
50 of Secondary School Principals, Gerald Tirozzi—who supports standards-based report cards—said that many educators and parents were far from ready to scrap letter grades, especially for older students, in part because they worry about the ripple effects on
55 things like the honor roll and class rank. "I think the present grading system—A, B, C, D, F—is ingrained in us," Mr. Tirozzi said. "It's the language which college admissions officers understand; it's the language which parents understand."
60 Outside San Francisco, the San Mateo-Foster City district delayed plans to expand standards-based report cards to its four middle schools from its elementary schools, where they have been used since 2006, after parents packed school board meetings and
65 collected more than 500 signatures in opposition.

Addressing these parental complaints, Pelham district officials said they planned to change the system next year to use benchmarks for each marking period—rather than a year-end standard—to give
70 more timely snapshots of students' progress (and allow many more students to earn 4's from the beginning). They also plan to bring back teacher comments, and are looking for ways to recognize student effort and attitude.

**CONTINUE**

**31**

As used in line 10, "feature" most nearly means

A) present.

B) attribute.

C) report.

D) promote.

**32**

It can be inferred that the author of Passage 1 believes that a standards-based report card

A) will be challenging for colleges and universities to evaluate.

B) provides a more specific way for teachers to evaluate students.

C) is unnecessarily complicated compared to a traditional report card.

D) is more effective for a student in third grade than a student in high school.

**33**

Which choice provides the best evidence for the answer to the previous question?

A) Lines 6–8 ("Some schools . . . standards")

B) Lines 9–13 ("Rather than . . . expectations")

C) Lines 13–18 ("As an . . . values")

D) Lines 18–23 ("Such a . . . averages")

**34**

According to the author of Passage 2, the use of standards-based report cards in elementary schools

A) led to plans for expansion into higher grades.

B) encountered much resistance.

C) has proven more accurate than other systems.

D) has been successfully implemented.

**35**

As used in line 53, "scrap" most nearly means

A) save.

B) fragment.

C) discard.

D) detach.

**36**

Passage 2 states that the new approach to grading

A) introduces a dilemma into the system.

B) does not truly measure whether learning has occurred.

C) is supported by experts in educational theory.

D) does not compare members of a class to each other.

**37**

Which choice provides the best evidence for the answer to the previous question?

A) Lines 38–44 ("Thomas R. Guskey . . . another")

B) Lines 44–46 ("The dilemma . . . anything")

C) Lines 46–48 ("They could . . . others")

D) Lines 72–74 ("They also . . . attitude")

**38**

The author of Passage 2 includes the quote by Thomas Guskey (lines 44–48) in order to address which concern not mentioned in Passage 1?

A) Colleges might favor traditional report cards over standards-based report cards.

B) Students might be disconcerted by a change from letter grades to number grades.

C) Student learning might be less accurately measured on a curve than by set criteria.

D) Traditional report cards might not provide information as specific as that in a standards-based report card.

**CONTINUE** ➡

**39**

Which best describes the overall relationship between Passage 1 and Passage 2?

A) Passage 2 examines different responses to the argument presented in Passage 1.

B) Passage 2 strongly challenges the point of view in Passage 1.

C) Passage 2 draws alternative conclusions from the evidence presented in Passage 1.

D) Passage 2 elaborates on the proposal presented in Passage 1.

**40**

The authors of both passages would most likely agree with which of the following statements about standards-based report cards?

A) Parental insistence on including traditional information has helped to improve the new system.

B) Despite encountering some resistance, standards-based report cards may provide more information than do previous systems.

C) Standards-based report cards remove the flawed system of grading on a curve.

D) Although concerns are understandable, standards-based report cards are superior to the alternatives.

**41**

How would the author of Passage 1 most likely respond to the points made in the final paragraph (lines 66–74) of Passage 2?

A) The author of Passage 1 would sympathize with the parental worries.

B) The author of Passage 1 would caution against the use of benchmarks.

C) The author of Passage 1 would agree with the proposed changes.

D) The author of Passage 1 would insist that intellectual character be included.

**CONTINUE**

**Questions 42–52 are based on the following passage and supplementary material.**

This passage is adapted from Nadav S. Bar, Sigurd Skogestad, Jose M. Marçal, Nachum Ulanovsky, and Yossi Yovel, "A Sensory-Motor Control Model of Animal Flight Explains Why Bats Fly Differently in Light Versus Dark," published 2015 by Public Library of Science. A series of flight experiments are performed with live and simulated bats.

Animal flight requires fine motor control. However, it is unknown how flying animals rapidly transform noisy sensory information into adequate
Line motor commands. Here we developed a sensorimotor
5 control model that explains vertebrate flight guidance with high fidelity. This simple model accurately reconstructed complex trajectories of bats flying in the dark.

To test our model, we used behavioral data
10 from Egyptian fruit bats (*Rousettus aegyptiacus*)—flying mammals that possess an advanced biosonar (echolocation) system, as well as an excellent visual system. We found that a simple model, which considers only the angle-to-target and its derivative,
15 was able to reconstruct complex, several-meter-long flight trajectories very accurately—with an average error of only 14.6 cm.

In reality, however, all organisms have sensory errors. To assess the effect of this sensory noise,
20 we tested two models of angle-dependent additive Gaussian noise, which mimic the sensory errors found in the auditory system of several vertebrates. As expected, sensory noise had strong implications for the convergence of the model: in many trials, adding the
25 noise resulted in increased maneuvering errors, and oftentimes led to complete failure to converge.

We therefore hypothesized that the bat must use a noise-suppression strategy and integrate (average) over several sensory measurements to overcome the
30 noise. An exponentially decaying integrator, which only takes into account the three to four most recent measurements, was found to outperform uniform and linearly decaying integrators. This simple exponential integrator exhibited successful noise suppression
35 and reproduced the bat's flight trajectories with high fidelity.

An important prediction of our model is that sensory noise determines motor performance. To test this hypothesis, we conducted new experiments in

40 which the same individual bats (five of the six bats) flew under a light level that is considered optimal for bat vision (1 lux), while performing the same landing task. We found that, as we hypothesized, the simulated bat exhibited significantly larger gain parameters in
45 light versus dark. Further, the simulated bat exerted significantly stronger forces when flying in the light. Moreover, flight trajectories in light conditions were more direct than in darkness, as quantified by their higher straightness index.

50 Taken together, these results imply the surprising conclusion that the highly curved flight trajectories often exhibited by bats in the dark are due to sensory limitations—not motor limitations.

**The Effect of Noise on Sensorimotor Control**

——— simulated without noise
----- original trajectory
----- simulated with noise

The figure above indicates the results of the experiments described in the 3rd and 4th paragraphs of the passage.

CONTINUE

**42**

The words "must," "exhibited," and "reproduced" in the fourth paragraph (lines 27–36) have what impact on the tone of the paragraph?

A) They display a hopeful tone that demonstrates the authors want the reader to agree with their uncertain results.

B) They display a confident tone that demonstrates the authors have faith in some elements of their conclusions.

C) They display an argumentative tone that demonstrates the authors disagree with researchers who conclude that bats do not use a noise-suppression strategy.

D) They display a commanding tone that demonstrates the authors desire to instruct others in the reproduction of simulated bat trajectories.

**43**

In line 49, the passage indicates that particular experiments resulted in a "higher straightness index." According to the passage, which of the following choices represents the theory these experiments were performed in order to verify?

A) In order to maintain experimental control conditions, it is vital to use the same bats in both the original and later experiments.

B) Inaccurate perceptions caused by common sensory errors have a significant detrimental impact on physical movements and coordination.

C) Mathematical models designed to test average measurements should always avoid uniform or linearly decaying integrators.

D) Bats which fly under light conditions that differ significantly from 1 lux, either brighter or darker, will not likely demonstrate optimal gain parameters.

**44**

Which choice provides the best evidence for the answer to the previous question?

A) Lines 30–33 ("An exponentially . . . integrators")

B) Lines 37–38 ("An important . . . performance")

C) Lines 38–43 ("To test . . . task")

D) Lines 43–45 ("We found . . . dark")

**45**

It can be inferred from the passage that including a simple exponential integrator countered what inaccuracy in the described experiments?

A) It can replace information the bats lose when they fly.

B) It accounted for sub-optimal light conditions.

C) It combined sensory input data for more accurate predictions.

D) It increased errors due to sensory noise.

**46**

Which choice provides the best evidence for the answer to the previous question?

A) Line 1 ("Animal flight . . . control")

B) Lines 6–8 ("This simple . . . dark")

C) Lines 33–36 ("This simple . . . fidelity")

D) Lines 50–53 ("Taken together . . . limitations")

**47**

As used in line 36, "fidelity" most nearly means

A) an accurate reproduction of the significant details.

B) a consistent performance of lower quality.

C) a complete perfection in all areas.

D) a rough, approximate similarity.

**48**

The main purpose of the fourth paragraph (lines 27–36) is to

A) describe a theory and experimental verification regarding the method a bat uses to handle imperfect perception.

B) suggest a trial in which three to four measurements are taken of several vertebrates to assess noise reduction.

C) introduce the probable pitfalls of the earlier theory briefly summarized in the following paragraph (lines 37–49).

D) detail the resulting data of a test that supports the authors' claim involving the accuracy of uniform integrators as applied to bat trajectories.

**49**

The authors assume that highly curved flight trajectories

A) are atypical of the *Rousettus aegyptiacus*.

B) never straighten for any brief period of time.

C) were not replaced by significantly straighter trajectories by bats flying in bright light.

D) were caused by physical limitations of the bat.

**50**

Based on the data in the figure, what is the best description of whether simulated trajectories with noise and a noise-suppression strategy reached the target?

A) All of the many trajectories reached the target.

B) The single trajectory smoothly reached the target.

C) The single trajectory wobbled, but reached the target.

D) None of the many trajectories reached the target.

**51**

Based on the data in the figure, which of the following trajectories most nearly matched the original trajectory?

A) The simulated trajectory with no noise and no integration

B) The simulated trajectory with no noise and integration

C) The simulated trajectory with noise and integration

D) The simulated trajectory with noise and no integration

**52**

Is the claim made by the authors that bat flight trajectories under optimal light conditions are more direct supported by the information in the figure?

A) Yes, because the simulated trajectories most nearly like the original trajectory are some of the 30 of those trajectories that included both noise and integration.

B) Yes, because the simulations with and without integration demonstrate that sensory noise caused bats to develop a compensating factor.

C) No, because they do not provide comparative data regarding the flights under optimal light conditions.

D) No, because the simulations with and without integration fail to clarify whether noise was a causal factor.

## STOP

**If you finish before time is called, you may check your work on this section only.**
**Do not turn to any other section in the test.**

**No Test Material On This Page**

# Writing and Language Test

## 35 MINUTES, 44 QUESTIONS

**Turn to Section 2 of your answer sheet to answer the questions in this section.**

### DIRECTIONS

Each passage below is accompanied by a number of questions. For some questions, you will consider how the passage might be revised to improve the expression of ideas. For other questions, you will consider how the passage might be edited to correct errors in sentence structure, usage, or punctuation. A passage or a question may be accompanied by one or more graphics (such as a table or graph) that you will consider as you make revising and editing decisions.

Some questions will direct you to an underlined portion of a passage. Other questions will direct you to a location in a passage or ask you to think about the passage as a whole.

After reading each passage, choose the answer to each question that most effectively improves the quality of writing in the passage or that makes the passage conform to the conventions of standard written English. Many questions include a "NO CHANGE" option. Choose that option if you think the best choice is to leave the relevant portion of the passage as it is.

**Questions 1–11 are based on the following passage.**

**The Agents of the FDA**

When you go to the grocery store, **1** can't it be fun to go with your friends and family? Why do you trust the chicken that you buy from the grocery store more than the chicken you could buy off the back of some guy's truck? Beyond common sense, the answer is pretty simple: the Food and Drug Administration, or FDA. The **2** agency's beginnings came in 1906, when politicians and consumer

**1**

Which choice provides the most appropriate introduction to the passage?

A) NO CHANGE

B) which way do you take when you drive or walk?

C) how is it possible to buy only the things that you need?

D) how do you know what you're buying is safe?

**2**

A) NO CHANGE

B) agency's beginning's

C) agencies beginnings

D) agencies' beginnings'

CONTINUE

advocates began to realize how harmful unregulated food, cosmetics, and drugs could be. The FDA **3** for we know it today was formally created in 1930.

The FDA is everywhere in American culture. **4** In fact, the FDA regulates nearly $1 trillion worth of American consumer goods. This $1 trillion constitutes approximately 25% of all that is bought and sold in the United States. A large portion of this money is devoted to goods imported into the United States. The FDA operates on a budget of nearly $5 billion a year, much of which is generated by user fees, **5** which come primarily from pharmaceutical companies, whose drugs require FDA approval.

**3**
A) NO CHANGE
B) how
C) as
D) DELETE the underlined portion.

**4**
In context, which choice best combines the underlined sentences?
A) In fact, the FDA regulates nearly $1 trillion worth of American consumer goods, approximately 25% of all that is bought and sold in the United States.
B) The FDA, in fact, which regulates nearly $1 trillion worth of American consumer goods, moreover regulates what amounts to 25% of all that is bought and sold.
C) A quarter of all that is bought and sold in the United States, which amounts to $1 trillion dollars approximately, is approved in some way by the FDA.
D) The $1 trillion dollars of goods in the United States, the same goods that constitute 25% of United States trade, are regulated by the FDA.

**5**
A) NO CHANGE
B) thus coming
C) those come
D) they come

CONTINUE

6 Still, while many people are familiar with the FDA's warning labels and health warnings, few know who actually *works* there. After all, an "agency" requires some agents, and the FDA must be a huge operation with all the food and pharmaceutical drugs needed in a population of hundreds of millions. The FDA is certainly large: 7 you've almost certainly seen its approvals on some of the products you use.

While the largest group of FDA employees comprises consumer safety officers, the central work of the FDA is conducted by scientists. 8 Relying on scientists makes sense, since the science of acceptable food is something most of us never think about. But how is it possible to know whether a type of food is safe for general consumption?

A) NO CHANGE

B) Stunningly,

C) Therefore,

D) For safety's sake,

Which choice best supports the statement made in the first part of the sentence?

A) NO CHANGE

B) it has played a large role in reducing the amount of tobacco use in the United States.

C) Teddy and Franklin Roosevelt were proud of it, and you should be too.

D) it has over 200 offices in the United States and employs many thousands of people.

At this point, the writer is considering adding the following sentence.

> The FDA employs nearly 1,000 chemists, 500 biologists, 300 pharmacologists, 40 epidemiologists, and many, many more.

Should the writer make this addition here?

A) Yes, because it lists the employment statistics for the FDA last year.

B) Yes, because it gives some data that will be elaborated upon later in the paragraph.

C) No, because it interrupts the paragraph's discussion of consumer safety officers.

D) No, because it does not account for the non-scientists who work at the FDA.

**CONTINUE**

How can one possibly be confident that a packaged good on a supermarket shelf will be safe **9** with confidence? This can't be a matter of taste: it must be a matter of chemistry, **10** biology, and a matter of physics. The average consumer simply does not have the knowledge to be able to assess the quality of food. The same goes for drugs. Imagine you were taking five prescription drugs at once—if the pills got mixed up, what would you do?

In short, the FDA is omnipresent in American life, even if it is a bit hidden. The truly remarkable thing about the FDA, other than its high rates of success, **11** are being the collection of expertise it has amassed among its workforce. Perhaps no other government agency requires such an incredible amount of brainpower on the cutting edge of scientific thought.

**9**

A) NO CHANGE

B) certainly?

C) with sureness?

D) DELETE the underlined portion and end the sentence with a question mark.

**10**

A) NO CHANGE

B) biology, including some

C) biology, and

D) biological sciences, and

**11**

A) NO CHANGE

B) have had

C) is

D) are

CONTINUE

**Questions 12–22 are based on the following passage.**

**Drop the Puck!**

For anyone aspiring to play ice hockey professionally, the National Hockey League (NHL) represents the pinnacle of hockey greatness in North America, if not the world. But how did the NHL rise to these remarkable ranks?

The story begins with that elusive trophy: the Stanley Cup. In many ways, this goal is as old as the history of professional hockey **12** its self. It was commissioned in 1892 as the Dominion Hockey Challenge Cup and was given to Canada's top-ranking amateur team each year. The name was later changed to commemorate the contributions of then-Governor General of Canada, Lord Stanley of Preston, **13** who did a great deal to grow the sport in the country.

**12**

A) NO CHANGE
B) themselves
C) itself
D) himself

**13**

Which choice provides the most logical conclusion to the sentence?

A) NO CHANGE
B) who was born in London and educated at Eton and Sandhurst.
C) who served as Governor General under British Queen Victoria.
D) DELETE the underlined portion and end the sentence with a period after the word *Preston*.

One of the early contenders for this prize was the National Hockey Association (NHA). When the NHA folded in 1917, it was replaced by the NHL that same year. Despite the name change, the NHL followed from the NHA in just about every way. Just as the NHA had before, **14** also competing annually for the Stanley Cup. This competition came against a variety of other professional and amateur teams and leagues, most notably the Pacific Coast Hockey Association (PCHA), which had formalized its relations with the NHA in 1915. The Boston Bruins, established in **15** 1924; they began the NHL's expansion into the United States.

By 1926, however, all other competing leagues had folded or merged, and the only remaining league was the NHL. **16** While other leagues and teams have issued challenges for the Cup, no non-NHL team has played for the Cup since that time. The NHL's sole dominion over Lord Stanley's Cup also symbolized its **17** supremacy in the world of professional hockey.

**14**
A) NO CHANGE
B) so too did the NHL compete
C) so too competed
D) so too was competing

**15**
A) NO CHANGE
B) 1924,
C) 1924. They
D) 1924:

**16**
The writer is considering deleting the previous sentence. Should the writer make this change?
A) Yes, because it breaks with the logical flow of the previous paragraph.
B) Yes, because it provides a topic sentence that would be better placed elsewhere in the passage.
C) No, because it contains the central argument of the passage as a whole.
D) No, because it provides a logical introduction and relevant information for this paragraph.

**17**
Which choice best maintains the tone established in the passage?
A) NO CHANGE
B) awesomeness
C) formality
D) swagger

CONTINUE →

This high position was firmly cemented in the 1940s when the "Original Six" NHL franchises competed with one another each year. **18** There were two Canadian teams that were especially ascendant, even dominant, and many of the players from the era are still considered all-time greats. The league has only continued to expand. Six more teams were added during the first expansion of 1967. Today, the league has 30 teams. **19**

**18**

A) NO CHANGE

B) Ascendant, even dominant, were the Canadian teams especially,

C) Canadian teams were especially ascendant, even dominant,

D) Canadian teams especially were dominant,

**19**

Which choice most logically follows the previous sentence?

A) There are even plans to expand the league to 32, with teams in Las Vegas and Quebec City.

B) My personal favorite team is the Philadelphia Flyers, who were part of the 1967 expansion.

C) Many of the "Original Six" teams have won the Stanley Cup in recent years.

D) It can seem a little bit odd to have hockey teams in places with no natural ice, but that's the way it goes.

**CONTINUE**

Since the early days of professional [20] hockey, but other leagues have come and gone. There are other [21] leagues. These, however, are "minor leagues," where young players develop the skills necessary for NHL play, or where players spend whole careers waiting for their chance at the big leagues. Still, while the NHL, made up of players from all over the world, [22] hold the sway that it does, the short history given here provides the important reminder that leagues come and go. The only thing that remains, the only unadulterated constant, is the passion both men and women have for the game.

A) NO CHANGE

B) hockey,

C) hockey;

D) hockey:

The writer is considering revising the underlined portion of the sentence to read:

leagues, such as the AHL, OHL, and QMJHL.

Should the writer add this information here?

A) Yes, because it lays the groundwork for the shift in this paragraph's focus.

B) Yes, because it provides examples of some current leagues other than the NHL.

C) No, because it suggests that the NHL is not such an important league after all.

D) No, because it provides details that should be given earlier in the passage.

A) NO CHANGE

B) holds the sway that they do,

C) hold the sway that they do,

D) holds the sway that it does,

CONTINUE

**Questions 23–33 are based on the following passage and supplementary material.**

**Is Sitting the New Smoking?**

[1] Health scientists have a new warning: "Sitting is the new smoking." [2] However, excessive sitting and stillness, particularly when it is interruptedly sedentary, can have terrible consequences for health. [3] Indeed, now that many Americans have accepted the health risks of smoking and **23** puffed away from that deadly pastime, researchers worry that the sedentary lifestyle of many Americans may have replaced smoking as a national health risk. [4] This may sound odd because everyone has to sit at some point, whether at a job, in class, or in a car. **24**

**25** Nearly 20 studies conducted in about as many years have confirmed this grim conclusion, and these studies have covered over 800,000 people overall. While this number does not cover the entire population, it is safely representative as a sample. In one study, researchers found a 46 percent increase in deaths from any cause among people who sat for more than four hours a day while watching television, **26** which is as compared to people who sat for only two. Other studies found links between excessive sitting and obesity, diabetes, and heart problems.

**23**

A) NO CHANGE
B) run
C) fired
D) veered

**24**

To make this paragraph most logical, sentence 4 should be placed

A) where it is now.
B) at the beginning of the paragraph.
C) before sentence 2.
D) before sentence 3.

**25**

Which choice most effectively combines the underlined sentences?

A) 800,000 is safely representative of the entire population, and that's precisely the number that nearly twenty studies used to confirm the grim conclusion that was mentioned above.
B) 20 tests used 800,000 subjects over the course of twenty or so years to confirm the grim conclusion and did so with a representative sample that was safe.
C) Nearly 20 studies conducted in about as many years have confirmed this grim conclusion, and these studies have covered over 800,000 people overall, a safely representative sample.
D) 800,000 people were safe from the grim conclusion of representative samples, as they were the 20 experiments of people in their 20s.

**26**

A) NO CHANGE
B) having
C) this is
D) DELETE the underlined portion.

**CONTINUE**

The problem, it seems, is that the human body has not evolved for this kind of idleness. Consider our primate [27] ancestors for example, if they were not incredibly active at all times, they would not have survived. Even many humans throughout history had to live actively— not just as hunters, but as farmers or machinists. Now, as most white-collar jobs involve sitting at a desk, human bodies aren't sure what to do with all the free time. And there is a lot of it, with some estimates showing that the average American is upright and active [28] for only 8 hours of a day. This data shows that the sitting epidemic is not restricted to the workplace: [29] standing desks have become increasingly popular in the American workplace.

**How Sedentary is the Typical American Each Day?**

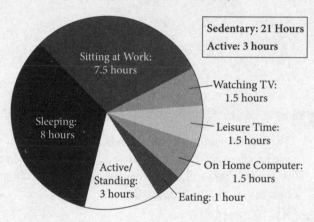

Sedentary: 21 Hours
Active: 3 hours

Sitting at Work: 7.5 hours
Watching TV: 1.5 hours
Sleeping: 8 hours
Leisure Time: 1.5 hours
On Home Computer: 1.5 hours
Active/ Standing: 3 hours
Eating: 1 hour

---

**27**

A) NO CHANGE
B) ancestors. For example,
C) ancestors, for example,
D) ancestors, for example:

**28**

Which choice offers an accurate interpretation of the data in the graph?

A) NO CHANGE
B) for only 3 hours of the 24-hour day.
C) for nearly one third of an average day.
D) for less than an hour a day.

**29**

Which choices offers an accurate interpretation of the data in the graph?

A) NO CHANGE
B) the sitting done at work accounts for more than half of all sitting on an average day.
C) the average American also eats far too much, sometimes for hours at a time.
D) less than half of all sitting during an average day is done at work.

**CONTINUE**

There may be a message of hope in this news, however. For one, this research suggests that much of the American obesity epidemic could be solved with a change in sitting habits rather than a change in eating habits. More walking (not to mention more running, biking, or other strenuous activity) can reduce weights significantly over time.

Also, the mantra that "sitting is the new smoking" may not apply to those 30 that, of all things, fidget. Researchers in the U.K. tracked the habits of nearly 13,000 women over the course of 12 years. In controlling for other factors, they found that the women who fidgeted—who moved their hands and feet in small, seemingly negligible ways—were less at risk for the perils of sitting than those who 31 sit perfectly still. The leader of the study, Janet Cade, says that fidgeting may not help with body-mass index, but it could improve metabolism.

Thus, while sitting is not likely to come with a warning label, we can see some of 32 their detrimental effects. We can also see, however, how easy those detrimental effects are to counteract. Perhaps you can't avoid sitting down on the job, but you can do yourself all kinds of favors by standing up, stretching out, or tapping your toes. 33 You don't have to take this national health threat sitting down.

30
A) NO CHANGE
B) who
C) we
D) which

31
A) NO CHANGE
B) went
C) are
D) sat

32
A) NO CHANGE
B) its
C) it's
D) they're

33

The writers wants a conclusion that acknowledges the problem of sitting but also encourages the reader to use this research in a proactive way. Which choice best accomplishes this goal?

A) NO CHANGE

B) You should also really go to the gym once in a while.

C) You might consider applying for a job that allows you to go outside sometimes.

D) There's not all that much you can do, frankly.

CONTINUE

**Questions 34–44 are based on the following passage.**

**It's So Rustic It's Chic**

For many people, "fashion"—the latest lines of shoes, suits, dresses, or **34** furniture; refers to new things. Increasingly, however, the new things are considered *less* fashionable than the old ones. Granted, "retro" has been popular for a long time, as people have sported the clothes and **35** furnished their homes with the knick-knacks of yesteryear. The newest style of all is both newer and older than mere "retro." This new style, rustic chic, rooted in the various attempts by the stylish to glorify old things, **36** seeks to take its proponents back even further to… well, no one's quite sure.

**34**

A) NO CHANGE
B) furniture
C) furniture,
D) furniture—

**35**

A) NO CHANGE
B) have furnished
C) furnish
D) furnishing

**36**

A) NO CHANGE
B) has sought
C) seek
D) seeking

**CONTINUE**

Poking fun at this trend, the creators of a popular comedy **37** show IFC's *Portlandia*, changed their early theme song "The Dream of the '90s is Alive in Portland." Back-dropped by men riding nineteenth-century bicycles, chipping their own ice, curing their own meats, and coiffing their handlebar **38** mustaches; these parts of the song jokes that the dream of the 1890s is alive in Portland. In fact, this joke is rooted in reality. Go into many coffee shops, restaurants, clothing stores, and furniture stores, and **39** the results may surprise you; salvaged furniture repainted in such a way that its age shows, handmade goods from artisans and craftspeople, and facial-hair configurations last seen on William Howard Taft.

This concept of rustic chic may seem a little odd. First, there's the question of economics. **40** Why, for instance, would anyone want to pay good money for a piece of furniture that is not only out of style but shows its signs of age? Or why would someone want to pay *more* money for something that is worn and broken than for something that is new?

**37**

A) NO CHANGE
B) show, IFC's *Portlandia*,
C) show, IFC's, *Portlandia*
D) show, IFC's, *Portlandia*,

**38**

A) NO CHANGE
B) mustaches, the song
C) mustaches. These parts of the song
D) mustaches. The song

**39**

Which choice most effectively sets up the examples that follow?
A) NO CHANGE
B) you'll notice something peculiar:
C) you'll see the look of yesteryear:
D) everything will be curiously expensive;

**40**

At this point, the writer is considering adding the following sentence.

> The effect of rustic chic on the American gross domestic product is yet to be determined.

Should the writer make this addition here?
A) Yes, because it adds a note of economic seriousness to the passage.
B) Yes, because the passage goes on to describe the global economy.
C) No, because it is not relevant to the main focus of the passage.
D) No, because it contradicts information given in the following paragraph.

**CONTINUE**

Moreover, rustic chic is difficult to understand because it does not have a clear **41** interest. At least we know that hippies are trying to dress like people from the 1960s and flappers are trying to dress like people from the 1920s. How about people who are interested in the rustic chic aesthetic? When people plan barn weddings, they do so because they want to get married like "they" did. **42** Why do you think people are getting married later now?

[1] These questions may be unanswerable, but that does not mean that we cannot speculate as to why rustic chic has become such a popular style. [2] Wear the clothes that men and women did *before* the existence of the fashion industry. [3] The simple answer would seem to be this: people want authenticity, so they want to free themselves of all the things that would seem to have created our contemporary, inauthentic world. [4] Have corporations ruined everything? [5] Buy from individual sellers and farmers. [6] Has the fashion industry ruined everything? **43**

In a culture wherein advertisements tell us every day to be ourselves, many have found that command to be restricting rather than liberating. Truly being yourself is the work of a lifetime. Even so, rustic chic provides one way to **44** prevent the capitalist system from turning us all into drones, though depending on whose side you're on, you might just think of it as more clutter.

**41**

A) NO CHANGE
B) choice.
C) fashion.
D) referent.

**42**

The writer wants to link this paragraph with the ideas that follow. Which choices best accomplishes this goal?

A) NO CHANGE
B) But who are "they"?
C) As it was famously said, "There's no accounting for the public's taste."
D) It's one thing to have a beard, but who actually likes mustaches?

**43**

To make this paragraph most logical, sentence 2 should be placed

A) where it is now.
B) after sentence 4.
C) after sentence 5.
D) after sentence 6.

**44**

A) NO CHANGE
B) reduce some of the clutter of contemporary life,
C) halt the military-industrial complex of today,
D) go off the grid and live a pure life,

# STOP

**If you finish before time is called, you may check your work on this section only.**
**Do not turn to any other section in the test.**

# Math Test – No Calculator

## 25 MINUTES, 20 QUESTIONS

Turn to Section 3 of your answer sheet to answer the questions in this section.

---

### DIRECTIONS

**For questions 1–15**, solve each problem, choose the best answer from the choices provided, and fill in the corresponding circle on your answer sheet. **For questions 16–20**, solve the problem and enter your answer in the grid on the answer sheet. Please refer to the directions before question 16 on how to enter your answers in the grid. You may use any available space in your test booklet for scratch work.

### NOTES

1. The use of a calculator **is not permitted**.
2. All variables and expressions used represent real numbers unless otherwise indicated.
3. Figures provided in this test are drawn to scale unless otherwise indicated.
4. All figures lie in a plane unless otherwise indicated.
5. Unless otherwise indicated, the domain of a given function $f$ is the set of all real numbers $x$ for which $f(x)$ is a real number.

### REFERENCE

$A = \pi r^2$
$C = 2\pi r$

$A = \ell w$

$A = \frac{1}{2} bh$

$c^2 = a^2 + b^2$

Special Right Triangles

$V = \ell wh$

$V = \pi r^2 h$

$V = \frac{4}{3} \pi r^3$

$V = \frac{1}{3} \pi r^2 h$

$V = \frac{1}{3}\ell wh$

The number of degrees of arc in a circle is 360.
The number of radians of arc in a circle is $2\pi$.
The sum of the measures in degrees of the angles of a triangle is 180.

---

**CONTINUE**

**1**

If $4s = 28$, what is the value of $8s + 13$ ?

A) 7

B) 56

C) 69

D) 84

**2**

Which of the following is equal to $b^{\frac{3}{4}}$, for all values of $b$ ?

A) $\sqrt[4]{b^3}$

B) $\sqrt[4]{b^{\frac{1}{3}}}$

C) $\sqrt[4]{b^{\frac{1}{4}}}$

D) $\sqrt[4]{b^4}$

**3**

A landscaper will sod $p$ plots of land with the same dimensions with a particular type of grass. The landscaper charges based on the equation $Cost = pGlw$, where $p$ is the number of plots, $G$ is a constant in dollars per square meter, $l$ is the length of a plot in meters, and $w$ is the width of a plot in meters. If the customers asks the landscaper to use a cheaper type of grass for sodding, the value of which of the following would change?

A) $p$

B) $G$

C) $l$

D) $w$

**4**

$$3x + 2y = -21$$
$$5x + 6y = -35$$

If $(x, y)$ is a solution to the system of equations above, what is $x + y$ ?

A) −14

B) −7

C) 14

D) 56

**CONTINUE**

**5**

The number of countries that were members of the European Union in 2008 was three times the number of countries in the European Union (then called the European Communities) in 1974. If the European Union had 27 members in 2008 and $m$ members in 1974, which of the following equations is true?

A) $m + 27 = 3$

B) $\dfrac{m}{3} = 27$

C) $3m = 27$

D) $27m = 3$

**6**

If $\dfrac{7}{y} = \dfrac{17}{y + 30}$, what is the value of $\dfrac{y}{7}$ ?

A) $\dfrac{1}{3}$

B) $3$

C) $7$

D) $21$

**7**

$$cx - 6y = 8$$
$$3x - 7y = 5$$

In the system of equations shown above, $c$ is a constant and $x$ and $y$ are variables. For what value of $c$ will the system of equations have no solution?

A) $\dfrac{24}{5}$

B) $\dfrac{18}{7}$

C) $-\dfrac{18}{7}$

D) $-\dfrac{24}{5}$

**8**

| $x$ | $g(x)$ |
|-----|--------|
| 0   | 2      |
| 1   | 5      |
| 3   | -1     |
| 7   | 0      |

The function $g$ is defined by a polynomial. Some of the values of $x$ and $g(x)$ are shown in the table above. Which of the following must be a factor of $g(x)$ ?

A) $x - 1$

B) $x - 2$

C) $x - 3$

D) $x - 7$

**CONTINUE**

**9**

The line $y = cx + 6$, where $c$ is constant, is graphed in the $xy$-plane. If the point $(r, s)$ lies on the line, where $r \neq 0$ and $s \neq 0$, which is the slope of the line, in terms of $r$ and $s$ ?

A) $\dfrac{r - 6}{s}$

B) $\dfrac{6 - s}{r}$

C) $\dfrac{6 - r}{s}$

D) $\dfrac{s - 6}{r}$

**10**

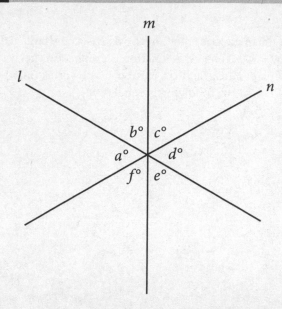

Note: Figure not drawn to scale.

In the figure above, lines $l$, $m$, and $n$ intersect at a single point. If $a + b = c + d$, which of the following must be true?

I.   $b = c$

II.  $e = f$

III. $a = e$

A) I and II only

B) II and III only

C) I and III only

D) I, II, and III

**CONTINUE** ➡

**11**

$$y = k(x - 4)(x + 12)$$

In the quadratic equation above, $k$ is a constant such that $k \neq 0$. When the equation is graphed in the $xy$-plane, the graph is a parabola with vertex $(m, n)$. Which of the following is equal to $n$?

A) $-24k$

B) $-36k$

C) $-48k$

D) $-64k$

**12**

In the $xy$-plane, a parabola defined by the equation $y = (x - 8)^2$ intersects the line defined by the equation $y = 36$ at two points, $P$ and $Q$. What is the length of $\overline{PQ}$?

A)  8

B)  10

C)  12

D)  14

**13**

$$F(C) = \frac{9}{5}C + 32$$

The function above describes the relationship between temperatures measured in degrees Fahrenheit, $F$, and in degrees Celsius, $C$. Based on the function, which of the following must be true?

I.   A temperature decrease of 1.8 degrees Celsius is equivalent to a temperature decrease of 1 degree Fahrenheit.

II.  A temperature decrease of 1 degree Celsius is equivalent to a temperature decrease of $\frac{9}{5}$ degrees Fahrenheit.

III. A temperature decrease of $\frac{5}{9}$ degrees Fahrenheit is equivalent to a temperature decrease of 1 degree Celsius.

A)  I only

B)  II only

C)  II and III only

D)  I, II, and III

CONTINUE

14

$$\frac{80x^2 + 84x - 13}{kx - 4} = -16x - 4 - \frac{29}{kx - 4}$$

The equation above is true for all values of $x = \dfrac{4}{k}$, where $k$ is a constant. What is the value of $k$ ?

A) −5

B) −2

C) 2

D) 5

15

What are the solutions to $5x^2 + 30x + 15 = 0$ ?

A) $x = -2 \pm 2\sqrt{6}$

B) $x = -2 \pm \sqrt{6}$

C) $x = -3 \pm \dfrac{\sqrt{60}}{10}$

D) $x = -3 \pm \sqrt{6}$

**CONTINUE**

## DIRECTIONS

**For questions 16–20,** solve the problem and enter your answer in the grid, as described below, on the answer sheet.

1.  Although not required, it is suggested that you write your answer in the boxes at the top of the columns to help you fill in the circles accurately. You will receive credit only if the circles are filled in correctly.

2.  Mark no more than one circle in any column.

3.  No question has a negative answer.

4.  Some problems may have more than one correct answer. In such cases, grid only one answer.

5.  **Mixed numbers** such as $3\frac{1}{2}$ must be gridded as 3.5 or 7/2. (If $\boxed{3\ 1\ /\ 2}$ is entered into the grid, it will be interpreted as $\frac{31}{2}$, not as $3\frac{1}{2}$.)

6.  **Decimal Answers:** If you obtain a decimal answer with more digits than the grid can accommodate, it may be either rounded or truncated, but it must fill the entire grid.

Answer: $\frac{7}{12}$    Answer: 2.5

Write answer in boxes. → Fraction line

Grid in result.

Decimal point

Acceptable ways to grid $\frac{2}{3}$ are:

Answer: 201 – either position is correct

**NOTE:** You may start your answers in any column, space permitting. Columns you don't need to use should be left blank.

CONTINUE ▶

**16**

If $\dfrac{21}{25}z - \dfrac{16}{25}z = \dfrac{1}{2} + \dfrac{3}{10}$, what is the value of $z$ ?

**17**

$$y^3(y^2 - 10) = -9y$$

If $y > 0$, what is one possible solution to the equation above?

**18**

At a music school, each long session lasts twenty minutes longer than each short session. If 3 long sessions and 4 short sessions last a total of 270 minutes, how many minutes does a long session last?

**19**

In triangle $UVW$, the measure of $\angle U$ is $90°$, $WV = 39$, and $UV = 36$. Triangle $XYZ$ is similar to triangle $UVW$, where $\angle X$, $\angle Y$, and $\angle Z$ correspond to $\angle U$, $\angle V$, and $\angle W$, respectively. If each side of triangle $XYZ$ is $\dfrac{3}{5}$ the length of its corresponding side of triangle $UVW$, what is the value of $\cos Z$ ?

**CONTINUE**

20

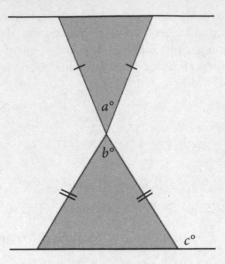

Note: Figure not drawn to scale.

Two isosceles triangles are shown above. If $b = 180 - 4a$ and $a = 35$, what is the value of $c$?

## STOP

**If you finish before time is called, you may check your work on this section only.**
**Do not turn to any other section in the test.**

**No Test Material On This Page**

# Math Test – Calculator

## 55 MINUTES, 38 QUESTIONS

**Turn to Section 4 of your answer sheet to answer the questions in this section.**

---

### DIRECTIONS

**For questions 1–30,** solve each problem, choose the best answer from the choices provided, and fill in the corresponding circle on your answer sheet. **For questions 31–38,** solve the problem and enter your answer in the grid on the answer sheet. Please refer to the directions before question 31 on how to enter your answers in the grid. You may use any available space in your test booklet for scratch work.

### NOTES

1.  The use of a calculator **is permitted**.
2.  All variables and expressions used represent real numbers unless otherwise indicated.
3.  Figures provided in this test are drawn to scale unless otherwise indicated.
4.  All figures lie in a plane unless otherwise indicated.
5.  Unless otherwise indicated, the domain of a given function $f$ is the set of all real numbers $x$ for which $f(x)$ is a real number.

### REFERENCE

$A = \pi r^2$
$C = 2\pi r$

$A = \ell w$

$A = \frac{1}{2} bh$

$c^2 = a^2 + b^2$

Special Right Triangles

$V = \ell wh$

$V = \pi r^2 h$

$V = \frac{4}{3}\pi r^3$

$V = \frac{1}{3}\pi r^2 h$

$V = \frac{1}{3}\ell wh$

The number of degrees of arc in a circle is 360.
The number of radians of arc in a circle is $2\pi$.
The sum of the measures in degrees of the angles of a triangle is 180.

**CONTINUE**

1

| | Eye color | | Total |
|---|---|---|---|
| Species | Yellow | Brown | |
| Grey wolf | 16 | 2 | 18 |
| Coyote | 7 | 5 | 12 |
| Total | 23 | 7 | 30 |

The table above shows the distribution by species and eye color for the 30 canids living in a nature conservancy. If one canid is selected at random, what is the probability that it will be either a grey wolf with yellow eyes or a coyote with brown eyes?

A) $\frac{11}{30}$

B) $\frac{17}{30}$

C) $\frac{21}{30}$

D) $\frac{23}{30}$

2

The graph below shows U.S. military spending, in billions of dollars, each year from 1992 through 2006.

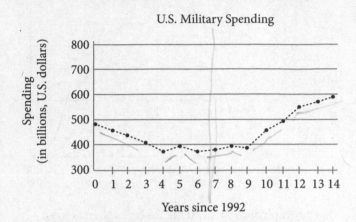

U.S. Military Spending

Years since 1992

Based on the graph, which of the following best describes the overall trend in U.S. military spending from 1992 through 2006 ?

A) Spending generally decreased in every year since 1992.

B) Spending generally increased in every year since 1992.

C) Spending generally remained constant in every year from 1992 through 2006.

D) Spending decreased until 1996 and increased after 2001.

CONTINUE

**3**

Eddie's Bike Ride

The graph above represents Eddie's distance from home during a 4-hour bike ride. He stopped for 40 minutes during his bike ride to repair a flat tire. According to the graph, which of the following is nearest to the time he finished repairing his flat tire and continued on his ride?

A)   11:10 A.M.

B)   11:50 A.M.

C)   12:10 P.M.

D)   12:50 P.M.

**4**

At the Acme automobile factory, approximately 4 percent of male employees and 6 percent of female employees received performance bonuses last month. If there were 648 male employees and 519 female employees at the Acme automobile factory last month, which of the following is closest to the total number of male and female employees at the Acme automobile factory who received performance bonuses last month?

A)   26

B)   31

C)   57

D)   113

**5**

What is the sum of the polynomials $4x^2 + 3x - 2$ and $2x^2 - 8x + 9$ ?

A)   $6x^2 - 5x - 7$

B)   $6x^2 - 5x + 7$

C)   $6x^4 - 5x - 7$

D)   $6x^4 - 5x + 7$

**CONTINUE**

**6**

| $k$ | 1 | 2 | 3 | 4 | 5 |
|-----|-----|-----|-----|-----|-----|
| $g(k)$ | –3 | 1 | 5 | 9 | 13 |

The table above shows selected values of the linear function $g$. Which of the following best defines $g$ ?

A)  $g(k) = k - 1$

B)  $g(k) = 2k - 4$

C)  $g(k) = 3k - 5$

D)  $g(k) = 4k - 7$

**7**

The total annual rainfall, in inches, in Brown County from 2005 to 2015 can be modeled by the equation $y = -0.14x + 7.8$, where $x$ is the number of years since 2005 and $y$ is the total annual rainfall. Which of the following best describes the meaning of the number $-0.14$ in the equation?

A)  The total annual rainfall in 2005

B)  The total annual rainfall in 2015

C)  The estimated difference between the total rainfall in 2005 and the total rainfall in 2015

D)  The estimated decrease in the average rainfall per year from 2005 to 2015

**8**

An insect crawls 30 inches in 16.3 minutes. If the insect continues to crawl at the same rate, approximately how many inches will it crawl in 6 hours?

A)  200

B)  300

C)  650

D)  960

CONTINUE

---

**9**

$$\frac{8}{5}v = \frac{7}{4}$$

In the equation above, what is the value of $v$ ?

A) $\dfrac{56}{20}$

B) $\dfrac{35}{32}$

C) $\dfrac{32}{35}$

D) $\dfrac{20}{56}$

---

**10**

The function $g$ has four distinct zeros. Which of the following could be the complete graph of $g$ in the $xy$-plane?

A)

B)

C)

D)

**CONTINUE**

**Questions 11 and 12 refer to the following information.**

| Substance | Specific heat capacity $\left(\dfrac{J}{g}\right)$ |
|-----------|:--:|
| Aluminum | 0.90 |
| Copper | 0.39 |
| Glass | 0.67 |
| Gold | 0.13 |
| Olive oil | 1.79 |
| Porcelain | 1.08 |
| Rubber | 1.25 |
| Water | 4.18 |

The chart above gives approximations for the specific heat capacity, in joules per gram $\left(\dfrac{J}{g}\right)$, for eight common substances. The heat energy required to raise the temperature of a substance by 1° Celsius can be represented by the expression $Q = mC$, where $Q$ is heat energy measured in joules (J), $m$ is the mass of the substance measured in grams (g), and $C$ is the specific heat capacity measured in $\dfrac{J}{g}$.

**11**

A piece of copper has a mass of 75 grams. How much heat energy, in joules, is needed to raise the temperature of the piece of copper by 1° Celsius?

A)  29.25

B)  50.25

C)  111.95

D)  192.30

**12**

A piece of porcelain requires 80 joules of heat energy to raise its temperature by 1° Celsius. If a piece of another substance with the same mass requires approximately 67 joules of heat energy to raise its temperature by 1° Celsius, the piece could be composed of which substance?

A)  Aluminum

B)  Glass

C)  Olive oil

D)  Rubber

**CONTINUE**

**13**

A medical study was conducted in order to determine whether product *K* could help people with hearing loss improve their hearing. The administrators of the study selected 200 subjects at random from a large group of people who had severe hearing loss. Half of the subjects were randomly assigned to be given product *K* and half were not. The resulting data demonstrated that subjects who were given product *K* had significantly improved hearing compared to those who were not given product *K*. Based on this study, which of the following conclusions is most appropriate?

A) Product *K* will enable all people who take it to significantly improve their hearing.

B) Product *K* is more effective than all other hearing-improvement products.

C) Product *K* will help people significantly improve their hearing.

D) Product *K* is likely to help people with severe hearing loss improve their hearing.

**14**

A car accelerates for *t* seconds at a constant rate of *a* meters per second squared $\left(\dfrac{m}{s^2}\right)$ until it reaches a velocity of *v* meters per second. The distance in meters the car travels is given by $d = vt - \dfrac{1}{2}at^2$. Which of the following gives *a* in terms of *v*, *d*, and *t* ?

A) $a = 2\left(v - \dfrac{d}{t}\right)$

B) $a = 2\left(v + \dfrac{d}{t}\right)$

C) $a = 2\left(\dfrac{v}{t} - \dfrac{d}{t^2}\right)$

D) $a = 2\left(\dfrac{v}{t} + \dfrac{d}{t^2}\right)$

**15**

A certain type of ribbon costs \$0.15 per inch. Which of the equations below gives the total price, *p*, in dollars, for *y* yards of ribbon? (1 yard = 36 inches)

A) $p = 0.15y + 36$

B) $p = 0.15(36y)$

C) $p = \dfrac{0.15y}{36}$

D) $p = \dfrac{36y}{0.15}$

**CONTINUE**

**Questions 16 and 17 refer to the following information.**

$$C(q) = 60q + 300$$

$$R(q) = 75q$$

The cost of producing a product and the revenue earned from selling a product are functions of the number of units sold. The functions shown above are the estimated cost and revenue functions for a certain product. The function $C(q)$ gives the total cost, in dollars, of producing a quantity of $q$ units of the product, and the function $R(q)$ gives the total revenue, in dollars, earned from selling a quantity of $q$ units of the product.

**16**

How will the total cost of producing $q$ units change if the quantity is decreased by 20 units?

A) The total cost will decrease by $1,200.

B) The total cost will decrease by $320.

C) The total cost will decrease by $20.

D) The total cost will increase by $1,200.

**17**

At what quantity will the cost of producing $q$ units equal the revenue earned from selling $q$ units?

A) 2

B) 15

C) 20

D) 45

**18**

The figure above shows the graphs of the functions $f$ and $g$ in the $xy$-plane. For which of the following values of $x$ is it true that $f(x) + g(x) = 1$ ?

A) −5

B) −4

C) −3

D) −2

**19**

Of the four types of depreciation shown below, which one would yield exponential decay in the value of an item?

A) The item loses 5% of its initial value in each successive year.

B) The item loses 6% of its current value in each successive year.

C) The value of the item decreases by $50 in each successive year.

D) The value of the item decreases by $60 in each successive year.

**CONTINUE**

**20**

A recipe for making lemonade states that one ounce of sugar is sufficient to make 30 imperial pints of lemonade. If an imperial pint is equivalent to $1\frac{1}{4}$ U.S. pints, approximately how many U.S. pints of lemonade can be made with 17 ounces of sugar?

A)    515

B)    640

C)  1,015

D)  1,280

**21**

Horizontal Distance versus Vertical Distance

Horizontal distance (inches)

For a physics experiment, Hussain made 18 long jumps, and his classmates recorded the results. The scatterplot above shows both the vertical and horizontal distance of each jump. A line of best fit for the data is also shown. For the jump with a horizontal distance of 230 inches, the vertical distance was approximately how many inches more than the distance predicted by the line of best fit?

A)  1.5

B)  3

C)  4.5

D)  6

**CONTINUE**

**22**

Mrs. Warren has *b* boxes of Girl Scout cookies that she wants to distribute to the members of her troop. If she gives each girl 4 boxes, she will have 11 boxes left over. If she wanted to give each student 5 boxes, she would need an additional 12 boxes. How many girls are in Mrs. Warren's Girl Scout troop?

A) 12

B) 23

C) 27

D) 32

**23**

When three numbers are added together, the result is 665. The largest number is one-third more than the sum of the other two numbers. What is the value of the largest number?

A) 95

B) 245

C) 350

D) 380

**24**

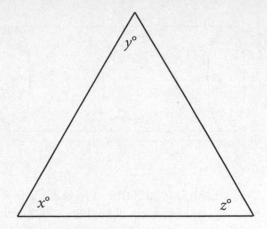

Note: Figure not drawn to scale.

In the triangle shown above, $\cos(x°) = \sin(z°)$. If $x = 3j - 19$ and $z = 5j - 15$, what is the value of $j$ ?

A) 8.5

B) 15.5

C) 34.5

D) 51.5

**25**

The length of a rectangle is decreased by 25 percent, and the width of the rectangle is increased by *k* percent. If the area of the rectangle increases by 5 percent, what is the value of *k* ?

A) 25

B) 30

C) 35

D) 40

**CONTINUE**

**26**

3 ft.

12 ft.

A space capsule is built from a right circular cylinder and two halves of a sphere with internal measurements as shown in the figure above. Which of the following is closest to the volume, in cubic feet, of the capsule?

A) 339.9

B) 396.3

C) 452.4

D) 565.6

**27**

The graph of line $\ell$ in the $xy$-plane passes through the origin and the points $(p, 4)$ and $(9, p)$. Which of the following is a possible value for $p$ ?

A) −6

B) −3

C) 0

D) 12

**28**

| | Decaffeinated | Caffeinated |
|---|---|---|
| Tea | | |
| Coffee | | |
| Total | 28 | 116 |

The partially completed table above shows all the drinks that were sold on one day at a coffee shop. The shop sold 3 times as many cups of caffeinated tea as it did decaffeinated tea, and it sold 5 times as many cups of caffeinated coffee as it did decaffeinated coffee. If 28 cups of decaffeinated beverages and 116 cups of caffeinated beverages were sold, and one cup is selected at random out of all the caffeinated beverages that were sold, which of the following is closest to the probability that this cup contains coffee?

A) 0.508

B) 0.583

C) 0.672

D) 0.690

**CONTINUE**

**29**

$$4x + j = 7x - 9$$
$$4y + k = 7y - 9$$

In the system of equations shown above, $j$ and $k$ are constants, and $j$ is $k$ plus $\dfrac{3}{2}$. Which of the following must be true?

A) $x$ is $y$ minus $\dfrac{1}{2}$

B) $x$ is $y$ plus $\dfrac{1}{2}$

C) $x$ is $y$ minus $\dfrac{3}{2}$

D) $x$ is $y$ plus $\dfrac{9}{2}$

**30**

Banerji currently owns 6,500 baseball cards. He is gradually selling his collection and estimates that the number of cards he owns will decrease by 20 percent every 6 months. Which of the following expressions best models Banerji's estimate of the number of baseball cards he will own $m$ months from now?

A) $6,500(0.2)^{\frac{m}{6}}$

B) $6,500(0.2)^{6m}$

C) $6,500(0.8)^{\frac{m}{6}}$

D) $6,500(0.8)^{6m}$

**CONTINUE**

## DIRECTIONS

**For questions 31–38,** solve the problem and enter your answer in the grid, as described below, on the answer sheet.

1. Although not required, it is suggested that you write your answer in the boxes at the top of the columns to help you fill in the circles accurately. You will receive credit only if the circles are filled in correctly.

2. Mark no more than one circle in any column.

3. No question has a negative answer.

4. Some problems may have more than one correct answer. In such cases, grid only one answer.

5. **Mixed numbers** such as $3\frac{1}{2}$ must be gridded as 3.5 or 7/2. (If $\boxed{3\,|\,1\,/\,2}$ is entered into the grid, it will be interpreted as $\frac{31}{2}$, not as $3\frac{1}{2}$.)

6. **Decimal Answers:** If you obtain a decimal answer with more digits than the grid can accommodate, it may be either rounded or truncated, but it must fill the entire grid.

Answer: $\frac{7}{12}$

Write answer in boxes. ← Fraction line

Grid in result.

Answer: 2.5 ← Decimal point

Acceptable ways to grid $\frac{2}{3}$ are:

Answer: 201 – either position is correct

**NOTE:** You may start your answers in any column, space permitting. Columns you don't need to use should be left blank.

CONTINUE →

**31**

If the expression $(6x^2 - 7x + 5) - 3(x^2 - 5x + 4)$ is written in the form $ax^2 + bx + c$, what is the value of $a$ ?

**32**

At a grocery store, potatoes are $0.30 each, and onions are $0.50 each. If Emeril plans to spend at least $2.00 but no more than $2.50 on $p$ potatoes and 1 onion, what is one possible value for $p$ ?

**33**

Height of 12 Infants in Mrs. Graham's Daycare Program

| Student | Height | Student | Height |
|---------|--------|---------|--------|
| Angela | 25 | Letitia | 22 |
| Benjamin | 22 | Moishe | 26 |
| Charles | 23 | Nancy | 30 |
| Denise | 27 | Sasha | 21 |
| Elaine | 24 | Tormund | 27 |
| Johanna | 30 | Walter | 25 |

The table above shows the heights, in inches, of 12 infants between the ages of 3 months and 6 months. According to the table, what is the mean height, in inches, of these infants? (Round your answer to the nearest tenth.)

**34**

In a certain course, students take 8 exams that are graded on a scale from 0 to 100, inclusive. Jacob received an average score of 65 on his first 4 exams. What is the lowest score he can receive on his 5th exam and still be able to score an average of 75 for all 8 exams?

**CONTINUE**

**35**

$$y \leq 20x + 3{,}500$$
$$y \leq -8x$$

The graph in the *xy*-plane of the solution set of the system of inequalities above contains the point $(j, k)$. What is the greatest possible value of $k$ ?

**36**

In the circle centered at $P$, the measure of central angle $QPR$ is $\dfrac{7\pi}{6}$ radians. The length of the arc defined by central angle $QPR$ is what fraction of the circumference of the circle?

**Questions 37 and 38 refer to the following information.**

According to a well-known statistics theorem, if patients enter a medical clinic at a rate of $m$ patients per minute and each stays at the clinic an average of $W$ minutes, the average number of patients, $L$, in the clinic at any point in time is given by $L = mW$.

The manager of the Kind Care clinic estimates that when the clinic is open, an average of 4 patients per minute enter the clinic and that on average, each of them stays 45 minutes. The manager uses the above theorem to estimate that at any point in time, there are 180 patients in the clinic.

**37**

A rival clinic, the Speedy Care clinic, recently opened across the street. The manager of this clinic estimates that, when the clinic is open, an average of 324 patients per <u>hour</u> enter the clinic and that, on average, each of them stays 40 minutes. The average number of patients in the Speedy Care clinic at any point in time is what percent greater than the average number of patients in the Kind Care clinic at any point in time? (Note: Disregard the percent sign when gridding in your answer. For example, if your answer is 38.4%, enter 38.4)

**CONTINUE**

**38**

The theorem above may be applied to any part of the clinic, such as the waiting room or a particular office. The manager observes that, when the clinic is open, approximately 36 patients per hour are being treated by a doctor, and that each of these patients spends an average of 15 minutes with his or her doctor. At any time when the clinic is open, approximately how many patients, on average, are being treated by a doctor at the Kind Care clinic?

▲

# STOP
**If you finish before time is called, you may check your work on this section only.**
**Do not turn to any other section in the test.**

# SAT Essay

## DIRECTIONS

The essay gives you an opportunity to show how effectively you can read and comprehend a passage and write an essay analyzing the passage. In your essay you should demonstrate that you have read the passage carefully, present a clear and logical analysis, and use language precisely.

Your essay must be written on the lines provided in your answer sheet booklet; except for the planning page of the answer booklet, you will receive no other paper on which to write. You will have enough space if you write on every line, avoid wide margins, and keep your handwriting to a reasonable size. Remember that people who are not familiar with your handwriting will read what you write. Try to write or print so that what you are writing is legible to those readers.

**You have <u>50 minutes</u> to read the passage and write an essay in response to the prompt provided inside this booklet.**

## REMINDER

— Do not write your essay in this booklet. Only what you write on the lined pages of your answer booklet will be evaluated.

— An off-topic essay will not be evaluated.

**CONTINUE** →

As you read the passage below, consider how Stiffler and Dubrow use

- evidence, such as facts or examples, to support claims.
- reasoning to develop ideas and to connect claims and evidence.
- stylistic or persuasive elements, such as word choice or appeals to emotion, to add power to the ideas expressed.

Excerpted from Lisa Stiffler and Aaron Dubrow, "Benefits and Risks of the 'Internet of Things'." © 2015 by National Science Foundation. Originally posted online on October 23, 2015.

1    Technology publications call 2015 "the year of the car hack."

2    This summer at DEF CON—one of the world's largest computer-hacker conferences— attendees tested the vulnerability of car computer systems at the first "Car Hacking Village." Members of Congress recently introduced the SPY Car Act, aimed at strengthening security in modern cars.

3    In other words, the rest of the world is catching up to the University of Washington's (UW) Security and Privacy Research Lab. Four years ago, with support from the National Science Foundation (NSF), the lab in the UW's Department of Computer Science & Engineering co-led an effort that first exposed weaknesses in car computer systems and demonstrated that hackers could remotely control a vehicle's brakes, door locks and other functions.

4    "We like to look in the places that no one else is looking yet," said computer science and engineering associate professor Yoshi Kohno, who founded the security lab. "You open that area up, and once people start to show up, you move on to the next thing."

5    That trailblazing strategy has put the lab, which Kohno runs jointly with assistant professor Franziska Roesner, at the forefront of computer security and privacy. The UW engineers are international leaders in addressing problems others haven't considered and helping guide the direction of the entire field. Their findings have driven security improvements in cars, medical devices, electronic voting machines and online browsing.

6    The lab's work is increasingly influential as computers are installed in countless everyday devices, making users' lives better and easier, but also putting them at risk for identity theft and even physical harm. This year alone, more than 530 security breaches have compromised more than 140 million records kept by credit card and insurance companies, hospitals, government agencies and others.

7    To combat these and other cyber threats, Kohno and Roesner investigate ways that people can co-opt a computerized product or use online information, warping it into something never intended. Take the car example: The UW researchers, in partnership with alumni Alexei Czeskis and Karl Koscher and computer scientists from the University of California

**CONTINUE**

at San Diego, were curious about the security of modern vehicles and their computerized systems. So the teams at each university bought cars and plugged their computers into the vehicles' computers to see if they could decode, and ultimately hijack, the cars' software. They did it by listening as the computer systems talked to each other.

8   "If I go to a foreign country and try to learn the language, one of the best ways to do this is to eavesdrop," Kohno said. Then, he said, you "try to repeat things, and see if you get the same reaction."

9   Once the engineers figured out how to talk to the cars' computers and manipulate their functions while plugged in, they moved to the next phase: controlling the cars remotely...

10   "We were surprised by how easy some things were" when it came to commandeering the vehicles, Roesner said. But up to that point, the carmakers hadn't thought to install systems that would make it difficult.

11   That's no longer the case. The car hacking experiments caught the attention of the National Highway Traffic Safety Administration, and the Society of Automotive Engineers created a cybersecurity taskforce. The federal car safety legislation can likewise be traced to the work by the UW lab. While the car hacking work garnered the most public attention, the lab has identified other important security weaknesses...

12   With Kohno's and Roesner's help, many of the UW Computer Science & Engineering students will graduate with a better understanding of risks posed by hackers. Professors there teach an undergraduate course in security and privacy that fills up almost instantly and has a waiting list of a dozen or more.

13   The course essentially turns traditional software development on its head by taking a finished product that works one way and asking how it could be twisted, potentially for nefarious purposes. "It's kind of a surprising mind switch," Roesner said. But, she added, it's important for students to grasp if the industry is going to get a handle on security threats.

14   "In order to build secure systems," she said, "you have to understand how to break them."

---

Write an essay in which you explain how Stiffler and Dubrow build an argument to advocate for the importance of research that includes hacking into systems. In your essay, analyze how Stiffler and Dubrow use one or more of the features listed in the box above (or features of your own choice) to strengthen the logic and persuasiveness of their argument. Be sure that your analysis focuses on the most relevant features of the passage.

Your essay should not explain whether you agree with the authors' claims, but rather explain how Stiffler and Dubrow build an argument to persuade their audience.

---

**END OF TEST**

**DO NOT RETURN TO A PREVIOUS SECTION.**

Completely darken bubbles with a No. 2 pencil. If you make a mistake, be sure to erase mark completely. Erase all stray marks.

**1.**

YOUR NAME: _____
(Print)
Last                    First                    M.I.

SIGNATURE: _____          DATE: __ / __ / __

HOME ADDRESS: _____
(Print)
Number and Street

_____
City          State          Zip Code

PHONE NO.: _____
(Print)

**IMPORTANT:** Please fill in these boxes exactly as shown on the back cover of your test book.

**2. TEST FORM**

**6. DATE OF BIRTH**

| Month | Day | | Year | |
|---|---|---|---|---|
| ○ JAN | | | | |
| ○ FEB | ⓪ | ⓪ | ⓪ | ⓪ |
| ○ MAR | ① | ① | ① | ① |
| ○ APR | ② | ② | ② | ② |
| ○ MAY | ③ | ③ | ③ | ③ |
| ○ JUN | | ④ | ④ | ④ |
| ○ JUL | | ⑤ | ⑤ | ⑤ |
| ○ AUG | | ⑥ | ⑥ | ⑥ |
| ○ SEP | | ⑦ | ⑦ | ⑦ |
| ○ OCT | | ⑧ | ⑧ | ⑧ |
| ○ NOV | | ⑨ | ⑨ | ⑨ |
| ○ DEC | | | | |

**3. TEST CODE**     **4. REGISTRATION NUMBER**

**7. SEX**
○ MALE
○ FEMALE

The **Princeton Review**®

**5. YOUR NAME**

| First 4 letters of last name | | | | FIRST INIT | MID INIT |
|---|---|---|---|---|---|

Test ③  Start with number 1 for each new section.
If a section has fewer questions than answer spaces, leave the extra answer spaces blank.

## Section 1—Reading

1. Ⓐ Ⓑ Ⓒ Ⓓ
2. Ⓐ Ⓑ Ⓒ Ⓓ
3. Ⓐ Ⓑ Ⓒ Ⓓ
4. Ⓐ Ⓑ Ⓒ Ⓓ
5. Ⓐ Ⓑ Ⓒ Ⓓ
6. Ⓐ Ⓑ Ⓒ Ⓓ
7. Ⓐ Ⓑ Ⓒ Ⓓ
8. Ⓐ Ⓑ Ⓒ Ⓓ
9. Ⓐ Ⓑ Ⓒ Ⓓ
10. Ⓐ Ⓑ Ⓒ Ⓓ
11. Ⓐ Ⓑ Ⓒ Ⓓ
12. Ⓐ Ⓑ Ⓒ Ⓓ
13. Ⓐ Ⓑ Ⓒ Ⓓ
14. Ⓐ Ⓑ Ⓒ Ⓓ
15. Ⓐ Ⓑ Ⓒ Ⓓ
16. Ⓐ Ⓑ Ⓒ Ⓓ
17. Ⓐ Ⓑ Ⓒ Ⓓ
18. Ⓐ Ⓑ Ⓒ Ⓓ
19. Ⓐ Ⓑ Ⓒ Ⓓ
20. Ⓐ Ⓑ Ⓒ Ⓓ
21. Ⓐ Ⓑ Ⓒ Ⓓ
22. Ⓐ Ⓑ Ⓒ Ⓓ
23. Ⓐ Ⓑ Ⓒ Ⓓ
24. Ⓐ Ⓑ Ⓒ Ⓓ
25. Ⓐ Ⓑ Ⓒ Ⓓ
26. Ⓐ Ⓑ Ⓒ Ⓓ
27. Ⓐ Ⓑ Ⓒ Ⓓ
28. Ⓐ Ⓑ Ⓒ Ⓓ
29. Ⓐ Ⓑ Ⓒ Ⓓ
30. Ⓐ Ⓑ Ⓒ Ⓓ
31. Ⓐ Ⓑ Ⓒ Ⓓ
32. Ⓐ Ⓑ Ⓒ Ⓓ
33. Ⓐ Ⓑ Ⓒ Ⓓ
34. Ⓐ Ⓑ Ⓒ Ⓓ
35. Ⓐ Ⓑ Ⓒ Ⓓ
36. Ⓐ Ⓑ Ⓒ Ⓓ
37. Ⓐ Ⓑ Ⓒ Ⓓ
38. Ⓐ Ⓑ Ⓒ Ⓓ
39. Ⓐ Ⓑ Ⓒ Ⓓ
40. Ⓐ Ⓑ Ⓒ Ⓓ
41. Ⓐ Ⓑ Ⓒ Ⓓ
42. Ⓐ Ⓑ Ⓒ Ⓓ
43. Ⓐ Ⓑ Ⓒ Ⓓ
44. Ⓐ Ⓑ Ⓒ Ⓓ
45. Ⓐ Ⓑ Ⓒ Ⓓ
46. Ⓐ Ⓑ Ⓒ Ⓓ
47. Ⓐ Ⓑ Ⓒ Ⓓ
48. Ⓐ Ⓑ Ⓒ Ⓓ
49. Ⓐ Ⓑ Ⓒ Ⓓ
50. Ⓐ Ⓑ Ⓒ Ⓓ
51. Ⓐ Ⓑ Ⓒ Ⓓ
52. Ⓐ Ⓑ Ⓒ Ⓓ

## Section 2—Writing and Language Skills

1. Ⓐ Ⓑ Ⓒ Ⓓ
2. Ⓐ Ⓑ Ⓒ Ⓓ
3. Ⓐ Ⓑ Ⓒ Ⓓ
4. Ⓐ Ⓑ Ⓒ Ⓓ
5. Ⓐ Ⓑ Ⓒ Ⓓ
6. Ⓐ Ⓑ Ⓒ Ⓓ
7. Ⓐ Ⓑ Ⓒ Ⓓ
8. Ⓐ Ⓑ Ⓒ Ⓓ
9. Ⓐ Ⓑ Ⓒ Ⓓ
10. Ⓐ Ⓑ Ⓒ Ⓓ
11. Ⓐ Ⓑ Ⓒ Ⓓ
12. Ⓐ Ⓑ Ⓒ Ⓓ
13. Ⓐ Ⓑ Ⓒ Ⓓ
14. Ⓐ Ⓑ Ⓒ Ⓓ
15. Ⓐ Ⓑ Ⓒ Ⓓ
16. Ⓐ Ⓑ Ⓒ Ⓓ
17. Ⓐ Ⓑ Ⓒ Ⓓ
18. Ⓐ Ⓑ Ⓒ Ⓓ
19. Ⓐ Ⓑ Ⓒ Ⓓ
20. Ⓐ Ⓑ Ⓒ Ⓓ
21. Ⓐ Ⓑ Ⓒ Ⓓ
22. Ⓐ Ⓑ Ⓒ Ⓓ
23. Ⓐ Ⓑ Ⓒ Ⓓ
24. Ⓐ Ⓑ Ⓒ Ⓓ
25. Ⓐ Ⓑ Ⓒ Ⓓ
26. Ⓐ Ⓑ Ⓒ Ⓓ
27. Ⓐ Ⓑ Ⓒ Ⓓ
28. Ⓐ Ⓑ Ⓒ Ⓓ
29. Ⓐ Ⓑ Ⓒ Ⓓ
30. Ⓐ Ⓑ Ⓒ Ⓓ
31. Ⓐ Ⓑ Ⓒ Ⓓ
32. Ⓐ Ⓑ Ⓒ Ⓓ
33. Ⓐ Ⓑ Ⓒ Ⓓ
34. Ⓐ Ⓑ Ⓒ Ⓓ
35. Ⓐ Ⓑ Ⓒ Ⓓ
36. Ⓐ Ⓑ Ⓒ Ⓓ
37. Ⓐ Ⓑ Ⓒ Ⓓ
38. Ⓐ Ⓑ Ⓒ Ⓓ
39. Ⓐ Ⓑ Ⓒ Ⓓ
40. Ⓐ Ⓑ Ⓒ Ⓓ
41. Ⓐ Ⓑ Ⓒ Ⓓ
42. Ⓐ Ⓑ Ⓒ Ⓓ
43. Ⓐ Ⓑ Ⓒ Ⓓ
44. Ⓐ Ⓑ Ⓒ Ⓓ

The Princeton Review®

**Test 3**

Start with number 1 for each new section.
If a section has fewer questions than answer spaces, leave the extra answer spaces blank.

## Section 3—Mathematics: No Calculator

1. Ⓐ Ⓑ Ⓒ Ⓓ
2. Ⓐ Ⓑ Ⓒ Ⓓ
3. Ⓐ Ⓑ Ⓒ Ⓓ
4. Ⓐ Ⓑ Ⓒ Ⓓ
5. Ⓐ Ⓑ Ⓒ Ⓓ
6. Ⓐ Ⓑ Ⓒ Ⓓ
7. Ⓐ Ⓑ Ⓒ Ⓓ
8. Ⓐ Ⓑ Ⓒ Ⓓ
9. Ⓐ Ⓑ Ⓒ Ⓓ
10. Ⓐ Ⓑ Ⓒ Ⓓ
11. Ⓐ Ⓑ Ⓒ Ⓓ
12. Ⓐ Ⓑ Ⓒ Ⓓ
13. Ⓐ Ⓑ Ⓒ Ⓓ
14. Ⓐ Ⓑ Ⓒ Ⓓ
15. Ⓐ Ⓑ Ⓒ Ⓓ

16.
17. 
18.
19.
20.

## Section 4—Mathematics: Calculator

1. Ⓐ Ⓑ Ⓒ Ⓓ
2. Ⓐ Ⓑ Ⓒ Ⓓ
3. Ⓐ Ⓑ Ⓒ Ⓓ
4. Ⓐ Ⓑ Ⓒ Ⓓ
5. Ⓐ Ⓑ Ⓒ Ⓓ
6. Ⓐ Ⓑ Ⓒ Ⓓ
7. Ⓐ Ⓑ Ⓒ Ⓓ
8. Ⓐ Ⓑ Ⓒ Ⓓ
9. Ⓐ Ⓑ Ⓒ Ⓓ
10. Ⓐ Ⓑ Ⓒ Ⓓ
11. Ⓐ Ⓑ Ⓒ Ⓓ
12. Ⓐ Ⓑ Ⓒ Ⓓ
13. Ⓐ Ⓑ Ⓒ Ⓓ
14. Ⓐ Ⓑ Ⓒ Ⓓ
15. Ⓐ Ⓑ Ⓒ Ⓓ
16. Ⓐ Ⓑ Ⓒ Ⓓ
17. Ⓐ Ⓑ Ⓒ Ⓓ
18. Ⓐ Ⓑ Ⓒ Ⓓ
19. Ⓐ Ⓑ Ⓒ Ⓓ
20. Ⓐ Ⓑ Ⓒ Ⓓ
21. Ⓐ Ⓑ Ⓒ Ⓓ
22. Ⓐ Ⓑ Ⓒ Ⓓ
23. Ⓐ Ⓑ Ⓒ Ⓓ
24. Ⓐ Ⓑ Ⓒ Ⓓ
25. Ⓐ Ⓑ Ⓒ Ⓓ
26. Ⓐ Ⓑ Ⓒ Ⓓ
27. Ⓐ Ⓑ Ⓒ Ⓓ
28. Ⓐ Ⓑ Ⓒ Ⓓ
29. Ⓐ Ⓑ Ⓒ Ⓓ
30. Ⓐ Ⓑ Ⓒ Ⓓ

31.
32.
33.
34.
35.
36.
37.
38.

# Chapter 8
# Practice Test 3:
# Answers and
# Explanations

# PRACTICE TEST 3 ANSWER KEY

## Section 1: Reading

| | | | |
|---|---|---|---|
| 1. | B | 27. | C |
| 2. | A | 28. | C |
| 3. | D | 29. | A |
| 4. | D | 30. | B |
| 5. | B | 31. | A |
| 6. | C | 32. | B |
| 7. | D | 33. | D |
| 8. | D | 34. | A |
| 9. | B | 35. | C |
| 10. | D | 36. | D |
| 11. | D | 37. | A |
| 12. | B | 38. | C |
| 13. | C | 39. | D |
| 14. | A | 40. | B |
| 15. | C | 41. | C |
| 16. | B | 42. | B |
| 17. | C | 43. | B |
| 18. | A | 44. | B |
| 19. | D | 45. | C |
| 20. | D | 46. | C |
| 21. | A | 47. | A |
| 22. | D | 48. | A |
| 23. | D | 49. | D |
| 24. | C | 50. | A |
| 25. | B | 51. | C |
| 26. | B | 52. | C |

## Section 2: Writing & Language

| | | | |
|---|---|---|---|
| 1. | D | 23. | D |
| 2. | A | 24. | C |
| 3. | C | 25. | C |
| 4. | A | 26. | D |
| 5. | A | 27. | D |
| 6. | A | 28. | B |
| 7. | D | 29. | D |
| 8. | B | 30. | B |
| 9. | D | 31. | D |
| 10. | C | 32. | B |
| 11. | C | 33. | A |
| 12. | C | 34. | D |
| 13. | A | 35. | A |
| 14. | B | 36. | A |
| 15. | B | 37. | B |
| 16. | D | 38. | B |
| 17. | A | 39. | C |
| 18. | D | 40. | C |
| 19. | A | 41. | D |
| 20. | B | 42. | B |
| 21. | B | 43. | D |
| 22. | D | 44. | B |

## Section 3: Math (No Calculator)

| | | | |
|---|---|---|---|
| 1. | C | 11. | D |
| 2. | A | 12. | C |
| 3. | B | 13. | B |
| 4. | B | 14. | A |
| 5. | C | 15. | D |
| 6. | B | 16. | 4 |
| 7. | B | 17. | 1 or 3 |
| 8. | D | 18. | 50 |
| 9. | D | 19. | $\frac{5}{13}$ |
| 10. | A | 20. | 110 |

## Section 4: Math (Calculator)

| | | | |
|---|---|---|---|
| 1. | C | 20. | B |
| 2. | D | 21. | A |
| 3. | B | 22. | B |
| 4. | C | 23. | D |
| 5. | B | 24. | B |
| 6. | D | 25. | D |
| 7. | D | 26. | C |
| 8. | C | 27. | A |
| 9. | B | 28. | D |
| 10. | B | 29. | B |
| 11. | A | 30. | C |
| 12. | A | 31. | 3 |
| 13. | D | 32. | 5 or 6 |
| 14. | C | 33. | 25.2 |
| 15. | B | 34. | 40 |
| 16. | A | 35. | 1,000 |
| 17. | C | 36. | $\frac{7}{12}$ or .583 |
| 18. | C | | |
| 19. | B | 37. | 20 |
| | | 38. | 9 |

For self-scoring assessment tables, please turn to page 957.

# PRACTICE TEST 3 EXPLANATIONS

## Section 1: Reading

1. **B**   This question asks for the best summary of the passage. Look for an answer choice that matches the passage as a whole; eliminate answer choices that are true but too specific. The first paragraph describes the party, the second paragraph gives the back story of the woman Lady Windermere is talking to, and the rest of the text relates their conversation. Choice (A) is true, but only refers to the last part of the text. Eliminate (A). Choice (B) could be true, as it reflects all three parts of the text. Keep (B) for now. Choice (C) is true, but only refers to the first part of the text. Eliminate (C). Choice (D) is both false and deceptive: This is her last reception before Easter, not her last reception ever, and she only jokingly refers to the need to flee danger. Eliminate (D). Choice (B) is the correct answer.

2. **A**   This question asks for the meaning of *smartest* in context. So find the word in context: *all the pretty women wore their smartest dresses*. Here, *smartest* has to do with a nice appearance. Choice (A), *most fashionable*, is possible; keep it for now. Choice (B), *most clever*, is another meaning of *smartest*. Eliminate (B). Choice (C), *most painful*, recalls another meaning of the verb "to smart." Eliminate (C). Choice (D), *brightest*, could be about appearance, so keep it for now. Compare the remaining answer choices: *most fashionable* is appropriately general, while *brightest* does not work in this context. Eliminate (D). Choice (A) is the correct answer.

3. **D**   This question is a general question followed by a best evidence question, so the Parallel POE strategy will work nicely here. Look at the answers for Q4 first and decide if any of them connect with the answers for Q3. Choice (4A) references Lady Windermere's *last reception before Easter*, which could initially connect to (3A). Draw a line between them. Choice (4B) does not support any of the answers for Q3, so eliminate it. Choice (4C) supports the idea that Lady Windermere is serious about the fortune-teller, which is not an idea presented in Q3, so eliminate (4C). Choice (4D) shows Lady Windermere's off-hand response to the Duchess's question about the chiromantist's fortunes. Her response is definitely not serious, so (4A) could connect with (3D). Without support from Q4, (3B) and (3C) can also be eliminated. Read the remaining pairs closely, looking for the one that best answers the question. Notice that (3A) says Lady Windermere is *nearing the end of her hostessing days*, while the text simply says it's the *last reception before Easter*. These two answers don't accurately support each other, so you can eliminate them. This leaves (3D) and (4D) as the correct answers.

4. **D**   (See explanation above.)

5. **B**   This question asks about the purpose of the description of *gorgeous peeresses ... violent Radicals, popular preachers ... eminent sceptics* and *a perfect bevy of bishops*. Look for that description in context. It is located in paragraph 1, following this sentence: *It was certainly a wonderful*

*medley of people. Medley* means *blend*, and so the description seems to support the claim that it was a wonderful mix of people. Choice (A) could be true, since political and artistic types are indeed two different groups. Choice (B) is even better, since the phrase *variety of people* can refer to *peeresses, Radicals, preachers, sceptics, and bishops.* Eliminate (A) for being too narrow in scope. Choice (C) is also narrow in scope, reducing the list to women and men, which is not the point of the description. Eliminate (C). Choice (D) can be eliminated because there is no explicit difference set up between any classes in the text. Choice (B) is the correct answer.

6.  **C**  This is a Vocab-in-Context question, so return to the text, find the word in question, and cross it out. Then use the surrounding text to fill in another word that fits the context. The Duchess is showing that she is surprised by something. *Start* must mean something that shows surprise. Choices (A), *opening*, and (B), *commencement*, refer to another meaning of start. Eliminate (A) and (B). Choice (C), *twitch*, refers to a movement that one might make when surprised, so keep it for now. Choice (D), *procedure*, is irrelevant, so eliminate (D). Choice (C) is the correct answer.

7.  **D**  This question asks what the narrator indicates about Princess Sophia, the Radicals, and the Royal Academicians. Find where they are mentioned, and see what the narrator actually says about them. They are mentioned in the middle of the first paragraph, which is describing the lively party with its different guests. Choice (A) could fit the Radicals, who are explicitly called violent, but the Royal Academicians are the ones who are disguised; the princess is neither violent nor disguised. Eliminate (A). Choice (B) fits the princess's laughter, but not necessarily anything else about her, and does not fit the Radicals or the Royal Academicians. Eliminate (B). Choice (C) could be true, but the text doesn't say so, so we don't know this. Choice (D) fits and has textual support in the sentence: *It was certainly a wonderful medley of people.* Choice (D) is the correct answer.

8.  **D**  This question asks what the narrator implies about Lady Windermere. To answer an inference question, look for what the narrator actually says about her. Choice (A) is in the text, but it is something Lady Windermere jokes about herself. It's not something the narrator says. Eliminate (A). Choice (B) again corresponds to a joke Lady Windermere makes rather than something the narrator says. Eliminate (B). Choice (C) could be true, but the text says nothing about this, so it has no support. Although Lady Windermere has been married several times, there is no indication that she will get another divorce. Eliminate (C). Choice (D) is supported by lines 18–19: *In fact, it was one of Lady Windermere's best nights.* Since this is the only answer choice with textual support, select it. Choice (D) is the correct answer.

9.  **B**  This question asks how the Duchess of Paisley is described in the passage. Be sure to read for descriptions of the Duchess, not Lady Windermere. Because Q10 is a best evidence question, those answer choices can be considered in tandem with Q9 using Parallel POE. First, consider (10A). Although those lines might initially seem to support (9D), that description is of Lady Windermere, not the Duchess. Eliminate (10A). Choice (10B) also describes Lady Windermere,

rather than the Duchess, so eliminate that answer. Choice (10C) is relevant to the Duchess, but the lines do not support anything from Q9. Eliminate (10C). Choice (10D) supports (9B). Because (9B) is the only answer in Q9 that has any support from Q10, eliminate (9A), (9C), and (9D). The correct answers are (9B) and (10D).

10.   **D**   (See explanation above.)

11.   **D**   This question asks how the first paragraph fits in with the rest of the passage. The opening paragraph gives an overview of the growing disparity between individuals of high and low SES. Eliminate (A) and (B), since neither mentions a disparity or discrepancy. Choice (C) does acknowledge a discrepancy, but there are no solutions offered throughout the course of the passage, making this choice incorrect. Choice (D) is correct because it highlights the discrepancy and mentions the research that permeates the rest of the passage.

12.   **B**   The question refers to advantages to higher SES. Look for clues in the question and try to locate the correct window. The advantages of higher SES are included in the second paragraph, which explicitly states that *individuals belonging to higher status positions in society benefit from greater access to material and social resources, increased workplace opportunities,* supporting (B). Choices (A) and (D) are incorrect because *stereotype threat* and *discrimination* are hindrances, not advantages. Similarly, (C) is incorrect because *political activism* may manifest in any individuals, regardless of SES or social category. Choice (B) is correct.

13.   **C**   This is a specific paired question, so locate the sentence that gave the answer in the previous question. The prediction for question 12 came from lines 31–35. Therefore, (C) is correct.

14.   **A**   The question asks for the function of the third paragraph, which is to explain the viewpoint of individuals of a higher socioeconomic status. These individuals attribute their successes to other aspects of life such as education and achievement based on merit. This fits (A), which states that these individuals cite reasons other than SES for their success. Choice (B) states that there is equal opportunity for both high and low SES, which contradicts the passage. Choice (C) is extreme and offensive, implying that the high SES individuals purposely repress those less fortunate, and (D) is too strong and over encompassing as well. Choice (A) is correct.

15.   **C**   This is a specific paired question, so locate the sentence that gave the answer in the previous question. The prediction for question 14 came from lines 42–45. Therefore, (C) is correct.

16.   **B**   This is a Vocab-in-Context question, so go back to line 47, find the word *bestow*, and cross it out. Then use the surrounding text to put in another word that makes sense based on the context. This part of the text talks about the *benefits* of *elevated social positions*. Something like *give* would also work in the sentence. Eliminate (A) because it's the opposite of *give*. Choice (B) might work, so hang on to it. Choice (C) might initially look attractive, but a closer reading of the window shows that these individuals try to explain their benefits as something earned, but they actually aren't. Eliminate (C). Choice (D) does not match the prediction. Choice (B) is the correct answer.

17.    **C**    This is a Vocab-in-Context question, so go back to line 65, find the word *aligns*, and cross it out. Then use the surrounding text to put in another word that makes sense based on the context. The text talks about the *present research* doing something with *mounting evidence* about *reliable predictors*. The missing word must mean something like *agree*. Now use the prediction to go through the answer choices and eliminate anything that doesn't match the prediction. Choice (A) can be eliminated because *arranges* has nothing to do with *agrees*. Choice (B) does not match the prediction and can be eliminated. Choice (C) matches the prediction. Keep it. Choice (D) can be eliminated, leaving (C) as the correct answer.

18.    **A**    This question asks about *supporting a conclusion* mentioned at the end of the passage. The correct answer must provide details that strengthen the conclusion that *social status is a reliable predictor of economic inequality*. Choice (A) talks about how *high status individuals* are more likely to *hold public office*, giving them *decision-making power on matters related to economic policy*. That connects strongly to the conclusion, so don't eliminate (A). Choice (B) states how individuals of different socioeconomic statuses perceive themselves, but does not support those differences predicting inequality. Eliminate (B). Choice (C) outlines a self-reflective study, not necessarily related to the inequality that exists between the two groups, making it incorrect as well. Choice (D) might initially look good because it mentions *social status predicts support for inequality*, but a closer reading of the text reveals that the conclusion itself is used as support for a call to action in this part of the text. Choice (D) can be eliminated. Choice (A) is correct.

19.    **D**    This question asks about data in the figure. Go straight to the figure and use the data points to POE. Find precise data points on the figure to support keeping or eliminating answer choices. Choice (A) can be eliminated because Panel B shows clearly that Democratic males are more likely to support the legislation than their female counterparts. Choices (B) and (C) are both incorrect because no information is given about the number of individuals who answered the polls to obtain this data. Choice (D) is supported by both Panel A and Panel B, making it the correct answer.

20.    **D**    The figures show an elected official's tendency to support or not support legislation supporting economic inequality, so a positive number would be more likely to support such legislation, while a negative number would be less likely to support it. Consistently, Republicans are in the positive range, while the Democrats are in the negative range, supporting (D). Choice (A) is incorrect because, while it may be true based on the passage, it is not supported by the figures. Several socioeconomic and social categories are mentioned in these figures, but they are not equally supporting or opposing such legislation. Choice (C) is also incorrect because Democratic females and individuals with low wealth are the most likely to *oppose* such legislation, not support it. Choice (D) is correct.

21.    **A**    This is a general question about the sequence of events in the passage, so save it until after the specific questions are answered. The passage begins with the songbirds' migration and then discusses experiments about the migration that provided some information but left other questions

unanswered. Choice (A) works because the observed phenomenon is the birds' nocturnal migration and decreased sleep need during migratory states. There is more research to be done, as the lab is a controlled environment and migration happens in the wild. Choice (B) is partially true, but the portion about inconclusive results makes it incorrect, since the study did reveal strong findings. Choice (C) is incorrect because nothing is revolutionized or disproved. Similarly, (D) is incorrect because there is never a second study mentioned in the passage. Therefore, (A) is correct.

22. **D** This is a Vocab-in-Context question, so go back to line 21, find the word *reconcile*, and cross it out. Then use the surrounding text to put in another word that makes sense based on the context of the passage. This part of the text talks about researchers trying to bring together conflicting observations that *sleep-deprived fliers appear no worse for wear* and that there's *evidence linking sleep deprivation to impaired neurobehavioral and physiological function*. The missing word must mean something like *bring together* or *make fit*. Choices (A) and (B) are both definitions of *reconcile*, but neither works in this context. Eliminate both of those answers. Choice (C) might initially sound good, because *clarify* might help researchers figure out the disparity between the observations, but it doesn't fit the context of needing to *bring together* the theories. Choice (D), *integrate*, does mean *bring together*. Choice (D) is the correct answer.

23. **D** This is a best evidence question, so it can be done in tandem with Q24. Consider the answer choices for Q24 and see if they support any of the answer choices for Q23. If the lines in Q24 don't support any of the answers to Q23, they can be eliminated. The lines in (24A) refer to the many miles the birds travel, which might initially look good for (23A) or (23D), but because those lines don't say anything about sleep, they don't actually support either of those answers. Choice (24A) can be eliminated. Choice (24B) mentions both the distance the birds flew as well as the birds having *little time for sleep*. This could support (23A), except (23A) mentions the birds' *evolutionary ancestors*. That idea isn't mentioned anywhere, so eliminate (24B). Choice (24C) could connect with (23D), so draw a line connecting those two answer choices. Choice (24D) connects with (23B), so draw a line connecting those two answer choices. Without support from Q24, (23A) and (23C) can be eliminated. The question asks about Benca's *central assumption in setting up her research*, which was about the birds sleeping while they migrate. While the birds' behavior in the lab cages is in the passage, it is not the central assumption. Eliminate (23B) and (24D). This leaves (23D) and (24C) as the correct answers.

24. **C** (See explanation above.)

25. **B** This question asks about Neils Rattenborg's findings and what they serve to do. Carefully read the fourth paragraph to see what Rattenborg found. His tests found that birds in the *nonmigrating state suffered cognitive deficits when sleep-deprived* but were able to *maintain cognitive function* when faced with *ongoing sleep loss in the migratory state*. These findings dovetail nicely with what Benca observed in the field. Eliminate any answers that have nothing to do with this prediction. Choice (A) can be eliminated because the results support the hypothesis rather

than upset it. Choice (B) is almost exactly what the prediction is, so keep it. Choice (C) can be eliminated, because no previous research was introduced. Choice (D) can be eliminated because there are no differences that are underscored. This leaves (B), which is the correct answer.

26.  **B**  Use the line reference to find the window for this question. Since the researchers noticed an *unprecedented ability to maintain cognitive function* during migratory states, they were able to draw a correlation between migratory states and decreased sleep without suffering cognitive deficits. The passage goes on to say that *Benca and colleagues concede it's impossible to know for sure without recording the birds in action.* The answer must have something to do with conceding a lack of information. Choice (A) might initially look good because it contains the word *impossible*, but that answer choice is too extreme. It's not impossible to know, just impossible to know without additional information. Eliminate (A). Choice (B) is a good paraphrase of the prediction, so keep it. Choice (C) can be eliminated because that observation happened before, not after. Choice (D) is not mentioned anywhere in the text. Choice (B) is the correct answer.

27.  **C**  This question asks about the factor that would necessitate further research. Using chronology, the answer to this question must come after the noted results from the research, so look around lines 50–56. The text says that the additional answers to the cognition question would be *impossible to know for sure without recording the birds in action.* The study tested the birds in a lab setting, so further research must require birds actually flying and migrating. Choice (C) is the only answer that addresses this and is the correct answer.

28.  **C**  This is a Vocab-in-Context question, so go back to line 68, find the word *improbable*, and cross it out. Then use the surrounding text to put in another word that makes sense based on the context of the passage. This part of the text talks about the *longstanding mysteries* of the *sleepless flight* of the migrating birds. The missing word must mean something like *mysterious* or *amazing*. Choices (A), (B), and (D) could be possible meanings for *improbable* in other contexts, but only (C), *remarkable*, fits the context of the passage. Choice (C) is the correct answer.

29.  **A**  This is a general question that comes at the end of the set of questions. After answering all the other questions, POE is very straightforward for the general questions. Go straight to the answers and see what can be eliminated about the songbirds based on the answers to prior questions. Choice (A) is exactly what many of the previous questions have been about, so don't eliminate it. Choice (B) is irrelevant—no mention of actual sleepwalkers occurred within the passage. Choice (C) might look good because of the word *impossible*, but the mechanisms are not actually *impossible to fully understand*, so (C) can be eliminated. Choice (D) is never mentioned, so eliminate it. This leaves (A) as the correct answer.

30.  **B**  This question asks about the best evidence to support the previous question, so simply eliminate any answer choices that don't support *activity levels correlating to migratory seasons.* Choice (A) is a rhetorical question introducing a question. Eliminate it. Choice (B) describes behavior

of songbirds. If there isn't a clear reason to eliminate an answer choice, keep it for now. Choice (C) mentions the birds' reduced sleep time, but that doesn't address the *activity level*. Choice (D) is irrelevant to Q29. Eliminate it. This leaves (B), which directly connects birds' activity levels (*hopping and wing flapping*) with *migratory seasons*. Choice (B) is the correct answer.

31.   **A**   This is a Vocab-in-Context question, so go back to line 10, find the word *feature*, and cross it out. Then use the surrounding text to put in another word that makes sense based on the context of the passage. Words like *have*, *give*, or *show* could work. Notice that the word is used as a verb. Choice (A), *present*, might look like the noun, but as a verb, it matches the prediction, so keep it. Choice (B), *attribute*, does not fit the prediction, so eliminate it. Choice (C), *report*, matches the prediction, so keep it. Choice (D), *promote*, does not fit the prediction, so eliminate it. Consider the remaining answer choices, (A) and (C). *Report* means to tell, to convey information; *present* more generally means to give or to show. Although these might initially seem very close, the report cards are not reporting the phrases. They are using the phrases to communicate performance expectations. Eliminate (C) and choose (A), which is the correct answer.

32.   **B**   This question asks for a reasonable inference about what the authors of Passage 1 believe about a standards-based report card. So look and see what they actually say about that topic. Paragraph 2 contains descriptions corresponding to the authors' claims, as opposed to reports about how other people think or feel about the new report cards: *Such a report card actually provides more detailed, specific information than a traditional grade....* Choice (A) is not necessarily an opinion of the authors, who report that *concerns have been expressed about how colleges might evaluate* these report cards. But whose concerns? You don't know, so eliminate (A). Choice (B) fits the prediction, so keep it. Choice (C) refers to an opinion not mentioned anywhere in the text; eliminate it. Choice (D) is deceptive; it compares third-graders and high-schoolers, both of whom are mentioned in the text, but who are not compared along the lines of this choice; eliminate (D). Select the remaining answer choice, (B), which is the correct answer.

33.   **D**   This question asks for the best evidence for the answer to Q32. Since the phrase *Such a report card actually provides more detailed, specific information than a traditional grade...* supported that answer, look for it in the answer choices here. Choice (A) is from the wrong paragraph; eliminate it; (B) and (C) are from the right paragraph, but do not contain the predicted phrase; eliminate them. Choice (D) fits the prediction and is the correct answer.

34.   **A**   This question asks what the author of Passage 2 says about the use of standards-based report cards in elementary schools. Since it is not clear from what part of the passage the answer will come, this question can be answered later. But then look for discussion of elementary schools in particular. There is no mention of elementary schools until paragraph 3, and elementary schools are not mentioned again in paragraph 4, so the correct answer has to be a restatement of something said in paragraph 3. Choice (A) matches paragraph 3's mention of *plans to expand standards-based report cards to its four middle schools from its elementary schools, where they have*

*been used since 2006*, even though the paragraph is about the delay of such plans. Keep it for now. Choice (B) is deceptive, because it matches the resistance encountered to instituting the report cards in the middle school, rather than the elementary school. Eliminate (B). Choice (C) is too strong: There is no comparison between the standards-based report cards and other systems in Passage 2. Eliminate (C). Choice (D) goes too far. You know that they have been implemented, but the text does not specify whether they have been successfully implemented in grade schools. Eliminate (D). Choice (A) is the correct answer.

35. **C** This is a Vocab-in-Context question, so go back to line 53, find the word *scrap*, and cross it out. Then use the surrounding text to put in another word that makes sense based on the context of the passage. Words like *get rid of* would work. Choices (A), *save*, (B), *fragment*, and (D), *detach*, do not fit this prediction, although they do recall the noun form meanings of the word *scrap*. Only (C), *discard*, fits the prediction and is therefore the correct answer.

36. **D** This question asks what Passage 2 states about the new approach to grading. Notice that Q37 is a best evidence question, so Q36 and Q37 can be answered in tandem. First, read over the answer choices to Q36. Next, look at the answer choices to Q37 to see whether they provide support for anything in Q36. Choice (37A) refers to a contrast between the new approach's criterion-based grading vs. grading on a curve. This supports (36D), so draw a line connecting them. Choice (37B) is deceptive: it refers to a dilemma, which would seem to support (36A), but the dilemma refers to the old, curve system, not the new one. Eliminate (37B). Choice (37C) again refers to the inferiority of the old, curve system. Eliminate (37C). Choice (37D) refers to plans to bring back teacher comments, and to recognize student effort and attitude. This does not support anything in Q36, so eliminate it. Since the only remaining choice in Q37 is (37A), select that answer and the answer it connects to, (36D). Both of these are the correct answers.

37. **A** (See explanation above.)

38. **C** This question asks why the author of Passage 2 uses a particular quote. It also asks what concern Passage 2 thereby addresses that Passage 1 does not address. First, locate the quote in context and predict an answer based on the text. In Passage 2, the quote in question describes a weakness of the older system of grading on a curve. So look for an answer choice that addresses this issue. Choices (A), (B), and (D) do not fit this specific prediction, but (C) does match it. Eliminate (A), (B), and (D). Since the concern about grading on a curve is indeed not mentioned in Passage 1, select (C), which is the correct answer.

39. **D** This question asks about the general relationship between Passage 1 and Passage 2. Answer it only after answering the specific questions about Passage 1 only and Passage 2 only. First, consider the tone and opinions of both passages. Both of them report on new report cards, and have a neutral-to-positive tone. Eliminate answer choices that misrepresent these facts. Choice (A) indicates a match in tone, but Passage 1 does not contain an argument, and Passage 2 does not contain responses to that argument. Eliminate (A). Choice (B) is completely wrong in tone,

so eliminate (B). Choice (C) could match in tone, but there are no alternative conclusions drawn in one passage versus the other. Eliminate (C). Choice (D) matches in tone, and Passage 2 does contain further information about the new report cards, so select (D), which is the correct answer.

40. **B** This question asks what the authors of both passages would likely agree on regarding standards-based report cards. To answer it, consider what the authors of both passages actually say about these report cards, and base the prediction on that evidence. Choice (A) references *parental insistence*, which sounds something like the parental complaints mentioned in Passage 2. But the only thing Passage 1 says about parents is that they *may find the change disconcerting*. Because Passage 1 provides no evidence about possible agreement with Passage 2 on this point, (A) can be eliminated. Choice (B) references *some resistance*, which both Passages 1 and 2 also do, and (B) states that the new report cards may provide more information than previous systems; both Passages 1 and 2 also do this. Since both passages state these things explicitly, it is reasonable to assume that both authors would agree on this point. Keep (B), but also keep checking, in case something better comes along. Choice (C) references *grading on a curve*, which is not mentioned in Passage 1, so eliminate (C) on that basis. Also, you do not know whether the new report cards *remove* the other system, so (C) is wrong on that count as well. Choice (D) sounds reasonable up to the comma, but the claim that the new report cards are *superior* to alternatives is not supported by statements in either passage. Eliminate (D). Select (B), which is the correct answer.

41. **C** This question asks how the author of Passage 1 would most likely respond to points made in the final paragraph of Passage 2. To answer this question, first review the final paragraph of Passage 2, which talks about responding to parental complaints by introducing benchmarks for each marking period, bringing back teacher comments, and looking for ways to recognize student effort and attitude. Then consider what the author of Passage 1 actually says that is relevant to these points. In the second paragraph of Passage 1, the author states that a standards-based report card provides more information than does a traditional report card, which shows clear support for the new system. But in the third paragraph of Passage 1, the author also shows support for report cards *that combine traditional grades and information about progress toward standards* and cites a researcher who supports including *teacher judgments about students' academic progress, growth, intellectual character, and work habits*. Based on this evidence, it seems the author of Passage 1 would support the changes mentioned in the fourth paragraph of Passage 2. Choice (A) could be true, but there isn't strong textual support for such sympathy. Keep (A) for now, just in case. Choice (B) can be eliminated: The author of Passage 1 would likely support the use of benchmarks, not oppose it. Choice (C) looks good, as it fits the evidence-based prediction made above, so keep it, and eliminate (A), as (C) is better. Choice (D) is too strong: The author of Passage 1 cites an author who supports including intellectual character. This is not the same thing as the author of Passage 1 *insist[ing]* that this factor be included. Eliminate (D). Select (C), which is the correct answer.

42.  **B**  This question asks about the impact of the words *must, exhibited,* and *reproduced* on the tone of the paragraph. Look for specific evidence in the text indicating the authors' goal of the paragraph. The paragraph is informational—the authors give straightforward information about a hypothesis and the observed results of the experiments. Choice (A) can be eliminated because the authors aren't *hopeful* or trying to convince readers of *uncertain results*. Choice (B) goes along with the prediction based on the text, so don't eliminate it. Choice (C) can be eliminated because the authors are straightforward but not argumentative. Choice (D) does not work because there is no indication that the authors want to *instruct others in the reproduction of simulated bat trajectories*. Choice (B) is the correct answer.

43.  **B**  This question mentions the key phrase *higher straightness index*, but that phrase is not actually a main part of the question. The question asks about the theory *experiments were performed in order to verify*. Use the key phrase to locate the necessary information in the passage. The experiments in the passage are about testing bats' *flight guidance* and *ability to fly in the dark*. Specifically, as written in paragraph 5, the theory is that *sensory noise determines motor performance*. Choice (A) does not address the issue of sensory noise. It may initially look attractive because the passage does mention using the same bats, but this answer does not address the theory the researchers are working on. Eliminate (A). Choice (B) looks good. It's a scientific paraphrase of the prediction. Keep it. Choice (C) has some words that look familiar from the text, but the words do not come together to say anything close to the prediction. Eliminate (C). Choice (D) can be eliminated because the text states that bats flew better in the light than they did in the dark. Also, the theory was about general sensory noise, not light versus dark specifically. Choice (B) is the correct answer.

44.  **B**  This is a best evidence question. Simply look at the line used to support the answer to the previous question. Choice (D) may initially look attractive, but it can be eliminated for the same reason (D) was eliminated in the previous question. Light versus dark was an experiment to test the theory, not the theory itself. Choice (C) can be eliminated for the same reason. It addresses the specifics of the experiment rather than the theory behind the experiment. The actual theory was about the sensory noise and motor performance. Choice (B) is the correct answer.

45.  **C**  This question asks about the role of the *single exponential integrator*. Read the window to determine what the integrator does. According to the text, the integrator is a *noise-suppression strategy* used by the bats used to *overcome the [sensory] noise*. Choice (A) can be eliminated because information is not lost. Choice (B) can be eliminated because it's too specific. The integrator deals with all sensory noise, not just *sub-optimal light*. Choice (C) can be kept because it's a solid rewording of the prediction. Choice (D) can be eliminated because it's the opposite of the prediction. Choice (C) is the best answer.

46.  **C**  This is a best evidence question. Consider the line(s) used to answer the previous question. Choice (C) is the correct answer.

47.    **A**    This is a Vocab-in-Context question. Go back to the text, find the word *fidelity*, and use the context to determine another word or phrase that would fit in place of *fidelity*. Something like *reproduced accurately* or *came closer than before* would work, based on the context. Choice (A) could work, so keep it. Choice (B) can be eliminated because the results were not *lower quality*. Choice (C) can be eliminated because there is no evidence of *complete perfection*. Choice (D) might look okay on its own, but (A) is better, because the correct answer should be as close to *really accurate* as possible. The *reproduction of details* matches the text's description that the integrator *reproduced…trajectories with high fidelity*. Choice (A) is the correct answer.

48.    **A**    This question asks about the *main purpose* of the fourth paragraph. Read the paragraph to determine what the main idea is. The researchers hypothesized that the bats were using *a noise-suppression strategy…to overcome the noise*. Then they determined this strategy was the *simple exponential integrator*. Choice (A) completely describes this, so keep it. Choice (B) is deceptive, using several words and phrases from the text without actually matching the prediction. Eliminate it. No *pitfalls of a theory* are mentioned, so eliminate (C). Choice (D) does not match the text since the authors found the simple exponential integrator outperformed the uniform integrator. Choice (A) is the correct answer.

49.    **D**    This question asks about the assumption made about *highly curved flight trajectories*. In the final sentence of the passage, the authors summarize their findings as a *surprising conclusion* that the curved trajectories *are due to sensory limitations—not motor limitations*. Therefore, the flight patterns are a result of a limitation the bat deals with. Choice (A) can be eliminated, because the trajectories were normal for bats with the introduction of sensory noise. Choice (B) can be eliminated because it's too extreme and not supported by the text. Choice (C) doesn't make sense. The researchers compared flight trajectories of bats in light and dark, but no flight trajectory replaced another one. Choice (D) matches the prediction because the authors were surprised that sensory limitations rather than motor limitations caused the curved trajectory, so they must have previously thought the curved trajectories were caused by the physicality of the bat. Choice (D) is the correct answer.

50.    **A**    This question asks about a simulated trajectory with noise and integration. Look at the second graphic. The lines that represent *simulated trajectory with noise* are the gray lines. There are many of them, so eliminate (B) and (C). In the *Integration* graphic, all the lines reach the target, so (A) is the correct answer.

51.    **C**    This question asks about the trajectory that most nearly *matches the original trajectory*. The *original trajectory* line is the dotted black line. Find the line that most closely follows that one. The *Integration* lines are all much closer to the original trajectory than any of the *No Integration* lines, so eliminate (A) and (D). Look to see which line most closely lines up with the *original trajectory* line in the *Integration* graphic. It's one of the gray lines, which are *simulated with noise*. Choice (C) is the correct answer.

52. **C** There is no evidence in the figure to show *optimal light conditions*. Eliminate (A) and (B). Choice (C) addresses the lack of information about optimal light conditions in the figure. Keep it. Choice (D) does not address optimal light specifically. Eliminate (D). Choice (C) is the correct answer.

## Section 2: Writing and Language

1. **D** The passage as a whole is about the FDA's role in ensuring that the goods we buy are safe for use. It does not concern family activities, as in (A), directions, as in (B), or family budgets, as in (C). The only appropriate introduction comes from (D), which addresses food safety.

2. **A** There are only two reasons to use an apostrophe: possession and contraction. The word *beginnings* does not fit within either of these categories, so there should be no apostrophe on this word. This eliminates (B) and (D). These *beginnings*, however, belong to the *agency*, so they should be described as the *agency's beginnings*, as in (A).

3. **C** When given the option to DELETE, give that option special consideration because it is often correct. In this case, however, the deletion of the word breaks up the commonly used phrase *as we know it* and makes the sentence incomplete. Eliminate (D). Choice (A) also makes the sentence incomplete, so eliminate it. The only choice that correctly completes the phrase, *as we know it,* is (C).

4. **A** Use POE! Choice (B) is not an effective combination, as it repeats the word *regulates* and uses too many commas. Choice (C) is not effective because it uses the passive voice awkwardly. Choice (D) also uses a passive construction and refers to *the $1 trillion dollars of goods* as if that amount has been cited previously in the passage. Choice (A) is the only effective combination that does not introduce new errors.

5. **A** While (A), (C), and (D) all seem to say roughly the same thing, notice that (C) and (D) contain subjects and verbs. The introduction of subjects and verbs into the underlined portions of (C) and (D) creates a comma splice within the sentence by separating two complete ideas with only a comma. The use of the word *thus* in (B) implies a cause and effect in the sentence where none is actually present. Only (A) remains, with the word *which* referring back to *fees* and creating a dependent idea.

6. **A** This paragraph marks a shift in tone, referring to the FDA's hidden role in our lives. The only one of the answer choices that effectively signals this shift is (A). Choices (B) and (D) are irrelevant in the context, and (C) suggests a continuation rather than a shift. Therefore, (A) is correct.

7. **D** The statement made in the first part of the sentence is the following: *The FDA is certainly large.* Therefore, a supporting statement should give some evidence of the FDA's large size. While (B)

uses the word *large*, it does so to describe the FDA's role in regulating the tobacco industry, not to describe the actual size of the agency. Choice (B) is irrelevant to the passage, as is (C). The best answer is (D), which lists some numbers that demonstrate the vast size of the FDA.

8.  **B**   The previous sentence refers to *consumer safety officers* but suggests that the bulk of the FDA's work is done by *scientists*. The sentence given in the question would help to elaborate upon that point by breaking down the number of scientists the FDA employs. The latter part of the paragraph actually goes on to describe some of the work of these various scientists. Choices (A) and (C) can be eliminated because the reasons are incorrect. Since the rest of the paragraph is concerned with scientists, not *non-scientists*, (D) can be eliminated as well. The sentence should be added for the reason given in (B).

9.  **D**   When given the option to DELETE, give that option special consideration because it is often correct. The information in (A), (B), and (C) is already given in the non-underlined portion of the sentence by way of the word *confidence*. Therefore, the best option is to DELETE this underlined portion altogether because none of the proposed choices add anything substantive to the sentence.

10. **C**   Make the items in a list consistent with one another. In this case, that list consists of the single-word names for various sciences: *chemistry, biology, and physics*. Choices (A), (B), and (D) all add unnecessary words to this list.

11. **C**   When there are verbs changing in the answer choices, find the subject. Here, the subject is *thing*, which is singular. Choices (A), (B), and (D) can all be eliminated because they contain plural verbs. The only singular verb in the list comes in (C), which is therefore the correct answer.

12. **C**   The pronoun in question refers to the noun *hockey*. This noun is neither a *them* nor a *he*, so (B) and (D) can be eliminated. Then, (A) can also be eliminated because it refers to the *self* of hockey rather than using the pronoun and conventional expression *itself*. Choice (C) provides the best answer in the context.

13. **A**   This sentence has not yet indicated why the Cup should be named after Lord Stanley of Preston, so the underlined portion should provide that information. Choices (B) and (C) may be true, but they do not explain why the Cup is named after Stanley and stray from the main idea of the passage. Choice (D) is worth considering, but this answer would delete a crucial piece of information. Therefore, the best answer is (A), which explains Lord Stanley's importance to the game of hockey.

14. **B**   This question is testing knowledge of the idiom *just as...so too*. Because these words need to exist in this pair, (A) can be eliminated. Of the remaining answer choices, only (B) mentions the NHL, which is needed to establish the movement from the NHA to the NHL that this sentence describes.

15. **B**   The underlined portion contains STOP punctuation, so use the vertical line test. The first part of the sentence is not complete, so eliminate (A) and (C). Choice (D) has a colon, which is HALF-STOP punctuation and also requires a complete idea before it. Eliminate (D). The phrase *established in 1924* is unnecessary to the meaning of the sentence, as implied by the comma after the word *Bruins*. Therefore, that phrase should be set off in a way consistent with the punctuation in the non-underlined portion. In this case, that punctuation is a comma, so the correct answer must be (B).

16. **D**   This sentence has a clear marker, *1926*, which places it in a consistent timeframe at this point in the passage. Eliminate (A) and (B). The sentence also contains relevant information that helps to develop the story about the emergence of the NHL. Eliminate (C), as the sentence contributes to the story of the emergence of the NHL but does not contain the entirety of the argument. The sentence does provide a logical introduction to the paragraph as well as relevant information, so (D) is the best answer.

17. **A**   The phrase *sole dominion* earlier in the passage suggests that the NHL has risen to a high position. Choice (A) effectively captures that high position. Choices (B) and (D) are too informal (i.e., they do not "maintain the tone established in the passage"), and (C) is irrelevant to the passage's meaning.

18. **D**   All four of these answer choices say similar things, but some do so in fewer words. Eliminate extra words when possible. In this case, *ascendant* and *dominant* are redundant, so any answer choices that include both of them can be eliminated. This leaves only (D), which contains all the same information as the other choices in the fewest words.

19. **A**   The previous sentence states, *Today, the league has 30 teams*. This is a continuation of the discussion of the league's expansion from six teams. The next sentence should therefore continue the discussion of expansion. Choices (B) and (D) are not relevant to that discussion and can be eliminated. Choice (C) discusses the league's *"Original Six"* teams but is out of place in the paragraph. Therefore, the best answer is (A), which discusses the league's plans to continue expanding.

20. **B**   Note the idea before the punctuation: *Since the early days of professional hockey*. This idea is incomplete, so it cannot be followed by the punctuation given in (A), (C), or (D). Semicolons require complete ideas on both sides. Colons require complete ideas beforehand, and the combination of a comma plus one of the coordinating conjunctions (for, and, nor, but, or, yet, so) requires a complete idea on both sides of the combination. Only (B) remains.

21. **B**   As it is, this sentence says merely, *There are other leagues*. This information is already given in the previous sentence, so this sentence must say something new. The proposed addition would help it to do so while adding relevant specificity to an otherwise too-general sentence. Eliminate (C) and (D) as they do not reflect the need for the additional information. Choice (A) incorrectly states that the paragraph changes focus. Eliminate (A) and choose (B), which accurately reflects the fact that the proposed revision adds relevant information.

22. **D** There are two main changes in the answer choices here: *hold/holds* and *it/they*. Both the verb *hold/ holds* and the pronoun *it/they* need to be consistent with other information in the sentence. The subject of the verb is *the NHL*, which is singular and therefore requires the singular verb *holds*. Eliminate (A) and (C). The referent for the pronoun is also *the NHL*, which requires the singular pronoun *it*. Therefore, (D) is correct.

23. **D** The word in the underlined portion should mean something like *turned*, describing how people *accepted the health risks of smoking* and then went *away from the deadly pastime*. Choices (A) and (C) might seem to be appealing because they appear to play off what one does with a cigarette, but they do not effectively signal that many Americans have abandoned the pastime. Between (B) and (D), (D) better reflects the sense of turning away from the behavior, while (B) suggests an urgency that is not fully supported by the passage. Eliminate (B) and choose (D).

24. **C** Sentence 4 starts with the idea that *This may sound odd because everyone has to sit at some point*. Therefore, the sentence that precedes it should contain information about how sitting is dangerous or unnatural. Sentence 1 contains the scientists' dictum that *Sitting is the new smoking*, so sentence 4 would follow logically from this idea. Additionally, sentences 1 and 2 are not contrasting ideas, but sentence 2 begins with the word *however*. Something needs to be inserted between sentences 1 and 2 for the non-underlined portion to make sense. Therefore, sentence 4 would best be placed before sentence 2, making (C) correct.

25. **C** Use POE! Choice (A) can be eliminated because it suggests that 800,000 was the target number for a representative sample, whereas the initial sentences indicate that it was merely the number of initial test subjects. Choice (B) reuses the word *safe* in a way that does not make sense in the context. Choice (D) refers to *people in their 20s*, which is not part of the initial sentences. Only (C) remains, which effectively combines the sentences by shortening them while preserving the initial meaning.

26. **D** When given the option to DELETE, give that option serious consideration because it is often correct. In this case, none of the proposed words in the underlined portion add to the sentence in a substantive way, so the best option is to DELETE them altogether, as in (D).

27. **D** Although it may not look like one at first glance, the idea *Consider our primate ancestors, for example* is in fact complete, so it should be set off from the next complete idea: *If they were not incredibly active at all times, they would not have survived*. Choices (A) and (C) do not have sufficient punctuation to separate two complete ideas. Choice (B) contains appropriate punctuation, but it attaches the *for example* to the wrong idea. Choice (D) is therefore the best possible answer in the context.

28. **B** Read the graph carefully. It estimates that the average human is "Active/Standing" for 3 hours a day, as (B) indicates. Keep (B), but check the other answer choices. Choice (A) incorrectly states this number as 8. Choice (C) misreads 3 hours as one-third of the 24 hours in a day. Choice (D) is not supported. Eliminate (A), (C), and (D) and choose (B).

29. **D** Read the graph carefully, and make sure that the information in the answers is supported. Choices (A) and (C) are not addressed in the graph, so eliminate them. Also, eliminate (B), which gives incorrect information based on the graph. Only (D) is supported, as only 7.5 of the 21 sitting hours in a day are done at work.

30. **B** The underlined word refers directly back to *those*, or those people who fidget. Therefore, (A) and (D) can be eliminated because they are not used to refer to people in this context. Choice (C) can also be eliminated because the word *we* is not used in this part of the passage. Choice (B) correctly refers to *those*.

31. **D** This sentence is in the past tense, as indicated by the earlier verb *were*. The need for past tense eliminates (A) and (C). Choice (B) can also be eliminated because the word *went* does not make sense in the given context. Choice (D) is the best answer, as it contains the correct meaning and tense.

32. **B** The underlined pronoun is a substitute for the word *sitting*. The phrase as a whole is concerned with the *detrimental effects of sitting*. Choices (A) and (D) can be eliminated because they are plural, while *sitting* is singular. Choice (C) can also be eliminated because it gives the contraction *it is*, while this sentence requires a possessive pronoun. Therefore, (B) is correct.

33. **A** Read the question carefully. It wants a conclusion that *acknowledges the problem of sitting but also encourages the reader to use this research in a proactive way*. Choices (B) and (C) do not acknowledge the problem of sitting, and (D) is not encouraging. Choice (A) contains both elements and is therefore the correct answer.

34. **D** The underlined portion contains STOP punctuation, so use the vertical line test. The first part of the sentence is incomplete, so eliminate (A). The phrase *the latest lines of shoes, suits, dresses, or furniture* is offset as unnecessary information, indicated by the dash after the word *fashion*. Keep the punctuation consistent by inserting another dash after the word *furniture*, as in (D).

35. **A** This word is part of a short list with the phrase *sported the clothes*. Keep this part of the list consistent. The underlined word should be consistent with the word *sported*, as in the word *furnished* in (A). Choice (B) also contains the word *furnished*, but it contains the unnecessary word *have*.

36. **A** The previous sentence is in the present tense, referring to *the newest style*. Because the sentence containing the underlined portion continues the discussion of that style, it should also be in the present tense, eliminating (B). Choice (D) would create a sentence fragment, so eliminate it. In order to choose between (A) and (C), find the subject of the verb. The subject is *style*, which is singular and therefore requires the singular verb *seeks*, given in (A).

37. **B** Because the information *IFC's Portlandia* is not essential to the completeness of the sentence, it should be offset with a pair of commas, thus eliminating (A) and (C). Choice (D) can also be

eliminated because it contains an unnecessary comma after the word *IFC's*. Only (B) has the proper number of commas.

38. **B** The idea before the punctuation (*Back-dropped by…mustaches*) is incomplete, so it cannot be followed by a semicolon or a period, eliminating (A), (C), and (D). Choice (B) is the only choice that correctly punctuates the first part of the sentence, regardless of what follows that punctuation.

39. **C** This sentence gives some examples of the "rustic chic" style, which is interested in using older styles. The underlined portion should therefore contain some mention of these older styles, as only (C) does. Choices (A) and (D) refer to examples of the rustic chic style as *results* and *expensive*, both of which are irrelevant. Choice (B) may be tempting, but it's referring to examples of the rustic chic style as *peculiar* before discussing the peculiarity of these items. This concept is elaborated on in the next paragraph, not this one, so (B) is not the best answer.

40. **C** While the previous sentence mentions economics, it is not doing so in a way that is literally concerned with rustic chic's influence on the global economy. The idea should therefore not be added, thus eliminating (A) and (B). Choice (D) can also be eliminated because the proposed sentence does not contradict other information in the passage. Only (C) remains as the correct answer.

41. **D** Use POE. Choice (A) can be eliminated because rustic chic has clearly generated *interest*, as the passage indicates throughout. Choice (B) can be eliminated because there is no discussion of rustic chic being a *choice*. Choice (C) can be eliminated because rustic chic *is a fashion*. Choice (D) correctly suggests that rustic chic can be confusing because it does not refer back to a clear or specific moment in history.

42. **B** As indicated by the topic sentence of this paragraph, rustic chic is a popular historically-minded style even though it does not refer back to a specific historical period. The sentence in the underlined portion should contain some indication of this lack of specificity, as (B) does. Additionally, (B) helps the preceding sentence make sense because it gives a context of what is meant by *"they."* Choices (A), (C), and (D) may have merit in other contexts, but they are not relevant here.

43. **D** Sentence 2 contains a directive that has something to do with the fashion industry. This directive is best used as an answer to the question posed in sentence 6. Placing sentence 2 after sentence 6 would also continue a pattern established by sentences 4 and 5. Sentence 2 is therefore best placed after sentence 6, as (D) indicates.

44. **B** Use POE. Choices (A), (C), and (D) may be attractive choices in other contexts, but in this essay, they are far too grandiose and negative to fit. Only (B) works because it contains the proper tone, and it matches with the mention of *clutter* at the end of the sentence.

# Section 3: Math (No Calculator)

1. **C** The question asks for the value of $8s + 13$, so determine the value of $s$. Since $4s = 28$, divide both sides by 4 to get $s = 7$. Therefore, $8s + 13 = 8(7) + 13 = 56 + 13 = 69$. Alternatively, since $4s = 28$, $8s = 2(4s) = 2(28) = 56$. Therefore, $8s + 13 = 56 + 13 = 69$. Using either method, the answer is (C).

2. **A** The question asks which choice is equal to $b^{\frac{3}{4}}$. By rule, fractional exponents express roots. Let the denominator of the fraction equal the root taken. Since the denominator is 4, take the 4th root. The numerator of the fraction remains as the exponent. Therefore, $b^{\frac{3}{4}} = \sqrt[4]{b^3}$, which is (A).

3. **B** The question asks for the value that will change if a cheaper type of grass is used. The only thing that has changed is that the customer has asked for a cheaper type of grass. A cheaper type of grass does not change the number of plots, the length of a plot, or the width of any plot, so the values $p$, $l$, and $w$ do not change. Eliminate (A), (C), and (D). Only (B) remains. Alternatively, note that it is only the price that changes and the only value whose units involve dollars is $G$, so this must be the value that changes. The answer is (B).

4. **B** When there is a system of equations, stack and add or subtract the two equations to get an equation. The goal is to find an equation in which the coefficients on $x$ and $y$ are the same as in the expression the question asks for the value of. In this case, since the question asks for $x + y$, the coefficients on $x$ and $y$ should be equal. Stack and add the two equations to get $8x + 8y = -56$. Divide both sides by 8 to get $x + y = -7$. The answer is (B).

5. **C** The question says that the number of countries in the European Union in 2008 was three times the number of countries in 1974. Translate this into an equation. Since the question says that the European Union had 27 members in 2008, translate *the number of countries in the European Union in 2008* to 27. Translate *was* to =. Translate *three times* to 3( ), leaving room between the parentheses for whatever follows in the sentence. What follows is *the number of countries in the European Union (then called the European Communities) in 1974*, which the question later says is $m$. Therefore the sentence translates to $27 = 3(m)$, or $3m = 27$, which is (C).

6. **B** The question asks for $\dfrac{y}{7}$, so solve for $y$. Since $\dfrac{7}{y} = \dfrac{17}{y + 30}$, cross-multiply to get $7(y + 30) = 17y$. Distribute the 7 to get $7y + 210 = 17y$. Subtract $7y$ from both sides to get $210 = 10y$. Divide both sides by 10 to get $21 = y$. Therefore, $\dfrac{y}{7} = \dfrac{21}{7} = 3$, which is (B).

7. **B** Since there are no exponents on $x$ or $y$ in either equation, the equations are linear. A system of linear equations has no solution if the two lines represented by the equations are parallel. Two lines are parallel when they have the same slope. To determine the slope of the lines, get each line in slope-intercept form: $y = mx + b$. Start with the second equation, $3x - 7y = 5$. Subtract

$3x$ from both sides to get $-7y = -3x + 5$. Divide both sides by $-7$ to get $y = \dfrac{3}{7}x - \dfrac{5}{7}$. In slope-intercept form, the slope is equal to $m$, so the slope of this line is $\dfrac{3}{7}$. Now get the slope of the other line, $cx - 6y = 8$. Subtract $cx$ from both sides to get $-6y = -cx + 8$. Divide both sides by $-6$ to get $y = \dfrac{c}{6}x - \dfrac{8}{6}$, so the slope of this line is $\dfrac{c}{6}$. Since these two slopes have to be equal, set $\dfrac{3}{7} = \dfrac{c}{6}$. Cross-multiply to get $7c = 18$. Divide both sides by 7 to get $c = \dfrac{18}{7}$. The answer is (B).

8. **D** A factor of a polynomial is used to find a solution, or a value of $x$ for which the corresponding value of the function is 0. When a function in factored form is set equal to 0, each factor can be set equal to 0 to get each solution. Since, according to the table, $g(7) = 0$, $x = 7$ is one solution of $g$. Therefore, it must also be the solution to an equation made by setting one of the factors equal to 0. To find this factor, get the equation $x = 7$ into the form of an equation with one side equal to 0. Subtract 7 from both sides to get $x - 7 = 0$. Therefore, $x - 7$ is one of the factors of $g$, and the answer is (D).

9. **D** A line whose equation is in the form $y = mx + b$ has slope $m$ and $y$-intercept $b$. In the equation $y = cx + 6$, the slope is $c$. Plug the point $(r, s)$ into the equation to get $s = cr + 6$. To find the slope, solve for $c$. First, subtract 6 from both sides to get $s - 6 = cr$. Now, divide both sides by $r$ to get $c = \dfrac{s - 6}{r}$. The correct answer is (D).

10. **A** The question asks for pairs of congruent angles. Start with the vertical angles. Vertical angles are non-adjacent angles formed by intersecting lines. The pairs of vertical angles in this figure are $a°$ and $d°$, $b°$ and $e°$, and $c°$ and $f°$. Since vertical angles are always congruent, $a = d$, $b = e$, and $c = f$. The question also states that $a + b = c + d$. Since $a = d$, it must also be the case that $b = c$. This shows that statement (I) is true, so (B) can be eliminated. Since $b = c$, $b = e$, and $c = f$, then $e$ must also equal $f$. Statement (II) is true, so eliminate (C). Statement (III) says that $a = e$. It has been determined that $b = c = e = f$ and that $a = d$, but so far nothing has shown that $a = e$. To be sure, plug in for $e$. Let $e = 30$. If $e = 30$, then $b = c = f = 30$, so $b + c + e + f = 30 + 30 + 30 + 30 = 120$. Since $a + b + c + d + e + f = 360$, then $a + d + 120 = 360$ and $a + d = 240$. Since $a = d$, then $a$ and $d$ are both equal to 120. Therefore, $a \neq e$. Cross off (III) and eliminate (D). The answer is (A).

11. **D** The graph asks for the $y$-coordinate of the vertex, which is the point of the parabola on the axis of symmetry. Therefore, the axis of symmetry is the line $x = m$. To determine the value of $m$, find a pair of points with the same $y$-coordinate, and get the midpoint of the segment between them. To make this easy, let $y = 0$ to get $0 = k(x - 4)(x + 12)$. Set each factor equal to 0 to get

$k = 0$, $x - 4 = 0$, and $x + 12 = 0$. Since the question says $k \neq 0$, reject the first equation. Solve the second equation, $x - 4 = 0$, by adding 4 to both sides to get $x = 4$. Solve the third equation, $x + 12 = 0$, by subtracting 12 from both sides to get $x = -12$. Therefore, the points $(4, 0)$ and $(-12, 0)$ are on the parabola. The midpoint of $(4, 0)$ and $(-12, 0)$ is $\left( \frac{4 + (-12)}{2}, 0 \right) = \left( \frac{-8}{2}, 0 \right) = (-4, 0)$. Therefore, $m = -4$. Since $(m, n)$ is a point on the parabola, $n = k(m - 4)(m + 12)$. To find $n$, plug in $m = -4$ to get $n = k(-4 - 4)(-4 + 12) = k(-8)(8) = -64k$. Another option would be to plug in for $k$ to get a quadratic, then complete the square on the $x$-terms to get the equation into the vertex form. Either way, the correct answer is (D).

12. **C** The question asks about points of intersection. Points of intersection are solutions to both equations. Since $y = (x - 8)^2$ and $y = 36$, set $(x - 8)^2 = 36$. To solve, take the square root of both sides to get $x - 8 = \pm 6$. Always remember to use $\pm$ when taking the square root of both sides of an equation. Consider both possible equations. If $x - 8 = 6$, add 8 to both sides to get $x = 14$. If $x - 8 = -6$, add 8 to both sides to get $x = 2$. Therefore, points $P$ and $Q$ are at coordinates $(2, 36)$ and $(14, 36)$. Since the endpoints of $\overline{PQ}$ share $y$-coordinates, the length of the segment is the difference in the $x$-coordinates of the endpoints. Therefore, $\overline{PQ} = 14 - 2 = 12$. The correct answer is (C).

13. **B** The question statements refer to equivalent decreases in Celsius and Fahrenheit. Test each of these statements by plugging in an example. Statement (I) refers to a decrease of 1.8 degrees Celsius. Use a simple example of such a decrease. Try $C = 1.8$ and $C = 0$. Since the formula includes fractions, convert 1.8 into a fraction in order to do the arithmetic. $\frac{1.8}{1.0} = \frac{18}{10} = \frac{9}{5}$, so $1.8 = \frac{9}{5}$. If $C = \frac{9}{5}$, then $F\left( \frac{9}{5} \right) = \frac{9}{5}\left( \frac{9}{5} \right) + 32 = \frac{81}{25} + 32 = 3\frac{6}{25} + 32 = 35\frac{6}{25}$. If $C = 0$, then $F(0) = \frac{9}{5}(0) + 32 = 32$. Since this is a decrease of more than 1, cross out (I) and eliminate any choice that includes (I): (A) and (D). Now look at the remaining choices. Since both remaining choices include (II), (II) must be true, so test (III) only. Statement (III) refers to a decrease of $\frac{5}{9}$ degrees Fahrenheit. Pick two easy values for $F$ with a difference of $\frac{5}{9}$. $F = \frac{5}{9}$ and $F = 0$ might appear easy, but the first step to solving will be to subtract 32, which is not convenient with $F = \frac{5}{9}$. Instead, use $F = 32\frac{5}{9}$ and $F = 32$. If $F = 32\frac{5}{9}$, then $32\frac{5}{9} = \frac{9}{5}C + 32$. Subtract

32 from both sides to get $\frac{5}{9} = \frac{9}{5}C$. Multiply both sides by $\frac{5}{9}$ to get $\frac{25}{81} = C$. If $F = 32$, then

$32 = \frac{9}{5}C + 32$. Subtract 32 from both sides to get $0 = \frac{9}{5}C$. Multiply both sides by $\frac{5}{9}$ to get

$0 = C$. Since this a decrease of less than 1, cross off (III) and eliminate (C). The answer is (B).

14.  **A**  This is a complicated algebra question, so look for a way to plug in. Since no calcula-

tor is allowed on this section, it is especially important to plug in an easy number. Try

$x = 1$. If $x = 1$, then $\dfrac{80(1)^2 + 84(1) - 13}{k(1) - 4} = -16(1) - 4 - \dfrac{29}{k(1) - 4}$. Simplify to get

$\dfrac{80 + 84 - 13}{k - 4} = -16 - 4 - \dfrac{29}{k - 4}$ and $\dfrac{151}{k - 4} = -20 - \dfrac{29}{k - 4}$. Add $\dfrac{29}{k - 4}$ to both sides to get

$\dfrac{151}{k - 4} + \dfrac{29}{k - 4} = -20$. Since the fractions on the right have the same denominator, add both

the numerators to get $\dfrac{180}{k - 4} = -20$. Multiply both sides by $(k - 4)$ to get $180 = -20(k - 4)$.

Distribute on the right side to get $180 = -20k + 80$. Subtract 80 from both sides to get

$100 = -20k$. Divide both sides by $-20$ to get $k = -5$, which is (A).

15.  **D**  To find the solutions to a quadratic equation, the first option is to factor. First, since 5

is a factor of each term, factor 5 to get $5(x^2 + 6x + 3) = 0$. Divide both sides by 5 to get

$x^2 + 6x + 3 = 0$. However, as the answer choices hint, factoring this equation further will be

difficult, so use the quadratic formula: $x = \dfrac{-b \pm \sqrt{b^2 - 4ac}}{2a}$. The standard form of a qua-

dratic equation is $ax^2 + bx + c = 0$, so $a = 1$, $b = 6$, and $c = 3$. Therefore, $x = \dfrac{-b \pm \sqrt{b^2 - 4ac}}{2a}$

$= \dfrac{-6 \pm \sqrt{6^2 - 4(1)(3)}}{2(1)} = \dfrac{-6 \pm \sqrt{36 - 12}}{2} = \dfrac{-6 \pm \sqrt{24}}{2}$. Simplify the square root by finding a

perfect square factor. Since $24 = 4 \times 6$, $\sqrt{24} = \sqrt{4} \times \sqrt{6} = 2\sqrt{6}$, so $x = \dfrac{-6 \pm 2\sqrt{6}}{2}$. Simplify

the fraction by dividing both terms in the numerator by 2 to get $x = -3 \pm \sqrt{6}$. The correct

answer is (D).

16.  **4**  To solve this equation, start by simplifying like terms on the left side. Since the denominators

are the same, subtract the numerators to get $\dfrac{5}{25}z = \dfrac{1}{2} + \dfrac{3}{10}$. Simplify the fraction on the left side of the equation to get $\frac{1}{5}z = \frac{1}{2} + \frac{3}{10}$. Now eliminate the fractions by multiplying both sides by a common multiple of all three denominators, such as 10. The result is $2z = 5 + 3$. Simplify the right side to get $2z = 8$. Divide both sides by 2 to get $z = 4$. The answer is 4.

17. **1 or 3** To solve a polynomial, get one side of the equation equal to 0. To do that in this case, add $9y$ to both sides to get $y^3(y^2 - 10) + 9y = 0$. Distribute $y^3$ to get $y^5 - 10y^3 + 9y = 0$. Since each term on the left includes $y$, factor $y$ to get $y(y^4 - 10y^2 + 9) = 0$. Now factor $(y^4 - 10y^2 + 9)$. Notice that this resembles a quadratic of the form $ax^2 + bx + c$ but with the exponents doubled. It can be factored the same way. The quadratic $(y^2 - 10y + 9)$ factors to $(y - 9)(y - 1)$, so $(y^4 - 10y^2 + 9)$ factors to $(y^2 - 9)(y^2 - 1)$. Notice that each of these factors is a difference of squares, so $(y^2 - 9) = (y - 3)(y + 3)$ and $(y^2 - 1) = (y - 1)(y + 1)$. Therefore, the equation $y(y^4 - 10y^2 + 9) = 0$ factors to $y(y - 3)(y + 3)(y - 1)(y + 1) = 0$. Set each of these factors equal to 0 to get $y = 0$, $y - 3 = 0$, $y + 3 = 0$, $y - 1 = 0$, and $y + 1 = 0$. Solve these equations to get $y = 0$, $y = 3$, $y = -3$, $y = 1$, and $y = -1$, respectively. Since the question specifies that $y > 0$, the only remaining possible solutions are $y = 3$ and $y = 1$. Grid-in either of these two answers.

18. **50** To solve this problem, translate each statement into an equation. Let $L$ represent the length of a long session and $S$ represent the length of a short session. Each long session lasts 20 minutes longer than each short session. *Each long session* translates to $L$. The word *lasts* is the main verb of the sentence, so it translates to $=$. The phrase *20 minutes longer* translates to ___ $+ 20$, leaving room on the left for whatever follows. What follows is *each short session*, which translates to $S$. Therefore, the first sentence translates to $L = S + 20$. Now translate the second sentence. The term *3 long sessions* translates to $3L$. The word *and* translates to $+$. The term *4 short sessions* translates to $4S$. The term *last a total of* translates to $=$. Therefore, the second sentence translates to $3L + 4S = 270$. To solve this system of equations, substitute $L = S + 20$ into the second equation to get $3(S + 20) + 4S = 270$. Distribute 3 to get $3S + 60 + 4S = 270$. Combine like terms to get $7S + 60 = 270$. Subtract 60 from both sides to get $7S = 210$. Divide both sides by 7 to get $S = 30$. This is not the answer. Don't forget to read the question, which asks for the length of a *long* session. Since $L = S + 20$, $L = 30 + 20 = 50$. The answer is 50.

19. $\frac{5}{13}$ The question asks for the value of cos $Z$. By definition, corresponding angles in similar triangles are congruent. Since $\angle Z$ corresponds to $\angle W$ in a similar triangle, $\angle Z$ is congruent to $\angle W$. Since congruent angles have equal cosines, cos $Z$ = cos $W$. Therefore, this question can be answered by ignoring triangle $XYZ$ and working exclusively with triangle $UVW$ to determine the value of cos $W$, and thus the value of cos $Z$. Draw triangle $UVW$, filling in $WV = 39$ and $UV = 36$.

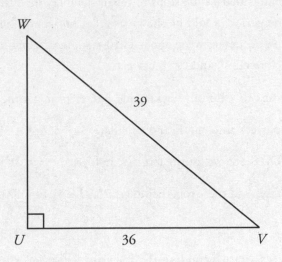

By definition, $\cos W = \dfrac{adj}{hyp}$. The hypotenuse is 39, but the adjacent side isn't given. The adjacent side can be solved for using the Pythagorean Theorem, but this is difficult with numbers this large and no calculator. Instead, look for a Pythagorean triple. The ratio 36:39, can be reduced by a factor of 3 to 12:13, so this is a 5:12:13 right triangle. Therefore the missing side, $\overline{UW}$, must have a length of $3 \times 5 = 15$. Thus, the adjacent side is 15, and $\cos W = \dfrac{adj}{hyp} = \dfrac{15}{39} = \dfrac{5}{13}$. The answer is $\dfrac{5}{13}$.

20. **110** Start with the equation $b = 180 - 4a$. Since $a = 35$, $b = 180 - 4(35) = 180 - 140 = 40$. Therefore, the two base angles of the lower triangle have a sum of $180° - 40° = 140°$. Since the two base angles are opposite equal sides, they must be equal, so each is 70°. The angle with measure $c$ combines with the base angle on the right to form a straight angle. Therefore, $70° + c° = 180°$, and $c = 110$. The answer is 110.

## Section 4: Math (Calculator)

1. **C** The probability of selecting a grey wolf with yellow eyes is $\dfrac{16}{30}$, and the probability of selecting coyote with brown eyes is $\dfrac{5}{30}$. Therefore, the probability of selecting one or the other is $\dfrac{16}{30} + \dfrac{5}{30} = \dfrac{21}{30}$, so (C) is correct.

2. **D** Use Process of Elimination. From 1992 to 1996 the graph shows a downward slope, which indicates a decrease in military spending. Therefore, eliminate (B) and (C). In 2001 the graph shows an upward slope, which indicates an increase in military spending. Eliminate (A). Choice (D) is correct.

3.  **B**  During the 40 minutes that Eddie stops to repair his bike, his distance does not change. On the graph, this time period would be shown as a flat horizontal line. The only flat horizontal portion of the graph occurs between about 11:10 A.M., just before noon. So, he finished repairing his bike just before noon, and (B) is correct.

4.  **C**  Use Bite-Sized Pieces to carefully tackle this one step at a time. Translate "4 percent" of the 648 male employees into math and calculate: $\frac{4}{100}(648) = 25.92$ male employees who received bonuses. Do the same for the female employees: $\frac{6}{100}(519) = 31.14$ female employees who received bonuses. Add these together to get $25.92 + 31.14 = 57.06$. This is closest to (C), so (C) is correct.

5.  **B**  Use Bite-Sized Pieces. Start by adding the $x^2$ terms: $4x^2 + 2x^2 = 6x^2$. Eliminate (C) and (D). Next, since the $x$ terms are the same in the remaining answers, add the constants: $-2 + 9 = 7$. Eliminate (A). Therefore, the correct answer is (B).

6.  **D**  Plug in. According to the table, when $k = 1$, $g(k) = -3$. Plug in 1 for $k$ in the answers and eliminate any answers that do not return a value of $-3$. Choice (A) becomes $1 - 1 = 0$. Eliminate (A). Choice (B) becomes $2(1) - 4 = -2$. Eliminate (B). Choice (C) becomes $3(1) - 5 = -2$. Eliminate (C). Choice (D) becomes $4(1) - 7 = -3$. Therefore, the correct answer is (D).

7.  **D**  Use Process of Elimination. Since $x$ represents the number of years since 2005, the $-0.14$ must somehow be related to the number of years. Eliminate (A) and (B) since the question states that $y$ represents the rainfall in any given year. Choice (C) would be represented by the $y$-value for 2005 minus the $y$-value for 2015, so eliminate (C). The correct answer is (D).

8.  **C**  There are $60(6) = 360$ minutes in 6 hours. To calculate the distance the insect crawls, set up the following proportion: $\frac{30 \text{ inches}}{16.3 \text{ min}} = \frac{x}{360 \text{ min}}$. Cross-multiply: $16.3x = 30(360)$. Solve for $x$, resulting in $16.3x = 10,800$ and $x = 662.577$. The question asks for an *approximate* answer, so choose the closest answer, which is (C).

9.  **B**  To isolate $v$, multiply both sides of the equation by $\frac{5}{8}$, resulting in $v = \frac{7}{4} \times \frac{5}{8} = \frac{35}{32}$. Choice (B) is correct.

10. **B**  The term *zero* means an $x$-intercept (a point where the curve crosses the $x$-axis. The only graph showing a curve that crosses the $x$-axis 4 times is (B), so (B) is correct.

11. **A**  According the information given, $Q = mC$ where $C = \frac{J}{g}$. The chart shows that the heat capacity $\left(\frac{J}{g}\right)$ for copper is 0.39, and the mass is 75. Therefore, $Q = 75(0.39) = 29.25$, which matches (A).

12.  **A**  According to the information given, $Q = mC$. The table indicates that for porcelain, $C = 1.08$. Find the mass of the porcelain by plugging in 80 for $Q$ and 1.08 for $C$, resulting in $80 = m(1.08)$. Solve for $m$ to get $m \approx 74$. To find the unknown substance, plug in 67 for $Q$ and 74 for $m$, resulting in $67 = 74C$. Solve for $C$ to get $C \approx 0.9054$. This approximates the value given for aluminum in the chart. Choice (A) is correct.

13.  **D**  Use Process of Elimination. The study was done on 200 people with severe hearing loss. Eliminate (A) because the study population doesn't deal with all people; it only deals with people who have severe hearing loss. Because no other hearing-improvement products were mentioned in the question, eliminate (B). In comparing (C) and (D), (C) is too broad, because it applies to people generally, rather than just to the people with severe hearing loss who were studied. Therefore, eliminate (C) and choose (D).

14.  **C**  Since the problem asks for an expression for $a$, rearrange the formula so that $a$ is alone on one side. First, subtract $vt$ from both sides, resulting in $d - vt = -\dfrac{1}{2}at^2$. Next, multiply both sides by $-2$, resulting in $-2(d - vt) = at^2$, then divide both sides by $t^2$, resulting in $\dfrac{-2(d - vt)}{t^2} = a$. To make the equation look like the answer choices, flip it around so the $a$ is on the left and apply the $t^2$ in the denominator to each part of the binomial in the parentheses. The equation becomes $a = -2\left(\dfrac{d}{t^2} - \dfrac{vt}{t^2}\right)$, and the second fraction can be reduced, resulting in $a = -2\left(\dfrac{d}{t^2} - \dfrac{v}{t}\right)$. Finally, apply the negative sign in front of the 2 to the terms in the parentheses and switch their order: $a = 2\left(\dfrac{v}{t} - \dfrac{d}{t^2}\right)$, which matches (C).

15.  **B**  The ribbon costs $0.15(36) = \$5.40$ per yard. There are variables in the answer choices, so plug in. If $y = 2$, then $p = 2(5.40) = 10.80$. Plug 2 in for $y$ in the answers to see which answer returns a value of 10.80. Choice (A) becomes $0.15(2) + 36 = 36.30$. Eliminate (A). Choice (B) becomes $0.15(36)(2) = 10.8$. Keep (B), but check (C) and (D) just in case. Choice (C) becomes $\dfrac{0.15(2)}{36} \approx 0.008$. Eliminate (C). Choice (D) becomes $\dfrac{36(2)}{0.15} = 480$. Eliminate (D). Choice (B) is correct.

16.  **A**  There are variables in the answer choices, so plug in. If $q = 40$, then $C = 60(40) + 300 = 2{,}700$. Now decrease $q$ by 20 units: if $q = 20$, then $C = 60(20) + 300 = 1{,}500$. $2{,}700 - 1{,}500 = 1{,}200$. Choice (A) is correct.

17.  **C**  To find the quantity at which revenues will equal costs, set the equations equal to each other: $60q + 300 = 75q$. Subtract $60q$ from each side to get $300 = 15q$, and $q = 20$, which matches (C).

18.  **C**  Look up the values for $f(x)$ and $g(x)$ for each of the $x$-values in the answer choices and see which pair adds up to 1. For (A), $f(-5) = -1$ and $g(-5) = -1$, and the sum of these values is $-2$. Eliminate (A). For (B), $f(-4)$ is a small negative number and $g(-4) = 0$, and the sum of these values is negative, so eliminate (B). For (C), $f(-3) = 0$ and $g(-3) = 1$, and the sum of these values is 1. Therefore, (C) is correct.

19.  **B**  Exponential decay provides increasingly greater or smaller changes in values as time progresses. Plug in to see what would happen in each situation. Let the initial value of the item equal $100. For (A), the item would lose $100 \times 0.05 = \$5$ every year. Eliminate (A), because the amount of value the item loses would be the same every year. For (B), the item would lose $100 \times 0.06 = \$6$ the first year. Therefore, the new item value would be $100 - 6 = \$94$. The second year, the item would lose $94 \times 0.06 = \$5.64$, and the new item value would be $94 - 5.64 = \$88.36$. Each successive year, the loss would be less than the loss the year before. This is an exponential decay; therefore, the correct answer is (B).

20.  **B**  First, calculate the number of imperial pints that can be made with 17 ounces of sugar. Set up

the following proportion: $\dfrac{1 \text{ ounce}}{30 \text{ I. pints}} = \dfrac{17 \text{ ounces}}{x}$. Cross-multiply to get $x = 510$ imperial pints.

Next, calculate the number of U.S. pints that are equivalent to 510 imperial pints by setting up

the following proportion: $\dfrac{1 \text{ I. pint}}{1\frac{1}{4} \text{ U.S. pints}} = \dfrac{510 \text{ I. pints}}{x}$. Simplify the left side of the equation to

$\dfrac{1}{\frac{5}{4}} = \dfrac{510}{x}$, or $\dfrac{4}{5} = \dfrac{510}{x}$. Cross-multiply, resulting in $4x = 2,550$. Solve for $x$ to get $x = 637.5$. The

closest approximation for 637.5 is 640. Choice (B) is correct.

21.  **A**  The actual plotted point at 230 inches is 49 yards. However, the line of best fit at 230 inches equals 47.5 inches. $49 - 47.5 = 1.5$. Therefore, (A) is correct.

22.  **B**  The question asks for a specific amount, so plug in the answers. Start with (B). If there are 23 girls in the troop, then Mrs. Warren currently has $23(4) + 11 = 103$ boxes. If she were to give 5 boxes to each girl, she would need $23(5) = 115$. Therefore, she is $115 - 103 = 12$ boxes short. Since this matches the information given in the problem, the correct answer is (B).

23.  **D**  Let $l$ = the largest number and $s$ = the sum of the other two numbers. According to the question, $l = \dfrac{4}{3}s$. Divide both sides by $\dfrac{4}{3}$ to get $\dfrac{3}{4}l = s$. Plug in the answers, starting with (B). If the largest number is 245, the sum of the other two numbers is $\dfrac{3}{4}(245) = 183.75$. The sum of all three numbers would be $245 + 183.75 = 428.75$. Eliminate both (A) and (B) because these values

are too small. Try (C). If the largest number is 350, then the sum of the other two numbers is $\frac{3}{4}(350) = 262.5$, and the sum of all three numbers is $350 + 262.5 = 612.5$. Eliminate (C). Since only (D) remains, it must be the correct answer.

24.  **B**  When the question asks for a specific value, plug in the answers. Start with (B) and make $j = 15.5$. The value of $x$ would then be $3(15.5) - 19 = 27.5$, and the value of $z$ would be $5(15.5) - 15 = 62.5$. Now use a calculator to check to if $\cos(27.5°) = \sin(62.5°)$. Both equal 0.887, so (B) is correct.

25.  **D**  First, plug in a length and a width for the rectangle. Let, $l = 12$ and $w = 10$. The area of this rectangle can be calculated as $A = lw = (12)(10) = 120$. In the new rectangle, the length is reduced by 25% or $\frac{1}{4}$, making the new length $12 - \left(\frac{1}{4}\right)(12) = 9$. The area of 120 is increased by 5%, so the new area is $120 + \left(\frac{5}{100}\right)(120) = 120 + 6 = 126$. Plug these new numbers into the area formula to get $126 = 9w$, then divide both sides by 9 to get $w = 14$. The width increased from 10 to 14, but the question asks for the percent increase, which is calculated as $\frac{difference}{original} \times 100$. In this case, that value is $\frac{14 - 10}{10}(100) = \frac{4}{10}(100) = 40$, so $k = 40\%$, and the correct answer is (D).

26.  **C**  The formula for the volume of a cylinder is $V = \pi r^2 h$. For the figure shown, $r = 3$ and $h = 12$. The volume of the cylinder portion of the capsule is $V = \pi(3^2)(12) = 108\pi$. The two ends of the capsule make up one complete sphere. The formula for the volume of a sphere is $V = \frac{4}{3}\pi r^3$. Again, $r = 3$. Therefore, the volume of spherical portion of the capsule is $V = \frac{4}{3}\pi(3)^3 = 36\pi$. The volume of the entire figure is $108\pi + 36\pi = 144\pi \approx 452.4$. The correct answer is (C).

27.  **A**  Given two points on a line, the slope is calculated as $\frac{y_2 - y_1}{x_2 - x_1}$. Use the points $(0, 0)$ and $(p, 4)$ to find the slope of the line: $\frac{4 - 0}{p - 0} = \frac{4}{p}$. Next, use the points $(0, 0)$ and $(9, p)$ to find the slope of the line: $\frac{p - 0}{9 - 0} = \frac{p}{9}$. Set the two expressions equal to each other to get $\frac{4}{p} = \frac{p}{9}$. Cross-multiply to get $p^2 = 36$. Solve for $p$ to get $p = \pm 6$. Only the $-6$ value appears in the answers, so (A) is correct.

28.  **D**  To fill in the table, write a system of equations using the information given. Call the number of decaffeinated teas $x$, so the number of caffeinated teas is $3x$. Call the number to decaffeinated coffees $y$, so the number of caffeinated coffees is $5y$. The two equations that can be written from this information and the table are $x + y = 28$ and $3x + 5y = 116$. When dealing with systems of equations, look for a way to stack and add the equations to eliminate one variable and solve for another.

To do this, multiply the first equation, $x + y = 28$, by $-3$ to get $-3x - 3y = -84$. Now stack and add the equations:

$$3x + 5y = 116$$
$$\underline{-3x - 3y = -84}$$
$$2y = \phantom{0}32$$

Divide by 2 to get $y = 16$. This means that $x = 28 - y = 28 - 16 = 12$. Use these values to fill in the chart.

|  | Decaffeinated | Caffeinated |
|---|---|---|
| Tea | $x = 12$ | $3x = 36$ |
| Coffee | $y = 16$ | $5y = 80$ |
| Total | 28 | 116 |

Now find the probability that a caffeinated beverage chosen at random is a coffee. Divide the number of caffeinated coffees, 80, by the total number of caffeinated beverages, 116, to get a probability of 0.69. Choice (D) is correct.

29. **B** Start by consolidating like terms. The top equation becomes $j = 3x - 9$, and the bottom equation becomes $k = 3y - 9$. In the first equation, replace $j$ with $k + 1.5$ to get $k + 1.5 = 3x - 9$. Solve this equation for $k$ to get $k = 3x - 10.5$. Set the two equations equal to each other to get $3y - 9 = 3x - 10.5$. Add 10.5 to both sides to get $3y + 1.5 = 3x$. Divide the entire equation by 3 to get $y + 0.5 = x$. Choice (B) is correct. Another approach would be to plug in numbers for $j$ and $k$ then solve for $x$ and $y$.

30. **C** The fastest way to solve this is to use the decay formula: *final amount = original amount* $(1 - r)^t$. In this case, the *original amount* = 6,500 and the $r = 0.2$. The *final amount* = $6,500(1 - 0.2)^t =$ $6,500(0.8)^t$. Eliminate (A) and (B). Next, plug in a value for $m$. If $m = 12$, then because the value of the baseball cards decreases every 6 months, $t = \dfrac{12}{6} = 2$. This matches (C). Of course, this question can also be solved without the formula, though not as quickly. Pick a value for $m$ that will make the number of baseball cards easy to calculate, such as $m = 6$. Banerji starts with 6,500 cards, and he will sell off 20% of them in those 6 months. Calculate 20% of 6,500, which is 1,300, then subtract that from 6,500 to get 5,200 cards. This is the target value. Plug in $m = 6$ in each of the answer choices to see which one equals 5,200. Only (C) matches this target value.

31. **3** Start by distributing the negative three to get $6x^2 - 7x + 5 - 3x^2 + 15x - 12$. Combine like terms to get $3x^2 + 8x - 7$. Therefore, $a = 3$.

32. **5 or 6** One onion costs $0.50. Subtract that from the total amounts that Emeril might spend to find that he can spend between $1.50 and $2 on potatoes. If he spends $1.50 on potatoes that cost $0.30 each, he can buy 5 potatoes. If he spends closer to $2.00 on potatoes, he can get 6 for $1.80. He can't get 7 potatoes, as that would put him over his $2 potato budget, so Emeril can get 5 or 6 potatoes.

33. **25.2** The mean of a list is the total divided by the number of items in the list. Here, the total of all the heights is 302, and there are 12 infants in the program. $\frac{302}{12} = 25.1\overline{6}$. Rounded to the nearest tenth, this becomes 25.2.

34. **40** For an average score of 75 on all 8 exams, Jacob needs to score a total of $75 \times 8 = 600$ points. Over the first 4 exams, he has already scored $65 \times 4 = 260$ points. To find the minimum score allowable for the 5th exam, maximize the scores on all of the other remaining exams. The most he can score on an exam is 100. If he got 100 on the 6th, 7th, and 8th exams that would be a total of 300 points. Add this to his current points: $300 + 260 = 560$ points, which means that on the 5th test, he would need to score a minimum of $600 - 560 = 40$.

35. **1,000** Draw a rough sketch of the graph of this system of inequalities to figure out what is going on here. It would look something like this:

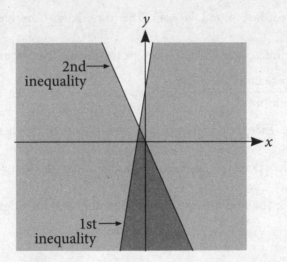

The area included in both inequalities represents the solution to the system. The question asks for the greatest value of $k$, which is the $y$-coordinate, so it would happen as close to the top of the graph as possible. For the area of overlap representing the solution, this happens at the point of intersection of the two lines. Find this point of intersection by setting the two equations $y = 20x + 3,500$ and $y = -8x$ equal to each other to get $20x + 3,500 = -8x$. Add $8x$ to both sides to get $28x + 3,500 = 0$, then subtract 3,500 from both sides to get $28x = -3,500$. Dividing both sides by 28 results in $x = -125$. This is the value for $j$, and it can be plugged back into either equation to get the value of $k$, the $y$-coordinate at that point. Use the easier equation, $y = -8x$ to get $k = -8(-125) = 1,000$.

36. $\dfrac{7}{12}$ or .583

There is a proportional relationship between the arc length, degree measure, and area of a section of a circle formed by two radii. For this question, the important aspects of the circle are the given angle measure of $\dfrac{7\pi}{6}$ radians and the arc the question asks about. Set up a proportion: $\dfrac{\text{arc}}{\text{circumference}} = \dfrac{\text{angle measure}}{\text{total radians}}$. This fractional part of the circumference in the first part of the proportion is what the question is asking for, so focus on the second part. The angle measure is given, and the total number of radians in a circle is $2\pi$. Fill in the second fraction to get $\dfrac{\text{arc}}{\text{circumference}} = \dfrac{\frac{7\pi}{6}}{2\pi}$. Dividing by a number is the same as multiplying by the reciprocal of the number, so the second fraction becomes $\dfrac{7\pi}{6} \times \dfrac{1}{2\pi} = \dfrac{7}{12}$.

37. **20** Start by calculating the average number of patients in the Kind Care clinic. According to the information provided, $m = 4$ and $W = 45$. Therefore, Kind Care has an average of $4(45) = 180$ patients in their clinic. Speedy Care sees 324 patients "per hour," so set up a proportion: $\dfrac{324 \text{ patients}}{60 \text{ minutes}} = \dfrac{m \text{ patients}}{1 \text{ minute}}$. Cross-multiply to get $60m = 324$, then divide by 60 to get $m = 5.4$ patients per minute. Therefore, the average number of patients in their clinic can be calculated as $L = 5.4(40) = 216$. To calculate a "percent greater than," use the following formula percent change formula: $\dfrac{\text{difference}}{\text{original}} \times 100$. In this case, the smaller number is the original, so the percent change is $\dfrac{216 - 180}{180} \times 100 = 20$.

38. **9** According to the question, the rate at which patients enter the clinic is defined as $m$ patients per minute. This question gives the rate of 36 patients "per hour," so set up a proportion: $\dfrac{36 \text{ patients}}{60 \text{ minutes}} = \dfrac{m \text{ patients}}{1 \text{ minute}}$. Cross-multiply to get $60m = 36$, then divide by 60 to get $m = 0.6$ patients per minute. Each stays with the doctor an average of 15 minutes, so to find the average number of patients being treated, $L$, use the formula to get $L = (0.6)(15) = 9$.

# Chapter 9
# Practice Test 4

# Reading Test

## 65 MINUTES, 52 QUESTIONS

**Turn to Section 1 of your answer sheet to answer the questions in this section.**

DIRECTIONS

Each passage or pair of passages below is followed by a number of questions. After reading each passage or pair, choose the best answer to each question based on what is stated or implied in the passage or passages and in any accompanying graphics (such as a table or graph).

**Questions 1–10 are based on the following passage.**

This passage is adapted from Ayn Rand, *Anthem.* © 1938. The protagonist, a street sweeper named Equality 7-2521, lives in a society in which the word "I" is forbidden.

*Note: Because the word "I" is forbidden in this society, the narrator refers to himself as "we."*

And as we all undress at night, in the dim light of the candles, our brothers are silent, for they dare not speak the thoughts of their minds. For all must agree
Line with all, and they cannot know if their thoughts are the
5 thoughts of all, and so they fear to speak. And they are glad when the candles are blown for the night. But we, Equality 7-2521, look through the window upon the sky, and there is peace in the sky, and cleanliness, and dignity. And beyond the City there lies the plain, and
10 beyond the plain, black upon the black sky, there lies the Uncharted Forest. We do not wish to look upon the Uncharted Forest. We do not wish to think of it. But ever do our eyes return to that black patch upon the sky. Men never enter the Uncharted Forest, for there is
15 no power to explore it and no path to lead among its ancient trees which stand as guards of fearful secrets. It is whispered that once or twice in a hundred years, one among the men of the City escape alone and run to the Uncharted Forest, without call or reason. These
20 men do not return. They perish from hunger and from the claws of the wild beasts which roam the Forest. But our Councils say that this is only a legend. We have heard that there are many Uncharted Forests over the land, among the Cities. And it is whispered that
25 they have grown over the ruins of many cities of the

Unmentionable Times. The trees have swallowed the ruins, and the bones under the ruins, and all the things which perished. And as we look upon the Uncharted Forest far in the night, we think of the secrets of the
30 Unmentionable Times. And we wonder how it came to pass that these secrets were lost to the world.

We have heard the legends of the great fighting, in which many men fought on one side and only a few on the other. These few were the Evil Ones and they were
35 conquered. Then great fires raged over the land. And in these fires the Evil Ones and all the things made by the Evil Ones were burned. And the fire which is called the Dawn of the Great Rebirth, was the Script Fire where all the scripts of the Evil Ones were burned, and with them
40 all the words of the Evil Ones. The words of the Evil Ones... The words of the Unmentionable Times... What are the words which we have lost? May the Council have mercy upon us! We had no wish to write such a question, and we knew not what we were doing till we
45 had written it. We shall not ask this question and we shall not think it. We shall not call death upon our head.

And yet . . . And yet . . . There is some word, one single word which is not in the language of men, but which had been. And this is the Unspeakable Word,
50 which no men may speak nor hear. But sometimes, and it is rare, sometimes, somewhere, one among men find that word. They find it upon scraps of old manuscripts or cut into the fragments of ancient stones. But when they speak it they are put to death.
55 There is no crime punished by death in this world, save this one crime of speaking the Unspeakable Word.

CONTINUE

**1**

In the passage, the narrator's focus shifts from

A) fear of exploring frontiers to preparation for it.

B) disquiet about the unknown to curiosity about it.

C) acknowledgement of an ancient city to dismissal of it.

D) repetition of the Council's rules to acceptance of them.

**2**

Which choice provides the best evidence for the answer to the previous question?

A) Lines 1–3 ("And as . . . minds")

B) Line 22 ("But our . . . legend")

C) Lines 35–37 ("And in . . . burned")

D) Lines 47–49 ("And yet . . . been")

**3**

As used in lines 3–4, "all must agree with all" most nearly means

A) truth is true.

B) language must be accurate.

C) thought must be uniform.

D) words match their meaning.

**4**

The sentence in lines 12–14 ("But ever . . . sky") mainly serves to

A) confirm that the narrator's job is to guard against outside threats.

B) show that some people find an object of mystery to be of recurring interest.

C) indicate that members of the narrator's society know everyone keeps looking at the horizon.

D) illustrate a repeated action stemming from a confusion about an unexplainable phenomenon.

**5**

The narrator states that a person who wished to navigate the Uncharted Forest would find

A) no source of electricity.

B) it impossible to locate objects within.

C) answers to many long-forgotten questions.

D) no clear trail through.

**6**

Which choice provides the best evidence for the answer to the previous question?

A) Lines 14–16 ("Men never . . . secrets")

B) Lines 20–21 ("They perish . . . Forest")

C) Lines 26–28 ("The trees . . . perished")

D) Lines 37–40 ("And the . . . Ones")

**7**

Which of the following most accurately expresses the narrator's perspective about exploring the secrets of the past?

A) Compelling but dangerous

B) Easily pursuable but illegal

C) Unavoidable but unexpectedly challenging

D) Appealing but inauthentic

**8**

The statement the narrator makes in lines 26–28 ("The trees . . . perished") can be most clearly inferred to mean that

A) people who ask questions in the narrator's society are banished to the Forest.

B) the trees grew in the streets of cities in the Unmentionable Times.

C) the visible traces of the past have been completely obscured.

D) the city buries its dead in the Forest.

**CONTINUE**

As used in lines 30–31, "how it came to pass" most nearly means

A) what crossed each other.

B) what went in circles.

C) what happened historically.

D) how time elapsed.

As used in line 39, "scripts" most nearly means

A) clothes.

B) habits.

C) screenplays.

D) writings.

CONTINUE

**Questions 11–21 are based on the following passage and supplementary material.**

The following excerpt is from The Economist, "Bring on the Hipsters: Gentrification Is Good for the Poor." © 2015 by The Economist.

In an old bar on U Street in Washington, DC—a place that was once a centre of black life and is now an inferno of hipsterdom—Jay, the bartender, is talking

*Line*  about how the area has changed over the past decade
5  or so. "They ain't got barmen any more," he says, with a grin. "They got mixologists." What happens in Washington, he explains, is that young white professionals move in, bars open, "and then you know that all the bodegas and liquor stores on every corner,
10  they ain't got long either."

Such gentrification obsesses the *bien-pensants*. In November the *New York Times* instructed its journalists to stop comparing everywhere to gentrified Brooklyn. A *Saturday Night Live* sketch showed a
15  young man in a tough neighborhood talking about his "bitches"—only to reveal that he runs a dog-walking business, and even knits matching sweaters for his bitches. In Philadelphia and San Francisco, presumed gentrifiers have been the target of protests and attacks.
20  Elsewhere, the term is used as an insult ("I would hate to be a gentrifier," says one young professional in Detroit). Yet the evidence suggests that gentrification is both rare and, on balance, a good thing.

The case against it is simple. Newcomers with
25  more money supposedly crowd out older residents. In Washington, according to a study by *Governing* magazine, 52% of census tracts that were poor in 2000 have since gentrified—more than in any other city bar Portland, Oregon. Young, mostly white singletons have
30  crowded into a district once built for families. Over the same period, housing in Washington has become vastly more expensive. And many black residents have left: between 1990 and 2010, the number of African-Americans in the District declined by almost 100,000,
35  falling from 66% of the population to 51%.

In New York and San Francisco, which both have rent-control rules, soaring property prices create an incentive for property owners to get rid of their tenants. Stories abound of unscrupulous developers
40  buying up rent-controlled properties and then using

legal loopholes or trickery to force residents to leave. Letting a building deteriorate so much that it can be knocked down is one tactic; bribing building inspectors to evict tenants illegally is another.

45  Yet there is little evidence that gentrification is responsible for displacing the poor or minorities. Black people were moving out of Washington in the 1980s, long before most parts of the city began gentrifying. In cities like Detroit, where gentrifiers are few and far
50  between and housing costs almost nothing, they are still leaving. One 2008 study of census data found "no evidence of displacement of low-income non-white households in gentrifying neighborhoods." They did find, however, that the average income of black people
55  with high-school diplomas in gentrifying areas soared.

Gentrifiers can make life better for locals in plenty of ways, argues Stuart Butler of the Brookings Institution, a think-tank. When professionals move to an area, "they know how to get things done." They
60  put pressure on schools, the police and the city to improve. As property prices increase, rents go up—but that also generates more property-tax revenue, helping to improve local services. In many cities, zoning laws force developers to build subsidized housing for the
65  poor as well as pricey pads for well-off newcomers, which means that rising house prices can help to create more subsidized housing, not less.

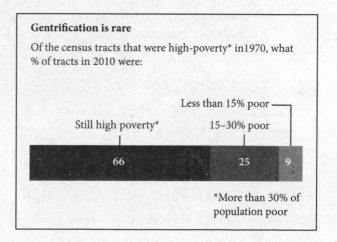

**Gentrification is rare**

Of the census tracts that were high-poverty* in 1970, what % of tracts in 2010 were:

| Still high poverty* | 15–30% poor | Less than 15% poor |
|:---:|:---:|:---:|
| 66 | 25 | 9 |

*More than 30% of population poor

**CONTINUE →**

The bigger problem for most American cities, says Mr. Butler, is not gentrification but the opposite: the
70 concentration of poverty. Of neighborhoods that were more than 30% poor in 1970, just 9% are now less poor than the national average (see chart), according to the City Observatory, a think-tank. In Chicago, yuppies can easily buy coffee and vinyl records in northern
75 neighborhoods such as Wicker Park. But the South Side, where racist housing policies created a ghetto in the 1950s and 1960s, remains violent and poor. In Brooklyn the most famously gentrified district, Williamsburg, was never all that poor in the first place.
80      However annoying they may be, hipsters help the poor. Their vintage shops and craft-beer bars generate jobs and taxes. So if you see a bearded intruder on a fixed-gear bike in your neighborhood, welcome him.

**11**

According to the passage, which choice best describes the case against gentrification?

A) New establishments catering to professionals threaten existing neighborhood stores.

B) As professionals move into neighborhoods, they displace previous residents.

C) Small businesses moving into the neighborhoods can create positive economic benefits for the area.

D) Discriminatory policies have led to the formation of minority-dominated ghettos.

**12**

Which choice provides the best evidence for the answer to the previous question?

A) Lines 5–6 ("They ain't . . . mixologists")

B) Lines 24–25 ("Newcomers with . . . residents")

C) Lines 46–48 ("Black people . . . gentrifying")

D) Lines 81–82 ("Their vintage . . . taxes")

**13**

According to the passage, members of which demographic moved into census tracts that were poor in 2000?

A) White singletons

B) Established families

C) African-Americans

D) Older residents

**14**

In line 37, "soaring" is closest in meaning to

A) flying.

B) suffering.

C) floating.

D) rising.

**15**

Which choice best summarizes the fifth paragraph of the passage (lines 45–55)?

A) Gentrification can lead to an increase in income for minority high-school graduates.

B) Minorities have been leaving cities like Washington and Detroit for decades.

C) Residents of poor minority households can be displaced by things other than gentrification.

D) Minorities have been profiting from gentrification in Washington and Detroit.

**CONTINUE**

**16**

The passage implies that gentrifiers moving into communities

A) cause property values to decrease to prohibitive levels.

B) put pressure on local police to remove low-income residents.

C) always crowd out older, established residents.

D) can effect positive change in their communities.

**17**

Which choice provides the best evidence for the answer to the previous question?

A) Lines 45–46 ("Yet there . . . minorities")

B) Lines 53–55 ("They did . . . soared")

C) Lines 61–63 ("As property . . . services")

D) Lines 68–70 ("The bigger . . . poverty")

**18**

As used in line 62, "generates" is closest in meaning to

A) powers.

B) ages.

C) creates.

D) increases.

**19**

The author of the passage would most likely consider the information in the chart to be

A) clear evidence to support an expert's opinion.

B) definitive proof for the main argument in the passage.

C) ambiguous data provided by a think-tank.

D) too limited to be useful.

**20**

According to the chart, most high-poverty census tracts in 1970 were characterized by

A) high poverty in 2010.

B) 15%–30% poverty in 2010.

C) less than 15% poverty in 2010.

D) increased poverty in 2010.

**21**

The chart suggests which of the following about poor areas?

A) One-tenth of gentrified areas have the lowest number of poor people.

B) One-fourth of poor areas might become gentrified.

C) One-third of poor areas might become gentrified.

D) Two-thirds of high-poverty areas may remain impoverished.

**CONTINUE**

**Questions 22–32 are based on the following passage and supplementary material.**

This passage is adapted from Schmitt et al., "Identifying the Volcanic Eruption Depicted in a Neolithic Painting at Çatalhöyük, Central Anatolia, Turkey." © 2014 by PLOS ONE.

A mural excavated at the Neolithic Çatalhöyük site (Central Anatolia, Turkey) has been interpreted as the oldest known map. Dating to around 6600 B.C.E.,
*Line*
5  it putatively depicts an explosive summit eruption of the Hasan Dağı twin-peaks volcano located about 130 km northeast of Çatalhöyük, and a birds-eye view of a town plan in the foreground. This interpretation, however, has remained controversial not least because independent evidence for a contemporaneous
10  explosive volcanic eruption of Hasan Dağı has been lacking.

Here, we document the presence of andesitic pumice veneer on the summit of Hasan Dağı, which we dated using (U-Th)/He zircon geochronology.
15  Collectively, our results reveal protracted intrusive activity at Hasan Dağı punctuated by explosive venting, and provide the first radiometric ages for a Holocene explosive eruption which was most likely witnessed by humans in the area. Geologic and
20  geochronologic lines of evidence thus support previous interpretations that residents of Çatalhöyük artistically represented an explosive eruption of Hasan Dağı volcano.

Starting from the discovery of the Neolithic
25  settlement of Çatalhöyük in the early 1960s by British archaeologist James Mellaart, the excavations at this location have provided unique insights into the living conditions of humans at the transition from hunter-gatherer to settled agriculture societies.
30  One outstanding find is a mural from level VII of Çatalhöyük famously described by its discoverer as depicting a volcanic eruption.

Similar interpretations, differing in detail, have been put forward since then, implicating this painting
35  not only as the oldest depiction of a volcanic eruption, but as a contender for being the first graphical representation of a landscape or a map. Detailed volcanological interpretations of the painting include reconstructions of the eruptive style with the summit
40  region showing "falling volcanic 'bombs' or large semiliquid lava." According to these interpreters, the most likely candidate for the erupting volcano depicted in the upper register of the painting is the twin-peak

volcano of Hasan Dağı, located about 130 km NE of
45  Çatalhöyük.

This view, however, has been contested, largely because of the extraordinary age of the mural, and the absence of any other landscape art or map until much later in history. The depiction of a leopard skin
50  underlain by geometric patterns has been proposed instead.

A testable prediction of the volcanic eruption hypothesis for the Çatalhöyük mural is a geologic record of an eruption that would fall into, or briefly
55  predate, the time when the Çatalhöyük mural was painted.

Protracted periods of oral tradition over 250 generations have been proposed for prehistoric native North American myths following the Mount Mazama
60  eruption at around 5700 B.C.E. For the Çatalhöyük map (and volcano) hypothesis to be plausible, however, we surmise that a brief line of oral tradition, or even an eyewitness portrayal, is perhaps more likely than tradition of a myth that detached itself from its
65  inspiration in the physical world. This is not to say that realism must prevail in Neolithic art, but many of the apparent details can be reasonably expected to become lost or obscured during a long period of oral tradition. A tradition that predated the settlement of Çatalhöyük
70  thus appears very unlikely, and hence we would predict a time period for the eruption between 7400 and 6600 B.C.E. based on the [14]C chronology of the Çatalhöyük cultural strata.

Neither proponents nor opponents of the "volcano"
75  hypothesis for the Çatalhöyük painting have thus far scrutinized if and when such a volcanic eruption might have occurred. The radiometric age, and the following geologic evidence, corroborates the "volcano" hypothesis.

CONTINUE ➡

## (U-Th)/He zircon

A — HD
xenocrysts (excluded)
eruption:
8.97±0.64 ka (2σ)
MSWD = 0.55
n = 12

HD = crystal particles from rim of volcano
HDA = crystal particles from flank of volcano

B
eruption:
28.9±1.5 ka (2σ)
MSWD = 1.2
n = 18

HDA

Ranked Order

Age (ka)
(Note: 1 ka = 1,000 years)

Figure 1: This table shows the (U-Th)/He zircon dated ages of sample particles removed from the rim and the flank of the Hasan Dağı volcano.

---

**22**

The main purpose of the passage is to

A) describe periods in Turkey's ancient geologic history.

B) explain the ways scientists use radiometric aging.

C) describe opposing views regarding an ancient mural and cautiously endorse one view.

D) explain how andesitic pumice veneer forms after volcanic eruptions.

---

**23**

Over the course of the passage, the focus shifts from

A) an explanation of a theory to a response to criticism of this theory.

B) a depiction of an event to its proof in oral history.

C) the use of (U-Th)/He zircon geochronology to a new method.

D) the use of radiometric aging to an examination of andesitic pumice veneer.

---

**24**

Which choice provides the best evidence for the answer to the previous question?

A) Lines 12–14 ("Here, we . . . geochronology")

B) Lines 46–49 ("This view . . . history")

C) Lines 60–65 ("For the . . . world")

D) Lines 77–79 ("The radiometric . . . hypothesis")

---

**25**

The author uses the phrase "it putatively depicts" (line 4) most likely to

A) detail the hands-on nature of the work done by those who study science.

B) emphasize the fact that scientists must always question theories.

C) underscore the need for clarification of the work of scientists.

D) bolster the idea that the evidence to support the claim is imperfect.

---

**26**

Where does the author indicate the Neolithic volcanic eruption most probably was located?

A) Near Central Anatolia, in Turkey

B) In the British Isles

C) In the Middle East

D) In the central region of North America

---

CONTINUE

**27**

Which choice provides the best evidence for the answer to the previous question?

A) Lines 1–6 ("A mural . . . Çatalhöyük")

B) Lines 24–29 ("Starting from . . . societies")

C) Lines 57–60 ("Protracted periods . . . B.C.E.")

D) Lines 60–65 ("For the . . . world")

**28**

As used in line 65, the phrase "This is not to say" implies that

A) the lost details are crucial for proving the truth.

B) oral traditions describe stories but not real events.

C) the scientists don't expect the mural to be completely true to life.

D) Neolithic artists used realism to portray the natural world.

**29**

Which choice best supports the claim that the mural was painted near the time of the volcanic eruption?

A) Lines 7–11 ("This interpretation . . . lacking")

B) Lines 49–51 ("The depiction . . . instead")

C) Lines 65–68 ("This is . . . tradition")

D) Lines 74–77 ("Neither proponents . . . occurred")

**30**

According to the data, the youngest Holocene eruption age for Hasan Dağı is approximately

A) 1.2 ka.

B) 8.97 ka.

C) 18 ka.

D) 28.9 ka.

**31**

The passage and the figure are in agreement that the chronology of the Çatalhöyük cultural strata predicts that the Hasan Dağı volcano erupted between

A) 9000 and 8000 B.C.E.

B) 7000 and 6000 B.C.E.

C) 6000 and 5000 B.C.E.

D) 4500 and 3500 B.C.E.

**32**

What statement is best supported by the data presented in the figure?

A) Xenocrysts are excluded from the data interpretation because the crystals are too new to be useful.

B) An oral tradition describing the eruption lasted for over 250 generations.

C) The dating method called (U-Th)/He zircon geochronology is the best way to determine the age of an artifact.

D) Particles on the rim of a volcano are more likely to be from recent eruptions than particles on the flank of the volcano.

**CONTINUE**

**Questions 33–42 are based on the following passages.**

Passage 1 is excerpted from Edmund Burke, *Reflections on the Revolution in France*. Originally published in 1790. Passage 2 is excerpted from Thomas Paine, *Common Sense*. Originally published in 1776.

**Passage 1**

A few years ago I should be ashamed to overload a matter so capable of supporting itself by the then unnecessary support of any argument; but this

Line

5   seditious, unconstitutional doctrine is now publicly taught, avowed, and printed.

The people of England will not ape the fashions they have never tried, nor go back to those which they have found mischievous on trial. They look upon the legal hereditary succession of their crown as among

10  their rights, not as among their wrongs; as a benefit, not as a grievance; as a security for their liberty, not as a badge of servitude. They look on the frame of their commonwealth, *such as it stands*, to be of inestimable value; and they conceive the undisturbed succession of

15  the crown to be a pledge of the stability and perpetuity of all the other members of our Constitution.

I shall beg leave, before I go any further, to take notice of some paltry artifices which the abettors of election as the only lawful title to the crown are

20  ready to employ, in order to render the support of the just principles of our Constitution a task somewhat invidious. These sophisters substitute a fictitious cause, and feigned personages, in whose favor they suppose you engaged, whenever you defend the inheritable

25  nature of the crown. It is common with them to dispute as if they were in a conflict with some of those exploded fanatics of slavery who formerly maintained, what I believe no creature now maintains, "that the crown is held by divine, hereditary, and indefeasible

30  right."

These old fanatics of single arbitrary power dogmatized as if hereditary royalty was the only lawful government in the world, just as our new fanatics of popular arbitrary power maintain that a popular

35  election is the sole lawful source of authority. The old prerogative enthusiasts, it is true, did speculate foolishly, and perhaps impiously too, as if monarchy had more of a divine sanction than any other mode of government; and as if a right to govern by inheritance

40  were in strictness *indefeasible* in every person who should be found in the succession to a throne, and under every circumstance, which no civil or political right can be.

**Passage 2**

But it is not so much the absurdity as the evil of

45  hereditary succession which concerns mankind. Did it ensure a race of good and wise men it would have the seal of divine authority, but as it opens a door to the FOOLISH, the WICKED, and the IMPROPER, it hath in it the nature of oppression. Men who look upon

50  themselves born to reign, and others to obey, soon grow insolent; selected from the rest of mankind their minds are early poisoned by importance; and the world they act in differs so materially from the world at large, that they have but little opportunity of knowing its true

55  interests, and when they succeed to the government are frequently the most ignorant and unfit of any throughout the dominions. Another evil which attends hereditary succession is, that the throne is subject to be possessed by a minor at any age; all which time the

60  regency, acting under the cover of a king, have every opportunity and inducement to betray their trust. The same national misfortune happens, when a king worn out with age and infirmity, enters the last stage of human weakness. In both these cases the public

65  becomes a prey to every miscreant, who can tamper successfully with the follies either of age or infancy.

The most plausible plea, which hath ever been offered in favour of hereditary succession, is, that it preserves a nation from civil wars; and were this true,

70  it would be weighty; whereas, it is the most barefaced falsity ever imposed upon mankind. The whole history of England disowns the fact. Thirty kings and two minors have reigned in that distracted kingdom since the conquest, in which time there have been

75  (including the Revolution) no less than eight civil wars and nineteen rebellions. Wherefore instead of making for peace, it makes against it, and destroys the very foundation it seems to stand on. ... In short, monarchy and succession have laid (not this or that kingdom

80  only) but the world in blood and ashes.

**CONTINUE**

**33**

In Passage 1, Burke indicates that the argument of those who support elected leaders is characterized by its

A) weakness and dishonesty.

B) universality and fanaticism.

C) antiquity and irrelevance.

D) hypocrisy and innovation.

**34**

As used in line 1, "overload" most nearly means

A) burden excessively.

B) cause to burst.

C) express emotionally.

D) short circuit.

**35**

As used in line 20, "employ" most nearly means

A) hire.

B) utilize.

C) reimburse.

D) work.

**36**

Passage 2 most strongly suggests that Paine believes leaderships by right of birth to be

A) illegitimate failures that cause devastating results.

B) useful means by which to avoid dangerously inferior governance.

C) complicated and passionate methods for expressing opinions.

D) valuable despite some historical setbacks.

**37**

In response to Burke's statement in lines 22–25 ("These sophisters . . . crown"), what would Paine most likely say?

A) He would indicate that it is important to address all possible reasons for supporting an unjust cause.

B) He would state that the argument against the divine right to rule is less important than the tendencies of rulers to arbitrarily provide favors to their supporters.

C) He would clarify that the argument against an accepted form of rule is based on results, not redirection.

D) He would deny that the old belief in an inherently granted right to rule a state has completely disappeared.

**38**

Which choice provides the best evidence for the answer to the previous question?

A) Lines 49–51 ("Men who . . . insolent")

B) Lines 57–59 ("Another evil . . . age")

C) Lines 67–69 ("The most . . . wars")

D) Lines 71–72 ("The whole . . . fact")

**39**

Which of the following types of responses would Burke most likely make to Paine's statements in the final paragraph of Passage 2?

A) One of disagreement, because conflicts do not necessarily indicate an unstable structure

B) One of agreement, because civil wars are a burden on a nation

C) One of acceptance, because excessive violence demonstrates a failure of a system

D) One of doubt, because Paine failed to provide details and dates of the wars and rebellions he cites

**CONTINUE**

Which choice provides the best evidence for the answer to the previous question?

A) Lines 6–8 ("The people . . . trial")

B) Lines 12–16 ("They look . . . Constitution")

C) Lines 31–35 ("These old . . . authority")

D) Lines 35–39 ("The old . . . government")

Which choice best states the relationship between the two passages?

A) Passage 2 underscores the concerns raised by Passage 1.

B) Passage 2 argues a point dismissed by Passage 1.

C) Passage 2 presents another method for resolving the issues delineated in Passage 1.

D) Passage 2 expands on the main position expressed and advocated in Passage 1.

## 42

The main purpose of both passages is to

A) evaluate the various benefits of parliamentary forms of government.

B) seek compromise on a passionately debated issue of importance.

C) reject an opposing view and a particular position.

D) prove that history is based on false beliefs.

**CONTINUE**

**Questions 43–52 are based on the following passage.**

This passage is excerpted from Heidi Ledford, "Where Could the First CRISPR Baby Be Born?" © 2015 by Nature.

They are meeting in China; they are meeting in the United Kingdom; and they met in the United States last week. Around the world, scientists are gathering to
Line  discuss the promise and perils of editing the genome
5  of a human embryo. Should it be allowed—and if so, under what circumstances?

The meetings have been prompted by an explosion of interest in the powerful technology known as CRISPR/Cas9, which has brought unprecedented ease
10  and precision to genetic engineering. This tool, and others like it, could be used to manipulate the DNA of embryos in a dish to learn about the earliest stages of human development. In theory, genome editing could also be used to "fix" the mutations responsible
15  for heritable human diseases. If done in embryos, this could prevent such diseases from being passed on.

The prospects have prompted widespread concern and discussion among scientists, ethicists and patients. Fears loom that if genome editing becomes acceptable
20  in the clinic to stave off disease, it will inevitably come to be used to introduce, enhance or eliminate traits for non-medical reasons. Ethicists are concerned that unequal access to such technologies could lead to genetic classism. And targeted changes to a
25  person's genome would be passed on for generations, through the germ line (sperm and eggs), fueling fears that embryo editing could have lasting, unintended consequences.

Adding to these concerns, the regulations in many
30  countries have not kept pace with the science.

*Nature* has tried to capture a snapshot of the legal landscape by querying experts and government agencies in 12 countries with histories of well-funded biological research. The responses reveal a wide range
35  of approaches. In some countries, experimenting with human embryos at all would be a criminal offense, whereas in others, almost anything would be permissible.

Concerns over the manipulation of human
40  embryos are nothing new. Rosario Isasi, a legal scholar at McGill University in Montreal, Canada, points to two key waves of legislation over the years: one sparked by concerns about the derivation of embryonic stem cells, which was largely deemed acceptable; the

45  other about reproductive cloning, which was largely prohibited for safety reasons.

But the research has already begun, and more is coming. Scientists in China announced in April that they had used CRISPR to alter the genomes of human
50  embryos, albeit ones incapable of producing a live baby (P. Liang, *et al.* Protein Cell 6, 363-372; 2015). Xiao-Jiang Li, a neuroscientist at Emory University in Atlanta, Georgia, who has used the technique in monkeys, says he has heard rumours that several
55  other Chinese laboratories are already doing such experiments. And in September, developmental biologist Kathy Niakan of the Francis Crick Institute in London applied to the UK Human Fertilisation and Embryology Authority for permission to use the
60  technique to study errors in embryo development that can contribute to infertility and miscarriage. No one so far has declared an interest in producing live babies with edited genomes, and initial experiments would suggest that it is not yet safe. But some suspect that it is
65  only a matter of time.

Tetsuya Ishii, a bioethicist at Hokkaido University in Sapporo, Japan, spent nearly a year analysing relevant legislation and guidelines in 39 countries, and found that 29 have rules that could be interpreted
70  as restricting genome editing for clinical use (M. Araki and T. Ishii Reprod. Biol. Endocrinol. 12, 108; 2014). Ishii predicts that countries with high rates of *in vitro* fertilization will be the first to attempt clinical applications. Japan, he says, has one of the highest
75  numbers of fertility clinics in the world, and has no enforceable rules on germline modification. The same is true for India.

Guoping Feng, a neuroscientist at the Massachusetts Institute of Technology in Cambridge,
80  hopes that with improvement, the technique could eventually be used to prevent genetic disease. But he argues that it is much too soon to be trying it in the clinic. "Now is not the time to do human-embryo manipulation," he says. "If we do the wrong thing,
85  we can send the wrong message to the public—and then the public will not support scientific research anymore."

**CONTINUE** ➡

**43**

The primary purpose of the passage is to

A) evaluate the findings of a long-term study.

B) present the background of a scientific discovery.

C) evaluate competing theories in a scientific field.

D) explain the prospects of a developing branch of science.

**44**

The author's attitude toward CRISPR/Cas9 technology is best described as one of

A) unconcerned ambivalence.

B) cautious optimism.

C) restrained fear.

D) unqualified exuberance.

**45**

As used in line 13, "editing" most nearly means

A) abridging.

B) altering.

C) revising.

D) polishing.

**46**

What does the author suggest about the prospects of human embryo editing?

A) They are limited by the expensive nature of monkey testing.

B) They are focused only on producing live babies with edited genomes.

C) They are not yet ready to be used on humans for ethical reasons.

D) They are ready for clinical trials in most countries.

**47**

Which choice provides the best evidence for the answer to the previous question?

A) Lines 13–16 ("In theory . . . on")

B) Lines 17–18 ("The prospects . . . patients")

C) Lines 35–38 ("In some . . . permissible")

D) Lines 52–56 ("Xiao-Jiang Li . . . experiments")

**48**

According to the passage, which of the following is true of CRISPR technology?

A) It is being researched at well-funded institutions.

B) It stems from months of previous genetic modification research.

C) It reduces the risk of passing on genetic mutations responsible for heritable diseases.

D) It has been used already in the United States.

**49**

Which choice provides the best evidence for the answer to the previous question?

A) Lines 13–16 ("In theory . . . on")

B) Lines 29–30 ("Adding to . . . science")

C) Lines 52–56 ("Xiao-Jiang Li . . . experiments")

D) Lines 74–77 ("Japan, he . . . India")

**50**

Which of the following does the author suggest about the "*in vitro* fertilization" mentioned in line 73?

A) Some human embryos have been genetically altered in China.

B) Japan will become the first country to produce a genetically mutated human.

C) It may be one of the first clinical applications of genetic editing in humans.

D) It will be the future of heritable disease prevention.

**CONTINUE**

## 51

The phrase "much too soon" (line 82) most directly suggests that

A) human genome editing has potential but is not yet ready for human trials.

B) human genome editing will soon be a valuable asset to heritable disease prevention.

C) human genome editing will prove to be financially insupportable.

D) human genome editing will be an inevitable failure that should not be attempted.

The most likely purpose of the quotations from Guoping Feng in lines 83–87 is to

A) reinforce an earlier point.

B) clarify an abstract concept.

C) define a theory.

D) refute a new hypothesis.

## STOP
If you finish before time is called, you may check your work on this section only.
Do not turn to any other section in the test.

**No Test Material On This Page**

# Writing and Language Test

## 35 MINUTES, 44 QUESTIONS

**Turn to Section 2 of your answer sheet to answer the questions in this section.**

---

**DIRECTIONS**

Each passage below is accompanied by a number of questions. For some questions, you will consider how the passage might be revised to improve the expression of ideas. For other questions, you will consider how the passage might be edited to correct errors in sentence structure, usage, or punctuation. A passage or a question may be accompanied by one or more graphics (such as a table or graph) that you will consider as you make revising and editing decisions.

Some questions will direct you to an underlined portion of a passage. Other questions will direct you to a location in a passage or ask you to think about the passage as a whole.

After reading each passage, choose the answer to each question that most effectively improves the quality of writing in the passage or that makes the passage conform to the conventions of standard written English. Many questions include a "NO CHANGE" option. Choose that option if you think the best choice is to leave the relevant portion of the passage as it is.

---

**Questions 1–11 are based on the following passage.**

**The New American Renaissance**

Since 1970 or so, the shape of the humanities has changed significantly. Before that time, it was rare to read books, look at paintings, or **1** watch plays by anyone other than white male European-American artists. While a bias still remains, there is no question that the canon, the group of accepted "classic" **2** works; has become much

**1**

A) NO CHANGE
B) rarer still was watching
C) to watch
D) DELETE the underlined portion.

**2**

A) NO CHANGE
B) works—
C) works
D) works,

CONTINUE →

more diverse. Still, in the United States, some groups have been **3** more vocal than others. There is no better example of such a marginalization than that of Native Americans.

Each century has had its figures—William Apess was a minister and autobiographer in the nineteenth century and Zitkala-Sa was a story writer and memoirist in the early twentieth. Still, these figures were never able to reach audiences as broad as those of their white contemporaries. Today, however, as the reclamation of heritage gains more traction, this public marginalization may be changing.

Literary critic Kenneth Lincoln identifies the change and **4** outlined a kind of historical timeline in his 1983 book *Native American Renaissance*. Throughout the nineteenth century, Native Americans were systematically eradicated throughout all parts of the growing United States. Much of their **5** repartee with white Americans came in the form of military campaigns. When the wars subsided, the American government started a similarly cruel program of assimilation, **6** often this involved the movement of Native American children from their homes to "Indian schools" that sought to remove any trace of tribal inheritance.

**3**

Which choice most effectively sets up the information that follows?

A) NO CHANGE
B) successful despite the obstacles.
C) forced to stay on the periphery.
D) content to stay out of the public eye.

**4**

A) NO CHANGE
B) outlining
C) was outlining
D) outlines

**5**

A) NO CHANGE
B) contact
C) chatting
D) badinage

**6**

A) NO CHANGE
B) it often involved
C) this type of thing often involved
D) often involving

**CONTINUE**

[7] There were lots of anti-war demonstrations in the 1960s and 1970s, an era of cultural reclamation, when the emphasis on "melting-pot"-style assimilation shifted toward an attitude of "multicultural society." [8] At this time, people from all races began to think it possible to live in the United States while at the same time identifying with a particular racial group. Around this time, after many of the "Indian schools" had closed, Native American children could gain English-language education closer to home. [9] Nevertheless, they could continue to identify with their cultural heritage while gaining an "American" education.

Which choice connects the sentence with the previous paragraph?

A) NO CHANGE

B) Kenneth Lincoln was just a young man

C) This practice of assimilation had begun to change

D) Many important things happened

At this point, the writer is considering adding the following sentence.

> This was not always the case as many groups have been marginalized throughout American history.

Should the writer make this addition here?

A) Yes, because it gives an important reminder that the United States is always changing.

B) Yes, because it shows that Native American writers have not always been popular.

C) No, because it makes a historical claim that the passage contradicts.

D) No, because it repeats information from earlier in the passage that is already implied in this paragraph.

A) NO CHANGE

B) And,

C) Because,

D) Moreover,

**CONTINUE** →

This shift led to more Native Americans attending colleges and universities, and more empathetic attitudes among the literary establishment allowed more **10** of them space for publication of poetry and fiction. **11** The result was an efflorescence of Native American writers, particularly in the 1970s and 1980s. During this period, writers like Leslie Marmon Silko, Gerald Vizenor, and Paula Gunn Allen became popular. These writers are now among the most respected in the country, and they have influenced countless others. While the literary establishment may have been centuries late in acknowledging the significant contributions that Native American culture can make to the world, we should nonetheless be glad that this influence is finally more widely available.

---

**10**

A) NO CHANGE
B) Native American writers
C) of these
D) from it

---

**11**

Which choice most effectively combines the underlined sentences?

A) Particularly in the 1970s and 1980s, writers like Leslie Marmon Silko, Gerald Vizenor, and Paula Gunn Allen became popular, a resultant efflorescence of Native American writers.

B) The result was an efflorescence of Native American writers, particularly in the 1970s and 1980s; in these decades, popularity was earned for writers including Leslie Marmon Silko, Gerald Vizenor, an Paula Gunn Allen.

C) Leslie Marmon Silko, Gerald Vizenor, and Paula Gunn Allen were three of the writers who became popular in this period of the 1970s and 1980s amid the resulting efflorescence of Native American writers.

D) The result, particularly in the 1970s and 1980s, was an efflorescence of Native American writers including Leslie Marmon Silko, Gerald Vizenor, and Paula Gunn Allen.

**CONTINUE**

**Questions 12–22 are based on the following passage.**

**Make Like a Tree and Change Leaves**

Anyone who lives in the Mid-Atlantic or New England [12] knows the flowering of spring and the lush greens of summer. The four seasons in these areas are most evident in the look of the trees. This is never more true than [13] when people are in the case of fall, when the trees are covered with beautiful swatches of red, yellow, and orange as the leaves change color. For many, this fall foliage represents the Northeast in [14] the state in which it is most pure.

People in this region have taken to the idea. Now, foliage tourism is as much a part of the region as beach season is for those on the coast. Many business [15] owners including, restaurant owners, hoteliers, and farmers, throughout the region depend on a boom in October and November.

---

**12**

A) NO CHANGE

B) bodes

C) foretells

D) indicates

---

**13**

A) NO CHANGE

B) considering

C) with the consideration

D) DELETE the underlined portion.

---

**14**

A) NO CHANGE

B) its purest state.

C) which it is in the purest possible state.

D) the state of purity rather than impurity.

---

**15**

A) NO CHANGE

B) owners, including

C) owners, including,

D) owners including:

---

However, there is a problem. Except in very odd circumstances, it will *always* be beach season in July and August. Foliage season, however, is a bit more difficult to predict. It is clear, **16** for instance, that the leaves tend to change in the last few months of the year, but when they change and how vivid their colors will be has long remained a mystery. Of course, many people would certainly like to know the cause. **17** Because of it, fall without the foliage is like a whole season of rainy beach days, at least from a tourism perspective.

A recent study published in *Proceedings of the National Academy of Sciences* has begun to uncover some of the factors behind the change. Scientists **18** have long known that climate conditions influence the changing of the leaves, but no one has ever been sure which aspect of the weather to privilege—moisture, temperature, frost, etc. **19** No previous explanation has been able to say why in one year the leaves were still a vibrant yellow on the first of November while the next year they had all fallen already.

**16**

A) NO CHANGE
B) nevertheless,
C) for all that,
D) on the other hand,

**17**

A) NO CHANGE
B) Subsequently,
C) After all,
D) Additionally,

**18**

A) NO CHANGE
B) long knows
C) long know
D) are long knowing

**19**

At this point, the writer is considering adding the following sentence.

> The Mount Washington Observatory reports that the average rainfall in the New Hampshire region is approximately 6-9 inches, depending on the month.

Should the writer make this addition here?

A) Yes, because it provides support for the passage's main claim that fall foliage can now be accurately predicted.

B) Yes, because it adds an important detail regarding the expected moisture levels in one region.

C) No, because it introduces the work of an organization that is not discussed elsewhere in the passage.

D) No, because it is not relevant to the paragraph's description of the general factors that influence fall foliage.

**CONTINUE**

The answer, it seems, is that **20** their is different factors in different places. This group of scientists analyzed two different New England ecosystems, one along the coast and one in the highlands. They found that both reacted to frosts in the fall, but only the highlands reacted to frosts in the spring. **21**

Combining these findings with climate-change predictions for the next century, **22** having suggested that the changes will come later in the year for the highlands and perhaps a bit earlier for the coasts. Should these predictions turn out to be true, it could be a major boon for the tourism industry in these areas and for the tourists who visit them.

**20**

A)  NO CHANGE

B)  their's

C)  their are

D)  there are

**21**

At this point, the writer wants to add another detail that adds to the findings described in this paragraph. Which choice most effectively accomplishes this goal?

A)  The forests along the coast, perhaps not surprisingly, were particularly sensitive to rain and other types of moisture.

B)  The leaves fall from the trees after they have changed, thus giving the name "fall" to the season.

C)  Except for the ocean breezes, temperatures along the water tend to be a bit higher than in the mountains.

D)  The leaves do not change color in the same way in the spring, but the blossoms of the trees create their own kind of beauty.

**22**

A)  NO CHANGE

B)  to suggest

C)  suggesting

D)  the researchers suggest

**CONTINUE**

**Questions 23–33 are based on the following passage and supplementary material.**

### (Almost) The Fifty-First State

When people refer to the "fifty-first state," they are usually referring to Puerto Rico or one of the contemporary U.S. holdings outside the fifty states. What many don't realize, however, is that the idea of extra states, particularly within U.S. borders, **23** is mainly the concern of academics. One early case is the state of Franklin. On a modern map, the state of Franklin would be bound by Tennessee to the west and south, Virginia to the north, and North Carolina to the southeast. **24**

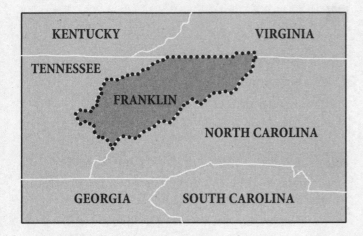

North Carolina, one of the original thirteen colonies, offered a few of its westernmost counties to the federal **25** government as payment for debts; those that had been incurred—for manpower and ammunition—during the Revolutionary War. As Congress decided what to do with the land, the North Carolinian legislature decided that the western counties were too valuable to let go, and the state soon retracted **26** it's offer of its' western counties.

**23**

Which choice most effectively completes the contrast in the sentence and is consistent with the information in the rest of the passage?

A) NO CHANGE

B) presents a fun historical challenge.

C) is actually quite an old idea.

D) is rather outdated in this day and age.

**24**

The writer wants the information in the passage to correspond as closely as possible with the information in the map. Given that goal and assuming that the rest of the previous sentence would remain unchanged, in which sequence should the three state names be discussed?

A) NO CHANGE

B) Virginia, Tennessee, North Carolina

C) North Carolina, Virginia, Tennessee

D) North Carolina, Tennessee, Virginia

**25**

A) NO CHANGE

B) government as payment for debts:

C) government as payment for debts

D) government-as payment for debts,

**26**

A) NO CHANGE

B) it's offer of its

C) its offer of it's

D) its offer of its

CONTINUE ➡

In the meantime, though, the counties in the northwest corner of the state had been developing a kind of regional identity. The three counties now called the State of Franklin **27** having been attempted to secede from North Carolina. Encouraged by the new federal government's quick creation of states from ceded lands, the three counties issued a declaration of **28** independence, yet their independence was rooted in particular in their distance from North Carolina's state capital.

[1] The secession was not recognized by Congress, and John Sevier and the leaders of the Franklin movement eventually took oaths of allegiance to the state of North Carolina. [2] This time, Congress acted quickly and accepted North Carolina's offer, interested as it was in pushing statehood further west from the thirteen colonies along the Atlantic coast. [3] Sevier and others led the administration of the ceded territories. [4] These territories were eventually granted statehood in 1796, though this time as something more recognizable—as the northeastern **29** boarder to the modern-day state of Tennessee. **30**

**27**

A) NO CHANGE
B) was attempting
C) were attempting
D) is attempting

**28**

A) NO CHANGE
B) independence, which
C) independence. Independence
D) independence, and independence

**29**

A) NO CHANGE
B) boarder from
C) border to
D) broader than

**30**

To improve the cohesion and flow of this paragraph, the writer wants to add the following sentence.

In 1789, however, North Carolina renewed its offer of the western counties to the federal government.

The sentence would most logically be placed after

A) sentence 1.
B) sentence 2.
C) sentence 3.
D) sentence 4.

CONTINUE

Today, Franklin is a distant memory, but its short-lived history provides a unique look into some of the early machinations of the newly formed American government. The contemporary fifty states may seem like they have always existed, but that is certainly not the case—just as national borders are artificial creations, **31** so too are state borders, and as such, they are always subject to change. It may have been nearly 150 years since a state, West Virginia, was carved out of another existing state, Virginia, but that does not mean that the map as it is drawn now will forever be so. The State of Franklin may be a mere historical **32** curiosity to some, but to others, it is a reminder that even a powerful, federally oriented nation is **33** usually made up of 50 or so states.

**31**

A) NO CHANGE

B) being

C) but also are

D) the same can be said of

**32**

The writer wants to convey an attitude of genuine interest and to avoid the appearance of mockery. Which choice best accomplishes this goal?

A) NO CHANGE

B) stumper

C) thing

D) mind-blower

**33**

Which choice most effectively concludes the sentence and paragraph?

A) NO CHANGE

B) very important in the world and in history.

C) a living, breathing thing, ever subject to change.

D) home to many things of historical interest.

CONTINUE

**Questions 34–44 are based on the following passage.**

**What's So Civil About Engineers Anyway?**

No matter where you live, you see their work everywhere. Whether you cross a bridge or drive on a highway, you **34** see the work of civil engineers. Civil engineering as a profession is centuries old and has long been necessary for the functioning of modern government. **35** As long as people need to get to school or work, civil engineers will continue to be **36** foundations of modern societies.

---

**34**

A) NO CHANGE

B) saw

C) have been seeing

D) sees

---

**35**

At this point, the writer is considering adding the following sentence.

> Few governments in the modern world could function without the work of civil engineers.

Should the writer make this addition here?

A) Yes, because it supports the information contained in the following paragraph.

B) Yes, because it provides an important reminder that governments are not made up of politicians alone.

C) No, because it is a mere restatement of an idea expressed in the previous sentence.

D) No, because it is a digression from the main point of the paragraph.

---

**36**

A) NO CHANGE

B) cornerstones

C) pillars

D) manipulators

---

CONTINUE

The American Society of Civil Engineers defines the profession as "the design and maintenance of public works such as roads, bridges, water, and energy systems as well as public facilities like ports, railways, and airports." **37** In other words, civil engineers design and maintain the components of energy and transportation systems in the modern world. The projects can be **38** large—like the Hoover Dam, the Holland Tunnel, or the interstate system that covers the whole country—or small—like local roads and power stations. Civil engineers see these projects through from start to finish: from the earliest stages of design and analysis to the final stages of completion and beyond.

**37**

A) NO CHANGE

B) On the other hand,

C) Nonetheless,

D) In the abstract,

**38**

A) NO CHANGE

B) large; like the Hoover Dam, the Holland Tunnel, or the interstate system that covers the whole country;

C) large: like the Hoover Dam, the Holland Tunnel, or the interstate system that covers the whole country,

D) large: like the Hoover Dam, the Holland Tunnel, or the interstate system that covers the whole country—

CONTINUE

[1] Civil engineers collaborate on large projects. [2] Their backgrounds tend to **39** vary—however, specialties can range from architecture to environmental engineering, from ecology to urban planning. [3] Those who want a greener country draw on the expertise of civil engineers in designing windmills and other sustainable sources of energy. [4] Environmental engineering has been particularly popular of late on both sides of the environmental debate. [5] Those who are less concerned with long-term energy sources have drawn on the help of civil engineers in mining oil and gas and in **40** creating delivery mechanisms that they make to get those resources all over the country. **41**

**39**

A) NO CHANGE

B) vary however specialties

C) vary, however, specialties

D) vary, however. Specialties

**40**

A) NO CHANGE

B) creating delivery mechanisms

C) creating delivery mechanisms by making them

D) fabricating and making mechanisms for delivery

**41**

To make this paragraph most logical, sentence 3 should be

A) placed where it is now.

B) placed after sentence 4.

C) placed after sentence 5.

D) DELETED from the paragraph.

CONTINUE

In either case, civil engineering is a fascinating field, and it is **42** full of interesting people. The Bureau of Labor Statistics predicts that the field will grow by nearly 20% between 2012 and 2022. The field offers incredible job security—regardless of changes in political power, civil engineering will continue to occupy a central place in the world. With every new development in energy or transportation, a civil engineer faces a new set of problems that **43** they have to solve for the country to reap the full benefits of these developments.

**44** Should you so choose the work of civil engineering it may not have the glory of political leadership, but it certainly does present opportunities to make a tangible difference in the city, state, or country in which you live. The work of civil engineers is always about the future. After all, it wouldn't make sense to build a bridge if it were only meant to stand for your own lifetime. The work of civil engineers is a gift to future generations in a way that few other types of work can be.

**42**

Which choice results in a sentence that best supports the point developed in this paragraph?

A) NO CHANGE

B) very complicated.

C) constantly growing.

D) difficult to describe.

**43**

A) NO CHANGE

B) they must solve

C) all of them really have to solve

D) he or she must solve

**44**

A) NO CHANGE

B) The career they call civil engineering

C) Civil engineering

D) Opting for a career in civil engineering

# STOP
**If you finish before time is called, you may check your work on this section only.**
**Do not turn to any other section in the test.**

# Math Test – No Calculator

## 25 MINUTES, 20 QUESTIONS

**Turn to Section 3 of your answer sheet to answer the questions in this section.**

---

### DIRECTIONS

**For questions 1–15,** solve each problem, choose the best answer from the choices provided, and fill in the corresponding circle on your answer sheet. **For questions 16–20,** solve the problem and enter your answer in the grid on the answer sheet. Please refer to the directions before question 16 on how to enter your answers in the grid. You may use any available space in your test booklet for scratch work.

### NOTES

1. The use of a calculator **is not permitted**.
2. All variables and expressions used represent real numbers unless otherwise indicated.
3. Figures provided in this test are drawn to scale unless otherwise indicated.
4. All figures lie in a plane unless otherwise indicated.
5. Unless otherwise indicated, the domain of a given function $f$ is the set of all real numbers $x$ for which $f(x)$ is a real number.

### REFERENCE

$$A = \pi r^2$$
$$C = 2\pi r$$

$$A = \ell w$$

$$A = \frac{1}{2}bh$$

$$c^2 = a^2 + b^2$$

Special Right Triangles

$$V = \ell wh$$

$$V = \pi r^2 h$$

$$V = \frac{4}{3}\pi r^3$$

$$V = \frac{1}{3}\pi r^2 h$$

$$V = \frac{1}{3}\ell wh$$

The number of degrees of arc in a circle is 360.
The number of radians of arc in a circle is $2\pi$.
The sum of the measures in degrees of the angles of a triangle is 180.

---

CONTINUE →

**1**

In the function $g(x) = \frac{5}{3}x + k$, $k$ is a constant. If $g(9) = 12$, what is the value of $g(-3)$?

A) −12

B) −8

C) −3

D) 2

**2**

$$3(k + 2) = h$$

$$\frac{h}{k} = 5$$

If the solution set to the system of equations shown above is $(h, k)$, what is the value of $k$?

A) 1

B) 3

C) 6

D) 15

**3**

Which of the following expressions is equal to 1 for some value of $y$?

A) $|2 - y| + 2$

B) $|y - 2| + 2$

C) $|y + 2| + 2$

D) $|2 - y| - 2$

**4**

If $\frac{x + y}{x}$ is equal to $\frac{6}{5}$, which of the following is true?

A) $\frac{y}{x} = \frac{1}{5}$

B) $\frac{y}{x} = \frac{11}{5}$

C) $\frac{x + y}{x} = \frac{1}{5}$

D) $\frac{x - 2y}{x} = -\frac{1}{5}$

**CONTINUE** →

**5**

$$g(x) = -4x - 7$$

The function $g$ is shown above. Which of the following is equal to $g(-2x)$ ?

A)  $8x - 7$

B)  $8x + 7$

C)  $8x^2 - 21x$

D)  $-8x - 7$

**6**

Which of the following expressions is equivalent to $4(3x - 2)(5x - 2)$ ?

A)  $12x$

B)  $7x^2 + 15x$

C)  $60x^2 + 16x$

D)  $60x^2 - 64x + 16$

**7**

If $k = 1$, which of the following is the solution set for

$x - 7 = \sqrt{x - k}$ ?

A)  $\{1\}$

B)  $\{5\}$

C)  $\{10\}$

D)  $\{5, 10\}$

**8**

While preparing for a weightlifting competition, Alexei plans a training program in which his heaviest lift of each day increases by a constant amount. If Alexei's training program requires that his heaviest lift on day 6 is 180 pounds and his heaviest lift on day 24 is 225 pounds, which of the following most accurately describes how the amount Alexei lifts changes from day 6 to day 24 in his training program?

A)  Alexei increases the weight of his heaviest lift by 2 pounds every 5 days.

B)  Alexei increases the weight of his heaviest lift by 2 pounds per day.

C)  Alexei increases the weight of his heaviest lift by 2.5 pounds per day.

D)  Alexei increases the weight of his heaviest lift by 5 pounds per day.

**CONTINUE**

**9**

$$y = -4x - 6$$

Which of the following is the equation of a line that is parallel to the line with the equation shown above?

A) $4x - y = 9$

B) $4x + 2y = 8$

C) $6x + 3y = 12$

D) $12x + 3y = 10$

**10**

$$y = (x - 7)(3x + 4)$$
$$x = 3y - 1$$

The solution set for the system of equations shown above contains how many ordered pairs?

A) Infinitely many

B) 2

C) 1

D) 0

**11**

Peggie and Joan each purchased a bouquet of flowers from a florist. The price of Peggie's bouquet was $d$ dollars, and the price of Joan's bouquet was $4 less than the price of Peggie's bouquet. If Peggie and Joan split the cost of the bouquets equally, and each paid 15% sales tax on her share, which of the following expressions gives the amount, in dollars, that each of them paid?

A) $1.15d - 2.3$

B) $2d - 1.15$

C) $2.15d - 2$

D) $2.3d - 4.6$

**12**

$$\frac{z - 3}{z + 3} = 8$$

What is the value of $z$ in the equation above?

A) $-\dfrac{27}{7}$

B) $-\dfrac{7}{2}$

C) $-3$

D) $-\dfrac{21}{9}$

CONTINUE

**13**

In the quadratic equation $x^2 - 3t = \dfrac{v}{3}x$, $t$ and $v$ are constants. What are the solutions for $x$ ?

A) $x = \dfrac{v}{3} \pm \dfrac{\sqrt{v^2 + 4t}}{3}$

B) $x = \dfrac{v}{3} \pm \dfrac{\sqrt{v^2 + 36t}}{6}$

C) $x = \dfrac{v}{6} \pm \dfrac{\sqrt{v^2 + 108t}}{6}$

D) $x = \dfrac{v}{6} \pm \dfrac{\sqrt{v^2 + 4t}}{6}$

**14**

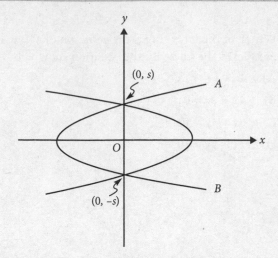

Two equations, $A$ and $B$, defined by $x = 18y^2 - 2$ and $x = -18y^2 + 2$, respectively, are graphed in the $xy$-plane above. The graphs of $A$ and $B$ intersect at the points $(0, s)$ and $(0, -s)$. What is the value of $s$ ?

A) 3

B) 1

C) $\dfrac{1}{3}$

D) $\dfrac{1}{9}$

**CONTINUE**

**15**

In the equation $\dfrac{18 + i}{4 + 3i} = a + bi$, where $a$ and $b$ are real numbers, what is the value of $a$?

(Note: $i = \sqrt{-1}$)

A)   2

B)   3

C)   $\dfrac{18}{4}$

D)   $\dfrac{11}{2}$

**CONTINUE**

## DIRECTIONS

**For questions 16–20**, solve the problem and enter your answer in the grid, as described below, on the answer sheet.

1. Although not required, it is suggested that you write your answer in the boxes at the top of the columns to help you fill in the circles accurately. You will receive credit only if the circles are filled in correctly.

2. Mark no more than one circle in any column.

3. No question has a negative answer.

4. Some problems may have more than one correct answer. In such cases, grid only one answer.

5. **Mixed numbers** such as $3\frac{1}{2}$ must be gridded as 3.5 or 7/2. (If ![grid showing 3 1 / 2] is entered into the grid, it will be interpreted as $\frac{31}{2}$, not as $3\frac{1}{2}$.)

6. **Decimal Answers:** If you obtain a decimal answer with more digits than the grid can accommodate, it may be either rounded or truncated, but it must fill the entire grid.

Answer: $\frac{7}{12}$  ← Write answer in boxes. ← Fraction line — Grid in result.

Answer: 2.5 ← Decimal point

Acceptable ways to grid $\frac{2}{3}$ are:

Answer: 201 – either position is correct

**NOTE:** You may start your answers in any column, space permitting. Columns you don't need to use should be left blank.

CONTINUE →

---

**16**

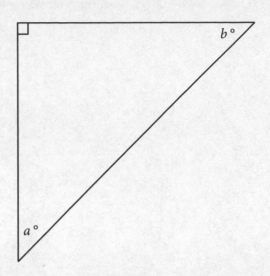

In the triangle above, the cosine of $a°$ is 0.625. What is the sine of $b°$ ?

---

**17**

Bridget owns a triangular patch of land. She decides to convert it into a garden with a paved walkway, as shown above. The long sides of the walkway are parallel to each other and to the base of the triangular patch of land. What is the width, $w$, in feet, of the walkway?

---

**18**

$$8x - 5y = 27$$
$$5x + 10y = 30$$

The solution set of the system of equations above is $(x, y)$. What is the value of $y$ ?

---

**CONTINUE** ➡

**19**

The epipelagic zone is the oceanic zone that extends from the surface down to a depth of approximately 650 feet below sea level. At a depth of 170 feet below sea level, the total pressure is 90 pounds per square inch. At a depth 215 feet below sea level, the total pressure is 110 pounds per square inch. For every additional 5 feet below sea level, the total pressure increases by $p$ pounds per square inch, where $p$ is a constant. What is the value of $p$ ?

**20**

If $x^3 - 4x^2 + 3x - 12 = 0$, what real value is a solution for $x$ ?

## STOP

**If you finish before time is called, you may check your work on this section only.
Do not turn to any other section in the test.**

**No Test Material On This Page**

# Math Test – Calculator

## 55 MINUTES, 38 QUESTIONS

**Turn to Section 4 of your answer sheet to answer the questions in this section.**

### DIRECTIONS

**For questions 1–30,** solve each problem, choose the best answer from the choices provided, and fill in the corresponding circle on your answer sheet. **For questions 31–38,** solve the problem and enter your answer in the grid on the answer sheet. Please refer to the directions before question 31 on how to enter your answers in the grid. You may use any available space in your test booklet for scratch work.

### NOTES

1. The use of a calculator **is permitted**.
2. All variables and expressions used represent real numbers unless otherwise indicated.
3. Figures provided in this test are drawn to scale unless otherwise indicated.
4. All figures lie in a plane unless otherwise indicated.
5. Unless otherwise indicated, the domain of a given function $f$ is the set of all real numbers $x$ for which $f(x)$ is a real number.

### REFERENCE

$A = \pi r^2$
$C = 2\pi r$

$A = \ell w$

$A = \frac{1}{2}bh$

$c^2 = a^2 + b^2$

Special Right Triangles

$V = \ell wh$

$V = \pi r^2 h$

$V = \frac{4}{3}\pi r^3$

$V = \frac{1}{3}\pi r^2 h$

$V = \frac{1}{3}\ell wh$

The number of degrees of arc in a circle is 360.
The number of radians of arc in a circle is $2\pi$.
The sum of the measures in degrees of the angles of a triangle is 180.

**CONTINUE**

## 1

To make the high school football team, Walter must be able to run a 40-yard dash in under 6 seconds. Walter currently runs the 40-yard dash in 7.2 seconds, and believes that with training he can reduce his time by 0.2 seconds per week. Which of the following represents the number of seconds in which Walter believes he will be able to run the 40-yard dash $w$ weeks from now?

A)  $0.2 - 7.2w$

B)  $6.0 - 0.2w$

C)  $7.2 + 0.2w$

D)  $7.2 - 0.2w$

## 2

A piece of yarn 4 yards long is cut in half, and each half is cut into fourths. What is the length, in inches, of each of the pieces of yarn? (1 yard = 36 inches)

A)   8

B)  18

C)  24

D)  36

## 3

A ride-sharing service charges a base fee of $2.40 per ride. The cost of gas is included in the base fee, but there is an additional charge of $0.30 per mile. For one ride, Edward paid $3.60. How many miles long was Edward's ride?

A)  2

B)  3

C)  4

D)  5

## 4

Yesterday Tiki cycled 13 fewer miles than Irina. If the two of them cycled a total of 51 miles yesterday, how many miles did Irina cycle?

A)  19

B)  32

C)  38

D)  64

**CONTINUE**

5

The resistance of a circuit is equal to the voltage applied to the circuit divided by the number of amps flowing through the circuit. How many amps are flowing through a circuit with a resistance of 9 ohms if 54 volts are applied to the circuit?

A) 486

B) 45

C) 6

D) 0.167

6

Florence interviewed a random sample of her first-year classmates in medical school to determine the statistical distribution of blood types among the students. Of the 75 students she interviewed, 38.7% had O-positive blood type. Based on this result, about how many of the 265 students in Florence's first-year class would be expected to have O-positive blood type?

A) 40

B) 80

C) 100

D) 110

CONTINUE

## Number of Viewers by Favorite Television Network

| Network | Age (years) | | | | | Total |
|---|---|---|---|---|---|---|
| | 18-24 | 25-34 | 35-44 | 45-64 | 65 and older | |
| A | 3,729 | 11,471 | 12,758 | 4,164 | 3,284 | 35,406 |
| B | 5,731 | 19,879 | 23,480 | 7,999 | 5,466 | 62,555 |
| C | 3,798 | 12,360 | 15,252 | 4,643 | 3,685 | 39,738 |
| D | 2,984 | 8,975 | 12,084 | 3,676 | 3,053 | 30,772 |
| Total | 16,242 | 52,685 | 63,574 | 20,482 | 15,488 | 168,471 |

A survey asked television viewers to name their one favorite network A, B, C, or D. The table above displays the number of surveyed viewers, categorized by age group and favorite network. According to the table, if a viewer who was 35 to 64 years old at the time of the survey is chosen at random, which of the following is nearest to the probability that the viewer preferred network D ?

A) 0.20

B) 0.35

C) 0.50

D) 0.75

CONTINUE

**8**

Custom Furniture Made in 2015

| Wood species | Furniture type | | | | |
|---|---|---|---|---|---|
| | Beds | Chairs | Desks | Tables | Total |
| Cherry | 9 | 7 | 0 | 15 | 31 |
| Maple | 12 | 6 | 9 | 0 | 27 |
| Walnut | 3 | 1 | 11 | 2 | 17 |
| Total | 24 | 14 | 20 | 17 | 75 |

The table above shows the 75 pieces of furniture that a custom furniture maker made in 2015, categorized by furniture type and wood species. What proportion of the furniture pieces are desks made of maple?

A) $\dfrac{2}{25}$

B) $\dfrac{3}{25}$

C) $\dfrac{4}{15}$

D) $\dfrac{9}{25}$

**9**

The graph of line $m$ in the $xy$-plane passes through Quadrants I, II, and III, but not Quadrant IV. Which of the following must be true about the slope of line $m$ ?

A) It is positive.

B) It is negative.

C) It is undefined.

D) It is zero.

**10**

The graph of the function $g$ in the $xy$-plane has $x$-intercepts at –2, 2, and 5. Which of the following could be the function $g$ ?

A) $g(x) = (x - 2)^2(x - 5)$

B) $g(x) = (x - 2)(x + 2)(x + 5)$

C) $g(x) = (x + 2)^2(x + 5)$

D) $g(x) = (x - 5)(x - 2)(x + 2)$

**CONTINUE**

**12**

Of the points labeled *P*, *Q*, *R*, and *S*, which point represents the species whose ratio of brain weight to body weight is the least?

A) *P*

B) *Q*

C) *R*

D) *S*

**Questions 11 and 12 refer to the following information.**

Body Weight Versus Brain Weight

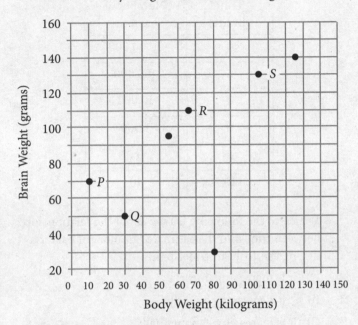

A researcher at a university made the scatterplot above to illustrate the relationship between the body weight and brain weight of 9 species of animals.

**11**

What is the brain weight, in grams, of the animal that has the greatest body weight?

A) 70

B) 125

C) 140

D) 160

**CONTINUE**

13

Which of the scatterplots below illustrates a relationship that is best modeled by the function $f(x) = \left(\dfrac{j}{x}\right)^k$, where $j$ is a positive constant and $k$ is a constant less than $-1$ ?

A)

B)

C)

D)

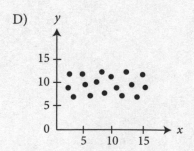

14

The estimated number of bacteria in a laboratory culture over a span of 10 hours is shown in the table below.

| Time (hours) | Number of bacteria |
|---|---|
| 0 | 1,000,000 |
| 2 | 100,000 |
| 4 | 10,000 |
| 6 | 1,000 |
| 8 | 100 |
| 10 | 10 |

Which of the following is true about the relationship between time and the estimated number of bacteria during the 10-hour time span?

A)   It is increasing linearly.

B)   It is decreasing linearly.

C)   It is increasing exponentially.

D)   It is decreasing exponentially.

CONTINUE

**15**

The expression $20{,}000\left(1+\dfrac{p}{400}\right)^4$ shows the value, in dollars, one year after purchase, of a savings bond that has an initial value of $20,000 and that pays an interest rate of $p$ percent, compounded quarterly. If Roger purchased a bond that pays an interest rate of 4 percent and Pete purchased a bond that pays an interest rate of 6 percent, which of the following expressions represents how much more Pete earned than Roger earned, after one year?

A) $20{,}000\left(1+\dfrac{6-4}{400}\right)^4$

B) $20{,}000\left(1+\dfrac{\frac{6}{4}}{400}\right)^4$

C) $20{,}000\left(1+\dfrac{6}{400}\right)^4 - 20{,}000\left(1+\dfrac{4}{400}\right)^4$

D) $\dfrac{20{,}000\left(1+\dfrac{6}{400}\right)^4}{20{,}000\left(1+\dfrac{4}{400}\right)^4}$

**Questions 16 and 17 refer to the following information.**

Stella is planning a vacation and deciding which travel package to purchase. The table below shows the cost of airfare, hotel, and car rental for three different travel packages.

| Travel package | Cost of air-fare, $A$ (in dollars) | Cost of hotel, $H$ (in dollars per day) | Cost of car rental, $R$ (in dollars per day) |
|---|---|---|---|
| $P$ | 400 | 85 | 60 |
| $Q$ | 550 | 75 | 50 |
| $R$ | 500 | 80 | 70 |

The total cost, $f(x)$, of a travel package for $x$ days is given by the function $f(x) = A + H(x-1) + Rx$, where $x \geq 2$.

**16**

If the relationship between the total cost, $f(x)$, of airfare, hotel, and car rental with travel package $R$ and the number of days, $x$, for the package is graphed in the $xy$-plane, the slope of the graph represents which of the following?

A) The combined daily cost of the hotel and car rental

B) The daily cost of the hotel

C) The daily cost of car rental

D) The total cost of airfare

**CONTINUE**

**17**

For how many days, $x$, will the total cost of travel package $Q$ be less than or equal to the total cost of travel package $P$ ?

A) $x \le 8$

B) $x \ge 8$

C) $x \le 9.4$

D) $x \ge 9.4$

**18**

A well-known projection known as Moore's law states that the maximum number of transistors that can be placed on an integrated circuit doubles every two years. Which of the following graphs is an accurate representation of Moore's law? (Note: In each graph below, $O$ represents $(0, 0)$.)

A)

B)

C)

D)

**CONTINUE**

## 19

Bob has a number of identical right circular cylindrical buckets, each with an inside diameter of 1 foot. He pours oil from a 55-gallon drum into each bucket until it is full. If the height of the oil in each bucket is approximately 1.5 feet, what is the greatest number of full buckets Bob can pour from one 55-gallon drum of oil? (Note: There are 0.133 cubic feet in 1 gallon.)

A)  6

B)  7

C)  9

D)  10

## 20

If $2x + 5 \leq 9$, what is the greatest possible value of $2x - 5$?

A)  −3

B)  −1

C)  0

D)  2

## 21

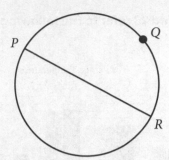

In the figure above, $\overline{PR}$ is a diameter. If the length of arc $\overparen{PQR}$ is $18\pi$, what is the length of $\overline{PR}$?

A)   6

B)  12

C)  18

D)  36

CONTINUE

**Questions 22 and 23 refer to the following information.**

The bar graph above shows the average temperature in degrees Fahrenheit for five select cities in 2000 and 2010.

**22**

In a scatterplot of this data where the average temperature of each city in the year 2000 is plotted along the x-axis and the average in the year 2010 is plotted along the y-axis, how many data points would be below the line $y = x$ ?

A)  1

B)  2

C)  3

D)  4

**23**

Of the following, which best approximates the percent increase in the average temperature of New York from 2000 to 2010 ?

A)  0.5%

B)  1%

C)  6%

D)  12%

CONTINUE

**24**

The tables below show the distribution of scores of recent quizzes in English and Physics given to the same 33 students of a particular class.

English Quiz

| Score | Frequency |
|-------|-----------|
| 1 | 5 |
| 2 | 7 |
| 3 | 8 |
| 4 | 7 |
| 5 | 6 |

Physics Quiz

| Score | Frequency |
|-------|-----------|
| 1 | 1 |
| 2 | 2 |
| 3 | 3 |
| 4 | 22 |
| 5 | 5 |

Which of the following is true about the data provided for the 33 students?

A) The standard deviation of the scores on the English quiz is larger.

B) The standard deviation of scores on the Physics quiz is larger.

C) The standard deviation of the scores on the English quiz is the same as that of the Physics quiz.

D) The standard deviation for the scores on the two quizzes cannot be calculated from the data provided.

**25**

Let $a$ and $b$ be numbers such that $b < a < -b$. Which of the following must be true?

I. $a < 0$

II. $b < 0$

III. $a < |b|$

A) I only

B) III only

C) I and II only

D) II and III only

CONTINUE

**26**

Time Spent on Internet (hours)

The scatterplot above shows scores on a recent quiz in a particular class and the number of hours the student spent on the Internet the day before. The line of best fit is also shown and can be described as $y = -12.408x + 31$. Which of the following best describes how the number 31 in the equation relates to the scatterplot?

A) On the quiz, even students who spend very little time on the Internet are unlikely to score above 31 on the quiz.

B) On the quiz, even students who spend very little time on the Internet never score above 31 on the quiz.

C) On the quiz, the lowest score was about 31% of the highest score.

D) On the quiz, the highest score on the test was 31.

**27**

$$r(x) = 3x^3 + 24x^2 + 21x$$
$$s(x) = x^2 + 8x + 7$$

The polynomials $r(x)$ and $s(x)$ are defined above. Which of the following polynomials is divisible by $3x + 4$ ?

A) $a(x) = r(x) + s(x)$

B) $b(x) = r(x) + 2s(x)$

C) $c(x) = r(x) + 4s(x)$

D) $d(x) = 2r(x) + 4s(x)$

**28**

The function $g(x) = x^3 - 2x^2 - 2x + \dfrac{4}{3}$ is graphed in the $xy$-plane above. If $c$ is a constant such that $g(x) = c$ has one real solution, which of the following could be the value of $c$ ?

A) 3

B) 1

C) 0

D) −1

**CONTINUE**

**29**

$$g(x) = (x - 10)(x + 4)$$

Which of the following is an equivalent of the function $g$ shown above in which the minimum value of $g$ appears as a constant or coefficient?

A) $g(x) = (x + 3)^2 - 31$

B) $g(x) = (x - 3)^2 - 49$

C) $g(x) = x^2 - 6x - 40$

D) $g(x) = x^2 - 40$

**30**

If $a$ is the average (arithmetic mean) of $4x$ and 7, $b$ is the average of $5x$ and 6, and $c$ is the average of $3x$ and 11, what is the average of $a$, $b$, and $c$, in terms of $x$ ?

A) $x + 4$

B) $x + 8$

C) $2x + 4$

D) $4x + 8$

**CONTINUE**

## DIRECTIONS

**For questions 31–38**, solve the problem and enter your answer in the grid, as described below, on the answer sheet.

1.  Although not required, it is suggested that you write your answer in the boxes at the top of the columns to help you fill in the circles accurately. You will receive credit only if the circles are filled in correctly.

2.  Mark no more than one circle in any column.

3.  No question has a negative answer.

4.  Some problems may have more than one correct answer. In such cases, grid only one answer.

5.  **Mixed numbers** such as $3\frac{1}{2}$ must be gridded as 3.5 or 7/2. (If ⟨3 1 / 2⟩ is entered into the grid, it will be interpreted as $\frac{31}{2}$, not as $3\frac{1}{2}$.)

6.  **Decimal Answers:** If you obtain a decimal answer with more digits than the grid can accommodate, it may be either rounded or truncated, but it must fill the entire grid.

Acceptable ways to grid $\frac{2}{3}$ are:

Answer: 201 – either position is correct

**NOTE:** You may start your answers in any column, space permitting. Columns you don't need to use should be left blank.

CONTINUE ➡

**31**

The target heart rate during moderate activity $R$, in beats per minute, for an adult who is $y$ years old can be estimated using the equation $R = \dfrac{3(220 - y)}{5}$. According to this estimate, for every increase of 2 years in age, by how many beats per minute will the target heart rate for adults engaged in moderate activity decrease?

**32**

At 1:00 P.M., a truck driver is 200 miles into a long journey to make a delivery. The driver continues on the journey and travels at an average speed of 60 miles per hour. How many total miles into the journey will the driver be at 8:00 P.M. ?

**33**

$$d = \frac{1}{2}at^2$$

The displacement $d$ of an object in a vacuum, starting from rest with an acceleration $a$ can be found using the formula above, where $t$ is the time the object has been moving. A physics student uses the formula to determine the displacement of an object in a vacuum accelerating from rest for time $t$ and an object with the same acceleration from rest for time $2.5t$. What is the ratio of the displacement of the object that accelerated for more time to the displacement of the object that accelerated for less time?

**34**

The *deben*, an ancient Egyptian unit of weight, is approximately equal to 3.21 ounces. It is also equivalent to 12 smaller Egyptian units called *shematies*. Based on these relationships, 488 shematies is equal to how many <u>pounds</u>, to the nearest hundredth? (16 ounces = 1 pound)

**CONTINUE**

**35**

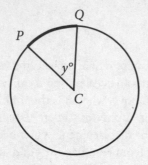

Note: Figure not drawn to scale.

The circle above has center $C$ and has a radius of 20. If the length of arc $\overset{\frown}{PQ}$ (shown in bold) is between 15 and 16, what is one possible <u>integer</u> value of $y$ ?

**36**

A toy store keeps marbles in the closet of its stock room. In the closet, 230 marbles are blue and 370 marbles are red. If 110 red marbles are added, how many blue marbles must be added to the closet so that $\frac{2}{5}$ of the marbles in the closet are blue?

**Questions 37 and 38 refer to the following information.**

A CD account contains $5,400 today. The account earns an annual interest of 7% for each of the next four years. The bank uses the equation $A = 5,400(r)^y$ to determine the amount of money in the account, $A$, after $y$ years if no other deposits or withdrawals are made.

**37**

What numerical value should the bank use for $r$ ?

**38**

To the nearest dollar, how much money will be in the CD account at the end of the four years? (Note: Disregard the $ sign when gridding your answer.)

## STOP
If you finish before time is called, you may check your work on this section only.
Do not turn to any other section in the test.

**No Test Material On This Page**

# SAT Essay

## DIRECTIONS

The essay gives you an opportunity to show how effectively you can read and comprehend a passage and write an essay analyzing the passage. In your essay you should demonstrate that you have read the passage carefully, present a clear and logical analysis, and use language precisely.

Your essay must be written on the lines provided in your answer sheet booklet; except for the planning page of the answer booklet, you will receive no other paper on which to write. You will have enough space if you write on every line, avoid wide margins, and keep your handwriting to a reasonable size. Remember that people who are not familiar with your handwriting will read what you write. Try to write or print so that what you are writing is legible to those readers.

**You have <u>50 minutes</u> to read the passage and write an essay in response to the prompt provided inside this booklet.**

## REMINDER

— Do not write your essay in this booklet. Only what you write on the lined pages of your answer booklet will be evaluated.

— An off-topic essay will not be evaluated.

CONTINUE →

As you read the passage below, consider how President Obama uses

- evidence, such as facts or examples, to support claims.
- reasoning to develop ideas and to connect claims and evidence.
- stylistic or persuasive elements, such as word choice or appeals to emotion, to add power to the ideas expressed.

**Excerpted from a speech given by President Barack Obama at the First Session of COP21, the United Nations Climate Change conference. The speech was delivered at Le Bourget in Paris, France on November 30, 2015.**

1   President Hollande, Mr. Secretary General, fellow leaders. We have come to Paris to show our resolve...

2   Nearly 200 nations have assembled here this week—a declaration that for all the challenges we face, the growing threat of climate change could define the contours of this century more dramatically than any other. What should give us hope that this is a turning point, that this is the moment we finally determined we would save our planet, is the fact that our nations share a sense of urgency about this challenge and a growing realization that it is within our power to do something about it.

3   Our understanding of the ways human beings disrupt the climate advances by the day. Fourteen of the fifteen warmest years on record have occurred since the year 2000—and 2015 is on pace to be the warmest year of all. No nation—large or small, wealthy or poor— is immune to what this means.

4   This summer, I saw the effects of climate change firsthand in our northernmost state, Alaska, where the sea is already swallowing villages and eroding shorelines; where permafrost thaws and the tundra burns; where glaciers are melting at a pace unprecedented in modern times. And it was a preview of one possible future—a glimpse of our children's fate if the climate keeps changing faster than our efforts to address it. Submerged countries. Abandoned cities. Fields that no longer grow. Political disruptions that trigger new conflict, and even more floods of desperate peoples seeking the sanctuary of nations not their own.

5   That future is not one of strong economies, nor is it one where fragile states can find their footing. That future is one that we have the power to change. Right here. Right now. But only if we rise to this moment. As one of America's governors has said, "We are the first generation to feel the impact of climate change, and the last generation that can do something about it."

6   I've come here personally, as the leader of the world's largest economy and the second-largest emitter, to say that the United States of America not only recognizes our role in creating this problem, we embrace our responsibility to do something about it.

**CONTINUE** ➡

7   Over the last seven years, we've made ambitious investments in clean energy, and ambitious reductions in our carbon emissions. We've multiplied wind power threefold, and solar power more than twentyfold, helping create parts of America where these clean power sources are finally cheaper than dirtier, conventional power. We've invested in energy efficiency in every way imaginable. We've said no to infrastructure that would pull high-carbon fossil fuels from the ground, and we've said yes to the first-ever set of national standards limiting the amount of carbon pollution our power plants can release into the sky.

8   The advances we've made have helped drive our economic output to all-time highs, and drive our carbon pollution to its lowest levels in nearly two decades...

9   And, my fellow leaders, accepting this challenge will not reward us with moments of victory that are clear or quick. Our progress will be measured differently—in the suffering that is averted, and a planet that's preserved. And that's what's always made this so hard. Our generation may not even live to see the full realization of what we do here. But the knowledge that the next generation will be better off for what we do here—can we imagine a more worthy reward than that? Passing that on to our children and our grandchildren, so that when they look back and they see what we did here in Paris, they can take pride in our achievement.

10  Let that be the common purpose here in Paris. A world that is worthy of our children. A world that is marked not by conflict, but by cooperation; and not by human suffering, but by human progress. A world that's safer, and more prosperous, and more secure, and more free than the one that we inherited.

11  Let's get to work. Thank you very much. (Applause.)

---

Write an essay in which you explain how President Obama builds an argument to advocate for world efforts to combat climate change. In your essay, analyze how Obama uses one or more of the features listed in the box above (or features of your own choice) to strengthen the logic and persuasiveness of his argument. Be sure that your analysis focuses on the most relevant features of the passage.

Your essay should not explain whether you agree with Obama's claims, but rather explain how Obama builds an argument to persuade his audience.

---

**END OF TEST**

**DO NOT RETURN TO A PREVIOUS SECTION.**

Completely darken bubbles with a No. 2 pencil.  If you make a mistake, be sure to erase mark completely.  Erase all stray marks.

**1.**
YOUR NAME: _____
(Print)          Last                          First                        M.I.

SIGNATURE: _____  DATE: ___ / ___ / ___

HOME ADDRESS: _____
(Print)                          Number and Street

_____
City                          State                        Zip Code

PHONE NO.: _____
(Print)

**IMPORTANT:** Please fill in these boxes exactly as shown on the back cover of your test book.

**2. TEST FORM**

**3. TEST CODE**

| 0 | Ⓐ | Ⓙ | 0 | 0 |
| 1 | Ⓑ | Ⓚ | 1 | 1 |
| 2 | Ⓒ | Ⓛ | 2 | 2 |
| 3 | Ⓓ | Ⓜ | 3 | 3 |
| 4 | Ⓔ | Ⓝ | 4 | 4 |
| 5 | Ⓕ | Ⓞ | 5 | 5 |
| 6 | Ⓖ | Ⓟ | 6 | 6 |
| 7 | Ⓗ | Ⓠ | 7 | 7 |
| 8 | Ⓘ | Ⓡ | 8 | 8 |
| 9 |   |   | 9 | 9 |

**4. REGISTRATION NUMBER**

| 0 | 0 | 0 | 0 | 0 | 0 | 0 |
| 1 | 1 | 1 | 1 | 1 | 1 | 1 |
| 2 | 2 | 2 | 2 | 2 | 2 | 2 |
| 3 | 3 | 3 | 3 | 3 | 3 | 3 |
| 4 | 4 | 4 | 4 | 4 | 4 | 4 |
| 5 | 5 | 5 | 5 | 5 | 5 | 5 |
| 6 | 6 | 6 | 6 | 6 | 6 | 6 |
| 7 | 7 | 7 | 7 | 7 | 7 | 7 |
| 8 | 8 | 8 | 8 | 8 | 8 | 8 |
| 9 | 9 | 9 | 9 | 9 | 9 | 9 |

**6. DATE OF BIRTH**

| Month |  | Day |  | Year |  |
|-------|--|-----|--|------|--|
| JAN |  |  |  |  |  |
| FEB | 0 | 0 | 0 | 0 |  |
| MAR | 1 | 1 | 1 | 1 |  |
| APR | 2 | 2 | 2 | 2 |  |
| MAY | 3 | 3 | 3 | 3 |  |
| JUN |  | 4 | 4 | 4 |  |
| JUL |  | 5 | 5 | 5 |  |
| AUG |  | 6 | 6 | 6 |  |
| SEP |  | 7 | 7 | 7 |  |
| OCT |  | 8 | 8 | 8 |  |
| NOV |  | 9 | 9 | 9 |  |
| DEC |  |  |  |  |  |

**7. SEX**
◯ MALE
◯ FEMALE

The **Princeton Review**®

**5. YOUR NAME**

| First 4 letters of last name |  |  |  | FIRST INIT | MID INIT |
|---|---|---|---|---|---|
| Ⓐ | Ⓐ | Ⓐ | Ⓐ | Ⓐ | Ⓐ |
| Ⓑ | Ⓑ | Ⓑ | Ⓑ | Ⓑ | Ⓑ |
| Ⓒ | Ⓒ | Ⓒ | Ⓒ | Ⓒ | Ⓒ |
| Ⓓ | Ⓓ | Ⓓ | Ⓓ | Ⓓ | Ⓓ |
| Ⓔ | Ⓔ | Ⓔ | Ⓔ | Ⓔ | Ⓔ |
| Ⓕ | Ⓕ | Ⓕ | Ⓕ | Ⓕ | Ⓕ |
| Ⓖ | Ⓖ | Ⓖ | Ⓖ | Ⓖ | Ⓖ |
| Ⓗ | Ⓗ | Ⓗ | Ⓗ | Ⓗ | Ⓗ |
| Ⓘ | Ⓘ | Ⓘ | Ⓘ | Ⓘ | Ⓘ |
| Ⓙ | Ⓙ | Ⓙ | Ⓙ | Ⓙ | Ⓙ |
| Ⓚ | Ⓚ | Ⓚ | Ⓚ | Ⓚ | Ⓚ |
| Ⓛ | Ⓛ | Ⓛ | Ⓛ | Ⓛ | Ⓛ |
| Ⓜ | Ⓜ | Ⓜ | Ⓜ | Ⓜ | Ⓜ |
| Ⓝ | Ⓝ | Ⓝ | Ⓝ | Ⓝ | Ⓝ |
| Ⓞ | Ⓞ | Ⓞ | Ⓞ | Ⓞ | Ⓞ |
| Ⓟ | Ⓟ | Ⓟ | Ⓟ | Ⓟ | Ⓟ |
| Ⓠ | Ⓠ | Ⓠ | Ⓠ | Ⓠ | Ⓠ |
| Ⓡ | Ⓡ | Ⓡ | Ⓡ | Ⓡ | Ⓡ |
| Ⓢ | Ⓢ | Ⓢ | Ⓢ | Ⓢ | Ⓢ |
| Ⓣ | Ⓣ | Ⓣ | Ⓣ | Ⓣ | Ⓣ |
| Ⓤ | Ⓤ | Ⓤ | Ⓤ | Ⓤ | Ⓤ |
| Ⓥ | Ⓥ | Ⓥ | Ⓥ | Ⓥ | Ⓥ |
| Ⓦ | Ⓦ | Ⓦ | Ⓦ | Ⓦ | Ⓦ |
| Ⓧ | Ⓧ | Ⓧ | Ⓧ | Ⓧ | Ⓧ |
| Ⓨ | Ⓨ | Ⓨ | Ⓨ | Ⓨ | Ⓨ |
| Ⓩ | Ⓩ | Ⓩ | Ⓩ | Ⓩ | Ⓩ |

**Test ④** Start with number 1 for each new section.
If a section has fewer questions than answer spaces, leave the extra answer spaces blank.

## Section 1—Reading

1. Ⓐ Ⓑ Ⓒ Ⓓ
2. Ⓐ Ⓑ Ⓒ Ⓓ
3. Ⓐ Ⓑ Ⓒ Ⓓ
4. Ⓐ Ⓑ Ⓒ Ⓓ
5. Ⓐ Ⓑ Ⓒ Ⓓ
6. Ⓐ Ⓑ Ⓒ Ⓓ
7. Ⓐ Ⓑ Ⓒ Ⓓ
8. Ⓐ Ⓑ Ⓒ Ⓓ
9. Ⓐ Ⓑ Ⓒ Ⓓ
10. Ⓐ Ⓑ Ⓒ Ⓓ
11. Ⓐ Ⓑ Ⓒ Ⓓ
12. Ⓐ Ⓑ Ⓒ Ⓓ
13. Ⓐ Ⓑ Ⓒ Ⓓ
14. Ⓐ Ⓑ Ⓒ Ⓓ
15. Ⓐ Ⓑ Ⓒ Ⓓ
16. Ⓐ Ⓑ Ⓒ Ⓓ
17. Ⓐ Ⓑ Ⓒ Ⓓ
18. Ⓐ Ⓑ Ⓒ Ⓓ
19. Ⓐ Ⓑ Ⓒ Ⓓ
20. Ⓐ Ⓑ Ⓒ Ⓓ
21. Ⓐ Ⓑ Ⓒ Ⓓ
22. Ⓐ Ⓑ Ⓒ Ⓓ
23. Ⓐ Ⓑ Ⓒ Ⓓ
24. Ⓐ Ⓑ Ⓒ Ⓓ
25. Ⓐ Ⓑ Ⓒ Ⓓ
26. Ⓐ Ⓑ Ⓒ Ⓓ
27. Ⓐ Ⓑ Ⓒ Ⓓ
28. Ⓐ Ⓑ Ⓒ Ⓓ
29. Ⓐ Ⓑ Ⓒ Ⓓ
30. Ⓐ Ⓑ Ⓒ Ⓓ
31. Ⓐ Ⓑ Ⓒ Ⓓ
32. Ⓐ Ⓑ Ⓒ Ⓓ
33. Ⓐ Ⓑ Ⓒ Ⓓ
34. Ⓐ Ⓑ Ⓒ Ⓓ
35. Ⓐ Ⓑ Ⓒ Ⓓ
36. Ⓐ Ⓑ Ⓒ Ⓓ
37. Ⓐ Ⓑ Ⓒ Ⓓ
38. Ⓐ Ⓑ Ⓒ Ⓓ
39. Ⓐ Ⓑ Ⓒ Ⓓ
40. Ⓐ Ⓑ Ⓒ Ⓓ
41. Ⓐ Ⓑ Ⓒ Ⓓ
42. Ⓐ Ⓑ Ⓒ Ⓓ
43. Ⓐ Ⓑ Ⓒ Ⓓ
44. Ⓐ Ⓑ Ⓒ Ⓓ
45. Ⓐ Ⓑ Ⓒ Ⓓ
46. Ⓐ Ⓑ Ⓒ Ⓓ
47. Ⓐ Ⓑ Ⓒ Ⓓ
48. Ⓐ Ⓑ Ⓒ Ⓓ
49. Ⓐ Ⓑ Ⓒ Ⓓ
50. Ⓐ Ⓑ Ⓒ Ⓓ
51. Ⓐ Ⓑ Ⓒ Ⓓ
52. Ⓐ Ⓑ Ⓒ Ⓓ

## Section 2—Writing and Language Skills

1. Ⓐ Ⓑ Ⓒ Ⓓ
2. Ⓐ Ⓑ Ⓒ Ⓓ
3. Ⓐ Ⓑ Ⓒ Ⓓ
4. Ⓐ Ⓑ Ⓒ Ⓓ
5. Ⓐ Ⓑ Ⓒ Ⓓ
6. Ⓐ Ⓑ Ⓒ Ⓓ
7. Ⓐ Ⓑ Ⓒ Ⓓ
8. Ⓐ Ⓑ Ⓒ Ⓓ
9. Ⓐ Ⓑ Ⓒ Ⓓ
10. Ⓐ Ⓑ Ⓒ Ⓓ
11. Ⓐ Ⓑ Ⓒ Ⓓ
12. Ⓐ Ⓑ Ⓒ Ⓓ
13. Ⓐ Ⓑ Ⓒ Ⓓ
14. Ⓐ Ⓑ Ⓒ Ⓓ
15. Ⓐ Ⓑ Ⓒ Ⓓ
16. Ⓐ Ⓑ Ⓒ Ⓓ
17. Ⓐ Ⓑ Ⓒ Ⓓ
18. Ⓐ Ⓑ Ⓒ Ⓓ
19. Ⓐ Ⓑ Ⓒ Ⓓ
20. Ⓐ Ⓑ Ⓒ Ⓓ
21. Ⓐ Ⓑ Ⓒ Ⓓ
22. Ⓐ Ⓑ Ⓒ Ⓓ
23. Ⓐ Ⓑ Ⓒ Ⓓ
24. Ⓐ Ⓑ Ⓒ Ⓓ
25. Ⓐ Ⓑ Ⓒ Ⓓ
26. Ⓐ Ⓑ Ⓒ Ⓓ
27. Ⓐ Ⓑ Ⓒ Ⓓ
28. Ⓐ Ⓑ Ⓒ Ⓓ
29. Ⓐ Ⓑ Ⓒ Ⓓ
30. Ⓐ Ⓑ Ⓒ Ⓓ
31. Ⓐ Ⓑ Ⓒ Ⓓ
32. Ⓐ Ⓑ Ⓒ Ⓓ
33. Ⓐ Ⓑ Ⓒ Ⓓ
34. Ⓐ Ⓑ Ⓒ Ⓓ
35. Ⓐ Ⓑ Ⓒ Ⓓ
36. Ⓐ Ⓑ Ⓒ Ⓓ
37. Ⓐ Ⓑ Ⓒ Ⓓ
38. Ⓐ Ⓑ Ⓒ Ⓓ
39. Ⓐ Ⓑ Ⓒ Ⓓ
40. Ⓐ Ⓑ Ⓒ Ⓓ
41. Ⓐ Ⓑ Ⓒ Ⓓ
42. Ⓐ Ⓑ Ⓒ Ⓓ
43. Ⓐ Ⓑ Ⓒ Ⓓ
44. Ⓐ Ⓑ Ⓒ Ⓓ

Completely darken bubbles with a No. 2 pencil. If you make a mistake, be sure to erase mark completely. Erase all stray marks.

**Test ④**  Start with number 1 for each new section.
If a section has fewer questions than answer spaces, leave the extra answer spaces blank.

## Section 3—Mathematics: No Calculator

1. (A) (B) (C) (D)
2. (A) (B) (C) (D)
3. (A) (B) (C) (D)
4. (A) (B) (C) (D)
5. (A) (B) (C) (D)
6. (A) (B) (C) (D)
7. (A) (B) (C) (D)
8. (A) (B) (C) (D)
9. (A) (B) (C) (D)
10. (A) (B) (C) (D)
11. (A) (B) (C) (D)
12. (A) (B) (C) (D)
13. (A) (B) (C) (D)
14. (A) (B) (C) (D)
15. (A) (B) (C) (D)

16. 17. 18. 19. 20.

## Section 4—Mathematics: Calculator

1. (A) (B) (C) (D)
2. (A) (B) (C) (D)
3. (A) (B) (C) (D)
4. (A) (B) (C) (D)
5. (A) (B) (C) (D)
6. (A) (B) (C) (D)
7. (A) (B) (C) (D)
8. (A) (B) (C) (D)
9. (A) (B) (C) (D)
10. (A) (B) (C) (D)
11. (A) (B) (C) (D)
12. (A) (B) (C) (D)
13. (A) (B) (C) (D)
14. (A) (B) (C) (D)
15. (A) (B) (C) (D)
16. (A) (B) (C) (D)
17. (A) (B) (C) (D)
18. (A) (B) (C) (D)
19. (A) (B) (C) (D)
20. (A) (B) (C) (D)
21. (A) (B) (C) (D)
22. (A) (B) (C) (D)
23. (A) (B) (C) (D)
24. (A) (B) (C) (D)
25. (A) (B) (C) (D)
26. (A) (B) (C) (D)
27. (A) (B) (C) (D)
28. (A) (B) (C) (D)
29. (A) (B) (C) (D)
30. (A) (B) (C) (D)

31. 32. 33. 34. 35.

36. 37. 38.

# Chapter 10
# Practice Test 4:
# Answers and
# Explanations

# PRACTICE TEST 4 ANSWER KEY

## Section 1:
### Reading

| | | | |
|---|---|---|---|
| 1. | B | 27. | A |
| 2. | D | 28. | C |
| 3. | C | 29. | C |
| 4. | B | 30. | B |
| 5. | D | 31. | B |
| 6. | A | 32. | D |
| 7. | A | 33. | A |
| 8. | C | 34. | A |
| 9. | C | 35. | B |
| 10. | D | 36. | A |
| 11. | B | 37. | C |
| 12. | B | 38. | D |
| 13. | A | 39. | A |
| 14. | D | 40. | B |
| 15. | C | 41. | B |
| 16. | D | 42. | C |
| 17. | C | 43. | D |
| 18. | C | 44. | B |
| 19. | A | 45. | B |
| 20. | A | 46. | C |
| 21. | D | 47. | B |
| 22. | C | 48. | D |
| 23. | A | 49. | C |
| 24. | B | 50. | C |
| 25. | D | 51. | A |
| 26. | A | 52. | A |

## Section 2:
### Writing & Language

| | | | |
|---|---|---|---|
| 1. | A | 23. | C |
| 2. | D | 24. | A |
| 3. | C | 25. | B |
| 4. | D | 26. | D |
| 5. | B | 27. | C |
| 6. | D | 28. | B |
| 7. | C | 29. | C |
| 8. | D | 30. | A |
| 9. | D | 31. | A |
| 10. | B | 32. | A |
| 11. | D | 33. | C |
| 12. | A | 34. | A |
| 13. | D | 35. | C |
| 14. | B | 36. | B |
| 15. | B | 37. | A |
| 16. | A | 38. | A |
| 17. | C | 39. | D |
| 18. | A | 40. | B |
| 19. | D | 41. | B |
| 20. | D | 42. | C |
| 21. | A | 43. | D |
| 22. | D | 44. | C |

## Section 3:
### Math (No Calculator)

| | |
|---|---|
| 1. | B |
| 2. | B |
| 3. | D |
| 4. | A |
| 5. | A |
| 6. | D |
| 7. | C |
| 8. | C |
| 9. | D |
| 10. | B |
| 11. | A |
| 12. | A |
| 13. | C |
| 14. | C |
| 15. | B |
| 16. | $\frac{5}{8}$ or .625 |
| 17. | 3 |
| 18. | 1 |
| 19. | $\frac{20}{9}$ or 2.22 |
| 20. | 4 |

## Section 4 :
### Math (Calculator)

| | | | |
|---|---|---|---|
| 1. | D | 20. | B |
| 2. | B | 21. | D |
| 3. | C | 22. | A |
| 4. | B | 23. | C |
| 5. | C | 24. | A |
| 6. | C | 25. | D |
| 7. | A | 26. | A |
| 8. | B | 27. | C |
| 9. | A | 28. | A |
| 10. | D | 29. | B |
| 11. | C | 30. | C |
| 12. | D | 31. | 1.2 |
| 13. | A | 32. | 620 |
| 14. | D | 33. | $\frac{25}{4}$, $\frac{50}{8}$, or 6.25 |
| 15. | C | | |
| 16. | A | | |
| 17. | B | | |
| 18. | D | | |
| 19. | A | | |
| | | 34. | 8.16 |
| | | 35. | 43, 44, or 45 |
| | | 36. | 90 |
| | | 37. | 1.07 |
| | | 38. | 7,078 |

For self-scoring assessment tables, please turn to page 957.

# PRACTICE TEST 4 EXPLANATIONS

## Section 1: Reading

1. **B** This is a general question that asks about the narrator's shift in focus through the passage. Save this question until the end of the set, because the big picture will be clearer after all the specific questions have been answered. At the beginning of the passage, the narrator is uneasy about the Uncharted Forest, but as the passage progresses he begins to say things like, *And we wonder*, or *We shall not ask this question... and yet....* Eliminate (A) because the narrator never prepares to explore a frontier. Choice (B) refers to a shift from *disquiet* to *curiosity*, which can be supported with the text. Keep (B). Choice (C) might look good initally, because the narrator does acknowledge the ancient city. He never dismisses it, though, so eliminate (C). Choice (D) can be eliminated because, although the narrator mentions the Council's rules, there's no shift from *repetition...to acceptance*. Choice (B) is the correct answer.

2. **D** This is a best evidence question, so consider the lines used to predict the answer to the previous question. The correct answer to this question should support *a shift* in the narrator's focus. Choice (A) can be eliminated because those lines don't refer to the narrator's focus. Choice (B) could refer to the *disquiet about the unknown*, but there's no support for a shift. Eliminate (B). Choice (C) does not refer to the narrator at all, so eliminate it. Choice (D) contains the phrase *and yet*, which indicates a change. In context, the lines show the narrator shifting from *we shall not ask this question* to wondering about that very question. This supports the answer to Q1. Choice (D) is the correct answer.

3. **C** This question asks about the meaning of the phrase *all must agree with all* in the context of the passage. Find evidence in the text to predict the answer. The text further explains the brothers are silent because they don't know if their *thoughts are the thoughts of all*. The phrase must mean something like *all in agreement*. Choice (A) can be eliminated because there's nothing in the text about whether the thoughts are actually true or not. Choices (B) and (D) can be eliminated for similar reasons because the text never talks about the accuracy or meaning of language. The brothers must simply agree, regardless of the truth. Choice (C), *thought must be uniform*, matches the prediction. Choice (C) is the right answer.

4. **B** This question asks about the role of the indicated sentence, so find evidence in the text to explain the function of the sentence. Before the sentence, the narrator mentions the *Uncharted Forest* and says *we do not wish to look upon...we do not wish to think of it. But ever do our eyes return to that black patch*. The *but* indicates a contrast, showing that even though the narrator may not wish to think about it, he definitely does. After the indicated sentence, the narrator provides evidence that the people know very little about the Uncharted Forest, and the only things he has heard have been dismissed as legend. Choice (A) can be eliminated because there is no indication that the Forest is an immediate threat or that the narrator's job is to guard anything. Choice (B)

matches the prediction, so don't eliminate it. Choice (C) does match the part that the narrator keeps looking at the horizon, but it doesn't address *why* he is looking in that direction. Eliminate (C). Choice (D) might initially look good because there is a repeated action and something unexplainable, but there's nothing in the text to support *confusion*. Eliminate (D). This leaves (B), which is supported by the text and is the correct answer.

5.   **D**   This question asks about a *person who wished to navigate the Uncharted Forest*. Find the reference and read the window. In the middle of the second paragraph, the narrator says *Men never enter the Uncharted Forest, for there is no power to explore it and no path to lead among its ancient trees*. The narrator is pretty clear that anyone wishing to navigate the Uncharted Forest is going to have a lot of trouble because there's no path, or map, or any good way to get through it. Choices (A) and (C) can be eliminated immediately because they have nothing to do with the prediction. Choice (B) doesn't quite match the prediction because the text focuses on the men getting lost in the Forest rather than on objects already lost in the woods. Eliminate (B). Choice (D) is the correct answer.

6.   **A**   These are the lines used to answer the previous question. Choice (A) is the correct answer.

7.   **A**   This question asks about the narrator's view of the secrets of the past. He knows the secrets exist, but he doesn't know the secrets themselves. He pays attention and wonders about the legends and stories. He equates seeking answers to the questions with *calling death upon our head*. The narrator is fascinated by the secrets of the past but also afraid of this curiosity because it is forbidden. Choice (A) matches this prediction, so keep it. Choice (B) can be eliminated because the text makes it clear that the answers to the secrets are not *easily pursuable*. Choice (C) does not match the prediction because the narrator is doing a very good job of avoiding exploring the secrets. Choice (D) can be eliminated because there is no mention of authenticity in the text. Choice (A) is the correct answer.

8.   **C**   This question asks about the inference that can be made from the given line. Find the line and carefully read the window around it to determine what clues are in the text about the meaning of the line. The Uncharted Forests have *grown over the ruins of many cities* and the *trees have swallowed...all things which perished*. The narrator means that anything that existed in the ancient cities is now covered up and destroyed by the growth of the Forests. Choice (A) can be eliminated because there's no stated connection in these lines between people in the narrator's society and the ancient cities. Choice (B) can be eliminated because the trees mentioned in the lines are covering the ancient cities, not living within them. Choice (C) matches the prediction, so don't eliminate it. Choice (D) can be eliminated because the text indicates that the Forest is forbidden, and there is no evidence that the Forest is used for any literal purpose. Choice (C) is the correct answer.

9.   **C**   This is a Vocab-in-Context question, so go back to the text, find the phrase *how it came to pass* in lines 30–31, and cross it out. Replace it with another phrase that makes sense in the sentence based on the context of the passage. The phrase means something like *what happened*

*back then*. Choices (A) and (B) can be eliminated because nothing is crossing anything else or going in a circle. Choice (C) matches the prediction. Choice (D) might initially look good because it connects to the passage of time, but the original phrase refers to what actually happened in the past, not how time moved from the past to the present. Choice (C) is the correct answer.

10.  **D**  This is a Vocab-in-Context question, so go back to the text, find the word *scripts* in line 39, and cross it out. Replace it with another word that makes sense in the sentence based on the context of the passage. The author refers to the *words of the Unmentionable Times*, so *scripts* must have to do with something written. Eliminate (A) and (B). There is no evidence in the text that the words are specifically screenplays, or even that there are movies at all, so (C) can be eliminated. Choice (D) is the correct answer.

11.  **B**  This question asks about the *case against gentrification* according to the passage. Notice that the next question is a best evidence question, so these two can be done in tandem. This is an efficient way to look for evidence in the text if there isn't a given line reference. Consider the answers for Q12 first to see if they support any of the answers in Q11. Choice (12A) is a quote from a bartender that *barmen* are now *mixologists*. That doesn't support any of the answers for Q11, so eliminate it. Choice (12B) talks about how the *newcomers crowd out older residents,* which is a direct paraphrase of (11B). Draw a line connecting those two answer choices. Choice (12C) does not support any of the answers to Q11, so it can be eliminated. Choice (12D) supports (11C), so connect those two answers. Because neither (11A) nor (11D) has support in Q12, those two answers can also be eliminated. Return to the question. It asks about a case *against* gentrification. While the (11C)/(12D) pair may be true, it provides a case *for* gentrification, so it can be eliminated. This leaves (11B) and (12B), which support each other and answer the question. Choices (11B) and (12B) are the correct answers.

12.  **B**  (See explanation above.)

13.  **A**  This question asks who moved into census tracts that were poor in 2000. Look for the year 2000, find it in paragraph three, and read the following: *In Washington, according to a study by Governing magazine, 52% of census tracts that were poor in 2000 have since gentrified—more than in any other city bar Portland, Oregon. Young, mostly white singletons have crowded into a district once built for families.* According to this evidence, the correct answer would be white singletons. Choose (A), and eliminate (B), (C), and (D). The correct answer is (A).

14.  **D**  This is a Vocab-in-Context question, so go back to the text, find the word *soaring* in line 37, and cross it out. Replace it with another word that makes sense in the sentence based on the context of the passage. Since it's prices doing the *soaring*, a word like *increasing* would make sense. Compare this prediction to the four answer choices: neither (A), (B), nor (C) fits the prediction, although two of them could mean *soaring* in another context. Choice (D), *rising*, fits the prediction perfectly. Choice (D) is the correct answer.

15.   **C**   This question asks for the best summary of paragraph five. So read paragraph 5, and then summarize the text before looking at the answer choices. This paragraph starts with a claim (*Yet there is little evidence that gentrification is responsible for displacing the poor or minorities*) and continues with three bits of evidence to support that claim. The paragraph concludes by noting that minorities' incomes in gentrified areas have soared. So the best summary of the paragraph will be one that conveys the idea that when poor minority populations leave cities, it's not always because of gentrification. Choice (A) is true, but too specific. This is a common trap for main idea questions. Choice (B) is deceptive: It mentions two cities that are in the paragraph, but tells a negative story rather than counters a negative story. Choice (C) fits the prediction that gentrification is not always the reason certain populations leave cities, so keep it. Choice (D) might look good initially because of the final sentence of the paragraph. However, there is only one detail in the paragraph that fits this story of profit, namely the detail about average incomes soaring, so (D) is too broad. Choice (C), on the other hand, fits the paragraph's opening claim as well as its overall purpose. Choice (C) is the correct answer.

16.   **D**   This question asks what the passage implies about gentrifiers moving into communities. Notice that Q17 is a best evidence question, so Q16 and Q17 can be answered in tandem. First, read over the answer choices to Q16. Next, look at the answer choices to Q17 to see whether they provide support for anything in Q16. Choice (17A) refers to text that implies that gentrifiers are not responsible for displacing the poor or minorities. This does not fit any of the answer choices in Q16, so eliminate (17A). Choice (17B) refers to text that discusses the increase in incomes of black people with high-school diplomas. This choice supports the idea that gentrification can be good, which (16D) indicates, so connect (17B) to (16D). Choice (17C) refers to text that discusses how the effects of gentrification include improving local services. This choice also supports the idea that gentrification can be good, which (16D) indicates, so connect (17C) to (16D). Choice (17D) refers to text that states that gentrification is not a problem, and that turns attention to another problem. This does not fit any of the answer choices in Q16, so eliminate (17D). At this point, the only answer choice with support in Q16 is (16D), so eliminate (16A), (16B), and (16C). Choice (16D) has two answers from Q17 connected to it, so go back to the text to see which one is most closely connected to the benefits of gentrifiers moving into communities. While (17B) is a positive thing, it's not directly connected to gentrifiers moving in. Choice (17C) is, however. Choices (16D) and (17C) are the correct answers.

17.   **C**   (See explanation above.)

18.   **C**   This is a Vocab-in-Context question, so go back to the text, find the word *generates* in line 62, and cross it out. Replace it with another word that makes sense in the sentence based on the context of the passage. A word like *makes* would make sense. Compare this prediction to the four answer choices. Neither (A), *powers*, (B), *ages*, nor (D), *increases*, means *makes*. Eliminate them. Choice (C), *creates*, means *makes*, so select it. The correct answer is (C).

19.   **A**   This question asks about the information in the chart and how the author would consider it. Go back to the chart and look at how the information in the chart fits with the passage. The chart has information about the change in poverty levels in certain census tracts from 1970 to 2010. It shows that a majority of the tracts remained in high poverty over that time span. Look above or below the chart in the passage to get information about the context of the information. The passage says that *Stuart Butler of the Brookings Institution, a think-tank...* says the bigger problem for most American cities is *the concentration of poverty*. The statistics in the chart support this idea. The correct answer to this question should be something like *support Butler's idea*. Choice (A) looks solid according to the prediction, so keep it. Choice (B) does mention *proof*, but the main argument in this passage is about gentrification, not poverty levels, so (B) can be eliminated. Choice (C) throws in the attractive phrase *think-tank,* but the data is not *ambiguous*. Eliminate (C). Choice (D) can be eliminated because Butler uses the data, so it is useful. Choice (A) is the correct answer.

20.   **A**   This question asks what the chart says about most high-poverty census tracts in 1970. So look at the chart. All data presented there concern high-poverty census tracts, so what is true about *most* of them? Sixty-six percent are listed as *still high poverty*, so the correct answer will fit this prediction. Choice (A) fits, so keep it. Choices (B) and (C) are both on the chart, but do not show *most* of the high poverty tracts. Eliminate these two answer choices. Consider (D) carefully. The percentage of *high poverty tracts* in 2010 was 66% of what it was in 1970, so the level of high poverty did not increase. Eliminate (D). Choice (A) is the correct answer.

21.   **D**   This question asks what the chart suggests about poor areas. Since the answer choices all contain fractions, the correct answer will match the numbers as well as the concepts presented in the chart. Choice (A) refers to the number of poor people. The chart does not give information about the numbers, so eliminate (A). Choices (B) and (C) both describe what might happen in the future; the chart compares areas from 1970 to 2010. Thus, both (B) and (C) are out of scope; eliminate them. Choice (D) refers to 2/3 of high-poverty areas, which fits the 66% in the graph, and (D) says that they *may remain impoverished*, which is also what the graph indicates. Choice (D) is the correct answer.

22.   **C**   This question asks about the main purpose of the passage, so don't answer it until after the other questions. The main purpose of the passage is to discuss how the authors investigated whether an ancient mural in Turkey depicts an actual eruption by proving that there was an eruption nearby at approximately the same time. Choice (A) can be eliminated because the passage doesn't discuss multiple geologic ages. Choice (B) can be eliminated because although the passage mentions radiometric aging, it never explains the ways in which it was used. It's also not the main idea. Choice (C) closely matches the prediction, so keep it. Choice (D) similarly doesn't explain how the pumice veneer forms nor is this the main idea, so this answer can be eliminated. Choice (C) is the correct answer.

23.  **A**  This question is a general question so answer it at the end of the question set. The passage primarily focuses on whether the mural could be a depiction of a real volcano and how the authors set about proving this, but the fifth paragraph states *This view, however, has been contested, largely because of the extraordinary age of the mural, and the absence of any other landscape art or map until much later in history. The depiction of a leopard skin underlain by geometric patterns has been proposed instead.* This is a criticism of the theory that the passage addresses. Choice (A) is a good description of this prediction, so don't eliminate it. Choice (B) might initially look good, since it addresses the idea that the volcano was depicted, but the discussion of oral history doesn't provide any sort of proof of the mural's purpose. This answer can be eliminated. Choice (C) uses complex words from the passage that may look attractive, but the passage doesn't shift from one aging method to another. Eliminate it. Choice (D) also uses scientific wording to make the answer possibly look good, but the content of the answer choice doesn't match the prediction because radiometric aging is mentioned throughout. Choice (A) is the correct answer.

24.  **B**  This is a best evidence question, so simply look at the lines used to answer the previous question. Choice (B) contains the line used to show the shift to a new focus: *This view, however, has been contested….* Choice (B) is the correct answer.

25.  **D**  This question asks about the phrase *it putatively depicts* in the context of the passage. The context reveals that it's not clear whether the mural shows an actual volcano or not, since no research has been done to determine whether it's even possible that someone during that time could have witnessed an eruption. Another word or phrase that could go into the passage here might be *possibly* or *theoretically.* Choice (A) describes what scientists do and has nothing to do with the doubt relayed, so it can be eliminated. Choices (B) and (C) are closer in that they mention the need for clarification and certainty that scientists rely upon, but they're both too general. Choice (B) says theories must *always* be questioned, but the text only discusses one theory. Choice (C) refers to *the work of scientists,* which is again too broad. Only (D) addresses the idea that this specific claim does not have enough evidence to be proven with a reasonable amount of satisfaction. Choice (D) is the correct answer.

26.  **A**  The passage states that the mural was found at the *Neolithic Çatalhöyük site (Central Anatolia, Turkey) and appears to show an eruption of the Hasan Dağı twin-peaks volcano located about 130 km northeast of Çatalhöyük.* Choice (A) is the correct answer.

27.  **A**  Refer to the lines used to answer the previous question. Choice (A) is the correct answer.

28.  **C**  This question asks about the meaning of the phrase *This is not to say* in the context of the passage. Prior to this sentence, the passage states *For the Çatalhöyük map (and volcano) hypothesis to be plausible, however, we surmise that a brief line of oral tradition, or even an eyewitness portrayal, is perhaps more likely than tradition of a myth that detached itself from its inspiration in the physical world.* Basically, for the map to be somewhat accurate, someone would have to have seen the eruption himself or the description could only have been relayed a couple times.

*This is not to say* clarifies that they wouldn't expect a Neolithic map to be completely accurate, but it should have details specific to that type of volcano. Choice (A) can be eliminated because it isn't stated that details were lost, nor does the passage state that details from the mural are crucial for proving the truth. Choice (B) is tempting since this sentence is near the discussion of oral histories, but the passage doesn't say that oral histories don't describe real events. Choice (C) closely matches the prediction, so don't eliminate it. Choice (D) is the opposite of the prediction, since the passage says *realism must not prevail in Neolithic art*, meaning that it wasn't important to the scientists that the drawing be realistic. Choice (C) is the correct answer.

29.  **C**  Although this question might initially look like a best evidence paired question, notice that the lines in the answers are all answers for this question. The question asks about evidence that supports the claim the *mural was painted near the time of the volcanic eruption*, so find evidence in the passage to support that. It would also be efficient to work backwards, using the lines given in the answers. Choice (A) does address the volcanic eruption, but it does not connect the eruption to the mural at all. Eliminate (A). Choice (B) has nothing to do with the volcano or the mural, so it can be eliminated. Choice (C) does connect time with accuracy, saying *but many of the apparent details can be reasonably expected to become lost or obscured during a long period of oral tradition.* That is, if the eruption happened and was described over many generations, the truth about the details would gradually change. Thus, the eruption must have happened close to the time of the painting of the mural. While it might not initially look perfect, there's no clear reason to eliminate it, so keep (C). Choice (D) focuses on the volcano and does not connect the eruption to the mural, so (D) can be eliminated. Choice (C) is the correct answer.

30.  **B**  On the table, two eruptions are marked: A and B. Notice the eruptions are labeled with the *ka* unit, which is defined as *age in thousands of years*. Therefore, the two eruptions are 8.97 ka, or 8970 years old, and 28.9 ka, or 28,900 years old. The question asks about the *youngest* eruption. Choice (B) is the correct answer.

31.  **B**  The passage states *we would predict a time period for the eruption between 7400 and 6600 B.C.E.* and the table indicates the eruption is roughly 8,970 years old. Going back in time just under 9,000 years would put the eruption roughly around 6,900 B.C. Choice (B) is the correct answer.

32.  **D**  This question asks about which statement would be supported by the data, so use the data to go through each of the four statements. Choice (A) is the opposite of what is in the table. The xenocrysts were older than the other particles. Eliminate (A). Choice (B) can be eliminated because there is nothing about the oral tradition in the graphic. Choice (C) does reference the dating method used for the crystals, but this answer can be eliminated because there is no indication that it's the *best way* to determine the age of an artifact. Choice (D) matches the data, indicating that the particles from HDA (the flank of the volcano) are older than the particles taken from the rim. Choice (D) is the correct answer.

33.  **A**  This question asks about Burke's opinion of the argument of those who support electing officials. In the text, Burke says that they use *paltry artifices* and *substitute a fictitious cause, and*

*feigned personages*, thereby using weak or untrue arguments. Choice (A) matches that prediction, so don't eliminate it. Choice (B) can be eliminated because even though Burke mentions *fanatics*, he isn't referring to the *sophisters*, and though *universality* might be understood, there's no support for it in the text. Choice (C) doesn't work because the argument, though weak, is current, not antiquated. Eliminate (C). Choice (D) can be eliminated because there is no mention anywhere of *innovation*. Choice (A) is the correct answer.

34.   **A**   This is a Vocab-in-Context question, so go back to the text, find the word *overload* in line 1, and cross it out. Replace it with another word that makes sense in the sentence based on the context of the passage. There is a time contrast in the sentence between *a few years ago* and *now* that can be used for context. Burke says *a few years ago* he would have been *ashamed to overload a matter...with unnecessary support* but now the doctrine is *publicly taught, avowed, and printed. Overload* must be referring to something that means *unnecessary support*. Choice (A) is a clear synonym of that phrase, whereas (B), (C), and (D) don't have anything to do with *unnecessary support*. Choice (A) is the correct answer.

35.   **B**   This is a Vocab-in-Context question, so go back to the text, find the word *employ* in line 20, and cross it out. Replace it with another word that makes sense in the sentence based on the context of the passage. *Employ* could easily be replaced with the word *use*, since the abettors are employing the artifices *in order to render the support...invidious*. POE anything that has nothing to do with *use*, leaving (B) as the correct answer.

36.   **A**   This question asks about Paine's beliefs about *leadership by right of birth*. He clearly has a negative view, as evidenced throughout Passage 2 with phrases such as *the evil of hereditary succession, minds early poisoned by importance,* and *monarchy and succession have laid but the world in blood and ashes*. Eliminate anything positive, including (B) because Paine does not view hereditary succession as useful and (D) because Paine does not see hereditary succession as valuable. Compare (A) and (C). Choice (A) might initially look extreme, but remember that a correct answer can contain extreme wording if the text has equally strong wording. Choice (C) can be eliminated because Paine doesn't believe leadership is about *expressing opinions*. Choice (A) is the correct answer.

37.   **C**   This is the first in a paired set of questions, so Parallel POE is a useful strategy here. Begin with the answers for Q38. Check and see if the indicated lines support any of the answers for Q37. Choice (38A) talks about men who consider themselves *born to reign* who *soon grow insolent*. While this might be an excellent argument against the crown, these lines don't support any of the answers to Q37. Eliminate (38A). Choice (38B) is another specific example of problems with the hereditary crown, but none of the answers for Q37 deal with specific examples. Choice (37A) is the closest thing, but that answer says *address all possible reasons* and that answer is just one reason. Eliminate (38B). Choice (38C) is an argument for the hereditary crown, which is the opposite of Paine's point. Eliminate it. Choice (38D) refers to an entire country denying a fact and believing something false. This supports (37C), so connect those

two answers. Without any support from Q38, (37A), (37B), and (37D) can all be eliminated. This leaves the pair of (37C) and (38D) as the correct answers.

38.  **D**  (See explanation above.)

39.  **A**  This question asks about Burke's likely response to Paine's statements in the final paragraph of Passage 2. Paine is clear that he believes the hereditary monarchy, instead of preserving *a nation from civil war*, actually causes wars and rebellions. Burke, on the other hand, says that the people of England *conceive the undisturbed succession of the crown to be a pledge of the stability and perpetuity...of our Constitution*. The two men clearly do not agree, so (B) and (C) can be eliminated. Compare (A) and (D). Whether or not Paine provides specifics about wars and rebellions is irrelevant to Burke's point, so (D) can be eliminated. This leaves (A), which matches the prediction and is the correct answer.

40.  **B**  These were the lines used for the prediction in the previous question. Choice (B) is the correct answer.

41.  **B**  The two passages do not agree, so (A) and (D) can be eliminated. Neither passage presents a method for *resolving the issues*, so (C) can be eliminated. Passage 2 discusses the specifics of England's violent history in relation to hereditary monarchy, a topic never discussed by Burke in Passage 1. Choice (B) is the correct answer.

42.  **C**  Both of these passages deal with hereditary succession and views about the validity of a crown passed down through families. However, this is not all they do. Burke argues for a hybrid of monarchy and elected officials (which is what Paine wants). As a result, their disagreement isn't really so extreme. Burke concedes, especially in the last paragraph, that pure hereditary monarchy is not all it's cracked up to be, while Paine addresses those who support the idea and explains why they are wrong. Choice (C) correctly identifies this purpose and is the correct answer.

43.  **D**  This question asks about the main idea of the passage. It is a general question, so save it for later until after the specific questions are answered. The passage is primarily about new possibilities of human genome editing, weighing the positives and potential dangers of this developing field in science. This supports (D). There is no one long-term study in the passage, making (A) incorrect. Choice (B) is also incorrect because, while there is some background information included in the passage, it is not the primary purpose. Choice (C) is incorrect as well because there are not any competing theories juxtaposed in the passage. Therefore, (D) is correct.

44.  **B**  This question asks about the author's attitude toward CRISPR/Cas9 technology. Attitude questions are general questions, and therefore should be saved until after the specific questions are answered. For tone/attitude questions, first decide whether the attitude is positive, negative, or neutral. Eliminate what doesn't match that general category, and then make a more specific decision from the remaining answers. The author of this passage is generally optimistic, noting CRISPR's potential for disease prevention while understanding the risks involved

at this current state of research. Eliminate any answer choices that are negative or neutral. Choice (A) can be eliminated because the author is concerned. Choice (B) is positive, so keep it. Choice (C) can be eliminated because it's negative. Choice (D) is also positive, so keep that. Compare (B) and (D) using the text. Choice (B) describes an understanding of risk (*cautious optimism*), while (D) takes the positivity to an extreme not matched in the passage. Therefore, (B) is correct.

45. **B** This is a Vocab-in-Context question, so go back to the text, find the word *editing* in line 13, and cross it out. Replace it with another word that makes sense in the sentence based on the context of the passage. In this case, *editing* refers to *changing* the human genetic material. Choices (A) and (C), *abridging* and *revising*, respectively, are both possible definitions of *editing*, but neither matches the context of the passage. No one is trying to shorten or improve the genetic material. Choice (D), *polishing*, does not make sense in context, leaving (B), *altering*, which most means *changing*. Therefore, (B) is correct.

46. **C** This is a paired question, so start with the best evidence question below to match evidence with the answer choices in this question. Choice (47A) does not support any of the choices in Q46, so eliminate it. Choice (47B) supports (46C), so connect both of these and check the other two choices in Q47. Choice (47C) does not pair with any of the choices in Q46, making it incorrect as well. Choice (47D) on first glance pairs with (46A) because both talk about monkey testing, but it does not provide evidence that monkey testing is expensive. Therefore, eliminate (47D). Eliminate (46A), (46B), and (46D) because they are unsupported by evidence in Q47. Since there is only one true pairing between (46C) and (47B), these are the correct answers.

47. **B** (See explanation above.)

48. **D** This is a paired question, so start with the best evidence question below to match evidence with the answer choices in this question. Choice (49A) pairs with (48C), so draw a line connecting these two answer choices. Choice (49B) does not pair with any of the choices in Q48, so it may be eliminated. Choice (49C) supports (48D) because these tests were done in Atlanta, Georgia in the United States, so draw a line connecting those two choices. Choice (49D) does not support any of the choices in Q48. Eliminate (48A) and (48B) because they are unsupported by evidence in Q49. Now, look back at Q48. Choice (48C) cannot be proven by the passage, eliminating this choice along with (49A). Therefore, (48D) and (49C) are correct.

49. **C** (See explanation above.)

50. **C** Use the key word and line reference to find the window for this question. The text states that countries with *high rates of in vitro* fertilization will be the first to attempt clinical applications, supporting (C). Choice (A) is incorrect because it is outside the window and is not related to *in vitro* fertilization. Choices (B) and (D) are incorrect as well because both predict the future, making them impossible to prove. Therefore, (C) is correct.

51. **A**   Since this question contains a specific phrase and line references, it is easy to find in the text, and therefore a good question to answer before more general questions. *Much too soon* refers to clinical trials of human genome editing, according to Guoping Feng at MIT. He says that it isn't *time to do human-embryo manipulation* and that doing the wrong thing could *send the wrong message to the public—and then the public will not support scientific research anymore.* The correct answer must have something to do with that statement. Choice (A) supports this prediction. Choice (B) might be tempting, but it does not answer the question. Choice (C) is not mentioned by the passage, making it incorrect, and (D) is too strong, stating that genome editing will be an *inevitable failure.* Therefore, (A) is correct.

52. **A**   Find the window for this question using the line references and quotations. This quote supports the previous statement that CRISPR technology is not ready for human testing yet. Therefore, it is not defining or refuting anything, eliminating (C) and (D). While the quote does clarify and go further into detail, Feng is not talking about an *abstract concept*, eliminating (B). Therefore, (A) is correct.

## Section 2: Writing and Language

1. **A**   In this sentence, the verb *watch* needs to be consistent with the other verbs in the list: *read* and *look.* Therefore, the single word *watch* is the most effective choice. Choices (B) and (C) add unnecessary words, and (D) removes a crucial component of the answer. Therefore, the correct answer is (A).

2. **D**   The phrase *the group of accepted "classic" works* should be offset as parenthetical in this sentence. In the absence of parentheses, use punctuation that will be consistent with the non-underlined parts of the sentence. In this case, there is a comma after the word *canon*, so the punctuation that concludes the parenthetical remark should also be a comma. Choices (A) and (B) mix the punctuation unnecessarily, and (C) discards it altogether. Choice (D) is correct.

3. **C**   The sentence that follows this idea is as follows: *There is no better example of such a marginalization than that of Native Americans.* The phrase *such a marginalization* suggests that some type of *marginalization* must be mentioned in the previous sentence. Choices (A), (B), and (D) mention other unrelated things, whereas (C) explicitly mentions the *periphery.*

4. **D**   Make the verbs within the sentence consistent. The nearest verb, and one that is used as part of this idea, is *identifies.* Therefore, the most consistent form of this present-tense verb is *outlines*, as (D) contains.

5. **B**   The underlined word must be something that could contain *military campaigns.* Choices (A), (C), and (D) all refer to types of pleasant conversation, so they are not likely to encompass military campaigns. Choice (B), *contact*, is neutral enough to encompass military campaigns, so even in the instance in which one or more of the other answers were unfamiliar words, (B) makes a good answer.

6. **D**    There is a comma after the word *assimilation*. If the sentence were written as in (A), it would contain a comma splice. The two ideas surrounding the comma—*When the wars subsided, the American government started a similarly cruel program of assimilation* and *often this involved the movement of Native American children from their homes to "Indian schools" that sought to remove any trace of tribal inheritance*—are complete, so they cannot be separated by the comma. Choices (B) and (C) would create run-on sentences. Therefore, only (D) fixes that error by giving an incomplete idea after the comma.

7. **C**    The previous paragraph describes the injustices suffered by Native Americans in the early nineteenth century. There is no mention of *anti-war demonstrations*, eliminating (A), or *Kenneth Lincoln*'s youth, eliminating (B). Between the remaining two choices, (C) is more effective because it connects to the idea of *assimilation*, whereas (D) is not sufficiently specific.

8. **D**    While the proposed sentence is true, it does not contribute in a substantive way to the information given in this paragraph. With questions like these, make sure that the proposed sentence is crucial to the meaning of the paragraph or passage before adding it. This sentence is not crucial, so it shouldn't be added, for the reason that (D) states.

9. **D**    The last two sentences of this paragraph further describe the positive changes that helped to create the conditions for the Native American Renaissance. These sentences agree with one another and point together toward positive change. The word *Nevertheless* suggests a contrast where none exists in the sentence, so (A) can be eliminated. Choices (B) and (C) point in the right direction rhetorically, but these conjunctions create sentence fragments made all the worse by the commas. Choice (D) is the only word that can work in the context with this particular punctuation.

10. **B**    When answer choices consist of three pronouns (*them*, *these*, and *it*, in this case) and one specific noun (*Native American writers*), the specific noun is almost always correct. The specific noun, given in (B), is correct in this case because it is the only choice that removes all ambiguity from the sentence.

11. **D**    When combining sentences, be sure to look for the shortest option that contains all the necessary information. Choices (B) and (C) are particularly long, and each contains some other issue. Choice (B) changes the punctuation to another form of STOP punctuation, but it does not combine the sentences in any other way. Choice (C) has an ambiguous meaning because of the many modifiers (*in this period, of the 1970s and 1980s*, *amid the resulting efflorescence*, and *of Native American writers*) that are strung together. Choice (A) creates ambiguity with the odd combination of words *a resultant efflorescence*. Choice (D) is the only choice that effectively combines and shortens the ideas without introducing new errors.

12. **A**    Choose the word that best fits the context. While the changing leaves may *bode, indicate*, or *foretell* the coming of winter, the verb in this sentence will describe the action of the subject, *Anyone who lives in the Mid-Atlantic or New England*. Therefore, the only verb that can apply in this context is the one given in (A), *knows*.

13. **D**    When given the option to DELETE an underlined portion, give it serious consideration: DELETE is often correct. In this case, deleting the underlined portion eliminates extraneous and awkward wording from the sentence, without introducing new errors. Therefore, (D), which says to delete the underlined portion, is the most effective choice.

14. **B**    All of the choices contain the same information; therefore, the most effective route is to choose the most concise of these answers. In this case, the most concise option is (B), which communicates in three words what the other choices communicate in seven or eight.

15. **B**    The phrase *including restaurant owners, hoteliers, and farmers* is a clarifying phrase, giving more detail to the words *business owners*. It should therefore be offset as parenthetical without adding any new commas. Choice (B) accomplishes this goal. Choice (D) cannot be used because the idea that precedes a colon must be complete, and *Many business owners including* is not complete.

16. **A**    The previous sentence states, *Foliage season, however, is a bit more difficult to predict*. This sentence expands on the previous sentence, providing an example or an instance of this difficulty. Therefore, (A), *for instance*, contains an effective transition in linking this idea to the previous one.

17. **C**    The previous idea states *Of course, many people would certainly like to know the cause* of how and why leaves change color in the fall. This sentence continues that idea, but since all the transitions signal continuation, use POE. Choice (A) can be eliminated because it introduces an ambiguous pronoun. Choice (B) can be eliminated because there is no indication that the ideas are happening in any kind of sequence. Choice (D) can be eliminated because it does not sufficiently address the connectedness of the ideas. Only (C) remains as the transition that best connects the two ideas.

18. **A**    This sentence indicates that *scientists* have always had some knowledge of how fall foliage works, so the verb must indicate a past knowledge that has continued into the future. Choices (B), (C), and (D) are all purely in the present, so they can be eliminated. Only (A), *have long known*, effectively communicates that the scientists' knowledge began in the past and continues into the present.

19. **D**    When asked to add an idea to a paragraph, make sure that there is a very good reason to do so. In general, it is best NOT to add new information to the passage. That is true here as well—the proposed sentence may be true, but it does not contribute in a substantive way to the larger purpose of the paragraph. Therefore, the sentence should not be added because it is irrelevant to the paragraph's focus, as stated in (D).

20. **D**    The subject of this verb is *factors*, thereby eliminating the singular verbs contained in (A) and (B). Choice (C) can also be eliminated because it contains the possessive pronoun *their* in a part of the sentence that does not indicate possession. Only (D) remains in giving the correct form of *there* and the appropriately plural verb.

21. **A**    The previous sentence states *They found that both reacted to frosts in the fall, but only the high-lands reacted to frosts in the spring.* The added detail should continue in this vein, as in (A). Choice (B) does not address climate, (C) does not address the leaves, and (D) is more focused on the spring than the fall.

22. **D**    Because the first idea of the sentence—*Combining these findings with climate-change predictions for the next century*—is an introductory idea, the second part of the sentence must contain a complete idea with a subject and a verb. Choices (A), (B), and (C) contain only verbs, so they can be eliminated. This leaves (D), which contains both a subject and a verb.

23. **C**    The previous sentence refers to *contemporary U.S. holdings*, so the best available contrast comes from (C), in which *quite an old idea* provides a contrast with *contemporary*. Choices (A), (B), and (D) are free of grammatical errors, but they are not adequately linked to the previous sentence or the next, which cites *One early case.*

24. **A**    Read the passage carefully. The regions are listed in this order: *west and south, north,* and *southeast.* The states shown in the map must be listed in that order as well: Tennessee is to the *west and south,* Virginia is to the *north,* and North Carolina is to the *southeast.* Choice (A) effectively matches the states to their appropriate regions.

25. **B**    The idea after the word *debts,* the idea from *those* to *the Revolutionary War* is not complete, so it cannot be preceded by a semicolon, as in (A). Choice (C) can be eliminated because this sentence should have some pause to break up the two parts of the sentence, and (D) can be eliminated because it contains too much punctuation, creating confusion with the other long dashes in this sentence. The best answer therefore is (B), which contains an appropriate colon and no extra punctuation.

26. **D**    Both uses of the word *its* refer back to *the state* of North Carolina, and both of the nouns in this part of the sentence—*offer* and *western counties*—belong to North Carolina, so both should take the possessive form of *its.* Choice (D) is therefore the best of the available answers. Remember, *it's* is a contraction of the words *it is.*

27. **C**    In keeping with the historical tone of the essay, the verb should be in the past tense, eliminating (D). Choice (A) creates an awkward sentence fragment, so it too can be eliminated. Then, the subject of this verb is *counties,* which is plural, meaning that between (B) and (C), the only possible verb is the plural *were* in (C).

28. **B**    Each answer contains essentially the same information, except for (A), which suggests a contrast that is not present in the sentence. When each answer contains the same information, choose the shortest. In this case, the shortest possible answer comes from (B), which fixes the sentence by removing the repetitive use of the word *independence.*

29. **C**    A *boarder* is someone who lives at a boarding house. This word has no logical place in this sentence, so (A) and (B) should be eliminated. The same could be said for the word *broader,*

which is an adjective meaning "more broad," eliminating (D). Only (C) remains in its use of the word *border*, which is the part or edge that forms the outer boundary of an area.

30.  **A**  Sentence 2 begins with the phrase *This time*, but that phrase does not clearly refer to anything in sentence 1. Therefore, the proposed sentence, with its mention of *1789*, should be placed before sentence 2, after sentence 1, because it will clarify the referent of *this time*. Therefore, (A) is correct.

31.  **A**  When the words *just as* are used to make a comparison within a sentence, they must be followed at some point by the words *so too*. This is an English idiom, a convention of usage that is particular to the language. The SAT tests these idioms but does not do so frequently. The best answer is therefore (A).

32.  **A**  Read the question carefully. It asks for a word that will *convey an attitude of genuine interest* and *avoid the appearance of mockery*. Choices (B) and (D) appear to be mocking, (B) because it is so informal and (D) because it is overstated. Choice (C) is not specific enough to convey an attitude of genuine interest. Choice (A) effectively meets the goal—when used in this way, *curiosity* conveys the sense of something meriting further inquiry.

33.  **C**  The final paragraph is a discussion of how the state of Franklin provides the reminder that the borders of and within the United States have often changed and that the shape and make-up of our current fifty states is not necessarily a permanent configuration. Choice (A) refers to only a minor aspect of this and implies a generalization to federally oriented states that may or may not be true. Choices (B) and (D) are not specific. Only (C) effectively fulfills the goal outlined in the question.

34.  **A**  The first two sentences are characterized by simple present-tense verbs: *live, see, cross, drive*. Therefore, the most logical verb in the underlined portion is *see*, as in (A), which has the same tense and format as the other verbs.

35.  **C**  The previous sentence states, *Civil engineering as a profession is centuries old and has long been necessary for the functioning of modern government*. The new proposed sentence, *Few governments in the modern world could function without the work of civil engineers*, is worded in a slightly different way, but it mainly restates the information contained in the previous sentence. The proposed sentence should therefore not be added because it does not give any new information, as stated in (C).

36.  **B**  Civil engineers are portrayed in a positive light, so the word *manipulators* in (D) would not have a place in this sentence. *Foundations* and *pillars*, particularly when referring to something about *society*, are typically used to describe principles (in abstract terms) or architectural structures (in more concrete terms). This eliminates (A) and (C). The best answer, therefore, is (B), *cornerstones*, which has a literal meaning as the stone at the corner of a foundation but also has a figurative meaning that describes any person or thing that is important to a structure.

37.  **A**  The information in this sentence restates the information from the quote. That is to say that it puts the quoted information *in other words*, making (A) the best possible answer. Choices (B) and (C) suggest a contrast, but there is no contrast between these two sentences. Choice (D) suggests a move to a different type of description, but this sentence is merely restating or rephrasing the information given in the quote. Therefore, (A) is correct.

38.  **A**  Use the context of the sentence. The information that expands upon the idea of *small* projects, *like local roads and power stations*, which is offset by a dash. Therefore, the information that is used the same way to describe *large* projects should also be offset with dashes, two in this case because it appears in the middle of the sentence. Choice (A) gives this punctuation most consistently.

39.  **D**  As written, the word *however* appears between two ideas that do not contrast. *Their backgrounds tend to vary* and *specialties can range from architecture to environmental engineering, from ecology to urban planning* are related sentences that move in the same direction. Therefore, the word *however* must be restricted to the first sentence, implying a contrast with some earlier idea. Choice (A) places the *however* in the second sentence, and (B) and (C) use the *however* explicitly to link the two sentences. Choice (D) is the only choice that provides another alternative by separating the ideas into two sentences and putting the word *however* in the first.

40.  **B**  When all four answers contain essentially the same meaning, choose the shortest that is free of grammatical errors. In this case, that answer is (B), *creating delivery mechanisms*, which communicates the same information as the other choices in the fewest words.

41.  **B**  Pay particular attention to the first few words of sentence 3: *Those who want a greener country*. These must come before the similarly worded beginning of sentence 5: *Those who are less concerned with long-term energy sources*. Both ideas must come after sentence 4, which is the first to discuss *environmental* concerns in a specific way. The best of the available answers, therefore, is (B).

42.  **C**  The following sentence states that *The Bureau of Labor Statistics predicts that the field will grow by nearly 20% between 2012 and 2022*. This sentence is concerned exclusively with the growth of the career, so the preceding sentence must signal some kind of preview of this *growth*. Choice (C) does so clearly with the words *constantly growing*. The other choices might sound fine in the context, but they do not fulfill the purpose outlined in the question.

43.  **D**  If the underlined portion contains a pronoun, that pronoun must be consistent with the noun to which it refers, *a civil engineer*. Choices (A), (B), and (C) all contain plural pronouns, which would not be consistent. Only (D) contains a singular pronoun.

44.  **C**  All four choices are concerned with *civil engineering*, but (A), (B), and (D) add a number of unnecessary words in referring to the profession. Therefore, the best of the available answers is (C), which states the information clearly and concisely.

# Section 3: Math (No Calculator)

1. **B**    Start by plugging in 9 for $x$ into the function to get $\frac{5}{3}(9) + k = 12$. Solve for $k$ to get

         $15 + k = 12$ and $k = -3$. Therefore, $g(x) = \frac{5}{3}x - 3$, and $g(-3) = \frac{5}{3}(-3) + (-3) = -5 - 3 = -8$,

         so the answer is (B).

2. **B**    Get rid of the fraction in the second equation by multiplying both sides of the equation by $k$ to
get $h = 5k$. Substitute $5k$ for $h$ in the first equation to get $3(k + 2) = 5k$. Distribute the 3 to get
$3k + 6 = 5k$. Solve for $k$ to get $6 = 2k$, and $3 = k$, which is (B).

3. **D**    Set the expressions in each of the answer choices equal to 1 and solve for $y$. Choice (A) becomes
$\left|2 - y\right| + 2 = 1$ or $\left|2 - y\right| = -1$. The result of an absolute value is always greater than or equal
to 0, so this doesn't work. Eliminate (A). The same thing happens with (B) and (C). Only (D)
works: $\left|2 - y\right| - 2 = 1$ or $\left|2 - y\right| = 3$, which happens when $y = -1$ or 5. Therefore, (D) is the
correct answer.

4. **A**    According to the question, $\frac{x + y}{x} = \frac{6}{5}$. Plug in an easy value for $x$, such as $x = 5$, and solve

         for $y$. The equation becomes $\frac{5 + y}{5} = \frac{6}{5}$, so $5 + y = 6$, and $y = 1$. Try these values in the answer

         choices to see which one works. Choice (A) becomes $\frac{1}{5} = \frac{1}{5}$. This is true, so keep (A), but

         check the rest of the answers to be sure. Choice (B) becomes $\frac{1}{5} = \frac{11}{5}$, (C) becomes $\frac{5 + 1}{5} = \frac{1}{5}$,

         and (D) becomes $\frac{5 - 2(1)}{5} = -\frac{1}{5}$. None of these are true, so eliminate (B), (C), and (D), and

         choose (A).

5. **A**    Plug $-2x$ in for $x$ in the function to get $g(-2x) = -4(-2x) - 7 = 8x - 7$, which is (A).

6. **D**    Use FOIL to expand the quadratic to get $4(15x^2 - 6x - 10x + 4)$. Use Bite-Sized Pieces to see
that the first term is $4(15x^2) = 60x^2$. Eliminate (A) and (B). Likewise, the last term must be
$4(4) = 16$. Therefore, eliminate (C). Choice (D) is correct.

7. **C**    Plug 1 in for $k$ to get $x - 7 = \sqrt{x - 1}$. Plug in the answers to solve. Start with $x = 5$ since 5

         appears in two of the answers. If $x = 5$, the equation becomes $5 - 7 = \sqrt{5 - 1}$. Solve both

         sides of the equation to get $-2 = \sqrt{4}$. The square root of a number is always its positive value.

         Therefore, this expression is untrue. Eliminate (B) and (D). Next, try $x = 1$. If $x = 1$, the equa-

         tion becomes $1 - 7 = \sqrt{1 - 1}$. Solve both sides of the equation to get $-6 = \sqrt{0}$. This is also

         untrue, so eliminate (A). The correct answer must therefore be (C).

8. **C** According to the question, Alexi increased the amount he lifted by 225 − 180 = 45 pounds over 24 − 6 = 18 days. Calculate his daily increase to get 45 ÷ 18 = 2.5 pounds per day, which is (C).

9. **D** In the slope-intercept from of an equation, $y = mx + b$, $m$ represents the slope. Therefore, the slope of the given line is −4. In the standard form of the equation $Ax + By = C$, the slope equals $-\dfrac{A}{B}$. For (A), the slope is $\dfrac{-4}{-1} = 4$. Eliminate (A). In (B), the slope is $-\dfrac{4}{2} = -2$. Eliminate (B). In (C), the slope is $-\dfrac{6}{3} = -2$. Eliminate (C). Therefore, the correct answer must be (D).

10. **B** The first equation is a parabola, because if FOILed out, it would contain an $x^2$ term, and the second equation is a line, because there is no exponent attached to $x$. The two can at most have two points of intersection, so eliminate (A). Next, draw a rough sketch of the parabola. Start by finding the roots of the equation by setting each of the binomials in the parentheses equal to 0. If $x − 7 = 0$, then $x = 7$. Therefore, one point on the parabola is (7, 0). If $3x + 4 = 0$, then $3x = −4$, and $x = -\dfrac{4}{3}$. Therefore, a second point on the parabola is $\left(-\dfrac{4}{3}, 0\right)$. Lastly, plug in 0 for $x$ to get $y = (0 − 7)[3(0) + 4] = (−7)(4) = −28$. Therefore, a third point on the graph is (0, −28). Connecting the three points will result in a sketch that looks roughly like this:

Next, draw the line. Rearrange the equation into slope-intercept form, $y = mx + b$, where $m$ stands for the slope and $b$ stands for the $y$-intercept. This is $y = \dfrac{1}{3}x + \dfrac{1}{3}$. So, the line has a slope of $\dfrac{1}{3}$, and a $y$-intercept of $\dfrac{1}{3}$. A rough sketch of the line would look like this:

It is clear from a rough drawing of the two equations that the line must cross the parabola twice, and the answer is (B).

11.   **A**   There are variables in the answer choices, so plug in. If $d$ = 10, then Joan's bouquet costs 10 − 4 = $6. The combined cost of both bouquets is 10 + 6 = $16, which means that each of them paid $16 ÷ 2 = $8 for the bouquets before the tax was added. The tax on each share is $8 × 0.15 = $1.20, which means that each of them paid a total of $8 + $1.20 = $9.20. Plug 10 in for $d$ in each of the answers to see which answer equals the target of $9.20. Choice (A) becomes 1.15(10) − 2.3 = 11.50 − 2.3 = 9.2. This matches the target, but check the remaining answers just in case. Choice (B) becomes 2(10) − 1.15 = 20 − 1.15 = 18.85. Eliminate (B). Choice (C) becomes 2.15(10) − 2 = 21.5 − 2 = 19.5. Eliminate (C). Choice (D) becomes 2.3(10) − 4.6 = 23 − 4.6 = 18.4. Eliminate (D). Therefore, the answer is (A).

12.   **A**   Multiply both sides of the equation by $(z + 3)$ to get $z − 3 = 8(z + 3)$. Distribute the 8 to get $z − 3 = 8z + 24$. Solve for $z$ to get $z = 8z + 27$, $−7z = 27$, and $z = -\dfrac{27}{7}$. Choice (A) is correct.

13.   **C**   Plug in, picking easy numbers. Let $x$ = 3, and $v$ = 6. The equation becomes $(3)^2 − 3t = \dfrac{6}{3}(3)$.

Solve for $t$ to get $9 − 3t = 6$, and $t = 1$. In the answers, plug in 6 for $v$ and 1 for $t$ to see which answer could return a value of 3 for $x$. Choice (A) becomes $\dfrac{6}{3} \pm \dfrac{\sqrt{6^2 + 4(1)}}{3} = 2 \pm \dfrac{\sqrt{40}}{3}$, which will not come out to an integer like 3. Eliminate (A). Choice (B) becomes

$\dfrac{6}{3} \pm \dfrac{\sqrt{6^2 + 36(1)}}{6} = 2 \pm \dfrac{\sqrt{72}}{6}$, which won't be an integer either. Eliminate (B). Choice (C)

becomes $\dfrac{6}{6} \pm \dfrac{\sqrt{6^2 + 108(1)}}{6} = 1 \pm \dfrac{\sqrt{144}}{6} = 1 \pm \dfrac{12}{6} = 1 \pm 2 = 3$. Keep (C), but check (D) just

in case. Choice (D) becomes $\dfrac{6}{6} \pm \dfrac{\sqrt{6^2 + 4(1)}}{6} = 1 \pm \dfrac{\sqrt{40}}{6}$. This won't be an integer, either, so

(C) is correct.

14. **C**    The two equations intersect at points on the *y*-axis, $(0, s)$ and $(0, -s)$. To find the value of *s*,

plug either of these points into either equation and solve for *s*. It is easier to use the first point

in equation *A* to avoid having to deal with negative signs. Plugging $(0, s)$ into $x = 18y^2 - 2$

results in $0 = 18s^2 - 2$. Add 2 to both sides to get $2 = 18s^2$, then divide both sides by 18 to get

$\dfrac{2}{18} = s^2$ or $\dfrac{1}{9} = s^2$. Take the square root of both sides to find that $s = \dfrac{1}{3}$, which is (C).

15. **B**    To get *i* out of the denominator of a fraction, multiply by the complex conjugate

of the denominator. Multiply the top and bottom of the fraction by $(4 - 3i)$ to get

$\dfrac{(18 + i)(4 - 3i)}{(4 + 3i)(4 - 3i)} = \dfrac{72 - 54i + 4i - 3i^2}{16 - 9i^2}$. Because $i = \sqrt{-1}$, $i^2 = -1$. Substitute $-1$ for $i^2$ to

get $\dfrac{72 - 54i + 4i - 3(-1)}{16 - 9(-1)} = \dfrac{72 - 50i + 3}{16 + 9} = \dfrac{75 - 50i}{25}$. The full equation becomes $3 - 2i =$

$a + bi$. Therefore, $a = 3$, and the answer is (B).

16.    $\dfrac{5}{8}$ or **0.625**

In a right triangle with angles $a°$ and $b°$, $\cos a = \sin b$. Knowing this fact about the complemen-

tary angles of a right triangle makes questions like this easier. Without that knowledge, plug-

ging in can help. Convert 0.625 to a fraction, which is $\dfrac{5}{8}$. Cosine is defined as $\dfrac{adj}{hyp}$, so label

the side next to *a* as 5 and the hypotenuse as 8. Sine is defined as $\dfrac{opp}{hyp}$, and the side opposite *b*

is the side that is 5. Therefore, $\sin a° = \dfrac{5}{8}$, or 0.625.

17.  **3**  Imagine the triangle as a right triangle with a height of 24 feet and a hypotenuse of $l + \frac{1}{4}l + \frac{3}{4}l = 2l$. The proportions that hold for the hypotenuse also hold for the height. To solve for the width, set $2l = 24$, which means that $l = 12$, and $\frac{1}{4}l = \left(\frac{1}{4}\right)(12) = 3$.

18.  **1**  Multiply the first equation by 2 to get $16x - 10y = 54$. Stack the two equations on top of each other and add them together to get:

$$16x - 10y = 54$$
$$+\ \underline{\ 5x + 10y = 30\ }$$
$$21x \qquad\quad = 84$$

Solve for $x$ to get $x = 4$. Plug 4 in for $x$ into the second equation to get $5(4) + 10y = 30$. Solve for $y$ to get $20 + 10y = 30$, $10y = 10$, and $y = 1$.

19.  $\dfrac{20}{9}$ or **2.22**

The difference in the known $p$ values is $110 - 90 = 20$. The difference in the depths for which the $p$ values are known is $215 - 170 = 45$ feet. Therefore, the pressure increase for every one foot of depth is $\dfrac{20}{45}$, which reduces to $\dfrac{4}{9}$. The question asks for the increase every 5 feet, though, so multiply this value by 5 to get $\dfrac{20}{9}$, or 2.22.

20.  **4**  Factor $x^2$ out of the first two terms to get $x^2(x - 4) + 3x - 12 = 0$. Factor a 3 out of the last two terms to get $x^2(x - 4) + 3(x - 4) = 0$. Rewrite the equation to get $(x^2 + 3)(x - 4) = 0$. Therefore, one of the solutions to the equation is $x - 4 = 0$. Solve for $x$ to get $x = 4$. The other solutions come from $x^2 + 3 = 0$, so $x^2 = -3$. This will yield imaginary solutions, so the only real solution is 4.

## Section 4: Math (Calculator)

1.  **D**  There are variables in the answer choices, so plug in. Let $w = 2$. In two weeks, his training time will be $7.2 - (0.2)(2) = 7.2 - 0.4 = 6.8$ seconds. Plug 2 in for $w$ in each of the answers to see which answer equals the target answer of 6.8. Choice (A) becomes $0.2 - 7.2(2) = 0.2 - 14.4 = -14.2$. Eliminate (A). Choice (B) becomes $6.0 - 0.2(2) = 6.0 - 0.4 = 5.6$. Eliminate (B). Choice (C) becomes $7.2 + 0.2(2) = 7.2 + 0.4 = 7.6$. Eliminate (C). Check (D) just to be sure: $7.2 - 0.2(2) = 7.2 - 0.4 = 6.8$. Therefore, the correct answer is (D).

2.  **B**  Start by converting the yards to inches by setting up the following proportion: $\dfrac{1 \text{ yard}}{36 \text{ inches}} = \dfrac{4 \text{ yards}}{x \text{ inches}}$. Cross-multiply to get $x = (36)(4) = 144$ inches. After the first cut, the yarn's length is $144 \div 2 = 72$. After the second cut, the yarn's length is $72 \div 4 = 18$, which is (B).

3. **C** Start by subtracting the base fee to get 3.60 − 2.40 = 1.20. Divide this amount by the cost per mile to get 1.20 ÷ 0.30 = 4 miles, so the correct answer is (C).

4. **B** Let $T$ represent the number of miles Tiki cycled and $I$ represent the number of miles Irina cycled. According to the question, $T + I = 51$, and $T = I − 13$. Substitute the second equation into the first to get $(I − 13) + I = 51$. Solve for $I$ to get $2I − 13 = 51$, $2I = 64$, and $I = 32$. Another approach is to plug in the answers. Either way, the correct answer is (B).

5. **C** According to the question, resistance = voltage applied ÷ number of amps. Plug the numbers given into the equation to get $9 = 54 ÷ x$. Solve for $x$ to get $x = 6$, which is (C).

6. **C** According to the sample, 38.7% of the class would be expected to have O-positive blood. $265 × 0.387 ≈ 103$. Therefore, the closest answer is (C).

7. **A** The total number of 35- to 64-year-old viewers is 63,574 + 20,482 = 84,056. The total number of viewers in that age range who preferred network $D$ is 12,084 + 3,676 = 15,760. Therefore, the probability that a viewer in this age group preferred Network $D$ is $\frac{15,760}{84,056} ≈ 0.2$, which is (A).

8. **B** According to the table, there were 75 total pieces of furniture made, of which 9 were desks made of maple. Therefore, the proportion of maple desks is $\frac{9}{75} = \frac{3}{25}$. The answer is (B).

9. **A** Eliminate (C) because a line that is undefined is parallel to the $y$-axis. Such a line would pass through exactly 2 quadrants. Likewise, eliminate (D) because a line with a slope equal to 0 is parallel to the $x$–axis. Such a line would pass through exactly 2 quadrants. Make a quick sketch of a line that goes through Quadrants I, II, III, such as:

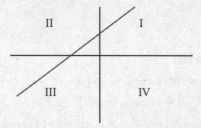

From the drawing, it is clear that the line has a positive slope, so the answer is (A).

10. **D** For the graph to have $x$-intercepts at −2, 2, and 5, the expression must equal 0 when $x = −2$, $x = 2$, and $x = 5$. For each answer choice, set each binomial equal to 0 to see if it results in these values for $x$. For (A) and (C), there is a squared binomial times another binomial. For (A), if $(x − 2) = 0$, $x = 2$, but that root will appear twice, leading to only 2 distinct roots. For this reason, eliminate (A) and (C). For (B), the first root is 2, then $(x + 2) = 0$ gives a root of $x = −2$,

and $(x + 5) = 0$ gives a root of $-5$. Eliminate (B). The roots for (D) will be 5, 2, and $-2$, respectively, so (D) is the answer.

11. **C**  The animal with the greatest body weight is the one furthest along the $x$-axis. That animal weighs approximately 125 kilograms. Look to the $y$-axis to see that the same animal has a brain weight of 140 grams. Therefore, (C) is the correct answer.

12. **D**  Remember that the brain weight is given in grams but the body weight is given in kilograms.

1 kilogram = 1,000 grams. Calculate the ratio of each of the points given in the answers in grams.

The ratio in (A) is $\dfrac{70}{10(1,000)} = \dfrac{7}{1,000} = 0.007$. The ratio in (B) is $\dfrac{50}{30(1,000)} = \dfrac{5}{3,000} = 0.001\overline{6}$.

Since this is less than the ratio in (A), eliminate (A). The ratio in (C) is $\dfrac{110}{65,000} = 0.00169$.

Since this is bigger than (B), eliminate (C). The ratio in (D) is $\dfrac{130}{105,000} = 0.00124$. Since this

is smaller than (B), eliminate (B) and choose (D).

13. **A**  First, because an exponent other than 1 is applied to the fraction, the function is not a linear

function. Because the scatterplots in (B) and (D) suggest a linear relationship between $x$ and $y$,

eliminate (B) and (D). Next, plug in some numbers to see what happens when $x$ gets larger. If

$x = 1, j = 4$, and $k = -2$, the function becomes $f(1) = \left(\dfrac{4}{1}\right)^{-2} = 4^{-2} = \dfrac{1}{4^2} = \dfrac{1}{16}$. If $x = 100, j = 4$,

and $k = -2$, the function becomes $f(100) = \left(\dfrac{4}{100}\right)^{-2} = \left(\dfrac{1}{25}\right)^{-2} = 625$. Therefore, according to

the function, as $x$ increases, $y$ also increases. Of the remaining answer choices, this is not true

for (C). Eliminate (C). The correct answer is (A). Another option would be to plug in some

values for the variables $j$ and $k$ and then graph the function on a graphing calculator.

14. **D**  Over time, the estimated number of bacteria is clearly decreasing. Therefore, eliminate (A) and
(C). If the number of bacteria were decreasing linearly, then it would be decreasing by the same
amount every hour. However, between hours and 0 and 2 the number of bacteria decreased
by 900,000, whereas between hours 2 and 4 the number of bacteria decreased by only 90,000.
Since the rate of decrease is not the same every hour, eliminate (B) and choose (D).

15. **C** The value of Pete's bond after one year would be $20,000\left(1 + \dfrac{6}{400}\right)^4$, and the value of Roger's

savings bond after one year would be $20,000\left(1 + \dfrac{4}{400}\right)^4$. The difference in the value of their

two bonds would be $20,000\left(1 + \dfrac{6}{400}\right)^4 - 20,000\left(1 + \dfrac{4}{400}\right)^4$. Since both of them started

with savings bonds in the same amount and held them over the same time period, the differ-

ence in the value of the bonds is equal to the difference in their earnings, so the answer is (C).

16. **A** To calculate the slope, plug in two values for $x$, for example, $x = 2$ and $x = 3$, and find the cor-

responding $y$-values. When $x = 2$, then $f(x) = 500 + 80(2 - 1) + 70(2) = 720$. When $x = 3$, then

$f(x) = 500 + 80(3 - 1) + 70(3) = 870$. Two points on the graph would then be (2, 720) and

(3, 870). Next, calculate the slope: $\dfrac{y_2 - y_1}{x_2 - x_1} = \dfrac{870 - 720}{3 - 2} = 150$. Now check the answer

choices: For (A), the combined daily cost of the hotel and car rental is $70 + 80 = 150$, so the

correct answer is (A).

17. **B** According to the equation given, the total cost of package $P$ is $400 + 85(x - 1) + 60x$, and the

total cost of package $Q$ is $550 + 75(x - 1) + 50x$, where $x$ is the number of days travelled.

Plug in the answers, starting with a value for a number of days that appears in (B). The cost

of package $P = 400 + 85(8 - 1) + 60(8) = 400 + 595 + 480 = 1,475$, and the cost of package

$Q = 550 + 75(8 - 1) + 50(8) = 550 + 525 + 400 = 1,475$. The cost of the two packages is the

same at 8 days, which fits the requirements of the question. Eliminate (D), since that range

does not include 8. Now test (A) by trying $x = 7$. Package $P$ would cost $400 + 85(6) + 60(7)$

$= 1,330$, and package $Q$ would cost $550 + 75(6) + 50(7) = 1,350$. Travel package $Q$ is not less

than or equal to the total cost of travel package $P$, so eliminate ranges that include 7. This

eliminates (A) and (C). Only (B) is left.

18. **D** Use Process of Elimination. According to Moore's Law, the maximum number of transistors

that can be placed on a circuit each year doubles. If there was 1 transistor to start, the next

year there would be 2, then 4, then 8, then 16. The number of transistors would increase more

and more rapidly over the years, which indicates exponential growth. Choice (A) is a flat, hori-

zontal line, showing no growth at all, and (B) has flat sections, showing periods of no growth.

Eliminate (A) and (B). Choice (C) shows growth, but it is a line, which indicates growth at a

constant rate. Eliminate (C). Only (D) shows growth that increases exponentially.

19. **A** The volume of a cylinder can be calculated as $V = \pi r^2 h$. According to the information given,

the radius of each bucket is 0.5 feet and the height of the oil in each bucket is 1.5 feet.

Therefore, the volume of the oil in each bucket is $\pi(0.25)(1.5) \approx 1.1781$ cubic feet. Set up the following proportion: $\frac{1 \text{ gallon}}{0.133 \text{ feet}^3} = \frac{x \text{ gallons}}{1.1781 \text{ feet}^3}$. Cross-multiply to get $0.133x = 1.1781$. Solve for $x$ to get $x = 8.858$ gallons per bucket. $55 \div 8.858 \approx 6.2$ buckets. Only round at the last step to ensure a correct answer when the choices are close together. The question asks for the number of full buckets, so round this down to 6, which is (A).

20.  **B**  There is no need to solve all the way for $x$. Just make the first inequality look like the second one. Solve for $2x$ to get $2x \le 4$. Subtract 5 from each side to get $2x - 5 \le 4 - 5$ or $2x - 5 \le -1$. Therefore, the greatest possible value is $-1$, and the answer is (B).

21.  **D**  The question says that the length of arc $\overparen{PQR}$ is $18\pi$. An arc formed by the diameter is a semicircle. The length of a semicircle is equal to half the circumference of the circle, so the circumference of the circle is $18\pi \times 2 = 36\pi$. The formula for the circumference of a circle is $C = \pi d$, so $36\pi = \pi d$. Divide both sides by $\pi$ to get $36 = d$. The question asks for the length of $\overline{PR}$, which is a diameter, so the length is 36. The answer is (D).

22.  **A**  The question asks which data points on a scatterplot are below the line $y = x$. To see what happens when a point is below a line, sketch a line on the coordinate plane and a point below it. Notice that the $y$-coordinate of the point is lower that the $y$-coordinate of the line at that same value of $x$. In case of the line $y = x$, a point is below the line if its $y$-value is less than its $x$-value. According to the question, the $y$-value is equal to a city's average temperature in 2010 and the $x$-value is equal to the city's average temperature in 2000, so find cities in which the average temperature in 2010 is less than its average temperature in 2000. The only city on the chart for which this is true is Miami. Since there is one such city, the answer is (A).

23.  **C**  The question asks for the approximate percent increase, so an estimate of the temperature will be enough. The top of the 2000 bar is between the 50 and 55 line, closer to 55, so call the average temperature 53. The top of the 2010 bar is between the 55 and 60 line, closer to 55, so call the average temperature 57. To calculate percent change, use the formula $\frac{difference}{original} \times 100$. The difference is $57 - 53 = 4$. Since the question asks for a percent *increase*, the original is the smaller value, which is 53. Therefore, the percent increase is about $\frac{4}{53} \times 100 \approx 7.55\%$. Since the closest choice is 6%, the answer is (C).

24.  **A**  The answer choices refer to standard deviation. All that is needed to compute standard deviation is the individual scores. Since this is provided by the table, eliminate (D). The formula to calculate standard deviation is very long and complicated. However, it is not necessary to use the formula here. Just understand that the standard deviation is a measure of how far apart the values are spread out. Notice that a strong majority of students received a 4 on the Physics quiz. Since most of

the students got the same score, the scores are not very spread out. Since the distribution of scores on the English quiz is more even, these scores are more spread out. Therefore, the standard deviation is higher for the English quiz. The answer is (A).

25. **D**    The question asks what *must be true*, so expect to plug in more than once. Plug in a value for $b$ such that $b < -b$. Let $b = -3$. If $b = -3$, then $-3 < a < 3$. Let $a = 2$. Go through each statement. Statement (I) says $a < 0$. Since $a = 2 > 0$, cross out (I) and eliminate the choices that include (I): (A) and (C). Since both remaining choices include (III), (III) must be true, so only worry about (II). Since $b = -3$, (II) is true, so keep (II) at least for now. Try to come up with a number a value of $b$ that will satisfy the inequality but make (II) false. Try a positive number. If $b = 4$, then $4 < a < -4$. Since 4 is not less than $-4$, do not use $b = 4$. Notice that any positive number leads to the same problem. Try $b = 0$. If $b = 0$, then $0 < a < 0$. Again, 0 is not less than 0, so do not use $b = 0$. Since positive numbers and 0 do not satisfy the inequality, only negative numbers do. Therefore, (II) must be true. Eliminate the remaining answer that does not include (II), which is (B). The answer is (D).

26. **A**    The question asks for how the number 31 relates to the scatterplot. The number 31 is the $y$-intercept of the line, or the point at which $x = 0$. The $x$-axis refers to the number of hours spent on the Internet, and the $y$-axis refers to the score on the quiz. Therefore, a student who spends no time on the Internet would be expected to score around a 31. Go through the answer choices. Choice (A) says that even students who spend very little time on the Internet are unlikely to score above a 31. This matches the prediction. Also, only one of the data points is above 31. Keep (A). Choice (B) says that even students who spend very little time on the Internet will never score above 31. This is more extreme than the prediction. Also, there is a data point above 31. Eliminate (B). Choice (C) says the lowest score was about 31% of the highest score. This doesn't match the prediction. Also, the highest score is about 34 and the lowest score is about 6, so the lowest score is $\frac{6}{34} \times 100 \approx 18\%$ of the highest score. Eliminate (C). Choice (D) says the highest score on the test was 31. Similar to (B), this is more extreme than the prediction. Also, there is a data point above 31. Eliminate (D). The answer is (A).

27. **C**    To determine which polynomial is divisible, plug in a value for $x$. Let $x = 2$. If $x = 2$, then $r(x) = r(2) = 3(2)^3 + 24(2)^2 + 21(2) = 162$, $s(x) = s(2) = 2^2 + 8(2) + 7 = 27$, and $3x + 4 = 3(2) + 4 = 10$. The question asks which choice is divisible by $3x + 4$, plug in $x = 2$ to each choice and eliminate any choice that isn't divisible by 10. Choice (A) is $r(2) + s(2) = 162 + 27 = 189$. This is not divisible by 10, so eliminate (A). Choice (B) is $r(2) + 2s(2) = 162 + 2(27) = 216$. This is not divisible by 10, so eliminate (B). Choice (C) is $r(2) + 4s(2) = 162 + 4(27) = 270$. This is divisible by 10, so keep (C).

Choice (D) is $2r(2) + 4s(2) = 2(162) + 4(27) = 432$. This is not divisible by 10, so eliminate (D). The only remaining choice is (C).

28. **A** The question asks for what value of $c$ does $g(x) = c$ have one real solution. Since $c$ is on the other side of the equals sign, it is the $y$-value. Therefore, if $g(x) = c$ has one real solution, it will intersect the line $y = c$ exactly once. Let each answer choice equal $c$ and draw the line $y = c$. Draw $y = 3$, $y = 1$, $y = 0$, and $y = -1$. Each line should be a horizontal line crossing the $y$-axis at 3, 1, 0, and $-1$, respectively. The lines $y = 1$, $y = 0$, and $y = -1$ cross the graph of $g$ at three points each. Therefore, if $c$ is any of these values, $g(x) = c$ has three real solutions. The line $y = 3$ crosses $g$ exactly once, so $g(x) = 3$ has exactly one real solution. Therefore, the answer is (A).

29. **B** The question asks for the form of a quadratic in which the minimum value appears. A parabola reaches its minimum (or maximum) value at its vertex, so get the equation into vertex form, which is $y = a(x - h)^2 + k$, where $(h, k)$ is the vertex. Choice (C) is not in this form, so eliminate it. To get $g$ into vertex form, expand using FOIL: $(x - 10)(x + 4) = x^2 + 4x - 10x - 40 = x^2 - 6x - 40$. Eliminate (D), which is not equivalent to this. Get the quadratic into vertex form by completing the square. The coefficient on the $x$ term is $-6$. Cut this value in half to get $-3$, and square the result to get 9. Add 9 to both sides (without combining like terms) to get $y + 9 = x^2 - 6x + 9 - 40$. Factor $(x^2 - 6x + 9)$ to get $y + 9 = (x - 3)^2 - 40$. Subtract 9 from both sides to get $y = (x - 3)^2 - 49$. Thus, the vertex is $(3, -49)$ and the minimum value is $-49$. Choice (B) is correct.

30. **C** There are variables in the answer choices, so plug in. Let $x = 2$. The question states that $a$ is the average of $4x$ and 7. The sum of $4x$ and 7 is $4(2) + 7 = 15$, so the average is $\frac{15}{2} = 7.5$. The question also states that $b$ is the average of $5x$ and 6. The sum of $5x$ and 6 is $5(2) + 6 = 16$, so the average is $\frac{16}{2} = 8$. Finally, the question states that $c$ is the average of $3x$ and 11. The sum of $3x$ and 11 is $3(2) + 11 = 17$, so the average is $\frac{17}{2} = 8.5$. The question asks for the average of $a$, $b$, and $c$. The sum of $a$, $b$, and $c$ is $7.5 + 8 + 8.5 = 24$, so the average is $\frac{24}{3} = 8$. Circle 8; this is the target number. Go through the answer choices and eliminate any choice that is not equal to 8. Choice (A) is $x + 4 = 2 + 4 = 6$, so eliminate (A). Choice (B) is $x + 8 = 2 + 8 = 10$, so eliminate (B). Choice (C) is $2x + 4 = 2(2) + 4 = 8$, so keep (C). Choice (D) is $4x + 8 = 4(2) + 8 = 16$, so eliminate (D). The answer is (C).

31. **1.2** The question asks how much of a decrease in target heart rate will occur if the person's age increases by 2 years. Plug in two values of $y$ that are 2 years apart. Start with $y = 20$. If $y = 20$, then $R = \dfrac{3(220 - 20)}{5} = 120$. Now try $y = 22$. If $y = 22$, then $R = \dfrac{3(220 - 22)}{5} = 118.8$. To determine the decrease, subtract the two values of $R$ to get $120 - 118.8 = 1.2$. The answer is 1.2.

32. **620** The question asks how many miles into the journey the driver will be at 8:00 P.M. From 1 P.M. to 8 P.M., the driver travels for 7 hours. To determine the distance traveled, use *distance = rate × time* to get $d = rt = $ (60 miles per hour)(7 hours) = 420 miles. This is not the answer. Note that at 1:00 P.M. the driver is already 200 miles into his journey. Therefore, the driver has traveled a total of 200 miles + 420 miles = 620 miles. The answer is 620.

33. $\dfrac{25}{4}, \dfrac{50}{8}$, or **6.25**

The variables in the question are given in terms of each other, so plug in. Let the first object travel at an acceleration of $a = 4$ for a time of $t = 10$. The displacement is $d = \dfrac{1}{2}(4)(10)^2 = 200$. The second object also has an acceleration of $a = 4$ but for a time of $2.5t = 2.5(10) = 25$. This displacement is $d = \dfrac{1}{2}(4)(25)^2 = 1{,}250$. The question asks for the ratio of velocity of the object that traveled for more time to the velocity of the object that traveled for less time. This is $\dfrac{1{,}250}{200}$. This requires more than four spaces on the answer sheet, so reduce the fraction to get $\dfrac{25}{4}$. (Note that $\dfrac{50}{8}$ is also an acceptable answer, as is 6.25.)

34. **8.16** The question asks for how many pounds are equivalent to 488 shematies. The question states that 12 shematies is equivalent to 1 deben, so set up the proportion $\dfrac{12 \text{ shematies}}{1 \text{ deben}} = \dfrac{488 \text{ shematies}}{x \text{ debens}}$. Cross-multiply to get $12x = 488$. Divide by 12 to get $x = 40.\overline{66}$, so 488 shematies is equivalent to $40.\overline{66}$ debens. The question also says that a deben is approximately equal to 3.21 ounces, so set up the proportion $\dfrac{3.21 \text{ ounces}}{1 \text{ deben}} = \dfrac{y \text{ ounces}}{40.66 \text{ debens}}$. Cross-multiply to get $y = 130.54$, so 488 shematies is equivalent to 130.54 ounces. Finally, the question states that 16 ounces is equivalent to one pound, so set up the proportion $\dfrac{16 \text{ ounces}}{1 \text{ pound}} = \dfrac{130.54 \text{ ounces}}{z \text{ pounds}}$. Cross-multiply to get $16z = 130.54$. Divide both sides by 16 to get $z = 8.15875$. The question asks for the answer to the nearest hundredth, so the answer is 8.16.

35. **43, 44,** or **45**

The question asks about arc, so use the arc formula, $\dfrac{arc}{circumference} = \dfrac{angle}{360}$. The radius is 20, so use the circumference formula to get that the circumference is $C = 2\pi r = 2\pi(20) = 40\pi$. The arc is between 15 and 16, so start with an arc of 15 to get $\dfrac{15}{40\pi} = \dfrac{y}{360}$. Cross-multiply to get $5{,}400 = 40\pi y$. Divide both sides by $40\pi$ to get $y = \dfrac{5{,}400}{40\pi} = \dfrac{135}{\pi} = 42.9718$. Now try an arc of 16 to get $\dfrac{16}{40\pi} = \dfrac{y}{360}$. Cross-multiply to get 5,760 = 40$\pi y$. Divide both sides by 40$\pi$ to get

$y = \dfrac{5,760}{40\pi} = \dfrac{144}{\pi} \approx 45.8366$. The angle is, therefore, in between these two values of $y$. The

question specifies that the answer must be an integer. Therefore, to get credit, grid-in one of the

following answers: 43, 44, or 45.

36. **90** The question says that $\dfrac{2}{5}$ of the marbles in the closet must be blue. At the beginning, there are 230

blue marbles and 370 red marbles, so there are a total of 230 + 370 = 600 marbles. 110 red marbles

are added, so there is now a total of 370 + 110 = 480 red marbles and 600 + 110 = 710 total mar-

bles. The question asks how many blue marbles must be added so that $\dfrac{2}{5}$ of the marbles are blue. If

$b$ blue marbles are added, there will be 230 + $b$ blue marbles and 710 + $b$ total marbles. Set up the

equation $\dfrac{230 + b}{710 + b} = \dfrac{2}{5}$. Cross-multiply to get 5(230 + $b$) = 2(710 + $b$). Distribute to get 1,150 + 5$b$

= 1,420 + 2$b$. Subtract 2$b$ from both sides to get 1,150 + 3$b$ = 1,420. Subtract 1,150 from both sides

to get 3$b$ = 270. Divide both sides by 3 to get $b$ = 90. The answer is 90.

37. **1.07** The question asks for the value of $r$ in the bank's interest formula. Interest is a type of exponential

growth. The formula for this is *final amount = original amount*(1 + *rate*)$^{number\ of\ changes}$. The original

amount is $5,400 and the rate of interest is 7%. In the formula, rate is in decimal form rather than

percent form, so the rate is 0.07. The bank pays annual interest, so the number of changes is the

number of years, which is $y$. The final amount is the amount in the bank after $y$ years, which is

$A$. Plug these into the exponential growth formula to get $A$ = 5,400(1 + 0.07)$^y$ or $A$ = 5,400(1.07)$^y$.

This is now in the same form as the equation provided by the question, $A$ = 5,400($r$)$^y$. Since the

question asks for the value of $r$ in the question's formula, which is in the same position as 1.07 in

the standard interest formula, the answer is 1.07.

38. **7,078** As discussed in the explanation for Q38, $r$ = 1.07, so $A$ = 5,400(1.07)$^y$. The question asks for the

value after four years, so $A$ = 5,400(1.07)$^4$. Enter this into a calculator to get about $7,078.29. The

question asks for the value to the nearest dollar (disregarding the dollar sign), so the answer is

7,078. Without the formula, it is still possible to get the answer. Just add 7% of 5,400 to get the

value after one year, 7% of that new value to get the value after two years, and do that 2 more

times to get the value after four years.

# Chapter 11
# Practice Test 5

# Reading Test

## 65 MINUTES, 52 QUESTIONS

**Turn to Section 1 of your answer sheet to answer the questions in this section.**

---

### DIRECTIONS

Each passage or pair of passages below is followed by a number of questions. After reading each passage or pair, choose the best answer to each question based on what is stated or implied in the passage or passages and in any accompanying graphics (such as a table or graph).

---

### Questions 1–10 are based on the following passage.

This passage is excerpted from Robert Louis Stevenson, *Treasure Island,* originally published in 1883. The narrator and his parents own an inn on the English coast.

The stranger kept hanging about just inside the inn door, peering round the corner like a cat waiting for a mouse. Once I stepped out myself into the road, but
Line he immediately called me back, and as I did not obey
5 quick enough for his fancy, a most horrible change came over his tallowy face, and he ordered me in with an oath that made me jump. As soon as I was back again he returned to his former manner, half fawning, half sneering, patted me on the shoulder, told me I
10 was a good boy and he had taken quite a fancy to me. "I have a son of my own," said he, "as like you as two blocks, and he's all the pride of my 'art. But the great thing for boys is discipline, sonny—discipline. Now, if you had sailed along of Bill, you wouldn't have stood
15 there to be spoke to twice—not you. That was never Bill's way, nor the way of sich as sailed with him. And here, sure enough, is my mate Bill, with a spy-glass under his arm, bless his old 'art, to be sure. You and me'll just go back into the parlour, sonny, and get
20 behind the door, and we'll give Bill a little surprise— bless his 'art, I say again."

So saying, the stranger backed along with me into the parlour and put me behind him in the corner so that we were both hidden by the open door. I was very
25 uneasy and alarmed, as you may fancy, and it rather added to my fears to observe that the stranger was certainly frightened himself. He cleared the hilt of his cutlass and loosened the blade in the sheath; and all the time we were waiting there he kept swallowing as if
30 he felt what we used to call a lump in the throat.

At last in strode the captain, slammed the door behind him, without looking to the right or left, and marched straight across the room to where his breakfast awaited him.

35 "Bill," said the stranger in a voice that I thought he had tried to make bold and big.

The captain spun round on his heel and fronted us; all the brown had gone out of his face, and even his nose was blue; he had the look of a man who sees a
40 ghost, or the evil one, or something worse, if anything can be; and upon my word, I felt sorry to see him all in a moment turn so old and sick.

"Come, Bill, you know me; you know an old shipmate, Bill, surely," said the stranger.

45 The captain made a sort of gasp.

"Black Dog!" said he.

"And who else?" returned the other, getting more at his ease. "Black Dog as ever was, come for to see his old shipmate Billy, at the Admiral Benbow Inn. Ah,
50 Bill, Bill, we have seen a sight of times, us two, since I lost them two talons," holding up his mutilated hand.

"Now, look here," said the captain; "you've run me down; here I am; well, then, speak up; what is it?"

"That's you, Bill," returned Black Dog, "you're
55 in the right of it, Billy. I'll have a glass of rum from this dear child here, as I've took such a liking to; and we'll sit down, if you please, and talk square, like old shipmates."

**CONTINUE** ➡

When I returned with the rum, they were already
60 seated on either side of the captain's breakfast-table—
Black Dog next to the door and sitting sideways so
as to have one eye on his old shipmate and one, as I
thought, on his retreat.

He bade me go and leave the door wide open.
65 "None of your keyholes for me, sonny," he said; and I
left them together and retired into the bar.

For a long time, though I certainly did my best to
listen, I could hear nothing but a low gattling; but at
last the voices began to grow higher, and I could pick
70 up a word or two, mostly oaths, from the captain.

"No, no, no, no; and an end of it!" he cried once.
And again, "If it comes to swinging, swing all, say I."

---

**1**

Which choice is the best synopsis of what happens in
the passage?

A) Two characters make a plan to surprise a third
   character.

B) One character shows another character how to
   properly behave in a parlour.

C) One character unpleasantly surprises another
   character with an unexpected reunion.

D) Two characters reminisce about their time
   together on a ship.

---

**2**

Which choice best describes the developmental
pattern of the passage?

A) A detailed analysis of an enthusiastic encounter

B) An inaccurate dictation of a notable conference

C) An apprehensive account of a contentious meeting

D) A dismissive description of an important
   homecoming

---

**3**

As it is used in line 5 and line 10, "fancy" most nearly
means

A) elaboration.

B) impatience.

C) imagination.

D) preference.

---

**4**

Which emotion does the narrator most sense from
the stranger regarding his imminent meeting with the
captain?

A) The stranger is fearful about the captain's reaction
   to seeing him.

B) The stranger is overjoyed to reunite with the
   captain.

C) The stranger is worried the captain won't
   remember him.

D) The stranger is concerned the captain will be more
   interested in his breakfast than in conversation.

---

**5**

Which choice provides the best evidence for the
answer to the previous questions?

A) Lines 24–27 ("I was . . . himself")

B) Lines 31–34 ("At last . . . him")

C) Lines 43–44 ("Come, Bill . . . stranger")

D) Line 71 ("No, no, . . . once")

---

**6**

In the passage, the stranger addresses the narrator
with

A) respect but not friendliness.

B) violence but not anger.

C) disgust but not hatred.

D) affection but not trust.

CONTINUE

The main purpose of the first paragraph is to

A) introduce a character.

B) criticize a belief.

C) describe a relationship.

D) investigate a discrepancy.

As it is used in line 51, "talons" most nearly means

A) weapons.

B) claws.

C) fingers.

D) hooks.

Why does the narrator describe the captain's face as something from which "all the brown had gone out of" (line 38)?

A) The captain has grown pale after being on land so long.

B) The captain has washed his face before the meal.

C) The captain has become ill during his walk.

D) The captain has gone pale with fright.

Which choice provides the best evidence for the answer to the previous question?

A) Lines 22–24 ("So saying . . . door")

B) Lines 39–42 ("he had . . . sick")

C) Lines 52–53 ("Now, look . . . is it")

D) Lines 59–63 ("When I . . . retreat")

**CONTINUE**

**Questions 11–21 are based on the following passage and supplementary material.**

This passage is adapted from Russell W. Belk, "It's the Thought that Counts." © 1976 by University of Illinois at Urbana-Champaign.

The phenomenon of selecting an object or service "X" to present as a gift to person "Y" on occasion "Z" is a unique and important act of consumer behavior.

Line Not only must the gift giver attempt to infer the
5 recipient's tastes, needs, desires, and reactions, the gift selection may also be affected by the information which it would appear to convey about the giver and the giver-recipient relationship. The ancient practice of gift-giving is still pervasive and significant in modern
10 cultures. For instance, Lowes, Turner, and Willis (1971) cite a series of British Gallup Polls from 1963-1967, in which it was found that over 90 percent of the adult population did some Christmas gift-giving each year. Another limited sample of middle and upper
15 income families in Montreal, Caron and Ward (1975) found that third- and fifth-grade children received an average of between five and six gifts for Christmas. Both because of its prevalence and because of its strong interpersonal meanings, gift-giving offers a potentially
20 rich area for consumer behavioral explanation.

Gift-giving has been treated from a variety of related theoretical perspectives, focusing primarily on the functions and effects of giving. The preeminent theoretical analysis of the gift-giving process is an essay
25 by French anthropologist-sociologist Marcell Mauss (1923). Based on his examination of gift-giving among numerous primitive, remote, or ancient societies, Mauss concluded that gift-giving is a self-perpetuating system of reciprocity. More specifically, Mauss outlined
30 three types of obligations, which perpetuate gift-giving:

    1. The obligation to give,
    2. The obligation to receive,
    3. The obligation to repay.

The obligation to give may be based on moral
35 or religious imperatives, the need to recognize and maintain a status hierarchy, the need to establish or maintain peaceful relations, or simply the expectation of reciprocal giving. These motives, which do not admit purely selfless giving, become institutionalized
40 in a society so that under appropriate conditions an individual is socially obligated to give. Receiving is seen as similarly obligatory, and avoiding or refusing

gifts is construed as an unfriendly or even hostile act. Mauss noted however that there is a certain tension
45 created in receiving a gift since acceptance is an implicit recognition of dependence on the giver. This tension may then be reduced by fulfilling the third obligation, the obligation to repay. Failure to repay or failure to repay adequately results in a loss of status
50 and self-esteem. Adequate or overly adequate repayment, on the other hand, creates an obligation to repay on the part of the original giver, and the cycle is reinitiated.

Schwartz (1967) noted that beyond the functions
55 served by the general process of gift exchange, the characteristics of the gift itself also act as a powerful statement of the giver's perception of the recipient. He also suggested that acceptance of a particular gift constitutes an acknowledgment and acceptance of the
60 identity that the gift is seen to imply. Among children this may lead to lasting changes in self-perceptions, but presumably gifts have less influence on the self-concept of an adult.

Nevertheless, the importance of this symbolic
65 function of gift selection appears clear enough in a gift shop's recent advertisement, which asks, "Do you want your gifts to tell someone how creative you are, how thoughtful you are, or just how big your Christmas bonus was? Do you buy with a specific
70 price or a specific personality in mind?" While the answers to such basic questions about gift selection may be personally evident, the underlying behavioral questions have not been addressed by empirical research.

75 There can be little doubt that gift-giving is a pervasive experience in human life and consumer behavior. Despite the additional variables which gift-giving introduces to conceptions of consumer behavior (e.g., characteristics of the recipient, gifter-
80 receiver similarity, nature of the occasion), the present findings suggest that preference for cognitive balance is a concept which can go far toward explaining gift selection and evaluation.

**CONTINUE** ▶

**GIFT-GIVING AS COMMUNICATION**

---

**11**

The author most likely uses the examples in lines 4–17 of the passage ("Not only . . . Christmas") to highlight the

A) recent increase in consumerism around Christmas time.

B) discrepancies in gift-giving between ancient and modern times.

C) apprehension between gift-givers and receivers.

D) pervasiveness of gift-giving on special occasions.

---

**12**

In line 20, the word "rich" most nearly means

A) opulent.

B) embellished.

C) fertile.

D) saccharine.

---

**13**

The author indicates that the self-perpetuating system of reciprocity

A) is a form of communication between gift-giver and recipient.

B) functions as a form of status hierarchy.

C) can wreak havoc on a child's concept of him- or herself.

D) requires equal participation in a relationship.

---

**14**

Which choice provides the best evidence for the answer to the previous question?

A) Lines 5–8 ("the gift . . . relationship")

B) Lines 34–38 ("The obligation . . . giving")

C) Lines 50–53 ("Adequate or . . . reinitiated")

D) Lines 60–63 ("Among children . . . adult")

---

**15**

Schwartz, mentioned in paragraph 4 (lines 54–63), would likely describe the process of gift exchange as

A) stressful.

B) unnerving.

C) intentional.

D) symbolic.

---

**16**

The fourth paragraph (lines 54–63) indicates that the acceptance of a gift may be

A) considerate.

B) influential.

C) authoritative.

D) immutable.

---

**17**

Which choice provides the best evidence for the answer to the previous question?

A) Lines 58–60 ("He also . . . imply")

B) Lines 60–63 ("Among children . . . adult")

C) Lines 66–69 ("Do you . . . was")

D) Lines 75–77 ("There can . . . behavior")

---

**CONTINUE**

**18**

As it is used in line 65, "function" most nearly means

A) purpose.

B) tradition.

C) occasion.

D) occupation.

**19**

The author refers to a gift shop's recent advertisement (lines 65–66) in order to

A) question a former claim.

B) offer a motive.

C) introduce a counter explanation.

D) support an argument.

**20**

The graph and the passage offer evidence that the communication process of gift-giving predicts that a gift will demonstrate

A) the receiver's self-concept.

B) the amount the gift-giver spent.

C) encoded meaning.

D) the thoughtfulness of the gift-giver.

**21**

The author would likely attribute the encoding and decoding phases of communication as represented in the graph to

A) an emerging form of conditional approval.

B) an inability to communicate effectively.

C) an increasing amount of pressure on gift-giving.

D) a component of implicit evaluation.

**CONTINUE**

**Questions 22–31 are based on the following passage and supplementary material.**

This passage is adapted from Nils Ekholm, "On the Variations of the Climate of the Geological and Historical Past and Their Causes." © 1901 by *Quarterly Journal of the Royal Meteorological Society*. Ekholm's studies are based on new mathematical calculations that show discrepancies among earlier scientists' findings in the study of historical changes in climate.

The atmosphere plays a very important part of a double character as to the temperature at the earth's surface. Firstly, the atmosphere may act like the glass of
Line a green-house, letting through the light rays of the sun
5 relatively easily, and absorbing a great part of the dark rays emitted from the ground, and it thereby may raise the mean temperature of the earth's surface. Secondly, the atmosphere acts as a heat store placed between the relatively warm ground and the cold space, and thereby
10 lessens in a high degree the annual, diurnal, and local variations of the temperature.

There are two qualities of the atmosphere that produce these effects. The one is that the temperature of the atmosphere generally decreases with the height
15 above the ground or the sea-level, owing partly to the dynamical heating of descending air currents and the dynamical cooling of ascending ones, as is explained in the mechanical theory of heat. The other is that the atmosphere, absorbing but little of the
20 insolation and most of the radiation from the ground, receives a considerable part of its heat store from the ground by means of radiation, contact, convection, and conduction, whereas the earth's surface is heated principally by direct radiation from the sun through
25 the transparent air.

It follows from this that the radiation from the earth into space does not go on directly from the ground, but on average from a layer of the atmosphere having a considerable height above sea-level. The
30 height of that layer depends on the thermal quality of the atmosphere, and will vary with that quality. The greater is the absorbing power of the air for heat rays emitted from the ground, the higher will that layer be. But the higher the layer, the lower is its temperature
35 relatively to that of the ground; and as the radiation from the layer into space is the less the lower its temperature is, it follows that the ground will be hotter the higher the radiating layer is.

Now if we are able to calculate or estimate how
40 much the mean temperature that layer is lower than the mean temperature of the ground, we may apply Table I for calculating the mean temperature of the ground, as soon as we know by direct measurements the quantity of solar heat absorbed by the ground.
45 Owing to the clouds and dust floating in the atmosphere, this heat is probably only about a third of that derived by using Langley's solar constant; and is thus about 360 calories per square centimeter during twenty-four hours. This gives, by means of Table I,
50 a temperature of −31°C to the radiating layer. But, according to Arrhenius's estimate, this is at a height of about 7600 meters; and assuming a corresponding decrease of 0.6°C per 100 meters, we find its temperature to be 46°C lower than that of the ground,
55 and thus the mean temperature of the ground equal to 15°C, as it is according to observations.

The table shows the loss of heat by radiation into space from a perfectly black body of the temperature $t°$ centigrade. In gram-calories per square centimeter per
60 24 hours at 7600 meters.

| $t$ | Loss of Heat | $t$ | Loss of Heat | $t$ | Loss of Heat |
|-----|-----|-----|-----|-----|-----|
| 100 | 2023 | 20 | 770 | −60 | 215 |
| 80 | 1624 | 0 | 581 | −80 | 145 |
| 60 | 1285 | −20 | 428 | −100 | 94 |
| 40 | 1003 | −40 | 308 | −120 | 57 |

**22**

A student claims that over half of solar radiation influences the ground temperature on the earth's surface. Which of the following statements in the passage contradicts the student's claim?

A) Lines 3–7 ("Firstly, the . . . surface")

B) Lines 13–18 ("The one . . . heat")

C) Lines 45–49 ("Owing to . . . hours")

D) Lines 49–50 ("This gives . . . layer")

**CONTINUE**

**23**

In the first paragraph (lines 1–11), what does the author claim is the atmosphere's importance to the temperature of the earth's surface?

A) The trapping of all hot air and energy from the sun

B) Controlling the heat energy that is admitted and released

C) The enclosure of all the earth's heat-producing mechanisms

D) The free passage of heat energy to and from the surface

**24**

The author uses the word "green-house" in line 4 to indicate that

A) the heat on the ground and in the atmosphere of the earth is provided exclusively by solar radiation.

B) most of the heat in the atmosphere comes from radiation from the ground.

C) the agricultural and botanical sectors of the economy are those most affected by climate fluctuations.

D) solar heat enters the atmosphere relatively unobstructed but the same does not apply as it leaves.

**25**

Based on the passage, the author's statement "the earth's surface is heated principally by direct radiation from the sun through the transparent air" (lines 23–25) implies that

A) when the sun is obscured by clouds the ground is heated principally by other sources of energy.

B) heat generated independently by the ground and by the sun is held in the atmosphere and released as cool air.

C) the heat from the sun that warms the ground must be partially absorbed by the earth's atmosphere.

D) the solar heat reflected back from the earth does not account for all the heat in the atmosphere.

**26**

The author's use of the words "if," "may," and "as soon as" in lines 39–43 functions mainly to

A) provide definitive evidence that the author's mathematical calculations predict the span of global warming with accuracy.

B) demonstrate that many of the author's conclusions rely on both observable and non-observable factors.

C) support the hypothesis that ground temperatures are warmer than higher temperatures.

D) warn against the indiscretion of earlier scientists who made incorrect claims with insufficient evidence.

**27**

The author's main purpose in noting the observations of ground temperature is to

A) indicate that the mathematical calculations given in this paragraph correspond to data recorded by others.

B) show the limitations of mathematical formulas in providing precise measurements of observable phenomena.

C) provide an example of one place in which the global temperature has risen because of human activity.

D) underline the importance of mathematical calculations in determining the influence of solar radiation.

**28**

Based on the table and passage, which choice gives the correct temperature on the ground when the loss of heat is approximately 300 gram-calories per square centimeter for 24 hours?

A) 40°C

B) 6°C

C) –6°C

D) –40°C

**CONTINUE**

Do the data in the table support the author's claim regarding the atmosphere as a heat store?

A) Yes, because at each given temperature, as the temperature decreases, the heat loss decreases as well but by larger and larger intervals.

B) Yes, because at each given temperature, as the temperature decreases, the heat loss decreases as well but by smaller and smaller intervals.

C) No, because at each given temperature, as the temperature decreases, the heat loss fluctuates according to an irregular pattern and series of intervals.

D) No, because at each given temperature, as the temperature decreases, the heat loss increases by larger and larger intervals.

## 30

According to the table, which of the following pairs of heat-loss values at different temperatures provide evidence in support of the answer to the previous question?

A) 2023 to 1624 and 2023 to 57

B) 1003 to 581 and 581 to 94

C) 1003 to 770 and 770 to 581

D) 308 to 94 and 581 to 57

Based on the passage and the table, does the temperature of the atmosphere of the earth stay the same or does it vary with distance from the earth, and which statement made by the authors is most consistent with this data?

A) The same; "Firstly, the . . . surface" (lines 3–7)

B) The same; "It follows . . . sea-level" (lines 26–29)

C) It varies; "Now if . . . ground" (lines 39–44)

D) It varies; "But, according . . . observations" (lines 50–56)

**CONTINUE**

**Questions 32–41 are based on the following passage.**

This passage is adapted from Frederick Douglass's speech "On Women's Suffrage" delivered in 1888 to a gathering of women's suffrage activists.

Mrs. President, Ladies and Gentlemen:— I come to this platform with unusual diffidence. Although I have long been identified with the Woman's Suffrage movement, and have often spoken in its favor, I am somewhat at a loss to know what to say on this really great and uncommon occasion, where so much has been said.

When I look around on this assembly, and see the many able and eloquent women, full of the subject, ready to speak, and who only need the opportunity to impress this audience with their views and thrill them with "thoughts that breathe and words that burn," I do not feel like taking up more than a very small space of your time and attention, and shall not. I would not, even now, presume to speak, but for the circumstance of my early connection with the cause, and of having been called upon to do so by one whose voice in this Council we all gladly obey. Men have very little business here as speakers, anyhow; and if they come here at all they should take back benches and wrap themselves in silence. For this is an International Council, not of men, but of women, and woman should have all the say in it. This is her day in court. I do not mean to exalt the intellect of woman above man's; but I have heard many men speak on this subject, some of them the most eloquent to be found anywhere in the country; and I believe no man, however gifted with thought and speech, can voice the wrongs and present the demands of women with the skill and effect, with the power and authority of woman herself. The man struck is the man to cry out. Woman knows and feels her wrongs as man cannot know and feel them, and she also knows as well as he can know, what measures are needed to redress them. I grant all the claims at this point. She is her own best representative. We can neither speak for her, nor vote for her, nor act for her, nor be responsible for her; and the thing for men to do in the premises is just to get out of her way and give her the fullest opportunity to exercise all the powers inherent in her individual personality, and allow her to do it as she herself shall elect to exercise them. Her right to be and to do is as full, complete and perfect as the right of any man on earth. I say of her, as I say of the colored people, "Give her fair play, and hands off." There was a time when, perhaps, we men could help a little. It was when this woman suffrage cause was in its cradle, when it was not big enough to go alone, when it had to be taken in the arms of its mother from Seneca Falls, N.Y., to Rochester, N.Y., for baptism. I then went along with it and offered my services to help it, for then it needed help; but now it can afford to dispense with me and all of my sex. Then its friends were few—now its friends are many. Then it was wrapped in obscurity—now it is lifted in sight of the whole civilized world, and people of all lands and languages give it their hearty support. Truly the change is vast and wonderful.

There may be some well-meaning people in this audience who have never attended a woman suffrage convention, never heard a woman suffrage speech, never read a woman suffrage newspaper, and they may be surprised that those who speak here do not argue the question. It may be kind to tell them that our cause has passed beyond the period of arguing. The demand of the hour is not argument, but assertion, firm and inflexible assertion, assertion which has more than the force of an argument. If there is any argument to be made, it must be made by opponents, not by the friends of woman suffrage. Let those who want argument examine the ground upon which they base their claim to the right to vote. They will find that there is not one reason, not one consideration, which they can urge in support of man's claim to vote, which does not equally support the right of woman to vote.

**32**

The main purpose of the passage is to

A) qualify the credentials of a speaker.

B) provide support for the suffrage movement.

C) argue for the equal rights of women.

D) compare the sufferings of women to those of African-Americans.

CONTINUE

**33**

The central claim of the passage is that

A) women should have the floor at this assembly.

B) men should act for women in this movement.

C) women and men have the same justification for voting.

D) the suffrage movement should be less obscure.

**34**

Douglass uses the word "cause" throughout the passage mainly to

A) clarify his early connection to the suffrage movement.

B) explain why the suffrage movement deserves support.

C) compare the suffrage movement to a baby in a cradle.

D) describe the suffrage movement.

**35**

According to the passage, Douglass

A) wants to give a great speech, because he has been identified with the suffrage movement.

B) is hesitant to speak, even though he has been identified with the suffrage movement.

C) does not want to speak, though he has been identified with the suffrage movement.

D) is hesitant to give a lengthy speech, since he has been identified with the suffrage movement.

**36**

Douglass indicates that men

A) should not be speakers in such a movement.

B) should not take too much time and attention.

C) should primarily listen at such a gathering.

D) should voice the wrongs of women publicly.

**37**

Which choice provides the best evidence for the answer to the previous question?

A) Lines 8–14 ("When I . . . not")

B) Lines 15–18 ("I would . . . obey")

C) Lines 18–21 ("Men have . . . silence")

D) Lines 24–31 ("I do . . . herself")

**38**

Douglass characterizes the "demands of women" in line 29 as related to injuries that

A) women can best describe and suggest solutions for.

B) men should speak about more eloquently.

C) the civilized world should support heartily.

D) men and women should both be responsible for.

**39**

Which choice provides the best evidence for the answer to the previous question?

A) Lines 25–27 ("but I . . . country")

B) Lines 32–34 ("Woman knows . . . them")

C) Lines 42–44 ("Her right . . . earth")

D) Lines 45–46 ("There was . . . little")

**CONTINUE** ➡

**40**

Which choice most closely captures the meaning of the figurative "cradle" referred to in line 47?

A) Nest

B) Rock

C) Hold

D) Beginnings

**41**

The surprise referred to in lines 58–74 mainly serves to emphasize how

A) some attendees may have expected different sorts of speeches.

B) male attendees may have expected more arguments than assertions.

C) audience members may not have expected speeches on women's suffrage.

D) speakers may have presented unexpected arguments for the right to vote.

**CONTINUE**

**Questions 42–52 are based on the following passages.**

Passage 1 is adapted from Michael B. McElroy and Xi Li, "Fracking's Future." © 2013 by *Harvard Monthly*. Passage 2 is adapted from Natural Resources Defense Council, "Unchecked Fracking Threatens Health, Water Supplies." © 2015.

### Passage 1

Supplies of natural gas now economically recoverable from shale in the United States could accommodate the country's domestic demand for
Line  natural gas at current levels of consumption for more
5  than a hundred years: an economic and strategic boon, and, at least in the near term, an important stepping-stone toward lower-carbon, greener energy.

The first step in extracting gas from shale involves drilling vertically to reach the shale layer, typically a
10  kilometer or more below the surface. Drilling then continues horizontally, extending a kilometer or more from the vertical shaft, and the vertical and horizontal components of the well are lined with steel casing, cemented in place. The horizontal extension of the
15  casing is then perforated, using explosives; thereafter, water, carrying sand and proprietary chemicals, is injected into the well at high pressure. The water encounters the shale through the perforations, generating a series of small fractures in the rock (hence
20  the nickname, "fracking"); the sand in the water keeps the cracks open, while the chemicals enhance release of gas from the shale. The injected water flows back up to the surface when the pressure in the well is released following completion of the fracking procedure. Then
25  the well starts to produce natural gas.

As many as 25 fracture stages (per horizontal leg) may be involved in preparing a single site for production, each requiring injection of more than 400,000 gallons of water—a possible total of more than
30  10 million gallons before the well is fully operational. A portion of the injected water flows back to the surface, heavily contaminated with the fracking chemicals and others it has absorbed from the shale. Depending on the local geology, this "return water" may also include
35  radioactive elements.

Drillers developing a well must take exceptional care to minimize contact between the wellbore and the surrounding aquifer—often the source of nearby residents' fresh water. Serious problems have arisen
40  in the past from failures to isolate the drilling liquids,

including cases where well water used for drinking became so contaminated that human and animal health was threatened. It is essential that monitoring be in place to ensure the continuing integrity of the seal
45  isolating the well from the aquifer even *after* the well has been fully exploited and abandoned.

### Passage 2

The oil and gas industry is rapidly expanding production across the nation, as new technology makes it easier to extract oil or gas from previously
50  inaccessible sites. Over the last decade, the industry has drilled hundreds of thousands of new wells all across the country. These wells are accompanied by massive new infrastructure to move, process, and deliver oil and gas, together bringing full-scale
55  industrialization to often previously rural landscapes.

The sector's growth is spurred by the use of hydraulic fracturing, or fracking, in which often-dangerous chemicals are mixed with large quantities of water (or other base fluid) and sand and injected
60  into wells at extremely high pressure. Unconventional development using advanced fracking methods poses threats to water, air, land, and the health of communities. Studies have shown dangerous levels of toxic air pollution near fracking sites; and oil and
65  gas extraction have caused smog in rural areas at levels worse than downtown Los Angeles. Oil and gas production have been linked to increased risk of cancer and birth defects in neighboring areas; as well as to a risk of increased seismic activity.
70  Constant massive truck traffic associated with large-scale development disrupts communities and creates significant hazards. The millions of gallons of water used in fracking operations not only strain water resources, but end up as vast amounts of contaminated
75  wastewater. Fracking has been reported as a suspect in polluted drinking water around the country. And methane—a potent climate change pollutant—leaks rampantly throughout the extraction, processing, and distribution of oil and gas.
80  Weak safeguards and inadequate oversight have allowed oil and gas producers to run roughshod over communities across the country with their extraction and production activities for too long, resulting in

**CONTINUE**

contaminated water supplies, dangerous air pollution,
85  destroyed streams, and devastated landscapes. Our
state and federal leaders have failed to hold them to
account, leaving the American people unprotected.
Many companies don't play by the few rules that do
exist; and industry has used its political power at every
90  turn to gain exemptions from environmental laws
designed to protect our air and water.

**42**

In lines 26–30, the author of Passage 1 mentions the
number of gallons of water primarily to

A)  warn of the inevitable dangers of industrial
fracking in small communities.

B)  show the variety of ways that natural gas and oil
can be extracted from shale.

C)  expand upon the idea that fracking uses only a few
basic elements.

D)  establish the size and scope of the industrial
equipment required for fracking.

**43**

The author of Passage 1 indicates that fracking could
have which positive effect?

A)  It could support small, local economies that do
not have other sources of income.

B)  It could alter the way scientists understand the
shale layer of the Earth.

C)  It could provide resources that meet the needs of
contemporary consumers.

D)  It could lower the price that large-scale industrial
firms pay for natural gas.

**44**

Which choice provides the best evidence for the
answer to the previous question?

A)  Lines 1–5 ("Supplies of . . . years")

B)  Lines 17–22 ("The water . . . shale")

C)  Lines 22–25 ("The injected . . . gas")

D)  Lines 30–35 ("A portion . . . elements")

**45**

What function does the discussion of the aquifer in
lines 36–46 serve in Passage 1?

A)  It outlines one significant risk involved in the
process described in earlier paragraphs.

B)  It addresses and disputes the concerns of those
whose attitude toward fracking is cautious.

C)  It extends a discussion of a significant term that
begins in the previous paragraph.

D)  It presents an unexpected new finding that
undermines industry arguments for a certain
practice.

**46**

As used in line 44, "integrity" most nearly means

A)  morality.

B)  impermeability.

C)  moisture.

D)  confidence.

**47**

The central claim of Passage 2 is that fracking mines
useful resources but

A)  the wells that have been built are not sufficiently
productive to justify all the cost.

B)  some experts believe that natural gas can be
acquired just as easily from other sources.

C)  it may lead some industry executives to believe
that they can mine resources from any place they
choose.

D)  it is currently not sufficiently regulated in a way
that is safe for local populations.

**CONTINUE** ➡

**48**

As used in line 81, "roughshod" most nearly means

A) productive.

B) rapid.

C) unregulated.

D) industrial.

**49**

Which statement best describes the relationship between the passages?

A) Passage 2 undermines the optimistic confidence of the author of Passage 1.

B) Passage 2 expands upon some of the concerns expressed less explicitly in Passage 1.

C) Passage 2 argues for certain regulations of which the author of Passage 1 does not approve.

D) Passage 2 describes the process discussed in Passage 1 but does so with more detail and statistics.

**50**

The author of Passage 2 would most likely respond to the discussion of drillers in lines 36–46, Passage 1, by claiming that these drillers

A) cite their successes in having grown the mining industry throughout the country.

B) often come from small towns themselves and are not likely to abuse the land.

C) have already caused irreparable harm to the American landscape.

D) can be difficult to contact when their work is conducted so far underground.

**51**

Which choice provides the best evidence for the answer to the previous question?

A) Lines 47–52 ("The oil . . . country")

B) Lines 56–60 ("The sector's . . . pressure")

C) Lines 66–72 ("Oil and . . . hazards")

D) Lines 80–85 ("Weak safeguards . . . landscapes")

**52**

Which point about the potential effects of fracking is implicit in Passage 2 and explicit in Passage 1?

A) The pollution caused by fracking can affect both the water and the air.

B) The process of fracking requires the use of many billions of gallons of water.

C) The process can contaminate drinking water and thus harm both animals and humans.

D) The economic costs of preparing wells can often cost more than the profits gained from mining.

## STOP
**If you finish before time is called, you may check your work on this section only.**
**Do not turn to any other section in the test.**

**No Test Material On This Page**

# Writing and Language Test

## 35 MINUTES, 44 QUESTIONS

**Turn to Section 2 of your answer sheet to answer the questions in this section.**

---

### DIRECTIONS

Each passage below is accompanied by a number of questions. For some questions, you will consider how the passage might be revised to improve the expression of ideas. For other questions, you will consider how the passage might be edited to correct errors in sentence structure, usage, or punctuation. A passage or a question may be accompanied by one or more graphics (such as a table or graph) that you will consider as you make revising and editing decisions.

Some questions will direct you to an underlined portion of a passage. Other questions will direct you to a location in a passage or ask you to think about the passage as a whole.

After reading each passage, choose the answer to each question that most effectively improves the quality of writing in the passage or that makes the passage conform to the conventions of standard written English. Many questions include a "NO CHANGE" option. Choose that option if you think the best choice is to leave the relevant portion of the passage as it is.

---

**Questions 1–11 are based on the following passage.**

**A Horse of a Different Doctor**

Although medical science has made huge bounds in understanding many parts of the body, the brain remains a kind of mystery. A heart attack, for instance, is much easier to identify and prevent than a brain stroke. And mental illness aside, **1** the variety of neurological disorders can make specific brain diagnoses complicated and often unreliable. As a result, the therapeutic resources available to neurologists and those with neurological disorders must necessarily be as vast and diverse as the patient base itself. Disciplines like art therapy, aromatherapy, and horticultural therapy have begun to gain some traction in the popular imagination. Some fields, however, are still awaiting **2** the okay from the people, although their achievements and successes are just as significant. One such field is that of hippotherapy.

**1**
A) NO CHANGE
B) the variety of different kinds of neurological disorders
C) the differing variety of disorders in neurology
D) disorders that show a variety of differences

**2**
A) NO CHANGE
B) broader public acceptance
C) something elusive from the public
D) a public to give the thumbs up

CONTINUE

Hippotherapy positions itself at the intersection of physical, occupational, and speech therapy. In this discipline, the characteristic movements of a horse (*hippo-* in Greek) **3** is used to build a foundation for improvements in human neurological functions and sensory processing. Its main difference from therapeutic horseback riding is that hippotherapy uses the movement of the horse as a way to treat a specific ailment. **4** Thus, it is more concerned with learning a skill set and establishing a bond between rider and horse.

**3**

A) NO CHANGE
B) has been used
C) are used
D) used

**4**

At this point, the writer is considering adding the following sentence.

> Therapeutic horseback riding teaches riding skills and is more concerned with emotional and behavioral disabilities.

Should the writer make this addition here?

A) Yes, because it makes the argument that hippotherapy is the more effective of the two disciplines.

B) Yes, because it further clarifies the difference between the two disciplines discussed in this paragraph.

C) No, because it undermines the point the author is trying to make about the validity of hippotherapy.

D) No, because a discussion of therapeutic horseback riding has no place in this particular paragraph.

**CONTINUE** ➡

[1] Many fields use the basic tenets of hippotherapy, but they each provide a unique spin on the practice. [2] Physical therapists may incorporate hippotherapy to manage a variety of disabilities and, hopefully, cure diseases. [3] Occupational therapists use many of the same features of the horse's movement, but they [5] are similarly plagued by the lack of laboratory support. [4] The research on the effectiveness of hippotherapy is still in the early stages of development, but therapists in a variety of fields, even including speech and language pathology, regularly achieve success with this technique and [6] eagerly to recommended it to their patients. [5] As the name suggests, these therapists are concerned mainly with the movement of the horse as it relates to physical aspects such as balance, posture, and strengthening the core. [7]

The American Hippotherapy Association can provide certification for those wishing to work in the discipline. Physical therapists, occupational therapists, and speech-language pathologists must have practiced for at least three years and had 100 hours of hippotherapy practice before they can sit for the Hippotherapy Clinical Specialty Certification Exam, and the certification lasts for five years. Because the discipline is relatively [8] new, certified, hippotherapists have stringent requirements for staying current on the research within the field.

---

**5**

Which choice provides a supporting example that reinforces the main point of the sentence?

A) NO CHANGE

B) use the therapy to develop the cognitive and fine motor skills.

C) work on different maladies and different parts of the body.

D) have a whole different set of requirements and backgrounds.

**6**

A) NO CHANGE

B) eager recommending of

C) eagerly recommending

D) eagerly recommend

**7**

To make this paragraph most logical, sentence 5 should be placed

A) where it is now.

B) before sentence 3.

C) before sentence 4.

D) at the beginning of the paragraph.

**8**

A) NO CHANGE

B) new, certified

C) new, and certified

D) new; certified

CONTINUE

Just as medical science is constantly evolving, **9** so are its alternatives. Hippotherapy may seem a bit out of the ordinary, but if it provides effective relief or treatment for people in pain, the skeptics **10** between doctors and researchers will not hesitate to embrace it. **11** Becoming a hippotherapist is pretty hard, as evidenced by all those hours one has to spend keeping up with the literature.

**9**

A) NO CHANGE

B) so too are its alternatives.

C) its alternatives also are.

D) its alternatives are, too.

**10**

A) NO CHANGE

B) above

C) within

D) among

**11**

The writer wants a concluding sentence that restates the main argument of the passage. Which choice best accomplishes that goal?

A) NO CHANGE

B) Hippotherapy has positioned itself at the crossroads of many disciplines, and it may just be the practice to provide relief in ways the other therapies have not done yet.

C) Many people used bloodletting and radiation regularly before the medical establishment showed how unsafe these practices were.

D) It makes you wonder whether the medical profession is ready for such a crazy discovery.

**CONTINUE**

**Questions 12–22 are based on the following passage and supplementary material.**

## The Call of the Wilderness

The way science textbooks teach about different ecosystems [12] elicit responses primarily from our visual and tactile senses. We have all seen pictures of the silent sands of the desert and can almost feel the heat radiating from the sands. We all know the ballet of fish and marine life coursing through the vast ocean. Some recent studies, however, have expanded our ideas about these ecosystems by incorporating another one of our senses: sound.

[13] It was Marco Polo who crossed the desert on his way to China, he described the sound he heard as "a variety of musical instruments." Researchers now understand that the curious sound that Polo heard, that odd confluence of pipe organ and [14] cello, probably resulted from the wind blowing across the sand dunes. In a study conducted in the deserts of California, scientists found that the "singing" dunes had dry, tightly-packed layers of sand, with dry sand on top of layers of damp sand. This variation creates an effect similar to that of a musical [15] instrument, a tonal quality coming from the trapping and release of certain frequencies.

**12**

A) NO CHANGE
B) elicits responses
C) illicit responses
D) illicits responses

**13**

A) NO CHANGE
B) Marco Polo crossed the desert
C) They called him Marco Polo, he who crossed the desert
D) As Marco Polo crossed the desert

**14**

A) NO CHANGE
B) cello;
C) cello—
D) cello: it has

**15**

A) NO CHANGE
B) instrument; a tonal quality coming from the trapping and release of certain frequencies.
C) instrument, a tonal quality that is said to be coming from the trapping and release of certain frequencies.
D) instrument, this quality comes from the trapping and release of certain frequencies.

**CONTINUE**

**16** From among the world's countless ecosystems and throughout that world, the ocean, too, has recently been given a kind of "voice." Although Jacques Cousteau referred to this body of water as *le monde du silence*—"the silent world"—recent research has shown the ocean to be anything but silent. University of Washington biologist Kate Stafford has, for the past five years, recorded sounds in the deep waters of the Bering Strait. **17** For Stafford, sound provides advantage that sight cannot: one can continue to record sound at night or underneath ice cover, and the challenges of deep-sea sound-recording are not nearly as problematic as those of deep-sea diving.

**16**

Which choice most smoothly and effectively introduces the writer's discussion of the sounds of the ocean in this paragraph?

A) NO CHANGE

B) Ecosystems are filled with sound, and one such sound in one such ecosystem is the "voice" of the ocean.

C) Another place that has recently been given a kind of "voice" is the ocean.

D) DELETE the underlined sentence.

**17**

At this point, the writer is considering adding the following sentence.

> If you go far enough from the coast, the only sounds you will hear are those of distant ships passing in the night.

Should the writer make this addition here?

A) Yes, because it creates a poetic image that complements the main idea of the paragraph.

B) Yes, because it supports the main idea of the passage as a whole.

C) No, because it undermines the argument made by the scientist described in this paragraph.

D) No, because it would be more appropriately placed at the beginning of the paragraph.

**CONTINUE**

According to Stafford's research, one of the most interesting aspects of the sound of the ocean is [18] its unwillingness to [19] not act so weird. Stafford's team found incredible inconsistencies among the sounds at any particular time of year. This may help to explain the [20] clear direct relationship in whale migrations between 2012-2013 and previous seasons. Recent data shows that it is not at all abnormal for nearly 40 whales to migrate on a single day when, on average, [21] only 14 whales would migrate on that same day. This gives some hint to how marine animals are and will be adapting to climate change in the future. It seems that those with the most flexibility will be those who are least affected.

This Season, Compared to the Averages of the Last Ten Seasons

Key
☐ Southbound Whales
☐ Northbound Whales

A) NO CHANGE
B) it's
C) their
D) they're

A) NO CHANGE
B) follow any discernible patterns.
C) chill out and be normal for a second.
D) play nice with others.

Which choice offers the most accurate interpretation of the data in the chart?
A) NO CHANGE
B) definable inverse relationship
C) absolute confluence
D) notable inconsistency

Which choice offers an accurate interpretation of the data in the chart?
A) NO CHANGE
B) most whales would typically migrate in the summer months.
C) many more whales migrate southward every single day.
D) over half that number migrate every day in the coldest winter months.

CONTINUE ➤

The work that Stafford and others are doing adds another dimension to how we understand different ecosystems. Sound may clarify the processes of these ecosystems in ways that were not available to researchers before. **22**

**22**

The writer wants a conclusion that points toward the role that sound might play in future research into different ecosystems. Which choice results in the passage having the most appropriate concluding sentence?

A) NO CHANGE

B) This is not, of course, to say that no research has ever been done on sound before; that would be an overstatement.

C) Researchers may have missed this sound component, but you have to hand it to them for covering the other parts as thoroughly as they have.

D) The vividness of soundscapes is nowhere more evident than in the experiences of the blind, who can use sound in much the way that sighted people use sight.

**CONTINUE**

**Questions 23–33 are based on the following passage.**

**Roosevelt's 100 Days**

In the 1932 presidential election, up-and-comer Franklin D. Roosevelt [23] won— in a landslide over the incumbent Herbert Hoover, who had done little to avert the crisis that would become known as the Great Depression. [24] And Hoover took office in 1929, the unemployment rate was a mere 3.2%. By 1932, that rate had skyrocketed to 25%.

[25] Roosevelt took office with a clear mandate for action. Even so, no one was quite ready for the legislative whirlwind that would follow. This period became known as Roosevelt's "100 Days." Roosevelt's first action came on March 5, 1933, when an executive order shut down all the nation's banks. At that time, he sent government workers to inspect each bank, [26] although determining which banks would be safe and sustainable to reopen. Four days later, the banks reopened and started business anew.

---

**23**

A) NO CHANGE
B) won;
C) won,
D) won

**24**

A) NO CHANGE
B) Because
C) When
D) DELETE the underlined portion and begin the sentence with a capital letter.

**25**

Which choice most effectively sets up the paragraph?
A) NO CHANGE
B) Politics could move a bit more quickly in those days.
C) That unemployment rate is remarkably low.
D) Hoover had given up all hope of ending the Depression.

**26**

A) NO CHANGE
B) for
C) thereby
D) whereupon

**CONTINUE**

Roosevelt's main goal was to lift the country from depression and to get the **27** economy operating again. In the 100 days, Roosevelt established programs to aid the poor, such as the $500 million Federal Emergency Relief Association. The Civilian Conservation Corps was established to give unemployed men six-month job assignments on environmental projects, such as national parks. In agricultural regions, Roosevelt sought to control supply as a way to level **28** with demand, and certain projects were geared toward electrifying until-then remote regions. The Tennessee Valley Authority brought dams to the non-coastal southern states, **29** including Tennessee itself, of course, but also the northern parts of Alabama and Mississippi.

---

**27**

Which choice provides the most specific information on the areas that Roosevelt hoped to stimulate?

A) NO CHANGE

B) industrial and agricultural sectors

C) whole thing

D) money flowing and the economy

---

**28**

A) NO CHANGE

B) on

C) off

D) to

---

**29**

Which choice gives an additional supporting detail that emphasizes the importance of the TVA in Roosevelt's larger economic project?

A) NO CHANGE

B) taking account of the fact that farming is difficult without a reliable large body of water.

C) establishing not only more reliable sources of water and work but electricity for millions of Americans.

D) one of many impressive public-works projects completed throughout Roosevelt's tenure.

CONTINUE ▶

Many of the programs, including the Tennessee Valley Authority, continue to exist to this day. Roosevelt's 100 Days were unique in that they not only jumpstarted the American economy at a time when a stimulus was most needed but also laid the groundwork for programs that could persist into the **30** future, past their own moment. Indeed, Roosevelt's "New Deal" remains new even though, at this point, **31** it's more than eighty years old.

Still, Roosevelt's 100 Days remain the subject of controversy. In Roosevelt's day, there was widespread criticism from those who thought government should play a smaller rather than a larger role in **32** people's day-to-day lives. For many others, Roosevelt's government interventions are a model for how governments should aid citizens in times of need. **33** Clearly, Roosevelt's unadulterated successes would seem odd in an era of political wrangling characterized by gridlock rather than swift action.

**30**

A) NO CHANGE
B) future.
C) future, which is to say after the present.
D) future, many years beyond when they were created.

**31**

A) NO CHANGE
B) its
C) they're
D) there

**32**

A) NO CHANGE
B) peoples'
C) peoples
D) peoples's

**33**

The writer wants to conclude the paragraph effectively without dismissing the debate described in this paragraph. Which choice best accomplishes this goal?

A) NO CHANGE
B) Unfortunately, even Roosevelt's obvious failures can
C) In either case, Roosevelt's achievements in the first 100 Days of his presidency
D) All of the things described above could accomplish this goal.

**CONTINUE**

**Questions 34–44 are based on the following passage.**

## Setsuko Hara: In and Out of the Tokyo Spotlight

One of the  34  hammiest board-treaders in the history of Japanese cinema was also one of the most mysterious. Setsuko Hara died in September 2015 at the age of 95, and while she is remembered as perhaps the most formidable actress in Japan's long cinematic tradition, no one had seen her in anything since the 1960s. The actress went into seclusion after the death of her longtime collaborator, the director Yasujiro Ozu.

Hara's first acting role came when she was only 15. The Japanese film industry had divided loyalties at the time,  35  despite its obvious debt to American cinema amid the increasing international tensions with the United States and others that would lead to World War II. Hara's first film, a German-Japanese production called *The Daughter of the Samurai* (1937), emerged among these tensions  36  using as it did the conventions of the American melodrama to promote an early version of what would become Axis propaganda. After her success in this film, Hara became one of the faces of the Japanese propaganda effort during the Second World War.

**34**

A) NO CHANGE

B) most exquisite thespians

C) most emotive of histrionists

D) greatest actresses

**35**

A) NO CHANGE

B) as evidenced by

C) contrasting with

D) enabled by

**36**

The writer is considering the deleting the underlined portion (ending the sentence with a period). Should the writer make this deletion?

A) Yes, because the information is provided in the previous sentence.

B) Yes, because the underlined portion undermines the paragraph's description of the Axis propaganda effort.

C) No, because the underlined portion gives a specific example of how the Axis powers conducted their propaganda campaign.

D) No, because the underlined portion provides information that clarifies an idea central to this paragraph.

CONTINUE

After Japan's defeat in the war, however, Hara's career changed significantly. Directors and audiences discovered her incredible talent acting in quieter dramas. The masterpieces in this mode were Ozu's *Late Spring* (1949) and *Tokyo Story* (1953), in which Hara plays a woman who is torn between the demands of various family members, who in turn **37** represented different generational expectations. Hara could reveal incredible emotion through subtle, almost imperceptible facial expressions and voice modulations. **38** Moreover, her compelling and unique beauty kept screen audiences eagerly engaged.

The subtle conflicts in *Late Spring* capture Hara's particular **39** style of acting in films. Even in the 1940s, Hollywood films were characterized by grand conflicts and even grander emotions. The films of Ozu's late period, especially his collaborations with Hara, however, worked with a much smaller canvas, usually with very few sets, limiting the scenes to a character's **40** office kitchen, living room, or garden. In *Late Spring*, Hara's character

**37**

A) NO CHANGE
B) would represent
C) had represented
D) represent

**38**

A) NO CHANGE
B) In sum,
C) Nevertheless,
D) Meanwhile,

**39**

A) NO CHANGE
B) acting style.
C) acting methods that were unique to her.
D) acting style in film and presumably in the theater.

**40**

A) NO CHANGE
B) office, kitchen, living,
C) office, kitchen, living
D) office, kitchen living,

CONTINUE ➡

Noriko is twenty-seven years old and has not married. Against the [41] council of her friends and family, she has instead chosen to care for her aging widowed father. The conflict and plot are that simple, [42] and Ozu's cinematography and Hara's expressive face show that sometimes the simplest and smallest domestic conflicts can have profound implications.

[1] Hara never formally announced her retirement, though she made her last film in 1963. [2] Rumors have always circulated about Hara's mysterious disappearance from the screen, and viewers' many theories show [43] their grief at having lost such a bright star. [3] Some believe that she had been going blind and did not want to do so in the public eye. [4] In either case, Hara left an indelible mark on the shape of world cinema. [5] Especially in a moment when all cinematic achievement seems to point toward bigger and louder, Setsuko Hara provides the important reminder that smaller and quieter can be just as powerful. [44]

41

A) NO CHANGE
B) council from
C) counsel with
D) counsel of

42

A) NO CHANGE
B) for
C) so
D) yet

43

A) NO CHANGE
B) one's
C) his
D) your

44

The writer plans to add the following sentence to this paragraph.

> Others believe that her grief over Ozu's death in 1963 kept her from returning to the cinema.

To make this paragraph most logical, the sentence should be placed

A) after sentence 2.
B) after sentence 3.
C) after sentence 4.
D) after sentence 5.

**STOP**
If you finish before time is called, you may check your work on this section only.
Do not turn to any other section in the test.

# Math Test – No Calculator

## 25 MINUTES, 20 QUESTIONS

**Turn to Section 3 of your answer sheet to answer the questions in this section.**

### DIRECTIONS

**For questions 1–15,** solve each problem, choose the best answer from the choices provided, and fill in the corresponding circle on your answer sheet. **For questions 16–20,** solve the problem and enter your answer in the grid on the answer sheet. Please refer to the directions before question 16 on how to enter your answers in the grid. You may use any available space in your test booklet for scratch work.

### NOTES

1. The use of a calculator **is not permitted**.
2. All variables and expressions used represent real numbers unless otherwise indicated.
3. Figures provided in this test are drawn to scale unless otherwise indicated.
4. All figures lie in a plane unless otherwise indicated.
5. Unless otherwise indicated, the domain of a given function $f$ is the set of all real numbers $x$ for which $f(x)$ is a real number.

### REFERENCE

$A = \pi r^2$
$C = 2\pi r$

$A = \ell w$

$A = \frac{1}{2} bh$

$c^2 = a^2 + b^2$

Special Right Triangles

$V = \ell wh$

$V = \pi r^2 h$

$V = \frac{4}{3} \pi r^3$

$V = \frac{1}{3} \pi r^2 h$

$V = \frac{1}{3} \ell wh$

The number of degrees of arc in a circle is 360.
The number of radians of arc in a circle is $2\pi$.
The sum of the measures in degrees of the angles of a triangle is 180.

**CONTINUE**

**1**

An editor is paid $25 an hour to edit 3 essays and an additional $50 bonus when the edits on all three essays are completed. If the edits on the essays are completed, what expression could be used to determine how much the editor earned?

A) $50y + 25$, where $y$ is the number of hours

B) $25y + 50$, where $y$ is the number of hours

C) $y(25 + 2) + 3$, where $y$ is the number of essays

D) $50y + (25 + 2)$, where $y$ is the number of essays

**2**

$$(-mn^2 + 2n^2 - 6m^2n) + (2mn^2 - 2n^2 + 3m^2n)$$

The expression above is equivalent to which of the following?

A) $mn^2 + 4n^2 - 9m^2n$

B) $mn^2 - 3m^2n$

C) $3mn^2 - 4n^2$

D) $3m^2n - mn^2$

**3**

$$\frac{1}{12}x - \frac{1}{12}y = 13$$
$$\frac{1}{3}x - \frac{1}{6}y = 20$$

Which ordered pair $(x, y)$ satisfies the equations above?

A) $(-35, 190)$

B) $(-36, -192)$

C) $(168, 25)$

D) $\left( \dfrac{752}{5}, \dfrac{304}{5} \right)$

**4**

Kelly is a salesperson at a shoe store, where she must sell a pre-set number of pairs of shoes each month. At the end of each workday, the number of pairs of shoes that she has left to sell that month is given by the equation $S = 300 - 15x$, where $S$ is the number of pairs of shoes Kelly still needs to sell and $x$ is the number of days she has worked that month. What is the meaning of the number 300 in this equation?

A) Kelly must sell 300 pairs of shoes per week.

B) Kelly must sell 300 pairs of shoes per day.

C) Kelly will sell the pairs of shoes in 300 days.

D) Kelly must sell 300 pairs of shoes each month.

**CONTINUE**

**5**

A certain amusement park sells half-day passes and all-day passes. The amusement park charges $40 for a half-day pass and $80 for an all-day pass. The amusement park sold a total of 70 passes one day for $4,600. How many all-day passes did the amusement park sell?

A) 25

B) 35

C) 45

D) 60

**6**

$$5x^2 + 7x - 6 = 0$$

If $a$ and $b$ are two solutions to the equation above and $a < b$, which of the following is the value of $b - a$?

A) $\dfrac{3}{5}$

B) $\dfrac{6}{5}$

C) $\dfrac{8}{5}$

D) $\dfrac{13}{5}$

**7**

Which of the following must be true if $\dfrac{t + u}{t} = \dfrac{12}{11}$ ?

A) $\dfrac{u}{t} = \dfrac{1}{11}$

B) $\dfrac{u}{t} = \dfrac{23}{11}$

C) $\dfrac{t - u}{t} = \dfrac{1}{11}$

D) $\dfrac{t + 2u}{t} = -\dfrac{8}{11}$

**8**

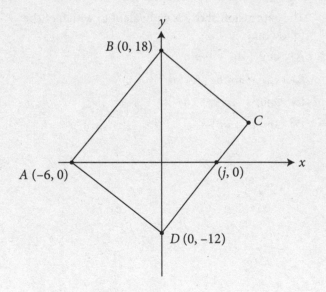

Parallelogram $ABCD$ is shown in the $xy$-plane above. What is the value of $j$ ?

A) 15

B) 12

C) 4

D) 3

CONTINUE

**9**

$$x = \frac{y(y-3)}{2}$$

The number of diagonals, $x$, that can be drawn within a polygon depends on the number of sides, $y$, of the polygon according to the formula above. If a polygon has at least 7 diagonals, what is the least number of sides it can have?

A) 7

B) 6

C) 5

D) 4

**10**

The value of a car decreases $500 for every 1,000 miles it is driven. The current value of the car is $23,000, and the car is driven an average of 10,000 miles per year. What will be the value of the car, in dollars, at a point in time $y$ years from now?

A) $23,000 – $5,000$y$

B) $23,000 – $500$y$

C) $23,000 – $0.02$y$

D) $23,000 – $0.0002$y$

**11**

$$7x - cy = 10$$
$$5x + 2y = 8$$

In the system of equations above, $x$ and $y$ are variables and $c$ is a constant. What must the value of $c$ be if the system of equations has no solution?

A) $\dfrac{14}{5}$

B) $\dfrac{27}{25}$

C) $-\dfrac{27}{25}$

D) $-\dfrac{14}{5}$

**12**

Which of the following complex numbers is equal to $\dfrac{4 - 7i}{6 + 3i}$ ? (Note: $i = \sqrt{-1}$)

A) $\dfrac{1}{15} + \dfrac{6i}{5}$

B) $\dfrac{1}{15} - \dfrac{6i}{5}$

C) $\dfrac{2}{3} - \dfrac{7i}{3}$

D) $\dfrac{2}{3} + \dfrac{7i}{3}$

**CONTINUE**

**13**

$$g(x) = 2(x^2 + 14x + 7) - 7(x + c)$$

In the polynomial $g(x)$ defined above, $c$ is a constant. If $g(x)$ is divisible by $x$, what is the value of $c$ ?

A)  −2

B)  0

C)  2

D)  5

**14**

If $3r - s = 10$, then which of the following is equivalent to $\dfrac{27^r}{3^s}$?

A)  $27^2$

B)  $9^4$

C)  $3^{10}$

D)  The value cannot be determined from the information given.

**15**

Which of the following is equivalent to $\dfrac{4n + 9}{n - 5}$ ?

A)  $4 + \dfrac{29}{n - 5}$

B)  $4 + \dfrac{9}{n - 5}$

C)  $4 - \dfrac{9}{5}$

D)  $-\dfrac{4 + 9}{5}$

**CONTINUE**

## DIRECTIONS

**For questions 16–20**, solve the problem and enter your answer in the grid, as described below, on the answer sheet.

1. Although not required, it is suggested that you write your answer in the boxes at the top of the columns to help you fill in the circles accurately. You will receive credit only if the circles are filled in correctly.

2. Mark no more than one circle in any column.

3. No question has a negative answer.

4. Some problems may have more than one correct answer. In such cases, grid only one answer.

5. **Mixed numbers** such as $3\frac{1}{2}$ must be gridded as 3.5 or 7/2. (If $\boxed{3\ 1\ /\ 2}$ is entered into the grid, it will be interpreted as $\frac{31}{2}$, not as $3\frac{1}{2}$.)

6. **Decimal Answers:** If you obtain a decimal answer with more digits than the grid can accommodate, it may be either rounded or truncated, but it must fill the entire grid.

Answer: $\frac{7}{12}$ — Write answer in boxes. — Fraction line — Grid in result.

Answer: 2.5 — Decimal point

Acceptable ways to grid $\frac{2}{3}$ are:

Answer: 201 – either position is correct

**NOTE:** You may start your answers in any column, space permitting. Columns you don't need to use should be left blank.

**CONTINUE** ➡

### 16

For what value of $x$ is $37 = \dfrac{x}{20} - 3$ ?

### 17

In the triangle above, the cosine of $p°$ is 0.8. What is the sine of $q°$ ?

### 18

If $a \neq 0$, what is the value of $\dfrac{9(5a)^2}{(3a)^2}$ ?

**CONTINUE**

## 19

Segment *HJ* intersects segment *IK* at *L* in the figure above. If $\overline{HI} \parallel \overline{JK}$, what is the length of segment *HJ*?

## 20

What is the value of *y* if $z = 5\sqrt{3}$ and $3z = \sqrt{3y}$?

## STOP

**If you finish before time is called, you may check your work on this section only.**
**Do not turn to any other section in the test.**

# Math Test – Calculator

## 55 MINUTES, 38 QUESTIONS

**Turn to Section 4 of your answer sheet to answer the questions in this section.**

---

### DIRECTIONS

**For questions 1–30**, solve each problem, choose the best answer from the choices provided, and fill in the corresponding circle on your answer sheet. **For questions 31–38**, solve the problem and enter your answer in the grid on the answer sheet. Please refer to the directions before question 31 on how to enter your answers in the grid. You may use any available space in your test booklet for scratch work.

### NOTES

1. The use of a calculator **is permitted**.
2. All variables and expressions used represent real numbers unless otherwise indicated.
3. Figures provided in this test are drawn to scale unless otherwise indicated.
4. All figures lie in a plane unless otherwise indicated.
5. Unless otherwise indicated, the domain of a given function $f$ is the set of all real numbers $x$ for which $f(x)$ is a real number.

### REFERENCE

$A = \pi r^2$
$C = 2\pi r$

$A = \ell w$

$A = \frac{1}{2} bh$

$c^2 = a^2 + b^2$

Special Right Triangles

$V = \ell wh$

$V = \pi r^2 h$

$V = \frac{4}{3} \pi r^3$

$V = \frac{1}{3} \pi r^2 h$

$V = \frac{1}{3} \ell wh$

The number of degrees of arc in a circle is 360.
The number of radians of arc in a circle is $2\pi$.
The sum of the measures in degrees of the angles of a triangle is 180.

**CONTINUE**

**1**

David has a mobile data plan for which the monthly fee is $20.00 and the data usage fee is $2.50 per gigabyte. Which of the following functions expresses David's cost, in dollars, for a month in which he uses $g$ gigabytes of data?

A) $f(g) = 22.50g$

B) $f(g) = 20g + 2.50$

C) $f(g) = 20 + 250g$

D) $f(g) = 20 + 2.50g$

**2**

Annual Profits

The line graph above shows the annual profit of a particular clothing store from 2000 to 2007. According to the graph, what was the greatest change (in absolute value) in the annual profit between two consecutive years?

A) $25,000

B) $30,000

C) $35,000

D) $40,000

**3**

In order to qualify for a fitness competition, a person must be able to complete 30 pull-ups in one minute. Jim can currently do 14 pull-ups in one minute and believes that he can increase that amount by 7 pull-ups each year. Which of the following represents the number of pull-ups that Jim believes he will be able to complete in one minute $y$ years from now?

A) $7y + 14$

B) $7y + 30$

C) $14y + 7$

D) $14 - 7y$

**4**

$$v = 17 + 2.5t$$

A constantly-accelerating particle is moving in a straight line. After $t$ seconds, the particle is moving at a velocity of $v$, in meters per second, as shown in the equation above. What is $t$ when $v$ is 67 ?

A) 184.5

B) 67

C) 33.6

D) 20

**CONTINUE**

**5**

When function $h$ is graphed in the $xy$-plane, it has $x$-intercepts at –4, 2, and 4. Which of the following could define $h$ ?

A) $h(x) = (x - 4)(x - 2)(x + 4)$

B) $h(x) = (x - 4)(x + 2)(x + 4)$

C) $h(x) = (x - 4)^2(x + 2)$

D) $h(x) = (x + 2)(x + 4)^2$

**6**

When three times a number $n$ is added to 9, the result is 3. What is the result when 4 times $n$ is added to 14 ?

A) –2

B) 3

C) 6

D) 22

**7**

A coffee shop is filling coffee cups from an industrial urn that contains 64 gallons of coffee. At most, how many 16-ounce cups of coffee can be filled from the urn? (1 gallon = 128 ounces)

A) 4

B) 512

C) 1,024

D) 2,048

**8**

What is the slope of the line in the $xy$-plane that passes through the points $\left(5, \frac{8}{3}\right)$ and $\left(1, -\frac{1}{3}\right)$ ?

A) –2

B) $-\frac{4}{3}$

C) $\frac{3}{4}$

D) 2

CONTINUE

9

Number of Fish in Each of 18 Tanks

Based on the histogram above, which of the following is closest to the average (arithmetic mean) number of fish per tank?

A) 5

B) 6

C) 7

D) 8

10

A telephone survey was conducted in order to determine if people in City C are more likely to work 9-to-5 office jobs than other jobs. The research team called 5,000 random people between 12 P.M. to 4 P.M. on a Thursday. Of the 5,000 people called, 3,000 did not answer, and 250 refused to participate. Which of the following was the biggest flaw in the design of the survey?

A) The time the survey was taken

B) Population size

C) Sample size

D) The fact that the survey was done by telephone

11

If the function $p$ has exactly four distinct roots, which of the following could represent the complete graph of $y = p(x)$ in the $xy$-plane?

A)

B)

C)

D)

CONTINUE

**12**

One morning in a particular restaurant, 85 percent of the customers ordered the brunch special. Which of the following could be the total number of customers in the restaurant that morning?

A) 40

B) 42

C) 44

D) 48

**13**

$$d = -8t^2 + vt + h$$

The equation above gives the distance, $d$, in meters, a projectile is above the ground $t$ seconds after it is released with an initial velocity of $v$ meters per second from an initial height of $h$ meters. Which of the following gives $v$ in terms of $d$, $t$, and $h$ ?

A)  $v = \dfrac{d-h}{t} + 8t$

B)  $v = \dfrac{d+h}{t} - 8t$

C)  $v = \dfrac{d-h+8}{t}$

D)  $v = d + h - 8t$

**14**

The histogram above shows the distribution of the scores of 22 students on a recent biology test. Which of the following could be the median score of the 22 students represented in the histogram?

A) 68

B) 71

C) 77

D) 84

**CONTINUE**

**Questions 15-17 refer to the following information.**

A survey of 130 randomly selected workers in a particular metropolitan area was conducted to gather information about average daily commute times. The data are shown in the table below.

|  | Commutes by public transit | Does not commute by public transit | Total |
|---|---|---|---|
| Less than 1 hour | 22 | 46 | 68 |
| At least 1 hour | 29 | 33 | 62 |
| Total | 51 | 79 | 130 |

In 2014, the population of the metropolitan area from the survey was about 13 million. If the survey results were used to estimate information about commute times throughout the metropolitan area, which of the following is the best estimate for the number of individuals who used public transit and had an average daily commute of at least one hour?

A)  290,000

B)  2,200,000

C)  2,900,000

D)  6,200,000

Which of the following is closest to the percent of those surveyed who commute using public transit?

A)  65%

B)  46%

C)  39%

D)  32%

Based on the data, how many times more likely is it for a person with a commute of less than 1 hour NOT to commute by public transit than it is for a person with a commute of at least one hour NOT to commute by public transit? (Round the answer to the nearest hundredth.)

A)  1.39 times as likely

B)  1.27 times as likely

C)  0.78 times as likely

D)  0.72 times as likely

CONTINUE

**18**

In order to determine the effect that caffeinated beverage C would have on sleep, researchers conducted a study. From a large population of people without sleep disorders, 500 subjects were randomly selected. Half the subjects were randomly selected to consume beverage C and the rest did not consume beverage C. The results of the study showed that the subjects who consumed beverage C slept less than those who did not consume beverage C. Based on the design and results of the study, which of the following statements is the best conclusion?

A) Beverage C will cause more loss in sleep than all other caffeinated beverages.

B) Beverage C will cause a substantial loss in sleep.

C) Beverage C is likely to reduce the amount of sleep of people without sleep disorders.

D) Beverage C will reduce sleep of anyone who consumes it.

**19**

The sum of four numbers is 1,764. One of the numbers, $n$, is 40% more than the sum of the other three numbers. What is the value of $n$ ?

A)     287

B)     735

C)  1,029

D)  1,260

**20**

Volume versus Mass

Selin weighs 14 different objects of similar density. The scatterplot shown above shows the volume of each object and the corresponding weight of each object. The line of best fit for the data is shown above. For the object that had a volume of 11.5 $m^3$, the actual mass was about how many kilograms more than the mass predicted by the line of best fit?

A)  1,000

B)  2,000

C)  3,000

D)  4,000

**CONTINUE**

**21**

Jessica owns a store that sells only laptops and tablets. Last week, her store sold 90 laptops and 210 tablets. This week, the sales, in number of units, of laptops increased by 50 percent, and the sales, in number of units, of tablets increased by 30 percent. By what percentage did total sales, in units, in Jessica's store increase?

A) 20 percent

B) 25 percent

C) 36 percent

D) 80 percent

**22**

Note: Figures not drawn to scale

For acute angles $P$ and $Q$ shown above, $\cos(x°) = \sin(y°)$. If $x = 3c - 23$ and $y = 7c - 42$, what is the value of $c$?

A) 24.5

B) 15.5

C) 9.0

D) 6.0

CONTINUE

## 23

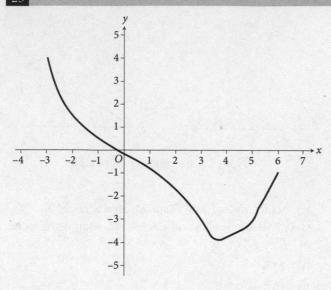

What is the maximum value of the function graphed in the $xy$-plane above, for $-3 \le x \le 6$ ?

A) 4

B) 5

C) 6

D) ∞

## 24

Matthew constructs a fence around a patch of grass in his backyard. The patch has a width that is 8 feet more than 4 times the length. What is the perimeter of the fence if Matthew's patch of grass has an area of 5,472 square feet?

A) 364 feet

B) 376 feet

C) 396 feet

D) 400 feet

## 25

In the $xy$-plane, the line determined by the points $(c, 3)$ and $(27, c)$ intersects the origin. Which of the following could be the value of $c$ ?

A) 0

B) 3

C) 6

D) 9

## 26

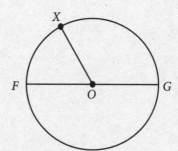

In the circle above, the length of arc $\overparen{FXG}$ is $14\pi$. If $\overline{FG}$ is a chord that passes through the circle's center, $O$, what is the length of the segment $\overline{XO}$ ?

A) 7

B) 14

C) 28

D) 56

**CONTINUE**

27

Let $p$ and $q$ be numbers such that $-|p| < q < |p|$. Which of the following must be true?

    I.   $p > 0$

    II.  $|p| > -q$

    III. $p > |q|$

A)  I only

B)  II only

C)  II and III only

D)  I, II, and III only

28

A rectangular container with a base that measures 10 feet by 10 feet is filled with jelly beans. The container is divided into regions each with the same height as the container and a square base with sides that measure 1 foot each. Sherman randomly selects ten of these regions and counts the number of blue jelly beans in each region. The results are shown in the table below.

| Region | Blue Jelly Beans | Region | Blue Jelly Beans |
|--------|------------------|--------|------------------|
| I | 20 | VI | 22 |
| II | 21 | VII | 25 |
| III | 27 | VIII | 24 |
| IV | 31 | IX | 28 |
| V | 19 | X | 23 |

Which of the following is a reasonable approximation of the number of blue jelly beans in the entire container?

A)  25,000

B)   2,500

C)     250

D)      25

**CONTINUE**

**29**

| Product Type | Flavor | |
| | Frozen Yogurt | Ice Cream |
| --- | --- | --- |
| Vanilla | | |
| Chocolate | | |
| Total | 32 | 152 |

The incomplete table above shows the sales for a particular sweet shop by product and flavor. There were 4 times as many vanilla ice creams sold as vanilla frozen yogurts, and there were 6 times as many chocolate ice creams sold as chocolate frozen yogurts. If there were a total of 32 frozen yogurts and 152 ice creams sold, and no flavors other than vanilla and chocolate were available, which of the following is closest to the probability that a randomly selected ice cream sold was vanilla?

A) 0.250

B) 0.435

C) 0.526

D) 0.667

**30**

$$\begin{cases} y \geq x \\ 3y < 2x - 3 \end{cases}$$

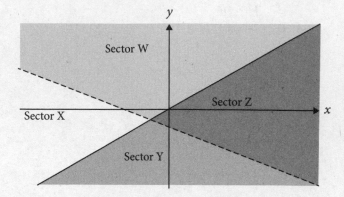

A system of inequalities is graphed above. Which sector or sectors on the graph could represent all of the solutions to the system shown?

A) Sectors Y and Z

B) Sectors W and Y

C) Sector W

D) Sector X

CONTINUE

## DIRECTIONS

**For questions 31–38**, solve the problem and enter your answer in the grid, as described below, on the answer sheet.

1. Although not required, it is suggested that you write your answer in the boxes at the top of the columns to help you fill in the circles accurately. You will receive credit only if the circles are filled in correctly.

2. Mark no more than one circle in any column.

3. No question has a negative answer.

4. Some problems may have more than one correct answer. In such cases, grid only one answer.

5. **Mixed numbers** such as $3\frac{1}{2}$ must be gridded as 3.5 or 7/2. (If $\boxed{3\ 1\ /\ 2}$ is entered into the grid, it will be interpreted as $\frac{31}{2}$, not as $3\frac{1}{2}$ .)

6. **Decimal Answers:** If you obtain a decimal answer with more digits than the grid can accommodate, it may be either rounded or truncated, but it must fill the entire grid.

Answer: $\frac{7}{12}$      Answer: 2.5

Write answer in boxes. ← Fraction line

Grid in result. ← Decimal point

Acceptable ways to grid $\frac{2}{3}$ are:

Answer: 201 – either position is correct

**NOTE:** You may start your answers in any column, space permitting. Columns you don't need to use should be left blank.

**CONTINUE** →

**31**

At a certain food truck, hamburgers are sold for $5 each and hot dogs are $3 each. If Martina buys one hamburger and $h$ hot dogs and spends at least $20 and no more than $25, what is one possible value of $h$ ?

**32**

| Number of States in 14 Federal Nations | | | |
|---|---|---|---|
| Nation | States | Nation | States |
| Australia | 6 | Micronesia | 4 |
| Austria | 9 | Nigeria | 36 |
| Brazil | 26 | Saint Kitts and Nevis | 2 |
| Germany | 16 | South Sudan | 10 |
| India | 29 | Sudan | 17 |
| Malaysia | 13 | United States | 50 |
| Mexico | 31 | Venezuela | 23 |

The table above lists the number of states in each of the 14 federal nations that have subdivisions called states. According to the table, what is the mean number of states of these nations? (Round your answer to the nearest tenth.)

**33**

In the $xy$-plane, the point $(-2, 6)$ lies on the graph of the function $g(x) = 2x^2 + kx + 18$. What is the value of $k$ ?

**34**

In a certain college dormitory, 108 students are assigned dorm rooms. The dormitory has 26 dorm rooms, each of which is assigned 3 or 5 students. How many of the dorm rooms will be assigned 3 students?

**CONTINUE**

## 35

### Population of Town A
### Each Decade from 1910 to 2000

According to the figure shown above, the population of Town A in 1970 was what fraction of the population of Town A in 2000 ?

## 36

16 centimeter

A wooden block is in the shape of the right circular cylinder shown above. If the volume of the wooden block is $64\pi$ cubic centimeters, what is the <u>diameter</u> of the base of the cylinder, in centimeters?

**Questions 37 and 38 refer to the following information.**

$\omega^2 = \omega_0^2 + 2\alpha\theta$    (angular position – angular velocity)

$\omega = \omega_0 + \alpha t$      (time – angular velocity)

$\theta = \omega_0 t + \dfrac{1}{2}\alpha t^2$  (time – angular position)

A carousel is rotating at an angular velocity of 90 degrees per second. The instant a particular point on the carousel reaches angular position $\theta = 0°$, the carousel operator flips a switch, causing the carousel at a constant angular acceleration to slow down and eventually change direction. The equations above describe the constant-acceleration motion of the carousel, where $\omega_0$ represents the initial angular velocity, $\omega$ is the angular velocity as it travels, $\theta$ is the angular position of the particular point on the carousel, $t$ is the time since the switch was flipped, and $\alpha$ is the constant angular acceleration $(-12.6°/s^2)$.

## 37

To the nearest degree, at what angular position will the carousel change direction?

## 38

To the nearest second, how long will it take the carousel to come to a complete stop before it changes direction?

# STOP

**If you finish before time is called, you may check your work on this section only.**
**Do not turn to any other section in the test.**

# SAT Essay

## DIRECTIONS

The essay gives you an opportunity to show how effectively you can read and comprehend a passage and write an essay analyzing the passage. In your essay you should demonstrate that you have read the passage carefully, present a clear and logical analysis, and use language precisely.

Your essay must be written on the lines provided in your answer sheet booklet; except for the planning page of the answer booklet, you will receive no other paper on which to write. You will have enough space if you write on every line, avoid wide margins, and keep your handwriting to a reasonable size. Remember that people who are not familiar with your handwriting will read what you write. Try to write or print so that what you are writing is legible to those readers.

**You have <u>50 minutes</u> to read the passage and write an essay in response to the prompt provided inside this booklet.**

## REMINDER

— Do not write your essay in this booklet. Only what you write on the lined pages of your answer booklet will be evaluated.

— An off-topic essay will not be evaluated.

CONTINUE ➡

As you read the passage below, consider how Jimmy Carter uses

- evidence, such as facts or examples, to support claims.
- reasoning to develop ideas and to connect claims and evidence.
- stylistic or persuasive elements, such as word choice or appeals to emotion, to add power to the ideas expressed.

**Adapted from Jimmy Carter, "The President's Proposed Energy Policy." The speech was televised and was delivered on April 18, 1977.**

1   Tonight I want to have an unpleasant talk with you about a problem unprecedented in our history. With the exception of preventing war, this is the greatest challenge our country will face during our lifetimes. The energy crisis has not yet overwhelmed us, but it will if we do not act quickly. It is a problem we will not solve in the next few years, and it is likely to get progressively worse through the rest of this century. We must not be selfish or timid if we hope to have a decent world for our children and grandchildren.

2   We simply must balance our demand for energy with our rapidly shrinking resources. By acting now, we can control our future instead of letting the future control us.

3   Two days from now, I will present my energy proposals to the Congress. Its members will be my partners and they have already given me a great deal of valuable advice. Many of these proposals will be unpopular. Some will cause you to put up with inconveniences and to make sacrifices. The most important thing about these proposals is that the alternative may be a national catastrophe. Further delay can affect our strength and our power as a nation.

4   Our decision about energy will test the character of the American people and the ability of the President and the Congress to govern. This difficult effort will be the "moral equivalent of war"—except that we will be uniting our efforts to build and not destroy. I know that some of you may doubt that we face real energy shortages. The 1973 gasoline lines are gone, and our homes are warm again. But our energy problem is worse tonight than it was in 1973 or a few weeks ago in the dead of winter. It is worse because more waste has occurred, and more time has passed by without our planning for the future. And it will get worse every day until we act.

5   The oil and natural gas we rely on for 75 percent of our energy are running out. In spite of increased effort, domestic production has been dropping steadily at about six percent a year. Imports have doubled in the last five years. Our nation's independence of economic and political action is becoming increasingly constrained. Unless profound changes are made to lower oil consumption, we now believe that early in the 1980s the world will be demanding more oil than it can produce.

CONTINUE

6 The world now uses about 60 million barrels of oil a day and demand increases each year about five percent. This means that, just to stay even, we need the production of a new Texas every year, an Alaskan North Slope every nine months, or a new Saudi Arabia every three years. Obviously, this cannot continue.

7 We must look back in history to understand our energy problem. Twice in the last several hundred years there has been a transition in the way people use energy. The first was about 200 years ago, away from wood—which had provided about 90 percent of all fuel—to coal, which was more efficient. This change became the basis of the Industrial Revolution. The second change took place in this century, with the growing use of oil and natural gas. They were more convenient and cheaper than coal, and the supply seemed to be almost without limit. They made possible the age of automobile and airplane travel. Nearly everyone who is alive today grew up during this age and we have never known anything different.

8 Because we are now running out of gas and oil, we must prepare quickly for a third change, to strict conservation and to the use of coal and permanent renewable energy sources, like solar power.

9 …Other generations of Americans have faced and mastered great challenges. I have faith that meeting this challenge will make our own lives even richer. If you will join me so that we can work together with patriotism and courage, we will again prove that our great nation can lead the world into an age of peace, independence, and freedom.

---

Write an essay in which you explain how Jimmy Carter builds an argument to convince his audience to support his proposed energy policy. In your essay, analyze how Carter uses one or more of the features listed in the box above (or features of your own choice) to strengthen the logic and persuasiveness of his argument. Be sure that your analysis focuses on the most relevant features of the passage.

Your essay should not explain whether you agree with Carter's claims, but rather explain how Carter builds an argument to persuade his audience.

---

**END OF TEST**

**DO NOT RETURN TO A PREVIOUS SECTION.**

The Princeton Review®

Completely darken bubbles with a No. 2 pencil. If you make a mistake, be sure to erase mark completely. Erase all stray marks.

**1.**

YOUR NAME: _____
(Print)                    Last                           First                    M.I.

SIGNATURE: _____          DATE: ___ / ___ / ___

HOME ADDRESS: _____
(Print)                         Number and Street

_____
City                    State                    Zip Code

PHONE NO.: _____
(Print)

IMPORTANT: Please fill in these boxes exactly as shown on the back cover of your test book.

**2. TEST FORM**

**3. TEST CODE**

**4. REGISTRATION NUMBER**

**6. DATE OF BIRTH**

| Month | Day | Year |
|-------|-----|------|
| ○ JAN | | |
| ○ FEB | ⓪ ⓪ | ⓪ ⓪ |
| ○ MAR | ① ① | ① ① |
| ○ APR | ② ② | ② ② |
| ○ MAY | ③ ③ | ③ ③ |
| ○ JUN | ④ | ④ ④ |
| ○ JUL | ⑤ | ⑤ ⑤ |
| ○ AUG | ⑥ | ⑥ ⑥ |
| ○ SEP | ⑦ | ⑦ ⑦ |
| ○ OCT | ⑧ | ⑧ ⑧ |
| ○ NOV | ⑨ | ⑨ ⑨ |
| ○ DEC | | |

**7. SEX**
○ MALE
○ FEMALE

The Princeton Review®

**5. YOUR NAME**

First 4 letters of last name | FIRST INIT | MID INIT

A B C D E F G H I J K L M N O P Q R S T U V W X Y Z

---

**Test 5**    Start with number 1 for each new section.
If a section has fewer questions than answer spaces, leave the extra answer spaces blank.

## Section 1—Reading

1. Ⓐ Ⓑ Ⓒ Ⓓ
2. Ⓐ Ⓑ Ⓒ Ⓓ
3. Ⓐ Ⓑ Ⓒ Ⓓ
4. Ⓐ Ⓑ Ⓒ Ⓓ
5. Ⓐ Ⓑ Ⓒ Ⓓ
6. Ⓐ Ⓑ Ⓒ Ⓓ
7. Ⓐ Ⓑ Ⓒ Ⓓ
8. Ⓐ Ⓑ Ⓒ Ⓓ
9. Ⓐ Ⓑ Ⓒ Ⓓ
10. Ⓐ Ⓑ Ⓒ Ⓓ
11. Ⓐ Ⓑ Ⓒ Ⓓ
12. Ⓐ Ⓑ Ⓒ Ⓓ
13. Ⓐ Ⓑ Ⓒ Ⓓ
14. Ⓐ Ⓑ Ⓒ Ⓓ
15. Ⓐ Ⓑ Ⓒ Ⓓ
16. Ⓐ Ⓑ Ⓒ Ⓓ
17. Ⓐ Ⓑ Ⓒ Ⓓ
18. Ⓐ Ⓑ Ⓒ Ⓓ
19. Ⓐ Ⓑ Ⓒ Ⓓ
20. Ⓐ Ⓑ Ⓒ Ⓓ
21. Ⓐ Ⓑ Ⓒ Ⓓ
22. Ⓐ Ⓑ Ⓒ Ⓓ
23. Ⓐ Ⓑ Ⓒ Ⓓ
24. Ⓐ Ⓑ Ⓒ Ⓓ
25. Ⓐ Ⓑ Ⓒ Ⓓ
26. Ⓐ Ⓑ Ⓒ Ⓓ
27. Ⓐ Ⓑ Ⓒ Ⓓ
28. Ⓐ Ⓑ Ⓒ Ⓓ
29. Ⓐ Ⓑ Ⓒ Ⓓ
30. Ⓐ Ⓑ Ⓒ Ⓓ
31. Ⓐ Ⓑ Ⓒ Ⓓ
32. Ⓐ Ⓑ Ⓒ Ⓓ
33. Ⓐ Ⓑ Ⓒ Ⓓ
34. Ⓐ Ⓑ Ⓒ Ⓓ
35. Ⓐ Ⓑ Ⓒ Ⓓ
36. Ⓐ Ⓑ Ⓒ Ⓓ
37. Ⓐ Ⓑ Ⓒ Ⓓ
38. Ⓐ Ⓑ Ⓒ Ⓓ
39. Ⓐ Ⓑ Ⓒ Ⓓ
40. Ⓐ Ⓑ Ⓒ Ⓓ
41. Ⓐ Ⓑ Ⓒ Ⓓ
42. Ⓐ Ⓑ Ⓒ Ⓓ
43. Ⓐ Ⓑ Ⓒ Ⓓ
44. Ⓐ Ⓑ Ⓒ Ⓓ
45. Ⓐ Ⓑ Ⓒ Ⓓ
46. Ⓐ Ⓑ Ⓒ Ⓓ
47. Ⓐ Ⓑ Ⓒ Ⓓ
48. Ⓐ Ⓑ Ⓒ Ⓓ
49. Ⓐ Ⓑ Ⓒ Ⓓ
50. Ⓐ Ⓑ Ⓒ Ⓓ
51. Ⓐ Ⓑ Ⓒ Ⓓ
52. Ⓐ Ⓑ Ⓒ Ⓓ

## Section 2—Writing and Language Skills

1. Ⓐ Ⓑ Ⓒ Ⓓ
2. Ⓐ Ⓑ Ⓒ Ⓓ
3. Ⓐ Ⓑ Ⓒ Ⓓ
4. Ⓐ Ⓑ Ⓒ Ⓓ
5. Ⓐ Ⓑ Ⓒ Ⓓ
6. Ⓐ Ⓑ Ⓒ Ⓓ
7. Ⓐ Ⓑ Ⓒ Ⓓ
8. Ⓐ Ⓑ Ⓒ Ⓓ
9. Ⓐ Ⓑ Ⓒ Ⓓ
10. Ⓐ Ⓑ Ⓒ Ⓓ
11. Ⓐ Ⓑ Ⓒ Ⓓ
12. Ⓐ Ⓑ Ⓒ Ⓓ
13. Ⓐ Ⓑ Ⓒ Ⓓ
14. Ⓐ Ⓑ Ⓒ Ⓓ
15. Ⓐ Ⓑ Ⓒ Ⓓ
16. Ⓐ Ⓑ Ⓒ Ⓓ
17. Ⓐ Ⓑ Ⓒ Ⓓ
18. Ⓐ Ⓑ Ⓒ Ⓓ
19. Ⓐ Ⓑ Ⓒ Ⓓ
20. Ⓐ Ⓑ Ⓒ Ⓓ
21. Ⓐ Ⓑ Ⓒ Ⓓ
22. Ⓐ Ⓑ Ⓒ Ⓓ
23. Ⓐ Ⓑ Ⓒ Ⓓ
24. Ⓐ Ⓑ Ⓒ Ⓓ
25. Ⓐ Ⓑ Ⓒ Ⓓ
26. Ⓐ Ⓑ Ⓒ Ⓓ
27. Ⓐ Ⓑ Ⓒ Ⓓ
28. Ⓐ Ⓑ Ⓒ Ⓓ
29. Ⓐ Ⓑ Ⓒ Ⓓ
30. Ⓐ Ⓑ Ⓒ Ⓓ
31. Ⓐ Ⓑ Ⓒ Ⓓ
32. Ⓐ Ⓑ Ⓒ Ⓓ
33. Ⓐ Ⓑ Ⓒ Ⓓ
34. Ⓐ Ⓑ Ⓒ Ⓓ
35. Ⓐ Ⓑ Ⓒ Ⓓ
36. Ⓐ Ⓑ Ⓒ Ⓓ
37. Ⓐ Ⓑ Ⓒ Ⓓ
38. Ⓐ Ⓑ Ⓒ Ⓓ
39. Ⓐ Ⓑ Ⓒ Ⓓ
40. Ⓐ Ⓑ Ⓒ Ⓓ
41. Ⓐ Ⓑ Ⓒ Ⓓ
42. Ⓐ Ⓑ Ⓒ Ⓓ
43. Ⓐ Ⓑ Ⓒ Ⓓ
44. Ⓐ Ⓑ Ⓒ Ⓓ

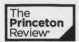

**Test 5** — Start with number 1 for each new section.
If a section has fewer questions than answer spaces, leave the extra answer spaces blank.

## Section 3—Mathematics: No Calculator

1. Ⓐ Ⓑ Ⓒ Ⓓ
2. Ⓐ Ⓑ Ⓒ Ⓓ
3. Ⓐ Ⓑ Ⓒ Ⓓ
4. Ⓐ Ⓑ Ⓒ Ⓓ
5. Ⓐ Ⓑ Ⓒ Ⓓ
6. Ⓐ Ⓑ Ⓒ Ⓓ
7. Ⓐ Ⓑ Ⓒ Ⓓ
8. Ⓐ Ⓑ Ⓒ Ⓓ
9. Ⓐ Ⓑ Ⓒ Ⓓ
10. Ⓐ Ⓑ Ⓒ Ⓓ
11. Ⓐ Ⓑ Ⓒ Ⓓ
12. Ⓐ Ⓑ Ⓒ Ⓓ
13. Ⓐ Ⓑ Ⓒ Ⓓ
14. Ⓐ Ⓑ Ⓒ Ⓓ
15. Ⓐ Ⓑ Ⓒ Ⓓ

16. 17. 18. 19. 20.

## Section 4—Mathematics: Calculator

1. Ⓐ Ⓑ Ⓒ Ⓓ
2. Ⓐ Ⓑ Ⓒ Ⓓ
3. Ⓐ Ⓑ Ⓒ Ⓓ
4. Ⓐ Ⓑ Ⓒ Ⓓ
5. Ⓐ Ⓑ Ⓒ Ⓓ
6. Ⓐ Ⓑ Ⓒ Ⓓ
7. Ⓐ Ⓑ Ⓒ Ⓓ
8. Ⓐ Ⓑ Ⓒ Ⓓ
9. Ⓐ Ⓑ Ⓒ Ⓓ
10. Ⓐ Ⓑ Ⓒ Ⓓ
11. Ⓐ Ⓑ Ⓒ Ⓓ
12. Ⓐ Ⓑ Ⓒ Ⓓ
13. Ⓐ Ⓑ Ⓒ Ⓓ
14. Ⓐ Ⓑ Ⓒ Ⓓ
15. Ⓐ Ⓑ Ⓒ Ⓓ
16. Ⓐ Ⓑ Ⓒ Ⓓ
17. Ⓐ Ⓑ Ⓒ Ⓓ
18. Ⓐ Ⓑ Ⓒ Ⓓ
19. Ⓐ Ⓑ Ⓒ Ⓓ
20. Ⓐ Ⓑ Ⓒ Ⓓ
21. Ⓐ Ⓑ Ⓒ Ⓓ
22. Ⓐ Ⓑ Ⓒ Ⓓ
23. Ⓐ Ⓑ Ⓒ Ⓓ
24. Ⓐ Ⓑ Ⓒ Ⓓ
25. Ⓐ Ⓑ Ⓒ Ⓓ
26. Ⓐ Ⓑ Ⓒ Ⓓ
27. Ⓐ Ⓑ Ⓒ Ⓓ
28. Ⓐ Ⓑ Ⓒ Ⓓ
29. Ⓐ Ⓑ Ⓒ Ⓓ
30. Ⓐ Ⓑ Ⓒ Ⓓ

31. 32. 33. 34. 35.

36. 37. 38.

# Chapter 12
# Practice Test 5:
# Answers and
# Explanations

# PRACTICE TEST 5 ANSWER KEY

| Section 1: Reading | | | Section 2: Writing & Language | | | Section 3: Math (No Calculator) | | | Section 4: Math (Calculator) | | |
|---|---|---|---|---|---|---|---|---|---|---|---|
| 1. | C | 27. | A | 1. | A | 23. | D | 1. | B | 11. | D |
| 2. | C | 28. | B | 2. | B | 24. | C | 2. | B | 12. | B |
| 3. | D | 29. | B | 3. | C | 25. | A | 3. | B | 13. | C |
| 4. | A | 30. | C | 4. | B | 26. | C | 4. | D | 14. | C |
| 5. | A | 31. | D | 5. | B | 27. | B | 5. | C | 15. | A |
| 6. | D | 32. | B | 6. | D | 28. | C | 6. | D | 16. | 800 |
| 7. | A | 33. | A | 7. | B | 29. | C | 7. | A | | |
| 8. | C | 34. | D | 8. | B | 30. | B | 8. | C | | |
| 9. | D | 35. | B | 9. | B | 31. | A | 9. | B | | |
| 10. | B | 36. | C | 10. | D | 32. | A | 10. | A | | |

**Section 1: Reading**

| | | | |
|---|---|---|---|
| 1. | C | 27. | A |
| 2. | C | 28. | B |
| 3. | D | 29. | B |
| 4. | A | 30. | C |
| 5. | A | 31. | D |
| 6. | D | 32. | B |
| 7. | A | 33. | A |
| 8. | C | 34. | D |
| 9. | D | 35. | B |
| 10. | B | 36. | C |
| 11. | D | 37. | C |
| 12. | C | 38. | A |
| 13. | A | 39. | B |
| 14. | A | 40. | D |
| 15. | D | 41. | A |
| 16. | B | 42. | D |
| 17. | A | 43. | C |
| 18. | A | 44. | A |
| 19. | D | 45. | A |
| 20. | C | 46. | B |
| 21. | D | 47. | D |
| 22. | C | 48. | C |
| 23. | B | 49. | B |
| 24. | D | 50. | C |
| 25. | D | 51. | D |
| 26. | B | 52. | C |

**Section 2: Writing & Language**

| | | | |
|---|---|---|---|
| 1. | A | 23. | D |
| 2. | B | 24. | C |
| 3. | C | 25. | A |
| 4. | B | 26. | C |
| 5. | B | 27. | B |
| 6. | D | 28. | C |
| 7. | B | 29. | C |
| 8. | B | 30. | B |
| 9. | B | 31. | A |
| 10. | D | 32. | A |
| 11. | B | 33. | C |
| 12. | B | 34. | D |
| 13. | D | 35. | B |
| 14. | A | 36. | D |
| 15. | A | 37. | D |
| 16. | C | 38. | A |
| 17. | C | 39. | B |
| 18. | A | 40. | C |
| 19. | B | 41. | D |
| 20. | D | 42. | D |
| 21. | A | 43. | A |
| 22. | A | 44. | B |

**Section 3: Math (No Calculator)**

| | | | |
|---|---|---|---|
| 1. | B | 11. | D |
| 2. | B | 12. | B |
| 3. | B | 13. | C |
| 4. | D | 14. | C |
| 5. | C | 15. | A |
| 6. | D | 16. | 800 |
| 7. | A | 17. | $\frac{8}{10}, \frac{4}{5}$, or 0.8 |
| 8. | C | 18. | 25 |
| 9. | B | 19. | 20 |
| 10. | A | 20. | 225 |

**Section 4: Math (Calculator)**

| | | | |
|---|---|---|---|
| 1. | D | 20. | D |
| 2. | B | 21. | C |
| 3. | A | 22. | B |
| 4. | D | 23. | A |
| 5. | A | 24. | B |
| 6. | C | 25. | D |
| 7. | B | 26. | B |
| 8. | C | 27. | B |
| 9. | A | 28. | B |
| 10. | A | 29. | C |
| 11. | D | 30. | D |
| 12. | A | 31. | 5 or 6 |
| 13. | A | 32. | 19.4 |
| 14. | D | 33. | 10 |
| 15. | C | 34. | 11 |
| 16. | C | 35. | $\frac{7}{12}$ |
| 17. | B | 36. | 4 |
| 18. | C | 37. | 321 |
| 19. | C | 38. | 7 |

For self-scoring assessment tables, please turn to page 957.

# PRACTICE TEST 5 EXPLANATIONS

## Section 1: Reading

1. **C** This is a general question about what happens in the passage as a whole. Leave it until the end of the questions because it will be easier to answer once all the specific questions for this passage have been answered. This passage is about a stranger showing up unexpectedly for an unhappy reunion with a former shipmate. Choice (A) might initially look attractive because the narrator and the stranger do hide and then surprise the captain, but there is no *plan* to surprise the captain. Eliminate (A). Choice (B) has nothing to do with the passage and can be eliminated. Choice (C) is a solid paraphrase of the prediction, so keep it. Choice (D) does mention two characters sharing time on a ship, but the passage does not indicate that the two men were reminiscing at all. Choice (C) is the correct answer.

2. **C** This is a general question that will be best answered after all of the more detail-oriented questions. Look at the second part of each answer choice. The *encounter* in the passage is not *enthusiastic*, so (A) can be eliminated. There is no *conference*, so (B) can also be eliminated. Choice (C) looks good because the narrator was worried, and the stranger and the captain fought, so keep (C). There is no *homecoming*, so eliminate (D). Choice (C) is the correct answer.

3. **D** This is a Vocab-in-Context question, so go back to the text, find the word *fancy* in lines 5 and 10, and cross it out. Replace it with another word that makes sense in the sentence based on the context of the passage. In the first case, the narrator says that he didn't step back inside *quick enough for his fancy*. *Fancy* could be replaced with *liking*. See if that also makes sense in the second occurrence. The stranger tells the narrator that he's *taken quite a fancy* to him because the narrator reminds him of his own son, or *the pride of [his] 'art*. *Liking* definitely fits in that context as well. Choices (A) and (C) can be eliminated immediately. Choice (B) might appear to match the context of the first occurrence of *fancy*, but *impatience* has nothing to do with the prediction of *liking*, so (B) can be eliminated. *Preference* means *liking*. Choice (D) is the correct answer.

4. **A** This question asks about the narrator's sense of the stranger's emotions regarding the coming meeting between him and the captain. Find evidence in the text to predict how the stranger feels about seeing the captain. In the second paragraph, there is plenty of evidence to predict that the stranger feels very bad about the upcoming meeting. The narrator is *uneasy and alarmed*, and he notices that the stranger is *certainly frightened himself*. The narrator goes on to say that the stranger readies his weapon and keeps *swallowing as if he felt…a lump in the throat*. The stranger is definitely not *overjoyed*, so eliminate (B). Choice (D) has nothing to do with the passage, so eliminate it. Choices (A) and (C) both have negative emotions, but the evidence in the text shows the stranger is clearly fearful, not just worried the captain won't recognize him. Choice (A) is the correct answer.

5.  **A**  This is a best evidence question, so simply refer to the lines used to predict the answer to the previous question. Choice (A) is the correct answer.

6.  **D**  This question asks about how the narrator is addressed by the stranger, so look for evidence in the text to predict what the answer might be. In the text used to answer previous questions, the stranger tells the narrator he has *taken a fancy* to him, but in that same paragraph the stranger swears at the boy *with an oath that made [him] jump*. Eliminate (A) because, while the stranger does address the narrator with friendliness at one point, he never addresses him with respect. Choice (B) is reversed—the stranger does address the boy with anger but he's never violent to him. Choice (C) does not match the prediction. *Affection* in (D) looks good, and later the stranger shows that he does not trust the narrator when he sends him for rum but tells him to leave the door open. Choice (D) is the correct answer.

7.  **A**  In order to determine the purpose of the first paragraph, simply look to see what's happening in that paragraph. Throughout the paragraph, the narrator creates a picture of the stranger, from how he looks to how he acts. Choice (A) is the correct answer.

8.  **C**  This is a Vocab-in-Context question, so go back to the text, find the word *talons* in line 51, and cross it out. Replace it with another word that makes sense in the sentence based on the context of the passage. Black Dog says he's lost two talons, and then he holds up *his mutilated hand*. *Talons* must mean *fingers*. Choice (C) is the correct answer.

9.  **D**  This question asks why the narrator uses a particular phrase (*all the brown had gone out of his face*), so go back to the text to see what's happening around that phrase. The narrator uses the phrase to describe the captain's reaction to seeing the stranger. Black Dog surprises the captain, who *spun round on his heel…he had the look of a man who sees a ghost, or the evil one, or something worse, if anything can be; and upon my word, I felt sorry to see him all in a moment turn so old and sick*. The narrator uses the phrase to show that the captain is reacting badly to the surprise of seeing Black Dog. Choice (A) does not match that prediction, so it can be eliminated. Choice (B) might be true, but isn't supported by the text. Choice (C) doesn't have any support in the text, either, so it can be eliminated. Choice (D) is a clear paraphrase of the prediction and is the correct answer.

10. **B**  This is a best evidence question, so simply refer to the lines used to predict the answer to the previous question. Choice (B) is the correct answer.

11. **D**  This question asks why the author mentions certain examples. Use the line reference to find the correct window and look for the claim the examples are meant to illustrate. The examples of gift giving are both recent and about Christmas, but they are offered to show that *the ancient practice of gift-giving is still pervasive and significant in modern cultures*. Eliminate (A), as there's no mention of a *recent increase*. Eliminate (B) and (C), since neither *discrepancies* nor *apprehension* is mentioned. Choice (D) matches the prediction and is the correct answer.

12.  **C**  This is a Vocab-in-Context question, so go back to the text, find the word *rich* in line 20, and cross it out. Replace it with another word that makes sense in the sentence based on the context of the passage. In this case, *rich* refers to the plethora of information that might help to explain consumer behavior. Choices (A) and (B) are actual definitions of the word *rich*, but they don't make sense based on the context. Both of these answers can be eliminated. Choice (C) could work, because when something is *fertile* it is *abundantly productive,* which fits the context of the passage. Choice (D) might connect with the idea of foods that are rich, but that doesn't make sense in this context. Eliminate (D), leaving (C) as the correct answer.

13.  **A**  This question asks about the *self-perpetuating system of reciprocity.* Notice that the following question is a best evidence question, so Q13 and Q14 can be answered in tandem. Look at the answers choices for Q14 first. Choice (14A) suggests that gift-giving conveys information, which supports (13A). Draw a line connecting those two answers. Choice (14B) deals specifically with the *obligation to give,* and (14C) deals with *repayment*—both refer only to part of the system of reciprocity, and neither supports an answer choice in Q13, so both can be eliminated. Choice (14D) might appear to support (13C), but the lines do not support the idea of wreaking *havoc,* so the relationship is weak. Eliminate (14D). Without any support from Q14, (13B), (13C), and (13D) can be eliminated. That leaves (13A) and (14A) as the correct answers.

14.  **A**  (See explanation above.)

15.  **D**  This question asks how Schwartz would view the gift-exchange process. The fourth paragraph presents Schwartz's insights about a gift's ability to reflect *the giver's perception of the recipient* and the implicit acceptance of that perception when a receiver accepts a gift. This point about the process matches well with (D), *symbolic.* Though it may be true that such a process could be *stressful* or *unnerving,* no evidence is given that Schwartz considers it to be so. Thus, (A) and (B) can be eliminated. While some givers and receivers may act *intentional[ly],* there's no evidence that the process always operates that way, so (C) can be eliminated. The best answer is (D).

16.  **B**  This question asks what the passage says about *the acceptance of a gift.* The fourth paragraph states that accepting a gift constitutes acceptance of the implied identity the gift conveys and that *this may lead to changes in self-perceptions.* The correct answer must have something to do with *a lot of power.* This prediction matches well with (B), *influential.* Eliminate (A), as there's no discussion of the idea that accepting a gift is *considerate.* Eliminate (C) because there is no indication that accepting a gift is *authoritative.* Choice (D) can be eliminated as well because, while accepting a gift may have influence on the recipient, there no evidence that it's *immutable.* Choice (B) is the best answer.

17.  **A**  This is a specific paired set with Q16, so simply look at the lines used to predict the answer to the previous question. Choice (A) is the correct answer.

18.   **A**   This is a Vocab-in-Context question, so go back to the text, find the word *function* in line 65, and cross it out. Replace it with another word that makes sense in the sentence based on the context of the passage. In this case, *function* refers to the purpose of gift selection, which supports (A). The *nevertheless* at the beginning of the sentence shows a continuation from the previous paragraph. The focus of the previous paragraph was how gift-giving *does* something, not *when* the gifts are given. Therefore, *function* in this context does not have to do with an event. Choices (B) and (C) can be eliminated. Choice (D), *occupation*, does not fit the context of the sentence. Choice (A) is the correct response.

19.   **D**   This question asks why the author mentions *a gift shop's recent advertisement*. Use the line reference to find the window and read for context. Here, the line reference points to the fourth paragraph and to the quoted advertisement. The ad does not question any prior claims or counter any explanations, eliminating (A) and (C). Choice (B) can be eliminated because the advertisement does not *offer a motive* for a certain behavior. The ad supports what was said in paragraph 3, making (D) the correct choice.

20.   **C**   The question asks about information in both the passage and the graph. Use the passage and the graph to answer it. The recipient's self-concept is not included in the graph, nor is the amount of money the giver spent, eliminating (A) and (B). Choice (D) does not work because the thoughtfulness is not measured by the graph. Rather, the graph shows the implicit communication between the gift-giver and recipient, and the passage supports this information in the last paragraph. Therefore, (C) is correct.

21.   **D**   This question asks about the author's thoughts on the graph. For graph-related questions, look at the graph and see what is also supported by the passage. The graph shows the various steps of communication and evaluation in the gift-giving process, as mentioned in the last lines of the passage. *Conditional approval* is not mentioned, making (A) incorrect. While (B) mentions communication, it does not state that parties cannot *communicate effectively*. Similarly, while (C) might be true, it is not supported by the passage, and therefore is incorrect. Choice (D) is supported by the graph and the last lines of the passage and therefore is the correct choice.

22.   **C**   This question asks for a piece of information that *contradicts* the student's claim that *over half of solar radiation influences the ground temperature*. Use the line references given in each of the answer choices to check. Choice (A) refers to a situation in which the atmosphere is *letting through the light rays of the sun relatively easily*, which would confirm rather than contradict the student's claim and should therefore be eliminated. Choice (B) mentions *the temperature of the atmosphere* but does not address solar radiation or ground temperature, so this answer can be eliminated. Choice (C) should be kept because it specifically contradicts the student's claim with these lines: *Owing to the clouds and dust floating in the atmosphere, this heat is probably only about a third of that derived by using Langley's solar constant.* In other words, the *clouds and dust floating in the atmosphere* block the sun's full energy. Choice (D) refers only to the table, not to

the conceptual information regarding the sun's radiation, so it too can be eliminated. Choice (C) is the correct answer.

23. **B** This question asks about the importance of the atmosphere as it influences the temperature of the earth. Use the given line reference to find the window. The relevant information is here: *the atmosphere may act like the glass of a green-house, letting through the light rays of the sun relatively easily, and absorbing a great part of the dark rays emitted from the ground, and it thereby may raise the mean temperature of the earth's surface.* A second purpose is cited here: *the atmosphere acts as a heat store placed between the relatively warm ground and the cold space, and thereby lessens in a high degree the annual, diurnal, and local variations of the temperature.* In other words, the atmosphere plays a crucial role in allowing certain heat in and trapping that heat so it influences ground temperature. Choice (A) is extreme in its use of the word *all*, particularly given that the text indicates that much of the heat is transferred back out of the atmosphere. Eliminate (A). Choice (B) should be kept because it captures the ideas from both quotations without overstating. Choice (C) can be eliminated because it neglects the role of solar radiation. Choice (D) can be eliminated because the words *free passage* are extreme—the passage indicates that the atmosphere absorbs *a great part of the dark rays emitted from the ground.* Choice (B) is the correct answer.

24. **D** This question asks why the author uses the word *green-house* to describe the effects in this passage. Use the given line reference to find the window. The relevant information is here: *like the glass of a green-house, letting through the light rays of the sun relatively easily, and absorbing a great part of the dark rays emitted from the ground.* In other words, the atmosphere is like a greenhouse in that it lets in more heat than it lets out. Choice (A) may be partially true (though it is extreme in its use of the word *only*), but it does not match the prediction because it does not answer the question as to why the word *green-house* is used. Eliminate (A). Choice (B) can also be eliminated because it neglects the role of solar radiation entirely. Choice (C) is deceptive in that it applies the term *green-house* literally rather than figuratively. Eliminate (C). Choice (D) matches well with the prediction and captures both the idea of solar radiation and the atmosphere's role in absorbing it. Choice (D) is the correct answer.

25. **D** This question asks which of the answers can be supported by the quoted statement and its surrounding context. Read the quotation carefully—the word *principally* indicates that most but not all of this energy comes from solar radiation. Choice (A) states a version of this, but there is no indication in the quotation or the passage that clouds block out solar radiation entirely, nor that ground heat does whatever heating solar energy cannot. Eliminate (A). Choice (B) correctly implies that heat can be generated by the sun and other sources, but this choice then goes on to state that the heat is held in the atmosphere and released as cool air, which is untrue. Eliminate (B). Choice (C) may seem plausible, but it overlooks the green-house effect described throughout this passage, which states that solar energy passes relatively unobstructed into the earth's atmosphere. Eliminate (C). Choice (D) takes proper account of the word *principally* by

stating that the heat in the atmosphere comes from the sun and other sources and that heat may be generated from non-solar sources. Choice (D) is thus the correct answer.

26. **B** This question asks why the author uses a few particular words in this context. The window is given by the line numbers in the passage. The cited lines read: *Now if we are able to calculate or estimate how much the mean temperature that layer is lower than the mean temperature of the ground, we may apply Table I for calculating the mean temperature of the ground, as soon as we know by direct measurements the quantity of solar heat absorbed by the ground.* The conditional language here implies that many factors must be considered as one calculates these values. Choice (A) overstates the confidence this language implies in the calculations, so this choice should be eliminated. Choice (B) is true, given the author's indication that the calculations will depend on mathematical formulas and constants in combination with some experimental observations. Choice (C) cannot be supported in the passage because it presumes the knowledge that the described calculations are setting out to find. Choice (D) identifies a harsh critique of earlier scientists where none is present in any part of the passage. Choice (D) can thus be eliminated. Choice (B) is the correct answer.

27. **A** This question asks why the author notes the observations of ground temperature. Using the chronology of previous questions, look for the lead words *observations* and *ground temperature* in the last paragraph. They appear in the last part of the last sentence: *assuming a corresponding decrease of 0.6°C per 100 meters, we find its temperature to be 46°C lower than that of the ground, and thus the mean temperature of the ground equal to 15°C, as it is according to observations.* Taken as a whole, the phrase *as it is according to observations* implies an agreement between the calculated data and the data observed by measurement. In this sense, the author cites the observations as a way to show the correctness of his calculations. Choice (A) captures the importance of the *observations*, so this answer should be kept. Choice (B) would undermine the importance of the mathematical calculations, when in fact the mention of *observations* is used to show the value of mathematical calculations. Eliminate (B). Choice (C) cites a contemporary theory of climate change, one that is not identified in the passage itself, so (C) should be eliminated. Choice (D) can be eliminated because it does not address the importance of the *observations* cited in the question. Choice (A) is the correct answer.

28. **B** This question asks for a combination of information from the table and passage. The relevant information in the passage is indicated by the data *1000 gram-calories per square centimeter for 24 hours.* This refers to the *Loss of Heat* columns in the chart, which are given in this unit. A *Loss of Heat* of 300 corresponds to a temperature of approximately −40°C. However, as the passage indicates, the figures given in the chart indicate the temperature at an elevation of *7600 meters.* Therefore, for the numbers given in the chart, *we find its temperature to be 46°C lower than that of the ground.* In other words, when the temperature on the chart is −40°C, the temperature on the ground must be approximately 6°C, or 46°C warmer, which corresponds with (B). Choices (A) and (D) pull the number directly from the chart but do not account for the information in the passage. Choice (C) confuses the negative signs. Choice (B) is the correct answer.

29. **B** This question asks whether the data from the chart support the author's claim regarding the atmosphere's *heat store*: *the atmosphere acts as a heat store placed between the relatively warm ground and the cold space*. This information is then expanded upon with the detail that *the higher the [atmospheric] layer, the lower is its temperature relatively to that of the ground*. Since this layer of atmosphere is located between the hot earth and cold space and the earth temperature gets colder with higher elevation, the loss of heat will be less as colder earth temperatures come nearer to space temperatures. Despite this technical explanation, this question can be answered with aggressive POE, particularly by looking at the given reasons rather than the "Yes" and "No" components of each answer. Choice (A) can be eliminated because it states that heat loss decreases at larger intervals at lower temperatures, which is not true. For each twenty-degree temperature interval, the heat-loss intervals shrink. In other words, whereas the heat loss at temperatures 100°C and 80°C goes down approximately 400, the heat loss at temperatures −100°C and −120°C goes down only 37. Choice (B) should be kept because it correctly establishes this relationship. Choices (C) and (D) can be eliminated because they cite incorrect relationships between temperature and loss of heat. Choice (B) is the correct answer.

30. **C** This question asks for a piece of information that will support the conclusion in the previous question. The correct answer to the previous question stated that *as the temperature decreases, the heat loss decreases as well but by smaller and smaller intervals*. This agrees with the information given in the chart. Choice (A) shows a widening gap between two heat-loss values, but it does not show the shrinking intervals mentioned in Q29. Eliminate (A). Choice (B) shows large intervals in heat-loss values, which make it difficult to form any conclusion. Eliminate (B). Choice (C) shows adjacent heat-loss values that decrease at smaller and smaller intervals, so keep this choice. Choice (D) shows decreasing values, but these are random and cannot be used to support a conclusion. Eliminate (D). The correct answer is (C).

31. **D** This question asks whether the temperature of the atmosphere varies relative to the distance from the ground. The chart does show variations in temperature, but it does not show variations in height. Therefore, the answer cannot be gleaned from the table alone and must be more explicitly stated within the passage. Choice (C) does hypothesize that temperatures may be different at the ground and at certain heights, but it does not offer conclusive proof and thus should be eliminated. Choice (D) offers conclusive proof of the relationship in the lines, *we find its temperature to be 46°C lower than that of the ground*. Choice (A) can be eliminated because it does not discuss different distances from the earth. Choice (B) can be eliminated for the same reason. Choice (D) is the correct answer.

32. **B** This question asks about the main purpose of the passage, or why this passage was composed. To answer it, ask why Douglass is speaking at this convention. He refers to his *early connection with the cause* as well as *having been called upon to do so by one whose voice in this Council we all gladly obey*. Now look for an answer choice that best fits these reasons. Choice (A) reflects a statement in paragraph 2 (*Men have very little business here as speakers, anyhow*), but does not fit this prediction. Choice (B) is consistent with the prediction. Choice (C) does not have

support in the passage, which explicitly states that *our cause has passed beyond the period of arguing.* Choice (D) reflects a statement in paragraph 2 (*I say of her, as I say of the colored people, "Give her fair play, and hands off"*), but does not fit this prediction. Choice (B) is the correct answer.

33. **A** This question asks for the central claim of the passage. To answer it, look for an answer choice that fits the most parts of the text, and eliminate answer choices that are true, but fit only part of the text. Choice (A) has support in paragraph 1 and several points of paragraph 2. Choice (B) contradicts the passage, which says that men *can neither speak for her, nor vote for her, nor act for her.* Choice (C) has support in the end of paragraph 3. Choice (D) slightly contradicts the passage, which indicates that the suffrage movement has become less obscure. It could be true that it should become less obscure still, but the passage doesn't say this, and so this cannot be the passage's central claim. Having eliminated (B) and (D), compare (A) and (C). Since (C) has less support, it is less likely to be the central claim; eliminate (C). Choice (A) is the correct answer.

34. **D** This question asks why Douglass uses the word *cause* throughout the passage. To answer it, find each time the word *cause* appears and take note of what Douglass is doing in each case. The first time, in paragraph 2, Douglass explains why he is speaking at this convention, and refers to his early connection to the cause. The second time, also in paragraph 2, he refers to the history of *this woman suffrage cause.* The third time, in paragraph 3, he refers to the convention of women and uses the phrase *our cause.* Putting these ideas together, it is clear that Douglass uses the word *cause* to refer to the women's suffrage movement. Now look for an answer choice that best fits this prediction, and eliminate answer choices that are either false, or true for only one instance of *cause.* (Remember, the question asks how Douglass uses the word *throughout* the passage.) Choice (A) could be true, since it refers to his early connection, but this better fits the first two uses of the word *cause.* Choice (B) goes beyond the scope of the passage: Douglass is not explaining why the movement deserves support; he assumes that it does, and that it is already clear to most people in attendance that it does. Eliminate (B). Choice (C) does not fit any of the uses of the word *cause.* Eliminate (C). Choice (D) could be true, since in each of the three uses of the word *cause* Douglass is referring to the suffrage movement. Now compare (A) and (D), and see that (A) kind of fits two out of three uses of the word, and that (D) completely fits three out of three uses of the word. Choice (D) is the correct answer.

35. **B** This question asks for something true about the passage. Notice that the first half of each answer choice addresses Douglass's speaking, and that the last half of each answer choice addresses his identification with the movement. Start by choosing the easier half and using POE. If that is the first half, begin by finding what the passage says about Douglass speaking. In paragraphs 1 and 2, Douglass indicates that he feels diffidence, that he is at a loss for words, and that men really have no business speaking here. Thus, (A) can be eliminated right away:

Douglass is not saying that he wants to give a great speech. Choice (C) also seems extreme, since he is in fact speaking. Eliminate (C). The first half of (B) and (D) are similar, and fit the text. Now look at the second half of (B) and (D). According to (B), he is hesitant to speak *even though* he is connected to the movement. That fits. According to (D), he is hesitant to speak *since* he is connected to the movement. This makes no sense. Eliminate (D). Choice (B) is the correct answer.

36. **C** This question is a excellent question for the Parallel POE strategy because it contains no line reference and no useful lead word. Douglass mentions *men* throughout the passage, so use the line references provided in the next question to help eliminate answer choices. Begin with (37A). Douglass says that he doesn't want to take *more than a very small space of... time and attention*. This could support (36B), so draw a line connecting those two answers. Choice (37B) talks about how he ended up speaking at the gathering, which doesn't support any of the answers from Q36. Eliminate (37B). Choice (37C) says that *men have very little business here as speakers* and that they should *take back benches and wrap themselves in silence*. This supports men *primarily listening*, so draw a line connecting this to (36C). Choice (37D) does not support any of the answers for Q36, so eliminate it. Without support from Q37, (36A) and (36D) can both be eliminated. Now compare the remaining pairs of (36B)/(37A) and (36C)/(37C). The question asks what Douglass indicates *about men*. While he does say that he doesn't want to take up much time, he's speaking specifically about himself and not men in general. The (36B)/(37A) pair can be eliminated. This leaves (36C)/(37C), which is consistent with the text and the question. The correct answers are (36C) and (37C).

37. **C** (See explanation above.)

38. **A** This question asks how the *demands of women* in line 29 are related to some kind of injuries. To answer it, find the phrase, and read a bit before and after to understand the context. Douglass says: *I believe no man, however gifted with thought and speech, can voice the wrongs and present the demands of women with the skill and effect, with the power and authority of woman herself.* He goes on to say that woman *knows and feels her wrongs as man cannot...* and *she is her own best representative.* Therefore, the demands of women are something that women can better speak about than men can. Look for an answer choice that fits this prediction. Choice (A) fits this prediction; keep it. Choice (B) can be eliminated because Douglass does not argue that the injuries are for men to speak about. Choice (C) can be eliminated because there is no evidence anywhere that the *world should support* injuries to women. Choice (D) may be true, but it doesn't fit the prediction. Choice (A) is the correct answer.

39. **B** This question asks for the best evidence to answer question 38. Look back at the lines used to predict the answer to the previous question. Lines 27–31 and 31–36 were used. Choice (B) is the correct answer.

40. **D** This question asks for the meaning of the word *cradle*, which the passage uses figuratively. Find the word in the passage, and read it in context: *It was when this woman suffrage cause*

*was in its cradle, when it was not big enough to go alone, when it had to be taken in the arms of its mother from Seneca Falls, N.Y., to Rochester, N.Y., for baptism.* Douglass is referring to the history of the movement, so the word *cradle* here means something like its early years. Choices (A), (B), and (C) have nothing to do with this prediction; eliminate them. Choice (D) fits this prediction exactly. Choice (D) is the correct answer.

41. **A** This question asks what the surprise referred to in lines 58–74 serves to emphasize. To do this, first find the word *surprise*, read it in context, and then determine what the author is trying to emphasize. Read the window: *There may be some…period of arguing.* Douglass says that some people attending were expecting arguments about women's suffrage, but were surprised to find no arguments. Look for an answer choice that fits this prediction. Choice (A) refers to *different sorts of speeches,* which could refer to *arguments* versus *no arguments.* Keep (A). Choice (B) may be attractive because of the reference to *more arguments than assertions,* but the text does not explicitly say what the gender of *some well-meaning people* is. Eliminate (B). Choice (C) can be eliminated. Although the phrase *may not have expected* might look good on its own, the answer as a whole clearly does not match the prediction. Choice (D) can be eliminated, because the arguments weren't *unexpected.* It was the lack of arguments that was surprising. Choice (A) is the correct answer.

42. **D** This question asks why the author mentions the number of gallons in discussing fracking. Use the given line reference to check: *As many as 25 fracture stages (per horizontal leg) may be involved in preparing a single site for production, each requiring injection of more than 400,000 gallons of water—a possible total of more than 10 million gallons before the well is fully operational.* Phrases like *as many as* and *more than* are there to draw attention to the size and scale of these numbers. Choice (A) can be eliminated because of the extreme language of the word *inevitable* and because it does not address the size of the fracking operation. Choice (B) can be eliminated because this passage discusses a single method, fracking, for extracting natural gas from shale. Choice (C) can be eliminated because while water might be described as a *basic element*, there is no indication that *only a few* of these basic elements are at play in fracking. Choice (D) should be kept because it reflects the passage's language of size and scale. Choice (D) is the correct answer.

43. **C** This question asks for some positive aspect of fracking in Passage 1. Notice that the following question is a best evidence question, so this question and Q44 can be answered in tandem. Look at the answers for Q44 first. The lines in (44A) mention that the natural gas from fracking can *accommodate the country's domestic demand for natural gas at current levels of consumption for more than a hundred years.* These lines match with (43C), which paraphrases that information. Connect these two answers. Next, consider the lines for (44B). These lines describe the way that high-pressure water is used to perforate the shale layer. The shale layer is mentioned in (43B), so those answers can be connected, though the connection is tentative. Next, consider the lines for (44C). These lines complete the description of how fracking extracts natural gas

from the shale layer, but the lines have no match in Q43, so (44C) can be eliminated. Next, consider the lines for (44D). These lines set up the discussion of water contamination and pollution in the next paragraph, but the lines have no match in Q43, so (44D) can be eliminated. Without any support from Q44, (43A) and (43D) can be eliminated. Consider the remaining pairs of answer choices in the context of the passage. The positive aspect of fracking is that it produces a lot of natural gas. Choices (43B) and (44B) can be eliminated because they do not contain this positive aspect. Choices (43C) and (44A) are the correct answers.

44. **A** (See explanation above.)

45. **A** This question asks why the author discusses the *aquifer* in the given lines. Use the line reference to find the window in which the *aquifer* is discussed. In the final paragraph of Passage 1, the aquifer is mentioned twice: *Drillers developing a well must take exceptional care to minimize contact between the wellbore and the surrounding aquifer—often the source of nearby residents' drinking water* and *It is essential that monitoring be in place to ensure the continuing integrity of the seal isolating the well from the aquifer even* after *the well has been fully exploited and abandoned.* In both sentences, the *aquifer* is mentioned as something that must be isolated and protected from the outflowing water used to frack. Choice (A) should be kept because it points to the *significant risk* that the aquifer could be contaminated. Choice (B) may address the concerns of those who worry about fracking, but it does not *dispute* those concerns, so (B) can be eliminated. Choice (C) can also be eliminated because the word *aquifer* does not appear before the final paragraph of Passage 1. Choice (D) can be eliminated because there is no indication that water contamination is a *new finding.* Choice (A) is the correct answer.

46. **B** This question asks for the meaning of the word *integrity* in this context. Remember the Vocab-in-Context strategy. Cross out the word, and use the surrounding context to fill in another word that makes sense based on the passage. Earlier sentences refer to the need to *minimize contact between the wellbore and the surrounding aquifer* and to *failures to isolate the drilling liquids.* The word in the blank should therefore mean something like "solidness," or any of a number of words that mean the opposite of "leakiness." Choice (A) does provide one definition of the word *integrity*, but that definition does not agree with the prediction based on the context above, so (A) can be eliminated. Choice (B) matches the prediction, so it should be kept. Choice (C) may be deceptive because this paragraph discusses water at such length, but the word *moisture* does not match the prediction and should be eliminated. Choice (D) provides another possible definition of the word *integrity*, but that definition does not match the context, so (D) can be eliminated. Choice (B) is the correct answer.

47. **D** This question asks for some aspect of Passage 2's main idea—something negative, as evidenced by the word *but* in the question. Because this question deals with Passage 2 as a whole, it is best to save it for later, after the more detail-oriented questions. The evidence appears throughout the passage—the first paragraph describes fracking's usefulness, but the remaining two paragraphs discuss its risks. The last paragraph is vicious in its criticism of *Weak safeguards*

*and inadequate oversight.* In short, the author of Passage 2 sees the potential value of fracking, but he does not consider it to be regulated in a way that protects local populations. Choice (A) does not address safety, only cost, so this answer can be eliminated. Choice (B) might be true, but it is not addressed in the passage, so it can be eliminated. Choice (C) is deceptive because while the author of Passage 2 does believe that industry executives flout the rules, there is no indication that these executives believe *they can mine resources from any place they choose.* This is extreme language that is not supported by the passage. Eliminate (C). Choice (D) effectively paraphrases the evidence presented in the passage, so it is the correct answer.

48.　**C**　This question asks for the meaning of the word *roughshod* in this context. Remember the Vocab-in-Context strategy. Cross out the word, and use the surrounding context to fill in another word that makes sense based on the passage. These lines continue the author's critique of industry leaders and overseers, who have created insufficient regulations and have been lax in enforcing the regulations that do exist. Therefore, the word in the blank should mean something like "without restriction" or "without care." Choice (A) could certainly describe the industries that have used fracking to generate a good deal of natural gas, but this does not match the prediction, so (A) can be eliminated. Choice (B) could also describe the industries that have quickly transformed certain rural landscapes, but this does not match with the prediction, so (B) can be eliminated. Choice (C) matches nicely with "without restriction" and "without care," so it should be kept. Choice (D) is deceptive because the sentence describes industrial processes, but the word in the blank should mean "without restriction," and (D) does not match. Choice (C) is the correct answer.

49.　**B**　This questions asks about the relationship between the two passages. This question should be done last because it asks about the main ideas of both passages. Passage 1 gives an overview of the process of fracking and hints at some of its dangers. Passage 2 is primarily concerned with these dangers and is less admiring of fracking's ability to extract natural resources. Choice (A) can be eliminated because Passage 1's author is not blind to the dangers of fracking and his attitude could not be described as *optimistic confidence.* Choice (B) should be kept because it offers a reasonable paraphrase of the relationship between the two passages. Choice (C) can be eliminated because there is no indication that the author of Passage 1 would disapprove of any particular regulations. Choice (D) can also be eliminated because Passage 2 is less concerned with the process of fracking than is Passage 1. Choice (B) is the correct answer.

50.　**C**　This question asks how the author of Passage 2 might respond to the referenced lines in Passage 1. The lines in Passage 1 discuss both the care that drillers must take to ensure that pollution does not occur and the risks associated with such pollution. Notice that the following question is a best evidence question, so this question and Q51 can be answered in tandem. Look at the answers in Q51 first. The lines in (51A) discuss the expansion of the mining industry. There is no match for this answer choice in Q50, so (51A) can be eliminated. Next, consider the lines for (51B), which continue the discussion of the proliferation of the practice of fracking. These lines match with (50A), which cites the mining industry's success and growth.

Connect these two answers. The lines for (51C) refer in a general way to increased industrial production, but they do not address the risks of drilling in particular. Choice (51C) can be eliminated because it does not match with any of the answers in Q50. Next, consider the lines for (51D). These lines match almost exactly with (50C), so these two answers should be connected. Without any support from Q51, (50B) and (50D) can be eliminated. Consider the remaining pairs of answer choices in the context of the passage. Passage 2's tone is overwhelmingly critical, so the author of Passage 2 is not likely to cite the successes of the mining industry in response to a claim about drillers' risks. Choices (50A) and (51B) can be eliminated because they are not sufficiently critical. Choices (50C) and (51D) are the correct answers.

51.  **D**  (See explanation above.)

52.  **C**  This question asks for something that is *implicit* (or implied) in Passage 2 and *explicit* (or stated outright) in Passage 1. Consider each answer separately and use POE. Choice (A) can be eliminated because Passage 2 explicitly states that fracking causes air and water pollution, and Passage 1 is concerned only with water pollution. Choice (B) can be eliminated because Passage 2 mentions the *millions of gallons of water used in fracking operations* but doesn't give any indication that it could also be *billions*. Passage 2 also focuses on the effects of fracking rather than the process. Choice (C) should be kept because Passage 2 addresses the effects of fracking on drinking water but does not specifically mention animals, whereas Passage 1 states explicitly, *Serious problems have arisen ... including cases where well water used for drinking became so contaminated that human and animal health was threatened*. Choice (D) can be eliminated because neither passage addresses the costs in setting up wells for drilling. Choice (C) is the correct answer.

# Section 2: Writing and Language

1.  **A**  The words *variety* and *difference* mean roughly the same thing in this context, so having versions of both words in the same answer would be redundant. The best choice is therefore (A), which contains only the word *variety*.

2.  **B**  All choices express essentially the same idea, so choose the one that expresses that idea in a way that is consistent with the tone of the passage. Choices (A) and (D) are too informal and can be eliminated. Choice (C) is too vague in its mention of *something elusive*. This leaves (B), which expresses a definitive idea and does so in a way that is in keeping with the tone of the passage.

3.  **C**  The subject of the underlined verb is *movements*, which is plural and therefore requires a plural verb, thus eliminating (A) and (B). Choice (D) would not make sense in the context, because it changes the meaning, saying that the movements *used* to do something. Instead, they are being used to do something. Only (C) remains, which matches the rest of the paragraph with its tense and the subject of the sentence with the plural verb *are*.

4.   **B**   As the paragraph now stands, its last sentence contains an ambiguous pronoun. It is unclear whether the *it* at the beginning of the last sentence refers to *difference, therapeutic horseback riding, hippotherapy, way,* or *ailment.* The addition of the new sentence would clarify that pronoun, so the sentence should be inserted, thus eliminating (C) and (D). In addition, the sentence helps to further clarify the differences between *therapeutic horseback riding* and *hippotherapy,* making (B) the correct answer.

5.   **B**   The first and second sentences of this paragraph describe the different applications of hippotherapy within different disciplines, stating that many fields *use the basic tenets of hippotherapy, but they each provide a unique spin on the practice.* Choice (A) would not contribute a useful detail in this regard, and (C) and (D) do not actually offer any specific examples. Choice (B) is therefore the best of the available answer choices in that it describes the work of occupational therapists by providing a specific example.

6.   **D**   The underlined verb should be consistent with the other verb in this part of the sentence, *achieve.* This eliminates all choices except for (D), which contains the verb *recommend,* which is in the simple present and matches *achieve.*

7.   **B**   The clues in this sentence are the references to *therapists* who are concerned with *physical aspects.* The only other sentence that discusses physical therapists is sentence 2. Sentence 4 should therefore go after sentence 1 because it refers *back* to the physical therapists mentioned earlier in the paragraph. Therefore, the best answer is (B).

8.   **B**   Although the underlined portion makes it seem that *new* and *certified* are both adjectives modifying a single noun, in fact, *new* is the end of the previous idea and *certified* is the beginning of the next one. The first idea, *Because the discipline is relatively new,* is incomplete and introduces the second idea, so there should be a comma after the word *new,* eliminating (D). There is no reason to insert a pause in the phrase *certified hippotherapists,* so the best available answer is (B).

9.   **B**   The words *Just as* at the beginning of the sentence require the words *so too* to complete the idiom, in the same way that *neither* requires *nor* or *not only* requires *but also.* Given the necessity of the words *so* and *too,* (A), (C), and (D) can all be eliminated, leaving only (B).

10.   **D**   In this sentence, choose a word that establishes the relationship between the *skeptics* and the *doctors and researchers.* Choices (B) and (C) can be eliminated because the relationship they create is illogical. Choice (A) can also be eliminated because it implies a division between doctors and researchers, where none is stated in the passage. Only (D) remains, suggesting that the *skeptics* are those *among* the medical community at large.

11.   **B**   Read the question carefully. It asks for a choice that *restates the main argument of the passage.* The passage as a whole is about hippotherapy, so this should be in the answer, eliminating (C). Choice (D) undermines the passage's claim that hippotherapy is gaining in popularity. Choice (A) mentions hippotherapy, but it can be eliminated because it is too informal and cites only

a minor detail rather than the passage's central argument. Only (B) remains, as it fulfills the goal outlined in the question.

12. **B** The word *elicit* is a verb meaning "to evoke or draw out." The word *illicit* is an adjective meaning "illegal." In this case, nothing illegal is being described, and the underlined part of speech is a verb, so (C) and (D) can be eliminated. Then, the subject of the underlined verb is *way*, which is singular, and thus requires the singular verb *elicits*, as in (B).

13. **D** Choice (A) creates a comma splice because it separates two complete ideas—*It was Marco Polo who crossed the desert on his way to China* and *he described the sound he heard as "a variety of musical instruments"*—with only a comma. Choices (B) and (C) create the same mistake. Only (D) fixes the mistake by making the first part of the sentence incomplete.

14. **A** The word *cello* is the last word in the phrase *that odd confluence of pipe organ and cello*. As the comma before the word *that* indicates, this phrase is meant to be set off as unnecessary information. Therefore, in order to remain consistent with the non-underlined part of the sentence, the entire phrase should be set off with commas, as in (A).

15. **A** Choice (B) can be eliminated because it uses a semicolon to set off a complete idea from an incomplete idea, when a semicolon should be used to separate only complete ideas. Choice (D) can be eliminated because it contains two complete ideas but insufficient punctuation—only a comma, not a semicolon or a period. Choices (A) and (C) state the same idea, but (A) does so more concisely, so (A) is the better of the two answers.

16. **C** This paragraph shifts the focus from the desert to the ocean, so there must be a phrase or sentence at the beginning to signal that shift, thus eliminating (D). Choices (A) and (B) provide this transition, but they do so in wordy, awkward ways. Choice (C) is relatively simple, but it does not contain any less information that (A) and (B), and it fulfills the purpose outlined in the question.

17. **C** The passage as a whole is all about sound—the sound of the seemingly silent desert sands or the seemingly silent ocean. The passage is mainly concerned with showing that these, especially the ocean, are actually noisy places. The proposed sentence goes against that general argument, so the sentence should not be added to the passage at all, thus making (C) the most appropriate answer.

18. **A** The underlined pronoun refers back to the word *ocean*, which is singular. The plural pronouns given in (C) and (D) can therefore be eliminated. Then, the sentence is referring to the *ocean's unwillingness*, so the possessive form *its* should be used, not the contraction *it's*. The best answer is thus (A).

19. **B** All four answers express essentially the same idea, but (A), (C), and (D) do so in oddly informal language. Only (B) is in keeping with the general tone of the passage and is therefore the best answer.

20. **D** The line graph and the bar graph on the chart show almost no consistency with one another, so the choices that describe a consistent relationship—(A), (B), and (C)—can be eliminated. Only (D) accurately describes the chart.

21. **A** Because the trends in this chart are so erratic, it is crucial to work with only single data points. At the point in March described earlier in the sentence, when there were 40 whale sightings, the average was approximately 14. Choice (A) captures this relationship. Choice (B) is not supported in the chart because summer months are not shown. Choice (C) is false by any measure. Choice (D) suggests that over 20 whales migrate every day in some other months (whatever those coldest winter months are), a claim which is not substantiated by information in the chart.

22. **A** Read the question carefully. It asks for *a conclusion that points toward the role that sound might play in future research into different ecosystems*. In fact, the paragraph already contains this information, so there is no reason to add a new sentence. In order words, that goal can be fulfilled most directly and concisely with NO CHANGE to the passage.

23. **D** Punctuation should only be used when it has a clear and definite purpose. In this case, there is no need for any punctuation, so the best available option is to eliminate punctuation entirely, as (D) does.

24. **C** When given the option to DELETE the underlined portion, give it serious consideration. It is often correct. In this case, however, the underlined portion must be kept—without it, there is only a comma separating two complete ideas. This eliminates (D). This sentence and the next one create a sequence—from 1929 to 1932. Therefore, the best of the available answers will be a word that indicates time, as only (C), *When*, does.

25. **A** This and all subsequent paragraphs are about Roosevelt and his legislative action when he took office in 1933. Of the four answers, the only one that mentions Roosevelt is (A), and this answer effectively sets up the information that is to follow.

26. **C** This sentence describes Roosevelt's action to send *government workers to inspect each bank*. The reports from these inspectors would allow government officials to determine *which banks would be safe and sustainable to reopen*. There is a cause-and-effect relationship established between these ideas, which (A) and (B) disrupt. Choice (D) provides the appropriate relationship, but this word cannot be used idiomatically with the non-underlined word, *determining*, that follows. Only (C) remains—it establishes the correct relationship and can be used in the context.

27. **B** Read the question carefully. It asks for the choice that *provides the most specific information on the areas that Roosevelt hoped to stimulate*. Choices (A), (C), and (D) may each be true, but none fulfills the question's demand for *specific information*. Only (B) does so in listing two specific sectors of the economy.

28. **C** This sentence refers to an action that would control *demand*. The best combination of words that refers to this action is *level off*, as in (C). Choice (A), *level with*, means "to be honest with." Choices (B) and (D) do not create idiomatically logical phrases.

29. **C** Read the question carefully. It asks for a detail that *emphasizes the importance of the TVA in Roosevelt's larger economic project*, a project, as the passage indicates, of stimulating the economy and reducing unemployment. Choices (A) and (D) do not fulfill any part of this purpose, and (B) gives a detail about the TVA but does not connect it to Roosevelt's larger project. Therefore, (C) most effectively fulfills the goal outlined in the question.

30. **B** All four answers express essentially the same idea, so the most effective answer will be the most concise. In this case, that answer is (B), which expresses in a single word what the other answers express in more.

31. **A** The underlined pronoun refers back to *Roosevelt's "New Deal,"* which is singular, thus eliminating (C), which is plural, and (D), which is not a pronoun. The underlined pronoun should be the contraction *it is*, as in (A). The possessive pronoun given in (B) would create a sentence fragment, in addition to the fact that the *it* is not in possession of anything.

32. **A** This sentence refers to the *day-to-day lives* belonging to *people*. Therefore, the best answer is (A), which gives the possessive form *people's*. Choice (C) is not possessive. With (B) and (D), remember that everything that comes before the apostrophe must be a word—*peoples* (when used in this way) is not a word.

33. **C** This paragraph describes a debate about the legacy of Roosevelt's legislative activity, citing arguments from those on either side of the issue. Only (C) remains neutral in this debate with the words *In either case*.

34. **D** All four choices express a similar idea, that of an actress who excels in some way. Choice (A) is informal and potentially sarcastic, so it can be eliminated. Choices (B) and (C) are unnecessarily elevated, as they are written in a tone that is not in keeping with that of the rest of the passage. Choice (D) is the most direct and keeps with the tone of the passage, in that it is sufficiently formal but not overblown in its use of language.

35. **B** This sentence states that *the Japanese film industry had divided loyalties at the time,* and it cites a *debt to American cinema* and *tensions with the United States and others,* which led to war. There is no contrast established in the sentence, eliminating (A) and (C). Nor was it the Japanese film industry's loyalties that *enabled* the tensions between nations that led to war, eliminating (D). Only (B) works effectively in this contrast by establishing the correct relationship between the ideas in the sentence.

36. **D** This paragraph mentions the Japanese film industry's divided loyalties and tensions between nations, and the underlined portion explains how these tensions played out in the particular

film. The underlined portion should be kept because this information is not given anywhere else in the passage, thus eliminating (A) and (B). The information in the underlined portion refers to something that *would become Axis propaganda* and is more general than specific, eliminating (C). Choice (D) is the correct answer in that it correctly states that the underlined portion should be kept because it clarifies the idea about divided loyalties that comes before it and connects to the sentence that follows it.

37. **D** This part of the sentence describes the film *Late Spring* in the present tense, as evidenced by the verbs *plays* and *is*. The underlined verb should therefore be in the present tense as well, eliminating (A), (B), and (C), leaving only (D) as the correct answer.

38. **A** This paragraph as a whole celebrates Hara's performance in *Late Spring*. The last sentence of the paragraph contributes to that celebration, so it should be introduced with a word that indicates a continuation, as only (A) does. Choice (B) can be eliminated because this sentence contains a detail, not a summation. Choice (C) can be eliminated because there is nothing in this sentence that contrasts with previous information. Choice (D) can be eliminated because it suggests a concurrent event, when in fact this sentence gives an additional detail about an event already being described.

39. **B** All four answers express essentially the same idea, so the most effective answer will be the most concise. In this case, that answer is (B), which expresses in a two words what the other answers express in more.

40. **C** This sentence refers to *very few sets*, suggesting that the terms in this list must each represent one of those sets. Choice (A) suggests that one of those sets is an *office kitchen*, which does not make sense. Choices (B) and (D) create similar errors in suggesting *living* and *kitchen living*, respectively, as possible sets. Only (C) creates a logical list by separating as possible sets an *office*, a *kitchen*, and a *living room*.

41. **D** The word *council* is used only as a noun and typically refers to a group of people brought together to deliberate a significant issue. The word *counsel* can be used as either a noun or a verb, and the word refers to either giving advice (in the verb form) or the advice itself (in the noun form). In this sentence, the word refers to the advice of *her friends and family*, so *counsel* must be used, eliminating (A) and (B). Then, the character is receiving the advice *of* this group, making (D) the better of the remaining answers.

42. **D** The first part of the sentence characterizes the plot and conflicts as *simple*, while the second part suggests that the plots are also very *profound*. As a result, the conjunction that links the ideas must indicate a contrast, eliminating (A), (B), and (C) and leaving only (D).

43. **A** The underlined pronoun refers back to the noun *viewers*, meaning that the pronoun must be plural. Of the available choices, only (A), *their*, provides such a pronoun. Though *your* can be plural, the viewers would not be referred to as "you."

44.  **B**  Note the first word of the proposed sentence: *Others*. This word must link with some first group. That group is indicated in sentence 3 by the word *Some*. Therefore, the most effective placement of the proposed sentence would be between sentences 3 and 4, or after sentence 3, as (B) states.

## Section 3: Math (No Calculator)

1.  **B**  Come up with the expression in bite-sized pieces. Notice that all of the choices use the variable *y*, which represents the number of hours for (A) and (B) but the number of essays for (C) and (D). The number of essays is given but the number of hours is not. Therefore, the variable has to represent the unknown value, the number of hours. Eliminate (C) and (D). The editor is paid $25 per hour. The total amount that the editor is paid for his or her time can be found by multiplying 25 by the number of hours. The remaining choices use *y* to represent the number of hours, so the product is 25*y*. Eliminate the remaining choice that doesn't include 25*y*, which is (A). Only one choice remains. To see why (B) is correct, note that the $50 bonus must be added to the editor's earnings for time spent. Also, the bonus is for *all three* essays rather than *each* essay, so it should only be added once. The answer is (B).

2.  **B**  Use bite-sized pieces and eliminate answer choices after each step. Start by combining $-mn^2 + 2mn^2$ to get $mn^2$, and use this to eliminate (C) and (D). Now combine the $2n^2$ terms, which cancel and should not appear in the correct answer. Use this to eliminate (A). The answer is (B).

3.  **B**  The question is made more complicated by fractions, so get rid of the fractions. Multiply both sides of the first equation by 12 to get $x - y = 156$. Multiply both sides of the second equation by 6 to get $2x - y = 120$. Subtract the first equation from the second equation.

$$
\begin{array}{r}
2x - y = \phantom{0}120 \\
-\underline{(x - y = \phantom{0}156)} \\
x \phantom{- y} = -36
\end{array}
$$

Eliminate any choice that doesn't include $x = -36$. Eliminate (A), (C), and (D). Only one choice remains. To see why $y = -192$, plug $x = -36$ into the non-fraction version of the first equation to get $-36 - y = 156$, and solve for *y*. The answer is (B).

4.  **D**  The problem discusses how many shoes Kelly must sell in a month. Eliminate (C) because 300 days does not fit the problem. Since *x* is the number of days she works each month, plug in $x = 0$ to see how many shoes she starts with at the beginning of the month. The value for *S* would be 300 at day 0. Therefore, (D) is the answer.

5.  **C**  Since there are actual numbers in the answer choices, plug in the answers, starting with one of the middle two choices. Start with (B), which is 35. The question asks for the number of all-day passes sold, so assume that there were 35 all-day passes sold. Since there were a total of 70

passes sold, there must have been a total of 70 − 35 = 35 half-day passes sold. The park sells all-day passes for $80 and half-day passes for $40. Since there were 35 of each sold, the park took in a total of $80 × 35 = $2,800 for all-day passes and $40 × 35 = $1,400 for half-day passes. Therefore, the park took in a total of $2,800 + $1,400 = $4,200. However, the question states that the park took in $4,600, so eliminate (B). Since the total should be greater, the park needs to sell more of the $80 tickets. Therefore, the number of all-day passes sold has to increase. Eliminate (A) as well. Only (C) and (D) remain. Since 60 is easier to work with than 45, try (D). If 60 all-day passes are sold, then 70 − 60 = 10 half-day passes are sold. The park takes in $60 × 80 = $4,800 from all-day passes. Since this is already too high, eliminate (D). Only one choice remains. The answer is (C).

6.   **D**   To find the solutions to a quadratic equation, either factor or use the quadratic formula. When

the coefficient on the $x^2$ term is not 1, factoring is more difficult than usual but not impossible.

Since 5 is prime, one factor will have $5x$ and the other will have $x$, so write $(5x \quad )(x \quad ) = 0$.

Now find two factors of 6 that fit the equation. Since the sign on 6 is negative, one factor is

negative and one is positive. To fit the equation, one of the factors must be multiplied by 5

and added to the other to get 7. The only pairs of factors of 6 are 1 and 6 and 2 and 3. Since

$5 \times 2 + (-3) = 7$, the equation can be factored as $(5x − 3)(x + 2) = 0$. Set each factor to 0 to

get $5x − 3 = 0$ and $x + 2 = 0$. Solve each factor to get $x = \dfrac{3}{5}$ and $x = -2$. Another way to

find the values for $x$ of a quadratic in the form $ax^2 + bx + c$ is to use the quadratic formula,

$x = \dfrac{-b \pm \sqrt{b^2 - 4ac}}{2a}$. In this case, $a = 5$, $b = 7$, and $c = -6$. Either way of solving yields the

solutions $\dfrac{3}{5}$ and $-2$. Since the question specifies that $a < b$, $a = -2$ and $b = \dfrac{3}{5}$. The question

asks for $b − a$, which is $\dfrac{3}{5} - (-2) = \dfrac{3}{5} + 2 = \dfrac{3}{5} + \dfrac{10}{5} = \dfrac{13}{5}$. The answer is (D).

7.   **A**   Look at the denominators of the fractions to find easy numbers to plug in. Try $t = 11$. Now look at the numerator to see that $t + u = 12$, so $u$ would then equal 1. Plug these values into the answers to see which is true. Only (A) works, so it must be the answer.

8.   **C**   Opposite sides of a parallelogram are parallel, and parallel lines have the same slope. Use

the slope formula: $\dfrac{y_1 - y_2}{x_1 - x_2}$. Segment $AB$ has a slope of $\dfrac{18 - 0}{0 - (-6)} = \dfrac{18}{6} = 3$. Segment $DC$ is parallel to $AB$ and must have the same slope, so $3 = \dfrac{0 - (-12)}{j - 0}$. Then $3 = \dfrac{12}{j}$, so $3j = 12$, and

$j = 4$. The answer is (C).

9.  **B**  Since the problem involves algebra and asks for the least possible value of $y$, plug in the answers

starting with the smallest number. Try (D). If $y = 4$, then $x = \dfrac{4(4 - 3)}{2} = \dfrac{4(1)}{2} = \dfrac{4}{2} = 2$, so a

polygon with 4 sides only has 2 diagonals. This is not at least 7, so eliminate (D) and try (C). If

$y = 5$, then $x = \dfrac{5(5 - 3)}{2} = \dfrac{5(2)}{2} = \dfrac{10}{2} = 5$. This is not at least 7, so eliminate (C) and try (B). If

$y = 6$, then $x = \dfrac{6(6 - 3)}{2} = \dfrac{6(3)}{2} = \dfrac{18}{2} = 9$. This is greater than 7, so choose (B).

10.  **A**  The question asks for the value of the car $y$ years from now. Determine the value of the car each

year. The car is driven 10,000 miles each year. Set up a proportion to determine the decrease

in the value each year. Since the car's value decreases \$500 for every 1,000 miles driven, set

up a proportion: $\dfrac{\$500}{1{,}000 \text{ miles}} = \dfrac{x}{10{,}000 \text{ miles}}$. Cross-multiply to get $1{,}000x = 5{,}000{,}000$.

Divide both sides by 1,000 to get $x = 5{,}000$. Therefore, the car's value decreases by \$5,000

each year. Plug in a value for $y$, such as $y = 2$, and calculate the value of the car. After 2 years,

the car's value decreases by \$10,000, so the value then would be \$13,000. Go through each

answer, plug in $y = 2$, and eliminate each choice that is not equal to \$13,000. Choice (A) is

$\$23{,}000 - \$5{,}000(2) = \$23{,}000 - \$10{,}000 = \$13{,}000$. Keep (A). Choice (B) is \$23,000 −

$\$500(2) = \$23{,}000 - \$1{,}000 = \$22{,}000$. Eliminate (B). Choice (C) is $\$23{,}000 - \$0.02(2) =$

$\$23{,}000 - \$0.04 = \$22{,}999.96$. Eliminate (C). Choice (D) is $\$23{,}000 - \$0.0002(2) = \$23{,}000$

$- \$0.0004 = \$22{,}999.9996$. Eliminate (D). The answer is (A).

11.  **D**  The problem states that the system of equations has no solution, which means that the lines

are parallel and the slopes are equal. The slope of a line in standard form $Ax + By = C$ is given

by $-\dfrac{A}{B}$, so the slope of the first line is $-\dfrac{7}{-c} = \dfrac{7}{c}$. The slope of the second line is $-\dfrac{5}{2}$. Set the slopes equal to each other to solve for $c$: $\dfrac{7}{c} = -\dfrac{5}{2}$. Now cross-multiply to get $-5c = 14$, and divide both sides by $-5$ to find that $c = -\dfrac{14}{5}$. Alternatively, convert each line into the form $y = mx + b$ to find the slopes and set them equal. In either case, the answer is (D).

12. **B**    Start by multiplying both the numerator and denominator of the given expression by the complex conjugate of the denominator: $\dfrac{4 - 7i}{6 + 3i} \times \dfrac{6 - 3i}{6 - 3i}$. Use FOIL to get $\dfrac{24 - 12i - 42i + 21i^2}{36 - 18i + 18i - 9i^2}$. Combine like terms to get $\dfrac{24 - 54i + 21i^2}{36 - 9i^2}$. Plug in $i^2 = -1$, since the problem says that $i = \sqrt{-1}$. This gives $\dfrac{24 - 54i + 21(-1)}{36 - 9(-1)} = \dfrac{24 - 54i - 21}{36 + 9} = \dfrac{3 - 54i}{45}$. To make this look like the answer choices, turn the expression into two fractions and reduce: $\dfrac{3}{45} - \dfrac{54i}{45} = \dfrac{1}{15} - \dfrac{6i}{5}$, which is (B).

13. **C**    If a polynomial is divisible by $x$, each term in the simplified form of the polynomial must have $x$ as a factor. Write $g(x)$ in simplified form. If $g(x) = 2(x^2 + 14x + 7) - 7(x + c)$, distribute to get $g(x) = 2x^2 + 28x + 14 - 7x - 7c$. Combine like terms to get $g(x) = 2x^2 + 21x + 14 - 7c$. The two terms without $x$ as a factor are 14 and $-7c$. In order for the polynomial to be divisible by $x$, $14 - 7c$ must equal 0, so that only the terms with $x$ as a factor remain. If $14 - 7c = 0$, add $7c$ to both sides to get $14 = 7c$. Divide both sides by 7 to get $c = 2$. The answer is (C).

14. **C**    Plugging in would normally be a good idea for a question like this, but this is the no-calculator section. Exponent questions are always easier to handle when the bases are the same, so rewrite 27 as $3^3$. Use the rules of exponents to work out the expression as $\dfrac{27^r}{3^s} = \dfrac{(3^3)^r}{3^s} = \dfrac{3^{3r}}{3^s}$. Now that the terms have the same base, remember the MADSPM rule that division means subtraction of the exponents, so $\dfrac{3^{3r}}{3^s} = 3^{3r - s}$. The problem states that $3r - s = 10$, so $3^{3r - s} = 3^{10}$ and (C) is the answer.

15. **A**    This question contains variables in the question and in the answer choices, so plug in. Use $n = 10$ so the calculations are straightforward. Then, $\dfrac{4n + 9}{n - 5} = \dfrac{4(10) + 9}{10 - 5} = \dfrac{40 + 9}{5} = \dfrac{49}{5}$. This is the target value, so plug 10 in for $n$ in the choices to find the one that matches the

target. Start with (A): $4 + \dfrac{29}{n-5} = 4 + \dfrac{29}{10-5} = 4 + \dfrac{29}{5} = \dfrac{20}{5} + \dfrac{29}{5} = \dfrac{49}{5}$. This matches the

target, so keep (A) but remember to check all four choices when plugging in. Move to (B):

$4 + \dfrac{9}{n-5} = 4 + \dfrac{9}{10-5} = 4 + \dfrac{9}{5} = \dfrac{20}{5} + \dfrac{9}{5} = \dfrac{29}{5}$. This doesn't match the target, so eliminate

(B). Try (C): $4 - \dfrac{9}{5} = \dfrac{20}{5} - \dfrac{9}{5} = \dfrac{11}{5}$. This doesn't match the target, so eliminate (C). Try (D):

$-\dfrac{4+9}{5} = -\dfrac{13}{5}$, which will be a negative number and won't match the target, so eliminate (D).

Choice (A) is the answer.

16. **800** To solve for $x$, isolate the variable. First, add 3 to both sides to get $40 = \dfrac{x}{20}$. Then, multiply both sides by 20 to get $x = 40 \times 20 = 800$. The answer is 800.

17. $\dfrac{8}{10}, \dfrac{4}{5}$, or **0.8**

In any triangle with angles of 90°, $x°$, and $y°$, $\cos x = \sin y$. Therefore, if $\cos p = 0.8$, then

$\sin q = 0.8$ as well. Alternatively, remember from SOHCAHTOA that the cosine of an angle

is the ratio of the adjacent side to the hypotenuse. The value 0.8 can also be written as $\dfrac{8}{10}$.

Plug in 8 as the base of the triangle (adjacent to $p°$) and 10 as the hypotenuse. Sine is opposite

over hypotenuse. To find the sine of $q°$, find the opposite side, which is 8, and the hypotenuse,

which is 10. The sine of $q°$ is therefore $\dfrac{8}{10}$, which can also be written as $\dfrac{4}{5}$ or 0.8. Any of these

are acceptable answers.

18. **25** Plug in a value for $a$ that will be easy to use without a calculator. If $a = 2$, then

$\dfrac{9(5a)^2}{(3a)^2} = \dfrac{9(5 \times 2)^2}{(3 \times 2)^2} = \dfrac{9(10)^2}{(6)^2} = \dfrac{9(100)}{36}$. Reduce this fraction now, rather than multiplying it

out, since 36 is divisible by 9. The fraction becomes $\dfrac{100}{4}$, which is 25. The answer is 25.

19. **20** Vertical angles are congruent, so $\angle HLI = \angle JLK$. Also, $\angle IHL = \angle KJL$ because $\overline{HI} \parallel \overline{JK}$. Like-

wise, $\angle HIL = \angle JKL$. These triangles are similar, and similar triangles have proportional side

lengths, so set up a proportion, which will help find $\overline{HJ}$: $\dfrac{3}{9} = \dfrac{5}{JL}$. Cross-multiply to find that

$45 = 3(\overline{JL})$, and divide both sides by 3 to find that $\overline{JL} = 15$. The question asks for the length of

$\overline{HJ}$, which is 5 (from $\overline{HL}$) plus 15 (from $\overline{JL}$) for a total length of 20, which is the answer.

20. **225**  Start by plugging $z = 5\sqrt{3}$ into the second equation to get $3(5\sqrt{3}) = \sqrt{3}y$. Distribute the 3 on the left side to get $15\sqrt{3} = \sqrt{3y}$. Square both sides to get rid of the square root signs: $225 \times 3 = 3y$. Divide both sides by 3 to get $225 = y$.

## Section 4: Math (Calculator)

1. **D**  Translate the information in the question into an expression in bite-sized pieces. The monthly fee is $20.00 and the data usage fee is $2.50 per gigabyte. Start with the fee for data usage. The usage is $2.50 per gigabyte used, so to get the fee in a month in which David used $g$ gigabytes, multiply $g$ by 2.50 to get $2.50g$. Eliminate any answer choice that doesn't include $2.50g$: (A), (B), and (C). Thus, only (D) remains. To determine why (D) is correct, note that the word *and* translates to +, so add 20 to $2.50g$ to get $20 + 2.50g$. The answer is (D).

2. **B**  The question asks for the greatest change between consecutive years. Go through each year and determine the change in each. From 2000 to 2001, there is a decrease of $50,000 – $40,000 = $10,000. From 2001 to 2002, there is an increase of $55,000 – $40,000 = $15,000. From 2002 to 2003, there is an increase of $60,000 – $55,000 = $5,000. From 2003 to 2004, there is an increase of $75,000 – $60,000 = $15,000. From 2004 to 2005, there is a decrease of $75,000 – $65,000 = $10,000. From 2005 to 2006, there is no change. From 2006 to 2007, there is an increase of $95,000 – $65,000 = $30,000. The greatest is $30,000, which is (B). Alternatively, ballpark. Look at the graph and notice that the change from 2006 to 2007 appears to be the steepest, so this difference would have to be the answer. The answer is (B).

3. **A**  There are variables in the answers, so plug in. Currently Jim can do 14 pull-ups in a minute. He believes that he can increase this amount by 7 each year. Therefore, he believes that in 1 year he can do $14 + 7 = 21$ pull-ups, and in 2 years he can do $21 + 7 = 28$ pull-ups. Now plug $y = 2$ into each of the choices and eliminate any that isn't equal to 28. Choice (A) is $7(2) + 14 = 28$, so keep (A). Choice (B) is $7(2) + 30 = 44$, so eliminate (B). Choice (C) is $14(2) + 7 = 35$, so eliminate (C). Choice (D) is $14 – 7(2) = 0$, so eliminate (D). The answer is (A).

4. **D**  The question gives an equation and a value for one of the variables in the equation. Plug in the given value to solve for the value of the other variable. If $v = 67$, the equation becomes $67 = 17 + 2.5t$. Subtract 17 from both sides to get $50 = 2.5t$. Divide both sides by 2.5 to get $t = 20$, so the answer is (D).

5. **A**  The question asks for the equation of a function that could possibly define $h$. Each of the equations in the choices is in factored form. If a factor of the equation of a function is in the form $(x – r)$, $r$ is one of the roots, or one of the $x$-intercepts. Since the roots of this function are $-4$, 2, and 4, the roots are $(x – (-4))$ or $(x + 4)$, $(x – 2)$, and $(x – 4)$. The only equation with all of these factors is (A), so the answer is (A).

6. **C** Translate the first statement into an equation. The phrase *three times a number n* translates to $3n$. The phrase *is added to* translates to +. The word *is* translates to =. Therefore, the sentence translates to $3n + 9 = 3$. Solve this for $n$: subtract 9 from both sides to get $3n = -6$, then divide both sides by 3 to get $n = -2$. This is (A). However, the question does not ask for the value of $n$, so (A) is a trap answer. The question asks for *the result when 4 times n is added to 14*. The phrase *4 times n* translates to $4n$. The phrase *is added to 14* translates to + 14. Therefore, *4 times n is added to 14* translates to $4n + 14$. Since $n = -2$, $4n + 14 = 4(-2) + 14 = -8 + 14 = 6$. The answer is (C).

7. **B** The question asks for how many 16-ounce cups can be filled from a 64-gallon urn. First, convert the 64 gallons into ounces. Use a proportion: $\dfrac{1 \text{ gallon}}{128 \text{ ounces}} = \dfrac{64 \text{ gallons}}{x \text{ ounces}}$. Cross-multiply to get $x = (128)(64) = 8{,}192$. Now determine the number of 16-ounce cups that can be filled from an 8,192-ounce urn. Use another proportion: $\dfrac{1 \text{ cup}}{16 \text{ ounces}} = \dfrac{y \text{ cups}}{8{,}192 \text{ ounces}}$. Cross-multiply to get $16y = 8{,}192$. Divide both sides by 16 to get $y = 512$. The answer is (B).

8. **C** To determine the slope of a line, use the slope formula, $slope = \dfrac{y_2 - y_1}{x_2 - x_1}$. Let $\left(1, -\dfrac{1}{3}\right)$ be $(x_1, y_1)$ and $\left(5, \dfrac{8}{3}\right)$ be $(x_2, y_2)$. The slope is $\dfrac{\dfrac{8}{3} - \left(-\dfrac{1}{3}\right)}{5 - 1} = \dfrac{\dfrac{8}{3} + \dfrac{1}{3}}{4} = \dfrac{\dfrac{9}{3}}{4} = \dfrac{3}{4}$. The answer is (C).

9. **A** The question asks for the average number of fish per tank. The average is $\dfrac{total}{number \text{ } of \text{ } things}$. The *things* in this case are the tanks. Since the title of the graph says that there are 18, the average is $\dfrac{total}{18}$. The *total* is the number of fish. To determine this, use the histogram. There are 2 tanks with 2 fish each, so these 2 tanks have a total of $2 \times 2 = 4$ fish. There are 4 tanks with 3 fish, so these 4 tanks have a total of $4 \times 3 = 12$ fish. There are no tanks with 4 fish, so ignore that column. There are 3 tanks with 5 fish, so these 3 tanks have a total of $3 \times 5 = 15$ fish. There are 5 tanks with 6 fish, so these 5 tanks have a total of $5 \times 6 = 30$ fish. There is 1 tank with 7 fish, so this 1 tank has a total of $1 \times 7 = 7$ fish. There are 3 tanks with 8 fish, so these 3 tanks have a total of $3 \times 8 = 24$ fish. Therefore, all the tanks have a total of $4 + 12 + 15 + 30 + 7 + 24 = 92$ fish, and the average number of fish per tank is $\dfrac{92}{18} = 5.\bar{1}$. The question asks for the *closest* choice, which is (A).

10. **A** The question asks for the design flaw in the survey. The survey was conducted to determine whether people in City C are more likely to work 9-to-5 office jobs than other jobs. The survey was conducted exclusively during the time in which people would be working at 9-to-5 office jobs.

Therefore, people at this type of job would be less likely to answer the call. Choice (A) matches the prediction, so keep (A). Choice (B) is population size. Population size is not necessarily a design flaw, since the population size is not given. Eliminate (B). Choice (C) is sample size. If the sample size were significantly less than the population size, this fact could lead to unreliable results. However, since population size is not known, sample size cannot be determined to be a design flaw. Eliminate (C). Choice (D) refers to the fact that the telephone was used. Since the problem does not mention telephone use by people with different types of jobs, there's no reason to believe that using a telephone to conduct the survey would make the results less reliable. Eliminate (D). The correct answer is (A).

11. **D** The question asks which graph could represent $y = p(x)$ and says that function $p$ has exactly four roots. A *root* of a function is an $x$-value for which the $y$-value is 0. The $y$-value is 0 for all points on the $x$-axis, so $p$ has to have exactly four $x$-intercepts (points where the graph intersects the $x$-axis). Go through each choice and determine the number of $x$-intercepts. Choices (A) and (C) have three $x$-intercepts, so eliminate these. Choice (B) has five intercepts. Since the question states that $p$ has *exactly* four roots rather than *at least* four, eliminate (B) as well. Only (D) has exactly four $x$-intercepts, so the answer is (D).

12. **A** The question states that 85% of the customers ordered the brunch special. Since the question asks for which choice could be the number of customers, plug in the answers by taking 85% of each choice. Eliminate any choice that doesn't result in a whole number of customers. Start with (A): 85% of 40 is $(0.85)(40) = 34$. Since this is a whole number, this could be the number of customers, so the answer is (A).

13. **A** The question includes variables and uses the phrase *in terms of*, so plug in. Since an equation is given with $d$ isolated, plug in for the other variables, $t$, $v$, and $h$, and calculate $d$. Let $t = 2$, $v = 10$, and $h = 20$. In this case, $d = -8t^2 + vt + h = -8(2)^2 + (10)(2) + 20 = 8$. The question asks for the value of $v$, so the target answer is 10. Go through the choices and eliminate any answer that is not 10. Choice (A) is $v = \dfrac{8 - 20}{2} + 8(2) = 10$, so keep (A). Choice (B) is $v = \dfrac{8 + 20}{2} - 8(2) = -2$, so eliminate (B). Choice (C) is $v = \dfrac{8 - 20 + 8}{2} = -2$, so eliminate (C). Choice (D) is $v = 8 + 20 - 8(2) = 12$, so eliminate (D). Only (A) matches, so the answer is (A).

14. **D** The question asks for what could be the median of 22 scores. The median of an even number of numbers is the average of the middle two when the numbers are listed in order. In this case, it is the average of the 11th and 12th score. Find the location of the 11th and 12th scores on the histogram. There is 1 score from 50 to 60. There are 4 scores from 60 to 70, so there are 5 scores from 50 to 70. There are 2 scores from 70 to 80, so there are 7 scores from 50 to 80. There are 11 scores from 80 to 90, so there are 18 scores from 50 to 90. Since the 11th and 12th scores were passed at the 80 to 90 interval, they must be in this interval. Therefore, the median must be within this interval, as well. The only choice within this interval is 84, so the answer is (D).

15. **C** The question asks for a percent, which is $\frac{part}{whole} \times 100$. The *part* is the total number of those surveyed who use public transit, which is 51, and the *whole* is the total number of those surveyed, which is 130. Therefore, the percent is $\frac{51}{130} \times 100 \approx 39$. The answer is (C).

16. **C** The proportion of people who fit the requirements in the survey can be expected to be the same proportion of people who will fit the requirements in the general population. First, find the number of commuters surveyed who used public transit and had an average daily commute of at least 1 hour. Find the column for *Commutes by Public Transit* and the row for *At least 1 hour*. At the intersection is 29, so this is the number of those surveyed who used public transit and had an average daily commute of at least 1 hour. Since the total number of those surveyed is 130 and the total population of the population is 13,000,000, set up the proportion $\frac{29}{130} = \frac{x}{13,000,000}$. Cross-multiply to get $130x = 377,000,000$. Divide both sides by 130 to get $x = 2,900,000$. The answer is (C).

17. **B** The question asks how many times more likely it is for a commuter whose average daily commute is less than 1 hour not to take public transit than it is for a commuter whose average daily commute is at least 1 hour not to take public transit. The term *more likely* refers to probability, so determine the probability of each. Go to the table and find the number of commuters who commute less than 1 hour and do NOT commute using public transit. Find the *Does Not Commute by Public Transit* column and the *Less than 1 hour* row. At the intersection is 46, so this is the number of commuters who commute less than 1 hour and do NOT commute using public transit. Now look in the same row under the *Total* column to find that the total number of commuters who commute less than 1 hour is 68. Therefore, the probability is $\frac{46}{68}$. Now do the same for the probability that someone who commutes at least one hour does not take public transit. Find the row for those who commute *At least 1 hour* and the columns for *Does Not Commute Using Public Transit* and *Total*. In this row, the number under *Does Not Commute by Public Transit* is 33 and the number under *Total* is 62, so the probability is $\frac{33}{62}$. The question asks *how many times more likely* is the first probability than the second. Set up the equation $\frac{46}{68} = \frac{33}{62}x$. Divide both sides by $\frac{33}{62}$ to get $x \approx 1.27$. The answer is (B).

18.   **C**   The question asks for the best conclusion from the study. The study takes a random sample of subjects without sleep disorders and gives half of them beverage *C*. The subjects who consume beverage *C* sleep less than the subjects who don't consume it. This would seem to indicate that beverage *C* caused people without sleep disorders to sleep less. Go through each of the choices. Choice (A) is incorrect because the study doesn't compare different caffeinated beverages. It only compares consuming beverage *C* to not consuming it. Choice (B) is incorrect, because the study does not indicate *substantial* loss is sleep. Furthermore, the sample only includes people without sleep disorders, so any conclusion must be restricted to this population. Choice (C) is similar to the prediction, so keep this choice. Choice (D), like (B), does not restrict the conclusion to people without sleep disorders. The answer is (C).

19.   **C**   The question involves algebra, asks for a value, and includes numbers in the answers, so plug in the answers. First, eliminate any answers that don't make sense: since *n* is 40% larger than the sum of the other three numbers, *n* will have to be greater than half of 1,764. Eliminate (A) and (B). Try one of the remaining answers, such as (D). If $n = 1,260$, then the remaining three numbers would add up to $1,764 - 1,260 = 504$. Since 1,260 is not 40% more than 504, eliminate (D) and choose (C). If desired, check (C): if $n = 1,029$, then the other three numbers add up to 735. Since 735 + 40% (735) = 735 + 294 = 1,029, (C) is the correct answer.

20.   **D**   The question asks how much more the 11.5 m³ object weighed than was predicted by the line of best fit. This question can be solved by determining the actual weight of the object and the weight predicted by the line of best fit. However, finding the actual amounts is not necessary. Instead, simply find the difference between the two. Volume is represented by the horizontal axis, so find 11.5 on the horizontal axis. Trace straight up to the data point. From that point, trace the line downward, counting the number of intervals to the line of best fit. There are four intervals. Go to the vertical axis to determine the number of kilograms per interval. The labels are 5,000 kilograms apart, and there are 5 intervals between each label. Therefore, each interval is $\frac{5,000}{5} = 1,000$, so 4 intervals are 4,000 kg. The answer is (D).

21.   **C**   The question asks the percent increase in total sales. Since the number of laptops and the number of tablets are different, don't just add the two percent increases. Thus, (D) is a trap answer. A percent change is always equal to the expression $\frac{difference}{original} \times 100$. The *original* is the total number of units sold last week, which is $90 + 210 = 300$. To get the difference, get the increase in laptops and the increase in tablets separately and then add. There is a fifty percent increase in laptop sales,

so the increase is $\dfrac{50}{100} \times 90 = 45$. There is a thirty percent increase in tablet sales, so the increase

is $\dfrac{30}{100} \times 210 = 63$. Therefore, the total *difference* is $45 + 63 = 108$, and the percent increase is

$\dfrac{108}{300} \times 100 = 36\%$. The answer is (C).

22.  **B**  According to the question, $\cos(x°) = \sin(y°)$. This can only be the case if the two angles are comple-mentary, meaning the measures of the two angles have a sum of 90°. The question asks for the value of $c$, and there are numbers in the answer choices, so plug in the answers. Start with (B). If $c = 15.5$, then $x = 3(15.5) - 23 = 23.5$ and $y = 66.5$, so $x + y = 23.5 + 66.5 = 90$. Thus, the two angles are complementary, and the answer is (B).

23.  **A**  The question asks for the maximum value for $-3 \le x \le 6$. This is the domain sketched in the graph, so only worry about the points on the sketch. The value of the function is equal to each $y$-value. Although the values of the function appear to be increasing toward $\infty$, they do not actually go to $\infty$ within the points sketched, so eliminate (D). Since the question asks for the maximum value of the function, which is the maximum $y$-value, find the highest point on the graph. This appears on the far left. Draw a horizontal line to the $y$-axis to see that this line crosses the $y$-axis at 4. Therefore, the $y$-value at this point, or the maximum value of the function, is 4. The answer is (A).

24.  **B**  The question says that the width is 8 feet more than 4 times the length. Take this statement and

translate it into an equation. Translate *the width* to $w$. Translate *is* to =. Translate *8 feet more than*

to _____ + 8, leaving room on the left for what follows. Translate *4 times the length* to $4l$. There-

fore, the statement translates to $w = 4l + 8$. The question also says that the area is 5,472. The area

of a rectangle can be found using the formula $A = lw$. Substitute $A = 5{,}472$ and $w = 4l + 8$ to get

$5{,}472 = l(4l + 8)$. Distribute the $l$ on the left side to get $5{,}472 = 4l^2 + 8l$. Since this is a qua-

dratic equation, get one side equal to 0 by subtracting 5,472 from both sides to get

$0 = 4l^2 + 8l - 5{,}472$. This is a difficult quadratic to factor, so use the quadratic formula,

$l = \dfrac{-b \pm \sqrt{b^2 - 4ac}}{2a}$, where $a = 4$, $b = 8$, and $c = -5{,}472$. Substitute these values to get

$l = \dfrac{-8 \pm \sqrt{8^2 - 4(4)(-5{,}472)}}{2(4)}$. Use a calculator to get that $8^2 - 4(4)(-5{,}472) = 87{,}616$ and that

$l = \dfrac{-8 \pm \sqrt{87{,}616}}{2(4)}$. Take the square root of 87,616 to get $l = \dfrac{-8 \pm 296}{2(4)} = \dfrac{-8 \pm 296}{8}$. Since

length can only be positive, don't take the negative into account and $l = \dfrac{-8 \pm 296}{8}$ becomes

$l = \dfrac{-8 + 296}{8} = \dfrac{288}{8} = 36$. If $l = 36$, then $w = 4l + 8 = 4(36) + 8 = 152$. To find the perimeter, use

$P = 2l + 2w = 2(36) + 2(152) = 376$. The answer is (B).

25.  **D**  The line intersects the origin as well as the points $(c, 3)$ and $(27, c)$. Questions about lines in the

xy-plane often involve slope, so determine the slope of this line. Any two points can be used to find

the equation of a line (including the slope). Note that since the line intersects the origin, it inter-

sects point $(0, 0)$ as well as the other two points. Use points $(0, 0)$ and $(c, 3)$ to calculate the slope:

$slope = \dfrac{y_2 - y_1}{x_2 - x_1} = \dfrac{3 - 0}{c - 0} = \dfrac{3}{c}$. The slope can also be determined using points $(0, 0)$ and $(27, c)$:

$\dfrac{c - 0}{27 - 0} = \dfrac{c}{27}$. Since these two slopes must be equal, $\dfrac{3}{c} = \dfrac{c}{27}$. Cross-multiply to get $c^2 = 81$. Take

the square root of both sides to get $c = \pm 9$. Since only 9 is a choice, the answer is (D).

26.  **B**  Since $\overline{FG}$ is a chord that includes the center, it is a diameter. Therefore, arc $\overset{\frown}{FXG}$ is a semicircle.
Since the length of the semicircular arc is $14\pi$, the circumference of the circle is $14\pi \times 2 = 28\pi$. The
formula for circumference is $C = 2\pi r$, so $28\pi = 2\pi r$. Divide both sides by $2\pi$ to get $r = 14$. The question asks for the length of the segment $\overline{XO}$. Since $\overline{XO}$ is a radius, the length is 14. The answer is (B).

27.  **B**  Since the question says *must be*, plug in multiple values of $p$ and $q$. Make sure that all values of $p$
and $q$ satisfy the inequality $-|p| < q < |p|$. Let $p = 4$ and $q = 2$. Go through each statement and
eliminate any statement that is false. Statement (I) is $4 > 0$, which is true, so keep statement (I).
Statement (II) is $|4| > -2$, which is true, so keep statement (II). Statement (III) is $4 > |2|$, which is
true, so keep statement (III). Try other values that might change the results. Since the question
involves absolute values, try negative numbers. Let $p = -4$ and $q = -2$. In this case, statement (I)
is $-4 > 0$, which is false, so cross out (I). Eliminate (A) and (D), since they include statement (I).
Since both remaining choices include statement (II), statement (II) must be true, and no more
testing of statement (II) is necessary. Test statement (III) using the same values of $p = -4$ and
$q = -2$: $-4 > |-2|$. This is false, so cross out statement (III), and eliminate (C). The answer is (B).

28.  **B**  The question asks for a reasonable estimate for the number of blue jelly beans in the entire container.

The number of blue jelly beans is given for each of ten regions. Determine the total number of regions in the container. The container has a base of 10 feet by 10 feet, so the area of the base of the entire container is $A = s^2 = (10)^2 = 100$. Each region has a base of 1 foot by 1 foot, so the area of the base of each region is $A = s^2 = (1)^2 = 1$. To get the number of regions, divide the area of the base of the container by the area of the base of each region to get $\frac{100}{1} = 100$. One way to get an estimate of the number of blue jelly beans in the entire container would be to find the average number of blue jelly beans in the counted regions and multiply that number by 100. The question asks for an approximation, though, and the answer choices are spread apart, so ballpark. All of the numbers in the table are around 25. Therefore, 25 is a reasonable estimate for the average number of blue jelly beans, and the total number of jelly beans should be about $25 \times 100 = 2,500$. The answer is (B).

29.  **C**  The question states that there are four times as many vanilla ice creams sold as vanilla frozen yogurts. Let $x$ be the number of vanilla frozen yogurts sold; therefore, $4x$ is the number of vanilla ice creams sold. The question also says that there are six times as many chocolate ice creams sold as chocolate frozen yogurts, so let $y$ be the number of chocolate frozen yogurts sold and $6y$ be the number of chocolate ice creams sold. Since there are a total of 32 frozen yogurts sold, $x + y = 32$. Since there are a total of 152 ice creams sold, $4x + 6y = 152$. Since there are two equations with two variables, it is possible to solve for the variables. Stack and add the two equations, trying to eliminate the chocolates to solve for the vanillas. Multiply both sides of the first equation by $-6$ to get $-6x - 6y = -192$, then stack and add the equations like this:

$$
\begin{array}{rcl}
4x + 6y &=& 152 \\
\underline{-6x - 6y} &=& \underline{-192} \\
-2x \phantom{+ 6y} &=& -40
\end{array}
$$

Divide both sides by $-2$ to get $x = 20$. The question asks for the probability that a randomly selected ice cream sold is vanilla, which will be calculated by dividing the number of vanilla ice creams sold ($4x$) by the total number of ice creams sold (152). Since $x = 20$, the number of vanilla ice creams sold is $4x = 4(20) = 80$. The probability that one ice cream is vanilla is $\frac{80}{152} \approx 0.526$. The answer is (C).

30.  **D**  To graph an inequality, start by graphing the equation. If the inequality sign is $\geq$, draw the equation as a solid line and shade above. If the inequality sign is $\leq$, draw the equation as a solid line and shade below. If the sign is $>$ or $<$, use the same rule as $\geq$ or $\leq$, respectively, but use a dashed line instead of a solid line. Use the inequalities given. Start with $y \geq x$. Since the inequality sign

is ≥ rather than >, the graph is the one with the solid line. Since the inequality sign is ≥, shade the solution above the line. Therefore, since only Sectors W and X are above the solid line, eliminate any choice that includes Y and Z. Eliminate (A) and (B). Now look at the inequality $3y < 2x - 3$. Divide both sides by 3 to get $y < \frac{2}{3}x - 1$. Since the inequality sign is <, the solution is below the dashed line. Since Sector W is above the dashed line, eliminate (C). The answer is (D).

31. **5 or 6** Martina spends between $20 and $25, inclusive, and she buys one hamburger at a cost of $5. This would leave her at least $20 − $5 = $15 and at most $25 − $5 = $20 for hot dogs. In the first case, $15 total divided by $3 per hot dog would get her 5 hot dogs, so 5 is one possible value for $h$. If she spent up to $20 on hot dogs, she could get $20 divided by $3 per hot dog for 6.67 hot dogs. She can only buy whole hot dogs, so 6 is another possible value of $h$. Therefore, the two possible correct answers are 5 and 6.

32. **19.4** The question asks for the average, so get the total and divide by the number of things. To get the total, add the number of states for each nation. The total is 6 + 9 + 26 + 16 + 29 + 13 + 31 + 4 + 36 + 2 + 10 + 17 + 50 + 23 = 272. Divide 272 by the 14 nations to get $\frac{272}{14} \approx 19.4285714$. Rounded to the nearest tenth, the answer is 19.4.

33. **10** The question gives the equation of a function and a point on the graph of the function. Plug the point into the equation. Substitute $x = -2$ and $y = g(x) = 6$ to get $6 = 2(-2)^2 + k(-2) + 18$. Simplify the right side to get $6 = 26 - 2k$. Subtract 26 from both sides to get $-20 = -2k$. Divide both sides by −2 to get $10 = k$. The answer is 10.

34. **11** The question asks how many rooms will be assigned three students. Consider the possibility that all rooms have three students. How many left over students would there be? If 26 rooms are assigned three students, then there are 26 × 3 = 78 students. However, the question says that there are 108 students, so there are 108 − 78 = 30 left over. These left over students have to be assigned to 5 student rooms. Since each room already has three students, to make five student rooms, pair the remaining students and add each pair to one of the three student rooms. Since there are 30 left over students, they make 15 pairs, so 15 rooms of three students become five-student rooms. Since there are a total of 26 rooms, there are 26 − 15 = 11 three-person rooms. The answer is 11.

35. $\frac{7}{12}$ The question asks for what fraction Town A's 1970 population was of Town A's 2000 population. To determine the population in 1970, find 1970 on the horizontal axis, trace straight up to the curve, then straight across to the vertical axis. It hits the vertical axis on the only line between 30 and 40, so the population in 1970 was 35,000. (Note that the vertical axis label indicates that the population is in thousands.) To determine the population in 2000, find 2000 on the horizontal

axis, trace straight up to the curve, then straight across to the vertical axis. It hits the vertical axis at 60, so the population in 2000 was 60,000. Therefore, the fraction is $\dfrac{35,000}{60,000} = \dfrac{35}{60} = \dfrac{7}{12}$. The answer is $\dfrac{7}{12}$.

36.    **4**    The question states that the volume of the cylinder is $64\pi$ cubic centimeters. The formula for volume of a cylinder is $V = \pi r^2 h$. Plug in $V = 64\pi$ and $h = 16$, as indicated by the figure, to get $64\pi = \pi r^2(16)$. Divide both sides by $16\pi$ to get $4 = r^2$. Take the square root of both sides to get $2 = r$. Note, however, that the question asks for the *diameter* and not the radius. Since the diameter is twice the radius, $d = 2r = 2(2) = 4$. The answer is 4.

37.    **321**    This question asks for angular position, which is in equation 1 and represented by $\theta$. Write down known variables and solve. When the carousel changes direction, the angular velocity is 0. Use the first equation, $\omega^2 = \omega_0^2 + 2\alpha\theta$. Plug in $\omega = 0$, $\omega_0 = 90$, and $\alpha = -12.6$ to get $0 = 90^2 + 2(-12.6)\theta$. Simplify the right side to get $0 = 8,100 - 25.2\theta$. Add $25.2\theta$ to both sides to get $25.2\theta = 8,100$. Divide both sides to get $\theta = 321.4286$. Rounded to the nearest degree, the answer is 321.

38.    **7**    The question asks for time. Write down known variables, then choose the equation that gives only time as the unknown. This is equation 2. When the carousel changes direction, the angular velocity is 0. Use the second equation, $\omega = \omega_0 + \alpha t$. Plug in $\omega = 0$, $\omega_0 = 90$, and $\alpha = -12.6$ to get $0 = 90 + (-12.6)t$. Simplify the right side to get $0 = 90 - 12.6t$. Add $12.6t$ to both sides to get $12.6t = 90$. Divide both sides by 12.6 to get $t = 7.1429$. Rounded to the nearest second, the answer is 7.

# Chapter 13
# Practice Test 6

# Reading Test

## 65 MINUTES, 52 QUESTIONS

**Turn to Section 1 of your answer sheet to answer the questions in this section.**

**DIRECTIONS**

Each passage or pair of passages below is followed by a number of questions. After reading each passage or pair, choose the best answer to each question based on what is stated or implied in the passage or passages and in any accompanying graphics (such as a table or graph).

**Questions 1–10 are based on the following passage.**

The following passage is from Charlotte Brontë, *Shirley*, originally published in 1849. Robert Moore is a mill owner and Reverend Helstone is the local parson.

Cheerfulness, it would appear, is a matter which depends fully as much on the state of things within as on the state of things without and around us. I
Line make this trite remark, because I happen to know
5 that Messrs. Helstone and Moore trotted forth from the mill-yard gates, at the head of their very small company, in the best possible spirits. When a ray from a lantern (the three pedestrians of the party carried each one) fell on Mr. Moore's face, you could
10 see an unusual, because a lively, spark dancing in his eyes, and a new-found vivacity mantling on his dark physiognomy; and when the rector's visage was illuminated, his hard features were revealed all agrin and ashine with glee. Yet a drizzling night, a somewhat
15 perilous expedition, you would think were not circumstances calculated to enliven those exposed to the wet and engaged in the adventure. If any member or members of the crew who had been at work on Stilbro' Moor had caught a view of this party, they
20 would have had great pleasure in shooting either of the leaders from behind a wall: and the leaders knew this; and the fact is, being both men of steely nerves and steady-beating hearts, were elate with the knowledge.
I am aware, reader, and you need not remind me,
25 that it is a dreadful thing for a parson to be warlike; I am aware that he should be a man of peace. I have

some faint outline of an idea of what a clergyman's mission is amongst mankind, and I remember distinctly whose servant he is, whose message he
30 delivers, whose example he should follow; yet, with all this, if you are a parson-hater, you need not expect me to go along with you every step of your dismal, downward-tending, unchristian road; you need not expect me to join in your deep anathemas, at once so
35 narrow and so sweeping, in your poisonous rancour, so intense and so absurd, against "the cloth;" to lift up my eyes and hands with a Supplehough, or to inflate my lungs with a Barraclough, in horror and denunciation of the diabolical rector of Briarfield.
40 He was not diabolical at all. The evil simply was— he had missed his vocation. He should have been a soldier, and circumstances had made him a priest. For the rest, he was a conscientious, hard-headed, hard-handed, brave, stern, implacable, faithful little man; a
45 man almost without sympathy, ungentle, prejudiced, and rigid, but a man true to principle, honourable, sagacious, and sincere. It seems to me, reader, that you cannot always cut out men to fit their profession, and that you ought not to curse them because their
50 profession sometimes hangs on them ungracefully. Nor will I curse Helstone, clerical Cossack as he was. Yet he was cursed, and by many of his own parishioners, as by others he was adored—which is the frequent fate of men who show partiality in friendship and bitterness
55 in enmity, who are equally attached to principles and adherent to prejudices.

CONTINUE

Helstone and Moore being both in excellent spirits, and united for the present in one cause, you would expect that, as they rode side by side, they would
60 converse amicably. Oh no! These two men, of hard, bilious natures both, rarely came into contact but they chafed each other's moods. Their frequent bone of contention was the war. Helstone was a high Tory (there were Tories in those days), and Moore was a
65 bitter Whig—a Whig, at least, as far as opposition to the war-party was concerned, that being the question which affected his own interest; and only on that question did he profess any British politics at all. He liked to infuriate Helstone by declaring his belief in the
70 invincibility of Bonaparte, by taunting England and Europe with the impotence of their efforts to withstand him, and by coolly advancing the opinion that it was as well to yield to him soon as late, since he must in the end crush every antagonist, and reign supreme.

**1**

Which choice best summarizes the passage?

A) A character becomes increasingly hostile as he travels with his fellow associate.

B) A character describes his reasons for disliking for another character.

C) Two characters in the same profession become increasingly competitive.

D) Two characters traveling together eagerly await confrontation.

**2**

The main purpose of the opening sentence of the passage is to

A) show the contrast between the clergymen's cheerfulness and the narrator's gloom.

B) provide an allegorical representation of the clergymen's journey.

C) issue a general statement that helps to clarify the characters' emotional states.

D) characterize the narrator's perspective on the characters' violent intentions.

**3**

During the course of the second paragraph, the narrator's focus shifts from

A) assessment of the reader's sentiment to the desire to chastise the clergymen.

B) acknowledgment that clergymen should be peaceful to admonition for anti-clergy prejudices.

C) reflection on the clergymen's behaviors to identification of their manners and appearance.

D) generalization about peaceful men to the details of two particular clergymen.

**4**

The references to "rancour" and "denunciation" at the end of the second paragraph mainly have which effect?

A) They reflect the narrator's fear of clergymen.

B) They reveal the reader's empathetic understanding of clergymen.

C) They illustrate the narrator's sense of dismay at clergymen.

D) They capture the reader's potential sense of disapproval of clergymen.

**5**

The passage indicates that Moore's behavior is mainly characterized by

A) attitudes that do not align with his profession.

B) indignation at his travel partner's political views.

C) a willingness to engage in confrontation.

D) impatience with his travel partner's apparent superiority.

**CONTINUE** ➡

## 6

The passage indicates that while the narrator acknowledges a certain evil in the third paragraph, Helstone is actually a

A) sympathetic clergyman.

B) harmless soldier.

C) righteous citizen.

D) ruthless warmonger.

## 7

Which choice provides the best evidence for the answer to the previous question?

A) Lines 7–14 ("When a . . . glee")

B) Lines 24–26 ("I am . . . peace")

C) Lines 42–47 ("For the . . . sincere")

D) Lines 51–56 ("Yet he . . . prejudices")

## 8

At the end of the third paragraph, the comparison of Helstone to a Cossack mainly has the effect of

A) illustrating his nature as soldier-like.

B) suggesting the likelihood of an altercation.

C) contrasting the natures of the two men.

D) conveying the belligerence of a course of action.

## 9

The passage indicates that, despite their excellent spirits, the men sometimes found each other's company to be

A) intolerable.

B) mundane.

C) vexing.

D) comforting.

## 10

Which choice provides the best evidence for the answer to the previous question?

A) Lines 24–26 ("I am . . . peace")

B) Lines 42–47 ("For the . . . sincere")

C) Lines 60–62 ("These two . . . moods")

D) Lines 63–65 ("Helstone . . . bitter Whig")

**CONTINUE**

**Questions 11–21 are based on the following passage and supplementary material.**

This passage is excerpted from John W. Murphy and John T. Pardeck, "The Current Political World-View, Education and Alienation." Originally published 1991.

In American society everything is a commodity and education is no exception. Of course, this means that every aspect of life is assumed to have a cash value and can be purchased for the right price. Also, every
5  person is a consumer, who enters the marketplace searching for a bargain. Although this scenario may be appropriate for describing the sale of shoes, when education is approached as a commodity the learning process may be seriously compromised.

10  Nonetheless, most students view education to be a product they are buying. Like good customers, students expect their education to meet their needs and assume a form they find palatable. Accordingly, students demand to have a significant amount of
15  control over their education, so as to guarantee the most favorable outcome possible. On the other hand, administrators must offer a competitive product, or revenues will decrease. Yet is the image of a buyer confronting a seller appropriate to describe how
20  students should relate to their school? The claim at this juncture is that education should not be exchanged in a manner similar to other products. Indeed, the worth of education is depreciated by this demarche.

In what ways do students participate in their
25  education? Usually their desires are voiced in the form of teacher evaluations. What is mostly revealed by this process is that students want, and demand, to be entertained. Like a competent sales representative, a teacher must be attractive, witty and capable of gaining
30  and retaining the attention of students. Additionally, material must not be dull or require much effort, or students will quickly become aggravated. For as every astute businessman knows, customers do not want to be hassled. Securing a favorable evaluation, therefore,
35  requires that a teacher adopt the demeanor of the television personalities who are invoked constantly to sell products to students.

Also similar to wise consumers, students strive to make the best deal possible. Translated into economic
40  terms, this means that the greatest rewards should be gained through the least amount of effort. Hence preparing students to take exams, organizing both their work and leisure time and summarizing their

reading assignments have become very profitable
45  businesses. Entrepreneurs who provide these and other services are well known to students. On the other hand, cheating has become rampant. Consistent with the ethos of consumerism, achieving some sort of advantage is considered to be essential to
50  beating the competition. Unfortunately the view has been conveyed that only through a series of dubious maneuvers can success be attained. In this climate, why should the message that becoming educated is hard work find a receptive audience?

55  From an administrative perspective, the curriculum offered by a school must be competitive. Creating an enticing array of courses is considered to be indispensable to attracting students and keeping enrollment figures high. Hence capitalizing on fads
60  has become normative, as witnessed by the recent proliferation of degrees and courses with captivating titles. In fact, many schools hire high paid advertising consultants to develop promotional material and discover untapped markets.

65  But education is trivialized when it is treated as a commodity. Content, in short, is replaced by form, for flash and glitter sell products. Difficult subjects are avoided, while the term relevant is reserved to describe the trendy courses that administrators have
70  begun to promote. Clearly the integrity of education is jeopardized when educational policies are dictated by the vagaries of the marketplace and ephemeral imagery is used to describe profound ideas that can be understood only through dedicated study.

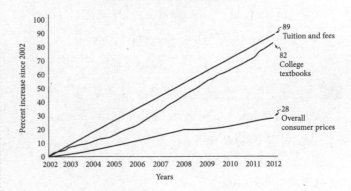

Estimated increases in New College Textbook Prices, College Tuition and Fees, and Overall Consumer Price Inflation, 2002–2012

Excerpted from the Government Accountability Office report to Congressional Committees from June 2013.

CONTINUE ▶

**11**

The main purpose of the passage is to

A) advocate for the marketing of education to students.

B) argue a position on a decidedly complex topic.

C) weigh the merits of educational products in the marketplace.

D) evaluate statistics about treating education as a commodity.

**12**

In the passage, the author makes which concession to the view that every person is a consumer in the marketplace of life?

A) The implied contract which exists between buyer and seller has educational value.

B) It may be valid when one is discussing the sale of some types of goods.

C) Students and administrators benefit from negotiating over the price of higher education.

D) A person engages with all aspects of a product when he or she assigns it monetary value.

**13**

Which choice provides the best evidence for the answer to the previous question?

A) Lines 2–4 ("Of course . . . price")

B) Lines 6–9 ("Although this . . . compromised")

C) Lines 11–13 ("Like good . . . palatable")

D) Lines 26–28 ("What is . . . entertained")

**14**

As used in line 13, "assume" most nearly means

A) guess intelligently.

B) pretend grudgingly.

C) suppose blindly.

D) take on readily.

**15**

The main purpose of the 4th paragraph (lines 38–54) is to

A) concede the logic of an attitude with which the author disagrees.

B) demonstrate that cheating results in serious consequences later in life.

C) provide a contrast to the view of teachers as salesmen.

D) argue against cheating or the use of educational preparation businesses.

**16**

As used in line 57, "enticing" most nearly means

A) pulling.

B) deceptive.

C) appealing.

D) suggestive.

**17**

Which choice best supports the authors' claim that schools have already begun to incorporate some facets of the popular marketplace into their educational materials?

A) Lines 16–18 ("On the…decrease")

B) Lines 59–62 ("Hence capitalizing…titles")

C) Lines 65–66 ("But education…commodity")

D) Lines 67–70 ("Difficult subjects…promote")

CONTINUE

**18**

The main idea of the final paragraph is that

A) focus on profit can undermine the effectiveness of true education.

B) ephemeral imagery cannot lead to an understanding of complex ideas.

C) education seems unimportant when it is present in the economic marketplace.

D) modern educators ignore difficult subjects in favor of trendy topics.

**19**

Data in the graph about estimated increases in prices from 2002 to 2012 most strongly support which of the following statements?

A) Overall consumer prices increased the same amount each year.

B) Overall consumer prices have not increased in the period since 2002.

C) Increases in college tuitions and fees exceed those of consumer prices.

D) Prices of college textbooks decreased from 2005 to 2006.

**20**

Data in the graph indicate that the greatest difference between the percent increase since 2002 of college tuition and fees and that of overall consumer prices occurred during which period?

A) 2004 to 2005

B) 2008 to 2009

C) 2010 to 2011

D) 2011 to 2012

**21**

Data in the graph provide most direct support for what idea in the passage?

A) Schools are interested in revenue.

B) Students have an expectation that school should be entertaining.

C) Teacher evaluations reflect the students' perceptions.

D) Content is replaced by flashy slogans.

**CONTINUE**

**Questions 22–32 are based on the following passages.**

Passage 1 is adapted from Connie Weaver, et al., "Contributions to Nutrition." ©2014 by the American Society for Nutrition. Passage 2 is from David Stuckler and Marion Nestle, "Big Food, Food Systems, and Global Health." © 2012 by PLOS Medicine.

**Passage 1**

Both fresh and processed foods make up vital parts of the food supply. Processed food contributes to both food security (ensuring that sufficient food is available)
*Line* and nutrition security (ensuring that food quality
5  meets human nutrient needs).

Nutrition scientists, public health professionals, agricultural economists, food scientists, and other professionals dedicated to meeting the food and nutritional needs of people around the globe recognize
10  that fresh, local foods cannot meet all nutritional requirements. Food processing is necessary.

Although nutritional security (quality) and food security (quantity) both depend on food processing, in recent years there has been considerable public
15  controversy over the nutritional contribution that processed foods make to the American diet.

If enrichment and fortification were not present, large percentages of the population would have had inadequate intakes of vitamins A, C, D, and E, thiamin,
20  folate, calcium, magnesium, and iron. When nutrients from enrichment and fortification were included, the percentages of the population with inadequate intakes decreased substantially for vitamin A, vitamin D, folate, and iron.

25  Clearly, this type of food processing, of adding nutrients to foods, has greatly benefitted nutrient intakes in the United States.

Thus, processed foods are nutritionally important to American diets. How, then, do we enhance the
30  contribution of processed food to nutritional security and food security?

Rather than limiting processed foods in the diet, it may be more productive to encourage the best available food options, namely, those that provide
35  fewer constituents to limit and more nutrients to encourage for the calories consumed.

One disadvantage of commercial food processing techniques is that they are poorly understood. Commercial food processing involves techniques that
40  are difficult for the general public to grasp and that

are out of their control, thus introducing a lack of transparency and generating suspicion and concerns about safety in some individuals.

In addition, concerns about the nutritional content
45  and other aspects of the production of processed foods, such as sustainability and cost, have led to criticisms of processed foods as "ultra-processed" and not compatible with good nutrition. However, the type and extent of processing do not necessarily correlate
50  with the nutritional content of the product.

**Passage 2**

Global food systems are not meeting the world's dietary needs. About one billion people are hungry, while two billion people are overweight. Underlying both is a common factor: food systems are not driven
55  to deliver optimal human diets but to maximize profits.

To understand who is responsible for these nutritional failures, it is first necessary to ask: *Who rules global food systems?* By and large it's "Big Food," by which we refer to multinational food and beverage
60  companies with huge and concentrated market power. Three-fourths of world food sales involve processed foods, for which the largest manufacturers hold over a third of the global market.

We see three possible ways to view this debate. The
65  first favors voluntary self-regulation, and requires no further engagement by the public health community. The second view favors partnerships with industry.

The third approach is critical of both. It recognizes the inherent conflicts of interest between corporations
70  that profit from unhealthy food and public health collaborations. Because growth in profit is the primary goal of corporations, self-regulation and working from within are doomed to fail.

We support the critical view, for several reasons.
75  Any partnership *must* create profit for the industry, which has a legal mandate to maximize wealth for shareholders. We also see no obvious, established, or legitimate mechanism through which public health professionals might increase Big Food's profits.

80  Big Food attains profit by expanding markets to reach more people, increasing people's sense of hunger so that they buy more food, and increasing profit margins through encouraging consumption of

CONTINUE ➤

products with higher price/cost surpluses. Although
in theory minimal processing of foods can improve
nutritional content, in practice most processing
is done so to increase palatability, shelf-life, and
transportability, processes that reduce nutritional
quality.

To promote health, industry would need to make
and market healthier foods so as to shift consumption
away from highly processed, unhealthy foods. Yet,
such healthier foods are inherently less profitable.
The only ways the industry could preserve profit is
either to undermine public health attempts to tax and
regulate or to get people to eat more healthy food while
continuing to eat profitable unhealthy foods. Neither is
desirable from a nutritional standpoint.

**22**

The authors of Passage 1 indicate which of the
following about the addition of nutrients to foods?

A) It has a helpful impact.

B) It should be increased significantly.

C) It may require further investigation.

D) It gives people unnecessary extra vitamins.

**23**

Which choice provides the best evidence for the
answer to the previous question?

A) Lines 2–5 ("Processed food . . . needs")

B) Lines 29–31 ("How then . . . security")

C) Lines 32–34 ("Rather than . . . options")

D) Lines 37–38 ("One disadvantage . . . understood")

**24**

The authors of Passage 1 indicate that food
enrichment methods

A) often involve industrial machinery.

B) lead to employment opportunities.

C) are the leading source of thiamin.

D) are not comprehended by all people.

**25**

As used in line 40, "grasp" most nearly means

A) comprehend.

B) clutch.

C) squeeze.

D) reach.

**26**

The authors of Passage 2 refers to "Big Food"
primarily to suggest that global food systems

A) result from a varied, competitive marketplace.

B) involve regions served by single companies.

C) should be simplified through local markets.

D) are largely dominated by a few extremely
influential companies.

**27**

According to the authors of Passage 2, what do profit
margins and price/cost surpluses have in common?

A) They typically coincide with ethical practices.

B) They are more important than other concerns
held by companies.

C) They are key elements of economic theory.

D) They are best increased through expanding
markets.

**28**

The possibilities offered in the final paragraph
(lines 90–97) of Passage 2 have primarily which
effect?

A) They show the only ways that industry could
promote health.

B) They demonstrate the unlikelihood of industry
marketing healthier foods.

C) They refer to government controls to illustrate
excessive regulation.

D) They supply positive steps to emphasize the
impossibility of corporate charity.

**CONTINUE** ➡

**29**

The main purpose of each passage is to

A) support a side in an argument about whether to promote vitamin intake through food.

B) discuss the nature of large-scale food production as it relates to nutrition.

C) compare the need for food security with the desire for nutrition security in the American diet.

D) emphasize the importance of sustainable processing in certain foods of the American diet.

**30**

Which choice best describes the relationship between the two passages?

A) Passage 2 discusses the underlying processes of a solution that Passage 1 describes in specific detail.

B) Passage 2 presents a plan to clarify the several misunderstood processes presented by Passage 1.

C) Passage 2 outlines an objective perspective that clashes with the opinions discussed in Passage 1.

D) Passage 2 explores the problematic nature of a system embraced by Passage 1.

**31**

On which of the following points would the authors of both passages most likely agree?

A) A thorough discussion of global food systems and content should address adequate nutrition.

B) Well-prepared, non-processed meals are generally more appealing than most processed foods.

C) Previous discussions of nutrition contained less suspicion of processed foods than those discussions do today.

D) People who avoid processed foods due to nutrient concerns are unlikely to be overweight.

**32**

Which choice provides the best evidence that the authors of Passage 2 would acknowledge some aspect of the statement made in lines 48–50 of Passage 1?

A) Lines 61–63 ("Three-fourths . . . market")

B) Lines 80–84 ("Big Food . . . surpluses")

C) Lines 84–89 ("Although in . . . quality")

D) Lines 90–92 ("To promote . . . foods")

CONTINUE

**Questions 33–42 are based on the following passage.**

The following passage is adapted from Bruce Ackerman and Jennifer Nou, "Hey, what about the 24th? The constitutional amendment about voting rights that the Supreme Court forgot." © 2008 in *Slate* online magazine.

Americans have long fought hard to protect the right to vote and a generation ago emphatically rejected the idea of paying for the ballot. As the civil rights revolution reached its peak, Congress and the states in 1964 enacted the 24th Amendment, forbidding any "poll-tax or other tax" in federal elections. Yet, remarkably enough, this basic text went unmentioned by the Supreme Court when it upheld Indiana's photo-ID law this week.

Indiana's law insists on a photo ID to vote, which in turn requires documents, like a birth certificate or passport, that verify identity. Getting these papers costs voters money as well as time and effort. This leads to the question the court failed to ask: Does the extra expense violate the absolute ban on all "taxes" imposed by the 24th Amendment?

The leading Supreme Court decision about this amendment provides a starting point. In *Harman v. Forssenius*, Virginia responded to the new constitutional prohibition by allowing citizens to escape its poll tax if they filed a formal certificate establishing their place of residence. Otherwise, they would be obliged to continue paying a state tax of $1.50 if they wanted to cast a ballot. Lars Forssenius refused to pay the tax or file the residency certificate and brought a class action suit attacking the statute as unconstitutional.

The Supreme Court agreed with Forssenius in 1965, only a year after the amendment came into force. Chief Justice Earl Warren emphasized that Virginia's escape clause for avoiding the $1.50 was unconstitutionally burdensome: "For federal elections," he explained, "the poll tax is abolished absolutely as a prerequisite to voting, and no equivalent or milder substitute may be imposed." Although the Roberts Court divided sharply this week over Indiana's voter ID law, Warren's opinion gained the support of all the sitting justices except the conservative Justice John Marshall Harlan—and even he concurred in the result.

*Harman* casts a shadow over Indiana's photo-ID law. On the face of things, Indiana provides identification free of charge, but so did Virginia when it required proof of residence. Like Virginians trying to avoid the tax, Indianans must file paperwork to get their IDs. And their burden is often heavier. It was enough for a Virginian to swear that he or she was a resident in front of witnesses or a notary public. Indianans must also travel to the Bureau of Motor Vehicles to get a photo ID as well as pay for supporting documents like a birth certificate or passport. They can escape the requisite fees only by casting a provisional ballot and then taking another trip to a local official to swear that they are too poor to comply. And they must repeat this humiliating procedure every time they cast a ballot.

Like Indiana, Virginia told the court that a certificate of residency was necessary to preserve the integrity of its elections. But in 1965, the justices would have none of it. According to *Harman*, the 24th Amendment could not be satisfied by a showing of "remote administrative benefits"—especially when other less burdensome devices were available for proving residency. In particular, the court pointed out that Virginia could ask voters to take an oath and rely on the threat of punishment to deter lying. The same is true today in Indiana.

We don't suggest that the Roberts Court isn't clever enough to find a way around *Harman*. Our point is that the justices didn't even try. They ignored the 24th Amendment and restricted themselves to the equal-protection clause of the 14th in deciding the Indiana case. Narrowing their vision didn't help them reach a consensus. The nine justices produced four very different opinions, none of which gained more than three votes.

This sort of thing doesn't happen every day in the life of the court—indeed, we can't think of another case in which the justices utterly failed to address the most obviously relevant provision of the constitutional text. If they had squarely confronted the law and language of the 24th Amendment, there is a fair chance that Justices Stevens and Anthony Kennedy would have switched sides, creating a new majority for striking down the Indiana law.

Perhaps the majority will choose to turn its back on *Harman* and uphold the state's exclusionary law. But at the very least, the justices should provide Indianans, and the rest of us, with an explanation for their decision to trivialize a solemn constitutional amendment enacted only 44 years ago.

**CONTINUE →**

**33**

The central problem that the authors describe in the passage is that Indiana's photo ID law

A) may run counter to a constitutional amendment, despite a Supreme Court ruling.

B) forces voters to spend time and money acquiring background checks.

C) divided the Roberts Court sharply on a matter of federal and state importance.

D) led the Supreme Court to take an overly wide view in ignoring the 24th amendment.

**34**

The authors use the phrase "remarkably enough" (line 7) mainly to emphasize the Supreme Court's

A) complete disregard for the U. S. Constitution.

B) partial ignorance of the Bill of Rights.

C) notable divergence from established law.

D) qualified reliance upon political polls.

**35**

The passage claims that which of the following casts doubt on the recent Supreme Court decision?

A) The civil rights movement

B) A later decision by the same Court

C) The views of Anthony Kennedy

D) The Department of Motor Vehicles

**36**

Which choice provides the best evidence for the answer to the previous question?

A) Lines 10–12 ("Indiana's law . . . identity")

B) Lines 24–27 ("Lars Forssenius . . . unconstitutional")

C) Lines 28–29 ("The Supreme . . . force")

D) Lines 48–50 ("Indianans must . . . passport")

**37**

As used in line 29, "force" most nearly means

A) violence.

B) power.

C) field.

D) effect.

**38**

As used in line 59, "have" most nearly means to

A) accept as legally reasonable.

B) obtain appropriate documents.

C) issue a ruling upon.

D) reread the relevant parts of the Constitution.

**39**

It can be reasonably inferred that "exclusionary" (line 86) is a term generally intended to

A) emphasize the difference between state and federal rights.

B) criticize a state law that may in fact be unconstitutional.

C) emphasize the solemnity of a trivialized amendment.

D) criticize the prejudiced actions of elected officials.

**40**

The authors contend that on the subject of voter-ID laws the present-day Supreme Court has

A) ruled in favor of Forssenius.

B) insisted on a heavier burden.

C) favored one amendment over another.

D) refused to explain its decision.

**CONTINUE**

**41**

Which choice provides the best evidence for the answer to the previous question?

A) Lines 28–29 ("The Supreme . . . force")

B) Line 45 ("And their . . . heavier")

C) Lines 69–72 ("They ignored . . . case")

D) Lines 87–90 ("But at . . . ago")

**42**

The eighth paragraph (lines 76–84) is primarily concerned with establishing a contrast between

A) the positions of Stevens and Kennedy.

B) a historical rule and a present anomaly.

C) a law in Virginia and a law in Indiana.

D) the decisions of Roberts and Warren.

**CONTINUE**

**Questions 43–52 are based on the following passage and supplementary material.**

The following excerpt is adapted from Ramez Naam, "Arctic Sea Ice: What, Why, and What Next." © 2012 by *Scientific American*.

On September 19th, NSIDC, the National Snow and Ice Data Center, announced that Arctic sea ice has shrunk as far as it will shrink this summer, and *Line* that the ice is beginning to reform, expanding the
5 floating ice cap that covers the North Pole and the seas around it. The Arctic Sea Ice extent this September was far smaller than the previous record set in 2007. At 3.4 million square kilometers of ice coverage, this year's Arctic minimum was 800,000 square kilometers
10 smaller than the 2007 record. That difference between the previous record and this year's is larger than the entire state of Texas. An ice-free summer in the Arctic, once projected to be more than a century away, now looks possible decades from now. Some say that it
15 looks likely in just the next few years.

Conditions in the Arctic change dramatically through the seasons. In the depths of winter, the Earth's tilt puts the Arctic in 24 hour-a-day darkness. Temperatures, cold year round, plunge even lower. The
20 sea surface freezes over. At the height of summer, the opposite tilt puts the Arctic in 24 hour-a-day sunlight. While it's a cold, cold place even at these times, the constant sunshine, warmer air, and influx of warm waters from further south serve to melt the ice. The ice
25 cap usually starts shrinking in March, and then reaches its smallest area in mid-September, before cooling temperatures and shorter days start the water freezing and the ice cap growing once again.

When scientists and reporters talk about an ice-
30 free Arctic, they're usually speaking of the Arctic in *summer*, and especially in September, when ice coverage reaches its minimum. The amount of ice left at that minimum has indeed been plunging. In 1980, the ice shrank down to just under 8 million square
35 kilometers before rebounding in the fall. This year's minimum extent of 3.4 million kilometers is less than half of what we saw in 1980. Strikingly, two thirds of the loss of ice has happened in the 12 years since 2000. The ice is receding, and the process, if anything,
40 appears to be accelerating.

Artic Sea Ice Minimum Area

Data: NSIDC. Graphic: Ramez Naam

Arctic sea ice coverage in September has dropped in half since 1980, and the drop appears to be accelerating.

As recently as a few years ago, most models of the Arctic ice anticipated that summers would remain icy until the end of the 21st century, and well into the 22nd century. But the trend line above makes that look
45 unlikely. The amount of ice remaining, this year, is about the same as the ice *lost* between the mid-1990s and today. If ice loss continued at that pace, we'd see an ice-free summer sometime around 2030, give or take several years.

50 Is that plausible? Opinions differ substantially, even among climate scientists. At one end of the spectrum are those who see the ice lasting in summer for another 20 or 30 years, or perhaps even a bit longer. For example, Lars-Otto Reierson, who leads the Arctic
55 Monitoring and Assessment Programme told Reuters that most models predict the summer ice disappearing by 2030 or 2040. Similarly, a paper published this year in *Geophysical Research Letters* by multiple scientists, including several from the National Snow and Ice Data
60 Center, found that an ice-free summer in the Arctic in the "next few decades" was a "distinct possibility." A recent assessment from Muyin Wang at the University of Washington and James Overland at the National Oceanographic and Atmospheric Administration,
65 using the most up to date Arctic ice models and data, projected a nearly ice-free Arctic around 2030. And Cecilia Bitz, a professor of Atmospheric Sciences at the University of Washington at part of the Polar Science Center sees a 50/50 chance that the Arctic will be ice-
70 free in summer in the next few decades.

**CONTINUE** ➡

On the other end of the spectrum are those who think the melt could happen much sooner. Peter Wadhams, who leads the Polar Ocean Physics Group at the University of Cambridge, has predicted since 2008
75 that the Arctic ice could be gone in summer by 2015. He now believes there's a chance that it could happen even sooner. Similarly, Mark Drinkwater, the European Space Agency's senior advisor on polar regions and a mission scientist for the CryoStat satellite that
80 measures arctic ice, believes that the Arctic could be ice-free in September by the end of this decade.

When will the ice melt? While the range of possibilities is wide today, it's shrunk dramatically from just a few years ago, when most climate scientists
85 expected the ice to survive through the 21st century. Now the question is whether it will be gone in decades —or in mere years.

**43**

The first paragraph serves mainly to

A) inform the reader that Arctic ice is starting to return.

B) compare the size of an Arctic area to a U. S. state.

C) illustrate dramatic changes in polar weather conditions over the last century.

D) present a trend that is occurring differently than expected.

**44**

As used in line 13, "projected" is closest in meaning to

A) hurled.

B) seen.

C) hypothesized.

D) illuminated.

**45**

According to Naam, the Earth's tilt is significant primarily because it

A) causes the sea surface to freeze and the ice cap to grow further.

B) accounts for seasonal differences in the Arctic.

C) explains why the ice-free summer is accelerating in recent years.

D) exposes the Arctic to constant daylight and melts portions of ice.

**46**

Which choice provides the best evidence for the answer to the previous question?

A) Lines 12–15 ("An ice-free . . . years")

B) Lines 16–21 ("Conditions in . . . sunlight")

C) Lines 29–32 ("When scientists . . . minimum")

D) Lines 37–40 ("Strikingly, two . . . accelerating")

**47**

As used in line 47, "pace" most nearly means

A) walk.

B) loss.

C) rate.

D) measure.

**CONTINUE**

**48**

Based on information in the passage, it can reasonably be inferred that climate scientists

A) agree that the polar ice is receding, but disagree about the rate of acceleration.

B) disagree that the polar ice is receding, but agree about the rate of deceleration.

C) are uncertain about whether the polar ice is receding, but agree that it should be studied.

D) are certain that the polar ice is receding, but cannot say whether it will rebound.

**49**

Which choice provides the best evidence for the answer to the previous question?

A) Lines 50–51 ("Is that . . . scientists")

B) Lines 57–61 ("Similarly, a . . . possibility'")

C) Lines 66–70 ("And Cecilia . . . decades")

D) Lines 77–81 ("Similarly, Mark . . . decade")

**50**

In the graph, what general trend in the area of Arctic sea ice is depicted?

A) An overall decline

B) A geometric series of rises and falls

C) An arithmetic series of dramatic changes

D) A temporary shrinkage

**51**

Which concept is supported by the passage and by the information in the graph?

A) The Arctic ice-free summer will be upon us within decades.

B) The Arctic ice-free summer may not be a scientific fact.

C) The Arctic ice-free summer may come sooner than the 22nd century.

D) The Arctic ice-free summer will not come as swiftly as some have predicted.

**52**

How does the graph support the author's point that Arctic ice is receding?

A) It shows that the change in ice from 2007 to 2012 is similar in size to the state of Texas.

B) It suggests that the amount of ice could drop to zero within a few years.

C) It indicates a loss of 3 million square kilometers of ice from 1980 to 1990.

D) It presents a trend of sharp and noticeable decline since 2000.

**STOP**
If you finish before time is called, you may check your work on this section only.
Do not turn to any other section in the test.

**No Test Material On This Page**

# Writing and Language Test

## 35 MINUTES, 44 QUESTIONS

**Turn to Section 2 of your answer sheet to answer the questions in this section.**

---

### DIRECTIONS

Each passage below is accompanied by a number of questions. For some questions, you will consider how the passage might be revised to improve the expression of ideas. For other questions, you will consider how the passage might be edited to correct errors in sentence structure, usage, or punctuation. A passage or a question may be accompanied by one or more graphics (such as a table or graph) that you will consider as you make revising and editing decisions.

Some questions will direct you to an underlined portion of a passage. Other questions will direct you to a location in a passage or ask you to think about the passage as a whole.

After reading each passage, choose the answer to each question that most effectively improves the quality of writing in the passage or that makes the passage conform to the conventions of standard written English. Many questions include a "NO CHANGE" option. Choose that option if you think the best choice is to leave the relevant portion of the passage as it is.

---

**Questions 1–11 are based on the following passage.**

**A Dirty Job Worth Having**

As people become more sensitive to the idea of preserving certain ecosystems, **[1]** yet more attention must be paid to the land. The central challenge of maintaining an ecosystem, especially by artificial means, is that ecosystems have a tendency to change, particularly with the dual influence of human **[2]** reacting and a

**1**

A) NO CHANGE
B) and
C) for
D) DELETE the underlined portion.

**2**

A) NO CHANGE
B) reacts
C) interacting
D) interaction

CONTINUE ➡

rapidly altering climate. **3** Still, one career that has grown by leaps and bounds in the last fifty years is that of the soil conservationist, whose land-use surveys guide both public and private entities as to how to work within sustainable ecosystems.

Take, for example, the factors that must be considered **4** when building a beach house. Coastal areas are particularly susceptible to the influence of **5** things eroding because of the water from the ocean and in the air. In this context, a soil conservationist might be asked to conduct a survey of the region in order to determine where it would be safest to build. After all, one's dream house would not be quite so ideal if it were at constant risk of collapsing, shifting, or **6** to deteriorate with the ground beneath it.

**3**

A) NO CHANGE
B) Nonetheless,
C) Finally,
D) Therefore,

**4**

Which choice most effectively sets up the subject discussed in this paragraph?
A) NO CHANGE
B) in performing these tasks.
C) with the changes in the seasons.
D) if you are doing soil conservation.

**5**

A) NO CHANGE
B) erosion
C) what erodes
D) the process of erosion

**6**

A) NO CHANGE
B) deteriorating
C) deteriorate
D) structures deteriorating

**CONTINUE**

In more agricultural communities, the work of a soil conservationist might take a different form. Farmers, after all, are not necessarily concerned with building structures on the land—instead, they are concerned with land that will yield reliable crops. **7** In these cases, soil conservationists employ a variety of techniques. Of these techniques each in its way is geared toward preserving or reviving land where crops are grown. The goal in these situations is to mimic the biology of "virgin land," or land that has never been farmed. Soil conservationists might advise on farming techniques **8** or chemical supplements that can help the land produce to its full potential. With the efforts of soil conservationists, no-till farmlands, lands that are not farmed with traditional plowing implements, **9** which has grown dramatically, nearly doubling in the fifteen years since 2000.

**7**

Which choice most effectively combines the underlined sentences?

A) Soil conservationists, in these cases, are ways of preserving or reviving land where cops are grown, and they will use a variety of techniques to do it.

B) In these cases, each one of them is geared toward the idea of preservation or revival as to crops, and the soil conservationists employ a variety of techniques to that end.

C) Geared toward preserving or reviving land where crops are grown, soil conservationists in these cases employ a variety of different techniques.

D) In these cases, soil conservationists employ a variety of techniques, each in its way geared toward preserving or reviving land where crops are grown.

**8**

At this point, the writer is considering adding the following information.

    —such as no-till or terrace methods—

Should the writer make this addition here?

A) Yes, because it demonstrates the advantages of the methods described later in the sentence.

B) Yes, because it gives specific instances of the techniques discussed in this sentence.

C) No, because it distracts from the sentence's main focus on soil conservationists.

D) No, because it provides an unnecessary detail that interrupts the sentence's flow.

**9**

A) NO CHANGE

B) which have

C) have

D) has

CONTINUE

Soil conservation can be applied to any ecosystem, but its details tend to be rather technical. As a result, most people who work as soil conservationists tend to study agricultural science or environmental studies in college. From there, however, the paths diverge. Clearly, someone working on the eastern seaboard would need a different knowledge base from that of someone working in the deserts of the Southwest, the **10** plains of the Midwest, or the forests of the Northwest. **11** In all cases, however, soil conservationists do truly fascinating work, seeking as they do to continue to strike the balance between natural spaces and the people who live in them.

**10**

A) NO CHANGE

B) areas without trees

C) plains-like ecosystems

D) barren wasteland

**11**

Which choice most clearly ends the passage with a restatement of the writer's claim?

A) NO CHANGE

B) In all of these places, soil conservationists do essential work, but just as much is required of the builders and contractors who accompany them.

C) Soil conservationists work in both the public and the private sectors, but the public is better because it can be enjoyed by all.

D) Because the desert is unique, the skills that soil conservationists learn in places like Arizona are valuable but difficult to transfer between regions.

**CONTINUE**

**Questions 12–22 are based on the following passage.**

**A Bigger Piece of the Peace**

—1—

Nobel Prizes have been given since 1901 as a way to honor outstanding achievements in Physics, Chemistry, Literature, Medicine, and Economics. There may be some controversy as to who earns these awards in many cases; **12** therefore, there can be no doubt that the winners are always accomplished in their fields and have contributed something significant to their **13** disciplines and the world at large.

**12**

A) NO CHANGE

B) for example,

C) however,

D) fightingly,

**13**

A) NO CHANGE

B) disciplines,

C) disciplines, it's

D) disciplines, for example

CONTINUE

—2—

The Nobel Peace Prize may be a good deal more controversial, but it is by no means any less significant. [14] The prize is given each year "to the person who shall have done the most or the best work for fraternity between nations, for the abolition or reduction of standing armies and for the holding and promotion of peace congresses." Time and again we see the [15] committee rewarded bravery in the face of adversity. This is a difficult thing to quantify, but the Peace Prize is as important as the other prizes and contributes to [16] their common goal: to make the world a better place.

[14]

At this point, the writer is considering adding the following sentence.

> One of the most important prizes of all time, the 1962 prize in Physiology, was given to Francis Crick, James Watson, and Hugh Wilkins, for their discovery of the structure of DNA.

Should the writer make this addition here?

A) Yes, because it cites an important moment in Nobel Prize-giving history.

B) Yes, because it explains the typical genetic makeup of a Nobel Prize winner.

C) No, because it implies that all Peace Prize winners must also be scientists.

D) No, because it distracts from the paragraph's main focus on another prize.

[15]

A) NO CHANGE

B) committee reward

C) committee's rewarding

D) committees' reward

[16]

A) NO CHANGE

B) they're common goal,

C) they're common goal;

D) their common goal;

CONTINUE

—3—

It is probably no surprise that Martin Luther King, Jr., won the award in 1964 amid his non-violent campaign for civil rights in the United States. By 1964, and certainly by the time of his death in 1968, Baptist **17** minister King's, influence spanned the globe, not only for people of color seeking civil rights, but also for all **18** those people's friends, family, and loved ones. King was also the first African-American man to gain this particular kind of stature in the United States and on the world stage.

—4—

**19** When given to first-year President Barack Obama, there was a good deal more controversy surrounding the award in 2009. In this case as in the others, however, the Nobel Peace Prize seeks to award the intangible, the unquantifiable, and the hopeful. Whether Burche, King, Obama, or the hundreds of other recipients, all winners provide the important reminder that people work every day to make the world a better place.

**17**

A) NO CHANGE
B) minister King's
C) minister, King's,
D) minister, King's

**18**

Which choice gives a specific supporting detail that is most similar to the details already in the paragraph?

A) NO CHANGE
B) the people throughout the world.
C) who thought the Nobel Prize should be awarded to someone who deserved it.
D) those who championed a cause in non-violent ways.

**19**

A) NO CHANGE
B) There was a good deal more controversy surrounding the award in 2009, when it was given to first-year President Barack Obama.
C) In 2009, when it was awarded, first-year President Barack Obama received the Prize with a good deal more controversy.
D) When it was awarded to first-year President Barack Obama in 2009, a good deal more controversy surrounded the award.

**CONTINUE**

—5—

King may be the most famous African-American recipient of the Nobel Peace **20** Prize. The honor was first given to a lesser known but no less illustrious figure, Ralph Bunche, in 1950. After a difficult childhood punctuated by an illustrious educational and political career, Bunche was one of the many tasked with trying to resolve the Arab-Israeli conflict that had erupted after World War II. The work began with a scare, as the UN's appointee, the Swedish Count Folke Bernadotte, was assassinated by members of the underground Lehi group. After this tragic event, Bunche, Bernadotte's chief aide, became the UN's chief mediator, and his long negotiations began with the Israeli representative Moshe Dayan. These negotiations, many of which were done while the two men shot pool, became the 1949 Armistice Agreements, concluding the 1948 Arab-Israeli Conflict and earning Ralph Bunche **21** the Nobel Peace Prize from the year 1950.

**Question 22 asks about the previous passage as a whole.**

**20**

Which choice most effectively combines the sentences at the underlined portion?

A) Prize: the

B) Prize, while the

C) Prize for the

D) Prize, yet the

**21**

Which choice most closely matches the stylistic pattern established earlier in the sentence?

A) NO CHANGE

B) 1950's Nobel Prize for Peace.

C) the 1950 Nobel Peace Prize.

D) the Nobel Prize for 1950's Peace.

**Think about the previous passage as a whole as you answer question 22.**

**22**

To make the passage most logical, paragraph 5 should be placed

A) where it is now.

B) after paragraph 1.

C) after paragraph 2.

D) after paragraph 3.

CONTINUE ➡

**Questions 23–33 are based on the following passage and supplementary material.**

### Conserving the Trees that Conserve the Earth

The most obvious facet of global warming is the rise in global temperatures. What many do not understand quite as well, **23** however, are the factors that contribute to that rise in global temperatures. The rise in carbon dioxide ($CO_2$) levels, for instance, is commonly cited as a reason, but what exactly does this chemical compound do?

For instance, every time you breathe, you inhale oxygen and a number of other compounds, and you exhale $CO_2$. Factories, cars, and other heavy machinery perform **24** functions that could be called analogous on a much larger scale. Because of the heavy output from this wide variety of industrial sources, the earth's atmosphere is bombarded **25** . This excess carbon dioxide creates what is known as a greenhouse effect, wherein heat enters the atmosphere but not all of it leaves. $CO_2$ does not absorb

**500** | 10 Practice Tests for the SAT

**23**

A) NO CHANGE

B) thereby,

C) correspondingly,

D) thus,

**24**

A) NO CHANGE

B) the functions of an analogy

C) functions that are like analogies

D) analogous functions

**25**

At this point, the writer is considering adding the following information

> with more $CO_2$ than it can process or release naturally back into the area outside the earth's atmosphere

Should the writer make this addition here?

A) Yes, because it defines the role that the trees in the Amazonian rainforest play in modulating the earth's $CO_2$ levels.

B) Yes, because it states why high levels of $CO_2$ can be a problem in the earth's atmosphere.

C) No, because it mentions the process of absorbing $CO_2$, which blurs the essay's focus on the Amazonian rainforest.

D) No, because it undermines the passage's central claim that the earth can absorb $CO_2$ naturally.

**CONTINUE**

heat energy from the sun, but where the compound is concerned, [26] it's always absorbing heat energy released from the earth. Here's the problem: while the carbon dioxide can release some of that heat into space, it also releases some back to the earth, creating a kind of self-perpetuating cycle of rising temperatures. Since 1960, carbon dioxide has increased at a steady rate, [27] as temperatures have increased along exactly the same curve.

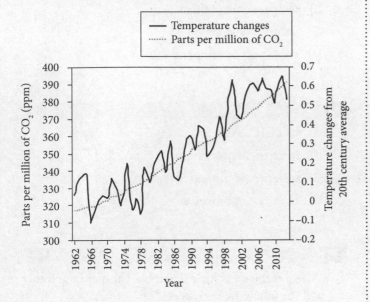

There are some earthly mechanisms to absorb and [28] chill out the levels of carbon dioxide in the atmosphere, but many of these industrial processes have depleted or overwhelmed these mechanisms. For instance, trees need carbon dioxide to perform their basic functions, but the number of trees required to offset carbon emissions is staggering. An independent analysis found that the number of trees required to offset the emissions of one modest coal plant [29] operating in a small city in Connecticut and would then require 52 million trees!

---

**26**

A) NO CHANGE

B) its

C) they're

D) there

**27**

Which choice offers an accurate interpretation of the data in the chart?

A) NO CHANGE

B) but the temperatures have shown no general increase despite the rising $CO_2$ levels.

C) whereas the temperature changes peaked in 1989 for no apparent reason.

D) and although temperatures have fluctuated, those have generally increased as well.

**28**

A) NO CHANGE

B) kill

C) reduce

D) mellow

**29**

A) NO CHANGE

B) operating in a small city in Connecticut, where it would

C) operating in a small city in Connecticut would

D) operating in a small city in Connecticut, it would

**CONTINUE** ➡

Still, there are lots of trees on the earth, and alongside many of the carbon caps that many countries and industries have begun to impose, people are starting to take the ideas of *re*forestation and conservation more seriously. A team of over 150 researchers produced the first comprehensive map of the Amazon rainforest's ecosystem and **30** said, "that half of the Amazon could be deforested by 2050.

[1] But there is a silver lining to the findings in this research. [2] Because of the team's efforts, as many as 57% of Amazon tree species could be eligible for the International Union for the Conservation of Nature's red list of threatened species. [3] Other polluting behaviors would need to change as well for significant emission reversals, but protecting the Amazon's trees could **31** temper some of those polluting behaviors in the meantime and into the future. [4] This could be a first major step in part of the much longer process, **32** or series, of processes, to get the earth's carbon levels back to appropriate ranges. **33**

**30**

A) NO CHANGE
B) said that
C) said, that
D) said—that

**31**

A) NO CHANGE
B) temper some of them
C) temper some of it
D) do its part by tempering them

**32**

A) NO CHANGE
B) or series of processes,
C) or series; of processes
D) or series, of processes

**33**

Where is the most logical place in this paragraph to add the following sentence?

This could go a long way toward reforesting the Amazon rainforest, adding a significant boost to the 390 billion individual trees that currently grow there.

A) Before sentence 1
B) Before sentence 2
C) Before sentence 3
D) Before sentence 4

**CONTINUE**

**Questions 34–44 are based on the following passage.**

**Original Adaptations and Rewrites**

Literary influence can take many forms. Therefore, the results of this influence can take many forms—novels, poems, critiques, and countless others. Every great writer works within a literary tradition established by the great writers who came before. Sometimes that influence is [34] formal, in any case—as in the case of a writer who uses the forms created by an earlier writer to discuss new topics. Sometimes that influence is more literal—as in the case of those writers who take marginal characters from earlier works [35] and sometimes poems or movies are included.

[1] Perhaps the most famous instance of such a work is the epic blank-verse poem *Paradise Lost*, written by John Milton and first published in 1667. [2] It was by this alternate route, Milton claimed, that he could help to "justify the ways of God to men." [3] This work retells the biblical story of Adam and Eve and their exile from the Garden of Eden. [4] With the framework set by the biblical story, *Paradise Lost* offers a unique interpretation, [36] just as the story focuses on the fallen angel Satan rather than on the human characters. [5] As such, *Paradise Lost* is considered essential reading for those interested in matters both aesthetic and theological. [37]

---

**34**

A) NO CHANGE

B) formal—

C) formal, nevertheless—

D) formal, therefore—

**35**

Which choice provides information that best supports the claim made by this sentence?

A) NO CHANGE

B) but don't cite the author's name at all.

C) and build new literary worlds around them.

D) yet still consider it entirely their own.

**36**

A) NO CHANGE

B) wherein

C) from which

D) into it

**37**

To make this paragraph most logical, sentence 2 should be placed

A) before sentence 2.

B) before sentence 3.

C) before sentence 4.

D) before sentence 5.

**CONTINUE**

The practice of adapting literary works, particularly the great classics of a [38] language; to unique ends has continued. The 1966 novel *Wide Sargasso Sea* was British author Jean Rhys's prequel to the 1847 novel *Jane Eyre*. Toward the end of *Jane Eyre*, it is revealed that one of the novel's central characters, Mr. Rochester, has a wife locked away in one of the rooms of his castle. Rhys's novel tells this wife's story, foregrounding the cruelty of British imperialism and the oppressive society that awaited women in England. As Milton had before, Rhys uses a well-known work to [39] overtake an alternate story.

More recently, Algerian writer Kamel Daoud [40] he adapted Albert Camus's novel *The Stranger* into his own unique work, *The Meursault Investigation*, first published in Algeria in 2013. Camus's novel centers on the protagonist Meursault, [41] who kills an anonymous Arab man for vague reasons. Daoud's novel starts with Camus's

**38**

A) NO CHANGE
B) language
C) language,
D) language—

**39**

A) NO CHANGE
B) tell
C) manifest
D) ideate

**40**

A) NO CHANGE
B) adapted
C) he adopted
D) adopted

**41**

A) NO CHANGE
B) he kills
C) whom killed
D) killing

CONTINUE

basic outline, but *The Meursault Investigation* is [42] deferent from *The Stranger* in that it writes the backstory of that man and gives him a name, Musa. [43] Daoud's narrative follows the observations of Musa's brother Harun and offers a critique of European views that refuse to acknowledge the existence of non-Europeans. "By claiming your own name," Daoud said in an interview, "you are also making a claim of your humanity and thus the right to justice."

Although some of these works may not seem quite as "original" as the original texts, they in fact make literal what all other texts merely imply [44] and do not state. Daoud refers to his novel as part of a "dialogue with Camus," but we should not forget that even the greatest works of literature are speaking to someone.

**42**

A) NO CHANGE
B) different, than
C) different than
D) different from

**43**

At this point, the writer is considering adding the following sentence

> The history of Franco-Algerian relations goes back centuries as France was the occupying colonial power in Algeria from 1830 to 1962.

Should the writer make this addition here?

A) Yes, because it situates Daoud's novel in an essential historical context.
B) Yes, because it gives an example of a global conflict that one writer might have drawn upon.
C) No, because it contradicts the passage's larger claim that literature cannot be defined by historical events.
D) No, because it strays from the paragraph's main focus with an idea that is not elaborated upon.

**44**

A) NO CHANGE
B) as well.
C) similarly.
D) DELETE the underlined portion, and end the sentence with a period.

**STOP**
If you finish before time is called, you may check your work on this section only.
Do not turn to any other section in the test.

# Math Test – No Calculator

## 25 MINUTES, 20 QUESTIONS

**Turn to Section 3 of your answer sheet to answer the questions in this section.**

---

### DIRECTIONS

**For questions 1–15,** solve each problem, choose the best answer from the choices provided, and fill in the corresponding circle on your answer sheet. **For questions 16–20,** solve the problem and enter your answer in the grid on the answer sheet. Please refer to the directions before question 16 on how to enter your answers in the grid. You may use any available space in your test booklet for scratch work.

### NOTES

1. The use of a calculator **is not permitted**.
2. All variables and expressions used represent real numbers unless otherwise indicated.
3. Figures provided in this test are drawn to scale unless otherwise indicated.
4. All figures lie in a plane unless otherwise indicated.
5. Unless otherwise indicated, the domain of a given function $f$ is the set of all real numbers $x$ for which $f(x)$ is a real number.

### REFERENCE

$A = \pi r^2$
$C = 2\pi r$

$A = \ell w$

$A = \frac{1}{2} bh$

$c^2 = a^2 + b^2$

Special Right Triangles

$V = \ell wh$

$V = \pi r^2 h$

$V = \frac{4}{3} \pi r^3$

$V = \frac{1}{3} \pi r^2 h$

$V = \frac{1}{3} \ell wh$

The number of degrees of arc in a circle is 360.
The number of radians of arc in a circle is $2\pi$.
The sum of the measures in degrees of the angles of a triangle is 180.

**CONTINUE** ➡

**1**

$$2x + 3y = -9$$
$$x - y = -2$$

Which of the following ordered pairs $(x, y)$ satisfies the system of equations above?

A) $(-3, -1)$

B) $(-1, -3)$

C) $(1, 3)$

D) $(3, 1)$

**2**

$$x = 4(x + y)$$

If $(x, y)$ is a solution to the equation above and $x \neq 0$, what is the value of $\dfrac{y}{x}$ ?

A) $\dfrac{3}{4}$

B) $\dfrac{1}{4}$

C) $-\dfrac{3}{4}$

D) $-\dfrac{5}{4}$

**3**

Note: Figure not drawn to scale.

Triangle $PQR$ is isosceles with $PR = QR$ and $PQ = 64$. If the ratio of $ST$ to $SU$ = 5:3, what is the length of $\overline{SQ}$ ?

A) 8

B) 24

C) 32

D) 40

**4**

Buster estimates the expected profit, in dollars, from one week's operation of his family's chocolate-covered banana stand using the expression $4cd - 200$, where $c$ is the number of expected customers of the banana stand each day, and $d$ is the number of days the banana stand will be open during that week. Which of the following is the best interpretation of the number 4 in the expression?

A) Each customer is expected to buy 4 chocolate-covered bananas.

B) The price of a banana increases by $4 every day.

C) The number of customers will increase by a factor of 4 every day.

D) The banana stand charges $4 for each chocolate-covered banana.

**CONTINUE** ➡

**5**

The number of Java Jim's coffee stores that existed in 2003 is approximately one-half the number of additional Java Jim's coffee stores that were added from 2004 to 2014. If approximately 700 Java Jim's coffee stores existed in 2003 and approximately $y$ Java Jim's stores were added from 2004 to 2014, which of the following equations is true?

A)  $\frac{1}{2}y = 700$

B)  $2y = 700$

C)  $700y = \frac{1}{2}$

D)  $700y = 2$

**6**

Stream Supreme, a streaming movie service, charges a monthly fee of $7 for membership and $1.75 per movie streamed. Another streaming movie service, Download Empire, charges a monthly fee of $4 for membership and $2.25 per movie streamed. If $m$ represents the number of movies streamed in a particular month, what are all the values of $m$ for which Stream Supreme's total monthly charge is less than that of Download Empire?

A)  $m < 4$

B)  $5 \leq m \leq 6$

C)  $6 \leq m \leq 7$

D)  $m > 6$

**7**

$$q = \frac{\left(p_e - p_{wf}\right)k}{\mu d}h$$

The formula above models the productivity index, $q$, in barrels per day, of an oil well with a pressure differential of $(p_e - p_{wf})$, a permeability of $k$, a pay zone thickness of $h$, a viscosity of $\mu$, and a drainage factor of $d$. Which of the following gives $h$ in terms of $q$, $p_e$, $p_{wf}$, $k$, $\mu$, and $d$ ?

A)  $h = \dfrac{\mu q d}{k}$

B)  $h = \dfrac{k}{\mu q d}$

C)  $h = \dfrac{\mu q d}{\left(p_e - p_{wf}\right)k}$

D)  $h = \dfrac{\left(p_e - p_{wf}\right)k}{\mu q d}$

**8**

$$s = 110 + 4C$$

The equation above is used to model the relationship between the number of scoops, $s$, of ice cream sold per day at a particular ice cream shop, and the temperature, $C$, in degrees Celsius. According to the model, what is the meaning of the 4 in the equation?

A)  For every increase of 1°C, four more scoops of ice cream will be sold.

B)  For every decrease of 1°C, four more scoops of ice cream will be sold.

C)  For every increase of 4°C, one more scoop of ice cream will be sold.

D)  For every decrease of 4°C, one more scoop of ice cream will be sold.

**CONTINUE**

**9**

While saving money to pay for graduate school, Stephan created a plan in which the amount of money he saves each month is increased by a constant amount. If Stephan's savings plan requires that he save $145 during month 3 and that he save $280 during month 12, which of the following describes how the money Stephan saves changes between month 3 and month 12 of his savings plan?

A) Stephan increases the amount he saves by $5 each month.

B) Stephan increases the amount he saves by $15 each month.

C) Stephan increases the amount he saves by $60 every 6 months.

D) Stephan increases the amount he saves by $45 every month.

**10**

Which of the following equations, when graphed in the $xy$-plane, will include only values of $y$ that are less than 2 ?

A) $y = -x^2 + 3$

B) $y = |-x| - 1$

C) $y = x^3 - 4$

D) $y = -(x - 1)^2 + 1$

**11**

If $f(x + 1) = 3x - 4$ for all values of $x$, what is the value of $f(-4)$ ?

A) $-19$

B) $-16$

C) $-13$

D) $-10$

**12**

$$\frac{5 - i}{2 - 3i}$$

If the expression above is rewritten in the form $a + bi$, where $a$ and $b$ are real numbers, what is the value of $a$ ? (Note: $i = \sqrt{-1}$)

A) $-2$

B) $-1$

C) $1$

D) $\dfrac{17}{13}$

**CONTINUE**

13

What is the sum of all values of $p$ that satisfy the equation $3p^2 + 24p - 6 = 0$ ?

A) $-6\sqrt{2}$

B) $-8$

C) $8$

D) $6\sqrt{2}$

14

The parabola with the equation $y = ax^2 + bx + c$, where $a$, $b$, and $c$ are constants, is graphed on the $xy$-plane. If the parabola passes through the point $(-1, -1)$, which of the following must be true?

A) $a - b + c = -1$

B) $a - b - c = -1$

C) $a + b = 1$

D) $b - c = -1$

15

If $(px + 5)(qx + 3) = 8x^2 + rx + 15$ for all values of $x$, and $p + q = 6$, what are the two possible values for $r$ ?

A) 2 and 4

B) 7 and 12

C) 22 and 26

D) 29 and 39

CONTINUE

## DIRECTIONS

**For questions 16–20,** solve the problem and enter your answer in the grid, as described below, on the answer sheet.

1. Although not required, it is suggested that you write your answer in the boxes at the top of the columns to help you fill in the circles accurately. You will receive credit only if the circles are filled in correctly.

2. Mark no more than one circle in any column.

3. No question has a negative answer.

4. Some problems may have more than one correct answer. In such cases, grid only one answer.

5. **Mixed numbers** such as $3\frac{1}{2}$ must be gridded as 3.5 or 7/2. (If ⟨3 1 / 2⟩ is entered into the grid, it will be interpreted as $\frac{31}{2}$, not as $3\frac{1}{2}$.)

6. **Decimal Answers:** If you obtain a decimal answer with more digits than the grid can accommodate, it may be either rounded or truncated, but it must fill the entire grid.

Answer: $\frac{7}{12}$ — Write answer in boxes. Fraction line. Grid in result.

Answer: 2.5 — Decimal point

Acceptable ways to grid $\frac{2}{3}$ are:

Answer: 201 – either position is correct

**NOTE:** You may start your answers in any column, space permitting. Columns you don't need to use should be left blank.

**CONTINUE** ➡

**16**

What is the value of $y$ if $(4y + 8) - (7y - 12) = 11$ ?

**17**

At a hotel, each double room has 25 more square feet of floor space than each single room. If 2 double rooms and 4 single rooms have a total of 1400 square feet of floor space, how many square feet of floor space does a double room have?

**18**

One angle of a right triangle measures $a°$, where $\cos a° = \dfrac{3}{5}$. What is $\sin(90° - a°)$ ?

**19**

If $x + 3$ is a factor $x^2 + kx + 2k$, where $k$ is a constant, what is the value of $k$ ?

**CONTINUE**

20

$$x^3 - 3x^2 + 5x - 15 = 0$$

What real value of $x$ is a solution to the above equation?

**STOP**
If you finish before time is called, you may check your work on this section only.
Do not turn to any other section in the test.

# Math Test – Calculator

## 55 MINUTES, 38 QUESTIONS

Turn to Section 4 of your answer sheet to answer the questions in this section.

---

### DIRECTIONS

**For questions 1–30**, solve each problem, choose the best answer from the choices provided, and fill in the corresponding circle on your answer sheet. **For questions 31–38**, solve the problem and enter your answer in the grid on the answer sheet. Please refer to the directions before question 31 on how to enter your answers in the grid. You may use any available space in your test booklet for scratch work.

### NOTES

1.  The use of a calculator **is permitted**.
2.  All variables and expressions used represent real numbers unless otherwise indicated.
3.  Figures provided in this test are drawn to scale unless otherwise indicated.
4.  All figures lie in a plane unless otherwise indicated.
5.  Unless otherwise indicated, the domain of a given function $f$ is the set of all real numbers $x$ for which $f(x)$ is a real number.

### REFERENCE

$A = \pi r^2$
$C = 2\pi r$

$A = \ell w$

$A = \frac{1}{2}bh$

$c^2 = a^2 + b^2$

Special Right Triangles

$V = \ell wh$

$V = \pi r^2 h$

$V = \frac{4}{3}\pi r^3$

$V = \frac{1}{3}\pi r^2 h$

$V = \frac{1}{3}\ell wh$

The number of degrees of arc in a circle is 360.
The number of radians of arc in a circle is $2\pi$.
The sum of the measures in degrees of the angles of a triangle is 180.

**CONTINUE**

**1**

A pizzeria sells pizzas in individual slices or in pies of 8 slices. On a certain day, the pizzeria sold a total of 364 slices, 84 of which were sold as individual slices. Which of the following shows the number of pies, $n$, sold on that day?

A)  $n = \dfrac{364 + 84}{8}$

B)  $n = \dfrac{364}{8} + 84$

C)  $n = \dfrac{364}{8} - 84$

D)  $n = \dfrac{364 - 84}{8}$

$N = \dfrac{364 - 84}{8}$

**2**

In the figure above, lines 1 and 2 are parallel, and lines 3 and 4 are parallel. If the measure of $\angle a$ is 125°, what is the measure of $\angle b$ ?

A)  40

B)  55

C)  110

D)  125

**3**

|  | Cream filling | No filling | Total |
|---|---|---|---|
| White chocolate | 5 | 15 | 20 |
| Dark chocolate | 7 | 3 | 10 |
| Total | 12 | 18 | 30 |

A box contains 30 pieces of chocolate, distributed as shown in the table above. Each piece is made of either white chocolate or dark chocolate, and each piece contains either cream filling or no filling. If one piece is selected at random, what is the probability that the piece is either white chocolate with cream filling or dark chocolate with no filling?

A)  $\dfrac{8}{30}$

B)  $\dfrac{12}{30}$

C)  $\dfrac{20}{30}$

D)  $\dfrac{22}{30}$

**CONTINUE**

**4**

An isosceles triangle has perimeter $T$ and sides of length $x$, $x$, and $y$. Which of the following represents $x$, in terms of $T$ and $y$?

A) $x = T - y$

B) $x = T - 2y$

C) $x = \dfrac{T - 2y}{2}$

D) $x = \dfrac{T - y}{2}$

**5**

$$2x + 3y = -6$$
$$x - 4y = 19$$

Which ordered pair satisfies the system of equations shown above?

A) $(-9, 4)$

B) $(-3, 4)$

C) $(-1, -5)$

D) $(3, -4)$

**6**

When 6 times the number $n$ is subtracted from 8, the result is 20. What is the result when 3 times the number $n$ is subtracted from 5?

A) $-2$

B) $8$

C) $11$

D) $20$

**7**

At 12 P.M. on Sunday, there are 25,000 people in a football stadium that holds 65,000. Every minute after 12 P.M., the number of people in the stadium increases by 550. If $m$ represents the time, in minutes, after 12 P.M., which of the inequalities below gives the set of minutes in which the football stadium is below capacity?

A) $550m < 25,000$

B) $550m < 65,000$

C) $550m + 25,000 < 65,000$

D) $25,000 - 550m < 65,000$

CONTINUE

Number of United States Residents
With Health Insurance in 2015, in Thousands

| Income in dollars | Age in years | | | | | | Total |
|---|---|---|---|---|---|---|---|
| | Under 19 | 19–25 | 26–34 | 35–44 | 45–64 | 65 and older | |
| Under 25,000 | 12,499 | 4,881 | 6,146 | 6,387 | 13,314 | 7,359 | 50,586 |
| 25,000–49,999 | 15,624 | 6,102 | 7,683 | 7,984 | 16,643 | 9,200 | 63,236 |
| 50,000–74,999 | 14,061 | 5,491 | 6,915 | 7,185 | 14,978 | 8,278 | 56,908 |
| 75,000–99,999 | 10,936 | 4,271 | 5,378 | 5,589 | 11,650 | 6,439 | 44,263 |
| 100,000 and above | 24,998 | 9,762 | 12,293 | 12,774 | 26,628 | 14,718 | 101,173 |
| Total | 78,118 | 30,507 | 38,415 | 39,919 | 83,213 | 45,994 | 316,166 |

The table above shows the number of U.S. residents with health insurance in 2015, in thousands, categorized by age group and annual income. According to these results, if a U.S. resident with health insurance who was 35-64 in 2015 is selected at random, what is the approximate probability that this resident had an income between $50,000 and $74,999 ?

A) 0.20

B) 0.25

C) 0.40

D) 0.80

**9**

A truck traveled at an average speed of 70 miles per hour for 4 hours and had a fuel efficiency of 18 miles per gallon. Approximately how many gallons of fuel did the truck use for the entire 4-hour drive?

A) 4

B) 10

C) 16

D) 20

**11**

$$t_b = 212 - 0.0018a$$

The temperature at which water boils varies with altitude. The formula above models the relationship between $t_b$, the temperature at which water boils, in degrees Fahrenheit, and $a$, the altitude, in feet. Which of the following equations expresses altitude in terms of the temperature at which water boils?

A) $a = \dfrac{0.0018}{t_b - 212}$

B) $a = \dfrac{t_b + 212}{0.0018}$

C) $a = \dfrac{t_b - 212}{0.0018}$

D) $a = \dfrac{212 - t_b}{0.0018}$

**10**

Distance Traveled

The scatterplot above shows the distances and times spent traveling for 22 trips by a driver. What is the time, in hours, of the trip represented by the data point farthest from the line of best fit (not shown)?

A) 4

B) 6

C) 8

D) 10

CONTINUE

**12**

Which scatterplot below expresses a positive association that is not linear? (Note: A positive association between two variables is one in which higher values in one variable correspond to higher values in the other variable, and vice versa.)

A)

B)

C)

D)

**13**

$$v = \frac{h - m}{t} + 4.9t$$

For an object thrown straight upward, the formula above gives the relationship between $v$, the initial speed in meters per second, $t$, the time in seconds after the object was thrown, $h$, the height after $t$ seconds, and $m$, the initial height from which the object was thrown. Which of the following expresses $h$, in terms of $v$, $t$, and $m$ ?

A)  $h = -4.9t^2 + vt - m$

B)  $h = -4.9t^2 + vt + m$

C)  $h = -4.9t^2 - vt + m$

D)  $h = 4.9t^2 - vt - m$

**14**

$$65x + y = 455$$

A grocery store receives a shipment of oranges and consistently sells the same number of oranges each day. The equation above models the number of oranges, $y$, that remain $x$ days after the shipment is received. What does it mean that $(7, 0)$ is a solution to the equation?

A)  It takes 7 days after the shipment until none of the oranges are remaining.

B)  There are 7 oranges in the shipment.

C)  It takes 7 days for oranges to be sold to 455 customers.

D)  After the shipment, 7 oranges are sold each day.

**CONTINUE**

**Questions 15 and 16 refer to the following information.**

A minor-league baseball player is offered a short-term contract by three teams: the Eagles, the Hawks, and the Jays. Each contract consists of a signing bonus, a daily salary, and a daily meal allowance, as shown in the table below.

| Team | Signing bonus, $b$ (in dollars) | Salary, $s$ (in dollars per day) | Meal allowance, $m$ (in dollars per day) |
| --- | --- | --- | --- |
| Eagles | 1400 | 140 | 40 |
| Hawks | 1200 | 160 | 50 |
| Jays | 1500 | 130 | 30 |

The player's total compensation, $C$, for each contract in terms of the number of days, $d$, is given by the formula $C = b + (s + m)d$.

$C = 1400 + (140 + 40)5$
$1400 + (180)5$

**15**

For what number of days, $d$, would the player's total compensation including signing bonus, salary, and meal allowance with the Eagles be greater than the total compensation with the Jays?

A) $d < 5$

B) $d > 5$

C) $d < 6$

D) $d > 6$

**16**

The relationship between the player's total compensation, $C$, for a contract with the Hawks as a function of the number of days, $d$, for which the contract lasts is graphed in the $xy$-plane, with $d$ on the $x$-axis and $C$ on the $y$-axis. What does the $y$-intercept of the graph represent?

A) The signing bonus

B) The daily salary

C) The daily meal allowance

D) The daily salary and meal allowance combined

**17**

The specific heat capacity of substance $K$, in calories per gram (cal/g), is approximately 30% less than that of methyl alcohol. The specific heat capacity of methyl alcohol is 0.60 cal/g. Which of the following is closest to the specific heat capacity, in cal/g, of substance $K$?

A) 0.18

B) 0.42

C) 0.56

D) 0.78

**CONTINUE**

**18**

In the $xy$-plane, if $(-1, 0)$ is a solution to the system of inequalities $y < x + c$ and $y < -x - d$, which of the following must be true about $c$ and $d$?

A) $c = d$

B) $c = -d$

C) $c < d$

D) $d < c$

**19**

### Percent Ad Time for Five Podcasts

A company advertises on five different podcasts: $P$, $Q$, $R$, $S$, and $T$. The graph above shows the amount of time used for the ad on the five different podcasts as a percentage of total run time. Each podcast runs for the same length of time, and the costs to advertise on podcasts $P$, $Q$, $R$, $S$ and $T$ are \$400, \$350, \$200, \$180, and \$150, respectively. Which of the following podcasts provides the most ad time per dollar?

A) $Q$

B) $R$

C) $S$

D) $T$

**20**

In quadrilateral $PQRS$ above, $PS = QR$, and $\overline{PQ}$ is parallel to $\overline{SR}$. If $PQ$ and $SR$ were both decreased by 75% and $PT$ were quadrupled, how would the area of $PQRS$ change?

A) The area of $PQRS$ would be quadrupled.

B) The area of $PQRS$ would be increased by 75%.

C) The area of $PQRS$ would be decreased by 75%.

D) The area of $PQRS$ would be unaffected.

**21**

Number of Times Watching the News per Week

|         | Never | 1–2 | 3–4 | More than 4 | Total |
|---------|-------|-----|-----|-------------|-------|
| Group A | 7     | 14  | 18  | 11          | 50    |
| Group B | 4     | 13  | 21  | 12          | 50    |
| Total   | 11    | 27  | 39  | 23          | 100   |

The table above shows the results of a survey in which 100 people were asked how often they watched the news. Group A consisted of people who were registered voters, and Group B consisted of people who were not registered to vote. If one person is randomly chosen from among those who watch the news fewer than three times a week, what is the probability that the person was a member of Group A ?

A) $\frac{21}{38}$

B) $\frac{4}{50}$

C) $\frac{21}{50}$

D) $\frac{38}{100}$

**22**

The bar graph above shows the distribution of randomly selected integers from 1 to 12. What is the mean of the list of numbers?

A)  5.5

B)  6.3

C)  7.0

D)  10.0

CONTINUE

**Questions 23–25 refer to the following information.**

A team of scientists measures the volume of various samples of different gases with a constant pressure of 0.1 atm and a constant temperature of 610 K. The graph below plots the volume of each sample against the amount of the gas.

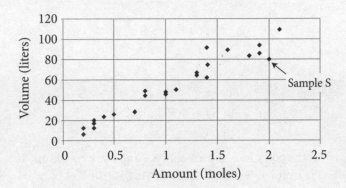

Volume-Amount Relationship
Among Samples of Gases

Sample S

The Ideal Gas Law predicts that at this pressure and temperature, the volume of an ideal gas can be modeled by the equation $V = 50n$, where $V$ is the volume in liters and $n$ is the amount of the substance, measured in moles. Assume that the relationship is valid for greater amounts of the substance than are shown in the graph. (A mole is approximately $6.022 \times 10^{23}$ molecules.)

---

**23**

According to the data provided, what is the volume, in <u>milliliters</u>, of Sample S ?

A) $8 \times 10^4$

B) $2 \times 10^3$

C) $8 \times 10^1$

D) $4 \times 10^1$

---

**24**

There are three samples shown of approximately 1.4 moles. Which of the following is closest to the range of volumes of these four samples, in liters?

A) 30

B) 20

C) 9

D) 3

---

**25**

Based on the ideal gas law, what is the volume, in liters, of a sample that contains 1,200 moles?

A) 6,000

B) 24,000

C) 36,000

D) 60,000

---

**CONTINUE**

**26**

Let the polynomials $f$ and $g$ be defined by $f(x) = 3x^3 + 6x^2 + 11x$ and $g(x) = 8x^2 + 15x + 7$. Which of the following polynomials is divisible by $3x + 7$ ?

A) $j(x) = 2f(x) + g(x)$

B) $k(x) = f(x) + g(x)$

C) $m(x) = f(x) + 2g(x)$

D) $n(x) = f(x) + 3g(x)$

**27**

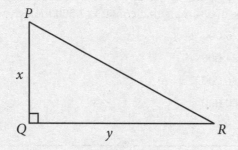

Given the right triangle $PQR$ above, which of the following is equal to $\dfrac{y}{x}$ ?

A) $\cos P$

B) $\cos Q$

C) $\tan P$

D) $\tan Q$

**28**

Let the function $f$ be defined by $f(x) = (x - 1)(x + 7)$. Which of the following is an equivalent form of $f$ in which the minimum value of $f$ appears as either a coefficient or a constant?

A) $f(x) = x^2 - 7$

B) $f(x) = x^2 + 6x - 7$

C) $f(x) = (x + 3)^2 - 16$

D) $f(x) = (x - 3)^2 - 20$

**29**

$$4a - j = 7a + 3$$
$$4b - k = 7b + 3$$

In the equations shown above, $j$ and $k$ are constants. If $j$ is $k$ plus 1, which of the following is true?

A) $a$ is $b$ plus $\dfrac{1}{3}$ .

B) $a$ is $b$ minus $\dfrac{1}{3}$ .

C) $a$ is $b$ minus 1.

D) $a$ is $b$ minus 3.

**CONTINUE**

**30**

If the average (arithmetic mean) of $3x$ and $11$ is $a$, the average of $4x$ and $6$ is $b$, and the average of $5x$ and $7$ is $c$, what is the average of $a$, $b$, and $c$, in terms of $x$ ?

A)  $x + 2$

B)  $x + 3$

C)  $2x + 4$

D)  $4x + 8$

CONTINUE ➡

## DIRECTIONS

**For questions 31–38**, solve the problem and enter your answer in the grid, as described below, on the answer sheet.

1. Although not required, it is suggested that you write your answer in the boxes at the top of the columns to help you fill in the circles accurately. You will receive credit only if the circles are filled in correctly.
2. Mark no more than one circle in any column.
3. No question has a negative answer.
4. Some problems may have more than one correct answer. In such cases, grid only one answer.
5. **Mixed numbers** such as $3\frac{1}{2}$ must be gridded as 3.5 or 7/2. (If $\boxed{3\ 1\ /\ 2}$ is entered into the grid, it will be interpreted as $\frac{31}{2}$, not as $3\frac{1}{2}$.)
6. **Decimal Answers:** If you obtain a decimal answer with more digits than the grid can accommodate, it may be either rounded or truncated, but it must fill the entire grid.

Answer: $\frac{7}{12}$     Answer: 2.5

Acceptable ways to grid $\frac{2}{3}$ are:

Answer: 201 – either position is correct

**NOTE:** You may start your answers in any column, space permitting. Columns you don't need to use should be left blank.

CONTINUE

**31**

A scientist estimates that the water level of a lake is dropping by 2.25 inches per year. If this trend continues, how many years will it take for the water level in the lake to drop by 27 inches?

**32**

A car factory that operates 24 hours a day and 7 days a week produces one car every 20 minutes. How many cars does the factory produce in 3 days?

**33**

Scores in the game of bowling range from 0 to 300 per game, inclusive. Vito's average score in the first 6 games of a bowling tournament was 200. What is the lowest score he can receive in his 7th game and still have an average score of at least 240 for the entire 12-game tournament?

**34**

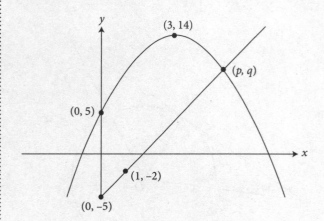

The $xy$-plane shows a point of intersection between a line and a parabola. The point of intersection has coordinates $(p, q)$. If the vertex of the parabola is at $(3, 14)$, what is the value of $p$ ?

CONTINUE

**35**

To purchase a car, Harry makes a down payment, and every month thereafter, he pays a fixed amount to the car dealer. The total amount, $T$, in dollars, that Harry has paid after $m$ months can be represented by the equation $T = 175m + 350$. According to this equation, how much, in dollars, was Harry's down payment? (Disregard the $ sign when gridding your answer.)

**36**

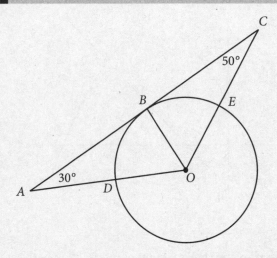

In the figure above, line segment $AC$ is tangent to the circle with center $O$ at point $B$. Line segments $AO$ and $CO$ intersect the circle at points $D$ and $E$, respectively. If the circumference of circle $O$ is 72, what is the length of minor arc $\overset{\frown}{DE}$ ?

**Questions 37 and 38 refer to the following information.**

The population of a small town is currently 800. A statistician estimates that the population of the town will decline by 14 percent per year for the next five years. The statistician models the population, $P$, of the town after $x$ years using the equation $P = 800(k)^x$.

**37**

In the equation above, what value should be used for $k$ ?

**38**

According to the statistician's model, what will the population of the town be, to the nearest whole number, after five years?

# STOP

**If you finish before time is called, you may check your work on this section only.**
**Do not turn to any other section in the test.**

**No Test Material On This Page**

# SAT Essay

**DIRECTIONS**

The essay gives you an opportunity to show how effectively you can read and comprehend a passage and write an essay analyzing the passage. In your essay you should demonstrate that you have read the passage carefully, present a clear and logical analysis, and use language precisely.

Your essay must be written on the lines provided in your answer sheet booklet; except for the planning page of the answer booklet, you will receive no other paper on which to write. You will have enough space if you write on every line, avoid wide margins, and keep your handwriting to a reasonable size. Remember that people who are not familiar with your handwriting will read what you write. Try to write or print so that what you are writing is legible to those readers.

**You have 50 minutes to read the passage and write an essay in response to the prompt provided inside this booklet.**

**REMINDER**

— Do not write your essay in this booklet. Only what you write on the lined pages of your answer booklet will be evaluated.

— An off-topic essay will not be evaluated.

CONTINUE ➡

As you read the passage below, consider how John Kerry uses

- evidence, such as facts or examples, to support claims.
- reasoning to develop ideas and to connect claims and evidence.
- stylistic or persuasive elements, such as word choice or appeals to emotion, to add power to the ideas expressed.

**The following is adapted from the article "Saving Our Future By Saving Our Oceans," written by John Kerry for National Geographic in June 2014.**

1   The ocean covers almost three-quarters of our planet and sustains life on Earth as we know it. But our ocean is at grave risk today—and we know the reason why.

2   Human activity threatens the world's ocean. Often illegal international fishing practices are decimating fisheries. A garbage patch twice the size of Texas floats in the Pacific Ocean, evidence of the trash we cast into our waterways. Rising carbon dioxide levels from emissions increase ocean acidity, endangering coral reefs and other marine life.

3   The warning could not be starker: Unless these trends are reversed, the effects across the planet will be profound. The damage will be felt whether you live on a coastline or hundreds of miles from the nearest ocean's edge. The ocean produces half the world's oxygen, creates the clouds that bring fresh water, and regulates our climate. More than a billion people eat fish as their primary source of protein. Fishing is a $500-billion global industry, and one in six jobs in the United States is marine related.

4   The good news is that we know what is behind the degradation of the ocean. We know the steps required to counter the dangers and restore the health of our ocean for this generation and those to come. We know the science to change the future for the ocean.

5   What we also know is that the global political will to address this urgent peril has yet to be summoned. We must change the equation. The plight of the ocean compels us to fight complacency and build consensus for action.

6   The United States has demonstrated that we can make progress. We have begun to restore fish stocks and sustain the livelihoods of our fishermen. We have reduced the flow of waste into the marine environment and launched intensive studies of the effects of rising acidity levels on sea life. Some other nations are also addressing the challenges in innovative ways.

7   But governments will not undertake this enormous campaign without prodding from the private sector—from businesses that depend on a healthy ocean, from nongovernmental organizations committed to saving the ocean, and from all of us who recognize that the ocean is a defining feature of life on our planet.

CONTINUE

8   That's why we will hold the State Department's first ocean conference on June 16 and 17. Government leaders from around the world—heads of state and foreign ministers—will join scientists, environmentalists, and business leaders to discuss the threat to our ocean and the steps that should be taken to reverse the damage and restore the balance.

9   We intend to create a global movement to protect the ocean and its resources. We will debate real solutions and come up with concrete plans for implementing them. We also have sent out a call to action that lays out the crucial steps all of us can take to ensure that a healthy ocean allows us to continue to enjoy its bounty.

10  Because I come from Massachusetts, the sea has been a constant in my life. But stewardship of the ocean is more than just a personal passion for those of us who hail from coastal communities. Just as this issue was a priority for me as a senator, it is a priority for me now as Secretary of State, because it means jobs, health, industry, and the safety of our planet.

11  I've been around enough to know that governments can't solve all of these problems alone. Just as we share a common dependence on the ocean, we must join together in a common endeavor to save the ocean from the damage caused by humans.

12  In a few days, I will ask leaders from around the world to take action to save our ocean. I'm convinced the ocean conference will be an important catalyst, that governments and experts can lead the way. But I know it will take more to win this crucial struggle

13  What we do as individuals will ultimately make the difference. Some acts are simple. Don't throw trash into waterways. Buy sustainable seafood. Volunteer at least one day a year to clean beaches or waterways in your community. Other acts require a sustained commitment by people everywhere to make certain saving the ocean is a priority for their governments.

14  In observing World Oceans Day yesterday, we recognized that protecting our ocean is not a luxury. It is a necessity that contributes to our economy, our climate, and our way of life. Working together, we can change the current course and chart a sustainable future.

---

Write an essay in which you explain how John Kerry builds an argument to persuade his audience that there are benefits to saving the oceans. In your essay, analyze how Kerry uses one or more of the features listed in the box above (or features of your own choice) to strengthen the logic and persuasiveness of his argument. Be sure that your analysis focuses on the most relevant features of the passage.

Your essay should not explain whether you agree with Kerry's claims, but rather explain how Kerry builds an argument to persuade his audience.

**END OF TEST**

**DO NOT RETURN TO A PREVIOUS SECTION.**

The Princeton Review®

Completely darken bubbles with a No. 2 pencil. If you make a mistake, be sure to erase mark completely. Erase all stray marks.

**1.**

YOUR NAME: _____
(Print)            Last                    First                    M.I.

SIGNATURE: _____    DATE: ___ / ___ / ___

HOME ADDRESS: _____
(Print)                          Number and Street

_____
City                    State                    Zip Code

PHONE NO.: _____
(Print)

IMPORTANT: Please fill in these boxes exactly as shown on the back cover of your test book.

**2. TEST FORM**

_____

**6. DATE OF BIRTH**

| Month | | Day | | Year | |
|---|---|---|---|---|---|
| ○ JAN | | | | | |
| ○ FEB | ⓪ | ⓪ | ⓪ | ⓪ | |
| ○ MAR | ① | ① | ① | ① | |
| ○ APR | ② | ② | ② | ② | |
| ○ MAY | ③ | ③ | ③ | ③ | |
| ○ JUN | | ④ | ④ | ④ | |
| ○ JUL | | ⑤ | ⑤ | ⑤ | |
| ○ AUG | | ⑥ | ⑥ | ⑥ | |
| ○ SEP | | ⑦ | ⑦ | ⑦ | |
| ○ OCT | | ⑧ | ⑧ | ⑧ | |
| ○ NOV | | ⑨ | ⑨ | ⑨ | |
| ○ DEC | | | | | |

**3. TEST CODE**

**4. REGISTRATION NUMBER**

**7. SEX**
○ MALE
○ FEMALE

The Princeton Review®

**5. YOUR NAME**

First 4 letters of last name    FIRST INIT    MID INIT

(bubbles A–Z)

**Test ⑥**    Start with number 1 for each new section.
If a section has fewer questions than answer spaces, leave the extra answer spaces blank.

## Section 1—Reading

1. Ⓐ Ⓑ Ⓒ Ⓓ
2. Ⓐ Ⓑ Ⓒ Ⓓ
3. Ⓐ Ⓑ Ⓒ Ⓓ
4. Ⓐ Ⓑ Ⓒ Ⓓ
5. Ⓐ Ⓑ Ⓒ Ⓓ
6. Ⓐ Ⓑ Ⓒ Ⓓ
7. Ⓐ Ⓑ Ⓒ Ⓓ
8. Ⓐ Ⓑ Ⓒ Ⓓ
9. Ⓐ Ⓑ Ⓒ Ⓓ
10. Ⓐ Ⓑ Ⓒ Ⓓ
11. Ⓐ Ⓑ Ⓒ Ⓓ
12. Ⓐ Ⓑ Ⓒ Ⓓ
13. Ⓐ Ⓑ Ⓒ Ⓓ
14. Ⓐ Ⓑ Ⓒ Ⓓ
15. Ⓐ Ⓑ Ⓒ Ⓓ
16. Ⓐ Ⓑ Ⓒ Ⓓ
17. Ⓐ Ⓑ Ⓒ Ⓓ
18. Ⓐ Ⓑ Ⓒ Ⓓ
19. Ⓐ Ⓑ Ⓒ Ⓓ
20. Ⓐ Ⓑ Ⓒ Ⓓ
21. Ⓐ Ⓑ Ⓒ Ⓓ
22. Ⓐ Ⓑ Ⓒ Ⓓ
23. Ⓐ Ⓑ Ⓒ Ⓓ
24. Ⓐ Ⓑ Ⓒ Ⓓ
25. Ⓐ Ⓑ Ⓒ Ⓓ
26. Ⓐ Ⓑ Ⓒ Ⓓ
27. Ⓐ Ⓑ Ⓒ Ⓓ
28. Ⓐ Ⓑ Ⓒ Ⓓ
29. Ⓐ Ⓑ Ⓒ Ⓓ
30. Ⓐ Ⓑ Ⓒ Ⓓ
31. Ⓐ Ⓑ Ⓒ Ⓓ
32. Ⓐ Ⓑ Ⓒ Ⓓ
33. Ⓐ Ⓑ Ⓒ Ⓓ
34. Ⓐ Ⓑ Ⓒ Ⓓ
35. Ⓐ Ⓑ Ⓒ Ⓓ
36. Ⓐ Ⓑ Ⓒ Ⓓ
37. Ⓐ Ⓑ Ⓒ Ⓓ
38. Ⓐ Ⓑ Ⓒ Ⓓ
39. Ⓐ Ⓑ Ⓒ Ⓓ
40. Ⓐ Ⓑ Ⓒ Ⓓ
41. Ⓐ Ⓑ Ⓒ Ⓓ
42. Ⓐ Ⓑ Ⓒ Ⓓ
43. Ⓐ Ⓑ Ⓒ Ⓓ
44. Ⓐ Ⓑ Ⓒ Ⓓ
45. Ⓐ Ⓑ Ⓒ Ⓓ
46. Ⓐ Ⓑ Ⓒ Ⓓ
47. Ⓐ Ⓑ Ⓒ Ⓓ
48. Ⓐ Ⓑ Ⓒ Ⓓ
49. Ⓐ Ⓑ Ⓒ Ⓓ
50. Ⓐ Ⓑ Ⓒ Ⓓ
51. Ⓐ Ⓑ Ⓒ Ⓓ
52. Ⓐ Ⓑ Ⓒ Ⓓ

## Section 2—Writing and Language Skills

1. Ⓐ Ⓑ Ⓒ Ⓓ
2. Ⓐ Ⓑ Ⓒ Ⓓ
3. Ⓐ Ⓑ Ⓒ Ⓓ
4. Ⓐ Ⓑ Ⓒ Ⓓ
5. Ⓐ Ⓑ Ⓒ Ⓓ
6. Ⓐ Ⓑ Ⓒ Ⓓ
7. Ⓐ Ⓑ Ⓒ Ⓓ
8. Ⓐ Ⓑ Ⓒ Ⓓ
9. Ⓐ Ⓑ Ⓒ Ⓓ
10. Ⓐ Ⓑ Ⓒ Ⓓ
11. Ⓐ Ⓑ Ⓒ Ⓓ
12. Ⓐ Ⓑ Ⓒ Ⓓ
13. Ⓐ Ⓑ Ⓒ Ⓓ
14. Ⓐ Ⓑ Ⓒ Ⓓ
15. Ⓐ Ⓑ Ⓒ Ⓓ
16. Ⓐ Ⓑ Ⓒ Ⓓ
17. Ⓐ Ⓑ Ⓒ Ⓓ
18. Ⓐ Ⓑ Ⓒ Ⓓ
19. Ⓐ Ⓑ Ⓒ Ⓓ
20. Ⓐ Ⓑ Ⓒ Ⓓ
21. Ⓐ Ⓑ Ⓒ Ⓓ
22. Ⓐ Ⓑ Ⓒ Ⓓ
23. Ⓐ Ⓑ Ⓒ Ⓓ
24. Ⓐ Ⓑ Ⓒ Ⓓ
25. Ⓐ Ⓑ Ⓒ Ⓓ
26. Ⓐ Ⓑ Ⓒ Ⓓ
27. Ⓐ Ⓑ Ⓒ Ⓓ
28. Ⓐ Ⓑ Ⓒ Ⓓ
29. Ⓐ Ⓑ Ⓒ Ⓓ
30. Ⓐ Ⓑ Ⓒ Ⓓ
31. Ⓐ Ⓑ Ⓒ Ⓓ
32. Ⓐ Ⓑ Ⓒ Ⓓ
33. Ⓐ Ⓑ Ⓒ Ⓓ
34. Ⓐ Ⓑ Ⓒ Ⓓ
35. Ⓐ Ⓑ Ⓒ Ⓓ
36. Ⓐ Ⓑ Ⓒ Ⓓ
37. Ⓐ Ⓑ Ⓒ Ⓓ
38. Ⓐ Ⓑ Ⓒ Ⓓ
39. Ⓐ Ⓑ Ⓒ Ⓓ
40. Ⓐ Ⓑ Ⓒ Ⓓ
41. Ⓐ Ⓑ Ⓒ Ⓓ
42. Ⓐ Ⓑ Ⓒ Ⓓ
43. Ⓐ Ⓑ Ⓒ Ⓓ
44. Ⓐ Ⓑ Ⓒ Ⓓ

The Princeton Review®

Completely darken bubbles with a No. 2 pencil. If you make a mistake, be sure to erase mark completely. Erase all stray marks.

**Test 6**  Start with number 1 for each new section.
If a section has fewer questions than answer spaces, leave the extra answer spaces blank.

## Section 3—Mathematics: No Calculator

1. Ⓐ Ⓑ Ⓒ Ⓓ
2. Ⓐ Ⓑ Ⓒ Ⓓ
3. Ⓐ Ⓑ Ⓒ Ⓓ
4. Ⓐ Ⓑ Ⓒ Ⓓ
5. Ⓐ Ⓑ Ⓒ Ⓓ
6. Ⓐ Ⓑ Ⓒ Ⓓ
7. Ⓐ Ⓑ Ⓒ Ⓓ
8. Ⓐ Ⓑ Ⓒ Ⓓ
9. Ⓐ Ⓑ Ⓒ Ⓓ
10. Ⓐ Ⓑ Ⓒ Ⓓ
11. Ⓐ Ⓑ Ⓒ Ⓓ
12. Ⓐ Ⓑ Ⓒ Ⓓ
13. Ⓐ Ⓑ Ⓒ Ⓓ
14. Ⓐ Ⓑ Ⓒ Ⓓ
15. Ⓐ Ⓑ Ⓒ Ⓓ

16. 17. 18. 19. 20.

## Section 4—Mathematics: Calculator

1. Ⓐ Ⓑ Ⓒ Ⓓ
2. Ⓐ Ⓑ Ⓒ Ⓓ
3. Ⓐ Ⓑ Ⓒ Ⓓ
4. Ⓐ Ⓑ Ⓒ Ⓓ
5. Ⓐ Ⓑ Ⓒ Ⓓ
6. Ⓐ Ⓑ Ⓒ Ⓓ
7. Ⓐ Ⓑ Ⓒ Ⓓ
8. Ⓐ Ⓑ Ⓒ Ⓓ
9. Ⓐ Ⓑ Ⓒ Ⓓ
10. Ⓐ Ⓑ Ⓒ Ⓓ
11. Ⓐ Ⓑ Ⓒ Ⓓ
12. Ⓐ Ⓑ Ⓒ Ⓓ
13. Ⓐ Ⓑ Ⓒ Ⓓ
14. Ⓐ Ⓑ Ⓒ Ⓓ
15. Ⓐ Ⓑ Ⓒ Ⓓ
16. Ⓐ Ⓑ Ⓒ Ⓓ
17. Ⓐ Ⓑ Ⓒ Ⓓ
18. Ⓐ Ⓑ Ⓒ Ⓓ
19. Ⓐ Ⓑ Ⓒ Ⓓ
20. Ⓐ Ⓑ Ⓒ Ⓓ
21. Ⓐ Ⓑ Ⓒ Ⓓ
22. Ⓐ Ⓑ Ⓒ Ⓓ
23. Ⓐ Ⓑ Ⓒ Ⓓ
24. Ⓐ Ⓑ Ⓒ Ⓓ
25. Ⓐ Ⓑ Ⓒ Ⓓ
26. Ⓐ Ⓑ Ⓒ Ⓓ
27. Ⓐ Ⓑ Ⓒ Ⓓ
28. Ⓐ Ⓑ Ⓒ Ⓓ
29. Ⓐ Ⓑ Ⓒ Ⓓ
30. Ⓐ Ⓑ Ⓒ Ⓓ

31. 32. 33. 34. 35.

36. 37. 38.

# Chapter 14
# Practice Test 6:
# Answers and
# Explanations

# PRACTICE TEST 6 ANSWER KEY

## Section 1: Reading

| | | | |
|---|---|---|---|
| 1. | D | 27. | B |
| 2. | C | 28. | B |
| 3. | B | 29. | B |
| 4. | D | 30. | D |
| 5. | C | 31. | A |
| 6. | C | 32. | C |
| 7. | C | 33. | A |
| 8. | A | 34. | C |
| 9. | C | 35. | B |
| 10. | C | 36. | C |
| 11. | B | 37. | D |
| 12. | B | 38. | A |
| 13. | B | 39. | B |
| 14. | D | 40. | C |
| 15. | A | 41. | C |
| 16. | C | 42. | B |
| 17. | B | 43. | D |
| 18. | A | 44. | C |
| 19. | C | 45. | B |
| 20. | D | 46. | B |
| 21. | A | 47. | C |
| 22. | A | 48. | A |
| 23. | A | 49. | A |
| 24. | D | 50. | A |
| 25. | A | 51. | C |
| 26. | D | 52. | D |

## Section 2: Writing & Language

| | | | |
|---|---|---|---|
| 1. | D | 23. | A |
| 2. | D | 24. | D |
| 3. | D | 25. | B |
| 4. | A | 26. | A |
| 5. | B | 27. | D |
| 6. | B | 28. | C |
| 7. | D | 29. | C |
| 8. | B | 30. | B |
| 9. | C | 31. | A |
| 10. | A | 32. | B |
| 11. | A | 33. | C |
| 12. | C | 34. | B |
| 13. | A | 35. | C |
| 14. | D | 36. | B |
| 15. | B | 37. | D |
| 16. | A | 38. | C |
| 17. | B | 39. | B |
| 18. | D | 40. | B |
| 19. | B | 41. | A |
| 20. | D | 42. | D |
| 21. | C | 43. | D |
| 22. | D | 44. | D |

## Section 3: Math (No Calculator)

| | | | |
|---|---|---|---|
| 1. | A | 11. | A |
| 2. | C | 12. | C |
| 3. | B | 13. | B |
| 4. | D | 14. | A |
| 5. | A | 15. | C |
| 6. | D | 16. | 3 |
| 7. | C | 17. | 250 |
| 8. | A | 18. | $\frac{3}{5}$ or 0.6 |
| 9. | B | 19. | 9 |
| 10. | D | 20. | 3 |

## Section 4: Math (Calculator)

| | | | |
|---|---|---|---|
| 1. | D | 20. | D |
| 2. | B | 21. | A |
| 3. | A | 22. | B |
| 4. | D | 23. | A |
| 5. | D | 24. | A |
| 6. | C | 25. | D |
| 7. | C | 26. | C |
| 8. | A | 27. | C |
| 9. | C | 28. | C |
| 10. | B | 29. | B |
| 11. | D | 30. | C |
| 12. | A | 31. | 12 |
| 13. | B | 32. | 216 |
| 14. | A | 33. | 180 |
| 15. | B | 34. | 5 |
| 16. | A | 35. | 350 |
| 17. | B | 36. | 20 |
| 18. | D | 37. | 0.86 |
| 19. | B | 38. | 376 |

For self-scoring assessment tables, please turn to page 957.

# PRACTICE TEST 6 EXPLANATIONS

## Section 1: Reading

1.  **D**  This question asks for the best summary of the passage, so save it until the end of the question set. To answer this question, look for an answer that fits the majority of the text and rely on POE. Choice (A) incorrectly states that a character *becomes increasingly hostile*; eliminate it. Choice (B) incorrectly states that a *character describes* something; the narrator does so. Eliminate (B). Choice (C) states that two characters are *in the same profession*, which is not true, and that they *become increasingly competitive*, which is not true; eliminate it. Choice (D) states that two characters are *traveling together*, which is true, and that they *eagerly await confrontation*, which may sound extreme, but which does fit the mention of a *frequent bone of contention* and that one character *liked to infuriate* the other. Choice (D) is the correct answer.

2.  **C**  This question asks for the main purpose of the opening sentence. To answer this question, go back to the first paragraph and carefully read the sentence to determine its purpose. The first sentence describes *cheerfulness* in general before the paragraph moves forward with specific descriptions of the cheerfulness of the characters. Eliminate any answers that have nothing to do with this prediction. Choice (A) incorrectly mentions a *contrast* and *the narrator's gloom*; eliminate it. Choice (B) refers to an *allegorical representation,* which is not present in the text. Eliminate this answer. Choice (C) matches the prediction, so keep it for now. Choice (D) incorrectly refers to *violent intentions*; eliminate it. Choice (C) is the correct answer.

3.  **B**  This question asks how the narrator's focus shifts in the second paragraph. To answer this question, carefully read the second paragraph to determine what's happening. At the beginning of the paragraph, the narrator says that it is *dreadful* for a parson to be *warlike* and that he remembers *distinctly whose servant he is*, so the narrator is referencing a parson being a *man of peace*. In the second half of the paragraph, the narrator continues by saying to the *parson-haters* that he will not go along *every step* of their *dismal, downward-tending, unchristian road*. The correct answer must have something to do with the shift from acknowledging the parson as a man of peace to disagreeing with those who are anti-parson. Choice (A) can be eliminated because the narrator does not want to chastise the clergy. Choice (B) matches the prediction, so keep it for now. Choice (C) can be eliminated because the second part of the paragraph has mention of the clergy's *manners and appearance*; eliminate it. Choice (D) is too general in its discussion of *peaceful men*; eliminate it. Choice (B) is the correct answer.

4.  **D**  Go back to the second paragraph to see how the words are used. The narrator says *if you are a parson-hater* he's not going to *go along* with the *poisonous rancor* and *horror and denunciation* toward a rector. The correct answer should have something to do with *showing strong anti-clergy sentiments*. Choice (A) can be eliminated because the narrator has no *fear* of clergymen. Choice (B) can be eliminated because it has nothing to do with the prediction. Choice (C) doesn't match the

prediction because the narrator is speaking to those who are anti-clergy, not illustrating his own *sense of dismay*. Eliminate this answer. Choice (D) mentions the *disapproval of clergymen* in the prediction, and the *reader* in the answer choice is supported by the narrator's use of *you*. Choice (D) is best supported by the text and is the correct answer.

5.  **C**  This question asks about *Moore's behavior*. The passage talks more about Helstone, but there is evidence in the passage to predict the answer for this question. In the first paragraph, the narrator says that both of the men knew that there were those who would have had *great pleasure in shooting either of [them]* and that the two men were *elate* with this knowledge. The final paragraph says *you would expect... they would converse amicably. Oh no!* and then goes on to say that Moore *liked to infuriate Helstone*. It's clear from the text that Moore likes to fight and pick fights, so the correct answer should reflect this. Choice (A) is deceptive: It contains words seen in the text but describes Helstone rather than Moore. Eliminate it. Choice (B) also describes Helstone rather than Moore, so it can be eliminated. Choice (C) is a solid paraphrase of the prediction, so keep it. Choice (D) is deceptive because the word *superiority* seems to match *reign supreme*, but that answer choice does not match the prediction. Eliminate it. This leaves (C) as the correct answer.

6.  **C**  The question asks how Helstone might be described and refers to the narrator's acknowledgement of *a certain evil* in the third paragraph. Look in the third paragraph to see that the narrator's larger point about Helstone is that he is not temperamentally suited to being a priest and *should have been a soldier*. On the whole, he is described positively, though some of his limitations are noted. Eliminate (A), as in the text he is described as *a man almost without sympathy*. Eliminate (B) because Helstone is not a *soldier*. Keep (C), as Helstone is described as *conscientious, true to principle* and *honourable*. Eliminate (D) because its tone is negative and there's no evidence to support such an extreme characterization. The correct answer is (C).

7.  **C**  The question asks for the best evidence to support the correct answer to the previous question. Look for the answer choice that refers to lines used for the prediction for Q6. Choices (A) and (B) can be eliminated, as those lines come from the first and second paragraphs, respectively. Choices (C) and (D) are both from the third paragraph and both describe Helstone, but (C) contains the list of characteristics that best supports that Helstone is a righteous citizen. Since the lines in (C) were useful in making the prediction in question 6, eliminate (D). Choice (C) is the best answer.

8.  **A**  This question asks the effect of comparing Helstone to a Cossack. To answer this question, look at the comparison in context. The narrator says, *"Nor will I curse Helstone, clerical Cossack as he was. Yet he was cursed...."* Thus, being a Cossack is something bad. Choice (A) could be true, so keep it for now. Choice (B) refers to an event, rather than a person; eliminate it. Choice (C) refers to two men, rather than only Helstone; eliminate it. Choice (D) refers to an action, rather than a person; eliminate it. The only remaining answer is (A), so select it. Choice (A) is the correct answer.

9.　**C**　This question asks how the men found each other's company sometimes. To answer this question, read paragraph 4 and find that they *chafed each other's moods*, had a *frequent bone of contention*, and that one *liked to infuriate* the other. There is no evidence that they found each other *intolerable*, only that they annoyed each other. Eliminate (A). Choice (B) is irrelevant to the text, so it can be eliminated. Choice (C) matches the idea that they annoyed each other, so don't eliminate it. Choice (D) can be eliminated because it's a positive word, and the two men were not *comforting* each other. Choice (C) is appropriately negative for the passage. Choice (C) is the correct answer.

10.　**C**　This question asks for the best evidence for the answer to Q9. To answer this question, start by eliminating choices that refer to the wrong paragraph: (A) refers to paragraph 2 and (B) refers to paragraph 3; eliminate both. Choices (C) and (D) refer to paragraph 4; compare them. Since (C) contains the phrase *chafed each other's moods*, keep it. While (D) does mention a difference between the two men that could potentially cause trouble, the lines themselves don't show that trouble. Eliminate (D). Choice (C) is the correct answer.

11.　**B**　This question asks about the main purpose of the passage. Because this is a general question, save it until the end of the question set. Choice (A) is the opposite of the text, so it can be eliminated. Choice (B) is possible, so keep it for now. Choice (C) is neutral, but the author of the passage definitely has a negative opinion about marketing education, so eliminate it. Choice (D) incorrectly states that the passage's focus is *to evaluate statistics,* so eliminate it. Choice (B) is the correct answer.

12.　**B**　The question asks about the *concession* the author makes to the view that people are *consumers in the marketplace of life.* That means the author disagrees with the view, but the correct answer will agree with it. Because this question is the first in a paired set, the answers to Q13 can be used to help with POE. Begin with Q13 and see if any connections can be made to answers in Q12. Choice (13A) says that every aspect of life has *cash value* and *can be purchased.* While this does agree with the view presented in the question, these lines do not support any of the answers for Q12, so (13A) can be eliminated. Choice (13B) says *this scenario may be appropriate for the sale of shoes....* This agrees with the idea that people are consumers, and these lines support (12B). Connect these two answers. Choice (13C) might initially seem to support (12C) because of the mention of *students*, *price*, and *customers*, but a careful reading shows these two answers don't actually support each other. Eliminate (13C). Choice (13D) talks about the students wanting *to be entertained*, which isn't mentioned in any of the choices for Q12. Eliminate (13D). Without support from Q13, (12A), (12C), and (12D) can be eliminated. Choices (12B) and (13B) are the correct answers.

13.　**B**　(See explanation above.)

14.　**D**　This question asks what *assume* means in context. To answer this question, find the word and read a few lines above and below. Substitute an alternate word or phrase that makes sense in the context, then compare that word to the answer choices. A phrase like "take on" could work well.

Choices (A), (B), and (C) all refer possible definitions of assume, but none of them fit the context of the passage, so eliminate them. Choice (D) fits the prediction and is the correct answer.

15.   **A**   This question asks about the main purpose of the fourth paragraph. To answer it, carefully read the fourth paragraph and determine why the author included it in the passage. In the paragraph, the author translates the educational experience into economic terms, presenting the idea that *achieving some sort of advantage is considered...essential to beating the competition.* He goes on to explain how cheating and *dubious maneuvers*, though *unfortunate*, have become rampant because that is an easier way to achieve success. Choice (A) matches the text because the author does explain the *logic of an attitude* (cheating) and he does disagree with that attitude. Choice (B) is something the author may agree with outside of the text, but that's not what the fourth paragraph is about. Eliminate it. Choice (C) has nothing to do with the paragraph and can be eliminated. Although he doesn't agree with cheating, the fourth paragraph does not argue against cheating, so (D) can be eliminated. Choice (A) is the correct answer.

16.   **C**   This question asks what *enticing* means in context. To answer this question, find the word and read a few lines above and below. Substitute a word or phrase that makes sense in the context, then compare that word or phrase to the answer choices. A word like "attractive" could work well. Choices (A), (B), and (D) do not fit this prediction; eliminate them. Choice (C) matches this prediction; select it. Choice (C) is the correct answer.

17.   **B**   This question asks for the best support for a particular claim (that schools have already begun to incorporate some facets of the popular marketplace into their educational materials). To answer this question, consider whether and how each answer choice would affect that claim. Choice (A) describes what administrators *must* do, rather than what they have already begun to do, so eliminate it. Choice (B) describes something that *has become normative*, so this could fit; keep it. Choice (C) is in the present tense and has the wrong tone, so eliminate it. Choice (D) refers to courses that administrators *have begun to promote*, so keep it. Now compare (B) and (D) to each other: (B) mentions a *proliferation of degrees and courses*, while (D) mentions *courses*. Choice (B) connects more specifically to the *advertising consultants* mentioned in paragraph 5. Choice (B) is the correct answer.

18.   **A**   This question asks what the main idea of the last paragraph is. To answer this question, read the paragraph and make a prediction of what that summary will be, such as, "education is hurt when it is treated like a commodity." Look for answers that match this prediction, and eliminate answers that express the main idea of some other paragraph, the main idea of the entire passage, or a secondary idea of the last paragraph. Choice (A) contains both ideas from the prediction (education hurt, treated like a commodity), so keep it. Choice (B) is true, but is a secondary point in the last paragraph. This answer is too narrow, so it can be eliminated. Choice (C) is tempting, as it has the correct tone, but *unimportant* is not the same as *hurt*; eliminate it. Choice (D) is deceptive, using concepts from the last paragraph to say something that the paragraph itself does not say; eliminate it. Choice (A) is the correct answer.

19.  **C**   This question asks what statement is supported by the data in the graph. To answer this question, look at the graph and notice any obvious trends, such as the following: all three lines show a positive increase, a small one with overall consumer prices and a big one with college textbooks and tuition and fees. Choice (A) mentions an increase, so keep it. Choice (B) says there is no increase, so eliminate it. Choice (C) mentions an increase, so keep it. Choice (D) says there is a decrease, so eliminate it. Now compare (A) and (C). Choice (A) does not match the graph because the line does not rise consistently, and (C) matches the information in the graph. Choice (C) is the correct answer.

20.  **D**   This question asks during which period the difference was largest between college tuition and fees and overall consumer prices. To answer this question, look at the graph and see that this was in 2012. Choice (D) is the correct answer.

21.  **A**   This question asks what idea in the passage is most directly supported by the graph. To answer this question, note that the graph is measuring prices. Now eliminate answers that do not concern prices, which are (B), (C), and (D). Choice (A) is the correct answer.

22.  **A**   This question asks what the authors of the first passage indicate about the addition of nutrients to food. This topic is covered throughout the whole passage, so there's no specific window to look for the answer. Notice that it's the first in a paired set, though, so this question can be done in tandem with Q23. Look at the lines given in the answers to Q23 first and see if they support any answer choices in Q22. Any answer choices that neither support nor have support can be eliminated. Start with (23A). The lines say that processed food contributes to *both food security... and nutrition security*. This could support (22A) because contributing to food and nutrition security is a helpful impact. Connect those two answers. Choice (23B) says that processed foods *are nutritionally important* and then goes on to ask how we can *enhance the contribution to...nutritional...and food security*. This refers to the securities mentioned in (23A), so connect this to (22A) as well. Choice (23C) presents a contrast between *limiting processed foods* and *encouraging best available food options*. These lines don't support any of the answers for Q22, so (23C) can be eliminated. Choice (23D) mentions a *disadvantage* in that the techniques *are poorly understood*. These lines may initially seem to support (22C), but there's no indication from the text that they *may require further investigation*. Even though it might make sense that something poorly understood would need further investigation, that's not in the text. Eliminate (23D). Without any support from Q23, (22B), (22C), and (22D) can be eliminated. There are two answer choices connected to (22A), so now go back and carefully reread each of the support lines. Choice (23A) is a statement of fact, clearly showing the *helpful impact*. Although (23B) also mentions the same ideas, those lines ask about how to enhance the contributions, rather than stating them as fact. Eliminate (23B). Choices (22A) and (23A) are the best answers.

23.  **A**   (See explanation above.)

24.   **D**   This question asks about food enrichment methods, which are mentioned throughout the first passage. Save this question until the others have been answered. Choice (A) can be eliminated because there is no information about how the food enrichment is done. Choice (B) can be eliminated because there is no mention of *employment opportunities. Thiamin* is mentioned in the fourth paragraph, so don't eliminate (C). Choice (D) can be supported by lines 37–38, which say that a disadvantage of the processing techniques is that they *are poorly understood.* Compare (C) and (D). Although thiamin is mentioned, there is no indication that processed foods are the *leading source* of thiamin. Choice (D) is directly supported by the text and is the correct answer.

25.   **A**   This question asks what *grasp* means in context. To answer this question, find the word and read a few lines above and below. Substitute a word or phrase that makes sense in the context, then compare that word or phrase to the answer choices. A word like "understand" could work well. Choice (A) matches that prediction; keep it. Choices (B) and (C) are definitions for *grasp*, but they don't fit the context of the passage. They can be eliminated. Choice (D) refers to physical grasping; eliminate it. Choice (A) is the correct answer.

26.   **D**   This question asks what Passage 2's reference to "Big Food" suggests about global food systems. To answer this question, see what the passage explicitly says: that a few companies rule global food systems. Choices (A) and (C) do not mention companies; eliminate them. Choice (B) refers to single companies that serve individual regions, and (D) refers to a few companies that dominate. Choice (D) most clearly matches what the text actually says; (D) is the correct answer.

27.   **B**   This question asks what profit margins and price/cost surpluses have in common in Passage 2. To answer this question, read paragraph 6, which mentions both things in a sentence that states that the main goals of these companies is to increase profits. So the profit margins and price/cost surpluses must have this in common: the goal of increasing profits. Choice (A) is not supported by this prediction; eliminate it. Choice (B) could be true; keep it. Choice (C) could be true; keep it. Choice (D) goes beyond what the passage says; the passage does not indicate that they are BEST increased by expanding markets; eliminate it. Compare (B) and (C). Choice (B) refers to the concerns of companies, and (C) refers to economic theory in general. The passage never treated economic theory in general, so (C) is too broad to answer the question. Choice (B) is the correct answer.

28.   **B**   This question asks what effect the possibilities mentioned in Passage 2 have. To answer this question, read the relevant selection in the context of the paragraph. The passage states that industry can only make profits by doing things that are not good nutritionally. Choice (A) uses words from the paragraph, but suggests the opposite of what the text says; eliminate it. Choice (B) supports the meaning of the last paragraph; keep it. Choices (C) and (D) do not fit the text; eliminate them. Choice (B) is the correct answer.

29.   **B**   This question asks about the main purpose of both passages. To answer this question, start by eliminating choices that are true for one passage only, or are not true for either passage.

Choice (A) is too specific and fits Passage 1 only; eliminate it. Choice (B) could be true; keep it. Choice (C) is too specific and fits some of Passage 1 only; eliminate it. Choice (D) is also too specific to be a main idea; eliminate it. Choice (B) is the correct answer.

30. **D** This question asks how Passages 1 and 2 are related to each other. To answer this question, consider the overall impression of both passages: Passage 1 says that American food processing is great, and Passage 2 says that global food systems are problematic. This does not involve *underlying processes* and there is no *solution* in Passage 1, so eliminate (A). Passage 2 does not present a *plan* relating to *processes* presented in Passage 1, so eliminate (B). Each passage seems to have an opinion, rather than *an objective perspective*, so eliminate (C). Choice (D) says that Passage 1 embraces a system, which matches the prediction, and that Passage 2 explores the problematic nature of a system, which also matches the prediction. Choice (D) is the correct answer.

31. **A** This question asks what the authors of both passages would most likely agree on. To answer this question, eliminate choices that fit only one passage (or neither). Choice (A) mentions adequate nutrition, which both passages examined, so this is possible, even though only Passage 2 concerned global food systems; keep it for now. Nothing matching (B) is mentioned in either passage; eliminate it. Almost nothing matching (C) is mentioned in either passage, although Passage 1 discusses *suspicion*; eliminate (C). Choice (D) is absent from Passage 2, and Passage 1 indicates the opposite to be true. Choice (A) is the correct answer.

32. **C** This question asks what in Passage 2 matches what is said in a specific part of Passage 1. To answer this question, first review the specific part of Passage 1, and note that it concerns *processing* and *nutritional content*. Choice (A) has processing, but no nutrition; eliminate it. Choice (B) has no processing and no nutrition; eliminate it. Choice (C) has processing and nutrition; keep it for now. Choice (D) has processing and mention of *healthier foods*; keep it for now. To decide between (C) and (D), review the specific part of Passage 1, and note that it focuses on processing and nutrition not necessarily correlating, which means that they might be independent of each other. Choice (C) states that processing *can improve nutritional content*, but that most processing actually serves to *reduce nutritional quality*. Choice (D) states that industry could make healthier foods. Choice (D) seems to point in one direction, whereas (C) points in two directions, which better fits the prediction. Choice (C) is the correct answer.

33. **A** This question asks what the central problem is regarding Indiana's photo law. To answer this question, select an answer choice that fits several paragraphs and eliminate answer choices that fit only one paragraph (or none of them). Choice (A) fits the last sentence of paragraph 1, as well as several parts of the passage afterwards; keep it for now. Choice (B) is true, but it is only mentioned in paragraphs 2 and 5. Choice (C) is true, but it is only mentioned in paragraph 4; eliminate (C). Choice (D) is only mentioned in paragraph 7, so it can be eliminated for that reason; it is also inaccurate, since the Supreme Court took a *restricted* view, not a *wide* one. Between (A) and (B), (A) is closer to the main idea of the entire passage. Choice (A) is the correct answer.

34.  **C**  This question asks what the phrase *remarkably enough* emphasizes about the Supreme Court. To answer this question, find the phrase in the first paragraph and read carefully for context. The author uses the phrase to indicate something notable or out-of-the-ordinary. Choice (A) can be eliminated because there is no evidence of *complete disregard* for the Constitution. The passage doesn't suggest *ignorance* of the Bill of Rights, just that it was surprising that the Supreme Court didn't use language that was previously very important. Eliminate (B). Choice (C) matches the prediction, so keep it. Choice (D) is irrelevant to the prediction, so eliminate it. Choice (C) is the correct answer.

35.  **B**  This question asks about a claim that casts doubt on the recent Supreme Court decision. Because this is the first in a paired set, use the answers from Q36 to work through answers for Q35. Eliminate any answer choices that don't provide support for other answers. Choice (36A) gives a specific details about Indiana's law, which aligns with the Supreme Court decision to uphold voter-ID laws. Eliminate (36A). Choice (36B) is an example of a specific individual who disagrees with the law, which could cast a small amount of doubt on the decision. There is no corresponding answer in Q35, though, so (36B) can be eliminated. Choice (36C) mentions that the Supreme Court agreed with the man who challenged the law. That would cast doubt on the decision, and it supports (35B). Connect those two answers. Choice (36D) is specific details about the process of getting an ID, which has nothing to do with whether or not the Supreme Court decision is a good one. Eliminate (36D). Without support, (35A), (35C), and (35D) can all be eliminated. This leaves (35B) and (36C) as the correct answers.

36.  **C**  (See explanation above.)

37.  **D**  This question asks what *force* means in context. To answer this question, find the word *force*, read a few lines above and below, and insert another word that would fit based on the context. Something like "effect" could work. Choices (A) and (B) refer to other meanings of force that don't match the context of the passage, and (C) is part of the term "force field." Choice (D) matches the prediction exactly, so pick it. Choice (D) is the correct answer.

38.  **A**  This question asks what *have* means in context. To answer this question, find the word *have*, read a few lines above and below, and insert another word that would fit based on the context. Something like "believe" could work. Choice (A) could fit; keep it for now. Choices (B), (C), and (D) do not fit this prediction, so eliminate them. Choice (A) is the correct answer.

39.  **B**  This question asks what the word *exclusionary* is used for. To answer this question, read in context to see that it refers to a state law. Choice (A) refers to a difference that is not the issue here. Choice (B) fits the prediction. Choice (C) could be true, but is not what the word in question is used for. Choice (D) does not fit anything in the passage. Choice (B) is the correct answer.

40.  **C**  This question asks what the authors claim (*contend*) the present-day Supreme Court has done regarding voter-ID laws. To answer this question, go back to the passage and see what is said about the present-day Supreme Court. Choice (A) refers to the past Supreme Court, so

eliminate it. Choice (B) is deceptive. Although the phrase *heavier burden* is in the text, it does not refer to the Supreme Court. That phrase refers to the burden on Indianans to get paperwork completed. Choice (C) is supported by paragraph 7, which states that the Supreme Court ignored the 24th Amendment and relied on the 14th. Choice (D) recalls paragraph 9 but is extreme: The passage does not say that the Supreme Court has *refused* to explain its decision. Choice (C) is the correct answer.

41. **C**  This question asks for the best evidence for the answer to Q40. To answer this question, simply refer back to the lines used to answer Q40. Choice (C) is from paragraph 7, is relevant, and it is the correct answer.

42. **B**  This question asks what contrast the eighth paragraph primarily makes. To answer this question, read the eighth paragraph and note the contrast, rewording if necessary. Something like "considering the Constitution versus not considering it" would work. Choices (A), (C), and (D) are not mentioned in paragraph 8; eliminate them. Choice (B) could fit as a summary of the prediction: The Constitution is the historical rule, and the anomaly is the current Court's not considering it. Choice (B) is the correct answer.

43. **D**  This question asks for the main purpose of the first paragraph. To answer this question, read the first paragraph, then summarize what the author uses this first paragraph to do. Several sentences indicate that the amount of ice is shrinking at a rate much faster than what was initially predicted. Look for an answer that matches this idea. Only one sentence talks about the ice reforming, so (A) is too specific; eliminate (A). Although the size is compared to a U.S. state in this paragraph, that's not the paragraph's main purpose; eliminate (B). Choice (C) may be tempting due to the first half, but it is flawed due to the second half; eliminate (C). Choice (D) fits, since the trend of the ice melting is occurring much faster than scientists originally predicted. Choice (D) is the correct answer.

44. **C**  This question asks for the meaning of *projected* in context. To answer this question, find the word and read a few lines above and below. Substitute a word or phrase that makes sense in the context, then compare that word or phrase to the answer choices. A word like "thought" could work well. Compare this prediction to the answer choices. Choice (A) is a different meaning of *projected*, and (B) and (D) do not fit the prediction. Choice (C) fits the prediction and is the correct answer.

45. **B**  This question asks why Naam says the Earth's tilt is significant. To answer this question, read paragraph 2, which says that the tilt puts the Arctic in complete darkness or complete sunlight in different seasons. The correct answer will have something to do with the tilt affecting sunlight and darkness in different seasons. Choices (A) and (D) are each only true for one season; eliminate them. Choice (C) is inaccurate, and (B) fits the prediction. Choice (B) is the correct answer.

46. **B**  This question asks for the best evidence for the answer to Q45. Since the evidence came from paragraph two, look at where the answer choices come from. Choices (A), (C), and (D) are

from the wrong paragraph, so eliminate them. Choice (B) is from paragraph two, and matches the prediction for Q45, so (B) is the correct answer.

47.   **C**   This question asks for the meaning of *pace* in context. To answer this question, find the word and read a few lines above and below. Substitute a word or phrase that makes sense in the context, then compare that word or phrase to the answer choices. A word like "rate" could work well. Compare this prediction to the answer choices. Choice (A) refers to a different meaning of *pace*; eliminate it. Choices (B) and (D) do not fit the prediction; (C) does. Choice (C) is the correct answer.

48.   **A**   This question asks about a reasonable inference that can be made about *climate scientists* based on the passage. There is no line reference, and climate scientists appear throughout the passage. Notice that this is the first question in a paired set, so use the best evidence answers in the next question to help with POE. Start with the answers to Q49 and eliminate any that don't support answers in Q48. Choice (49A) states that *opinions differ substantially... among climate scientists.* It's not clear from the line what those opinions are, but the answers in Q48 do have *agree* and *disagree* options, so these lines could work. Don't eliminate (49A). Choice (49B) mentions a paper in which *multiple scientists* agree about the possibility of *an ice-free summer.* No disagreement or uncertainty is mentioned, so these lines can't support any answer choices for Q48. Eliminate (49B). Both (49C) and (49D) mention specific scientists by name. Neither of those choices is broad enough to support any answers for Q48, so they can both be eliminated. This leaves (49A), but there's no clear connection to any of the answers in Q48. Go back to the text and read the window for this line to determine what the scientists' differing opinions are. Just before that line reference, the text discusses the amount of ice and what would happen if it continued to melt at its current pace. Therefore, the differing opinions must have something to do with the rate of ice melt. Eliminate (48C) and (48D). Compare the remaining two choices. Choice (48A) correctly matches the information in the text. Choices (48A) and (49A) are the correct answers.

49.   **A**   (See explanation above.)

50.   **A**   This question asks how the graph depicts the general trend in the area of Arctic sea ice. To answer this question, look at the graph and draw a line that best fits the overall trend. The amount of sea ice overall goes down over time, with some fluctuations up and down. Choice (A) could fit; keep it. Choice (B) could be tempting, but it is not a *geometric series;* eliminate it. Choice (C) exaggerates the changes, which are not *dramatic;* eliminate it. Choice (D) is not supported, since the graph does not show that the shrinkage is temporary. Choice (A) is the correct answer.

51.   **C**   This question asks which concept is supported by the passage and by the information in the graph. To answer this question, consider both the passage, which indicates that the ice is shrinking and will be gone at some point in the future, and the graph, which shows the amount of ice dropping over a 30-year period. Choices (B) and (D) are contradicted by both the passage and the graph; eliminate them. Choice (A) is possible, but is not necessarily true

based on information in the passage or the graph. Choice (C) has the best support from both the passage and the graph. Choice (C) is the correct answer.

52. **D** This question asks how the graph supports the author's point that Arctic ice is receding. To answer this question, go back to the text to see the specific points made by the author, then see how the graph relates to those points. Although (A) fits the text, it does not fit the graph; eliminate it. Choice (B) is mentioned in the passage as a possibility, but this is not a point the author makes; thus, eliminate it. Choice (C) does not accurately depict the graph; eliminate it. Choice (D) fits both the author's point and the graph. Choice (D) is the correct answer.

## Section 2: Writing and Language

1. **D** Choose DELETE unless there is some very good reason not to. In this case, (A), (B), and (C) add unnecessary transitions to a sentence that already contains a transition in the word *As*. Additionally, *yet*, *and*, and *for* are all FANBOYS, and when used with a comma, these words operate as STOP punctuation, which links only complete ideas. The phrase *As people become more sensitive to the idea of preserving certain ecosystems* is incomplete, so it cannot be followed by STOP punctuation. The best option is therefore to DELETE the underlined portion, as (D) suggests.

2. **D** The odd pairs of *human reacting* and *human reacts*, as in (A) and (B), can be eliminated because they do not make sense in this or any other context. The same can be said for (C), *human interacting*. Choice (D) presents the most viable option, *human interaction*, and is therefore the best answer.

3. **D** In order to choose an appropriate transition word, consider the ideas that must be linked. The idea that precedes the transition word reads as follows: *The central challenge of maintaining an ecosystem, especially by artificial means, is that ecosystems have a tendency to change, particularly with the dual influence of human interaction and a rapidly altering climate.* The idea that comes after the transition word reads as follows: *one career that has grown by leaps and bounds in the last fifty years is that of the soil conservationist.* These ideas agree with one another, especially given the first sentence's claim that people have *become more sensitive to the idea of preserving certain ecosystems.* Of the available transition words, the only one that signals agreement in this way is (D), *Therefore.*

4. **A** The question asks which answer most effectively sets up the subject of the paragraph, so start by figuring out the subject of the paragraph. This paragraph is primarily concerned with the role a soil conservationist might play in helping to *determine where it would be safest to build a dream house* in a *coastal area.* Choices (B) and (D) are not specific, so they can be eliminated. Choice (C) does not address the coastal region, so it too can be eliminated. Choice (A) mentions *building a beach house*, so it is the only choice that is adequately specific and germane to the topic of the paragraph.

5. **B** All four choices refer to the same idea, that of erosion, so the best answer will be the most concise. Choice (B), *erosion*, provides that conciseness because it expresses the idea in a single word.

6. **B** The items in a list must be consistent with one another. In this case, the first two items in the list are *collapsing* and *shifting*, so the only consistent option is (B), *deteriorating*. Choice (D) also contains this word, but this choice adds the unnecessary word *structures*. Choice (B) is therefore the correct answer.

7. **D** For long combination questions like this one, use POE on answers that do not make sense. Choice (A) can be eliminated because it says that soil conservationists *are ways of preserving land*, when in fact the soil conservationists *provide* these ways. Choice (B) can be eliminated because the phrase *each one of them* is ambiguous. Choice (C) is awkwardly phrased because of the excessive phrases *in these cases* and *a variety of different*. Choice (D) is therefore the best of the available answers because it states the idea directly and without excess or ambiguity.

8. **B** The phrase *farming techniques* could be clarified by the proposed information, so that information should be added. The mention of *no-till farming* does not demonstrate the advantages of the method, however, so (A) can be eliminated. Choice (B) is more effective: *no-till farming* and *terrace methods* provide specific examples of the *farming methods* mentioned in the sentence.

9. **C** The subject of the underlined verb is *farmlands*, which is plural. Choices (A) and (D) contain singular verbs, so these choices can be eliminated. The word *which* in (B) creates a sentence fragment, so this too can be eliminated. Choice (C) is the correct answer: It contains a verb that agrees with the non-underlined subject and does not add unnecessary words.

10. **A** Choice (A) seems good, but check the other answer choices to see if one is better. Choice (D) is offensive to people living in the Midwest, so it should be eliminated. Choices (A), (B), and (C) each express similar ideas, so the best answer will be the most concise and the most consistent with the phrasing of the other items in the list, *deserts of the Southwest* and *forests of the Northwest*. In this case, the most concise of the answers is (A), *plains*.

11. **A** The passage as a whole is concerned with describing the work of soil conservationists and the importance of the work these conservationists do. Choice (A) encapsulates that idea effectively. Choice (B) undermines the importance of soil conservationists, and (C) gives a value judgment that the passage has not discussed and that is unfair to one group of soil conservationists. Choice (D) is too concerned with a particular ecosystem. Choice (A) is therefore the best answer.

12. **C** In order to choose an appropriate transition word, consider the ideas that must be linked. The idea that precedes the transition word reads as follows: *There may be some controversy as to who earns these awards in many cases.* The idea that comes after the transition word reads as follows: *there can be no doubt that the winners are always accomplished in their fields and have contributed something to their disciplines and the world at large.* These ideas contrast, especially given the words *controversy* and *no doubt*, and the only word that effectively signals this contrast is (C), *however*.

13. **A** Use POE to eliminate words that don't belong in the context. Choice (C) creates an ambiguous pronoun in its use of the word *it*. Choice (D) anticipates an example, but no example is forthcoming. Choice (B) cuts out these words, but it creates a new problem—the phrase *the world at large* now has no clear place within the sentence. The best answer is therefore (A), which establishes that the work of Nobel recipients is significant to their disciplines *and* to the world at large.

14. **D** If there is no good reason to add new information, don't add it. This new information about Watson and Crick is interesting, but it does not belong in this paragraph, which focuses on the Nobel Peace Prize. Choices (A) and (B) can be eliminated, then, because they suggest that the sentence should be added. Choice (C) correctly states that the sentence should not be added, but its reason is untrue. Choice (D) better captures the reason the sentence should not be added: The sentence does not contribute in a significant way to the main idea of the paragraph.

15. **B** As the verb *see* indicates, this sentence should be in the present tense, eliminating (A). Choice (D) can be eliminated because there is no indication that multiple committees give the award. Choices (B) and (C) express essentially the same idea, but (B) does so in a more direct way that avoids the awkward *-ing* construction in (C). Choice (B) is therefore the best of the available answers.

16. **A** This sentence refers to a *common goal* belonging to some group—in other words, *their common goal*. The form given in (B) and (C), *they're*, is the contraction *they are*, which has no place in this sentence. Choices (B) and (C) can be eliminated. Choice (D) can also be eliminated because it contains a semicolon, which cannot be used with anything other than complete ideas. The idea *to make the world a better place* is not a complete idea, so the semicolon cannot punctuate this sentence. Only (A) can work, as it uses the correct form of the pronoun and punctuation that is appropriate to the context. A colon must come after a complete idea, but what comes after it can be either complete or incomplete.

17. **B** Unless there is a reason to use a comma, don't use one. In this case, the word *King's* is needed to make the sentence complete. Because it is essential to the completeness of the sentence, it should not be offset with any commas. Choice (B) is therefore the best of the answers.

18. **D** The question asks for a supporting detail that is most similar to the detail already in the paragraph. This sentence mentions *people of color seeking civil rights*, but it also mentions that King's influence *spanned the globe*. Choice (A) does not fit with these large ideas, (B) is not adequately specific, and (C) undermines King's importance. Only (D) adequately fulfills the question's requirement of a *specific supporting detail* and ties this sentence to the *non-violent campaign* mentioned in the previous sentence.

19. **B** When faced with long, confusing sentences, use POE aggressively. In this case, the incorrect answers—(A), (C), and (D)—all create misplaced or dangling modifiers. Choice (C), for example, contains the modifier *when it was awarded*, but that modifier seems to be describing *first-year President Barack Obama*, which does not make sense. Choice (B) is the only choice that is free of any such incoherence and is therefore the best answer.

20.  **D**  Choice (A) changes the punctuation but does not combine the sentences in a meaningful way. Choice (B) introduces the transition word *while*, which does not create the desired contrast between the two sentences. Choice (C) introduces the transition *for*, which makes it seem that King is famous *because* Bunche was the first. Only (D) is truly effective at combining the ideas, stating that King was the most famous *yet* Bunche was the first African-American to win the prize.

21.  **C**  Use the other similarly phrased items in the sentence to determine the best form of the underlined portion. These other items are *the 1949 Armistice Agreements* and *the 1948 Arab-Israeli conflict*. The choice that best preserves this format is (C).

22.  **D**  Martin Luther King, Jr., is discussed in paragraph 3. Paragraph 5 begins with the idea that *King may be the most famous African-American recipient of the Nobel Peace Prize*, thus suggesting that paragraph 5 must come after paragraph 3. This eliminates (B) and (C). Choice (A) can also be eliminated because paragraph 4 must come at the end—it describes a recent recipient of the Nobel Peace Prize and offers some concluding remarks. The best placement for paragraph 5, therefore, would be directly after paragraph 3, as (D) suggests.

23.  **A**  The first two sentences of this paragraph establish a contrast between the *most obvious facet* and *What many do not understand quite as well*. These two phrases require a contrasting transition, so *however* in (A) is the best response.

24.  **D**  Since all four answer choices express the same idea, choose the shortest that does not introduce any grammatical errors. In this case, the shortest answer is (D), *analogous functions*, which accomplishes what the other answers do in the fewest words.

25.  **B**  The idea given in the passage, *Because of the heavy output from this wide variety of industrial sources, the earth's atmosphere is bombarded*, is complete grammatically. However, the meaning of the word *bombarded* is not entirely clear. The proposed insertion could clarify the word *bombarded*, so it should be added. The insertion is not helpful in defining anything about the *Amazonian rainforest*, which is not mentioned in the passage, so (A) can be eliminated. Choice (B), however, states the value of the inserted idea and correctly states that the idea should be inserted. Choice (B) is therefore the correct answer.

26.  **A**  The underlined pronoun refers back to $CO_2$, which is singular. The pronoun should be consistent with this singular noun, thus eliminating (C) and (D). (In fact, *there* is not a pronoun at all.) Of the remaining two pronouns, *it's* is the contraction *it is*, and *its* provides a possessive pronoun. This phrase should read *it is always absorbing heat energy*, indicating the need for the contraction given in (A).

27.  **D**  According to the graph, carbon-dioxide parts per million have increased with almost linear consistency. Temperature changes have also increased, though in an irregular pattern. Choice (A) can be eliminated for stating that the two curves are *exactly the same*. Choice (B) states that

temperatures have not increased at all, when the graph shows that they have. Choice (C) is untrue. Only (D) is consistent with the information in the graph and is therefore the correct answer.

28.  **C**  Choose the word that best fits the style and tone of the passage. Choices (A) and (D) are too informal for the tone of the passage. Choice (B) is also a bit informal and overstates the idea of the sentence. Only (C) works in the context in a way that is consistent with the passage's style and tone.

29.  **C**  This long sentence may seem to require additional punctuation or linking words, but pay attention to the verb *would*, which the answer choices do not change. The subject of this verb is the word *number*, from *the number of trees required to offset the emissions of one modest coal plant operating in a small city in Connecticut*. Quite a long phrase! Even so, that phrase should not be broken up by any punctuation, nor should the subject and verb be split by transition words such as those found in (A) and (B). Choice (D) adds the word *it*, which stands in for the subject *number* again, but has no transition. Only (C) appropriately leaves out extra words and punctuation.

30.  **B**  Use the context. If this is an actual quotation, a second set of punctuation marks should appear at the end of the quote. No second set appears, thus eliminating (A). In fact, this sentence does not need any punctuation at all—the comma in (C) and the long dash in (D) break up the flow of the sentence unnecessarily. When there is no need for punctuation, don't add it! Choice (B) is the best of the available answers.

31.  **A**  The main differences among the answer choices have to do with the pronouns. The word *temper* remains essentially the same. The choice is instead between *those polluting behaviors* in (A); *them* in (B) and (D); and *it* in (C). Pronouns are concise substitutes, but they are never as precise as specific nouns. Therefore, when, as in this question, the answers list three pronouns and one specific noun, choose the specific noun. Choice (A) contains that specific noun, and this answer provides the best option because there is no room for ambiguity.

32.  **B**  The underlined portion is offset as unnecessary information, which is included to clarify the statement made in this passage about the *longer process* of getting the Earth's carbon levels *back to appropriate ranges*. As such, the whole phrase, *or series of processes*, should be offset by commas (as it is in this sentence), thus eliminating (C) and (D). Choice (A) has too many commas, splitting up the phrase unnecessarily. Choice (B) is therefore the best of the available answers.

33.  **C**  Use the language of the sentence. The first word is *This*, which refers to something that could *go a long way toward reforesting the Amazon rainforest*. As such, the previous sentence must contain some plan or course or action. Sentence 2 provides exactly that in its mention of the trees that could be placed on the *list of threatened species*. The proposed sentence should therefore be placed after sentence 2 and before sentence 3, as (C) indicates.

34.  **B**  Look at the changes among the answer choices. There are three choices with transition words and one without. For the sake of conciseness, if the sentence can stand without the transition

words, don't include them! In this case, the sentence is complete without the transition words, so the best answer is (B).

35. **C** Read the question carefully. It asks for a sentence that best supports this sentence's claim. There's not a tremendous amount of context in this sentence, *Sometimes that influence is more literal—as in the case of those writers who take marginal characters from earlier works.* Use POE. Choices (A) and (B) are irrelevant, so they can be eliminated. Choice (D) can also be eliminated because the word *it* creates ambiguity within the sentence. As a result, the best of the available answers is (C), which continues the thought established in the beginning of the sentence without creating new grammatical errors.

36. **B** On questions that test idioms and odd transitions words, use POE. Choice (A) can be eliminated because the phrase *just as* means "at that exact moment," which would not apply here. Choice (C) can be eliminated because this construction would imply that the story focuses *from* the interpretation, which does not make sense. Choice (D) can be eliminated because the word *it* in this context would be awkward and ambiguous. Only (B) remains, suggesting that *in* the story's interpretation, the characters act in a certain way.

37. **D** The key words in sentence 2 are *this alternate route*. Sentences 1 and 2 do not contain any mention of alternatives, but sentence 4 does with the words *rather than*. Sentence 4 describes how Milton's *Paradise Lost* was an alternate take on a biblical story, so the words *this alternate route* in sentence 2 must refer directly back to sentence 4, as (D) does.

38. **C** The words *particularly the great classics of the language* are offset in this sentence as unnecessary or parenthetical information. There are three ways to offset this information—with commas, dashes, or parentheses—so the underlined portion should have punctuation that is consistent with the rest of the sentence. The phrase *particularly the great classics of the language* is initially offset with a comma, so it should be concluded with a comma as well, as in (C).

39. **B** Choose a word that is consistent in style and tone with the rest of the passage. Use POE to eliminate words that don't make sense in the context, such as *overtake*, in (A). Choice (C) can also be eliminated because the word *manifest* means "to show or demonstrate," and one cannot *manifest a story*. Choice (D) may be unfamiliar (*ideate* means "to form an idea of"), but (B) works appropriately in the context and does not elevate the level of vocabulary in the context. Choice (B) is therefore the better answer, whatever the definition of *ideate* may be.

40. **B** To *adopt* is "to take on or assume," as an idea or a name. The word can also refer to taking on the legal guardianship of children. To *adapt* is "to suit to a new purpose" or "to modify." In this sentence, the latter definition applies, eliminating (C) and (D). Choice (A) can also be eliminated because the word *he* repeats the subject of the sentence unnecessarily. Choice (B) is therefore the best of the available answer choices.

41. **A** Although the answer choices are relatively short, this problem is testing a wide variety of concepts, so the most effective option is to use POE. Choice (B) creates a comma splice because

it makes the sentence's second idea, *he kills an anonymous Arab man for vague reasons*, into a complete idea. The sentence is written in the present tense, so (C) is incorrect as well. Choice (D) creates an ambiguous modifier, making the sentence sound as if *Camus's novel* is doing the *killing*. Only (A) remains as a viable answer, as it gives the correct tense and the pronoun *who* refers clearly back to *Meursault*.

42.　**D**　The word *deferent* means "respectful," and it takes the preposition *to*, so (A) can be eliminated. Choices (B) and (C) can also be eliminated because the word *different* always takes the preposition *from*. The word *than* is used for comparisons—for example, this apple is bigger *than* that apple. Because the word *different* is not used in this kind of comparison (can one thing be *differenter* than another?), it does not take the preposition *than* but rather *from*. Choice (D) is the only one of the answers that uses the correct preposition.

43.　**D**　If there is no good reason to add new information, don't add it. This new information about Franco-Algerian relations is interesting, but it does not *have* to be in this paragraph. Choices (A) and (B) can be eliminated because they say the sentence should be added. Choice (C) can also be eliminated because there is nothing in the passage to suggest that it is making a larger claim about the separation of literature and historical events. Choice (D) is therefore the best answer, correctly giving a viable reason for why the sentence should not be added.

44.　**D**　Choose DELETE unless there is a very good reason not to. In this case, (A) can be eliminated because *do not state* is redundant with the word *imply*. Choices (B) and (C) give information that is already implied in the phrase *all other texts*. The best option, therefore, is to DELETE the underlined portion, as (D) states.

## Section 3: Math (No Calculator)

1.　**A**　The question involves algebra and has numbers in the answers, so plug in the answers. Start with (B). Using the values given in (B), the first equation becomes $2(-1) + 3(-3) = -9$. Solve the left side of the equation to get $-2 - 9 = -9$ or $-11 = -9$. This isn't true, so eliminate (B). Whether to go up or down may not be clear, so just choose a direction. Using the values given in (A), the first equation becomes $2(-3) + 3(-1) = -9$. Solve the left side of the equation to get $-6 - 3 = -9$, or $-9 = -9$. That works, so plug the values into the second equation to get $-3 - (-1) = -2$. Solve the left side of the equation to get $-3 + 1 = -2$, and $-2 = -2$. Since the values given in (A) work in both equations, the correct answer is (A).

2.　**C**　The question gives an equation in terms of $x$ and $y$ and asks for an expression involving both. To solve this, plug in for one variable and solve for the other. Since there are two instances of the variable $x$ in the equation, plug in for $x$. Let $x = 4$. Plug this into the equation to get $4 = 4(4 + y)$. Distribute the 4 to get $4 = 16 + 4y$. Subtract 16 from both sides to get $-12 = 4y$. Divide both sides by 4 to get $y = -3$. The question asks for $\dfrac{y}{x}$, which is $-\dfrac{3}{4}$. The answer is (C).

3.  **B**  The question involves multiple triangles and ratios. This is often an indication that the question involves similar triangles. The question gives the ratio of the lengths of $\overline{ST}$ and $\overline{SU}$. Since these two segments are sides of triangles $PST$ and $QSU$, respectively, determine whether these two triangles are similar. All that is needed to prove that two triangles are similar is to find two pairs of congruent corresponding angles. Since both triangles have a right angle, there is one pair. Also, the question states that triangle $PQR$ is isosceles with $\overline{PR} = \overline{QR}$. In an isosceles triangle, equal angles are opposite equal sides, so $\angle P \cong \angle Q$. Thus, triangles $PST$ and $QSU$ have a second pair of congruent corresponding angles and are similar. Therefore, all corresponding sides have the same ratio. The question asks for the length of $\overline{SQ}$, which is opposite the right angle. Since $\overline{PS}$ is also opposite a right angle, $\overline{PS}$ and $\overline{SQ}$ are corresponding. Therefore, their lengths are in a ratio of 5:3. On any ratio question, use the ratio box to keep track of the parts of a total and the actual numbers. Draw a 3 × 3 table, and label the columns $\overline{PS}$, $\overline{SQ}$, and $\overline{PQ}$, respectively. The top row of a ratio box is the ratio, so fill in the ratio with 5 under $\overline{PS}$ and 3 under $\overline{SQ}$. The bottom row is for actual numbers. Since the actual length of $\overline{PQ}$ is 64, fill in 64 in the third row under $\overline{PQ}$. The result is below.

| $\overline{PS}$ | $\overline{SQ}$ | $\overline{PQ}$ |
|---|---|---|
| 5 | 3 | |
| | | |
| | | 64 |

The numbers in the top row form an addition equation, so add 3 and 5 to get 3 + 5 = 8 and fill in 8 in the top row under $\overline{QR}$. Each column in the ratio box forms a multiplication equation. Since 8 × 8 = 64, fill in the middle row under $\overline{PQ}$ with 8. This is the multiplier for all parts of the ratio, so fill in 8's across the middle row.

| $\overline{PS}$ | $\overline{SQ}$ | $\overline{PQ}$ |
|---|---|---|
| 5 | 3 | 8 |
| 8 | 8 | 8 |
| | | 64 |

The question asks for the length of $\overline{SQ}$. Multiply the ratio number for $\overline{SQ}$, which is 3, by the multiplier of 8 to get an actual length of 24. The answer is (B).

4.  **D**  Use Process of Elimination. Profit = Revenue − Expenses. According to the question, profit = $4cd - 200$. Therefore, the expression $4cd$ must be related to the revenue the chocolate-covered banana stand brings in. Since $c$ represents the number of expected customers, and $d$ is the number of days, the 4 must be related to revenue dollars. Eliminate (A) and (C) since neither of these answers is related to dollars. The question does not say that the price of bananas increases on any given day, so it's safe to assume that the price of a chocolate-covered banana remains the same irrespective of the day it is bought. Therefore, eliminate (B). The correct answer is (D).

5. **A** According to the question, 700 coffee stores existed in 2003, which is one-half of the number of coffee stores that were added from 2004 to 2014. Therefore, $2 \times 700 = 1,400$ stores were added from 2004 to 2014. Plug $y = 1,400$ into each of the answer choices to see which one works. Choice (A) becomes $\frac{1}{2}(1,400) = 700$, or $700 = 700$. Since this equation works, keep it, but check the other answers. You'll see that only (A) works, so (A) is the correct answer.

6. **D** Plugging in could work on this question, but it may take a few tries to get down to one answer choice. A faster way to the answer is to translate the information in the question into an inequality and solve it. The question asks for values of $m$ for which Stream Supreme's monthly cost is less than Download Empire's. *Less than* translates into <, not ≤, so eliminate (B) and (C). To watch $m$ movies, the cost with Stream Supreme would be $7 for the monthly fee plus $1.75 for each movie, or $7 + $1.75$m$. The cost with Download Empire would be $4 + $2.25$m$. Therefore, the inequality is $7 + $1.75$m$ < $4 + $2.25$m$. Subtract $4 from both sides to get $3 + $1.75$m$ < $2.25$m$, then subtract $1.75$m$ from both sides to get $3 < $0.50$m$. Divide both sides by $0.50 to get $6 < m$, so the answer is (D).

7. **C** Solve the equation for $h$. Start by multiplying both sides of the equation by $\mu d$ to get $q\mu d = (p_e - p_{wf})kh$. Next, divide both sides by $(p_e - p_{wf})k$ to get $\dfrac{q\mu d}{(p_e - p_{wf})k} = h$. The correct answer, (C), simply reorders the variables in the numerator, which is permissible since numbers can be multiplied in any order.

8. **A** The question asks for the relationship between $s$ and $C$. Plug in values for $C$ to determine the effect on $s$. To start, plug in $C = 4$ and $C = 0$ to determine what happens where there is an increase or decrease of 4°C. If $C = 0$, then $s = 110 + 4(0) = 110$. If $C = 4$, then $s = 110 + 4(4) = 126$. As the temperature, $C$, increases by 4 degrees from 0 to 4, there is an increase in $s$ of $126 - 110 = 16$, so eliminate (C). Also, as $C$ decreases by 4 degrees from 4 to 0 there is a decrease in $s$ of 16, so eliminate (D). Now, test a temperature change of 1°C. Plug in $C = 1$ to compare the results to those from $C = 0$. If $C = 1$, then $s = 110 + 4(1) = 114$. Therefore, as the temperature decreases from $C = 1$ to $C = 0$, there is a decrease in the number of scoops sold of $114 - 110$. Choice (B) says there would be an increase, so eliminate (B). On an increase from $C = 0$ to $C = 1$, there is an increase of 4. This is what is described in (A), so the answer is (A).

9. **B** Information is given about Stephan's plan over a period of 9 months. Find the increase in savings over that time: $280 - $145 = $135 increase in savings over the 9-month period. Find the increase each month: $135 ÷ 9 = $15 additional savings per month, which best matches (B).

10. **D** Since graphing on a calculator is not an option, try plugging in some numbers. Let $x = 10$. Choice (A) becomes $y = -(10^2) + 3 = -100 + 3 = -97$. Since $y$ is less than 2, leave (A), but check

the remaining answers just in case. Choice (B) becomes $y = |-10| - 1 = 10 - 1 = 9$. Since $y$ is greater than 2, eliminate (B). Choice (C) becomes $y = 10^3 - 4 = 1000 - 4 = 996$. Eliminate (C). Choice (D) becomes $y = -(10 - 1)^2 + 1 = -81 + 1 = -80$. Since this value for $y$ is less than 2, keep (D). When plugging in more than once, try some weird numbers too. Next, try $x = 0$ in the remaining answer choices. Choice (A) becomes $y = -(0^2) + 3 = 0 + 3 = 3$. Since this is a value greater than 2, eliminate (A). Therefore, the correct answer is (D).

11.  **A**  The question asks for the value of $f(-4)$. If the function equation were given in $f(x)$ form, $-4$ would replace $x$. However, the function is written in $f(x + 1)$ form, so $-4$ replaces $x + 1$. Since $-4 = x + 1$, subtract 1 from both sides to get $x = -5$. Therefore, $f(-4) = 3(-5) - 4 = -15 - 4 = -19$. The answer is (A).

12.  **C**  To get rid of the fractions, get the $i$ out of the denominator by multiplying the expression by the conjugate of the denominator. Multiplying the expression by $\dfrac{2 + 3i}{2 + 3i}$ is the same as multiplying by 1, so it won't change the value. This becomes $\dfrac{(5 - i)(2 + 3i)}{(2 - 3i)(2 + 3i)} = \dfrac{10 + 15i - 2i - 3i^2}{4 + 6i - 6i - 9i^2} = \dfrac{10 + 13i - 3i^2}{4 - 9i^2}$. Since $i = \sqrt{-1}$, $i^2 = -1$. Substitute $-1$ for $i^2$ to get $\dfrac{10 + 13i - 3(-1)}{4 - 9(-1)} = \dfrac{10 + 13i + 3}{4 + 9} = \dfrac{13 + 13i}{13}$. Divide by 13 to get $1 + i$. Therefore, if $a + bi = 1 + i$, then $a = 1$, and the answer is (C).

13.  **B**  For all quadratic equations in the form $y = ax^2 + bx + c$, the sum of the roots equals $-\dfrac{b}{a}$. In the equation given, $-\dfrac{b}{a} = -\left(\dfrac{24}{3}\right) = -8$. Without that handy trick, it is still possible to answer the question using the quadratic formula to find the roots. Then add them together to get $-8$. Either way, the answer is (B).

14.  **A**  The parabola passes through the point $(-1, -1)$, so plug $x = -1$ and $y = -1$ into the equation of the parabola. The equation of the parabola is $y = ax^2 + bx + c$, so $-1 = a(-1)^2 + b(-1) + c$. Simplify this equation to get $-1 = a(1) + b(-1) + c$ and $-1 = a - b + c$. The correct answer is (A).

15.  **C**  Start by expanding the left side of the equation to get $pqx^2 + 3px + 5qx + 15 = 8x^2 + rx + 15$. Subtract 15 from both sides of the equation to get $pqx^2 + 3px + 5qx = 8x^2 + rx$. The two $x$ terms on the left can be combined as $(3p + 5q)x$. When two quadratics are equal to each other, the coefficients on the $x^2$ terms on both sides are equal, and the coefficients on the $x$ terms on both sides are equal. From this, it can be determined that $pq = 8$ and $3px + 5qx = rx$. Simplify the second equation by dividing by $x$ to get $3p + 5q = r$. Given that $2 \times 4 = 8$ and that the problem states that $p + q = 6$, one of the values for either $p$ or $q$ could be 2 and the other could be 4. If $p = 2$ and $q = 4$, then $3(2) + 5(4) = r$.

Solve the right side of the equation to get $6 + 20 = r$, and $26 = r$. The only choice with 26 as one of its answer is (C).

16. **3** To solve for $y$, isolate the variable. First, distribute the negative sign to get $4y + 8 - 7y + 12 = 11$. Combine like terms to get $-3y + 20 = 11$. Subtract 20 from both sides to get $-3y = -9$. Divide both sides by $-3$ to get $y = 3$. The answer is 3.

17. **250** Let $d$ represent the square footage of a double room, and $s$ represent the square footage of a single room. According to the question, $d = s + 25$. Solve the equation for $s$ to get $s = d - 25$. According to the question, $2d + 4s = 1,400$. Substitute $d - 25$ in for $s$ to get $2d + 4(d - 25) = 1,400$. Distribute the 4 to get $2d + 4d - 100 = 1,400$. Combine like terms to get $6d - 100 = 1,400$. Solve for $d$ to get $6d = 1,500$, so $d = 250$.

18. $\dfrac{3}{5}$ **or 0.6**

There is a useful trigonometry rule that states $\cos \theta = \sin(90 - \theta)$. Therefore, $\sin(90 - a^\circ) = \cos a^\circ = \dfrac{3}{5}$. Without knowing that rule, it is still possible to answer this question. Draw a right triangle and label one of the acute angles as $a^\circ$ and the other as $(90 - a^\circ)$. If $\cos a^\circ = \dfrac{3}{5}$, the side adjacent to the angle with $a^\circ$ is 3 and the hypotenuse is 5. Now find $\sin(90 - a^\circ)$: it is the value of the side opposite $(90 - a^\circ)$ over the hypotenuse, or $\dfrac{3}{5}$. This can also be entered as 0.6 in the grid-in box.

19. **9** The question says that $x + 3$ is a factor of $x^2 + kx + 2k$. By definition, this means that $x^2 + kx + 2k = 0$ if $x + 3 = 0$. If $x + 3 = 0$, subtract 3 from both sides to get $x = -3$. Plug this value in for $x$ into the equation $x^2 + kx + 2k = 0$ to get $(-3)^2 + (-3)k + 2k = 0$. Simplify the equation to get $9 - 3k + 2k = 0$. Combine like terms to get $9 - k = 0$. Add $k$ to both sides to get $9 = k$. The answer is 9.

20. **3** Factor $x^2$ out of the first two terms to get $x^2(x - 3) + 5x - 15 = 0$. Factor 5 out of the last two terms to get $x^2(x - 3) + 5(x - 3) = 0$. Factor out the $(x - 3)$ from both parts of the left side and rewrite the equation as $(x^2 + 5)(x - 3) = 0$. If $x^2 + 5 = 0$, then $x^2 = -5$, which results in 2 imaginary values for $x$: $\sqrt{-5}$ and $-\sqrt{-5}$. Therefore, the real value of $x$ is when $x - 3 = 0$, and $x = 3$.

## Section 4: Math (Calculator)

1. **D** Translate the information in the question into an equation. The question asks for the number of pies sold. The store sold a total of 364 slices, 84 of which were individual slices. Since individual slices sold do not affect the number of pies sold, these 84 slices should not be counted. In order not to count them, subtract them from the total to get the total number of slices sold as parts of pies. Therefore, eliminate any choice that does not include $364 - 84$. This

eliminates (A), (B), and (C). Only (D) remains. To determine why (D) is correct, note that 364 − 84 represents the number of slices sold in pies. To get the number of pies, divide this total by the number of slices in each pie, which is 8. Therefore, the number of pies sold is $\frac{364 - 84}{8}$. The answer is (D).

2. **B** In this scenario, parallel lines are cut by another set of parallel lines, and two kinds of angles are created—big and small. All the small angles are equal to each other, all the large angles are equal to each other, and any large angle plus any small angle equals 180°. The given angle, $\angle a$, is a big angle, and $\angle b$ is a small angle. So $125 + \angle b = 180$, and angle $\angle b = 55°$, which is (B).

3. **A** According to the table, there are 5 white chocolate pieces with cream filling, 3 dark chocolate pieces with no filling, and 30 total pieces in the box. Therefore, the probability of selecting a piece that is either white chocolate with cream filling or dark chocolate with no filling is $\frac{5 + 3}{30} = \frac{8}{30}$, which is (A).

4. **D** The perimeter of a triangle is the sum of the individual sides. Plug in for the sides. The question says that the sides have length $x$, $x$, and $y$, so let $x = 3$ and $y = 4$. Thus, the perimeter is $T = 3 + 3 + 4 = 10$. The question asks for the value of $x$, which is 3, so this is the target number. Plug $T = 10$ and $y = 4$ into each choice and eliminate any that are not equal to 3. Choice (A) is $3 = 10 − 4$. Since this is false, eliminate (A). Choice (B) is $3 = 10 − 2(4)$. Since this is false, eliminate (B). Choice (C) is $3 = \frac{10 − 2(4)}{2}$. Since this is false, eliminate (C). Choice (D) is $3 = \frac{10 − 4}{2}$. Since this is true, the answer is (D).

5. **D** To solve a system of equations, stack and then add them to try to make a variable disappear. To do this, it may be necessary to manipulate the equations first. In this case, multiply the second equation by −2 to get $−2x + 8y = −38$. Stack and add the equations.

$$\begin{array}{rcr} 2x + 3y = & −6 \\ \underline{−2x + 8y = } & \underline{−38} \\ 0x + 11y = & −44 \end{array}$$

Therefore, the result is $11y = −44$. Divide both sides by 11 to get $y = −4$. Eliminate any answer choice for which the $y$-coordinate is not −4: (A), (B), and (C). Only (D) remains. To determine why the $x$-coordinate is 3, plug $y = −4$ into one of the equations. Try the original form of the second equation. If $x − 4y = 19$, then $x − 4(−4) = 19$, and $x + 16 = 19$. Subtract 16 from both sides to get $x = 3$. The answer is (D).

6. **C**  Translate the question. The first part of the question indicates that $8 - 6n = 20$. Solve for $n$ to get $-6n = 12$, and $n = -2$. The question is asking for the value of $5 - 3n$. Substitute $-2$ for $n$ to get $5 - 3(-2) = 5 + 6 = 11$. Choice (C) is correct.

7. **C**  Translate the question. Given that there are 25,000 attendees at 12 P.M and the number of attendees increases by 550 every minute, the number of attendees $m$ minutes after 12 P.M. can be expressed as $25,000 + 550m$. The full capacity of the stadium is 65,000. To calculate the time prior to the stadium reaching full capacity, the equation would read $25,000 + 550m < 65,000$. Choice (C) is correct.

8. **A**  According to the table, the total number of residents between the ages of 35 and 64 who have an income between $50,000 and $74,999 is $7,185 + 14,978 = 22,163$. These numbers are all in the thousands, but the total will be as well. Those extra zeros cancel out when making the probability, so don't worry about them. The total number of residents between the ages of 35 and 64 is $39,919 + 83,213 = 123,132$. Therefore, the approximate probability that a resident randomly selected in this age range has an income between $50,000 and $74,999 is $\frac{22,163}{123,132} = 0.18$. The closest answer is 20%, which is (A).

9. **C**  The question says the truck traveled at an average speed of 70 miles per hour for 4 hours. If the speed and time are given, multiply them to get the distance, so $d = (70 \text{ mph})(4 \text{ hours}) = 280$ miles. The truck has a fuel efficiency of 18 miles per gallon. Set up a proportion: $\frac{1 \text{ gallon}}{18 \text{ miles}} = \frac{g \text{ gallons}}{280 \text{ miles}}$. Cross-multiply to get $280 = 18g$. Divide both sides by 18 to get $g \approx 15.56$. The question says *approximately*, so select the closest choice, which is (C).

10. **B**  The question asks about the data point farthest from the best fit line, so draw an estimate of the best fit line onto the graph itself. It should look something like this.

Distance Traveled

Notice that one point is far away from the line, the point at about (6, 220). The question asks for the time of the trip represented by this data point. Since time is represented by the $x$-axis, the time is 6 hours. The answer is (B).

11. **D** Start by subtracting 212 from both sides of the equation to get $t_b - 212 = -0.0018a$. Multiply

both sides of the equation by $-1$ to get $-t_b + 212 = 0.0018a$. Divide both sides by 0.0018 to get

$\dfrac{-t_b + 212}{0.0018} = a$. Reorder the terms in the numerator to get $\dfrac{212 - t_b}{0.0018} = a$. This matches (D).

12. **A** The question asks for the scatterplot with a positive association that is not linear. First, eliminate any answer that does not have a positive association. In a positive association, $y$ increases as $x$ increases, so eliminate any choice for which this is not true. Eliminate (C), since it doesn't appear to have a clear positive or negative association. Eliminate (D), since it decreases then increases, so it's not consistently increasing. The question asks for the one that is not linear, so eliminate the answer that is linear. A linear association is one in which a line rather than a curve best fits the data points. In (B), the data points roughly form a linear pattern, so eliminate this choice. The answer is (A).

13. **B** Start by multiplying the entire equation by $t$ to get $vt = h - m + 4.9t^2$. Isolate the $h$ by adding $m$ and subtracting $4.9t^2$ on both sides to get $vt + m - 4.9t^2 = h$. Reorder the terms to get $-4.9t^2 + vt + m = h$, which is (B).

14. **A** The question says that $x$ refers to the number of days after the shipment is received and $y$ refers to the number of oranges that remain. Therefore, since (7, 0) is a solution, there are 0 oranges remaining 7 days after the shipment. Go through each choice and determine whether it reflects this information. Choice (A) seems to be consistent with this, so keep (A). Choice (B) says that there are 7 oranges, but 7 refers to days rather than oranges, so eliminate (B). Choice (C) refers to 455 customers, but since there is no information about how many oranges are sold to each customer, the number of customers cannot be determined. Eliminate (C). Similar to (B), (D) refers to 7 oranges rather than 7 days, so eliminate (D). The answer is (A).

15. **B** There are variables in the answer choices, so plug in. Let $d = 4$. The player's total compensation if he played for the Eagles would be $1,400 + (140 + 40)4 = 1,400 + 720 = 2,120$, and his compensation if he played for the Jays would be $1,500 + (130 + 30)4 = 1,500 + 640 = 2,140$. Given that his compensation would be higher with the Jays, eliminate (A) and (C). Next, try $d = 6$. His compensation with the Eagles would be $1,400 + (140 + 40)6 = 1,400 + 1,080 = 2,480$, and his compensation with the Jays would be $1,500 + (130 + 30)6 = 1,500 + 960 = 2,460$. Given that his compensation is greater with the Eagles, eliminate (D). The correct answer is (B).

16. **A** The question states that days are on the $x$-axis and compensation is on the $y$-axis. The $y$-intercept is where the line crosses the $y$-axis, at a point where $x = 0$. Plug in 0 for days, and the function becomes $y = b + (s + m)0$. Simplify the function to get $y = b$. Therefore, when $x = 0$, $y$ is equal to $b$, which is the signing bonus. Choice (A) is correct.

17. **B** Start by using Process of Elimination. The question states that substance $K$ has a heat capacity that is lower than that of methyl alcohol. Eliminate (D) since it is greater than 0.6. To calculate the heat capacity of substance $K$, find 30% of 0.6, which is $0.3 \times 0.6 = 0.18$. Therefore, the heat capacity of substance $K$ is $0.6 - 0.18 = 0.42$, so (B) is correct.

18. **D** If a point is a solution to two inequalities, it means that point is on the graphs of both. Plug $x = -1$ and $y = 0$ into both inequalities and solve them for $c$ and $d$, respectively. The first inequality becomes $0 < -1 + c$. Add 1 to both sides to get $1 < c$. The second inequality becomes $0 < -(-1) - d$ or $0 < 1 - d$. Add $d$ to both sides to get $d < 1$. If $d < 1$ and $c > 1$, then $d < c$, and the correct answer is (D).

19. **B** The question asks for which podcast had the most ad time per dollar. To get this for each podcast that is a choice, divide the amount of ad time by the cost of the ad. To get the amount of ad time, take the percent of ad time multiplied by the length of each podcast. However, since the length of each podcast is the same, the percent can be used rather than the amount itself. The ad times per dollar for $Q$, $R$, $S$, and $T$, respectively, are $\dfrac{30}{\$350} = 0.086$ per dollar, $\dfrac{25}{\$200} = 0.125$ per dollar, $\dfrac{20}{\$180} = 0.111$ per dollar, and $\dfrac{15}{\$150} = 0.1$ per dollar. Since $R$ has the greatest result, the answer is (B).

20. **D** The formula for the area of a trapezoid is $A = \dfrac{1}{2}(b_1 + b_2)h$, where $b_1$ and $b_2$ represent the two bases, or the two parallel sides on the trapezoid, and $h$ represents the height, or the perpendicular distance between the two bases. Plug in for the bases and height. Let $b_1 = 4$, $b_2 = 8$, and $h = 3$. The area is $A = \dfrac{1}{2}(4 + 8)(3) = 18$. The question says that $PQ$ and $SR$ are decreased by 75% and $PT$ is quadrupled. Since $PQ$ and $SR$ are parallel, they are $b_1$ and $b_2$. Decrease each of these by 75%. 75% of 4 is $\dfrac{75}{100}(4) = 3$, so decrease by 3 to get $b_1 = 4 - 3 = 1$. 75% of 8 is $\dfrac{75}{100}(8) = 6$, so decrease by 6 to get $b_2 = 8 - 6 = 2$. Since $PT$ is perpendicular to the two bases, it is the height. Since the height is quadrupled, the new height is $4 \times 3 = 12$. Therefore, the new area is $A = \dfrac{1}{2}(1 + 2)(12) = 18$. Since the area is unchanged, the answer is (D).

21. **A** According to the table, 11 people never watch the news, and 27 people watch between 1 and 2 times a week, which makes $11 + 27 = 38$ people who watch the news fewer than 3 times a week. Of those viewers, there are $7 + 14 = 21$ people who belong to Group A. Therefore, the probability that a person randomly chosen from among those who watch fewer than 3 times a week is a member of Group A is $\dfrac{21}{38}$. Choice (A) is correct.

22. **B** Use the graph to determine the frequency of each integer. There are four 4's, one 5, one 6, one 7, two 9's, and one 11. To get the mean, take the sum of these numbers and divide by the number of terms. The sum is $4 + 4 + 4 + 4 + 5 + 6 + 7 + 9 + 9 + 11 = 63$. Count the numbers to get that there are 10 numbers. Therefore, the average is $\frac{63}{10} = 6.3$. The answer is (B).

23. **A** Find the point representing Sample S on the graph. The volume of the sample is represented by the vertical axis, so trace the horizontal line from Sample S to the vertical axis at 80. However, this is 80 liters and the question asks for milliliters. The answer should begin with an 8, so eliminate (B) and (D). There are 1,000 milliliters in a liter, so set up the proportion $\frac{1{,}000 \text{ mL}}{1 \text{ L}} = \frac{x \text{ mL}}{80 \text{ L}}$. Cross-multiply to get $x = 80{,}000$. The choices are in scientific notation. Since 80,000 is an 8 followed by four 0's, it is equal to $8 \times 10^4$. The answer is (A).

24. **A** The question asks for the range, or the difference between the greatest and least values, of the volume of the three samples of approximately 1.4 moles. The horizontal axis represents amount. Go just to the left of the line representing 1.5 moles, trace a line straight upward and cross three points. To determine the volume of the sample represented by each point, trace a line directly to the left of each point and see where it crosses the vertical axis, which represents volume. The highest point is between 80 and 100 liters, closer to 100, so it is between 90 and 100. The lowest is between 60 and 80 liters, closer to 60, so it is between 60 and 70. Therefore, the range must be greater than $90 - 70 = 20$ and less than $100 - 60 = 40$. The only choice in this range is 30, so the answer is (A).

25. **D** According to the ideal gas law prediction given, $V = 50n$, where $V$ is the volume and $n$ is the number of moles. The question asks about a sample with 1,200 moles, so the volume is $V = 50(1{,}200) = 60{,}000$. The answer is (D).

26. **C** There is a variable in the question, so plug in. If $x = 2$, $f(x) = 3(2^3) + 6(2^2) + 11(2) = 24 + 24 + 22 = 70$, $g(x) = 8(2^2) + 15(2) + 7 = 32 + 30 + 7 = 69$, and $3x + 7 = 3(2) + 7 = 13$. In the answers, plug in 70 for $f(x)$ and 69 for $g(x)$ to see which answer is divisible by 13. Choice (A) becomes $j(x) = 2(70) + 69 = 140 + 69 = 209$, which is not divisible by 13. Eliminate (A). Choice (B) becomes $k(x) = 70 + 69 = 139$, which is not divisible by 13. Eliminate (B). Choice (C) becomes $m(x) = 70 + 2(69) = 70 + 138 = 208$. $208 \div 13 = 16$. Keep (C), but check (D) just in case. Choice (D) becomes $n(x) = 70 + 3(69) = 70 + 207 = 277$, which is not divisible by 13. Eliminate (D); the answer is (C).

27. **C** The question asks for which of the trigonometric function in the choices is equal to $\frac{y}{x}$. The answer choices include two different functions and two different angles, so use POE (Process of Elimination) and Bite-Sized Pieces. The function cosine is equal to $\frac{opp}{hyp}$. Since neither $x$ nor $y$ is the hypotenuse, eliminate the choices that use cosine, (A) and (B). The only two remaining choices use tangent, which is $\frac{opp}{adj}$. Therefore, $\frac{opp}{adj} = \frac{y}{x}$. Since $P$ is opposite side $y$, $\frac{y}{x} = \tan P$. The answer is (C).

28.  **C**  The given equation of $f(x)$ is a quadratic equation which when graphed will be a parabola. The minimum value of a parabola is the vertex. The vertex form of a quadratic equation is $y = a(x - h)^2 + k$, where $(h, k)$ is the vertex. Eliminate (B), since it is not in the vertex form of the equation. Expand the function to get $f(x) = x^2 + 7x - x - 7 = x^2 + 6x - 7$. Eliminate (A), since it is not an equivalent form of this quadratic. Set the quadratic to 0 to get $x^2 + 6x - 7 = 0$. Complete the square to get $(x^2 + 6x + 9) - 7 = 0 + 9$. Factor the equation to get $(x + 3)^2 - 7 = 9$. Subtract 9 from both sides to get $f(x) = (x + 3)^2 - 16$. The correct answer is (C).

29.  **B**  Simplify the top equation to get $-j = 3a + 3$. Multiply both sides of the equation by $-1$ to get $j = -3a - 3$. Substitute $k + 1$ for $j$ to get $k + 1 = -3a - 3$. Solve for $k$ to get $k = -3a - 4$. Simplify the bottom equation to get $-k = 3b + 3$. Multiply both sides of the equation by $-1$ to get $k = -3b - 3$. Therefore, $-3a - 4 = -3b - 3$. Solve for $a$ to get $-3a = -3b + 1$, and $a = b - \dfrac{1}{3}$. Choice (B) is correct.

30.  **C**  There are variables in the question and answer choices, so plug in. If $x = 3$, $3x = 9$, $4x = 12$, and $5x = 15$. Use these values to find the values of $a$, $b$, and $c$. *Average = total ÷ number of things*, so $a = \dfrac{9 + 11}{2} = \dfrac{20}{2} = 10$, $b = \dfrac{12 + 6}{2} = \dfrac{18}{2} = 9$, and $c = \dfrac{15 + 7}{2} = \dfrac{22}{2} = 11$. Now take the average of $a$, $b$, and $c$: $\dfrac{10 + 9 + 11}{3} = \dfrac{30}{3} = 10$. Plug $x = 3$ into the answers to see which one matches this target number. Choice (A) becomes $3 + 2 = 5$, (B) becomes $3 + 3 = 6$, (C) becomes $2(3) + 4 = 10$, and (D) becomes $4(3) + 8 = 20$. Choice (C) is correct.

31.  **12**  Let $y$ represent number of years. Set up the following equation: $2.25y = 27$. Divide both sides by 2.25 to get $y = 12$.

32.  **216**  Given that the car factory produces one car every 20 minutes, it produces 3 cars in 1 hour. Since the car factory operates 24 hours a day, the factory produces $3 \times 24 = 72$ cars per day. Therefore, in 3 days the factory produces $72 \times 3 = 216$ cars.

33.  **180**  To average 240 over all 12 games, Vito must score a total of $240 \times 12 = 2,880$ points. In his first 6 games, Vito scored a total of $6 \times 200 = 1,200$ points. To find the least number of points he would need to earn on his 7th game, calculate the maximum number of points Vito could get on his last 5 games. If he bowled a perfect game for the last 5 games, he would receive a total of $5 \times 300 = 1,500$ additional points. Add this to the total of his first 6 games to get $1,200 + 1,500 = 2,700$ points scored. Therefore, the minimum number of points Vito must score on his 7th game is $2,880 - 2,700 = 180$ points.

34.  **5**  Only two points on the parabola are given. However, one of the points is the vertex, so use the vertex form of the equation of a parabola: $y = a(x - h)^2 + k$, where $(h, k)$ is the vertex. Plug the point

(3, 14) in as the vertex to get $y = a(x - 3)^2 + 14$. To determine the value of $a$, plug in the other point, (0, 5), to get $5 = a(0 - 3)^2 + 14$. Simplify the parentheses to get $5 = a(-3)^2 + 14$, and square $-3$ to get $5 = 9a + 14$. Subtract 14 from both sides to get $-9 = 9a$. Divide by 9 to get $a = -1$. Therefore, the equation of the parabola is $y = -(x - 3)^2 + 14$. To determine the point of intersection, find the equation of the line, which contains the points (0, -5) and (1, -2). The equation of a line can be put into the form $y = mx + b$, where $m$ is the slope and $b$ is the $y$-intercept. The $y$-intercept is the point at which $x = 0$. Since (0, -5) is on the line, the $y$-intercept is -5. Now get the slope by using the formula $m = \dfrac{y_2 - y_1}{x_2 - x_1}$ . Let $(x_1, y_1) = (0, -5)$ and $(x_2, y_2) = (1, -2)$, so $m = \dfrac{-2 - (-5)}{1 - 0} = \dfrac{-2 + 5}{1} = -2 + 5 = 3$. Therefore, the equation of the line is $y = 3x - 5$. Now set the two equations equal to each other to get $-(x - 3)^2 + 14 = 3x - 5$. FOIL $(x - 3)^2$ to get $-(x^2 - 6x + 9) + 14 = 3x - 5$. Distribute the negative to get $-x^2 + 6x - 9 + 14 = 3x - 5$. Combine like terms to get $-x^2 + 6x + 5 = 3x - 5$. To solve a quadratic, get one side equal to 0. Subtract $3x$ from and add 5 to both sides to get $-x^2 + 3x + 10 = 0$. Divide both sides by $-1$ to get $x^2 - 3x - 10 = 0$. Factor to get $(x - 5)(x + 2) = 0$. Set both factors equal to 0 to get $(x - 5) = 0$ and $(x + 2) = 0$. Solve the two equations to get $x = 5$ and $x = -2$. Since the point $(p, q)$ is in Quadrant I, the $x$-coordinate is positive, so use $x = 5$. Since $p$ is the $x$-coordinate, the answer is 5.

35. **350** The total amount paid = monthly payments + his down payment. In the function given, the $175m$ represents the monthly payments, which means his down payment must have been the 350 dollars.

36. **20** A line of tangency is always perpendicular to the radius of the circle. Therefore, $\angle ABO = 90°$ and $\angle CBO = 90°$. Given that the interior angles of a triangle add up to 180°, $\angle AOB = 60°$, and $\angle BOC = 40°$. The interior angle $\angle AOC = 60° + 40° = 100°$. To determine the circumference of minor arc $\overset{\frown}{DE}$ set up the following proportion: $\dfrac{\text{angle}}{360°} = \dfrac{\text{minor arc}}{\text{circumference}}$. In this case, $\dfrac{100°}{360°} = \dfrac{x}{72}$. Cross-multiply to get $360x = 7{,}200$. Divide both sides by 360 to get $x = 20$.

37. **0.86** The decay formula states that *final amount = original amount* × $(1 - rate)^n$. The rate is 14% per year, which is written as a decimal in the decay formula. Therefore, $k = 1 - 0.14 = 0.86$.

38. **376** Use the decay formula, *final amount = original amount* × $(1 - rate)^n$, and the value for $k$ found in the last question to find the population in 5 years. Plug 800 in for the original amount, 0.86 in for $k$, and 5 in for $x$ to get $P = 800(0.86)^5 \approx 376$. Without the formula, it is still possible to get this question right. Just use a calculator to find the population after 1 year, which would be $800 - 0.14(800) = 688$. Then do it again for the population after 2 years: $688 - 0.14(688) = 591.68$. Continue the process 3 more times to find the population after five years, which will round to 376.

# Chapter 15
# Practice Test 7

# Reading Test

## 65 MINUTES, 52 QUESTIONS

**Turn to Section 1 of your answer sheet to answer the questions in this section.**

**DIRECTIONS**

Each passage or pair of passages below is followed by a number of questions. After reading each passage or pair, choose the best answer to each question based on what is stated or implied in the passage or passages and in any accompanying graphics (such as a table or graph).

**Questions 1–10 are based on the following passage.**

The passage is adapted from Saki, "The Background." Originally published in 1911.

"That woman's art-jargon tires me," said Clovis to his journalist friend. "She's so fond of talking of certain pictures as 'growing on one,' as though they were a sort
Line of fungus."
5      "That reminds me," said the journalist, "of the story of Henri Deplis. Have I ever told it to you?"
Clovis shook his head.
"Henri Deplis was by birth a native of the Grand Duchy of Luxemburg. On maturer reflection he
10  became a commercial traveller. His business activities frequently took him beyond the limits of the Grand Duchy, and he was stopping in a small town of Northern Italy when news reached him from home that a legacy from a distant and deceased relative had
15  fallen to his share.
"It was not a large legacy, even from the modest standpoint of Henri Deplis, but it impelled him towards some seemingly harmless extravagances. In particular it led him to patronize local art as
20  represented by the tattoo-needles of Signor Andreas Pincini. Signor Pincini was, perhaps, the most brilliant master of tattoo craft that Italy had ever known, but his circumstances were decidedly impoverished, and for the sum of six hundred francs he gladly undertook
25  to cover his client's back, from the collar-bone down to the waist-line, with a glowing representation of the Fall of Icarus. The design, when finally developed,

was a slight disappointment to Monsieur Deplis, who had suspected Icarus of being a fortress taken by
30  Wallenstein in the Thirty Years' War, but he was more than satisfied with the execution of the work, which was acclaimed by all who had the privilege of seeing it as Pincini's masterpiece.
"It was his greatest effort, and his last. Without even
35  waiting to be paid, the illustrious craftsman departed this life, and was buried under an ornate tombstone, whose winged cherubs would have afforded singularly little scope for the exercise of his favourite art. There remained, however, the widow Pincini, to whom the
40  six hundred francs were due. And thereupon arose the great crisis in the life of Henri Deplis, traveller of commerce. The legacy, under the stress of numerous little calls on its substance, had dwindled to very insignificant proportions, and when a pressing wine
45  bill and sundry other current accounts had been paid, there remained little more than 430 francs to offer to the widow. The lady was properly indignant, not wholly, as she volubly explained, on account of the suggested writing-off of 170 francs, but also at the
50  attempt to depreciate the value of her late husband's acknowledged masterpiece. In a week's time Deplis was obliged to reduce his offer to 405 francs, which circumstance fanned the widow's indignation into a fury. She cancelled the sale of the work of art, and a few
55  days later Deplis learned with a sense of consternation that she had presented it to the municipality of Bergamo, which had gratefully accepted it. He left the

**CONTINUE** ➡

neighbourhood as unobtrusively as possible, and was genuinely relieved when his business commands took

60 him to Rome, where he hoped his identity and that of the famous picture might be lost sight of.

"But he bore on his back the burden of the dead man's genius. On presenting himself one day in the steaming corridor of a vapour bath, he was at once

65 hustled back into his clothes by the proprietor, who was a North Italian, and who emphatically refused to allow the celebrated Fall of Icarus to be publicly on view without the permission of the municipality of Bergamo. Public interest and official vigilance

70 increased as the matter became more widely known, and Deplis was unable to take a simple dip in the sea or river on the hottest afternoon unless clothed up to the collar-bone in a substantial bathing garment. Later on the authorities of Bergamo conceived the idea that

75 salt water might be injurious to the masterpiece, and a perpetual injunction was obtained which debarred the muchly harassed commercial traveller from sea bathing under any circumstances. Altogether, he was fervently thankful when his firm of employers found

80 him a new range of activities in the neighbourhood of Bordeaux. His thankfulness, however, ceased abruptly at the Franco-Italian frontier. An imposing array of official force barred his departure, and he was sternly reminded of the stringent law which forbids the

85 exportation of Italian works of art.

---

**1**

Which choice best summarizes the passage?

A) A man is unable to display a work of art.

B) A man is forced to consider whether or not to obey the law.

C) A man finds his choices restricted because of the result of an unpaid debt.

D) A man tries to steal art to please a deceased relative.

---

**2**

The passage most clearly suggests that Henri Deplis' financial status before receiving the legacy was

A) chaotic.

B) meager.

C) wealthy.

D) destitute.

---

**3**

Which choice provides the best evidence for the answer to the previous question?

A) Lines 8–9 ("Henri Deplis . . . Luxemburg")

B) Lines 16–18 ("It was . . . extravagances")

C) Lines 21–25 ("Signor Pincini . . . back")

D) Lines 42–44 ("The legacy . . . proportions")

---

**4**

In line 38, "exercise" most nearly means

A) express beliefs.

B) increase strength.

C) practice repeatedly.

D) ability to perform.

---

**5**

The journalist implies that the cherubs on Pincini's tombstone were

A) artistic subjects.

B) religious icons.

C) particularly tiny.

D) plain stone.

---

CONTINUE →

**6**

The journalist indicates that Deplis reduced his offer to 405 francs because he

A) thought he could trick Pincini's widow.

B) could no longer afford the 430 francs.

C) wanted to annoy the widow.

D) thought she would accept a lower offer.

**7**

The author's statement that the widow "cancelled the sale of the work of art" (line 54) chiefly serves to

A) show that Deplis had to return the art.

B) preview Deplis' inability to travel.

C) demonstrate the unpleasant temper of the widow.

D) introduce an unexpected shift in perspective.

**8**

In line 67, "celebrated" most nearly means

A) welcomed.

B) famous.

C) decorated.

D) endless.

**9**

As presented in the passage, the trouble Henri Deplis encountered due to his tattoo is most accurately described as

A) socially awkward but well intended.

B) well-deserved but clearly cruel.

C) obviously absurd but persistently troublesome.

D) uncomfortably restrictive but secretly flattering.

**10**

Which choice provides the best evidence for the answer to the previous question?

A) Lines 57–61 ("He left . . . of")

B) Lines 62–63 ("But he . . . genius")

C) Lines 78–81 ("Altogether, he . . . Bordeaux")

D) Lines 82–85 ("An imposing . . . art")

**CONTINUE**

**Questions 11–20 are based on the following passage and supplementary material.**

This passage is excerpted from Marianne Lavelle, "Forcing Gas Out of Rock With Water." © 2010 by National Geographic News.

Harlan Shober remembers how cars lined Hickory Ridge Road in the spring of 2008 with curiosity-seekers hoping for a glimpse of the first Marcellus
Line shale gas flare in Chartiers Township, Pennsylvania.
5 "I live on an opposite hill, where I could see the top of the flare, and my house was rumbling, it was that loud," recalls Shober, president of the township board of supervisors. "It was overcast, and the flame would bounce up against the clouds. You could see the glow
10 from Pittsburgh," 25 miles away.

The eerie sight heralded the arrival of a new phase of life in this rural community of 7,200 people—one of the hottest spots in Pennsylvania's Marcellus shale boom, with more than 40 natural gas wells drilled
15 here in the past two years. But the fiery scene that takes place above ground after wells are completed in certain circumstances—a controlled burn-off of initial gas for several days—is not as dramatic as what is happening more than a mile beneath the
20 surface. There, a new combination of old oil industry technologies has unlocked a giant resource geologists thought was unattainable for 75 years.

The conventional way to produce natural gas is to drill and extract it out of "traps," or folds and
25 pockets in underground sandstone layers. Scientists have long known there was also natural gas in the soft rock layer called shale, formed by millions of years of heat and pressure from dead algae that mixed with mud at the deep bottom of ancient seas that
30 once covered land in Pennsylvania and elsewhere. Geologists believe the gas found in sandstone traps seeped out of this rich source rock. When it became clear that gas companies were successfully tapping the largest such rock formation in North America,
35 the Marcellus shale, in December 2007, Pennsylvania State University geologist Terry Engelder did the calculations based on 54,000 square miles (14 million hectares) of rock he gauged to be the right geological age for gas prospecting. "I remember thinking,
40 'Merry Christmas, America, you don't know what's out there,'" he says. "It's going to be a real treat." But in this well, which had seemed such a good prospect,

the drillers came up with nothing. "Well, nobody likes a dry hole, but it was an expensive dry hole,"
45 Zagorski says. "We were kind of at a crossroads on what to do."

In 2002, a bigger firm, Devon Energy, had purchased Mitchell's company. Now, a year later, Devon attacked the shale by combining fracking with
50 another technique that was its specialty—horizontal drilling. The results were stupendous. By continuing to drill sideways after a vertical well had reached its geological target, it was possible to reach far more rock surface area. Long touted as a method that
55 reduced the environmental footprint on the surface, horizontal drilling also allowed a company to reach huge volumes of gas from just one well.

Due to numerous uncertainties, estimates of the total potential of the Marcellus shale formation range
60 from 50 trillion cubic feet to 500 trillion cubic feet. Even at the low end of that large range, it would be one of the most significant reservoirs of natural gas in the world. Zagorski marvels at the Marcellus, together with the other shales around the United
65 States: Barnett in Texas, Haynesville in Louisiana, Fayetteville in Arkansas. "The gas shales—these have been the most significant oil and gas finds I've ever seen in my whole career," he says. He's confident that similar shales will be found elsewhere in the world,
70 possibly in Europe, which for many years has been dependent on Russia for imports of natural gas.

The township has had public meetings to learn about the fracking process, and is reviewing its ordinances aimed at minimizing disturbance to
75 neighbors. Although Shober still fields complaints about noisy compressors and the like, he feels the township's residents have welcomed the gas industry. "Any time change comes in, the first thing is you are fearful," he says. "But once you understand, and
80 you have the knowledge and you know what's going on, you tend to accept the change and you move forward."

CONTINUE ▶

U.S. Natural Gas Production in 2014

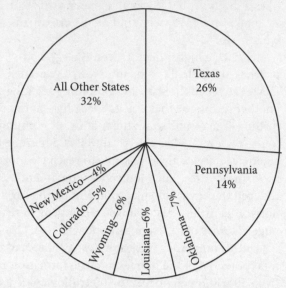

World's Top Producers of Natural Gas in 2014

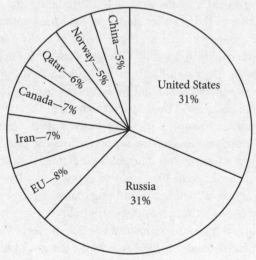

Data from U.S. Energy Information Administration

Which choice provides the best evidence for the answer to the previous question?

A) Lines 11–15 ("The eerie . . . years")

B) Lines 43–45 ("Well, nobody . . . says")

C) Lines 66–68 ("The gas . . . career")

D) Lines 68–71 ("He's confident . . . gas")

Which choice best supports the conclusion that horizontal drilling is not a completely new technique?

A) Lines 1–4 ("Harlan Shober . . . Pennsylvania")

B) Lines 20–22 ("There, a . . . years")

C) Lines 51–54 ("By continuing . . . area")

D) Lines 75–77 ("Although Shober . . . industry")

As used in line 33, "tapping" most nearly means

A) beating.

B) drumming.

C) knocking.

D) opening.

The central idea of the third paragraph (lines 23–46) is that

A) the Marcellus shale is one of the most significant reservoirs of natural gas in the world.

B) natural gas is produced by underground sandstone layers.

C) gas deposits, even when plentiful, aren't always easy to reach.

D) the geography of present-day Pennsylvania has changed significantly over the past million years.

Which choice does the author explicitly cite as a known location of shales?

A) Russia

B) Europe

C) North Carolina

D) Pennsylvania

**CONTINUE**

**16**

Which choice provides the best evidence for the answer to the previous question?

A) Lines 25–30 ("Scientists have . . . elsewhere")

B) Lines 32–39 ("When it . . . prospecting")

C) Lines 41–43 ("But in . . . nothing")

D) Lines 61–63 ("Even at . . . world")

**17**

What function does the fourth paragraph (lines 47–57) serve in the passage as a whole?

A) It provides additional details about a single method mentioned in the previous paragraph.

B) It describes a drilling method that is more effective than a previously described method.

C) It offers context for the environmentalists' argument against a particular drilling technique.

D) It champions an alternate drilling technique that taps fewer reserves of natural gas.

**18**

As used in line 75, "fields" most nearly means

A) stops.

B) returns.

C) handles.

D) retrieves.

**19**

Which choice is supported by the data in the first figure?

A) Louisiana and Pennsylvania combined produce more gas than Texas.

B) Four states produce more than half of the country's gas.

C) No individual state produces more than a quarter of the country's natural gas.

D) Texas produces less gas than Wyoming, Oklahoma, and Louisiana combined.

**20**

The two figures together suggest that

A) Oklahoma and Iran produce the same amount of natural gas.

B) Texas and Pennsylvania combined produce more gas than any country except for the United States and Russia.

C) two countries produce exactly half of the world's natural gas.

D) Canada and Iran combined produce the same amount of natural gas as Pennsylvania.

**CONTINUE**

**Questions 21–30 are based on the following passage.**

This passage is adapted from Virginia Hughes, "Like in Humans, Genes Drive Half of Chimp Intelligence, Study Finds." © 2014 by National Geographic.

Chimpanzees and other great apes are known for their intelligence: They can learn words, play with objects, and even seem to mourn the deaths of their
Line friends. But just as for humans, cognitive abilities vary
5 from one animal to the next.

Now, in one of the largest studies ever conducted on chimp cognition, researchers report that those individual differences are due in no small part to genetic makeup. Genes determine about
10 half of the variability in chimp intelligence and environmental factors the other half, according to primatologist William Hopkins, of the Yerkes National Primate Research Center in Atlanta, Georgia, and colleagues.

15 Research on animal learning has been focused almost entirely on the contribution from the environment. For most of the 20th century, scientists held that animals were like robots, behaving in predictable ways based only on environmental cues,
20 such as reward and punishment. This new study adds to growing evidence that animals are not passive machines but rather are sharp, active thinkers.

Chimps can be surprising in their cognitive abilities, Hopkins noted. Several decades ago, a
25 chimpanzee Hopkins was studying figured out that he could watch real-time video of himself on a nearby television monitor. A video camera was recording the chimp's actions. The chimp, named Austin, opened his mouth wide to look at his teeth, but couldn't see
30 them well. "So he went and got a flashlight and shined it into his mouth to see farther down his throat," said Hopkins.

Austin was the smartest chimp Hopkins ever encountered, he said. But he also saw a lot of variability
35 among the animals. "When you're out there working with them all the time, you definitely form some opinions about whether you think they're smart or not so smart," he said. To find out how much of that variability is due to genetics, Hopkins and his
40 team assessed the cognitive abilities of 99 captive

chimpanzees. They used a battery of 13 tests measuring various manifestations of intelligence, such as how the animals dealt with the physical world, reacted to sound, and used tools.

45 The group of chimps tested had an expansive family tree, ranging from full siblings to fourth and fifth cousins. This allowed the researchers to calculate how well scores on cognitive traits aligned with genetic relatedness.

50 Two categories of tasks were significantly heritable: those related to spatial cognition, such as learning physical locations, and those that required social cognition, such as grabbing a person's attention. Some chimps are quite clever, making kissing sounds
55 or clapping their hands to draw an experimenter's attention, Hopkins said. "This one is a real measure of intelligence and innovative behavior."

That the study found spatial cognition to be heritable also makes sense, noted Josep Call, a
60 comparative psychologist at the University of St. Andrews in Scotland, who was not involved in the study. "Thinking about space is extremely important for a number of animals. It's evolutionarily ancient," he said.

65 Puzzlingly, though, the study found that other cognitive skills, such as understanding causality and using tools, are not particularly heritable. "Why do they find it for space, why do they find it for social cognition, but they don't find it for tool use?" Call
70 wondered. The ability to use tools, after all, would have also been an important skill for survival. Although Hopkins and colleagues found a strong genetic component to chimp intelligence, there were equally strong effects from environmental influences, which
75 are malleable over time.

These results are similar to those in human studies, noted Ajit Varki, distinguished professor of medicine at the University of California, San Diego, who was not part of the new study. What's more, the power of
80 the environment may be underestimated by studies like these, Varki said. "In the impoverished and stereotyped setting of long-term captivity," he said, "the critical influence of environmental variability could be markedly blunted."

**CONTINUE**

**21**

Which choice best describes the organization of the information presented in the passage?

A) An outline of an area of study is presented; research proving exceptions to an earlier assumption is described and analyzed.

B) A discrepancy is revealed and explored scientifically; perspectives both supporting and rejecting the findings are described, and new theories are provided.

C) A general overview of a topic is provided along with specific examples; a study exploring that topic is described, and implications are briefly discussed in broader context.

D) An attempt to answer a difficult evolutionary question is rejected; a study is described that explains why some elements of evolutionary theory will remain a mystery.

**22**

As used in line 18, "held" most nearly means

A) grasped.

B) embraced.

C) restrained.

D) contended.

**23**

In the fourth paragraph (lines 23–32), the description of Austin's surprising action is provided primarily in order to

A) describe a humorous action to lighten the tone.

B) illustrate a relatable action that conveys a surprising level of intelligence.

C) introduce a significant subject in the subsequently described study.

D) show Hopkins' basis for his later study's hypothesis.

**24**

Which statement most accurately reflects an assumption underlying the research performed by Hopkins' team?

A) Chimpanzees' use of human-made tools indicates a higher level of intelligence.

B) Chimpanzee extended-family relationships can be statistically compared to those same relationships in human families.

C) Environmental factors have a much greater impact on intelligence than genetic factors.

D) Tests performed on animals that cannot speak can nonetheless provide insight into some aspects of the animals' mental capabilities.

**25**

Which choice provides the best evidence for the answer to the previous question?

A) Lines 38–41 ("To find . . . chimpanzees")

B) Lines 41–44 ("They used . . . tools")

C) Lines 45–47 ("The group . . . cousins")

D) Lines 71–75 ("Although Hopkins . . . time")

**26**

According to the passage, researchers were able to compare cognitive scores with "genetic relatedness" (lines 48–49), because the researchers had

A) observed surprisingly intelligent behavior in some of the specific chimpanzees.

B) tested chimpanzees with a broad variety of genetic relationships.

C) used 13 different tests to study the chimpanzees' intelligence.

D) found that both spatial and social cognition were genetically heritable.

**CONTINUE**

**27**

The passage presents which of the following as an indication of a task related to social cognition?

A) Making a sound to draw attention

B) Reactions to sounds produced by human researchers

C) The use of flashlights

D) Recognition of a video image

**28**

As used in line 68, "find" most nearly means

A) show.

B) locate.

C) prove.

D) search.

**29**

The passage most clearly implies which of the following statements about animals in captivity?

A) They are likely to have close contact with extended family members.

B) They display more social cognition than do animals in the wild.

C) Studies on them may not reveal elements which may play significant roles.

D) Inferences drawn from studies on them can be easily applied to wild animals.

**30**

Which choice provides the best evidence for the answer to the previous question?

A) Lines 17–20 ("For most . . . punishment")

B) Lines 45–47 ("The group . . . cousins")

C) Lines 58–62 ("That the . . . study")

D) Lines 81–84 ("In the . . . blunted")

CONTINUE

**Questions 31–41 are based on the following passages.**

Passage 1 is adapted from a letter from Thomas Jefferson to John Adams, October 28th 1813. Passage 2 is adapted from a letter from John Adams to Thomas Jefferson, November 15th 1813. Jefferson and Adams are discussing whether aristocracy is inherited.

**Passage 1**

For I agree with you that there is a natural aristocracy among men. The grounds of this are virtue and talents.

There is also an artificial aristocracy founded on
5  wealth and birth, without either virtue or talents; for with these it would belong to the first class. The natural aristocracy I consider as the most precious gift of nature, for the instruction, the trusts, and government of society. And indeed it would have
10  been inconsistent in creation to have formed man for the social state, and not to have provided virtue and wisdom enough to manage the concerns of the society. May we not even say that that form of government is the best which provides the most effectually for a pure
15  selection of these natural aristoi into the offices of government? The artificial aristocracy is a mischievous ingredient in government, and provision should be made to prevent its ascendancy.

I think the best remedy is exactly that provided by
20  all our constitutions, to leave to the citizens the free election and separation of the aristoi from the pseudo-aristoi, of the wheat from the chaff. In general, they will elect the really good and wise. In some instances, wealth may corrupt, and birth blind them; but not
25  in sufficient degree to endanger the society. But even in Europe a change has sensibly taken place in the mind of Man. Science had liberated the ideas of those who read and reflect, and the American example had kindled feelings of right in the people. An insurrection
30  has consequently begun, of science, talents and courage against rank and birth, which have fallen into contempt.

This however we have no right to meddle with. It suffices for us, if the moral and physical condition
35  of our own citizens qualifies them to select the able and good for the direction of their government, with a recurrence of elections at such short periods as will enable them to displace an unfaithful servant before the mischief he meditates may be irremediable.

**Passage 2**

40  We are now explicitly agreed, in one important point, that "there is a natural aristocracy among men; the grounds of which are virtue and talents."

But though we have agreed in one point, in words, it is not yet certain that we are perfectly agreed in
45  sense. Fashion has introduced an indeterminate use of the word "talents." Education, wealth, strength, beauty, stature, birth, marriage, graceful attitudes and motions, gait, air, complexion, and physiognomy are talents, as well as genius and science and learning. Any one of
50  these talents, that in fact commands or influences true votes in society, gives to the man who possesses it the character of an aristocrat, in my sense of the word.

Your distinction between natural and artificial aristocracy does not appear to me well founded. Birth
55  and wealth are conferred on some men as imperiously by Nature, as genius, strength or beauty. The heir is honors and riches, and power has often no more merit in procuring these advantages than he has in obtaining a handsome face or an elegant figure.
60  When aristocracies are established by human laws, and honor, wealth, and power are made hereditary by municipal laws and political institutions, then I acknowledge artificial aristocracy to commence: but this never commences, till corruption in elections
65  becomes dominant and uncontrollable. But this artificial aristocracy can never last. The everlasting envies, jealousies, rivalries and quarrels among them, their cruel rapacities upon the poor ignorant people their followers, compel these to set up Caesar, a
70  demagogue to be a monarch and master. Here you have the origin of all artificial aristocracy, which is the origin of all monarchy. And both artificial aristocracy, and monarchy, and civil, military, political and hierarchical despotism, have all grown out of the
75  natural aristocracy of "virtues and talents."

Your distinction between the aristoi and pseudo aristoi, will not help the matter. I would trust one as soon as the other with unlimited power. The law wisely refuses an oath as a witness in his own cause to the
80  saint as well as to the sinner.

CONTINUE ➔

**31**

As used in line 20, "free" most nearly means

A) complimentary.

B) available.

C) unrestricted.

D) gratuitous.

**32**

It can be inferred that the author of Passage 1 believes the best way to prevent the rise of the artificial aristocracy is to

A) allow those with power to pass that power to their children.

B) run America the same way the Europeans run their countries.

C) require voters to vote only for the best and wisest candidates.

D) allow voters to choose their own leaders.

**33**

Which choice provides the best evidence for the answer to the previous question?

A) Lines 4–6 ("There is . . . class")

B) Lines 16–18 ("The artificial . . . ascendancy")

C) Lines 19–22 ("I think . . . chaff")

D) Lines 25–27 ("But even . . . Man")

**34**

As used in line 45, "fashion" most nearly means

A) convention.

B) demeanor.

C) model.

D) construction.

**35**

According to the author of Passage 2, an artificial aristocracy begins only when

A) laws give one group power over another.

B) all people are given the right to vote.

C) a democracy turns into a monarchy.

D) those who are virtuous and talented control the government.

**36**

In Passage 2, the author claims that political advantages come mainly from

A) birth and wealth.

B) a wide range of characteristics.

C) physical attributes.

D) municipal laws and political institutions.

**37**

Which choice provides the best evidence for the answer to the previous question?

A) Lines 40–42 ("We are . . . talents")

B) Lines 49–52 ("Any one . . . word")

C) Lines 54–56 ("Birth and . . . beauty")

D) Lines 60–65 ("When aristocracies . . . uncontrollable")

**38**

In lines 76–80, the author of Passage 2 refers to a statement made in Passage 1 in order to

A) question the working vocabulary of the author of Passage 1.

B) argue against the central theme of Passage 1.

C) agree with the logic of the proposal outlined in Passage 1.

D) point out a perceived flaw in the argument made in Passage 1.

**CONTINUE** →

**39**

Which best describes the overall relationship between Passage 1 and Passage 2?

A) Passage 2 further develops a distinction presented in Passage 1.

B) Passage 2 disagrees with a key assumption of Passage 1.

C) Passage 2 considers the historical context of statements made in Passage 1.

D) Passage 2 redefines key terms used in the argument in Passage 1.

**40**

The authors of both passages would most likely agree with which of the following statements about advantages people may have over each other?

A) Those born talented and virtuous have an advantage over those who aren't.

B) Wealth and power are more important than beauty and talent.

C) Advantages one gains later in life are more powerful than those one is born with.

D) There is a clear distinction between those who earn their power and those who have it handed to them.

**41**

How would the author of Passage 1 most likely respond to the points made in Passage 2 (lines 60–75)?

A) Passing power down through families will lead to governments run like those in Europe.

B) Although a few who are unfit may be elected, leaving the decisions in the hands of the voters will ultimately keep the system balanced.

C) Rank and birth are more highly prized than science and talent.

D) The setup of the American system could allow for an unfaithful leader to cause irremediable damage.

**CONTINUE**

**Questions 42–52 are based on the following passage and supplementary material.**

This passage is adapted from Nicolaas Bouwes et al., "Ecosystem Experiment Reveals Benefits of Natural and Simulated Beaver Dams to a Threatened Population of Steelhead (*Oncorhynchus mykiss*)." © 2016 by Scientific Reports.

Beaver in Eurasia and North America were once abundant and ubiquitous. Their dense and barbed fur has great felting properties, and as early as the
*Line*
5   1500s, intense trapping to provide pelts mainly for making hats occurred throughout Eurasia. When Lewis and Clark explored the Pacific Northwest in 1805, salmon and steelhead coexisted with beavers in very high densities. When the British and United States jointly occupied the Oregon Territories (which
10   included the Columbia River Basin), the Hudson Bay Company implemented their "scorched earth" or "fur desert" policy to eliminate all fur-bearing animals, in an attempt to discourage American settlement. As a result, beaver were nearly extirpated from the region
15   by 1900.

Around this time, a decrease in the great harvests of Pacific salmon and steelhead was first perceived. Anadromous salmon and steelhead populations have since declined precipitously in the Columbia
20   River Basin, leading to their listing under the U.S. Endangered Species Act (ESA). Human activities, including the removal of beaver, have exacerbated the occurrence of stream channel incision, where a rapid down-cutting of the stream bed disconnects
25   the channel from its floodplain. We hypothesized that beaver dams or simulated beaver dams that we construct (referred to as beaver dam analogs or BDAs) can greatly accelerate the incision recovery process.

BDAs were built by pounding wooden fence posts
30   vertically into the channel bed and potential floodplain surfaces. Willow branches were woven between the posts, and bed sediment was used to plug the base of structures. The addition of BDAs into Bridge Creek led to an immediate and rapid increase in the number
35   of natural beaver dams, not only in our treatment areas but throughout much of Bridge Creek. Whether their dam-building activities increased because of a demographic or behavioral response is somewhat immaterial, because the modification of the stream
40   ecosystem, rather than the beavers themselves, likely caused the fish population response.

BDAs and beaver dams led to large changes in both fish and beaver habitat, and the steelhead population response largely followed our hypothesized pathways.
45   We found compelling evidence that beavers increased the quantity of juvenile habitat.

Increasing habitat complexity may also partially explain the observed increase in total juvenile abundance, survival and productivity. Increased
50   habitat complexity provides fish a greater selection of locations at which to forage, rest, and avoid predation and high flow events, while reducing migration distances required to conduct these activities for multiple life-stages. Thus, we suspect that an increase
55   in habitat complexity is partly responsible for the observed positive steelhead population responses.

## Number of Dams Over Time

Panel represents the total number of dams for the Bridge Creek (dotted line), the sum of all treatment (solid line) and all control (dashed line) reaches. Black vertical line represents when BDAs were initially installed.

**42**

As used in line 22, "removal" most nearly means the

A) significant reduction of a population.

B) surgical extraction of an item.

C) complete extinction of a species.

D) physical relocation of an individual beaver.

CONTINUE ➡

**43**

In line 56, the authors state that certain hypothesized results were largely consistent with "steelhead population responses." According to the passage, which of the following best represents the broader hypothesis the authors tested in order to obtain those results?

A) Artificial beaver dams can be constructed by the placement of wooden posts and cross-woven willow branches without obstructing the development of natural dams.

B) Reconnecting a stream's channel and floodplain can occur more quickly through the construction of natural or artificial beaver dams.

C) The removal of an animal from its habitat can lead to unexpected results throughout an ecosystem.

D) Stream channel incision, caused by the rapid down-cutting of a stream bed, is exacerbated by the presence of unexpectedly large numbers of beaver dams.

**44**

Which choice provides the best evidence for the answer to the previous question?

A) Lines 16–17 ("Around this . . . perceived")

B) Lines 21–25 ("Human activities . . . floodplain")

C) Lines 25–28 ("We hypothesized . . . process")

D) Lines 29–31 ("BDAs were . . . surfaces")

**45**

The primary purpose of the third paragraph (lines 29–41) is to

A) illustrate methods and results of research to determine the impact of beaver dams on stream ecosystems.

B) detail the findings of research designed to investigate beaver responses to competition from other dams.

C) describe the plan that will be followed by the hypothetical experiment referenced in the fifth paragraph (lines 47–56).

D) suggest a method by which a potential experiment could be carried out in the future in order to test the strength of beaver dams.

**46**

The passage most clearly indicates that the authors' Bridge Creek BDA building efforts had which of the following indirect effects?

A) They temporarily disturbed the local wildlife populations.

B) They reduced the downstream water flow.

C) They prompted beavers to build more natural dams.

D) They increased local beaver populations.

**47**

Which choice provides the best evidence for the answer to the previous question?

A) Lines 13–15 ("As a . . . 1900")

B) Lines 33–36 ("The addition . . . Creek")

C) Lines 36–41 ("Whether their . . . response")

D) Lines 49–54 ("Increased habitat . . . life-stages")

CONTINUE

**48**

The words "partially," "suspect," and "partly" in the fifth paragraph (lines 47–56) have which effect on the tone of the paragraph?

A) They indicate an insecure tone that displays the depth of the authors' nervousness about how the new research will be received.

B) They indicate an objective tone that states facts while also allowing for the possibility that other factors may be important.

C) They indicate a conceding tone that grudgingly accepts unwelcome results of the conducted research on the effects of artificial dams.

D) They create a suspicious tone that suggests the authors are afraid that they may have missed crucial implications of their research.

**49**

An unstated assumption of the experiment described in the passage is that habitat complexity

A) was at its greatest before 1900.

B) is always increased by the addition of dams.

C) is detrimental to most types of predator populations in stream-based ecosystems.

D) was not maximized before the construction of the BDAs.

**50**

According to the data in the figure, what was the greatest number of dams on Bridge Creek during the twenty years prior to the installation of BDAs?

A) 105 dams

B) 125 dams

C) 150 dams

D) 225 dams

**51**

Based on the data in the figure, which of the following years represents the last year during which a control reach had a greater number of dams than a treatment reach?

A) 1995

B) 2000

C) 2007

D) 2012

**52**

Does the graphic support the author's claim that increasing the number of real or simulated beaver dams leads to an increase in steelhead populations?

A) Yes, because the initial construction of BDAs led directly and significantly to steep increases in natural dams along all the treated stream systems.

B) Yes, because the data in the figure indicate that the construction of BDAs led to an increase in the steelhead populations.

C) No, because the data do not provide a link between the number of dams and the quality of steelhead habitats.

D) No, because the data do not show that floodplain access is significantly increased by the presence of dams.

# STOP
**If you finish before time is called, you may check your work on this section only.
Do not turn to any other section in the test.**

**No Test Material On This Page**

# Writing and Language Test

## 35 MINUTES, 44 QUESTIONS

**Turn to Section 2 of your answer sheet to answer the questions in this section.**

---

### DIRECTIONS

Each passage below is accompanied by a number of questions. For some questions, you will consider how the passage might be revised to improve the expression of ideas. For other questions, you will consider how the passage might be edited to correct errors in sentence structure, usage, or punctuation. A passage or a question may be accompanied by one or more graphics (such as a table or graph) that you will consider as you make revising and editing decisions.

Some questions will direct you to an underlined portion of a passage. Other questions will direct you to a location in a passage or ask you to think about the passage as a whole.

After reading each passage, choose the answer to each question that most effectively improves the quality of writing in the passage or that makes the passage conform to the conventions of standard written English. Many questions include a "NO CHANGE" option. Choose that option if you think the best choice is to leave the relevant portion of the passage as it is.

---

**Questions 1–11 are based on the following passage.**

**Paternal Instincts: The Case for Paternity Leave**

From high-rise office buildings to massive manufacturing plants, the main focus in any workplace is generally on what employees are being paid to do, but **1** the personal needs of workers must also be addressed for a modern company to maximize its potential for success. After all, it is no longer the dawn of the Industrial Age. Children are no longer used as part of the workforce, paid days off are commonplace, and a safe working environment is the rule rather than the exception. Contemporary employers **2** of today understand that providing for the safety and security of an employee, and an employee's family, can improve not only quality of life, but also the company's production.

**1**

Which choice provides the most appropriate introduction to the passage?

A) NO CHANGE

B) work isn't the only thing.

C) many companies also care about profit as well.

D) companies could do everything possible to make all employees happy.

**2**

A) NO CHANGE

B) today

C) of right now

D) DELETE the underlined portion.

CONTINUE ⟶

There is no more important event for a family than the birth of a child, and many companies offer paid maternity leave to mothers in order to ease the natural burden that families experience during this time. However, significantly fewer companies offer the male equivalent— paid paternity leave. A 2012 study conducted **3** from the United States Department of Labor found that only 13 percent of men who took paternity leave received pay compared to 21 percent of women who took maternity leave. The same study found that maternity leave averages six to twelve weeks in length. Of the men who reported taking leave following the birth of a child, 70 percent indicated that they took a paternity leave **4** they are at most ten days long.

**3**

A) NO CHANGE
B) by
C) of
D) DELETE the underlined portion.

**4**

A) NO CHANGE
B) that was
C) they were
D) those being

**CONTINUE**

This pronounced deficit in leave **5** is important for two reasons. The first is that companies might not only increase the happiness of their workforce, but also retain high-skilled workers who could be tempted to leave for another company offering better paternity benefits. A 2014 study by the U.S. Bureau of Labor and Statistics found that nine out of ten men considered paternity leave to be a factor of at least marginal importance when considering employment opportunities. **6** Others considered it to be less important. **7** Clearly, this is becoming a more important issue to the newest additions to the workforce.

A) NO CHANGE

B) are

C) is being

D) had been

Which choice best supports the statement made in the previous sentence?

A) NO CHANGE

B) But not as important as mothers having time off.

C) But others did not seem to think it mattered.

D) Six out of ten considered it to be extremely important.

At this point, the writer is considering adding the following sentence.

> The younger a male respondent was, the more likely he was to rate the issue of paternity leave as important when considering employment.

Should the writer make this addition?

A) Yes, because it provides a reason for the assertion made in the last sentence of the paragraph.

B) Yes, because it supplies qualitative data that is challenged in the remainder of the paragraph.

C) No, because it interrupts the discussion of what is important to older fathers.

D) No, because it does not take into account whether workers were actually fathers or not.

**CONTINUE**

**8** However, paternity leave is not just about what potential employees want. There is a second reason that paternity leave policies are so important; they bring attention to a larger societal issue. Not enough emphasis has been placed on the importance of both **9** parent's being involved in the earliest stages of a child's life. Paternity leave allows fathers to bond with their children earlier, participate in the household more **10** actively, and, raise children with a greater sense of gender equality. **11** In other words, paternity leave not only benefits a lone employee and his or her family—it improves society as a whole.

**8**

In context, which choice best combines the underlined sentences?

A) However, another reason that paternity leave is so important is that they bring attention to a larger societal issue that is also what potential employees want.

B) However, a second reason is about what potential employees want and paternity leave having an impact on an entire society.

C) Beyond being something potential employees desire, paternity leave policies are also important because they highlight a larger societal issue.

D) Employees want paternity leave, so another important reason to take it seriously in our society is that these policies involve a larger societal issue.

**9**

A) NO CHANGE

B) parent's being involved in the earliest stages of a childs life.

C) parents being involved in the earliest stages of a child's life.

D) parents being involved in the earliest stages' of a childs life.

**10**

A) NO CHANGE

B) active, and raise children

C) actively, and raise children

D) actively and raising

**11**

A) NO CHANGE

B) Otherwise,

C) Completely,

D) Alternatively,

**CONTINUE**

**Questions 12–22 are based on the following passage.**

### The Divided Elections of America

The cyclical nature of American federal elections is one aspect of American life common to all fifty states. However, once you move past the cycle and look at the voting mechanisms themselves, similarities are hard to come by. **12** One major difference among the states pertaining to elections for federal offices, for example presidential or congressional **13** candidates. Is whether a state holds a primary or a caucus. These two systems, primaries and caucuses, are meant to accomplish the same **14** goal; nominate major-party candidates for office.

**12**

Which choice provides the most logical introduction to the sentence?

A) NO CHANGE

B) All states vote for the same offices on the same cycle

C) The main questions for all democratic nations and their elections,

D) DELETE the underlined portion, and begin the sentence with a capital letter.

**13**

A) NO CHANGE

B) candidates:

C) candidates; is

D) candidates, is

**14**

A) NO CHANGE

B) goal nominate

C) goal, and

D) goal:

CONTINUE

Because the goal of each of these systems is the same, it can be surprising how fundamentally different primaries and caucuses are. Caucuses, for example, are strictly limited to the members of a single political party. If a caucus is the preferred method of election, these state-level party members will convene a meeting, called a caucus, to select candidates or decide policy. At this caucus, members of that single political party meet in person at an appointed time and location to discuss the candidates and debate their merits based on the party platform. **15** The voting for candidates then happens manually.

Primaries, on the other hand, involve an election that narrows the field of major-party candidates before an election for office. Additionally, primaries may be declared as "open," which means that they are not limited to participation by a single political party as caucuses are. In primaries, non-affiliated and affiliated voters may present **16** themselves at their respective precincts and cast their votes privately.

**15**

The writer is considering revising the underlined sentence to read:

> The voting for candidates then happens manually, either by a raised hand count or by separating into groups for a tally.

Should the writer add this information here?

A) Yes, because it provides examples of why caucuses are more effective than primaries.

B) Yes, because it further explains the assertion made in the sentence.

C) No, because it should be placed later in the passage.

D) No, because it contradicts the main claim of the passage.

**16**

A) NO CHANGE

B) himself or herself

C) their selves

D) oneself

**CONTINUE**

Historically, caucuses made a great deal of practical sense. **17** In the late eighteenth century it was difficult for candidates to share information with potential voters or campaign on a large geographical scale. **18** Much of the voting population had limited, if any, knowledge of the candidates or party platforms before traveling to designated centers to actually cast a vote. Caucuses allowed voters who were limited in their knowledge to learn firsthand from representatives of the candidates what the party platform was and what positions the candidates had on issues within that platform. Voters then selected representatives who were pledged to the candidate the voters had chosen. **19**

**17**

The writer is considering deleting the previous sentence. Should the writer make this change?

A) Yes, because it does not logically follow from the previous paragraph.

B) Yes, because it introduces information that is irrelevant at this point in the passage.

C) No, because it provides a specific example in support of arguments made elsewhere in the passage.

D) No, because it provides a logical introduction to the paragraph.

**18**

A) NO CHANGE

B) Much of the voting population, had limited if any knowledge

C) Much of the voting population had, limited, if any, knowledge

D) Much of the voting population had limited if any knowledge,

**19**

Which choice most logically follows the previous sentence?

A) The man who received the most votes would become president.

B) Of course, not everyone who came voted in the same way.

C) Functionally, voters directly voted for their caucus representatives, not the actual candidates.

D) Local elections rarely used this system because candidates were always well known.

CONTINUE →

Over time, especially in this era of mass and social media, primaries have been steadily surpassing caucuses in popularity. Out of the fifty voting states and commonwealths, only 13 currently hold caucuses. This is due in part to the **20** horrid nature of caucuses in comparison to primaries. Not only are they difficult to keep organized, **21** it is also difficult to keep civil. In addition, caucuses have come to be perceived as less democratic because **22** it is an election of representatives rather than direct elections of candidates.

Which choice best maintains the tone established in the passage?

A) NO CHANGE

B) deplorable

C) litigious

D) inconvenient

A) NO CHANGE

B) but also they are

C) but, also, they can be

D) also they were

A) NO CHANGE

B) it has been an election

C) they are elections

D) those have been an election

**CONTINUE**

**Questions 23–33 are based on the following passage and supplementary material.**

### The Sloth: Nature's Layabout or Efficient Mammal?

Many people believe that the sloth is an extremely lazy animal. This popular image of the sloth has its roots in both history and etymology. European explorers in South America, **23** they noticed the sloth's slow and **24** lackadaisical movements, named the creature after one of the "Seven Deadly Sins." **25** Recently, the sloth's image is reinforced by Blue Sky Studios' 2002 movie *Ice Age*. In this movie, Sid, a sloth, sleeps through the migration of his community and is nearly left behind. However, while it is true that the sloth typically moves slowly and spends a significant portion of **26** its day sleeping, this slow rate of activity is not due to laziness. Rather, the sloth has evolved this lifestyle in order to adapt to the particular challenges of consuming leaves located high in the rainforest canopy.

**23**

A) NO CHANGE
B) that
C) which
D) who

**24**

A) NO CHANGE
B) careless
C) inactive
D) leisurely

**25**

Which choice most effectively combines the underlined sentences?

A) Sid, a sloth in the 2002 movie *Ice Age*, sleeps through the migration of his community and is nearly left behind, which reinforces the sloth's image recently by Blue Sky Studios.

B) Blue Sky Studios' 2002 movie *Ice Age* reinforces this image by featuring a sloth, Sid, who sleeps through the migration of his community and is nearly left behind.

C) Blue Sky Studios' Sid, a sloth, sleeps through the migration of his community and is nearly left behind recently in *Ice Age*, reinforcing the sloth's image.

D) A sloth, Sid, sleeps through Blue Sky Studios' 2002 movie *Ice Age*, reinforcing the sloth's image and being left behind through the migration of his community.

**26**

A) NO CHANGE
B) it's
C) there
D) their

CONTINUE

[1] The sloth is categorized as a folivore because the bulk of its diet consists of the leaves, buds, and tender shoots of *Cercropia*, [27] that is a tree found in the tropical regions of Central and South America. [2] Take the sloth's [28] stomach for example, it is very large with multiple compartments. [3] These compartments contain bacteria that break down the leafy material. [4] It may take a sloth over a month to digest a meal of *Cercropia* leaves. [5] However, leaves and other non-fruit parts of trees are nutritionally poor, so the sloth has various adaptations to help it thrive on this diet. [6] Another, perhaps even more amazing dietary adaptation is the sloth's unusually low body temperature. [29]

**27**

A) NO CHANGE

B) it is

C) being

D) DELETE the underlined portion.

**28**

A) NO CHANGE

B) stomach, for example,

C) stomach. For example,

D) stomach, for example:

**29**

To make this paragraph most logical, sentence 5 should be placed

A) where it is now.

B) after sentence 1.

C) after sentence 3.

D) after sentence 6.

CONTINUE

Most mammals regulate their body temperature in part by creating heat through metabolic processes. Through normal body processes, heat is generated (more in the core organs than in the extremities), and this heat is spread throughout the body. This process of heat generation requires nutrition, and, as mentioned above, the sloth survives predominantly on tree products that are poor in nutrition. As the graph shows, this in part explains why the sloth has a body temperature **30** approximately five degrees Celsius lower than the other mammals shown, even when active. Furthermore, the sloth does not keep its body temperature in as limited a range as, for instance, a dog **31** has. A healthy dog's temperature will remain within 0.4 degrees Celsius of its average, whereas a healthy sloth's temperature can be as much as 2 degrees Celsius warmer or cooler than its average body temperature when active. This means that **32** a healthy sloth's active body temperature can be greater than that of a healthy dog. This lower body temperature helps the sloth thrive on a nutritionally poor diet. The sloth's slow and steady lifestyle is therefore not the result of laziness, but rather the result of **33** popular culture's stereotypes about this animal as seen through the movie *Ice Age*.

### Average Body Temperature of Various Mammals

Adapted from Gary Meisner, "Golden Ratio in Body Temperatures." Originally published May 13, 2012 by Goldennumber.net.

**30**

Which choice offers an accurate interpretation of data in the graph?

A) NO CHANGE

B) approximately equal to

C) approximately five degrees greater than

D) approximately half that of

**31**

A) NO CHANGE

B) will.

C) did.

D) does.

**32**

Which choice offers an accurate interpretation of the data in the graph?

A) NO CHANGE

B) a healthy dog's body temperature is greater than that of any mammal shown in the graph.

C) a healthy dog's body temperature will be greater than that of a sloth, even when the sloth is active.

D) a healthy, active sloth will have a body temperature equal to that of a healthy dog.

**33**

The writer wants a conclusion that conveys how the sloth's inactivity is the result of adaptations to its diet. Which choice best accomplishes this goal?

A) NO CHANGE

B) the unfortunate name given to the sloth by Europeans exploring the South American rainforest.

C) keeping its body temperature lower than that of most other mammals.

D) needing to survive off of a food source that, while abundant, is not a rich source of nutrients.

**CONTINUE**

**Questions 34–44 are based on the following passage.**

**Milton Babbitt: A Punny Composer**

Typically, a pun is a form of word play suggesting that there are multiple interpretations of a word or phrase. Some puns—Oscar Wilde's "The Queen is not a [34] subject," for example use words that have multiple meanings. Other puns, such as the comedian George Carlin's observation that "Atheism is a non-prophet organization," [35] relies on words with different definitions, but that sound alike. From Shakespeare's plays to Abbott and Costello's *Who's on First?* to even the [36] Bible, wordsmiths have used puns for humorous and rhetorical effect. However, puns aren't just limited to words. One [37] punster, American composer, Milton Babbitt, has imported the use of puns into music.

---

**34**

A) NO CHANGE

B) subject," for example,

C) subject," for example;

D) subject," for example—

---

**35**

A) NO CHANGE

B) rely

C) has relied

D) relying

---

**36**

A) NO CHANGE

B) Bible. These wordsmiths

C) Bible. Wordsmiths

D) Bible; these wordsmiths

---

**37**

A) NO CHANGE

B) punster, American composer Milton Babbitt,

C) punster, American composer, Milton Babbitt

D) punster American composer Milton Babbitt,

---

**CONTINUE**

Two of Babbitt's works for percussion, *Homily* and *Beaten Paths*, show how he [38] writes effectively for the instruments chosen. *Homily*, for snare drum, uses dynamics (how loudly or softly a note is played) and timbre (the "color" of the note, changed by using different drumsticks) to change how similar musical phrases are audibly perceived. The musical phrase is [39] modified in such a way that different interpretations of the phrase are possible, much in the same way that verbal puns rely on concurrent interpretations of a word. Similarly, *Beaten Paths*, for marimba, also uses dynamics to create different musical meanings.

Which choice most effectively sets up the examples that follow?

A) NO CHANGE

B) has fun with the music in his compositions.

C) creates puns in music by using the same musical idea in multiple ways.

D) shows the absurdity of translating ideas from one type of work to another.

A) NO CHANGE

B) twisted

C) doctored

D) refined

CONTINUE →

*Beaten Paths* uses pitch to not only create repeated musical motifs, but also **40** reshaped the audience's perception of the music. **41** Beyond his music, Babbitt's use of puns even **42** extends to the titles of his works.

A) NO CHANGE

B) reshape

C) have reshaped

D) reshaping

At this point, the writer is considering adding the following sentence.

> Babbitt was one of the first to work in electronic music, producing his *Composition for Synthesizer* in 1961.

Should the writer make this addition here?

A) Yes, because it helps to explain Babbitt's interest in puns.

B) Yes, because it links Babbitt's music to literature.

C) No, because it provides background information that is irrelevant to the paragraph.

D) No, because it fails to indicate whether Babbitt wrote for other instruments besides the synthesizer.

The writer wants to link the second paragraph to the ideas that follow. Which choice best accomplishes this goal?

A) NO CHANGE

B) helps his listeners understand his musical ideas.

C) makes his music both funny and persuasive.

D) makes similar sounding ideas mean different things.

**CONTINUE** ➡

[1] *Beaten Paths* refers both to the repetition of musical ideas and the use of the marimba, which is struck to create sound. [2] The pun contained in *Homily* is a bit less obvious. [3] The music of both *Beaten Paths* and *Homily* originate in another work of Babbitt's, *My Complements to Roger*, the title of which contains a pun on the word "compliments"/"complements." [4] A homily is a religious sermon, and a quote from a homily by St. John Chrysostom is included in the score: "And why, it is asked, are there so many snares? That we may not fly low, but seek the things that are above." [5] Other works by Babbitt also contain puns, such as *All Set*, *About Time*, and *Autobiography of the Eye*. [6] Milton Babbitt, by **43** using percussion instruments in novel ways, enhances listener enjoyment through the creation of different layers of meaning. **44**

**43**

A) NO CHANGE

B) playing around with the meanings of words,

C) using puns in both the music and titles of his compositions,

D) having his performers use dynamics and timbre in unusual ways,

**44**

To make this paragraph most logical, sentence 4 should be placed

A) where it is now.

B) after sentence 1.

C) after sentence 2.

D) after sentence 5.

## STOP
**If you finish before time is called, you may check your work on this section only.
Do not turn to any other section in the test.**

**No Test Material On This Page**

# Math Test – No Calculator

## 25 MINUTES, 20 QUESTIONS

Turn to Section 3 of your answer sheet to answer the questions in this section.

---

**DIRECTIONS**

**For questions 1–15,** solve each problem, choose the best answer from the choices provided, and fill in the corresponding circle on your answer sheet. **For questions 16–20,** solve the problem and enter your answer in the grid on the answer sheet. Please refer to the directions before question 16 on how to enter your answers in the grid. You may use any available space in your test booklet for scratch work.

**NOTES**

1. The use of a calculator **is not permitted**.
2. All variables and expressions used represent real numbers unless otherwise indicated.
3. Figures provided in this test are drawn to scale unless otherwise indicated.
4. All figures lie in a plane unless otherwise indicated.
5. Unless otherwise indicated, the domain of a given function $f$ is the set of all real numbers $x$ for which $f(x)$ is a real number.

**REFERENCE**

$A = \pi r^2$
$C = 2\pi r$

$A = \ell w$

$A = \frac{1}{2}bh$

$c^2 = a^2 + b^2$

Special Right Triangles

$V = \ell wh$

$V = \pi r^2 h$

$V = \frac{4}{3}\pi r^3$

$V = \frac{1}{3}\pi r^2 h$

$V = \frac{1}{3}\ell wh$

The number of degrees of arc in a circle is 360.
The number of radians of arc in a circle is $2\pi$.
The sum of the measures in degrees of the angles of a triangle is 180.

---

**CONTINUE**

**1**

Which of the following is equal to $m^{\frac{5}{2}}$, for all values of $m$?

A) $\sqrt{m^5}$

B) $\sqrt{m^{\frac{1}{5}}}$

C) $\sqrt[5]{m^2}$

D) $\sqrt[5]{m^{\frac{1}{2}}}$

**2**

A sealcoating company will seal $d$ driveways with the same size and shape in a subdivision using a specific type of sealant. The company's fee can be calculated by the expression $dClw$, where $d$ is the number of driveways, $C$ is a constant with units in dollars per square meter, $l$ is the length of each driveway in meters, and $w$ is the width of each driveway in meters. If the homeowners' association asks the company to use a less expensive type of sealant, which of the factors in the expression would change?

A) $l$

B) $d$

C) $w$

D) $C$

**3**

If $4x = 20$, what is the value of $12x - 4$?

A) 5

B) 36

C) 56

D) 60

**4**

If $\dfrac{2}{z} = \dfrac{8}{z + 42}$, what is the value of $\dfrac{z}{2}$?

A) 14

B) 7

C) 2

D) $\dfrac{1}{7}$

**CONTINUE**

**5**

$$3r - 5s = -17$$
$$5r - 3s = -7$$

If $(r, s)$ is a solution to the system of equations above, what is the value of $r - s$ ?

A)  10

B)  −3

C)  −10

D)  −24

**6**

The number of scripted shows produced for streaming services between 2012 and 2013 is triple the number of scripted shows the services produced between 2009 and 2010. If 24 scripted shows were produced between 2012 and 2013 and $s$ shows were produced between 2009 and 2010, which of the following equations is true?

A)  $3s = 24$

B)  $24s = 3$

C)  $\dfrac{s}{3} = 24$

D)  $s + 24 = 3$

**7**

The line $y = cx - 2$, where $c$ is a constant, is graphed in the $xy$-plane. If the line contains the point $(m, n)$, where $m \neq 0$ and $n \neq 0$, what is the slope of the line, in terms of $m$ and $n$ ?

A)  $\dfrac{2 - m}{n}$

B)  $\dfrac{2 - n}{m}$

C)  $\dfrac{m + 2}{n}$

D)  $\dfrac{n + 2}{m}$

**8**

$$3x - 2y = 5$$
$$cx - 7y = 12$$

In the system of equations above, $c$ is a constant and $x$ and $y$ are variables. For what values of $c$ will the system of equations have no solution?

A)  $-\dfrac{21}{2}$

B)  $-\dfrac{36}{5}$

C)  $\dfrac{36}{5}$

D)  $\dfrac{21}{2}$

**CONTINUE**

**9**

| $x$ | $p(x)$ |
|-----|--------|
| 0   | −1     |
| 1   | 0      |
| 2   | 3      |
| 5   | 4      |

The function $p$ is defined by a polynomial. Some values of $x$ and $p(x)$ are shown in the table above. Which of the following must be a factor of $p(x)$ ?

A) $x - 1$

B) $x - 2$

C) $x - 3$

D) $x - 4$

**10**

$$y = a(x - 3)(x + 5)$$

In the quadratic equation above, $a$ is a nonzero constant. The graph of the equation in the $xy$-plane is a parabola with vertex $(s, t)$. Which of the following is equal to $t$ ?

A) $-2a$

B) $-10a$

C) $-15a$

D) $-16a$

**11**

In the $xy$-plane, the parabola with equation $(x - 9)^2$ intersects the line with the equation $y = 36$ at two points, $F$ and $G$. What is the length of $\overline{FG}$ ?

A) 10

B) 12

C) 15

D) 25

**12**

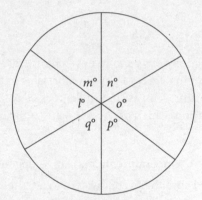

Note: Figure not drawn to scale.

In the figure above, three lines intersect at a point in a circle. If $l + m = n + o$, which of the following statements must be true?

I. $l = n$

II. $m = q$

III. $p = q$

A) I only

B) II only

C) II and III only

D) I, II, and III

CONTINUE ▶

**13**

What are the solutions to $2x^2 + 12x + 8 = 0$ ?

A)   $-3 \pm \dfrac{\sqrt{58}}{2}$

B)   $-3 \pm \sqrt{5}$

C)   $-8 \pm \sqrt{5}$

D)   $-8 \pm 8\sqrt{5}$

**14**

$$D = \frac{5}{6}(212 - F)$$

The equation above shows how a temperature $F$, measured in degrees Fahrenheit, relates to the temperature $D$, measured in degrees Delisle. Based on the equation, which of the following must be true?

I.   A temperature increase of $\dfrac{5}{6}$ degree Fahrenheit is equivalent to a temperature decrease of 1 degree Delisle.

II.   A temperature increase of 1 degree Delisle is equivalent to a temperature decrease of 1.2 degrees Fahrenheit.

III.   A temperature increase of 1 degree Fahrenheit is equivalent to a temperature decrease of $\dfrac{5}{6}$ degree Delisle.

A)  II only

B)  III only

C)  II and III only

D)  I, II, and III

**15**

The equation $\dfrac{36y^2 + 43y - 25}{ky - 3} = -9y - 4 - \dfrac{37}{ky - 3}$ is true for all values of $y = \dfrac{3}{k}$, where $k$ is a constant.

What is the value of $k$ ?

A)   27

B)    4

C)   −4

D)  −27

CONTINUE

## DIRECTIONS

**For questions 16–20**, solve the problem and enter your answer in the grid, as described below, on the answer sheet.

1. Although not required, it is suggested that you write your answer in the boxes at the top of the columns to help you fill in the circles accurately. You will receive credit only if the circles are filled in correctly.

2. Mark no more than one circle in any column.

3. No question has a negative answer.

4. Some problems may have more than one correct answer. In such cases, grid only one answer.

5. **Mixed numbers** such as $3\frac{1}{2}$ must be gridded as 3.5 or 7/2. (If $\boxed{3\ 1\ /\ 2}$ is entered into the grid, it will be interpreted as $\frac{31}{2}$, not as $3\frac{1}{2}$.)

6. **Decimal Answers:** If you obtain a decimal answer with more digits than the grid can accommodate, it may be either rounded or truncated, but it must fill the entire grid.

Answer: $\frac{7}{12}$      Answer: 2.5

Write answer in boxes.    Fraction line

Grid in result.    Decimal point

Acceptable ways to grid $\frac{2}{3}$ are:

Answer: 201 – either position is correct

**NOTE:** You may start your answers in any column, space permitting. Columns you don't need to use should be left blank.

CONTINUE

**16**

If $\dfrac{9}{10}z - \dfrac{7}{10}z = \dfrac{1}{3} + \dfrac{7}{15}$, what is the value of $z$?

**17**

In triangle $LMN$, the measure of $\angle M$ is 90°, $LN = 26$, and $MN = 24$. Triangle $OPQ$ is similar to triangle $LMN$, where each side of triangle $OPQ$ is $\dfrac{1}{5}$ the length of the corresponding side of triangle $LMN$ and vertices $O$, $P$, and $Q$ correspond to vertices $L$, $M$, and $N$, respectively. What is the value of $\cos O$?

**18**

At a bakery, each pecan braid has 30 more milligrams of sodium than each chocolate pastry. If 3 pecan braids and 4 chocolate pastries have a total of 1840 milligrams of sodium, how many milligrams of sodium does a pecan braid have?

**19**

$$a^3(a^2 - 25) = -144a$$

If $a > 0$, what is one possible solution to the equation above?

**CONTINUE** →

20

Note: Figure not drawn to scale.

Two isosceles triangles are shown above. If
$180 - f = 2g$ and $g = 65$, what is the value of $h$?

## STOP
If you finish before time is called, you may check your work on this section only.
Do not turn to any other section in the test.

Practice Test 7 | **605**

# Math Test – Calculator

## 55 MINUTES, 38 QUESTIONS

**Turn to Section 4 of your answer sheet to answer the questions in this section.**

---

### DIRECTIONS

**For questions 1–30**, solve each problem, choose the best answer from the choices provided, and fill in the corresponding circle on your answer sheet. **For questions 31–38**, solve the problem and enter your answer in the grid on the answer sheet. Please refer to the directions before question 31 on how to enter your answers in the grid. You may use any available space in your test booklet for scratch work.

### NOTES

1. The use of a calculator **is permitted**.
2. All variables and expressions used represent real numbers unless otherwise indicated.
3. Figures provided in this test are drawn to scale unless otherwise indicated.
4. All figures lie in a plane unless otherwise indicated.
5. Unless otherwise indicated, the domain of a given function $f$ is the set of all real numbers $x$ for which $f(x)$ is a real number.

### REFERENCE

$A = \pi r^2$
$C = 2\pi r$

$A = \ell w$

$A = \frac{1}{2} bh$

$c^2 = a^2 + b^2$

Special Right Triangles

$V = \ell wh$

$V = \pi r^2 h$

$V = \frac{4}{3}\pi r^3$

$V = \frac{1}{3}\pi r^2 h$

$V = \frac{1}{3}\ell wh$

The number of degrees of arc in a circle is 360.
The number of radians of arc in a circle is $2\pi$.
The sum of the measures in degrees of the angles of a triangle is 180.

CONTINUE

## 1

| Size | Color | | Total |
| --- | --- | --- | --- |
| | Red | Blue | |
| Small | 16 | 6 | 22 |
| Large | 7 | 21 | 28 |
| Total | 23 | 27 | 50 |

The table above shows the number of marbles of different colors and sizes in a bag of 50 marbles. If a marble is chosen from the bag at random, what is the probability that the marble selected will be either a small, red marble or a large, blue marble?

A) $\dfrac{9}{50}$

B) $\dfrac{17}{50}$

C) $\dfrac{21}{50}$

D) $\dfrac{37}{50}$

## 2

The graph below shows the balance of Jerry's bank account, in thousands of dollars, for each month from January through December of 2012.

Jerry's Bank Account Balance in 2012

Months since January 2012

Based on the graph, which of the following best describes the general trend of Jerry's bank account balance in 2012 ?

A) The balance generally decreased each month in 2012.

B) The balance generally decreased until July, then increased.

C) The balance was generally constant throughout 2012.

D) The balance generally increased each month in 2012.

CONTINUE

**3**

Hot Air Balloon Ride

The graph above shows the altitude of a hot air balloon over the course of a 5-hour flight. During the flight, the balloon floated at a constant altitude for 1 hour in order to best view a historic landmark. Based on the graph, what time did the hot air balloon begin viewing the historic landmark?

A) 10:30 A.M.

B) 11:30 A.M.

C) 12:30 P.M.

D) 1:00 P.M.

**4**

Every spring, Lowland High School administers a standardized test that includes only math and science questions at various levels of difficulty. On the standardized test, approximately 6 percent of the math questions and 9 percent of the science questions are categorized as very difficult questions. If the test included 153 math questions and 267 science questions, which of the following is the closest to the total number of very difficult questions on this standardized test?

A) 9

B) 17

C) 24

D) 33

**5**

What is the sum of $6y^3 - 3y^2 + 7$ and $5y^3 - 2y^2 - 3$ ?

A) $11y^6 - 5y^4 + 4$

B) $11y^6 + 5y^4 + 4$

C) $11y^3 - 5y^2 + 4$

D) $11y^3 + 5y^2 + 4$

**6**

| $x$ | $g(x)$ |
|---|---|
| 2 | −4 |
| 3 | −2 |
| 4 | 0 |
| 5 | 2 |
| 6 | 4 |

The table above shows some values of the linear function $g$. Which of the following defines $g$ ?

A) $g(x) = x - 6$

B) $g(x) = 2x - 8$

C) $g(x) = 3x - 10$

D) $g(x) = 4x - 12$

**CONTINUE**

**7**

Paul can run 144 meters in 72 seconds. If he runs at this same rate, which of the following is closest to the distance he can run in 16 minutes?

A)    200 meters

B)    500 meters

C)  1,000 meters

D)  2,000 meters

**8**

If $\dfrac{2}{7}z = \dfrac{5}{2}$, what is the value of $z$ ?

A)  $\dfrac{35}{4}$

B)  $\dfrac{5}{7}$

C)  $\dfrac{4}{35}$

D)  $\dfrac{7}{5}$

**9**

Each year, the average number of legal cases per attorney at Gary's law firm can be modeled by the equation $y = 1.74x + 15.3$, where $x$ represents the number of years that Gary's firm has been in operation since it opened in 2000, and $y$ represents the average number of legal cases per attorney. Which of the following best describes the meaning of the number 1.74 in the equation?

A)  The average number of cases per attorney in 2000

B)  The approximate increase in the average number of legal cases per attorney each year

C)  The total number of legal cases that Gary's firm handled in 2000

D)  The approximate difference between the number of legal cases Gary's firm handled in 2000 and in 2005

**CONTINUE**

**10**

The function *m* has 4 distinct zeros. Which of the following graphs could represent the graph of *m* in the *xy*-plane?

A)

B)

C)

D)

**Questions 11 and 12 refer to the following information.**

| | Spring Constant $\left(\dfrac{N}{m}\right)$ |
|---|---|
| Spring #1 | 0.7 |
| Spring #2 | 0.9 |
| Spring #3 | 1.2 |
| Spring #4 | 4.7 |
| Spring #5 | 0.6 |
| Spring #6 | 3.3 |
| Spring #7 | 2.1 |

The chart above shows the spring constants in newtons per meter $\left(\dfrac{N}{m}\right)$ for 7 different springs in a laboratory. The force required to stretch a spring can be found by using the formula $F = km$, where $F$ is the applied force measured in newtons, $k$ is the spring constant measured in $\dfrac{N}{m}$, and $m$ is the distance that spring is stretched measured in meters.

**11**

What is the force, in newtons, required to stretch Spring #2 a distance of 5 meters?

A)  3.5

B)  4.5

C)  5.5

D)  6.5

**CONTINUE**

**12**

A force of 7 newtons is applied to stretch Spring #4. Which spring would stretch the same distance when a force of 5 newtons is applied?

A)  Spring #3

B)  Spring #5

C)  Spring #6

D)  Spring #7

▲

**13**

A secretarial business bills corporations $0.30 per minute to type reports. Which of the following equations represents the total bill $b$, in dollars, for a corporation needing $t$ hours of typing?

A)  $b = \dfrac{60t}{0.30}$

B)  $b = (0.30)(60)(t)$

C)  $b = 60t + 0.30$

D)  $b = \dfrac{0.30t}{60}$

**14**

Graphs of the functions $j$ and $k$ are shown in the $xy$-plane above. For which of the following values of $x$ does $j(x) + k(x) = 0$ ?

A)  1

B)  2

C)  3

D)  4

**15**

$$e = 0.5mv^2 + 10mh$$

The equation above gives the approximate energy $e$ in joules associated with a rollercoaster cart that has mass $m$ in kilograms, speed $v$ in meters per second, and height $h$ in meters. Which of the following gives $h$, in terms of $e$, $m$, and $v$ ?

A)  $h = \dfrac{e}{10m} - 0.05v^2$

B)  $h = \dfrac{e - 0.5v^2}{10m}$

C)  $h = e + 0.05v^2 + 1$

D)  $h = \dfrac{e}{10m} + 0.05v^2$

**CONTINUE**

16

A group of scientists designed a study to test the effectiveness of pesticide P at eradicating aphids from rose gardens. From a large group of botanists, 400 participants with aphid-infested rose gardens were randomly selected to participate in the study. Half of the 400 botanists sprayed their rose gardens with pesticide P, and the other half did not. The data showed that the rose gardens sprayed with pesticide P had significantly fewer aphids as compared to those that were not sprayed with pesticide P. Which of the following is an appropriate conclusion of the study?

A) Pesticide P will decrease the number of aphids in any rose garden.

B) Pesticide P is the best pesticide available for decreasing the number of aphids in a garden.

C) Pesticide P will likely decrease the number of aphids in aphid-infested rose gardens.

D) Pesticide P will kill substantial numbers of aphids present in a garden.

**Questions 17 and 18 refer to the following information.**

$$C(x) = 3x + 75$$
$$R(x) = 8x$$

The cost of manufacturing a product and the revenue generated by that product are functions of the number of products manufactured and sold. The functions above are the cost and revenue functions for a certain product. The function $C(x)$ gives the cost, in dollars, of manufacturing $x$ products and the function $R(x)$ gives the revenue, in dollars, generated when those $x$ products are sold.

17

How many units of product must be manufactured and sold in order for the cost of manufacturing a product to equal the revenue generated by selling the product?

A) 8

B) 10

C) 12

D) 15

18

How will the cost of manufacturing change if 5 additional units of product are manufactured?

A) The cost will decrease by $15.

B) The cost will increase by $3.

C) The cost will increase by $15.

D) The cost will increase by $75

**CONTINUE**

**19**

Number of Bacteria Colonies versus Temperature

Sixteen samples of bacteria were each incubated for 24 hours. The scatterplot above shows the number of colonies present at the end of the incubation period and the temperature of the incubator. The line of best fit for the data is also shown. For the sample incubated at 40°C, the actual number of colonies was about how many more than the number predicted by the line of best fit?

A)   0

B)   10

C)   20

D)   40

**20**

Of the following four geographically distinct communities, which community would exhibit exponential growth of the population?

A)   Each successive year, the community increases by 5% of the original population.

B)   Each successive year, the community increases by 4% of the original population and 300 new individuals are added to the community.

C)   Each successive year, 300 new individuals are added to the community.

D)   Each successive year, the community increases by 3% of the current population.

**21**

Glucose, which is an important component of growth media for cultured cells, is so energy rich that 1 milliliter can feed up to 9 Petri dishes of cells. If a Petri dish has an area of approximately $7\frac{1}{4}$ square centimeters, about how many square centimeters of cells could 115 milliliters of glucose feed?

A)   140

B)   1,000

C)   6,500

D)   7,500

**22**

In the triangle shown above, $\sin(c°) = \cos(d°)$. If $c = 6m - 9$ and $d = 8m - 6$, what is the value of $m$ ?

A)   5.4

B)   7.5

C)   10.5

D)   13.5

CONTINUE

**23**

A behavioral biologist has a bag containing *t* treats that she is using to train a group of animals. If she gives 4 treats to each animal, she will have 6 treats left over. In order to give each animal 5 treats, she will need an additional 8 treats. How many animals are in the behavioral biologist's training group?

A) 2

B) 8

C) 14

D) 16

**24**

The sum of three numbers is 738. One of the numbers, *k*, is 20% less than the sum of the other two numbers. What is the value of *k* ?

A) 328

B) 267

C) 215

D) 144

**25**

In the *xy*-plane, line *l* passes through the origin and contains points $(4, r)$ and $(r, 16)$. Which of the following could be the value of *r* ?

A) 12

B) 8

C) 4

D) 0

**26**

A triangle was modified by increasing its base by 20 percent and decreasing its height by *h* percent. If these modifications decreased the area of the triangle by 28 percent, what is the value of *h* ?

A) 48

B) 40

C) 30

D) 28

**CONTINUE**

**27**

A time capsule is constructed from two rectangular pyramids and a rectangular solid with measurements indicated in the figure above. Of the following, which is the closest to the volume of the time capsule, in cubic inches?

A) 1,386

B) 1,173

C)  960

D)  426

**28**

$$2a + x = 4a - 8$$
$$2b + y = 4b - 8$$

In the equation above, $x$ and $y$ are constants. If $x$ is $y$ minus $\frac{1}{4}$, which of the following is true?

A)  $a$ is $b$ minus $\frac{1}{2}$

B)  $a$ is $b$ minus $\frac{1}{4}$

C)  $a$ is $b$ minus $\frac{1}{8}$

D)  $a$ is $b$ plus $\frac{1}{4}$

**29**

In order to plan for his family's future, Michael has decided to invest some of his money into a mutual fund that, starting from the present, his broker estimates will increase by 15 percent every 4 years. If Michael invests $20,000 into the mutual fund, which of the following expressions represents his broker's estimate of his mutual fund's worth $t$ years from now?

A)  $20,000(1.15)^{\frac{t}{4}}$

B)  $20,000(0.15)^{\frac{t}{4}}$

C)  $20,000(1.15)^{4t}$

D)  $20,000(0.15)^{4t}$

**30**

| | Varsity Soccer | Varsity Basketball |
|---|---|---|
| Juniors | | |
| Seniors | | |
| Total | 108 | 32 |

The unfinished table above shows the number of juniors and seniors at Woodsfield High School who participate in either varsity soccer or varsity basketball. There are 4 times as many junior varsity soccer players as there are junior varsity basketball players, and there are 3 times as many senior varsity soccer players as there are senior varsity basketball players. If there is a total of 108 varsity soccer players and 32 varsity basketball players at Woodsfield High, which of the following is closest to the probability that a randomly chosen varsity basketball player is a junior? (Note: Assume that no student plays both varsity soccer and varsity basketball.)

A)  0.086

B)  0.134

C)  0.247

D)  0.375

**CONTINUE**

## DIRECTIONS

**For questions 31–38**, solve the problem and enter your answer in the grid, as described below, on the answer sheet.

1. Although not required, it is suggested that you write your answer in the boxes at the top of the columns to help you fill in the circles accurately. You will receive credit only if the circles are filled in correctly.

2. Mark no more than one circle in any column.

3. No question has a negative answer.

4. Some problems may have more than one correct answer. In such cases, grid only one answer.

5. **Mixed numbers** such as $3\frac{1}{2}$ must be gridded as 3.5 or 7/2. (If ⟨3 .1 / 2⟩ is entered into the grid, it will be interpreted as $\frac{31}{2}$, not as $3\frac{1}{2}$.)

6. **Decimal Answers:** If you obtain a decimal answer with more digits than the grid can accommodate, it may be either rounded or truncated, but it must fill the entire grid.

Answer: $\frac{7}{12}$          Answer: 2.5

Write answer in boxes. → Fraction line

Grid in result.

Decimal point

Acceptable ways to grid $\frac{2}{3}$ are:

Answer: 201 – either position is correct

**NOTE:** You may start your answers in any column, space permitting. Columns you don't need to use should be left blank.

**CONTINUE →**

**31**

Enrollment per Course at Riverview College—
Spring Semester of 2001

| Course | Number of Students Enrolled | Course | Number of Students Enrolled |
|--------|------|--------|------|
| Sociology | 98 | U.S. History | 27 |
| Psychology | 37 | Anthropology | 33 |
| Economics | 85 | Marketing | 68 |
| Calculus | 45 | Political Science | 79 |
| Biology | 42 | Linguistics | 16 |
| Accounting | 64 | Chemistry | 52 |

The above table lists the number of students enrolled in 12 different courses at Riverview College during its spring semester of 2001. According to the table, what is the mean class size of these selected courses at Riverview College in the spring semester of 2001 ? (Round your answer to the nearest tenth.)

**32**

A fruit stand sells pints of blueberries for $3 each and pints of strawberries for $5 each. If John spends at least $23 but no more than $27 on $b$ pints of blueberries and 1 pint of strawberries, what is one possible value of $b$ ?

**33**

Jasmine's algebra teacher gives pop quizzes that are scored between 0 and 50 points, inclusive. After the first 5 quizzes, Jasmine's quiz average (arithmetic mean) is 35. What is the lowest score Jasmine can receive on the 6th quiz and still be able to have an average of at least 45 for the first 20 quizzes?

**34**

$$(-4z^2 + 3z - 7) - 3(z^2 - 5z - 2)$$

If the expression above is rewritten in the form $az^2 + bz + c$, where $a$, $b$, and $c$ are constants, what is the value of $b$ ?

**CONTINUE**

**35**

$$y \geq -12x + 384$$

$$y \geq 4x$$

In the $xy$-plane, if a point with coordinates $(f, g)$ lies in the solution set of the system of inequalities above, what is the minimum value of $g$ ?

**36**

In a circle with center $C$, central angle $XCY$ has a measure of $\dfrac{3\pi}{2}$ radians. The major arc $XY$ formed by central angle $XCY$ is what fraction of the circumference of the circle?

**Questions 37 and 38 refer to the following information.**

In telecommunication networks, the transmission time is the amount of time required for a message to be successfully transmitted from beginning to end. If a message is transmitted at a rate of $r$ bytes per second with a transmission time of $T$ seconds, then the size of the message in $b$ bytes can be found by the formula $b = rT$.

The CEO of Relay Communications estimates that the average global transmission time of a message is 2.5 seconds and that the average transmission rate is 1,000 bytes per second. The CEO uses the above formula to estimate that the average global message size at his company is 2,500 bytes.

**37**

The CEO of Relay Communications decides to study transmission times in a rural geographical region that his company serves. In this region, the CEO estimates that the average transmission rate rises to 75,000 bytes per <u>minute</u> and that the average transmission time is 1.6 seconds. The average message size in this region is what percent less than the average global message size? (Note: Ignore the percent symbol when entering your answer. For example, if the answer is 24.1%, enter 24.1.)

**CONTINUE**

38

Transmission times can vary depending on population, geographical region, or the type of material used in the telecommunication wires. The CEO realizes that in a heavily populated city, the transmission rate drops to 45,000 bytes per minute. If the average transmission time of a message being transmitted in this heavily populated city is 4.2 seconds, what is the average size of a message transmitted by Relay Communications in this heavily populated city?

▲

# STOP

**If you finish before time is called, you may check your work on this section only.**
**Do not turn to any other section in the test.**

# SAT Essay

## DIRECTIONS

The essay gives you an opportunity to show how effectively you can read and comprehend a passage and write an essay analyzing the passage. In your essay you should demonstrate that you have read the passage carefully, present a clear and logical analysis, and use language precisely.

Your essay must be written on the lines provided in your answer sheet booklet; except for the planning page of the answer booklet, you will receive no other paper on which to write. You will have enough space if you write on every line, avoid wide margins, and keep your handwriting to a reasonable size. Remember that people who are not familiar with your handwriting will read what you write. Try to write or print so that what you are writing is legible to those readers.

**You have 50 minutes to read the passage and write an essay in response to the prompt provided inside this booklet.**

## REMINDER

— Do not write your essay in this booklet. Only what you write on the lined pages of your answer booklet will be evaluated.

— An off-topic essay will not be evaluated.

CONTINUE ➔

As you read the passage below, consider how Ruth Reichl uses

- evidence, such as facts or examples, to support claims.
- reasoning to develop ideas and to connect claims and evidence.
- stylistic or persuasive elements, such as word choice or appeals to emotion, to add power to the ideas expressed.

**Adapted from Ruth Reichl, "The F.D.A.'s Blatant Failure on Food." © 2014 by The New York Times. Originally published July 30, 2014.**

1   Every year, antibiotic-resistant infections kill at least 23,000 Americans and make another two million sick, according to the Centers for Disease Control and Prevention. That's why a recent ruling by the United States Second Circuit Court of Appeals is so appalling.

2   It allows the federal Food and Drug Administration to leave an antibiotic used in animal feed on the market even if the agency openly states that the drug's use is not safe and increases the risk of antibiotic resistance in people. This means that the dangerous misuse of antibiotics in industrial livestock and poultry can continue unabated.

3   For years industrial meat and poultry producers have fed healthy animals antibiotics to fatten them up fast. The antibiotics also prevent disease in what are often overcrowded, unsanitary conditions. This practice breeds antibiotic-resistant bacteria that threaten us all.

4   The F.D.A. has issued a toothless voluntary guidance document for the industry, which requires no action to reduce antibiotic use and will therefore do little to nothing to stop the spread of antibiotic-resistant superbugs.

5   Why should we be concerned? Because the superbugs bred on industrial farms can easily travel to us in our food—as in the recent antibiotic-resistant salmonella outbreak linked to Foster Farms chicken that has sickened over 600 people. The superbugs also get into our water and our soil. Some of the antibiotic-resistant bacteria can cause life-threatening infections.

6   While prescribing unnecessary antibiotics to people is one widely known cause of the problem, the C.D.C. and leading medical groups have identified the misuse of drugs in livestock and poultry operations as another important contributor. Dr. Thomas R. Frieden, the C.D.C. director, has said of antibiotic resistance, "If we don't act now, our medicine cabinet will be empty and we won't have the antibiotics we need to save lives." That's a truly terrifying prospect.

CONTINUE ➡

7   And it's one we don't need to face. Although many industrial farmers claim that cleaning up their act will cost the rest of us at the cash register, responsible producers from Missouri to Denmark are already raising healthy livestock and poultry at competitive prices without the use of unnecessary drugs. Some mainstream food companies and their suppliers are starting to move in that direction, but it's time all of the big meat and poultry firms joined them.

8   A fifth-generation pork producer, Russ Kremer of Missouri, is showing the way. In 1989, after an antibiotic-resistant infection from one of his pigs nearly killed him, he realized the danger of his antibiotic-dependent methods and decided to start over. He now raises pigs the natural way—free-roaming and without drugs—for his company, Heritage Acres Food. Today, buyers of his pork include Chipotle and Costco. He also leads a thriving pork cooperative, showing dozens of producers that they, too, can make similar conversions at a profit.

9   And Mr. Kremer is hardly alone. In Denmark, one of the world's largest pork exporters, industrial farmers have cut overall antibiotic use by more than 40 percent while increasing production. The European Union, with its additional 27 member nations, also prohibits the misuse of growth-promoting antibiotics.

10  While the F.D.A. continues to drag its feet, it's time for cooks and consumers to step in. We can play an important, proactive role in protecting against superbugs by changing the marketplace. Insist that your supermarkets stock meat and poultry raised without antibiotics. Demand that your restaurants do the same. An increasing number of major food companies, including Whole Foods, Chick-fil-A, Chipotle, Applegate and Panera Bread, have gotten on board, proof that as we vote with our wallets and our roasting pans, producers will rise to meet us.

11  Food should be delicious. It should also be good for you. We shouldn't have to worry that we're endangering our health each time we put a morsel of meat into our mouths. Rather than protecting the unsafe practices of the country's animal agriculture industry, it's time the F.D.A. followed its mandate and put America's health first.

---

Write an essay in which you explain how Ruth Reichl builds an argument to persuade her audience to take a proactive role in protecting against superbugs. In your essay, analyze how Reichl uses one or more of the features listed in the box above (or features of your own choice) to strengthen the logic and persuasiveness of her argument. Be sure that your analysis focuses on the most relevant features of the passage.

Your essay should not explain whether you agree with Reichl's claims, but rather explain how Reichl builds an argument to persuade her audience.

**END OF TEST**

**DO NOT RETURN TO A PREVIOUS SECTION.**

Completely darken bubbles with a No. 2 pencil. If you make a mistake, be sure to erase mark completely. Erase all stray marks.

**1.**

YOUR NAME: _____
(Print)
Last          First          M.I.

SIGNATURE: _____          DATE: __ / __ / __

HOME ADDRESS: _____
(Print)
Number and Street

_____
City          State          Zip Code

PHONE NO.: _____
(Print)

IMPORTANT: Please fill in these boxes exactly as shown on the back cover of your test book.

**2. TEST FORM**

**6. DATE OF BIRTH**

| Month | | Day | | Year | |
|---|---|---|---|---|---|
| ○ JAN | | | | | |
| ○ FEB | ⓪ | ⓪ | ⓪ | ⓪ | |
| ○ MAR | ① | ① | ① | ① | |
| ○ APR | ② | ② | ② | ② | |
| ○ MAY | ③ | ③ | ③ | ③ | |
| ○ JUN | | ④ | ④ | ④ | |
| ○ JUL | | ⑤ | ⑤ | ⑤ | |
| ○ AUG | | ⑥ | ⑥ | ⑥ | |
| ○ SEP | | ⑦ | ⑦ | ⑦ | |
| ○ OCT | | ⑧ | ⑧ | ⑧ | |
| ○ NOV | | ⑨ | ⑨ | ⑨ | |
| ○ DEC | | | | | |

**3. TEST CODE**

**4. REGISTRATION NUMBER**

**7. SEX**
○ MALE
○ FEMALE

The **Princeton Review**®

**5. YOUR NAME**

First 4 letters of last name | FIRST INIT | MID INIT

(A)(B)(C)(D)(E)(F)(G)(H)(I)(J)(K)(L)(M)(N)(O)(P)(Q)(R)(S)(T)(U)(V)(W)(X)(Y)(Z)

**Test ⑦**   Start with number 1 for each new section.
If a section has fewer questions than answer spaces, leave the extra answer spaces blank.

## Section 1—Reading

1. Ⓐ Ⓑ Ⓒ Ⓓ
2. Ⓐ Ⓑ Ⓒ Ⓓ
3. Ⓐ Ⓑ Ⓒ Ⓓ
4. Ⓐ Ⓑ Ⓒ Ⓓ
5. Ⓐ Ⓑ Ⓒ Ⓓ
6. Ⓐ Ⓑ Ⓒ Ⓓ
7. Ⓐ Ⓑ Ⓒ Ⓓ
8. Ⓐ Ⓑ Ⓒ Ⓓ
9. Ⓐ Ⓑ Ⓒ Ⓓ
10. Ⓐ Ⓑ Ⓒ Ⓓ
11. Ⓐ Ⓑ Ⓒ Ⓓ
12. Ⓐ Ⓑ Ⓒ Ⓓ
13. Ⓐ Ⓑ Ⓒ Ⓓ
14. Ⓐ Ⓑ Ⓒ Ⓓ
15. Ⓐ Ⓑ Ⓒ Ⓓ
16. Ⓐ Ⓑ Ⓒ Ⓓ
17. Ⓐ Ⓑ Ⓒ Ⓓ
18. Ⓐ Ⓑ Ⓒ Ⓓ
19. Ⓐ Ⓑ Ⓒ Ⓓ
20. Ⓐ Ⓑ Ⓒ Ⓓ
21. Ⓐ Ⓑ Ⓒ Ⓓ
22. Ⓐ Ⓑ Ⓒ Ⓓ
23. Ⓐ Ⓑ Ⓒ Ⓓ
24. Ⓐ Ⓑ Ⓒ Ⓓ
25. Ⓐ Ⓑ Ⓒ Ⓓ
26. Ⓐ Ⓑ Ⓒ Ⓓ
27. Ⓐ Ⓑ Ⓒ Ⓓ
28. Ⓐ Ⓑ Ⓒ Ⓓ
29. Ⓐ Ⓑ Ⓒ Ⓓ
30. Ⓐ Ⓑ Ⓒ Ⓓ
31. Ⓐ Ⓑ Ⓒ Ⓓ
32. Ⓐ Ⓑ Ⓒ Ⓓ
33. Ⓐ Ⓑ Ⓒ Ⓓ
34. Ⓐ Ⓑ Ⓒ Ⓓ
35. Ⓐ Ⓑ Ⓒ Ⓓ
36. Ⓐ Ⓑ Ⓒ Ⓓ
37. Ⓐ Ⓑ Ⓒ Ⓓ
38. Ⓐ Ⓑ Ⓒ Ⓓ
39. Ⓐ Ⓑ Ⓒ Ⓓ
40. Ⓐ Ⓑ Ⓒ Ⓓ
41. Ⓐ Ⓑ Ⓒ Ⓓ
42. Ⓐ Ⓑ Ⓒ Ⓓ
43. Ⓐ Ⓑ Ⓒ Ⓓ
44. Ⓐ Ⓑ Ⓒ Ⓓ
45. Ⓐ Ⓑ Ⓒ Ⓓ
46. Ⓐ Ⓑ Ⓒ Ⓓ
47. Ⓐ Ⓑ Ⓒ Ⓓ
48. Ⓐ Ⓑ Ⓒ Ⓓ
49. Ⓐ Ⓑ Ⓒ Ⓓ
50. Ⓐ Ⓑ Ⓒ Ⓓ
51. Ⓐ Ⓑ Ⓒ Ⓓ
52. Ⓐ Ⓑ Ⓒ Ⓓ

## Section 2—Writing and Language Skills

1. Ⓐ Ⓑ Ⓒ Ⓓ
2. Ⓐ Ⓑ Ⓒ Ⓓ
3. Ⓐ Ⓑ Ⓒ Ⓓ
4. Ⓐ Ⓑ Ⓒ Ⓓ
5. Ⓐ Ⓑ Ⓒ Ⓓ
6. Ⓐ Ⓑ Ⓒ Ⓓ
7. Ⓐ Ⓑ Ⓒ Ⓓ
8. Ⓐ Ⓑ Ⓒ Ⓓ
9. Ⓐ Ⓑ Ⓒ Ⓓ
10. Ⓐ Ⓑ Ⓒ Ⓓ
11. Ⓐ Ⓑ Ⓒ Ⓓ
12. Ⓐ Ⓑ Ⓒ Ⓓ
13. Ⓐ Ⓑ Ⓒ Ⓓ
14. Ⓐ Ⓑ Ⓒ Ⓓ
15. Ⓐ Ⓑ Ⓒ Ⓓ
16. Ⓐ Ⓑ Ⓒ Ⓓ
17. Ⓐ Ⓑ Ⓒ Ⓓ
18. Ⓐ Ⓑ Ⓒ Ⓓ
19. Ⓐ Ⓑ Ⓒ Ⓓ
20. Ⓐ Ⓑ Ⓒ Ⓓ
21. Ⓐ Ⓑ Ⓒ Ⓓ
22. Ⓐ Ⓑ Ⓒ Ⓓ
23. Ⓐ Ⓑ Ⓒ Ⓓ
24. Ⓐ Ⓑ Ⓒ Ⓓ
25. Ⓐ Ⓑ Ⓒ Ⓓ
26. Ⓐ Ⓑ Ⓒ Ⓓ
27. Ⓐ Ⓑ Ⓒ Ⓓ
28. Ⓐ Ⓑ Ⓒ Ⓓ
29. Ⓐ Ⓑ Ⓒ Ⓓ
30. Ⓐ Ⓑ Ⓒ Ⓓ
31. Ⓐ Ⓑ Ⓒ Ⓓ
32. Ⓐ Ⓑ Ⓒ Ⓓ
33. Ⓐ Ⓑ Ⓒ Ⓓ
34. Ⓐ Ⓑ Ⓒ Ⓓ
35. Ⓐ Ⓑ Ⓒ Ⓓ
36. Ⓐ Ⓑ Ⓒ Ⓓ
37. Ⓐ Ⓑ Ⓒ Ⓓ
38. Ⓐ Ⓑ Ⓒ Ⓓ
39. Ⓐ Ⓑ Ⓒ Ⓓ
40. Ⓐ Ⓑ Ⓒ Ⓓ
41. Ⓐ Ⓑ Ⓒ Ⓓ
42. Ⓐ Ⓑ Ⓒ Ⓓ
43. Ⓐ Ⓑ Ⓒ Ⓓ
44. Ⓐ Ⓑ Ⓒ Ⓓ

The Princeton Review®

**Test 7**  Start with number 1 for each new section.
If a section has fewer questions than answer spaces, leave the extra answer spaces blank.

## Section 3—Mathematics: No Calculator

1. Ⓐ Ⓑ Ⓒ Ⓓ
2. Ⓐ Ⓑ Ⓒ Ⓓ
3. Ⓐ Ⓑ Ⓒ Ⓓ
4. Ⓐ Ⓑ Ⓒ Ⓓ
5. Ⓐ Ⓑ Ⓒ Ⓓ
6. Ⓐ Ⓑ Ⓒ Ⓓ
7. Ⓐ Ⓑ Ⓒ Ⓓ
8. Ⓐ Ⓑ Ⓒ Ⓓ
9. Ⓐ Ⓑ Ⓒ Ⓓ
10. Ⓐ Ⓑ Ⓒ Ⓓ
11. Ⓐ Ⓑ Ⓒ Ⓓ
12. Ⓐ Ⓑ Ⓒ Ⓓ
13. Ⓐ Ⓑ Ⓒ Ⓓ
14. Ⓐ Ⓑ Ⓒ Ⓓ
15. Ⓐ Ⓑ Ⓒ Ⓓ

16. 17. 18. 19. 20.

## Section 4—Mathematics: Calculator

1. Ⓐ Ⓑ Ⓒ Ⓓ
2. Ⓐ Ⓑ Ⓒ Ⓓ
3. Ⓐ Ⓑ Ⓒ Ⓓ
4. Ⓐ Ⓑ Ⓒ Ⓓ
5. Ⓐ Ⓑ Ⓒ Ⓓ
6. Ⓐ Ⓑ Ⓒ Ⓓ
7. Ⓐ Ⓑ Ⓒ Ⓓ
8. Ⓐ Ⓑ Ⓒ Ⓓ
9. Ⓐ Ⓑ Ⓒ Ⓓ
10. Ⓐ Ⓑ Ⓒ Ⓓ
11. Ⓐ Ⓑ Ⓒ Ⓓ
12. Ⓐ Ⓑ Ⓒ Ⓓ
13. Ⓐ Ⓑ Ⓒ Ⓓ
14. Ⓐ Ⓑ Ⓒ Ⓓ
15. Ⓐ Ⓑ Ⓒ Ⓓ
16. Ⓐ Ⓑ Ⓒ Ⓓ
17. Ⓐ Ⓑ Ⓒ Ⓓ
18. Ⓐ Ⓑ Ⓒ Ⓓ
19. Ⓐ Ⓑ Ⓒ Ⓓ
20. Ⓐ Ⓑ Ⓒ Ⓓ
21. Ⓐ Ⓑ Ⓒ Ⓓ
22. Ⓐ Ⓑ Ⓒ Ⓓ
23. Ⓐ Ⓑ Ⓒ Ⓓ
24. Ⓐ Ⓑ Ⓒ Ⓓ
25. Ⓐ Ⓑ Ⓒ Ⓓ
26. Ⓐ Ⓑ Ⓒ Ⓓ
27. Ⓐ Ⓑ Ⓒ Ⓓ
28. Ⓐ Ⓑ Ⓒ Ⓓ
29. Ⓐ Ⓑ Ⓒ Ⓓ
30. Ⓐ Ⓑ Ⓒ Ⓓ

31. 32. 33. 34. 35.

36. 37. 38.

# Chapter 16
# Practice Test 7:
# Answers and
# Explanations

# PRACTICE TEST 7 ANSWER KEY

| | Section 1:<br>Reading | | Section 2:<br>Writing & Language | | Section 3:<br>Math (No Calculator) | | Section 4 :<br>Math (Calculator) |
|---|---|---|---|---|---|---|---|
| 1. C | 27. A | 1. A | 23. D | 1. A | 11. B | 1. D | 20. D |
| 2. B | 28. A | 2. D | 24. D | 2. D | 12. C | 2. B | 21. D |
| 3. B | 29. C | 3. B | 25. B | 3. C | 13. B | 3. A | 22. B |
| 4. D | 30. D | 4. B | 26. A | 4. B | 14. C | 4. D | 23. C |
| 5. C | 31. C | 5. A | 27. D | 5. B | 15. C | 5. C | 24. A |
| 6. B | 32. D | 6. D | 28. D | 6. A | 16. 4 | 6. B | 25. B |
| 7. D | 33. C | 7. A | 29. B | 7. D | 17. $\frac{5}{13}$ | 7. D | 26. B |
| 8. B | 34. A | 8. C | 30. A | 8. D | | 8. A | 27. A |
| 9. C | 35. A | 9. C | 31. D | 9. A | 18. 280 | 9. B | 28. C |
| 10. D | 36. B | 10. C | 32. C | 10. D | 19. 3 or | 10. A | 29. A |
| 11. D | 37. B | 11. A | 33. D | | 4 | 11. B | 30. D |
| 12. A | 38. D | 12. A | 34. D | | 20. 115 | 12. C | 31. 53.8 |
| 13. B | 39. B | 13. D | 35. B | | | 13. B | 32. 6 or |
| 14. D | 40. A | 14. D | 36. A | | | 14. D | 7 |
| 15. C | 41. B | 15. B | 37. B | | | 15. A | 33. 25 |
| 16. C | 42. A | 16. A | 38. C | | | 16. C | 34. 18 |
| 17. B | 43. B | 17. D | 39. A | | | 17. D | 35. 96 |
| 18. C | 44. C | 18. A | 40. B | | | 18. C | 36. $\frac{3}{4}$ |
| 19. B | 45. A | 19. C | 41. C | | | 19. C | or |
| 20. B | 46. C | 20. D | 42. A | | | | .75 |
| 21. C | 47. B | 21. B | 43. C | | | | 37. 20 |
| 22. D | 48. B | 22. C | 44. C | | | | 38. 3,150 |
| 23. B | 49. D | | | | | | |
| 24. D | 50. A | | | | | | |
| 25. A | 51. C | | | | | | |
| 26. B | 52. C | | | | | | |

For self-scoring assessment tables, please turn to page 957.

# PRACTICE TEST 7 EXPLANATIONS

## Section 1: Reading

1.  **C**  This question asks *which choice best summarizes the passage*, indicating that it is a general question that should be done after all of the specific questions. Whether it is referred to as worth *six hundred francs due, 430 francs to offer*, or simply *the burden he bore on his back*, the passage is mainly concerned with Deplis' tattoo and how he would pay for it, so an accurate summary would address this debt and the troubles he faced because of it. Choice (A) says that he is *unable to display a work of art*. While it does describe his troubles, it is a specific detail and does not mention the debt, which was the prediction. Eliminate (A). Choice (B) mentions *whether or not to obey the law*, which does not match the prediction, so eliminate it. Choice (C) mentions the *unpaid debt* and that he *finds his choices restricted*. Both of these ideas match the prediction, so keep (C). Choice (D) states that he *tries to steal art to please a deceased relative*, which never happened and doesn't match the prediction, so eliminate it. Choice (C) is the correct answer.

2.  **B**  This question asks for *Henri Deplis' financial status before receiving the legacy*. Notice that the question that follows is a best evidence question, so this question and Q3 can be answered in tandem. Look at the answers for Q3 first. The lines in (3A) only mention his place of birth and do not mention anything about Deplis' financial status, and therefore do not support any of the answer choices for Q2. Eliminate (3A). Choice (3B) mentions that his financial situation was *modest*, so look to see whether those lines support any answers in Q2. Choice (2B) is a close match, so draw a line connecting (3B) and (2B). Choice (3C) mentions *impoverished circumstances*, but the lines given refer to Signor Pincini rather than Deplis, so eliminate (3C). Choice (3D) refers to the *legacy dwindling to insignificant proportions*, but the question asks about his financial status before the legacy, so eliminate (3D). Without any support from Q3, (2A), (2C), and (2D) can be eliminated. Choices (2B) and (3B) are the correct answers.

3.  **B**  (See explanation above.)

4.  **D**  This question asks for the meaning of the word *exercise* as it is used in the text. Cross out the word, and use the surrounding information to fill in another word that makes sense based on the passage. According to the text, the tattoo on Deplis' back was *Pincini's masterpiece* and *his greatest effort*, and lines 34–38 ("Without even...art") state that the *little scope* of the tombstone cherubs would not be a good place to *exercise his favorite art*—tattooing. A good replacement word in this case would be something like "perform," which would indicate how Pincini approached his tattoos as masterpieces. Choices (A) and (B) have no relation to performance and can be eliminated. Choice (C) is close, but a *masterpiece* is original and would not be done *repeatedly*; eliminate (C). *Ability to perform* matches the prediction. Choice (D) is the correct answer.

5.  **C**  This question asks about a detail regarding *the cherubs on Pincini's tombstone.* Use the lead words *cherubs* and *tombstone* to find the window to read. Lines 36–37 include the phrase *under an ornate tombstone, whose winged cherubs.* Pincini is a tattoo artist, so *the exercise of his favorite art* refers to tattooing. The passage describes Deplis' tattoo as covering his client's back, *from the collar-bone down to the waist-line,* which is a big tattoo. The *winged cherubs would have afforded singularly little scope,* offering a surface area much smaller than that of a human back, so the correct answer will have something to do with the small size of the cherubs. Choice (A) might initially look attractive, but Pincini is a tattoo artist, not a sculptor, so the cherubs themselves aren't the works of art; furthermore, the passage is not suggesting that Pincini would actually use the cherubs as artistic subjects, since he is already buried underneath the tombstone. Neither (B) nor (D) mentions small size, so eliminate those answers. Choice (C) matches the prediction, and it is the correct answer.

6.  **B**  This question asks why *Deplis reduced his offer to 405 francs.* Look for the lead words *405 francs* in the text; they appear in line 52. Earlier in the paragraph, Deplis' *legacy had dwindled* and *there remained little more than 430 francs to offer to the widow.* In this context *obliged* means he had to, so Deplis reduced the offer because his funds continued to dwindle. Eliminate anything that doesn't match this prediction. The paragraph indicates that Deplis was running out of money, not that he had an inclination to *annoy* or *trick Pincini's widow;* eliminate (A) and (C). While it is true that Deplis wanted Pincini's widow to *accept a lower offer,* there is no indication he *thought she would,* so eliminate (D). The paragraph indicates that Deplis' funds had been dwindling, so it is reasonable that they would continue to do so. Choice (B) is the correct answer.

7.  **D**  The question asks what the phrase *cancelled the sale of the work of art* does in the context of the passage. The widow *was properly indignant* and Deplis' *offer of 405 francs fanned the widow's indignation into a fury.* However, after the matter-of-fact phrase *she cancelled the sale of the work of art,* there is no further reference to the widow in the entire passage, beyond that *she had presented [the work of art] to the municipality of Bergamo, which had gratefully accepted it.* The tattoo has already been done, so her decision to cancel the sale and give the artwork to Bergamo is unrealistic. The correct answer should reflect this idea of the widow's unrealistic decision. Choices (A) and (B) refer to Deplis, not the widow, and can be eliminated. *The unpleasant temper of the widow* may be mentioned in the passage, but does not match the prediction, so eliminate (C). Choice (D) mentions an *unexpected shift in perspective,* which matches the unexpected idea that the widow has canceled the sale of the completed tattoo and offered the art to Bergamo. Choice (D) is the correct answer.

8.  **B**  This question asks for the meaning of the word *celebrated* as it is used in the text. Cross out the word, and use the surrounding information to fill in another word that makes sense based on the passage. In lines 69–70, *Public interest and official vigilance increased as the matter became more widely known.* The vapour bath proprietor had already been aware of *the celebrated Fall of Icarus,* so the correct answer must mean something like "known." Choices (A) and (C) might look like possible definitions of *celebrated,* but they do not match the

prediction. Eliminate them. Choice (D) does not match the prediction at all and can be eliminated. *Famous* matches the predicted answer of "known." Choice (B) is the correct answer.

9. **C**   This question asks for a description of the trouble Henri Deplis encountered due to his tattoo. Notice that the question that follows is a best evidence question, so this question and Q10 can be answered in tandem. Look at the answers for Q10 first. Choice (10A) describes how he snuck out *as unobtrusively as possible* and *hoped his identity and that of the famous picture might be lost*, implying that the tattoo was trouble that he hoped to hide. Look to see whether those lines support any answers in Q9. In (9C), the phrase *persistently troublesome* is a good match, but (10A) does not support *obviously absurd*, so it's not a good connection. Choice (10A) does not support any of the other answers for Q9, so it can be eliminated. Choice (10B) mentions that the tattoo is a *burden*, which could support *socially awkward* in (9A) or *persistently troublesome* in (9C), but neither *well intended* nor *obviously absurd* is supported by (10B), so eliminate it. Choice (10C) says that he was fervently thankful to go to *the neighbourhood of Bordeaux*. Like (10A), this shows that he hoped to get away and hide, so eliminate it for the same reason: It supports *persistently troublesome* but not *obviously absurd*. Choice (10D) states that *an array of official force barred his departure* because of a *stringent law which forbids the exportation of Italian works of art*, which means he couldn't leave the country because the tattoo on his back technically belonged to Italy. These lines support (9C) because *absurd* is a match for *unusual*, and the situation is clearly troublesome. Draw a line to connect (10D) and (9C). Without any support from Q10, (9A), (9B), and (9D) can be eliminated. Choices (9C) and (10D) are the correct answers.

10. **D**   (See explanation above.)

11. **D**   This question asks for the location that the *author explicitly cite[s] as a known location of shales*. Notice that the next question is a best evidence question, so this question and Q12 can be answered in tandem. Look at the answers for Q12 first. Choice (12A) says *one of the hottest spots in Pennsylvania's Marcellus shale boom*, so look to see whether those lines support any answers in Q11. Choice (11D) is Pennsylvania, so connect (12A) and (11D). Choice (12B) provides no details regarding location, so eliminate it. Choice (12C) references gas shales mentioned in a previous sentence, but it does not provide any location evidence itself. In addition, none of the locations mentioned in the previous sentence are answers for Q11. Eliminate (12C). Choice (12D) mentions shales being found *possibly in Europe*, and it also mentions that Europe imports natural gas from Russia. However, the author does not explicitly state that the gas comes from a *known location of shales*. Eliminate (12D). Without any support from Q12, (11A), (11B), and (11C) can be eliminated. Choices (11D) and (12A) are the correct answers.

12. **A**   (See explanation above.)

13. **B**   This question asks for support *that horizontal drilling is not a completely new technique*, so the correct answer will show that *horizontal drilling* happened in the past. A personal memory

from *the spring of 2008* does not prove drilling occurred in the past, so eliminate (A). Choice (B) talks about *a new combination of old oil industry technologies*, and *horizontal drilling* fits that category, so keep (B). Choice (C) discusses *drilling sideways*, or horizontal drilling, but does not discuss whether the technique is old or new, so eliminate it. Whether *residents have welcomed the gas industry* does not discuss whether the technique is old or new, so eliminate (D). Choice (B) is the correct answer.

14. **D** This question asks for the meaning of the word *tapping* in this context. Cross out the word, and use the surrounding information to fill in another word that makes sense based on the passage. According to the sentences preceding line 31, *gas [was] found in sandstone traps. Gas companies* want to get into the rock in order to get the gas, so a good replacement word would be something like "piercing" or "mining." Even though (A), (B), and (C) are all definitions of *tapping*, none of these answers match the prediction. *Opening* is a method of getting into something. Choice (D) is the correct answer.

15. **C** This question asks for the *central idea of the third paragraph*. Notice that the question that follows is a best evidence question, so this question and Q16 can be answered in tandem. Look at the answers for Q16 first. Choice (16A) mentions that the scientist knew there was *natural gas in the soft rock layer called shale*, that the gas formed from *dead algae that mixed with mud*, and that *ancient seas...once covered land in Pennsylvania and elsewhere*. Look to see whether those lines support any answers in Q15. Choice (15B) might be tempting, but the gas is formed *in* the sandstone, not *by* the sandstone. Choice (15D) might be tempting, but the passage only states that there were *ancient seas*, and not that *the geography changed significantly over the past million years*. Without any match from Q15, (16A) can be eliminated. Choice (16B) mentions that the Marcellus shale is the *largest such rock formation in North America* and that *gas companies were successfully tapping* it. Look to see whether those lines support any answers in Q15. Choice (15A) may be tempting, but it's deceptive. The fact that the Marcellus shale is *the largest such rock formation in North America* does not match with *the most significant reservoirs of natural gas in the world*, which is stated in the fifth paragraph, not the third. Without any match from Q15, (16B) can be eliminated. Choice (16C) mentions that the well *had seemed such a good prospect* but that *drillers came up with nothing*. Look to see whether those lines support any answers in Q15. Choice (15C) is a close match because even though they knew the gas was there, their calculations were incorrect and all they found was a dry hole. Connect (16C) and (15C). Choice (16D) is in the fifth paragraph and does not share any themes with the third paragraph, so it can be eliminated. Without any support from Q16, (15A), (15B), and (15D) can be eliminated. Choices (15C) and (16C) are the correct answers.

16. **C** (See explanation above.)

17. **B** The question asks about the function of the fourth paragraph in the context of the entire passage, so do it after all of the specific questions. Return to the passage and determine how the fourth paragraph fits into the general structure of the whole passage. In the previous

paragraph, it is clear that drilling in the Marcellus shale had not been a success. The fourth paragraph shows that an alternative tactic *attacked the shale by combining fracking with another technique that was its specialty—horizontal drilling,* and that *the results were stupendous.* The correct answer will show that a solution to this problem had been found. Choice (A) mentions *additional details about a single method mentioned in the previous paragraph,* but the paragraph discusses an alternative tactic that was used. Eliminate (A). Choice (B) mentions a *method that is more effective than a previously described method,* which matches the prediction, so keep it. No *environmentalists* are mentioned, so eliminate (C). Choice (D) mentions *an alternate drilling technique,* which matches the prediction. However, it also states that the technique taps fewer reserves, which is not mentioned. Since the choice is partly wrong, eliminate (D). Choice (B) is the correct answer.

18. **C**   This question asks for the meaning of the word *fields* in this context. Cross out the word, and use the surrounding information to fill in another word that makes sense based on the passage. According to the text, *public meetings* were held to address *minimizing disturbance to neighbors.* From this information, it can be predicted that a good replacement word would be something like "answers" or "addresses." Choices (A), (B), and (D) have no relation to answering concerns and can be eliminated. *Handles* matches the prediction. Choice (C) is the correct answer.

19. **B**   This question asks for *data supported in the first figure,* so the correct answer will be provable from the graph. Louisiana (6%) and Pennsylvania (14%) add up to 20%, which is less than Texas's 26%, so eliminate (A). Louisiana (6%), Oklahoma (7%), Pennsylvania (14%), and Texas (26%) make up a total of 53% of U.S. production, so keep (B). The 26% produced by Texas is more than *one-quarter of the country's natural gas,* so eliminate (C). Wyoming (6%), Oklahoma (7%), and Louisiana (6%) add up to 19%, which is less than Texas's 26%, so eliminate (D). Choice (B) is the correct answer.

20. **B**   This question asks what is supported by the two *figures together,* so the correct answer will be provable from the graphs. Although both Oklahoma and Iran are labeled 7%, they do not produce the *same amount of natural gas.* The percents are of different totals. Even though the specific totals aren't listed, the United States is one part of the second graph, so the entire total of the United States fits inside the world's production. Oklahoma makes up 7% of the United States's production, but Iran makes up 7% of the world's production. Eliminate (A). For (B), Texas (26%) and Pennsylvania (14%) combine to over one-third of the United States's oil production. Since the United States produces about 30% of the world's oil, Texas and Pennsylvania combined produce roughly 10% of the world's oil. This is more than any country shown in the graph *except for the United States and Russia,* so keep (B). There is no combination of two countries on the graph that add to exactly 50%, nor does this answer combine information from both graphs, so eliminate (C). Choice (D) can be eliminated for the same reason as (A): The percents are of different totals, so 14% of the United States's production does not equal 14% of the world's production. Choice (B) is the correct answer.

21.　**C**　This question asks *which choice best describes the organization of the...passage*, indicating it is a general question that should be done after all of the specific questions. The passage begins with the idea that *genes determine about half of the variability in chimp intelligence and environmental factors the other half*. This is followed by a description of studies on chimps to prove this hypothesis. However, in the eighth paragraph the author puts the findings of the study in context by quoting a comparative psychologist who states, *"Thinking about space is extremely important for a number of animals. It's evolutionarily ancient."* From this information, the correct answer should reflect this evolution of thought from the introduction of a new finding to the experiments conducted that prove the finding and then the context for the finding. Eliminate (A) because *research proving exceptions to an earlier assumption* does not match the prediction. Eliminate (B) because *perspectives both supporting and rejecting the findings* does not match the prediction. Keep (C) because it closely matches the prediction. Eliminate (D) because *An attempt to answer a difficult evolutionary question is rejected* does not match the prediction. Choice (C) is the correct answer.

22.　**D**　This question asks for the meaning of the word *held* in this context. Cross out the word, and use the surrounding information to fill in another word that makes sense based on the passage. Since research *has been focused almost entirely on the contribution from the environment, scientists* "believed" or "claimed" *that animals were like robots, behaving in predictable ways based only on environmental cues.* Choices (A), (B), and (C) do not mean "believed" or "claimed," so they can be eliminated. *Contended* matches the prediction. Choice (D) is the correct answer.

23.　**B**　The question asks why the *description of Austin's surprising action* is provided. The last sentence of the third paragraph states that there is *growing evidence that animals are not passive machines but rather are sharp, active thinkers. Austin's surprising action* is an example of a sharp, active thinker, and the answer will reflect this relationship. *Lighten the tone* does not match the prediction, so eliminate (A). *Illustrate a...level of intelligence* matches the prediction, so keep (B). The idea of a *subsequently described study* does not match the prediction, so eliminate (C). Mentioning a *later study's hypothesis* does not match the prediction, so eliminate (D). Choice (B) is the correct answer.

24.　**D**　This question asks for the *assumption underlying the research*. Notice that the question that follows is a best evidence question, so this question and Q25 can be answered in tandem. Look at the answers for Q25 first. Choice (25A) mentions that *Hopkins and his team assessed the cognitive abilities of 99 captive chimpanzees*, so look to see whether those lines support any answers in Q24. Choice (24D) says that *Tests performed on animals that cannot speak can nonetheless provide insight into some aspects of animals' mental capabilities.* This is a close match, since animals that cannot speak matches chimpanzees, and mental capabilities matches cognitive abilities, so draw a line connecting (25A) and (24D). Choice (25B) mentions that they tested *how the animals dealt with the physical world, reacted to sound, and used tools,* so look to see whether those lines support any answers in Q24. Choice (24A) mentions tools, but the use of these tools indicating a *higher level of intelligence* is not supported, so eliminate (25B). Choice (25C) discusses the chimps' *expansive family tree,* so look to see whether those lines support any answers in Q24. Choice (24B) mentions *chimpanzee extended-family relationships* but compares them to *relationships in human families,* which was not mentioned in (25C). Therefore, eliminate (25C) because it has no match. Choice (25D) mentions a *strong genetic component* and *strong effects from environmental influences,* so look to see whether those lines support any answers in Q24. Choice (24C) says that *Environmental factors have a much greater impact,* which is not supported, so eliminate (25D) because it doesn't have a match. Without any support from Q25, (24A), (24B), and (24C) can be eliminated. Choices (24D) and (25A) are the correct answers.

25.   **A**   (See explanation above.)

26.   **B**   This question asks about a specific detail regarding why *researchers were able to compare cognitive scores with "genetic relatedness."* Return to the passage and read the necessary window around lines 43–54 to predict the correct answer. The passage states that *the group of chimps tested had an expansive family tree,* so it can be predicted that the answer will reference this broad family tree. Eliminate (A) because *surprisingly intelligent behavior* does not match the prediction. Keep (B) because *a broad variety of genetic relationships* matches the prediction. Eliminate (C) because *13 different tests* does not match the prediction. Eliminate (D) because *spatial and social cognition* does not match the prediction. Choice (B) is the correct answer.

27.   **A**   This question asks about a specific detail regarding *an indication of a task related to social cognition.* There is no given line reference, so look for the lead words *social cognition.* Because the questions roughly follow chronological order, look to the previous and subsequent questions for clues about the reference window. Q26 has a line reference in paragraph 6 and Q28 has a line reference in paragraph 9, so the window for this question should be between those two paragraphs. Return to the passage and read the necessary window around lines 50–57. Paragraph 7 mentions *two categories of tasks,* including *those that required social cognition, such as grabbing a person's attention.* The next sentence continues to say that *Some chimps are quite clever, making kissing sounds or clapping their hands to draw attention.* From this information, it can be predicted that the answer will have something to do with these sounds. Keep (A) because *Making a sound* matches the prediction. It is not the *human researchers* who *produced sounds,* so eliminate (B). Eliminate (C) because *use of flashlights* does not match the prediction. Eliminate (D) because *video image* does not match the prediction. Choice (A) is the correct answer.

28.   **A**   This question asks for the meaning of the word *find* in this context. Cross out the word, and use the surrounding information to fill in another word that makes sense based on the passage. According to the sentence before line 68, *the study found that other skills…are not particularly heritable.* The sentences discuss the results of the study, so the prediction should be what the studies "reveal" or "indicate." Choices (B) and (D) have no relation to the prediction, so eliminate them. Choice (A) is a close match to the prediction, so keep it. Choice (C) is close but too

extreme. The scientist doesn't anticipate that the study will *prove* the relationship, just that it will *show* it to be the case in the study. Eliminate (C). Choice (A) is the correct answer.

29. **C** This question asks about *animals in captivity*. Notice that the question that follows is a best evidence question, so this question and Q30 can be answered in tandem. Look at the answers for Q30 first. The lines in (30A) reference the scientists' belief that animals are *like robots, behaving in predictable ways*. There is nothing specific in these lines about animals *in captivity*, and these lines don't support any of the answers for Q29. Eliminate (30A). Choice (30B) talks about the chimps that were tested and their *expansive family tree*. This might initially seem to support (29A) because of the mention of *extended family members*, but the lines don't give any indication about whether or not the chimps were in *close contact* with those family members. Eliminate (30B). Choice (30C) references the researchers finding *spatial cognition to be heritable*, which does not support any of the answers for Q29. Eliminate (30C). Now left with only (30D), see if those lines support any of the answers for Q29. The lines say that the *impoverished...setting of captivity* can blunt the influence of environmental variability. Choice (29C) is almost a direct paraphrase of those lines, so connect (30D) and (29C). None of the other answers in Q29 are supported, so they can be eliminated. This leaves (29C) and (30D) as the correct answers.

30. **D** (See explanation above.)

31. **C** This question asks for the meaning of the word *free* in the context of the passage. Cross out the word, and use the surrounding information to fill in another word that makes sense based on the passage. According to the sentence after line 20, Jefferson believes *In general, [the citizens] will elect the really good and wise*. It is the *free election* that will create this situation, so it can be predicted that a good replacement word for *free* would be something like "open" or "unhindered." *Complimentary* means without cost, so eliminate (A). The election is not extra, or *gratuitous*, so eliminate (D). While the election would indeed be *available*, the key distinction is that it is available to all, "unrestricted," so eliminate (B). Choice (C) is the correct answer.

32. **D** This question asks for the *best way to prevent the rise of the artificial aristocracy*. Notice that the question that follows is a best evidence question, so this question and Q33 can be answered in tandem. Look at the answers for Q33 first. Choice (33A) only defines the term *artificial aristocracy*, but provides no *way to prevent the rise*. This doesn't connect to any answer choices in Q32, so eliminate (33A). Similarly, (33B) only says *provision should be made to prevent its ascendancy* without prescribing a *best way*. The answers for Q32 all offer specific plans, so (33B) does not support any of the answers for Q32. Eliminate (33B). Choice (33C) refers to *the best remedy*, which is *to leave to the citizens the free election*. Look to see whether those lines support any answers in Q32. Choice (32D) says to *allow voters to choose their own leaders*, which is a close match. Connect (33C) and (32D). Choice (33D) says *a change has sensibly taken place in the mind of Man*. Look to see whether those lines support any answers in Q32. None of the choices in Q32 mention this idea, so eliminate (33D). Without any support from Q33, (32A), (32B), and (32C) can be eliminated. Choices (32D) and (33C) are the correct answers.

33.  **C**  (See explanation above.)

34.  **A**  This question asks for the meaning of the word *fashion* in the context of the passage. Cross out the word, and use the surrounding information to fill in another word that makes sense based on the passage. The author claims that *Fashion has introduced an indeterminate use of the word "talents."* The use of quotes indicates that he doesn't believe them to be talents at all. The next sentence lists the so-called talents, *beauty, stature...graceful attitudes and motions, gait, air, complexion,* which are all more trendy attributes. The prediction is a word that means something like "trend." *Convention* matches the prediction, so keep (A). *Demeanor, model,* and *construction* don't mean anything like "trend"; eliminate (B), (C), and (D). Choice (A) is the correct answer.

35.  **A**  This question asks when *an artificial aristocracy begins.* Since there is no given line reference, search for the lead words *artificial aristocracy* in Passage 2. That phrase is mentioned several times in paragraph 7, so read the necessary window around lines 57–68 to predict the correct answer. In the fourth sentence of the paragraph, Adams says *When aristocracies are established by human laws, and honor, wealth, and power are made hereditary by municipal laws and political institutions, then I acknowledge artificial aristocracy to commence.* Therefore, the correct answer will reference this list of conditions. *Laws [that] give one group power over another* matches the prediction, so keep (A). *All people are given the right to vote* does not match the prediction, so eliminate (B). *A democracy turns into a monarchy* does not match the prediction, so eliminate (C). The *virtuous and talented control the government* does not match the prediction, so eliminate (D). Choice (A) is the correct answer.

36.  **B**  This question asks where *political advantages come mainly from.* Notice that the question that follows is a best evidence question, so this question and Q37 can be answered in tandem. Look at the answers for Q37 first. Choice (37A) discusses the *natural aristocracy among men* but not *political advantages.* These lines do not support any of the answers for Q36, so (37A) can be eliminated. Choice (37B) mentions *commands or influences true votes in society* and that the influence comes from *any one of these talents.* Look to see whether those lines support any answers in Q36. Choice (36B) mentions *a wide range of characteristics,* which is a close match. Connect (37B) and (36B). Choice (37C) mentions that some are born with *birth and wealth* and some with *genius, strength or beauty,* but does not relate these attributes to *political advantage.* Because these lines do not support any of the answers for Q36, (37C) can be eliminated. Choice (37D) mentions that the *artificial aristocracy* will take power only when *corruption in elections becomes dominant and uncontrollable.* Look to see whether those lines support any answers in Q36. Choice (36D) might be tempting because it mentions *municipal laws and political institutions,* but that's deceptive language. The author states that it is *corruption* that gives rise to *political advantages.* Eliminate (37D) because it does not have a match. Without any support from Q37, (36A), (36C), and (36D) can be eliminated. Choices (36B) and (37B) are the correct answers.

37.  **B**  (See explanation above.)

38. **D** The question asks why *the author of Passage 2 refers to a statement made in Passage 1*. Return to the passage and read the necessary window around lines 71–80. From the final paragraph, it is clear that Adams would trust neither of the groups defined by Jefferson and believes Jefferson's *distinction...will not help the matter.* From this information, it can be predicted that Adams refers to the statement in order to disagree with this particular statement by Jefferson. Choice (A) can be eliminated because there is no mention of Jefferson's *working vocabulary.* While Adams takes issue with Jefferson's *distinction between the aristoi and pseudo aristoi,* he is not quarreling with Jefferson's *central theme.* In fact, the second passage begins with *We are now explicitly agreed.* Eliminate (B). Choice (C) begins with *agree,* which is the opposite of the prediction. Eliminate (C). Choice (D) matches the prediction and is the correct answer.

39. **B** This question asks *which best describes the overall relationship between Passage 1 and Passage 2,* indicating that it is a general question that should be done after all of the specific questions. Adams responds to Jefferson's claim in Passage 1 and in the opening two sentences of Passage 2, Adams outlines his position: *We are now explicitly agreed, in one important point...but...it is not yet certain that we are perfectly agreed in sense.* It can therefore be predicted that Passage 2 provides a qualification, but not a complete alternative to Jefferson's stance in Passage 1. *Further develops* and *considers the historical context* do not match the prediction of a disagreement, so eliminate (A) and (C). While Adams addresses Jefferson's *key terms,* he disagrees with them rather than *redefines* them, so eliminate (D). Choice (B) is the correct answer.

40. **A** The question asks what statement the authors of both passages would agree with regarding *advantages people may have over each other,* indicating that it is a general question that should be done after all of the specific questions. In each passage's opening sentence, the authors agree that *there is a natural aristocracy among men,* so it can be predicted that both would agree there are advantages that are innate. Choice (A) mentions *born talented,* which matches the prediction of natural or innate, so keep it. The phrases *Wealth and power* and *beauty and talent* are deceptive language. The authors do not agree that one is *more important* than the other, so eliminate (B). Eliminate (C) because that statement *Advantages one gains later in life are more powerful* is the opposite of the prediction. Eliminate (D) because neither *those who earn their power* nor *those who have it handed to them* matches the prediction of natural or innate advantage. Choice (A) is the correct answer.

41. **B** The question asks how *the author of Passage 1 would respond to the points made in* lines 60–75. Since this is a question about both passages, it should be done last. Return to the text and read the necessary window ("Birth and wealth...talents"). Adams' position is that human laws lead to *artificial aristocracy, which is the origin of all monarchy.* Jefferson would disagree because he believes that if we *leave to the citizens the free election...they will elect the really good and wise.* It can be predicted that the correct answer will discuss free elections. Eliminate (A) because *Passing power down through families* is not the same as a free election, so it does not match the prediction. Keep (B) because *leaving the decisions in the hands of the voters will ultimately keep the system balanced* is a direct description of a free election. Eliminate (C) because *Rank and*

*birth* and *science and talent* and the order in which they are admired have nothing to do with the prediction. Eliminate (D) because the *American system could allow for an unfaithful leader* is the opposite of the prediction. Choice (B) is the correct answer.

42.  **A**  This question asks for the meaning of the word *removal* in the context of the passage. Cross out the word, and use the surrounding information to fill in another word that makes sense based on the passage. According to the end of the paragraph preceding line 22, *the Hudson Bay Company implemented their "scorched earth" or "fur desert" policy to eliminate all fur-bearing animals…As a result, beaver were nearly extirpated*, so a good replacement word would be something that means "nearly eliminated." The *removal* was not *of an individual beaver*, nor was it a *surgical extraction*; eliminate (B) and (D). The phrase *complete extinction* is too extreme, so eliminate (C). Choice (A) is the correct answer.

43.  **B**  This question asks for a *broader hypothesis* that was tested to obtain results *consistent with "steelhead population responses."* Notice that the question that follows is a best evidence question, so this question and Q44 can be answered in tandem. Look at the answers for Q44 first. Choice (44A) states that *a decrease…was first perceived.* This is an observation, not a hypothesis, and it does not support any of the answers for Q43, so eliminate (44A). Choice (44B) mentions *the removal of beaver…exacerbated the occurrence of stream channel incision, where a rapid downcutting of the stream bed disconnects the channel from its floodplain.* Look to see whether those lines support any answers in Q43. Choice (43D) may be tempting, but it contains deceptive language. It states that *Stream channel incision…is exacerbated by…large numbers of beaver dams*, which is the opposite of what the passage states. Eliminate (44B) because it has no match. Choice (44C) mentions what was *hypothesized*, so look to see whether those lines support any answers in Q43. Choice (43B) says *Reconnecting a stream's channel and floodplain can occur more quickly through the construction of natural or artificial beaver dams*, which matches *beaver dams or simulated beaver dams that we construct…can greatly accelerate the incision recovery process* in (44C) and with "the steelhead population responses" because *BDAs and beaver dams led to large changes in both fish and beaver habitat.* Connect (44C) and (43B). Choice (44D) mentions how *BDAs were built* but does not discuss a broader hypothesis, so eliminate it. Without any support from Q44, (43A), (43C), and (43D) can be eliminated. Choices (43B) and (44C) are the correct answers.

44.  **C**  (See explanation above.)

45.  **A**  The question asks for *the primary purpose of the third paragraph* in the context of the entire passage. Return to the passage and read the necessary window around lines 24–46. The paragraph begins with *BDAs were built*, which describes the experiment that was conducted. It then states *The addition of BDAs into Bridge Creek led to an immediate and rapid increase in the number of natural beaver dams*, which describes the results of the experiment. From this information, it can be predicted that the purpose of the paragraph is to describe an experiment and

its results. Keep (A) because *illustrate methods and results of research* closely matches the prediction. Choice (B) seems tempting because *detail the findings of research* closely matches the prediction. However, the experiment was not *designed to investigate beaver responses* but rather to investigate *fish population response.* If a choice is slightly wrong, it's all wrong, so eliminate (B). Eliminate (C) because the paragraph does not *describe the plan that will be followed* but an actual experiment with results. For the same reason, eliminate (D). The paragraph does not suggest a *potential experiment could be carried out in the future.* Choice (A) is the correct answer.

46. **C** This question asks for an indirect effect of building BDAs in Bridge Creek. Notice that the question that follows is a best evidence question, so this question and Q47 can be answered in tandem. Look at the answers for Q47 first. Choice (47A) mentions that *beaver were nearly extirpated,* so look to see whether those lines support any answers in Q46. None of the choices are supported by the lines, so eliminate (47A). Choice (47B) mentions a *rapid increase in the number of natural beaver dams,* so look to see whether those lines support any answers in Q46. Choice (46C) is a close match, so connect (47B) and (46C). Choice (47C) mentions that the BDAs *caused the fish population response,* so look to see whether those lines support any answers in Q46. Since none of the answers for Q46 are supported by those lines, eliminate (47C). Choice (47D) mentions that BDAs provide *fish a greater selection of locations…while reducing migration distances,* so look to see whether those lines support any answers in Q46. Since none of the choices match that idea, eliminate (47D). Without any support from Q47, (46A), (46B), and (46D) can be eliminated. Choices (46C) and (47B) are the correct answers.

47. **B** (See explanation above.)

48. **B** The question asks what effect the words *"partially," "suspect,"* and *"partly"* have on the *tone of the paragraph.* Return to the passage and read the necessary window around lines 42–61. In the previous paragraph, it is clear that the experiment provided *compelling evidence that beavers increased the quantity of juvenile habitat. Compelling* is directly in contrast to the words *"partially," "suspect,"* and *"partly"* in the fifth paragraph, so these words were used to show the conclusions in this paragraph were less compelling. There is no indication of *the authors' nervousness* or them being *afraid,* so eliminate (A) and (D). There is also no indication that these are *unwelcome results,* so eliminate (C). *That other factors may be important* matches the prediction stating these conclusions were less compelling. Choice (B) is the correct answer.

49. **D** This question asks for an unstated assumption about *habitat complexity.* Even though the question asks for an *unstated assumption,* the correct answer will still be supported by the text. The passage states that an *increase in habitat complexity* is partly responsible for the increases in the steelhead population. Therefore, the correct answer should somehow connect to the idea that increasing complexity positively affects the populations. The complexity increased with the construction of the BDAs, which happened well after 1900, so (A) can be eliminated. Choice (B) might initially look attractive because it mentions *the addition of dams,* but notice the *always* in the answer choice. That is a strong word that is not supported by equally strong

wording in the text, so (B) can be eliminated. The prediction has nothing to do with negative effects of habitat complexity on predators, so (C) can be eliminated. Choice (D) is not specifically mentioned, but if increasing habitat complexity increases steelhead population, and the steelhead population increased after the construction of the BDAs, the complexity was not maximized prior to that construction. Choice (D) is the correct answer.

50. **A** This question asks for *the greatest number of dams on Bridge Creek during the twenty years prior to the installation of BDAs, according to the figure.* Look at the figure to see the highest point for the Bridge Creek line *before* the black vertical line. The high point is about 100 dams in 1992. Choice (A) at 105 is close, while anything 125 and above is too high, so eliminate (B), (C), and (D). Choice (A) is the correct answer.

51. **C** This question asks for *the last year a control reach had a greater number of dams than a treatment reach,* so look at the figure to see the last time the dashed line was above the solid line. The answer will be somewhere between 2005 and 2010. Choice (C) is the correct answer.

52. **C** This question asks whether *the graphic [supports] the author's claim that increasing the number of real or simulated beaver dams leads to an increase in steelhead populations,* so look at the figure to see if there are any connections that can be drawn. While the correlation is drawn in the passage, there is no reference at all to steelhead population numbers in the figure, so the correct answer will be "no." Eliminate (A) and (B). Whether or not the graphic mentions *floodplain access* has no relation to the *steelhead populations,* so eliminate (D). That *the data do not provide a link between the number of dams and the quality of steelhead habitats* matches the prediction. Choice (C) is the correct answer.

# Section 2: Writing and Language

1. **A** Note the question! The question asks what the most appropriate introduction to the passage is, so it is testing consistency. If the content of the underlined portion is consistent with the topics presented in the passage, then it is correct. The passage discusses paternity leave and the need to provide both men and women time off with newborn children. The *personal needs of workers* are discussed in (A), so keep it. Choice (B) is vague and does not address what workers need, so eliminate (B). Choice (C) is focused on profit as opposed to worker needs; eliminate (C). Although (D) addresses worker needs, it is too broad and references *all employees.* Since the passage is focused primarily on paternity leave for male employees, (D) can be eliminated. The correct answer is (A).

2. **D** The phrase after *contemporary workers* is changing in the answer choices, so the question is testing either precision or concision. First, determine whether the phrase is necessary. The sentence already begins with the words *contemporary employers,* which means the employers of

today. There is no need to repeat that idea. Eliminate any choices that are redundant. Choices (A), (B), and (C) each repeat the idea of *contemporary*, so eliminate them. The correct answer is (D).

3.   **B**   The vocabulary is changing in the answers, so this question is testing word choice. The correct choice will match *a 2012 study conducted* to the group that conducted the study, *the United States Department of Labor*. The study was not conducted *from* or *of* the Department of Labor, so eliminate (A) and (C). The sentence would not be complete without a connecting word between *a study conducted* and *the United States Department of Labor*; eliminate (D). Choice (B) is the correct answer.

4.   **B**   Pronouns are changing in the answer choices, so the question is testing consistency of pronouns. A pronoun must be consistent in number and case with the noun it is replacing. The pronoun refers to the noun *paternity leave*, which is singular. *They* and *those* are plural, so eliminate (A), (C), and (D). The correct answer is (B).

5.   **A**   Verbs are changing in the answer choices, so the question is testing consistency of verbs. A verb must be consistent with its subject and with the other verbs in the paragraph. The subject of the verb is the *deficit*, which is singular (ignore the prepositional phrase *in leave* between the subject and the verb). To be consistent, the verb in the answer choices must also be singular. Eliminate (B) since *are* is a plural verb. The verb form must also be consistent with the tense of other verbs in the sentence. The sentence immediately following this sentence uses the present verb *is*. Eliminate (D) because *had been* is a past tense verb. Choice (C) is not as concise as (A), so it can be eliminated as well. The correct answer is (A).

6.   **D**   Note the question! The question asks for the choice that best supports the statement in the previous sentence, so it's testing consistency. If the content of the underlined portion is consistent with the previous sentence in the passage, then it is correct. The previous sentence discusses the results of a study and states that *nine out of ten men considered paternity leave to be a factor of at least marginal importance*, so the best answer should be consistent with that information. Choice (B) discusses mothers having time off and that is not relevant to whether paternity leave is an important factor, so eliminate (B). Choice (C) goes against the claim that paternity leave is important; eliminate (C). Although (A) is consistent with the point being made, (D) offers a more precise supporting statement. Choice (D) is the correct answer.

7.   **A**   Note the question! The question asks whether the sentence should be added, so it's testing consistency. If the content of the new sentence is consistent with the ideas surrounding it, then it should be added; otherwise, it should not be added. The paragraph discusses the results of a study conducted by the U.S. Department of Labor. The new sentence indicates that *The younger a male individual respondent was, the more likely he was to rate the issue of paternity leave as important when considering employment,* so it is consistent with the ideas in the paragraph. The sentence should be added. Eliminate (C) and (D). Eliminate (B) because there is no challenge presented to this information in the last sentence of the paragraph. The correct answer is (A).

8. **C** Note the question! The question asks about combining sentences, so it's testing consistency and concision. Choice (A) inaccurately combines the *larger societal issue* with *what employees want*. Additionally, *they,* which is plural, refers incorrectly to the singular noun *paternity leave;* eliminate (A). Choice (B) also inaccurately combines *what potential employees want* and *paternity leave having an impact,* so eliminate (B). Choice (D) never mentions that these are reasons paternity leave is important and is therefore not consistent; eliminate (D). Choice (C) correctly orders the reasons, so it is the most concise and consistent. The correct answer is (C).

9. **C** Apostrophes are changing in the answer choices, so the question is testing apostrophe usage. When used with a noun, an apostrophe indicates possession. In this sentence, the parents are not possessing anything, so eliminate (A) and (B). The child does possess its own life, so that apostrophe is necessary; eliminate (D). The correct answer is (C).

10. **C** Commas are changing in the answer choices, so the question is testing the four ways to use a comma on the SAT. The sentence contains a list of three things: 1) *bond with their children earlier,* 2) *participate in their household more actively,* and 3) *raise children with a greater sense of gender equality.* There should be a comma between the items in the list, so eliminate (D) because this answer does not include a comma after *actively.* There should not be a comma after *and,* so eliminate (A). In (B), the adverb *actively* has been changed to the adjective *active.* *Actively* modifies the verb *participate,* so an adverb is needed. Since adjectives can only modify nouns, eliminate (B). The correct answer is (C).

11. **A** Introductory phrases are changing in the answer choices, so the question is testing the consistency of that introduction. The sentence states that *paternity leave not only benefits a lone employee and his or her family—it improves society as a whole.* This sentence summarizes the points made in the paragraph, so the answer should be consistent with that summary. Eliminate (B) and (D) as they change direction and are therefore inconsistent with the summary and paragraph. While the passage is in fact complete, nothing rhetorically has been completed, so *completely* is incorrect; eliminate (C). The correct answer is (A).

12. **A** Note the question! The question asks about the most logical introduction to the sentence, so it is testing consistency. The correct answer must be consistent with the rest of the paragraph. The prior portion of the paragraph is focused on the lack of similarities among states with regard to federal elections. Choice (A) mentions *one major difference among the states pertaining to elections for federal offices,* which is consistent with the beginning of the paragraph. Choice (B) is focused on states having the same election cycle, which is inconsistent with the rest of the paragraph. Choice (C) discusses *all* democratic nations, while this passage is focused only on the United States. Choice (D) makes the presidential and congressional candidates, rather than the state elections, the focus of the sentence and also, in the process, makes the sentence incomplete. Choice (A) is the correct answer.

13. **D** The punctuation is changing in the answer choices, so the question is testing STOP and GO punctuation. Use the vertical line test, and identify the ideas on either side of the vertical line as

complete or incomplete. Draw the vertical line between the words *candidate* and *Is*. The phrase *One of the major differences among the states when it comes to elections for federal offices, for example presidential or congressional candidates* is an incomplete idea, and the phrase *Is whether a state holds a primary or a caucus* is an incomplete idea. To connect an incomplete idea to an incomplete idea, GO punctuation is needed. A period is STOP punctuation, so eliminate (A). The colon is HALF-STOP punctuation, so eliminate (B). A semicolon is STOP punctuation, so eliminate (C). A comma is GO punctuation, so keep (D). The correct answer is (D).

14. **D**  The punctuation is changing in the answer choices, so the question is testing STOP and GO punctuation. Use the vertical line test, and identify the ideas on either side of the vertical line as complete or incomplete. Draw the vertical line between the words *goal* and *nominate*. The phrase *These two systems, primaries and caucuses, are meant to accomplish the same goal* is a complete idea. The phrase *nominate major-party candidates for office* is an incomplete idea. To connect a complete idea to an incomplete idea, GO or HALF-STOP punctuation is necessary. The semicolon is STOP punctuation, so eliminate (A). The comma + FANBOYS is STOP punctuation, so eliminate (C) as well. Choice (B) has no punctuation, which can only be used between two incomplete ideas or between a complete idea and a necessary incomplete idea. The incomplete idea here is unnecessary, so it must be separated from the complete idea with HALF-STOP punctuation; eliminate (B). The colon is HALF-STOP punctuation, which is acceptable when it is preceded by a complete idea. The correct answer is (D).

15. **B**  Note the question! The question asks if an addition should be made, so it is testing consistency and precision. If the content of the new sentence is consistent with the ideas surrounding it, then it should be added. The paragraph describes how caucuses work, and this new addition to the sentence discusses the two ways votes can be counted at caucuses. This content is consistent with the ideas in the text and provides more precise information. The sentence should be added. Therefore, eliminate (C) and (D). Eliminate (A) because it states that *caucuses are more effective than primaries,* which is not consistent with the information in either the sentence or paragraph. The correct answer is (B).

16. **A**  Pronouns are changing in the answer choices, so the question is testing consistency. A pronoun must be consistent in number with the noun it is replacing. The plural pronoun *themselves* refers to the noun *voters*, which is plural. To be consistent, the pronoun in the correct answer choice must also be plural. Eliminate (B) and (D) because both answers present singular pronouns. The pronoun *their* is a possessive pronoun that should not be placed together with the word *selves*; eliminate (C). The correct answer is (A).

17. **D**  Note the question! The question asks whether the sentence should be deleted, so it's testing consistency and concision. If the content of the current sentence is consistent with the ideas surrounding it, then it should not be deleted. The paragraph discusses the history and reasoning for caucuses. The sentence at the beginning of the paragraph states that *Historically, caucuses made a great deal of practical sense.* Therefore, the sentence is consistent with the ideas in

the paragraph, and the sentence should not be deleted. Eliminate (A) and (B). The sentence does not provide any *specific example*, so eliminate (C). The sentence serves as an introduction to the discussion in this paragraph, so keep (D). The correct answer is (D).

18.  **A**  Commas are changing in the answer choices, so the question is testing the four ways to use a comma on the SAT. The phrase *if any* is unnecessary information, so it should be surrounded by commas. Eliminate (B) and (D) because they each contain only one comma. Eliminate (C) because it includes an unnecessary additional comma after *had*. The correct answer is (A).

19.  **C**  Note the question! The question asks which of the following logically follows the previous sentence, so it is testing consistency. The paragraph discusses the historical reasoning behind and manner in which caucuses function, so the correct answer will further explain one of these two concepts. The previous sentence in particular defines how voters *selected representatives*, not the candidates themselves. The only answer choice that addresses this functionality of caucuses is (C). The correct answer is (C).

20.  **D**  Note the question! The question asks which choice best maintains the tone established in the passage, so it is testing consistency. The tone of the passage is informative and neutral, so the correct answer should be consistent with that tone. Eliminate (A) and (B) because *horrid* and *deplorable* are both negative words that do not match the neutral tone of the passage. Although (C) is neutral, *litigious* is not consistent with the information provided in the passage as there is no discussion of settling legal disputes in the paragraph. Choice (D) is consistent with the passage, as the paragraph discusses what is difficult about caucuses as compared to primaries. According to the following sentence, caucuses are *difficult to keep organized* and *difficult to keep civil*. The correct answer is (D).

21.  **B**  Verbs are changing in the answer choices, so the question is testing consistency of verbs. A verb must be consistent with its subject and with the other verbs in the sentence. The subject of the sentence is *caucuses*, which is plural, so the verb must also be plural. Eliminate (A) because of the singular verb *is*. The verb in the non-underlined portion of the sentence is the present tense verb *are*. The correct answer must also be in the present tense. For this reason, eliminate (D), which uses the past tense *were*. Choice (C) includes unnecessary commas around the word *also*; eliminate (C). The correct answer is (B).

22.  **C**  Pronouns are changing in the answer choices, so the question is testing consistency of pronouns. A pronoun must be consistent in number with the noun it is replacing. The singular pronoun *it* refers to the noun *caucuses*, which is plural. To be consistent, the pronoun in the correct answer must also be plural. Eliminate (A) and (B). The rest of the paragraph is in the present tense and there is no reason to change the tense. Choice (D) changes the tense to *have been*, so eliminate (D). The correct answer is (C).

23.  **D**  Pronouns are changing in the answer choices, so the question is testing consistency of pronouns. The pronouns refer to *European explorers*, so the correct answer must be a plural

pronoun that can refer to multiple people in order to be consistent with the non-underlined portion of the sentence. Both (B) and (C) refer to things, not people, so eliminate both. *They* makes the phrase *they noticed the sloth's slow and lackadaisical movements* a complete idea. The commas in this sentence surround unnecessary information, and a phrase providing unnecessary information such as this cannot be a complete idea; eliminate (A). The correct answer is (D).

24.  **D**  The vocabulary is changing in the answer choices, so this question is testing word choice. Use Process of Elimination to determine which answer is most consistent with the rest of the text, most notably the words *lazy* and *slow*. Choice (B), *careless*, can be eliminated because *slow* and *lazy* do not necessarily mean careless. *Lackadaisical* means to be carelessly lazy; it can be eliminated for the same reason, so eliminate (A). The sentence is describing *the sloth's slow and ____ movements*; describing *movements* as *inactive* would be contradictory, so eliminate (C). Only (D), *leisurely*, which means lazy, is consistent with *slow*. The correct answer is (D).

25.  **B**  Note the question! The question asks which option best combines the two sentences, so it's testing precision and concision. Look for the answer that combines the sentences while maintaining the meaning of the originals. The movie *Ice Age* was produced by *Blue Sky Studios*, so these two phrases should be next to each other to make this meaning precise. Eliminate (A) and (C). Choice (D) changes the meaning by stating that *Sid sleeps through the movie*, not *the migration of his community*. Eliminate (D). The correct answer is (B).

26.  **A**  Pronouns are changing in the answer choices, so the question is testing pronoun choice. The pronouns refer to *the sloth*, which is singular, so the answer must also be singular. Eliminate (D), *their*, which is plural. Choice (C), *there*, can also be eliminated, as *the sloth* is not a place. With pronouns, apostrophes create contractions. "It is" does not make sense in the sentence, so eliminate (B). The pronoun *Its* is correct because *day* is possessed by *the sloth*, so the possessive form of the pronoun should be used. The correct answer is (A).

27.  **D**  The words are changing in the answer choices, with the option to DELETE the underlined portion in (D). This question is testing precision and concision. Carefully consider the option to DELETE, as it is often correct because it is the most concise answer. In this case, both (A) and (B) make the phrase after the comma a complete idea. *The sloth is categorized as a folivore because the bulk of its diet consists of the leaves, buds, and tender shoots of Cercropia* is also a complete idea, so that would require STOP punctuation in between the two ideas. Since the non-underlined portion of the sentence includes a comma between the ideas, eliminate both (A) and (B). Choice (C), *being*, makes the sentence less precise because it confuses whether the subject of the sentence is *the sloth* or *the leaves, buds, and tender shoots of Cercropia*, so eliminate it. The best option is to delete the underlined portion. The correct answer is (D).

28.  **D**  The punctuation is changing in the answer choices, so the question is testing STOP and GO punctuation. Use the vertical line test and identify the ideas on either side as complete or incomplete. There are two complete ideas here: *Take the sloth's stomach, for example,* and *it is very large with multiple compartments.* The example is *the sloth's stomach,* so the phrase *for example*

should be with that idea and not *it is very large with multiple compartments*; eliminate (C). Because there are two complete ideas, there needs to be STOP or HALF-STOP punctuation between the ideas. Eliminate (A) and (C) because they each contain a comma, which is GO punctuation. Keep (D) because the colon is HALF-STOP punctuation. The correct answer is (D).

29.  **B**  Note the question! The question asks for the best placement of sentence 5, so determine where the sentence should be to maximize consistency and precision. The first part of sentence 5 refers to *leaves* being *nutritionally poor*, so this sentence should come after the reference to eating leaves in sentence 1. The second part refers to *various adaptations*, so sentence 5 should come before any talk about adaptations. Sentence 1 discusses the idea of the sloth eating leaves, and sentence 2 introduces the adaptations of the sloth's stomach. To make the meaning precise and the paragraph consistent, sentence 5 should go between sentences 1 and 2. The correct answer is (B).

30.  **A**  Note the question! The question asks for the choice that accurately interprets the graph, so this question is testing consistency. The sentence compares the sloth's body temperature to the other mammals in the graph. In the graph, the other mammals have body temperatures between 36.5 and 39.7 degrees Celsius, whereas the sloth's body temperature is only 32 degrees Celsius. The sloth's body temperature is clearly lower than those of the other mammals in the graph; (B) and (C) are inconsistent with this, so eliminate them. The sloth's temperature is between 4.5 and 7.7 degrees below the temperature of the other mammals, which is consistent with *approximately five degrees Celsius lower*. Keep (A). The sloth's temperature is not half that of the other temperatures, so eliminate (D). The correct answer is (A).

31.  **D**  Verb tense is changing in the answer choices, so the question is testing the consistency of verbs. Select the choice that is consistent with the other verbs in the sentence. The first part of the sentence states *the sloth does not keep its temperature in as limited a range*. Match the tense and meaning closest to *does not*. Choice (B), *will*, is future tense and (C), *did*, is past tense; eliminate them. *Has* confers a different meaning than *does not*, so eliminate (A). Choice (D), *does*, matches *does not*. The correct answer is (D).

32.  **C**  Note the question! The question asks for the choice that is most consistent with the graph. Use Process of Elimination! Choice (A) says that *a healthy sloth's active body temperature can be greater than that of a healthy dog*. However, according to the graph the average body temperature of an active sloth is 32 degrees Celsius, whereas the average body temperature of a healthy dog is 38.9 degrees Celsius. The sentence does say that a sloth's temperature can vary by 2 degrees and a dog's by 0.4 degrees, which gives a possible high temperature of 34 degrees Celsius for the sloth and a possible low temperature of 38.5 degrees Celsius for the dog. The dog's temperature is still higher; eliminate (A) because it is inconsistent with the data. Choice (B) says that *a healthy dog's body temperature is greater than that of any mammal shown in the graph*, but both the cat's and the goat's body temperatures are higher; eliminate (B). The work

from (A) shows that the dog's body temperature will always be higher than the sloth's, so keep (C). Choice (D) can be eliminated based on the same work from (A). The correct answer is (C).

33.  **D**  Note the question! The question asks for the choice that *conveys how the sloth's inactivity is the result of adaptations to its diet*. Choose the answer most consistent with this goal. Choices (A), (B), and (C) do not refer to the sloth's diet. Choice (D) discusses the sloth's *food source*, which is consistent with *its diet*, and claims that its diet *is not a rich source of nutrients*, which is the cause of *the sloth's inactivity*. The correct answer is (D).

34.  **D**  Punctuation is changing in the answer choices, so the question is testing STOP and GO punctuation. It is also testing consistency. Earlier in the sentence there is a dash before the phrase *Oscar Wilde's "The Queen is not a subject," for example.* This phrase is unnecessary information, so it should be surrounded by either commas or dashes. Because a dash is used before the phrase, a dash must also be used afterwards in order to be consistent. The only choice that uses a dash is (D). The correct answer, therefore, is (D).

35.  **B**  The form of the verb *relies* is changing in the answer choices, so the question is testing consistency of verbs. A verb must be consistent with its subject, which in this case is *puns*. The verb should be plural in order to be consistent with this subject. Eliminate (A), *relies*, and (C), *has relied*, because both are singular. Choice (D), *relying*, makes the sentence incomplete because *relying* cannot be the main verb. Only (B), *rely*, is consistent with the subject and makes the sentence complete. The correct answer is (B).

36.  **A**  Punctuation is changing in the answer choices, so the question is testing STOP and GO punctuation. Use the vertical line test. Draw a vertical line between *Bible* and *wordsmiths*. *From Shakespeare's plays to Abbott and Costello's Who's on First? to even the Bible* is an incomplete idea, so STOP punctuation cannot be used. Eliminate (B), (C), and (D), all of which include STOP punctuation. The only answer without STOP punctuation is (A). The correct answer is (A).

37.  **B**  Commas are changing in the answer choices, so the question is testing four ways to use a comma. When commas surround a phrase, check to see if that phrase is necessary or unnecessary to the sentence. *American composer Milton Babbitt* is unnecessary information; if it is removed from the sentence, the sentence is still grammatically correct and the meaning does not change. Therefore, commas must surround this phrase. Eliminate (C) and (D) because neither of these answers include commas both before and after this phrase. There is no reason to place a comma between *composer* and *Milton*; eliminate (A). The correct answer is (B).

38.  **C**  Note the question! The question is testing consistency by asking for the option that *sets up the examples that follow*. Eliminate any answer choices that are inconsistent with the examples that follow this sentence. The example of *Homily* is used to show how Babbitt *change[s] how similar musical phrases are audibly perceived* and writes the piece so *different interpretations of the phrase are possible, much in the same way that verbal puns rely on concurrent interpretations of a word*. *Beaten Paths* also *create[s] different musical meanings*. Choice (A) focuses on the instruments,

not the different interpretations or meanings; eliminate it. Choice (B) discusses *fun* with the music. Puns may be fun, but fun isn't the point in these examples; eliminate (B). Choice (C) mentions how Babbitt uses puns in his music. This fits the examples, so keep (C). Choice (D) contradicts the point the passage is trying to make of how Babbitt takes the concept of the pun from language and uses it in music; eliminate (D). The correct answer is (C).

39.   **A**   The words are changing in the answer choices, so this question is testing word choice. Look for a word that is consistent with the rest of the passage. The previous sentence discusses how Babbitt *change[s] how similar musical phrases are audibly perceived*, so the correct choice will be consistent with *change*. *Modified* means "to change somewhat in form." This is consistent with the context of the sentence, so keep (A). Choice (B), *twisted*, means "to force out of its natural shape; distort." The changes in the music discussed in the paragraph are positive, not negative, so eliminate (B). Choice (C), *doctored*, means "to change in order to deceive." While different simultaneous interpretations are intended, there is no deception in the music; eliminate (C). Choice (D), *refined*, means "to improve." While the music is being changed, there is no indication that it is being improved. Eliminate (D). The correct answer is (A).

40.   **B**   Verbs are changing in the answer choices, so the question is testing consistency of verbs. Choose the answer that is consistent with other verbs in the sentence. The sentence contains a list: *not only create repeated musical motifs, but also _____* . The blank should be consistent with the other verb in the list, *create*. Choice (B), *reshape*, is the only answer with the same verb tense as *create*. The correct answer is (B).

41.   **C**   Note the question! The question is asking whether to add the proposed sentence to the passage, so it is testing consistency. If the content of the new sentence is consistent with the ideas surrounding it, then it should be added; otherwise, it should not, as leaving the sentence out will be the most concise option. The paragraph is about how Babbitt creates puns in his music, whereas the proposed sentence introduces a new composition without discussing puns. Since it does not relate to the rest of the paragraph, the new sentence should not be added. Eliminate (A) and (B). Choice (D) discusses *other instruments,* which is not the reason that the sentence was inconsistent with the paragraph. Eliminate (D). Choice (C) accurately describes how the proposed sentence provides irrelevant information. The correct answer is (C).

42.   **A**   Note the question! The question is asking for the option that links the second paragraph to the ideas in the following paragraph, so it is testing consistency. The second paragraph is about Babbitt's puns in music, and the final paragraph is about puns in the titles of Babbitt's music. Only (A) discusses the titles of Babbitt's compositions. The correct answer is (A).

43.   **C**   The phrase is changing in the answer choices, so the question is testing consistency. The passage is about how Milton Babbitt uses puns both within his music and in the titles of his works. Choice (A) discusses novel uses of percussion instruments. Babbitt used percussion in *Homily* and *Beaten Path*, but the passage doesn't indicate whether it was new, nor is this phrase consistent with the passage overall. Eliminate (A). Choice (B) talks about playing with words,

but doesn't include music. This is inconsistent with the passage's point about Babbitt, so eliminate (B). Choice (C) includes puns in both the music and titles, so keep (C). Choice (D), like (A), includes information about *unusual* performance practices, which is not the point of the passage. Eliminate (D). The correct answer is (C).

44. **C** Note the question! The question is asking for the best placement of sentence 4, so it is testing consistency. Determine what placement would make the paragraph most consistent. Sentence 4 gives information about the word *homily* and a quote contained in the score. This sentence should therefore be near the discussion of *Homily* in sentence 2. Eliminate (A) and (D). Sentence 2 introduces the puns in the meaning of the title *Homily*. Because sentence 4 explains those puns, sentence 4 should be after sentence 2. The correct answer is (C).

# Section 3: Math (No Calculator)

1. **A** For fractional exponents, the denominator indicates the root, and the numerator indicates the exponent power. In other words, fractional exponents are Power over Root. Therefore, the 2 in the denominator indicates a square root. Eliminate (C) and (D). The 5 in the numerator indicates that $m$ should be raised to the 5th power. Eliminate (B). The correct answer is (A).

2. **D** Use Process of Elimination. The question asks about which factor would change if a less expensive type of sealant were used. The length of the driveway, $l$, the number of driveways, $d$, and the width of each driveway, $w$, are values that will remain the same irrespective of what price of sealant is used. Eliminate (A), (B), and (C). The correct answer is (D).

3. **C** The question asks for the value of $12x - 4$ and gives you $4x = 20$. Multiply both sides of this equation by 3 to get $12x = 60$. Subtract 4 from both sides to get $12x - 4 = 56$. The correct answer is (C).

4. **B** Cross-multiply to get $2(z + 42) = 8z$. Distribute the 2 to get $2z + 84 = 8z$. Solve for $z$ to get $6z = 84$ and $z = 14$. The question is asking for the value of $\frac{z}{2}$, which is $\frac{14}{2} = 7$. Therefore, the correct answer is (B).

5. **B** The question asks for the value of $r - s$, so Stack and Add the equations first to see if that gets closer to the goal. Set the equations on top of each other and add them together to get:

$$\begin{array}{r} 3r - 5s = -17 \\ + \quad 5r - 3s = -7 \\ \hline 8r - 8s = -24 \end{array}$$

Divide the resulting equation by 8 to get $r - s = -3$. The correct answer is (B).

6.  **A**  From 2012 to 2013, 24 scripted shows were produced. This is three times the number of scripted shows produced between 2009 and 2010, so $24 \div 3 = 8$ shows were produced between 2009 and 2010. Therefore, $s = 8$. Plug 8 in for $s$ in the answers and eliminate any answer that isn't true. Choice (A) becomes $3(8) = 24$. The equation works, so keep (A). Choice (B) becomes $24(8) = 3$ or $192 = 3$. This is false; eliminate (B). Choice (C) becomes $\frac{8}{3} = 24$, which is false; eliminate (C). Choice (D) becomes $8 + 24 = 3$, or $32 = 3$. This is also false; eliminate (D). The correct answer is (A).

7.  **D**  The slope-intercept form of the line equation is $y = mx + b$, where $m$ stands for the slope, $b$ stands for the $y$-intercept, and $x$ and $y$ are points on the line. Therefore, in the equation $y = cx - 2$, the slope is $c$. Substitute the point $(m, n)$ into the equation given to get $n = cm - 2$. Solve for $c$ to get $n + 2 = cm$ and $c = \frac{n + 2}{m}$. The correct answer is (D).

8.  **D**  In the equation $Ax + By = C$, the slope is equal to $-\frac{A}{B}$. Therefore, the slope of the first equation given is $-\left(\frac{3}{-2}\right) = \frac{3}{2}$, and the slope of the second equation is $-\left(\frac{c}{-7}\right) = \frac{c}{7}$. A system of linear equations will have no solution when the lines are parallel, meaning that they have equal slopes. Set the slopes of the two equations equal to each other to get $\frac{c}{7} = \frac{3}{2}$. Cross-multiply to get $2c = 21$. Solve for $c$ to get $c = \frac{21}{2}$. Therefore, the correct answer is (D).

9.  **A**  Factors are used to find the roots of a function, which are the places where the function crosses the $x$-axis. At these places, $y = 0$. For example, if the equation was $y = x^2 - 2x - 3$, factoring it to $(x - 3)$ and $(x + 1)$ and setting those factors equal to 0 would give roots of 3 and –1. On the table, $y$ or $p(x)$ is 0 when $x = 1$. Therefore, $x = 1$ is a solution of $p(x)$, and $(x - 1)$ is a factor of $p(x)$. The correct answer is (A).

10. **D**  There are variables in the answer choices, so plug in. Usually, it's good to avoid plugging in 1, because it could result in multiple correct answers. However, the math will be much more straightforward on this particular question if $a = 1$, so try that first. The equation becomes $y = (x - 3)(x + 5)$. Expand the quadratic to get $y = x^2 + 2x - 15$. To answer the question, it is necessary to get this equation into vertex form, $y = (x - h)^2 + k$, in which the vertex is $(h, k)$. To do this, set the equation equal to 0, move the constant over to the left, and complete the square. The equation becomes first $0 = x^2 + 2x - 15$, then $15 = x^2 + 2x$. To complete the square, take half the coefficient on the $x$-term, square it, and add it to both sides to get $15 + 1 = x^2 + 2x + 1$. Add the numbers on the left side, and convert the right side into the square term, so the equation becomes $16 = (x + 1)^2$. Finally, subtract 16 from both sides and replace the $y$ to get $y = (x + 1)^2 - 16$. The vertex is $(1, -16)$, and the value of $t$ is –16. Plug $a = 1$ into the answer choices to find the one that equals –16. The correct answer is (D).

11. **B** The parabola intersects the line $y = 36$ when the two are equal to one another, so $(x - 9)^2 = 36$. Both sides are squares, so take the square root of both sides to get $(x - 9) = \pm 6$. Now solve the two equations: if $x - 9 = 6$, then $x = 15$, and if $x - 9 = -6$, $x = 3$. Therefore, the parabola crosses the line $y = 36$ when $x = 15$ and when $x = 3$. In other words, the parabola intersects the line $y = 36$ at the points $(3, 36)$ and $(15, 36)$. The distance between these points will be the difference in the $x$-values: $15 - 3 = 12$. If taking the square root of both sides of the equation is not an immediately obvious approach, it is also possible to get the values of $x$ using FOIL. Expand the left side of the equation to get $x^2 - 18x + 81 = 36$. Set the equation equal to 0: $x^2 - 18x + 45 = 0$. Factor the equation to get $(x - 15)(x - 3) = 0$. Either way, the correct answer is (B).

12. **C** Angles $l$ and $o$ are vertical angles, or opposite angles made by two intersecting lines. Therefore, $l = o$. Since $l + m = n + o$, subtracting $l$ from the left side and $o$ from the right side (which is possible because $l = o$) shows that $m = n$. Since vertical angles are equal to each other, it is also true that $m = p$ and $n = q$. This means that $m = n = p = q$. Therefore, both statements II and III must be true. The correct answer is (C).

13. **B** Start by dividing the entire equation by 2 to get $x^2 + 6x + 4 = 0$. This doesn't factor nicely, and the answer choices are simplified versions of the quadratic formula. Therefore, use the quadratic formula, $x = \dfrac{-b \pm \sqrt{b^2 - 4ac}}{2a}$, to solve for $x$. In this case $a = 1$, $b = 6$, and $c = 4$. The resulting equation is $x = \dfrac{-6 \pm \sqrt{6^2 - 4(1)(4)}}{2(1)}$. Simplify the right side of the equation to get $x = \dfrac{-6 \pm \sqrt{36 - 16}}{2} = \dfrac{-6 \pm \sqrt{20}}{2} = \dfrac{-6 \pm 2\sqrt{5}}{2} = -3 \pm \sqrt{5}$. The correct answer is (B).

14. **C** The question asks about changes to different temperatures, but no values are given. Plug in numbers and test each statement. To test statement I, plug $F = 2$ into the equation to get $D = \dfrac{5}{6}(212 - 2) = \dfrac{5}{6}(210) = 175$. Plug in again using $F = 2 + \dfrac{5}{6} = \dfrac{17}{6}$. Using this new value, $D = \dfrac{5}{6}(212 - \dfrac{17}{6}) \approx 174.3$. Since the value of $D$ did not decrease by 1 when $F$ increased by $\dfrac{5}{6}$, statement I is not true. Eliminate (D). Go to statement II. Plug $D = 5$ into the equation to get $5 = \dfrac{5}{6}(212 - F)$. Solve for $F$ to get $6 = 212 - F$, and $F = 206$. Next, plug $D = 6$ into the equation to get $6 = \dfrac{5}{6}(212 - F)$. Solve for $F$ to get $7.2 = 212 - F$, and $F = 204.8$. Subtract the two values of $F$ to get $206 - 204.8 = 1.2$. Statement II is true. Therefore, eliminate (B). Finally, test statement III. Plug $F = 2$ into the equation to get $D = \dfrac{5}{6}(212 - 2) = \dfrac{5}{6}(210) = 175$. Next, plug in $F = 3$ to get $D = \dfrac{5}{6}(212 - 3) = \dfrac{5}{6}(209) = 174\dfrac{1}{6}$. Subtract the two values of $D$ to get $175 - 174\dfrac{1}{6} = \dfrac{5}{6}$. Since statement III is true, eliminate (A). The correct answer is (C).

15.  **C**  This is a complicated algebra question, but the equation is true for almost all values of $y$, so look for a way to plug in. Since use of a calculator is not allowed on this section, it is especially important to plug in an easy number. Try $y = 1$. If $y = 1$, then $\dfrac{36(1)^2 + 43(1) - 25}{k(1) - 3} = -9(1) - 4 - \dfrac{37}{k(1) - 3}$. Simplify to get $\dfrac{36 + 43 - 25}{k - 3} = -9 - 4 - \dfrac{37}{k - 3}$ and then $\dfrac{54}{k - 3} = -13 - \dfrac{37}{k - 3}$. Add $\dfrac{37}{k - 3}$ to both sides to get $\dfrac{54}{k - 3} + \dfrac{37}{k - 3} = -13$. Since the fractions on the left have the same denominator, add both the numerators to get $\dfrac{91}{k - 3} = -13$. Multiply both sides by $(k - 3)$ to get $91 = -13(k - 3)$. Distribute on the right side to get $91 = -13k + 39$. Subtract 39 from both sides to get $52 = -13k$. Divide both sides by $-13$ to get $k = -4$, which is (C).

16.  **4**  First, clear out the fractions by multiplying the entire equation by 30. The resulting equation is $27z - 21z = 10 + 14$. Combine like terms to get $6z = 24$. Divide both sides by 6 to get $z = 4$.

17.  $\dfrac{5}{13}$  Draw the two triangles and label the sides. Given the information in the question, $PQ = \dfrac{24}{5}$ and $OQ = \dfrac{26}{5}$.

The values for triangle $OPQ$ aren't easy numbers to work with. However, since the triangles are similar, the corresponding angles have the same measurements. Therefore, $\cos O = \cos L$. Just work with the larger triangle to find the cosine of $L$. $\text{Cos} = \dfrac{adjacent}{hypotenuse}$, so find the length of side $LM$, which is adjacent to angle $L$. The Pythagorean Theorem is a way to find the third side of a right triangle, but this is a Pythagorean triple: It's the 5:12:13 triangle with each side doubled. Therefore, $LM = 10$, and $\cos L = \dfrac{10}{26} = \dfrac{5}{13}$. Since $\cos L = \cos O$, the answer is $\dfrac{5}{13}$.

18. **280** Translate the information in the question into equations that can be solved. Let $p$ represent the amount of sodium in a pecan braid and $c$ represent the amount of sodium in a chocolate pastry. Then, according to the question, $p = c + 30$. Solve for $c$ to get $c = p - 30$. The question also states that $3p + 4c = 1840$. Substitute $p - 30$ for $c$ to get $3p + 4(p - 30) = 1840$. Distribute the 4 to get $3p + 4p - 120 = 1840$. Solve for $p$ to get $7p - 120 = 1840$, $7p = 1960$, and $p = 280$.

19. **3 or 4** Divide both sides of the equation by $a$ to get $a^2(a^2 - 25) = -144$. Distribute the $a^2$ to get $a^4 - 25a^2 = -144$. Set the equation to 0 to get $a^4 - 25a^2 + 144 = 0$. Factor the equation to get $(a^2 - 9)(a^2 - 16) = 0$. Factor further to get $(a - 3)(a + 3)(a - 4)(a + 4) = 0$. The question specifies that $a > 0$, so the factors with subtraction will give the possible values of $a$. Therefore, one of the possible solutions for the equation is $a - 3 = 0$ or $a = 3$. The other possible solution is $a - 4 = 0$ or $a = 4$.

20. **115** Plug 65 in for $g$ in the equation to get $180 - f = 2(65)$. Solve for $f$ to get $180 - f = 130$ and $f = 50$. The three angles in a triangle add up to $180°$. Therefore, the other two interior angles of the top triangle will add up to $180 - 50 = 130°$. Because the top triangle is isosceles and the unknown angles are opposite equal sides, the other two angles in the top triangle will be equal to each other. Therefore, each of the other angles in the top triangle is equal to $130 \div 2 = 65°$. Given that a straight line is equal to $180°$, $h = 180 - 65 = 115°$.

## Section 4: Math (Calculator)

1. **D** Probability is defined as $\dfrac{\# \text{ of outcomes that fit requirements}}{\text{total } \# \text{ of possible outcomes}}$. The outcomes that fit the requirements are small red marbles and large blue marbles. From the table, there are 16 small red marbles, 21 large blue marbles, and 50 total marbles. So the probability of getting either a small red marble or a large blue marble is $\dfrac{16 + 21}{50} = \dfrac{37}{50}$. The correct answer is (D).

2. **B** Look at trends in the graph and use Process of Elimination. The graph shows a negative slope until month 6, which means that the amount of money in his bank account was decreasing until July, the 6th month after January. Eliminate (C) and (D). After July, the line shows a positive slope, which means that the amount of money in his bank account was increasing. Eliminate (A). The correct answer is (B).

3. **A** According to the question, the balloon floated at a constant altitude for 1 hour while getting the best view of the historic landmark. Since the $y$-axis is the altitude, the constant altitude is represented by a straight horizontal line. The only horizontal portion of the graph begins at about 10:30 A.M. Therefore, the correct answer is (A).

4.  **D**  According to the problem, approximately 6 percent of the math questions are very difficult, so there are approximately $\frac{6}{100} \times 153 \approx 9$ very difficult math questions. Approximately 9 percent of the science questions are considered very difficult, so there are approximately $\frac{9}{100} \times 267 \approx 24$ very difficult science questions. Therefore, the total number of very difficult questions is $9 + 24 = 33$. The correct answer is (D).

5.  **C**  Rather than take the time to add every term, work the problem in bite-sized pieces and use Process of Elimination after each step. Start by adding the first terms of the two expressions to get $6y^3 + 5y^3 = 11y^3$. Eliminate (A) and (B), which don't contain this term. Next, add the second terms of the two expressions to get $-3y^2 + (-2y^2) = -5y^2$. Eliminate (D). The correct answer is (C).

6.  **B**  The chart gives values of $x$ that will result in corresponding values of $y$, so plug in numbers from the chart. The chart states that when $x = 2$, $g(x) = -4$. Plug 2 into each of the answer choices to see which answer returns a value of $-4$. Choice (A) becomes $g(x) = 2 - 6 = -4$. Keep (A), but always check the other answers. Choice (B) becomes $g(x) = 2(2) - 8 = -4$. Keep (B). Choice (C) becomes $g(x) = 3(2) - 10 = -4$. Keep (C). Choice (D) becomes $g(x) = 4(2) - 12 = -4$. Keep (D). Since all the answers are true when $x = 2$, try a different value of $x$, such as $x = 4$. The correct answer will then equal 0, according to the chart. Choice (A) becomes $4 - 6 = -2$. Eliminate (A). Choice (B) becomes $2(4) - 8 = 0$. Keep (B). Choice (C) becomes $3(4) - 10 = 2$. Eliminate (C). Choice (D) becomes $4(4) - 12 = 4$. Eliminate (D). The correct answer is (B).

7.  **D**  The question gives time in seconds and minutes, so convert the units. There are 60 seconds in one minute. Therefore, 16 minutes = $16 \times 60 = 960$ seconds. To find the distance that Paul can run in that amount of time, set up the following proportion: $\frac{x \text{ meters}}{960 \text{ seconds}} = \frac{144 \text{ meters}}{72 \text{ seconds}}$. Cross-multiply to get $72x = 138,240$. Divide both sides by 72 to get $x = 1,920$. The closest answer to 1,920 is (D).

8.  **A**  When given two fractions equal to each other, cross-multiplying will help to solve the equation. In this question, that is tricky with the $z$ multiplied by the first fraction. Rewrite the equation so that the $z$ is in the numerator of the fraction: $\frac{2z}{7} = \frac{5}{2}$. Now cross-multiply to get $4z = 35$. Divide both sides by 4 to get $z = \frac{35}{4}$. Therefore, the correct answer is (A).

9.  **B**  Label the parts of the equation and use Process of Elimination. According to the question, $y$ represents the average number of cases per attorney and $x$ represents the years. Eliminate (A) because the average number of cases per attorney is represented by $y$, not the 1.74. Neither the question nor the equation mentions the total number of cases. For this reason, eliminate both (C) and (D). The correct answer is (B).

10. **A** The term *zero* is synonymous with *x*-intercept, or where the graph intersects the *x*-axis. Therefore, a function that has 4 distinct zeros will intersect the *x*-axis at 4 distinct points. Graph (A) intersects the *x*-axis at 4 distinct points. Graph (B) intersects the *x*-axis at 2 distinct points. Graphs (C) and (D) intersect the *x*-axis at 3 distinct points. Therefore, the correct answer is (A).

11. **B** According to the question, $F = km$, where $F$ stands for force, $k$ stands for the spring constant, and $m$ stands for the distance the spring is stretched in meters. So, $m = 5$, and for Spring #2, $k = 0.9$. Therefore, $F = (0.9)(5) = 4.5$. The correct answer is (B).

12. **C** Start by finding the distance that Spring #4 is stretched. According to the question, $F = km$, where $F$ stands for force, $k$ stands for the spring constant, and $m$ stands for the distance the spring is stretched in meters. For Spring #4, $k = 4.7$. To find the distance the spring is stretched, plug $F = 7$ and $k = 4.7$ into the equation $F = km$ to get $7 = 4.7x$. Divide both sides by 4.7 to get $x \approx 1.49$ meters. The question asks for the spring that would stretch the same distance under 5 newtons of force, so plug 5 in for $F$ and 1.49 for $m$ and solve for $k$. Start with $5 = 1.49k$, then divide both sides by 1.49 to get $k = 3.3$. According to the table, Spring #6 has a spring constant of 3.3. Therefore, the correct answer is (C).

13. **B** There are variables in the answer choices, so plug in. Let $t = 3$ hours. Set up the following proportion to convert hours to minutes: $\dfrac{1 \text{ hour}}{60 \text{ minutes}} = \dfrac{3 \text{ hours}}{x \text{ minutes}}$. Cross-multiply to get $x = 180$ minutes. Each minute will cost the corporation $0.30, so multiply 180 by $0.30 to get a cost of $54.

Plug 3 in for $t$ in the answer choices to see which answer choice equals $54. Choice (A) becomes $\dfrac{60(3)}{0.3} = 600$. Eliminate (A). Choice (B) becomes $(0.30)(60)(3) = 54$. Keep (B), but always check the remaining answers. Choice (C) becomes $60(3) + 0.30 = 180.30$. Eliminate (C). Choice (D) becomes $\dfrac{0.30(3)}{60} = 0.015$. Eliminate (D). The correct answer is (B).

14. **D** The question asks about a specific value, so plug in the answers. Start with (B). In (B), $x = 2$. On the graph, $j(2) = 3$ and $k(2) = 6$. Because $3 + 6 \neq 0$, eliminate (B). If it is not clear whether $x$ needs to be larger or smaller, just pick a direction. In (C), $x = 3$, $j(3) \approx -2$, and $k(3) \approx 4$. Because $-2 + 4 \neq 0$, eliminate (C). In (D), $x = 4$, $j(4) = -3$, and $k(4) = 3$. Because $-3 + 3 = 0$, the correct answer is (D).

15. **A** Solve the equation for $h$. Start by subtracting $0.5mv^2$ from both sides of the equation to get $e - 0.5mv^2 = 10mh$. Divide the entire equation by $10m$ to get $\dfrac{e}{10m} - \dfrac{0.5mv^2}{10m} = h$. Simplify the second term to get $\dfrac{e}{10m} - 0.05v^2 = h$. Therefore, the correct answer is (A).

16. **C** Questions like this, in which no math is involved, are best handled with Process of Elimination. The word *any* in (A) is problematic. The study does not state whether pesticide P would reduce the number of aphids in a garden that was not infested with aphids. Eliminate (A). The phrase *best pesticide* in (B) is problematic. The study only evaluated pesticide P. It is possible that another

pesticide exists that is even better at treating aphid infestation. The phrase *kill substantial numbers of aphids* in (D) is problematic. The study showed that pesticide P led to a reduction in the number of aphids, but this does not necessarily mean that there was a *substantial* decrease in the number of aphids in the gardens that were sprayed with pesticide P. Furthermore, the answer references *a garden*, not specifically a *rose garden*, which extends the conclusion further than the study would indicate. Therefore, the best answer is (C).

17. **D** The question states that the cost must equal the revenue. Since the question asks for a specific value, Plugging In the Answers could work. However, that may be more time consuming than just solving for $x$ in this case. To do that, set the two equations given equal to each other to get $3x + 75 = 8x$. Subtract $3x$ from both sides to get $75 = 5x$. Divide both sides by 5 to get $x = 15$. The correct answer is (D).

18. **C** The question asks about the effect of changes in cost, but it does not give any specific number of products. Therefore, plug in values for the number of products. First, plug in $x = 2$ to find that $C(2) = 3(2) + 75 = 6 + 75 = 81$. Since the question asks for 5 additional units, next plug in $x = 7$ to find that $C(7) = 3(7) + 75 = 21 + 75 = 96$. The cost increased by $96 - 81 = 15$. Therefore, the correct answer is (C).

19. **C** Use the graph to look up the number of bacteria colonies at 40°. The actual number of colonies present, as shown by the dot, was 420. The line of best fit predicts 400 colonies at 40°. The difference is $420 - 400 = 20$ colonies. The correct answer is (C).

20. **D** The question doesn't give any numbers, so plug in and use Process of Elimination. When a population grows exponentially, it is increasing by a constant percent of the current population, not by a constant amount. Say that the original population is 100 people. In (A), the growth every year would be $100 \times 0.05 = 5$ people. Eliminate (A) since the growth rate does not change. Likewise, in (B), the growth rate would be $(100 \times 0.04) + 300 = 304$ people every year. Eliminate (B). In (C), the growth rate is 300 people every year. Eliminate (C). In (D), the growth rate is $100 \times 0.03 = 3$ people the first year. However, the second year the growth rate would be $103 \times 0.03$. In subsequent years, the growth rate would continue to increase. The correct answer is (D).

21. **D** The question states that one milliliter of glucose can feed up to 9 Petri dishes of cells. If each Petri dish has an area of $7\frac{1}{4}$ square centimeters, then 9 Petri dishes would have a total area of $9 \times 7\frac{1}{4} = 65\frac{1}{4}$ square centimeters. That is just for 1 milliliter of glucose, but the question asks about 115 milliliters of glucose. Multiply the area 1 milliliter can feed by 115 to get $65\frac{1}{4} \times 115 = 7,503.75$ square centimeters. The closest answer is therefore (D).

22. **B** The question asks for a specific value, so plug in the answers. Start with (B). If $m = 7.5$, then $c = 6(7.5) - 9 = 36$, and $d = 8(7.5) - 6 = 54$. Next, use a calculator to see whether, $\sin(c°) = \cos(d°)$. Given that $\sin(36°) = \cos(54°)$, it is true that $m = 7.5$. The correct answer is (B).

23. **C** The question asks for a specific value, so plug in the answers. Start with (B), and assume the biologist has 8 animals. According to the question, if she gives each animal 4 treats, she will have 6 treats left over. This means she has $(8 \times 4) + 6 = 38$ treats. If she gave each of the animals 5 treats, she would need $8 \times 5 = 40$ treats. This would mean she would be $40 - 38 = 2$ treats short. Given that the question states she would be 8 treats short in this second scenario, eliminate (B). It may not be clear which direction to go from here, so pick a direction. In (C), the biologist has 14 animals. This means she has $(14 \times 4) + 6 = 62$ treats. If she were to give each animal 5 treats, she would need $14 \times 5 = 70$ treats. This would mean that she would be $70 - 62 = 8$ treats short, which matches the information given in the question. The correct answer is (C).

24. **A** The question asks for a specific value, so plug in the answers. Start with (B). If $k = 267$, the sum of the other two numbers is $738 - 267 = 471$. According to the question, $k$ is 20% less than the sum of the other two numbers. This can be calculated as $471 - (0.2)(471) = 376.8$. In this case, the two values for $k$ are not the same, so eliminate (B). It may not be clear which direction to go next, so just pick a direction. In (A), $k = 328$, making the sum of the other two numbers $738 - 328 = 410$. Next, 20% less than 410 is $410 - (0.2)(410) = 328$. Since the two values for $k$ are equal, the correct answer is (A).

25. **B** When given two points on a line, finding the slope of the line is often the key to answering the question. The equation to find the slope of a line containing points $(x_1, y_1)$ and $(x_2, y_2)$ is $slope = \dfrac{y_2 - y_1}{x_2 - x_1}$. Given the point $(4, r)$ and the origin $(0, 0)$, the slope of the line is $\dfrac{r - 0}{4 - 0} = \dfrac{r}{4}$. Given the point $(r, 16)$ and the origin, the slope is $\dfrac{16 - 0}{r - 0} = \dfrac{16}{r}$. Since both points are on the same line, the slopes are equal. Therefore, $\dfrac{r}{4} = \dfrac{16}{r}$. Cross-multiply to get $r^2 = 64$. Take the square root of both sides to find that $r = \pm 8$. The correct answer is (B).

26. **B** No information is given about the dimensions of the triangle, so plug in. Let the base and the height of the original triangle equal 10. The formula for the area of a triangle is $A = \dfrac{1}{2}bh$. The area of the triangle would be $A = \dfrac{1}{2}(10)(10) = 50$. The base of the modified triangle is equal to $10 + (0.2)(10) = 12$. The area of the modified triangle can be calculated as $50 - (0.28)(50) = 50 - 14 = 36$. Plug these values into the formula for the area of a triangle to get $36 = \dfrac{1}{2}(12)(h)$. Solve for $h$ to get $36 = 6h$, and $h = 6$. The formula to find a percent decrease is $\dfrac{difference}{original} \times 100$. The height of the original triangle was 10, and the height of the modified triangle is 6. Therefore, the percent decrease $= \dfrac{10 - 6}{10} \times 100 = \dfrac{4}{10} \times 100 = 40$. The correct answer is (B).

27. **A** To find the volume of the capsule, first find the volume of each part, and then add them together. The formula for the volume of a right rectangular pyramid, found in the reference box at the beginning of each math section, is $V = \frac{1}{3}lwh$. Therefore, the volume of each of the pyramids at the ends of the capsule is $V = \frac{1}{3}(8)(10)(8) = \frac{1}{3}(640) \approx 213$. The volume of a rectangular solid is given by the formula $V = lwh$. Therefore, the volume of the rectangular solid part of the capsule is $V = (12)(10)(8) = 960$. The total approximate volume of the capsule is $213 + 960 + 213 = 1,386$. The closest answer is (A).

28. **C** The question gives information about the relationship between $x$ and $y$, so start by solving the two equations for $x$ and $y$, respectively. Subtract $2a$ from both sides of the first equation to get $x = 2a - 8$. Subtract $2b$ from each side of the second equation to get $y = 2b - 8$. The question states that $x = y - \frac{1}{4}$. Substitute in the expressions for $x$ and $y$ to get $(2a - 8) = (2b - 8) - \frac{1}{4}$. All of the choices are in terms of $a$, so solve for $a$. Add 8 to both sides to get $2a = 2b - \frac{1}{4}$. Divide both sides by 2 to get $a = b - \frac{1}{8}$. The correct answer is (C).

29. **A** The growth rate formula states that *final amount = initial amount*$(1 \pm rate)^n$, where $n$ is the number of times interest will be calculated. In this problem, the initial amount is \$20,000, the rate is 15%, or 0.15 when expressed as a decimal, and interest will be calculated every 4 years. Since the question is asking about interest after $t$ years, $n = \frac{t}{4}$. Plugging all of the values into the growth equation results in the portfolio's worth as $20,000(1.15)^{\frac{t}{4}}$. Therefore, the correct answer is (A).

30. **D** The question asks for a probability, which is defined as $\frac{\text{\# of outcomes that fit requirements}}{\text{total \# of possible outcomes}}$. The number of varsity basketball players, the *total # of possible outcomes* in this case, is given as 32. The question gives very few other actual numbers to work with, so create some variables to stand in for the missing numbers. The number of soccer players is given in relation to the number of basketball players. Let $j$ represent the number of junior varsity basketball players and $s$ represent the number of senior varsity basketball players. Fill in the chart according to the information given in the question. In the junior row, fill in $4j$ under varsity soccer and $j$ under varsity basketball. In the senior row, fill in $3s$ in the varsity soccer column and $s$ in the varsity basketball column. Given the information in the chart, $4j + 3s = 108$, and $j + s = 32$. The question asks about juniors, so try

to eliminate the seniors in the equations. Multiply the second equation by $-3$ to get $-3j - 3s = -96$.

Stack the two equations on top of each other and add them together.

$$
\begin{aligned}
4j + 3s &= 108 \\
-3j - 3s &= -96 \\
\hline
j &= 12
\end{aligned}
$$

Therefore, there are 12 junior varsity basketball players. Now calculate the probability that a randomly chosen varsity basketball player is a junior: $\dfrac{\text{junior varsity basketball players}}{\text{total varsity basketball players}} = \dfrac{12}{32} = 0.375$. The correct answer is (D).

31. **53.8** For questions about mean, use the Average Pie. $Average = \dfrac{total}{\# \ of \ things}$, so add up all of the enrolled students and put that number in the *Total* part at the top of the Average Pie. The total enrollment of all of the classes is 646. There are 12 classes listed, so put that in the *# of things* part on the bottom left of the Average Pie. Divide the total by 12 to get $646 \div 12 = 53.833$ as the average. Rounded to the nearest tenth, the correct answer is 53.8.

32. **6 or 7** The problem states that John bought 1 pint of strawberries, which costs $5, and spent a total amount between $23 and $27, inclusive. Therefore, he spent between $23 - $5 = $18 and $27 - $5 = $22 on blueberries. Let $b$ represent a pint of blueberries. Given that a pint of blueberries costs $3, set up the following equation to solve for the number of pints of blueberries John bought: $18 \leq 3b \leq 22$. Solve for $b$ to get $6 \leq b \leq 7.33$. Since he can only buy whole pints of blueberries, John bought either 6 or 7 pints of blueberries.

33. **25** For questions about averages, $Average = \dfrac{total}{\# \ of \ things}$, so the $total = (average)(\# \ of \ things)$. Over 20 tests, Jasmine wants an average of 45 points. This means that Jasmine will need to score a total of $20 \times 45 = 900$ points. For the first 5 tests, Jasmine has scored a total of $5 \times 35 = 175$ points. This means she needs to score an additional $900 - 175 = 725$ points on the remaining 15 tests. To find the minimum required score on the 6th test, maximize the number of points that Jasmine can score on the other 14 remaining tests. The maximum score for any one test is 50 points, so Jasmine can score a maximum of $14 \times 50 = 700$ on the 14 remaining tests. Since $725 - 700 = 25$, Jasmine can score 25 on the 6th test and keep her average at 45. The correct answer is 25.

34. **18** Rather than take the time to multiply out every term in this expression, use Bite-Sized Pieces. The question asks for the value of $b$, which is the coefficient on the $z$ term, so just add the $z$ terms. This becomes $(3z) - 3(-5z) = 3z + 15z = 18z$. Therefore, $b = 18$.

35. **96** Use a calculator to graph the inequalities to get a better understanding of the relationship. Each inequality will create a line that is shaded on one side. The solution set is the area where the shaded regions overlap. For these inequalities, the solution set forms a "V," so the minimum $y$-value will be the vertex of the "V" where the two lines intersect. To find the point of intersection, set the two expressions equal to each other: $4x = -12x + 384$. Add $12x$ to both sides to get $16x = 384$. Then divide both sides by 16 to get $x = 24$. Plug this value for $x$ into the second equation to get $y \geq 4(24)$ and $y \geq 96$. Therefore, the smallest value for $y$ is 96.

36. $\dfrac{3}{4}$ or **.75**

To find the arc, set up the *part to whole* relationship. The total circle has $2\pi$ radians, so $\dfrac{part}{whole} = \dfrac{arc}{circumference} = \dfrac{angle}{2\pi}$. The angle forming the arc is $\dfrac{3\pi}{2}$ radians, so

$\dfrac{arc}{circumference} = \dfrac{angle}{2\pi} = \dfrac{\frac{3\pi}{2}}{2\pi} = \dfrac{3}{4}$. Therefore, the arc is $\dfrac{3}{4}$, or 0.75, of the circumference.

37. **20** The question asks about the size of a message, or the value for $b$. The equation for transmission time is $b = rT$, where $r$ represents the rate of transmission and $T$ represents the time. Both $r$ and $T$ are measured in seconds, but the question gives a rate of 75,000 bytes *per minute*, or per 60 seconds. To convert this rate into seconds, set up a proportion: $\dfrac{75{,}000 \text{ bytes}}{60 \text{ seconds}} = \dfrac{r \text{ bytes}}{1 \text{ second}}$. Cross-multiply to get $60r = 75{,}000$. Divide both sides by 60 to get $r = 1{,}250$. To find the size of the file, plug this value and $T = 1.6$ seconds into the formula to get $b = (1{,}250)(1.6) = 2{,}000$ bytes. When asked for a *percent less than* something, use the formula for percent change: $\dfrac{difference}{original} \times 100$. The average global transmission time is 2,500 bytes. Therefore, the message size in this region is $\dfrac{2{,}500 - 2{,}000}{2{,}500} \times 100 = \dfrac{500}{2{,}500} \times 100 = 20\%$ less than the average global message size.

38. **3,150** The question asks for the size of the message, or the value for $b$. The equation for transmission time is $b = rT$, where $r$ represents the rate of transmission and $T$ represents the time. Both $r$ and $T$ are measured in seconds, but the question gives a rate of 45,000 bytes *per minute*, or per 60 seconds. To convert this rate into seconds, set up a proportion: $\dfrac{45{,}000 \text{ bytes}}{60 \text{ seconds}} = \dfrac{r \text{ bytes}}{1 \text{ second}}$. Cross-multiply to get $60r = 45{,}000$. Divide both sides by 60 to get $r = 750$. To find the value of $b$, plug this value and $T = 4.2$ seconds into the formula to get $b = (750)(4.2) = 3{,}150$. This is the correct answer.

# Chapter 17
# Practice Test 8

# Reading Test

## 65 MINUTES, 52 QUESTIONS

**Turn to Section 1 of your answer sheet to answer the questions in this section.**

---

### DIRECTIONS

Each passage or pair of passages below is followed by a number of questions. After reading each passage or pair, choose the best answer to each question based on what is stated or implied in the passage or passages and in any accompanying graphics (such as a table or graph).

---

### Questions 1–10 are based on the following passage.

This passage is adapted from R. O'Grady, "But Once a Year." © 1917 by The Reilly & Britton Co.

A shabby little woman detached herself from the steadily marching throng on the avenue and paused before a shop window, from which solid rows of
Line electric bulbs flashed brilliantly into the December
5 twilight. The ever-increasing current of Christmas shoppers flowed on. Now and then it rolled up, like the waters of the Jordan, while a lady with rich warm furs about her shoulders made safe passage from her car to the tropic atmosphere of the great department store.
10 Wax figures draped with rainbow-tinted, filmy evening gowns caught her passing admiration, but she lingered over the street costumes, the silk-lined coats and soft, warm furs.

With her wistful gaze still fixed upon her favorite,
15 she had begun to edge her way through the crowd at the window. At the same instant, she caught the scent of fresh-cut flowers and looked up into the eyes of a tall young girl in a white-plumed velvet hat, with a bunch of English violets in her brown mink fur. As
20 their glances met, the shabby little woman checked a start, and half-defensively dropped her lids. There had flashed over the mobile face beneath the velvet hat a look of personal interest, an unmistakable impulse to speak.
25 The thrill of response that set the woman's pulses throbbing died suddenly. The red that mottled her grayish cheeks was the red of shame. Through the window, in a mirrored panel cruelly ablaze with light,

she saw herself: her made-over turban, her short,
30 pigeon-tailed jacket of a style long past, and her old otter cape with its queer caudal decorations and its yellowed cracks grinning through the plucked and ragged fur. As the white plume came nearer and nearer, the tremulous little woman regained her self-control.
35 It was but one of the coincidences of the city, she told herself, turning resolutely away.

The door slammed shut behind her. She glanced at her fingers, stained to an oily, bluish grime by the cheap dye of the garments that furnished her daily
40 work. Mechanically, she rose to wash. While her hands were immersed in the lather of rankly perfumed toilet soap, there came a gentle knock at the door.

"Come in," invited the woman, expecting some famine-pressed neighbor for a spoonful of coffee or a
45 drawing of tea.

The woman, having absently hung her towel on the doorknob, stared dazedly at the visitant. She could hardly credit her eyes. It was indeed the girl with the white ostrich plume and the bouquet of violets in her
50 brown mink fur.

"Do you know, I've such a silly excuse for coming." She laughed, and the laugh brought added music to her voice. "I noticed you had a rare fur-piece" her vivid glance returned to the pile of wraps on the chair" and
55 I want to ask a very great favor of you. Now please don't be shocked—I've been ransacking the city for something like it, and," with a determined air of taking the plunge, "I should like to buy it of you!"

**CONTINUE** ➡️

"It, it's a rare pattern, you know," groped the girl,
60 her sweet tones assuming an eloquent, persuasive
quiver, "and you don't know how glad I'd be to have it."

The indignant color faded out of the woman's face.
"If you really want the thing"—abruptly she put her
bizarre possession into her strange visitor's lap—"If
65 you really want it, but I don't see"—yearning crept into
her work-dimmed eyes, a yearning that seemed to
struggle with disillusionment. "Tell me," she broke off,
"is that all you came here for?"

Apparently oblivious to the question, the young
70 woman rose to her feet. "You'll sell it to me then!" she
triumphed, opening her gold-bound purse.

"But, see here," demurred the woman, "I can't, it
ain't worth…"

The girl's gloved hands went fumbling into her
75 purse, while the old fur cape hung limply across one
velvet arm.

"You leave it to me," she commanded, and smiled,
a radiant, winning smile. The girl was gone and all at
once the room seemed colder and dingier than it ever
80 had before. But the woman was not cold. As she sat
huddled on the cot, warmth and vitality glowed within
her, kindled by the memory of a recent kindly human
touch.

The following evening, after working hours, the
85 shabby woman, wearing a faded scarf about her neck
to replace the old fur collar, diffidently accosted a
saleslady at the Sixth Avenue department store.

It was unusual to sell expensive furs to such a
customer. But people might send what freaks of
90 servants they pleased to do their Christmas shopping,
provided they sent the money, too. In this case, the
shabby little woman was prepared. She produced three
crisp ten-dollar bills—the fabulous sum which the
girl had left in her hand at parting—and two dollars
95 more from the savings in her worn little purse. Then,
hugging the big flat box against the tight-fitting bosom
of her jacket, she triumphantly left the store.

---

**1**

The author uses the image of the "waters of the
Jordan" (line 7) most likely to

A) claim the crowd approaching the window will
never ebb.

B) assert that the little woman was drowning in the
throng.

C) describe the method and magnitude of the crowd's
movement.

D) illustrate how a rich lady arrived at the
department store.

**2**

As used in line 16, "caught" most nearly means

A) chased.

B) grabbed.

C) stopped.

D) noticed.

**3**

Which choice best supports the claim that the shabby
little woman was at first excited by the tall young girl?

A) Lines 16–19 ("At the . . . fur")

B) Lines 19–21 ("As their . . . lids")

C) Lines 25–26 ("The thrill . . . suddenly")

D) Lines 29–33 ("she saw . . . fur")

**4**

According to the passage, why does the woman invite
the visitor to come in?

A) She plans to help someone in need.

B) No one has ever been refused entry.

C) She expects the young girl to drop by.

D) She is dazed and cannot see.

CONTINUE

**5**

In the context of the conversation between the young girl and the woman, the girl's comments in lines 51–58 ("Do you . . . you!") mainly serve to

A) persuade the woman to sell the fur at a discount.

B) emphasize the desire that inspired the girl's action.

C) laugh at the shabby woman for being indignant.

D) demand that the shabby woman surrender her wrap.

**6**

The girl uses the word "ransacking" (line 56) mainly to emphasize that her search was

A) comprehensive.

B) disruptive.

C) shocking.

D) silly.

**7**

It can reasonably be inferred from the passage that the shabby woman initially declines to sell the fur mainly because

A) the young woman is only interested in rare fur pieces.

B) she yearns for the young woman to appreciate her work more.

C) the young woman offers too high of a price.

D) she doesn't believe that it has much value.

**8**

Which choice provides the best evidence for the answer to the previous question?

A) Lines 63–67 ("If you . . . disillusionment")

B) Lines 72–73 ("But, see . . . worth")

C) Lines 84–87 ("The following . . . store")

D) Lines 88–89 ("It was . . . customer")

**9**

The passage states that after the girl's departure the shabby woman felt

A) cold.

B) dingy.

C) tired.

D) warmth.

**10**

The main purpose of the last paragraph is to

A) claim that stores only reluctantly sold to people like the shabby woman.

B) contrast common occurrences with the shabby woman's experience.

C) highlight the shabby woman's greatest triumph.

D) show how servants like the shabby woman go Christmas shopping.

CONTINUE

**Questions 11–20 are based on the following passages.**

Passage 1 is from Winston Churchill's first election broadcast, June 4, 1945, reproduced with permission of Curtis Brown, London, on behalf of the Estate of Winston S. Churchill. Copyright © The Estate of Winston S. Churchill. Passage 2 is from Albert Einstein, "Why Socialism?" Originally published by *Monthly Review* in 1949.

**Passage 1**

My friends, I must tell you that a Socialist policy is abhorrent to the British ideas of freedom. Although it is now put forward in the main by people who have
*Line*
5 a good grounding in the Liberalism and Radicalism of the early part of this century, there can be no doubt that Socialism is inseparably interwoven with Totalitarianism and the abject worship of the State. It is not alone that property, in all its forms, is struck at, but that liberty, in all its forms, is challenged by the
10 fundamental conceptions of Socialism. Look how even today they hunger for controls of every kind, as if these were delectable foods instead of war-time inflictions and monstrosities. There is to be one State to which all are to be obedient in every act of their lives. This State
15 is to be the arch-employer, the arch-planner, the arch-administrator and ruler, and the arch-caucus boss.

A Socialist State once thoroughly completed in all its details and its aspects—and that is what I am speaking of—could not afford to suffer opposition.
20 Socialism is, in its essence, an attack not only upon British enterprise, but upon the right of the ordinary man or woman to breathe freely without having a harsh, clumsy, tyrannical hand clapped across their mouths and nostrils. A Free Parliament—look at
25 that—a Free Parliament is odious to the Socialist doctrinaire.

But I will go farther. I declare to you, from the bottom of my heart, that no Socialist system can be established without a political police. Many of those
30 who are advocating Socialism or voting Socialist today will be horrified at this idea. That is because they are short-sighted, that is because they do not see where their theories are leading them. No Socialist Government conducting the entire life and industry
35 of the country could afford to allow free, sharp, or violently-worded expressions of public discontent. They would have to fall back on some form of Gestapo, no doubt very humanely directed in the first instance. And this would nip opinion in the bud; it would stop

40 criticism as it reared its head, and it would gather all the power to the supreme party and the party leaders, rising like stately pinnacles above their vast bureaucracies of Civil servants, no longer servants and no longer civil. And where would the ordinary simple
45 folk—the common people, as they like to call them in America—where would they be, once this mighty organism had got them in its grip?

**Passage 2**

The economic anarchy of capitalist society as it exists today is, in my opinion, the real source of
50 the evil. We see before us a huge community of producers the members of which are unceasingly striving to deprive each other of the fruits of their collective labor—not by force, but on the whole in faithful compliance with legally established rules. In
55 this respect, it is important to realize that the means of production—that is to say, the entire productive capacity that is needed for producing consumer goods as well as additional capital goods—may legally be, and for the most part are, the private property of
60 individuals.

Private capital tends to become concentrated in few hands, partly because of competition among the capitalists, and partly because technological development and the increasing division of labor
65 encourage the formation of larger units of production at the expense of the smaller ones. The result of these developments is an oligarchy of private capital the enormous power of which cannot be effectively checked even by a democratically organized political
70 society. This is true since the members of legislative bodies are selected by political parties, largely financed or otherwise influenced by private capitalists who, for all practical purposes, separate the electorate from the legislature. The consequence is that the
75 representatives of the people do not in fact sufficiently protect the interests of the underprivileged sections of the population. Moreover, under existing conditions, private capitalists inevitably control, directly or indirectly, the main sources of information (press,
80 radio, education). It is thus extremely difficult, and indeed in most cases quite impossible, for the individual citizen to come to objective conclusions and to make intelligent use of his political rights.

**CONTINUE**

This crippling of individuals I consider the worst
85  evil of capitalism. Our whole educational system
suffers from this evil. An exaggerated competitive
attitude is inculcated into the student, who is trained
to worship acquisitive success as a preparation for his
future career.

90      I am convinced that there is only one way to
eliminate these grave evils, namely through the
establishment of the socialist economy, accompanied
by an educational system which would be oriented
toward social goals. Nevertheless, it is necessary to
95  remember that a planned economy is not yet socialism.
A planned economy as such may be accompanied
by the complete enslavement of the individual. The
achievement of socialism requires the solution of some
extremely difficult socio-political problems: how is it
100 possible, in view of the far-reaching centralization of
political and economic power, to prevent bureaucracy
from becoming all-powerful and overweening? How
can the rights of the individual be protected and
therewith a democratic counterweight to the power of
105 bureaucracy be assured?

**11**

In Passage 1, Churchill implies that those who
advocate for a socialist state have which quality?

A) They fundamentally deny the expression of
freedom.

B) They ignore economic consequences for the
individual.

C) They advocate a position contrary to their
education.

D) They demand that no one should ever own
property.

**12**

Which choice provides the best evidence for the
answer to the previous question?

A) Lines 1–2 ("My friends . . . freedom")

B) Lines 2–7 ("Although it . . . State")

C) Lines 20–24 ("Socialism is . . . nostrils")

D) Lines 24–26 ("A Free . . . doctrinaire")

**13**

As used in line 11, "hunger" most nearly means

A) yearn.

B) inspire.

C) need.

D) starve.

**14**

The statement in lines 29–31 ("Many of . . . idea")
primarily serves which role in Passage 1?

A) It acknowledges that Churchill's opponents argue
for a broadly undesirable outcome.

B) It explains a situation that Churchill's opponents
do not prefer.

C) It highlights a fear held by many supporters of
socialism.

D) It emphasizes the impact of Churchill's preferred
turn of events.

**15**

As used in line 47, "grip" most nearly means

A) reach.

B) control.

C) squeeze.

D) handle.

**16**

In Passage 2, Einstein suggests that a planned
economy could

A) permit the destruction of free choice.

B) eliminate deadly perils and consequences.

C) be more beneficial to society than freedom.

D) lead to only journalistic uses of the media.

CONTINUE

**17**

Which choice provides the best evidence for the answer to the previous question?

A) Lines 77–80 ("Moreover, under . . . education")

B) Lines 84–85 ("This crippling . . . capitalism")

C) Lines 90–94 ("I am . . . goals")

D) Lines 96–97 ("A planned . . . individual")

**18**

The primary purpose of each passage is to

A) define circumstances that determine the relative benefits of socialism.

B) debate whether free choice is more supported by socialism or capitalism.

C) consider the most appropriate form of government for a developing nation.

D) discuss the impact of governing philosophy on the individual.

**19**

Based on the passages, it is most strongly supported that Churchill would consider Einstein's question in lines 99–102 ("how is . . . overweening") to be

A) appalling for free-minded people in a democracy to consider.

B) a sound criticism of an otherwise plausible suggestion.

C) indicative of a core reason to reject socialism.

D) a fair question to consider in open discussion.

**20**

Based on the passages, a similarity in the perspectives of Churchill and Einstein toward an independent legislature is that

A) both view the institution as compatible with their own perspectives.

B) both see any threat to the institution as a challenge to its existence.

C) neither considers the institution to be particularly worthy of mention.

D) neither believes that changes in societal structure will impact the institution.

**CONTINUE**

**Questions 21–30 are based on the following passage and supplementary material.**

This passage is adapted from Wendy Koch, "Has the U.S. Really Reached an Epic Turning Point in Energy?" © 2016 by National Geographic.

Line

The United States is setting new milestones that suggest a fundamental, and possibly permanent, shift in its energy economy…. Consider what happened last year alone. The amount of electricity from coal-fired
5    power plants hit a record low while that from natural gas generators hit a record high. Also, renewable energy added the most new power to the electric grid, and annual carbon emissions reached a 20-year low.

"2015 clearly marked a turning point for American
10   energy…. We've entered a new era here in the United States," says Lisa Jacobson, president of the Business Council for Sustainable Energy, which released the fourth annual *Sustainable Energy in America Factbook* in partnership with Bloomberg New Energy Finance.
15   Colleen Regan, a senior BNEF analyst, expects many of the key changes will likely be "permanent shifts, rather than temporary adjustments."

Indeed, in recent years, the U.S. oil and natural gas boom has sparked much talk about an American
20   energy renaissance. Yet as prices for oil, wind and solar have plunged, the most recent U.S. short-term forecast doesn't see production growth for all three. Rather, it sees oil falling for the next two years but solar and wind rising. What this means is an energy mix in the
25   world's largest economy that's increasingly efficient and clean with fewer heat-trapping carbon emissions. For example, energy productivity—the ratio of U.S. gross domestic product to energy consumed—continues to improve. It rose 2.3 percent from 2014 to 2015, up
30   from a 1.1 percent increase the prior year, according to the BNEF Factbook. This shows that the economy can grow without increasing energy use.

Coal-fired power plants, which have seen a record number of closures, are producing much
35   less electricity. Last year, through November—the most recent month for which government data are available—they generated 33.6% of U.S. electricity, down from 39 percent for all of 2014 and 50 percent in 2005.

40   In contrast, cheap natural gas is surging. Last year, through November, its generators produced 32.5 percent of U.S. electricity and could actually overtake coal when December figures are published later this month by the Energy Information Administration.
45   This shift has climate benefits, because natural gas emits half as much carbon as coal when burned. So also does the boom in wind and solar power, which emits zero carbon. Solar panels added a record amount of capacity to the power grid last year, and
50   wind farms saw their capacity jump 65 percent as developers sought to take advantage of a federal tax credit slated to expire, according to the BNEF data. In December, Congress renewed wind and solar tax credits for another five years. As a result of the growth
55   in both natural gas and renewables, the U.S. power sector recorded the lowest yearly carbon emissions— down 4.3 percent from 2014—since 1995. In fact, these emissions are now 17.8% below 2005 levels, the benchmark against which the Environmental
60   Protection Agency's Clean Power Plan set a goal of a 32% emissions cut by 2030….

However, some of the world's major carbon emitters such as India are developing countries that have done little to curb fossil fuel use despite severe
65   air pollution. "This group of countries has greatly expanded its use of fossil fuels," says a new study by three prominent economists. They say global consumption of fossil fuels rose 7.5 percent for oil, 24 percent for coal, and 20 percent for natural gas
70   from 2005 to 2014. "In the absence of substantial greenhouse gas policies, the U.S. and the global economy are unlikely to stop relying on fossil fuels as the primary source of energy," write Thomas Covert and Michael Greenstone of the University of Chicago
75   and Christopher R. Knittel of the Massachusetts Institute of Technology. In the short- and middle-term, they say solar and wind are unlikely to "play a major role in base-load electricity capacity or in replacing petroleum-fueled internal combustion engines."
80   Their calculations are ominous. They figure that burning the currently known fossil fuels would increase global average temperatures by at least 10° to 15° Fahrenheit. They say that whether the voluntary agreements in the UN climate accord, reached in
85   December in Paris, can help developing countries adopt cleaner energy "will be determined in the coming years and decades."

**CONTINUE ▶**

U.S. Coal Power Plant Retirements
(Completed and Announced)

■ Retirement Completed   ■ Retirement Announced

Source: Bloomberg Finance LP and the Business Council for Sustainable Energy.

Figure 1

U.S. Electricity Generation by Fuel
(thousand megawatthours/day)

— Coal   — Natural Gas   ······· Nuclear   ····· Renewables

Source: EIA, Short-Term Energy Outlook, January 2017.

Figure 2

**21**

The passage is written from the point of view of a(n)

A) politician advocating for a specific policy.

B) economist evaluating the effects of new data.

C) environmentalist protesting technological changes.

D) journalist assessing the implications of certain trends.

**22**

As used in line 19, "sparked" most nearly means

A) flickered.

B) begun.

C) scrapped.

D) brightened.

**23**

It can most reasonably be inferred from the passage that, prior to 2015, U.S. energy sources were

A) relatively less expensive than newer sources will be.

B) more likely to be derived from natural gas than either wind or solar.

C) directly tied to an increase in severe air pollution.

D) producing more carbon emissions, making those sources inefficient and dirty by comparison.

**24**

Which choice provides the best evidence for the answer to the previous question?

A) Lines 6–7 ("Also, renewable . . . grid")

B) Lines 24–26 ("What this . . . emissions")

C) Lines 31–32 ("This shows . . . use")

D) Lines 33–35 ("Coal-fired power . . . electricity")

**25**

According to the passage, prices for various energy sources will likely

A) reach record highs and record lows.

B) plunge significantly across the board.

C) experience some variance from source to source.

D) lead to power plant closures.

CONTINUE ➤

**26**

Which choice provides the best evidence for the answer to the previous question?

A) Lines 4–6 ("The amount . . . high")

B) Lines 20–22 ("Yet as . . . three")

C) Lines 22–24 ("Rather, it . . . rising")

D) Lines 35–39 ("Last year . . . 2005")

**27**

As used in line 52, "slated" most nearly means

A) scheduled.

B) billed.

C) reserved.

D) listed.

**28**

The last sentence of the passage mainly serves to

A) predict an outcome that is likely to occur.

B) document a recommended change to energy production.

C) indicate that more choices remain to be made.

D) insist all nations follow through on an agreement.

**29**

According to Figures 1 and 2, which type of fuel generated the least electricity in the same year that the most coal plant retirements were completed?

A) Renewables

B) Nuclear

C) Natural Gas

D) Coal

**30**

According to Figure 2, in what year did electricity generated by coal first equal electricity generated by natural gas?

A) 2011

B) 2013

C) 2015

D) 2017

**CONTINUE**

**Questions 31–41 are based on the following passage and supplemental material.**

This passage is excerpted from Maxwell T. Boykoff and Jules M. Boykoff, "Balance as bias: global warming and the US prestige press." Originally published in 2004. University of Colorado Boulder.

The mass media play an important role in the construction of environmental issues and problems. Accordingly, prestige-press coverage of global warming
Line is not just a collection of news articles; it is a social
5 relationship between people that is mediated by news articles. The parameters of this social relationship are defined, in large part, by the many journalistic norms and values that both affect what is deemed news and influence how that news is framed. The
10 United States prestige press—by which we mean the *New York Times,* the *Washington Post,* the *Los Angeles Times,* and the *Wall Street Journal*—has contributed in significant ways to failed discursive translations regarding global warming. These press outlets have
15 done this by adhering to the journalistic norm of balanced reporting, offering a countervailing "denial discourse"—"a voluble minority view [that] argues either that global warming is not scientifically provable or that it is not a serious issue"—roughly equal space
20 to air its suppositions. The 'balancing' of scientific findings and the counter-findings results, in large part, from an accumulation of tactical media responses and practices guided by widely accepted journalistic norms and values.
25 In fact, when it comes to coverage of global warming, balanced reporting can actually be a form of informational bias. Despite the highly regarded United Nations-sponsored Intergovernmental Panel on Climate Change's (IPCC's) consistent assertions
30 that global warming is a serious problem with a "discernible" human component that must be addressed immediately, balanced reporting has allowed a small group of global warming skeptics to have their views amplified.
35 Ross Gelbspan has asserted, "[t]he professional canon of journalistic fairness requires reporters who write about a controversy to present competing points of view. When the issue is of a political or social nature,

fairness—presenting the most compelling arguments
40 of both sides with equal weight—is a fundamental check on biased reporting. But this canon causes problems when it is applied to issues of science. It seems to demand that journalists present competing points of view on a scientific question as though they
45 had equal scientific weight, when actually they do not."
The IPCC has asserted that global warming is a serious problem that has anthropogenic* influences, and that it must be addressed immediately. In the managerial scientific discourse represented by the
50 IPCC, a remarkably high level of scientific consensus has emerged on these two particular issues. D. James Baker, administrator of the US National Oceanic and Atmospheric Administration, has said about global warming that "[t]here's a better scientific consensus on
55 this than on any issue I know—except maybe Newton's second law of dynamics."
However, on December 3, 2002, the *Washington Post* cited "numerous uncertainties [that] remain about global warming's cause and effect," echoing
60 George W. Bush's call "for a decade of research before the government commits to anything more than voluntary measures to stem carbon dioxide and other greenhouse gas emissions." This statement was not only a backhanded swipe at the findings of scientists
65 concerned about global warming, but it was also the spectacular culmination of a complex and perpetually unfolding discursive process propagated by the prestige press in the United States.
The continuous juggling act journalists engage
70 in often mitigates against meaningful, accurate, and urgent coverage of the issue of global warming. Since the general public garners most of its knowledge about science from the mass media, investigating the mass media's portrayal of global warming is crucial. The
75 disjuncture above is one illustration that—through the filter of balanced reporting—popular discourse has significantly diverged from the scientific discourse. To date, this disconnection has played a significant role in the lack of concerted international action to curb
80 practices that contribute to global warming.

* anthropogenic = caused by human beings

U.S. Prestige-Press Coverage of Action
Regarding Global Warming

Credit: Maxwell T. Boykoff and Jules M. Boykoff

Figure 1

**31**

The main purpose of the passage is to

A) question the journalistic ideal of balanced coverage regarding scientific reporting.

B) demonstrate the bias of scientific journalists covering environmental stories.

C) analyze the antagonistic relationship between the elite press and local news outlets.

D) discuss ideals of objectivity in relation to journalism.

**32**

According to the passage, which expectation do reporters covering controversy face?

A) They should present only the most objective reporting of the issues.

B) They should persist in unearthing the truth, no matter the consequences.

C) They should offer equal consideration to opposing perspectives.

D) They should promote constructive solutions to environmental problems.

**33**

Which choice provides the best evidence for the answer to the previous question?

A) Lines 1–2 ("The mass . . . problems")

B) Lines 6–9 ("The parameters . . . framed")

C) Lines 35–38 ("Ross Gelbspan . . . view")

D) Lines 48–51 ("In the . . . issues")

**34**

As used in line 51, "particular" most nearly means

A) local.

B) specific.

C) appropriate.

D) peculiar.

**35**

The authors most likely include the quotation in lines 54–56 to

A) contrast the consensus of scientific authorities with the reporting in prestige publications.

B) propose possible models for accurate reporting.

C) criticize the gullibility of readers of partisan media outlets.

D) demonstrate the importance of scientific facts for public discourse.

**36**

The authors indicate that the work of journalists may involve

A) independent research concerning the trustworthiness of sources.

B) questioning one's own conscience when investigating controversial topics.

C) relating socially to interview subjects for stories.

D) prioritizing balanced reporting of viewpoints over covering the facts.

**CONTINUE**

**37**

Which choice provides the best evidence for the answer to the previous question?

A) Lines 3–6 ("Accordingly, prestige-press . . . articles")

B) Lines 57–63 ("However, on . . . emissions'")

C) Lines 63–68 ("This statement . . . States")

D) Lines 69–71 ("The continuous . . . warming")

**38**

As used in line 79, "curb" most nearly means

A) bend.

B) limit.

C) delay.

D) edge.

**39**

Based on the table, in what year was the coverage of action tactics regarding global warming most similar?

A) 1989

B) 1993

C) 1994

D) 1999

**40**

Which statement is best supported by information in the graph?

A) Between 1989 and 1999, the number of "cautious/voluntary" accounts of global warming declined dramatically, but then rose significantly.

B) Between 1995 and 2000, the number of "immediate/mandatory" accounts of global warming remained the same.

C) Between 1988 and 2002, the number of "balanced" accounts of global warming tended to increase.

D) Between 1988 and 2001, the number of all accounts of global warming doubled.

**41**

The 2001 data in the table best serve as evidence that

A) "coverage of global warming is not just a collection of news articles" (lines 3–4).

B) "balanced reporting can actually be a form of informational bias" (lines 26–27).

C) "global warming is a serious problem that has anthropogenic influences" (lines 46–47).

D) "through the filter of balanced reporting—popular discourse has significantly diverged from the scientific discourse" (lines 75–77).

**CONTINUE**

**Questions 42–52 are based on the following passage.**

This passage is adapted from Jef Akst, "Silent Canopies."
©2016 by The Scientist.

In late September, Kimberly Williams-Guillén, an assistant professor at the University of Washington Bothell and a conservation scientist for the Nicaraguan environmental NGO Paso Pacífico, received a report that a handful of howler monkeys (genus Alouatta) had been found dead at an eco-resort in Nicaragua. Bizarrely, the monkeys showed no signs of trauma or disease. "They seemed to be in fairly good condition," she recalls.

Over the next couple of months, Williams-Guillén and her colleagues continued to receive news that howler monkeys were dying. Then, around mid-January, the reports really started to flood in.

When it became clear that this was not just an isolated incident, Williams-Guillén hopped on a plane to Nicaragua to see for herself. "I saw many healthy-looking monkeys, but I also saw many visibly unwell monkeys," she says. "They were thin and very lethargic, often solitary and nonresponsive. There were several that I was able to walk up to and grab them out of a bush."

Although the mortality rate seems to have slowed since mid-February, the researchers are anxious to understand what's going on. Williams-Guillén speculates that the deaths may be linked to the drought that has struck Nicaragua and other areas of Central and South America this year. "The deaths are all really concentrated in the areas worst hit by drought," she says. "Even just going to the other side of the mountain, where it's slightly more humid, there's a lot fewer deaths, and there's visibly more potential howler monkey food, whereas the areas that have the highest rates of mortality, the trees are just bare—there's hardly a leaf or flower to be eaten."

Kenneth Glander of Duke University agrees that limited food availability is likely a contributing factor, though the cause of death may not be starvation per se. Rather, the lack of food may drive the monkeys to consume plants with high levels of certain toxins that aren't part of their normal diet. In the 1970s, Glander witnessed a handful of dead or dying howler monkeys in Costa Rica, including two that displayed convulsions similar to those reported in Nicaraguan monkeys this year. "When we did autopsies on them, I was able to determine [that] their stomachs were full of leaves that they'd never eaten before." He then collected a sample of those leaves from trees at his study site and brought them back to Duke for analysis, finding that they were chock-full of toxic alkaloids.

A good test of this hypothesis would be to see how other animals in the areas are faring, says Pedro Américo Dias of the University of Veracruz in Mexico. "If there are no reports of deaths in other frugivorous primates and other frugivorous animals, perhaps [food availability] doesn't have to do with it," he says.

Another possible cause for the howler monkey die-offs is disease. Although Nicaragua is currently believed to be free of yellow fever, Dias points out that outbreaks of the viral disease devastated howler monkey populations in the late 1940s and into the 1950s. Some researchers even speculate that yellow fever may be a cause of the relatively low genetic diversity among Central American howler monkeys, Dias says. "Yellow fever in the past could have caused important bottlenecks."

Williams-Guillén thinks that disease is an unlikely cause of the recent monkey deaths, however. While she and her colleagues are still waiting to export blood and tissue samples to U.S. labs for further analysis, she notes that a Nicaraguan researcher has done virus diagnostics on some of the samples. And, so far, none have tested positive for yellow fever, Zika, chikungunya, or dengue viruses. "Between that and the lack of any necrosis of the liver in the dead animals, [disease] is unlikely," Williams-Guillén says.

For now, however, the cause of the recent howler monkey deaths remains a mystery. Williams-Guillén suspects that no one hypothesis will be correct. "There's probably an interaction of factors," she says. "Animals that might have had some clinical or secondary infections that normally aren't that problematic…got into a situation where they were extremely food- and water-stressed, and that might have been enough to tip them into mortality."

**CONTINUE** →

**42**

The primary purpose of the passage is to

A) portray the concerns, actions, and theories of an investigation.

B) discuss and assess contradictory results regarding an aberration.

C) demonstrate the unusual persistence of a researcher's efforts toward a problem.

D) examine the methodology and questions raised by a hypothesis.

**43**

According to the passage, Williams-Guillén's ultimate hypothesis rests most strongly on which kind of evidence?

A) Genealogical evidence

B) Authoritative opinions

C) Unreliable descriptions

D) Multiple tests

**44**

As used in line 15, "hopped on" most nearly means

A) avoided.

B) flew.

C) jumped.

D) entered.

**45**

Which statement regarding howler monkeys is most strongly supported by the passage?

A) They are less affected by ecological changes than other species would be.

B) They cannot easily be captured by researchers when healthy.

C) They share some known dietary similarities with other species.

D) They prefer the taste of non-toxic foods.

**46**

According to the author, an early consideration regarding howler monkey deaths was whether they

A) could be prevented through food distribution.

B) were simply random occurrences.

C) impacted howler monkeys of all ages.

D) were impacting the entire population.

**47**

Which theory provided by the passage supports Williams-Guillén's belief that "no one hypothesis will be correct" (line 78)?

A) The unusual monkey deaths have since ceased to be a problem.

B) The assumption that the impact of drought on the health of the monkey population was more significant than that of any other factor.

C) Lack of food in the past has led some monkeys to consume lethal alkaloids.

D) Yellow fever was the cause of a previous outbreak of disease that had afflicted the howler monkey population.

**48**

Which choice provides the best evidence for the answer to the previous question?

A) Lines 22–24 ("Although the . . . on")

B) Lines 27–29 ("'The deaths . . . says")

C) Lines 29–34 ("Even just . . . eaten")

D) Lines 35–40 ("Kenneth Glander . . . diet")

**CONTINUE →**

**49**

The primary purpose of the seventh and eighth paragraphs (lines 56–75) is to

A) define Williams-Guillén's method.

B) demonstrate Williams-Guillén's expertise.

C) underscore Williams-Guillén's assumptions.

D) provide Williams-Guillén's perspective.

**50**

In indicating that yellow fever may have created "bottlenecks" (line 65), the author most likely means that the fever

A) reduced the monkey's opportunities to breed with genetically different partners.

B) led to the current howler monkey deaths.

C) introduced a prohibitively large number of virus-free monkeys into the ecosystem.

D) caused a greater degree of competition between monkeys.

**51**

According to the passage, Williams-Guillén's investigation provides an answer to which of the following questions?

A) What factor is unlikely to have contributed to howler monkey deaths?

B) Why do monkeys insist on continuing to consume toxic leaves?

C) How do yellow fever outbreaks affect genetic diversity among howler monkeys?

D) How can howler monkey populations return to normal following this outbreak of deaths?

**52**

Which choice provides the best evidence for the answer to the previous question?

A) Lines 61–64 ("Some researchers . . . says")

B) Lines 66–67 ("Williams-Guillén thinks . . . however")

C) Lines 71–73 ("And, so . . . viruses")

D) Lines 80–84 ("Animals that . . . mortality")

# STOP

**If you finish before time is called, you may check your work on this section only.**
**Do not turn to any other section in the test.**

**No Test Material On This Page**

# Writing and Language Test

## 35 MINUTES, 44 QUESTIONS

**Turn to Section 2 of your answer sheet to answer the questions in this section.**

### DIRECTIONS

Each passage below is accompanied by a number of questions. For some questions, you will consider how the passage might be revised to improve the expression of ideas. For other questions, you will consider how the passage might be edited to correct errors in sentence structure, usage, or punctuation. A passage or a question may be accompanied by one or more graphics (such as a table or graph) that you will consider as you make revising and editing decisions.

Some questions will direct you to an underlined portion of a passage. Other questions will direct you to a location in a passage or ask you to think about the passage as a whole.

After reading each passage, choose the answer to each question that most effectively improves the quality of writing in the passage or that makes the passage conform to the conventions of standard written English. Many questions include a "NO CHANGE" option. Choose that option if you think the best choice is to leave the relevant portion of the passage as it is.

**Questions 1–11 are based on the following passage.**

**Wake Up!**

If you've ever been driving on a long stretch of highway late at **1** night or, early in the morning, you almost certainly know the feeling. Even though you're in a heavy machine hurtling forward at an extraordinary rate, you just can't stay awake. You know that driving requires your full attention, but your eyelids are just too heavy.

If you haven't had this experience, you're lucky, but you're in the minority. Charles Czeisler, from the Division of Sleep Medicine at Harvard, says that as many as 56 million Americans a month "admit that they drive when they haven't gotten enough sleep." This may seem like a harmless enough problem, but as many as one seventh of these drivers admit to falling asleep at the **2** wheel. Causing more than a million crashes each year, including 50,000 injuries and 6,400 deaths.

**1**
A) NO CHANGE
B) night or early in the morning you,
C) night or early in the morning, you
D) night, or early in the morning you

**2**
A) NO CHANGE
B) wheel, causing
C) wheel, this causes
D) wheel. Which causes

CONTINUE

**3** These may sound like drunk-driving numbers and with good cause. At a recent forum, Czeisler suggested that driving on fewer than two hours of sleep is the equivalent of driving while **4** intoxicated. Judgment is—similarly compromised, and reactions are correspondingly slowed. The numbers speak for themselves, so Czeisler and the committee are attempting now to implement changes in the law code to address sleep deprivation. **5**

**3**

Which choice provides the best transition from the previous paragraph to this one?

A) NO CHANGE

B) Auto-accident fatalities are among the leading causes of death every year.

C) Medical professionals regularly hold forums to share their findings and discover new findings.

D) Drunk driving remains a difficult problem in this country, even though the penalties for it are strict.

**4**

A) NO CHANGE

B) intoxicated, judgment is

C) intoxicated. Judgment is:

D) intoxicated: judgment is

**5**

At this point, the writer wants to add a specific proposal that Czeisler's group has made based on the information in this paragraph. Which choice best accomplishes this goal?

A) Some of Czeisler's colleagues have already organized new conferences on sleep apnea and other sleep disorders.

B) The invention of self-driving cars could potentially reduce the risks of sleep-deprived driving.

C) Czeisler has had a long and illustrious career teaching people about how to observe their own unconscious behavior.

D) Czeisler and his colleagues are trying to get sleep-deprived driving added to the list of criminal statutes.

**CONTINUE** ➡

Some of the group's findings make obvious sense. They argue that people who work night shifts never quite regulate their sleep, regardless of how regular their sleep schedules are. **6** In addition, night-shift workers with sleep disorders are at a particular risk of which they are unaware. One major sleep disorder for which this is especially true is sleep apnea. Czeisler's group estimates that approximately 85% of sleep apnea cases go undiagnosed and untreated. Individuals with sleep apnea don't rest deeply even when they are asleep, and the disorder, given all of its negative side effects, **7** was doubling the risk of sleep-related crashes.

**6**

Which choice most effectively combines the underlined sentences?

A) In addition, night-shift workers with sleep disorders are at a particular risk of which they are unaware; moreover, one major sleep disorder for which this is especially true is sleep apnea.

B) In addition, night-shift workers with sleep disorders, especially sleep apnea, are at a particular risk of which they are unaware.

C) In addition, night-shift workers with sleep disorders are at a particular risk of which they are unaware: among them are sleep apnea especially.

D) In addition, night-shift workers with sleep disorders are at a particular risk of which they are unaware; one major sleep disorder for which this is especially true is sleep apnea.

**7**

A) NO CHANGE
B) are doubling
C) is doubling
D) doubles

**CONTINUE**

The findings regarding young people, [8] nevertheless, were not quite so obvious. Young people have a tendency to think that they can operate at a high level with less sleep. [9] This may be anecdotally true, but the science suggests that in fact quite the opposite is true. A set of chemicals in the hypothalamus region of the brain produces the cells that help the transition from wakefulness to sleep. In younger people, these cells are [10] highly developed, whereas in older people, many of the cells have died or function at a lower level. As a result, a younger person is more at risk for uncontrollable lapses in engagement [11] adding too attention because brain function between wakefulness and sleep is more easily blurred. So next time you think you're okay to drive after a late night, use some of those brain cells and call a cab or take a nap instead.

**8**

A) NO CHANGE
B) however,
C) furthermore,
D) thus,

**9**

Which choice most effectively cites commonly-held views while previewing what is to come in this paragraph?

A) NO CHANGE
B) Young people's susceptibility to alcoholism is also much higher than that of adults.
C) It's also well known that young people tend to drive faster than older people.
D) Everyone's different, and maybe you are one of the lucky few who doesn't need that much sleep.

**10**

A) NO CHANGE
B) firing on all cylinders,
C) going off,
D) off the chain,

**11**

A) NO CHANGE
B) and attention lapses also
C) plus attention as well
D) and attention

CONTINUE ➡

**Questions 12–22 are based on the following passage.**

### To Preserve, but Not to Reconstruct

Although the building served a variety of functions, the Parthenon's original construction remained more or less intact for over two millennia. The enormous temple to the goddess Athena Parthenos that stands in ruins today was completed in 432 B.C.E. **12** Nevertheless, it served its original purpose for a thousand years, until it was turned into a church by the Byzantines in the 6th century and then into a mosque by the Ottoman Empire in the mid-15th century. The shift of the building's religious affiliation involved some minor architectural changes, but until the late 17th **13** century, the building, largely retained its majestic, classical profile.

The first major catastrophe in the Parthenon's history came during a war between the Ottoman Empire and the Venetian army in 1687: the Ottomans used the Parthenon as a gunpowder storehouse **14** for storing ammunition, which exploded when it was hit by a Venetian cannon. **15** Additionally, three hundred people died in the explosion.

---

**12**

A) NO CHANGE
B) Remarkably,
C) As a result,
D) Therefore,

**13**

A) NO CHANGE
B) century, the building largely
C) century: the building largely
D) century the building, largely,

**14**

A) NO CHANGE
B) where they stored ammunition,
C) —a place to store ammunition—
D) DELETE the underlined portion.

**15**

At this point, the writer is considering adding the following sentence.

> The roof of the building collapsed, along with many sculptures and several dozen columns.

Should the writer make this addition here?

A) Yes, because it provides an important detail about the effect of the explosion.
B) Yes, because it helps to explain the facts presented later in the passage.
C) No, because it repeats information presented later in the passage.
D) No, because it is not directly related to the main idea of the paragraph.

**CONTINUE**

Over the course of the 18th century, the ruins of the Parthenon were largely neglected by the local government, **16** though interest in the building grew in Britain. The first major effort at what might be called preservation came in the years 1801-1812 when Thomas Bruce, the Earl of Elgin, systematically removed most of the extant sculpture from the Parthenon and shipped it all to Britain, where it remains today.

In the 1890s, the first major push to restore the Parthenon began when Nikolaos Balanos was charged with restoring **17** its iconic column's. Unfortunately, Balanos's restoration efforts ultimately caused more harm than good. Most disastrously, the iron clamps that he **18** used holding pieces of masonry together corroded after years of exposure to the **19** weather, eventually it caused even more damage to the already fragile building.

**16**

Which choice best supports the main point of the paragraph?

A) NO CHANGE

B) which makes it all the more remarkable that the government later sponsored restoration efforts.

C) and the building was even briefly used as an army barracks.

D) but it became a very popular subject of paintings and engravings.

**17**

A) NO CHANGE

B) it's iconic column's.

C) its iconic columns.

D) it's iconic columns.

**18**

A) NO CHANGE

B) used to hold

C) using to hold

D) used in the holding of

**19**

A) NO CHANGE

B) weather; eventually causing

C) weather, eventually causing

D) weather, eventually it causing

**CONTINUE**

[1] The most recent restoration effort was begun in 1975, and conservation work continues today. [2] As a result of this painstaking work, the restoration is proceeding at far slower pace than the original construction, which took only sixteen years. [3] The project has taken so long partly because the first step was to undo the misguided earlier restoration attempt. [4] Workers then catalogued tens of thousands of pieces of marble and used computer programs to try to match each piece to its specific location. [5] The **20** shadows of each column's design are incredibly sophisticated, and pieces match one another by fractions of millimeters. **21**

The goal of the current restoration is not, however, to entirely rebuild the structure. "We wanted to preserve the beauty of what has survived these past 2,500 years," says Manolis Korres, **22** who is the project's chief architect. "It's a reminder of man's power to create, as well as to destroy."

**20**

A) NO CHANGE
B) tininess
C) suggestions
D) nuances

**21**

To make this paragraph most logical, sentence 2 should be

A) placed after sentence 3.
B) placed after sentence 4.
C) placed after sentence 5.
D) DELETED from the paragraph.

**22**

A) NO CHANGE
B) being
C) the architect is
D) DELETE the underlined portion.

CONTINUE

**Questions 23–33 are based on the following passage and supplementary material.**

## Today is Brought to You by Big Data

Ask anyone what the next big thing in business is, and it's very likely they'll say "big data." The term refers to all the information that the digital age allows companies and organizations to collect: how many items an online shopper looks at before deciding to make a purchase, exactly how much time a delivery truck spends idling in [23] traffic, or, how the weather affects which books patrons check out from the library. Some of this glut of data comes from increasingly sophisticated and connected sensors on everything from cars and trucks to appliances and light bulbs. [24] Consequently, a huge portion of it comes from social media posts that can't be analyzed in traditional ways. This means that new ways of [25] digging online activity for information are constantly being developed.

Data analysts are the people who develop new ways of looking at such information, in fields ranging from healthcare to the nonprofit [26] sector too manufacturing. Although many companies have long employed financial analysts or market research analysts, the need for even more data analysts is quickly growing. Job seekers with degrees in computer science mathematics are likely to be attracted to data analysis jobs, because there is no standard requirement for a graduate degree or certification.

**23**

A) NO CHANGE
B) traffic, or
C) traffic: or
D) traffic; or

**24**

A) NO CHANGE
B) Additionally,
C) However,
D) Therefore,

**25**

A) NO CHANGE
B) checking out
C) mining
D) taking a peek at

**26**

A) NO CHANGE
B) sector to
C) section, to
D) section to

**CONTINUE**

Salaries are also attractive: the average starting salary of a data analyst is almost $50,000 more than [27] that as a computer programmer.

[28] Another draw of the field of data analytics is that specialized knowledge of a particular field is not necessarily a requirement. While it may seem that a background in healthcare would be prerequisite for making sense of medical data, the analyst's job is very much a collaborative one. Doctors and epidemiologists, for example, work alongside data analysts, who can design algorithms tailored to the needs of particular research projects. An expert in statistics can open researchers' eyes to new ways of using [29] his or her information, and such collaborations ultimately lead to innovations that benefit society at large.

[30] According to Bureau of Labor Statistics, related

---

**27**

A) NO CHANGE
B) that of
C) those of
D) DELETE the underlined portion.

**28**

Which choice is the best introduction to the paragraph?

A) NO CHANGE
B) More and more schools are offering degree programs in data analytics.
C) Epidemiology is one example of a field in which data analytics is of fundamental importance.
D) Some companies are creating new positions for data analysts, while others are adding the duties to positions that already exist.

**29**

A) NO CHANGE
B) there
C) they're
D) their

**30**

At this point, the writer is considering adding the following sentence:

> Since there is no standard certification or job title for those who analyze big data, it can be difficult to quantify exactly how much the field is growing.

Should the writer make this addition here?

A) Yes, because it introduces an issue that is further discussed in the paragraph.
B) Yes, because it offers additional details about a point made in the previous paragraph.
C) No, because it strays from the main focus of the paragraph.
D) No, because it contradicts the ideas presented later in the paragraph.

CONTINUE ➡

job **31** titles (including operations research analyst and statistician) have projected growth rates of up to 34% over the next ten years.

**32** Big data is already used to schedule our UPS deliveries and to recommend music and movies for us to stream. Within the next decade it will no doubt become a part of nearly every other aspect of our **33** goings-on.

Projected Increase in Jobs Related to Data Analytics, 2014–2024

|  | 2014 Number | 2024 Number (predicted) | Projected Growth Rate |
|---|---|---|---|
| Statistician | 30,000 | 40,100 | 34% |
| Operations Research Analyst | 91,300 | 118,900 | 30% |
| Market Research Analyst | 495,500 | 587,800 | 19% |
| Management Analyst | 758,000 | 861,400 | 14% |
| Financial Analyst | 277,600 | 309,900 | 12% |

Data from Bureau of Labor Statistics, Occupational Outlook Handbook, http://www.bls.gov/ooh/

**31**

A) NO CHANGE

B) titles: including operations research analyst and statistician,

C) titles including operations research analyst, and statistician,

D) titles, including operations research analyst and statistician

**32**

At this point, the writer is considering adding the following sentence.

> In fact, operations research analyst is projected to have the greatest number of jobs in the field by 2024.

Should the writer make this addition?

A) Yes, because it includes surprising data that makes the argument more interesting.

B) Yes, because it summarizes the central thesis of the passage.

C) No, because it is only tangentially related to the main idea of the passage.

D) No, because it is not supported by the data presented in the table.

**33**

A) NO CHANGE

B) habits.

C) usual procedure.

D) daily lives.

CONTINUE

**Questions 34–44 are based on the following passage.**

**The Near-Death and Rebirth of Rock**

Every generation can be defined by its music: the GI Generation is sometimes called the Jazz Generation. The Silent Generation had big band and swing, and Baby Boomers, of course, had rock and roll. But there was a time during the **34** delayed 50s and early 60s when it seemed that rock and roll might be a short-lived fad.

The film *Blackboard* **35** *Jungle,* which featured the song "Rock Around the Clock" by Bill Haley and his Comets—catapulted popular culture into the rock and roll era in 1955. The movie sparked controversy, **36** moreover, with some theaters cutting the iconic opening song, others refusing to show it at all, and large crowds of teenagers flocking to see it wherever they could. The following year, Elvis Presley **37** will appear on the Ed Sullivan show, thrilling and scandalizing audiences nationwide with his pompadour and his hip-swiveling dance moves.

**34**

A) NO CHANGE
B) tardy
C) behind
D) late

**35**

A) NO CHANGE
B) *Jungle*—
C) *Jungle*:
D) *Jungle*;

**36**

A) NO CHANGE
B) and,
C) however,
D) as a result,

**37**

A) NO CHANGE
B) appearing
C) appeared
D) was appearing

**CONTINUE**

Rock and roll was widely embraced as the [38] symbol, of a new, rebellious generation. Chuck Berry, Little Richard, Buddy Holly, and Jerry Lee Lewis expanded on the groundwork laid by Bill Haley and Elvis, bringing bluesy rhythms and exuberant, danceable energy to popular music. [39] Les Paul's innovations in developing a solid-body electric guitar helped make this kind of music possible.

A) NO CHANGE

B) symbol of a

C) symbol: of a

D) symbol of, a

The writer wants a conclusion to the paragraph that logically completes the discussion of the popularity of early rock and provides an effective transition into the next paragraph. Which choice best accomplishes these goals?

A) NO CHANGE

B) Popular new dance moves, such as the Hand Jive, popped up alongside the new style of music.

C) The television show American Bandstand, which focused exclusively on Top 40 hits, helped popularize rock music.

D) It seemed as if the rise of rock and roll was unstoppable.

**CONTINUE** ➡

But in the late 50s, one by one, [40] rock musicians began to expand their musical styles, incorporating elements of gospel and classical music. Buddy Holly was killed in a plane crash. Elvis was drafted. Little Richard abandoned music and became a preacher. Others were marred by scandal: Jerry Lee Lewis married his 13-year-old cousin, and Chuck Berry [41] debuted his signature duck walk, hopping across the stage on one foot while playing the guitar. As the big stars dropped off, it was as if those who viewed rock and roll as dangerous and degenerate had been correct: nothing good was coming of it.

[40]

Which choice most effectively sets up the main idea of the paragraph?

A) NO CHANGE

B) the icons of early rock disappeared from the music scene.

C) rock musicians began to write their own songs instead of just playing covers of already-established hits.

D) British rock bands began to gain popularity in the United States.

[41]

Which choice is most consistent with the examples in the previous sentences?

A) NO CHANGE

B) opened some of the first integrated music clubs in St. Louis.

C) served time in jail for having improper relations with a minor.

D) combined blues, country, and R&B in an innovative new way.

**CONTINUE**

The Beatles changed everything in 1963, when their songs were first aired on American radio. In early 1964, two of The **42** Beatles' album's, were released in the United States, followed quickly by an appearance on the Ed Sullivan show and their first American tour. The Beatles had been inspired by Buddy Holly, and young American audiences loved these new stars even more than they had loved **43** those of the late 50s. **44** Elvis's dance moves had met with disapproval from older generations. The Beatles' shaggy hairdos were seen as a symbol of rebellion by parents of the band's fans. Young fans, however, embraced everything The Beatles stood for, and the band members relished their roles as leaders of a revolutionary youth culture. Over the course of the 1960s, the band's music became increasingly experimental and political, reflecting the changing interests of its audience, but rock's popularity never again waned.

**42**

A) NO CHANGE

B) Beatles' albums

C) Beatles album's

D) Beatle's album's

**43**

A) NO CHANGE

B) them

C) these

D) DELETE the underlined portion.

**44**

Which choice most effectively combines the underlined sentences?

A) Just as Elvis's dance moves had met with disapproval from older generations, The Beatles' shaggy hairdos were seen as a symbol of rebellion by parents of the band's fans.

B) Elvis's dance moves had met with disapproval from older generations, even though The Beatles' shaggy hairdos were seen as a symbol of rebellion by parents of the band's fans.

C) In the same way that Elvis's popular dance moves made older generations disapproving in their style, The Beatles' hairdos, which were seen by many parents as shaggy, were widely taken by the band's fans to be a symbol of rebellion.

D) The Beatles' hairdos were met with disapproval from parents of the band's fans in being shaggy and rebellious, just as Elvis's dance moves had met with disapproval from older generations.

# STOP

**If you finish before time is called, you may check your work on this section only.**
**Do not turn to any other section in the test.**

# Math Test – No Calculator

## 25 MINUTES, 20 QUESTIONS

Turn to Section 3 of your answer sheet to answer the questions in this section.

---

### DIRECTIONS

**For questions 1–15**, solve each problem, choose the best answer from the choices provided, and fill in the corresponding circle on your answer sheet. **For questions 16–20**, solve the problem and enter your answer in the grid on the answer sheet. Please refer to the directions before question 16 on how to enter your answers in the grid. You may use any available space in your test booklet for scratch work.

### NOTES

1. The use of a calculator **is not permitted**.
2. All variables and expressions used represent real numbers unless otherwise indicated.
3. Figures provided in this test are drawn to scale unless otherwise indicated.
4. All figures lie in a plane unless otherwise indicated.
5. Unless otherwise indicated, the domain of a given function $f$ is the set of all real numbers $x$ for which $f(x)$ is a real number.

### REFERENCE

$A = \pi r^2$
$C = 2\pi r$

$A = \ell w$

$A = \frac{1}{2} bh$

$c^2 = a^2 + b^2$

Special Right Triangles

$V = \ell wh$

$V = \pi r^2 h$

$V = \frac{4}{3}\pi r^3$

$V = \frac{1}{3}\pi r^2 h$

$V = \frac{1}{3}\ell wh$

The number of degrees of arc in a circle is 360.
The number of radians of arc in a circle is $2\pi$.
The sum of the measures in degrees of the angles of a triangle is 180.

**CONTINUE**

### 1

What is the sum of the complex numbers $3 + 6i$ and $7 + 2i$, where $i = \sqrt{-1}$ ?

A)  $10 + 8i$

B)  $21 + 12i$

C)  $18$

D)  $18i$

### 2

Abigail creates a pricing plan for her job as a piano instructor. She charges a one-time registration fee to every client in order to begin instruction. The equation $C = 40h + 100$ represents the total amount $C$, in dollars, that Abigail charges for $h$ hours of lessons. What does 100 represent in the equation?

A)  The amount of the registration fee, in dollars

B)  The total amount, in dollars, Abigail will charge for one hour

C)  The total amount, in dollars, Abigail will charge for any number of hours

D)  The price of one hour, in dollars

### 3

A jeweler obtains two samples of gold. Sample F weighs 220 ounces and Sample G weighs 140 ounces. The samples bought by the jeweler contain a total of 150 ounces of pure gold. Which equation models this relationship, where $a$ is the percent of pure gold, expressed as a decimal, of Sample F and $b$ is the percent of pure gold, expressed as a decimal, of Sample G ?

A)  $1.4a + 2.2b = 150$

B)  $2.2a + 1.4b = 150$

C)  $140a + 220b = 150$

D)  $220a + 140b = 150$

### 4

If $a = \dfrac{4}{5}b$ and $b = 15$, what is the value of $4a - 5$ ?

A)  $8$

B)  $10$

C)  $12$

D)  $43$

**CONTINUE**

## 5

$$(cy - d)(cy + d) = 25y^2 - 16$$

Which of the following could be the value of $c$ in the equation above, where $c$ and $d$ are constants?

A)  4

B)  5

C)  16

D)  25

## 6

If $\sqrt{49} = \sqrt{y} - \sqrt{16}$, what is the value of $y$?

A)  121

B)  65

C)  11

D)  $\sqrt{11}$

## 7

Which of the following is the graph of the equation $y = \dfrac{1}{3}x - 2$ in the $xy$-plane?

A)

B)

C)

D)

**CONTINUE**

**8**

A wedding band uses the equation $F = 300nh$ to estimate the fee $F$, in dollars, it charges for a wedding that requires $n$ musicians and lasts $h$ hours. Which of the following correctly expresses $h$, in terms of $F$ and $n$?

A) $h = \dfrac{F}{300 + n}$

B) $h = \dfrac{F}{300n}$

C) $h = \dfrac{n}{300F}$

D) $h = \dfrac{300}{nF}$

**9**

| s | r(s) | t(s) |
|---|------|------|
| 0 | −1 | −1 |
| 1 | 2 | 1 |
| 2 | 3 | 1 |
| 3 | −1 | −3 |
| 4 | −2 | 3 |

The table above shows some values for the functions $r$ and $t$. For which value of $s$ is $r(s) \times t(s) = s$?

A) 0

B) 1

C) 2

D) 3

**10**

Which of the following is equivalent to $\dfrac{2y^2 + 5y}{2y + 7}$?

A) $y - 1 + \dfrac{7}{2y + 7}$

B) $y + \dfrac{7}{2y + 7}$

C) $y + 2$

D) $y$

**11**

Renee is taking a calculus class. Her goal is to have the average score on her 3 tests be at least a 90. She scored 99 on the first test and 83 on the second test. Which inequality can be used to represent the score, $s$, that Renee could receive on the 3rd test to meet her goal?

A) $\dfrac{99}{3} + \dfrac{83}{3} + s \geq 90$

B) $99 + 83 + s \geq 3(90)$

C) $\dfrac{99 + 83}{2} + s \geq 90$

D) $99 + 83 \geq s(90)$

**CONTINUE**

**12**

$y = ax^2 - k$

The vertex of the parabola in the $xy$-plane above is $(0, -c)$. Which of the following is true about the parabola with the equation $y = -a(x + j)^2 - k$ ?

A) The graph opens downward and the vertex is $(j, -k)$.

B) The graph opens upward and the vertex is $(j, -k)$.

C) The graph opens downward and the vertex is $(-j, -k)$.

D) The graph opens upward and the vertex is $(-j, -k)$.

**13**

Which of the following is equivalent to $\left(\dfrac{x}{2} - y\right)^2$ ?

A) $\dfrac{x^2}{2} + y^2$

B) $\dfrac{x^2}{4} + y^2$

C) $\dfrac{x^2}{4} - xy + y^2$

D) $\dfrac{x^2}{2} - \dfrac{xy}{2} + y^2$

**14**

$$4x^2 - 5x = k$$

In the equation above, $k$ is a constant. If the equation has two real solutions, which of the following could be the value of $k$ ?

A) $-4$

B) $-3$

C) $-2$

D) $-1$

**15**

A clothing store is buying T-shirts and pairs of jeans from a wholesaler. The clothing store wants to buy at least three times as many T-shirts as pairs of jeans. The store will spend no more than \$200 on the order. Each T-shirt that is ordered costs the store \$1.25, and each pair of jeans that is ordered costs the store \$9.75. Let $t$ represent the number of T-shirts ordered and $j$ represent the number of pairs of jeans ordered, where $t$ and $j$ are nonnegative integers. Which of the following systems of inequalities best expresses this situation?

A) $t \geq 3j$

$\quad 3.75t + 9.75j \leq 200$

B) $3t \geq j$

$\quad 3.75t + 9.75j \leq 200$

C) $t \geq 3j$

$\quad 1.25t + 9.75j \leq 200$

D) $3t \geq j$

$\quad 1.25t + 9.75j \leq 200$

**CONTINUE**

## DIRECTIONS

**For questions 16–20,** solve the problem and enter your answer in the grid, as described below, on the answer sheet.

1. Although not required, it is suggested that you write your answer in the boxes at the top of the columns to help you fill in the circles accurately. You will receive credit only if the circles are filled in correctly.

2. Mark no more than one circle in any column.

3. No question has a negative answer.

4. Some problems may have more than one correct answer. In such cases, grid only one answer.

5. **Mixed numbers** such as $3\frac{1}{2}$ must be gridded as 3.5 or 7/2. (If [3 1 / 2] is entered into the grid, it will be interpreted as $\frac{31}{2}$, not as $3\frac{1}{2}$.)

6. **Decimal Answers:** If you obtain a decimal answer with more digits than the grid can accommodate, it may be either rounded or truncated, but it must fill the entire grid.

**NOTE:** You may start your answers in any column, space permitting. Columns you don't need to use should be left blank.

**16**

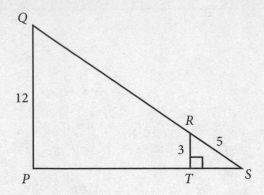

In the figure above, $\overline{PQ}$ is parallel to $\overline{RT}$. What is the length of $\overline{PS}$?

**17**

If $r^{\frac{s}{2}} = 64$ for positive integers $r$ and $s$, what is one possible value of $s$?

**18**

Points $P$ and $Q$ lie on a circle with radius 2, and arc $\widehat{PQ}$ has length $\dfrac{\pi}{6}$. What fraction of the circumference is the length of arc $\widehat{PQ}$?

**19**

$$\frac{4}{7}a = \frac{7}{2}$$

What value of $a$ is the solution to the equation above?

CONTINUE

**20**

How many gallons of a juice mix that is 60% orange juice must be added to 5 gallons of a juice mix that is 30% orange juice to obtain a juice mix that is 40% orange juice?

## STOP
**If you finish before time is called, you may check your work on this section only.**
**Do not turn to any other section in the test.**

# Math Test – Calculator

## 55 MINUTES, 38 QUESTIONS

**Turn to Section 4 of your answer sheet to answer the questions in this section.**

### DIRECTIONS

**For questions 1–30**, solve each problem, choose the best answer from the choices provided, and fill in the corresponding circle on your answer sheet. **For questions 31–38**, solve the problem and enter your answer in the grid on the answer sheet. Please refer to the directions before question 31 on how to enter your answers in the grid. You may use any available space in your test booklet for scratch work.

### NOTES

1. The use of a calculator **is permitted**.
2. All variables and expressions used represent real numbers unless otherwise indicated.
3. Figures provided in this test are drawn to scale unless otherwise indicated.
4. All figures lie in a plane unless otherwise indicated.
5. Unless otherwise indicated, the domain of a given function $f$ is the set of all real numbers $x$ for which $f(x)$ is a real number.

### REFERENCE

$A = \pi r^2$
$C = 2\pi r$

$A = \ell w$

$A = \frac{1}{2}bh$

$c^2 = a^2 + b^2$

Special Right Triangles

$V = \ell wh$

$V = \pi r^2 h$

$V = \frac{4}{3}\pi r^3$

$V = \frac{1}{3}\pi r^2 h$

$V = \frac{1}{3}\ell wh$

The number of degrees of arc in a circle is 360.
The number of radians of arc in a circle is $2\pi$.
The sum of the measures in degrees of the angles of a triangle is 180.

**CONTINUE**

## 1

Laura went out for a run. After running for a while, she stopped to sit on park bench and rest. When she started running again, she was tired, and ran at a slower rate than she had initially. Which of the following graphs could model the distance Laura ran versus time?

A)

B)

C)

D)

## 2

What expression is equivalent to
$(3y^2 - 2) - (-5y^2 + 3y - 6)$ ?

A) $-2y^2 + 3y - 4$

B) $-2y^2 - 3y - 4$

C) $8y^2 + 3y - 4$

D) $8y^2 - 3y + 4$

## 3

The graph above shows the temperature of two different blocks of metal that are being cooled in a freezer to a temperature of 0 degrees Fahrenheit. Both blocks lose heat at a constant rate, and Block B started at a lower initial temperature to decrease the time required to cool it. Block A took 8 minutes to cool to 0 degrees Fahrenheit and Block B took 12 minutes to cool to 0 degrees Fahrenheit. According to the graph, what was the difference, in degrees Fahrenheit, between the initial temperatures of Block A and Block B ?

A) 10

B) 15

C) 20

D) 25

**CONTINUE**

**4**

**Who is Your Internet Service Provider?**

| Internet Service Provider | Percent of Households |
|---|---|
| Corporate Cable | 47% |
| Speedy Connections | 21% |
| Global Networks | 17% |
| Dave's Dial-Up | 12% |
| Other | 3% |

The table above summarizes a census of 2,800 households within a small community. Based on the table, how many households receive their Internet service from either Corporate Cable or Global Networks?

A) 1,792

B) 1,843

C) 1,904

D) 2,039

**5**

An office supply vendor that delivers printer ink to companies charges a subscription fee of $230 for its services plus $x$ dollars for each carton of ink. If a company paid $1,364 for 18 cartons of ink, including the subscription fee, what is the value of $x$ ?

A) 46

B) 52

C) 63

D) 78

**6**

$$16a + 20b > 12$$

Which of the following inequalities is equivalent to the inequality above?

A) $5b + 4a > 4$

B) $5a + 4b > 3$

C) $a + b > 4$

D) $4a + 5b > 3$

**7**

In May of 1937, American aviation pioneer Amelia Earhart attempted to circumnavigate the globe. According to flight logs, the first stage of the trip was 110 nautical miles less than the second stage of the trip, and the two stages combined totaled 676 nautical miles. How many nautical miles was the first stage?

A) 249

B) 283

C) 327

D) 390

**CONTINUE** ➡

**8**

The total weight of a carton of oranges is 27.3 pounds, of which 9.6 pounds is the weight of the carton itself. If a fruit vendor pays $46.25 for a carton of oranges, which of the following is closest to the cost of the oranges, in dollars per pound?

A) $6.50

B) $4.80

C) $2.60

D) $1.70

**9**

The board of directors at a natural history museum decided to survey all of its scientists to determine if the new wing in the museum should feature an aquatic exhibit. The board met with a sample group of 30 marine biologists. The majority of the sample group were in favor of featuring an aquatic exhibit in the new wing. Which of the following is true about the board's survey?

A) The sample group should have included more marine biologists.

B) It concludes that a majority of the scientists are in favor of featuring an aquatic exhibit in the new wing.

C) The sample group is biased because it is not representative of all scientists.

D) The sample group should have consisted only of scientists who are not marine biologists.

**10**

Adopted Animal Characteristics

|  |  | Species | |
|---|---|---|---|
|  |  | Dogs | Cats |
| Color | Brown | 13 | 9 |
|  | Black | 21 | 7 |

An animal shelter held an adoption event to find new homes for a group of dogs and cats. The table above shows the number and color of dogs and cats that were adopted at the event. Each animal was classified as only one color. Of the cats that were adopted, what fraction were black?

A) $\dfrac{7}{16}$

B) $\dfrac{9}{16}$

C) $\dfrac{7}{50}$

D) $\dfrac{16}{50}$

**CONTINUE**

**Questions 11–13 refer to the following information.**

| Artic Sea Ice | |
|---|---|
| Study Year | Extent (million km²) |
| 0 | 5.98 |
| 1 | 6.18 |
| 2 | 6.08 |
| 3 | 5.59 |
| 4 | 5.95 |
| 5 | 4.32 |
| 6 | 4.73 |
| 7 | 5.39 |
| 8 | 4.81 |
| 9 | 4.22 |
| 10 | 3.63 |
| 11 | 5.35 |
| 12 | 5.29 |
| 13 | 4.68 |
| 14 | 4.72 |

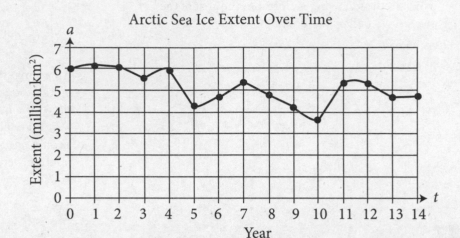

Arctic Sea Ice Extent Over Time

A team of research climatologists conducted a 14-year study to determine the change in the area of the Arctic sea covered with ice, termed the Arctic sea ice extent. The graph and table above model the extent $a$, in millions of square kilometers, of Arctic sea ice $t$ years after the study began.

**11**

The function $a$, defined by $a(t) = c - dt$, where $c$ and $d$ are constants, models the extent, in millions of square kilometers, of Artic sea ice $t$ years after the start of the study during a period in which the change is approximately linear. What does $d$ represent?

A) The predicted total decrease in extent, in millions of square kilometers, of Arctic sea ice during the period

B) The predicted decrease in extent, in millions of square kilometers, of Arctic sea ice per year during the period

C) The predicted extent, in millions of square kilometers, of Arctic sea ice at the beginning of the period

D) The predicted extent, in millions of square kilometers, of Arctic sea ice at the end of the period

**12**

The rate of decrease of Artic sea ice extent from Year 7 to Year 10 is nearly constant. On this interval, which of the following best models the extent $a$, in millions of square kilometers, of Arctic sea ice $t$ years after the study began?

A) $a = 5 - 0.21t$

B) $a = 7 - 0.13t$

C) $a = 10 - 0.64t$

D) $a = 15 - 1.82t$

**13**

Over which time period is the average decrease of Arctic sea ice extent the greatest?

A) Year 4 to Year 5

B) Year 7 to Year 8

C) Year 9 to Year 10

D) Year 12 to Year 13

**CONTINUE**

**14**

$$9c + 5d = 22$$
$$7c - 5d = 10$$

For the solution $(c, d)$ to the system of equations above, what is the value of $c + d$ ?

A) $-\dfrac{6}{5}$

B) $\dfrac{6}{5}$

C) $\dfrac{7}{5}$

D) $\dfrac{14}{5}$

**15**

Triangle $WXY$ is shown above. Which of the following is equal to the ratio $\dfrac{WZ}{WX}$ ?

A) $\dfrac{XZ}{XY}$

B) $\dfrac{XY}{XZ}$

C) $\dfrac{XZ}{YZ}$

D) $\dfrac{YZ}{XY}$

**16**

| $s$ | $t$ |
|---|---|
| $-2$ | $\dfrac{7}{2}$ |
| $-1$ | $\dfrac{19}{2}$ |
| $0$ | $\dfrac{31}{2}$ |
| $1$ | $\dfrac{43}{2}$ |
| $2$ | $\dfrac{55}{2}$ |

Which of the following equations relates $t$ to $s$ for the values in the table above?

A) $t = \dfrac{31}{2} \cdot (6)^s$

B) $t = 6s + \dfrac{31}{2}$

C) $t = \dfrac{1}{4} \cdot \left(\dfrac{31}{2}\right)^s$

D) $t = \dfrac{1}{6} s - 4$

CONTINUE

**Questions 17–19 refer to the following information.**

Note: Figure not drawn to scale.

When designing stacked displays of different types of crackers for sale, a manufacturer can use the box size formula $h + 3w = 30$, where $h$ is the height of each box of crackers, in inches, and $w$ is the width of each box of crackers, in inches. For any given stacked display, the height and width of each box displayed is the same.

The height of each level in the stacked display is equal to the height of the boxes of crackers in the display. For example, there are 2 levels in the figure above, each with a height of $h$. The total height of the stacked display is the sum of each level's height as shown in the figure.

**17**

Some cracker manufacturing companies require that, for wheat crackers, the box height must be at least 12 inches and the box width must be at least 3 inches. According to the box size formula, which of the following inequalities represents the set of all possible values for the box width that meets this size requirement?

A)  $6 \leq w \leq 12$

B)  $3 \leq w \leq 6$

C)  $w \geq 3$

D)  $0 \leq w \leq 3$

**18**

A manufacturer wants to use the box size formula to design a stacked display that has a total height of 7 feet, holds boxes with a height between 8 and 10 inches, and contains an even number of levels. With the manufacturer's constraints, which of the following must be the width, in inches, of the box? (1 foot = 12 inches)

A)  6.8

B)  7.2

C)  8.4

D)  10

**19**

Which of the following expresses the box width in terms of the box height?

A)  $w = \dfrac{1}{3}(30 - h)$

B)  $w = \dfrac{1}{3}(30 + h)$

C)  $w = -\dfrac{1}{3}(30 - h)$

D)  $w = -\dfrac{1}{3}(30 + h)$

**CONTINUE**

**20**

A study was done on the circumferences of different types of trees in a forest. A random sample of trees were measured and each tree was marked to guarantee that no tree was measured twice. The sample contained 250 red maple trees, of which 40% had a circumference less than 35 inches. Which of the following conclusions is best supported by the data?

A) The average circumference of all the trees in the forest is approximately 35 inches.

B) Approximately 40% of all the trees in the forest have circumferences less than 35 inches.

C) Approximately 40% of all the red maple trees in the forest have circumferences less than 35 inches.

D) The majority of all the trees in the forest have circumferences larger than 35 inches.

**21**

What is the product of the solutions to $(y + 4)(y - 0.3) = 0$ ?

A) −1.2

B) −3.7

C) 3.7

D) 1.2

**22**

Height versus Time for a Trampolining Gymnast

To break a height record in a trampolining competition, a gymnast repeatedly bounced on a trampoline using increasing amounts of force to achieve greater heights. The graph above represents the relationship between the time elapsed after the start of the jumps and the height of the gymnast above the trampoline. How many times was the gymnast at a height of 15 feet?

A) Three

B) Two

C) One

D) None

**23**

A writer's salary was $81.34 per assignment. After a promotion and a raise, her salary is now $88.51 per assignment. To the nearest tenth of a percent, by what percent did the writer's salary increase?

A) 7.2%

B) 8.1%

C) 8.8%

D) 9.3%

CONTINUE

**24**

| x | 1 | 3 | 7 |
|---|---|---|---|
| h(x) | −3 | 5 | 21 |

Some values of the linear function *g* are shown in the table above. What is the value of *h*(6) ?

A)  14

B)  15

C)  16

D)  17

**25**

Number of U.S. Presidents Aged 60 or
Younger when Inaugurated

| Age | Frequency |
|-----|-----------|
| 42 | 1 |
| 43 | 1 |
| 46 | 2 |
| 47 | 2 |
| 48 | 1 |
| 49 | 2 |
| 50 | 1 |
| 51 | 5 |
| 52 | 2 |
| 54 | 5 |
| 55 | 4 |
| 56 | 3 |
| 57 | 4 |
| 58 | 1 |
| 60 | 1 |

There are 35 U.S. Presidents who were 60 years old or younger when they were inaugurated, as shown in the table above. Based on the table, what was the median age for these 35 presidents?

A)  51

B)  52

C)  54

D)  55

**26**

In the *xy*-plane, the graph of $4x^2 + 20x + 4y^2 - 12y = 110$ is a circle. What is the radius of the circle?

A)  $\sqrt{55}$

B)  34

C)  12

D)  6

**27**

The resistor ratio *a*:*b* is the ratio of the current, in amperes, through two resistors connected in a parallel circuit. The ratio of resistance, in ohms, of two resistors connected in a parallel circuit is *b*:*a*. In the diagram below, the circuit is powered by a battery that passes current through Resistors X, Y, and Z.

If Resistor X has a resistance of 24 ohms, what is the resistance of Resistor Z ?

A)    8

B)   32

C)   72

D)  240

**CONTINUE**

**28**

Satellites orbit Earth so that it takes $P$ seconds to complete one orbit when the satellite is $a$ meters from the center of the planet, where $P = 36 \times 10^{-8}\ a\sqrt{a}$. Which of the following gives the approximate orbital ratio, in seconds per meter, for a satellite $a$ meters away from the center of Earth?

A) $6 \times 10^{-4}\ \sqrt{a}$

B) $\dfrac{36 \times 10^{-8}}{\sqrt{a}}$

C) $36 \times 10^{-8}\ a$

D) $36 \times 10^{-8}\ \sqrt{a}$

**29**

The scatterplot below shows the number of soft drinks sold, in thousands of gallons, by fast food restaurants over a 15-year period.

Soft Drinks Sold by Fast Food Restaurants

Of the following equations, which best models the data in the scatterplot?

A) $y = 2.138x^2 - 38.44x + 483.27$

B) $y = 2.138x^2 + 38.44x - 483.27$

C) $y = -2.138x^2 - 38.44x - 483.27$

D) $y = -2.138x^2 - 38.44x + 483.27$

**30**

On a number line, two different points are both 5 units from the point with coordinate −6. The solution to which of the following equations gives the coordinates of both points?

A) $\left|y - 6\right| = 5$

B) $\left|y + 6\right| = 5$

C) $\left|y - 5\right| = 6$

D) $\left|y + 5\right| = 6$

CONTINUE

## DIRECTIONS

**For questions 31–38**, solve the problem and enter your answer in the grid, as described below, on the answer sheet.

1. Although not required, it is suggested that you write your answer in the boxes at the top of the columns to help you fill in the circles accurately. You will receive credit only if the circles are filled in correctly.

2. Mark no more than one circle in any column.

3. No question has a negative answer.

4. Some problems may have more than one correct answer. In such cases, grid only one answer.

5. **Mixed numbers** such as $3\frac{1}{2}$ must be gridded as 3.5 or 7/2. (If [3 1 / 2] is entered into the grid, it will be interpreted as $\frac{31}{2}$, not as $3\frac{1}{2}$.)

6. **Decimal Answers:** If you obtain a decimal answer with more digits than the grid can accommodate, it may be either rounded or truncated, but it must fill the entire grid.

Acceptable ways to grid $\frac{2}{3}$ are:

Answer: 201 – either position is correct

**NOTE:** You may start your answers in any column, space permitting. Columns you don't need to use should be left blank.

CONTINUE →

**31**

A baking company produces ice cream cones, each with an internal radius at the opening of 4 centimeters and an internal height between 14.75 centimeters and 15 centimeters. What is one possible volume, rounded to the nearest cubic centimeter, of an ice cream cone produced by this company?

**32**

A group of coworkers decided to buy their boss a $400 birthday gift and to split the cost equally among themselves. When three of the coworkers decided not to contribute, those remaining still divided the $400 birthday gift equally, but each coworker's share of the cost increased by $30. How many coworkers were in the group originally?

**33**

$$3(4k - 10) - (26 + 5k) = 21$$

What value of $k$ satisfies the equation above?

**34**

The line with the equation $-\dfrac{3}{4}x + \dfrac{5}{6}y = 1$ is graphed in the $xy$-plane. What is the $y$-coordinate of the $y$-intercept of the line?

**CONTINUE**

**35**

| Height (feet) | | | | |
|---|---|---|---|---|
| Robert | 3.9 | 6.1 | 4.4 | 5.3 | 5.8 |
| Louis | $h$ | 4.5 | 5.7 | 4.2 | 3.8 |

Robert and Louis each have five rose bushes, and the heights of the bushes are shown in the table above. The mean of the heights of Robert's rose bushes is 0.3 feet greater than the mean of the heights of Louis's rose bushes. What is the value of $h$ ?

**36**

In the $xy$-plane, the graph of $y = -4x^2 + 25x$ intersects the graph of $y = x$ at the points $(0, 0)$ and $(c, c)$. What is the value of $c$ ?

**37**

John is analyzing the monthly expenditures of his business to determine whether his expenses exceeded his predicted budget. Of the money he spent this month, 10% was for office supplies, 40% was for employee salaries, 35% was for rent, and the remaining $450 was for utilities. How much more money did John spend on rent than on office supplies?

**38**

An elementary school had $k$ kindergarten students enrolled at the beginning of the 2011 school year. The number of kindergarten students enrolled tripled each year until 2014, when the elementary school had 540 kindergarten students enrolled. What is the value of $k$ ?

# STOP

If you finish before time is called, you may check your work on this section only.
Do not turn to any other section in the test.

No Test Material On This Page

CONTINUE

# SAT Essay

## DIRECTIONS

The essay gives you an opportunity to show how effectively you can read and comprehend a passage and write an essay analyzing the passage. In your essay you should demonstrate that you have read the passage carefully, present a clear and logical analysis, and use language precisely.

Your essay must be written on the lines provided in your answer sheet booklet; except for the planning page of the answer booklet, you will receive no other paper on which to write. You will have enough space if you write on every line, avoid wide margins, and keep your handwriting to a reasonable size. Remember that people who are not familiar with your handwriting will read what you write. Try to write or print so that what you are writing is legible to those readers.

**You have <u>50 minutes</u> to read the passage and write an essay in response to the prompt provided inside this booklet.**

## REMINDER

— Do not write your essay in this booklet. Only what you write on the lined pages of your answer booklet will be evaluated.

— An off-topic essay will not be evaluated.

CONTINUE →

As you read the passage below, consider how Brian Handwerk uses

- evidence, such as facts or examples, to support claims.
- reasoning to develop ideas and to connect claims and evidence.
- stylistic or persuasive elements, such as word choice or appeals to emotion, to add power to the ideas expressed.

**Adapted from Brian Handwerk, "Sustainable Earth: Water." Originally published by National Geographic News; reprinted with permission.**

1    Clean water is essential for life, but most people in the developed world don't think much about the water they use for drinking, food preparation, and sanitation. In developing nations, however, the search for safe drinking water can be a daily crisis. Millions of people die each year, most of them children, from largely preventable diseases caused by a lack of access to clean water and proper sanitation.

2    Sandra Postel, director of the Global Water Policy Project and the National Geographic Society's freshwater fellow, said freshwater scarcity presents a growing problem to be addressed during the United Nations Conference on Sustainable Development (Rio+20) in Brazil from June 20 to 22. "It manifests itself in the depletion of groundwater, and the drying up of rivers and lakes upon which people depend for irrigation to grow their food," she said. "The intersection of water scarcity, food security, and a changing climate on top of it all raises a suite of water concerns that urgently need to be addressed."

3    Much progress is possible. In fact, due to the dedicated efforts of governments and NGOs since the 1992 Earth Summit, safe drinking water has been made available to some 1.7 billion people around the world, with projects ranging from modern piped plumbing to rainwater collection and storage.

4    But an estimated 880 million people still don't have regular access to clean water. "And we haven't made nearly as much progress on sanitation," Postel said. "Something like 2.7 billion people are without adequate sanitation, so that challenge still looms very large." Policymakers will struggle to lower both numbers even as the planet's population rises by an expected three billion over the next 50 to 75 years.

5    About 5,000 children die each day due to preventable diarrheal diseases such as cholera and dysentery, which spread when people use contaminated water for drinking or cooking. A lack of water for personal hygiene leads to the spread of totally preventable ailments like trachoma, which has blinded some six million people.

6    Water woes also trap many low-income families in a cycle of poverty and poor education— and the poorest suffer most from lack of access to water. People who spend much of their time in ill health, caring for sick children, or laboriously collecting water at distances averaging 3.75 miles (6 kilometers) a day are denied educational and economic opportunities to better their lives.

**CONTINUE** ➡

7    Competition can be fierce for this precious commodity. Agriculture claims the lion's share of freshwater worldwide, soaking up some 70 percent, and industrial uses consume another 22 percent. Watersheds and aquifers don't respect political borders and nations don't always work together to share common resources—so water can be a frequent source of international conflict as well.

8    Day-by-day demand keeps growing, further draining water sources, from great rivers to underground aquifers. "We're going deeper into debt on our groundwater use," Postel said, "and that has very significant impacts for global water security. The rate of groundwater depletion has doubled since 1960."

9    Some of Earth's groundwater is fossil water, created when Earth's climate was far different. Today such water is as finite as petroleum. Other aquifers are renewable. "But we're pumping many of them out faster than precipitation is recharging them," Postel explained. "This is the case underneath the breadbasket of India, underneath the wheat and cornfields on the plains of north China, under California's Central Valley. We need to bring withdrawals into balance with recharge."

10   Humanity's growing thirst also poses a major problem for aquatic ecosystems. "When we take water from rivers, floodplains, and watersheds, those ecosystems bear the brunt of water scarcity and begin to be degraded or disappear," she said. "And that also creates a cost to us, not just to nature, because we also depend upon those ecosystems."

11   The silver lining, Postel noted, is that many opportunities exist to use the water we do have more productively. Change begins with more efficient management of water resources.

12   "Seventy percent of all the water we use globally is for agriculture, so that's where we first have to become a lot more efficient through methods like drip irrigation and growing crops that are more suitable to the local climate," Postel said. "We still have too few incentives for farmers to use water more efficiently. Farmers are good businesspeople; they respond to incentives that affect their bottom line."

13   The United National General Assembly has recognized "the right to safe and clean drinking water and sanitation as a human right that is essential for the full enjoyment of life and all human rights." Making that right become a universal reality, and providing each person on the planet with affordable access to the 20 to 50 liters of daily water required to sustain life, is a clear goal for the decades ahead.

---

Write an essay in which you explain how Brian Handwerk builds an argument to persuade his audience to fight to conserve freshwater. In your essay, analyze how Handwerk uses one or more of the features listed in the box above (or features of your own choice) to strengthen the logic and persuasiveness of his argument. Be sure that your analysis focuses on the most relevant features of the passage.

Your essay should not explain whether you agree with Handwerk's claims, but rather explain how Handwerk builds an argument to persuade his audience.

---

**END OF TEST**

**DO NOT RETURN TO A PREVIOUS SECTION.**

The Princeton Review®

Completely darken bubbles with a No. 2 pencil. If you make a mistake, be sure to erase mark completely. Erase all stray marks.

**1.**

YOUR NAME: _____
(Print)     Last          First          M.I.

SIGNATURE: _____     DATE: ___ / ___ / ___

HOME ADDRESS: _____
(Print)          Number and Street

_____
City          State          Zip Code

PHONE NO.: _____
(Print)

**IMPORTANT:** Please fill in these boxes exactly as shown on the back cover of your test book.

**2. TEST FORM**

**6. DATE OF BIRTH**

| Month | Day | Year |
|-------|-----|------|
| ○ JAN |     |      |
| ○ FEB | ⓪ ⓪ | ⓪ ⓪ |
| ○ MAR | ① ① | ① ① |
| ○ APR | ② ② | ② ② |
| ○ MAY | ③ ③ | ③ ③ |
| ○ JUN | ④ ④ | ④ ④ |
| ○ JUL | ⑤ ⑤ | ⑤ ⑤ |
| ○ AUG | ⑥ ⑥ | ⑥ ⑥ |
| ○ SEP | ⑦ ⑦ | ⑦ ⑦ |
| ○ OCT | ⑧ ⑧ | ⑧ ⑧ |
| ○ NOV | ⑨ ⑨ | ⑨ ⑨ |
| ○ DEC |     |      |

**3. TEST CODE**     **4. REGISTRATION NUMBER**

**7. SEX**
○ MALE
○ FEMALE

The Princeton Review®

**5. YOUR NAME**

First 4 letters of last name | FIRST INIT | MID INIT

**Test 8**

Start with number 1 for each new section.
If a section has fewer questions than answer spaces, leave the extra answer spaces blank.

## Section 1—Reading

1. Ⓐ Ⓑ Ⓒ Ⓓ
2. Ⓐ Ⓑ Ⓒ Ⓓ
3. Ⓐ Ⓑ Ⓒ Ⓓ
4. Ⓐ Ⓑ Ⓒ Ⓓ
5. Ⓐ Ⓑ Ⓒ Ⓓ
6. Ⓐ Ⓑ Ⓒ Ⓓ
7. Ⓐ Ⓑ Ⓒ Ⓓ
8. Ⓐ Ⓑ Ⓒ Ⓓ
9. Ⓐ Ⓑ Ⓒ Ⓓ
10. Ⓐ Ⓑ Ⓒ Ⓓ
11. Ⓐ Ⓑ Ⓒ Ⓓ
12. Ⓐ Ⓑ Ⓒ Ⓓ
13. Ⓐ Ⓑ Ⓒ Ⓓ
14. Ⓐ Ⓑ Ⓒ Ⓓ
15. Ⓐ Ⓑ Ⓒ Ⓓ
16. Ⓐ Ⓑ Ⓒ Ⓓ
17. Ⓐ Ⓑ Ⓒ Ⓓ
18. Ⓐ Ⓑ Ⓒ Ⓓ
19. Ⓐ Ⓑ Ⓒ Ⓓ
20. Ⓐ Ⓑ Ⓒ Ⓓ
21. Ⓐ Ⓑ Ⓒ Ⓓ
22. Ⓐ Ⓑ Ⓒ Ⓓ
23. Ⓐ Ⓑ Ⓒ Ⓓ
24. Ⓐ Ⓑ Ⓒ Ⓓ
25. Ⓐ Ⓑ Ⓒ Ⓓ
26. Ⓐ Ⓑ Ⓒ Ⓓ
27. Ⓐ Ⓑ Ⓒ Ⓓ
28. Ⓐ Ⓑ Ⓒ Ⓓ
29. Ⓐ Ⓑ Ⓒ Ⓓ
30. Ⓐ Ⓑ Ⓒ Ⓓ
31. Ⓐ Ⓑ Ⓒ Ⓓ
32. Ⓐ Ⓑ Ⓒ Ⓓ
33. Ⓐ Ⓑ Ⓒ Ⓓ
34. Ⓐ Ⓑ Ⓒ Ⓓ
35. Ⓐ Ⓑ Ⓒ Ⓓ
36. Ⓐ Ⓑ Ⓒ Ⓓ
37. Ⓐ Ⓑ Ⓒ Ⓓ
38. Ⓐ Ⓑ Ⓒ Ⓓ
39. Ⓐ Ⓑ Ⓒ Ⓓ
40. Ⓐ Ⓑ Ⓒ Ⓓ
41. Ⓐ Ⓑ Ⓒ Ⓓ
42. Ⓐ Ⓑ Ⓒ Ⓓ
43. Ⓐ Ⓑ Ⓒ Ⓓ
44. Ⓐ Ⓑ Ⓒ Ⓓ
45. Ⓐ Ⓑ Ⓒ Ⓓ
46. Ⓐ Ⓑ Ⓒ Ⓓ
47. Ⓐ Ⓑ Ⓒ Ⓓ
48. Ⓐ Ⓑ Ⓒ Ⓓ
49. Ⓐ Ⓑ Ⓒ Ⓓ
50. Ⓐ Ⓑ Ⓒ Ⓓ
51. Ⓐ Ⓑ Ⓒ Ⓓ
52. Ⓐ Ⓑ Ⓒ Ⓓ

## Section 2—Writing and Language Skills

1. Ⓐ Ⓑ Ⓒ Ⓓ
2. Ⓐ Ⓑ Ⓒ Ⓓ
3. Ⓐ Ⓑ Ⓒ Ⓓ
4. Ⓐ Ⓑ Ⓒ Ⓓ
5. Ⓐ Ⓑ Ⓒ Ⓓ
6. Ⓐ Ⓑ Ⓒ Ⓓ
7. Ⓐ Ⓑ Ⓒ Ⓓ
8. Ⓐ Ⓑ Ⓒ Ⓓ
9. Ⓐ Ⓑ Ⓒ Ⓓ
10. Ⓐ Ⓑ Ⓒ Ⓓ
11. Ⓐ Ⓑ Ⓒ Ⓓ
12. Ⓐ Ⓑ Ⓒ Ⓓ
13. Ⓐ Ⓑ Ⓒ Ⓓ
14. Ⓐ Ⓑ Ⓒ Ⓓ
15. Ⓐ Ⓑ Ⓒ Ⓓ
16. Ⓐ Ⓑ Ⓒ Ⓓ
17. Ⓐ Ⓑ Ⓒ Ⓓ
18. Ⓐ Ⓑ Ⓒ Ⓓ
19. Ⓐ Ⓑ Ⓒ Ⓓ
20. Ⓐ Ⓑ Ⓒ Ⓓ
21. Ⓐ Ⓑ Ⓒ Ⓓ
22. Ⓐ Ⓑ Ⓒ Ⓓ
23. Ⓐ Ⓑ Ⓒ Ⓓ
24. Ⓐ Ⓑ Ⓒ Ⓓ
25. Ⓐ Ⓑ Ⓒ Ⓓ
26. Ⓐ Ⓑ Ⓒ Ⓓ
27. Ⓐ Ⓑ Ⓒ Ⓓ
28. Ⓐ Ⓑ Ⓒ Ⓓ
29. Ⓐ Ⓑ Ⓒ Ⓓ
30. Ⓐ Ⓑ Ⓒ Ⓓ
31. Ⓐ Ⓑ Ⓒ Ⓓ
32. Ⓐ Ⓑ Ⓒ Ⓓ
33. Ⓐ Ⓑ Ⓒ Ⓓ
34. Ⓐ Ⓑ Ⓒ Ⓓ
35. Ⓐ Ⓑ Ⓒ Ⓓ
36. Ⓐ Ⓑ Ⓒ Ⓓ
37. Ⓐ Ⓑ Ⓒ Ⓓ
38. Ⓐ Ⓑ Ⓒ Ⓓ
39. Ⓐ Ⓑ Ⓒ Ⓓ
40. Ⓐ Ⓑ Ⓒ Ⓓ
41. Ⓐ Ⓑ Ⓒ Ⓓ
42. Ⓐ Ⓑ Ⓒ Ⓓ
43. Ⓐ Ⓑ Ⓒ Ⓓ
44. Ⓐ Ⓑ Ⓒ Ⓓ

Completely darken bubbles with a No. 2 pencil.  If you make a mistake, be sure to erase mark completely.  Erase all stray marks.

**Test 8**   Start with number 1 for each new section.
If a section has fewer questions than answer spaces, leave the extra answer spaces blank.

## Section 3—Mathematics: No Calculator

## Section 4—Mathematics: Calculator

# Chapter 18
# Practice Test 8:
# Answers and
# Explanations

# PRACTICE TEST 8 ANSWER KEY

| Section 1: Reading | | Section 2: Writing & Language | | Section 3: Math (No Calculator) | | Section 4: Math (Calculator) | |
|---|---|---|---|---|---|---|---|
| 1. C | 27. A | 1. C | 23. B | 1. A | 11. B | 1. C | 20. C |
| 2. D | 28. C | 2. B | 24. C | 2. A | 12. C | 2. D | 21. A |
| 3. C | 29. A | 3. A | 25. C | 3. D | 13. C | 3. B | 22. B |
| 4. A | 30. C | 4. D | 26. B | 4. D | 14. D | 4. A | 23. C |
| 5. B | 31. A | 5. D | 27. B | 5. B | 15. C | 5. C | 24. D |
| 6. A | 32. C | 6. B | 28. A | 6. A | 16. 16 | 6. D | 25. C |
| 7. D | 33. C | 7. D | 29. D | 7. A | 17. 1, 2, | 7. B | 26. D |
| 8. B | 34. B | 8. B | 30. A | 8. B | 3, 4, | 8. C | 27. A |
| 9. D | 35. A | 9. A | 31. A | 9. D | 6, or | 9. C | 28. D |
| 10. B | 36. D | 10. A | 32. D | 10. A | 12 | 10. A | 29. A |
| 11. C | 37. D | 11. D | 33. D | | | 11. B | 30. B |
| 12. B | 38. B | 12. B | 34. D | | 18. $\frac{1}{24}$, | 12. C | 31. 247, |
| 13. A | 39. C | 13. B | 35. B | | .041, | 13. A | 248, |
| 14. A | 40. C | 14. D | 36. C | | or | 14. D | 249, |
| 15. B | 41. D | 15. A | 37. C | | .042 | 15. A | 250, |
| 16. A | 42. A | 16. A | 38. B | | | 16. B | or |
| 17. D | 43. D | 17. C | 39. D | | 19. $\frac{49}{8}$, | 17. B | 251 |
| 18. D | 44. D | 18. B | 40. B | | 6.12, | 18. B | 32. 8 |
| 19. C | 45. C | 19. C | 41. C | | or | 19. A | 33. 11 |
| 20. A | 46. B | 20. D | 42. B | | 6.13 | | 34. $\frac{6}{5}$ |
| 21. D | 47. C | 21. C | 43. A | | 20. $\frac{5}{2}$ or | | or |
| 22. B | 48. D | 22. D | 44. A | | 2.5 | | 1.2 |
| 23. D | 49. D | | | | | | 35. 5.8 |
| 24. B | 50. A | | | | | | 36. 6 |
| 25. C | 51. A | | | | | | 37. 750 |
| 26. C | 52. C | | | | | | 38. 20 |

For self-scoring assessment tables, please turn to page 957.

# PRACTICE TEST 8 EXPLANATIONS

## Section 1: Reading

1.   **C**   This question asks why the author uses the image of the *waters of the Jordan*. Use the given line reference to find the window to read. The answer should come from a window of approximately lines 1–10. The passage states that *The ever-increasing current of Christmas shoppers flowed on. Now and then it rolled up, like the waters of the Jordan*. The image is used to describe the movement of the crowd. Find an answer that matches this prediction. Choice (A) includes the word *never*, which is extreme language. The passage does not suggest that the crowd *will never ebb*. Eliminate (A). Choice (B) can be eliminated because there is no indication in the passage that *the little woman was drowning in the throng*. Choice (C) matches the prediction, so hang on to it. The image of the *waters of Jordan* is used to describe the movement of the crowd, not the movements of one person. Eliminate (D). The correct answer is (C).

2.   **D**   This question asks for the meaning of the word *caught* as it is used in the text. Cross out the word, and use the surrounding information to fill in another word that makes sense based on the passage. Use context clues to fill in another word that makes sense. The text says the woman *caught the scent of fresh-cut flowers.* In other words, the woman "became aware of" the scent. Find an answer that means something similar to becoming aware of. The only answer that matches this meaning is (D). The other answers might initially look attractive because they all relate to the word "caught," but none of the other three answers match the context of the passage. The correct answer is (D).

3.   **C**   This question asks about supporting the claim that *the shabby little woman was at first excited by the tall young girl*. Use the line references in the answer choices. The lines for (A) state that the shabby little woman *caught the scent of fresh-cut flowers and looked up into the eyes of a tall young girl in a white-plumed velvet hat, with a bunch of English violets in her brown mink fur.* These lines are an objective description of the young girl. There is no indication in these lines of how the woman feels. Eliminate (A). The lines for (B) state that *As their glances met, the shabby little woman checked a start, and half-defensively dropped her lids.* This description of the woman notes that she is startled and somewhat defensive. However, the question asks which lines show that the woman was excited. Eliminate (B). The lines for (C) state that *The thrill of response that set the woman's pulses throbbing died suddenly.* The phrase *The thrill of response that sent the woman's pulses throbbing* indicates that the woman was initially excited. Keep (C). The lines for (D) describe how the woman saw herself. These lines do not relate to how the woman felt at meeting the tall young girl. Eliminate (D). The correct answer is (C).

4.   **A**   This question asks why the woman invites the visitor to come in. Use chronology to find the answer. The answer to question 3 was in the third paragraph, and the line reference for question 5 is in the seventh paragraph. Therefore, scan between the third and seventh paragraph

for a description of the woman inviting a visitor. The fifth paragraph provides the following description. *"Come in," invited the woman, expecting some famine-pressed neighbor for a spoonful of coffee or a drawing of tea.* Look for an answer that matches the idea of the woman *expecting* someone in need. Choice (A) matches that idea, so keep it. Choice (B) can be eliminated because, though she does invite this person in, there's no evidence that the woman allows everyone in. Eliminate (C) because there is no indication that the woman expected *the young girl to drop by.* The passage also does not suggest that the woman *cannot see,* so eliminate (D). The correct answer is (A).

5. **B** This question asks about the purpose of the girl's comments in lines 51–58. The passage describes the young girl as saying *"I've such a silly excuse for coming.... I noticed you had a rare fur-piece...and I want to ask a very great favor of you. Now please don't be shocked—I've been ransacking the city for something like it, and...I should like to buy it of you."* Find an answer that matches the idea of the girl explaining why she has come to the apartment. Choice (A) can be eliminated: while the girl seeks to persuade the woman to sell her the fur, there is no indication that she wants *a discount.* Choice (B) is a solid paraphrase of the prediction, so keep it. The girl is not laughing at the shabby woman, nor does she demand *the shabby woman surrender her wrap,* so (C) and (D) can both be eliminated. The correct answer is (B).

6. **A** The question asks why the girl uses the word *ransacking.* In the passage the young girl says *"I noticed you had a rare fur-piece...and I want to ask a very great favor of you. Now please don't be shocked—I've been ransacking the city for something like it, and...I should like to buy it of you."* In context, *ransacking the city* means that the girl has been looking everywhere in the city for a similar rare fur piece. Find an answer that matches this prediction. Only (A) matches the context of the passage. The girl has searched everywhere in the city for the same fur piece so her search can be described as *comprehensive.* The correct answer is (A).

7. **D** This question asks why *the shabby woman initially declines to sell the fur.* In lines 72–73, the women first expresses confusion about the girl's request, but then says, *"I can't, it ain't worth…"* The woman doesn't think the fur is worth anything. Eliminate (A) because the question asks about the woman's thoughts, not the young girl's. Choice (B) has nothing to do with the passage, so eliminate it. Choice (C) does mention the worth of the piece, but there is no discussion about the actual price. Eliminate (C). Choice (D) is a solid paraphrase of the prediction. The correct answer is (D).

8. **B** Because this is the second question in a paired set, look at the lines used to answer question 7. The correct answer is (B).

9. **D** This question asks how the shabby woman felt after the girl's departure. Use chronology to find the answer. The answer to question 8 came from lines 72–73. Start reading after these lines to find how the woman felt. According to the passage, *As she sat huddled on the cot, warmth and vitality glowed within her, kindled by the memory of a recent kindly human touch.* Find an answer

that matches the prediction. The only answer that matches the positive feeling that the woman has after the young girl leaves is (D), *warmth*. The correct answer is (D).

10.  **B**  This question asks what the purpose of the last paragraph is. According to the last paragraph, *It was unusual to sell expensive furs to such a customer. But…[i]n this case, the shabby little woman was prepared. She produced three crisp ten-dollar bills…and two dollars more from the savings in her worn little purse.* Find an answer that matches the idea of the purchase being different than what normally happened. Choice (A) is a detail. Although the first sentence of the paragraph states that *it was unusual to sell expensive furs to such a customer*, this is not the purpose of the paragraph as a whole. Eliminate (A). Choice (B) matches the prediction, so keep it. Choice (C) uses extreme language. While the last paragraph describes the shabby woman as *triumphantly* leaving the store, there is no indication in the passage that the purchase was the shabby woman's *greatest triumph*. Eliminate (C). Choice (D) does not match the prediction. According to the passage, the sale of the furs to the shabby woman is described as *unusual*. Therefore, the last paragraph does not illustrate how servants *go Christmas shopping*. Eliminate (D). The correct answer is (B).

11.  **C**  The question asks what Churchill implies about *those who advocate for a Socialist State*. Notice that this is the first question in a paired set, so it can be done in tandem with question 12. Start with the best evidence answer choices for Q12. The lines for (12A) state that *a Socialist policy is abhorrent to the British ideas of freedom*. While it may be tempting to connect this answer with (11A), this is the opinion of Churchill and not a quality of *those who advocate for a Socialist state*. Eliminate (12A). In the lines for (12B), Churchill states that *Although [Socialist policy] is now put forward in the main by people who have a good grounding in the Liberalism and Radicalism of the early part of this century, there can be no doubt that Socialism is inseparably interwoven with Totalitarianism and the abject worship of the State*. This supports (11C). Those who advocate for socialism have a foundational knowledge of liberalism and radicalism, which are positions counter to socialism. Connect (12B) with (11C). The lines for (12C) say that *Socialism is, in its essence an attack not only upon British enterprise, but upon the right of the ordinary man or woman to breathe freely*. These lines do not discuss a quality that is possessed by *those who advocate for a Socialist State*. Eliminate (12C). The lines for (12D) say that *A Free Parliament is odious to the Socialist doctrinaire*. This does not support any of the answers in Q11. Eliminate (12D). The correct answers are (11C) and (12B).

12.  **B**  (See explanation above.)

13.  **A**  This question asks for the meaning of the word *hunger* as it is used in the text. Cross out the word, and use the surrounding information to fill in another word that makes sense based on the passage. In the context of the passage, *Socialists* desire controls of every kind. Look for an answer choice that means something like "desire." Only (A), *yearn,* means the same thing as "desire." Both (C), *need,* and (D), *starve,* may seem like tempting answers since they are definitions for the word *hunger*. However, these meanings do not work in the context with which *hunger* is used in the passage. The correct answer is (A).

14. **A** The question asks about the primary purpose of the statement in lines 29–31. According to Churchill, *no Socialist system can be established without a political police. Many of those who are advocating Socialism or voting Socialist today will be horrified at this idea.* Find an answer that matches this prediction. Churchill's opponents are those who are advocating socialism. However, according to Churchill the socialist system requires a political police, which is a *broadly undesirable outcome.* Keep (A). Choice (B) might initially look attractive because being *horrified* would definitely indicate *not prefer[ring]*, but those lines do not *[explain] a situation.* Eliminate (B). Choice (C) can be eliminated because the lines do not highlight a fear held by supporters of socialism. Eliminate (D) because these lines do not mention what the impact of not voting for the socialist party would be. The correct answer is (A).

15. **B** This question asks for the meaning of the word *grip* as it is used in the text. Cross out the word, and use the surrounding information to fill in another word that makes sense based on the passage. The word *grip* is used in the context of a *mighty organism* that has got the common people *in its grip.* The mighty organism is socialism. According to Churchill, socialism would *nip opinion in the bud; it would stop criticism as it reared its head, and it would gather all the power to the supreme party and the party leaders....* In other words, socialism amasses power to control the common people. *Grip* in the context of the passage means *control,* which is (B). Both (C), *squeeze,* and (D), *handle,* may seem like tempting answers. However, both of these offer a different definition of *grip* than the context in which the word is used. The correct answer is (B).

16. **A** This question asks what Einstein suggests about a *planned economy.* Notice that this is the first question in a paired set, so it can be done in tandem with question 17. Start with the best evidence answer choices for Q17. The lines for (17A) state that *under existing conditions, private capitalists inevitably control, directly or indirectly, the main sources of information.* Although that is a discussion of the media and might seem to support (16D), the lines do not discuss a *planned economy.* Eliminate (17A). In the lines for (17B), Einstein states that *This crippling of individuals I consider the worst evil of capitalism.* Einstein is not talking about a *planned economy.* Eliminate (17B). In the lines for (17C), Einstein argues for the establishment of a *socialist economy, accompanied by an educational system which would be oriented to social goals.* This answer does not support any of the answers in Q16. Eliminate (17C). The lines for (17D) state that *A planned economy as such may be accompanied by the complete enslavement of the individual.* This supports (16A). Connect (17D) with (16A). The correct answers are (16A) and (17D).

17. **D** (See explanation above.)

18. **D** This question asks about the primary purpose of each passage. Because this is a general question about both passages, it should be done after all the questions for each individual passage. Passage 1 argues against socialist policy and goes on to describe what a socialist state is like. In the last paragraph of the passage, Churchill states that a socialist government *would nip opinion in the bud; it would stop criticism as it reared its head, and it would gather all the power to the*

*supreme party and the party leaders, rising like stately pinnacles above their vast bureaucracies of Civil servants, no longer servants and no longer civil.* Passage 2 describes the capitalist society. It argues that in a capitalist society *Private capital tends to become concentrated in few hands,* which makes it *extremely difficult...for the individual citizen to come to objective conclusions and to make intelligent use of his political rights.* In the last paragraph, Einstein argues that the only way to eliminate the evils of capitalism is *through the establishment of the socialist economy.* Find an answer that matches both passages. Choice (A) does not match Passage 1: according to Churchill, socialism provides no benefits. Choice (B) does not match Passage 2: Einstein does not debate whether *free choice is more supported by socialism or capitalism.* Choice (C) does not match either passage: Neither passage discusses *a developing nation.* Choice (D) matches both passages: Churchill discusses the impact of socialism on the individual, and Einstein discusses the impact of capitalism on the individual. The correct answer is (D).

19. **C** This question asks how *Churchill would consider Einstein's question in lines 99–102.* Because this question asks about both passages, it should be done after all the questions that ask about the individual passages. In the lines cited, Einstein asks *how is it possible, in view of the far-reaching centralization of political and economic power, to prevent bureaucracy from becoming all-powerful and overweening.* In Passage 1, it is clear that Churchill is entirely opposed to a socialist-style centralization of political and economic power, and he argues that a socialist government would *gather all the power to the supreme party and the party leaders, rising like stately pinnacles above their vast bureaucracies of Civil servants, no longer servants and no longer civil.* Find an answer that is consistent with what Churchill says. Choice (A) uses extreme language. While Churchill finds socialism appalling, he doesn't find the consideration of socialism appalling. Eliminate (A). Churchill does not find socialism a *plausible suggestion.* Eliminate (B). Churchill does argue that one of the reasons to reject socialism is the centralization of power. Keep (C). Churchill is completely opposed to socialism and therefore would not consider the question a fair one that would require *open discussion.* Eliminate (D). The correct answer is (C).

20. **A** This question asks about the *similarity in the perspectives of Churchill and Einstein toward an independent legislature.* Because this question asks about both passages, it should be done after all the questions that ask about the individual passages. In Passage 1, Churchill describes the socialist state as being tyrannical. He states that *A Free Parliament is odious to the Socialist doctrinaire.* Given that Churchill is opposed to all things socialist, it can be inferred that Churchill is in favor of a free parliament. In the last paragraph of Passage 2, Einstein is concerned about preventing a socialist bureaucracy from *becoming all-powerful and overweening.* He wants the rights of the individual to be protected. Therefore, the authors of both passages are in favor of an independent legislature. The only answer that aligns with the idea that both authors favor an independent legislature is (A). The correct answer is (A).

21. **D** This question asks about the point of view of the passage. Since this is a general question, it should be answered after the specific questions. The passage begins by stating that *the United States is setting new milestones that suggest a...shift in its energy economy* and the majority of the

passage discusses these milestones, before introducing the contrasting information that *some of the world's major carbon emitters...have done little to curb fossil fuel use.* Look for an answer choice that matches this information. The passage is neither *advocating for a specific policy* nor *protesting technological changes*, so eliminate (A) and (C). While the author does discuss new power sources, effects of data moving forward are not evaluated; eliminate (B). *Assessing the implications of certain trends* matches the discussion of the United States' clean energy milestones in contrast with the actions of the major carbon emitters. The correct answer is (D).

22.   **B**   This question asks for the meaning of the word *sparked* as it is used in the text. Cross out the word, and use the surrounding information to fill in another word that makes sense based on the passage. The text says that *in recent years, the U.S. oil and natural gas boom has sparked much talk about an American energy renaissance.* Therefore, *sparked* must mean something like "kicked off" or "started." *Flickered* and *brightened* both refer to the electrical meanings of "sparked," so eliminate (A) and (D). *Begun* matches "kicked off" or "started," so keep (B). *Scrapped* means "thrown away," so eliminate (C). The correct answer is (B).

23.   **D**   This question asks what can be inferred about U.S. energy sources prior to 2015. Since this is the first question in a paired set, it can be done in tandem with Q24. Look at the answer choices for Q24 first. The lines for (24A) say that *renewable energy added the most new power to the electric grid,* but refer to data from 2015, not prior to it; eliminate (24A). The lines for (24B) indicate that the U.S. energy mix is *increasingly efficient and clean,* following the opening of the paragraph stating that the information in this section pertains to recent years, which would be prior to 2015. This information matches (23D), indicating *that, prior to 2015, U.S. energy sources were producing more carbon emissions, making those sources inefficient and dirty by comparison.* Connect (24B) and (23D). The lines for (24C) mention only *that the economy can grow without increasing energy use,* but have no correlation to *U.S. energy sources*; eliminate (24C). The lines in (24D) provide information regarding *a record number of [coal-fired power plant] closures,* which pertains to *U.S. energy sources prior to 2015.* However, coal is not mentioned in any of the answer choices for Q23, so eliminate (24D). The correct answers are (23D) and (24B).

24.   **B**   (See explanation above.)

25.   **C**   This question asks what various energy source prices will likely do, according to the passage. Although there isn't a line reference, use chronology to look for the lead word *prices.* The third paragraph states that *prices for oil, wind and solar have plunged,* before continuing to say that *the most recent U.S. short-term forecast...sees oil falling for the next two years but solar and wind rising.* The correct choice will match this prediction. *Reach record highs and record lows, plunge significantly across the board,* and *lead to power plant closures* do not match the prediction; eliminate (A), (B), and (D). *Experience some variance from source to source* matches the prediction. The correct answer is (C).

26. **C** This question *asks which choice provides the best evidence for the answer to the previous question.* Because Q25 was a specific question, simply look at the lines used to answer it. The evidence came from lines 22–24. The correct answer is (C).

27. **A** This question asks for the meaning of the word *slated* as it is used in the text. Cross out the word, and use the surrounding information to fill in another word that makes sense based on the passage. The passage states that *developers sought to take advantage of a federal tax credit slated to expire.* From this information it can be predicted that *slated* means something like "about" or "ready." *Scheduled* fits this prediction, so keep (A). Of the choices, *billed, reserved,* and *listed* do not match the prediction, so eliminate (B), (C), and (D). The correct answer is (A).

28. **C** This question asks what purpose the last sentence of the passage mainly serves. The last paragraph says *that burning the currently known fossil fuels would increase global average temperatures by at least 10° to 15° Fahrenheit* and *that whether the voluntary agreements in the UN climate accord, reached in December in Paris, can help developing countries adopt cleaner energy "will be determined in the coming years and decades."* Thus, the main idea of the last paragraph is a warning about the potential consequences of continuing to burn fossil fuels and a reminder that the ultimate outcome is not yet decided. While there is a forecast regarding the outcome of continued fossil fuel usage, *likely to occur* is too extreme for what is only a possible outcome; eliminate (A). The paragraph does not *recommend change* or *insist all nations follow through on an agreement,* so eliminate (B) and (D). *Indicate that more choices remain to be made* matches the prediction. The correct answer is (C).

29. **A** This question asks *which type of fuel generated the least electricity in the same year that the most coal plant retirements were completed,* and that this is *according to Figures 1 and 2.* First begin by locating the year with the most coal plant retirements in Figure 1. According to Figure 1, there were 11 coal plant retirements completed in 2015, surpassing the individual total of any other year. Then, look at the electricity generation by fuel trend lines for the year 2015 in Figure 2. In 2015 renewables generated the least amount of electricity. The correct answer is (A).

30. **C** This question asks when *electricity generated by coal first [equaled] electricity generated by natural gas,* and that this is *according to Figure 2.* Locate the trend lines for coal and natural gas in Figure 2. Then, identify where the two lines first intersect. They first intersect in 2015. The correct answer is (C).

31. **A** This question asks for the *main purpose of the passage.* Because this is a general question, it should be done after all the specific questions. Beginning from the opening sentence, the passage states that the *mass media play a role in the construction of environmental issues and problems.* The second paragraph states that *when it comes to coverage of global warming, balanced reporting can be a form of informational bias.* The correct answer will reflect this information. *Question the journalistic ideal of balanced coverage regarding scientific reporting* matches the prediction, so keep (A). The passage does not focus solely on the *bias of scientific journalists,* so eliminate (B).

There is no analysis of *the antagonistic relationship between the elite press and local news outlets*, so eliminate (C). The *ideals of objectivity* are not just discussed, they are questioned; eliminate (D). The correct answer is (A).

32.  **C**  The question asks what expectation *reporters covering controversy face*. Notice that this is the first question in a paired set, so it can be done in tandem with question 33. Start with the best evidence answer choices for Q33. The lines for (33A), (33B), and (33D) talk about *the mass media*, *journalistic norms and values*, and *scientific consensus*, respectively, but not specifically *reporters*; eliminate (33A), (33B), and (33D). The fact that *journalistic fairness requires reporters who write about a controversy to present competing points of view* in the lines for (33C) matches the idea that *reporters should offer equal consideration to opposing perspectives*. The correct answers are (32C) and (33C).

33.  **C**  (See explanation above.)

34.  **B**  This question asks for the meaning of the word *particular* as it is used in the text. Cross out the word, and use the surrounding information to fill in another word that makes sense based on the passage. The passage states that *a remarkably high level of scientific consensus has emerged on these two issues*. In the previous sentence, *these two issues* are defined as the facts *that global warming is a serious problem that has anthropogenic influences, and that it must be addressed immediately*. In the context of the passage *particular* means something like "defined" or "exact." *Local* can mean "exact," but only in reference to place or position; eliminate (A). *Specific* means "defined" or "exact," so keep (B). *Appropriate* means "suitable," not exact; eliminate (C). *Peculiar* means "strange" or "different," so eliminate (D). The correct answer is (B).

35.  **A**  The question asks why the authors include the quotation in lines 54–56. Use the given line reference to find the window. The sentence prior to the quotation says that *a remarkably high level of scientific consensus has emerged on these two particular issues*. This references the issues from the prior sentence *that global warming is a serious problem that has anthropogenic influences, and that it must be addressed immediately*, so it can be predicted that the quotation highlights this *remarkably high level of scientific consensus*. This high level of *consensus of scientific authorities* does *contrast...with the reporting in prestige publications*, as mentioned in the beginning of the fifth paragraph, so keep (A). The quote does not *propose models for accurate reporting*, *criticize readers*, nor *demonstrate the importance of scientific facts*; eliminate (B), (C), and (D). The correct answer is (A).

36.  **D**  The question asks what *the work of journalists may involve*. Notice that this is the first question in a paired set, so it can be done in tandem with question 37. Start with the best evidence answer choices for Q37. The lines for (37A) discuss *prestige-press coverage of global warming* as *a social relationship between people*. The only paired answer discussing social aspects of journalists' work is (36C), but it specifically mentions an unsupported claim about the journalists *relating socially to interview subjects*; eliminate (37A). The lines for (37B) and (37C) are related to concerned scientists and scientific discourse, not *the work of journalists*; eliminate

(37B) and (37C). The lines for (37D) indicate that journalists engage in a *continuous juggling act [that] often mitigates against meaningful, accurate, and urgent coverage of the issue of global warming*. This provides evidence to support (36D), stating that the *work of journalists* is *prioritizing balanced reporting of viewpoints over covering the facts*. The correct answers are (36D) and (37D).

37. **D** (See explanation above.)

38. **B** This question asks for the meaning of the word *curb* as it is used in the text. Cross out the word, and use the surrounding information to fill in another word that makes sense based on the passage. The passage states that a *disconnection has played a significant role in the lack of concerted international action to* do something to the *practices that contribute to global warming*. From the overall passage, it is known that journalism has not helped to stop global warming. Therefore, *curb* must mean something like "stop" or "restrict" in the context of the passage. Neither *bend* nor *edge* matches this prediction, so eliminate (A) and (D). *Limit* means "restrict," so keep (B). *Delay* is a close answer that means "slow down" rather than "stop" or "restrict," so eliminate (C). The correct answer is (B).

39. **C** The question asks *in what year was the coverage of action tactics regarding global warming most similar,* based on the table. Check the answer choices against the table, looking for a year where the three lines are closest together. In 1989, the lines for balanced accounts and immediate/mandatory action are close together, but the line for cautious/voluntary action is not; eliminate (A). In 1993 and 1999, the lines for cautious/voluntary action and immediate/mandatory action are close together, but the line for balanced accounts is not; eliminate (B) and (D). In 1994, all three lines, for balanced accounts, immediate/mandatory action, and cautious/voluntary action, are close together. The correct answer is (C).

40. **C** The question asks *which statement is best supported by information in the graph*. Check the answer choices against the table. *Between 1989 and 1999, the number of "cautious/voluntary" accounts of global warming* did decline *dramatically*, but then never *rose significantly*; eliminate (A). *Between 1995 and 2000, the number of "immediate/mandatory" accounts of global warming* may not have varied as much as the number of balanced accounts regarding action, but they didn't remain *the same* either; eliminate (B). Overall, *the number of "balanced" accounts of global warming* did increase between 1988 and 2002, so keep (C). There is no indication that the information from the graph includes *all accounts of global warming*, so eliminate (D). The correct answer is (C).

41. **D** The question asks what *the 2001 data in the table best serve as evidence* of. Check the table for where the coverage of action lines lie in 2001 to predict that in 2001 balanced accounts regarding global warming action had peaked. The graph provides no information regarding the composition of *coverage of global warming* or *anthropogenic influences;* eliminate (A) and (C). Choice (B) refers to *balanced reporting*, but the table has no reference to *informational bias*; eliminate (B). Choice (D) also refers to *balanced reporting*, and states that *popular discourse*

*has significantly diverged from the scientific discourse.* According to the passage, *balanced reporting* is the *popular discourse,* and according to the table, in 2001 the line for *balanced reporting* diverged the most from the other types of reporting. The correct answer is (D).

42.   **A**   This question asks about the *primary purpose of the passage.* Because this is a general question, it should be done after all the specific questions. The passage starts with the report of the death of howler monkeys in Nicaragua, goes on to present different theories on why the howler monkeys died, and concludes by stating that the *cause of the recent howler monkey deaths remains a mystery* and that there is *probably an interaction of factors.* Choice (A) is consistent with this structure. The passage presents concerns for the howler monkey deaths, portrays the actions of the researchers, and raises several theories for why the howler monkeys died. Choice (B) can be eliminated because are no *contradictory results* presented in the passage. The passage simply raises various theories as to why the howler monkeys died. Eliminate (C) because there is no indication in the passage that the researchers are *unusual[ly]* persistent. Choice (D) can be eliminated because the passage does not examine the researcher's *methodology.* The correct answer is (A).

43.   **D**   This question asks what type of evidence *Williams-Guillén's ultimate hypothesis* rests on. In the eighth paragraph of the passage, the author states that *William-Guillén thinks that disease is an unlikely cause of the recent monkey deaths,* and that *she and her colleagues are still waiting to export blood and tissue samples to U.S. labs for further analysis.* Therefore, Williams-Guillén's ultimate hypothesis rests on laboratory tests, which is (D). The correct answer is (D).

44.   **D**   This question asks for the meaning of the phrase *hopped on* as it is used in the text. Cross out the phrase, and use the surrounding information to fill in another word or phrase that makes sense based on the passage. According to the passage, *William-Guillén hopped on a plane to Nicaragua.* In this context, *hopped on* would mean something like "boarded" a plane. Look for an answer that could mean "boarded." The only answer that could have a similar meaning is (D), *entered.* Choice (B), *flew,* may seem tempting. However, there is no indication in the passage that William-Guillén is a pilot. The correct answer is (D).

45.   **C**   This question asks what the passage states about *howler monkeys.* Given that the entire passage is about the howler monkeys, this is a general question that should be done after all the specific questions. For (A), there is no indication in the passage that howler monkeys *are less affected by ecological changes than other species would be.* In fact, the passage states that drought may have played a role in the death of the howler monkeys. Eliminate (A). For (B), although the third paragraph describes sick monkeys being easily captured, it never describes how difficult it is to capture healthy howler monkeys. Eliminate (B). For (C), look to the sixth paragraph of the passage, which states that one way to test whether limited food availability was a factor in the howler monkeys' deaths is to *see how other animals in the area are faring...If there are no reports of deaths in other frugivorous primates and other frugivorous animals, perhaps [food availability]*

*doesn't have to do with it.* This suggests that howler monkeys *share some known dietary similarities with other species.* Keep (C). Choice (D) can be eliminated, because while the passage suggests that the howler monkeys may have eaten toxic food as a result of not having enough food available, it does not indicate whether the howler monkeys *prefer the taste of non-toxic foods.* The correct answer is (C).

46. **B** This question asks for *an early consideration regarding howler monkey deaths.* Given that the question is asking about an *early consideration,* the answer is likely to be found toward the beginning of the passage. According to the first paragraph, in late September Williams-Guillén received the first report that *a handful of howler monkeys…had been found dead at an eco-resort in Nicaragua.* According to the second paragraph, *Over the next couple of months, Williams-Guillén and her colleagues continued to receive news that howler monkeys were dying. Then around mid-January, the reports really started to flood in.* According to the third paragraph, *When it became clear that this was not just an isolated incident, Williams-Guillén hopped on a plane to Nicaragua to see for herself.* Therefore, an early consideration was whether the deaths were an isolated incident. Isolated incidents can also be thought of as *random occurrences,* which matches (B). The passage doesn't provide any suggestions on what could prevent the howler monkey deaths. Eliminate (A). The passage does not state that *all ages* of howler monkeys were impacted. Eliminate (C). The passage does not suggest that *the entire population* of howler monkeys was impacted. Eliminate (D). The correct answer is (B).

47. **C** The question asks which theory provided by the passage *supports William-Guillén's belief that "no one hypothesis will be correct."* Notice that this is the first question in a paired set, so it can be done in tandem with Q48. Start with the best evidence answer choices for Q48. The lines for (48A) state that *although the mortality rate seems to have slowed since mid-February, the researchers are anxious to understand what is going on.* These lines do not discuss the accuracy of any hypotheses. Eliminate (48A). The lines for (48B) state that *the deaths are all really concentrated in the areas worst hit by drought.* This does not support any of the answers in Q47. Eliminate (48B). The lines for (48C) state that in areas where it is *slightly more humid, there's a lot fewer deaths, and there's visibly more potential howler monkey food, whereas the areas that have the highest rates of mortality, the trees are just bare.* This does not support any of the answers in Q47. Eliminate (48C). The lines for (48D) state that *limited food availability is likely a contributing factor, though the cause of death may not be starvation per se. Rather, the lack of food may drive the monkeys to consume plants with high levels of certain toxins that aren't part of their normal diet.* This supports (47C). Connect (48D) and (47C). Any unsupported answers for Q47 can be eliminated. The correct answers are (47C) and (48D).

48. **D** (See explanation above.)

49. **D** This question asks about the *primary purpose of the seventh and eighth paragraphs (lines 56–75).* The seventh paragraph introduces disease as a possible cause for the howler monkeys' deaths and provides the historical impact of yellow fever on howler monkeys. The eighth paragraph

discusses Williams-Guillén's thoughts that *disease is an unlikely cause of the recent monkey deaths*. According to the eighth paragraph, none of the virus diagnostics done tested positive for yellow fever. Find an answer consistent with this prediction. Choice (A) does not match the prediction. Neither paragraph 7 nor paragraph 8 discusses Williams-Guillén's methodology. Choice (B) can be eliminated because there is no discussion of Williams-Guillén's *expertise* in either the seventh or eighth paragraph. Choice (C) can also be eliminated because in the eighth paragraph Williams-Guillén rules out disease as a cause for the howler monkey deaths. However, there is no assumption that is underscored in either paragraph. Choice (D) matches the prediction. Williams-Guillén's perspective is that disease was not responsible for the howler monkey deaths. The seventh paragraph provides background on the historical impact of yellow fever on the howler monkeys, while the eighth paragraph rules yellow fever out as a cause for the current howler monkey deaths. The correct answer is (D).

50.    **A**    This question asks what the author means when he indicates that *yellow fever may have created bottlenecks* in line 65. According to Dias, *yellow fever may be a cause of the relatively low genetic diversity among Central American howler monkeys. 'Yellow fever could have caused important bottlenecks.'* Find an answer that matches this prediction. Choice (A) matches the prediction. The bottleneck is related to the *relatively low genetic diversity*. Choice (B) can be eliminated because, although the passage states that yellow fever *devastated howler monkey populations into the late 1940s and into the 1950s*, there is no indication that yellow fever *led to the current howler monkey deaths*. In fact, later in the passage yellow fever is specifically ruled out as a cause of the howler monkey deaths. Eliminate (C) because nowhere in the passage is it suggested that a *prohibitively large number of virus-free monkeys* were introduced into the ecosystem. Choice (D) can be eliminated because there is no discussion of *competition between monkeys*. The correct answer is (A).

51.    **A**    This question asks what question Williams-Guillén's investigation answers. Notice that this is the first question in a paired set, so it can be done in tandem with question 52. Start with the best evidence answer choices for Q52. The lines for (52A) state that *Some researchers even speculate that yellow fever may be a cause of the relatively low genetic diversity among Central American howler monkeys.* It may be tempting to connect this answer with (51C). However, these lines do not relate to the findings of Williams-Guillén's investigation. For this reason, eliminate (52A). The lines for (52B) state that *Williams-Guillén thinks that disease is an unlikely cause of the recent monkey deaths.* This might initially seem to connect with (51A). Keep it if there isn't a clear reason to immediately eliminate it. The lines for (52C) state that *so far, none [of the howler monkeys] have tested positive for yellow fever, Zika, chikungunya, or dengue viruses.* This solidly supports (51A). The listed diseases are unlikely to have contributed to howler monkey deaths. Connect (52C) with (51A). The lines for (52D) state that *Animals that might have had some clinical or secondary infections that normally aren't that problematic...got into a situation where they were extremely food- and water-stressed, and that might have been enough to tip them into mortality.* This does not support any of the answers in Q51. Eliminate (52D).

Compare the remaining answers. While both (52B) and (52C) address the issue of whether disease caused the howler monkey deaths, (52B) only provides a hypothesis—*Williams-Guillén thinks.* Choice (52C), on the other hand, provides concrete evidence of disease not being present. The correct answers are (51A) and (52C).

52.   **C**   (See explanation above.)

## Section 2: Writing and Language

1.   **C**   Commas are changing in the answer choices, so the question is testing the four ways to use a comma. The phrase *or early in the morning* is necessary information, so it should not be surrounded by commas; eliminate (A). Since none of the other choices incorrectly surrounds the phrase with commas, use the vertical line test to identify the ideas in the other choices as *complete* or *incomplete*. For (B), draw the vertical line between the words *you* and *almost*. The phrase *If you've ever been driving on a long stretch of highway late at night or early in the morning you* is an incomplete idea, and the phrase *almost certainly know the feeling* is also an incomplete idea. To connect two incomplete ideas no punctuation is needed, so eliminate (B). For (C), draw the vertical line between the words *morning* and *you*. The phrase *If you've ever been driving on a long stretch of highway late at night or early in the morning* is an incomplete idea, while the phrase *you almost certainly know the feeling* is a complete idea. A comma is GO punctuation that can join a complete idea with an incomplete idea, so keep (C). For (D), draw the vertical line between the words *night* and *or*. The phrase *If you've ever been driving on a long stretch of highway late at night* is an incomplete idea, and the phrase *or early in the morning you almost certainly know the feeling* is also an incomplete idea; eliminate (D). The correct answer is (C).

2.   **B**   The punctuation is changing in the answer choices, so the question is testing STOP and GO punctuation. Use the vertical line test, and identify the ideas as complete or incomplete. Draw the vertical line between the words *wheel* and *causing*. The phrase *This may seem like a harmless enough problem, but as many as one seventh of these drivers admit to falling asleep at the wheel* is a complete idea, but the phrase *Causing more than a million crashes each year, including 50,000 injuries and 6,400 deaths* is an incomplete idea. To connect an incomplete idea with a complete idea, GO punctuation is needed; eliminate (A) and (D). Adding the subject-verb pair *this causes* to *more than a million crashes each year, including 50,000 injuries and 6,400 deaths* makes it a complete idea, which cannot be joined to another complete idea using GO punctuation, so eliminate (C). The correct answer is (B).

3.   **A**   Note the question! The question asks which sentence *provides the best transition from the previous paragraph*, so it is testing consistency. If the content of an answer choice is more consistent with the ideas surrounding it, then it should be added; otherwise it should not, because leaving the sentence as is will be the most consistent option. The end of the previous paragraph states that drivers *falling asleep at the wheel* cause *more than a million crashes each year* and the

following sentence says that *driving on fewer than two hours of sleep is the equivalent of driving while intoxicated*. The statement *these (numbers) may sound like drunk driving numbers and with good cause* combines both of these concepts, so keep (A). There is no reason to mention *the leading causes of death every year*, *medical professionals*, or *drunk driving penalties* in general so eliminate (B), (C), and (D). The correct answer is (A).

4.  **D**  The punctuation is changing in the answer choices, so the question is testing STOP and GO punctuation. Use the vertical line test, and identify the ideas as complete or incomplete. Draw a vertical line between the words *intoxicated* and *judgment*, as well as the words *is* and *similarly*. The phrase *judgment is* is an incomplete idea, and *similarly compromised, and reactions are correspondingly slowed* is also an incomplete idea. To connect two incomplete ideas no punctuation is needed, so eliminate (A) and (C). Now evaluate the vertical line between the words *intoxicated* and *judgment*. *At a recent forum, Czeisler suggested that driving on less than two hours of sleep is the equivalent of driving while intoxicated* is a complete idea, and the phrase *Judgment is similarly compromised, and reactions are correspondingly slowed* is also a complete idea. To connect two complete ideas, STOP punctuation is needed, so eliminate (B). The correct answer is (D).

5.  **D**  Note the question! The question asks which of the following accomplishes the goal of adding a *specific proposal that Czeisler's group has made,* so it is testing consistency. The previous sentence indicates that *Czeisler and the committee are now attempting to implement changes in the law code to address sleep deprivation*, so it can be predicted that the correct answer should provide a legal proposal to address sleep deprivation. *Conferences*, *risks of sleep-deprived driving*, and *Czeisler's career* do not match the prediction, so eliminate (A), (B), and (C). *Trying to get sleep-deprived driving added to the list of criminal statutes* is a proposed change *in the law code to address sleep deprivation*. The correct answer is (D).

6.  **B**  Note the question! The question asks *which option best combines the two sentences*, so it's testing precision and concision. Look for the answer that combines the sentences while maintaining the meaning of the originals. The two sentences each repetitively use the phrase *sleep disorder*, so the correct answer will eliminate this redundancy without introducing another. Choices (A) and (D) maintain the redundancy, so eliminate them. *Among them are* redundantly refers to the *sleep disorders*, and contains plural phrasing that does not match the singular noun *sleep apnea*; eliminate (C). The correct answer is (B).

7.  **D**  Verbs are changing in the answer choices, so the question is testing verb consistency. A verb must be consistent with its subject and with the other verbs in the sentence. According to information from earlier in the sentence, *individuals with sleep apnea don't rest deeply even when they are asleep*. Since this information is in the present tense, the action of the *disorder* should also be in the present tense; eliminate (A). The subject of the plural verb *are doubling* is the singular *disorder*, which refers to *sleep apnea*; eliminate (B). *Is doubling* changes the intended meaning of the sentence by making the *disorder* different from *sleep apnea*, so eliminate (C).

*The disorder, given all of its negative side effects, doubles the risk of sleep-related crashes* correctly indicates that *sleep apnea* is presently the risk factor. The correct answer is (D).

8. **B**  Transition words are changing in the answer choices, so the question is testing the consistency of that transition and the ideas it connects. The sentence surrounding the transition indicates that *the findings regarding young people were not quite so obvious*, so the correct answer should be something like "on the contrary" to indicate a contrast with other ideas already presented in the passage. *Nevertheless* can reflect a change in direction, but indicates that things ultimately stayed the same; eliminate (A). *Furthermore* and *thus* are same direction transitions, so eliminate (C) and (D). *However* matches "on the contrary." The correct answer is (B).

9. **A**  Note the question! The question asks which of the following *most effectively cites commonly-held views while previewing what is to come in this paragraph*, so it is testing consistency. Before the underlined portion, it is stated that *young people have a tendency to think that they can operate at a high level with less sleep*. The rest of the paragraph after the underlined portion then explains that this thought regarding young people and sleep deprivation is actually a misconception, so the correct answer will address this "misconception." That *science suggests the opposite is true* matches the prediction, so keep (A). The notions that young people drive faster and are susceptible to alcoholism are both irrelevant to the paragraph, so eliminate (B) and (C). Whether *you are one of the lucky few who doesn't need sleep* is irrelevant to the paragraph and too casual, so eliminate (D). The correct answer is (A).

10. **A**  The vocabulary is changing in the answer choices, so this question is testing word choice. Look for a phrase that has a definition consistent with the other ideas in the sentence. The cells in younger people are being compared to the same cells in older people that *have died or function at a lower level*. Therefore, it can be predicted that the cells in younger people could accurately be described as "alive" and "high functioning." *Firing on all cylinders, going off,* and *off the chain* are all slang phrases that would not be used to describe the "high functioning" nature of cells; eliminate (B), (C), and (D). The correct answer is (A).

11. **D**  The phrase after *a younger person is more at risk for uncontrollable lapses in engagement* is changing in the answers, so the question is testing precision and concision. The *attention* relates to the lapses in engagement, so the correct answer will be similar in meaning to "lapses in engagement." *Attention* is not actually being added to the *lapses in engagement*, so eliminate (A) and (C). *Attention lapses also* accurately defines the underlined portion as similar to *lapses in attention*, but is not as concise as *and attention*, which also correctly indicates that the lapses are in both *engagement and attention*; eliminate (B). The correct answer is (D).

12. **B**  The transition word is changing in the answer choices, so the question is testing consistency of ideas. Read the sentences before and after the underlined portion to determine how the ideas connect. The previous sentence states that the temple that *stands in ruins today was completed in 432 B.C.E.* The next sentence states that it *served is original purpose for a thousand years.* These

ideas are similar but *nevertheless* indicates a contrast, so eliminate (A). The fact that it was completed in 432 B.C.E. did not cause it to serve its purpose, so eliminate (C) and (D). Two thousand years is a long time, and is quite remarkable. The correct answer is (B).

13. **B** The punctuation is changing in the answer choices, so the question is testing STOP and GO punctuation. Use the vertical line test, and identify the ideas as complete or incomplete. Draw the vertical line between the words *century* and *the building*. The phrase before the *until the late 17th century* is an incomplete idea and the phrase *the building largely retained its majestic, classical profile* is a complete idea, so GO punctuation is needed. The colon is HALF-STOP punctuation, so eliminate (C). The commas are changing in the remaining choices, so the question is testing the four ways to use a comma. Look for a list and for unnecessary information. This sentence does not contain a list. The phrase *the building* is necessary for the sentence, so eliminate (A). Putting the word *largely* in commas would change the meaning of the sentence, so eliminate (D). The correct answer is (B).

14. **D** The words and punctuation are changing in the choices with the option to DELETE. Consider the DELETE option carefully as it is often the correct answer. The sentence already states that the Parthenon was used as a *gunpowder storehouse*. The phrase *for storing ammunition* is redundant, so the phrase should be deleted. Eliminate (A), (B), and (C), which all repeat the idea. The correct answer is (D).

15. **A** Note the question! The question asks whether the sentence should be added, so it's testing consistency. If the content of the new sentence is consistent with the ideas surrounding it, then it should be added; otherwise, it should not be added. The previous sentence states that the Parthenon exploded. The next sentence starts with the word *additionally*, which indicates more information about the results of the explosion. The sentence to be added discusses the results of the explosion. Therefore, it's consistent with the surrounding ideas and should be added. Eliminate (C) and (D). The sentence does not explain later facts, so eliminate (B). The correct answer is (A).

16. **A** Note the question! The question asks for the choice that best supports the main point of the paragraph, so it's testing consistency of ideas. The only other sentence in the paragraph states that Britain took the first steps to preserve the Parthenon, so the correct answer should contain that idea. Only (A) mentions Britain. The correct answer is (A).

17. **C** Apostrophes are changing in the choices, so the question is testing apostrophe usage. When used with a pronoun, the apostrophe indicates a contraction. In this sentence, *it* refers to the Parthenon, which is possessing the *iconic columns*. The possessive pronoun does not use the apostrophe, so eliminate (B) and (D). When used with a noun, the apostrophe indicates possession. In this sentence, the *columns* are plural and are not possessing anything, so the apostrophe is not needed. Eliminate (A). The correct answer is (C).

18. **B**    The verbs are changing in the answer choices, so the question is testing verb consistency. A verb must be consistent with the other verbs in the sentence. The verb *corroded* is in the past tense, so the verb *used* must also be in the past tense. Eliminate (C). The proper phrase is *used to*, so eliminate (A) and (D). The correct answer is (B).

19. **C**    The punctuation is changing in the answer choices, so the question is testing STOP and GO punctuation. Use the vertical line test, and identify the ideas as complete or incomplete. Draw the vertical line between the words *weather* and *eventually*. The words after the vertical line are also changing, so check each choice separately. For (A), the phrase before the vertical line is a complete idea and the phrase after is a complete idea, so STOP or HALF-STOP punctuation is needed. The comma is GO punctuation, so eliminate (A). For (B), the phrase before the vertical line is a complete idea and the phrase after is an incomplete idea, so GO punctuation is needed. The semicolon is STOP punctuation, so eliminate (B). For (C), the phrase before the vertical line is a complete idea and the phrase after is an incomplete idea, so GO punctuation is needed. The comma is GO punctuation, so keep (C). For (D), the phrase before the vertical line is a complete idea and the phrase after is an incomplete idea, so GO punctuation is needed. The comma is GO punctuation, so keep (D). The verbs are changing in the remaining choices, so it's testing verb form. The phrase *it causing* is not the correct form of the verb, so eliminate (D). The correct answer is (C).

20. **D**    The vocabulary is changing in the answer choices, so this question is testing word choice. Look for a word whose definition is consistent with the other ideas in the sentence. The sentence states that the pieces are *incredibly sophisticated* and *match by fractions of millimeters*, so the word should mean something like "small details." *Shadows* means "areas of less light," so eliminate (A). *Tininess* means "small" but does not capture the intricacies of the details, so eliminate (B). *Suggestions* means "hints" or "possible ideas," so eliminate (C). *Nuances* means "slight difference or variation," so keep (D). The correct answer is (D).

21. **C**    Note the question! The question asks where sentence 2 should be placed, so it's testing consistency. Determine the subject matter of the sentence, and find the other sentence that also discusses that information. Sentence 2 discusses *a result of this painstaking work*, so it should follow the description of the work. Sentence 5 states that the work is hard because the *design is incredibly sophisticated, and pieces match one another by fractions of millimeters*. Therefore, sentence 2 should be placed after sentence 5. The correct answer is (C).

22. **D**    The words are changing in the choices with the option to DELETE. Consider the DELETE option carefully as it is often the correct answer. The sentence contains the name *Manolis Korres* followed by a description of who that person is. Only a comma is needed to link the name and the description, so the sentence could read *Manolis Korres, the project's chief architect*. The correct answer is (D).

23. **B**    The punctuation is changing in the answer choices, so the question is testing STOP and GO punctuation. Use the vertical line test, and identify the ideas as complete or incomplete. Draw

the vertical line between the words *traffic* and *or*. The sentence already contains a colon. The phrase after the colon contains a list, so a comma should be used to connect the items in the list. Eliminate (C) and (D). In a list, the comma is needed before the *or* but not after. Eliminate (A). The correct answer is (B).

24. **C** The transition word is changing in the answer choices, so the question is testing consistency of ideas. The previous sentence discusses one of the sources of the *glut of data: sensors*. The next sentence introduces a different source—*social media posts*—which *can't be analyzed in traditional ways*. This indicates a shift in ideas, so the transition word should indicate a shift. Eliminate (A), (B), and (D). The correct answer is (C).

25. **C** The vocabulary is changing in the answer choices, so this question is testing word choice. Look for a word whose definition is consistent with the other ideas in the sentence. The previous sentence states that *social media posts can't be analyzed in traditional ways*. This sentence highlights that *new ways of "digging" online activity* are needed. Therefore, the word should mean something like "analyzing" or "studying." *Digging* means either "to burrow under the earth" or "to really like something," so eliminate (A). *Checking out* means "to look at," so keep (B). *Mining* means "to extract a desired material or information," so keep (C). *Take a peek at* means "to look at for a brief time," so eliminate (D). *Checking out* is too informal for this passage and doesn't indicate analysis, so eliminate (B). The correct answer is (C).

26. **B** The vocabulary is changing in the answer choices, so this question is testing word choice. Look for a word whose definition is consistent with the other ideas in the sentence. The sentence is using the comparison *from* this *to* that. The word *too* means "also" and is not correct. Eliminate (A). *Sector* means "a distinct part or area," so keep (B). *Section* means "part that is cut off or separated," so eliminate (C) and (D). The correct answer is (B).

27. **B** The pronouns are changing in the answer choices with the option to DELETE, so the question is testing consistency and precision of meaning. Consider the option to DELETE carefully since it is often the answer. The sentence contains the phrase *$50,000 more than* which is intended to compare the *average starting salary*. In this case, the pronoun cannot be deleted because the meaning would change. Eliminate (D). The pronoun must refer to the *salary*, which is singular. The pronoun *those* is plural, so eliminate (C). Finally, the preposition is changing, so the question is testing consistency. The beginning of the sentence says "salary *of* a data analyst," so the answer should say "that *of* a computer programmer." Eliminate (A). The correct answer is (B).

28. **A** Note the question! The question asks for the best introduction to the paragraph, so it's testing consistency of ideas. The rest of the paragraph discusses how the analyst works with other experts in the field, thus the analyst doesn't need to be an expert in everything. The correct answer should be consistent with this idea. Stating that *specialized knowledge of a particular field is not necessarily a requirement* is consistent, so keep (A). *Schools are offering degree programs* is

not consistent, so eliminate (B). *A field in which data analytics is of fundamental importance* is not consistent, so eliminate (C). *Creating new positions* is not consistent, so eliminate (D). The correct answer is (A).

29. **D**  Pronouns are changing in the answer choices, so the question is testing precision. Determine the subject of the pronoun, and choose an answer that makes the meaning consistent and precise. The subject of the *information* is *researchers*, which is plural. The pronoun must also be plural, so eliminate (A). *There* does not refer to people, so eliminate (B). The apostrophe in *they're* indicates the conjunction "they are," while the pronoun *there* indicates possession. The information belongs to the researchers, so the possessive pronoun is needed. Eliminate (C). The correct answer is (D).

30. **A**  Note the question! The question asks whether the sentence should be added, so it's testing consistency. If the content of the new sentence is consistent with the ideas surrounding it, then it should be added; otherwise, it should not be added. The sentence to be added discusses *how much the field is growing*. The rest of the paragraph discusses how *related jobs have projected growth rates of up to 34% over the next ten years* and that the *big data will no doubt become a part of nearly every other aspect* of our society. Thus, the sentence is consistent with the rest of the paragraph, so it should be added. Eliminate (C) and (D). The sentence *introduces an issue that is further discussed in the paragraph*, so keep (A). The sentence does not *offer additional details about a point made in the previous paragraph*, so eliminate (B). The correct answer is (A).

31. **A**  The punctuation is changing in the answer choices, so the question is testing STOP and GO punctuation. Use the vertical line test, and identify the ideas as complete or incomplete. Draw the vertical line between the words *title* and *including*. The phrase before the vertical line is an incomplete idea and the phrase after is an incomplete idea, so GO punctuation is needed. The colon is HALF-STOP punctuation, so eliminate (B). The phrase *including operations research analyst and statistician* is unnecessary information, so it should have the same punctuation both before and after it. Choice (A) has parentheses both before and after, so keep (A). Choice (C) has a comma after but not before, so eliminate (C). Choice (D) has a comma before but not after, so eliminate (D). The correct answer is (A).

32. **D**  Note the question! The question asks whether the sentence should be added, so it's testing consistency. If the content of the new sentence is consistent with the ideas surrounding it, then it should be added; otherwise, it should not be added. The sentence to be added states that *operations research analyst is projected to have the greatest number of jobs in the field by 2024*. The rest of the paragraph discusses the *projected growth rates* of analysts, so the content is consistent. However, the claim is not supported by the table. The number of *operations research analyst* in 2024 is projected to be 587,800, and the number of *management analysts* is projected to be 861,400. The new sentence is not supported by the table, so it should not be added. Eliminate (A) and (B). The sentence is related to the topic, so eliminate (C). The correct answer is (D).

33. **D** The vocabulary is changing in the answer choices, so this question is testing word choice. Look for a word whose definition is consistent with the other ideas in the sentence. The previous sentence states *big data is used in deliveries and to recommend music and movies*. The next sentence discusses how the use of big data will grow in the next decades. The word should mean something like other aspects of our "lives" or "society." *Goings-on* is too informal for this passage, so eliminate (A). *Habits* means "a reoccurring practice," so eliminate (B). *Usual procedures* means "common course of action," so eliminate (C). *Daily lives* means "everyday society," so keep (D). The correct answer is (D).

34. **D** The vocabulary is changing in the answer choices, so this question is testing word choice. Look for a word whose definition is consistent with the other ideas in the sentence. The sentence is discussing time periods and mentions the *early 60s*. Therefore, the word must mean something like "late" or "latter." *Delayed* means "to postpone," so eliminate (A). *Tardy* means "to be behind schedule," so eliminate (B). *Behind* means "to come after," so eliminate (C). *Late* means "at the end," so keep (D). The correct answer is (D).

35. **B** The punctuation is changing in the answer choices, so the question is testing STOP and GO punctuation. Use the vertical line test, and identify the ideas as complete or incomplete. Draw the vertical line between the words *Jungle* and *which*. The phrase before the vertical line is an incomplete idea and the phrase after is an incomplete idea, so GO punctuation is needed. The comma is GO punctuation, so keep (A). The colon is HALF-STOP punctuation, so eliminate (C). The semicolon is STOP punctuation, so eliminate (D). The long dash is HALF-STOP punctuation. However, the sentence also contains another long dash, so consider whether the sentence contains unnecessary information. The phrase *which featured the song "Rock Around the Clock" by Bill Haley and his Comets* is not necessary, so it should have the same punctuation both before and after it. Eliminate (A). The correct answer is (B).

36. **C** The conjunction is changing in the answer choices, so the question is testing consistency of ideas. The previous sentence mentions that the film *catapulted popular culture*. The next sentence states that the *movie sparked controversy*. The two ideas are contrasting, so the conjunction should indicate a contrast. *Moreover, and,* and *as a result* all indicate similar ideas, so eliminate (A), (B), and (D). The correct answer is (C).

37. **C** Verbs are changing in the choices, so the question is testing verb consistency. A verb must be consistent with the other verbs in the sentence. Both the sentence before and after this one have verbs in the past tense: *movie sparked controversy* and *rock and roll was widely embraced*. To be consistent, the answer choice must also be in the past tense. Eliminate (A), (B), and (D). The correct answer is (C).

38. **B** The punctuation is changing in the answer choices, so the question is testing STOP and GO punctuation. Use the vertical line test, and identify the ideas as complete or incomplete. Draw the vertical line between the words *symbol* and *of*. The phrase before the vertical line is a complete idea and the phrase after is an incomplete idea, so GO or HALF-STOP punctuation is

needed. None of these can be eliminated at this point. Consider the sentence as a whole. *Rock and roll was widely embraced as the symbol of a new, rebellious generation.* The entire sentence is a complete idea, so no punctuation is needed. Eliminate (A), (C), and (D). The correct answer is (B).

39. **D** Note the question! The question asks for the choice that *logically completes the discussion of the popularity of early rock and provides an effective transition into the next paragraph*, so it's testing consistency of ideas. The paragraph discusses the rise in the popularity of rock and roll and the artists that propelled it to popularity. The next paragraph begins with *but in the late 50s*, which indicates a shift in ideas. The paragraph goes on to say that many of the popular artists were disappearing from the rock and roll scene. The concluding sentence should end on a very positive note about the popularity of rock and roll. The type of *guitar* is not consistent with the popularity of the music, so eliminate (A). The type of *dance moves* is not consistent with the popularity of the music, so eliminate (B). The *American Bandstand* does add to the popularity of the music, so keep (C). The *rise of rock and roll was unstoppable* is consistent with the popularity of the music, so keep (D). Choice (C) is another detail about the music, but it is not a concluding summary that is then contrasted in the next paragraph. Eliminate (C). The correct answer is (D).

40. **B** Note the question! The question asks for the choice that *most effectively sets up the main idea of the paragraph,* so it's testing consistency of ideas. The paragraph discusses how many of the popular artists were leaving the rock and roll scene. The correct answer will be consistent with this idea. *Expand their musical styles* is not consistent with leaving the scene, so eliminate (A). *Icons of early rock disappeared from the music scene* is consistent, so keep (B). *Write their own songs* is not consistent with leaving the scene, so eliminate (C). *British rock bands* are not consistent with leaving the scene, so eliminate (D). The correct answer is (B).

41. **C** Note the question! The question asks for the choice that is *most consistent with the examples in the previous sentences*, so it's testing consistency of ideas. All the other examples are negative situations that caused artists to leave the rock and roll scene. The correct answer will be consistent with this idea. *Debuted his signature move* is not consistent with leaving the scene, so eliminate (A). *Opened some of the first integrated music clubs* is not consistent with leaving the scene, so eliminate (B). *Served time in jail* is consistent with leaving the scene, so keep (C). *An innovative new way* is not consistent with leaving the scene, so eliminate (D). The correct answer is (C).

42. **B** Apostrophes are changing in the choices, so the question is testing apostrophe usage. When used with a noun, the apostrophe indicates possession. In this sentence, The Beatles are possessing the albums, but the albums are not possessing anything. Therefore, *albums* does not need an apostrophe. Eliminate (A), (C), and (D). The correct answer is (B).

43. **A** The pronouns are changing in the choices with the option to DELETE, so the question is testing consistency and precision of meaning. Consider the option to DELETE carefully, as

it is often the correct answer. The pronoun refers to the *stars*, so it cannot be deleted without changing the meaning of the sentence. Eliminate (D). The pronoun must be a subject pronoun, but *them* is an object pronoun, so eliminate (B). The *stars of the late 50s* is a subject that is discussed in the past. *These* indicates something near and in the present, so eliminate (C). *Those* indicates something distant or in the past. The correct answer is (A).

44. **A**  Note the question! The question asks for the choice that *combines the underlined sentences*, so it's testing consistency of ideas. The first sentence mentions that Elvis was *met with disapproval*, and the second sentence mentions that The Beatles were *seen as a symbol of rebellion*. These two ideas are similar examples of the same phenomenon, so the combination should be consistent with this comparison. *Just as* indicates two similar ideas, so keep (A). *Even though* indicates opposite ideas, so eliminate (B). The sentence is supposed to convey that *parents* not *the band's fans* viewed The Beatles' hairdos as a symbol of rebellion; eliminate (C). In (D), it is unclear what is *shaggy and rebellious*, so eliminate (D). The correct answer is (A).

## Section 3: Math (No Calculator)

1. **A**  To get the sum of complex numbers, add the real parts and the imaginary parts separately. Therefore, $(3 + 6i) + (7 + 2i) = (3 + 7) + (6i + 2i) = 10 + 8i$. The correct answer is (A).

2. **A**  The question asks for the meaning of a constant in an equation, so use Bite-Sized Pieces. The 100 in the equation is added separately and not multiplied by $h$, which is the number of hours. Because it is not multiplied by the number of hours, eliminate any choice that relates to hours. Eliminate (B), (C), and (D). Only one choice remains. To further see why (A) is correct, think about what part of the charge would be added unrelated to the number of hours. This would have to be the registration fee. Therefore, the correct answer is (A).

3. **D**  The question asks to model a relationship, so use Bite-Sized Pieces. In all four choices, 150 is given on the right side as a result of addition on the left side. Since 150 is the total number of ounces of gold, determine what is added to get the total number of ounces. Because there are two samples, the number of ounces of gold in each sample is added to get 150. Since $a$ represents the percent, as a decimal, of pure gold in Sample F, which weighs 220 ounces, the number of ounces of gold in Sample F is $220a$. Eliminate any choice that does not include this quantity. Eliminate (A), (B), and (C). Only one choice remains. To better see why (D) is correct, follow a similar line of reasoning to get that the number of ounces of gold in Sample B is $140b$. This must be added to $220a$ to get 150. The correct answer is (D).

4. **D**  Plug $b = 15$ into $a = \frac{4}{5}b$ to get $a = \frac{4}{5} \times \frac{15}{1}$. Cancel a 5 from the numerator and denominator to make the math easier: $a = \frac{4}{1} \times \frac{3}{1} = 12$. The question asks for $4a - 5$, so plug in $a = 12$ to get $4(12) - 5 = 48 - 5 = 43$. The correct answer is (D).

5. **B** The question asks for the value of $c$, which appears on the left side of the question. Notice that the left side is in the form of one of the common quadratics: $a^2 - b^2 = (a + b)(a - b)$ with $a = cy$ and $b = d$. Therefore, $(cy - d)(cy + d) = (cy)^2 - d^2 = c^2y^2 - d^2$. Since $25y^2 - 16 = c^2y^2 - d^2$, $c^2 = 25$ and $d^2 = 16$. The question asks for the value of $c$, so take the square root of both sides in $c^2 = 25$ to get $c = \pm5$. Only $+5$ is a choice, so the correct answer is (B).

6. **A** The question asks for the value of $y$, so isolate $y$ in the equation $\sqrt{49} = \sqrt{y} - \sqrt{16}$. Add $\sqrt{16}$ to both sides to get $\sqrt{49} + \sqrt{16} = \sqrt{y}$. Now simplify the equation. Since $\sqrt{49} = 7$ and $\sqrt{16} = 4$, the equation simplifies to $7 + 4 = \sqrt{y}$. Add on the left side to get $11 = \sqrt{y}$. Square both sides to get $y = 121$. The correct answer is (A).

7. **A** To find the graph of an equation in the form $y = mx + b$, use the fact that $m$ is the slope and $b$ is the $y$-intercept. In the equation $y = \frac{1}{3}x - 2$, the $y$-intercept is $-2$, so eliminate any choice that crosses the $y$-axis at a point other than $-2$. Eliminate (B) and (D). The slope of $y = \frac{1}{3}x - 2$ is $\frac{1}{3}$. Because the slope is positive, the graph increases as it goes from left to right. Eliminate (C), which decreases as it goes from left to right. The correct answer is (A).

8. **B** The question asks for $h$, in terms of $F$ and $n$. Isolate $h$ in the equation $F = 300nh$ by dividing both sides by $300n$ to get $\frac{F}{300n} = h$. The correct answer is (B).

9. **D** The question asks for the value of $s$, and there are numbers in the choices, so plug in the answers. Eliminate any choice for which $r(s) \times t(s)$ is not equal to $s$. For (A), $s = 0$, so $r(s) \times t(s) = r(0) \times t(0) = (-1) \times (-1) = 1$. Since this is not equal to 0, eliminate (A). For (B), $s = 1$, so $r(s) \times t(s) = r(1) \times t(1) = 2 \times 1 = 2$. Since this is not equal to 1, eliminate (B). For (C), $s = 2$, so $r(s) \times t(s) = r(2) \times t(2) = 3 \times 1 = 3$. Since this is not equal to 2, eliminate (C). For (D), $s = 3$, so $r(s) \times t(s) = r(3) \times t(3) = (-1) \times (-3) = 3$. Since this is equal to the value of $s$, the correct answer is (D).

10. **A** There are variables in the question and choices, so plug in. Let $y = 2$. If $y = 2$, then $\frac{2y^2 + 5y}{2y + 7} = \frac{2(2)^2 + 5(2)}{2(2) + 7} = \frac{2(4) + 5(2)}{4 + 7} = \frac{8 + 10}{11} = \frac{18}{11}$. Plug $y = 2$ into each of the choices and eliminate any that are not equal to the target value of $\frac{18}{11}$. Choice (A) is $2 - 1 + \frac{7}{2(2) + 7} = 1 + \frac{7}{11} = \frac{18}{11}$. Keep (A), but try the other answers just in case. Choice (B) is $2 + \frac{7}{2(2) + 7} = 2 + \frac{7}{11} = \frac{29}{11}$. Eliminate (B). Choice (C) is $2 + 2 = 4$. Eliminate (C). Choice (D) is 2. Eliminate (D). The correct answer is (A).

11.  **B**  The question asks for an inequality that can represent *s* in an average, so use Bite-Sized Pieces and an Average Pie. The number of things, in this case the number of tests, goes in the lower left space, and the average goes in the lower right. The total will be 99 + 83 + *s*. Fill these values into the pie.

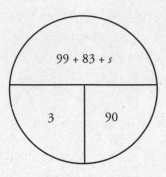

In an Average Pie, the total is the number of things multiplied by the average, or in this case, 99 + 83 + *s* = 3(90). Since Renee wants her average to be *at least* 90, the equal sign must be changed to the ≥ symbol, making the inequality 99 + 83 + *s* ≥ 3(90). The correct answer is (B).

12.  **C**  The question asks for what is true about the parabola given by the equation $y = -a(x + j) - k$. Use Bite-Sized Pieces. First, notice $-a$. The negative sign on the *a* means the parabola opens downwards. Eliminate (B) and (D). The equation $y = -a(x + j)^2 - k$ is in vertex form, so it is straightforward to determine the vertex. In vertex form $a(x - h)^2 + k$, the vertex is $(h, k)$. Therefore, the vertex in the given equation is $(-j, -k)$. Eliminate (A). The correct answer is (C).

13.  **C**  There are variables in the question and choices, so plug in. Let $x = 4$ and $y = 5$. Make $x = 4$ and

$y = 5$ to get $\left(\dfrac{x}{2} - y\right)^2 = \left(\dfrac{4}{2} - 5\right)^2 = \left(2 - 5\right)^2 = \left(-3\right)^2 = 9$. Plug $x = 4$ and $y = 5$ into each of

the choices, and eliminate any that are not 9. Choice (A) is $\dfrac{4^2}{2} + 5^2 = \dfrac{16}{2} + 25 = 8 + 25 = 33$,

so eliminate (A). Choice (B) is $\dfrac{4^2}{4} + 5^2 = \dfrac{16}{4} + 25 = 4 + 25 = 29$, so eliminate (B). Choice

(C) is $\dfrac{4^2}{4} - (4)(5) + 5^2 = \dfrac{16}{4} - 20 + 25 = 4 - 20 + 25 = -16 + 25 = 9$, so keep (C). Choice (D)

is $\dfrac{4^2}{4} - \dfrac{(4)(5)}{2} + 5^2 = \dfrac{16}{2} - \dfrac{20}{2} + 25 = 8 - 10 + 25 = -2 + 25 = 23$, so eliminate (D). The cor-

rect answer is (C).

14.  **D**  The question asks for a specific value, and there are numbers in the choices, so plug in the

answers. Start with one of the middle choices. Try (C). If $k = -2$, then $4x^2 - 5x = -2$. Add 2 to both sides to get $4x^2 - 5x + 2 = 0$. Determine whether this has two real solutions. This may be difficult to factor, so use the quadratic formula. To find the solutions to a quadratic in the form $ax^2 + bx + c = 0$, use the formula $x = \dfrac{-b \pm \sqrt{b^2 - 4ac}}{2a}$. Plug in $a = 4$, $b = -5$, and $c = 2$ to get $x = \dfrac{-(-5) \pm \sqrt{(-5)^2 - 4(4)(2)}}{2(4)} = \dfrac{5 \pm \sqrt{25 - 32}}{8} = \dfrac{5 \pm \sqrt{-8}}{8}$. However, since $\sqrt{-8}$ does not have any real values, this does not have any real solutions. Eliminate (C). In order to get a positive number under the square root, a smaller number must be subtracted from $b^2$. Try (D). If $k = -1$, then $4x^2 - 5x = -1$. Add 1 to both sides to get $4x^2 - 5x + 1 = 0$. Plug in $a = 4$, $b = -5$, and $c = 1$ into the quadratic formula to get $x = \dfrac{-(-5) \pm \sqrt{(-5)^2 - 4(4)(1)}}{2(4)} = \dfrac{5 \pm \sqrt{25 - 16}}{8} = \dfrac{5 \pm \sqrt{9}}{8} = \dfrac{5 \pm 3}{8}$. Therefore, $x = \dfrac{5 + 3}{8} = \dfrac{8}{8} = 1$ or $x = \dfrac{5 - 3}{8} = \dfrac{2}{8} = \dfrac{1}{4}$. Because there are two real solutions, the correct answer is (D).

15. **C**   The question asks for a system of inequalities, so use Bite-Sized Pieces. Start with the simplest piece. The store wants to buy at least three times as many T-shirts as pairs of jeans. Since the number of T-shirts must be at least 3 times the number of pairs of jeans, $t \geq 3j$. Eliminate (B) and (D), which don't include this inequality. The store wants to spend no more than $200. Set what the store spends as $\leq 200$. Because the store spends $1.25 on each of the $t$ T-shirts, the store spends a total of $1.25t$ dollars on T-shirts. Even though the number of T-shirts is at least 3 times the number of pairs of jeans, there is no need to multiply this number by 3. Eliminate (A), which does not include $1.25t$. Only one choice remains. To better see why (C) is correct, note that the store spends $9.75 on each of the $j$ pairs of jeans it buys, so it spends a total of $9.75j$ dollars on jeans. Therefore, it spends a total of $1.25t + 9.75j$ on T-shirts and jeans. Set this sum less than or equal to 200 to get $1.25t + 9.75j \leq 200$. The correct answer is (C).

16. **16**   The question asks for the length of $\overline{PS}$, which is the longer leg of the larger triangle. Because $\overline{PQ}$ is parallel to $\overline{RT}$, the two triangles are similar, making their corresponding sides proportional. Notice that the smaller right triangle has a leg with length 3 and a hypotenuse of 5. Therefore, this is a 3:4:5 right triangle with $\overline{ST}$ measuring 4. Since $\overline{PQ}$ corresponds to $\overline{RT}$ and $\overline{PS}$ corresponds to

$\overline{ST}$, set up the proportion $\frac{PQ}{RT} = \frac{PS}{ST}$. Substitute the known lengths to get $\frac{12}{3} = \frac{PS}{4}$. To make the math easier, reduce the left fraction to get $4 = \frac{PS}{4}$. Multiply both sides by 4 to get $PS = 16$. The correct answer is 16.

17. **1, 2, 3, 4, 6,** or **12**

Because the question asks for *one possible value of s* rather than *the value of s*, there is more than one possible answer. Since only one value is needed, plug in a possible value of $r$. To make this as easy as possible, put the two sides of the equation in the same form. Because the left side of the equation is a base raised to an exponent, rewrite the right side as $64^1$ to get $r^{\frac{s}{2}} = 64^1$. Since both sides are bases raised to exponents, the two bases could be equal and the two exponents could be equal, so set $r = 64$ and $\frac{s}{2} = 1$. To find the value of $s$, multiply both sides of $\frac{s}{2} = 1$ by 2 to get $s = 2$. Therefore, one possible answer is 2. There is no need to continue, but other correct answers are $s = 1$ when $r = 4{,}096$, $s = 3$ when $r = 16$, $s = 4$ when $r = 8$, $s = 6$ when $r = 4$, and $s = 12$ when $r = 2$. All these value of $s$ are correct answers.

18. $\frac{1}{24}$, **.041,** or **.042**

The question asks what fraction of the circumference is the length of arc $PQ$, so set up the fraction $\frac{arc}{circumference}$. The question says that the arc length is $\frac{\pi}{6}$, so put this into the numerator to get $\dfrac{\frac{\pi}{6}}{circumference}$. Now find the circumference. The formula for circumference is $C = 2\pi r$. Since the question says that the radius is 2, plug $r = 2$ into the formula to get $C = 2\pi(2) = 4\pi$. Plug this into the denominator to get $\dfrac{\frac{\pi}{6}}{4\pi}$. Rewrite the denominator as a fraction to get $\dfrac{\frac{\pi}{6}}{\frac{4\pi}{1}}$. To divide fractions, multiply the numerator by the reciprocal of the denominator to get $\frac{\pi}{6} \times \frac{1}{4\pi} = \frac{\pi}{24\pi}$. Cancel $\pi$ in the numerator and denominator to get $\frac{1}{24}$. The correct answer is $\frac{1}{24}$.

19. $\dfrac{49}{8}$, **6.12**, or **6.13**

   To find the value of $a$, divide both sides by the coefficient of $a$. Because the coefficient is a fraction, dividing by the coefficient is the same as multiplying by the reciprocal. Multiply both sides by $\dfrac{7}{4}$ to get $a = \dfrac{7}{2} \times \dfrac{7}{4} = \dfrac{49}{8}$. The correct answer is $\dfrac{49}{8}$.

20. $\dfrac{5}{2}$ or **2.5**

   The question asks how many gallons of the juice mix that is 60% orange juice must be added. Let this amount be $x$. A juice mix of $x$ gallons that contains 60% orange juice has $\dfrac{60}{100} x$ gallons of orange juice. The 5 gallons of a juice mix that have 30% orange juice contains $\dfrac{30}{100}(5)$ gallons of orange juice. The solutions are added to a new solution that contains $\dfrac{60}{100} x + \dfrac{30}{100}(5)$ gallons of orange juice. Because the combined juice mix has $x + 5$ total gallons and is 40% orange juice, it contains $\dfrac{40}{100}(x + 5)$ gallons of orange juice. Set the two equal to get $\dfrac{60}{100} x + \dfrac{30}{100}(5) = \dfrac{40}{100}(x + 5)$. Multiply both sides by 100 to get $60x + 30(5) = 40(x + 5)$. Simplify the left side and distribute the 40 on the right side to get $60x + 150 = 40x + 200$. Subtract $40x$ from both sides to get $20x + 150 = 200$. Subtract 150 from both sides to get $20x = 50$. Divide both sides by 20 to get $x = \dfrac{50}{20}$. Because this requires more than four spaces to grid in, reduce the fraction. Divide the numerator and denominator by 10 to get that the correct answer is $\dfrac{5}{2}$.

## Section 4: Math (Calculator)

1. **C** Look at the graphs in the answer choices and use process of elimination to find the answer. Choice (D) shows that Laura's distance did not change over time. Since this isn't true, eliminate (D). Choice (A) indicates that after resting on the park bench, Laura didn't run any more. This isn't true either, so eliminate (A). The question states that after resting, Laura *ran at a slower rate than she had initially*. This means that her change in distance over time would be less after she rested. The graph in (B) shows that Laura's change in distance over time before and after resting is the same. This doesn't match the statement in the question, so eliminate (B). In (C), Laura's change in distance is less after resting than it was before resting. The correct answer is (C).

2. **D**  The question asks to simplify the expression. Start by finding the first term, which is $3y^2 - (-5y^2) = 3y^2 + 5y^2 = 8y^2$. Eliminate (A) and (B), since neither has $8y^2$ as the first term. Now find the last term, which is $-2 - (-6) = -2 + 6 = 4$. Eliminate (C) since it has $-4$ as the last term. The correct answer is (D).

3. **B**  The question asks for the difference between the initial temperatures of Block A and Block B. Since the temperature is found on the $y$-axis, look for the temperature of each block at time $t = 0$. Block B has an initial temperature of 40 and Block A has an initial temperature of 25. The difference is $40 - 25 = 15$. The correct answer is (B).

4. **A**  The question asks how many households receive their Internet service from either Corporate Cable or Global Networks. Corporate Cable serves 47% of households and Global Networks serves 17% of households. Add these to get 47% + 17% = 64%. Since the total number of households is 2,800, take 64% of that to get $2,800 \times \dfrac{64}{100} = 1,792$. The correct answer is (A).

5. **C**  The question asks for a specific amount, so plug in the answers. Start with (B) and plug in 52 for the value of $x$. If the cost of the cartridges is $52, 18 cartridges would cost $52 \times 18 = $936. Add on the subscription fee of $230 to get a total of $936 + $230 = $1,166. This is not enough, so eliminate (B) and also (A), which is even smaller. The total was only slightly too small, so try (C) next. If the cartridges cost $63 each, 18 cost $63 \times 18 = $1,134. With the subscription fee, the total is $1,134 + $230 = $1,364. This matches the information in the question. The correct answer is (C).

6. **D**  Simplify the inequality to find the answer. Since each term has a greatest common factor of 4, divide each term by 4 to get $4a + 5b > 3$. This inequality matches (D). The correct answer is (D).

7. **B**  The question asks for a specific amount, so plug in the answers. Start with (B) and plug in 283 for the number of nautical miles in the first stage. If the first stage was 283 nautical miles, then the second stage was 283 + 110 = 393 nautical miles. Add the two stages together to get 283 + 393 = 676 nautical miles. This matches the information in the question. The correct answer is (B).

8. **C**  Use Bite-Sized Pieces to solve this question. The total weight of the carton of oranges is 27.3 pounds, but 9.6 of those pounds represent the weight of the carton itself. Since 27.3 − 9.6 = 17.7 pounds, the oranges by themselves weigh 17.7 pounds. The question asks for the cost of the oranges in dollars per pound, and the cost of the carton is $46.25. Divide to find $\dfrac{\$46.25}{17.7 \text{ pounds}} = \$2.61$ per pound. This is closest to (C). The correct answer is (C).

9. **C**  The question asks what information is true about the board's survey. Since only marine biologists were included in the sample group, the results of the survey cannot be extrapolated to all scientists. Even though a majority of the marine biologists were in favor of the aquatic exhibit, this does not

mean that a majority of all the scientists would also be in favor of the aquatic exhibit. Because of this, eliminate (B). For the survey to be truly representative of all the scientists, the sample group needs to include other scientists besides marine biologists. Adding more marine biologists would not make the sample group more representative, so eliminate (A). Using a sample group that contains no marine biologists at all would also not be representative, so eliminate (D). Since the sample group used in the survey was not representative of all the scientists, the survey was biased. The correct answer is (C).

10.  **A**  This question asks for the fraction of adopted cats that were black. First, find the total number of adopted cats, which is $9 + 7 = 16$. Of those 16 cats, 7 were black. Therefore, the fraction of adopted cats that were black is $\frac{7}{16}$. The correct answer is (A).

11.  **B**  The question asks for the meaning of $d$ in the function $a(t) = c - dt$. Label what is known in the equation. The function $a$ is the extent, in millions of square kilometers, of Arctic sea ice. The variable $t$ represents the number of years since the study began. Next, use Process of Elimination. Constant $d$ is multiplied by $t$. In a linear equation, the coefficient on the variable is the slope, which is the rate of change. Choice (A), (C), and (D) refer to a specific amount, not the change *per year*. Only (B) indicates that $d$ is the rate of change. The correct answer is (B).

12.  **C**  The question asks for the best linear model for the extent from Year 7 to Year 11. Plug in values from the table during this period. Since the extent in Year 7 was 5.39, plug in $t = 7$ into each choice, and eliminate any for which $a$ is not close to 5.39. Choice (A) is $a = 5 - 0.21(7) = 3.53$. This is not close to 5.39, so eliminate (A). Choice (B) is $a = 7 - 0.13(7) = 6.09$. This is not close to 5.39, so eliminate (B). Choice (C) is $a = 10 - 0.64(7) = 5.4$. This is close to 5.39, so keep (C). Choice (D) is $a = 15 - 1.82(7) = 2.26$. This is not close to 5.39, so eliminate (D). The correct answer is (C).

13.  **A**  To determine the period with the greatest change in rate, check the years in the answer choices and Ballpark. A great decrease would be a line that slopes down sharply from left to right. Choice (A) shows a sharp decrease from Year 4 to Year 5, so keep (A). Choice (B) also shows a decrease from Year 7 to Year 8, but it is not as steep as the one in (A). Eliminate (B). Choice (C) shows a decrease from Year 9 to Year 10, but it is not as steep as the one in (A). Eliminate (C). Choice (D) shows a decrease from Year 12 to Year 13, but it is not as steep as the one in (A). Eliminate (D). The correct answer is (A).

14.  **D**  This question asks for the solution to the system of equations. Since the equations have the same coefficient on the $d$ terms with opposite signs, add the two equations together to eliminate $d$.

$$\begin{array}{r} 9c + 5d = 22 \\ +\ 7c - 5d = 10 \\ \hline 16c \qquad = 32 \end{array}$$

Divide both sides by 16 to get $c = 2$. Plug $c = 2$ back into the top equation to get $9(2) + 5d = 22$.

Simplify to $18 + 5d = 22$. Subtract 18 from both sides to get $5d = 4$. Divide both sides by 5 to get $d = \dfrac{4}{5}$. Make sure to read the full question to see that it asks for the value of $c + d$, which is $2 + \dfrac{4}{5} = \dfrac{10}{5} + \dfrac{4}{5} = \dfrac{14}{5}$. The correct answer is (D).

15.  **A**   Start this question by filling in the missing angle measurements for $\angle WXZ$ and $\angle YXZ$ by using the rule that there are 180° in a triangle. $\angle WXZ$ is 28° and $\angle YXZ$ is 62°. Since triangle $WXZ$ and triangle $XYZ$ have identical angle measurements, they are similar triangles. Start by determining what the numerator of the ratio represents. Side $WZ$ is the side opposite the 28° angle in triangle $WXZ$ and corresponds to side $XZ$ of triangle $XYZ$, since side $XZ$ is opposite the 28° angle in triangle $XYZ$. Therefore, $WZ$ corresponds to $XZ$. Eliminate (B) and (D), since these answers do not have the correct numerator. As for the denominator of the ratio, side $WX$ represents the hypotenuse of triangle $WXZ$. In triangle $XYZ$, the hypotenuse is represented by $XY$. Therefore, $WX$ corresponds to $XY$. Taken together, $\dfrac{WZ}{WX} = \dfrac{XZ}{XY}$. The correct answer is (A).

16.  **B**   There are variables in the answer choices, so plug in values from the table to find the correct equation. Choose an easy number to plug in, like $s = 0$, and look for an equation that gives $t = \dfrac{31}{2}$. Choice (A) becomes $t = \dfrac{31}{20} \cdot (6)^0 = \dfrac{31}{2}(1) = \dfrac{31}{2}$. This equals $\dfrac{31}{2}$, so keep (A). Choice (B) becomes $t = 6(0) + \dfrac{31}{2} = 0 + \dfrac{31}{2} = \dfrac{31}{2}$. This equals $\dfrac{31}{2}$, so keep (B). Choice (C) becomes $t = \dfrac{1}{4} \cdot \left(\dfrac{31}{2}\right)^0 = \dfrac{1}{4}(1) = \dfrac{1}{4}$. This does not equal $\dfrac{31}{2}$, so eliminate (C). Choice (D) becomes $t = \dfrac{1}{6}(1) - 4 = \dfrac{1}{6} - 4 = -\dfrac{23}{6}$. This does not equal $\dfrac{31}{2}$, so eliminate (D). Plug in a second time to see if the answer is (A) or (B). Choose another easy value to plug in, like $s = 1$, and look for an equation that gives $t = \dfrac{43}{2}$. Choice (A) becomes $t = \dfrac{31}{2}(6)^1 = \dfrac{31}{2}(6) = \dfrac{186}{2}$. This does not equal $\dfrac{43}{2}$, so eliminate (A). Choice (B) becomes $t = 6(1) + \dfrac{31}{2} = 6 + \dfrac{31}{2} = \dfrac{43}{2}$. Since (B) equals $\dfrac{43}{2}$, the correct answer is (B).

17.  **B**   The question asks for all the possible values for box width. The question states that the box width must be at least 3 inches. Use this information to eliminate (D), since it allows for box widths that are less than 3 inches. Now, determine what possible box dimensions meet the requirements of a

width of at least 3 inches and a height of at least 12 inches using the box size formula, $h + 3w = 30$. If the width of the box is 3 inches, then the height is $h + (3)(3) = 30$, or $h + 9 = 30$. Subtract 9 from both sides to get $h = 21$. This means that when a box has a width of 3 inches, the height of the box is 21 inches. Since 21 inches is more than 12 inches, these dimensions meet the requirement. Therefore, 3 inches is a possible width for this requirement. Use this information to eliminate (A), since 3 inches is not included in this answer choice. According to the box size formula, as the width of the box increases, the height of the box decreases. Therefore, to find the maximum possible width of the box, plug in the least possible height of 12 inches to get $12 + 3w = 30$. Subtract 12 from both sides to get $3w = 18$. Divide both sides by 3 to get $w = 6$. Therefore, 6 inches is a possible box width, and it is also the greatest possible box width given the restrictions in the question. Since 6 inches must be the greatest possible width, eliminate (C), which allows for unlimited box widths. The correct answer is (B).

18. **B** The question asks for a specific amount, so plug in the answers. The answer choices represent possible values for the width of the box in the stacked display. Use the box size formula, $h + 3w = 30$, to find the corresponding height for each answer choice. The question states that this height must be between 8 and 10 inches. Start with (B) and make $w = 7.2$ inches. The box size formula becomes $h + 3(7.2) = 30$, which simplifies to $h + 21.6 = 30$. Subtract 21.6 from both sides to get $h = 8.4$. Since 8.4 is between 8 and 10, keep (B). Now use the other information in the question to determine if the answer is (B). The question says that the stacked display has a total height of 7 feet, which is $7 \times 12 = 84$ inches. Since the height of the boxes is equal to the height of each level, divide the total height of the stacked display by the height of the box to find the number of levels. Remember that the question stated that the stacked display must have an even number of levels. If the boxes have a height of 8.4 inches, divide to find $\frac{84}{8.4} = 10$ levels. This is an even integer, and because plugging in (B) satisfies all other requirements in the question, the correct answer is (B).

19. **A** This question asks for the box width in terms of the box height. To find the answer, rearrange the box size formula in terms of $w$. The formula states that $h + 3w = 30$. Start by subtracting $h$ from both sides to get $3w = 30 - h$. Divide both sides by 3 to get $w = \dfrac{30 - h}{3} = \dfrac{1}{3}(30 - h)$. This matches (A). The correct answer is (A).

20. **C** The question asks for the conclusion that is best supported by the data. The main result of the study was that of the 250 red maple trees measured in the sample, 40% had a circumference less than 35 inches. This data is specific to one type of tree, the red maple tree, and cannot be extrapo-

lated to other types of trees or generalized to all the trees in the forest. Use this logic to eliminate (A), (B), and (D), which draw conclusions for *all the trees in the forest*. The data from the study can only be used to support conclusions about red maple trees. Since (C) is the only choice that specifically references red maple trees, the correct answer is (C).

21. **A** To solve the equation in the question, set each binomial to 0 and solve. For the first binomial, $y + 4 = 0$, so subtract 4 from both sides to get $y = -4$. For the second binomial, $y - 0.3 = 0$, so add 0.3 to both sides to get $y = 0.3$. Therefore, there are two solutions to the equation, $y = -4$ or 0.3. Make sure to read the full question and see that the question asks for the product of the solutions. Multiply to get $-4 \times 0.3 = -1.2$. The correct answer is (A).

22. **B** The question asks how many times the gymnast was at a height of 15 feet. Find 15 feet on the $y$-axis and draw a line across. Look for the number of times this line intersects with the graph. It intersects twice: once at about 4 seconds and a second time at about 5.5 seconds. Since the gymnast was at a height of 15 feet exactly two times, the correct answer is (B).

23. **C** The question asks by what percent the writer's salary increased. The question asks for a specific amount, so plug in the answers. Look for the answer choice that gives the writer's new salary of $88.51. Start with (B). If the writer's original salary of $81.34 increased by 8.1%, her salary would increase by $81.34 \times \dfrac{8.1}{100} = \$6.59$. Add this increase to her original salary to get a new salary of $81.34 + \$6.59 = \$87.93$. This is not equal to new salary of $88.51, so eliminate (B). Additionally, since the salary calculated with (B) is too small, eliminate (A) as well. Try (C) next. If the writer's original salary of $81.34 increased by 8.8%, her salary would increase by $81.34 \times \dfrac{8.8}{100} = \$7.16$. Add this increase to her original salary to get a new salary of $81.34 + \$7.16 = \$88.50$. This is closest to the new salary of $88.51. The correct answer is (C).

24. **D** The question states that the function is a linear function and asks for the value of $h(6)$, or the value of $y$ when $x = 6$. Use two points to find the slope of the line, which is defined as $\dfrac{y_1 - y_2}{x_1 - x_2}$. Using the second and third points on the table, $slope = \dfrac{21 - 5}{7 - 3} = \dfrac{16}{4} = 4$. Plug this value and point $(3, 5)$ into $y = mx + b$ to get $5 = 3(4) + b$ or $5 = 12 + b$. Therefore, $b = -7$ and the equation of the line is $y = h(x) = 4x - 7$. Now find $h(6)$, which is $4(6) - 7 = 24 - 7 = 17$. The correct answer is (D).

25. **C** The question asks for the median age, and the median is defined as the middle number in a numerical list. The table contains 35 numbers for age, but displays them as frequency. Because there are 35 numbers for age, the middle age will be the 18th age in the table. Start counting from the left, adding up the frequency for each age: $1 + 1 + 2 + 2 + 1 + 2 + 1 + 5 + 2 = 17$. This list

includes all ages up to and including 52. The 18th age is 54, so the median age in the table is 54. The correct answer is (C).

26. **D** This question gives an equation of a circle and asks for the radius of the circle. Start by simplifying the equation by dividing each term by 4 to get $x^2 + 5x + y^2 - 3y = 27.5$. The standard form for the equation of a circle with center $(h, k)$ and radius $r$ is $(x^2 - h)^2 + (y^2 - k)^2 = r^2$. In order to factor this expression into standard form, complete the square. For each $x$ and $y$, take half of the coefficient of the middle term, square it, and add it to both sides. For the $x$-terms, $x^2 + 5x$, add $\left(\dfrac{5}{2}\right)^2 = 6.25$ to both sides. For the $y$-terms, $y^2 - 3y$, add $\left(-\dfrac{3}{2}\right)^2 = 2.25$ to both sides. The new equation will be $(x^2 + 5x + 6.25) + (y^2 - 3y + 2.25) = 27.5 + 6.25 + 2.25$. The simplified expression in standard form is $(x^2 + 2.5)^2 + (y^2 - 1.5)^2 = 36$. Therefore, $r^2 = 36$ and $r = 6$. The correct answer is (D).

27. **A** Use Bite-Sized Pieces to approach this question. The question gives the resistance of X and asks for the resistance of Z. Focus on Resistors X and Z since the question does not ask about Resistor Y. Start with the information in the figure, which shows that the current through Resistor X is 5 amperes and the current through Resistor Z is 15 amperes. According to the question, this means that the current ratio, $a{:}b$, is 5:15, which can be reduced to 1:3. Therefore, the current ratio of Resistor X to Resistor Z is 1:3. However, the question is asking about the resistance. The resistance ratio is defined as $b{:}a$. Since the current ratio, $a{:}b$, is 1:3, the resistance ratio, $b{:}a$, is 3:1. Therefore, the resistance ratio of Resistor X to Resistor Z is 3:1. The question states that the resistance of Resistor X is 24 ohms. Use the resistance ratio to find the resistance of Resistor Z: $\dfrac{3}{1} = \dfrac{24}{x}$. Cross-multiply to get $3x = 24$, then divide both sides of the equation by 3 to get $x = 8$. The resistance of Resistor Z is 8. The correct answer is (A).

28. **D** Remember to read the full question, which asks for the *orbital ratio, in seconds per meter.* Label the variables given in the equation, where $P$ is seconds and $a$ is meters. To get *seconds per meter,* divide $P$ by $a$ to get $\dfrac{36 \times 10^{-8} a\sqrt{a}}{a}$. Cancel the $a$ in the numerator and the $a$ in the denominator to get $36 \times 10^{-8}\sqrt{a}$. The correct answer is (D).

29. **A** This question asks for the equation that best models the data in the scatterplot. All the equations in the answer choices are parabolas, and this matches the shape of the data in the scatterplot. The scatterplot data is shaped as a parabola opening upwards. Since a parabola that opens upwards

must have a positive $x^2$ term, eliminate (C) and (D). Now check the constant term in the equations. For an equation in the $xy$-plane, a positive constant term means that the graph crosses the $y$-axis above the $x$-axis, and a negative constant term means that the graph crosses the $y$-axis below the $x$-axis. Since the graph of the scatterplot data would cross the $y$-axis well above the $x$-axis, the constant term must be positive. Eliminate (B), since the constant term is −483.27. Choice (A) has a positive constant term of 483.27. The correct answer is (A).

30.  **B**  The question asks for the coordinates of the two points on the number line. Each point is 5 units away from the point −6. Since −6 + 5 = −1 and −6 − 5 = −11, the two points on the number line must be −1 and −11. Plug these values in for $y$ and use Process of Elimination to find the answer. Start with −1. Choice (A) becomes $|-1 - 6| = 5$, which simplifies to $|-7| = 5$. Since this is false, eliminate (A). Choice (B) becomes $|-1 + 6| = 5$, which simplifies to $|5| = 5$. Since this is true, keep (B). Choice (C) becomes $|-1 - 5| = 6$, which simplifies to $|-6| = 6$. Since this is true, keep (C). Choice (D) becomes $|-1 + 5| = 6$, which simplifies to $|4| = 6$. Since this is false, eliminate (D). Now test −11 in (B) and (C). Choice (B) becomes $|-11 + 6| = 5$, which simplifies to $|-5| = 5$. Since this is true, keep (B). Choice (C) becomes $|-11 - 5| = 6$, which simplifies to $|-16| = 6$. Since this is false, eliminate (C). The correct answer is (B).

31.  **247, 248, 249, 250,** or **251**

This question asks for the volume of the ice cream cone. The reference box at the beginning of the math section gives the formula for the volume of a cone as $V = \frac{1}{3}\pi r^2 h$. The question states that $r$ is 4 centimeters and that $h$ is between 14.75 and 15 centimeters. Choose a value of $h$ to work with, for example, 14.8. Plug the known values into the formula to get $V = \frac{1}{3}\pi(4)^2(14.8)$. Solve to get $V = 247.97$ or 248. Depending on which value is used for height, the correct answer could be 247, 248, 249, 250, or 251.

32.  **8**  This question asks for the number of coworkers in the original group. Plug-and-play, trying different numbers for this value to solve the question. Try 10, since $400 divides evenly among 10 people. This would make the cost $40 per person. The question states that after 3 people decide not to contribute, the cost increases by $30 per person. In this scenario, that would mean the new cost should be $70 per person. However, after 3 people decide not to contribute, 7 people remain, and the $400 is divided by 7, making each person's share approximately $57. Since $57 is smaller than $70, 10 people is incorrect. Try a smaller number to make each person's share greater. Try 8 people, which would make the original cost per person $50. If 3 people drop out, the cost should

increase by $30 per person. In this scenario, that would mean the new cost is $80 per person. After 3 people decide not to contribute, 5 people remain, and the $400 is divided by 5, making each person's share $80. Since $80 is equal to $80, 8 people is correct. The correct answer is 8.

33. **11**   This questions asks to solve the equation. Simplify the equation by distributing the 3 and negative sign to get $12k - 30 - 26 - 5k = 21$. Combine like terms to get $7k - 56 = 21$. Add 56 to both sides to get $7k = 77$. Divide by 7 to get $k = 11$. The correct answer is 11.

34.   $\dfrac{6}{5}$ or **1.2**

The question asks for the $y$-coordinate of the $y$-intercept of the line. The $y$-intercept is the point where $x = 0$. To find the $y$-intercept, plug in 0 for $x$. This gives $-\dfrac{3}{4}(0) + \dfrac{5}{6}y = 1$, which can be simplified to $\dfrac{5}{6}y = 1$. Multiply both sides by 6 to get $5y = 6$. Divide both sides by 5 to get $y = \dfrac{6}{5}$. The $y$-intercept is $\left(0, \dfrac{6}{5}\right)$, and its $y$-coordinate is $\dfrac{6}{5}$. The answer is $\dfrac{6}{5}$.

35.   **5.8**   The question asks for the value of $h$ in the table. Start by finding the mean of the heights of Robert's rose bushes by using the Average Pie. Put the total in the top section and the number of things in the lower left section.

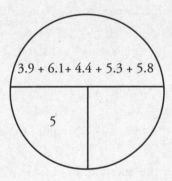

The average is the total divided by the number of things, so average = $\dfrac{3.9 + 6.1 + 4.4 + 5.3 + 5.8}{5} = \dfrac{25.5}{5} = 5.1$. The mean of the heights of Robert's rose bushes is 5.1, and the question states that this value is 0.3 feet greater than the mean of the heights of Louis's rose bushes. Since $5.1 - 0.3 = 4.8$, the mean of the heights of Louis's rose bushes is 4.8. Now use the Average Pie again to solve for the value of $h$ in the table.

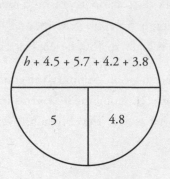

Therefore, $\dfrac{h + 4.5 + 5.7 + 4.2 + 3.8}{5}$ = 4.8. Simplify to get $\dfrac{h + 18.2}{5}$ = 4.8. Multiply both sides by 5 to get $h$ + 18.2 = 24. Subtract 18.2 from both sides to get $h$ = 5.8. The correct answer is 5.8.

36.   **6**   This question asks for the value of $c$. Since the point $(c, c)$ can be found on the graph of $y = -4x^2 + 25x$, plug in $c$ for both $x$ and $y$. This gives $c = -4c^2 + 25c$. Subtract $25c$ from both sides to get $-24c = -4c^2$. Divide both sides by $-4c$ to get $6 = c$. The correct answer is 6.

37.   **750**   The question asks how much more money John spent on rent than on office supplies. Add up the percents that have already been allocated to get 10% + 40% + 35% = 85%. Notice that 15% remains unaccounted for. This 15% represents the $450 that was spent on utilities. This means that 15% of John's total monthly expenditures equaled $450. Set up an equation to find John's total monthly expenditures: $\left(\dfrac{15}{100}\right)$ *total* = $450. Simplify to get (0.15)*total* = $450. Divide by 0.15 to get *total* = 3,000. Now answer the question. John spent 35% of his monthly expenditures on rent, which is $\left(\dfrac{35}{100}\right)$ ($3,000) = $1,050. He spent 10% of his monthly expenditures on office supplies, which is $\left(\dfrac{10}{100}\right)$ ($3,000) = $300. The difference between rent and office supplies is $1,050 – $300 = $750. The correct answer is $750.

38.   **20**   The question asks for the value of $k$, which represents the number of kindergarten students enrolled in 2011. Since the enrollment triples each year, divide by 3 to find the number of students enrolled each year. If there were 540 student enrolled in 2014, then there were $\dfrac{540}{3}$ = 180 students enrolled in 2013. This means that there were $\dfrac{180}{3}$ = 60 students enrolled in 2012 and $\dfrac{60}{3}$ = 20 student enrolled in 2011. Since this represents the value of $k$, the correct answer is 20.

# Chapter 19
# Practice Test 9

# Reading Test

## 65 MINUTES, 52 QUESTIONS

**Turn to Section 1 of your answer sheet to answer the questions in this section.**

---

### DIRECTIONS

Each passage or pair of passages below is followed by a number of questions. After reading each passage or pair, choose the best answer to each question based on what is stated or implied in the passage or passages and in any accompanying graphics (such as a table or graph).

---

**Questions 1–10 are based on the following passage.**

This passage is adapted from Wright Morris, *Ceremony in Lone Tree.* ©1959 by Wright Morris.

From the highway a half mile to the north, the town sits on the plain as if delivered on the flatcar—as though it were a movie set thrown up during the
Line  night. Dry as it is, something about it resembles an
5  ark from which the waters have receded. In the winter it appears to be locked in a sea of ice. In the summer, like the plain around it, the town seems to float on a watery surface, stray cattle stand knee-deep in a blur of reflections, and waves of light and heat flow across the
10  highway like schools of fish. Everywhere the tongue is dry, but the mind is wet. According to his daughters, who should know, the dirt caked around Tom Scanlon's teeth settled there in the thirties when the dust began to blow. More of it can be seen, fine as talcum, on the
15  linoleum floor in the lobby, where the mice raised in the basement move to their winter quarters in the cobs behind the stove.

To the east, relatively speaking, there is much to see, a lone tree, a water tank, sheets of rain and heat
20  lightning: to the west a strip of torn screen blurs the view. The effect is that of now-you-see-it, now-you-don't. As a rule, there is nothing to see, and if there is, one doubts it. The pane is smeared where Scanlon's nose has rubbed the glass. The fact that there is little
25  to see seems to be what he likes about it. He can see what he pleases. It need not please anybody else. Trains come from both directions, but from the east they

come without warning, the whistle blown away by the wind. From the west, thin and wild or strumming
30  like a wire fastened to the building, the sound wakes Scanlon from his sleep before the building rocks. It gives him time, that is, to prepare himself. The upgrade freights rock the building and leave nothing but the noise in his head, but the downgrade trains leave a
35  vacuum he sometimes raises the window to look at. A hole? He often thought he might see one there. A cloud of dust would veil the caboose, on the stove one of the pots or the lids would rattle, and if the lamp was lit, the flame would blow as if in a draft.

40  One day as the dust settled he saw a team of mares, the traces dragging, cantering down the bank where the train had just passed. On the wires above the tracks, dangling like a scarecrow, he saw the body of Emil Bickel, in whose vest pocket the key-wound
45  watch had stopped. At 7:34, proving the train that hit him had been right on time.

To the west the towns are thin and sparse, like the grass, and in a place called Indian Bow the white faces of cattle peer out of the soddies on the slope across the
50  dry bed of the river. They belong to one of Scanlon's grandchildren who married well. On the rise behind the soddies are sunken graves, one of the headstones bearing the name of Will Brady, a railroad man who occasionally stopped off at Lone Tree. Until Brady married and went
55  east, Scanlon thought him a sensible man.

Down the grade to the east the towns are greener and thicker, like the grass. The town of Polk, the

**CONTINUE**

home of Walter McKee, who married Scanlon's eldest
daughter, Lois, has elm-shaded streets and a sign on
60 the highway telling you to slow down. There is also
a park with a Civil War cannon, the name of Walter
McKee carved on the breech and that of his friend,
Gordon Boyd, on one of the cannon balls. In the
house where Walter McKee was born grass still grows
65 between the slats on the porch, and the neighbor's
chickens still lay their eggs under the stoop. At the
corner of the porch a tar barrel catches and stores the
rain from the roof. At the turn of the century, when
McKee was a boy, he buried the white hairs from a
70 mare's tail in the rain barrel, confident they would turn
up next as garter snakes. In the middle of the century
that isn't done, and a TV aerial, like a giant Martian
insect, crouches on the roof as if about to fly off with
the house. That is a change, but on its side in the yard
75 is a man's bicycle with the seat missing. The small boy
who rides it straddles it through the bars: he never
sits down. He mounts it slantwise, like a bareback
rider, grease from the chain rubbing off on one leg
and soiling the cuff of the pants leg rolled to the knee.
80 Gordon Boyd still bears the scar where the teeth of
the sprocket dug into his calf. Bolder than McKee, he
liked to ride on the gravel around the patch of grass in
the railroad station, leaning forward to hold a strip of
berry-box wood against the twirling spokes.

---

**1**

Over the course of the passage, the primary focus
shifts from

A) the death of Tom Scanlon's acquaintance to a tense
relationship.

B) explanations of how to navigate an area to
elements of Tom Scanlon's history.

C) a presentation of an area and its surroundings to
the details of a nearby town.

D) a description of a scene to the thoughts of
characters in another town.

---

**2**

The main purpose of the first paragraph is to

A) specify the time period of the passage through
recognizable events.

B) introduce an illustrative sequence by describing a
setting and a person.

C) begin a writing style that will shift in later
paragraphs.

D) illustrate the main character by describing things
that bother him.

---

**3**

It can be reasonably inferred that Scanlon has time to
"prepare himself" (line 32) because

A) he sets an alarm.

B) he wakes to the sound of a train whistle.

C) he has memorized the nightly train schedules.

D) he is made anxious by train noise.

---

**4**

Scanlon's frequent observation about the "downgrade
trains" (line 34) is that they

A) are noticeably louder than the upgrade trains.

B) may have damaged his window.

C) deliver dry goods to town.

D) are followed by silence.

---

**5**

Which choice provides the best evidence for the
answer to the previous question?

A) Lines 29–31 ("From the . . . rocks")

B) Lines 35–36 ("A hole? . . . there")

C) Lines 36–39 ("A cloud . . . draft")

D) Lines 40–42 ("One day . . . passed")

---

**CONTINUE** ➡

**6**

The author indicates that the area to the west of Scanlon's town is

A) where Emil Bickel used to live before he died.

B) less interesting to Scanlon than is the area to the east.

C) full of cattle ranches and frontier towns.

D) dry and relatively less densely populated.

**7**

The primary impression left by the author's description of Will Brady in lines 51–55 is that Will Brady was a

A) businessman and a disappointment.

B) preacher and martyr.

C) traveler and husband.

D) resident and loner.

**8**

The information in the final paragraph suggests that Polk

A) is the home of people who are connected to Scanlon.

B) is a town which contains a large number of children.

C) contains people who like to be reminded of historical events.

D) is a town with an unusually long history.

**9**

Which choice best supports the idea that a contrast between the old and the new can be found in Polk?

A) Lines 74–75 ("That is . . . missing")

B) Lines 75–77 ("The small . . . down")

C) Lines 77–79 ("He mounts . . . knee")

D) Lines 81–84 ("Bolder than . . . spokes")

**10**

As used in line 80, "bears" most nearly means

A) conveys.

B) transports.

C) shoulders.

D) possesses.

CONTINUE ➡

**Questions 11–20 are based on the following passage and supplementary material.**

This passage is adapted from John Byers, et al, "The Groupon Effect on Yelp Ratings: A Root Cause Analysis." Submitted to ACM EC '12 ACM X, X, Article X (February 2012).

In previous work examining Groupon, we measured and evaluated aspects of Groupon's operational strategy, as well as observed the impact
*Line* of customer behaviors including word-of-mouth
5   effects and how running a Groupon offer affects a merchant's reputation. One specific finding that received significant interest and attention was that Yelp reviews that contained the word "Groupon" provided, on average, significantly lower ratings than reviews
10  that did not, to the extent that it significantly lowered the average rating for businesses that used Groupon. In the original paper, we did not examine reasons to explain this finding, leaving it to future work. Our analysis met with a variety of reactions, ranging
15  from disbelief, to a number of plausible explanations for why this phenomenon should be expected: for example, Groupon users are fussy reviewers, Groupon businesses provide worse service than their peers, businesses discriminate by providing worse service
20  specifically to Groupon customers, and Groupon users are less of a good fit for the businesses where they redeem Groupons.

In this paper, we return to our finding of a sharp decline in Yelp ratings scores that coincides with
25  Groupon offers, a phenomenon we term the *Groupon effect*, and consider possible explanations through the lens of data analysis, based on an extensive dataset we gathered from Groupon and Yelp. Through this undertaking, we learn significantly more about the
30  daily deals model, including the behavior of Groupon users and businesses. *A priori*, one or more of the suggested explanations might be valid, and as such we examine where data provides positive and negative evidence for each.

35  However, we also suggest and provide evidence for an alternative explanation that we have not heard previously. It is well known that a potential problem with review sites is that businesses may actively solicit positive reviews for their business, either through
40  unscrupulous means such as hiring people to write positive reviews for them, or by less questionable means such as encouraging reviews from obviously enthusiastic customers. (In some cases, they may also attempt to place negative reviews for their competitors,
45  although this is arguably a less effective strategy.) Indeed, Yelp filters its reviews to prevent "spam reviews" from affecting its ratings.

Our hypothesis is that one reason for the discrepancy in review scores is that reviews that
50  mention Groupon correspond almost exclusively to reviews written by actual customers who use the service, and that other reviews are significantly more likely to be "fake" or otherwise introduced in an arguably artificial manner. Hence, we suggest that, at
55  least in part, the issue is not that reviews mentioning Groupon are somehow unusually low, but that the baseline of other reviews is on average artificially high, most likely because of actions taken by businesses designed specifically to generate high-scoring reviews.

60  We investigate the question of whether one class of reviewers is generally more critical than another. A more critical class of reviewers would review all businesses more critically on average, irrespective of whether they ran a Groupon. The fairest comparison
65  to isolate this effect is to compare evaluation on non-Groupon businesses. The results are surprising. We do not see strong evidence that Groupon reviewers are much more critical on average. Instead, they are more moderate! They provide fewer 1- and 5-star ratings
70  than their non-Groupon counterparts and more 3- and 4-star ratings.

Our interpretation is that this evidence strongly points not to critical reviewers, but to unrealized expectations between reviewers and merchants.
75  Moreover, while this mismatch appears to occur relatively infrequently, when it does occur, the result is a much more negative review than is typical for that reviewer.

We have examined a number of hypotheses for
80  explaining what we have dubbed the Groupon effect. While there remain challenges in trying to exactly quantify the different issues at play, we have shown that a combination of poor business behavior, Groupon user experimentation, and an artificially high baseline
85  all play a role.

Our compilation of evidence about Groupon users highlights that on average, Groupon users provide detailed reviews that are valued more highly by their Yelp peers. Contrary to what some would believe, the

**CONTINUE** ➡

90 evidence suggests that Groupon users are no more critical than their peers, although they may well be experimenting with a new business when using a Groupon. Although it seems obvious, we would advise businesses to treat Groupon customers as well as (or
95 possibly better than?) their other customers to avoid negative reputational impact.

Distribution of Yelp Star-Ratings by User and Review Type

— Groupon Businesses, Groupon User, Does Not Mention Groupon
— Non-Groupon Businesses, Groupon User
···■··· Non-Groupon Businesses, Standard User
– ■ – Groupon Businesses, Groupon User, Mentions Groupon

**11**

Over the course of the passage, the main focus shifts from describing a known phenomenon and potential theories for its existence to

A) an evaluation of evidence that addresses the possibility of several hypotheses.

B) an explanation of the method used to detect the original observation.

C) a critical review of the research and its implicit results.

D) an absolute reason for the previously identified dynamic.

**12**

The authors of the passage suggest that the *Groupon effect* may be defined by

A) ascribing great importance to Yelp ratings instead of multiple reviews.

B) combining disparate causes rather than just a single factor.

C) providing "spam reviews" more often than honest customer opinions.

D) speculating about Groupon users' behavior as compared to that of the general public.

**13**

Which choice provides the best evidence for the answer to the previous question?

A) Lines 29–31 ("we learn . . . businesses")

B) Lines 43–45 ("In some . . . strategy")

C) Lines 72–74 ("Our interpretation . . . merchants")

D) Lines 81–85 ("While there . . . role")

**14**

As used in line 53, "fake" most nearly means

A) plastic.

B) imaginary.

C) counterfeit.

D) planted.

**15**

Which action would best address a concern regarding the introduction of artificial Yelp reviews?

A) Requiring a verifiable receipt image to submit a review

B) Decreasing the scale from five stars to three stars

C) Implementing baseline ratings for online businesses

D) Soliciting only positive opinions of participating businesses

CONTINUE ➤

**16**

Which choice best describes the "unrealized expectations" (lines 73–74)?

A) Lines 1–5 ("we measured . . . effects")

B) Lines 17–22 ("Groupon users . . . Groupons")

C) Lines 37–43 ("It is . . . customers")

D) Lines 86–89 ("Our compilation . . . peers")

**17**

As used in line 86, "compilation" most nearly means

A) collection.

B) summary.

C) anthology.

D) yearbook.

**18**

According to the figure, which category of Yelp user showed the most evenly distributed star ratings?

A) Standard users of non-Groupon businesses

B) Groupon users of Groupon businesses who mention Groupon

C) Groupon users of Groupon businesses who do not mention Groupon

D) Groupon users of non-Groupon businesses

**19**

In the figure, which Yelp rating is a non-Groupon user most likely to give a business?

A) 1 star

B) 2 stars

C) 4 stars

D) 5 stars

**20**

Data presented in the figure most directly support which idea from the passage?

A) The patterns of Yelp star ratings are directly correlated to the type of business the customers are patronizing.

B) The customers most likely to post reviews on Yelp are those that produce "spam reviews."

C) The Yelp scores of Groupon users are more moderate than non-Groupon user reviews of the same businesses.

D) The number of Groupon mentions in a review directly correlates with the relative ranking of that review.

**CONTINUE** ➤

**Questions 21–31 are based on the following passage.**

This passage is adapted from Malcolm Macleod, "Some Salt with Your Statin, Professor?" ©2014 by PLOS Biology.

We know that clinical trials sponsored by the pharmaceutical industry are likely to exaggerate benefit and minimize harms. But do these biases extend to
Line their sponsorship of non-human animal research?
5 Are the findings of such studies credible? And how do those findings compare with "proper" research conducted by dispassionate academics?

These are important questions, but how could we find this stuff out? In the same way that it would
10 be difficult to conduct a randomized controlled trial of the effect of living in Scotland on your chance of having a stroke, it is difficult to do an experiment to test whether the funding source for a study influences the outcome. Since clinical trials sponsored by the
15 pharmaceutical industry seem to be at greater risk of bias than others, a lazy assumption might be that their non-human animal research is similarly confounded, as they seek to rush compounds to market to maximize profitability.

20 However, a few straws in the wind hint this might not be the case. One way companies identify drug targets is by reading what's out there in the literature and, if something looks interesting, seeking to replicate the findings. Bayer scientists found inconsistencies
25 in 43 of 65 studies when they tried to replicate them in-house. Implementation of good laboratory practice standards is much more advanced in industry labs, and for some types of experiments these standards are a legal requirement. So, could it be that industry-
30 sponsored research is actually more rigorous than academic research?

Taking the example of statin treatments for atheroma, David Krauth, Andrew Anglemyer, Rose Philipps, and Lisa Bero address this issue head-on.
35 Using systematic review, they identified non-human animal studies describing the efficacy of statins. Focusing on those studies where sponsorship status was known, they found that the results of nine of 19 industry-sponsored studies (43%) and 18 of 28
40 non-industry-sponsored studies (72%) supported

the efficacy of statins. As interesting, however, is the analysis of the interpretation placed on the findings in each of the included studies. Of 19 industry-sponsored studies, the conclusion of 18 favored the use of statins
45 (95%), while of 28 non-industry-sponsored studies, only 21 did so (75%).

It does therefore appear that findings from research sponsored by industry are more conservative than those sponsored by non-industry sources, but
50 the interpretation of those data is, in contrast, less conservative. Why might this be?

In my view it is likely that the impact of approaches to research management and the regulatory environment that apply to some parts of industry—
55 particularly standards for internal reporting—extends to most of the non-human animal research activity with which they are involved, whether or not it is performed in-house. That is, non-human animal work sponsored by industry is likely to be performed and
60 reported to a higher quality, and to be at lower risk of bias, than work sponsored by others. This would explain the difficulty industry has in replicating the results of research conducted in academic labs. However, the interpretation, or "spin," with which
65 industry-sponsored work is presented does appear to be an issue, with exaggeration of the conclusions to favor the drug being tested.

This makes sense—for industry there is a clear financial interest in being absolutely secure in the non-
70 human animal data for a compound before embarking on a clinical trial, so there is a real motivation to get the preclinical data as good as they can be. But when that money has been spent (and for statins it largely has been), the motivation is to present an analysis of
75 the available data that is most supportive for clinical use. So, if a drug is a turkey, try to find that out before spending a fortune taking it to clinical trial—and if it's too late for that, try to convince everyone that the non-human animal and clinical trial data supporting an
80 efficacy for *Meleagris gallopavo* (commonly known as the wild turkey) are more convincing than they might at first appear.

**CONTINUE** ➡

**21**

As used in line 3, "extend" most nearly means

A) reach.

B) require.

C) apply.

D) stretch.

**22**

The questions posed in lines 3–7 are chiefly intended to

A) introduce a set of considerations that may not have been investigated in prior research.

B) show confusion about the nature of results provided by similar forms of research.

C) declare that non-human animal research is an improper method of conducting trials.

D) stir controversy about the quality of research performed by academics.

**23**

Which question was the research of Bero's team primarily intended to answer?

A) Does industry-sponsored research make it more difficult to analyze statins than academic research sponsored by non-industry sources?

B) Do experiments funded by invested corporations get performed with a greater level of attention to detail than those that are not?

C) What prevents industry-sponsored research from being conducted with the same level of rigor as academic research?

D) Does non-human animal research funded by industry sources lead to fewer clinical trials than research performed by academics?

**24**

Which choice provides the best evidence for the answer to the previous question?

A) Lines 29–31 ("So could . . . research")

B) Lines 32–34 ("Taking the . . . head-on")

C) Lines 37–41 ("Focusing on . . . statins")

D) Lines 61–63 ("This would . . . labs")

**25**

The main purpose of the fourth paragraph (lines 32–46) is to

A) question the implications of the surprising findings of Bero's team.

B) note significant results of Bero's team's study regarding sources of research.

C) shift from a description of Bero's team's study to an overview of a question.

D) connect research performed on human subjects to research performed on non-human animals.

**26**

As used in line 48, "conservative" most nearly means

A) old-fashioned.

B) dramatic.

C) traditional.

D) reserved.

**27**

According to the passage, when compared to non-human animal research sponsored by industry, the non-human research sponsored by others

A) shows a lower risk of bias.

B) is easier to accurately reproduce in clinical trials.

C) is not always performed at as high a quality.

D) costs more to complete.

**CONTINUE**

**28**

According to the passage, the findings of Bero's team are surprising because they

A) give support to an obvious conclusion.

B) apparently contradict a sensible assumption.

C) undermine the studies of clinical trials.

D) confirm the existence of unknown statistics.

**29**

Which choice provides the best evidence for the answer to the previous question?

A) Lines 24–26 ("Bayer scientists . . . in-house")

B) Lines 43–46 ("Of 19 . . . (75%)")

C) Lines 47–51 ("It does . . . be")

D) Lines 64–67 ("However, the . . . tested")

**30**

The author of the passage would most likely agree that industry-sponsored research may be rigorous because it

A) applies standards of internal reporting to employees who cut corners.

B) hires scientists who excel in their respective fields.

C) risks scrutiny from legislators if it fails to adhere to adequate standards.

D) utilizes elements of documentation that are also applied to purposes other than research.

**31**

Which choice provides the best evidence for the answer to the previous question?

A) Lines 35–36 ("Using systematic . . . statins")

B) Lines 41–43 ("As interesting . . . studies")

C) Lines 47–51 ("It does . . . conservative")

D) Lines 52–58 ("In my . . . in-house")

**CONTINUE**

**Questions 32–42 are based on the following passages.**

Passage 1 is adapted from P. G. Hubert, "Occupations for Women." Originally published in 1894. Passage 2 is adapted from Virginia Penny, *Think and Act*. Originally published in 1869.

## Passage 1

The fact that women are paid less than men for apparently the same service seems to disturb a great many people, who find here a conspiracy upon the part of man to keep women out of the wage-earning field so far as this can be done. The maxim, "Business is business," applies here with as much force as anywhere. Both men and women earn, as a rule, just what they are worth. The law of supply and demand comes into play as relentlessly here as elsewhere. If a woman wants more money than a man, she has only to do better and more work in the long run than the man, and she will get more pay as surely as business rules remain in force in the business world.

There are some reasons for the apparent discrepancy between the pay of men and women, which may serve to clear away some of the false impressions that have grown up about this question. In the first place, women as a class of workers are beginners, comparatively speaking, in the great field of industry; they lack the hereditary instinct for such work, and as beginners their wages are low. Woman's preparation for work is seldom so thorough as with a man, and long technical training for any work is often considered superfluous for a woman because she may marry. Even should she remain a wage earner, the woman has seldom the strong incentive of others dependent upon her; the man has a wife and children who will suffer, should he relax his efforts; the woman is usually alone.

A curious feature of work by women is that, while in this century and in America work and money-earning have always been considered to be proper in every way for men, there is still some slight social stigma pertaining to money-getting by women. This may be trusted to die out as fast as women show that they can retain all the most attractive attributes of womanhood and yet earn their own living.

The old-time fiction to the effect that woman was a tender flower, blooming only when sheltered from the world, and likely either to droop or lose its fragrance when brought into contact with a vulgar, work-a-day, money-grubbing world, has been called into question before now. Some eminent thinkers and essayists, such as Mr. Frederic Harrison, the English writer, dread the effect of political, professional, and business life upon woman. They fear the appearance of the mannish woman upon the scene.

## Passage 2

In woman's work and wages the times are a century or more behind the improvements made in science and art. Society is tardy, dragging, in the matter. A woman may be defined to be a creature that receives half price for all she does, and pays full price for all she needs. She earns as a child — she pays as a man. Besides, her sex, if not barbarous custom, cuts her off from the best rewarded colleges. Her hands, feet, and brain are clogged. We ask our readers to pause and inquire if this is not true.

It requires just as much to support a woman as a man. Her dress requires more. Often infirm, sick, or aged parents are relying on her for a support, or, it may be, orphan brothers and sisters. Or, even if it were not so, a woman needs to lay up something for times of sickness, old age, and want of employment, as well as a man. When men and women are employed in the same establishments, women have not the lightest, most healthy, and most pleasant parts of the labor. They have the hardest, worst paid, and most unhealthy work. In civilized countries it is a remnant of the former degradation of the sex. Over-work and under-pay are the curse of workwomen. While they last, the poverty, and suffering, of women, will continue.

To pay women better prices for labor will give it a dignity in public estimation. The effect will prove beneficial not only to workers, pecuniarily and socially, but its influence will extend to those indirectly affected. If women were paid in proportion to the quality and quantity of their work, at the same rate that men are paid, there could be no reasonable objection to women entering any occupation they desire to. It is unmanly and unjust to cut short a woman's wages merely because she is a woman.

**CONTINUE**

**32**

In Passage 1, Hubert makes which point about working women relative to working men?

A) Women make disturbingly less than men, and women also supply more conspiracies than men.

B) Women are able to earn as much as men, but women choose to become parents more often than men.

C) Women are newer to the workforce than men, and women have less training than men.

D) Women can currently perform as well as men, but women receive less pay than men.

**33**

Which choice provides the best evidence for the answer to the previous question?

A) Lines 1–5 ("The fact . . .. done")

B) Lines 18–25 ("In the . . . marry")

C) Lines 25–29 ("Even should . . . alone")

D) Lines 30–34 ("A curious . . . women")

**34**

In Passage 1, Hubert implies that the wage gap between women and men is

A) inevitable, because women's genes do not prepare them for the same work as men's.

B) avoidable, because women and men can either support themselves or marry.

C) misunderstood, because workers are paid based on experience.

D) regrettable, because women and men deserve fair treatment in the working world.

**35**

As used in line 28, "relax" most nearly means

A) lessen.

B) chill.

C) recuperate.

D) calm.

**36**

As used in line 30, "curious" most nearly means

A) interested.

B) nosy.

C) mischievous.

D) peculiar.

**37**

What is Penny's central claim in Passage 2?

A) Women must protest the gender-based wage gap.

B) Society should progress by reducing the gender-based wage gap.

C) Women should not have to pay full price when they are paid half price.

D) Societies that underpay women while overpaying men will be punished.

**38**

In Passage 2, Penny makes which point about women's working conditions?

A) They are similar to the working conditions of children.

B) They may involve lighter tasks than those expected of men in similar jobs.

C) They can involve harder and less pleasant tasks than men are asked to do.

D) They have been improved through acts of civil disobedience.

CONTINUE ▶

**39**

Which choice provides the best evidence for the answer to the previous question?

A) Line 50 ("Society is . . . matter")

B) Lines 59–61 ("Often infirm . . . sisters")

C) Lines 64–66 ("When men . . . labor")

D) Lines 73–75 ("The effect . . . affected")

**40**

Which choice best states the relationship between the two passages?

A) Passage 2 promotes several theories offered in Passage 1.

B) Passage 2 outlines the results of a plan defended in Passage 1.

C) Passage 2 supports changing a discrepancy discussed in Passage 1.

D) Passage 2 offers reasons for a view presented in Passage 1.

**41**

Based on the passages, both authors would agree with which of the following claims?

A) Businesses often overwork and underpay women.

B) Social disapproval of working women may decline over time.

C) The wage gap between men and women is more apparent than real.

D) Educated women should earn higher salaries.

**42**

Hubert would most likely have reacted to lines 72–73 ("To pay . . . estimation") of Passage 2 with

A) disagreement, because men and women are paid fairly according to the labor market.

B) panic, because affirmative action amounts to reverse discrimination.

C) empathy, because women deserve this sort of respect as much as men do.

D) elation, because pay raises for working women will remove the stigma that working women currently suffer from.

**CONTINUE** ➡

**Question 43–52 are based on the following passage and supplementary material.**

This passage is adapted from Jennifer Ackerman, "Food: How Altered?" © 2015 by National Geographic.

Most people in the United States don't realize that they've been eating genetically engineered foods since the mid-1990s. More than 60 percent of all processed
Line foods on U.S. supermarket shelves—including pizza,
5 chips, cookies, ice cream, salad dressing, corn syrup, and baking powder—contain ingredients from engineered soybeans, corn, or canola.

In the past decade or so, the biotech plants that go into these processed foods have leaped from hothouse
10 oddities to crops planted on a massive scale—on 130 million acres (52.6 million hectares) in 13 countries, among them Argentina, Canada, China, South Africa, Australia, Germany, and Spain. On U.S. farmland, acreage planted with genetically engineered crops
15 jumped nearly 25-fold from 3.6 million acres (1.5 million hectares) in 1996 to 88.2 million acres (35.7 million hectares) in 2001. More than 50 different "designer" crops have passed through a federal review process, and about a hundred more are undergoing
20 field trials….

Genetic modification is not novel. Humans have been altering the genetic makeup of plants for millennia, keeping seeds from the best crops and planting them in following years, breeding and
25 crossbreeding varieties to make them taste sweeter, grow bigger, last longer. In this way we've transformed the wild tomato, *Lycopersicon*, from a fruit the size of a marble to today's giant, juicy beefsteaks. From a weedy plant called teosinte with an "ear" barely an inch long
30 has come our foot-long (0.3-meter-long) ears of sweet white and yellow corn….

But the technique of genetic engineering is new, and quite different from conventional breeding. Traditional breeders cross related organisms whose
35 genetic makeups are similar. In so doing, they transfer tens of thousands of genes. By contrast, today's genetic engineers can transfer just a few genes at a time between species that are distantly related or not related at all.

40 Genetic engineers can pull a desired gene from virtually any living organism and insert it into virtually any other organism. They can put a rat gene into lettuce to make a plant that produces vitamin C or splice genes from the cecropia moth into apple plants,
45 offering protection from fire blight, a bacterial disease that damages apples and pears. The purpose is the same: to insert a gene or genes from a donor organism carrying a desired trait into an organism that does not have the trait.

50 The engineered organisms scientists produce by transferring genes between species are called transgenic. Several dozen transgenic food crops are currently on the market, among them varieties of corn, squash, canola, soybeans, and cotton, from
55 which cottonseed oil is produced. Most of these crops are engineered to help farmers deal with age-old agriculture problems: weeds, insects, and disease….

"Eight hundred million people on this planet are malnourished," says Channapatna Prakash, a native
60 of India and an agricultural scientist at the Center for Plant Biotechnology Research at Tuskegee University, "and the number continues to grow."

Genetic engineering can help address the urgent problems of food shortage and hunger, say Prakash and
65 many other scientists. It can increase crop yields, offer crop varieties that resist pests and disease, and provide ways to grow crops on land that would otherwise not support farming because of drought conditions, depleted soils, or soils plagued by excess salt or high
70 levels of aluminum and iron. "This technology is extremely versatile," Prakash explains, "and it's easy for farmers to use because it's built into the seed. The farmers just plant the seeds, and the seeds bring new features in the plants."

75 Some critics of genetic engineering argue that the solution to hunger and malnutrition lies in redistributing existing food supplies. Others believe that the ownership by big multinational companies of key biotechnology methods and genetic information
80 is crippling public-sector efforts to use this technology to address the needs of subsistence farmers…. All of this bodes ill, say critics, for farmers in the developing world….

CONTINUE

Whether biotech foods will deliver on their promise
85 of eliminating world hunger and bettering the lives of
all remains to be seen. Their potential is enormous,
yet they carry risks—and we may pay for accidents or
errors in judgment in ways we cannot yet imagine. But
the biggest mistake of all would be to blindly reject or
90 endorse this new technology. If we analyze carefully
how, where, and why we introduce genetically altered
products, and if we test them thoroughly and judge
them wisely, we can weigh their risks against their
benefits to those who need them most.

**Adoption of genetically engineered crops in the U. S.**

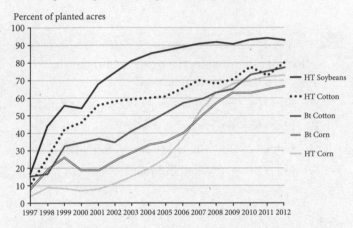

Data for each crop category include varieties with both HT and Bt (stacked) traits.
Source: USDA, Economic Research Service.

Figure 1

**Adoption of genetically engineered corn in the United States, by trait, 2000–16**

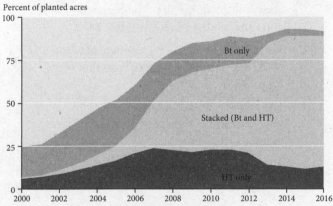

Source: USDA, Economic Research Service using data from USDA,
National Agricultural Statistics Service, *June Agricultural Survey*.

Figure 2

Note: HT crops are genetically-engineered to be herbicide-tolerant, allowing farmers to use more herbicides to fight weeds. Bt crops are genetically-
engineered to be pest-resistant.

---

**43**

According to the passage, a unique benefit of genetic
engineering is the ability to

A) combine more traits than through conventional
breeding.

B) create plants that are larger or sweeter than their
previous generations.

C) cure the problem of world hunger.

D) produce more crops on smaller plots of land.

**44**

As used in line 21, "novel" most nearly means

A) bookish.

B) written.

C) common.

D) modern.

**45**

Which statement best expresses a relationship
between conventional breeding and genetic
engineering that is presented in the passage?

A) Both alter the genetic makeup of an organism, but
genetic engineering allows tens of thousands of
genes to be shared rather than only a few.

B) Both encourage the development of favorable
characteristics, but conventional breeding only
allows cross-breeding between genetically-similar
organisms.

C) Both can improve plant hardiness and longevity,
but the plants used in conventional breeding are
different from those used in genetic engineering.

D) Both allow engineers to combine individual genes
from various species, isolating only the traits they
want to develop.

CONTINUE

**46**

Which choice provides the best evidence for the answer to the previous question?

A) Lines 21–26 ("Humans have . . . longer")

B) Lines 32–33 ("But the . . . breeding")

C) Lines 36–39 ("By contrast . . . all")

D) Lines 40–42 ("Genetic engineers . . . organism")

**47**

As used in line 65, "yields" most nearly means

A) rewards.

B) earnings.

C) outputs.

D) benefits.

**48**

According to Prakash, the technology behind genetically-engineered crops is "easy for farmers to use" (lines 71–72) because

A) no additional work or training is required for its distribution.

B) farmers already have systems in place to deal with drought conditions.

C) salt, aluminum, and iron are provided by the engineers.

D) it provides a network to help farmers redistribute existing food supplies.

**49**

Which choice best reflects the perspective of the "critics" (line 75) in regard to genetic engineering?

A) It is the only way to assist subsistence farmers competing against multinational companies.

B) It will result in eight hundred million people losing direct access to valuable food resources.

C) It will have a negative impact on the fight against world hunger.

D) Its potential effectiveness is severely limited by other influences.

**50**

Which choice provides the best evidence for the answer to the previous question?

A) Lines 63–65 ("Genetic engineering . . . scientists")

B) Lines 65–70 ("It can . . . iron")

C) Lines 77–81 ("Others believe . . . farmers")

D) Lines 84–86 ("Whether biotech . . . seen")

**51**

Which statement is best supported by the information provided in Figure 1?

A) The percentage of HT cotton planted acres increased at a constant rate from 1997–2012.

B) The percentage of Bt corn planted acres was consistently higher than the percentage of Bt cotton planted acres from 1997–2012.

C) From 2001–2007, the percentage of planted acres of HT corn increased more than that of any other crop shown.

D) From 2008–2012, no single crop consistently maintained the highest percentage of acres planted.

**CONTINUE**

52

Which of the following claims is supported by Figure 2?

A) Corn that is only resistant to pests never had the highest percent of acres planted.

B) In 2016, more corn was planted that was both resistant to pests and tolerant of herbicides than corn that was only either resistant to pests or tolerant of herbicides.

C) In 2014, Bt-only and HT-only corn had roughly the same combined percentage of acres planted as stacked (Bt and HT) corn.

D) Corn that was both resistant to pests and tolerant of herbicides did not exist until 2004.

## STOP

**If you finish before time is called, you may check your work on this section only.**
**Do not turn to any other section in the test.**

# Writing and Language Test

## 35 MINUTES, 44 QUESTIONS

**Turn to Section 2 of your answer sheet to answer the questions in this section.**

### DIRECTIONS

Each passage below is accompanied by a number of questions. For some questions, you will consider how the passage might be revised to improve the expression of ideas. For other questions, you will consider how the passage might be edited to correct errors in sentence structure, usage, or punctuation. A passage or a question may be accompanied by one or more graphics (such as a table or graph) that you will consider as you make revising and editing decisions.

Some questions will direct you to an underlined portion of a passage. Other questions will direct you to a location in a passage or ask you to think about the passage as a whole.

After reading each passage, choose the answer to each question that most effectively improves the quality of writing in the passage or that makes the passage conform to the conventions of standard written English. Many questions include a "NO CHANGE" option. Choose that option if you think the best choice is to leave the relevant portion of the passage as it is.

**Questions 1–11 are based on the following passage.**

**Lions and Tigers and... Deer?**

A large majority of the six million auto accidents each year are preventable. Many are caused by the traditional risks, like cell-phone use, drunk driving, or excessive speed. **1**

**1**

At this point, the writer is considering adding the following sentence.

> Statistics show that people are 23 times more likely to be involved in collisions when they are texting and driving.

Should the writer make this addition here?

A) Yes, because it provides a useful transition from the previous sentence to the next.

B) Yes, because it provides evidence for a claim made in the paragraph's first sentence.

C) No, because it gives a detail that contradicts the paragraph's main focus.

D) No, because it deviates from the paragraph's main topic and argument.

CONTINUE ➡

A recent set of research findings, however, [2] has been suggesting that nearly one sixth of these accidents could be prevented by a single factor: mountain lions.

[3] We probably want to start conjuring funny images of mountain lions with speed guns or a taste for cell phones. Before we do that, let's back up a bit. The fact is that nearly 1.2 million collisions each year occur between automobiles and deer. [4] The eastern part of the United States is at a special risk for these collisions because deer tend to roam freely and plentifully around the region. For all their adaptations to human life, deer have not developed a way to deal with traffic. If you drive regularly in the northeast, you know that the proof is usually on the side of the road.

[2]

A) NO CHANGE
B) would suggest
C) have suggested
D) suggests

[3]

Which choice most effectively combines the underlined sentences?

A) Before we start conjuring funny images of mountain lions with speed guns or a taste for cell phones, let's back up a bit.

B) Let's back up a bit before we start conjuring images like the funny ones we want of mountain lions with speed guns or a taste for cell phones.

C) We probably want to start conjuring funny images of mountain lions with speed guns or a taste for cell phones; before we do that, however, let's back up a bit.

D) Let's back up a bit before we can talk about mountain lions with speed guns and a taste for cell phones that we conjured in funny ways.

[4]

The writer is considering deleting the underlined sentence. Should the sentence be kept or deleted?

A) Kept, because it provides a detail that explains the statistic given in the previous sentence.

B) Kept, because it helps to explain why car travel is so dangerous in the United States.

C) Deleted, because it skews the passage's focus on the more serious causes of auto accidents.

D) Deleted, because it undermines the passage's claim that deer are useful members of an ecosystem.

CONTINUE

[1] Part of the reason that deer populations have grown as much as **5** they have is that deer face no natural predators in the eastern states. [2] Large-scale development and hunting have eliminated this threat. [3] In areas where these predators continue to exist, such as California, deer-related collisions are significantly lower. [4] Deer are thus able to reproduce without restriction. **6**

For a kind of natural solution to this problem, University of Washington wildlife biologist Laura Pugh has proposed reintroducing mountain lions into ecosystems along the eastern seaboard. The shock for the carnivorous cats would not be so significant because these species of mountain lion are actually indigenous to the area. Pugh **7** opines the mountain lion populations of the west as evidence **8** that these big cats "can coexist in close proximity with people, with very few conflicts."

**5**

A) NO CHANGE

B) we have

C) it has

D) one has

**6**

To make this paragraph most logical, sentence 4 should be placed

A) before sentence 1.

B) after sentence 1.

C) after sentence 2.

D) where it is now.

**7**

A) NO CHANGE

B) cites

C) says

D) proclaims

**8**

A) NO CHANGE

B) or

C) which

D) when

CONTINUE →

Obviously, it will be difficult to get public sentiment on her side. The thought of encountering mountain lions in the wild chills most of us to the bone, and it doesn't seem that introducing this fierce animal back into the wild would be beneficial enough to offset its terrorizing costs. [9] Therefore, Pugh and her team say, these predators could save approximately five times as many people from deer-related deaths as they might endanger through unprovoked attacks.

The question now is whether the data are [10] sufficiently overcoming public concerns. If we've accepted the risks of driving tons of metal many miles an hour down the road, is it possible that [11] our fear of mountain lions could be the next human instinct to be cast aside?

9
A) NO CHANGE
B) Still,
C) Inevitably,
D) Furthermore,

10.
A) NO CHANGE
B) a good amount in overcoming
C) enough to overcome
D) enough for overcoming

11
A) NO CHANGE
B) its
C) one's
D) their

**CONTINUE**

**Questions 12–22 are based on the following passage.**

## The Original Music of New Orleans

The city of New Orleans, Louisiana, has always been a kind of national treasure with **12** routes in French, American, African, and indigenous cultures. This has become even more apparent since 2005, when Hurricane Katrina nearly wiped the city off the map. **13** For example, Katrina brought new attention to the city, demonstrating how much would be lost if New Orleans were to disappear.

While the city has always been praised as the place to "let the good times roll," its status in the popular imagination has changed significantly over the years and **14** shifts with broader national interests. Today, for instance, New Orleans is seen as the birthplace of jazz music. **15** Louis Armstrong was born in New Orleans in 1901 and began playing trumpet at an early age. The annual Jazzfest celebrates this heritage, and groups like the New Orleans Preservation Hall Jazz Band continue to commemorate the long tradition of jazz in the city.

**12**

A) NO CHANGE
B) roots in
C) roots of
D) routes of

**13**

A) NO CHANGE
B) However,
C) Thus,
D) DELETE the underlined portion.

**14**

A) NO CHANGE
B) have shifted
C) shifted
D) shifting

**15**

The writer is considering deleting the underlined sentence. Should the sentence be kept or deleted?

A) Kept, because it supports the passage's claim that jazz is a significant part of musical history.

B) Kept, because it adds a crucial detail about a resident of New Orleans that supports the passage's main idea.

C) Deleted, because it suggests that the type of music discussed in the passage is insignificant.

D) Deleted, because it introduces a piece of information that is only vaguely related to the paragraph's main idea.

**CONTINUE** ➡

The musical history of New Orleans does not stop here, however. In a way, jazz gets the attention because it is a kind of national **16** music has roots all over the American South, the East Coast, and the Midwest. But there is at least one style of music that is unique to New Orleans and the areas to the south: zydeco. **17** Some people find this name curious, and you may be one of them. If you are, you're not alone. Scholars disagree on its origins, though most believe that it comes from some combination of words in creole French, the dialect spoken by the early European settlers of Louisiana.

Wherever the name comes from, one of its earliest recorded uses is on the 1929 recording "It Ain't Gonna Rain No' Mo'" by the Zydeco Skillet Lickers. This song is one of the earliest examples of a genre that has **18** remained and impressively stayed both durable and adaptable with the changing times and technologies. Early zydeco music was primarily performed with a button or piano accordion and a washboard, and it was **19** influenced by the polkas and waltzes of the late nineteenth century.

**16**

A) NO CHANGE
B) music that it has
C) music, with
D) music, which

**17**

Which choice most effectively combines the underlined sentences?

A) Finding this name curious as many people do means that you're not alone.
B) If you find this name curious, you're not alone.
C) You're not alone if you find this name a curious one like many people.
D) Like many people who find this name curious, you're not alone if you do.

**18**

A) NO CHANGE
B) remained, impressively stayed
C) remained
D) remained and stayed

**19**

A) NO CHANGE
B) influenced, by the polkas and waltzes,
C) influenced by the polkas and waltzes—
D) influenced by the polkas and waltzes,

CONTINUE

The form changed throughout the twentieth century, perhaps crystallizing in the work of the "King of Zydeco" Clifton **20** Chenier. Today, groups like **21** BeauSoleil continue to help zydeco to evolve, incorporating rock and country influences as well. As a testament to the endurance and popularity of zydeco music, the Grammys even introduced a new category in 2007: Best Zydeco or Cajun Music Album.

Zydeco is a pleasure to listen to, but it is just as important as a cultural **22** memorial. Indeed, zydeco provides an important reminder that a region is never merely defined by its most popular exports. Lots of things go into creating "local color," and the "local" in any place is much richer than we typically recognize.

**20**

Which choice adds the most relevant supporting information to the paragraph?

A) Chenier, born in the Creole-French speaking town of Opelousas, Louisiana.

B) Chenier, who infused the uptempo music with blues and jazz from the region.

C) Chenier; he is best known for how well he played the accordion and once won a Grammy.

D) Chenier, who was greatly respected at the time of his death in 1987.

**21**

A) NO CHANGE

B) BeauSoleil continue to help zydeco, to evolve

C) BeauSoleil continue, to help zydeco, to evolve

D) BeauSoleil, continue to help zydeco to evolve,

**22**

A) NO CHANGE

B) agreement.

C) victory.

D) artifact.

CONTINUE →

**Questions 23–33 are based on the following passage and supplementary material.**

### Between Land and Sea

The separation between land and water seems a relatively simple one. Land is for walking, for cars, and for trains, whereas water is for swimming, for bathing, and for ships. The two come into contact in riverbeds, on banks, and on beaches, but the separation between them is clear. Or is it?

[23] Excavations in San Francisco, conducted over the past fifty years have revealed that the boundary between land and water is not so distinct. Digging into the surface of San Francisco's downtown Financial District has unearthed some unlikely building foundations: ships. [24] In fact, one of the tunnels for San Francisco's subway system, the BART, passes right through one of these interred ships. How did those massive vessels all get down there?

[25] The answer may seem counterintuitive. San Francisco manufactured a bit of its land. If this seems odd, consider that many cities throughout the world—among them Chicago, Singapore, and New York—have created landmasses in this way. The solution may seem bizarre until we consider that one of the major problem in cities is overcrowding. What better way to ease this problem than to create more land?

**CONTINUE →**

**23**

A) NO CHANGE

B) Excavations—in San Francisco conducted over the past fifty years—

C) Excavations, in San Francisco conducted, over the past fifty years,

D) Excavations in San Francisco conducted over the past fifty years

**24**

At this point, the writer is considering adding the following information.

> The area that was to become San Francisco was for many years known as Yerba Buena.

Should the writer make this addition here?

A) Yes, because it gives an interesting detail that delves further into San Francisco's history.

B) Yes, because it explains why so many ships should be buried in San Francisco's downtown.

C) No, because it obscures the focus of the passage by introducing a detail that does not have an obvious connection.

D) No, because the passage is primarily concerned with the importance of mass transit in San Francisco.

**25**

Which choice most effectively combines the underlined sentences?

A) San Francisco, an answer that may seem counterintuitive, manufactured some of its land.

B) The answer may seem counterintuitive, so San Francisco manufactured some of its land.

C) Even though the answer may be seeming counterintuitive, San Francisco was a place that manufactured some of its land.

D) The answer may seem counterintuitive: San Francisco manufactured some of its land.

[1] One outgrowth of these recent discoveries has been a blurring of traditional scholarly boundaries. [2] Each of these disciplines has historically stuck to **26** its own area of expertise. [3] What happens, though, when geologists want to study landmasses containing man-made items such as ships and building fragments? [4] Both groups of experts are starting to work together on many projects, as it becomes clear that, particularly in the last 150 years, humans have shaped their natural environments to such an extent that nothing can be considered purely "natural" any longer. [5] For example, archaeology focused on human history, while geology concerned itself with natural history. **27**

Researchers have called this new layer of land the "archaeosphere." **28** Because we may think of the ground as something that is relatively constant, the archaeosphere suggests that quite the opposite is true.

**26**

A) NO CHANGE

B) our

C) their

D) his

**27**

To make this paragraph most logical, sentence 5 should be placed

A) where it is now.

B) after sentence 1.

C) after sentence 2.

D) after sentence 3.

**28**

A) NO CHANGE

B) But

C) While

D) Since

**CONTINUE**

On the one hand, this is disturbing because it shows that the solid ground [29] built on by them may not be so solid after all. On the other hand, the classification and study of the archaeosphere could be beneficial and not just for the work of archaeologists and geologists. [30] In a sense, some companies in Scandinavia have begun to mine the archaeosphere for [31] resources that may have been wasted or discarded in earlier ages. Perhaps the world is not running out of resources in the way that we believed. Maybe it has instead found [32] its' own way to recycle those resources, and we just need to catch up.

Cross-section of Waste Deposits

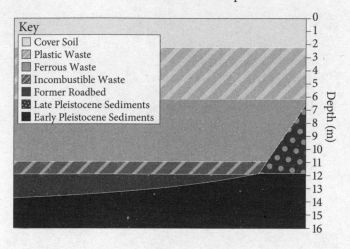

**Question [33] asks about the graphic.**

---

**29**

A) NO CHANGE

B) they build on

C) built on by us

D) we build on

**30**

A) NO CHANGE

B) Nonetheless,

C) For example,

D) Therefore,

**31**

A) NO CHANGE

B) resources to have been

C) resources, they have been

D) resources, being

**32**

A) NO CHANGE

B) they're

C) it's

D) its

**33**

Which choice offers an accurate interpretation of the data in the figure?

A) The cover soil is made up primarily of human and industrial waste products.

B) The soil as deep as 14 meters below the surface contains traces of human development.

C) The soil above 14 meters deep is made up of approximately 75% human and industrial waste products.

D) At depths of less than 10 meters below the surface, there is some human influence, but at depths greater than 10 meters, there is none.

**CONTINUE** →

**Questions 34–44 are based on the following passage.**

## The Sequence

Advances in the medical sciences have saved countless lives and made the lives of many, even the seriously ill, much more **34** healthy and medical. Since the Human Genome Project declared its work complete in 2003, genetic sequencing has begun to reveal some of its most significant contributions, and the breadth of those contributions is likely to extend well beyond what is currently known.

**35** One affect, genetic sequencing, as it relates to family history and lifetime health, has spawned a whole new field of wellness. Genetic counseling enables expectant parents to estimate the risks of having children based on hereditary patterns. This growing field is primarily concerned with the transmission of potentially harmful genes from parents to their offspring. **36** Children are particularly susceptible to illness just after birth. A large category of patients are expectant mothers, who seek prenatal testing to predict the likelihood of **37** medical risks, transmittable diseases, inborn illnesses, and birth defects for their unborn children.

**34**

A) NO CHANGE
B) tolerable and manageable.
C) complicated and expensive.
D) patient and tolerant.

**35**

A) NO CHANGE
B) An affect
C) Effecting
D) In effect

**36**

Which choice most effectively sets up the examples in the following sentences?

A) NO CHANGE
B) Patients of genetic counselors can be of any age.
C) Little is known about the range of inheritable diseases.
D) Parents' behaviors can often influence their children's health.

**37**

A) NO CHANGE
B) the dark side of medicine,
C) unpleasant things,
D) DELETE the underlined portion.

**CONTINUE**

If she decides to continue with the pregnancy after a potential risk has been identified, [38] a mother might seek the guidance of a genetic counselor to help manage a child with inborn medical issues. Older parents might even consider genetic testing before trying to conceive, thus [39] reducing the risks associated with: conceptions after the primary maternal or paternal periods of fertility.

As in the case of expectant mothers, genetic counseling has many [40] facets, the two primary divisions are diagnosis and support. The diagnostic side of genetic counseling involves the actual testing of genes and an estimation of risk. The support side involves managing and assessing risks to the child and mother that are associated with certain medical conditions. The work of these groups is often [41] complicated, particularly since modern adults more frequently have children in their 30s and 40s.

[38]

A) NO CHANGE

B) a genetic counselor who can advise how to manage a child with inborn medical issues may be sought.

C) a child with inborn medical issues may be born to a mother who seeks the help of a genetic counselor.

D) advice of a genetic counselor may be sought by a mother who fears inborn medical issues.

[39]

A) NO CHANGE

B) reducing the risks, associated with

C) reducing the risks associated with

D) reducing the risks: associated with

[40]

A) NO CHANGE

B) facet's;

C) facet's—

D) facets:

[41]

Which choice most effectively suggests that the "two primary divisions" are often not separate from one another?

A) NO CHANGE

B) specialized,

C) intertwined,

D) enriching,

For all of genetic counseling's benefits, **42** therefore, the field and its accomplishments are still not widely known. The National Society of Genetic Counselors was founded in 1979, and the field has had some breakthroughs (such as prenatal testing for Down syndrome) become popular knowledge. **43** Even so, there remains abundant opportunity for publicity and many genetic counselors are determined to get the word out—not only to patients, but also the general public.

[1] The field is perfect for those with an interest in science and education. [2] How effectively they communicate their findings can, at the most basic level, be a matter of life and death. [3] The technical aspects can be gained with a Master of Science in genetic counseling. [4] The ability to share these findings with patients, however, requires a special skill set. [5] Genetic counselors, like addiction or employment counselors, are fundamentally educators. **44**

**42**

A) NO CHANGE

B) for instance,

C) thus,

D) however,

**43**

At this point, the writer is considering adding the following sentence.

> The number of children born with Down syndrome has decreased significantly since this type of genetic prediction became available in the mid-1970s.

Should the writer make this addition here?

A) Yes, because it offers an important reminder for those who believe that genetic counseling is not a morally demanding job.

B) Yes, because it provides evidence that genetic counseling has resulted in new diagnostic possibilities.

C) No, because it gives an example that is inconsistent with the work of genetic counselors as they are described in the passage.

D) No, because it offers an illustration that does not have a significant bearing on this particular paragraph.

**44**

For the sake of the logic and cohesion of the paragraph, sentence 2 should be

A) placed where it is now.

B) placed before sentence 1.

C) placed after sentence 5.

D) DELETED from the paragraph.

# STOP

**If you finish before time is called, you may check your work on this section only.
Do not turn to any other section in the test.**

**No Test Material On This Page**

# Math Test – No Calculator

## 25 MINUTES, 20 QUESTIONS

**Turn to Section 3 of your answer sheet to answer the questions in this section.**

---

### DIRECTIONS

**For questions 1–15**, solve each problem, choose the best answer from the choices provided, and fill in the corresponding circle on your answer sheet. **For questions 16–20**, solve the problem and enter your answer in the grid on the answer sheet. Please refer to the directions before question 16 on how to enter your answers in the grid. You may use any available space in your test booklet for scratch work.

### NOTES

1. The use of a calculator **is not permitted**.
2. All variables and expressions used represent real numbers unless otherwise indicated.
3. Figures provided in this test are drawn to scale unless otherwise indicated.
4. All figures lie in a plane unless otherwise indicated.
5. Unless otherwise indicated, the domain of a given function $f$ is the set of all real numbers $x$ for which $f(x)$ is a real number.

### REFERENCE

$A = \pi r^2$
$C = 2\pi r$

$A = \ell w$

$A = \frac{1}{2} bh$

$c^2 = a^2 + b^2$

Special Right Triangles

$V = \ell wh$

$V = \pi r^2 h$

$V = \frac{4}{3} \pi r^3$

$V = \frac{1}{3} \pi r^2 h$

$V = \frac{1}{3} \ell wh$

The number of degrees of arc in a circle is 360.
The number of radians of arc in a circle is $2\pi$.
The sum of the measures in degrees of the angles of a triangle is 180.

---

**CONTINUE** ➡

## 1

What are the solutions of the quadratic equation $-3x^2 - 3x + 18 = 0$ ?

A) $x = -3$ and $x = 2$

B) $x = -3$ and $x = -2$

C) $x = 3$ and $x = -2$

D) $x = 3$ and $x = 2$

## 2

Which of the following is an equation of line $m$ ?

A) $x = -2$

B) $y = -2$

C) $y = 2x - 2$

D) $y = 2x + 2$

## 3

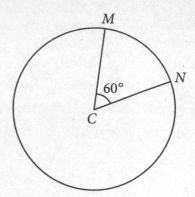

The circle above with center $C$ has an area of 48. What is the area of sector $\overset{\frown}{MN}$ ?

A) 48

B) 16

C) 12

D) 8

## 4

Which of the following is equivalent to the sum of the expressions $x^2 + x$ and $-x - 2$ ?

A) $x - 2$

B) $2x - 2$

C) $x^2 - 2$

D) $x^3 - x^2 - 2$

**CONTINUE**

**5**

Which of the following CANNOT be an example of a function whose graph in the *xy*-plane has two *x*-intercepts?

A) A function with an absolute value and real zeros

B) A cubic polynomial with only real zeros

C) A quadratic function with real zeros

D) A quadratic function with no real zeros

**6**

$$\sqrt{c-1} - t = 0$$

In the equation above, *c* is a constant. If $t = 4$, what is the value of *c* ?

A) 17

B) 15

C) 5

D) 3

**7**

$$x = y^2$$
$$6x + 9 = -3(2y - 3)$$

If $(x, y)$ is a solution to the system of equations above and $y < 0$, what is the value of $xy$ ?

A) −2

B) −1

C) 1

D) 3

**8**

Richard either walks or rides his bicycle everywhere he goes. When he walks, he burns 50 calories per mile, and when he rides his bicycle, he burns 25 calories per mile. Richard can travel no more than 15 miles per day, but he wants to burn at least 500 calories per day. Which of the following systems of inequalities represents the situation in terms of *w* and *b*, where *w* is the number of miles he walks and *b* is the number of miles he rides his bicycle?

A) $50w + 25b \le 500$
$w + b \le 15$

B) $50w + 25b \ge 500$
$w + b \le 15$

C) $50w + 25b \ge 500$
$w + b \ge 15$

D) $50w + 25b \le 500$
$w + b \ge 15$

**CONTINUE**

**9**

The Rankine scale is an alternate scale for measuring temperature where the unit of temperature is a Rankine, $R$. The conversion from degrees Celsius, $C$, to degrees Rankine, $R$, is given by the function $R(C) = 1.8C + 491.67$. Which of the following statements is the best interpretation of the number 491.67 in this context?

A) The increase in degrees Rankine that corresponds to a 1-degree Celsius increase in temperature

B) The increase in degrees Rankine that corresponds to a 1.8-degree Celsius increase in temperature

C) The temperature in degrees Rankine at 1.8 degrees Celsius

D) The temperature in degrees Rankine at 0 degrees Celsius

**10**

Which of the following is equivalent to $4^{\frac{5}{6}}$ ?

A) $2\sqrt[3]{4}$

B) $\sqrt[3]{2}$

C) $\sqrt[5]{4}$

D) $\sqrt[6]{4}$

**11**

If $x^2 + y^2 = c$ and $-xy = b$, which of the following is equivalent to $c + 2b$ ?

A) $(-2x - y)^2$

B) $(-x - y)^2$

C) $(x - y)^2$

D) $(x + y)^2$

**12**

The volume of cone C is 12 cubic millimeters. What is the volume, in cubic millimeters, of a cone with one-third the radius and triple the height of cone C ?

A) 2

B) 4

C) 12

D) 36

**CONTINUE**

**13**

Marcy spends an average of $42 on coffee each month. She buys special pods of coffee that cost $7 each. Recently, Marcy decided that she wanted to reduce the amount of coffee she drinks per month by 9 cups. Assuming these pods can brew four cups of coffee at a time, which equation can Marcy use to determine how many dollars, $d$, she will save each month?

A) $\dfrac{4}{7}d = 9$

B) $\dfrac{4}{7}d = 33$

C) $\dfrac{7}{4}d = 9$

D) $\dfrac{7}{4}d = 33$

**14**

At a juice bar, $s$ servings of banana smoothie are made by adding $b$ bananas to a blender. If $s = b - 4$, how many additional servings of banana smoothie can be made with each additional banana?

A) One

B) Two

C) Three

D) Four

**15**

$$g(x) = 2 - 3^x$$

The function $g(x)$ is defined by the equation above. Which of the following is the graph of $y = -g(x)$ in the $xy$-plane?

A)

B)

C)

D)

**CONTINUE**

## DIRECTIONS

**For questions 16–20**, solve the problem and enter your answer in the grid, as described below, on the answer sheet.

1. Although not required, it is suggested that you write your answer in the boxes at the top of the columns to help you fill in the circles accurately. You will receive credit only if the circles are filled in correctly.

2. Mark no more than one circle in any column.

3. No question has a negative answer.

4. Some problems may have more than one correct answer. In such cases, grid only one answer.

5. **Mixed numbers** such as $3\frac{1}{2}$ must be gridded as 3.5 or 7/2. (If is entered into the grid, it will be interpreted as $\frac{31}{2}$, not as $3\frac{1}{2}$.)

6. **Decimal Answers:** If you obtain a decimal answer with more digits than the grid can accommodate, it may be either rounded or truncated, but it must fill the entire grid.

Acceptable ways to grid $\frac{2}{3}$ are:

Answer: 201 – either position is correct

**NOTE:** You may start your answers in any column, space permitting. Columns you don't need to use should be left blank.

CONTINUE →

**16**

$$\frac{1}{3}(5m - n) = \frac{31}{3}$$

$$n = 3m$$

The system of equations above has solution $(m, n)$. What is the value of $m$ ?

**17**

Asaf plans to start working out at a gym. The gym membership costs $50 per month, and he will also have to pay a $30 one-time registration fee. Asaf wants to spend no more than $555 for the membership and the registration fee. If gym memberships are only available for a whole number of months, what is the maximum number of months for which Asaf can have his gym membership?

**18**

Intersecting lines $l$, $m$, and $o$ are shown below.

What is the value of $c$ ?

CONTINUE

**19**

$$9(s - 2) + 3(s + 2) = 7s$$

What value of $s$ is the solution of the equation above?

**20**

$$\frac{4c + 1}{(2c - 3)^2} - \frac{2}{(2c - 3)}$$

The expression above is equivalent to $\dfrac{x}{(2c - 3)^2}$, where $x$ is a positive constant and $c \neq \dfrac{3}{2}$. What is the value of $x$?

# STOP

**If you finish before time is called, you may check your work on this section only.
Do not turn to any other section in the test.**

# Math Test – Calculator

## 55 MINUTES, 38 QUESTIONS

**Turn to Section 4 of your answer sheet to answer the questions in this section.**

---

### DIRECTIONS

**For questions 1–30,** solve each problem, choose the best answer from the choices provided, and fill in the corresponding circle on your answer sheet. **For questions 31–38,** solve the problem and enter your answer in the grid on the answer sheet. Please refer to the directions before question 31 on how to enter your answers in the grid. You may use any available space in your test booklet for scratch work.

### NOTES

1. The use of a calculator **is permitted**.
2. All variables and expressions used represent real numbers unless otherwise indicated.
3. Figures provided in this test are drawn to scale unless otherwise indicated.
4. All figures lie in a plane unless otherwise indicated.
5. Unless otherwise indicated, the domain of a given function $f$ is the set of all real numbers $x$ for which $f(x)$ is a real number.

### REFERENCE

$A = \pi r^2$
$C = 2\pi r$

$A = \ell w$

$A = \frac{1}{2} bh$

$c^2 = a^2 + b^2$

Special Right Triangles

$V = \ell wh$

$V = \pi r^2 h$

$V = \frac{4}{3} \pi r^3$

$V = \frac{1}{3} \pi r^2 h$

$V = \frac{1}{3} \ell wh$

The number of degrees of arc in a circle is 360.
The number of radians of arc in a circle is $2\pi$.
The sum of the measures in degrees of the angles of a triangle is 180.

---

**CONTINUE** →

**1**

Sam's Special Hot Chocolate recipe calls for 4.5 fluid ounces of cream for every serving of hot chocolate. How many <u>cups</u> of cream are needed to make 24 servings of hot chocolate?
(1 cup = 8 fluid ounces)

A) 108

B) 36

C) 28.5

D) 13.5

**2**

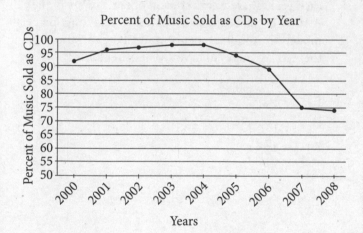

Percent of Music Sold as CDs by Year

According to the line graph above, between which two consecutive years was there the greatest change in the percent of music sold as CDs?

A) 2000–2001

B) 2003–2004

C) 2006–2007

D) 2007–2008

**3**

| $x$ | $g(x)$ |
|---|---|
| 2 | 11 |
| 4 | 17 |
| 6 | 23 |

Some values of the linear function $g$ are shown in the table above. Which of the following defines $g$ ?

A) $g(x) = 2x + 7$

B) $g(x) = 3x + 5$

C) $g(x) = 4x + 3$

D) $g(x) = 5x + 1$

**4**

A souvenir store sells postcards and magnets. Each postcard costs \$1, and each magnet costs \$3. If Annalee purchased a total of 10 postcards and magnets that cost a total of \$22 before tax, how many magnets did she purchase?

A) 3

B) 4

C) 5

D) 6

CONTINUE

**5**

If $7(x - y) = 4$, what is the value of $x - y$ ?

A) $\dfrac{4}{7}$

B) $\dfrac{7}{4}$

C) 4

D) 7

**6**

The average annual precipitation in Orlando is

approximately $\dfrac{13}{10}$ of the precipitation in Columbus.

The average annual precipitation in Saint Cloud is

approximately $\dfrac{7}{10}$ of the precipitation in Columbus.

If the average annual precipitation in Columbus is

1,000 millimeters, approximately how many more

millimeters of precipitation fall in Orlando than in

Saint Cloud each year?

A) 600

B) 700

C) 1,150

D) 1,300

**7**

Which of the following is an equivalent form of $(2.6a - 3.5)^2 - (7.3a^2 - 4.1)$ ?

A) $-2.1a^2 - 2.9$

B) $-2.1a^2 + 11.1$

C) $-0.54a^2 - 18.2a - 8.15$

D) $-0.54a^2 - 18.2a + 16.35$

**8**

The American Association of University Women (AAUW) hopes to expand its reach by starting a total of $t$ student organizations on college campuses each year. There were $s$ student organizations in the AAUW at the beginning of 2015. Which function best models the total number of student organizations, $y$, the AAUW hopes to have $x$ years after 2015 ?

A) $y = s(t)^x$

B) $y = t(s)^x$

C) $y = tx + s$

D) $y = tx - s$

**CONTINUE**

**9**

The resistance $R$ of a conductor is found by dividing the voltage $V$ across the conductor by the current $I$ through the conductor. Which of the following gives the voltage $V$ in terms of $R$ and $I$ ?

A)  $V = \dfrac{R}{I}$

B)  $V = \dfrac{I}{R}$

C)  $V = R - I$

D)  $V = IR$

**10**

In 1893, the Major League Baseball pitching distance from the pitcher's plate to home base was increased from 50 feet to 60.5 feet. Which of the following is closest to the increase in the pitching distance in Major League Baseball, in meters? (1 meter is approximately 3 feet.)

A)  3.50

B)  3.25

C)  3.00

D)  2.75

**11**

| Area of Focus | Highest Level of Education | | Total |
|---|---|---|---|
| | Master's Degree | Doctoral Degree | |
| Pediatric | 157 | 221 | 378 |
| Adult | 129 | 22 | 151 |
| Total | 286 | 243 | 529 |

In a survey, 529 social workers focusing on pediatric or adult services indicated their highest level of education. If one of the social workers is selected at random, which of the following is closest to the probability that the selected social worker is a pediatric social worker whose highest level of education is a doctoral degree?

A)  0.297

B)  0.418

C)  0.459

D)  0.541

**12**

$$-3x + 4y = 5$$

In the $xy$-plane, the graph of which of the following equations is perpendicular to the graph of the equation above?

A)  $3x + 6y = 5$

B)  $3x + 8y = 2$

C)  $4x + 3y = 5$

D)  $4x + 6y = 5$

**CONTINUE**

**13**

$$2 = -\frac{1}{3}x + y$$

$$6 = \frac{1}{3}x$$

The system of equations above has solution $(x, y)$. What is the value of $y$ ?

A)  8

B)  6

C)  $\frac{9}{2}$

D)  4

**14**

A community advocacy group recently polled 500 people who were selected at random from a small town and asked each person, "Are you in favor of the referendum to increase the property tax rate?" Of those surveyed, 67 percent stated that they were opposed to the property referendum. Which of the following statements must be true based on the results of the poll?

  I.  If another 500 people selected at random from the town were polled, 67 percent of them would state they are opposed to the property tax referendum.

 II.  If 500 people selected at random from a different town were polled, 67 percent of them would report they are opposed to the property tax referendum.

III.  Of all the people in the town, 67 percent are opposed to the property tax referendum.

A)  I only

B)  I and III only

C)  II and III only

D)  None

**15**

$$4x - 1 \le y$$

$$2 > x + y$$

Which of the following ordered pairs $(x, y)$ satisfies the system of inequalities above?

A)  $(-3, -1)$

B)  $(2, -5)$

C)  $(3, 1)$

D)  $(4, -1)$

**CONTINUE**

**Questions 16–18 refer to the following information.**

| Type of Exercise | Burn Rate |
|---|---|
| Shooting baskets | 3.0 |
| Boxing punching bag | 4.5 |
| Light aerobics | 2.0 |
| Speed walking | 5.0 |
| Doubles tennis | 2.5 |
| Yoga | 1.5 |
| Moderate walking | 3.5 |
| Running sprints | 7.5 |

One method of calculating the calories a person will burn by doing a particular exercise is to multiply the number of minutes doing the exercise by a constant called the burn rate for that exercise. The table above gives the burn rate for a 100-pound person for eight types of exercise.

**16**

Two 100-pound people have each been exercising for 1 hour, one speed walking and one doing yoga. Which of the following will be closest to the difference of their total exercise times, in minutes, when they have each burned an additional 20 calories? (1 hour = 60 minutes)

A)  9.2

B)  9.3

C)  9.4

D)  9.6

**17**

According to the information in the table, what is the approximate number of calories that will be burned by a 100-pound person shooting baskets for 30 minutes?

A)    60 calories

B)    70 calories

C)    90 calories

D)  120 calories

**18**

Calories Burned versus Time

The scatterplot above gives the time spent exercising plotted against calories burned for 20 100-pound people doing a particular exercise. The burn rate of this exercise is closest to that of which of the following exercises?

A)  Boxing punching bag

B)  Light aerobics

C)  Moderate walking

D)  Running sprints

**CONTINUE**

**19**

Time

The figure on the left above shows an electric fan with a spot of paint on one of its blades. The electric fan is sitting on a flat desk and is switched on to a constant low setting, causing the blades to rotate in a clockwise direction. The graph of $y = f(t)$ on the right could represent which of the following as a function of time from when the electric fan was turned on?

A) The distance traveled by the spot of paint

B) The distance of the spot of paint from the center of the electric fan

C) The distance of the spot of paint from the desk

D) The speed at which the blades of the fan are moving

**20**

$$h = \frac{f - g}{g}$$

In the equation above, if $f$ is positive and $g$ is negative, which of the following must be true?

A) $h = 1$

B) $h > 1$

C) $h = -1$

D) $h < -1$

**21**

In quadrilateral *LMNO* above, what is the length of $\overline{LM}$ ?

A) 8

B) $4\sqrt{3}$

C) $4\sqrt{2}$

D) 4

CONTINUE

**Questions 22 and 23 refer to the following information.**

| Neighborhoods in Forest City | | |
|---|---|---|
| Neighborhood Name | Population | Area (square miles) |
| Cedar Vale | 12,000 | 57 |
| Fir Fen | 2,000 | 22 |
| Maple Mall | 122,000 | 442 |
| Old Oaks | 85,000 | 312.5 |
| Poplar Park | 78,000 | 288 |

Forest City consists of five different neighborhoods, listed in the table above. The table above shows the population of each neighborhood and area, in square miles, as of January 1, 2015. Over the past decade, Forest City has redrawn the borders of its neighborhoods two times in an attempt to balance school enrollments.

**22**

Due to redrawing of borders, the population of the Maple Mall neighborhood increased by 30% from January 1, 2010 to January 1, 2012. That population then increased a further 20% by January 1, 2014. No other changes in the population of Maple Mall have occurred since 2014. Which of the following best approximates the population of Maple Mall on January 1, 2010 ?

A) 83,700

B) 81,300

C) 78,200

D) 62,500

**23**

The relationship between the area $A$, in square miles, and the population $n$, in <u>thousands</u> of residents, of a neighborhood as of January 1, 2015 can be represented by a linear function. Which of the following functions represents the relationship?

A) $A(n) = 2n + 18$

B) $A(n) = 2.5n - 300$

C) $A(n) = 3.5n + 15$

D) $A(n) = 4.5n - 107$

**24**

In County C, the 132 employees at the small business Perfect Paper Products were surveyed and 62.9 percent of the employees responded that they had less than $1,000 in savings. The average small business size in the county is 132 employees. If the employees at Perfect Paper Products are representative of employees in the county's small businesses and there are 270 small businesses in the county, which of the following best estimates the number of small business employees in the county who have at least $1,000 in savings?

A) 12,700

B) 13,220

C) 22,400

D) 35,640

**CONTINUE**

**25**

The volume of a cube is $V = \dfrac{1}{8}c^3$, where $c$ is a positive constant. Which of the following gives the surface area of the cube?

A) $6\left(\dfrac{c}{2}\right)^2$

B) $6\left(\dfrac{c^2}{2}\right)$

C) $6c^2$

D) $12c^2$

**26**

The mean weight of 6 people in an elevator is 160.5 pounds. If the person with the lowest weight gets off, the mean weight of the remaining 5 people becomes 168 pounds. What is the lowest weight, in pounds?

A) 89

B) 123

C) 140

D) 297

**27**

A sociologist designed an experiment to examine the likelihood of a person to favor members of a group to which that person belongs. In the experiment, 400 students from several different colleges watched a series of video-taped interviews in a random order. Each interview featured an actor identified as a professor from each of those colleges discussing issues affecting students. Each student was then asked to select the most trustworthy interviewee. Of the first 200 students, $s$ students chose the interviewee associated with their college. Among the remaining 200 students, 58 chose the interviewee associated with their college. If less than 25% of all students chose the interviewee associated with their college, which of the following inequalities best describes the possible value of $s$ ?

A) $s - 58 < 0.25(400)$, where $0 \le s \le 200$

B) $s + 58 < 0.25(400)$, where $0 \le s \le 200$

C) $s < 0.25(400 - 58)$, where $0 \le s \le 200$

D) $s < 0.25(400 + 58)$, where $0 \le s \le 200$

**28**

$$y = c - x^2$$

The graph of the equation above forms a parabola in the $xy$-plane. If $c$ is a positive constant, which of the following is an equivalent form of the equation?

A) $y = (c - x)^2$

B) $y = (c - x)(c + x)$

C) $y = \left(\dfrac{c}{2} - x\right)\left(\dfrac{c}{2} + x\right)$

D) $y = \left(\sqrt{c} - x\right)\left(\sqrt{c} + x\right)$

**CONTINUE**

**29**

The graph of the linear function $r$ is shown in the $xy$-plane above. The slope of the graph of the linear function $s$ is $\frac{1}{6}$ the slope of the graph of $r$. If the graph of $s$ passes through the point $(0, 2)$, what is the value of $s(15)$ ?

A) 5

B) 7

C) 10

D) 15

**30**

$$x^2 + 16x + y^2 - 12y = -19$$

The equation above defines a circle in the $xy$-plane. What are the coordinates of the center of the circle?

A) $(16, -12)$

B) $(8, -6)$

C) $(-8, 6)$

D) $(-16, 12)$

**CONTINUE**

## DIRECTIONS

**For questions 31–38**, solve the problem and enter your answer in the grid, as described below, on the answer sheet.

1. Although not required, it is suggested that you write your answer in the boxes at the top of the columns to help you fill in the circles accurately. You will receive credit only if the circles are filled in correctly.

2. Mark no more than one circle in any column.

3. No question has a negative answer.

4. Some problems may have more than one correct answer. In such cases, grid only one answer.

5. **Mixed numbers** such as $3\frac{1}{2}$ must be gridded as 3.5 or 7/2. (If [3 1 / 2] is entered into the grid, it will be interpreted as $\frac{31}{2}$, not as $3\frac{1}{2}$.)

6. **Decimal Answers:** If you obtain a decimal answer with more digits than the grid can accommodate, it may be either rounded or truncated, but it must fill the entire grid.

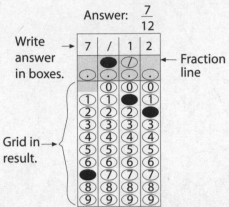

Acceptable ways to grid $\frac{2}{3}$ are:

Answer: 201 – either position is correct

**NOTE:** You may start your answers in any column, space permitting. Columns you don't need to use should be left blank.

**CONTINUE** →

**31**

The flag that was raised in 1814 at Fort McHenry, the original "Star Spangled Banner," was rectangular in shape with height 30 feet and length 42 feet. If a reproduction is made where each dimension is $\frac{1}{9}$ the corresponding original dimension, what is the length of the reproduction, in feet?

**32**

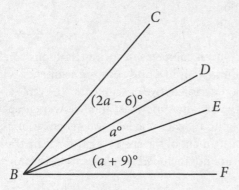

Note: Figure not drawn to scale.

In the figure above, $\angle CBD = \angle EBF$. What is the measure of $\angle CBF$, in degrees?

**33**

The square mile and the acre are units of measure of land area that are directly proportional. If 7 square miles are equal to 4,480 acres, how much area, in acres, is equal to 4 square miles?

**34**

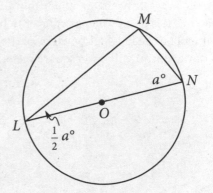

Point $O$ is the center of the circle in the figure above. What is the value of $a$ ?

**CONTINUE**

**35**

The point (4, 3) lies on the graph of the function $h(x)$ in the $xy$-plane. If $h(x) = \frac{1}{2}x^2 - a$, where $a$ is a constant, what is the value of $a$ ?

**36**

An artist is creating a rectangular mural. The height of the mural is to be 4 meters shorter than the width. What will be the height, in meters, of the mural if the area of the mural will be 96 square meters?

**Questions 37 and 38 refer to the following information.**

Ms. McQueen's Sprint Triathlon Performance

| Segment of triathlon | Average moving speed for segment (mph) | Distance (miles) |
|---|---|---|
| From start of race to end of swimming stage | 2 | 0.25 |
| From end of 1st transition to end of biking stage | 20 | 12.4 |
| From end of 2nd transition to end of running stage | 8 | 3.1 |

Ms. McQueen competes in sprint triathlons consisting of swimming, biking, and running segments, with a transition period between segments. The table above shows the distance, in miles, and her average speed, in miles per hour, when she is between transition periods, for each segment of the sprint triathlon. The transition periods are not included in her speed or distance numbers.

**CONTINUE**

**37**

When Ms. McQueen uses her triathlon bike to compete, she can complete a sprint triathlon at her average moving speed for each segment of the competition. When her triathlon bike is broken, she must use her hybrid bike instead. In those cases, the time it takes her to complete the biking segment of the sprint triathlon increases by 30% due to increased drag, but the time for each of the other segments of the competition does not change. Based on the table, how many more <u>minutes</u> did Ms. McQueen take to complete a sprint triathlon when she used her hybrid bike than when she used her triathlon bike? (Round your answer to the nearest minute.)

**38**

At one sprint triathlon, Ms. McQueen completed the course in 75 minutes, not including the time spent in transitions. What was her average speed, in miles per hour, during the sprint triathlon?

▲

**STOP**
**If you finish before time is called, you may check your work on this section only.**
**Do not turn to any other section in the test.**

# SAT Essay

**ESSAY BOOK**

## DIRECTIONS

The essay gives you an opportunity to show how effectively you can read and comprehend a passage and write an essay analyzing the passage. In your essay you should demonstrate that you have read the passage carefully, present a clear and logical analysis, and use language precisely.

Your essay must be written on the lines provided in your answer sheet booklet; except for the planning page of the answer booklet, you will receive no other paper on which to write. You will have enough space if you write on every line, avoid wide margins, and keep your handwriting to a reasonable size. Remember that people who are not familiar with your handwriting will read what you write. Try to write or print so that what you are writing is legible to those readers.

**You have 50 minutes to read the passage and write an essay in response to the prompt provided inside this booklet.**

## REMINDER

— Do not write your essay in this booklet. Only what you write on the lined pages of your answer booklet will be evaluated.

— An off-topic essay will not be evaluated.

CONTINUE →

As you read the passage below, consider how Nick Bilton uses

- evidence, such as facts or examples, to support claims.
- reasoning to develop ideas and to connect claims and evidence.
- stylistic or persuasive elements, such as word choice or appeals to emotion, to add power to the ideas expressed.

Adapted from Nick Bilton, "Reclaiming Our (Real) Lives from Social Media." © 2014 by New York Times. Originally published July 16, 2014.

1    One day in the early 1920s, a young Ernest Hemingway rushed along the streets of Paris seeking shelter from a downpour. He soon came upon a warm cafe on the Place St.-Michel and ducked inside. Hemingway ordered a café au lait, pulled out a notepad and pencil from his pocket and began writing. Before long he had fallen into a trancelike state, oblivious to his surroundings as he penned the first chapter of his memoir, "A Moveable Feast." If Hemingway were alive in 2014, he probably wouldn't have even put a pen to paper. Instead, he might have ducked into the cafe, pulled out his smartphone and proceeded to waste an entire afternoon on social media. Perhaps he would update his Facebook, snap a picture of his café au lait to post on Instagram and then lose the rest of the afternoon to Twitter.

2    While my early adventures on social sites were exciting and novel, increasingly, my time spent on these services is starting to feel like a lot of wasted time. Like a virus slowly invading its victim, social media has methodically started to consume every hour of my day. Now, it's all social media all the time. Numerous reports estimate that 18- to 34-year-olds spend as much as 3.8 hours a day on social media. These days 35- to 49-year-olds don't fare much better, racking up 3 hours a day on social sites.

3    I'm not blaming the Internet for procrastination. Yet I am blaming the Internet for sucking people into a cacophony of links, videos and pictures that leave us all feeling a little bit empty inside. Neil Fiore, a psychologist and author of four books on productivity, said that while procrastination can be a good thing, helping stave off anxiety about an impending project, today we tend to procrastinate in online labyrinths that are difficult to climb out of.

4    Most alarmingly, some of these social sites have also learned they can affect our mood. Last month Facebook came under heavy fire after news surfaced that its data scientists had manipulated the news feed for 689,003 users to see if they could affect how people feel. "When positive expressions were reduced, people produced fewer positive posts and more negative posts; when negative expressions were reduced, the opposite pattern occurred," wrote Adam Kramer, a data scientist at Facebook. Mr. Kramer added that Facebook found it could cause "massive-scale contagion via social networks." While this was a sole experiment, you don't need to be a Facebook researcher to realize that its news feed changes how we feel.

**CONTINUE** →

5     For a while people have been trying to push back against online distractions. Some install software like SelfControl or Cold Turkey on their computer that will block access to certain sites, including Facebook, Twitter and Instagram. This month, a Dutch nonprofit put forth an initiative called "99 Days of Freedom," which urges people to abstain from Facebook for three months to see if their mood improves as a result. But for many people, it's not that easy to just quit for three months. Social media is entwined in daily life, and abandoning Facebook and Twitter would be like trying to quit driving in protest of oil companies, or giving up electricity as a way of objecting to Con Edison's environmental policies.

6     For me, I'm making a change—albeit a small one. Rather than wake up in the morning and get lost on social media for an hour or more, I've started spending the early hours of my mornings reading a book. So far, I feel so much more fulfilled. I'm reading two to three books a week. This week I started "A Moveable Feast." And even if I spend the rest of my day on social media, I still feel as if I've done something enriching. You don't have to quit social media; the trick is finding balance.

---

Write an essay in which you explain how Nick Bilton builds an argument to persuade his audience that today's adults need to limit their time spent on social media sites. In your essay, analyze how Bilton uses one or more of the features listed in the box above (or features of your own choice) to strengthen the logic and persuasiveness of his argument. Be sure that your analysis focuses on the most relevant features of the passage.

Your essay should not explain whether you agree with Bilton's claims, but rather explain how Bilton builds an argument to persuade his audience.

---

**END OF TEST**

**DO NOT RETURN TO A PREVIOUS SECTION.**

The **Princeton Review**®

Completely darken bubbles with a No. 2 pencil. If you make a mistake, be sure to erase mark completely. Erase all stray marks.

**1.**

YOUR NAME: _____
(Print)      Last          First          M.I.

SIGNATURE: _____  DATE: __ / __ / __

HOME ADDRESS: _____
(Print)                 Number and Street

_____
City          State          Zip Code

PHONE NO.: _____
(Print)

**IMPORTANT:** Please fill in these boxes exactly as shown on the back cover of your test book.

**2. TEST FORM**

**6. DATE OF BIRTH**

| Month | Day | Year |
|-------|-----|------|
| ○ JAN | | |
| ○ FEB | ⓪ ⓪ | ⓪ ⓪ |
| ○ MAR | ① ① | ① ① |
| ○ APR | ② ② | ② ② |
| ○ MAY | ③ ③ | ③ ③ |
| ○ JUN | ④ | ④ ④ |
| ○ JUL | ⑤ | ⑤ ⑤ |
| ○ AUG | ⑥ | ⑥ ⑥ |
| ○ SEP | ⑦ | ⑦ ⑦ |
| ○ OCT | ⑧ | ⑧ ⑧ |
| ○ NOV | ⑨ | ⑨ ⑨ |
| ○ DEC | | |

**3. TEST CODE**

**4. REGISTRATION NUMBER**

**7. SEX**
○ MALE
○ FEMALE

The **Princeton Review**®

**5. YOUR NAME**

First 4 letters of last name | FIRST INIT | MID INIT

**Test ⑨**  Start with number 1 for each new section.
If a section has fewer questions than answer spaces, leave the extra answer spaces blank.

## Section 1—Reading

1. Ⓐ Ⓑ Ⓒ Ⓓ
2. Ⓐ Ⓑ Ⓒ Ⓓ
3. Ⓐ Ⓑ Ⓒ Ⓓ
4. Ⓐ Ⓑ Ⓒ Ⓓ
5. Ⓐ Ⓑ Ⓒ Ⓓ
6. Ⓐ Ⓑ Ⓒ Ⓓ
7. Ⓐ Ⓑ Ⓒ Ⓓ
8. Ⓐ Ⓑ Ⓒ Ⓓ
9. Ⓐ Ⓑ Ⓒ Ⓓ
10. Ⓐ Ⓑ Ⓒ Ⓓ
11. Ⓐ Ⓑ Ⓒ Ⓓ
12. Ⓐ Ⓑ Ⓒ Ⓓ
13. Ⓐ Ⓑ Ⓒ Ⓓ
14. Ⓐ Ⓑ Ⓒ Ⓓ
15. Ⓐ Ⓑ Ⓒ Ⓓ
16. Ⓐ Ⓑ Ⓒ Ⓓ
17. Ⓐ Ⓑ Ⓒ Ⓓ
18. Ⓐ Ⓑ Ⓒ Ⓓ
19. Ⓐ Ⓑ Ⓒ Ⓓ
20. Ⓐ Ⓑ Ⓒ Ⓓ
21. Ⓐ Ⓑ Ⓒ Ⓓ
22. Ⓐ Ⓑ Ⓒ Ⓓ
23. Ⓐ Ⓑ Ⓒ Ⓓ
24. Ⓐ Ⓑ Ⓒ Ⓓ
25. Ⓐ Ⓑ Ⓒ Ⓓ
26. Ⓐ Ⓑ Ⓒ Ⓓ
27. Ⓐ Ⓑ Ⓒ Ⓓ
28. Ⓐ Ⓑ Ⓒ Ⓓ
29. Ⓐ Ⓑ Ⓒ Ⓓ
30. Ⓐ Ⓑ Ⓒ Ⓓ
31. Ⓐ Ⓑ Ⓒ Ⓓ
32. Ⓐ Ⓑ Ⓒ Ⓓ
33. Ⓐ Ⓑ Ⓒ Ⓓ
34. Ⓐ Ⓑ Ⓒ Ⓓ
35. Ⓐ Ⓑ Ⓒ Ⓓ
36. Ⓐ Ⓑ Ⓒ Ⓓ
37. Ⓐ Ⓑ Ⓒ Ⓓ
38. Ⓐ Ⓑ Ⓒ Ⓓ
39. Ⓐ Ⓑ Ⓒ Ⓓ
40. Ⓐ Ⓑ Ⓒ Ⓓ
41. Ⓐ Ⓑ Ⓒ Ⓓ
42. Ⓐ Ⓑ Ⓒ Ⓓ
43. Ⓐ Ⓑ Ⓒ Ⓓ
44. Ⓐ Ⓑ Ⓒ Ⓓ
45. Ⓐ Ⓑ Ⓒ Ⓓ
46. Ⓐ Ⓑ Ⓒ Ⓓ
47. Ⓐ Ⓑ Ⓒ Ⓓ
48. Ⓐ Ⓑ Ⓒ Ⓓ
49. Ⓐ Ⓑ Ⓒ Ⓓ
50. Ⓐ Ⓑ Ⓒ Ⓓ
51. Ⓐ Ⓑ Ⓒ Ⓓ
52. Ⓐ Ⓑ Ⓒ Ⓓ

## Section 2—Writing and Language Skills

1. Ⓐ Ⓑ Ⓒ Ⓓ
2. Ⓐ Ⓑ Ⓒ Ⓓ
3. Ⓐ Ⓑ Ⓒ Ⓓ
4. Ⓐ Ⓑ Ⓒ Ⓓ
5. Ⓐ Ⓑ Ⓒ Ⓓ
6. Ⓐ Ⓑ Ⓒ Ⓓ
7. Ⓐ Ⓑ Ⓒ Ⓓ
8. Ⓐ Ⓑ Ⓒ Ⓓ
9. Ⓐ Ⓑ Ⓒ Ⓓ
10. Ⓐ Ⓑ Ⓒ Ⓓ
11. Ⓐ Ⓑ Ⓒ Ⓓ
12. Ⓐ Ⓑ Ⓒ Ⓓ
13. Ⓐ Ⓑ Ⓒ Ⓓ
14. Ⓐ Ⓑ Ⓒ Ⓓ
15. Ⓐ Ⓑ Ⓒ Ⓓ
16. Ⓐ Ⓑ Ⓒ Ⓓ
17. Ⓐ Ⓑ Ⓒ Ⓓ
18. Ⓐ Ⓑ Ⓒ Ⓓ
19. Ⓐ Ⓑ Ⓒ Ⓓ
20. Ⓐ Ⓑ Ⓒ Ⓓ
21. Ⓐ Ⓑ Ⓒ Ⓓ
22. Ⓐ Ⓑ Ⓒ Ⓓ
23. Ⓐ Ⓑ Ⓒ Ⓓ
24. Ⓐ Ⓑ Ⓒ Ⓓ
25. Ⓐ Ⓑ Ⓒ Ⓓ
26. Ⓐ Ⓑ Ⓒ Ⓓ
27. Ⓐ Ⓑ Ⓒ Ⓓ
28. Ⓐ Ⓑ Ⓒ Ⓓ
29. Ⓐ Ⓑ Ⓒ Ⓓ
30. Ⓐ Ⓑ Ⓒ Ⓓ
31. Ⓐ Ⓑ Ⓒ Ⓓ
32. Ⓐ Ⓑ Ⓒ Ⓓ
33. Ⓐ Ⓑ Ⓒ Ⓓ
34. Ⓐ Ⓑ Ⓒ Ⓓ
35. Ⓐ Ⓑ Ⓒ Ⓓ
36. Ⓐ Ⓑ Ⓒ Ⓓ
37. Ⓐ Ⓑ Ⓒ Ⓓ
38. Ⓐ Ⓑ Ⓒ Ⓓ
39. Ⓐ Ⓑ Ⓒ Ⓓ
40. Ⓐ Ⓑ Ⓒ Ⓓ
41. Ⓐ Ⓑ Ⓒ Ⓓ
42. Ⓐ Ⓑ Ⓒ Ⓓ
43. Ⓐ Ⓑ Ⓒ Ⓓ
44. Ⓐ Ⓑ Ⓒ Ⓓ

The Princeton Review®

Completely darken bubbles with a No. 2 pencil. If you make a mistake, be sure to erase mark completely. Erase all stray marks.

**Test 9**  Start with number 1 for each new section.
If a section has fewer questions than answer spaces, leave the extra answer spaces blank.

## Section 3—Mathematics: No Calculator

1. Ⓐ Ⓑ Ⓒ Ⓓ
2. Ⓐ Ⓑ Ⓒ Ⓓ
3. Ⓐ Ⓑ Ⓒ Ⓓ
4. Ⓐ Ⓑ Ⓒ Ⓓ
5. Ⓐ Ⓑ Ⓒ Ⓓ
6. Ⓐ Ⓑ Ⓒ Ⓓ
7. Ⓐ Ⓑ Ⓒ Ⓓ
8. Ⓐ Ⓑ Ⓒ Ⓓ
9. Ⓐ Ⓑ Ⓒ Ⓓ
10. Ⓐ Ⓑ Ⓒ Ⓓ
11. Ⓐ Ⓑ Ⓒ Ⓓ
12. Ⓐ Ⓑ Ⓒ Ⓓ
13. Ⓐ Ⓑ Ⓒ Ⓓ
14. Ⓐ Ⓑ Ⓒ Ⓓ
15. Ⓐ Ⓑ Ⓒ Ⓓ

16. 17. 18. 19. 20.

## Section 4—Mathematics: Calculator

1. Ⓐ Ⓑ Ⓒ Ⓓ
2. Ⓐ Ⓑ Ⓒ Ⓓ
3. Ⓐ Ⓑ Ⓒ Ⓓ
4. Ⓐ Ⓑ Ⓒ Ⓓ
5. Ⓐ Ⓑ Ⓒ Ⓓ
6. Ⓐ Ⓑ Ⓒ Ⓓ
7. Ⓐ Ⓑ Ⓒ Ⓓ
8. Ⓐ Ⓑ Ⓒ Ⓓ
9. Ⓐ Ⓑ Ⓒ Ⓓ
10. Ⓐ Ⓑ Ⓒ Ⓓ
11. Ⓐ Ⓑ Ⓒ Ⓓ
12. Ⓐ Ⓑ Ⓒ Ⓓ
13. Ⓐ Ⓑ Ⓒ Ⓓ
14. Ⓐ Ⓑ Ⓒ Ⓓ
15. Ⓐ Ⓑ Ⓒ Ⓓ
16. Ⓐ Ⓑ Ⓒ Ⓓ
17. Ⓐ Ⓑ Ⓒ Ⓓ
18. Ⓐ Ⓑ Ⓒ Ⓓ
19. Ⓐ Ⓑ Ⓒ Ⓓ
20. Ⓐ Ⓑ Ⓒ Ⓓ
21. Ⓐ Ⓑ Ⓒ Ⓓ
22. Ⓐ Ⓑ Ⓒ Ⓓ
23. Ⓐ Ⓑ Ⓒ Ⓓ
24. Ⓐ Ⓑ Ⓒ Ⓓ
25. Ⓐ Ⓑ Ⓒ Ⓓ
26. Ⓐ Ⓑ Ⓒ Ⓓ
27. Ⓐ Ⓑ Ⓒ Ⓓ
28. Ⓐ Ⓑ Ⓒ Ⓓ
29. Ⓐ Ⓑ Ⓒ Ⓓ
30. Ⓐ Ⓑ Ⓒ Ⓓ

31. 32. 33. 34. 35.

36. 37. 38.

# Chapter 20
# Practice Test 9:
# Answers and
# Explanations

# PRACTICE TEST 9 ANSWER KEY

| | Section 1:<br>Reading | | | Section 2:<br>Writing & Language | | | Section 3:<br>Math (No Calculator) | | | Section 4 :<br>Math (Calculator) | |
|---|---|---|---|---|---|---|---|---|---|---|---|
| 1. C | 27. C | 1. D | 23. D | 1. A | 11. C | 1. D | 20. D |
| 2. B | 28. B | 2. D | 24. C | 2. C | 12. B | 2. C | 21. C |
| 3. B | 29. C | 3. A | 25. D | 3. D | 13. A | 3. B | 22. C |
| 4. D | 30. D | 4. A | 26. A | 4. C | 14. A | 4. D | 23. C |
| 5. B | 31. D | 5. A | 27. B | 5. D | 15. D | 5. A | 24. B |
| 6. D | 32. C | 6. C | 28. C | 6. A | 16. $\frac{31}{2}$ | 6. A | 25. A |
| 7. C | 33. B | 7. B | 29. D | 7. B | or | 7. D | 26. B |
| 8. A | 34. C | 8. A | 30. C | 8. B | 15.5 | 8. C | 27. B |
| 9. A | 35. A | 9. B | 31. A | 9. D | 17. 10 | 9. D | 28. D |
| 10. D | 36. D | 10. C | 32. D | 10. A | 18. 117 | 10. A | 29. B |
| 11. A | 37. B | 11. A | 33. B | | 19. $\frac{12}{5}$ | 11. B | 30. C |
| 12. B | 38. C | 12. B | 34. B | | or | 12. C | 31. $\frac{42}{9}$, |
| 13. D | 39. C | 13. D | 35. D | | 2.4 | 13. A | $\frac{14}{3}$, |
| 14. D | 40. C | 14. C | 36. B | | 20. 7 | 14. D | 4.66, |
| 15. A | 41. B | 15. D | 37. D | | | 15. A | or |
| 16. B | 42. A | 16. C | 38. A | | | 16. B | 4.67 |
| 17. A | 43. A | 17. B | 39. C | | | 17. C | |
| 18. B | 44. D | 18. C | 40. D | | | 18. B | 32. 63 |
| 19. C | 45. B | 19. A | 41. C | | | 19. C | 33. 2,560 |
| 20. C | 46. C | 20. B | 42. D | | | | 34. 60 |
| 21. C | 47. C | 21. A | 43. D | | | | 35. 5 |
| 22. A | 48. A | 22. D | 44. C | | | | 36. 8 |
| 23. B | 49. D | | | | | | 37. 11 |
| 24. A | 50. C | | | | | | 38. 12.6 |
| 25. B | 51. C | | | | | | |
| 26. D | 52. B | | | | | | |

For self-scoring assessment tables, please turn to page 957.

# PRACTICE TEST 9 EXPLANATIONS

## Section 1: Reading

1. **C**   This question asks how the primary focus shifts over the course of the passage. Because this is a general question, it should be done after all the specific questions. The first three paragraphs describe the town that Tom Scanlon lives in with a particular focus on the railroad. The fourth paragraph describes the area to the west of the town Scanlon lives in. The last paragraph is devoted to describing the town of Polk, which lies to the east of the town in which Scanlon lives. Find an answer that matches this prediction. Nowhere in the passage is *a tense relationship* described, so (A) can be eliminated. Eliminate (B) because the passage provides no explanation on *how to navigate an area*. The passage does describe the town Scanlon lives in, then goes on to describe the area to the west of where Scanlon lives, and finally describes the town of Polk, which lies to the east of where Scanlon lives, so keep (C). Eliminate (D) because the passage does not provide *the thoughts of characters in another town.* The correct answer is (C).

2. **B**   This question asks about the *main purpose of the first paragraph.* The first paragraph describes a town as currently being dry and then goes on to describe what the town is like in winter and summer. In the last sentences of the first paragraph, Tom Scanlon is introduced. Find an answer that matches this prediction. Eliminate (A) because the first paragraph does not *specify the time period.* The first paragraph describes the town and Tom Scanlon, so keep (B). Eliminate (C) because the *writing style* remains unchanged throughout the passage. Eliminate (D) because the first paragraph does not mention anything that bothers Tom Scanlon. The correct answer is (B).

3. **B**   This question asks why *Scanlon has time to "prepare himself."* Use the given line reference to find the window to read. According to the passage, *Trains come from both directions, but from the east they come without warning, the whistle blown away by the wind. From the west, thin and wild or strumming like a wire fastened to the building, the sound wakes Scanlon from his sleep before the building rocks.* Therefore, the sound of the whistle gives Scanlon time to prepare himself. Eliminate (A) because no mention is made of Scanlon setting an alarm. It is the sound of the train that wakes Scanlon from his sleep, so keep (B). Eliminate (C) because there is no mention in the passage of Scanlon's having memorized the train schedule. There is also no indication in the passage that the train noise makes Scanlon *anxious,* so (D) can be eliminated. The correct answer is (B).

4. **D**   This question asks what observation Scanlon frequently makes about the "downgrade trains." Notice that this is the first question in a paired set, so it can be done in tandem with Q5. Look at the best evidence answer choices for Q5 first. The lines for (5A) describe the noise that the upgrade trains make. Given that the question is about the *downgrade trains*, eliminate (5A). The lines for (5B) state that Scanlon often thought he might see a hole outside of his window

as a result of the lack of noise the downgrade trains made. This answer matches (4D). Connect answers (5B) and (4D). The lines for (5C) describe the train by stating that *A cloud of dust would veil the caboose, on the stove one of the pots or the lids would rattle, and if the lamp was lit, the flame would blow as if in a draft.* This description matches none of the answers in Q4. Eliminate (5C). The lines for (5D) state that Scanlon *saw a team of mares…cantering down the bank where the train had just passed.* These lines do not describe the train and do not support any of the answers in Q4. Eliminate (5D). The correct answers are (4D) and (5B).

5.  **B**   (See explanation above.)

6.  **D**   This question asks what the author indicates about the area to the west of Scanlon's town. Use the lead word *west* and chronology to answer the question. According to the passage, *To the west the towns are thin and sparse, like the grass, and in a place called Indian Bow the white faces of cattle peer out of the soddies on the slope across the dry bed of the river.* Find an answer that matches this prediction. While Emil Bickel is mentioned in an earlier paragraph, the passage provides no information on where Emil Bickel lived, so eliminate (A). Eliminate (B) because, while the west is described as *thin and sparse,* the passage does not indicate that the west is *less interesting to Scanlon.* The passage states that the west is *thin and sparse,* which would indicate that it is not *full of* any sort of settlement or town. Eliminate (C). Choice (D) matches the prediction. The passage describes the *dry bed of the river* in the west and states that the towns were *thin and sparse,* which suggests few people lived there. The correct answer is (D).

7.  **C**   This question asks what the author's description of Will Brady suggests about Will Brady. Use the given line reference to find the window to read. According to the passage, Will Brady was *a railroad man who occasionally stopped off at Lone Tree.* The passage also states that Will Brady *married and went out East.* Look for an answer that matches this prediction. Choice (A) can be eliminated because there is no indication in the passage that Will Brady is a *disappointment.* Eliminate (B) because there is no indication in the passage that Will Brady is either a *preacher* or a *martyr.* Choice (C) looks good because in the passage Will Brady is described as having been *a railroad man who occasionally stopped off at Lone Tree.* In other words, he was a *traveler.* Also, the passage states that *he married and went west* which means he is a *husband.* Keep (C). The passage describes Will Brady as having been *a railroad man who occasionally stopped off at Lone Tree.* This means that he was a visitor, not a resident. There is no indication in the passage that Will Brady was a *loner.* Eliminate (D). The correct answer is (C).

8.  **A**   The question asks what the final paragraph suggests about Polk. Polk is described as *the home of Walter McKee, who married Scanlon's eldest daughter, Lois.* Choice (A) matches the prediction. In the final paragraph, Polk is described as the home of Walter McKee, who married Scanlon's eldest daughter, Lois, and his friend Gordon Boyd. The family connection makes McKee and Boyd people who are connected to Scanlon. Eliminate (B) because there is no indication in the paragraph that Polk *contains a large number of children.* Choice (C) can be eliminated because, while the paragraph describes historical events, there is no indication that

the residents of Polk *like to be reminded of historical events.* Eliminate (D) because, while the paragraph describes some of the events that have happened in Polk, there is no indication that the town has *an unusually long history.* The correct answer is (A).

9.  **A**  This question asks which choice best supports the idea that there is a contrast between the old and the new in Polk. Use the line references in the answer choices to find the window. The lines for (A) describe the *middle of the century...TV aerial* as *a change* contrasted with the *man's bicycle with the seat missing.* Keep (A). The lines for (B) and (C) describe how a boy rides a bicycle with a missing seat. These lines do not contain a contrast and can both be eliminated. The lines for (D) describe how Boyd was bolder than McKee in riding his bicycle. Although there is a contrast here, the contrast mentioned is not between the old and the new. Eliminate (D). The correct answer is (A).

10.  **D**  This question asks what the word *bears* most nearly means, as used in line 80. Cross out the word *bears* and replace it with another word that makes sense based on the context of the sentence. The word *bears* is used in the context of Gordon Boyd having a *scar where the teeth of the sprocket dug into his calf.* Find an answer that means something like "having." Only (D), *possesses,* provides a meaning similar to "having." Choices (A), *conveys,* and (C), *shoulders,* may seem tempting since both of these answers are related to a definition of *bears.* However, these answers do not work in the context of having a scar. The correct answer is (D).

11.  **A**  This question asks how the main focus of the passage shifts. Because this is a general question, it should be done after all the specific questions. The authors evaluate the evidence for whether Groupon users are more critical in their reviews than non-Groupon users, and then suggest some hypotheses about why Groupon reviews yield lower ratings. Choice (A) summarizes this shift, so keep (A). Eliminate (B) because the original observation was that *Yelp reviews that contained the word "Groupon" provided, on average, significantly lower ratings than reviews that did not.* The authors do not discuss the method used to detect this. Choice (C) can be eliminated because the passage provides no review of the research itself. Eliminate (D) because the authors conclude that there are a number of reasons that combine to create the Groupon effect. Hence, there is no *absolute* reason. Note, too, that the word *absolute* is an extreme word that does not have similarly extreme support in the text. The correct answer is (A).

12.  **B**  This question asks how the *Groupon effect* may be defined. Notice that this is the first question in a paired set, so this question can be done in tandem with Q13. Look at the best evidence answer choices for Q13 first. The lines for (13A) state that by looking at a dataset from Groupon and Yelp, the authors learned *significantly more about the daily deals model.* These lines do not describe the Groupon effect and do not support any of the answers in Q12. Eliminate (13A). The lines for (13B) state that in some cases, businesses *may also attempt to place negative reviews for their competitors.* These lines support (12C), but that pair does not answer the question and can ultimately be eliminated. The lines for (13C) describe *unrealized expectations between reviewers and merchants.* This does not support any of the answers in Q12. Eliminate

(13C). The lines for (13D) state that the authors have *shown that a combination of poor business behavior, Groupon user experimentation, and an artificially high baseline all play a role* in describing the Groupon effect. This supports (12B). Connect answers (13D) and (12B). The correct answers are (12B) and (13D).

13. **D** (See explanation above.)

14. **D** This question asks what the word *fake* means, as used in line 53. Cross out the word *fake* and replace it with another word that makes sense based on the context of the sentence. The word *fake* in the passage is used in the context of a review being introduced *in an arguably artificial manner.* Look for an answer that means something like being introduced in an artificial manner. Only (D), *planted,* has that meaning. To plant information means to secretly place the information for publication or dissemination. Choices (A), (B), and (C) may all seem tempting because all of these answers relate to a definition of the word *fake.* However, none of these answers relate to introducing a review *in an arguably artificial manner.* The correct answer is (D).

15. **A** This question asks, *Which action would best address a concern regarding the introduction of artificial Yelp reviews.* Use the reference word *artificial* and chronology to find the window to read. The passage states that reviews that mention Groupon are written by actual customers, while other reviews *are significantly more likely to be "fake" or otherwise introduced in an arguably artificial manner.* Therefore, the problem is that not all reviews are being written by actual customers who use the service. Find an answer that addresses this concern. Choice (A) addresses the concern. If a *verifiable receipt image* were required, the reviews would be entirely submitted by customers who used the service. None of the other answers would help ensure that only those who had used the services could write reviews. The correct answer is (A).

16. **B** This question asks which choice best describes the *"unrealized expectations"* between reviewers and merchants. Use the line references in the answer choices as the windows to read. Look for an answer that mentions both the reviewers and the merchants. The lines for (A) describe the research methodology the author used. This information is unrelated to the unrealized expectations between reviewers and merchants. The lines for (B) describe Groupon users as *fussy reviewers* and businesses as *providing worse service specifically to Groupon customers.* This describes a mismatch between reviewers and merchants. Keep (B). The lines for (C) describe how businesses attempt to gain more positive reviews. However, these lines say nothing about the reviewers themselves. Eliminate (C). The lines for (D) state that *Groupon users provide detailed reviews that are valued more highly by their Yelp peers.* However, this answer provides no information about the merchants. Eliminate (D). The correct answer is (B).

17. **A** This question asks what the word *compilation* means, as used in line 86. Cross out the word *compilation* and replace it with another word that makes sense based on the context of the sentence. The word describes a group of data about Groupon users. Look for an answer choice that means "a group." Only (A), *collection,* means a group. Choice (B), *summary,* may seem

tempting. However, while the data has been collected, it is not clear from the passage that it has been summarized. The correct answer is (A).

18. **B**  This question asks *which category of Yelp user showed the most evenly distributed star ratings*, according to the figure. In the figure, the *x*-axis shows the star rating and the *y*-axis shows the frequency of any given star rating. The user group with the flattest line is the one with the most evenly distributed star ratings. The flattest relative line in the graph belongs to the Groupon Businesses, Groupon User, Mentions Groupon, which is (B).

19. **C**  This question asks which Yelp rating a non-Groupon user is most likely to give. Look at the two lines for non-Groupon businesses. Both lines for the non-Groupon business users peak at 4 stars. Therefore, the correct answer is (C).

20. **C**  This question asks what idea from the passage is most directly supported from the passage. The data in the figure provide no information on the correlation between the type of business and the pattern of Yelp star ratings. Eliminate (A). The data in the figure provide no information on customers who produce "spam reviews." Eliminate (B). The data in the figure provide no information on the number of Groupon mentions in a review. Eliminate (D). The only answer that can be deduced from the figure is (C). The figure shows Yelp scores of Groupon users relative to Yelp scores of non-Groupon users. The correct answer is (C).

21. **C**  This question asks what the word *extend* most nearly means, as used in line 3. Cross out the word *extend* and replace it with another word that makes sense based on the context of the sentence. The word *extend* refers to the statement in the previous sentence that *We know that clinical trials sponsored by the pharmaceutical industry are likely to exaggerate benefit and minimize harms* related to *their sponsorship of non-human animal research*. So *extend* should mean something like "relate." *Reach*, *require*, and *stretch* do not mean "relate," so eliminate (A), (B), and (D). *Apply* means "to make relevant," which matches the prediction. The correct answer is (C).

22. **A**  This question asks what the questions posed in lines 3–7 chiefly intend to do. Read the window to find that the questions, *do these biases extend to their sponsorship of non-human animal research? Are the findings of such studies credible? And how do those findings compare with "proper" research conducted by dispassionate academics?* are asked before being described as "important questions" to begin the second paragraph. The questions intend to show what type of information could be determined by the proposed investigation of pharmaceutical clinical trials. *Introduce a set of considerations that may not have been investigated in prior research* matches the prediction, so keep (A). There is no reference to *confusion about the nature of results*, *an improper method of conducting trials*, or *controversy about the quality of research performed by academics*; eliminate (B), (C), and (D). The correct answer is (A).

23. **B** This question asks which question *the research of Bero's team* primarily intended to answer. Notice that this is the first question in a paired set, so this question can be done in tandem with Q24. Look at the best evidence answer choices for Q24 first. The lines for (24A) ask *could it be that industry-sponsored research is actually more rigorous than academic research?* This matches *do experiments funded by invested corporations get performed with a greater level of attention to detail than those that are not*, so connect (24A) with (23B). The lines for (24B) and (24C) discuss statins, so they might initially seem to connect to (23A), but neither set of lines actually answers the question in (23A). Eliminate (24B) and (24C). The lines for (24D) address *the difficulty industry has in replicating the results of research conducted in academic labs*, but there is no indication that something explicitly *prevents industry-sponsored research from being conducted with the same level of rigor as academic research* in (23C); eliminate (24D). The correct answers are (23B) and (24A).

24. **A** (See explanation above.)

25. **B** This question asks about the *main purpose of the fourth paragraph*. The fourth paragraph describes the systematic review of statin treatments for atheroma, *focusing on those studies where sponsorship status was known* before presenting the results of the studies. So the main purpose of the fourth paragraph is to show the results of the studies of sponsorship status. The fourth paragraph does not *question the implications of the surprising findings, shift from a description of Bero's team's study to an overview of a question*, or *connect research performed on human subjects to research performed on non-human animals*, so eliminate (A), (C), and (D). *Note significant results of Bero's team's study* matches the prediction. The correct answer is (B).

26. **D** This question asks what the word *conservative* most nearly means, as used in line 48. Cross out the word *conservative* and replace it with another word that makes sense based on the context of the sentence. The study in the previous paragraph shows *that findings from research sponsored by industry are more conservative than those sponsored by non-industry sources, but the interpretation of those data is, in contrast, less conservative*. Additionally, in the previous paragraph, industry-supported studies find less evidence supporting the use of statins, but are more likely to ultimately favor their use. So *conservative* means something like "reserved in interpretation." Because *old-fashioned, dramatic*, and *traditional* do not mean "reserved in interpretation," eliminate (A), (B), and (C). *Reserved* matches the prediction. The correct answer is (D).

27. **C** This question asks about *non-human research sponsored by others compared to non-human animal research sponsored by industry*. The author states in the sixth paragraph that *non-human animal work sponsored by industry is likely to be performed and reported to a higher quality, and to be at lower risk of bias, than work sponsored by others*. Subsequently, the passage mentions *the difficulty industry has in replicating the results of research conducted in academic labs*. Find an answer choice that matches the information from the text. *Non-human research sponsored by others shows a lower risk of bias* reverses this relationship, so eliminate (A). Choice (B) might initially look attractive because the passage does talk about research that is easier to reproduce,

but read the question carefully. The question asks about *non-human research sponsored by others,* which the passages says industry has *difficulty replicating.* Eliminate (B). Choice (C) is directly supported by the passage, so keep that answer. There is no comparison of the *costs,* so (D) can be eliminated. The correct answer is (C).

28. **B**    This question asks why *the findings of Bero's team are surprising.* Notice that this is the first question in a paired set, so this question can be done in tandem with Q29. Look at the best evidence answer choices for Q29 first. The lines for (29A) and (29B) provide the study results alone without any indication as to why they *are surprising,* so eliminate (29A) and (29B). The lines for (29C) indicate that *It does appear that findings from research sponsored by industry are more conservative than those sponsored by non-industry sources, but the interpretation of those data is, in contrast, less conservative,* before asking *why might this be?* This contradiction indicates the findings are surprising and *apparently contradict a sensible assumption,* so connect (29C) with (28B). The lines for (29D) reference *exaggeration of conclusions,* but this doesn't match any of the choices for Q28; eliminate (29D). The correct answers are (28B) and (29C).

29. **C**    (See explanation above.)

30. **D**    This question asks why the author of the passage would most likely agree that *industry-sponsored research may be rigorous.* Notice that this is the first question in a paired set, so this question can be done in tandem with Q31. Look at the best evidence answer choices for Q31 first. The lines for (31A), (31B), and (31C) make no reference to the level of rigor with which *industry-sponsored research* is conducted; eliminate (31A), (31B), and (31C). *Standards for internal reporting* would refer to the rigor with which *non-human animal research* is conducted by industry and matches *elements of documentation that are also applied to purposes other than research.* The correct answers are (30D) and (31D).

31. **D**    (See explanation above.)

32. **C**    This question asks what point Hubert makes about *working women relative to working men.* Notice that this is the first question in a paired set, so this question can be done in tandem with Q33. Look at the best evidence answer choices for Q33 first. The lines for (33A) state that *The fact that women are paid less than men for apparently the same service seems to disturb a great many people who find here a conspiracy upon the part of the man to keep women out of the wage-earning field.* This matches none of the answers in Q32. It may be tempting to connect this answer with (32A) because (32A) includes both the words *disturbingly* and *conspiracies.* However, the passage does not state that women *supply more conspiracies than men.* Eliminate (33A). The lines for (33B) state that *women as a class of workers are beginners, comparatively speaking in the great field of industry…Woman's preparation for work is seldom so thorough as with a man, and long technical training for any work is considered superfluous for a woman….* This matches (32C). Connect answers (33B) and (32C). The lines for (33C) state that *the woman has seldom the strong incentive of others dependent upon her; the man has a wife and children who will suffer, should he relax his efforts; the woman is usually alone.* This answer matches none of the

answers in Q32. Eliminate (33C). The lines for (33D) state that *while in this century and in America work and money-earning have always been considered to be proper in every way for men, there is still some slight social stigma pertaining to money-getting by women.* This matches none of the answers in Q32. Eliminate (33D). The correct answers are (32C) and (33B).

33.   **B**   (See explanation above.)

34.   **C**   This question asks what Hubert implies about the *wage gap between women and men*. Scan the passage for where the author discusses the wage gap. The second paragraph discusses the *reasons for the apparent discrepancy between the pay of men and women*. Use the second paragraph as the window to read. According to the second paragraph, *There are some reasons for the apparent discrepancy between the pay of men and women, which may serve to clear away some of the false impressions that have grown up about this question. In the first place, women as a class of workers are beginners comparatively speaking, in the great field of industry; they lack the hereditary instinct for such work, and as beginners their wages are low.* Find an answer that matches this prediction. Choice (A) can be eliminated because at no point in the passage does the author suggest that the wage gap is *inevitable*. In fact, the first paragraph states that *If a woman wants more money than a man, she has only to do better and more work in the long run than the man.* In other words, the author does not preclude a woman from earning as much as a man. Choice (B) can be eliminated because the passage does not indicate that the reason the wage gap is *avoidable* is because *women and men can either support themselves or marry*. Choice (C) matches the prediction. The author states that there are *false impressions* about the apparent discrepancy between the pay of men and women, and that women get paid less because they are *beginners*. The implication is that one gets paid more if one has more experience. Eliminate (D) because the author never indicates that he finds the wage gap *regrettable*. The correct answer is (C).

35.   **A**   This question asks what the word *relax* most nearly means, as used in line 28. Cross out the word *relax* and replace it with another word that makes sense based on the context of the sentence. The word *relax* is used in the sentence that states *the man has a wife and children who will suffer, should he relax his efforts.* Within the context of the passage *relax his efforts* means something like reducing the amount of work he does. Find an answer that has a meaning close to "reducing." Choice (A), *lessen,* is the only answer that means to reduce. Choices (B), *chill,* and (D), *calm,* may seem tempting because they are alternate definitions of the word *relax*. However, given that *relax* is used in this passage as meaning to "reduce effort" these answers do not work in context. The correct answer is (A).

36.   **D**   This question asks what the word *curious* most nearly means, as used in line 30. Cross out the word *curious* and replace it with another word that makes sense based on the context of the sentence. The word *curious* is used to describe a feature of *work by women*. The sentence states that *while in this century and in America work and money-earning have always been considered to be proper in every way for men, there is still some slight social stigma pertaining to money-getting by women.* In context, the word *curious* means "odd." It is odd that it is proper for men to

make money by working, but not proper for women to do so. Look for an answer that means something like "odd." The only answer that means something similar to odd is (D), *peculiar.* Choice (A), *interested,* may seem tempting because that is a definition of *curious,* however, it does not work in the context of the sentence. The correct answer is (D).

37. **B** This question asks what *Penny's central claim* is in Passage 2. Because this is a general question, it should be done after all of the specific questions for Passage 2. In the first paragraph, the author notes that *a woman...receives half price for all she does.* In the second paragraph, the author goes on to state that *It requires just as much to support a woman as a man,* and that when women are employed *they have the hardest, worst paid, and most unhealthy work.* The passage concludes with the author stating that the effect of paying women better *will prove beneficial not only to workers...but its influence will extend to all those directly affected.* Choice (A) can be eliminated because at no point in the passage does the author suggest that *women must protest.* Choice (B) matches the prediction since the central claim of the passage is that women should get paid more. Choice (C) may be tempting because the first paragraph states that *a woman may be defined to be a creature that receives half price for all she does, and pays full price for all she needs.* However, the author does not state that women shouldn't pay full price. The central claim of the passage is that women should be paid more. Choice (D) can be eliminated because there is no call in the passage for punishing *societies that underpay women.* The correct answer is (B).

38. **C** This question asks what point Penny makes about *women's working conditions* in Passage 2. Notice that this is the first question in a paired set, so this question can be done in tandem with Q39. Look at the best evidence answer choices for Q39 first. The line for (39A) states that *Society is tardy, dragging, in the matter.* This does not support any of the answers in Q38. Eliminate (39A). The lines for (39B) state that *often infirm, sick, or aged parents are relying on her for a support, or, it may be, orphan brothers and sisters.* This matches none of the answers in Q38. Eliminate (39B). The lines for (39C) state that *When men and women are employed in the same establishments, women have not the lightest, most healthy, and most pleasant parts of the labor.* This supports (38C). Connect answer (39C) with (38C). The lines for (39D) discuss the beneficial effect of paying women better prices for their labor. This answer is unrelated to women's working conditions. Eliminate (39D). The correct answers are (38C) and (39C).

39. **C** (See explanation above.)

40. **C** This question asks about the *relationship between the two passages.* Because this question is a general question about both passages, it should be done after the questions that pertain to each individual passage. Passage 1 describes the reasons that women are paid less than men. Passage 2 argues that women should get paid the same as men. Find an answer that connects the two passages. Passage 1 provides several theories of why women do not get paid the same as men, but these theories are not discussed in Passage 2, so eliminate (A). Choice (B) can be eliminated because there is no plan defended in Passage 1. Choice (C) matches the passages:

Passage 1 discusses the reasons for the discrepancies in the wages between men and women. Passage 2 argues that women should get paid more, which if it came to pass would lessen the discrepancy. Choice (D) can be eliminated: Passage 1 provides reasons for why women do not get paid as much as men. Passage 2 does not address these reasons. The correct answer is (C).

41.  **B**  This question asks what both authors would agree on. Because this is a general question about both passages, it should be done after the questions that pertain to each individual passage. While the author of Passage 2 states that when men and women work in the same establishments women have *the hardest, worst paid, and most unhealthy work*, the author of Passage 1 does not state that businesses *overwork* women. For this reason, eliminate (A). The authors of both passages agree that there is a real *wage gap* between men and women. For this reason, eliminate (C). Neither passage discusses whether educated *women should earn higher salaries*. For this reason, eliminate (D). The correct answer is (B).

42.  **A**  This question asks how the author of Passage 1 would most likely have reacted to lines 72–73 of Passage 2. Because this question is about both passages, it should be done after the questions that pertain to each individual passage. According to the author of Passage 1, there are a number of valid reasons that women do not get paid as much as men. These include that *women as a class of workers are beginners;* that *woman's preparation for work is seldom so thorough as with a man;* and that *the woman has seldom the strong incentive of others dependent on her* that a man does. Therefore, the author would not agree with the statement that *To pay women better prices for labor will give it a dignity in public estimation*. Eliminate (C) and (D) because *empathy* and *elation* would suggest that the author of Passage 1 agrees with the author of Passage 2. In (B), *panic* is too extreme. The author of Passage 1 does not indicate that he is in any way panicked. Choice (B) is also incorrect since neither passage discusses reverse discrimination. The correct answer is (A).

43.  **A**  This question asks about a *unique benefit* of genetic engineering. Because there is no line reference and the entire passage is about genetic engineering, this question should be done after the other specific questions. In the fourth paragraph, the author begins to describe genetic engineering in detail and explains how it's different from conventional breeding. Because this question asks about a *unique benefit*, the correct answer will be something specific to genetic engineering. Choice (A) is supported by the text in the fourth paragraph: *By contrast, today's genetic engineers can transfer just a few genes at a time between species that are distantly related or not related at all.* The *by contrast* at the beginning of the sentence indicates this is a characteristic specific to genetic engineering. Keep (A). Choice (B) is a benefit of genetic engineering, but it's also true of conventional breeding. *Humans have been altering the genetic makeup of plants for millennia…to make them taste sweeter, grow bigger, last longer.* Eliminate (B). Choice (C) can be eliminated because it's too extreme. While genetic engineering could help the problem, it will not solve it entirely. Choice (D) might look attractive because genetic engineering can *increase crop yields*, but there's no indication that is a characteristic *unique* to genetic engineering. The correct answer is (A).

44. **D** This question asks for the meaning of the word *novel* as it is used in the text. Cross out the word, and use the surrounding information to fill in another word that makes sense based on the passage. The text says that genetic modification is *not novel* and that humans have been altering plants' genetic makeup *for millennia*. Therefore, *novel* must mean something like "new" or "cutting-edge." Choices (A) and (C) can be eliminated because they are the opposite of the prediction. Choice (B) may initially look attractive because a novel can also be a piece of *written* literature, but that isn't consistent with the use of the word in the passage. Eliminate (B). Choice (D), *modern*, means "new" or "cutting-edge." The correct answer is (D).

45. **B** This question asks about the relationship between *conventional breeding and genetic engineering*, as presented in the passage. Notice that this is the first question in a paired set, so it can be done in tandem with Q46. Read the lines for (46A) first. These lines reference humans *altering the genetic makeup of plants for millennia…breeding varieties to make them taste sweeter, grow bigger….* These lines only refer to conventional breeding, and they don't support any of the answer choices in Q45. Eliminate (46A). The lines in (46B) mention that *genetic engineering is…quite different from conventional breeding.* Although the lines mention both conventional breeding and genetic engineering, they don't provide specifics to support any of the answers in Q45. Eliminate (46B). The lines in (46C) say that genetic engineers can *transfer just a few genes…between species that…are not related at all.* In addition, the lines begin with *By contrast*, indicating that this is different from what's possible with conventional breeding. These lines support (45B). Draw a line connecting the two answers. The lines for (46D) only mention genetic engineering, which doesn't support any of the answers for Q45. Eliminate (46D). The correct answers are (45B) and (46C).

46. **C** (See explanation above.)

47. **C** This question asks for the meaning of the word *yields* as it is used in the text. Cross out the word, and use the surrounding information to fill in another word that makes sense based on the passage. The passage talks about how genetic engineering can *help address…food shortage and hunger* by *increas[ing] crop yields.* The missing word must mean something like "harvests" or "production." Choices (A) and (D) can be eliminated because they are both positive words that have similar meanings. Neither word is consistent with the prediction, and if two answer choices are very close in meaning, they can both be eliminated. Eliminate (B) because there is no indication the farmers are making more money, simply that more food is grown. Choice (C), *outputs*, matches the prediction of "production." The correct answer is (C).

48. **A** This is a specific question that asks why Prakash says the technology is *easy for farmers to use*. Use the line reference to find the window and read carefully. In the next sentence, Prakash continues by saying that *The farmers just plant the seeds, and the seeds bring new features….* The correct answer should have something to do with the farmers simply having to plant the seeds. Choice (A) matches that prediction. Keep it. Choice (B) can be eliminated because whether

the farmers have systems in place to deal with drought has nothing to do with the prediction. Choice (C) uses familiar words from the passage such as *salt, aluminum,* and *iron,* but the answer itself has nothing to do with the text. Eliminate (C). Choice (D) can be eliminated because the technology of the seed has nothing to do with redistribution networks. The correct answer is (A).

49.   **D**   This question asks about the *perspective of the "critics."* Use the line reference to find the window and read carefully to find a prediction. The passage says that the critics argue that *the solution to hunger and malnutrition lies in redistributing existing food supplies.* Make sure to read the whole window, because the passage goes on to say that *Others believe that the ownership by big multinational companies of key biotechnology methods and genetic information is crippling…efforts to use this technology to address the needs of subsistence farmers.* Look for an answer that addresses both or either of these beliefs. Choice (A) might initially look attractive because it mentions *subsistence farmers* and *multinational companies,* but there is no indication in the passage that critics consider genetic engineering the *only* solution. Eliminate (A). Choice (B) is not supported by the text and can be eliminated. Choice (C) is both extreme and counter to the ideas of the critics mentioned in the passage. Eliminate (C). Choice (D) is a paraphrase of the prediction: genetic engineering could be much more effective if more farmers had access to the technology. The correct answer is (D).

50.   **C**   This question is the best evidence question in a paired set. Because Q49 was a specific question, simply look at the lines used to answer the previous question. Two different sets of lines were used in the prediction: *the solution to hunger and malnutrition lies in redistributing existing food supplies* and *Others believe that the ownership by big multinational companies of key biotechnology methods and genetic information is crippling…efforts to use this technology to address the needs of subsistence farmers.* Of these two sets of lines, only the second one is an answer choice. The correct answer is (C).

51.   **C**   This question asks which statement is supported by Figure 1. Work through each answer choice using the figure. Choice (A) can be eliminated because HT cotton decreased from 2010–2011. Choice (B) can be eliminated because for most of the time in the given range, the percentage of planted acres of Bt corn was lower than the percentage of planted acres of Bt cotton. Choice (C) is supported by the graph, so keep it. Choice (D) can be eliminated because HT soybeans consistently had the highest percentage of planted acres throughout the entire time period. The correct answer is (C).

52.   **B**   This question asks which claim is *supported by Figure 2.* Make sure to read the note under the figure. Bt-only corn is engineered to be pest-resistant, HT-only is engineered to be herbicide-tolerant, and stacked is engineered to be both. Work through each answer choice using the figure. Choice (A) can be eliminated because in 2000, Bt-only corn had the highest percentage of acres planted. Choice (B) mentions 2016, so only look at that year. In 2016, more acres

of stacked corn were planted than either of the other types. Keep (B). Choice (C) can be eliminated because in 2014 HT-only looks to be about 10% and Bt-only is only about 4 or 5%. Meanwhile, stacked is closer to 70%, which is significantly more than HT-only and Bt-only combined. Choice (D) can be eliminated because the graph shows that, while it was a small percentage, stacked corn was planted before 2004, so corn that was both resistant to pests and tolerant of herbicides must have existed before 2014. The correct answer is (B).

## Section 2: Writing and Language

1. **D** Note the question! The question asks whether the sentence should be added, so it is testing consistency. If the content of the new sentence is consistent with the topics presented in the passage, then it should be added. The previous sentences discuss preventable auto accidents and lists their causes; the following sentence introduces *A recent set of research findings* pertaining to a single potential preventative factor, mountain lions. The proposed sentence would add information stating that *Statistics show that people are 23 times more likely to be involved in collisions when they are texting and driving*, which is not relevant to the topic of research findings on mountain lions; eliminate (A) and (B). However, the sentence does not *contradict the paragraph's main focus*, so eliminate (C). The additional sentence does *deviate from the paragraph's main topic*. The correct answer is (D).

2. **D** Verbs are changing in the answer choices, so the question is testing consistency of verbs. A verb must be consistent with its subject and with the other verbs in the sentence. Later in the sentence it is stated that *accidents could be prevented by a single factor*. Since this information is present tense, the action of *A recent set of research findings* should also be present tense; eliminate (A) and (C). *Would suggest* is partially redundant and incorrectly indicates that there is a condition tied to the suggestion provided by *a recent set of research findings*, so eliminate (B). The *set of findings* is a collective noun, so the verb should be present and singular. The correct answer is (D).

3. **A** Note the question! The question asks which option best combines the two sentences, so it's testing precision and concision. Look for the answer that combines the sentences while maintaining the meaning of the originals. The sentences use the repetitive phrasing *We probably want to start* and *before we do that*, so the correct answer will eliminate this redundancy without introducing another. Choice (A) eliminates the redundancy without introducing any other errors, so keep it. *Images* and *funny ones* are redundant, so eliminate (B). Choice (C) does not eliminate the original redundancy, so eliminate it. Choice (D) uses the subject *we* twice, so eliminate it. The correct answer is (A).

4. **A** Note the question! The question asks whether the sentence should be kept or deleted, so it is testing consistency. If the content of the underlined sentence is not consistent with the topics presented in the passage, then it should be deleted. The sentence states that *The eastern part of the United States is at a special risk for these collisions because deer tend to roam freely and*

*plentifully around the region.* The sentence mentions *these collisions*, which refers directly to the *1.2 million collisions each year between automobiles and deer* from the previous sentence. Therefore, the sentence should be kept; eliminate (C) and (D). The sentence is only about accidents involving deer, not why all *car travel is so dangerous in the United States*; eliminate (B). The information in the sentence *does provide a detail that explains the statistic in the previous sentence.* The correct answer is (A).

5. **A** Pronouns are changing in the answer choices, so the question is testing consistency of pronouns. The pronoun refers to the plural *deer populations*, so the correct choice must be plural. *They* is a plural pronoun, so keep (A). *We* is a first person pronoun that includes the reader, so eliminate (B). *It* and *one* are singular, so eliminate (C) and (D). The correct answer is (A).

6. **C** Note the question! The question asks where sentence 4 should be placed, so it's testing consistency. Determine the subject matter of the sentence, and find the other sentence that also discusses that information. Sentence 4 states that *Deer are thus able to reproduce without restriction*, so this sentence should come after the reason deer can reproduce freely. Sentence 2 states *development and hunting have eliminated this threat*, mentioned in sentence 1, *that deer face no natural predators in the eastern states.* Sentence 4 must come directly after the elimination of the threat, allowing for increased reproduction. The correct answer is (C).

7. **B** The vocabulary is changing in the answer choices, so this question is testing word choice. Look for a word whose definition is consistent with the other ideas in the sentence. According to the context of the sentence, *the mountain lion populations of the west* are mentioned *as evidence*, so the underlined word should mean something like "uses" or "references." *Opines* means "express an opinion," so eliminate (A). *Cites* means "quotes," which matches the prediction, so keep (B). *Says* means "states," which is not the same as "uses," so eliminate (C). *Proclaims* means "announces," so eliminate (D). The correct answer is (B).

8. **A** Pronouns are changing in the answer choices, so the question is testing consistency of pronouns. The pronoun refers to the singular *evidence* supporting the claim *these big cats "can coexist in close proximity with people."* *That* is a singular pronoun, so keep (A). *Or* is a conjunction that cannot refer to another idea, so eliminate (B). *Which* is not precise because it does not refer to one specific noun, so eliminate (C). *When* refers only to time, so eliminate (D). The correct answer is (A).

9. **B** Introductory transitions are changing in the answer choices, so the question is testing the consistency of that introduction. The sentence before the introduction states that *it doesn't seem that introducing this fierce predator into the wild would be beneficial enough to offset its terrorizing costs.* In contrast, the following sentence states that *Pugh and her team say these predators could save approximately five times as many people from deer-related deaths as they might endanger through unprovoked attacks.* Therefore, a change in direction introductory transition is needed, so eliminate (A), (C), and (D). *Still* is a change of direction transition. The correct answer is (B).

10.   **C**   The words are changing in the answer choices, so the question is testing precision. Given the choice between *sufficiently*, *a good amount*, and *enough*, the phrase *a good amount* does not work in this context, so eliminate (B). When using the word *enough*, it is necessary to say *enough to* accomplish something, not *enough for* accomplishing something, so eliminate (D). The phrase in (A) is awkward and not as straightforward as that in (C), so eliminate (A). The correct answer is (C).

11.   **A**   Pronouns are changing in the answer choices, so the question is testing consistency of pronouns. The beginning of the sentence says *we've accepted the risks*, so the subject is plural. Eliminate (B) and (C), which contain singular possessive pronouns. The possessive pronoun *their* is used for the subject *they*, and *our* is used for the subject *we*. Eliminate (D). The correct answer is (A).

12.   **B**   The vocabulary is changing in the answer choices, so this question is testing word choice. Look for a phrase whose definition is consistent with the other ideas in the sentence. According to the context of the sentence, it can be predicted that *New Orleans has always been a kind of national treasure with* something like "bases" or "origins" *in French, American, African, and indigenous cultures. Routes* means "way" or "manner of travel," but New Orleans does not include a way through these various cultures; eliminate (A) and (D). *Roots* in context means "origins" that reside *in* the various cultures, not *of* them; eliminate (C). The correct answer is (B).

13.   **D**   The words are changing in the answer choices, with the option to DELETE the underlined portion in (D). This question is testing precision and concision. Consider the option to DELETE carefully, as it is often correct because it is the most concise answer. Since the previous sentence already says that *Hurricane Katrina nearly wiped the city off the map,* it is unnecessary to reintroduce *Katrina* as an example; eliminate (A). *However* indicates a change of direction that is not necessary, so eliminate (B). *Thus* would incorrectly indicate that Katrina was a result of Katrina, so eliminate (C). The best option is to delete the underlined portion. The correct answer is (D).

14.   **C**   Verbs are changing in the answer choices, so the question is testing the consistency of verbs. A verb must be consistent with its subject and with the other verbs in the sentence. According to information from earlier in the sentence, *the city has always been praised* and *its status in the popular imagination has changed*. Since this information is past tense, the action to be paired *with broader national interests* should also be past tense; eliminate (A) and (D). *Its status in the popular imagination* is singular, so eliminate (B). The correct answer is (C).

15.   **D**   Note the question! The question asks whether the sentence should be kept or deleted, so it is testing consistency. If the content of the underlined sentence is not consistent with the topics presented in the passage, then it should be deleted. The sentence states that *Louis Armstrong was born in New Orleans in 1901 and began playing trumpet at an early age*. This is the only reference to Louis Armstrong in the entire passage and is not consistent with the paragraph, so eliminate (A) and (B). The sentence does not *suggest that the type of music discussed in the*

*passage is insignificant*, so eliminate (C). However, it *is only vaguely related to the paragraph's main idea*. The correct answer is (D).

16. **C**    Commas are one thing that is changing in the answer choices, so the question is testing the four ways to use a comma. One way is to connect a complete idea with an incomplete idea. The phrase *In a way, jazz gets the attention because it is a kind of national music* is a complete idea, and the phrase *has roots all over the American South, the East Coast, and the Midwest* is an incomplete idea. To connect an incomplete idea with a complete idea, GO punctuation is needed; eliminate (A) and (B). A comma is GO punctuation, and the phrase *with roots all over the American South, the East Coast, and the Midwest* is still an incomplete idea; keep (C). Inserting the word *which* makes it unclear as to what the roots belonged to, so eliminate (D). The correct answer is (C).

17. **B**    Note the question! The question asks which option best combines the two sentences, so it's testing precision and concision. Look for the answer that combines the sentences while maintaining the meaning of the originals. The phrases *you may be one of them* and *you aren't alone* use repetitive phrasing, so the correct answer will eliminate this redundancy without introducing another. *Finding this name curious* is passive and is to be avoided, so eliminate (A). Choice (B) eliminates the redundancy without introducing any other errors, so keep it. *You're not alone* and *like many people* are redundant phrases, so eliminate (C) and (D). The correct answer is (B).

18. **C**    The phrase after *remained* is changing in the answer choices, so the question is testing precision and concision. First, determine whether the phrase is necessary. The sentence already states that the genre *has remained...durable and adaptable*, so there is no need to repeat that idea. Eliminate any choices that are redundant. Choices (A), (B), and (D) each repeat the idea of *remained* by adding *stayed*, so eliminate them. The correct answer is (C).

19. **A**    Commas are changing in the answer choices, so the question is testing the four ways to use a comma. The phrase *by the polkas and waltzes* is necessary information that shouldn't be bracketed by commas, so eliminate (B). In the non-underlined portion of the sentence, there is a comma after *washboard*. However, the phrase *and it was influenced by the polkas and waltzes* is also still necessary information that cannot be bracketed by commas or dashes; eliminate (C) and (D). The correct answer is (A).

20. **B**    Note the question! The question asks *which choice adds the most relevant supporting information*, so it is testing consistency. The start of the paragraph says that *the work of the "King of Zydeco" Clifton Chenier* changed (musical) forms, so the correct choice will explain how Chenier changed zydeco music. That Chenier was *born in...Opelousas, once won a Grammy*, and *was greatly respected at the time of his death* does not explain how he changed zydeco music; eliminate (A), (C), and (D). That he *infused the uptempo music with blues and jazz* explains how Chenier changed zydeco music. The correct answer is (B).

21.  **A**  Commas are changing in the answer choices, so this question is testing the four ways to use a comma. The phrase *Today, groups like BeauSoleil continue to help zydeco to evolve* is a complete idea that does not need to be broken up by any commas, so keep (A). Choices (B) and (C) add a comma after *zydeco*, so eliminate them. Choice (D) adds a comma after BeauSoliel, so eliminate (D). The correct answer is (A).

22.  **D**  The vocabulary is changing in the answer choices, so this question is testing word choice. Look for a word whose definition is consistent with the other ideas in the paragraph. The sentence before the underlined portion states that *Zydeco is a pleasure to listen to, but it is just as important* culturally. The next sentence continues to state that *zydeco provides an important reminder.* The correct choice will be something like "important cultural thing." *Memorial* means "monument" or "tribute" and can be important culturally, but a memorial is mostly about the person or thing it commemorates; eliminate (A). Neither *agreement* nor *victory* match the prediction, so eliminate (B) and (C). A *cultural artifact* is in fact something important to a culture. The correct answer is (D).

23.  **D**  Commas are the main thing changing in the answer choices, so the question is testing the four ways to use a comma. In (C), the phrase *in San Francisco conducted* is surrounded by commas. This phrase is necessary, however, so eliminate (C). A pair of em-dashes can also surround unnecessary information, but the em-dashes in (B) are around necessary information. Eliminate (B). The difference between (A) and (D) is that there are no commas in (D). There is no need to pause anywhere in this sentence, so there's no need for a comma; eliminate (A). The correct answer is (D).

24.  **C**  Note the question! The question asks whether the sentence should be added, so it is testing consistency. If the content of the new sentence is consistent with the topics presented in the passage, then it should be added. The surrounding sentences discuss *unlikely building foundations: ships,* and that *San Francisco's subway...passes right through one.* The proposed sentence would add information stating that *San Francisco was for many years known as Yerba Buena,* which is not relevant to the main topic of the paragraph, so eliminate (A) and (B). However, the passage isn't *primarily concerned with mass transit,* so eliminate (D). The sentence *obscures the focus of the passage by introducing a detail that does not have an obvious connection.* The correct answer is (C).

25.  **D**  Note the question! The question asks which option best combines the two sentences, so it's testing precision and concision. The previous sentence mentions a surprising discovery of ships underground. This sentence needs to explain the reason for that, so it must come in the form of something like "the reason is…." Choice (A) refers to San Francisco as *an answer,* but San Francisco is a location of the mystery, not an answer. Eliminate (A). Choice (B) makes more sense, but by including the word *so* between the parts of the sentence, it makes it seem like San Francisco manufactured land because of *the answer.* Eliminate (B). Choice (C) includes the phrase *Even though,* but a contrast is not needed. Eliminate (C). Choice (D) states *The answer* for the underground ships in a way that connects the ideas precisely. The correct answer is (D).

26. **A** Pronouns are changing in the answer choices, so the question is testing consistency of pronouns. The pronoun refers to *each discipline*, which is singular, so keep (A). *Our* and *their* are plural pronouns, so eliminate (B) and (C). *His* refers to a male and each discipline lacks gender specificity, so eliminate (D). The correct answer is (A).

27. **B** Note the question! The question asks where sentence 5 should be placed, so it's testing consistency. Determine the subject matter of the sentence, and find the other sentences that also discuss that information. Sentence 5 states that in a classical sense, archaeologists study human history, and geologists study natural history, so look for another sentence about *archaeologists and geologists*. Sentence 2 references *Each of these disciplines*, and in the current order of the passage only *sciences* in general are mentioned by sentence 1. Therefore, at least a pair of disciplines should be mentioned prior to sentence 2. Sentence 5 provides those disciplines. The correct answer is (B).

28. **C** Introductory transitions are changing in the answer choices, so the question is testing the consistency of that introduction. The sentence after the introduction says that *we may think of the ground as something that is relatively constant*, but after a comma the sentence changes direction to say that *the archaeosphere suggests that the opposite is true*. Therefore, there needs to be an introduction indicating this change of direction. *Because* and *since* are each same direction transitions, so eliminate (A) and (D). *But* directly indicates an exception rather than previewing one, so eliminate (B). *While* is a change of direction transition. The correct answer is (C).

29. **D** Pronouns and verbs are changing in the answer choices, so the question is testing consistency of those pronouns and verbs. In the previous sentence, it is stated that *we may think of the ground as something constant*, so the passage uses the first person plural voice. *Them* and *they* are each third person pronouns that incorrectly change the voice of the passage, so eliminate (A) and (B). *Built on by us* is passive voice that is less concise than the active *we build on*; eliminate (C). The correct answer is (D).

30. **C** Introductory transitions are changing in the answer choices, so the question is testing the consistency of that introduction. The sentence after the introduction says *some companies in Scandinavia have begun to mine the archaeosphere*, which is provided to support information in the prior sentence stating that *the classification and study of the archaeosphere could be beneficial and not just for the work of archaeologists and geologists*. Therefore, the correct choice will introduce supporting evidence. *In a sense*, *nonetheless*, and *therefore* do not introduce supporting evidence, so eliminate (A), (B), and (D). *For example* introduces supporting evidence. The correct answer is (C).

31. **A** Verbs are changing in the answer choices, so the question is testing the consistency of verbs. A verb must be consistent with its subject and with the other verbs in the sentence. The verb *may have been wasted* refers to resources that *some companies in Scandinavia have begun to mine the archaeosphere for*, so keep (A). The resources were not *to have been wasted* nor were the *resources*,

*being wasted*, so eliminate (B) and (D). Inserting *they* makes the phrase after the comma a complete idea and a comma is GO punctuation that cannot come between two complete ideas; eliminate (C). The correct answer is (A).

32. **D** Pronouns are changing in the answer choices, so the question is testing consistency of pronouns. The pronoun refers to the subject *it* that begins the sentence. That it a little vague, so look back to the previous sentence to see that *it* refers to *the world*. This sentence is about the way the world can recycle resources, so the correct choice will be singular and possessive. *Its'* incorrectly uses an apostrophe, and *it's* is the contraction for "it is," so eliminate (A) and (C). *They're* is the plural possessive pronoun, so eliminate (B). *Its* is the singular possessive pronoun. The correct answer is (D).

33. **B** Note the question! The question asks for the choice which *offers an accurate interpretation of the data in the figure*. Choose the answer most consistent with this goal. There is no information in the figure regarding the proportion *of human and industrial waste products* in the *cover soil*, so eliminate (A) and (C). According to the figure, *there is some human influence at depths greater than 10 meters*. In fact, that influence goes *as deep as 14 meters below the surface;* eliminate (D). The correct answer is (B).

34. **B** The vocabulary is changing in the answer choices, so this question is testing word choice. Look for a phrase whose definition is consistent with the other ideas in the sentence. The opening of passage states that scientific endeavors purporting to better the human condition *have saved countless lives* and that this science in turn has done something similar for *the lives of many, even the seriously ill*. From the context of the passage, the phrase should be something like "better their personal condition." *Healthy* matches this prediction, but *medical* means "pertaining to medicine" instead of the patient's own condition; eliminate (A). *Tolerable and manageable* matches, so keep (B). Neither *complicated and expensive* nor *patient and tolerant* match "better their personal condition," so eliminate (C) and (D). The correct answer is (B).

35. **D** The words are changing in the answer choices, so this question is testing precision. To decide between *affect* and *effect*, consider whether a verb (*affect*) or a noun (*effect*) is needed. Genetic sequencing is not *affecting* anything, so eliminate (A) and (B). Choice (C) takes the noun *effect* and adds an *-ing*, making it a verb. Eliminate (C). The correct answer is (D).

36. **B** Note the question! The question asks which *most effectively sets up the examples in the following sentences*, so it is testing consistency. The example after the underlined sentence is *a large category of patients—expectant mothers*, so the correct choice will be related to the category of *expectant mothers*. *Children* and *inheritable diseases* are not related to the category of *expectant mothers*, so eliminate (A) and (C). That *Patients of genetic counselors can be of any age* could be narrowed down to the *large category of patients* that is *expectant mothers*, so keep (B). *Parents' behaviors* are not mentioned in the passage, so eliminate (D). The correct answer is (B).

37. **D** The words are changing in the answer choices, with the option to DELETE the underlined portion in (D). This question is testing precision and concision. Consider the option to DELETE carefully, as it is often correct because it is the most concise answer. *Medical risks* is redundant because each of the items in the subsequent list—*transmittable diseases, inborn illnesses, and birth defects*—is a medical risk; eliminate (A). *The dark side of medicine* is unrelated and *unpleasant things* is also redundant, so eliminate (B) and (C). The correct answer is (D).

38. **A** The entire second half of the sentence is changing in the answer choices, so this question is testing precision and concision. The subject of the underlined section should match *she* in the non-underlined beginning of the sentence. Based on the previous sentence, it can be predicted that *she* is a mother. Eliminate (B), (C), and (D). The correct answer is (A).

39. **C** The punctuation is changing in the answer choices, so the question is testing STOP and GO punctuation. Use the vertical line test, and identify the ideas as complete or incomplete. Draw the vertical line between the words *with* and *conceptions*. The phrase *Older parents might even consider genetic testing before trying to conceive, thus reducing the risks associated with* is an incomplete idea, and the phrase *conceptions after the primary maternal or paternal periods of fertility* is also an incomplete idea. No punctuation is needed to connect an incomplete idea with another incomplete idea, so eliminate (A). Choice (B) adds another comma that results in the phrase *thus reducing the risks* being bracketed by commas. This phrase is necessary information that cannot be surrounded by commas, so eliminate (B). The phrase also cannot be surrounded by a comma and a colon, so eliminate (D). The correct answer is (C).

40. **D** The punctuation is changing in the answer choices, so the question is testing STOP and GO punctuation and apostrophes. Use the vertical line test, and identify the ideas as complete or incomplete. Draw the vertical line between the words *facets* and *the*. The phrase *As in the case of expectant mothers, genetic counseling has many aspects* is a complete idea, and the phrase *the two primary divisions are diagnosis and support* is also a complete idea. To connect two complete ideas, STOP punctuation is needed; eliminate (A). In the context of the passage, the *facets* belong to *genetic counseling* rather than possessing something themselves. Therefore, an apostrophe is not needed for *facets*; eliminate (B) and (C). A colon is HALF-STOP punctuation that can come between two complete ideas. The correct answer is (D).

41. **C** Note the question! The question asks *which most effectively suggests that the "two primary divisions" are not often separate* with different vocabulary in the answer choices, so it is testing consistency and word choice. From the question, the correct choice will mean something like "not separate from each other." *Complicated* means "difficult to understand," so eliminate (A). *Specialized* means "specifically tailored," so eliminate (B). *Intertwined* means "tied together," so keep (C). *Enriching* means "adding value to," so eliminate (D). The correct answer is (C).

42. **D** Transitions are changing in the answer choices, so the question is testing the consistency of that transition. The sentence after the transition states that *the field and its accomplishments are still*

*not widely known*, which is in spite of *all genetic counseling's benefits*. Therefore, a change of direction transition is necessary. *Therefore* and *thus* are same direction transitions, so eliminate (A) and (C). The fact that *the field and its accomplishments are not widely known* is not an example of a phenomenon, so eliminate (B). *However* is a change of direction transition. The correct answer is (D).

43. **D** Note the question! The question asks whether the sentence should be added, so it is testing consistency. If the content of the new sentence is consistent with the topics presented in the passage, then it should be added. The surrounding sentences discuss *the work of genetic counselors* in general and how this work is *still not widely known*. The proposed sentence would add information stating that *the number of children born with Down syndrome has decreased significantly since this type of genetic prediction became available in the mid-1970s*. The sentence is not relevant to the main topic of the paragraph, so eliminate (A) and (B). However, the example is not *inconsistent with the work of genetic counselors*, so eliminate (C). The additional sentence *does not have a significant bearing on this paragraph*. The correct answer is (D).

44. **C** Note the question! The question asks where sentence 2 should be placed, with the option to DELETE the underlined portion in (D). This question is testing precision and concision. Consider the option to DELETE carefully, as it is often correct because it is the most concise answer. Determine the subject matter of the sentence, and determine if there are other sentences also discussing that information. Sentence 2 says that *How effectively they communicate their findings can...be a matter of life and death*. Based on the context of the passage, the *they* in this sentence refers to *genetic counselors*, so look for another sentence about *genetic counselors*. Sentence 5 is the only sentence in the paragraph to mention *genetic counselors*, so eliminate (A) and (B). Sentence 2 provides new information directly related to the content of sentence 5, so eliminate (D). The correct answer is (C).

## Section 3: Math (No Calculator)

1. **A** The question asks for a specific amount, so plug in the answers. Pick a value that appears in more than one answer, such as $x = -3$. Plug $-3$ into the equation for $x$ to get $-3(-3)^2 - 3(-3) + 18 = 0$ or $-3(9) + 9 + 18 = 0$. This becomes $-27 + 27 = 0$, which is true. Eliminate (C) and (D), which do not contain the value $x = -3$. Now try $x = 2$ to get $-3(2)^2 - 3(2) + 18 = 0$ or $-3(4) - 6 + 18 = 0$. This becomes $-12 + 12 = 0$, which is true, so eliminate (B). The correct answer is (A).

2. **C** To find the equation of a line that pertains to this specific graph, plug an $x$-value from the graph into the equation and see if it gives the correct $y$-value. The point $(1, 0)$ is on the graph of $m$, so plug in $x = 1$ and $y = 0$. Choice (A) becomes $1 = -2$, which is not true, so eliminate (A). Choice (B) becomes $0 = -2$, so eliminate (B). Choice (C) becomes $0 = 2(1) - 2 = 2 - 2 = 0$. This is true, so keep (C), but check (D) just in case. Choice (D) becomes $0 = 2(1) + 2 = 2 + 2 = 4$, so eliminate (D). The correct answer is (C).

3.  **D**  A full circle is 360°, and angle MN measures 60°. Set up the proportion $\frac{60°}{360°} = \frac{\text{sector}}{48}$. Reduce the fraction on the left to get $\frac{1}{6} = \frac{\text{sector}}{48}$, then cross-multiply to get 6(sector) = 48. Divide both sides by 6 to get sector = 8. The correct answer is (D).

4.  **C**  The word *sum* indicates addition, so add the two expressions to get $x^2 + x - x - 2 = x^2 - 2$. The correct answer is (C).

5.  **D**  Zeros are also known as *x*-intercepts, so find the answer choice that cannot have two zeros. An absolute value function with real zeros will have two *x*-intercepts. Eliminate (A). Cubic functions can have up to three real zeros, so eliminate (B). A quadratic function with real zeros can have up to two real zeros, so eliminate (C). Only a function with no real zeros or just one real zero CANNOT have two *x*-intercepts. Choice (D) is the correct answer.

6.  **A**  Plug in $t = 4$ into the given equation to get $\sqrt{c-1} - 4 = 0$. Now plug in the answers to see which one makes this equation true. Start with (B) and plug in 15 for *c*. The equation becomes $\sqrt{15-1} - 4 = 0$, or $\sqrt{14} - 4 = 0$. This is not true, so eliminate (B). The square root of 14 would be less than the square root of 16, or less than 4, so the left side of the equation would give a negative value with (B). A larger value is needed for *c,* so eliminate (C) and (D). The correct answer is (A).

7.  **B**  To solve this system of equations, substitute $y^2$ into the second equation for *x* to get $-3(2y - 3) = 6y^2 + 9$. Distribute the $-3$ across the terms on the left side to get $-6y + 9 = 6y^2 + 9$. Subtract 9 from both sides to get $-6y = 6y^2$. Divide both sides by 6*y* to get $y = -1$. Now, plug the value for *y* back into the first equation to get $x = (-1)^2 = 1$. The question asks for the value of *xy*, so multiply the two values: $(-1)(1) = -1$. The correct answer is (B).

8.  **B**  Use Bite-Sized Pieces to break the word problem into manageable chunks. Start with a straightforward piece of information, such as the total number of miles. This value will be made up of the miles Richard walks, *w*, and the miles he bikes, *b*, so it translates to $w + b$. The total miles must be *no more than 15*, which translates to $w + b \leq 15$. Eliminate (C) and (D) because they do not include this inequality. Now compare the remaining answers. Both have the same numbers and variables, and the only difference is the direction of the inequality sign. These inequalities relate to the other part of the question, the calories burned, which should be *at least 500. At least* is represented by the $\geq$ symbol, so eliminate (A). The correct answer is (B).

9.  **D**  Label what is known about the equation. The left side is Rankine degrees and the *C* on the right side is Celsius degrees. The number 491.67 is on the right side, so it has something to do with Rankine degrees. However, all the answers refer to Rankine degrees, so it is difficult to eliminate anything at this time. Plug-and-play to see how the variables relate. Since this is the No Calculator section, start with the easiest plug in, which will be in (D). If $C = 0$, then $R(0) = 1.8(0) + 491.67 = 491.67$. Therefore, at 0 degrees Celsius, the temperature in degrees Rankine is 491.67. This matches the information in (D), so the correct answer is (D).

10.  **A**  The key to solving exponent questions is often to rewrite the base in a different form. The number 4 can be rewritten as $2^2$, so the expression becomes $\left(2^2\right)^{\frac{5}{6}}$. Use the MADSPM rules to combine the exponents to get $2^{\frac{10}{6}} = 2^{\frac{5}{3}}$. With fractional exponents, the numerator is the power and the denominator is the root, so this can be rewritten as $\sqrt[3]{2^5}$. There are five 2's under the root sign, and for every three, one of them can come out. The expression becomes $2\sqrt[3]{2^2} = 2\sqrt[3]{4}$. Choice (A) is the correct answer.

11.  **C**  To find the value of $c + 2b$, first find the value of $2b$, which is $2b = -2xy$. Add that to the expression for $c$, $x^2 + y^2$, to get $x^2 + y^2 - 2xy$. None of the answer choices are of this form, so factor the expression to make it look like the answers. It becomes $x^2 - 2xy + y^2 = (x - y)^2$. The correct answer is (C).

12.  **B**  The formula for the volume of a cone is given at the beginning of the Math sections as $V = \frac{1}{3}\pi r^2 h$. There aren't explicit values for the radius and height given in the problem, so ratios will be necessary to find the new value. The new radius is one-third the original, so the value will be written as $\frac{r}{3}$. The new height is triple the original, so it will be written as $3h$. Plug these new values in the formula for the volume of a cone to get $V = \frac{1}{3}\pi r^2 h = \frac{1}{3}\pi\left(\frac{r}{3}\right)^2(3h) = \frac{1}{3}\pi\left(\frac{1}{9}\right)r^2(3)h = \frac{1}{3}\pi r^2 h\left(\frac{1}{9}\right)(3) = \frac{1}{3}\pi r^2 h\left(\frac{1}{3}\right)$. The value of $\frac{1}{3}\pi r^2 h$ is the volume of the original cone, 12 cubic millimeters. Plug this value into the formula for the new cone to get $(12)\left(\frac{1}{3}\right) = 4$. Choice (B) is the correct answer.

13.  **A**  This question gives the cost of one pod, which is $7, and the number of cups that each pod brews, which is 4. Then the question asks how much Marcy will save if she drinks 9 fewer cups. Set up a proportion of $\frac{\text{cups}}{\text{dollars}}$ to figure out how much 9 cups of coffee will cost her: $\frac{4}{7} = \frac{9}{d}$. To make this look like the answer choices, multiply both sides by $d$ to get $\frac{4}{7}d = 9$. Choice (A) is the correct answer.

14.  **A**  Plug in to see how the variables are related in order to solve this question. Start with $b = 6$ bananas and solve for the number of servings of smoothie. The equation becomes $s = 6 - 4 = 2$. Now plug in $b = 7$ for the additional banana to get $s = 7 - 4 = 3$. The difference in number of servings of smoothie from 2 bananas to 3 bananas is $3 - 2 = 1$ serving. The correct answer is (A).

15.  **D**  Take advantage of the fact that the equation has been given and plug in $x = 0$ to find the $y$-intercept of the function. The equation becomes $2 - 3^0 = 2 - 1 = 1$. The $y$-intercept of $g(x)$ is 1, so multiply this value by $-1$ to find the $y$-intercept of $-g(x)$: $(-1)(1) = -1$. The only graph that has a $y$-intercept at $-1$ is (D), so the correct answer is (D).

16.     $\dfrac{31}{2}$ or **15.5**

To solve this system of equations, plug the value of $n$ given in the second equation into the first equation to get $\dfrac{1}{3}(5m - 3m) = \dfrac{31}{3}$. Multiply both sides of the equation by 3 to eliminate the fractions, and combine like terms to get $2m = 31$. Divide both sides by 2 to get $m = \dfrac{31}{2}$. The correct answer is $\dfrac{31}{2}$.

17.    **10**    Set up an inequality using Bite-Sized Pieces. Asaf must pay a rate of $50 per month for the membership, so this must be multiplied by a number of months, and the first piece of the inequality is $50m$. Next, Asaf must pay a one-time fee of $30 dollars, so this must be added to the first piece to get $50m + 30$. Finally, the total must not exceed $555, so the complete inequality is $50m + 30 \le 555$. Subtract 30 from both sides to get $50m \le 525$, and divide both sides by 50 to get $m \le 10.5$. The problem asks for an answer as a whole number of months, so round down to 10. The correct answer is 10.

18.    **117**    There are 180° in a line, so use this to find the angle to the left of the one that measures 97°: 180° − 97° = 83°. The sum of the internal angles of a triangle must equal 180°, so add 83° and 34° and subtract this from 180° to find the measure of the third angle, which is 180° − (83° + 34°) = 63°. The angle marked $c°$ is next to the one that is 63°, so they add up to 180, and 180° − 63° = 117°. The correct answer is 117.

19.     $\dfrac{12}{5}$ or **2.4**

To solve this problem, distribute the numbers across the terms on the left-hand side of the equation to get $9s - 18 + 3s + 6 = 7s$. Next, combine like terms on the left to get $12s - 12 = 7s$. Subtract $7s$ from both sides to get $5s - 12 = 0$, then add 12 to both sides to get $5s = 12$. Divide both sides by 5 to get $s = \dfrac{12}{5}$. This fits in the grid-in box, so enter it in. The correct answer can also be entered as 2.4.

20.    **7**    The word *equivalent* means that these two expressions need to be equal, so write an equation to show this: $\dfrac{4c + 1}{(2c - 3)^2} - \dfrac{2}{(2c - 3)} = \dfrac{x}{(2c - 3)^2}$. Multiply $\dfrac{2}{(2c - 3)}$ by $\dfrac{(2c - 3)}{(2c - 3)}$, so that the two expressions on the left have a common denominator and can be combined. The left side of the equation becomes $\dfrac{4c + 1}{(2c - 3)^2} - \dfrac{4c - 6}{(2c - 3)^2}$ or $\dfrac{4c + 1 - 4c + 6}{(2c - 3)^2}$. Combine like terms in the numerator to get $\dfrac{7}{(2c - 3)^2}$. The left-side of the equation must equal the right, so $\dfrac{7}{(2c - 3)^2} = \dfrac{x}{(2c - 3)^2}$. Because both sides have the same denominator, set the numerators equal to one another, so $x = 7$. The correct answer is 7.

# Section 4: Math (Calculator)

1. **D**    Start by determining how many fluid ounces are needed for 24 servings of hot chocolate by multiplying: $4.5 \times 24 = 108$ fluid ounces. Next, convert to cups by making a proportion: $\dfrac{1 \text{ cup}}{8 \text{ fluid ounces}} = \dfrac{x \text{ cups}}{108 \text{ fluid ounces}}$. Cross-multiply to get $8x = 108$. Divide both sides by 8 to get $x = 13.5$ cups of cream. The correct answer is (D).

2. **C**    This graph is great for Ballparking. There are many small changes from year-to-year and one very large change from 2006 to 2007. Since the question asks for the greatest change from year-to-year, the answer must be 2006–2007. The correct answer is (C).

3. **B**    Plug in values of $x$ from the table and eliminate choices that do not match the given value of $g(x)$. Start with the first row. When $x = 2$, $g(2) = 11$. Choice (A) becomes $2(2) + 7 = 4 + 7$, which is 11. Keep (A). Choice (B) becomes $3(2) + 5 = 6 + 5$, which is 11. Keep (B). Choice (C) becomes $4(2) + 3 = 8 + 3$, which is 11. Keep (C). Choice (D) becomes $5(2) + 1 = 10 + 1$, which is 11. Keep (D). Since all the answers worked, try another pair of numbers from the table. When $x = 4$, $g(x) = 17$. Choice (A) becomes $2(4) + 7 = 8 + 7$, which is 15. This doesn't match the target value of 17, so eliminate (A). Choice (B) becomes $3(4) + 5 = 12 + 5$, which is 17. This matches the target value, so keep (B). Choice (C) becomes $4(4) + 3 = 16 + 3$, which is 19. Eliminate (C). Choice (D) becomes $5(4) + 1 = 20 + 1$, which is 21. Eliminate (D). The correct answer is (B).

4. **D**    The question asks for a specific value and there are numbers in the answer choices, so plug in the answers. Start with (B), which indicates that Annalee purchased 4 magnets. Those 4 magnets would cost $\$3(4) = \$12$. She bought 10 items, so if she bought 4 magnets, she bought 6 postcards. Those cost $\$1$ each, so that adds $\$6$ to her total cost to get $\$12 + \$6 = \$18$. The question states that she paid $\$22$, so this value is not enough. Annalee must have purchased more magnets to increase the total cost. Eliminate (A) and (B). Try (C) and assume she bought 5 magnets. The magnets would cost $\$3(5) = \$15$. She would also buy 5 postcards, adding $\$5$ to her total to get $\$20$. This is still not enough, so eliminate (C). The correct answer is (D).

5. **A**    Start by reading the full question. The question asks for $x - y$, so look to isolate that expression. Clear the 7 by dividing both sides of the equation by 7 to get $\dfrac{7(x - y)}{7} = \dfrac{4}{7}$, so $x - y = \dfrac{4}{7}$. The correct answer is (A).

6. **A**    Break the question down into bite-sized pieces. To find the average annual precipitation in Orlando, multiply the precipitation in Columbus by $\dfrac{13}{10}$ to get $\dfrac{13}{10}(1{,}000) = 1{,}300$ millimeters. To get the average annual precipitation in Saint Cloud, multiply the precipitation in Columbus by $\dfrac{7}{10}$

to get $\dfrac{7}{10}$ (1,000) = 700 millimeters. The difference in precipitation in the two cities is 1,300 – 700 = 600 millimeters. The correct answer is (A).

7. **D**  Use FOIL and Bite-Sized Pieces to determine which answer matches the original expression. Start with the first term of the squared expression: $(2.6a)^2 = 6.76a^2$. Next, subtract the $a^2$ term from the second expression to get $6.76a^2 – 7.3a^2 = –0.54a^2$. Eliminate (A) and (B) because they do not contain this term. Next, find another term in the expansion. Both (C) and (D) have the term $–18.2a$, so find the terms without $a$: $(–3.5)^2 = 12.25$, and $12.25 – (–4.1) = 12.25 + 4.1 = 16.35$. This only appears in (D), so eliminate (C). The correct answer is (D).

8. **C**  This is a translation problem. To solve this problem, use Bite-Sized Pieces. The AAUW plans to increase the number of student organizations by $t$ per year for $x$ years, so multiply $t$ by $x$ to get $tx$. Since (A) and (B) do not include $tx$, eliminate those answers. The number of student organizations is increasing, so the value $tx$ must be added to the total number of student organizations. The equation needs to include addition, so eliminate (D). The correct answer is (C).

9. **D**  The question states that the resistance, $R$, of a conductor is found by dividing the voltage, $V$, by the current, $I$. Therefore, $R = \dfrac{V}{I}$. To solve this equation in terms of $V$, it is necessary to get $V$ by itself. Multiply both sides by $I$ to get $IR = V$. Flip the equation to get $V = IR$. The correct answer is (D).

10. **A**  The pitching distance increased from 50 feet to 60.5 feet, for an increase of $60.5 – 50 = 10.5$ feet. The question asks for a conversion from feet to meters, so set up a proportion: $\dfrac{1 \text{ meter}}{3 \text{ feet}} = \dfrac{x \text{ meters}}{10.5 \text{ feet}}$. Cross-multiply to get $3x = 10.5$. Divide both sides by 3 to get $x = 3.5$ meters. The correct answer is (A).

11. **B**  This question asks about probability, which is defined as $\dfrac{want}{total}$. Since the social worker is selected at random, the total number of possible outcomes is the total number of social workers: 529. The question asks for the probability that the social worker is a pediatric social worker whose highest level of education is a doctoral degree, so find this number on the chart, which is 221. Put this into the probability definition to get $\dfrac{221}{529} \approx 0.418$. The correct answer is (B).

12. **C**  Perpendicular lines have slopes that are opposite reciprocals. The given equation and the answer choices are all in standard form: $Ax + By = C$. In standard form, the slope of the line is $-\dfrac{A}{B}$. Therefore, the slope of the given line is $-\dfrac{(-3)}{4}$ or $\dfrac{3}{4}$. The perpendicular slope will be $-\dfrac{4}{3}$.

Determine the slope of each answer choice to see which one matches this value. For (A), the slope is $-\dfrac{3}{6} = -\dfrac{1}{2}$. This is not equal to the target slope, so eliminate (A). For (B), the slope is $-\dfrac{3}{8}$. Eliminate (B). For (C), the slope is $-\dfrac{4}{3}$, which is matches the target slope. The correct answer is (C).

13.   **A**   The question asks for the value of $y$, so look for the most direct way to find that. The goal is to make the $x$-terms disappear. In the two equations, the coefficients of the $x$-terms have the same value with opposite signs. Therefore, if the two equations were added together, the $x$-terms would cancel each other out. Stack and add the equations:

$$2 = -\frac{1}{3}x + y$$
$$+\,6 = \;\;\frac{1}{3}x$$
$$\overline{\phantom{+6 = }}$$
$$8 = \qquad y$$

Therefore, the correct answer is (A).

14.   **D**   This question asks which of the statements *must be true*. With statistics, the only things that can definitively be stated are about the survey or poll itself. Statement (I) says that another poll would have the exact same results, but there is no way to know this, so eliminate (A) and (B). Next, statement (II) says that another survey conducted with people in a different town would have the same results, but again, there is no way to know this. Eliminate (C). Thus, the correct answer is (D).

15.   **A**   There are variables in the question and numbers in the answer choices, so plug in the answers. The setup states that the ordered pairs are arranged such that the first term is $x$ and the second term is $y$. Start with (B) and plug in $x = 2$ and $y = -5$ in the first equation to get $4(2) - 1 \le -5$ or $8 - 1 \le -5$. This is not true, so eliminate (B). The number on the left side of the inequality was too big, so the value of $x$ needs to be smaller. Choice (A) has a negative value for $x$, so try it next. The first inequality becomes $4(-3) - 1 \le -1$ or $-12 - 1 \le -1$. This is true, so check the second inequality, which becomes $2 > -3 + (-1)$ or $2 > -4$. This is also true. Thus, the correct answer is (A).

16.   **B**   The question asks for the difference in time it takes for the two people to burn an additional 20 calories each. The 1 hour that the people have already exercised is irrelevant; only the time it takes to burn an additional 20 calories matters. Use the formula *calories* = (*time in minutes*) × (*burn rate*) to calculate the time for each person. For the person who is speed walking, the formula becomes $20 =$ (*time in minutes*) × (5.0). Divide both sides of the formula by 5 to get *time in minutes* = 4. For the person who is doing yoga, the formula becomes $20 =$ (*time in minutes*) × (1.5). Divide both sides by 1.5 to get *time in minutes* = $13\frac{1}{3}$. The difference between these times is $13\frac{1}{3} - 4 = 9\frac{1}{3}$. This is closest to 9.3, so the correct answer is (B).

17. **C** According to the information above the question, the number of calories burned is equal to the time in minutes multiplied by the burn rate for that exercise. The time is given as 30 minutes, and the burn rate for shooting baskets is 3.0. Therefore, *calories burned* = (30)(3.0) = 90 calories. The correct answer is (C).

18. **B** Since there are so many data points and the burn rates for all four exercises are very different, use Ballparking. Pick any point that looks like it intersects a known value on each axis, such as 15 minutes and 30 calories. To calculate the burn rate in calories per minute, divide the calories by the time to get $\dfrac{30 \text{ calories}}{15 \text{ minutes}}$ = 2.0. This value is closest to the burn rate of light aerobics, so the correct answer is (B).

19. **C** Without a label on the vertical axis of the graph, it is difficult to predict what the graph might represent. Go right to the answers and use Process of Elimination. Choice (A) considers the total distance traveled by the spot of paint, which should always be increasing. The graph of $f(t)$ oscillates, so this does not match. Eliminate (A). Choice (B) describes the distance the spot of paint is from the center of the fan, but the spot is traveling in a circular path with the center of the fan as its center. Therefore, the distance between the spot and the center will not change. Eliminate (B). If (C) is true, it indicates that in this scenario the spot would start at a certain distance above the table, go a maximum distance from the table, decrease to a minimum distance close to the table, and return toward the starting point. This matches the graph on the right, so keep (C), but check out (D) just in case. Choice (D) mentions the speed of the fan blades, but the question states that the fan is at a constant low setting, meaning the speed does not change. Eliminate (D). Therefore, the correct answer is (C).

20. **D** There are variables in the question and the answer choices, so plug in. Make $f = 2$ and $g = -2$. The equation becomes $h = \dfrac{2 - (-2)}{-2} = \dfrac{2 + 2}{-2} = \dfrac{4}{-2} = -2$. Now, plug this value of $h$ into the answer choices. Choice (A) says $-2 = 1$, which is false, so eliminate (A). Choice (B) says $-2 > 1$, which is false, so eliminate (B). Choice (C) says $-2 = -1$, which is false, so eliminate (C). Choice (D) says $-2 < -1$, which is true. The correct answer is (D).

21. **C** At the beginning of the Math sections, the relationship between the sides of a 45°-45°-90° triangle is listed. Use this information whenever a triangle question contains these values for angles. The hypotenuse is opposite the 90° angle, and its length is the length of one of the legs multiplied by $\sqrt{2}$. The leg given is 4, so *MO* is $4\sqrt{2}$. Sides *MO* and *LM* are legs of a second 45°-45°-90° triangle, so they are congruent. Therefore, the length of *LM* is also $4\sqrt{2}$. The correct answer is (C).

22. **C** When a question asks for a specific amount and gives numbers in the answer choices, plug in the answers. Here, the answers are approximated, but they are spread apart, so PITA will still work. Start with (B) and calculate the increase of 30 percent: $81{,}300 + \frac{30}{100}(81{,}300) = 81{,}300 + 24{,}390 = 105{,}690$. Next, calculate the increase of 20 percent: $105{,}690 + \frac{20}{100}(105{,}690) = 105{,}690 + 21{,}138 = 126{,}828$. Choice (B) is too big, since the chart indicates a current population of 122,000 for Maple Mall. Eliminate (B) and also (A), which is even bigger. Since the population wasn't too far off with (B), try (C) next using the same steps. If the 2011 population was 78,200, the 30% increase would bring it to 101,660. The 20% increase would bring the population to 121,992. This is very close to 122,000, so the correct answer is (C).

23. **C** Use the data in the table to test the equations in the answer choices by plugging in. Choose the data for Fir Fen because it has the smallest population, making it easier to work with. Use Bite-Sized Pieces to translate the question. The population $n$ is actually in terms of <u>thousands</u> of people, so convert the population of Fir Fen to thousands, which would be 2. Plug 2 into the answer choices to see which one results in the target answer of 22. Choice (A) becomes $A(2) = 2(2) + 18 = 4 + 18 = 22$. This matches the target value of 22, so keep (A), but check the remaining answers just in case. Choice (B) becomes $A(2) = 2.5(2) - 300 = 5 - 300 = -295$. Eliminate (B). Choice (C) becomes $A(2) = 3.5(2) + 15 = 7 + 15 = 22$. Keep (C). Choice (D) becomes $A(2) = 4.5(2) - 107 = 9 - 107 = -98$. Eliminate (D). Since both (A) and (C) worked, try another point, such as Cedar Vale's $n = 12$ and $A(12) = 57$. Choice (A) becomes $A(12) = 2(12) + 18 = 24 + 18 = 42$. This doesn't match the target value of 57, so eliminate (A). The correct answer is (C).

24. **B** Use Bite-Sized Pieces. It is stated that 62.9 percent of the employees at the small business have less than $1,000 in savings, but the question asks about the number of small business employees in the whole county who have *at least* $1,000 in savings. To find the percentage of employees who have at least that much in savings, subtract 62.9% from the total to get $100\% - 62.9\% = 37.1\%$. Now, calculate the total number of employees working at small businesses in the county by multiplying the number of small businesses by the average number of employees at each small business to get $270 \times 132 = 35{,}640$ total small business employees. Now take 37.1% of this total: $\frac{37.1}{100}(35{,}640) \approx 13{,}222$. This is closest to (B), so the correct answer is (B).

25.  **A**   This question gives the volume of a cube and asks for the surface area of the cube. The Geometry Basic Approach says to write out any formulas needed. The reference box at the start of the Math sections gives the formula for the volume of a rectangular solid as $V = lwh$, but on a cube, all the dimensions are the same, so the volume of a cube is $V = s^3$. There are variables in the question and answers, so plug in a value for $c$ to find the volume of the cube. If $c = 4$, the volume is $V = \dfrac{1}{8}(4^3) = \dfrac{1}{8}(64) = 8$. Set this equal to the volume formula for a cube to solve for $s$. If $V = s^3 = 8$, take the cube root of both sides to get $s = 2$. Now find the surface area of the cube, which is the area of one face times the number of faces. For this cube, that value is $SA = (2 \times 2) \times 6 = 24$. This is the target value. Plug $c = 4$ into the answer choices to see which one equals 24. Choice (A) becomes $6\left(\dfrac{4}{2}\right)^2 = 6(2)^2 = 24$. This matches the target, so keep (A), but check the remaining answers just in case. Choice (B) becomes $6\left(\dfrac{4^2}{2}\right) = 6\left(\dfrac{16}{2}\right) = 6(8) = 48$. Eliminate (B). Choice (C) becomes $6(4^2) = 6(16) = 96$. Eliminate (C). Choice (D) will be even larger, so eliminate (D). The correct answer is (A).

26.  **B**   This question uses the word *mean*, so use the Average Pie. Starting with the information in the first sentence, put the number of things in the lower left spot and the average in the lower right spot. Multiply them together to get the total: $6 \times 160.5 = 963$. Put this number in the upper spot on the pie.

Now follow the same steps with the information in the second sentence. The second total will be 5 × 168 = 840.

The original total was 963, and the new total is 840, so the change in total is 963 − 840 = 123. Because the only difference between the two groups is the weight of the person that gets off the elevator, the weight of that person must have been 123, so the correct answer is (B).

27. **B** This is a translation question, so use Bite-Sized Pieces and Process of Elimination. The first piece of information is that *s* students chose the interviewee associated with their college, so the correct answer choice needs to include *s*. All the choices have *s*, so nothing can be eliminated. The question also states that 58 more people chose the interviewee associated with their college, so that translates to *s* + 58. This eliminates all choices except for (B), so the correct answer is (B).

28. **D** The word *equivalent* means "the same," so the expressions in the answer choices need to equal $y = c - x^2$ when expanded. Start with (A) and use FOIL to get $y = (c - x)(c - x) = c^2 - cx - cx + x^2$. This does not match the given expression, so eliminate (A). Choice (B) becomes $y = (c - x)(c + x) = c^2 + cx - cx + x^2$. Eliminate (B). Choice (C) becomes $y = \left(\dfrac{c}{2} - x\right)\left(\dfrac{c}{2} + x\right) = \dfrac{c^2}{4} + \dfrac{cx}{2} - \dfrac{cx}{2} - x^2$. Eliminate (C). Therefore, the correct answer is (D).

29. **B** This question asks for the value of $s(15)$, but no equation is given for $s(x)$. The slope of *s* is described in terms of the slope of *r*, so start there. The graph shows line *r* going through points (1, 0) and (0, −2). To calculate the slope of $s(x)$, use slope = $\dfrac{y_2 - y_1}{x_2 - x_1}$. Therefore, the slope is $\dfrac{0 - (-2)}{1 - 0} = \dfrac{2}{1} = 2$. The slope of $s(x)$ is $\dfrac{1}{6}$ times the slope of $r(x)$, or $\dfrac{1}{6}$ (2) = $\dfrac{2}{6} = \dfrac{1}{3}$. Now, find the equation for $s(x)$. The slope-intercept form is $y = mx + b$, where *m* is the slope and *b* is the *y*-intercept. The *y*-intercept

is the $y$-value when $x = 0$. The question states that $s$ passes through the point $(0, 2)$, so the $y$-intercept is 2. Therefore, $s(x) = \frac{1}{3}x + 2$. The question asks for the value of $s(15)$, so plug in 15 for $x$. The equation becomes $s(15) = \frac{1}{3}(15) + 2 = 5 + 2 = 7$. Thus, the correct answer is (B).

30. **C** The standard form of a circle is $(x - h)^2 + (y - k)^2 = r^2$, where the center is point $(h, k)$. In order to find the center, convert this equation to standard form by completing the square. First, group the $x$- and $y$-terms together to get $(x^2 + 16x) + (y^2 - 12y) = -19$. Next, divide the coefficient on the $x$-term, 16, by two and square it to get 64. Add this number to the $x$-terms and to the other side of the equation to get $(x^2 + 16x + 64) + (y^2 - 12y) = -19 + 64$. Next, divide the coefficient on the $y$-term, $-12$, by two and square it to get 36. Now, add this number to the $y$-terms and to the other side of the equation to get $(x^2 + 16x + 64) + (y^2 - 12y + 36) = -19 + 64 + 36$. Factor the $x$ and $y$ expressions to get $(x + 8)^2 + (y - 6)^2 = -19 + 64 + 36$. According to the standard form, $h = -8$ and $k = 6$, so the center must be $(-8, 6)$. The correct answer is (C).

31. $\frac{42}{9}, \frac{14}{3}$, **4.66, or 4.67**

This is a conversion problem where both dimensions of the flag are multiplied by $\frac{1}{9}$. Use this information, and multiply the original length by the fraction to get $\frac{1}{9}(42) = \frac{42}{9}$. This fits in the grid-in box, so the correct answer is $\frac{42}{9}$.

32. **63** The question states that $\angle CBD = \angle EBF$, so $2a - 6 = a + 9$. Add 6 to both sides to get $2a = a + 15$. Subtract $a$ from both sides to get $a = 15$. Use this value for $a$ to find the value of either $\angle CBD$ or $\angle EBF$, since they are equal. It is easier to find $\angle EBF$, which is $15 + 9 = 24$. Add the three angles together to get the measure of $\angle CBF$, which is $24 + 15 + 24 = 63$. The correct answer is 63.

33. **2,560** The question states that the two measurements are proportional, so use the information given in the problem to set up a proportion: $\frac{7 \text{ square miles}}{4{,}480 \text{ acres}} = \frac{4 \text{ square miles}}{x \text{ acres}}$. Cross-multiply to get $7x = 17{,}920$, then divide both sides by 7 to get $x = 2{,}560$ acres. The correct answer is 2,560.

34. **60** In the given triangle, $\angle LMN$ is inscribed in the circle, with points $L$ and $N$ as its endpoints. Points $L$ and $N$ are also the endpoints of a diameter of the circle, since line $\overline{LN}$ passes through center $O$. When this happens, the inscribed angle has a measure of $90°$, so $\angle LMN = 90°$. There are $180°$ in a triangle, so set up an equation to solve for $a$: $\frac{1}{2}a + a + 90 = 180$. Combine like terms to get $\frac{3}{2}a + 90 = 180$, then subtract 90 from both sides to get $\frac{3}{2}a = 90$. Multiply both sides by $\frac{2}{3}$ to get $a = 60$. The correct answer is 60.

35. **5** When dealing with functions, $x$-values are the inputs, and $y$-values are the outputs of the function. Plug in 4 for $x$ and 3 for $h(x)$ to get $3 = \frac{1}{2}(4^2) - a$ or $3 = 8 - a$. Add $a$ to both sides to get $3 + a = 8$. Subtract 3 from both sides to get $a = 8 - 3 = 5$. Therefore, the correct answer is 5.

36. **8** Use the Geometry Basic Approach. Draw a rectangle and label the sides. The question asks for the height, which is 4 meters shorter than the width, so label the height $h$ and label the width $h + 4$. Write any of the formulas that are mentioned in the problem, so *area = height × width*. The area is given as 96 square meters, so the formula becomes $96 = h(h + 4)$. Expand the right side of the equation to get $96 = h^2 + 4h$, then subtract 96 from both sides to get $0 = h^2 + 4h - 96$. Now, factor the right side of the equation into $0 = (h - 8)(h + 12)$. Set each factor equal to 0 and solve to get $h = 8$ and $h = -12$. Since the value for height must be positive, the correct answer is 8.

37. **11** Because only one portion of the sprint triathlon has a different time to complete, it is only necessary to calculate the time it takes Ms. McQueen to complete the biking stage. If she uses her triathlon bike, she can complete the distance of the biking stage, 12.4 miles, at her average speed in miles per hour, which is 20. Use the Rate Pie to find the time in hours.

Divide to get the time in hours: $12.4 \div 20 = 0.62$ hours. Multiply this by 60 to get a time of about 37.2 minutes. If Ms. McQueen uses her hybrid bike, the biking stage will take 30% more time, so multiply $37.2 \times 0.3$ to get an additional time of about 11.2 minutes. Since the question says to round the answer to the nearest minute, the correct answer is 11.

38. **12.6** To find Ms. McQueen's average speed in miles per hour, start by finding the total number of miles she traveled, which is 0.25 + 12.4 + 3.1 = 15.75 miles. To find the average speed in miles per hour, first convert 75 minutes to hours by dividing by 60 to get a time of 1.25 hours. Next, use the Rate Pie. Put the distance in the upper portion and the time in the lower right portion.

To find the average moving speed, divide the distance by the time to get 15.75 ÷ 1.25 = 12.6 miles per hour. The correct answer is 12.6.

# Chapter 21
# Practice Test 10

# Reading Test

## 65 MINUTES, 52 QUESTIONS

**Turn to Section 1 of your answer sheet to answer the questions in this section.**

**DIRECTIONS**

Each passage or pair of passages below is followed by a number of questions. After reading each passage or pair, choose the best answer to each question based on what is stated or implied in the passage or passages and in any accompanying graphics (such as a table or graph).

**Questions 1–10 are based on the following passage.**

This passage is excerpted from Gloria Steinem, *My Life on the Road.* © 2015 by Random House. The narrator, a writer, recalls her childhood in the United States of America.

There were only a few months each year when my father seemed content with a house-dwelling life. Every summer, we stayed in the small house he had
Line  built across the road from a lake in rural Michigan,
5  where he ran a dance pavilion on a pier over the water. Though there was no ocean within hundreds of miles, he had named it Ocean Beach Pier, and given it the grandiose slogan "Dancing Over the Water and Under the Stars."
10     On weeknights, people came from nearby farms and summer cottages to dance to a jukebox. My father dreamed up such attractions as a living chess game, inspired by his own love of chess, with costumed teenagers moving across the squares of the dance floor.
15  On weekends, he booked the big dance bands of the 1930s and 1940s into this remote spot. People might come from as far away as Toledo or Detroit to dance to this live music on warm moonlit nights. Of course, paying the likes of Guy Lombardo or Duke Ellington
20  or the Andrews Sisters meant that one rainy weekend could wipe out a whole summer's profits, so there was always a sense of gambling. I think my father loved that, too.
       But as soon as Labor Day had ended this precarious
25  livelihood, my father moved his office into his car. In the first warm weeks of autumn, we drove to nearby

country auctions, where he searched for antiques amid the household goods and farm tools. After my mother, with her better eye for antiques and her reference
30  books, appraised them for sale, we got into the car again to sell them to roadside antique dealers anywhere within a day's journey. I say "we" because from the age of four or so, I came into my own as the wrapper and unwrapper of china and other small items that
35  we cushioned in newspaper and carried in cardboard boxes over country roads. Each of us had a role in the family economic unit, including my sister, nine years older than I, who in the summer sold popcorn from a professional stand my father bought her.
40     But once the first frost turned the lake to crystal and the air above it to steam, my father began collecting road maps from gas stations, testing the trailer hitch on our car, and talking about such faraway pleasures as thin sugary pralines from Georgia, all-
45  you-can-drink orange juice from roadside stands in Florida, or slabs of salmon fresh from a California smokehouse.
       Then one day, as if struck by a sudden whim rather than a lifelong wanderlust, he announced that it was
50  time to put the family dog and other essentials into the house trailer that was always parked in our yard, and begin our long trek to Florida or California.
       Sometimes this leave-taking happened so quickly that we packed more frying pans than plates, or left a
55  kitchen full of dirty dishes and half-eaten food to greet us like Pompeii on our return. My father's decision

**CONTINUE**

always seemed to come as a surprise, even though his fear of the siren song of home was so great that he refused to put heating or hot water into our small
60 house. If the air of early autumn grew too chilly for us to bathe in the lake, we heated water on a potbellied stove and took turns bathing in a big washtub next to the fireplace. Since this required the chopping of wood, an insult to my father's sybaritic soul, he had invented
65 a wood-burning system all his own: he stuck one end of a long log into the fire and let the other protrude into the living room, then kicked it into the fireplace until the whole thing turned to ash. Even a pile of cut firewood in the yard must have seemed to him a
70 dangerous invitation to stay in one place.

   After he turned his face to the wind, my father did not like to hesitate. Only once do I remember him turning back, and even then my mother had to argue strenuously that the iron might be burning its way
75 through the ironing board. He would buy us a new radio, new shoes, almost anything rather than retrace the road already traveled.

---

**1**

Over the course of the passage, the main focus shifts from

A) a description of the narrator's father to a portrayal of a significant place the family often visited.

B) a depiction of the family's settled life to a description of the family's life on the road.

C) an allegorical display of domesticity to an example of its rejection by the narrator's father.

D) an anecdote about the poverty of the narrator's childhood to a speculation concerning the causes of that poverty.

---

**2**

The main purpose of the second paragraph (lines 10–23) ("On weeknights . . . too") is to

A) analyze the source of the father's compulsive desire to travel.

B) introduce the figures who play a role in the narrator's remembrances.

C) illustrate the father's delusions of grandeur that harmed the family's financial well-being.

D) describe the father's unique approach to living life that is expanded upon later in the passage.

---

**3**

The word "precarious" is used in line 24 to

A) emphasize the danger inherent to dancing over the water.

B) caution against burning firewood in an unapproved manner.

C) underscore the joy that this dancehall brought to so many.

D) highlight the uncertainty regarding the summer profits.

---

**4**

The narrator indicates that she participated in the family business

A) in a way that matched her age and abilities.

B) much less than her older siblings.

C) despite not being paid for her work.

D) on a volunteer basis until her teenage years.

## 5

With which of the following statements about her father would the narrator most likely agree?

A) He objected to train travel as a mode of transportation.

B) He had no consideration for his family's wishes.

C) He feared the expense of installing a heater into the family home.

D) He seemed mostly discontent with a settled, domestic life.

## 6

Which choice provides the best evidence for the answer to the previous question?

A) Lines 1–2 ("There were . . . life")

B) Lines 22–23 ("I think . . . too")

C) Lines 36–39 ("Each of . . . her")

D) Lines 59–60 ("he refused . . . house")

## 7

As used in line 48, "struck" most nearly means

A) battered.

B) boycotted.

C) inspired.

D) disturbed.

## 8

It can reasonably be inferred from the passage that the main reason that the narrator's father started the cross-country trip is because

A) he was struck by a sudden desire to escape the monotony of the house.

B) his desire to travel stemmed from a basic personality trait.

C) the family had already depleted the resources at one site.

D) he was surprised by the sudden change in the weather.

## 9

Which choice provides the best evidence for the answer to the previous question?

A) Lines 25–28 ("In the . . . tools")

B) Lines 40–47 ("But once . . . smokehouse")

C) Lines 48–52 ("Then one . . . California")

D) Lines 53–56 ("Sometimes this . . . return")

## 10

Which statement best characterizes the mother's role in the family?

A) She resented the father's impulsive nature.

B) She shared the father's wanderlust equally.

C) She sometimes played a more practical role than the father did.

D) She rescued the family's possessions from the flames.

**CONTINUE**

**Questions 11–21 are based on the following passage and supplementary material.**

This passage is adapted from "Stanford researchers uncover patterns in how scientists lie about their data," by Bjorn Carey, originally published in November 2015 by Stanford University.

Even the best poker players have "tells" that give away when they're bluffing with a weak hand. Scientists who commit fraud have similar, but even more subtle,
Line tells, and a pair of Stanford researchers have cracked
5 the writing patterns of scientists who attempt to pass along falsified data. The work, published in the *Journal of Language and Social Psychology*, could eventually help scientists identify falsified research before it is published.

10 There is a fair amount of research dedicated to understanding the ways liars lie. Studies have shown that liars generally tend to express more negative emotion terms and use fewer first-person pronouns. Fraudulent financial reports typically display higher
15 levels of linguistic obfuscation—phrasing that is meant to distract from or conceal the fake data—than accurate reports.

To see if similar patterns exist in scientific academia, Jeff Hancock, a professor of communication
20 at Stanford, and graduate student David Markowitz searched the archives of PubMed, a database of life sciences journals, from 1973 to 2013 for retracted papers. They identified 253, primarily from biomedical journals, that were retracted for documented fraud and
25 compared the writing in these to unretracted papers from the same journals and publication years, and covering the same topics.

They then rated the level of fraud of each paper using a customized "obfuscation index," which
30 rated the degree to which the authors attempted to mask their false results. This was achieved through a summary score of causal terms, abstract language, jargon, positive emotion terms and a standardized ease of reading score.

35 "We believe the underlying idea behind obfuscation is to muddle the truth," said Markowitz, the lead author on the paper. "Scientists faking data know that they are committing a misconduct and do not want to get caught. Therefore, one strategy to evade this may be
40 to obscure parts of the paper. We suggest that language can be one of many variables to differentiate between fraudulent and genuine science."

The results showed that fraudulent retracted papers scored significantly higher on the obfuscation index
45 than papers retracted for other reasons. For example, fraudulent papers contained approximately 1.5 percent more jargon than unretracted papers. "Fraudulent papers had about 60 more jargon-like words per paper compared to unretracted papers," Markowitz said.
50 "This is a non-trivial amount."

The researchers say that scientists might commit data fraud for a variety of reasons. Previous research points to a "publish or perish" mentality that may motivate researchers to manipulate their findings or
55 fake studies altogether. But the change the researchers found in the writing, however, is directly related to the author's goals of covering up lies through the manipulation of language. For instance, a fraudulent author may use fewer positive emotion terms to curb
60 praise for the data, for fear of triggering inquiry.

In the future, a computerized system based on this work might be able to flag a submitted paper so that editors could give it a more critical review before publication, depending on the journal's threshold
65 for obfuscated language. But the authors warn that this approach isn't currently feasible given the false-positive rate. "Science fraud is of increasing concern in academia, and automatic tools for identifying fraud might be useful," Hancock said. "But much more
70 research is needed before considering this kind of approach. Obviously, there is a very high error rate that would need to be improved, but also science is based on trust, and introducing a 'fraud detection' tool into the publication process might undermine that trust."

Frequencies of Language Categories in Publications, Reviewed by Markowitz and Hancock

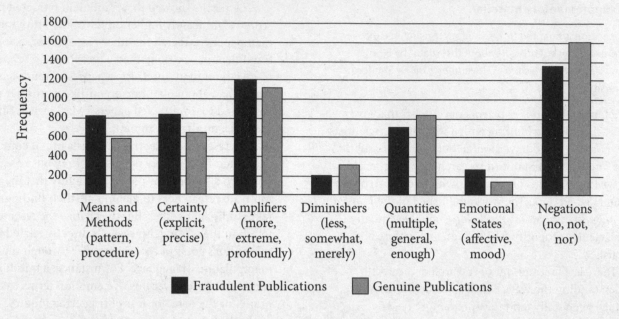

Fraudulent Publications     Genuine Publications

Data sourced from "Linguistic Traces of a Scientific Fraud: The Case of Diederik Stapel," © David M. Markowitz and Jeffrey T. Hancock, August 25, 2014. http://journals.plos.org/plosone/article/figure?id=10.1371/journal.pone.0105937.t001

**11**

The primary purpose of this passage is to

A) defend scientists who have incorporated fraudulent data into their reports in order to succeed in a competitive field.

B) contrast various methodologies for spotting false information in different industries and research fields.

C) describe an experiment designed to find the differences between fraudulent and genuine scientific data and caution against a possible solution.

D) reveal the secrets of those who successfully convince others of the veracity of false information.

**12**

The first paragraph serves mainly to

A) introduce a concept at the foundation of the research discussed in the passage.

B) propose additional applications for the results of the study in the passage.

C) introduce the development of general methods of fraud detection.

D) present an idea about scientific development that will be questioned later in the passage.

**13**

As used in line 10, "fair" most nearly means

A) ample.

B) lawful.

C) equal.

D) favorable.

CONTINUE ➡

**14**

As used in line 40, "obscure" most nearly means

A) hide.

B) blind.

C) distort.

D) characterize.

**15**

The passage indicates that scientific papers with fraudulent data can potentially be spotted by looking for

A) references to research studies that did not happen.

B) writing that uses deliberately distracting and confusing words and phrases.

C) results that differ from those of other studies by more than 1.5 percent.

D) authors who have published more than 60 papers in academic journals.

**16**

Which choice provides the best evidence for the answer to the previous question?

A) Lines 31–34 ("This was . . . score")

B) Lines 43–45 ("The results . . . reasons")

C) Lines 58–60 ("For instance . . . inquiry")

D) Lines 61–65 ("In the future . . . language")

**17**

Which hypothetical situation would Hancock most likely agree could be a consequence of action without further research into science fraud?

A) A scientist runs his paper through a computer program to check for confusing language before publication.

B) A scientist includes fraudulent data in a paper that does not affect the conclusion of the experiment.

C) A scientist publishes a genuine paper in a journal that has been known to publish fraudulent papers.

D) A scientist is less likely to submit a paper to a journal that uses automatic tools to detect fraud.

**18**

Which choice provides the best evidence for the answer to the previous question?

A) Lines 39–40 ("Therefore, one . . . paper")

B) Lines 52–55 ("Previous research . . . altogether")

C) Lines 65–67 ("But the . . . rate")

D) Lines 71–74 ("Obviously, there . . . trust")

**19**

According to the graph, the greatest difference between the language used in fraudulent and genuine research occurred in which category?

A) Means and Methods

B) Amplifiers

C) Quantities

D) Emotional States

**CONTINUE**

Which of the following statements is supported by the graph?

A) Scientists who published fraudulent data were more likely to use quantities-related language in their papers than were scientists who published genuine data.

B) Scientists who published fraudulent data used means and methods-related language nearly as often as they used certainty-related language.

C) Scientists who used more negation-related language were more likely to have published fraudulent data than scientists who used less negations-related language.

D) Scientists who used more amplifiers and diminishers were more likely to publish genuine data than scientists who used fewer amplifiers and diminishers.

Based on information in the graph and passage, which statement from the passage best supports the claim that jargon would be classified as "means and methods?"

A) Lines 2–6 ("Scientists who . . . data")

B) Lines 11–13 ("Studies have . . . pronouns")

C) Lines 47–49 ("Fraudulent papers . . . said")

D) Lines 69–71 ("But much . . . approach")

**CONTINUE**

**Questions 22–31 are based on the following passage and supplementary material.**

This passage is adapted from "The Story of YInMn Blue," originally published by Mas Subramanian, Joseph Tang, and Oregon State University.

YInMn Blue, or "MasBlue" as it is commonly referred to at Oregon State University ("OSU"), is a serendipitous discovery of a bright blue pigment
Line by scientists led by Mas Subramanian at OSU while
5 researching materials for electronics applications. The pigment contains the elements Yttrium, Indium, Manganese, and Oxygen.

In 2009, graduate student Andrew Smith was exploring the electronic properties of manganese oxide
10 by heating it to approximately 1,200°C (~2,000°F). Instead of a new, high-efficiency electronic material, what emerged from the furnace was a brilliant blue compound—a blue that Subramanian knew immediately was a research breakthrough. "If I hadn't
15 come from an industry research background—DuPont has a division that developed pigments and obviously they are used in paint and many other things—I would not have known this was highly unusual, a discovery with strong commercial potential," he says.

20 Blue pigments dating back to ancient times have been notoriously unstable—many fade easily and contain toxic materials. The fact that this pigment was synthesized at such high temperatures signaled to Subramanian that this new compound was extremely
25 stable, a property long sought in a blue pigment, he says. . . .

The chemical formula of YInMn Blue is $YIn_{1-x}Mn_xO_3$. These compositions adopt a crystal structure in which the chromophore responsible for
30 the intense blue color ($Mn^{3+}$) resides in the trigonal bipyramidal site. The intensity of the color can be systematically tuned by adjusting the In:Mn ratio. . . .

By measuring the spectral properties of this series, it was found that $YIn_{1-x}Mn_xO_3$ exhibits high absorbance
35 in the UV region and high reflectivity in the near-infrared region when compared to currently-used Cobalt Blue pigments. . . .

In May 2012, the Subramanian team received a patent with the U.S. Patent Office for the new pigment
40 (US82822728). Shepherd Color Co. subsequently began rigorous testing of the pigment. They concluded that the increased UV absorbance and stability in outdoor weathering and heat buildup tests demonstrate that YInMn blue is superior to Cobalt
45 Blue ($CoAl_2O_4$). In addition, the high solar reflectance (compared to similarly colored pigments) indicates that this 'cool pigment' can find use in a variety of exterior applications by reducing surface temperatures, cooling costs, and energy consumption. As a result of
50 this testing, Shepherd Color Co. has licensed the patent for commercialization efforts.

Recently, several local artists (including OSU art students) have used this pigment in their own professional endeavors, utilizing it in watercolors and
55 drypoint.

The excitement of discovering a brilliant blue, heat reflecting, thermally stable, and UV absorbing pigment did not stop them from exploring beyond the blues. Since then, Subramanian and his team have expanded
60 their research and have made a range of new pigments to include almost every color, from bright oranges to shades of purple, turquoise and green.

They continue to search for a new stable, heat reflecting, and brilliant red, the most elusive color to
65 synthesize.

CONTINUE

Reflectance vs. Wavelength

**Figure 1**

UV: 200–400 nm
Near-IR: 700–2500 nm

**Figure 2**

UV: 200–400 nm
Near-IR: 700–2500 nm

Images provided courtesy of Oregon State University.

**CONTINUE**

**22**

One main idea of the passage is that

A) chemically-engineered substances can be both beneficial and dangerous.

B) unexpected findings can have significant implications.

C) pigments can be described most effectively in terms of chemical composition.

D) increased UV absorbance is directly related to pigment stability.

**23**

Which choice best describes the overall structure of the passage?

A) A description of a discovery, a scientific explanation, and the practical applications of the discovery

B) A comparison of the properties of a synthetic compound and the presentation of a natural compound alternative

C) A historical account of several accidental discoveries and an unbiased critique of the resulting products

D) A listing of chemical compounds, a description of how those compounds work together, and a comparison of the benefits of each compound

**24**

As used in line 5, "applications" most nearly means

A) requests.

B) forms.

C) uses.

D) industries.

**25**

Which choice provides the best evidence for the claim that Smith did not intend for his experiment to produce the results that it did?

A) Lines 6–7 ("The pigment . . . Oxygen")

B) Lines 11–14 ("Instead of . . . breakthrough")

C) Lines 49-51 ("As a . . . efforts")

D) Lines 63–65 ("They continue . . . synthesize")

**26**

As used in line 21, "unstable" most nearly means

A) impermanent.

B) threatening.

C) careless.

D) antiquated.

**27**

According to the passage, researchers have identified which of the following factors as most indicative of stable pigments?

A) Toxic materials

B) Oxygenated indium

C) Extreme temperatures

D) High pressure

CONTINUE

28

Based on the passage, which choice best describes the relationship between the new YInMn Blue pigment and the Cobalt Blue pigment currently used?

A) Cobalt Blue is superior for exterior conditions, while YInMn Blue is preferred for interior conditions.

B) YInMn Blue was specifically engineered to provide a color that can be chemically-adjusted for intensity, while Cobalt Blue was not.

C) YInMn Blue pigment is as hard to synthesize as purple pigment is, while Cobalt Blue is simpler.

D) Cobalt Blue has a lower UV absorbency and infrared reflectivity than does YInMn Blue.

29

Which choice provides the best evidence for the answer to the previous question?

A) Lines 20–22 ("Blue pigments . . . materials")

B) Lines 34–37 ("$YIn_{1-x}Mn_xO_3$ exhibits . . . pigments.")

C) Lines 41–45 ("They concluded . . . ($CoAl_2O_4$)")

D) Lines 56–58 ("The excitement . . . blues")

30

According to Figure 2, at which of the following wavelengths does $CoAl_2O_4$ have a reflectance of 0.4%?

A) 2400 nm

B) 1800 nm

C) 1200 nm

D) 600 nm

31

Based on information in the passage and the graph, which of the following ranges of wavelengths most clearly illustrates the thermal advantages of YInMn Blue over Cobalt Blue?

A) 200–400

B) 400–600

C) 800–1000

D) 1200–1400

CONTINUE

## Questions 32–41 are based on the following passages.

Passage 1 is adapted from President Grover Cleveland's *1895 Annual Message to the Congress of the United States*. Passage 2 is adapted from William Jennings Bryan's speech at the 1896 Democratic National Convention. The Coinage Act of 1873 ended the United States' federal policy of accepting both gold- and silver-backed currency, establishing a gold monetary standard. This decision was a primary point of contention in the 1896 presidential race.

### Passage 1

While I have endeavored to make a plain statement of the disordered condition of our currency and the present dangers menacing our prosperity and to suggest a way which leads to a safer financial system, I
5  have constantly had in mind the fact that many of my countrymen, whose sincerity I do not doubt, insist that the cure for the ills now threatening us may be found in the single and simple remedy of the free coinage of silver. They contend that our mints shall be at once
10  thrown open to the free, unlimited, and independent coinage of both gold and silver dollars of full legal-tender quality, regardless of the action of any other government and in full view of the fact that the ratio between the metals which they suggest calls for 100
15  cents' worth of gold in the gold dollar at the present standard and only 50 cents in intrinsic worth of silver in the silver dollar.

Were there infinitely stronger reasons than can be adduced for hoping that such action would secure for
20  us a bimetallic currency moving on lines of parity, an experiment so novel and hazardous as that proposed might well stagger those who believe that stability is an imperative condition of sound money.

No government, no human contrivance or act of
25  legislation, has ever been able to hold the two metals together in free coinage at a ratio appreciably different from that which is established in the markets of the world.

Those who believe that our independent free
30  coinage of silver at an artificial ratio with gold of 16 to 1 would restore the parity between the metals, and consequently between the coins, oppose an unsupported and improbable theory to the general belief and practice of other nations; and to the
35  teaching of the wisest statesmen and economists of the world, both in the past and present, and, what is far more conclusive, they run counter to our own actual experiences.

Twice in our earlier history our lawmakers,
40  in attempting to establish a bimetallic currency, undertook free coinage upon a ratio which accidentally varied from the actual relative values of the two metals not more than 3 per cent. In both cases, notwithstanding greater difficulties and cost
45  of transportation than now exist, the coins whose intrinsic worth was undervalued in the ratio gradually and surely disappeared from our circulation and went to other countries where their real value was better recognized.
50  Acts of Congress were impotent to create equality where natural causes decreed even a slight inequality.

### Passage 2

If they tell us that the gold standard is the standard of civilization, we reply to them that this, the most enlightened of all nations of the earth, has never
55  declared for a gold standard, and both the parties this year are declaring against it. If the gold standard is the standard of civilization, why, my friends, should we not have it? So if they come to meet us on that, we can present the history of our nation. More than that, we
60  can tell them this, that they will search the pages of history in vain to find a single instance in which the common people of any land ever declared themselves in favor of a gold standard. They can find where the holders of fixed investments have.
65  Mr. Carlisle said in 1878 that this was a struggle between the idle holders of idle capital and the struggling masses who produce the wealth and pay the taxes of the country; and my friends, it is simply a question that we shall decide upon which side the
70  Democratic Party shall fight. Upon the side of the idle holders of idle capital, or upon the side of the struggling masses? That is the question that the party must answer first; and then it must be answered by each individual hereafter. The sympathies of the
75  Democratic Party, as described by the platform, are on the side of the struggling masses, who have ever been the foundation of the Democratic Party.

There are two ideas of government. There are those who believe that if you just legislate to make the
80  well-to-do prosperous, that their prosperity will leak through on those below. The Democratic idea has been

**CONTINUE**

that if you legislate to make the masses prosperous their prosperity will find its way up and through every class that rests upon it.

85     You come to us and tell us that the great cities are in favor of the gold standard. I tell you that the great cities rest upon these broad and fertile prairies. Burn down your cities and leave our farms, and your cities will spring up again as if by magic. But destroy our farms

90 and the grass will grow in the streets of every city in the country.

---

**32**

As used in line 3, "present" most nearly means

A) prompt.

B) current.

C) instant.

D) gifted.

---

**33**

What does Passage 1 suggest about the proponents of implementing a bimetallic system of currency?

A) They doubt the use of gold to back a currency in any situation.

B) They have an honest belief in the potential of their proposed solution.

C) They would rather Congress become impotent than submit to bimetallic currency.

D) They resent the great cities that are pushing the gold standard on the people of the prairies.

---

**34**

Which choice provides the best evidence for the answer to the previous question?

A) Lines 4–9 ("I have . . . silver")

B) Lines 9–13 ("They contend . . . government")

C) Lines 29–34 ("Those who . . . nations")

D) Lines 37–38 ("they run . . . experiences")

---

**35**

In the final sentence of Passage 1, the main purpose of Cleveland's reference to "Acts of Congress" is to

A) emphasize a disparity between government forces and market forces.

B) summarize Congress's argument for implementing the gold standard.

C) propose a natural alternative to the complex problem facing the nation.

D) assert that only the passage of a law could solve a seemingly intractable debate.

---

**36**

As used in line 66, "idle" most nearly means

A) abandoned.

B) ambitious.

C) inactive.

D) cheap.

---

**37**

Based on Passage 2, Bryan would be most likely to agree with which claim about the controversy over the gold standard?

A) It would only be settled if gold were the preferred standard of civilization.

B) It has consistently lacked support from large segments of society.

C) It motivated further investigation of the silver standard worldwide.

D) It could have been avoided if Congress had not listened to the prosperous.

**CONTINUE** ➡

**38**

Which choice provides the best evidence for the answer to the previous question?

A) Lines 56–58 ("If the . . . it")

B) Lines 59–63 ("More than . . . standard")

C) Lines 74–77 ("The sympathies . . . Party")

D) Lines 78–81 ("There are . . . below")

**39**

Both passages discuss the issue of the gold standard in relationship to

A) Congress.

B) the Democratic Party.

C) economists.

D) other nations.

**40**

In the context of each passage as a whole, the historical references in line 39 of Passage 1 and line 65 of Passage 2 primarily function to help each speaker

A) establish that a debate has been ongoing.

B) cite established precedent to support a position.

C) challenge the gold standard status quo.

D) question whether progress has been made.

**41**

Which choice identifies a central tension between the two passages?

A) Cleveland advocates for new legislation to enact the gold standard, but Bryan questions the necessity of such a move without elite support.

B) Cleveland questions the validity of a proposed solution, but Bryan argues that the alternative is an even more unreasonable path forward.

C) Cleveland demands gold standard proponents reconsider their position, and Bryan defends the specifics of that position.

D) Cleveland presents studies in support of the gold standard, and Bryan asserts that the sources of the evidence are biased.

**CONTINUE**

**Questions 42–52 are based on the following passage.**

This passage is adapted from "Zombie ant fungi 'know' brains of their hosts," originally published on August 22, 2014 by Chuck Gill, Penn State College of Agricultural Sciences.

A parasitic fungus that reproduces by manipulating the behavior of ants emits a cocktail of behavior-controlling chemicals when encountering the brain
Line of its natural target host, but not when infecting other
5 ant species, a new study shows. The findings, which suggest that the fungus "knows" its preferred host, provide new insights into the molecular mechanisms underlying this phenomenon, according to researchers. "Fungi are well known for their ability to secrete
10 chemicals that affect their environment," noted lead author Charissa de Bekker, a Marie Curie Fellow in Penn State's College of Agricultural Sciences, and Ludwig Maximilian of the University of Munich. "So we wanted to know what chemicals are employed to
15 control so precisely the behavior of ants."

The research focused on a species from the genus *Ophiocordyceps* — known as "zombie ant fungi" — which control their ant hosts by inducing a biting behavior. Although these fungi infect many insects,
20 the species that infect ants have evolved a mechanism that induces hosts to die attached by their mandibles to plant material, providing a platform from which the fungus can grow and shoot spores to infect other ants. To study this mechanism, the researchers combined
25 field research with a citizen-scientist in South Carolina, infection experiments under laboratory conditions, and analysis using metabolomics, which is the study of the chemical processes associated with the molecular products of metabolism. The scientists used a newly
30 discovered fungal species from North America— initially called *Ophiocordyceps unilateralis sensu lato* while it awaits a new name—that normally controls an ant species in the genus *Camponotus*. To test whether a species of fungus that has evolved to control the
35 behavior of one ant species can infect and control others, they infected nontarget hosts from the same ant genus and another genus (*Formica*).

They found that this obligate killer can infect and kill nontarget ants, but it cannot manipulate their
40 behavior. "The brain of the target species was the key to understanding manipulation," de Bekker said. The researchers next removed ant brains, keeping the organs alive in special media. The fungus then was grown in the presence of brains from different
45 ant species to determine what chemicals it produced for each brain. "This was 'brain-in-a-jar' science at its best," said co-author David Hughes, assistant professor of entomology and biology, Penn State. "It was necessary to reduce the complexity associated
50 with the whole, living ant, and just ask what chemicals the fungus produces when it encounters the ant brain. "You don't get to see a lot of behavior with fungi," he said. "You have to infer what they are doing by examining how they grow, where they grow and most
55 important, what chemicals they secrete."

"We could see in the data that the fungus behaved differently in the presence of the ant brain it had co-evolved with," said de Bekker, whose Penn State co-authors also included Andrew Patterson, assistant
60 professor of molecular toxicology, and Phil Smith, director of the Metabolomics Core Facility. The researchers found thousands of unique chemicals, most of them completely unknown. This, according to Hughes, is not surprising, since little previous work has
65 mined these fungi for the chemicals they produce. But what did stand out were two known neuromodulators, guanobutyric acid (GBA) and sphingosine. These both have been reported to be involved in neurological disorders and were enriched when the fungus was
70 grown in the presence of brains of its target species. "There is no single compound that is produced that results in the exquisite control of ant behavior we observe," de Bekker said. "Rather, it is a mixture of different chemicals that we assume act in synergy. "But
75 whatever the precise blend and tempo of chemical secretion," she said, "it is impressive that these fungi seem to 'know' when they are beside the brain of their regular host and behave accordingly."

Noted Hughes, "This is one of the most complex
80 examples of parasites controlling animal behavior because it is a microbe controlling an animal—the one without the brain controls the one with the brain. By employing metabolomics and controlled laboratory infections, we can now begin to understand how the
85 fungi pull off this impressive trick." The research also is notable, the scientists contend, because it is the first extensive study of zombie ants in North America.

**CONTINUE**

**42**

The primary purpose of the passage is to

A) correct a misconception about the interactions between fungi and host organisms.

B) present the findings of a study that is one of the first of its kind.

C) detail a research study that discovered a new genus of ant.

D) explain the difference between a symbiotic relationship and a parasitic relationship.

**43**

According to the passage, which statement best explains why the fungi have evolved to control the behavior of the ants?

A) When the infected ant bites a non-infected ant, the fungus is able to spread and grow.

B) When an infected ant dies while biting a plant, the fungus can reproduce more easily.

C) When the infected ant dies on the ground, its corpse is an ideal breeding ground for the fungus.

D) There is no evolutionary benefit for the fungus to control the ant's behavior.

**44**

In line 37, the mention of the *Formica* genus primarily serves to

A) introduce another ant genus newly-discovered to be controlled by the fungus.

B) provide the scientific name of the ant genus most affected by the fungus.

C) present a new finding about a specific genus of fungus.

D) name a genus of ant that scientists tested to extend their research on the fungus.

**45**

The use of phrases such as "exquisite control" (line 72), "most complex examples" (lines 79–80), and "impressive trick" (line 85) in the passage communicate a tone that is

A) amused.

B) informative.

C) critical.

D) admiring.

**46**

Which choice describes a scenario in which the zombie ant fungi would NOT successfully reproduce?

A) Fungus spores infect both *Camponotus* and *Formica* ants.

B) An infected *Camponotus* ant attaches to a twig and dies.

C) A spore-releasing stalk grows from the head of a dead, infected *Camponotus* ant.

D) An infected *Formica* ant dies on a plant-free patch of soil.

**47**

As used in line 43, "media" most nearly means

A) communications.

B) material.

C) channels.

D) periodicals.

CONTINUE

Based on the passage, which part of the research process was the most effective for obtaining an unprecedented amount of information?

A) The researchers grew the fungus in the presence of isolated ant brains.

B) The researchers infected ants not normally targeted by the fungus.

C) The researchers removed the brains from the ants.

D) The researchers observed how the fungus behaved while in the ant brains.

Which choice provides the best evidence for the answer to the previous question?

A) Lines 29–33 ("The scientists . . . *Camponotus*")

B) Lines 43–46 ("The fungus . . . brain")

C) Lines 61–63 ("The researchers . . . unknown")

D) Lines 65–67 ("But what . . . sphingosine")

Based on the passage, a unique outcome of the chemicals produced by the fungus is

A) a reaction from the host organism that could only be reproduced in the lab.

B) a contagious infection that could not be controlled in the lab.

C) a parasitic relationship notably different from those usually found in nature.

D) a result that can be applied to neurological disorders in human patients.

Which choice provides the best evidence for the answer to the previous question?

A) Lines 16–19 ("The research . . . behavior")

B) Lines 38–40 ("They found . . . behavior")

C) Lines 56–58 ("We could . . . de Bekker")

D) Lines 79–82 ("This is . . . brain")

Based on the passage, in studying the zombie ants, the research team made the most extensive use of which type of evidence?

A) Observation of the interplay between the ant and the fungus in the natural world

B) Predictions based on research obtained from experiments with a different genus of ant

C) Chemical analysis of the brains of fungi

D) Data obtained from laboratory experiments designed to isolate particular factors

# STOP
If you finish before time is called, you may check your work on this section only.
Do not turn to any other section in the test.

**No Test Material On This Page**

# Writing and Language Test

## 35 MINUTES, 44 QUESTIONS

Turn to Section 2 of your answer sheet to answer the questions in this section.

---

### DIRECTIONS

Each passage below is accompanied by a number of questions. For some questions, you will consider how the passage might be revised to improve the expression of ideas. For other questions, you will consider how the passage might be edited to correct errors in sentence structure, usage, or punctuation. A passage or a question may be accompanied by one or more graphics (such as a table or graph) that you will consider as you make revising and editing decisions.

Some questions will direct you to an underlined portion of a passage. Other questions will direct you to a location in a passage or ask you to think about the passage as a whole.

After reading each passage, choose the answer to each question that most effectively improves the quality of writing in the passage or that makes the passage conform to the conventions of standard written English. Many questions include a "NO CHANGE" option. Choose that option if you think the best choice is to leave the relevant portion of the passage as it is.

---

**Questions 1–11 are based on the following passage and supplementary material.**

### Fast Fashion Slows Down

In most US cities, the presence of blue recycling bins alongside the ubiquitous black trash bins is no longer **1** an innovation. Most people are used to separating recyclable materials from their landfill-bound trash, even in public waste bins. In many cities composting is even becoming a standard third component of waste separation, but one area that is just **2** kicking off is textile recycling.

**1**

A) NO CHANGE
B) a deviation.
C) a novelty.
D) a miracle.

**2**

Which choice best maintains the style and tone of the passage?

A) NO CHANGE
B) fixing to start
C) getting in gear
D) gaining traction

CONTINUE ➡

A few cities have begun to collect textiles as part of their curbside recycling programs, along with the more customary cardboard and glass, but such programs generally require specially-designed multi-compartment recycling **3** trucks—(which most cities don't have). Many areas that don't have curbside textile recycling instead have designated drop-off bins where residents can recycle unwanted clothing and other household textiles, such as sheets and towels.

Textile recycling is in its infancy, but it has the potential to make a big impact. The average American discards 70 pounds of **4** clothing each year, only 15% of which is recycled. Of the most commonly recycled materials, only **5** rubber and leather are recycled at a higher rate than is clothing. Not only can cities save on trash pick-up and disposal costs by encouraging their

**3**

A) NO CHANGE

B) trucks which

C) trucks—which

D) trucks (which

**4**

The writer wants to include information from the graph that is consistent with the description of textiles in the passage. Which choice most effectively accomplishes this goal?

A) NO CHANGE

B) paper each year, only 45%

C) rubber and leather each year, only 15%

D) wood each year, only 9%

**5**

The writer wants to support the paragraph's main idea with accurate, relevant information from the graph. Which choice most effectively accomplishes this goal?

A) NO CHANGE

B) plastic and wood are recycled at a lower

C) yard trimmings are recycled at a higher

D) glass is recycled at a higher

**CONTINUE** ➡

residents to recycle unwanted textiles, [6] and re-using clothing can also save resources by reducing the amount of new clothing that needs to be manufactured.

[7] For example, producing enough virgin cotton for one pair of jeans requires 1,800 gallons of water; buying a pair of jeans second-hand saves that water.

Estimated Recycling Rates in the United States

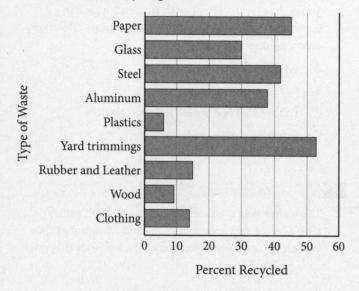

Percent Recycled

So-called "fast fashion" chains that produce trendy, low-cost (and, according to critics, low-quality) clothing, are often singled out as one of the primary causes of the increase in clothing waste in the U.S. in recent decades. But at least one such chain, the Swedish retailer H&M, is also trying to [8] rain in, clothing waste by offering 15% off coupons to consumers who bring unwanted clothing, of any brand, to their stores for recycling. Since the program began in 2013, H&M has collected over 44,000 tons of clothing to recycle. The company's goal is to eventually collect 25,000 tons of clothing for recycling each year.

6

A) NO CHANGE
B) yet
C) but
D) for

7

A) NO CHANGE
B) Surprisingly,
C) However,
D) Moreover,

8

A) NO CHANGE
B) rain in
C) rein in,
D) rein in

**CONTINUE**

[9] Hopefully other retailers will institute similar programs. The first step is reuse: any items still in useable condition are sold second-hand. Non-useable items are shredded for use as insulation, [10] they are repurposed as cleaning rags, or recycled to make fabric for new clothing.

The technology for recycling textile fibers into new fabrics [11] are currently limited, however. The ultimate goal of H&M and other environmentally-conscious retailers is to establish a "closed loop" manufacturing system, in which 100% of the fibers they use to create their clothing can be recycled into new clothing. This may seem like a lofty goal, but it is worth pursuing.

**9**

Which choice provides the most effective transition from the previous paragraph?

A) NO CHANGE

B) Recycling that quantity of clothing is done in several steps.

C) Low-quality fast fashion should make that goal easily attainable.

D) Offering a bigger discount might help H&M meet its goal.

**10**

A) NO CHANGE

B) repurposed as cleaning cloths,

C) cleaning cloths are repurposed,

D) alternatively they are repurposed as cleaning cloths,

**11**

A) NO CHANGE

B) is

C) were

D) have been

CONTINUE

**Questions 12–22 are based on the following passage.**

## Celebrating Death

At dusk on the night of November 1, Lake Pátzcuaro in the southern Mexican state of Michoacán begins to glow as residents float across the lake in candlelit boats. The people are going to the island of Janitzio for an all-night vigil at the cemeteries where [12] its loved ones are buried. This vigil is the culmination of the Day of the Dead celebrations that begin with the construction of [13] *ofrendas. Ofrendas* are altars that honor the dead. The festivities begin in early October, when towns host markets [14] dedicated to the bright skeleton decorations and colorful flowers used to adorn the altars.

[1] The origins of the Mexican Day of the Dead tradition date back nearly 3,000 years to pre-Columbian times, when dead ancestors were celebrated in rituals that lasted for an entire month in the late summer of the Aztec calendar. [2] After Europeans brought Catholicism to North America, the Aztec rituals were combined with the Christian tradition of All Souls Day and moved to November 1–2. [3] During these two days, the spirits of the dead are believed to come back to the land of the living to visit their families. [4] The Aztec tradition was that the dead would be offended by mourning, [15] but it's sad when family members die. [5] The *ofrendas* that help to

---

**12**

A) NO CHANGE
B) it's
C) they're
D) their

---

**13**

Which choice most effectively combines the sentences at the underlined portion?

A) *ofrendas*, in Spanish; those are
B) *ofrendas*; the Spanish word *ofrendas* means
C) *ofrendas*,
D) *ofrendas*; moreover, *ofrendas* are

---

**14**

A) NO CHANGE
B) dedicated, to the bright skeleton decorations,
C) dedicated to the bright, skeleton, decorations,
D) dedicated to the bright skeleton decorations—

---

**15**

Which choice most effectively completes the explanation of the Aztec tradition?

A) NO CHANGE
B) so they are remembered in a spirit of celebration rather than sadness.
C) though it can be difficult to tell whether an invisible spirit is offended.
D) and the Aztec didn't want to disrespect the wishes of the dead.

---

**CONTINUE**　▶

celebrate the dead often have items similar to [16] those found on church altars, such as candles and pictures. [17]

Many Day of the Dead altars are built in private homes, but they can also be found in cemeteries, at churches, in government buildings, and in public squares. Some public altars are meant to call attention to a specific cause. Others are built by local artists, [18] of which many are best known for their elaborate *ofrendas*.

For many families, preparing an *ofrenda* is similar to preparing for a visit from living relatives. The bright colors and fragrance of marigolds are said to lead spirits back to their families. Altars are loaded with food and drink [19] (which smell delicious) and sometimes include pillows and blankets (which provide a resting spot for the spirits). Some families put personal items that belonged to the deceased on the altars, and altars dedicated to children

---

**16**

A) NO CHANGE

B) church altars,

C) churches and altars,

D) the structures of church altars,

**17**

To make this paragraph most logical, sentence 3 should be placed

A) where it is now.

B) before sentence 1.

C) before sentence 2.

D) before sentence 5.

**18**

A) NO CHANGE

B) many

C) many of whom

D) many of them

**19**

Which choice provides information that is most consistent in style and content with the information about why pillows and blankets are included on the altars?

A) NO CHANGE

B) (including *pan de muerto*)

C) (which are often homemade)

D) (which provide sustenance for the travelling spirits)

CONTINUE ➡

often include toys. **20** It's more work to provide food for living relatives than for dead ones.

Many of the same items that decorate altars are also part of the cemetery vigils on Janitzio. Graves are covered with candles and **21** marigolds, and families bring ample picnics to sustain both themselves and the spirits of the departed through the night. Living family members spend the night eating, drinking, singing, and telling stories. Rather than focusing on the finality of death, **22** the people's merriment celebrates life.

**20**

Which choice most effectively concludes the paragraph?

A) NO CHANGE

B) Regardless of what specifically is included on an altar, the dead are always welcomed home, just as they were when they were alive.

C) The toys for children can be new or old.

D) Some altars include religious items such as crucifixes and images of saints.

**21**

A) NO CHANGE

B) marigolds just as altars are,

C) marigolds like those that also decorate altars,

D) marigolds that attract spirits with their bright colors,

**22**

A) NO CHANGE

B) life is celebrated by the people through their merriment.

C) the merriment of the people celebrates life.

D) the people celebrate life through their merriment.

CONTINUE ➡

**Questions 23–33 are based on the following passage and supplementary material.**

## Bank Tellers: Machine v. Human

When automated teller machines (ATMs) were first installed in the 1970s, there were widespread predictions that the machines would replace human bank tellers. Such predictions did not immediately come true, however. [23] In fact, throughout the 1990s, as the number of ATMs increased most quickly, the number of human bank tellers also increased.

[1] While many simple bank transactions now happen at ATMs, people still rely on human tellers to cash [24] checks, transfer money between accounts; provide specific bill denominations, and dispense information about bank products and services. [2] Some of these duties, particularly the marketing aspect of advising customers about bank services, have changed with the advent of ATMs. [3] They also limit the amount of cash a customer can get in a single day, place restrictions on how soon funds from deposits are available, and generally don't offer much choice in currency denominations. [4] Before the rise of banking machines, tellers were primarily responsible for handling cash, but machines have proven to be faster and [25] more rock solid with cash than people are.

---

**23**

A) NO CHANGE
B) As a result,
C) For example,
D) Therefore,

**24**

A) NO CHANGE
B) checks; transfer money between accounts;
C) checks; transfer money between accounts,
D) checks, transfer money between accounts,

**25**

Which choice best fits with the tone of the rest of the passage?
A) NO CHANGE
B) more impeccable
C) more reliable
D) safer

CONTINUE

**26** [5] On the other hand, ATMs are far more vulnerable to theft. **27**

---

**26**

At this point, the writer is considering adding the following graph.

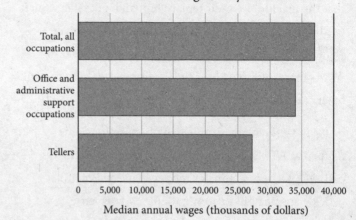

Annual Wage Comparison:
Tellers versus Other Occupations
Median annual wages, May 2016

Median annual wages (thousands of dollars)

Note: All Occupations includes all occupations in the U.S. Economy.
Source: U.S. Bureau of Labor Statistics, Occupational Employment Statistics

Should the writer make this addition here?

A) Yes, because it provides evidence that supports the idea that the number of bank tellers is rising.

B) Yes, because it effectively contradicts the idea that ATMs are faster at counting money than people are.

C) No, because it does not make a comparison between wages for tellers and those for loan officers.

D) No, because it gives information that distracts from the paragraph's focus on the duties performed by tellers.

---

**27**

To make this paragraph most logical, sentence 3 should be placed

A) where it is now.

B) after sentence 1.

C) after sentence 4.

D) after sentence 5.

**CONTINUE** ➤

With the rise of tech-savvy customers who are increasingly [28] custom to using their smartphones in all aspects of life, mobile banking apps are the latest mechanized challenge to the need for human bank tellers. Apps are also beginning to improve upon some banking functions that had largely been taken over by ATMs. Mobile apps [29] are used consistently by only about 50% of smartphone owners. Apps also usually offer less waiting time before funds from a check deposit are available for use, but they cannot handle cash. That doesn't mean there's a need for human tellers, [30] though. Without a teller, customers can still go to a traditional ATM to deposit or withdraw cash.

A) NO CHANGE

B) accustomed for

C) accustomed to

D) custom at

Which choice provides the best supporting example for the main idea of the paragraph?

A) NO CHANGE

B) can quickly and easily perform the more complex balance inquiries and transfers that not all ATMs are capable of.

C) are not always designed well, though user ratings through an app store can help consumers decide which one is best.

D) are also highly susceptible to theft or fraud, particularly when they are used over public Wi-Fi networks.

Which choice most effectively combines the sentences at the underlined portion?

A) though: customers

B) though, because it's true that customers

C) though, without them customers

D) though; it's the case that customers

CONTINUE

Physical banks have begun to respond to the rising popularity of mobile banking by replacing their old-fashioned teller windows **31** with an automated kiosk that combine all the functions of both mobile banking apps and ATMs.

Such kiosks are not replacing ATMs, nor are they replacing humans altogether. What they are doing is changing, again, the job description of human bank employees. Todd Barnhart, head of branch distribution for PNC bank, stresses the continued need for humans in bank branches. Employees are now trained to answer questions about how to use mobile apps, **32** as well as trained to handle deposits and provide loan advice. "We're not building branches with teller lines but with places where customers and employees can have meaningful conversations," he said. So while the old-fashioned notion of a bank teller may be on the way **33** out, machines are not yet close to replacing human bank employees altogether.

**31**

A) NO CHANGE
B) to an automated kiosk
C) each for automated kiosks
D) with automated kiosks

**32**

A) NO CHANGE
B) as well as handle
C) also to answer questions about
D) and in addition to handle

**33**

A) NO CHANGE
B) out; machines
C) out. Machines
D) out, nevertheless machines

CONTINUE ➔

**Questions 34–44 are based on the following passage.**

**Bacteria in Space**

Ever since antibiotics began to be widely used in the 1940s, scientists have been engaged in an arms race against bacteria. Bacteria continue to evolve and develop resistance to antibiotics; **34** as a result, scientists must continually develop newer, stronger antibiotics to overcome the resistant bacteria. Since scientists generally want to **35** count the number of bacteria mutations, it may seem strange that they would intentionally make bacteria more aggressive, but researchers from Arizona State University (ASU) are doing just that by sending some strains of bacteria to the International Space Station to be studied.

NASA scientists first began studying bacteria and other pathogens in space because they wanted to keep astronauts healthy. Extended trips to space **36** that last a long time have long been understood to weaken astronauts' immune systems, so studies were designed to determine whether pathogens, including bacteria, are similarly affected by microgravity. Scientists were surprised

**34**
A) NO CHANGE
B) however,
C) nevertheless,
D) for example,

**35**

Which choice most effectively establishes scientists' goal, related to information presented earlier in the paragraph?
A) NO CHANGE
B) facilitate
C) stay ahead of
D) shoot at

**36**
A) NO CHANGE
B) that are extensive
C) continuing for many weeks
D) DELETE the underlined portion.

**CONTINUE**

to find that pathogens of any kind [37] mutated more rapidly and became more virulent in space. A team led by Cheryl Nickerson of the Biodesign Institute at ASU [38] speculated that microgravity would cause a fluid shear stress reduction (the friction between cells and the fluids they interact with). Fluid shear stress affects gene expression in pathogens, and reducing it allows mutations to occur more quickly. The ASU scientists believe that microgravity mimics the reduced fluid shear stress conditions that bacteria encounter inside the human body [39] .

Although pathogen studies in space were initially intended just to help protect astronauts' health during flight, the implications of these [40] subjects now have a much broader application. Scientists are looking more closely at the specific mechanics of various pathogens'

---

**37**

A) NO CHANGE

B) had mutated more rapidly and had become

C) mutates more rapidly and becomes

D) mutate more rapidly and becomes

**38**

A) NO CHANGE

B) thought that fluid shear stress would be reduced by microgravity

C) speculated that microgravity reduces fluid shear stress

D) believed that microgravity lessens the shear stress caused by fluid

**39**

At this point, the writer is considering adding the following.

> so that studying something like *Salmonella* in space allows, in effect, a glimpse into how that pathogen behaves in the human digestive tract

Should the writer make this addition here?

A) Yes, because it makes clear that researchers cannot actually see inside the human digestive tract.

B) Yes, because it further explains the benefits of conducting bacteria studies in space.

C) No, because it repeats information stated earlier in the paragraph.

D) No, because it is not relevant to the discussion of what fluid shear stress is.

**40**

Which choice provides the most precise description of the proceeding depicted in the first part of the sentence?

A) NO CHANGE

B) examinations

C) experiments

D) tests

CONTINUE

mutations so that they **41** could have developed treatments, especially vaccines, that attack those changes. Nickerson and her team are working on developing a vaccine for *Salmonella*. The virus is one of the leading **42** causes of food-borne illness, in the United States and one of the leading causes of infant mortality worldwide, so an effective vaccine has the potential to have a major impact on public health.

**43** *Salmonella* is already playing an important role in vaccine research, though in an unexpected way. A promising new vaccine technology, recombinant attenuated *Salmonella* vaccine (RASV), uses a genetically modified form of *Salmonella* as a delivery vehicle. RASVs quickly and efficiently deliver **44** antigens, substances, that stimulate the production of antibodies to multiple body systems with just a single dose, and can be taken orally, eliminating the need for more expensive vaccine shots. Such a vaccine already exists for *Streptococcus pneumonia*, the bacterium responsible for pneumonia and meningitis among other things. Next up on the researchers' list: an RASV to guard against *Salmonella* itself.

**41**
A) NO CHANGE
B) can develop
C) were developing
D) developed

**42**
A) NO CHANGE
B) causes of food-borne illness in the United States
C) causes, of food-borne illness in the United States
D) causes of food-borne illness, in the United States,

**43**
Which choice provides the most effective transition between ideas in the paragraph?
A) NO CHANGE
B) Such a vaccine hasn't yet been developed for *Salmonella*, however.
C) Researchers would also like to be able to develop better vaccines against a number of other particularly nasty bacteria.
D) This potential positive impact is part of the reason the *Salmonella* studies have expanded beyond the International Space Station.

**44**
A) NO CHANGE
B) antigens, substances that stimulate the production of antibodies, to multiple body systems
C) antigens, substances that stimulate the production of antibodies to multiple body systems,
D) antigens substances that stimulate the production of antibodies to multiple body systems

# STOP

**If you finish before time is called, you may check your work on this section only.
Do not turn to any other section in the test.**

# Math Test – No Calculator

## 25 MINUTES, 20 QUESTIONS

**Turn to Section 3 of your answer sheet to answer the questions in this section.**

---

### DIRECTIONS

**For questions 1–15,** solve each problem, choose the best answer from the choices provided, and fill in the corresponding circle on your answer sheet. **For questions 16–20,** solve the problem and enter your answer in the grid on the answer sheet. Please refer to the directions before question 16 on how to enter your answers in the grid. You may use any available space in your test booklet for scratch work.

### NOTES

1.  The use of a calculator **is not permitted**.
2.  All variables and expressions used represent real numbers unless otherwise indicated.
3.  Figures provided in this test are drawn to scale unless otherwise indicated.
4.  All figures lie in a plane unless otherwise indicated.
5.  Unless otherwise indicated, the domain of a given function $f$ is the set of all real numbers $x$ for which $f(x)$ is a real number.

### REFERENCE

$A = \pi r^2$
$C = 2\pi r$

$A = \ell w$

$A = \frac{1}{2} bh$

$c^2 = a^2 + b^2$

Special Right Triangles

$V = \ell wh$

$V = \pi r^2 h$

$V = \frac{4}{3}\pi r^3$

$V = \frac{1}{3}\pi r^2 h$

$V = \frac{1}{3}\ell wh$

The number of degrees of arc in a circle is 360.
The number of radians of arc in a circle is $2\pi$.
The sum of the measures in degrees of the angles of a triangle is 180.

---

**CONTINUE**

**1**

Time (minutes)

In a certain game, players start with a certain number of coins and then spend their coins. The graph above shows the number of coins, $c$, possessed by Erica at $m$ minutes. Which of the following equations correctly relates $c$ and $m$ ?

A) $c = -\dfrac{1}{7}m$

B) $c = -m$

C) $c = -m + 7$

D) $c = -7m + 7$

**2**

$$\dfrac{2A + B + 2C}{5} = D$$

Based on the number of pages of algebra homework, $A$, biology homework, $B$, and chemistry homework, $C$, she is assigned, Katerina uses the above formula to determine the amount of time, $D$, in hours, she spends per page of homework assigned by her teachers. Which of the following correctly gives $B$ in terms of $A$, $C$, and $D$ ?

A) $B = \dfrac{2A + 2C - D}{5}$

B) $B = \dfrac{D - 2A - 2C}{5}$

C) $B = 2A + 2C - 5D$

D) $B = 5D - 2A - 2C$

**3**

$$a + a - 9 = 4a + a + a - 3 - 1$$

In the equation above, what is the value of $a$ ?

A) $-1$

B) $\dfrac{9}{4}$

C) $\dfrac{13}{5}$

D) $5$

**CONTINUE**

**4**

$$3y < 7$$
$$x < 3y + 4$$

Which of the following consists of the *x*-coordinates of all the points that satisfy the system of inequalities above?

A) $x < \dfrac{7}{3}$

B) $x < 3$

C) $x < \dfrac{19}{3}$

D) $x < 11$

**5**

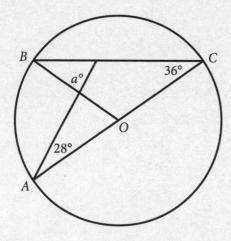

In the figure above, *O* is the center of the circle. What is the value of *a* ?

A) 100

B) 80

C) 72

D) 64

**6**

A traffic island is shaped like an isosceles triangle. The equal sides each have a length of *s* meters, and the third side is 4 meters shorter than the equal sides. Which of the following represents the perimeter, in meters, of the traffic island in terms of *s* ?

A) $2s - 4$

B) $\dfrac{s^2 - 4s}{2}$

C) $3s - 4$

D) $\dfrac{s - 4}{2}$

**7**

Point *A* has coordinates $(-11, 1)$, point *B* has coordinates $(-11, 7)$, and $\overline{AB}$ is the diameter of a circle. What is the equation of that circle?

A) $(x - 11)^2 + (y + 4)^2 = 9$

B) $(x + 11)^2 + (y - 1)^2 = 36$

C) $(x - 11)^2 + (y - 7)^2 = 36$

D) $(x + 11)^2 + (y - 4)^2 = 9$

**8**

$$a - 6 = \sqrt{8a - 7} - 4$$

What is the solution set of the equation above?

A) $\{0\}$

B) $\{1\}$

C) $\{11\}$

D) $\{1, 11\}$

**CONTINUE**

**9**

$$h(a) = a^2 + a - 20$$
$$k(a) = a^3 - 16a$$

Which of the following is equal to $\dfrac{h(a)}{k(a)}$, for $a > 4$ ?

A) $\dfrac{a+5}{a(a+4)}$

B) $\dfrac{a+5}{a(a-4)}$

C) $\dfrac{a+5}{a+4}$

D) $a+5$

**10**

Which of the following could be the equation of the graph above?

A) $y = -x(x-1)(x+2)$

B) $y = -x(x+1)(x-2)$

C) $y = -x(x-1)^2(x+2)$

D) $y = -x(x+1)^2(x-2)$

**11**

If $\dfrac{x}{3y} = 3$, what is the value of $\dfrac{y}{x}$ ?

A) $\dfrac{1}{9}$

B) $\dfrac{1}{3}$

C) 3

D) 9

**12**

Taylor's garden produced 296 tomatoes, and he is preserving all the tomatoes in jars that hold either 3 or 5 tomatoes each. Taylor has a total of 80 jars. If he uses all the jars and preserves all the tomatoes, exactly how many of the jars hold 3 tomatoes?

A) 50

B) 52

C) 54

D) 56

**13**

$$f(x) = 2 - [g(x)]^2$$
$$g(x) = 3x - 3$$

The functions $f$ and $g$ are defined above. Which of the following is the value of $f(0)$ ?

A) $-7$

B) $-3$

C) 2

D) 11

**CONTINUE** ➡

**14**

The population of Bulgaria was approximately 9 million people in 1989. Bulgaria's population decreased to 7.4 million people in 2011. If the decrease in population was linear, which of the following linear functions $P$ best models the population of Bulgaria, in millions of people $x$ years after the year 1989?

A) $P(x) = -\dfrac{74}{220}x + 9$

B) $P(x) = -\dfrac{16}{220}x + 9$

C) $P(x) = \dfrac{16}{220}x + 9$

D) $P(x) = \dfrac{74}{220}x + 9$

**15**

$$y = x^2 + 2x + k$$
$$y = 2x$$

If the system of equations above has exactly one real solution, which of the following is the value of $k$ ?

A) $-4$

B) $0$

C) $2$

D) $4$

**CONTINUE**

## DIRECTIONS

**For questions 16–20,** solve the problem and enter your answer in the grid, as described below, on the answer sheet.

1. Although not required, it is suggested that you write your answer in the boxes at the top of the columns to help you fill in the circles accurately. You will receive credit only if the circles are filled in correctly.

2. Mark no more than one circle in any column.

3. No question has a negative answer.

4. Some problems may have more than one correct answer. In such cases, grid only one answer.

5. **Mixed numbers** such as $3\frac{1}{2}$ must be gridded as 3.5 or 7/2. (If $\boxed{3\ 1\ /\ 2}$ is entered into the grid, it will be interpreted as $\frac{31}{2}$, not as $3\frac{1}{2}$.)

6. **Decimal Answers:** If you obtain a decimal answer with more digits than the grid can accommodate, it may be either rounded or truncated, but it must fill the entire grid.

Acceptable ways to grid $\frac{2}{3}$ are:

Answer: 201 – either position is correct

**NOTE:** You may start your answers in any column, space permitting. Columns you don't need to use should be left blank.

CONTINUE

**16**

When $a^2 + 2a + 4$ is subtracted from $3a^2 - 4a + 27$, the result can be written in the form $xa^2 + ya + z$, where $x$, $y$, and $z$ are constants. What is the value of $y + z$?

**17**

$$n^2 - n - 30 = 0$$

What is the positive solution to the equation above?

**18**

A student is modeling the number of assignments she has completed in a semester. She models the number of completed assignments by writing an equation in the form $y = mx + b$, where $y$ is the number of assignments she has completed and $x$ is the number of weeks since the start of the month. If at the start of the month she has completed 12 assignments and she completes 3 assignments per week, what is the value of $m$?

**CONTINUE**

**19**

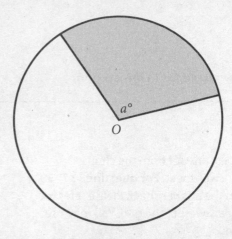

Note: Figure not drawn to scale.

In the figure above, $O$ is the center of the circle and $a = 110$. If the area of the circle is 72, what is the area of the shaded region?

**20**

$$9x + 2y = 17.75$$
$$x + 2y = 3.75$$

If $(x, y)$ is the solution to the system of equations above, what is the value of $x$ ?

## STOP
**If you finish before time is called, you may check your work on this section only.**
**Do not turn to any other section in the test.**

# Math Test – Calculator

## 55 MINUTES, 38 QUESTIONS

**Turn to Section 4 of your answer sheet to answer the questions in this section.**

---

### DIRECTIONS

**For questions 1–30**, solve each problem, choose the best answer from the choices provided, and fill in the corresponding circle on your answer sheet. **For questions 31–38**, solve the problem and enter your answer in the grid on the answer sheet. Please refer to the directions before question 31 on how to enter your answers in the grid. You may use any available space in your test booklet for scratch work.

### NOTES

1. The use of a calculator **is permitted**.
2. All variables and expressions used represent real numbers unless otherwise indicated.
3. Figures provided in this test are drawn to scale unless otherwise indicated.
4. All figures lie in a plane unless otherwise indicated.
5. Unless otherwise indicated, the domain of a given function $f$ is the set of all real numbers $x$ for which $f(x)$ is a real number.

### REFERENCE

$$A = \pi r^2$$
$$C = 2\pi r$$

$$A = \ell w$$

$$A = \frac{1}{2}bh$$

$$c^2 = a^2 + b^2$$

Special Right Triangles

$$V = \ell wh$$

$$V = \pi r^2 h$$

$$V = \frac{4}{3}\pi r^3$$

$$V = \frac{1}{3}\pi r^2 h$$

$$V = \frac{1}{3}\ell wh$$

The number of degrees of arc in a circle is 360.
The number of radians of arc in a circle is $2\pi$.
The sum of the measures in degrees of the angles of a triangle is 180.

---

CONTINUE

**1**

The figure below shows the total number of tenants living in an apartment building between January 1st of 2005 and January 1st of 2010.

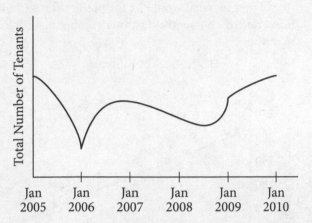

During which of the following years of operation does the number of tenants in the building increase the fastest?

A) 2005

B) 2006

C) 2007

D) 2009

**2**

A doctor randomly selects 500 residents of an island and finds that 4 of these residents have a specific gene mutation. Based on these results, approximately how many of the island's 15,000 residents likely have this mutation?

A) 75

B) 90

C) 105

D) 120

**3**

Chris buys one box of cookies for $n$ dollars. At this rate, how much does he pay, in dollars, for 4 boxes of cookies?

A) $\dfrac{n}{4}$

B) $\dfrac{4}{n}$

C) $4n$

D) $n + 4$

**4**

In the figure above, lines $l_1$ and $l_2$ are parallel and $a = 110$. What is the value of $b$ ?

A) 40

B) 70

C) 80

D) 140

CONTINUE

**5**

A newspaper sells both paper and digital subscriptions. The newspaper reports that 1,800 total subscriptions were sold last month and the total revenue from those subscription sales was $20,760. The digital subscriptions, $d$, cost $8 a month, and the paper subscriptions, $p$, cost $20 a month. Which of the following systems of equations could be used to solve for the number of each type of subscription that was sold by the newspaper last month?

A)  $d + p = 1,800$
    $20d + 8p = 20,760$

B)  $d + p = 1,800$
    $8d + 20p = 20,760$

C)  $d + p = 20,760$
    $8d + 20p = 1,800$

D)  $d + p = 1,800$
    $8d (20p) = 20,760$

**6**

A study tracked the maximum heart rate for runners competing in a marathon. The data and line of best fit are shown in the scatterplot below. Based on the line of best fit, what would be the predicted maximum heart rate of a 60-year-old runner competing in the marathon?

Heart Rates of Runners

A)  166.5

B)  170.7

C)  183.4

D)  216.9

**7**

$$\frac{3}{c-2} = c - 2$$

Which of the following values of $c - 2$ satisfies the equation above?

A)  5

B)  3

C)  $\sqrt{3}$

D)  $\sqrt{3} - 2$

CONTINUE

**8**

Which of the following equations, when graphed in the $xy$-plane, results in a line with a $y$-intercept of $-1$ ?

A) $y = x - \dfrac{1}{2}$

B) $y = \dfrac{1}{2}x - 1$

C) $y = -x$

D) $y = 2x + 1$

**9**

Sarah works at an art school and is purchasing canvases for $6 each and bottles of paint for $4 each. She budgets a total of $1,700 for canvases and paint. She goes over-budget, but purchases more than 360 items. Which of the following systems of inequalities represents all the possible values for the number of canvases, $a$, and the number of paint bottles, $b$, that she buys?

A) $6a + 4b < 1,700$
   $a + b > 360$

B) $6a + 4b < 1,700$
   $a + b < 360$

C) $6a + 4b > 1,700$
   $a + b < 360$

D) $6a + 4b > 1,700$
   $a + b > 360$

**Questions 10–12 refer to the following information.**

800 ml

$3n$

$n$

A beaker that can be filled to a maximum volume of 800 milliliters is shown above. For safety reasons, it cannot be filled above the 800-milliliter line. The radius of the base is equal to the diameter of the top, and the volume in cubic inches of the beaker is given by the equation $V = \dfrac{21\pi n^3}{12}$.

**10**

How many beakers of this size, filled to the 800-milliliter line, would be needed to hold 4 liters of a solution? (1 liter = 1000 mL)

A) 2

B) 4

C) 5

D) 8

**CONTINUE**

## 11

Given that the volume of 800 milliliters of liquid is approximately 13.2 cubic inches, which of the following is closest to the radius of the base of the beaker?

A)  1.34 inches

B)  2.28 inches

C)  4.23 inches

D)  8.04 inches

## 12

The beaker is filled with a solution to the 800-milliliter line and then left outside in the sun where the solution evaporates at a constant rate. The graph of the height of the solution remaining in the beaker over time would have which of the following shapes?

A)

B)

C)

D)

## 13

The amount of work done to move an object is equal to the product of the mass of the object, in kilograms; the distance the object moves, in meters; and the gravitational constant of 9.8 meters per second squared. What is the power rating of a machine that can move a 100-kilogram object 3.6 meters in 18 seconds?  (Power is work per unit time.)

A)  196

B)   54

C)   19.6

D)    5.4

## 14

If $y = \dfrac{1}{x^3}$ , which of the following gives $x$ in terms of $y$ ?

A)  $y^{\frac{1}{3}}$

B)  $y^{-\frac{1}{3}}$

C)  $-y^3$

D)  $y^3$

CONTINUE

**15**

The function $f(x) = \dfrac{5}{x^2 - 5x + 4}$ is graphed in the

$xy$-plane. Which of the following values of $x$ is NOT

in the domain of $f(x)$ ?

A) −1

B) 0

C) 1

D) 5

**16**

Number of Eggs Laid by Chickens

| Number of Eggs | 8 | 7 | 6 | 5 | 4 | 2 |
|---|---|---|---|---|---|---|
| Frequency | 1 | 3 | 8 | 5 | 2 | 5 |

A farmer has 24 chickens. At the end of a week he counts the total number of eggs each chicken laid that week. The table above shows the distribution of the number of eggs laid by the chickens. Which of the following statements about the mean, median, and mode of the number of eggs laid is true?

A) The mean is greater than both the mode and the median.

B) The mean is less than both the mode and the median.

C) The mean is greater than the mode but less than the median.

D) The mean is equal to both the mode and the median.

**17**

A Human Resources department seeking to increase employee retention commissioned a study to determine the relationship between job tasks and employee satisfaction. The scatterplot above shows the relationship for employees in a particular field between the number of work hours spent on creative tasks per week and their overall job satisfaction. The line of best fit is shown on the figure.

An employee that works in the same field but was not part of the study indicates that he spends 12 hours a week on creative tasks. Which of the following is the best approximation of his predicted job satisfaction based on the line of best fit?

A) 68%

B) 75%

C) 80%

D) 84%

CONTINUE

18

### Effectiveness of Ad Campaign

| | Favorable | Not Favorable | Total |
|---|---|---|---|
| New Ad | 120 | 130 | 250 |
| Previous Ad | 85 | 165 | 250 |
| Total | 205 | 295 | 500 |

The table above shows the results of a study on the effectiveness of a new ad campaign. In a randomly selected sample of 500 participants, 250 were shown the new ad campaign for a car while the rest were shown the previous ad campaign. The participants then reported whether their opinion of the car was favorable or not. What proportion of participants who watched the new ad campaign had a favorable opinion?

A) $\dfrac{12}{25}$

B) $\dfrac{41}{100}$

C) $\dfrac{6}{25}$

D) $\dfrac{24}{41}$

**Questions 19 and 20 refer to the following information.**

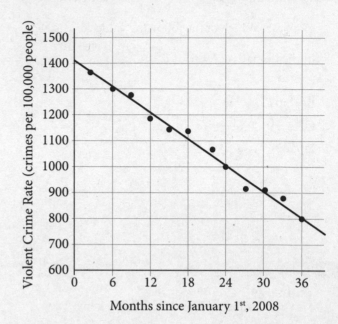

Months since January 1$^{st}$, 2008

On January 1$^{st}$, 2008, a city implemented a new program to combat crime. The graph above shows the violent crime rate in the city, measured in violent crimes per 100,000 residents, from January 1$^{st}$, 2008, to the end of 2010. The line of best fit has the equation $y = 1{,}412 - 16.8x$, where $y$ is the violent crime rate and $x$ is the number of months since the implementation of the program.

19

Which of the following is closest to the percent decrease in the violent crime rate in the city from January 1$^{st}$, 2010, to January 1$^{st}$, 2011?

A)    8%

B)    20%

C)    80%

D)   140%

**CONTINUE**

**20**

What does the coefficient 16.8 represent in the line of best fit equation?

A) The number of months since the crime reduction program was implemented

B) The average crime rate per month since January 2008

C) The average monthly reduction in the violent crime rate during the first three years that the crime reduction program was in place

D) The violent crime rate in January 2008

---

**21**

Samuel's annual salary is $49,500. If he completes an MBA program with a tuition of $73,320, his annual salary will be $64,500. If $n$ represents the number of years that Samuel works at his job after completing his MBA, which of the following inequalities demonstrates the value of $n$ for which his total additional income exceeds the cost of the tuition?

A) $n > \dfrac{73,320}{(64,500 - 49,500)}$

B) $n < \dfrac{73,320}{(64,500 - 49,500)}$

C) $n > \dfrac{(73,320 - 49,500)}{64,500}$

D) $n < \dfrac{(73,320 - 49,500)}{64,500}$

**22**

Polynomial function $g$ is graphed in the $xy$-plane. This function has zeroes at $-4$ and 2, and its range is the set of all real numbers such that $g(x) \geq -3$. Which of the following graphs represents function $g$ ?

A)

B)

C)

D)

**CONTINUE**

**23**

To determine support for a proposition on the state ballot, residents were called on the phone. Of those residents called, 20% did not answer the phone. Approximately 35% of the residents who did answer were contacted on a landline and the other 65% were contacted on a cell phone. Approximately 55% of the respondents contacted on a landline and 30% of the respondents contacted on a cell phone supported the proposition. Which of the following conclusions is best supported by the poll results?

A) The proposition will pass if voter turnout is high on Election Day.

B) Voters over 35 years old were more likely to support the proposition than voters between 18 and 35 were.

C) Participants that were reached on their cell phones were less likely to support the bill than participants that were reached on a landline.

D) If only voters that own a landline vote on Election Day, the proposition will pass.

**24**

The weight $w$, in grams, of a newborn panda can be approximated with the equation $w = 109(1.12)^n$, where $n$ represents the number of days since birth. Which of the following equations models the weight, in grams, of a newborn panda $x$ weeks after the panda is born?

A) $w = 109(2.21)^{\frac{x}{7}}$

B) $w = 109(1.12)^{\frac{x}{7}}$

C) $w = 109(1.84)^x$

D) $w = 109(1.12)^{7x}$

**25**

An activist group wants to determine how frequently the average resident of a county uses the library. The group plans to ask everybody that enters one of the library branches on a Saturday to estimate how many times per year they visit a library. Based on these responses, the group will estimate the number of library visits that the average resident makes each year. Which of the following statements is true?

A) The proposed survey has a small sample size and therefore the results will likely be an unreliable estimate of the average library use of the county's residents.

B) The proposed survey will likely produce a reliable estimate of the average library use of the county's residents only if the group conducts it on both a Saturday and a weekday.

C) The proposed survey will likely produce a reliable estimate of the average library use of the county's residents if the group conducts the survey at the busiest library in the county.

D) Due to a flawed sampling method, the proposed survey will likely produce a biased estimate of the average library use of the county's residents regardless of the sample size and the days of the week on which the survey is conducted.

**CONTINUE**

**26**

The point $(c, d)$ lies on a line with a slope of 2 in the $xy$-plane. The point $(3, 2d)$ lies on a different line with a slope of $-3$. If the two lines have the same $y$-intercept and $\dfrac{c}{d} = \dfrac{3}{2}$, what is the value of $d$ ?

A) $-\dfrac{9}{4}$

B) $-\dfrac{2}{3}$

C) $\dfrac{3}{2}$

D) $\dfrac{9}{2}$

**27**

Unemployment Rate in Country X

| Year | 2010 | 2013 |
|------|------|------|
| Unemployment Rate | 11.5% | 13% |

The table above shows the unemployment rate for Country X in 2010 and 2013. If the unemployment rate and year have a linear relationship, which of the following expressions best approximates the unemployment rate of the country $n$ years after 2010?

A) $1.5n + 11.5$

B) $0.5(n - 2{,}010) + 11.5$

C) $0.5n + 11.5$

D) $-1.5n + 11.5$

**28**

A pool has 750 gallons of water in it when a hose begins adding water at a constant rate. The pool contains 60% more water after the hose has run for 5 hours. Which of the following expressions gives the number of gallons of water in the pool after the hose has run for a total of $t$ hours?

A) $750 + 90t$

B) $750 + 5t$

C) $750(1.6)^{\frac{t}{5}}$

D) $750(1.6)^{5t}$

**CONTINUE**

**29**

A table of values for function $f(x)$ and the graph of function $h(x)$ are shown below. If the vertex of $h(x)$ is $(a, b)$, what is $f(h(a))$ ?

| $x$ | $-3$ | $-2$ | $-1$ | $0$ | $1$ | $2$ | $3$ |
|---|---|---|---|---|---|---|---|
| $f(x)$ | 11 | 8 | 5 | 2 | $-1$ | $-4$ | $-7$ |

A)  $-1$

B)  2

C)  5

D)  11

**30**

Researchers allowed 15 participants in a study to get a full night's sleep, while another 15 were awoken after only 3 hours of sleep. The researchers then gave the participants a series of mental tasks and calculated each participant's average completion time. The results are shown below.

Completion time (sec)
Normal Sleep

Completion time (sec)
Reduced Sleep

If the participants with normal sleep make up Group A and the participants with 3 hours of sleep make up Group B, which of the following statements regarding the standard deviations and ranges of the groups is true?

A)  The range of Group B is larger than the range of Group A.

B)  The standard deviation of Group B is smaller than the standard deviation of Group A.

C)  The standard deviation of Group B is equal to the standard deviation of Group A.

D)  The range of Group B is equal to the range of Group A.

**CONTINUE**

## DIRECTIONS

**For questions 31–38**, solve the problem and enter your answer in the grid, as described below, on the answer sheet.

1. Although not required, it is suggested that you write your answer in the boxes at the top of the columns to help you fill in the circles accurately. You will receive credit only if the circles are filled in correctly.

2. Mark no more than one circle in any column.

3. No question has a negative answer.

4. Some problems may have more than one correct answer. In such cases, grid only one answer.

5. **Mixed numbers** such as $3\frac{1}{2}$ must be gridded as 3.5 or 7/2. (If is entered into the grid, it will be interpreted as $\frac{31}{2}$, not as $3\frac{1}{2}$.)

6. **Decimal Answers:** If you obtain a decimal answer with more digits than the grid can accommodate, it may be either rounded or truncated, but it must fill the entire grid.

Answer: $\frac{7}{12}$   Answer: 2.5

Write answer in boxes.   Fraction line   Decimal point

Grid in result.

Acceptable ways to grid $\frac{2}{3}$ are:

Answer: 201 – either position is correct

**NOTE:** You may start your answers in any column, space permitting. Columns you don't need to use should be left blank.

CONTINUE

**31**

$$nx - 8y = 18$$
$$7x - 4y = 9$$

The equations above both represent line $l$ in the $xy$-plane. If $n$ is a constant, what is the value of $n$ ?

**32**

One liter of a solution contains one milligram of Solute A and three milligrams of Solute B. How many milligrams of Solute B are there in 22 liters of the solution?

**33**

$$\frac{1}{3}c + x = 0$$

The equation above is true when $x = -3$. What is the value of $c$ ?

**34**

The function $p$ is defined by the equation

$p(x) = \frac{1}{3}(x - 9)^2 - 18$. A portion of the graph of $p$

is shown above. Function $q$ (not shown) is defined

by the equation $q(x) = 15 - 5x$. If $p(x)$ intersects the

graph of $q(x)$ at the point $(r, s)$ where $r > 0$, what

is the value of $r$ ?

**CONTINUE**

**35**

In the figure above, if cos ($\angle DBA$) = 0.3, what is the value of cos ($\angle DBA$) + sin ($\angle DBC$) ?

**36**

October 28 and 29, 1929 are known as Black Monday and Black Tuesday, respectively. During two days of trading the Dow Jones Industrial Average lost 68.9 points. If there were 5 hours of trading during each of the two days, on average how many points per <u>minute</u>, to the nearest hundredth, did the Dow Jones Industrial Average lose during those two days?

**CONTINUE**

**Questions 37 and 38 refer to the following information.**

Days since germination

| Days since germination | 0 | 2 | 4 | 6 | 8 | 10 |
|---|---|---|---|---|---|---|
| Average mass per plant (milligrams) | 5.0 | 6.6 | 8.4 | 11.1 | 14.4 | 18.8 |

Once a seed has germinated and the first leaves begin producing carbohydrates through photosynthesis, a plant grows rapidly until it begins flowering or its growth is restricted by a lack of nutrients or light. An agriculture class grew *Zea mays L.* (sweet corn) in its greenhouse and measured the mass of each plant every other day. The average mass per plant was determined and presented in the graph and table above.

**37**

$$H(d) = 5.0r^{\frac{d}{2}}$$

The students in the class modeled the average mass per plant using the above function $H$, where $H$ is average mass in grams $d$ days after germination, and $r$ is a constant. The students found their model matched the data collected within 0.1 grams. To the nearest tenth, what is the value of $r$?

**38**

According to the table, what is the positive difference on average, in grams, between a group of 4 plants that germinated 4 days ago and a group of 3 plants that are germinated 8 days ago?

**STOP**

If you finish before time is called, you may check your work on this section only.
Do not turn to any other section in the test.

# Experimental: Writing and Language Skills

## 20 MINUTES, 18 QUESTIONS

**Turn to Section 5 of your answer sheet to answer the questions in this section.**

DIRECTIONS

The passage below is accompanied by a number of questions. For some questions, you will consider how the passage might be revised to improve the expression of ideas. For other questions, you will consider how the passage might be edited to correct errors in sentence structure, usage, or punctuation. A passage or a question may be accompanied by one or more graphics (such as a table or graph) that you will consider as you make revising and editing decisions.

Some questions will direct you to an underlined portion of the passage. Other questions will direct you to a location in the passage or ask you to think about the passage as a whole.

After reading the passage, choose the answer to each question that most effectively improves the quality of writing in the passage or that makes the passage conform to the conventions of standard written English. Many questions include a "NO CHANGE" option. Choose that option if you think the best choice is to leave the relevant portion of the passage as it is.

**CONTINUE**

**Questions 1–18 are based on the following passage.**

**Metric Mayhem**

[1] In the fall of 1999, the metric system caused the $125 million Mars Climate Orbiter to crash on Mars **1** . [2] Somehow, neither group realized the units were different, and the result was that the trajectory of the probe was miscalculated and it crashed. [3] This, at least, is the argument of **2** people who are against adopting the metric system in the U.S. [4] The problem was that two different groups that worked on the project used different systems of measurement. [5] One group used pounds of force per second, a U.S. Customary measurement, and the other group **3** uses newtons, the equivalent metric measurement of force. **4**

**1**

At this point, the writer is considering adding the following.

> instead of going into orbit around the planet to collect and transmit data

Should the writer make this addition here?

A) Yes, because it gives details that clarify that the crash was unexpected.

B) Yes, because it establishes an important shift in focus in the paragraph's discussion of the Mars Climate Orbiter.

C) No, because it contains information that is not directly related to the main focus of the paragraph.

D) No, because it repeats information given later in the paragraph.

**2**

A) NO CHANGE

B) them

C) they

D) those ones

**3**

A) NO CHANGE

B) had used

C) used

D) will have used

**4**

To make this paragraph most logical, sentence 2 should be placed

A) where it is now.

B) after sentence 3.

C) after sentence 4.

D) after sentence 5.

**CONTINUE**

The history of the metric system in the Western world began soon after the replacement of Roman numerals with the base-ten Arabic numbering **5** system. The replacement of Roman numerals with Arabic numerals happened in the 15th century. The earliest known treatise promoting the **6** idea, of a decimal, or base-ten system of measurement was printed in 1586. The foundations of the metric system as we know it today were developed over the next two **7** centuries, as commerce, across great distances, became more common. A universal system makes trade vastly simpler because weights and prices can be easily understood, **8** so cheating is difficult.

**5**

Which choice most effectively combines the sentences at the underlined portion?

A) system; this replacement

B) system, which

C) system—the adoption of Arabic numerals

D) system, an occurrence that largely

**6**

A) NO CHANGE

B) idea of a decimal, or base-ten,

C) idea, of a decimal or base-ten,

D) idea of a decimal—or base-ten,

**7**

A) NO CHANGE

B) centuries as commerce, across great distances

C) centuries as commerce, across great distances,

D) centuries as commerce across great distances

**8**

Which choice most effectively completes the explanation of how the metric system was important for trade over long distances?

A) NO CHANGE

B) since different currencies make long-distance trade hard enough.

C) regardless of whether buyers and sellers are from the same place.

D) whether the goods are spices, wine, or textiles.

CONTINUE →

France was the first country to officially adopt the metric system in the late 18^th century, and **9** they organized several international conferences to establish what the universal standards would be. Much of Europe **10** got on board with the metric system quickly on the heels of France, with the exception of Britain. **11** Since the American colonies were part of the British Empire, they used the British Imperial System of measurement. When the United States was established, the Constitution specified that Congress had the power to "fix the Standard of Weights and Measures," and Thomas Jefferson and Ben Franklin were both among the proponents of **12** sacrificing the British system in favor of the metric system.

**9**

A) NO CHANGE

B) they were organizing

C) it organized

D) it had organized

**10**

Which choice best maintains the style and tone of the passage?

A) NO CHANGE

B) singled out

C) adopted

D) pinned down

**11**

A) NO CHANGE

B) Although

C) Therefore,

D) Nevertheless,

**12**

A) NO CHANGE

B) ducking

C) evading

D) abandoning

**CONTINUE**

In the late 18th century, [13] for example, politics and distance turned out to be insurmountable roadblocks to adopting the metric system in the U.S. Although France had been an American ally during the Revolutionary [14] War. It quickly turned hostile towards the U.S. as diplomatic relations between the U.S. and Britain warmed after the war. There was also concern in the U.S. about the cost of sending a delegation to France [15] for learn about the metric system and worry that political upheaval within France might mean the quick demise of the new system. In the end, the British system was retained, though we now know it as the U.S. Customary System.

[16] There have been multiple attempts over the years to establish the metric system in the U.S. In fact, the metric system was made legal (though not mandatory) by Congress in 1866, and our standards for yards and pounds are defined as fractions of meters and kilograms,

---

**13**

A) NO CHANGE
B) moreover,
C) thus,
D) however,

**14**

A) NO CHANGE
B) War, it
C) War; it
D) War: it

**15**

A) NO CHANGE
B) to
C) by
D) of

**16**

Which choice provides the best introduction to this paragraph?

A) NO CHANGE
B) The metric system continued in France, despite Napoleonic rule.
C) Congress deals with a lot of issues that might not seem like they have a big impact on everyday life.
D) Political upheaval also happens in the United States.

CONTINUE

respectively. When Congress passed the Metric Conversion Act in 1975, [17] metric enthusiasts who admired that system were optimistic that the U.S. was finally going to make the switch. But the bill was later amended to make metric conversion voluntary, [18] which is why our speed limit signs are in miles per hour instead of kilometers per hour, and at least in part why the Mars Climate Orbiter crashed.

[17]

A) NO CHANGE

B) those in enthusiastic favor of the metric system

C) metric enthusiasts

D) enthusiastic metric system admirers

[18]

Which choice most effectively concludes the essay?

A) NO CHANGE

B) but even though it isn't official, many school children learn about the metric system from an early age.

C) so some businesses have opted to go metric, while most government agencies haven't fully made the switch.

D) which means no one is motivated to make the change even though it wouldn't be that hard.

**END OF TEST**

**DO NOT RETURN TO A PREVIOUS SECTION.**

The Princeton Review®

Completely darken bubbles with a No. 2 pencil. If you make a mistake, be sure to erase mark completely. Erase all stray marks.

**1.**
YOUR NAME: _____
(Print)          Last          First          M.I.

SIGNATURE: _____     DATE: ___/___/___

HOME ADDRESS: _____
(Print)                    Number and Street

_____
City          State          Zip Code

PHONE NO.: _____
(Print)

IMPORTANT: Please fill in these boxes exactly as shown on the back cover of your test book.

**2. TEST FORM**

**3. TEST CODE**

**4. REGISTRATION NUMBER**

**5. YOUR NAME**
First 4 letters of last name | FIRST INIT | MID INIT

(A B C D E F G H I J K L M N O P Q R S T U V W X Y Z bubbles for each column)

**6. DATE OF BIRTH**

| Month | Day | Year |
|-------|-----|------|
| JAN | | |
| FEB | 0 0 | 0 0 |
| MAR | 1 1 | 1 1 |
| APR | 2 2 | 2 2 |
| MAY | 3 3 | 3 3 |
| JUN | 4 | 4 4 |
| JUL | 5 | 5 5 |
| AUG | 6 | 6 6 |
| SEP | 7 | 7 7 |
| OCT | 8 | 8 8 |
| NOV | 9 | 9 9 |
| DEC | | |

Test code bubbles: 0-9, A-I, J-R

**7. SEX**
○ MALE
○ FEMALE

The Princeton Review®

**Test ⑩**   Start with number 1 for each new section.
If a section has fewer questions than answer spaces, leave the extra answer spaces blank.

## Section 1—Reading

1. A B C D
2. A B C D
3. A B C D
4. A B C D
5. A B C D
6. A B C D
7. A B C D
8. A B C D
9. A B C D
10. A B C D
11. A B C D
12. A B C D
13. A B C D
14. A B C D
15. A B C D
16. A B C D
17. A B C D
18. A B C D
19. A B C D
20. A B C D
21. A B C D
22. A B C D
23. A B C D
24. A B C D
25. A B C D
26. A B C D
27. A B C D
28. A B C D
29. A B C D
30. A B C D
31. A B C D
32. A B C D
33. A B C D
34. A B C D
35. A B C D
36. A B C D
37. A B C D
38. A B C D
39. A B C D
40. A B C D
41. A B C D
42. A B C D
43. A B C D
44. A B C D
45. A B C D
46. A B C D
47. A B C D
48. A B C D
49. A B C D
50. A B C D
51. A B C D
52. A B C D

## Section 2—Writing and Language Skills

1. A B C D
2. A B C D
3. A B C D
4. A B C D
5. A B C D
6. A B C D
7. A B C D
8. A B C D
9. A B C D
10. A B C D
11. A B C D
12. A B C D
13. A B C D
14. A B C D
15. A B C D
16. A B C D
17. A B C D
18. A B C D
19. A B C D
20. A B C D
21. A B C D
22. A B C D
23. A B C D
24. A B C D
25. A B C D
26. A B C D
27. A B C D
28. A B C D
29. A B C D
30. A B C D
31. A B C D
32. A B C D
33. A B C D
34. A B C D
35. A B C D
36. A B C D
37. A B C D
38. A B C D
39. A B C D
40. A B C D
41. A B C D
42. A B C D
43. A B C D
44. A B C D

Completely darken bubbles with a No. 2 pencil. If you make a mistake, be sure to erase mark completely. Erase all stray marks.

**Test 10**    Start with number 1 for each new section.
If a section has fewer questions than answer spaces, leave the extra answer spaces blank.

## Section 3—Mathematics: No Calculator

16.    17.    18.    19.    20.

## Section 4—Mathematics: Calculator

31.    32.    33.    34.    35.

36.    37.    38.

## Section 5—Experimental: Writing and Language Skills

# Chapter 22
# Practice Test 10:
# Answers and
# Explanations

# PRACTICE TEST 10 ANSWER KEY

## Section 1: Reading

| | | | |
|---|---|---|---|
| 1. | B | 27. | C |
| 2. | D | 28. | D |
| 3. | D | 29. | B |
| 4. | A | 30. | B |
| 5. | D | 31. | D |
| 6. | A | 32. | B |
| 7. | C | 33. | B |
| 8. | B | 34. | A |
| 9. | C | 35. | A |
| 10. | C | 36. | C |
| 11. | C | 37. | B |
| 12. | A | 38. | B |
| 13. | A | 39. | D |
| 14. | C | 40. | A |
| 15. | B | 41. | B |
| 16. | B | 42. | B |
| 17. | D | 43. | B |
| 18. | D | 44. | D |
| 19. | A | 45. | D |
| 20. | B | 46. | D |
| 21. | C | 47. | B |
| 22. | B | 48. | A |
| 23. | A | 49. | B |
| 24. | C | 50. | C |
| 25. | B | 51. | D |
| 26. | A | 52. | D |

## Section 2: Writing & Language

| | | | |
|---|---|---|---|
| 1. | C | 23. | A |
| 2. | D | 24. | D |
| 3. | D | 25. | C |
| 4. | A | 26. | D |
| 5. | B | 27. | D |
| 6. | C | 28. | C |
| 7. | A | 29. | B |
| 8. | D | 30. | A |
| 9. | B | 31. | D |
| 10. | B | 32. | B |
| 11. | B | 33. | A |
| 12. | D | 34. | A |
| 13. | C | 35. | C |
| 14. | A | 36. | D |
| 15. | B | 37. | A |
| 16. | A | 38. | C |
| 17. | A | 39. | B |
| 18. | C | 40. | C |
| 19. | D | 41. | B |
| 20. | B | 42. | B |
| 21. | A | 43. | A |
| 22. | D | 44. | B |

## Section 3: Math (No Calculator)

| | | | |
|---|---|---|---|
| 1. | C | 13. | A |
| 2. | D | 14. | B |
| 3. | A | 15. | B |
| 4. | D | 16. | 17 |
| 5. | B | 17. | 6 |
| 6. | C | 18. | 3 |
| 7. | D | 19. | 22 |
| 8. | C | | |
| 9. | A | | |
| 10. | C | | |
| 11. | A | | |
| 12. | B | | |

20. $\frac{14}{8}$, $\frac{7}{4}$, or 1.75

## Section 4: Math (Calculator)

| | | | |
|---|---|---|---|
| 1. | B | 20. | C |
| 2. | D | 21. | A |
| 3. | C | 22. | C |
| 4. | A | 23. | C |
| 5. | B | 24. | D |
| 6. | A | 25. | D |
| 7. | C | 26. | A |
| 8. | B | 27. | C |
| 9. | D | 28. | A |
| 10. | C | 29. | D |
| 11. | A | 30. | B |
| 12. | A | 31. | 14 |
| 13. | A | 32. | 66 |
| 14. | B | 33. | 9 |
| 15. | C | 34. | 6 |
| 16. | B | 35. | 0.6 |
| 17. | B | 36. | 0.11 |
| 18. | A | 37. | 1.3 |
| 19. | B | 38. | 9.6 |

## Section 5: Experimental (Writing & Language)

| | | | |
|---|---|---|---|
| 1. | A | 10. | C |
| 2. | A | 11. | A |
| 3. | C | 12. | D |
| 4. | D | 13. | D |
| 5. | B | 14. | B |
| 6. | B | 15. | B |
| 7. | D | 16. | A |
| 8. | C | 17. | C |
| 9. | C | 18. | A |

For self-scoring assessment tables, please turn to page 957.

# PRACTICE TEST 10 EXPLANATIONS

## Section 1: Reading

1. **B** This question asks how the main focus of the passage shifts from the beginning to the end. Because this is a general question, it should be done after the specific questions. The passage begins with the narrator's description of her family's *house-dwelling life* in a house built *across the road from a lake*. She continues with a description of the family's business running a *dance pavilion* with live music and dancing throughout the summer. In the third paragraph, the story focus changes when her father *moved his office into his car* and they drove around buying and selling antiques. The narrator describes her father's *lifelong wanderlust* and how he would suddenly decide it was time to go somewhere else. Eliminate any answer choices that are not consistent with this structure. Choice (A) can be eliminated because there is no *portrayal of a significant place the family often visited* in the passage. Choice (B) is consistent with the shift from her description of life in the summer house to life on the road. Choice (C) can be eliminated because the descriptions in the first part of the passage are concrete descriptions of the narrator's childhood rather than an *allegorical display of domesticity*. Choice (D) can be eliminated because the passage is not an examination of the narrator's childhood financial situation. The correct answer is (B).

2. **D** This question asks about the main purpose of the second paragraph. Carefully read the paragraph to determine what the central focus is. Throughout the paragraph, the narrator describes the dance pavilion her father ran during the summer. He *dreamed up such attractions as a living chess game* and *booked the big dance bands of the 1930s and 1940s*. She says that people would come from *as far away as Toledo or Detroit*, but that *paying the likes of Guy Lombardo or Duke Ellington…meant that one rainy weekend could wipe out a whole summer's profits*. This paragraph establishes the idea that the narrator's father is a man with big ideas who doesn't always play it safe. Eliminate any answer choices that aren't consistent with this idea. Choice (A) can be eliminated because there is no discussion of the father's *compulsive desire to travel* in this paragraph. Choice (B) can also be eliminated, because no one important to the *narrator's remembrances* is *introduced* in this paragraph. Choice (C) might initially look good, but the father is actually bringing in the famous acts rather than suffering *delusions of grandeur*, and while his decisions *could wipe out* the *summer's profits*, that's a risk that is being described rather than an actual negative outcome. Eliminate (C). Choice (D) is consistent with the prediction. The correct answer is (D).

3. **D** This question asks what the word *precarious* does in line 24. Use the line reference to find the window, and read carefully. The narrator describes the family's livelihood as *precarious* after saying that her father's business decisions could *wipe out a whole summer's profits*, which always gave them *a sense of gambling*. The word *precarious* describes their livelihood as "risky" or "a

gamble." Eliminate anything that is not consistent with this prediction. Choices (A) and (B) can be eliminated because there is no mention of their family's financial situation in either answer. Choice (C) might be true in the life of the narrator, but the word *precarious* is used here to highlight the riskiness of the financial situation, so eliminate (C). Choice (D) is a clear paraphrase of the prediction. The correct answer is (D).

4.  **A**  This question asks about the narrator's participation in the *family business*. Use chronology to find the window that talks about the family business and read carefully. The narrator says that *from the age of four*, she *came into [her] own as the wrapper and unwrapper of china*. She goes on to say that each of the family members *had a role in the family economic unit*, including her older sister, who *sold popcorn from a professional stand*. The correct answer should be consistent with the idea of the narrator having her own job within the family business from a young age. Choice (A) is consistent with this idea, so keep it. Choice (B) might be initially attractive, but there is no mention in the text of the time either sister spent doing her job. Choices (C) and (D) can be eliminated because there is no mention in the passage of money, getting paid, or volunteering. The correct answer is (A).

5.  **D**  This question asks which statement the narrator's father would most likely agree with. Notice that this is the first question in a paired set, so it can be done in tandem with Q6. Begin with the answers to Q6. The lines for (6A) say that there were only *a few months each year* when her father was *content with a house-dwelling life*. These lines support (5D), so draw a line connecting those two answer choices. The lines for (6B) say that her father loved the risks of the summer business. These lines do not support any of the answer choices for Q5, so eliminate (6B). The lines for (6C) say that everyone *had a role in the family economic unit* and then go on to explain her sister's role. These lines don't support any of the answers for Q5, so eliminate (6C). The lines for (6D) say that he *refused to put heating or hot water* in their house. Those lines might initially seem to support (5C), but read carefully. The father is not concerned about *the expense* of the water heater; he is concerned about the permanence of it. Eliminate (6D). Without support from Q6, (5A), (5B), and (5C) can all be eliminated. The correct answers are (5D) and (6A).

6.  **A**  (See explanation above.)

7.  **C**  This question asks what *struck* most nearly means in line 48. Go back to the text, find the word *struck*, and cross it out. Carefully read the surrounding text to determine another word that would fit based on the context. The narrator describes how her father is preparing to travel by *collecting road maps…, testing the trailer hitch…, and talking about faraway pleasures*. Then she says he announces it's time to go *as if struck by a sudden whim rather than a lifelong wanderlust*. The missing word must mean "suddenly decided" or "just realized." Eliminate anything that isn't consistent with this prediction. Choice (A), *battered*, is a definition of *struck*, but it doesn't mean "suddenly decided." Eliminate (A). Choice (B), *boycotted*, means "abstained from buying," which does not match the prediction. Eliminate (B). Choice (C), *inspired*, is consis-

tent with the prediction, so keep it. Choice (D), *disturbed*, can be eliminated because it does not mean "suddenly decided" or "just realized." The correct answer is (C).

8.  **B**  This question asks why the father started the cross-country trip. Notice that it is the first question in a paired set, so it can be done in tandem with Q9. Begin with the answers to Q9. The lines for (9A) refer to the family's antiquing business, driving to *nearby country auctions* to search for antiques. There is no mention of the *cross-country trip*, so these lines do not support any of the answers for Q8. Eliminate (9A). The lines for (9B) describe the father's specific actions as he prepares for the trip, including *collecting road maps…, testing the trailer hitch…, and talking about faraway pleasures*. These lines provide details about the trip, but they do not give the *reason* the trip started. Eliminate (9B). The lines for (9C) refer to the father's *lifelong wanderlust* when he announces it's time to go. These lines support (8B), so draw a line connecting those two answers. The lines for (9D) describe the speed of the *leave-taking*, but do not offer a reason for it. Eliminate (9D). Without support from Q9, (8A), (8C), and (8D) can all be eliminated. The correct answers are (8B) and (9C).

9.  **C**  (See explanation above.)

10. **C**  This question asks about the mother's role in the family. Carefully read the window where the mother is mentioned. She is first mentioned in line 28 when the narrator discusses the family antiquing business. She says that her mother had a *better eye for antiques and reference books* and was the one who *appraised them for sale*. Then, in the last paragraph (lines 71–77), the narrator again mentions her mother as the one who remembered the iron was still on and *might be burning its way through the ironing board*. The correct answer should have something to do with the mother being reasonable and practical in the family. Choice (A) can be eliminated because there is no evidence that she *resented* her husband's *impulsive nature*. Choice (B) can also be eliminated because she goes along with her husband, but there is no evidence in the text that she *shared the…wanderlust equally*. Choice (C) is consistent with the prediction, so keep it. Choice (D) can be eliminated because, although she was worried about the iron, it did not actually set the house on fire. The correct answer is (C).

11. **C**  This question asks about the primary purpose of the passage. Because it is a general question, it should be done after the specific questions have been completed. The passage begins by introducing the idea that liars and bluffers have *tells* that indicate when they aren't being truthful. The passage then expands this idea into a discussion about a pair of Stanford researchers who identified patterns that show up in reports with falsified data and could potentially be used to spot fraudulent papers. The passage ends with a warning that systems designed to detect fraudulent papers by simply counting words could have negative repercussions. The correct answer should be consistent with this prediction. Eliminate (A) because this passage is not *defend*[ing] anyone. Choice (B) can also be eliminated because the passage is focused on scientific publications, not *different industries and research fields*. Choice (C) is consistent with the prediction, so keep it. Eliminate (D) because the passage is about research into detecting fraud,

not *reveal[ing] secrets* of those who successfully lie. The correct answer is (C).

12.  **A**  This question asks about the function of the first paragraph. Carefully read the paragraph to determine the author's reason for including the given information. The paragraph begins by mentioning how *poker players* have "tells" that give away *when they're bluffing*. The paragraph goes on to say that this idea of *tells* can also happen with *scientists* who *commit fraud* by attempting to *pass along falsified data*. The paragraph ends by saying *a pair of Stanford researchers* have *cracked the writing patterns* of the tells, which could help *identify falsified research* before it is published. The paragraph is there to provide context for research discussed later in the passage. Eliminate any answer choices that are not consistent with that prediction. Choice (A) is consistent with the prediction, as the paragraph introduces the concept of *tells*, which is what the later research is about. Keep (A). Choice (B) can be eliminated because there is no mention in the paragraph of *additional applications* of the research results. Choice (C) can be eliminated: although there is mention of *fraud detection*, the paragraph does not introduce *general methods* of fraud detection. Choice (D) can be eliminated because the idea is not *questioned* later in the passage, but expanded upon. The correct answer is (A).

13.  **A**  This question asks what the word *fair* means in line 10. Go back to the text, find the word *fair*, and cross it out. Carefully read the surrounding text to determine another word that would fit in the blank based on the context of the passage. The text says that there is a *fair amount of research* dedicated to understanding how liars lie. The text continues with a mention of the results of some of these studies. The missing word must mean something like "enough" or "plenty." Eliminate any answer choices that aren't consistent with that prediction. Choice (A), *ample*, is consistent with "plenty," so keep it. Choice (B), *lawful*, can be eliminated because there is no mention in the text about the legality of the evidence. Choice (C) can be eliminated because the amount of research is not compared to anything else, so it can't be *equal*. Choice (D) can be eliminated because the text focuses on the amount of research, not the quality of the research or whether the outcomes were positive or negative. The correct answer is (A).

14.  **C**  This question asks what the word *obscure* means in line 40. Go back to the text, find the word *obscure*, and cross it out. Carefully read the surrounding text to determine another word that would fit in the blank based on the context of the passage. The passage says that scientists who don't want to get caught *committing a misconduct* may *obscure parts of the paper*. The text also says that these same fraudsters may *muddle the truth*. Therefore, the missing word must mean something like "muddle" or "confuse." Eliminate anything that isn't consistent with this prediction. Choice (A) might initially look good because the scientists would want to *hide* the fact that they are lying. However, *hide* does not mean "muddle" or "confuse," and the scientists aren't actually hiding parts of their papers. Eliminate (A). Choice (B), *blind*, can be eliminated because the scientists are trying to make parts of their papers "confusing," not *blind[ing]*. Choice (C), *distort*, is consistent with "muddle" or "confuse," so keep it. Choice (D), *characterize*, is not consistent with the predictions at all. Eliminate (D). The correct answer is (C).

15.  **B**  This question asks how papers with fraudulent data can be spotted. Notice that this is the first question in a paired set, so it can be done in tandem with Q16. Begin with the answers to Q16 first. The lines for (16A) say that the [rating] was done through *summary score of causal terms, abstract language, jargon, positive emotion terms and…an ease of reading score.* These lines explain how the obfuscation index was determined, but there are no specifics about how to spot the papers that are fraudulent. These lines do not support any of the answers for Q15, so eliminate (16A). The lines for (16B) say that *fraudulent retracted papers scored significantly higher on the obfuscation index.* These lines indicate that a fraudulent paper will have a higher obfuscation index, which would mean more *abstract language and jargon.* These lines could support (15B), so draw a line connecting those two answers. The lines for (16C) say that a *fraudulent author* may use *fewer positive emotion terms.* While this could be a way to spot a fraudulent paper, these lines do not support any of the answer choices for Q15. Eliminate (16C). The lines for (16D) talk about a *computerized system* that might be able to *flag a submitted paper.* These lines don't give any specifics about how to spot the paper, so these lines don't support any of the answers for Q15. Eliminate (16D). Without support from Q16, eliminate (15A), (15C), and (15D). The correct answers are (15B) and (16B).

16.  **B**  (See explanation above.)

17.  **D**  This question asks which hypothetical situation Hancock would most likely agree could be a consequence of action without further research. Notice that this is the first question in a paired set. Although *Hancock* could be a good lead word, the whole passage is about his experiment, so his ideas are not in once place. Do this question in tandem with Q18. Begin with the answer choices for Q18. The lines for (18A) refer to avoiding getting caught publishing fraudulent data by *obscur[ing] parts of the paper.* These lines don't support any of the answers for Q17, so eliminate (18A). The lines for (18B) talk about the *publish or perish* mentality that motivates researchers to publish manipulated or fake findings. These lines do not support any of the answers for Q17, so eliminate (18B). The lines for (18C) warn of the *false-positive rate* of the computerized fraud-detection system. These lines might seem to connect to (17A) because both mention *computer programs,* but there is no connection between the ideas or to the question. Eliminate (18C). The lines for (18D) refer back to the *high error rate,* and also say that *science is based on trust* and if a publication introduces a *fraud detection tool,* it might *undermine that trust.* These lines support (17D), so draw a line connecting those two answers. Without support from Q18, (17A), (17B), and (17C) can all be eliminated. The correct answers are (17D) and (18D).

18.  **D**  (See explanation above.)

19.  **A**  This question asks which category of language had the greatest difference between *language used in fraudulent and genuine research,* according to the graph. The difference between the two in Means and Methods is a little over 200, so keep (A) for now. The difference between them in Amplifiers is less than 100, so eliminate (B). Quantities has a difference of about 125,

so eliminate (C). Emotional States has a difference of about 75, so eliminate (D). The correct answer is (A).

20.  **B**  This question asks which of the statements is supported by the graph. Go through each of the answer choices and eliminate anything not supported by the graph. Eliminate (A) because *Quantities* is higher in Genuine Publications rather than Fraudulent ones. Keep (B) because the bars for *Means and Methods* and *Certainty* are about the same for Fraudulent publications. Eliminate (C) because the Genuine publications have higher occurrences of *Negations* than the Fraudulent publications. Eliminate (D) because there is no consistency for *Amplifiers* and *Diminishers*. The correct answer is (B).

21.  **C**  This question asks which statement supports the idea that *jargon* could be classified as *means and methods*, using both the graph and the passage. Carefully read each answer choice and eliminate any that do not address the connection between *jargon* and *means and methods*. Choice (A) can be eliminated because it is only a general statement that scientists who falsify data have certain writing patterns they use. There is no specific connection to *jargon* or the graph. Choice (B) mentions a specific characteristic of the writing of liars in general, but there is no connection to the study discussed in the passage. Eliminate (B). Choice (C) says that the *fraudulent papers* had *60 more jargon-like words per paper*. The graph shows that fraudulent papers contain more *Means and Methods* language than genuine papers, so that could support the idea in question. Keep (C). Choice (D) simply says that *more research is needed*, with no specifics about types of language or types of papers. Eliminate (D). The correct answer is (C).

22.  **B**  This question asks about a main idea of the passage. Because this is a general question, it should be done after the specific questions have been completed. The passage begins with an introduction of a new, blue pigment, a *serendipitous discovery* made while *researching materials for electronics applications*. The passage then goes on to describe how the pigment was discovered, what makes the pigment particularly notable, and ends with a discussion of further discoveries that have resulted from the discovery of this pigment. Eliminate any answers that are inconsistent with the ideas in the passage. Choice (A) can be eliminated because there is no discussion of how the pigment is *dangerous*. Choice (B) is consistent with the idea of a *serendipitous discovery* of a *superior* new pigment. Choice (C) is consistent with the passage naming the new pigment by its chemical composition, but that is not the *main idea* of the passage, nor is there mention of the chemical composition being the *most effective* way to describe a pigment. Eliminate (C). Choice (D) can be eliminated because it is too narrow: The relationship between *UV absorbance* and *pigment stability* is mentioned in the passage, but it is not the *main idea*. The correct answer is (B).

23.  **A**  This question asks about the *overall structure of the passage*. Because this is a general question, it should be done after the specific questions have been completed. The passage begins with an introduction of a new pigment, goes on to describe how the pigment was discovered and what makes the pigment particularly notable, and then ends with a discussion of further discoveries

that have resulted from the discovery of this pigment. Eliminate any answer choices that aren't consistent with this prediction. Choice (A) is similar to the prediction, so keep it. Choice (B) can be eliminated because the focus of the passage is the new, synthetic pigment. There is no *natural alternative* presented. Choice (C) can also be eliminated because only one accidental discovery is mentioned, rather than *several accidental discoveries*. Choice (D) can be eliminated because there is no discussion about how compounds *work together* in the passage. The correct answer is (A).

24.   **C**   This question asks what the word *applications* means in lines line 5. Go back to the text, find the word *applications*, and cross it out. Carefully read the surrounding text to determine another word that would fit in the blank based on the context of the passage. The text says that a scientist discovered the pigment while *researching materials for electronics applications*. It goes on to say that the researchers were trying to create a *high-efficiency electronic material*. The missing word must mean something like "functions" or "materials." Eliminate (A), *requests*, because it does not mean "functions." Choice (B), *forms*, can also be eliminated because it is not consistent with the prediction. Choice (C), *uses*, is consistent, so keep it. Choice (D), *industries*, might initially look attractive, but the text says that they were trying to develop *material* rather than "businesses." Eliminate (D). The correct answer is (C).

25.   **B**   This question asks for the best evidence that Smith did not intend for his experiment to produce the results it did. Carefully read each of the lines provided and eliminate any that do not answer the question. Choice (A) can be eliminated because the lines simply describe the pigment, not an experiment or results. Choice (B) answers the question, saying that *instead of… high-efficiency material, what emerged…was a brilliant blue compound*. Keep (B). Choice (C) can be eliminated because the patent process is not related to the discovery process. Choice (D) can also be eliminated because those lines indicate the researchers are continuing to research the accidental discovery, hoping to find additional new pigments. The correct answer is (B).

26.   **A**   This question asks what the word *unstable* means in line 21. Go back to the text, find the word *unstable*, and cross it out. Carefully read the surrounding text to determine another word that would fit in the blank based on the context of the passage. The text describes blue pigments as *notoriously unstable* and then goes on to say that they *fade easily*. The missing word must mean something like "fades easily" or "doesn't last." Eliminate any answer choices that are inconsistent with this prediction. Choice (A), *impermanent*, means "doesn't last." Keep (A). Choice (B) can be eliminated because the pigments are not *threatening*. Choice (C) can be eliminated because *careless* does not mean the same thing as "doesn't last." Choice (D) might initially look attractive because the passage does mention *ancient times*, but *antiquated* does not mean "doesn't last." Eliminate (D). The correct answer is (A).

27.   **C**   This question asks which factor has been identified as *most indicative of stable pigments*. In lines 22–25, the author says that the fact that *this pigment was synthesized at such high temperatures*

signaled to researchers that *this new compound was extremely stable.* Therefore, synthesis at high temperatures indicates a stable compound. The correct answer is (C).

28. **D** This question asks about the relationship between the *YInMn Blue pigment and the Cobalt Blue pigment currently used.* The fifth paragraph, lines 33–37, discusses the relationship between the two pigments. The paragraph says that $YIn_{1-x}Mn_xO_3$ *exhibits high absorbance in the UV region and high reflectivity in the near-infrared region when compared to currently-used Cobalt Blue pigments.* Therefore, Cobalt Blue has *lower UV absorbency* and *lower reflectivity in the near-infrared region.* Eliminate any answer choices that aren't consistent with this prediction. Eliminate (A): although the text mentions *outdoor weathering,* YInMn is superior to Cobalt Blue for exterior applications. Choice (B) can be eliminated because, although *YInMn* can be *chemically-adjusted,* it was not *specifically engineered* to be so. Choice (C) can be eliminated because there is no discussion of the comparative difficulty of engineering purple, YInMn, or Cobalt Blue. Choice (D) is consistent with the prediction. The correct answer is (D).

29. **B** This is the best evidence for a specific question, so simply look at the lines used to answer Q28: $YIn_{1-x}Mn_xO_3$ *exhibits high absorbance in the UV region and high reflectivity in the near-infrared region when compared to currently-used Cobalt Blue pigments.* This statement is in lines 34–37. Although (C) mentions *increased UV absorbance,* there is no mention of *infrared reflectivity,* so (C) is not the best evidence to support Q28. The correct answer is (B).

30. **B** This question asks at which wavelength $CoAl_2O_4$ has a reflectance of 0.4%. Go to Figure 2 and find the reflectance of 0.4. Draw a line across the graph and see which wavelengths correspond to that reflectance. There are several places where $CoAl_2O_4$ has a reflectance of 0.4%, but the only one that is an answer choice is 1800 nm. The correct answer is (B).

31. **D** This question asks which range of wavelengths illustrates the thermal advantages of YInMn Blue over Cobalt Blue based on both the graph and the passage. The passage says that *high solar reflectance [of YInMn Blue] indicates that this 'cool pigment' can find use in a variety of exterior applications by reducing surface temperatures, cooling costs, and energy consumption.* Eliminate any answer choices that aren't consistent with this prediction. Choices (A), (B), and (C) all offer wavelength ranges in which the reflectance for YInMn Blue and Cobalt Blue are similar. This would not give YInMn Blue any thermal advantages, so eliminate all three. Choice (D), 1200–1400, gives a range in which the reflectance of YInMn Blue is much higher than Cobalt Blue, which, according to the passage, would give YInMn Blue an advantage. The correct answer is (D).

32. **B** This question asks what the word *present* means in line 3. Go back to the text, find the word *present,* and cross it out. Carefully read the surrounding text to determine another word that would fit in the blank based on the context of the passage. The author says that he is trying to be clear about the *disordered condition of…currency and the present dangers,* while also trying to *suggest a way which leads to a safer financial system.* He is contrasting the current situation with what he hopes will be a better situation in the future. The missing word must mean something

like "at this moment" or "at this time." Eliminate any answers that aren't consistent with that prediction. Choice (A), *prompt*, means that something happens right away, but not necessarily "at this time." Eliminate (A). Eliminate (C) for the same reason. Choice (B), *current*, is consistent with "at this time," so keep (B). Choice (D) can be eliminated because *present* and *gifted* might seem similar, but *gifted* does not mean "at this time." The correct answer is (B).

33. **B**  This question asks what Passage 1 suggests about those who support implementing the bimetallic system of currency. Notice that this is the first question in a paired set, so it can be done in tandem with Q34. Read the lines for Q34 first. The lines for (34A) say that *many countrymen…insist that the cure for the ills* is *the free coinage of silver*. These lines support (33B), so draw a line connecting those two answers. The lines for (34B) say that those who support the bimetallic system think *mints shall be…thrown open to the free, unlimited, and independent coinage of both gold and silver*. These lines don't support any of the answers to Q33, so eliminate (34B). The lines for (34C) say that those who believe *independent coinage…would restore the parity between the metals…oppose an unsupported and improbable theory*. While these lines do describe those who support the bimetallic system, these lines don't support any of the answers for Q33. Eliminate (34C). The lines for (34D) say that the ideas *run counter to our own actual experiences*. These lines give the author's feelings about the system, but not about those who support the system. The lines don't support any of the answers for Q33, so eliminate (34D). Without support from Q34, (33A), (33C), and (33D) can be eliminated. The correct answers are (33B) and (34A).

34. **A**  (See explanation above.)

35. **A**  This question asks why Cleveland refers to Acts of Congress, which is in line 50. Go back to the text and carefully read the window to determine why he mentions them. The line says that the Acts of Congress were *impotent to create equality where natural causes decreed even a slight inequality*. The correct answer must have something to do with the idea that the Acts of Congress could not create equality when outside forces set up an inequality. Choice (A) is a direct paraphrase of this prediction, so keep it. Choice (B) can be eliminated, because Cleveland mentions the acts to show a contrast, not to *summarize* anything. Choice (C) can be eliminated because the acts would not be a viable *alternative* if they are *impotent to create equality*. Choice (D) can be eliminated for the same reason as (C). The correct answer is (A).

36. **C**  This question asks what the word *idle* means in line 66. Go back to the text, find the word *idle*, and cross it out. Carefully read the surrounding text to determine another word that would fit in the blank based on the context of the passage. The text contrasts the *idle holders of idle capital* with the *struggling masses who produce the wealth and pay the taxes*. Therefore, the missing word must mean something like "not working" or "not producing anything." Eliminate any answer choices that aren't consistent with that prediction. Choice (A) can be eliminated, because the holders of the capital have not *abandoned* anything. Choice (B) might initially make sense, because those who hold a great deal of money are likely to be *ambitious*, but *ambitious*

does not mean "not producing anything." Eliminate (B). Choice (C), *inactive*, is consistent with "not working." Keep (C). Choice (D), *cheap*, is not consistent with the prediction, so it can be eliminated. The correct answer is (C).

37.  **B**  This question asks which claim Bryan would most likely agree with about the gold standard controversy. Notice that this is the first question in a paired set, so it can be done in tandem with Q38. Begin with the answers to Q38 first. The lines for (38A) say that if the gold standard is the standard of civilization, *should we not have it?* Those lines could support (37A), so draw a line connecting those two answers. The lines for (38B) say that a person could *search the pages of history in vain to find a single instance in which the common people…declared themselves in favor of a gold standard.* Those lines support (37B), so draw a line connecting those two answer choices. The lines for (38C) say that *the sympathies of the Democratic Party…are on the side of the struggling masses.* These lines don't mention anything about Bryan's views about the gold standard controversy, and these lines don't support any of the answer choices for Q37. Eliminate (38C). The lines for (38D) say what others believe about legislation to make the *well-to-do prosperous*, but there is no mention of Bryan's thoughts about the gold standard controversy. Eliminate (38D). Go back to the remaining pairs of answer choices and reread the question. The question asks which statement *Bryan would be most likely to agree with.* Choices (37A) and (38A) present an idea that Bryan refutes later in the passage, so eliminate those two answer choices. The correct answers are (37B) and (38B).

38.  **B**  (See explanation above.)

39.  **D**  This question asks how both passages discuss the issue of the gold standard. Because this question asks about both passages, it should be done after the questions are done for each individual passage. Use POE to go through the answers one passage at time. Passage 1 mentions *Acts of Congress* in line 50, *economists* in line 35, and *other nations* in line 34. Because Passage 1 does not mention *the Democratic Party*, eliminate (B). Now look for the remaining three answers in Passage 2. Passage 2 does not mention *Congress* or *economists*, so eliminate (A) and (B). Passage 2 mentions *all nations of the earth* in line 54. The correct answer is (D).

40.  **A**  This question asks how the two historical references mentioned help each speaker. The reference in Passage 1 says that *twice in our earlier history* and the Passage 2 reference says that someone *said in 1878 that this was a struggle.* Both of these references show this debate occurring in the past, which allows both speakers to say something to the effect of, "We've been talking about this for a while now." Eliminate any answer choice that is not consistent with this prediction. Choice (A) is a direct paraphrase of the prediction, so keep it. Choice (B) can be eliminated because there is no *established precedent*, just an idea that's been discussed previously. Choices (C) and (D) can be eliminated because the lines neither *challenge* nor *question* any of the ideas in the debate. The correct answer is (A).

41.  **B**  This question asks about a *central tension* between the passages. Because this is a general question about both passages, it should be done after all the other questions have been completed.

Use POE to go through the answers one passage at a time. Choice (A) can be eliminated because Cleveland is not advocating for *new legislation to enact the gold standard*. He is against the gold standard and says that *Acts of Congress were impotent to create equality* when the market said otherwise. Choice (B) looks good for Passage 1, because Cleveland is *questioning* the validity of the *free coinage bimetallic* proposal, so keep (B) for now. Choice (C) can be eliminated because Cleveland does not *demand gold standard proponents reconsider their position*. Choice (D) can be eliminated, because Cleveland never *presents studies*. The correct answer is (B).

42. **B** This question asks about the primary purpose of this passage. Because this is a general question, it should be done after the specific questions are complete. The passage begins with introducing the discovery of *a parasitic fungus* that manipulates *the behavior of ants*. The passage goes on to describe the research and the fungus. The primary purpose of the passage is to explain a new discovery. Eliminate any answers that aren't consistent with this prediction. Choice (A) can be eliminated because the passage was not written to *correct* any *misconception*. The first part of (B), *present the findings*, is consistent with the prediction, and the second part of the answer choice is supported by the final sentence of the passage (*The research also is... the first extensive study of zombie ants in North America*). Choice (C) can be eliminated because a new fungus has been discovered, not a new ant. Choice (D) can be eliminated because the passage is not explaining differences between types of relationships. The correct answer is (B).

43. **B** This question asks why fungi have evolved to control the behavior of the ants. Go back to the text and find the window in which the author discusses how the fungi works. In the second paragraph, the author says that the fungus species that infects ants *induces hosts to die attached by their mandibles to plant material*. The author goes on to say that the dead ant attached to the plant provides *a platform from which the fungus can grow and shoot spores to infect other ants*. Find an answer that is consistent with this information. Choice (A) can be eliminated because the fungus spreads through spores, not through bite wounds. Choice (B) is consistent with the information in the text, so keep it. Choice (C) can be eliminated because the text says the fungus wants the ant to die attached to a plant. Choice (D) can be eliminated because it is the opposite of what the text says. The correct answer is (B).

44. **D** This question asks about the role of the *Formica* ant in the passage. Use the lead word to find the window and read carefully to determine why the author mentioned the *Formica* ant. In line 37, the author mentions the *Formica* ant as *another genus* of ant not normally targeted by the fungus. Researchers infected the *Formica* ants as well as ants from the *Camponotus* genus, the genus typically targeted by the fungus. Eliminate any answer choices that aren't consistent with the prediction. Choice (A) can be eliminated because the scientists already know that the *Formica* ants are *nontarget ants*. Choice (B) can be eliminated for the same reason as (A): *Formica* ants aren't *most affected* because they are *nontarget ants*. Choice (C) can be eliminated because it doesn't address the role of the ant in the research. Choice (D) is consistent with the prediction. The correct answer is (D).

45. **D** This question asks what tone the author communicates with the use of phrases such as *exquisite control…, most complex examples…,* and *impressive trick.* Use the lines provided to find the window, and read carefully for context. The phrases come from a quote from one of the researchers talking about how evolved the fungus is. The use of the words *exquisite* and *impressive* gives a positive tone, so eliminate (B) and (C). There is no evidence that the researcher is *amused* by the fungus, but he is impressed. Eliminate (A). The correct answer is (D).

46. **D** This question asks about a scenario in which zombie ant fungi would not successfully reproduce. Carefully read the second paragraph, in which the fungus reproduction is explained. The fungus infects *Camponotus* ants and *induces [them] to die attached by their mandibles to plant material.* The dead ant, attached to the plant, provides *a platform from which the fungus can grow and shoot spores to infect other ants.* Remember, because this is a *NOT* question, cross out the *NOT* and mark each answer choice as "true" or "false." Choice (A) is true. Although the fungus cannot control the *Formica* ant, it can infect and kill it. Keep (A). Choice (B) is true, so keep it. Choice (C) is true, so keep it. Choice (D) is false. A *Formica* ant that doesn't die on a plant will not provide any sort of platform for the fungus to grow from. The correct answer is (D).

47. **B** This question asks what the word *media* means in line 43. Go back to the text, find the word *media,* and cross it out. Carefully read the surrounding text to determine another word that would fit in the blank based on the context of the passage. The text describes the experiment and how the researchers *removed ant brains* and then kept them *alive in special media.* The missing word must mean something like "material" or "substance." Eliminate anything that is not consistent with this prediction. Choice (A), *communications,* might initially seem to be consistent with the word *media,* but it does not mean "substance" or "material." Eliminate (A). Choice (B) is consistent with the prediction, so keep it. Choice (C), *channels,* and (D), *periodicals,* may also be tempting because of the connection with *media,* but neither of those words is consistent with the prediction. The correct answer is (B).

48. **A** This question asks which part of the research was *most effective for obtaining an unprecedented amount of information.* The text says that the *researchers found thousands of unique chemicals, most of them completely unknown.* That is the *unprecedented information,* but remember that the question is asking about the *part of the research* that allowed them to obtain that information. Carefully read the window. The researchers were able to find out this information by growing the fungus *in the presence of brains from different ant species to determine what chemicals it produced for each brain.* Eliminate any answer choice that is not consistent with this prediction. Choice (A) is an exact paraphrase of the prediction, so keep it. Choice (B) was a part of the process, but not the one that allowed them to obtain all the information. Eliminate it. Choice (C), as with (B), was a part of the research, but not the key piece. Eliminate (C). Choice (D) might initially look attractive, but the scientists weren't actually looking at the fungus *in the ant brains.* Eliminate (D). The correct answer is (A).

49. **B** This is the best evidence question for a specific question, so simply look at the lines used to answer Q48. Remember, although (C) might look attractive, the question asks about the *part of the research* that allowed them to *obtain unprecedented information*, not the information itself. The correct answer is (B).

50. **C** This question asks about a unique outcome of the chemicals produced by the fungus. Notice that this is the first question in a paired set, so it can be done in tandem with Q51. Consider the answer for Q51 first. The lines for (51A) introduce the fungus, but don't mention anything about the chemicals the fungus produces. Eliminate (51A). The lines for (51B) say that the killer *can infect and kill nontarget ants* but cannot *manipulate their behavior*. These lines do not support any of the answers for Q50. Eliminate (51B). The lines for (51C) say *the fungus behaved differently in the presence of the ant brain it had co-evolved with*. These lines could look attractive on their own, but they do not support any of the answers for Q50. Eliminate (51C). The lines for (51D) say that the fungus/ant relationship is *one of the most complex examples of parasites controlling animal behavior*. These lines support the idea in (50C) that the complexity of this relationship is different than those *usually found in nature*. Draw a line connecting those two answers. Without support from Q51, (50A), (50B), and (50D) can be eliminated. The correct answers are (50C) and (51D).

51. **D** (See explanation above.)

52. **D** This question asks what type of evidence the team mostly used while studying the zombie ants. Most of their work took place in the lab, so eliminate (A). Choice (B) can also be eliminated because researchers were making observations rather than *predictions*. Choice (C) might initially look attractive, but the researchers were using the brains of *ants* in their research. Choice (D) is consistent with information in the passage. The correct answer is (D).

## Section 2: Writing and Language

1. **C** The vocabulary is changing in the answer choices, so this question is testing word choice. Look for a word whose definition is consistent with the other ideas in the passage. The sentence discusses the *presence of blue recycling bins*, and the next sentence says that *most people are used to separating recyclable materials*. The underlined portion is preceded by *no longer*, so the definition should mean "out of the ordinary." An *innovation* is "a new way of doing something." While this is close, it is not the bins themselves that were an innovation, so eliminate (A). A *deviation* is "a departure from the norm." While this is close, the bins were not "going against the system," so eliminate (B). A *novelty* is "something new and unusual." The presence of the bins is now a normal, everyday sight, so keep (C). A *miracle* is "an extraordinary event," so eliminate (D). The correct answer is (C).

2. **D** The vocabulary is changing in the answer choices, so this question is testing word choice. All of the choices have similar meanings, so choose the answer whose tone best matches the passage.

Choices (A), (B), and (C) are too informal, so eliminate them. The correct answer is (D).

3.  **D**   The punctuation is changing in the answer choices, so the question is testing STOP and GO punctuation. However, notice that the sentence ends with a closed parenthesis. Therefore, the phrase must start with an open parenthesis; eliminate (B) and (C). There is no reason to use a dash to separate an idea already separated by parentheses, so eliminate (A). The correct answer is (D).

4.  **A**   Note the question! The question asks for information that is *consistent with the description of textiles*. *Clothing* is a type of textile, so keep (A). *Paper, rubber,* and *wood* are not textiles, so eliminate (B), (C), and (D). The correct answer is (A).

5.  **B**   Note the question! The question asks for information that is supported by the graph. The sentence is comparing the recycling rate of clothing to that of the other items in the graph. First, look up clothing on the graph and find that its rate is about 15%. Then look up each choice to see whether it's true, keeping in mind that the underlined part follows the word *only*. The rate for rubber and leather is about 16%, which is higher than that of clothing, but many other materials are also recycled at higher rates than clothing. Since rubber and leather aren't the only ones with higher rates, eliminate (A). The rate for plastic is 5% and wood is 9%, which is lower than that of clothing, so keep (B). The rate for yard trimmings is 53%, which is higher than that of clothing. Again, it is not the only higher rate, so eliminate (C). The rate for glass is 30%, which is another rate higher than that of clothing, so eliminate (D). It is true that *only* plastics and wood are lower. The correct answer is (B).

6.  **C**   The conjunction is changing in the answer choices, so the question is testing consistency of ideas. Determine how the ideas before and after the conjunction relate to each other and select the appropriate transition. The sentence begins with *Not only*, which should be followed by *but also*. The correct answer is (C).

7.  **A**   The transitional phrase is changing in the answer choices, so the question is testing consistency of ideas. Determine how the ideas before and after the transitional phrase relate to each other and select the appropriate transition. The previous sentence says that *re-using clothing can also save resources*. The next sentence says that *buying a pair of jeans second-hand saves that water*. The second sentence is similar in idea to the first, so eliminate (B) and (C) because they indicate a change of idea. *Moreover,* indicates a new idea that is similar to the first, but the second sentence is a specific example of the general idea in the first sentence; eliminate (D). The correct answer is (A).

8.  **D**   First, commas are changing in the answer choices, so the question is testing the four ways to use a comma. The sentence does not contain a list, and the phrase *clothing waste by offering 15% off coupons to consumers who bring unwanted clothing* is a necessary part of the sentence. Therefore, there is no reason to use a comma; eliminate (A) and (C). Next, the vocabulary is changing, so the question is testing word choice. The meaning of the sentence is that *H&M*

*is trying to* "reduce" *clothing waste. Rain* means "water that falls from clouds," so eliminate (B). *Rein* means to "control." The correct answer is (D).

9. **B** Note the question! The question asks for the most effective transition from the previous paragraph. Determine the subject of each paragraph to determine how they should be linked. The previous paragraph discusses H&M's desire to reduce clothing waste and the beginning of its plan to collect and recycle unwanted clothing. The next paragraph discusses the specific steps taken to recycle the clothing. The correct answer will connect these two ideas. Introducing *other retailers* does not connect the ideas, so eliminate (A). Introducing the *several steps* of recycling does connect the ideas, so keep (B). Introducing *low-quality fast fashion* does not connect the ideas, so eliminate (C). Introducing *a bigger discount* does not connect the ideas, so eliminate (D). The correct answer is (B).

10. **B** The phrases are changing in the answer choices, so the question is testing consistency and precision. Notice that the sentence contains a list. Therefore, all of the items in the list should be in a consistent format. The first part of the list says that items are *shredded*; the third part of the list says the items are *recycled*. Therefore, the underlined portion must be consistent in this verb phrasing. Choice (B), *repurposed*, is consistent with *shredded* and *recycled*. No other choice starts with the consistent verb phrasing. The correct answer is (B).

11. **B** Verbs are changing in the answer choices, so the question is testing consistency of verbs. A verb must be consistent with its subject and with the other verbs in the sentence. The subject of the verb is *the technology*, which is singular. To be consistent, the verb in the answer choices must also be singular. Eliminate (A), (C), and (D) because they are plural. The correct answer is (B).

12. **D** Apostrophes are changing in the answer choices, so the question is testing apostrophe usage. In this sentence, the pronoun refers to *people*, who possess the *loved one*. Therefore, the apostrophe is not needed because possessive pronouns do not use apostrophes. Eliminate (B) and (C). Next, pronouns are changing in the choices, so the question is testing consistency of pronouns. A pronoun must be consistent in number with the noun it is replacing. Since *people* is plural, the pronoun must also be plural. Eliminate (A). The correct answer is (D).

13. **C** Note the question! The question asks for the choice that combines the sentences, so it's testing precision and concision. Select the choice that keeps the intended meaning of the sentences using the fewest words. Consider (C) first because it's the shortest. The choice ends with *ofrendas*, and then a comma, and then the non-underlined portion is a modifier that describes the *ofrendas*. This creates a sentence that is both precise and concise. The correct answer is (C).

14. **A** Commas are changing in the answer choices, so the question is testing the four ways to use a comma. The sentence does not contain a list, so check for unnecessary information. Read the sentence with the phrases between the commas removed to see if the sentence retains the same meaning without it. In this case, all of the phrases are necessary, so there's no need for com-

mas. Eliminate (B) and (C). The long dash cannot be followed by *and*, so eliminate (D). The correct answer is (A).

15. **B** Note the question! The question asks for the explanation of the Aztec tradition, so it's testing consistency of ideas. The first part of the sentence says that *the dead would be offended by mourning*. The correct answer must be consistent with a "tradition" that would not offend the dead. Eliminate (A) because it describes an emotion (*sad*) but not a tradition. Keep (B) because it describes a tradition of *celebration rather than sadness*. Eliminate (C) and (D) because neither describes a tradition. The correct answer is (B).

16. **A** The phrases are changing in the answer choices, so the question is testing consistency and precision. The sentence uses the phrase *similar to*, so it's comparing two things. The "thing" in the underlined portion must be consistent with the "thing" in the non-underlined portion. The sentence says that *ofrendas ... have items*. Thus, the correct answer must reference the "items" on *church altars*. The pronoun *those* could refer to the *items*, so keep (A). Choices (B) and (C) only mention the *altars* and not the *items* on the altars, so eliminate them both. Eliminate (D) because it mentions the *structures* and not the *items*. The correct answer is (A).

17. **A** Note the question! The question asks where sentence 3 should be placed, so it's testing consistency. Determine the subject matter of the sentence, and find the other sentence that also discusses that information. Sentence 3 says *During these two days*, so it should be placed after a sentence that references two days. Sentence 2 discusses *November 1–2*, so sentence 3 should be placed after sentence 2. The correct answer is (A).

18. **C** The pronouns are changing in the answer choices, so the question is testing consistency. The pronoun must be consistent with the noun it is referring to. The phrase *are best known for their elaborate ofrendas* refers to the *local artists*, so the pronoun should also refer to the artists. Eliminate (A) because *which* refers to things, and not people. Eliminate (B) because it creates two complete ideas which are separated by a comma; STOP punctuation is needed. Keep (C) because *whom* refers to people. Although *them* can refer to people, (D) also creates two complete ideas separated by a comma. Eliminate (D). The correct answer is (C).

19. **D** Note the question! The question asks for information that is most consistent in style and content with the information about why pillows and blankets are included on the altars, so it's testing consistency of ideas. The sentence includes the phrase *pillows and blankets (which provide a resting spot for the spirits)*, which describes their function or use. *Smells delicious* describes a characteristic but not a function, so eliminate (A). *Pan de muerto* is an example but not a function, so eliminate (B). *Homemade* describes a characteristic but not a function, so eliminate (C). *Provide sustenance* describes a function, so keep (D). The correct answer is (D).

20. **B** Note the question! The question asks for the choice that best concludes the paragraph, so it's testing consistency of ideas. The first sentence of the paragraph says that the celebration of the dead is *similar to preparing for a visit from living relatives*. The remaining sentences discuss the

many items placed on the altars. Therefore, a concluding sentence should be consistent with each of those ideas. Claiming that it is *more work* would highlight how the situations are different, not similar; since it's not consistent, eliminate (A). Mentioning both what is *included on an altar* and the similarity to *when they were alive* is consistent, so keep (B). The *toys* is consistent with the items on the altars but does not conclude the paragraph by discussing the similarities for *preparing for a visit from living relatives*; eliminate (C). Eliminate (D) for the same reason as (C). The correct answer is (B).

21. **A** The phrases are changing in the answer choices, so the question is testing precision and concision. Select the shortest answer whose meaning is clear. Keep (A) because it does not contain any words after marigolds, so it is probably correct. The first sentence already states that *Many of the same items that decorate altars are also part of the cemetery vigils*, so there's no need to repeat that idea. Eliminate (B) and (C) because they are redundant. The phrase *that attract spirits with their bright colors* does not play a precise role in the sentence, so eliminate (D). The correct answer is (A).

22. **D** The phrases are changing in the answer choices, so the question is testing precision. The beginning of the sentence (*focusing on the finality of death*) is a modifying phrase that does not have a subject. Therefore, the subject must be placed immediately after the comma. In (A) and (C), it is the *merriment* that is *focusing on the finality of death*; this is not the correct meaning, so eliminate (A) and (C). In (B), it is *life* that is *focusing on the finality of death*; this is not the correct meaning, so eliminate (B). In (D), it is *the people* who are *focusing on the finality of death*. This is the precise intended meaning. The correct answer is (D).

23. **A** The transitional phrase is changing in the answer choices, so the question is testing consistency of ideas. Determine how the ideas before and after the transitional phrase relate to each other and select the appropriate transition. The previous sentence states that the *predictions that the machines would replace human bank tellers...did not immediately come true*. The next sentence states that *the number of human bank tellers also increased*. The second idea supports the first with evidence. *In fact* indicates support, so keep (A). *As a result* indicates an effect of a previous cause, so eliminate (B). *For example* is close, but the second sentence is not a specific example but rather general evidence; eliminate (C). *Therefore* indicates causality, so eliminate (D). The correct answer is (A).

24. **D** The punctuation is changing in the answer choices, so the question is testing punctuation. After reading the sentence, it should be clear that the sentence contains a list. The non-underlined portion of the list is separated by a comma: *provide specific bill denominations, and dispense information*. Therefore, all the items in the list must be separated by commas. Eliminate (A), (B), and (C) because they contain semicolons. The correct answer is (D).

25. **C** The vocabulary is changing in the answer choices, so the question is testing word choice. The sentence intends to say that *machines* are "more accurate" *with cash than people are*. The meaning of *rock solid* is unclear and the phrase is too informal for the passage, so eliminate (A).

*Impeccable* means "without blame or fault," so eliminate (B). *Reliable* means "accurate," so keep (C). *Safer* means "protected" or "more secure," so eliminate (D). The correct answer is (C).

26. **D** Note the question! The question asks whether the graph should be added, so it's testing consistency of ideas. The graph should be added only if the information in the graph is consistent with the information in the passage. The passage compares and contrasts the services provided by human tellers and ATMs. The graph shows the income for different groups of people. The information is not consistent, so the graph should not be added; eliminate (A) and (B). The passage does not contrast *tellers and loan officers*, so eliminate (C). The wage data does *distract from the paragraph's focus*. The correct answer is (D).

27. **D** Note the question! The question asks where sentence 3 should be placed, so it's testing consistency. Determine the subject matter of the sentence, and find the other sentence that also discusses that information. Sentence 3 says that *They also limit the amount of cash...*, which lists another downside of ATMs. Thus, sentence 3 should follow another sentence about the downside of ATMs. Sentence 5 gives a downside when it states *ATMs are far more vulnerable to theft*. The correct answer is (D).

28. **C** The vocabulary is changing in the answer choices, so the question is testing word choice. The sentence intends to say that *tech-savvy customers are increasingly* "familiar with" *their smart phones. Custom* means "personalized," so eliminate (A) and (D). *Accustomed* means "familiar with" or "used to," so keep (B) and (C). The proper idiom is *accustomed to*. The correct answer is (C).

29. **B** Note the question! The question asks for a supporting example for the main idea of the paragraph, so it's testing consistency of ideas. The paragraph as a whole compares and contrasts human tellers, ATMs, and mobile apps. The previous sentence contrasts mobile apps with ATMs by claiming that the apps are better at some tasks, so the underlined portion must be consistent with that idea. The percentage of people using the app is not consistent, so eliminate (A). Comparing the mobile apps to what *ATMs are capable of* is consistent, so keep (B). Stating that mobile apps are *not always designed well* and stating that they are *highly susceptible to theft or fraud* is not consistent with the apps outperforming ATMs, so eliminate (C) and (D). The correct answer is (B).

30. **A** Note the question! The question asks for the most effective combination of the two sentences, so it's testing precision and concision. Select the shortest answer that keeps the intended meaning of the sentence. Choice (A) is the shortest answer. It keeps the intended meaning of the sentence and uses proper punctuation — the colon is HALF-STOP punctuation which can separate two complete ideas. The correct answer is (A).

31. **D** First, nouns are changing in the answer choices, so the question is testing consistency of nouns. A noun must be consistent in number with the other nouns in the sentence. The sentence contains the noun *teller windows*, which is plural. To be consistent, the noun in the answer choice

must also be plural. Eliminate (A) and (B) because they contain the singular noun *kiosk*. Next, the adjoining phrase is changing, so the question is testing precision of language. The proper idiom is *replacing...with*, so the banks are *replacing* teller windows *with* kiosks. The correct answer is (D).

32.  **B**  First, the transitions are changing in the answer choices, so the question is testing consistency. The sentence states what the employees are *trained* to do: they are *trained to answer questions* and to *handle deposits and provide loan advice*. The phrases *as well as* can join the phrases, so keep (A) and (B). *Also* cannot join the phrases, so eliminate (C). The *comma + and* acts as STOP punctuation. In this case, it would separate a complete idea and an incomplete idea, which is not allowed; eliminate (D). Next, the difference between (A) and (B) is the number of words, so the question is testing concision and precision. Both choices have the same meaning, so select the more concise answer. Eliminate (A). The correct answer is (B).

33.  **A**  The punctuation is changing in the answer choices, so the question is testing STOP and GO punctuation. Use the vertical line test, and identify the ideas as complete or incomplete. Draw the vertical line between the words *out* and *machines*. The first phrase is an incomplete idea, and the second phrase is a complete idea. Therefore, GO punctuation is needed. The semicolon and the period are STOP punctuation, so eliminate (B) and (C). The sentence starts with *So while*, so there is no need to add *nevertheless*. Eliminate (D). The correct answer is (A).

34.  **A**  The transitional phrase is changing in the answer choices, so the question is testing consistency of ideas. Determine how the ideas before and after the transitional phrase relate to each other and select the appropriate transition. The first sentence states that there is *an arms race against bacteria*. Then it says that *Bacteria...develop resistance to antibiotics* and follows with *scientists must continually develop newer, stronger antibiotics*. The second is an effect of the first. *As a result* indicates an effect, so keep (A). *However* and *nevertheless* indicate opposite ideas, so eliminate (B) and (C). Developing new antibiotics is not an *example* of bacterial resistance, so eliminate (D). The correct answer is (A).

35.  **C**  Note the question! The question asks for the scientists' goal, so it's testing consistency of ideas. Earlier in the paragraph it says that *scientists have been engaged in an arms race against bacteria* and that they need to *overcome the resistant bacteria*, so the correct answer must be consistent with "outcompete." *Count the number* is not consistent, so eliminate (A). *Facilitate* means "to help," which is not consistent, so eliminate (B). *Stay ahead of* is consistent, so keep (C). *Shoot at* is too literal of the arms race and is not consistent with "outcompete," so eliminate (D). The correct answer is (C).

36.  **D**  The phrases are changing in the answer choices with the option to DELETE, so the question is testing concision and precision. Consider the option to DELETE carefully, as it is often correct. The sentence already says *extended trips*, so there's no reason to repeat that idea. Choices (A), (B), and (C) are each redundant and unnecessary, so eliminate them. The correct answer is (D).

37. **A** Verbs are changing in the answer choices, so the question is testing consistency of verbs. A verb must be consistent with its subject and with the other verbs in the sentence. The subject of the verb is *pathogens*, which is plural. Therefore, the verbs must also be plural. *Becomes* is singular, so eliminate (C) and (D). Next, check the other verbs in the sentence for consistency. The non-underlined verb *were surprised* is past tense, so the correct answer should also be in the past tense. *Mutated* and *became* are past tense, so keep (A). *Had mutated* and *had become* are the past perfect tense, but the non-underlined verb does not contain *had*. Eliminate (B) because it's not consistent with the sentence. The correct answer is (A).

38. **C** The order of the phrases is changing in the answer choices, so the question is testing precision. To create precise meaning, the modifying phrase must be placed immediately next to the thing that it modifies. The modifier in the following parentheses (*the friction between cells and the fluids they interact with*) is describing the *fluid shear stress*. Therefore, the *fluid shear stress* must be placed just before the parentheses. Only one choice places *fluid shear stress* last. The correct answer is (C).

39. **B** Note the question! The question asks whether the phrase should be added, so it's testing consistency and concision. The phrase should be added only if the information is consistent with the information in the passage and is not redundant. The first part of the sentence states how scientists believe microgravity will affect *bacteria inside the human body*. The new phrase says that studying this allows for *a glimpse into how that pathogen behaves in the human digestive tract*. The idea is consistent and is not redundant, so it should be added. Eliminate (C) and (D). The new phrase shifts from what scientists believe to actually studying it. The correct answer is (B).

40. **C** Note the question! The question asks for the most precise description of the proceeding depicted in the first part of the sentence, so it's testing precision. The first part of the sentence discusses the *studies*, so the correct answer should match that precisely. *Subject* could mean "ideas" or "participants." Neither matches "studies," so eliminate (A). *Examinations* means "inspections," so eliminate (B). *Experiments* means "studies" or "acts of discovery," so keep (C). *Tests* means "methods to assess," so eliminate (D). The correct answer is (C).

41. **B** Verbs are changing in the answer choices, so the question is testing consistency of verbs. A verb must be consistent with its subject and with the other verbs in the sentence. The subject of the verb is *they*, which is plural. Since all the answers are plural, check the other verbs. The other verbs in the sentence are *are looking* and *attack*, which are present tense. Choices (A), (C), and (D) are past tense, so eliminate them. The correct answer is (B).

42. **B** Commas are changing in the answer choices, so the question is testing the four ways to use a comma. The sentence does not contain a list, so check for unnecessary information. Removing any of the phrases between the commas would cause the sentence to not make sense. The information is necessary, so there is no need to use commas. The correct answer is (B).

43. **A**  Note the question! The question asks for the most effective transition, so it's testing consistency of ideas. Determine how the ideas before and after the sentence relate to each other and select the appropriate transition. The previous sentences discuss the need for *developing a vaccine for Salmonella*. The following sentences discuss using *Salmonella as a delivery vehicle* for another vaccine. The correct transition will shift from needing a vaccine to cure *Salmonella* to using *Salmonella* as a vaccine to cure some other illness. *Salmonella...playing an important role in vaccine research... in an unexpected way* connects the two ideas, so keep (A). Stating that a *vaccine hasn't yet been developed* does not connect to the second part, so eliminate (B). Wanting to *develop better vaccines against... other* illnesses connects to the second part, but doesn't mention *Salmonella*, so eliminate (C). *Studies...beyond the International Space Station* do not connect the ideas, so eliminate (D). The correct answer is (A).

44. **B**  Commas are changing in the answer choices, so the question is testing the four ways to use a comma. The sentence does not contain a list, so check for unnecessary information. Removing only the word *substances* would change the meaning of the sentence to mean that some *antigens stimulate the production of antibodies*, while others do not; eliminate (A). Removing the phrase *substances that stimulate the production of antibodies* would not change the meaning of the sentence, and is therefore unnecessary; keep (B). Removing the phrase *substances that stimulate the production of antibodies to multiple body systems* would change the meaning of the sentence; the antigens would no longer be delivered to multiple body systems. Eliminate (C). Choice (B) is better than (D) because it separates the unnecessary information from the rest of the sentence with commas. The correct answer is (B).

## Section 3: Math (No Calculator)

1. **C**  The question asks for an equation that represents a graph. To find the best equation, compare features of the graph to the answer choices. The graph for this question has a $y$-intercept of 7 and a negative slope. Eliminate answer choices that do not match this information. All the choices are already in $y = mx + b$ form, in which $m$ is the slope and $b$ is the $y$-intercept. Choices (A) and (B) have $y$-intercepts of 0; eliminate (A) and (B). The difference between (C) and (D) is the slope, so calculate slope using the formula $slope = \dfrac{y_2 - y_1}{x_2 - x_1}$. The graph goes through the points (0, 7) and (7, 0), so $slope = \dfrac{0 - 7}{7 - 0}$, which is $\dfrac{-7}{7}$ or $-1$. Eliminate (D). The correct answer is (C).

2. **D**  The question asks for an equation in terms of a specific variable. Although there are variables

in the answer choices, plugging in on this question would be difficult, given the lack of calculator use and the four different variables. Instead, solve for *B*. To begin to isolate *B*, start by multiplying both sides by 5 to get $2A + B + 2C = 5D$. Next, subtract $2A$ and $2C$ from both sides to get $B = 5D - 2A - 2C$. The correct answer is (D).

3. **A** The question asks for the value of *a*. Although there are numbers in the answer choices, plugging in the answers would be difficult, given the lack of calculator use and the fractions in (B) and (C). Instead, solve for *a*. To begin to isolate *a*, combine like terms on both sides of the equation to get $2a - 9 = 7a - 4$. Next, subtract $2a$ from both sides to get $-9 = 5a - 4$. Add 4 to both sides to get $-5 = 5a$. Divide both sides to get $-1 = a$. The correct answer is (A).

4. **D** The question asks for the value of a variable in a system of inequalities. There are variables in the answer choices, so plug in. Find a value of *y* that works in the first equation, such as $y = 2$. Plug this in to the second inequality to get $x < 3(2) + 4$, which is $x < 10$. Use this inequality to plug in for *x*. Make $x = 9$. Next, plug in this value for *x* into each answer choice and eliminate any choice that is not true when $x = 9$. Choice (A) becomes $9 < \frac{7}{3}$. This is false; eliminate (A). Choice (B) becomes $9 < 3$; eliminate (B). Choice (C) becomes $9 < \frac{19}{3}$; eliminate (C). Choice (D) becomes $9 < 11$; keep (D). The correct answer is (D).

5. **B** The question asks for the value of an angle on a figure. Use the geometry basic approach. Start by labeling the figure with the given information. Because *O* is the center of the circle, *BO* and *CO* are both radii, so $BO = CO$, and triangle *BOC* is an isosceles triangle. Therefore, angle *CBO* is also equal to 36°; mark this in the figure. The angles in a triangle add up to 180°, so the third angle in the triangle with angles 28° and 36° must equal $180 - 28 - 36 = 116$°. Label this angle in the diagram:

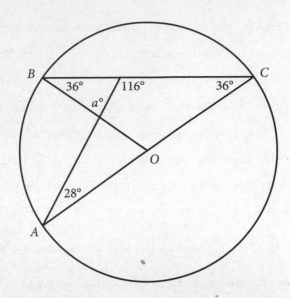

A straight angle has 180°, so the angle adjacent to the 116° must be 180 − 116 = 64°; label this in the diagram. Finally, the triangle containing the angle with measure $a°$ has 180°, so $a$ must be 180 − 36 − 64 = 80°. The correct answer is (B).

6.  **C**  The question asks for the perimeter of the traffic island. Use the geometry basic approach. Start by drawing an isosceles triangle. Next, label the figure. Because there are variables for the side lengths, plug in. Make $s = 6$. Label the two equal sides as having a length of 6. The third side is *4 meters shorter than the equal sides*, so the third side must be 6 − 4 = 2 meters. Label that side. The perimeter is the sum of the sides: 6 + 6 + 2 = 14. This is the target value; circle it. Next, make $s = 6$ in each answer and eliminate any answer that does not equal the target value. Choice (A) becomes 2(6) − 4, which is 12 − 4 or 8. This does not equal the target value; eliminate (A). Choice (B) becomes $\frac{(6)^2 - 4(6)}{2}$, which is $\frac{36 - 24}{2}$ or $\frac{12}{2}$, which is 6. Eliminate (B). Choice (C) becomes 3(6) − 4, which is 18 − 4 or 14. Keep (C), but check (D) just in case. Choice (D) becomes $\frac{6 - 4}{2}$, which is $\frac{2}{2}$ or 1. Eliminate (D). The correct answer is (C).

7.  **D**  The question asks for the equation of a circle given the endpoints of the diameter. The equation of a circle in standard form is $(x − h)^2 + (y − k)^2 = r^2$, where $(h, k)$ is the center and $r$ is the radius. Since the endpoints have the same $x$-coordinate, the length of the diameter is the difference in the $y$-coordinates. Therefore, the diameter is 7 − 1 = 6, and the radius is 3. This means that $r^2 = 9$. Eliminate (B) and (C), which have $r^2 = 36$. Be careful of sign changes with the coordinates of the center of the circle. In this circle equation, the $h$ is −11, so the first part of the equation is $[x − (−11)]^2$, or $(x + 11)^2$. Eliminate (A). The correct answer is (D).

8. **C** The question asks for the solution set of the equation. Since the question asks for a specific value and the answers contain numbers, plug in the answers. Begin by labeling the answers as $a$ and start with (B). If $a = 1$, the equation becomes $1 - 6 = \sqrt{8(1) - 7} - 4$, which is $-5 = \sqrt{1} - 4$ or $-5 = -3$. This is false; eliminate (B) and (D) because both answers include 1. There must be a positive number or 0 under the square root; eliminate (A) because if $a = 0$, there would be a negative number under the radical. Only one choice remains, but test it to be sure. If $a = 11$, then the equation becomes $11 - 6 = \sqrt{8(11) - 7} - 4$, which is $5 = \sqrt{81} - 4$ or $5 = 9 - 4$. This is true. The correct answer is (C).

9. **A** The question asks for an equivalent form of an expression when one function is divided by another. There are variables in the answer choices, so plug in. Make $a = 5$. The first function becomes $h(5) = 5^2 + 5 - 20 = 25 + 5 - 20 = 10$. The second function becomes $k(5) = 5^3 - 16(5)$ $= 125 - 80 = 45$. The question asks for $\dfrac{h(a)}{k(a)}$, so plug these values in to get $\dfrac{10}{45}$. This is the target value; circle it. Now plug $a = 5$ into the answer choices to see which one matches the target value. Choice (A) becomes $\dfrac{5 + 5}{5(5 + 4)} = \dfrac{10}{5(9)} = \dfrac{10}{45}$. This matches the target, so keep (A) but check the remaining answers just in case. Choice (B) becomes $\dfrac{5 + 5}{5(5 - 4)} = \dfrac{10}{5(1)} = \dfrac{10}{5}$. Eliminate (B). Choice (C) becomes $\dfrac{5 + 5}{5 + 4} = \dfrac{10}{9}$. Eliminate (C). Choice (D) becomes $5 + 5 = 10$. Eliminate (D). The correct answer is (A).

10. **C** The question asks for an equation that represents a graph. One option would be to pick a point that is on the graph and plug it into the answer choices to see which ones are true. The answers are all in factored form, however, which shows the roots or solutions of a function. If $(x - a)$ is a factor of a polynomial, then $a$ is a solution, and the graph will cross the $x$-axis at $a$. This graph crosses the $x$-axis at $-2$, 0, and 1, so the factors must include $(x + 2)$, $x$, and $(x - 1)$. Eliminate (B) and (D) because they do not contain these factors. Compare the remaining answers, (A) and (C). They have the same factors, so plugging in the points will result in true statements for both. Instead, pick an $x$-value that is not a root, such as $x = -1$. The exact $y$-value is not clear, but it must be positive. Choice (A) becomes $y = -(-1)(-1 - 1)(-1 + 2)$ or $y = 1(-2)(1)$. This becomes $y = -2$, which does not match the graph. Eliminate (A). The correct answer is (C).

11. **A** The question asks for the value of an expression given an equation. Because the question includes a relationship between the variables, plug in. Start by plugging in for $y$ and solving for $x$ in the first equation. Make $y = 2$. The equation becomes $\dfrac{x}{3(2)} = 3$, which is $\dfrac{x}{6} = 3$. Multiply

both sides by 6 to get $x = 18$. Next, plug $y = 2$ and $x = 18$ into $\frac{y}{x}$ to get $\frac{2}{18}$, which is $\frac{1}{9}$. The correct answer is (A).

12. **B** The question asks for the number of jars that hold 3 tomatoes. Since the question asks for a specific value and the answers contain numbers in increasing order, plug in the answers. Begin by labeling the answers as "jars with 3 tomatoes" and start with (B), 52. If 52 jars hold 3 tomatoes each, then these jars hold a total of $52 \times 3 = 156$ tomatoes. Because there are 80 jars, there are $80 - 52 = 28$ jars that hold 5 tomatoes each, for a total of $28 \times 5 = 140$ tomatoes in these jars. This gives a total of $156 + 140 = 296$ tomatoes, which matches the value given in the question, so stop here. The correct answer is (B).

13. **A** The question asks for the value of a function. In function notation, the number inside the parentheses is the $x$-value that goes into the function, and the value that comes out of the function is the $y$-value. Plug $x = 0$ into the $f$ function to get $f(0) = 2 - [g(0)]^2$. Now plug $x = 0$ into the $g$ function to get $g(0) = 3(0) - 3 = 0 - 3 = -3$. Plug this value into the $f$ function for $g(0)$ to get $f(0) = 2 - [-3]^2 = 2 - (9) = -7$. The correct answer is (A).

14. **B** The question asks for an equation that models a specific situation. Translate the question in bite-sized pieces and eliminate after each piece. One piece of information says that the population of Bulgaria is decreasing. This will translate to a negative slope, so eliminate (C) and (D), which have positive slopes. Compare the remaining answers. The difference between (A) and (B) is the slope, so calculate slope using the formula $slope = \frac{y_2 - y_1}{x_2 - x_1}$. The question states that the population was approximately 9 million people in 1989 and 7.4 million people in 2011. Because $x$ is years after the year 1989 and $P(x)$ is in millions of people, the points are $(0, 9)$ and $(22, 7.4)$. Use the slope formula to get $slope = \frac{7.4 - 9}{22 - 0}$, which is $-\frac{1.6}{22}$. Both answers have slopes with a denominator of 220, so multiply by $\frac{10}{10}$ to get a slope of $-\frac{16}{220}$. The correct answer is (B).

15. **B** The question asks for the value of $k$ in the system of equations. Since the question asks for a specific value, plug in the answers. With two equations, it may be hard to tell if a value that doesn't work is too big or too small, so start with any of the answers. Since 0 is an easy number to work with, start with (B). If $k = 0$, the first equation becomes $y = x^2 + 2x + 0$ or $y = x^2 + 2x$. The second equation states that $y = 2x$, so the right sides of the two equations can be set equal to get $2x = x^2 + 2x$. Subtract $2x$ from both sides to get $x^2 = 0$. Take the square root of both sides to get $x = 0$. There is only one solution when $k = 0$. The correct answer is (B).

16. **17** The question asks for the sum of $y$ and $z$, which are two of the coefficients in the expression

$xa^2 + ya + z$. This expression comes from subtracting the first polynomial ($a^2 + 2a + 4$) from the second polynomial ($3a^2 - 4a + 27$), so the resulting expression is $(3a^2 - 4a + 27) - (a^2 + 2a + 4)$. Work in bite-sized pieces. It is unnecessary to know what $x$ is to solve the question, so ignore the $a^2$ terms. Subtracting the $a$ terms gives $-4a - 2a = -6a$, so $y = -6$. Subtracting the constants gives $27 - 4 = 23$, so $z = 23$. Therefore, $y + z = -6 + 23$, which is 17. The correct answer is 17.

17.  **6**   The question asks for the positive solution of a quadratic. When given a quadratic in standard form, which is $ax^2 + bx + c$, it is often necessary to factor it to solve the question. Find two numbers that add to –1 and multiply to –30. These are –6 and 5. Therefore, the equation factors to $(n - 6)(n + 5) = 0$. Set each factor equal to 0 and solve to find the solutions. If $n - 6 = 0$, then $n = 6$. If $n + 5 = 0$, then $n = -5$. The question asks for the positive solution, so $n = 6$. The correct answer is 6.

18.  **3**   The question asks for the value of a variable in the context of a model. In the form $y = mx + b$, $m$ is the slope and $b$ is the $y$-intercept. Therefore, this question asks for the slope of the equation, so calculate slope using the formula $slope = \dfrac{y_2 - y_1}{x_2 - x_1}$. The question states that *at the start of the month she has completed 12 assignments* and $x$ is *the number of weeks since the start of the month*, so when $x = 0$, $y = 12$. Additionally, the question states that *she completes 3 assignments per week*, so when $x = 1$, $y = 12 + 3$, or 15. Therefore, two points are (0, 12) and (1, 15). The slope formula gives *slope* = $\dfrac{15 - 12}{1 - 0}$, which is $\dfrac{3}{1}$ or 3. The correct answer is 3.

19.  **22**   The question asks for the area of a sector of the circle. The parts of a circle have a proportional relationship, so the fraction of the degrees in the shaded region is the same as the fraction of the sector area out of the total area. Set up the proportion $\dfrac{\text{degrees}}{360} = \dfrac{\text{sector area}}{\text{total area}}$, then plug in the given information to get $\dfrac{110}{360} = \dfrac{\text{sector area}}{72}$. Since calculator use is not allowed, reduce the fraction on the left to $\dfrac{11}{36}$ before cross-multiplying to get $11(72) = 36(\textit{sector area})$. Rather than doing the awkward multiplication on the left, divide both sides by 36 first to get $11(2) = \textit{sector area}$. Therefore, the shaded region has an area of 22. The correct answer is 22.

20.  $\dfrac{14}{8}$, $\dfrac{7}{4}$ **or 1.75**

The question asks for the value of a variable given a system of equations. Try to make the other variable disappear. Because the unwanted variable has the same coefficient in both equations, stack the equations and subtract:

$$9x + 2y = 17.75$$
$$- [x + 2y = 3.75]$$
$$8x \phantom{+ 2y} = 14$$

Divide both sides by 8 to get $x = \dfrac{14}{8}$. Since this answer fits in the grid, there is no need to reduce. The correct answer is $\dfrac{14}{8}$, $\dfrac{7}{4}$, or 1.75.

# Section 4: Math (Calculator)

1. **B**   The question asks for the year when the number of tenants in the building increased the fastest. Use ballparking and estimation to eliminate incorrect answers. The graph represents the total number of tenants on the $y$-axis and years on the $x$-axis. For the number of tenants to increase the fastest, the line should have a great positive slope. In 2005 and 2007, the slope is negative; eliminate (A) and (C). In 2006, the slope of the line is steeper than in 2009; eliminate (D). The correct answer is (B).

2. **D**   The question asks about population based on information about a study of a sample from that population. Since the residents were randomly selected, the incidence of the gene mutation found in the study should match that of the larger population. To extrapolate the study results, set up a proportion. In this case, the proportion is based on the number of mutations out of the total of each group: $\dfrac{4}{500} = \dfrac{x}{15,000}$. Cross-multiply to get $500x = 60,000$. Divide both sides by 500 to get $x = 120$. The correct answer is (D).

3. **C**   The question asks for an algebraic expression to represent a situation. There are variables in the answer choices, so plug in. Make $n = 2$. If each box of cookies costs $2, then 4 boxes of cookies will cost $2 \times 4 = \$8$. This is the target value; circle it. Now plug $n = 2$ into the answer choices to see which one matches the target value. Choice (A) becomes $\dfrac{2}{4}$, which reduces to $\dfrac{1}{2}$. This does not match the target, so eliminate (A). Choice (B) becomes $\dfrac{4}{2}$, which reduces to 2. Eliminate (B). Choice (C) becomes $4(2) = 8$. Keep (C), but check (D) just in case. Choice (D) becomes $2 + 4 = 6$. Eliminate (D). The correct answer is (C).

4. **A**   The question asks for the value of an angle on a figure. Use the geometry basic approach. Start by labeling the figure with the given information. Mark lines $l_1$ and $l_2$ as parallel and the angle marked $a°$ as 110. It may not be immediately obvious how to get the value of $b$, so see what else

can be determined. There are 180° in a triangle, so the angle to the right of $a$ is 180 − 110 − 30 = 40°. When two parallel lines like $l_1$ and $l_2$ are cut by a third line, like the one to the right of the 40° angle and the angle marked $b°$, two kinds of angles are created: big and small. All small angles are equal, and both these angles are small angles. Therefore, $b$ = 40. The correct answer is (A).

5.   **B**   The question asks for a system of equations that models a specific situation. Translate the question in bite-sized pieces and eliminate after each piece. One piece of information says that the total number of digital and paper subscriptions was 1,800, so one of the equations must be $d + p = 1,800$. Eliminate (C), which does not contain this equation. Compare the remaining answer choices. All are equal to 20,760, which is the total revenue from the sale of subscriptions. Find the other information related to money. Digital subscriptions cost \$8, so $8d$ must be part of the equation. This does not appear in (A), so eliminate it. The revenue from the digital subscriptions must be added to the revenue from the paper subscriptions to get the total revenue, but (D) multiplies the values. Eliminate (D). The correct answer is (B).

6.   **A**   The question asks for the predicted value given a graph. This specific value will be based on the line of best fit, but the maximum heart rate of a 60-year-old runner is not on the graph. Use either the equation or the graph of the line of best fit to determine the value. In the equation, the $x$-value is the age and the $y$-value is the heart rate. The equation becomes $y$ = −0.84(60) + 216.9 or $y$ = −50.4 + 216.9 = 166.5. To use the graph instead, continue the line of best fit off the right side of the graph a bit, then estimate where an age of 60 years would fall along the horizontal axis. From this point, trace up to find the intersection with the line of best fit, using the answer sheet as a straight edge if necessary. It is between the horizontal gridlines for 160 and 170 on the maximum heart rate axis. Only the value in (A) falls between 160 and 170. The correct answer is (A).

7.   **C**   The question asks for the value of $c − 2$ in the given equation. Since the question asks for a specific value and the answers contain numbers in increasing order, plug in the answers. Begin by labeling the answers as "$c − 2$" and start with (B), 3. If $c − 2$ = 3, then the equation becomes $\frac{3}{3}$ = 3 or 1 = 3. This is not true, so eliminate (B). A smaller value of $c − 2$ is needed to make the two sides of the equation closer to the same value, so try (C) next. If $c − 2 = \sqrt{3}$, the equation becomes $\frac{3}{\sqrt{3}} = \sqrt{3}$. Multiply both sides by $\sqrt{3}$ to get 3 = $\sqrt{3} \times \sqrt{3}$ or 3 = 3. This is true. The correct answer is (C).

8.   **B**   The question asks for an equation with a $y$-intercept of −1. To find the equation, look for the $y$-intercept in each answer choice. Each answer choice is already in slope-intercept form: $y = mx + b$, where $m$ represents the slope and $b$ represents the $y$-intercept. Therefore, the correct answer must have a $b$ term of −1. Choices (A), (C), and (D) have $y$-intercepts of $-\frac{1}{2}$, 0, and 1, respectively; eliminate them. The correct answer is (B).

9.   **D**   The question asks for a system of inequalities that models a specific situation. Translate the question in bite-sized pieces and eliminate after each piece. One piece of information says that Sarah purchases *more than 360 items*. The items she purchases are canvases ($a$) and paint bottles ($b$), so one inequality must be $a + b > 360$. Eliminate (B) and (C) because they do not contain this inequality. Compare the remaining answer choices. The difference between (A) and (D) is which way the inequality sign is pointing. The question states that Sarah *goes over-budget*, so she spent more than $1,700. The expression on the left is therefore greater than the cost. This does not fit (A), so eliminate it. The correct answer is (D).

10.  **C**   The question asks for the number of beakers needed to hold 4 liters of solution. Since the question asks for a specific value and the answers contain numbers in increasing order, plug in the answers. Begin by labeling the answers as "number of beakers" and start with (B), 4. If there are 4 beakers each holding 800 milliliters, they can hold a total of $4 \times 800 = 3,200$ milliliters. There are 1,000 milliliters in a liter, so 3,200 milliliters is equivalent to 3.2 liters. There are 4 liters of solution, so there are not enough beakers. Eliminate (B) and (A), which are too small. Try (C) next. If there are 5 beakers, they can hold $5 \times 800 = 4,000$ milliliters or 4 liters. This matches the question. The correct answer is (C).

11.  **A**   The question asks for the radius of the beaker, in inches. Since the question asks for a specific value and the answers contain numbers in increasing order, plug in the answers. Begin by labeling the answers as "radius" and start with (B), 2.28 inches. If $n = 2.28$, the volume becomes $\frac{21\pi(2.28)^3}{12} \approx \frac{21\pi(11.85)}{12} \approx \frac{782}{12} \approx 65$ cubic inches. The question states that the volume of 800 milliliters is 13.2 cubic inches, so this is much too large. Eliminate (B), (C), and (D). The correct answer is (A).

12.  **A**   The question asks for the graph that models a specific situation. To find the best graph, read the question carefully and compare features of the graphs in the answer choices, then use Process of Elimination. The question states that the beaker was full of a solution which then evaporated over time. Therefore, the height of the solution in the beaker must be decreasing. Choice (C) shows a constant height over time. Eliminate (C). Choice (D) shows a linear decrease over time. Although the solution evaporates at a constant rate, the odd shape of the beaker would make the height of the solution change in a non-linear way. Eliminate (D). Since the beaker is narrower at the top, the height of the solution will decrease quickly at first then more slowly near the wide base of the beaker. Eliminate (B), which shows the height decreasing more quickly near the end of the evaporation period. The correct answer is (A).

13.  **A**   The question asks for the power rating of a machine given that power is work per unit time. Set up the power equation: $power = \frac{work}{time}$. Now find the information about work and time. Work is defined as *the product of the mass of the object, in kilograms; the distance the object moves, in meters;*

*and the gravitational constant of 9.8 meters per second squared.* Put this into the power formula to get $power = \dfrac{(mass)(distance)\left(9.8\,\frac{m}{s^2}\right)}{time}$. The time is given as 18 seconds, the mass as 100 kilograms, and the distance as 3.6 meters. Plug these values into the formula to get $\dfrac{(100\text{ kg})(3.6\text{ m})\left(9.8\,\frac{m}{s^2}\right)}{18\text{ s}} = \dfrac{3{,}528}{18} = 196$. The correct answer is (A).

14.  **B**  The question asks for one variable in terms of another. There are variables in the answer choices, so plug in. Make $x = 2$. This is the target value; circle it. Use this to find the value of $y$: $y = \dfrac{1}{2^3} = \dfrac{1}{8}$. Now plug $y = \dfrac{1}{8}$ into the answer choices to see which one matches the target value. Use a calculator if needed to find the values. Choice (A) becomes $\left(\dfrac{1}{8}\right)^{\frac{1}{3}} = \sqrt[3]{\dfrac{1}{8}} = \dfrac{1}{2}$. This does not match the target value, so eliminate (A). A negative exponent flips the base to its reciprocal, so (B) becomes $\left(\dfrac{1}{8}\right)^{-\frac{1}{3}} = (8)^{\frac{1}{3}} = \sqrt[3]{8} = 2$. Keep (B), but check the remaining answer choices just in case. Choice (C) becomes $-\left(\dfrac{1}{8}\right)^3 = -\left(\dfrac{1}{512}\right)$, and (D) becomes $\left(\dfrac{1}{8}\right)^3 = \left(\dfrac{1}{512}\right)$. Eliminate (C) and (D). The correct answer is (B).

15.  **C**  The question asks for the value of $x$ that is not in the domain of $f(x)$, which is a value of $x$ that does not work in the equation. Since the question asks for a specific value and the answers contain numbers in increasing order, plug in the answers. Begin by labeling the answers as $x$ and start with (B), 0. If $x = 0$, the function becomes $f(0) = \dfrac{5}{0^2 - 5(0) + 4}$, which is $\dfrac{5}{4}$. This is a value for $f(x)$ that works, so $x = 0$ is in the domain of $f(x)$; eliminate (B). It can be tricky to determine whether a larger or smaller number is needed when working with quadratics, so just pick a direction. Try (C). If $x = 1$, the function becomes $f(1) = \dfrac{5}{1^2 - 5(1) + 4}$, which is $\dfrac{5}{1 - 5 + 4}$ or $\dfrac{5}{0}$. This is undefined, so $x = 1$ must not be in the domain of $f(x)$. The correct answer is (C).

16.  **B**  The question asks about the mean, median, and mode of a set of data. The mean or average is defined as $\dfrac{total}{\#\ of\ things}$. The number of things is 24, since the farmer took the total for each of the 24 chickens for the week. To find the total, take each number of eggs times the frequency for that

number, then add all the results together. The total is $8(1) + 7(3) + 6(8) + 5(5) + 4(2) + 2(5) = 8 + 21 + 48 + 25 + 8 + 10 = 120$. Therefore, the mean is $\frac{120}{24} = 5$. The median of a list of numbers is the middle number when all values are arranged in order. In lists with an even number of items, the median is the average of the middle two numbers. There are 24 chickens, so the median number of eggs will be the average of the eggs laid by the 12th and 13th chickens. The number of eggs are already listed in order, so start counting from the 1st chicken, which laid 8 eggs. The 2nd, 3rd, and 4th chickens laid 7 eggs each. The next 8 chickens, the 5th through the 12th, laid 6 eggs and the 13th chicken laid 5 eggs. Therefore, the median number of eggs is $\frac{6+5}{2} = 5.5$. This is greater than the mean, so eliminate (A) and (D). Now find the mode, which is the most common number in a set of data. In this set, the number of eggs with the highest frequency is 6, so the mode is 6. This is also greater than the mean, so eliminate (C). The correct answer is (B).

17. **B** The question asks for a certain value on a graph. *Hours* are listed along the horizontal axis, so find 12 on that axis. From this point, trace up to find the intersection with the line of best fit, using the answer sheet as a straight edge if necessary. It is between the horizontal gridlines for 70% and 80% on the *Job Satisfaction* axis. Only the value in (B) falls between 70% and 80%. The correct answer is (B).

18. **A** The question asks for a proportion, which is defined as $\frac{part}{whole}$. Read the table carefully to find the numbers to make the proportion. There were 250 participants who watched the new ad, so that is the *whole*. Of these participants, 120 had a favorable opinion, so that is the *part*. Therefore, the proportion is $\frac{120}{250} = \frac{12}{25}$. The correct answer is (A).

19. **B** The question asks for a percent decrease based on data. Percent change is defined as $\frac{difference}{original} \times 100$. Set it up, then find the numbers on the table. The question asks *for the percent decrease…from January 1st, 2010, to January 1st, 2011*. The graph lists time as *Months since January 1st 2008*. There are two years or 24 months from January 1st, 2008 to January 1st, 2010, so the crime rate for January 1st, 2010 is at 24 months on the horizontal axis. From this point, trace up to find the intersection with the line of best fit, using the answer sheet as a straight edge if necessary. It is at a crime rate of 1,000. There is one more year or an additional 12 months between January 1st, 2010 and January 1st, 2011, so the crime rate for January 1st, 2011 is at 36 months on the vertical

axis. This intersects the line of best fit at a crime rate of 800. Therefore, the percent decrease is $\dfrac{1,000 - 800}{1,000} \times 100 = \dfrac{200}{1,000} \times 100 = 0.2 \times 100 = 20\%$. The correct answer is (B).

20.  **C**  The question asks for the meaning of a coefficient in context. Start by reading the full question, which asks for the meaning of the number 16.8. Then label the parts of the equation with the information given. The question states that $y$ is the violent crime rate in the city and $x$ is the number of months since the crime prevention program began. The number 16.8 is multiplied by months and subtracted from 1,412, so it must have something to do with the decrease in the crime rate over time. Next, use Process of Elimination to get rid of answer choices that are not consistent with the labels. Choice (A) refers to the number of months, but $x$ represents time in the equation, so eliminate (A). Choice (B) refers to the average crime rate, but $y$ represents the crime rate in the equation, so eliminate (B) also. Choice (C) refers to a *reduction* in the crime rate over time, so keep (C). Choice (D) refers to the exact crime rate in 2008, when the program began. To check this, plug in $x = 0$. The equation becomes $y = 1,412 - 16.8(0) = 1,412 - 0 = 1,412$. Therefore, the crime rate at the start of the program in January 2008 was 1,412. Eliminate (D). The correct answer is (C).

21.  **A**  The question asks for an inequality that models a specific situation. Translate the question in bite-sized pieces and eliminate after each piece. One piece of information says that Samuel's salary will increase from \$49,500 to \$64,500 once he completes the MBA program. Therefore, the *additional income* each year will be $(64,500 - 49,500)$, so eliminate (C) and (D), which do not include this term. Compare the remaining answer choices. The difference between (A) and (B) is the direction of the inequality symbol. The question states that the *total additional income* should *exceed the cost of tuition*. Therefore, the additional income per year times the number of years will be greater than the tuition. This translates to $(64,500 - 49,500)n > 73,320$. The answer choices isolate $n$, so divide both sides by $(64,500 - 49,500)$ to get $n > \dfrac{73,320}{(64,500 - 49,500)}$. The correct answer is (A).

22.  **C**  The question asks for the graph of a function given a description of that function. The *zeroes* of a polynomial are the points where it crosses the $x$-axis, or where $y = 0$. Therefore, the graph of this polynomial will contain the points $(-4, 0)$ and $(2, 0)$. Look at the graphs and eliminate any that do not include these points. Choice (A) has zeroes at $(-4, 0)$, $(-1, 0)$, and $(2, 0)$. Choice (A) also has a third zero not mentioned in the question, so check the remaining answers. Choice (B) has zeroes at $(-4, 0)$ and $(2, 0)$. Keep (B) as well. Choice (C) has zeroes at $(-4, 0)$ and $(2, 0)$. Keep (C) as well. Choice (D) has zeroes at $(-2, 0)$ and $(4, 0)$. Eliminate (D). The question also states that the graph should only contain values for $y$ that are greater than or equal to $-3$. Choices (A) and (B) contain values of $y$ less than $-3$. Eliminate (A) and (B). The correct answer is (C).

23.  **C**  The question asks for a statement that is supported based on the results of a poll that was con-

ducted. Read each answer carefully and use Process of Elimination. Choice (A) refers to high voter turnout on Election Day. It is impossible to know whether additional voters will be for or against the proposition, since only one poll was conducted. Furthermore, no information is given regarding the number of people polled or how they were selected. The poll sample may be too small or too biased to draw conclusions about the larger population. Eliminate (A). Choice (B) refers to the ages of voters. No information was given about the ages of the poll participants, so no conclusion can be drawn about voters based on age. Eliminate (B). Choice (C) refers to the method in which the poll participants were reached. This applies directly to the poll, so it could contain a reasonable conclusion. The percent of participants contacted by cell phone who supported the proposition was 30%, whereas 55% of all participants contacted by landline supported it. Since the percent is higher for landline participants, (C) is true. Keep it, but check (D) just in case. Choice (D) refers to only the landline users, but it has the same problem as (A) in that no information is given to determine if these participants make up a representative sample. Eliminate (D). The correct answer is (C).

24. **D** The question asks for an equation that models a specific situation. There are variables in the answer choices, so plug in. Make $n = 14$ days in the original equation, so $x = 2$ weeks in the answer choices. The original equation becomes $w = 109(1.12)^{14} \approx 109(4.887) \approx 532.7$. This is the target value; circle it. Now plug $x = 2$ into the answer choices to see which one matches the target value. Choice (A) becomes $w = 109(2.21)^{\frac{2}{7}} \approx 109(1.254) \approx 137$. This does not match the target, so eliminate (A). Choice (B) becomes $w = 109(1.12)^{\frac{2}{7}}$, which will be even smaller than (A). Eliminate (B). Choice (C) becomes $w = 109(1.84)^2 = 109(3.3856) \approx 369$. Eliminate (C). Choice (D) becomes $w = 109(1.12)^{7(2)} \approx 109(4.887) \approx 532.7$. The correct answer is (D).

25. **D** The question asks for a true statement regarding the results of a study that was conducted. Read each answer carefully and use Process of Elimination. Choice (A) refers to the size of the sample. Generally, the larger the sample, the more reliable the study results. No numbers are given regarding the sample size or number of residents, so this is difficult to determine. Keep (A) for now, but check the other answers. Choice (B) refers to the days that the study was conducted. While doing the study two days instead of one would improve the results, there is no way to tell if that will make the result completely reliable. Again, keep (B) but see if there is a better answer. Choice (C) refers to the location of the study. Again, a busier location may help get more respondents, but it is unclear if that will make the study reliable. Eliminate (C). Choice (D) refers to bias in the study, which means that the group involved might be more inclined to a certain outcome. Since the study only involved people entering the library, the results are likely to favor library-use more than if randomly selected people had participated. Since exact numbers were not given, the sample size is less of a problem than the bias in the sample. Eliminate (A). The correct answer is (D).

26. **A** The question asks for the value of $d$ in point $(c, d)$. Start by determining the value of $c$ in terms of $d$.

The question states that $\dfrac{c}{d} = \dfrac{3}{2}$. Cross-multiply to get $2c = 3d$. Divide both sides by 2 to get $c = \dfrac{3d}{2}$. Next, use the given information to determine the equation of the lines. Use slope-intercept form: $y = mx + b$, where $(x, y)$ is a point on the line, $m$ is the slope, and $b$ is the $y$-intercept. The first line contains point $(c, d)$ and has a slope of 2, so its equation is $d = 2c + b$. Substitute $\dfrac{3d}{2}$ for $c$ to get $d = 2\left(\dfrac{3d}{2}\right) + b$, which becomes $d = 3d + b$ or $-2d = b$. The second line contains the point $(3, 2d)$, has a slope of $-3$, and the same $y$-intercept as the first equation, so its equation is $2d = -3(3) + b$, or $2d = -9 + b$. Substitute $-2d$ for $b$ to get $2d = -9 - 2d$. Add $2d$ to both sides to get $4d = -9$. Divide both sides by 4 to get $d = -\dfrac{9}{4}$. The correct answer is (A).

27.   **C**   The question asks for the relationship between two variables. When given a table of values and asked for the correct equation, plug values from the table into the answer choices to see which one works. In the answers, $n$ is *years after 2010*. Therefore, according to the table, $n = 3$ when the unemployment rate was 13%. Choice (A) becomes $1.5(3) + 11.5$, which is $4.5 + 11.5$ or 16. This does not match the unemployment rate; eliminate (A). Choice (B) becomes $0.5(3 - 2,010) + 11.5$, which is $0.5(-2,007) + 11.5$ or $-1,003.5 + 11.5$, which is $-992$. Eliminate (B). Choice (C) becomes $0.5(3) + 11.5$, which is $1.5 + 11.5$ or 13. Keep (C), but check (D) just in case. Choice (D) becomes $-1.5(3) + 11.5$, which is $-4.5 + 11.5$ or 7. Eliminate (D). The correct answer is (C).

28.   **A**   The question asks for the model that best fits the data. The question states that water is added *at a constant rate*. Therefore, the rate of increase is linear rather than exponential. Eliminate (C) and (D), which are equations for exponential growth. Next, find a value from the data to plug in to the remaining answers. The pool *contains 60% more water after the hose has run for 5 hours*. The pool initially contained 750 gallons, so after 5 hours it contains $750 + 750 \times \dfrac{60}{100} = 1,200$ gallons. Therefore, when $t = 5$, the answer should equal 1,200. Choice (A) becomes $750 + 90(5)$, which is $750 + 450$ or 1,200. This is true, so the correct answer is (A).

29.   **D**   The question asks for the value of a function. In function notation, the number inside the parentheses is the $x$-value that goes into the function, and the value that comes out of the function is the $y$-value. The vertex of the graph of function $h$ is at $(-1, -3)$, so $a = -1$ and $h(a) = h(-1) = -3$. Substitute to get $f(h(a)) = f(-3)$. Use the table to determine that $f(-3) = 11$. The correct answer is (D).

30.   **B**   The question asks for a true statement based on the data. Consider each answer and use Process of Elimination. Choice (A) compares the ranges of Group A and Group B. The range of a list of values is the greatest value minus the least value. In Group A, the greatest value is 9 and the least value is 3, so the range is $9 - 3$, which is 6. In Group B, the greatest value is 13 and the least value is 8, so the range is $13 - 8 = 5$. Eliminate (A), which says the range of Group B is larger. Also

eliminate (D), which says the ranges are equal. Choices (B) and (C) compare the standard deviation of the two groups. Standard deviation is a measure of how close together the data points are in a group of numbers; a list with numbers close together has a small standard deviation, whereas a list with numbers spread out has a large standard deviation. In Group A, the data points are evenly distributed, whereas in Group B most of the data points are around 12. Therefore, the standard deviation of Group B must be less than the standard deviation of Group A. Eliminate (C). The correct answer is (B).

31. **14** The question asks for the value of $n$ if the two equations represent the same line. Make the second equation equal to the first by multiplying the second equation by 2 to get $14x - 8y = 18$. Both equations are equal, so $n$ must equal 14. The correct answer is 14.

32. **66** The question asks for a measurement and gives conflicting units. When dealing with scale maps or models, make a proportion, being sure to match up units. The proportion is $\dfrac{1 \text{ liter}}{3 \text{ milligrams}} = \dfrac{22 \text{ liters}}{x \text{ milligrams}}$. Cross-multiply to get $x = 66$. The correct answer is 66.

33. **9** The question asks for the value of $c$ in the equation. Start by substituting $-3$ for $x$ to get $\dfrac{1}{3}c + (-3) = 0$. Add 3 to both sides of the equation to get $\dfrac{1}{3}c = 3$. Multiply both sides by 3 to get $c = 9$. The correct answer is 9.

34. **6** The question asks for the value of a variable in a system of equations. Since $p(x) = q(x)$ where the two functions intersect, one way to solve this would be to graph both functions on a graphing calculator and trace to find the intersections. Another method is to solve algebraically by setting the equations equal to one another. This gives $15 - 5x = \dfrac{1}{3}(x - 9)^2 - 18$. Add 18 to both sides to get $33 - 5x = \dfrac{1}{3}(x - 9)^2$. Clear the fraction by multiplying both sides by 3 to get $99 - 15x = (x - 9)^2$. FOIL the right side to get $99 - 15x = x^2 - 9x - 9x + 81$, which is $99 - 15x = x^2 - 18x + 81$. Add $15x$ to both sides to get $99 = x^2 - 3x + 81$. Subtract 99 from both sides to get $0 = x^2 - 3x - 18$. Factor by finding two numbers that add to $-3$ and multiply to $-18$. Those numbers are $-6$ and 3, so the equation becomes $0 = (x - 6)(x + 3)$. Set each factor equal to 0 and solve to get $x - 6 = 0$ or $x = 6$ and $x + 3 = 0$ or $x = -3$. The question asks for the positive $x$ value. The correct answer is 6.

35. **0.6** The question asks for the value of the sum of two trigonometric functions. The functions of sine and cosine usually apply to right angles and give the ratio of the side opposite or adjacent the angle, respectively, to the hypotenuse. This question has a right angle, but the angles in question are not the other two angles of triangle $ABC$. The angles $\angle DBA$ and $\angle DBC$ add together to make the right angle, so use the fact that $\sin(x°) = \cos(90° - x°)$. If $\angle DBC$ is $x°$, then $\angle DBA$ is $(90° - x°)$ and

sin(∠DBC) = cos(∠DBA) = 0.3. Therefore, cos(∠DBA) + sin(∠DBC) = 0.3 + 0.3 = 0.6. The correct answer is 0.6.

36. **0.11**  The question asks for a rate in terms of points per minute.  Begin by reading the question to find information on the average number of points lost.  The question states that *during two days of trading the Dow Jones Industrial Average lost 68.9 points* and that *there were 5 hours of trading during each of the two days combined*. Therefore, there were 2 × 5 = 10 hours of trading. There are 60 minutes in an hour, so 10 hours is 60 × 10 = 600 minutes. To determine rate, divide amount by time: $\frac{68.9 \text{ points}}{600 \text{ minutes}} \approx 0.1148$ points per minute. The question asks for the rate to the nearest hundredth of a point per minute, so round to 0.11. The correct answer is 0.11.

37. **1.3**  The question asks for the value of $r$ in the function. Use the table to fill in the other variables and solve. Choose a point that makes the math easier. Because the exponent is divided by 2 in the function, choose 2 days. At 2 days after germination, the plants weighed 6.6 grams, so $d = 2$ and $H(2) = $ 6.6. The function becomes $6.6 = 5.0r^{\frac{2}{2}}$, which is $6.6 = 5.0r^1$ or $6.6 = 5.0r$. Divide both sides by 5.0 to get $r = 1.32$. The question asks for the value of $r$ rounded to the nearest tenth, so round 1.32 to 1.3. The correct answer is 1.3.

38. **9.6**  The question asks for the difference between the masses of two groups of plants. Start by determining the mass of the 4 plants that germinated 4 days ago. According to the table, plants that germinated 4 days ago have a mass of 8.4 grams per plant, so 4 plants would have a mass of 4 × 8.4 = 33.6 grams. Next, find the mass of the 3 plants that germinated 8 days ago. These plants have an average mass of 14.4 grams, so their total mass is 3 × 14.4 = 43.2 grams. To find the difference, subtract: 43.2 − 33.6 = 9.6 grams. The correct answer is 9.6.

## Section 5: Experimental

1. **A**  Note the question! The question asks whether the phrase should be added, so it's testing consistency of ideas and precision. If the phrase is consistent with the first part of the sentence and it plays a precise role, then it should be added. The first part of the sentence states that the Orbiter crashed on Mars. The new phrase states that it should have gone *into orbit around the planet to collect and transmit data*. This explains what the Orbiter's mission was supposed to be, so it's consistent and plays a precise role. The phrase should be added, so eliminate (C) and (D). The phrase does *give details that clarify that the crash was unexpected*, so keep (A). The phrase does not *establish an important shift in focus*, so eliminate (B). The correct answer is (A).

2. **A**  The change in the answer choices is from a noun to different pronouns, so the question is testing

precision. Determine the subject of the pronoun, and choose an answer that makes the meaning consistent and precise. The underlined portion must establish who is *against adopting the metric system*. At this point in the passage, no specific party has been established, so the most precise answer will be the specific noun, not the general pronoun. *People* is a specific noun, so keep (A). *They*, *them*, and *those* are general pronouns, so eliminate (B), (C), and (D). The correct answer is (A).

3. **C** Verbs are changing in the answer choices, so the question is testing consistency of verbs. A verb must be consistent with its subject and with the other verbs in the sentence. All the answer choices are consistent with the subject of the verb, *the other group*, so look for other verbs. The first part of the sentence states that *one group used*, so the underlined portion must be consistent with that verb. Only *used* is consistent. Eliminate (A), (B), and (D). The correct answer is (C).

4. **D** Note the question! The question asks where sentence 2 should be placed, so it's testing consistency. Determine the subject matter of the sentence, and find the other sentence that also discusses that information. Sentence 2 states that *neither group realized*, so it should be placed after the sentence that mentions the two groups. Only sentence 5 mentions *one group...* and *the other group*, so sentence 2 should be placed after sentence 5. The correct answer is (D).

5. **B** Note the question! The question asks for the best combination, so it's testing concision. Select the shortest choice that eliminates the redundancy present in the original sentences. Evaluate (B) first because it's the shortest. The pronoun *which* refers to the *replacement of Roman numerals with the base-ten Arabic numbering* in the first part of the sentence. Because *which* replaces that same phrase in the second part of the sentence, the redundancy has been eliminated and the answer is concise. The correct answer is (B).

6. **B** The number and placement of the commas is changing in the answer choices, so the question is testing comma usage. The commas are changing in two places (and there's a dash), so check for unnecessary information. Because *decimal* and *base-ten* mean the same thing, it is unnecessary to say it twice. Therefore, there should be either commas or dashes before and after the phrase *or base-ten*. The comma and the dash cannot be used together, so eliminate (D). Eliminate (A) and (C) because the commas are in the wrong place. The correct answer is (B).

7. **D** The number and placement of the commas is changing in the answer choices, so the question is testing comma usage. The sentence does not contain a list, so check for unnecessary information. Removing any of the phrases between the commas creates an incomplete sentence. Therefore, all the phrases are necessary, and there is no reason to use a comma. The correct answer is (D).

8. **C** Note the question! The question asks for the explanation of how the metric system was important for trade over long distances, so it's testing consistency of ideas. Select the choice that is consistent with *important for trade over long distances*. *Cheating* is not consistent with *long distances*, so eliminate (A). Although (B) mentions *long-distance*, *different currencies* is not consistent with the *metric system*; eliminate (B). The *buyers and sellers* not being *from the same place* is consistent with *trade*

*over long distances*, so keep (C). The type of *goods* is not consistent, so eliminate (D). The correct answer is (C).

9.  **C**  First, the pronouns are changing in the answer choices, so the question is testing consistency. The pronoun must be consistent in number with the noun it is replacing. The noun is *France*, which is singular. Thus, the pronoun must also be singular. Eliminate (A) and (B), which are plural. Next, the verbs are changing, so the question is testing consistency. A verb must be consistent with its subject and with the other verbs in the sentence. The sentence states that *France was*, which is the simple past tense. Thus, the underlined portion must also be in the simple past tense. *Organized* is the simple past, so keep (C). *Had organized* includes the unnecessary helping verb *had*, so eliminate (D). The correct answer is (C).

10. **C**  Note the question! The question asks for the choice that maintains the style and tone of the passage, so it's testing consistency. The overall tone of the passage is semi-formal and educational, so the correct answer should be consistent with this tone. Choices (A), (B), and (D) are too informal. The correct answer is (C).

11. **A**  The transition phrase is changing in the answer choices, so the question is testing consistency of ideas. The sentence contains two phrases separated by a comma, so evaluate those two ideas to determine how they should be connected. The first part states that *the American colonies were part of the British Empire*, and the second part states that *they used the British Imperial System of measurement*. These ideas are similar, so eliminate (B) and (D) because they indicate opposite ideas. Using *therefore* would create two complete ideas separated by a comma. GO punctuation cannot separate two complete ideas, so eliminate (C). The correct answer is (A).

12. **D**  The vocabulary is changing in the answer choices, so this question is testing word choice. Look for a word whose definition is consistent with the other ideas in the sentence. The sentence is trying to state that both Jefferson and Franklin were proponents of "getting rid of" the British system, so the correct answer must be consistent with this idea. *Sacrificing* means "to kill or destroy something as an offering," so eliminate (A). *Ducking* means "to get out of the way of something," so eliminate (B). *Evading* means "to avoid something," so eliminate (C). *Abandoning* means to "give something up" or to "leave something behind." This is consistent with the rest of the sentence. The correct answer is (D).

13. **D**  The transition phrase is changing in the answer choices, so the question is testing consistency of ideas. Evaluate the ideas that come before and after the transition to determine how they should be connected. The prior idea is that both Jefferson and Franklin were proponents of adopting the metric system. The next idea is that there were *insurmountable roadblocks to adopting the metric system*. These are opposite ideas, so a transition that changes direction is needed. *For example, moreover*, and *thus* all indicate the same direction, so eliminate (A), (B), and (C). *However* indicates a change in direction. The correct answer is (D).

14. **B**  The punctuation is changing in the answer choices, so the question is testing STOP and GO

punctuation. Use the vertical line test, and identify the ideas as complete or incomplete. Draw the vertical line between the words *War* and *it*. The first phrase is an incomplete idea, and the second phrase is a complete idea. STOP punctuation can only come between two complete ideas, so eliminate (A) and (C), which both contain STOP punctuation. HALF-STOP punctuation must come after a complete idea, so eliminate the colon in (D). A comma is GO punctuation, which can separate an incomplete idea from a complete idea. The correct answer is (B).

15.  **B**  The vocabulary is changing in the answer choices, so the question is testing word choice. The correct choice will match the idea of *sending a delegation to France* to the purpose of the trip. The purpose was not *by learn* or *of learn*, so eliminate (C) and (D). If the word *for* is used, the phrase should say *for learning*, so eliminate (A). The purpose was *to learn about the metric system*. The correct answer is (B).

16.  **A**  Note the question! The question asks for the best introduction to this paragraph, so it's testing consistency of ideas. The previous paragraph ends by stating that the U.S. kept the British system. This paragraph discusses a few times that the U.S. tried and failed to convert to the metric system. The correct answer will be consistent with this idea. *Multiple attempts...to establish the metric system* is consistent, so keep (A). Discussing *France* is not consistent, so eliminate (B). Eliminate (C) because it does not mention the metric system. The topic of *political upheaval* is not consistent, so eliminate (D). The correct answer is (A).

17.  **C**  The phrases are changing in the answer choices, so the question is testing concision and precision. Select the shortest choice whose meaning is precise. The terms *enthusiasts* and *admirers* mean the same thing, so that idea should not be repeated. Eliminate (A) and (D) because they are redundant. Choices (B) and (C) mean the same thing, so select the more concise choice. The correct answer is (C).

18.  **A**  Note the question! The question asks for the conclusion of the essay, so it's testing consistency of ideas. The essay started by stating that some people believe the metric system caused the Mars Climate Orbiter to crash, and it ended by stating that the United States had been unable to make the metric system mandatory. The correct answer must be consistent with these ideas. Choice (A) states that our *speed limit signs are* not in *kilometers per hour* and revisits the *Mars Climate Orbiter crash*, so keep it. Stating what *school children learn* is not consistent, so eliminate (B). Discussing *businesses* in relation to *government agencies* is not consistent, so eliminate (C). Stating that *no one is motivated to make the change* is not consistent, so eliminate (D). The correct answer is (A).

## RAW SCORE CONVERSION TABLE   SECTION AND TEST SCORES

| Raw Score (# of correct answers) | Math Section Score | Reading Test Score | Writing and Language Test Score | Raw Score (# of correct answers) | Math Section Score | Reading Test Score | Writing and Language Test Score |
|---|---|---|---|---|---|---|---|
| 0 | 200 | 10 | 10 | 30 | 530 | 28 | 29 |
| 1 | 200 | 10 | 10 | 31 | 540 | 28 | 30 |
| 2 | 210 | 10 | 10 | 32 | 550 | 29 | 30 |
| 3 | 230 | 11 | 10 | 33 | 560 | 29 | 31 |
| 4 | 240 | 12 | 11 | 34 | 560 | 30 | 32 |
| 5 | 260 | 13 | 12 | 35 | 570 | 30 | 32 |
| 6 | 280 | 14 | 13 | 36 | 580 | 31 | 33 |
| 7 | 290 | 15 | 13 | 37 | 590 | 31 | 34 |
| 8 | 310 | 15 | 14 | 38 | 600 | 32 | 34 |
| 9 | 320 | 16 | 15 | 39 | 600 | 32 | 35 |
| 10 | 330 | 17 | 16 | 40 | 610 | 33 | 36 |
| 11 | 340 | 17 | 16 | 41 | 620 | 33 | 37 |
| 12 | 360 | 18 | 17 | 42 | 630 | 34 | 38 |
| 13 | 370 | 19 | 18 | 43 | 640 | 35 | 39 |
| 14 | 380 | 19 | 19 | 44 | 650 | 35 | 40 |
| 15 | 390 | 20 | 19 | 45 | 660 | 36 | |
| 16 | 410 | 20 | 20 | 46 | 670 | 37 | |
| 17 | 420 | 21 | 21 | 47 | 670 | 37 | |
| 18 | 430 | 21 | 21 | 48 | 680 | 38 | |
| 19 | 440 | 22 | 22 | 49 | 690 | 38 | |
| 20 | 450 | 22 | 23 | 50 | 700 | 39 | |
| 21 | 460 | 23 | 23 | 51 | 710 | 40 | |
| 22 | 470 | 23 | 24 | 52 | 730 | 40 | |
| 23 | 480 | 24 | 25 | 53 | 740 | | |
| 24 | 480 | 24 | 25 | 54 | 750 | | |
| 25 | 490 | 25 | 26 | 55 | 760 | | |
| 26 | 500 | 25 | 26 | 56 | 780 | | |
| 27 | 510 | 26 | 27 | 57 | 790 | | |
| 28 | 520 | 26 | 28 | 58 | 800 | | |
| 29 | 520 | 27 | 28 | | | | |

*Please note that these scores are best approximations and that actual scores on the SAT may slightly vary, depending on individual adaptations made by the College Board.

## CONVERSION EQUATION 1   SECTION AND TEST SCORES

## CONVERSION EQUATION 2 · SECTION AND TEST SCORES

## CONVERSION EQUATION 3 · SECTION AND TEST SCORES

## CONVERSION EQUATION 4 · SECTION AND TEST SCORES

## CONVERSION EQUATION 5   SECTION AND TEST SCORES

## CONVERSION EQUATION 6   SECTION AND TEST SCORES

## CONVERSION EQUATION 7   SECTION AND TEST SCORES

## CONVERSION EQUATION 8 SECTION AND TEST SCORES

## CONVERSION EQUATION 9 SECTION AND TEST SCORES

## CONVERSION EQUATION 10 SECTION AND TEST SCORES

# NOTES

# NOTES

# NOTES

# NOTES

# NOTES

# NOTES

**NOTES**

Are you an international student looking to study in the U.S.A.?

Visit us at
**https://www.princetonreview.com/global**